Author's Note

Facts, figures and statistics, including team line-ups, have been largely omitted from the chronological narrative, and instead have been concentrated in the extensive statistical Appendices.

Photographs have been chosen until two criteria ; firstly that they were not included in the two Pictorial Histories of the Club, published during the previous decade.   Copies of Rovers Recalled, Volumes 1 and 2, remain available for sale, and each contains 100 pages of photographs which, in the main, are not included in this book.

The second criterion is that photographs of the 200 players who have made most appearances for Raith Rovers are included, either individually, or prominently in team groups.   That explains the indifferent quality of some of the photographs, which were the best obtainable for some of the players from the early years of the club's history.

For those wishing to explore particular areas of the club's history, or that of its players, there are suggestions in the closing pages for further reading, and the Sources of Information and Acknowledgements, also at the end of the book, will also be useful in that respect.

There shall, inevitably, be errors and omissions in the pages which follow.   I would be grateful to learn of these, by email (progm@hotmail.com) or post (c/o 4 Ben Ledi Road, Kirkcaldy KY2 5RP). All corrections and additions will be posted on the website www.pmfc.co.uk (click on Football History and follow subsequent links from that page).

John Litster
Kirkcaldy
September 2008

Illustrations

On page one (overleaf), Andy Young, Ernie Till, Malcolm McLure and stand-in goalkeeper Willie Penman combine to prevent Leith Athletic from scoring in a Scottish Cup tie at Meadowbank in January 1949

Opposite, above, Lochgelly United v Raith Rovers, Scottish Qualifying Cup Second Round replay at Lochgelly on 22nd September 1906.   Below, the final act of the 1994 League Cup Final ; Scott Thomson saves Paul McStay's penalty kick.

Published in 2008 by Programme Monthly, PO Box 3236, Norwich, NR7 7BE
01603 449237   progm@hotmail.com   www.pmfc.co.uk

Printed in the UK by hswprint, Tonypandy CF40 2XX

ISBN : 978-0-95346-822-5

£25.95

I t was far from a typical late Sunday morning in Kirkcaldy. Apart from the unseasonally bright, still weather, the streets were busier than usual. The normal, light traffic of a Sunday morning, church goers, dog owners and the drowsy walk of those going out for the morning papers and rolls, was multiplied hundreds of times over. The newcomers to this Sunday morning promenade were dressed for a day out, as they made their way to their cars and buses. Most carried scarves, predominantly navy blue, with touches of red and white. All over the town, there were individuals and small groups of people, like a Lowry painting, moving slowly but purposefully. It was Sunday November 27th 1994, and around 8,000 of the town's 50,000 inhabitants were on their way to Glasgow, where 2,000-or-so exiled Langtonians would join them in the Govan Stand at Ibrox Park, to see Raith Rovers contest only the third major final in their long and largely unsuccessful history.

Eighty-one years earlier, there had been a similar exodus, to the opposite end of Glasgow's great divide, to see Rovers lose to Falkirk in the Scottish Cup Final. In 1949, the process was repeated, this time to Hampden, where Rovers set the tone for the first 111 years of the club's existence, with an undeserved defeat by Rangers in the League Cup Final. Far too late, and far too infrequently, the club was back in a Final, from a place in the second tier of Scottish football, and this time the opponents were Celtic.

The perfectly still and peaceful Sunday morning by the Firth of Forth, developed into an enthralling, exciting and thrilling afternoon's football on the banks of the Clyde, and culminated in unbridled joy in the dusk of a late autumn Glasgow evening. In 120 minutes, followed by a penalty shoot-out at Ibrox, 13 young (and, well, not so young) men, five Fifers amongst them, played the game of their lives, and on that day changed forever the history of Raith Rovers Football Club.

No longer the club which built up the hopes and expectations of successive generations of supporters, only to fall short or, at best, stumble at the final hurdle, leaving their supporters with the inadequate consolation of rueing hard luck, bad decisions or missed chances, as they endured the downturn which inevitably followed the ascent which stopped just short of the summit. No longer the plucky or unlucky losers, best known as a nursery to some of the game's greatest talents, or the nursing home to others playing out once-glorious careers. No longer the losers.

For those who had doggedly supported the club though decades of little achievement, dwindling crowds and the apathetic cynicism of their fellow townsmen and women, that pleasant Sunday morning was a prelude to a sequence of indelible memories. The sight of people all over the town on the way to the match ; the team lined up before kick off, in front of a packed crowd ; Stevie Crawford's opening goal ; the heroics of the entire team as they defended the lead, and their tenuous grasp on the match after Celtic equalised ; Gordon Dalziel's unlikely equaliser as the green and white ribbons were being tied on the old trophy ; the knuckle-biting tension of the penalty shootout, culminating in Scott Thomson's save of the Celtic's captain's penalty kick ; the look of disbelief on David Narey's face as it dawned on him that he had unexpectedly won a final winner's medal at the end of a long and highly decorated career ; and the sight of Gordon Dalziel, the Raith Rovers captain, being presented with the Scottish League Cup. The handful of Raith Rovers supporters in the official areas of the Main Stand were gifted an additional memory to moisten the eyes and bring a lump to the throat ; the view of 10,000 celebrating Raith Rovers supporters in the stand opposite.

Those Rovers supporters may have been outnumbered 3 to 1 by Celtic fans, but the underdogs were willed on by tens of thousands more, who watched over the game from another place.

In the moment of the penalty save, and in the celebrations and ceremonies immediately afterwards, there were other memories, of those not there to witness the joyous scenes. Fathers and mothers, brothers and sisters, uncles and aunts, grandfathers and grandmothers, cousins, friends and neighbours, all with a love of the club which had been passed down through generations of Kirkcaldy families, and who had not, in long or tragically short lives, had the privilege of seeing anything approaching the scenes witnessed by their successors that afternoon. Tears of regret and loss mixed with the tears of joy, an outpouring of emotion unimaginable to the dozen or so Linktown laddies who literally kicked it all off 125 years ago. This is their story, and of those who followed them.

A photograph of the club's first ever ground, or at least the backdrop to it. This is Peter Purves' school which stood back from Sands Brae, providing a rare open space in the teeming housing, commercial and industrial Linktown of Abbotshall. The youths of Linktown first kicked a football in the flat area in front of the school in 1883. Purves came to Kirkcaldy as a gardener in 1822, became an Elder of Bethelfield Church in Nicol Street, and was very well read and a man of letters. He was encouraged to open a Sunday School in 1831, and the building which overlooked the Firth of Forth was used for that purpose.

The Laird of Raith at the time of Rovers formation was Mr Ronald Crauford Munro Ferguson, born in 1860, MP for Leigh Burghs, who inherited the family estates at 8 years of age when his father died. Mr W. Ferguson acquired the lands of Raith from the Melville family in 1707 and his grand-nephew, Lieutenant-Colonel Robert Ferguson, got the estate of Novar, near Evanton in Ross-shire through his marriage to Miss Jean Munro of Novar.

1881 - St Brycedale Church opened ; John Barry, Ostlere & Co formed.
1883 - Raith Church on Links Street rebuilt ; Parcel Post was introduced to Kirkcaldy
1884 - Pathhead Hall opened

The "Presbyterie Booke of Kirkcaldy" records that in 1630 a man was summoned before the Presbytery on a charge of having played "futtball" on the Sabbath Day. Having, in spite of the rebuke by his minister, obstinately continued in his evil ways, the man was ordered to go to the local session and suffer censure.

In the same year, the minister of Kinghorn complained to the Presbytery that some of his parishioners played football on Sundays on the ground of Balmourto. It was ordained that one or two elders should visit the laird and request him to see that "no such thing be done in time coming."

To the despair and delight of their successors, Langtonians continued down the centuries to hone their skills with boot and ball, until they could follow the example set by those to the west and south, and present their pastime as a spectator sport to fill the recently granted Saturday half holiday.

Football with a semblance of organisation first emerged in Kirkcaldy in 1880, three years before the birth of its most enduring practitioner. Before that, spectator sports were restricted to the cramped confines of the quoiting green, the cricket fields of Kirkcaldy and Dunnikier, and the rugby pitch. Kirkcaldy Rugby Club played at Newtown Park (hereafter referred to in its corrupted version, Newton), situated to the west of Nicol Street, between what are now Ava Street and Munro Street, running towards Novar Crescent. In 1880, however, rugby was regarded by the bulk of the town's population as "a toff's game" and far from a mass participation or spectator sport.

The round ball game was enthusiastically practiced by the town's youngsters on the sands and on grassy parklands, but it was not until 1880, from an example shown in West Fife, that Kirkcaldy Wanderers Football Club was formed

After a few desultory kick-abouts in the evenings, the Wanderers club was properly constituted at a meeting held in the People's Club and Institute, and Joe Turner was elected their first captain. He had

previously played for the Hanover Club in Edinburgh and, like several of his team-mates, worked for A. Beveridge, Printers, where he was a bookbinder.. His vice captain was James Pollock, a very popular and learned young man who had a local reputation as a humorous character vocalist and actor, who brought with him his workmates from A. McIntosh, Cabinetmakers.

Turner was a real enthusiast for the game, and played at centre forward and in other positions for Wanderers over five seasons, as well as acting in various official capacities, including the vital role of secretary. Marriage (on the occasion of which the Club presented him with a handsome marble clock) finished his playing career, but he acted as match secretary for another seven years. Joseph Turner was the father of association football in Kirkcaldy.

Councillor Robert Stark, who for many years carried on a licensed business at the West Bridge, generously placed a grazing field leased by him (from the Laird of Raith) on Callochy Brae at the disposal of the Wanderers, free of charge, and so in the spring of 1881 the pioneer club moved into the field now known throughout the football world as Stark's Park.

It would be recognisable today purely for its location. The ground was undulating - not unlike Thornton Hibs' Memorial Ground today - and there was a sudden and precipitous fall from the touchline to the entrance gate at the bottom (south east) corner. Many an unwary winger disappeared from view following a robust challenge in that part of the pitch.

Provost Munro Ferguson became a patron of the club in 1882, along with Mr Wemyss of Wemyss Castle, Charles Bond, and Bailie Hendry. Season 1883-84 saw a very rapid development of football in Kirkcaldy, thanks in the main to the activities of the Wanderers over the previous two years.

1883 opened with news in the "Fife Free Press and Kirkcaldy Guardian" that a Dock and Harbour was proposed for Seafield, the land being owned by the Raith Estate. "For many generations the Raith family and Kirkcaldy have been closely connected, and the interesting event of last week is a measure of the friendly connection which still exists. The present proprietor, who has already made himself popular, is likely to bulk largely in our future history."

Indeed on the Wednesday evening, it was reported that "servants of the Raith Estate, and a number of ladies and gentlemen of Kirkcaldy, were entertained to a supper in the large granary at Raith." Within the year, Kirkcaldy's Provost would have a football club named after his estate and lairdship.

New Year's entertainment, in the sporting sense, seems to have been confined to "an interesting quoiting match", which took place on New Year's Day "in Stark's quoiting ground, West Bridge, between Henry Hutchison, Gallatown, and John Campbell, Kirkcaldy, for £5 a side." Hutchison won 61-52

Wanderers did not play exclusively at

Stark's Park, however. On 28th April they staged a match between 1st and 2nd Elevens, billed for "Southerton Park, head of Newton. Admission 1d. Kick off at 3.30. A full turn out of members requested." Shortly afterwards, the cricket season got underway, with Kirkcaldy playing their matches at Newton Park and, like their football counterparts, they charged 1d admission.

A local newspaper editorial bemoaned the state of Sands Road ; "in the absence of a public park, would a little bit of money not keep 'Neptune at bay' and lay out some public land for the people to roam - in the absence of a millionaire such as enjoyed by Dunfermline." Round about that time, a group of young men from the Links area of the town started kicking a ball about Sands Brae, in the area behind Peter Purvis's school on Links Street.

Kirkcaldy was a growing town, with booming industry. The Fife Free Press reported that in 1882, the value of floorcloths (linoleum) exported from Kirkcaldy was £546,375, an increase of 53% since 1878. To put that figure into modern context, the same newspaper advertised a "GRAND FOOTBALL MATCH. Wanderers v Rossend, Burntisland will take place at Stark's Park, West Bridge, on Saturday, kick off 4pm. Admission 2d, Ladies Free."

Comparing the 2d admission charge in 1883, to the £12 asked in 2005 (a 1680-fold increase) the current value of Kirkcaldy's linoleum exports in 1883 would be nearly £918 million. That was just the exports, and the linen trade was even larger. The town's landscape was dominated by factory chimneys, and in the absence of public transport, the workers lived nearby, cramped into two storey terraced houses which rang along the coast from the Tiel Burn, across the Den Burn, and up the Path to Pathhead. The railway was built where it was in 1847 because that was the northern edge of the town, hence the town's nickname.

The game soon caught on in the Lang Toun, and junior and juvenile clubs sprang up, particularly in the western part of the town. They had an uncertain and precarious existence, forever searching for players and a playing surface. Once they had scraped up enough funds to purchase a coveted football, they either practiced on very rough ground, or on the Sands when the tide was out. Players were more likely to be blinded by the wind-blown sand than the brilliance of the football skills on show. A farmer's stubble field was held to be superior accommodation, but provided as much security of tenure as the tidal sands. Most of these teams had very brief existences, and only one has survived.

The Kirkcaldy Times of Wednesday 19th December 1883 made its first mention of a name that was to become familiar. "Football - a match was played on Saturday in Mr Kinninmonth's park between the 1st West End Rangers and the 1st Raith Rovers. Rangers 5 goals Rovers nothing." The ground was also known as "The Skating Pond", and a return match was played at Rovers' pitch near Windygates Farm, in the approximate area of the present day golf clubhouse at Balwearie.

Rovers sprung from very modest beginnings. In 1883, a number of youths from the Links area, impressed by the example of Kirkcaldy Wanderers. desired to move on from their kick-abouts on Sands Brae with a bundle of rags and paper bound with string.

Legend has it that a football was found by one of them in the branches of a tree, when he was searching for birds' eggs. Given the youth of the club's founders, and the publication of their Illysian genesis during their lifetime, there may be some substance to this romantic tale.

Prominent amongst them were Jimmy and Willie Pringle, whose mother kept a little shop at the top of Hendry's Wynd, opposite the old Music Hall, the site of which is now occupied by the Raith Church building. Jimmy and Davie Tod were also in the group, and they asked their father to purchase a football.

Mr Tod pointed out that it would be better if all members of the group contributed a share of the cost. James Tod senior's guidance benefitted the Rovers for many more years, and his son was secretary/director of the club when they reached the Scottish Cup Final in 1913.

The youngsters' first formal meeting was convened at the Linktown Pottery kiln, the principal point of discussion being the name by which they were to be known. Rovers was chosen because no other local club had that appellation ; they added the name of the local landowner in the hope of gaining his patronage, which would give the club additional standing in a deferential community, and there was also the prospect of an annual donation from its well-heeled patron.

The new football was kicked about on the harrow strip of foreshore behind Peter Purvis' School (when the tide was in) and on the sands (when the tide was out). Four stout pieces of wood were used as goalposts, and the Tod brothers obtained a couple of lengths of web from their father's girth factory to stretch between the posts to take the place of crossbars, which were virtually unheard of even in senior football. Most clubs, including Wanderers, used tape between the tops of their posts.

Their burgeoning ambitions required a better pitch than the open field in the Tiel Valley, and they secured the use of a field at the old clay hole behind the railway, which was afterwards converted into a refuse depot, and is now the site of the handsome row of houses in Balwearie Road. One of the first residents in those houses was the aforementioned Mr James Tod and several subsequent club directors were amongst the

Robert Stark was born in Mid Calder in 1828 and moved to Kirkcaldy to became a ropemaker, conducting his business from his offices at 155 High Street. In due course, he was licensee of the "People's House" at the corner of Links Street and Bridge Street. He and his family, sons Andrew (also a ropemaker), Robert (a clerk in the pottery works) and two daughters lived next door what became Stark's Bar, at 326 Links Street.

He was elected to Kirkcaldy Town Council in November 1879, at the same time as Henry Morton Barnet (ironmonger) and John Barnet (upholsterer).

He was on the Corn Exchange and Slaughter Houses committees, and among his colleagues were Provost Swan, Bailies Hendry, Barnet, Dowie and Beveridge, councillors Lockhart, Stocks, Westwater, Young, Douglas, Nairn, Yule, Davidson, Hutchison, Shepherd, Wishart, Mitchell, Hunter, Pratt, Gourlay, Herd and Ramsay.

He served as a councillor until resigning, through ill health, on 4th March 1889. Andrew Nicol, a flesher, was elected to replace him on the council, defeating Andrew Beattie, a Linktown draper, and James Scott, grocer.

He lived a further 21 years, outliving his wife, a son and a daughter

early house owners.

Rovers beat West End Rangers 2-1 in a return fixture on the latter's ground on 16th February 1884, and despite indifferent results in local competitions and friendly matches, the ambition of those young men was undimmed. Led by secretary Bob Donaldson, they approached the Laird of Raith's factor, with some trepidation, to enquire about leasing a pitch at Robbie's Park. The factor's house was well known to them in their playing around Linktown, as it was located in Mill Street, beneath the steep slope to the Wanderers' ground on Councillor Stark's park (and later used as the offices for Sievewright's dairy).

They were well received, and returned jubilant from having secured a pitch for four months of the year, for a very reasonable rent.

Their first match at Robbie's Park was on 29th March 1884, when they "unexpectedly" beat Whitebank Engineers, a team made up from the "black squad" of Key's engineering works, 2-0. This semi-enclosure allowed them to charge admission money, initially 1d, and their first gate amounted to 3s 9d (in other words 45 people paid to watch).

The money was collected by a club official who stood by the wicket gate on Boglily Road. Having emptied his pockets, he alternately put one penny in his right pocket, muttering "a penny for the Rovers" and the next one in his left pocket, with the words "a penny for the [opponents]".   Sometimes the sequence was disturbed by conversation : it was long rumoured that Rovers were always careful to put a right-hander on the gate !

Around that time, Wanderers, taking their responsibilities as Kirkcaldy's senior club very seriously, introduced a Badge competition for Juvenile clubs.   This was keenly anticipated by the following clubs who entered the draw : Our Boys, Wemyss v St Brycedale ; St Clair Dysart v Kirkcaldy Rangers ; Raith Rovers v Thistle, Kirkcaldy. Kirkcaldy Albion were given a bye.

The knock-out competition prompted other clubs to form, and join the contest in later years. These included Pathhead United, Ramblers, Union, Fern, Blackburn and Star. It is quite possible that all of the ties were played at Wanderers ground at Stark's Park, which was certainly the venue for the last tie of the first round, on 25th October 1884, when Thistle beat Raith Rovers 2-1. Starting as generations of disappointed fans would ruefully insist they meant to carry on, Rovers lost their first ever cup tie.

Kirkcaldy Rangers were playing their home matches at Newton Park, used by Kirkcaldy Cricket Club during the summer months. There they beat Rovers 3-0. On the same afternoon, the second elevens met on Rovers ground, Rangers winning 9 (plus 3 disputed goals) to nil.

A few weeks later, Rovers' second eleven were at home to their Kirkcaldy Albion counterparts "at Bogie", and lost 7 (plus 2 disputed goals) to nil.   There was ample consolation the following week, the clash of

the first teams ending 1-0 to Rovers.

Fixtures were being fulfilled on a weekly basis, and on 6th December 1884 they beat Wanderers' third team 4-0 at Robbie's Park.   Despite being a man short against Townsend Swifts at home, they won 4-3.

As the popularity of football spread throughout the burgh and the wider district, more teams appeared.   Raith Rovers started 1885 with matches against 2nd Blues of Wemyss, and Randolph Rangers from Gallatown (the matches won 4-1 and 3-2 respectively).   Abden, Shield, Caledonian, Fitzroy (the latter from Dysart) and Denburn Rovers from Pathhead all appeared.

For two of Kirkcaldy's juvenile clubs, all attention was focused on the final of Wanderers' badge competition, as anticipated in the Fifeshire Advertiser of 7th February 1885 :

"The Kirkcaldy Wanderers Football Club have presented a set of silver badges for the winners in a competition among the junior clubs in Kirkcaldy district. The badges, which have been made by J & J Preston of Birmingham, are in the form of a Maltese cross, with an enamelled centre, bearing the motto "Labore e honore" and on the back the initials of the Wanderers club and the date ["K.W.F.C.J.C. 1885"].   The Albion and the Thistle Clubs play off the final tie on the 21st inst.   The badges are on view at the shop of Mr John Bryson, bookseller."

While Albion and Thistle were looking forward to their Badge final, Rovers were winning 5-0 against Denburn at Dunnikier Park, and the second eleven match between the clubs ended 15-0 in favour of Rovers.   The first eleven beat The Rose from Burntisland at home in a "rough game". Rovers could clearly look after themselves, as their secretary's report of the match against Union shows : "after a rough and well contested game, resulted in a win for the Rovers by 1 goal and 1 dispute to 1 goal." A report sent in by the Union says the match was a draw, and that the "Rovers play was rough." Both club secretaries filed reports on that particular fixture ; sometimes neither did, and the result was lost for posterity.   Results in newspapers depended on Secretaries filing them (on time).

Rovers visited Newton Park on 12th September 1885, and their second eleven beat Kirkcaldy's third team 3-0, with the following team : T, Laing ; W. Clark, R. Chalmers ; A. Heron, R. Donaldson ; D. Galloway, J. Litster, J. Russell, J. Brown, A. Holborn, A. Elder.

Those names, and the first elevens which began to be reported in the local papers from the start of season 1885/86, allow us to track down the men (or more accurately the boys) who formed Raith Rovers, A search of the 1881 and 1891 censuses indicates the addresses, and ages, of the club's founding fathers in 1883. Two main features emerge ; how young they were, and how close together they lived.

Rovers won the second, third and fourth competitions of the Kirkcaldy Junior

Cup, and the increasingly competitive nature of local football can be discovered by the following excerpt from the Kirkcaldy Mail newspaper on 3rd November 1885 :

"A correspondent complains of the conduct of some of the members of a football club at a match on Saturday, who booed their opponents out on the field. Such conduct must be exceptional, and ought to be left for political meetings."

The Fife Free Press summarised the state of football in the Lang Toun in their edition of September 19th 1885. "That the game of football has become thoroughly popularised in the Lang Toun, is not far to seek. The enthusiasm displayed last season, and the excellent arrangements for the forthcoming season speaks volumes for itself. The association game, inaugurated some time ago by the Kirkcaldy Wanderers, has now developed itself so much that we have nearly a score of promising young clubs. Handicapped to a certain extent by the want of a public park or recreation ground, several of our more ardent players have had to adjourn to the beach   The step taken by the Kirkcaldy Wanderers and the Kirkcaldy Rugby Clubs in amalgamating with a view of obtaining the Newton Park, is, I am sure, a step in the right direction. The combination will have the effect of increasing the interest in the game, and getting together a capital team. The success attending the competition for the silver badges for the junior clubs ought to warrant a further continuance of the same, or what would be more acceptable in these full times, a Charity Cup Competition might be got us, the "gates" derived from the same being handed over for some charitable object."

Amongst the junior teams, Raith Rovers were beginning to establish a reputation. Early in 1885/86, they defeated Royal Albert 1-0 in Dunfermline and beat Thistle 2-1 at Robbie's Park. Included in the Thistle team were two future stalwarts of the Rovers, William Hazels, a labourer who lived at 10 Bute Wynd, and William Dall, a floorcloth printer, who lived further afield, at 7 Elgin Cottages, Nairn Street.

As 1885 drew to a close, the expanding football scene in Kirkcaldy was making good use of the Laird of Raith's grazing ground at Robbie's Park. Both Raith Rovers and Kirkcaldy Star were using the flat, grassed land as their home pitches, and on November 14th 1885 it was reported that "The Albion open their new ground at Southerton today", signifying the marking-out of yet another pitch on Boglily Road.

The last Saturday of the year saw the established club in the town, Kirkcaldy FC, entertain the upwardly mobile Raith Rovers at Newton Park. "Since their defeat in the badge ties, the Rovers have made great improvements in their play, and with the addition of one or two of the Thistle in their ranks they have come well to the front among the junior teams in the district, and the fact that they have never been defeated this season yet, caused a good deal of interest to be taken in the game. Having beaten the

Albion, and drawn with Rangers, it was expected they would give the senior team a lot of trouble."   The "one or two" from Thistle actually amounted to four, Lyall, Russell, Nelson and Chalmers. No wonder Thistle's tackles were a little keener when they met their former colleagues in Rovers' colours.

The experience of the home side prevailed, and Kirkcaldy won 4-1. They had much more than local domination to be proud of.   At their annual soiree at the Assembly Rooms, Mr R.C. Lockhart, president of the Club, pointed to the great stimulus that they had given to sport in the district. There were no fewer than 23 football teams active in the area, many with second elevens, providing a level of regular athletic pursuit never seen before in Kirkcaldy.

With such a level of participation, came keen local rivalry.

In early February 1886, "Wanderer" in the Fife Free Press reported that "A meeting of the junior clubs in the town was held on Thursday evening in Morrison's Hall. About fifty members were present, representing 16 clubs. It was unanimously agreed to form a junior association, and the various office-bearers were appointed accordingly. The advantages accruing from such an association are too numerous to mention, and are so apparent to all interested in football that it is useless for me to refer to them. That the association will prove a great success, and be heartily supported by all the junior clubs, is the confident wish of Wanderer."

The teams represented were : Albion, Rovers, Union, Dunnikier, Fern, Royal Oak, Crown, Eastern, Kirkcaldy Star, Thistle, St Clair Blues, Blackburn, Parkhill, Abden, Ramblers, Ravenscraig Rangers. By the time the first round of the inaugural Kirkcaldy Junior Cup was drawn a fortnight later, five more clubs had joined, Rosslands (Kinghorn), Eclipse, Loughborough Swifts, Giffen Park (Dysart) and St Clair Star.

"On the motion of [the secretary of Raith Rovers] it was agreed to form an Association for Kirkcaldy, to include Dysart and Kinghorn. It was agreed that all members of junior clubs who have played in senior cup ties be debarred from membership, and also all members of senior clubs." The office bearers were : President, David Lonie, Albion ; Vice President James Snadden, Dunnikier, Treasurer ; John Litster, Raith Rovers, who proposed at the meeting that no protests with regard to ground or colours be entertained this season, given the clubs have had so short notice, and this was unanimously carried.

The need for a greater level of governance was illustrated the following week, when part of the large crowd "broke in" at the match between Albion and Rovers at

It was believed that Kirkcaldy Wanderers followed the example of Dunfermline Football Club, formed by John and Davie Brown, which inspired
Joseph Turner (pictured above in a Kirkcaldy Wanderers team photograph of 1883) to form a rival team in Kirkcaldy.

On April 27th 1885 Wanderers held their annual meeting at the Institute, and after presenting Mrs Stark with a beautiful silver epergne to acknowledge the help given to the club by her husband, Joe Turner reported on the conditions under which the Wanderers could amalgamate with the Kirkcaldy Rugby Club. Wanderers had their eyes on Newton Park, and the proposal won a majority of the club's 63 members.   The flatter, more centrally located Newton Park, was not only attractive to the town's senior football club, but it was also prime building land.   In due course, the playing pitches were built upon, the Rugby and Cricket clubs relocated, but the football club could not find a suitable alternative, and eventually folded, being supplanted in the town's affections by their successors as tenants of Stark's Park. Had Wanderers remained in the Links in 1884, the world of football would likely never have heard of Raith Rovers, and the town would have been represented by Kirkcaldy FC. The first meeting of the combined club took place in Morrison's Hall on 27th August, and it was agreed that the teams of both codes would play under the name "Kirkcaldy".

The earliest known photograph of Raith Rovers was taken in 1887, four years after the club's formation. In 1896 an Ordnance Survey map of Linktown was published. Together with the 1881 and 1891 Census returns, we can see how close together the original Raith Rovers' lived - and how young they were in 1883.

The map also shows the location of the club's first ever "playing field", in front of Peter Purves' school (1). Their latest resting place, Stark's Park, is marked (2).

Among those early pioneers who are not in the picture is Robert Donaldson, who was 14 years old in 1883, about to start work as a block cutter, and who lived at 153 Links Street (40). The Tod brothers, Jimmy and Davie, were 10 and 13 respectively, and lived at 154 Links Street (12)

Those pictured in 1887 (aged below in 1883), standing at the back were
Alex Ness, not identified in the 1881 or 1891 Census returns
(3) William Jarvis, 15 years old, a Manufacturer's Clerk who lived at 114 Links Street with his widowed mother, who was a herring net worker in a factory.
(32) Jimmy Russell, 15 years old, Glednie Cottage, 14 Bute Wynd, his father a sack sewer
Charlie Ramsay, not identified in the 1881 or 1891 Census returns
(31) Peter Hazel, 15 years old, Glednie House, 12 Bute Wynd., a winder at a spinning mill.
(4) Peter Lyle, 15 years old, 117 Links Street, his father a cabinet maker
Sitting in the middle row were
(15) Tom Nelson, a 15 year old pottery boy who lived at 111 Links Street
(6) Alex Holburn, 15 years old, lived at 13 Gas Wynd, a jigarman's boy in the pottery
(19) John Litster, 15 years old, lived at 15 Gas Wynd, his father a clay potter
(7) David Clark, 15 years old, a potter painter and gilder who lived at 3 Pottery Road
(8) Tom Chalmers, 13 years old, 1 Hendrie's Wynd, his father a linen warehouseman
On either side of the Kirkcaldy Junior Cup were
(3) David Jarvis, 14 year old brother of William, an apprentice in a linen factory
Bill Clark, not identified in the 1881 or 1891 Census returns
         Other players from the early years of the club who lived locally included :
(9) Andrew Hepburn, 17 years old, who lived in Muckerie's Land in Gas Wynd
(10) David Hepburn, 17 years old, a pottery worker who lived at 103 Links Street
(11) William Henderson, 9 years old in 1883, lived at 124 Links Street, his father a sailor
(13) David Cairns, 18 years old, a housewright who lived at 88 Links Street
(13) John Cairns, 10 year old younger brother of David, his father a flaxdresser
(14) David Neilson, 13 years old, father a blacksmith who lived at 3 Hendrie's Wynd
(14) James Neilson, 10 year old younger borther of David, who went on to run Neilson's cycle factory in Hendrie's Wynd, the area in front of it being named Neilson's square
(15) Willie Dall, 11 years old in 1883, lived with his uncle, William Chalmers, a flax yard dyer, at 140 Links Street. In the 1891 Census, the 19 year old Dall was listed as a journeyman upholsterer.
(16) John Lambert -there were two on Links Street at the time of the 1881 Census. The 10 year old in 1883 lived at 162 Links Street with his widowed mother, who ran a grocery shop. A 12 year old of the same name lived at 208 Links Street (17), his father was a slater.

(18) Robert Stark, a 55 year old ropemaker master, lived at 326 Links Street, and owned the licensed premises at 328.

(20) David Galloway, 14 years old, 136 Links Street, his father a hemp spinning mill manager

(21) Andrew Elder, 14 years old, lived at Back of Pottery (near Watery Wynd), his father a pottery worker

(22) Duncan Menzies, 7 years old, lived at 245 Links Street, his 33 year old father a linen powerloom tender

(23) Alex Hall, lived at Palm Villa, between 111 and 113 Links Street

(24) John Cameron, 10 years old, lived at 113 Links Street, his father a plasterer

(25) Henry Clunie, 11 years old, lived at 150 Links Street, his father a floorcloth printer

(26) David Stewart, 7 years old, lived at 28 Buchanan Street

(27) John Eckford, 7 years old, 69 Links Street, a flax mill worker by the time of 1891 Census

(28) Charlie Moodie, lived at 130 Links Street

(29) James Mackie, lived at 118 Links Street

In the years which followed, future players Andrew Baxter, Andrew Grieve, Andrew Marshall, Robert Robertson and Alex Oag all lived on Links Street ; and Henry Simpson lived on Sands Road.

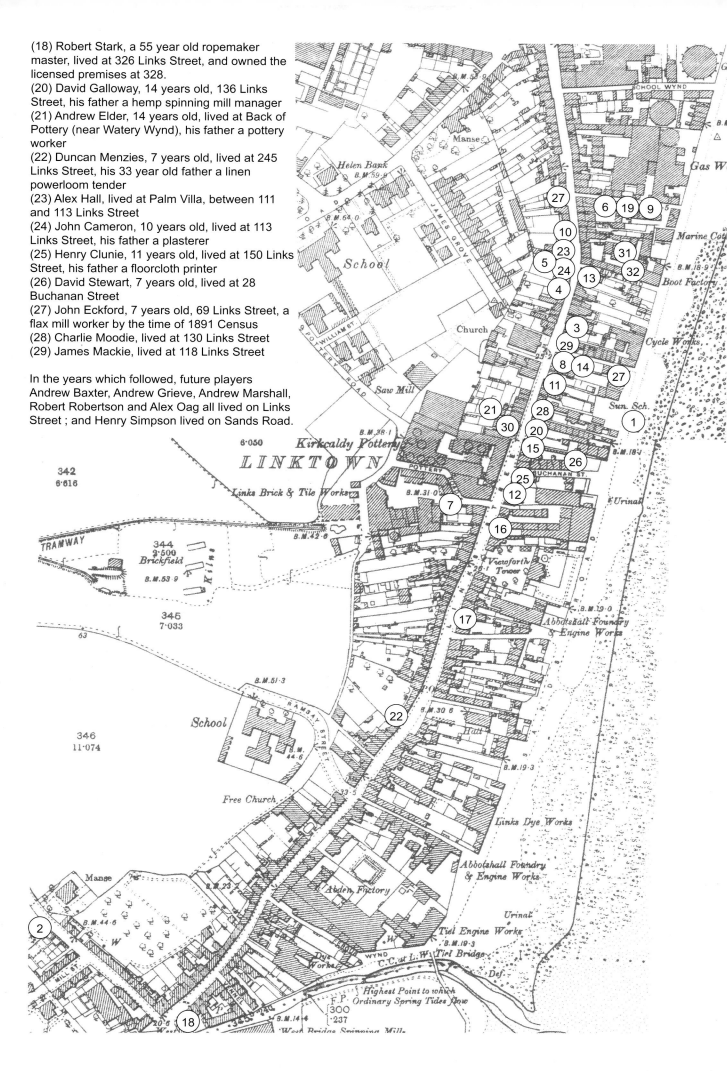

Newton Park was initially a large, open area, which could accommodate simultaneous games on adjoining pitches.

Shortly after moving to the ground, the Football Club soon discovered that the attention of spectators was only transferred to the round ball game when the egg-chasers were having their half-time break.

The Association team opened their season on 12 September 1885 with a home match against Lochleven Rangers, while the second eleven met the Albion at Bogie.

Matches between Rovers and Union, who played at Kinninmonth's Park, seemed to be the most unruly of the annual fixture list.

In November 1885, it was reported that "owing to (Union's) rough playing pugilistic inclinations, the Rovers left the field after seventeen minutes play."

The Union Secretary wrote to the Fifeshire Advertiser the following week blaming Raith Rovers, who won the match 1-0 with a first minute goal.

1886 - Kirkcaldy Chamber of Commerce was revived in March ; Opening of YMCA 1887 - Caledonian Works on Forth Avenue sold to John Barry, Ostlere & Co

At the meeting of the Kirkcaldy Junior FA at the People's Club & Institute on 15th December 1886, the following select team was selected to meet Edinburgh club Dalry Albert on Christmas Day.

Nicol (Royal Oak), W, Clark (Rovers), Adamson (Dunnikier) ; Russell, captain (Rovers), Ramsay (Albion), Jarvis (Rovers) ; left Chalmers & Clark (both Rovers), centre Ritchie (Albion) ; right Henderson (Union), Nelson (Rovers).

The match was played on the Rovers' ground at Robbie's Park, and ended in a 7-2 victory for the visitors.

Robbie's Park. "Wanderer" suggested they should follow the lead of Kirkcaldy FC and have a rope round the field.

In early March 1886, "Wanderer" reported in the Fife Free Press : "It is pleasing to note that Sir George Campbell, MP, has become a patron of the Junior Football Association. Surely some of our local gentlemen will follow his example and allow their names to be put on the patron list. Such conduct would only tend to encourage our youthful players. If such was to be the case all impediments to the procuring of a cup would be overcome and might, I presume, that in the course of a few years a splendid park might follow suit. It is an undeniable fact that all lovers of the game have experienced the greatest difficulty in securing a place in which to play. This is all the more to be regretted seeing that football has become more and more the popular game in Scotland."

The MP made a donation towards the cost of a trophy, as did Mr H C Darney, Braehead House, Kinghorn, who consented to become honorary president of the Junior F.A.

On 30th March, the new Junior Association selected a team, and reserves, to play Kirkcaldy FC, although it was noted that several of the best players would be otherwise deployed that afternoon, Raith Rovers visiting Kirkcaldy Rangers at Stark's Park. The 4-1 defeat was a surprise to Rovers, with Litster off form in attack, and the scoreline would have been worse but for an heroic performance by Peter Lyall in goal. 500 watched the other match at Newton Park, which Kirkcaldy won 8-1.

Towards the end of March, the following Raith Rovers team lined up for the much-anticipated semi final of the Kirkcaldy Junior Cup, against Albion at neutral Newton Park : G. Chapman ; W. Clark, D. Jarvis ; J.Russell, W.Jarvis ; (right wing) T. Nelson, A. Holburn ; (left wing) T. Chalmers, D. Clark ; (centre) J. Norval, J. Litster. Six forwards were the norm in the early years of the game.

George Chapman had taken over from Peter Lyall in goal, Alex Holburn and Peter Hazells were in competition for a midfield place, otherwise it was a settled side.

Despite torrential rain, the match attracted record receipts for a football attendance in Kirkcaldy. Albion, wearing red and blue, were 2-0 ahead at half time and scored another three goals after the interval. Some spectators encroached on the field ; the referee blew his whistle to urge them off, and several of the players thought it was time and ran off the field, but were soon brought back. The Rovers, however, refused to start again, and the referee awarded the match to the Albion (5-0).

Rovers lodged a protest, which was upheld by the Kirkcaldy Junior Football Association, on the grounds of the pitch being unfit for play. They limbered up for the replay with a Wednesday evening friendly match at Kirkcaldy FC on the same ground, which ended in a 2-2 draw. Albion won the replayed match 1-0, and won the Final

against Union by 4-1 in front of an attendance of over 1,000. There was no presentation ceremony, however, as the trophy had not yet been purchased by the Kirkcaldy Junior FA. The Association was in funds, its annual income of £21 4s 10d comfortably exceeding expenditure of £10 4d 1/2d.

The replayed semi final between Albion and Rovers saw two great individual performances, from Jimmy Russell, the Rovers accomplished half-back and Peter Connolly, right back of the Albion. He was a brilliant player either at centre forward or back. A watchmaker to trade, he secured a good job at Woolwich Arsenal and was a stalwart in the early games of the Arsenal Football Club, formed by another early pioneer of Kirkcaldy football, David Danskin. Although both men played for several Kirkcaldy clubs, Raith Rovers was not one of them.

The season finished with a Junior five-a-sides tournament at Stark's Park in late May. The Raith Rovers quintet beat Albion Athletics in the first round but lost to Strathforth in the second. The competition was won by Albion Strollers.

The close season was enlivened by an exchange of letters in the town's newspapers disputing who was the best Junior side in Kirkcaldy. The Albion president wrote : "It is a well known fact that the reason why the Rovers have been so strong this season is that they have been strengthened by the pick of another west end club."

Footballers spent the summer months at local athletics meetings, and at five-a-side competitions. Raith Rovers, for instance, played in Dysart Horticultural Society's 5-a-sides at Stark's Park in late August 1886. They were beaten by the appropriately named Rose in the semi finals. The full eleven returned to the Callochy Brae pitch a week later, to play an away match with Union. The game went to pre-match expectations, Rovers winning 4-1.

The growing confidence, and organisation, of the club was illustrated by a notice printed on the front page of the Fife Free Press on Saturday August 21st 1886.

FOOTBALL
A GENERAL MEETING of the RAITH ROVERS FOOTBALL CLUB will be held in Morrison's Hall on MONDAY first, at 7.30pm. New Members Enrolled.

By the start of 1886/87, some of the teams had moved grounds. Union took up residence at Rangers' old ground at Councillor Stark's Park, having previously shared Robbie's Park with Rovers, Thistle and occasionally Albion ; Albion had finished the previous season at Milton Road Park, which they shared with Blackburn. Dunnikier played at Dunnikier Park and Ravenscraig Rangers at Hutchison's Park,

Teams, players and grounds came around with remarkable frequency. It was later recalled that "nearly every wynd in the Links had its football 'club', and as in those days there were no hard binding agreements, and each player was practically a law unto himself, the fancy dress matches which later came into vogue were not a patch on the fearful and wonderful appearance of some of the young teams.

"Clubs vied as to which would have the most "rory" and glaring colours of jersey, and as the players shifted about perpetually from one club to another the conglomeration of colours when two rival teams met was something to remember ! One full back in red, white and blue stripes would be partnered by another in a harlequin-looking quartered-body of orange and green.

"One half back, with his ordinary trousers suspended by a precariously small number of buttons, would be partnered by another whose thick worsted drawers were secured by a muffler that would persist in coming untied. Almost every one wore tackety boots that left their mark on tender shins, and to guard against this it was not uncommon to see players, whose finances did not run the length of proper shin-guards, with their legs swathed in several thicknesses of "packsheet"."

Gloves for goalkeepers were unknown ; they rarely had time to catch the ball before being barged over their goal line by an on-rushing forward. The best goalkeepers were the ones who could punch the ball furthest. Rovers were adept at the tactic of charging the goalkeeper. Their two wingers, Tommy Nelson and Tommy Chalmers, excelled in crossing the ball into the goal-area, where the muscular Johnny Litster would engage with the hapless goalkeeper.

Tam Nicol, the lanky Albion goalkeeper, was ready for this tactic in one match against the Rovers. Nelson dropped a cross right in front of the goalkeeper, and the Rovers' centre forward bore down. Nicol ignored the ball, stooped down, lifted Litster on his shoulders and, walking behind the goal to the wire that separated the pitches at Robbie's Park, dropped him none too gently on top of the wire !

The major change to the team was the introduction of George 'Dod' Ramsay at centre forward. Holburn and Hazells were both accommodated, Norval moving on to pastures new.

On October 23rd, the Fife Free press reported : Through the kindness and courtesy of their secretary I have just had forward to me an admission ticket and card of fixtures for the Raith Rovers, for which allow me to return my warmest thanks. It is pleasing to note that this enterprising and most promising junior club has successfully negotiated for and obtained a piece of Robbie's Park for their private use all the year round. They enter upon their new ground upon the 11th November. This will be most advantageous, both from a financial point of view, and for the comfort of players and spectators alike. The match card is well arranged, and for the first eleven eight events have been arranged. The clubs they are to meet are Dunnikier,

Caroline (Granton), Claremount Park (Edinburgh), Thistle (Kirkcaldy), Albion (Kirkcaldy), Rose (Burntisland), Vale of Eden (Cupar), Union (Kirkcaldy), Bridgend Athletics (Perth), Albert (Dalry, Edinburgh), Heather Bell (Leith), Woodburn (Edinburgh) and St Vincent (Edinburgh) Twenty-seven events are also arranged for the second eleven, the most of our local junior clubs having to be met by them. Altogether, the Rovers are to be congratulated on the excellent programme provided, and in the coming season I only hope they may sustain their well-known reputation."

The new ground was positioned in what is now Beveridge Park, on the site now occupied by the Park gardener's house and a portion of the ornamental gardens, near the corner of Boglily Road and Southerton Road. The new pitch was opened with a match against Kirkcaldy Albion, for the benefit of the widows and families of two Kirkcaldy men, Robert Rodger and John Traill, killed in Edinburgh on 2nd November, by the falling of a gable at Royston Terrace Rovers won 5-2 and £6 was expected to be handed over to the fund.

The first rounds of both cup competitions saw Rovers record huge victories. Thistle were beaten 11-0 in the Kirkcaldy Junior Cup, while the club's debut in the Scottish Junior Cup, impressively arranged within a couple of months of the national association being formed, resulted in a 9-1 victory over Edinburgh club St Clair.

The visitors decided to drown their sorrows after the match, and made a tour of the Lang Toun's hostelries. Thus fortified, they tore off the window shutter of one shop and heaved it over the wall of the Whytehouse Grounds, aimed at the "craw trees". Other shops were raided and their goods carried off, but Police Sergeant John Rhynd was soon on their track and several of the Edinburgh footballers found themselves in the cells in Tolbooth Street. They then spent a week in Cupar jail. Suitably warned, another Edinburgh club learned from this and came prepared for the second round - Woodburn beat Rovers 7-0 at Robbie's Park..

The result came as a surprise in Kirkcaldy, as the following week's Fife Free Press exclaimed : "Is it possible ? Something must have been far wrong. The Woodburn are undoubtedly a smart set of fellows, but their tactics are, to say the least of it, very questionable. There is a tendency to roughness, and I certainly do not like to see an Umpire coaching on his team in the manner the Edinburgh representative was doing." Rovers lodged a protest on the grounds of rough play, to no avail. The visitors were, in fact, the leading Junior team in Edinburgh, and a regular supplier of players to senior clubs on both sides of the border. They were a big, strapping team, and in outside right Willie Cox, later of Hibs, possessed an irresistible force. Rovers principal tactic, in response, was for Tommy Nelson, the outside right, to run single-handedly against the Woodburn defence, but

GEORGE RAMSAY

On January 16th 1886, Kirkcaldy seconds drew 1-1 with Rovers at Robbie's Park - according to the Kirkcaldy Times. The Fife Free Press, however, reported a 2-1 victory for the visitors, Raith's first defeat of the season on their own ground.
A week later, the match between Albion and Rovers, staged for the benefit of a Raith player who was unwell (and therefore off work, with no money coming into his house), was abandoned. Albion led 1-0 at half time, but Johnny Litster equalised, and "scored" again. After disputing the matter for a considerable time, the teams left the field after only 65 minutes of play.

A 3-3 draw between Rovers and Thistle "contrary to the expectations of the wearers of the blue and white", brought this censure from a local journalist early in 1886 : "The Thistle should not be so rough in their play, while the Rovers should study the rules of etiquette."
The sporting ethos did not stretch to Loughborough Swifts, who found themselves 4-1 down to the Rovers in short time at Veitch's Park, Loughborough Road, which they shared with St Clair Star. "After playing about half-an-hour ...., the Swifts declined to play any longer, having got enough of the Rovers, and evidently wishing to keep down their goal register."
The Kirkcaldy Times suggested that there had been a "dispute about an offside goal"

The match against St Leonards of Cowdenbeath kicked off at 5pm (it was billed for 4.15) owing to the late arrival of the visitors. Kirkcaldy Albion, for long handicapped by the lack of a suitable pitch, had secured the tenancy of a field in the upper reaches of Robbie's Park.

They and Rovers were joined in the vicinity by Ramblers, Thistle having moved to Milton Road Park. Meanwhile "The Rovers appeared in their new uniform, quarter-bodied jerseys, which looked very neat" The new strip inspired a 4-1 victory over Edinburgh club Blackford.

An enduring mystery in the history of Kirkcaldy football is the failure of Dysart to produce a prominent team. On October 1st 1887, Rovers were invited to open Blairhill Park, and bore few gifts in beating their hosts 14-0. A local journalist optimistically predicted : "I have no doubt, if the Dysart men keep together, they will come to be as good as the Rovers." Alas, the club's life was short and unspectacular, and it remains something of an anomaly that the ancient Saut Burgh, which has produced so many notable men in various walks of life, has signally failed to nurture any footballer of great note.

The Kirkcaldy Directory 1886/87, "containing the names of all householders in the extended burgh" with official and trade lists., published by John Bryson at the Advertiser Office, estimated the Burgh's population to be 26,000, the 1881 census having counted it as 23,306.

By Parish, this was broken down as Invertiel 1996, Abbotshall 4536, Kirkcaldy 5761, St James' 2762, Dysart (3rd Ward) 8251.

The Raith Rovers entry in the Directory noted President William Innes, Captain William Clark, Vice Captain David Clark, Treasurer William Jarvis Secretary - John Litster, 10 Factory Square,

the strong play of Gibson and Turner at full back was too much for him.

The result was Rovers heaviest defeat at Robbie's Park although there was some consolation in their conquerors advancing to the first ever Scottish Junior Cup Final, which they lost 3-1 to Fairfield at Argyle Park, Govan.

The following week a "miserable and discouraging attendance of spectators "watched Rovers lose to Burntisland Thistle at Robbie's Park. The Fife Free Press thought the small crowd would "teach them a lesson that footballers expect some return for their money paid at the gate" - an early lesson that spectators' loyalty is determined by recent results.

Rovers' dip in form following their exit from the Scottish Junior Cup was reflected in the Kirkcaldy Junior select team to play an Edinburgh select. Full back Clark and forward Litster were the only Rovers players picked, and Russell was the sole nominee for the reserve selection. In the event, Rovers were unrepresented as they had to replay their Cup semi final on the day of the fixture.

Quite often progress in the cup competition was as much due to advocacy in the committee room, as prowess on the pitch. On 24th February, at a meeting of the Kirkcaldy Junior Football Association, a protest by Union against Rovers was sustained, and the semi final tie was to be replayed.

"In the first half the Rovers, playing up the hill, scored 1 goal to the Union's nothing, and in the second half both teams scored 1 each. The Union disputed the last goal scored by the Rovers on the ground that the ball went over the bar, but the referee decided against them. The Union refused to continue the game, and a general melee ensued. During the game the Union players indulged in hacking and tripping. The referee, Mr D. Macrae, St Vincent, Edinburgh, decided the tie in favour of the Rovers by 2 goals to 1." W. Lynch, captain of Union, wrote to the Fifeshire Advertiser, denying rough play by his side, and he would have been heartened by the Advertiser's reporter who thought that the ball had gone over the bar.

The "general melee" involved a pitch invasion, with supporters of both clubs squaring up for a fight. Just as hostilities were about to start, Mr Stark junior released a young bull from the byre at the north end of Stark's Park. An eye witness recalled : "In an instant the crowd scattered in all directions, and as the bull trotted round, gathering speed and lowering its horns as it went, there was a wild stampede. Many made a bee-line for the dyke and dropped over into Pratt Street, many others scrambled headlong up the embankment to the railway, and in the shortest time on record the bovine invader was left in solitary possession of the field." Strangely, over the ensuing 120 years, Mr Stark's crowd control methods were not repeated.

The Kirkcaldy Junior Football

Association sustained Union's protest, and ordered the tie to be replayed. Rovers, in a fit of pique, withdrew their players from the Association team to play Edinburgh, to save them for the replayed tie, and watched with some glee as the Lang Toun select lost 4-0. Russell scored the only goal of the replayed match, refereed by Mr McFadden of Hibs. Union protested again, but an impatient Fife Free Press reported that "The Association have overthrown all petty objections and have rightly adhered to the decision given by the referee." The referee reported that Union had made no protest during or after the game.

The Final, against holders Kirkcaldy Albion, was keenly anticipated in the Lang Toun. It was played on March 26th at Newton Park. Albion had reached the final by beating Ravenscraig Rangers 4-0, Rosslands 8-0, and Dunnikier 10-2. Rovers were represented by Lyall, Jarvis, Clark, Hazells, Russell, Jarvis, Nelson, Holburn, Litster, Clark, Chalmers. Mr McFadden was the referee, and the Umpires came from Cowdenbeath, Messrs Dougray and Paterson.

The largest crowd ever seen for a football match in the district witnessed a poor game. Neilson Deuchars opened the scoring for Albion but Litster equalised before half time. Chalmers and Litster again gave Rovers the lead, but Barker and Sinclair scored for Albion, for the match to finish 3-3.

The replay, at the same venue the following week, saw Rovers win surprisingly comfortably, by 4-0. Their only change was Charlie Ramsay taking over from Peter Lyall in goal. The club's first ever trophy was celebrated in the following manner :
"The members of the Raith Rovers, along with a large number of friends, met in a social capacity on Saturday evening in the Anchor Tavern, and celebrated their victory in winning the Kirkcaldy Junior Association Cup. Mr Ness presided, and a happy evening was spent."

There was a double header for football fans at Robbie's Park on April 23rd. Rovers first eleven lost 2-1 to Dalry Albert, immediately followed by a 1-1 draw between the Second Eleven, and Newburgh. There was probably greater interest in the end of season match played against Wanderers, to benefit James Taylor, Rovers' groundsman who later became something of a legendary groundsman to Kirkcaldy Cricket Club over several decades when they played in Beveridge Park. Both teams were at full strength, and Peter Connelly, later to star for Woolwich Arsenal, scored two lovely goals ; but Rovers won 4-2, having led 3-0 at the interval. Another great Arsenal man, John McBean, scored an own goal. It was Rovers' first ever victory over the senior club.

The Fife Free Press announced on May 7th : "The Rovers are to have a great blow out on Friday night in the Public Buildings. The Junior Cup holders are pretty jubilant over their victory this year. Why not ? They are making every preparation to make the turn-out a regular "swell" affair. The programme is a long and varied one, and its get up is worthy of note., Several amusing illustrations relative to the dribbling code are very well done, but the cleverest bit of all is the representation of an infuriated bull chasing a crowd out of a field, designated "an amusing incident in our club's history." Its appearance no doubt will bring the memory of that eventful day in Stark's Park vividly before the minds of those who were present on that occasion."

To everyone's surprise, Rovers drew 2-2 with Norton Park the following afternoon. The energetic young men found the energy to participate in the Trades Band Sports senior 5-a-side competition, where they lost by 1 goal and 2 points to 2 points in the first round to Lochies No. 1, and many of the players participated in the club's first Grand Amateur Athletic Sports at Robbie's Park, on 18th and 25th June

It was the custom to enjoy end of season friendlies further afield, the results reflecting the extent of the festivities. Thus, on 21st May, Rovers' second eleven lost 1-0 to Newburgh at the Cricket Park, near Clunie bleachfield, while the first team made the long trip to Hydepark, Springburn in Glasgow, only to lose 3-1 to Campbellfield.

Complaints about the brief nature of the football close season are nothing new. On Saturday July 16th, Rovers played a team comprising former Kirkcaldy Rangers players at Stark's Park in a benefit match in aid of Mr W. Mackie "who has been ill for the last six months" Rovers won 6-2, in very hot conditions, but it was noted that Rangers could only muster 10 players for the first half, and nine for part of the second half. Following their general meeting of the members held in Burleigh Street Hall on Monday August 8th 1887 at 7.30pm – "full attendance appreciated" – Rovers opened the season on 20th August with a visit from St Bernards' second eleven, anticipated by the Fifeshire Advertiser in the following terms.

"During the recess the Rovers have not been idle. Their field has been greatly enhanced by the erection of a large pavilion, which will afford much needed comfort to both the visitors and the home team. The work has been executed by Mr David Clephane, Nicol Street, to the design of Mr Robert Graham, one of the members of the committee. The field is looking well just now, and Mr Litster has been busy in his attempts to provide some good sport to the lovers of the popular game."

Come the day of the match, disappointment : "The attendance was not so large as was anticipated, this being accounted for by other attractions, notably the Kirkcaldy Flower Show …" and St Bernards won 6-2.

Rovers faced St Leonards of Cowdenbeath in the first round of the Scottish Junior Cup, in a match billed as Kirkcaldy Cup winners v Cowdenbeath Cup winners. Rovers won 5-3, and had Ramsay in place of Lyall in goal, Adamson came in at full back with Dave Jarvis moving to centre forward, although Bill Henderson had spells in that

position at the start, and end, of the season.

Northern Western of Edinburgh were beaten 2-1 in the second round, prompting the influential "Scottish Umpire" newspaper to feature "the energetic secretary of the Raith Rovers." After complimenting the Rovers on their successful overthrow of the North Western, the notice goes on to say "Such a result, I am sure, must be indeed pleasing to Mr James H McLeod, who, in the capacity of secretary, has done much to raise the Rovers to their present position. Chiefly through his exertions, Robbie's Park has this season been enhanced by the erection of a large pavilion, which tends greatly to the comfort of the players. The team is exceedingly well-balanced this season by the inclusion of Henderson of the Union, in the centre, Litster being shifted to Holburn's place inside right, and Adamson, of the late Dunnikier, at back. The officials are of the right mettle., and so long as they are at the head of affairs the team is bound to prosper."

To emphasise the claim, the team beat Dysart 9-0 in a Kirkcaldy Junior Cup tie, followed by a much savoured 2-0 win over Albion, Dave Jarvis scoring both goals. The Fife Free Press intoned :

" The secret of the Rovers success is due to the fact that they have kept together. It is only a pity to think that such excellent players as Litster, Nelson, W. Jarvis, Russell and Hazels should not see their way to throw off the cover of juniordom and improve our senior team. Should they continue much longer in this state there will be a lurking suspicion that they are merely playing football for pecuniary gain, and not for the mere love of it."

The New Year's holiday fixtures brought two Glasgow clubs to Robbie's Park. On the Monday, Elderslie won 6-1 in a one sided match, partly attributable to David Clark and Tom Nelson being absent from the Rovers team. The following day saw another six goals conceded, to Roseburn, although Dave Jarvis scored three of Rovers four goals on a pitch covered with several inches of snow. The Glaswegians turned up a man short, and Sinclair of Albion made up their numbers.

Those results did not give much promise for the visit of Wishaw Thistle in the third round of the Scottish Junior Cup. The Secretary of the Scottish Junior Football Association, Mr AS McIntosh, refereed the fixture.

The fears of the home fans were confirmed as Wishaw took a 3-1 half time lead, but Nelson and Dave Jarvis scored in the second half. Unfortunately, Wishaw scored another goal to win the tie 4-3. Once again, Rovers' Junior Cup conquerors advanced to the final, Wishaw Thistle beating Maryhill 3-1 at Ibrox. Now known simply as Wishaw, the Lanarkshire club are the oldest surviving winners of the national trophy. The following week, old rivals Albion were visited across the ropes at Robbie's Park, but the 1-1 draw was devoid of recent acrimony. The Fife Free Press concluded : "One

CHARLIE RAMSAY
Goalkeepers wore the same jerseys as their outfield team-mates and were usually distinguished by their bunnet.

The widening interest in the sport was illustrated by an advert in the Kirkcaldy Times on 3rd November 1886. Football followers could purchase the special football edition of the Evening Dispatch every Saturday night by the last train, at James Burt's booksellers, 201 High Street, Kirkcaldy.

As season 1886/87 drew to a close, the various tournaments were beginning to appear. On Saturday April 16, Kirkcaldy FC organised a tournament for the benefit (ie in lieu of payment) of Messrs A. Napier and J.Pirie, gatekeeper and groundsman, at Newton Park. Rovers were drawn against Albion, Dunnikier v Thistle ; United and Union byes. Albion beat Rovers by 1 goal and 3 corners to 1 goal and 1 corner, but Union won the tournament.

Albion gained some revenge against the same Rovers eleven who had beaten them in the Cup Final. The Fife Free Press were less than enthusiastic in their praise : "It must be admitted the Albion was greatly strengthened by the new acquisitions (three players brought in) , as the result shows the Rovers being beat by two minor points. In ordinary circumstances, however, the result was a draw."

JOHN FLANDERS

The last weekend of January 1888 should have seen a first meeting between Rovers and Dunfermline Athletic (although it was to be the latter's second eleven). The game was cancelled when Athletic fixed up a home fixture against 3rd LRV (Third Lanark) and Rovers had to settle for a 4-3 victory over Dunfermline Albion at Lady's Mill Park. A 2-0 defeat by Woodburn was an improvement on the previous season's 7-0 beating by the Edinburgh club, particularly as Dave Jarvis was absent from the team.

Rovers were well represented in the Kirkcaldy Junior FA team selected to play Kirkcaldy Wanderers on March 31st. Ramsay (Raith Rovers) ; Clark (Raith Rovers), Downie (Kirkcaldy Albion) ; Skinner (Union) ; Russell (Raith Rovers), Henderson (Pathhead United) ; Chalmers (Raith Rovers), Elder (Pathhead United), Henderson (Raith Rovers), Yule (Union), Nelson (Raith Rovers)

Reserves :
Currie (Pathhead United), Napier (Union), Masterton (Pathhead United), Jarvis (Raith Rovers), Millar (Fern), Sinclair (Kirkcaldy Albion) ; Philp (Pathhead United), Walker (Union), Gossling (Kirkcaldy Albion) Umpire J.R. Litster (Raith Rovers).

Wanderers, who had been without their star-player, London-bound Peter Connelly, since November, won the match 6-1, and there were several changes from the initial selection. Napier of Union was at right back, Millar of Fern at right half, Litster of Raith Rovers at left half, and Philp of Pathhead United at centre forward

desirable thing that ought to be fostered is more friendliness between the teams. Each team accuses the other of coldness, but why not take up the moral side of the question, and let bygones be bygones."

On 17th March "The long vexed question as to which was the superior team, the Rovers or Wanderers, has been set at rest ...." The senior team won 6-3 at Newton Park with goals from Mathie, Hughes, Miller, Lawson, Doig and Napier. Chalmers, Litster and David Clark scored for the junior team.

The following week, a record attendance at Elder's Park saw Rovers draw 1-1 with Pathhead United in the semi final of the Kirkcaldy Junior Cup, Chalmers scoring for Raith, Burnett for United. Another record crowd was set for the replay at Robbie's Park, which Rovers won 4-1 with goals from Nelson, Litster (2) and Philp. Earlier in the month, Fern had beaten Abden in the other semi final. The final was played on 14th April at Albion's ground in Robbie's Park. The first half was scoreless, but Rovers outplayed their younger opponents in the second half, and won 4-0.

Despite poor results against senior opposition in friendly matches, the Rovers members recognised that they had outgrown junior football, and decided to join the senior ranks for 1888/89 season. The Fife Free Press of 21st April commented :

"The Rovers ... now leave the field of juniordom to the younger and most promising teams in the district. Merit, we know, is a progressive agency, and now that the Rovers have secured the highest stage they can reach in junior football in Kirkcaldy, they ought to be penalised with seniorism. The Rovers have certainly done much to advance the cause of junior football in the district, but they must not shut their eyes to the fact that by continuing to compete for the cup, they will retard its progress, and keep back numerous young clubs who will know that they have no chance against such an experienced team as the Rovers"

Infused with the pioneering spirit, Rovers ventured north of the Tay to play Nomads at Gayfield Park, Arbroath. They were beaten 5-1, and discovered the hazards of playing at the picturesque ground by the North Sea. "The weather was bitterly cold [this was April 21st !], and a strong variable wind blew from the north east, rendering shooting extremely difficult."

On Friday May 4th, the club's second annual soiree, concert and assembly was held at the Corn Exchange. Dr J M Campbell, the club's Honorary President, remarked in his address that "they had one of the finest pitches in the country and the best pavilion belonging to any junior club he knew" The first eleven had won 19 and drawn 4 of their 36 matches, scoring 121 goals and conceding 81. The second eleven had won 11 and drawn 3 of their 18 games, scoring 52 and conceding 29 goals.

"In the course of the evening Mr Charles Robertson was presented by Mr Andrew Ness, in the name of the club, with a handsome silver albert in recognition of the services he had rendered the club by acting as MC at their weekly dance practice. Dancing afterwards took place, when about 50 couples "tripped it lightly" to music supplied by Mr Johnston's quadrille band."

Andrew Ness, secretary to Messrs Douglas & Grant Ltd., and the esteemed conductor of the Ian Hay Choir, was one of the best and most popular of Rovers' officials. A former player recalled, some twenty years later : "Mr Ness was always keen on elevating the tone of football and football players, and I well remember when he formed a Literary Society in connection with the club. The meetings were held in the club pavilion on Robbie's Park and papers on a variety of subjects were read by members of the club, the players, officials and ordinary members contributing. The Literary Society flourished fairly well so long as the players were composed practically entirely of local chaps, but when young fellows from Dundee and elsewhere were introduced, it gradually became defunct. It was a very praiseworthy institution, and was only one example of the enthusiasm and high tone which characterised Mr Ness' efforts for the good of the Rovers, as it has done with everything he has taken up."

There seemed a reluctance to end the season. Adventurers were beaten 4-0 at Robbie's Park on 12th May, and the following week the Kirkcaldy Junior FA were beaten 4-0 by their Cowdenbeath equivalents at Station Park, Cowdenbeath. Rovers' Second Annual Amateur Athletics Sports at Robbie's Park was advertised for 9th and 16th June, when Rovers lost to Leith Athletic in the football tournament, having beaten Edinburgh club Primrose in the first round. Leith beat North End 2-0 in Final. In the 5-a-side tournament the following week, Rovers lost to Union in the first round, but John Litster won the 100 yards race for players in sports

The Annual Meeting at Burleigh Street Hall on July 6th, had ""Important Business. Full attendance requested." and the following Monday there was a social evening at the National Hotel in the High Street for full back Mr William Clark who was leaving for Australia. He was presented with "a handsome gold albert, briar pipe & case, tobacco pouch and silver match box. With song and sentiment a very happy evening was spent."

Some of the happiness may have been caused by the surprise decision at the AGM to remain in junior football. It is unlikely that this was due to lack of ambition, more a realisation that the team had to raise its game before it could compete at the higher level.

Rovers opened 1888/89 season at South End Park, Cowdenbeath, on August 18th. Minus four of their first eleven, they lost 5-3. For the all important cup ties, when a full first eleven was fielded, Thomson replaced Bill Clark at back, Willie Dall replaced Litster and, confusingly, two separate inside forwards, both called A Marshall, took the place of Hazells.

Local rivalries were rejoined, with a match at Pathhead United. Despite Rovers winning 5-0, there was `crowd trouble at the end following a melee involving Dave Jarvis, Henderson and Mathie of United. "There is no doubt that the referee was in a great measure to blame. We would suggest to our local teams to procure an entirely neutral and competent person to act as referee when they intend to play each other."

The Fife Free Press reported : "Towards the close a most disgraceful scene ensured, members of both teams indulging in stand up fights. It is certainly a matter of regret that two such teams should have indulged in such conduct. Should such conduct be tolerated, football, instead of being popularised, will degenerate ...." The bad feeling engendered between the clubs filled the letters columns of the local papers in the following weeks.

In the Cowdenbeath Cup, Rovers travelled with a full strength team to "Little Chicago" to play North End, and won 9-0. There was a major shock a fortnight later in the first round of the Scottish Junior Cup when Rovers ventured up The Path to Elder's Park   Burnett, Elder and Bogie scored for Pathhead United to give them a 3-1 half time lead, Dall scoring for Rovers.   Instead of the expected fightback, the second half produced "a poor exhibition of football, consisting mainly of the long kick-and-rush style. Ramsay in the Rovers goal did not have much extra work, but it might have been better done. The first and third goals were, indeed, very soft ones. The forward rank seldom played a worst game, and the less said about them the better"

The grip that football had taken on the menfolk of Kirkcaldy was illustrated by the lengthy and prolonged correspondence printed in the town's four weekly newspapers. Those of a bardic bent were also given column space.   Mr J Hughes (pace Burns) sent in some lines on the Raith Rovers, in the course of which he said

Yer daffin tricks micht weel astoun'
The gentry o' yer ain laing toun ;
Od ! lang yer fame be trumpit roun'
Our hilly mountains,
An' mak' yer hearts a'envy doon,
Like bristlin' fountains.
Ye still may boast the richt tae weer
The laureate's croon - the laur-ate's gear, *
An' mak' a'clues yer name tae fear
In future dangling ;
Nae ane can boast o' sic a rear
O' awfu' fangling
Allusion to cup

An indication that playing fortunes were improving came with a 2-1 win over Burntisland Thistle, who had been an extremely strong team in Fife senior football for several years.   Revenge was exacted on Pathhead United, with a visit to Elder's Park in the Kirkcaldy Junior Cup producing a 4-0 win for Rovers, in front of another record crowd for the third ward enclosure.

The dawning of the New Year (1889) brought the first sighting of what was to be a persistent and long-running speculation. "Rumour hath it that another month will see an amalgamation of the Rovers and the Wanderers. Nothing could be better for the game in Kirkcaldy. Then we could have a team worthy of the "lang toon". Should this little arrangement come about, several of the county clubs would be made to sit up, aye, and some of our friends over the "dub" as well."

A Second Eleven Cup had been established in the town, and in that competition the following Raith Rovers team beat Fern 6-2. Muir, Morton, Buchanan, Hepburn, Neilson, Williamson, Webster, Cameron, Norval, Ross, Leitch.   When the Second Eleven Cup Final was played in mid February Rovers won 3-2.   Hazel replaced Hepburn, and Elder, who scored twice, played instead of Norval.   Leitch scored the winning goal in the second half

Most of the town's attention, however, was focussed on the final of the Kirkcaldy Junior Cup, between the old and bitter rivals, Rovers (winners for the past two seasons) and Albion (winners of the first competition in 1886).   "That the event was attracting no small share of attention was quite evident during the week, it being the chief theme of conversation among young men," said the Fife Free Press. "Where is the rejoicing to be on Saturday night ? Along the Links or down about the Volunteers Green ?"

The venue was Newton Park and despite Wanderers increasing the rental, the Kirkcaldy Junior Association had little option but to pay.   Robbie's Park was obviously ruled out because of the competing teams ; Elder's Park was unsuitable, as was Stark's Park, whose new tenants, Links Fern, had been victims of a protest from their opponents earlier in the season that their new pitch was "not a private ground".   Henderson opened the scoring in just two minutes, and then a minute into the second half scored direct from a corner kick. Rovers won a poor game 2-0. At the close of the game the Albion lodged a protest on the grounds of encroachment of spectators, and that time was not up when the game was stopped. The protest was unanimously dismissed at Association meeting on Wednesday evening.   It had to be acknowledged that " the Albion have been most unfortunate with their players since they became a club. If such players as Connolly, Gosling, Myles, Macbean and Mathie were still in their ranks, they would about run out anything in the "Kingdom"".

Adverse weather thwarted the Kirkcaldy sporting public on 2nd February. Rovers first eleven were due to play Fern at Stark's Park, but neither team turned up, such were the conditions.   The second elevens of Albion and Rovers should have contested the final of the Second Eleven Cup, but poor ground conditions caused the match to be played as a friendly, which was drawn 3-3. The choice of Raith Rovers to be Pathhead United's visitors for a benefit match for John

WILLIE DALL
with the King Cup

Before taking their planned leave of junior football, Rovers had some domestic matters to attend to in May 1888. Benefit matches were played at Robbie's Park on successive Saturdays for their gatekeeper, Mr McPhee, who had secured the services of Muirhouse Rovers from Davidson's Mains, and groundsman, Jimmy Taylor, for whom Mr Ross of St Bernards selected a team under the banner of Edinburgh Crusaders. Rovers won the first match 7-0 and drew the second 2-2, the attendance for the latter regarded as disappointing considering the deserving beneficiary. The cricket team had taken over Newton Park for the summer, and Kirkcaldy Wanderers had to play Lassodie, recent winners of the Fife Cup, at Albion's Robbie's Park.

Early in 1889, Kirkcaldy Wanderers had arranged a friendly against one of Rangers' elevens, the Swifts, and "The rumour that the Wanderers were to play some of the Rovers men, added to a hint given in certain quarters of a proposed amalgamation of the Rovers and the Wanderers, created no little interest". Ramsay and Nelson of Rovers played

1888 - Weslyan Methodist Church opened
1890 - Cottage Hospital gifted by Michael Barker Nairn

The members of the Kirkcaldy Junior FA met in a social capacity on Friday 22nd January 1889 in the "Duke of Edinburgh" restaurant. Mr James Mullen (Albion) president of the Association, occupied the chair, while Mr Robertson (Rovers) acted as croupier." Financial problems had been resolved, due mainly to support from Mr Ferguson MP and badges could now be awarded to finalists. The Rovers had the cup presented to them for the third successive year.

The path of fixture scheduling was a bumpy one, as reported in the Fifeshire Advertiser on March 22nd. "The Albion and Raith Rovers were advertised to play their Cowdenbeath Cup tie at Elder's Park on Saturday. The Albion's "social" came off on Friday night, and they therefore thought they were entitled to have the tie postponed for a week, seeing they had been humbugged so long by the Cowdenbeath Association before that. The Association committee, in order to secure any gate which might be going, brought down the St Leonards from Cowdenbeath to play the Rovers [at Elder's Park]" Albion preferred a trip to Anstruther.

The annual (1889) soiree in the Corn Exchange saw Mr Charles Robertson presented with a pipe and tobacco pouch for giving preparatory dancing lessons to members.

On 29th March 1890 it was announced that : "Raith Rovers Football Club intend holding an Evening Trades Tournament. Entries - 3s per team - close on April 14th with R. Donaldson, 42 Links Street, from whom particulars can be had."

The April Holiday Monday saw Rovers compete in the Dunnikier Band Tournament, alongside Burntisland Thistle, Lassodie and Cowdenbeath. The Junior competition featured Pathhead United, Wemyss Athletic, Kirkcaldy Albion and Hearts of Beath.

Oliphant, who had his leg broken in a match against Glasgow club Haghill on 1st January, owed more to the expectation of a large gate than the promise of a trouble-free afternoon. The Fife Free Press drew solace from the fact "that the game is to be under the superintendence of Doctors Smith and Campbell, and Mr Landale, is a sufficient guarantee that it should be well conducted, all rough play being put aside. The appearance of Mr Smith, a gentleman who has donned the jersey and sustained the glory of Scotland in more than one International, should certainly be an incentive to both teams to play their best." John Smith, recently settled in the town, refereed a pulsating match which ended in favour of United, 5-3.

Meanwhile, the Rovers had been ordered to replay their Cowdenbeath Cup tie with Lochgelly Athletic owing to the captain of the Rovers failing to hand the referee a list of his players' names before the game commenced. "They may well thank their lucky stars that they got off so lightly." The technicalities properly observed, Rovers won 7-2, despite local criticism of the team's prolific centre forward. "Dave Jarvis delights too much in his easy-going, hands-in-pockets style. It won't do."

Perhaps the forward's demeanour was indicative of his unrest at Robbie's Park ? Not long afterwards, he and his brother William decamped to Kirkcaldy Wanderers.

A third Raith Rovers eleven had been formed, and it was reported that they lost 3-1 to Victoria Thistle at Robbie's Park The Spring Holiday Monday (1st April) was filled with a junior eleven a side tournament on Rovers' ground at Robbie's Park, under the auspices of the Dunnikier Band. Entries were 3d per team, and there were prizes of silver and gold badges. The competing teams were : Rovers 1st, Rovers 2nd, Albion, Fern, Hearts of Fife (Dunfermline), Northern Rangers (Thornton), St Leonards, Thistle, United. Albion beat Hearts of Fife in the Final.

Also advertised was a Juvenile 11-a-side Badge competition, to be played during April under the auspices of Raith Rovers. This was for Under 18s only, no Junior Cup players, at a cost of 2s per team

Perhaps it was the late kick off time (4.30) or maybe the Kirkcaldy footballing public were becoming jaded with meeting between Rovers and Albion, but the semi final of the Cowdenbeath Cup, when played at Newton Park on 6th April, attracted a smaller than expected crowd. Those who stayed away missed a great game. Rovers led 3-2 at the interval with goals from Henderson and Norval (2). Rovers claimed a fourth goal, but, in the days before goal-nets, Albion protested that the ball had gone past the post, and the Referee agreed. Ritchie equalised for Albion after the interval, and Deuchars scored the winner in the last minute.

Rovers had the consolation of hosting the final at Robbie's Park, which Albion won 4-2, but the result was protested on account of the rough play of Millar, and the Association sustained the protest. The

replay finished with the same scoreline. The Fifeshire Advertiser claimed a "scoop" with the story "We believe the Rovers have agreed to become seniors next season, under the name of the Raith Athletic. How two senior teams will thrive in the town is what we can't make out. What we need is an amalgamation of some sort between two or three of the clubs in town, so that a team might be got together to uphold the honour of the "lang toun""

The notice calling the Annual General Meeting at Burleigh Street Hall on Monday 6th May warned of "Business important", and it was agreed at the meeting to join the Senior Associations for season 1889/90. Robert Donaldson, 42 Links Street, was appointed honorary and match secretary. It was also agreed to keep a team into the Junior Associations, and J. Norval was appointed match secretary "the junior team to be named the Raith Athletic." The Advertiser got the details slightly wrong, but time proved their sentiments correct.

Kirkcaldy had discovered five-a-side football by 1889, and the craze among the town's footballers lasted for many years. Wanderers, Rovers, Albion, the Trades' Band and Dunnikier Brass Band all staged annual tournaments, inviting such as Leith Ivanhoe, Edinburgh Woodburn, Corinthians, Bellstane Birds, Burntisland Spiders, Dunfermline St Leonards, Hearts, St Bernards, Cardross, Strathforth and Muirhouse Rovers.

Robbie's Park and Newton Park reverberated with the excitement of these contests, notably one held by the Rovers for which several clubs crossed the Forth by paddle steamer, beaching on the sands. Many of the teams were selected on the day, and there was a demand for contrasting strips, some of which were shared by a number of teams, having been hung out to dry on the fences surrounding Robbie's Park.

That football was played throughout the summer months at Robbie's Park was shown by the press announcement of 29th June.
"RAITH ROVERS FOOTBALL CLUB will hold a Grand ELEVEN-A-SIDE FOOTBALL COMPETITION on SATURDAY, 6th July, and the following well-known Clubs have accepted invitations :- Cowdenbeath, Kirkcaldy Wanderers, Burntisland Thistle, Bellstane Birds, Adventurers (Edinburgh) and Cameron Highlanders. For further particulars see Bills." Cowdenbeath beat Wanderers in the final.

On Saturday August 24th 1889, there was a double bill for the football followers of the town. Dr John Smith used his influence to attract Queen's Park ("the premier club in Scotland") to play Wanderers, although this was to be played at Albion's ground as Newton Park was needed for a cricket fixture. Jack McBean, now of Royal Arsenal, was to play left half for his former club. Kick off was 5.30, and at 3.15, the holders of the Dundee Charity Cup were due at Rovers pitch.

"The Raith Rovers, who appear this season before the public as seniors, open their ground today by engaging the Dundee Wanderers. The Rovers for sometime back occupied the proud position of being about the best junior team in the county, and certainly now they have aspired to higher ideas. We wish them all success. Being the possessors of one of the best pitches in the kingdom, with plenty of talent to draw from, and under good management, we are confident that they will take a prominent stand this season."

Rovers had some difficulty in enticing some of their players to move to the senior grade, as there was no monetary incentive, professionalism not yet having been adopted in Scotland. In place of those who remained in Kirkcaldy Junior football were Henderson and Clark from Burntisland Thistle, and Stewart and Sturrock from Arbroath. Rovers lost 3-0, and later that evening Queen's Park beat Wanderers 5-0. On Wednesday August 28th, Rovers and Pumpherston Union were admitted as members of the East of Scotland Football Association. The draw for the first round of Shield matched Rovers and Kirkcaldy Wanderers, but first Rovers had to make their debut in the Scottish Cup, at home to Dunfermline Athletic.

The best juniors preferred to remain in junior football, as it allowed them to continue to compete in the lucrative close-season five-a-side competitions. In the days leading up to the Dunfermline game Rovers were still short of a centre forward, and in some desperation, prevailed upon a notable sprinter, Jimmy Barker, to appear. Jimmy was certainly fast, but had no stamina, and finished the match on the touchline, exhausted, watching his beleaguered team-mates. Tom Cook scored the only goal of the first half for Rovers, but Bruce scored twice after the interval for the visitors.

The move from junior to senior did not bring about a transformation in paperwork ; there were no registrations or contracts, and clubs were at the mercy of their players, as reported in the wake of the Dunfermline cup defeat.

"The Rovers were disappointed by Henderson of the Thistle not turning up on Saturday. It is rather bad of a player to promise to assist a club, and then fail to turn up without giving the club any warning as to his intention. It is a true saying "a bird in the hand is worth two in the bush", and unless the Rovers can depend on their men turning up, they would be better to put in players they are sure of, even although they are not quite so good as the shaky ones. Several of our juniors are having a quiet chuckle to themselves, over some of the Rovers' men entering the senior ranks now." The reporter concluded, enigmatically : "Wonder if a certain local "agent" will seek to carry on any more of his "poaching" operations after the fright he got on Saturday ?"

In due course, Alex Hall, John Cameron, G.C. Buchanan and Robert Urquhart all became first team regulars, and Morton usurped John Cairns as the regular goalkeeper.

Rovers, wearing striped shirts, lost the Shield tie at Newton Park by 4-0. They may have been consoled by their share of the £11 gate, but Dave Jarvis' two goals would have been keenly felt. "The Rovers played pluckily, but even the keenest partisan could not fail to see a vast difference between the teams on the day's play."

In those days before the Forth Rail Bridge was built, there was an understandable reluctance to venture outside Fife for matches. On 28th September 1889, Rovers played Norton Park in Edinburgh and had to cross from Granton in a luggage boat, and walk home from Burntisland, arriving back in Kirkcaldy in the small hours of Sunday morning. At that time to walk from Burntisland was commonplace, the difficult task being to get to this side of the Forth. Rovers were having a hard time of it, losing 3-2 to their former Junior colleagues Kirkcaldy Albion. There was worse to come in the first round of the Fife Cup – Cowdenbeath won 8-2 at Robbie's Park. On October 19th Rovers entertained Townhill, and the press report said "Whether it was on account of the cold weather or the obscurity of the visitors, we know not, but the attendance was small." It might have had something to do with the wretched form of their favourites, although Rovers cheered their stalwart fans with an 8-1 win.

Following another defeat at the hands of Albion, the newspapers announced : "We believe the Rovers have re-arranged their team. Tynie has not given satisfaction, and consequently has been shunted."

There was a glimmer of better things to come, as one local paper reported in November : "Handicapped to a large extent by teams not keeping their engagement, the Rovers have not been so actively engaged this season as they would have been otherwise. Their appearance on Saturday was therefore all the more refreshing and the fact that they were only beat by a goal by such an excellent combination as the Celtic Reserves, shows that they are in rare form just now."

The fans may not have agreed, with a low attendance for the visit of St Johnstone the following week. "The turn-out of spectators was extremely poor, and not nearly up to our expectations. In fact, we begin to think the people of Kirkcaldy are not taking so great an interest in the game as they formerly did ; at least one thing is certain, the efforts of our local football committees to bring teams of good standing are not being encouraged as they ought to be."

Graham ("who is an old Preston North End man - at least, so the knowing ones at Robbie's Park say") played full back. "We hope, however, the Rovers' Committee, after Saturday's exhibition, will have got quite enough of imported demons, and will try some of our own manufacture the next time there is a blank in the team." John Thomson moved position to replace Alex Hall "who is suffering from an extreme kick"

Robert Donaldson, pictured in 1907, 24 years after he was credited with finding a football on a tree while bird-nesting, and being a central figure in forming Raith Rovers. He was the last secretary of the club before it became a Limited Liability Company.

The Fife Free Press on Saturday May 25 1889 opined "The Rovers' sports today, which take place at Robbie's Park promise to be a source of great attraction, The football competition bulks largely in the programme, and some good teams have entered. The other events [under SAAA rules], which include several races and a tug-of-war competition, should go to make up a splendid afternoon's sport, and with the anticipation of good weather the gathering should prove to be a great success." The players John Thomson and TomChalmers got among the prizes at the sports and Rovers beat Burntisland Thistle in the 5-a-side tournament "and won the clocks".

The Fife Free Press was not amused by the cavalier administration of some of the matches at Robbie's Park early in 1889/90 "The game was advertised to begin at 3.15, but it was about half an hour after that before a start was made. Why this should be, as both teams are local, we fail to see, it being anything but pleasant to stand for half-an-hour in the cold wind on Saturday, and await the pleasure of the teams turning up. See to this late starting, somebody !"

The Christmas and New Year holiday period brought brighter prospects to local football followers. "There will be great excitement at Robbie's Park tomorrow. A Scottish Junior tie at one end of the field, and a struggle between the two local seniors [Wanderers and Rovers] at the other." Rovers played Rangers on the holiday Wednesday afternoon. Rangers' Ibrox XI (ie not their first team) out-passed Rovers and won 4-0 on New Year's Day, but once again "a much larger turnout of spectators was expected. The game was a very pleasant and enjoyable one. That the best team won few will deny, the only wonder was that they did not score oftener". The previous Saturday, Rovers had the satisfaction of beating Wanderers 6-2, while Albion beat Dalry Albert 6-2 at the other end of Robbie's Park.

1890 - Forth Rail Bridge opened

The Fife Free Press of 22nd September 1888 included the Notice : "Raith Rovers' Football Club Dance Practice will commence on Wednesday, 26th September, at 8 o'clock, in Oswald's Wynd Hall. Gentlemen 6d ; Ladies Free."

Early Kirkcaldy Junior Club Grounds

Ravenscraig Rangers played at Ingleside ; Ramblers at Kinninmonth's Park. Thistle and Albion at Robbie's Park ; St Clair Blues at Hutchison's Park ; Blackburn at Mr Aitken's Park ; Union at Stark's Park. Fern at Tyrie

RAITH ROVERS FOOTBALL CLUB

THE FOURTH ANNUAL CONCERT and ASSEMBLY, under the auspices of the above Club, will be held on FRIDAY, 8th May [1891], in the CORN EXCHANGE. Assembly tickets 3s per couple. Concert tickets - Reserved Seats 1s ; back seats 6d each.

Dance Practice for above on Wednesday evening in Oswald's Wynd Hall

Results against more established opponents remained poor. Cowdenbeath ejected Rovers from the King Cup with a 6-2 scoreline, and Dunfermline Athletic inflicted a 7-3 defeat, albeit against a weakened Raith side. There was no reserve strength either ; Albion beat Raith Athletic 10-0 in the Cowdenbeath Junior Cup.

Rovers' difficult first season amongst the seniors was not helped by Wanderers enjoying good fortune, and attracting top teams to their superior ground. They drew 4-4 with Hibs, and dominated the sports coverage in the local papers. Rovers appeared to be struggling to keep up with their older rivals. Only Henderson was selected (at left half) for the Fifeshire team to meet Stirlingshire, although there was surprise in Kirkcaldy that Hall and Dall were not also in the team.

Of much more importance, although it was not immediately realised, was the news of Provost Beveridge's death on 4th March, aged 54 ; nor did Rovers' men appreciate the looming consequences of his bequest to the town of the massive sum of £50,000. Rovers had been planning a benefit match for James Russell, the veteran half back "laid low for a considerable time through illness. Wanderers had been approached, but it was Cowdenbeath who ultimately provided the opposition. Unfortunately "The visitors were fully half-an-hour late in arriving, an incident which was severely condemned by the large assemblage, who had to stand waiting in a drizzling rain." The considerable sum of £20 was handed over to Russell, who had been off work for seven months.

There was plenty of football-related gossip to fill several columns of the Fifeshire Advertiser on 4th April. "There is some talk of the Kirkcaldy Football and Bicycle Clubs being amalgamated, and an athletic club formed. There is much need of something of this sort in Kirkcaldy."

The Town Council were in earnest discussion about how to spend Provost Beveridge's legacy, or more particularly where to spent it. One of three potential sites was rather too close to home for Rovers. "Should the Town Council select the Southerton ground for the public park the Albion and the Rovers will require to clear out. What will the cricketers do after all the expense they have been at in laying out a pitch in Robbie's Park ?" The map which accompanied the article showed the whole of Robbie's Park to be roughly the same area as what we now know as Beveridge Park, and all of it outside the burgh boundary.

The other three sites under consideration were ; (1) Farm at Sauchenbush on Bennochy estate, sloping upwards from the railway station to the Long Braes and the farm cottages. (2) The ground between the cemetery and Hendry Road on the west, and Dunnikier Road on the east, from the railway up to Hayfield farm. (3) The land north of Hayfield, including the upper Den.

The Rovers Smoking Concert in

Burleigh Street Hall was reported in the Fifeshire Advertiser of April 18th. Mr Alex Strachan presided, and stated that Rovers decision to go senior had been vindicated by performances. "Mr Rintoul purveyed in a satisfactory manner".

A less optimistic view was tendered at the Third Annual reunion of Pathhead United, at the new Town Hall in Pathhead. Mr W.G. Landells, the honorary President of the club, believed that Kirkcaldy "should support one strong Junior and one strong senior club, achieved by amalgamation." He did not hold out much hope for this, however, and he also referred to the bad press which football received. "During the evening only temperance refreshments were obtainable. This is certainly a step in the right direction."

A game between Rovers and Leith Athletic "was far below the standard of Robbie's Park. The Rovers were not fully represented, one or two of their seconds being pressed into service." Rovers had expected Leith's 1st eleven, but Friday's newspapers showed that Leith had arranged to play Motherwell. The notice on the front page of the Fife Fress Press of 26th April 1890 was stark enough : "Albion v Rovers. Match Declared Off. Rovers Refusing to Play." They preferred a match against Burntisland Thistle.

"We have been requested to take notice of the very unsportsmanlike treatment of the Kirkcaldy Albion by their townsmen, Raith Rovers. We are informed that on Thursday morning last week the Secretary of the Albion received a postcard from the Secretary of the Rovers arranging a match for last Saturday. The Rovers issued bills throughout the town announcing the match ; but on Friday afternoon another postcard reached the Albion cancelling the fixture, and the bills were withdrawn from the shops, another announcing Raith Rovers v Burntisland Thistle being substituted, while the excuse for so doing given by the Rovers Secretary was that his committee had ordered him to declare the match off with the Albion. To say the least of it, the whole affair is discreditable, and some further explanation is required. It cannot by any means be regarded as sportsmanlike. The following are the copies of the post cards sent to the Rovers – the one announcing the fixture and the other declaring it off.

153 Links Street 23/4/1890 – Dear Sir, We will play you on our ground on Saturday ; kick off 3.30pm, half gate terms. Yours truly, R. Donaldson, Raith Rovers

153 Links Street 24/4/1890 – Dear Sir, I am very sorry, I have been instructed by my committee to put off the fixture on Saturday. I am very sorry for disappointing you, but it is no fault of mine, as I would have liked very much to have played the Albion. Yours, in haste, R. Donaldson."

Henderson retained his place in the Fifeshire select, and had the dubious distinction of captaining the side beaten 12-1 by Linlithgowshire at Broxburn. Rovers organised an 11-a-side tournament for 14th

June, involving Hearts, Broxburn and Wanderers. The hosts beat Wanderers 4-3 but lost 7-2 to Hearts in the Final. McWee of Dundee Wanderers and McAulay of Burntisland Thistle played for Rovers, but the promised guests from Dumbarton did not show up. Rovers published the correspondence to emphasise their innocence in the omission.

"Dumbarton 13/6/1890
Dear Sir, I am very sorry, but it is impossible for me to come, Bell and McMillan go to a wedding to-night, and will not play. I tried Mair and Galbraith, but they will not come without the others. I am very sorry I have caused you so much inconvenience, but I could do no better.
Yours sincerely, John McLeod
PS Our team is also to be photographed on Saturday."

A fortnight later, there was worse news for Rovers – they were about to become homeless. The Town Council voted on the three possible sites for the Beveridge Park on Monday June 23rd 1890, Robbie's Park receiving 16 votes, north of Hayfield 7, and Sauchenbush 2. In early July, Robbie's Park was purchased from Mr Ferguson of Raith for around £15,000. It was a very generous price. Southerton House and offices were purchased for an additional £1,000 ; and Messrs Methven's clay rights for another £1,000.

Despite the late finish to the previous season, there was an early start to 1890/91, the Fifeshire Advertiser of Friday 8th August reporting : "Tomorrow will see a commencement made in local football circles for another season. The Raith Rovers are first to set the ball a-rolling, and it is only a pity the match clashes with the flower show and football competition at Dysart."

St Bernards led 2-0 at the interval, but Rovers scored four times without reply in the second half to record a very encouraging victory. "The Rovers are to be complimented on their victory, which proves a hearty stimulus for renewed effort. With improved forward play and the back division of Saturday, last, they would be hard to beat anywhere."

Starring against his former club was Willie McKay, who had also played for Hearts and Burnley. Although not designated as such, he was effectively the club's first player coach, using his experience to influence by play and example. He quickly became a huge favourite at Robbie's Park, and his presence in the team, either at centre half or centre forward, gave his team-mates the confidence that was to propel them to greater deeds.

McKay was the start of an inevitable process which saw the club recruit players from beyond its locality, in order to advance in Scottish football. It took another 15 years before the majority of the team came from outwith the district, however, and for 1890/91, McKay apart, the team strengthening came from local sources. George Webster took over from John Cameron at wing half,

and Leitch came in at inside right. William Cowan, Alex Bogie and Neilson Deuchars joined the sole remaining forward from the previous season, Willie Dall.

Alas, the Scottish Cup draw was not kind to Rovers, away to Hearts, who won 7-2. The Kirkcaldy men were attracting some attention in the senior game, however, as reported by the Fifeshire Advertiser : "Hall, of the Raith Rovers, has been well pestered by the St Bernards since they took a notion of him. Sandy will stick by the Rovers, however."

The match against Lassodie resulted in an 8-2 victory for Rovers, but there were two or three fights amongst the players in the second half, the referee being judged to be too lenient.

This probably coloured the anticipation of the first local derby of the season. "The meeting of the Kirkcaldy Wanderers and Raith Rovers at Newton Park to-day is the all absorbing topic among football enthusiasts. Weighed individually, we are inclined to give the Wanderers the advantage, although in respect to combination there is very little to choose between the opposing teams. It is only to be hoped that in the excitement of the moment the players will not allow their judgement to be led away." Hall and Mackay of Rovers had been selected in the East of Scotland FA eleven to meet Cleveland at Middlesbrough. Three thousand watched the match at Newton Park, and Wanderers "the best team" won 3-0. Local rivalry was fierce. An onlooker later remembered : "It was no uncommon thing of an evening for members of the rival clubs to stroll, with a great show of unconcern and innocence, into the haunts of their opponents - the People's Club, or the "Duke" for instance - and wave the red rag before each other's faces.

"When the Rovers were due to play on Newton Park, nothing in the world would induce them to don their football togs in the Wanderers' pavilion. They would change in their own pavilion and march in full war paint along the railway line and drop down on the foe like a pack of Indian warriors storming the stockades of a pale-face settlement."

The second round of the King Cup took Rovers to Kingcavil, a mining village near Linlithgow, to play Champfleurie. The pitch was at the back of the miners rows, and the attendance comprised the home team's players' wives and mothers, whose shouts of approval and derision rather upset the Rovers' players.

Just before Christmas, Rovers came down to earth with a bump when they played Lassodie in the semi finals of the Fife Cup. "So the Rovers have lost the Fife Cup when it was almost within their grasp. It was expected that Lassodie would run them hard for victory, but it was never imagined that they would beat them to the tune of 5 goals to 1." It was a bitter below, particularly in the light of the Friendly match played between the clubs three months earlier, when Rovers had beaten the Miners 8-2. Nevertheless, three

WILLIE MCKAY
A native of Edinburgh (he lived in that city's High Street while he played for Rovers), he was a first team player with Hearts in the mid 1880s, then played in the Football League for Burnley in 1887-88. After a brief spell with Newcastle West End he joined St Bernards, and became Rovers' first significant signing from beyond Fife.

On 3rd January 1890, the famous English team Corinthians visited Newton Park in a match arranged through Dr Smith. "The fact that the Kirkcaldy footballers were to be so signally honoured has caused a great deal of talk in football circles throughout Scotland", and the attendance of 3,000 (paying £54 10/- at gate and stand) was reached thanks to a special train run from Edinburgh. Wanderers team was augmented by players from Hibs, St Bernards, Cowdenbeath and Walter Arnot of Queen's Park – but none from their Kirkcaldy neighbours. Corinthians won 5-3 and the local team was "not disgraced".
Following the excitement of the holiday fixtures, no matches were arranged for 4th January 1890. "Football was at a discount in the district on Saturday last, not a single match taking place". Rovers were also without a game the following Saturday, Hearts 2nd XI calling off at the last minute, so four of the players assisted Pathhead United in their 3-2 defeat by Wanderers, who themselves were dependent upon three Albion men and three of their second eleven.

ALEX BOGIE
A prolific goalscorer who lived at 41 Bridgeton, not quite The Links but not far from it. He played for two seasons with Rovers, scoring 40 goals in the first of them and 8 in 9 matches in 1891/92 before he moved south to Ardwick.

Rovers had drawn 1-1 with Lochgelly United in a Fife Cup tie late in1890, but there was a protest by Lochgelly "that a full list of players had not been presented to their captain by Raith Rovers." The protest was dismissed, and Rovers won the replay 7-2 at Robbie's Park. This was followed by a 6-3 victory at Dunfermline Athletic. "The doings of the Rovers have been such as to keep up the prestige of Kirkcaldy football"

In December, Rovers stepped in to fill a sudden gap in Pathhead United's fixture list, but they started with 10 men "McKay being fully 20 minutes late in arriving". Rovers won 4-1, but not before another unseemly incident. "Semi-darkness had now set in, and it was impossible to follow the game accurately. Another goal fell to the Rovers, and then ensued a disgraceful scene in the mouth of the United's goal. Currie and McKay seemed to be the cause of the dispute, and blows were exchanged. Spectators at once rushed on to the field of play, and a scene of confusion ensued. Ultimately the ground was cleared, and the game proceeded, but feeling was running high, and some questionable tactics were engaged in by both teams."

defeats in the 17 games played that season pointed to an upsurge in Rovers' fortunes. Wanderers had lost 6 of their 14.

The unpredictable Scottish weather conspired against Rovers' hopes of scaling a new peak in their ascent of the Scottish football range, and it also put paid to the visit of Celtic to Robbie's Park on New Year's Day. On Saturday January 31st 1891, Bathgate Rovers were the visitors in the semi final of the King Cup.

".... the visitors arrived all right. The elements, however, ruthlessly tossed aside all arrangements, and the game has yet to be fought out. The referee had walked over the ground and declared it playable. Both teams had therefore to turn out, but only a quarter of an hour was played when it was agreed to stop. The spectators had their money returned or received tickets to admit them next Saturday." At the other end of Robbie's Park, Kirkcaldy Albion managed to finish their Scottish Junior Cup 4th round tie against East Benhar Heatherbell

When the game was replayed a fortnight later, Bathgate opened the scoring, but Bogie equalised and a goal from a scrimmage, and one from Cowan, gave Rovers a 3-1 interval league. Cowan and Bogie both scored two apiece in the second half, Hall one and Murnin for the visitors to settle the tie 8-2 in Rovers favour.

The final of the King Cup against Armadale was played at Logie Green in Edinburgh. Chalmers opened the scoring for Armadale, but Leitch ensured parity at half time. In the second half, Rovers scored from a scrimmage and added a third goal by Cowan to win the King Cup 3-1, Willie Dall being the decisive figure on the park. The Fife Free Press of Saturday March 7th reported Rovers' triumph as follows :

THE KING CUP FINAL : THE TROPHY BROUGHT TO KIRKCALDY
First Fife winners of the trophy.
300 travelling fans

"A happy meeting took place in the pavilion after the match, when the cup was presented by Mr Percival King to the Rovers, whom he complimented on their well won victory. Arriving home about nine o'clock, the team received a glorious reception. Thousands of people lined the entrance to the station. On alighting hearty cheers were raised for the victorious team, while individual congratulations were showered on them from all sides. So great was the demonstration that the players and officials of the team experienced great difficulty in making for the vehicles ready to convey them to the rendezvous. The Trades Band had also turned out to honour the occasion, and welcomed the team by playing "See the conquering heroes come." Mr Strachan, president of the club, and other officials, with the cup in their possession, got into a cab, while the team and friends were accommodated in a large brake. A torchlight procession was then formed, headed by the

band, and they marched to the town. As it wended its way, the procession was greatly increased in numbers, and it was with difficulty it could be kept moving, all being anxious to catch a glimpse of the trophy, which was held out of the window of the machine several times. On arriving at the High Street, it proceeded westwards to the club's rendezvous, where a pleasant hour was spent in social congratulations."

The winning Raith Rovers team was : Harry Clunie ; Tom Nelson and Jack Thomson ; Sandy Hall, Willie McKay, George Webster ; Alex Leitch, Willie Dall, Bill Cowan, Alex Bogie and Neil Deuchars.

In late March 1891, most people in the Links and West End of Kirkcaldy were pre-occupied with the opening of Abbotshall School, on Monday 16th March, but there was a significant result for their football team. Johnstone Wanderers visited Robbie's Park, where they had previously seen off the upstarts from Kirkcaldy when they were known as Dundee Wanderers. A measure of Rovers' progress was that their visitors returned north nursing a 5-0 defeat. The following month, Rovers showed their ambition by entering Lord Rosebery's Charity Cup, an action which potentially put them at odds with the East of Scotland FA. "The Rovers have shown a great amount of pluck in throwing away all chance of competing for the King Cup next year, and of taking part in the Charity ties. Their action will bring them all the more into prominence." They played Leith Athletic at Tynecastle Park, in front of an attendance which "would not exceed 1000 persons" and lost 4-2, but the consensus was that they had played well, deserved better, and gave notice of their growing ability.

At the end of the week in which it was announced that 27,152 people were counted in Kirkcaldy in the 1891 census, an increase of 3847 in ten years, Rovers journeyed to play Dunfermline Athletic and won 5-3, the Dunfermline Advertiser sourly noting that "Rovers had their full eleven" Hearts Second Eleven were then beaten 8-1 and Rovers opened Johnstone Wanderers' new ground at Clepington by winning 2-1 On May 23rd there was a return visit to Dunfermline, to meet Athletic in the final of the Fife Charity Cup. The Fife Free Press match report was headlined "Disgraceful Scene", and went on to describe the events surrounding Rovers' equaliser to make the scoreline 2-2 : .

"Cree got a shot which he caught and ran back several yards with, and then threw it out. The Rovers claimed a goal, and the Athletic disputed the point, maintaining that the leather was over the bar when Cree caught it. Mr Robertson of the Queen's Park, who was referee, at once consulted the umpires, Mr G. Wilson of the Kirkcaldy FC, gave a goal, while the other umpire admitted that he could not say what it was. Mr Robertson being of opinion that it was a goal from where he was standing, gave the goal to the Rovers. On the ball being centred, G. Wilson, having again taken up his position, he was soon surrounded by people, and with the crowd breaking in, Robertson was soon also besieged by the excited spectators. A scene of great confusion ensured, the officials being jostled about very unceremoniously. The police came to their rescue, and they were safely escorted to the pavilion. The game being stopped, the crowd waited for some time to see what the result of the conclave with the committee would be, but, the players beginning to dress, it was evident there was to be no more game that day. On Wilson and Robertson leaving the pavilion they were followed into town by a large crowd of people, who kept booing and shouting all the way, Wilson coming in for most attention on that score. An escort of police, however, was in attendance, and nothing of a serious nature transpired. The action of the crowd in breaking in cannot be condoned in the slightest. After the referee, who by the bye is the party appointed to settle all disputes, gave his decision the game should have been renewed, the Athletic reserving the right to protest to the Association. Such scenes as witnessed on Saturday only tend to degrade the national game, and lower it in the estimation of respectable, right-mind people."

In the replay at Newton Park a fortnight later, Rovers raced to a 3-1 half time lead with two goals from Bogie and one from a scrimmage. Leitch and Cowan scored in the second half to secure the trophy with a 5-2 scoreline. Before they could think about strengthening the team to retain the trophies won during 1890/91, Rovers had to find a home for them.

SPORTS AND RECREATION IN THE BEVERIDGE PARK

"Now that operations for the laying out of the Beveridge Park have got fairly under way, it seems to us a suitable time for considering what position that important element in the arranging of all public parks, sport and recreation, is to occupy. ...

"It is certainly, in a sense, a pity, so far as sport is concerned, that that part of the field at Raith Gate, known as "Robbie's Park", should have been included in the public park, seeing it contained two of the finest football pitches in the town, and also the cricket ground."

The article went on to consider the merits of football "... it has its great drawbacks, the chief of which is that in very many instances it seems to be a means of, one might almost say, brutalising our young men."

The Fife Free Press opened their coverage of season 1891/92 with the following words, on August 15th :

"The football season, at any rate so

far as the Association code was concerned, opened on Saturday afternoon. The inauguration of the Alliance and Federation matches took place. These bodies are new organisations in Scotland, and it will be interesting to watch their effect as regards the popularity of the game". [They were effectively regionalised Second Divisions of the Scottish League, which started the previous season, two years after the first football league in the world was established in England.]

"To-day our local football campaign begins in earnest. Unfortunately the taking over of Robbie's Park by the Council to convert it into the Beveridge Public Park, has greatly interfered with the Rovers and Albion. Ground is so scarce that both teams have been greatly perplexed to procure suitable enclosures. The Rovers have got Stark's Park, but the Albion have not been so fortunate, and a feeling is prevalent that they should amalgamate with the Wanderers, and play on the lower pitch in Newton Park." Leagues were the new fashion in Scottish football, following the great success of the inaugural season of the Scottish Football League. Rovers joined one, and opened their season against Grangemouth in the Scottish Midland Alliance, with a team similar to that which brought great success the previous season. "Nelson is said to be wishing to retire, but it is to be hoped he will be got to go through another campaign. His experience, tact and judgement is not easily dispensed with ...." Wanderers joined the Eastern Alliance, as clubs rushed to join Leagues and not be left behind.

The need to fulfil League fixtures probably explained why both clubs played in opposition to the biggest event in the town's calendar, the Band Contest held on the grounds of Raith House. It was reported that over 20,000 were present, as the people of Kirkcaldy enjoyed their annual picnic on the Laird's sweeping front lawn.

With goals from Cowan and Dall, Rovers beat Grangemouth 2-1 in their new surroundings ".... but this enclosure is not to

The crowds gather at the annual picnic in the grounds of Raith House. The Brass Band Contest attracted tens of thousands of spectators each year and Rovers avoided playing at home in opposition.

The trip to Alva for a Midland League fixture on 3rd October 1891 was not without incident. The travelling party arrived at Alloa, only to find there was no train to Hillfoot for two hours – and the game was due to begin in half an hour's time. A cabby, who said he belonged to Kirkcaldy and knew some of the party by sight, offered to drive them to Alva and back for 1/- a head. After half an hour, and no Alva in sight, he was asked if he was on the right road. He answered that he "thought so". Quarter of an hour later they came to a small town, but it was Tillicoultry, two miles from Alva. They arrived at Alva to find the players had been on the field for 30 minutes, decided Rovers' weren't turning up, and gone to the hotel and got changed. They were good sports, however, and got stripped again, only to be beaten by the odd goal in eleven.

An East of Scotland Shield tie against Adventurers, from Slateford, saw Rovers line up with nine men, Leitch and Nelson joining their colleagues "several minutes after kick off" It was 2-2 at half time, and Dall scored the winner for Rovers in the second half.

ALEX HALL
Born in Leslie, he first played for Rovers in 1889, and was right half in the legendary Hall, Dall and Cowper half back line. He lived at Palm Villa and on Links Street.

Dunfermline Athletic were beaten 5-3 in the second round of the King Cup on 5th December 1891, the vanquished then protesting that Rovers were late in turning out. The match was replayed three weeks later and Rovers, timeously, won 5-1. In between, Rovers had to make the trip to St Bernards in the East of Scotland Shield without Dall, "seized with illness earlier in the week."

"Rovers fully justified expectations by the grand fight they gave the Saints at Logie Green on Saturday, and the result is bound to do this rising young club a world of good, and invest their future visits to Edinburgh with increased interest." The Referee considered "Raith Rovers are about the best team that has appeared at Logie Green this season." They did, however, lose 2-3.

Rovers protested at the end of the game on account of the darkness. A report stated "the game ought certainly to have been stopped at least thirteen minutes from the finish, as the ball could not be followed - not even from the grandstand - unless on rare occasions, and that only when the leather was "skied". In fact, towards the closing stages the players were observed "squatting" all over the field in their endeavours to follow the ball." The "powers that be" met the following Wednesday evening and the protest was dismissed by 11 votes to 3.

be compared with the one they previously had. No small satisfaction was felt, therefore, when the team turned out to almost a man that brought the King Cup to Kirkcaldy." Rovers first away match in the Midland League, at Alloa, had to be undertaken with just ten men., although they won 2-1. There was great anticipation at Rovers' Scottish Cup tie at Broxburn on 5th September, and arrangements were made to have the : "Result of Football Match at Broxburn between Raith Rovers and Broxburn at Prince of Wales, Tavern, High Street", as advertised in that morning's newspaper. Alas, it was a disappointment. Missing only Hall from their full team, Rovers lost 2-1. With increasing national interest in League and Cup ties, C. Mackay's at 157 Links Street had arranged to receive "telegrams of principal Scotch and English matches." There was little need for such arrangement for the 1st round tie in the East of Scotland Shield, as the Raith Rovers v Lochgelly United match was played at the western end of Links Street. Gentlemen paid 3d and Boys 2d for the match which kicked off at 3.45pm, and was won 5-1 by Rovers. Hall and Bogie were selected for the East of Scotland FA match against Linlithgowshire at Tynecastle Park.

The club's committee were smart enough to prioritise their limited resources in a political fashion when it came to developing their new ground. "With commendable forethought, the Raith Rovers have attended to the comfort of the representatives of the press. A splendid press-box has now been provided, and is both ample and commodious. To all connected with the getting up of this valuable acquisition is due the best thanks of the "scribes of the pencil." This was described as resembling "a fair-sized cupboard on four wooden poles, erected on the side of the field next the railway embankment." Although crowded with three occupants, it was weather-proof, and it was immediately noticed that Rovers match reports were three times longer than they used to be. In the meantime, the paying spectators were left at the mercy of the elements.

Rovers discovered, probably for the first time, that success on the field came at a price – the best players signed for bigger teams. The former inside left Alex Bogie was making a name for himself at Ardwick (later known as Manchester City) and Alex Hall left for Sheffield United. Bill Kaye had come in at right back, Robert Nicholson started the season at wing half, and John Cowper came in on the other side of midfield. New forwards were Bill Cowan and Wishart, while in the spring Walker and Jimmy Nelson joined them, at the same time as Cairns replaced Harry Clunie in goal. John Cairns, later a director of the club, was a great servant to Kirkcaldy Wanderers, and memorably took a goal kick against London Caledonians in one of their glamour friendly matches, struck Watty Arnott, guesting for Wanderers, on the back, resulting in the great Queen's Park and Scotland player scoring an own goal at

Newton Park.

In advance of the King Cup tie at Burntisland Thistle, the influential "The Referee" sports paper had this to say about Rovers : "If there is one club above all others which is making rapid strides towards first class rank that club is Raith Rovers. Their football is far removed from the wild style of most of our country clubs, and before the end of the season we expect them to frighten some of the leading clubs in the Shield ties. The Rovers hold premier position in the Midland League, and bid fair to defy opposition." Mercifully, the praise was justified with a 4-1 win at Lammerlaws, Burntisland, although the first Midland League defeat was suffered the following week at Camelon

This early success did not rub off on their landlord. Robert Stark stood for election to the Town Council for the 1st Ward, in which there were three vacancies. The result of the poll, on a voters roll of 1,543, was Joseph Hunter, Merchant 493. James Lockhart, manufacturer 492, Andrew Pratt, manufacturer 252, William J L Taylor, cabinet maker 227, Robert Stark, spirit merchant 218.

The ownership of football grounds, past and present, was a subject of keen discussion in Kirkcaldy as 1891 drew to a close. There was considerable, and belated, speculation as to why Kirkcaldy Corporation had paid Mr Munro-Ferguson £150 per acre for his 85 acres at Robbie's Park, when the cost of such land had been £50 per acre for the previous 50 years.

While Stark's Park was not as well appointed as their former ground, Rovers were at least grateful for a home to call their own. Clubs coveted a patch of flat grassland, and there was great interest in the feuing of "Milton Lands", with the comment : "There is also a park to the west of the North British Railway, immediately overlooking the public park." At juvenile level, there was respite with the playing fields at the new Beveridge Park being opened, with Kirkcaldy Rangers early users.

The local junior grade was struggling to cope with the untimely demise of Kirkcaldy Albion. Pathhead United and Raith Athletic (effectively Raith Rovers' second eleven) were the two prominent teams, and the latter in particular nurtured many players who would go on to star for Rovers, including Jack Eckford, Jimmy Nelson, Duncan Menzies and Andrew Hood. Eckford (to Tottenham) and Menzies (to Bradford) later played in the Football League.

The visit of Lochgelly United in the semi final of the Fife Cup brought a 4-0 victory for Rovers, and the inevitable protest, over the state of the pitch. The Fifeshire Advertiser admitted : "The ground was in a very heavy state, and good football was an impossibility." Rovers followed this with a 7-1 demolition of Alloa Athletic in a League match, Cowan scoring four and Neilson three, but the Midland League was not progressing smoothly. At a meeting held in the Crown

Hotel, Alloa, the previous Saturday, Cowdenbeath withdrew from the League as they could not raise a team on a regular basis. They were fined £3.

Kirkcaldy Wanderers did not have an enjoyable Spring Holiday weekend. They lost 2-1 at Stark's Park on Saturday, when Gentlemen paid 3d and Boys 2d to see Rovers wear red jerseys, and were thumped 8-0 by Queen's Park at Newton Park on Monday.

The former match was "the whole theme of conversation in the football radius of the Lang Toun," and it inevitably led to the "a" word being trotted out once again in the letters pages of the local press. "The Future of Football In Kirkcaldy, by "Union" ... nothing would be more calculated to improve the conditions of football here, than amalgamation. .... union would be strength, and ... the result would be beyond our most sanguine expectations."

"Non Union" replied the following week by stating that those in favour of amalgamation were looking to their own positions, and were it to happen, it would last a season at most. "If there isn't room for two senior clubs in our midst, let the older club, which has been struggling away for the last 10 or 11 years and never getting out of the bit, stand down and give the younger club the chance. They have done very creditably during their short term as seniors, and deserve every encouragement and support."

To prove the point, Rovers became the first Kirkcaldy club to win the Fife Cup, beating Cowdenbeath (holders for the previous three years) 3-1 in the final at East End Park, Dunfermline. A special train ran from Kirkcaldy, adding to the crowd of between two and three thousand who watched Cowan and Neilson give Rovers a half-time lead. Neilson made it 3-0 on the hour, and Drummond's 85th minute goal for Cowdenbeath was by way on consolation

A shortage of suitable grounds began to affect the fixture schedule. Rovers were due at Dunfermline in a top-of-the-table League match on 7th May, but East End Park was staging the Consolation Cup Final, so the match was postponed, and Rovers had a blank Saturday despite having six pending fixtures.

When the game was eventually played on 28th May, it was meaningless, Rovers beat Alva 7-0 at Stark's Park, and clinched the Midland League Championship with a 5-0 win at Grangemouth, allowing the luxury of a 3-2 defeat at Dunfermline in the final League game. All that remained was a couple of promised local friendlies, shoe-horned in before the close of the season on 31st May. The day before, Pathhead United were beaten 4-1, and on the last day of the month Rovers won 3-1 at Newton Park.

Those fund-raising fixtures, at the end of a long and demanding season for players and spectators alike, were at least three games too far, starting with a match at Pathhead United on Monday 23rd May which was described as "purely a farce, only four of

the Rovers first eleven appearing, accompanied by five substitutes drawn from various sources. The United were even more handicapped, and could only muster up three of their first string, while several former players in the United team and one of their second eleven completed the lot - nine men a side." Only two thirty minutes were played, in extremely unpleasant weather.

The Kirkcaldy Times reported : "One of the Rovers subs sought the friendly shelter of the pavilion in the second half, and it would have been a wise act on the part of the other players had they followed suit, but they preferred to brace the elements and at the finish several of them looked more like n****** than anything else in consequence of their frequent hugging tendencies towards "mother earth" which was of a very clinging nature." A week later, two halves of 35 minutes were played at Elder's Park, in drier conditions.

The close season lasted barely six weeks, time enough for Rovers players to distinguish themselves in the club's annual Sports Day. Although Albion beat Kinghorn in the final of the 5-a-sides, John Thomson of Rovers won the 100 yards race, with James Neilson third. Both held the same positions in the 300 yards race confined to Rovers players, with Willie Dall second.

Because of the late end to season 1891/92, the Secretary engineered a delayed start to the following season, save for a match on 7th August at Cowdenbeath, which was won 5-4 by Rovers. The players then enjoyed a fortnight off, before losing to King's Park in the final of Dunfermline's 11-a-side tournament. Stark's Park was opened for the season on 3rd September with the visit of Grangemouth, who replaced Johnstone Wanderers at short notice, and won 3-2. In pre-registration days, footballers were somewhat promiscuous in dispensing their favours around local clubs, as noted by a Fife Free Press correspondent, who reported that Coan and Bonella appeared to be promised to both Rovers and Kirkcaldy FC, on the same afternoon.

"It is rather strange, though not uncommon, and by no means a manly thing, for footballers now-a-days to promise to throw in their lot with a couple, or even three different clubs, However, today will set the minds of a few at rest as to which team shall have the luck (shall we say ?) in securing the services of the above-mentioned players, for assuredly the majority of players are as fickle as some of our Parliamentary candidates - they will promise everything, but the fulfilment is very remote."

Rovers sprang a surprise when they listed their team for the friendly match against Broxburn on 10th September. "According to the above list D. Walker, who played for Kirkcaldy in the Scottish tie at Galashiels on Saturday last, rejoins his last love by playing centre for the Rovers. Truly the ways of footballers are past finding out - here today and there tomorrow. They are like so many bees flitting from flower to flower in search of "honey !" We hope our local ramblers will

WILLIAM COWAN

DAVID WALKER
"India Rubber- man"
(and trophy man !) with the
five cups Rovers won in 1898

Rovers sartorial elegance was remarked upon a month later when they won 3-2 at Dunfermline Athletic in the King Cup. "Rovers wore blue shirts with white collars and cuffs ; Athletic turned out in "Penny numbers". Their results were equally impressive, losing just twice in the opening 20 fixtures of the 1892/93 season. In advance of the Shield quarter final against Lochgelly United, the (Edinburgh) Evening News remarked :" ... whether they win or lose today the Rovers have done relatively better work in friendly matches than any club in the (Fife) Association. and whether they win or lose today the Rovers have borne themselves with great credit to their club and their town."

Stark's Park being frost-bound, the teams agreed to play two thirty minute halves as a friendly and Lochgelly returned a fortnight later to lose 8-2. The week before the friendly, despite the Stark's Park pitch being hard with frost, both captains agreed that the Fife Cup tie should proceed, and Rovers beat Kirkcaldy 4-1. The inevitable protest followed, on the grounds of darkness, which was sustained, with a replay ordered for Stark's Park. "This should draw more grist to the mill for both teams."

settle down to a resting place some day." Walker did indeed play, and score, for Rovers.

Both Davie and Jimmy Walker opened the season with Rovers. The latter developed into a great right wing flyer who could always be depended upon to play a skilful and speedy game, and was held in great respect by opposing backs and half backs – indeed, that was the only thing they could hold about the speedy and clever winger.

Davie Walker soon became known as the "India rubber man" from the elusive and tricky manner in which he could evade the attentions of opposing defenders. He was a clever centre forward, slim and slippery, and it was a good centre half that could keep him in check.

Andrew Grieve replaced Clunie in goal. Deuchars moved from the forward line to right half, while Alex Suttie came in at inside left

The opening rounds of the major cup competitions came very early in the season, which meant that several clubs were ill-prepared for such season-defining fixtures. Rovers looked to have no such concerns when they beat Lassodie 14-0 in the first round of the East of Scotland Shield, but were shocked the following week when Smithston Hibernians of `Dunbartonshire won 3-1 at Stark's Park in the second round of the Scottish Cup. The gate of the latter fixture (24th September) was not helped by the counter attraction of the official opening of the Beveridge Park, and Rovers, who enjoyed most of the play, particularly in the second half, were left to rue Walker's absence, he being cup-tied.

The bold Davie scored two and helped Dall to a hat-trick, and Suttie to two goals, in Rovers 7-0 demolition of Coupar Angus in the October holiday fixture, although Rovers had to rely on four players from Raith Athletic to complete their eleven.

Kirkcaldy Wanderers went into the second round Shield tie at Stark's Park in confident mood, happy at the "new blood" in their team. Rovers took the field looking "very smart in their new dress of blue, with 'collar and cuff' attachment," and Suttie gave them a half-time lead. The roof fell in on Wanderers in the second half, Rovers winning the tie 6-0.

"In Memorium" cards were in their infancy, and young Rovers players pooled their money and had printed cards which bore the inscription "In Memory of the Kirkcaldy Wanderers, who died at the feet of Raith Rovers," etc.etc. The printer, a keen Wanderers supporter, made the young jokers swear not to divulge his name. They engaged a boy to go to Newton Park the following Saturday and distribute the cards amongst the Wanderers' spectators, bearding the lion in his den with a vengeance !

Alex Arnot, the first chronicler of the Rovers history, recalled in a newspaper article in 1925 a friend of his who started work as an apprentice tailor around that time. "On his first day at work, the foreman (a staunch

supporter of the Wanderers) asked him which club he supported. "The Rovers," he modestly replied. The foreman regarded the youthful recruit to the sartorial art sternly for a moment, and then said slowly and distinctly. "Weel, my man, just let me hear tell of you going to Stark's Park as long as you sit on THIS board ! This is a Wanderers' shop !"

Those were heady days for Kirkcaldy football followers. Rovers were winning matches and scoring goals by the barrow-load, and on Monday 2nd January 1893 Renton, one of the great Dunbartonshire clubs from the early days of Scottish football, visited Stark's Park. Admission was raised to 6d, Boys 3d, with Ladies free. Wanderers were not enjoying the same success as Rovers, but their impressive ground could still attract top teams for friendly matches over the holiday period. The visit of Dumbarton was described as "the match of the season", while Corinthians and Casuals made their by now customary visits.

Before all that "Mr Thomas Nelson, the well-known back of the Raith Rovers was entertained to supper by his club-mates and a few friends, in the Harbourhead Hotel, on the occasion of his approaching marriage." Mr Alex Strachan, President, was in the chair and the honorary president, Dr Campbell, was in attendance. A gift of a suitably inscribed easy chair was given to Nelson, and a silver cruet & tea-kettle. Nelson had been with the club since its origin, but for a short period of "rest."

Dr Campbell congratulated Rovers on being semi finalists in the Shield. "There was only one danger of this success, and that was the English agent disease." He hoped, however, they would all remain loyal, and (to applause) "treat those gentlemen in the way their young friend Mr Dall did."

The weather intervened to stall Rovers' progress in the King Cup. On 7th January, "... the referee, after an inspection of the ground, declared it unplayable. The Raith team were on the field prepared to play the tie, but the Bathgate declined. The home team, however, offered to play a friendly, but this the visitors refused to do. Before leaving the field the captain of the Raith Rovers intimated to the referee that he would claim the tie."

The following week saw Rovers and Kirkcaldy reconvene at Stark's Park for the replayed Fife Cup tie. A frozen pitch meant that a friendly was played, of two 30 minutes, must to the disgust of the spectators. A further week hence, the tie was finally decided, albeit in very slippery and treacherous conditions. Jimmy Walker scored a hat-trick in Rovers' 7-2 victory. There was no such good fortune in the King Cup, in which Bathgate won 2-1 at Stark's Park, after a 1-1 draw over the Forth.

Rovers next major cup tie was the semi final of the East of Scotland Shield, in which they entertained St Bernards. A letter to the Fife Free Press suggested that Rovers move the tie to Newton Park, where they would have use of a grandstand, enjoy better facilities, and would be better for spectators.

Stark's Park it was, however, and the Scottish League team won 3-1, to leave Rovers with just the Fife Cup to look forward to in the closing months of the season.

The amalgamation question was not just confined to the local press. Reporting on the St Bernards match, the Evening Dispatch commented : "It seems a great pity that the Raith Rovers and Kirkcaldy should not unite. There is not sufficient interest in the "Lang Toon" to support two football clubs, and if the two were to come together they would form a powerful team."

There was still much for the players to enjoy with the programme of friendly matches, not least the annual trip to the Granite City. On March 18th Rovers played Victoria United, one of the three clubs who, in 1902, amalgamated to form the present Aberdeen FC. An attendance in excess of 2,000 at Wellington Grounds saw Rovers win 4-2, "dressed in blue jerseys, which, to avoid confusion, caused the United to don white semmits for the nonce."

The following week, Wishaw Thistle, holders of the Lanarkshire Cup, were welcomed to Stark's Park, with an earlier kick off of 3.15 scheduled to allow the visitors to catch the 6 o'clock train. Rovers won 5-0, Davie Walker and Willie Dall scoring two apiece and Alex Suttie completing the scoring. The same scorers, and quantities saw off Lochgelly United, this time 5-3, in the semi final of the Fife Cup a week later.

The importance of the fixture can be assessed from the following Fifeshire Advertiser report. : "Immediately on the whistle sounding, Mr Waugh, the referee, was surrounded by the Lochgelly team and several of their supporters, who attempted to put their spite out upon him. McKay and the home team were, however, successful in getting Mr Waugh safely into the pavilion, but not before he had been subjected to the Lochgelly team, one of whom struck him in the face."

The good burghers of Kirkcaldy may have been engaged in the debate for the location of the Adam Smith & Beveridge Halls (the High Street site was now out of the running, with Mr Sang's site considered to be the best, rather than the nearby Parish Church glebe site) ; but they had a free scoring football club to enjoy in their midst.

The Fife Cup Final, between Rovers and Cowdenbeath, was staged at Newton Park, the Fifeshire FA and Dunfermline Athletic being at loggerheads. "With the exception of the first five minutes the Rovers were out of it, their display being one of the poorest witnessed this season." The 2-2 draw was therefore fortuitous, but Rovers lost the replay 2-1 at East End Park, peace having broken out between Dunfermline and the Fife FA.

"The game was well contested throughout, and, in the first half especially, the Rovers played a grand game, having nearly all the play, and for a considerable portion of this half Cowdenbeath were seldom past mid-field. In the second half, however, the miners

played up finely, and stood the pace much better than their opponents, who completely fell away towards the close of the game. At the finish of the game Mackay lodged a protest on the ground that Hynd, having only lately returned from England, was illegible, but at a meeting of the Association this week the protest was dismissed."

A season of progress ended in defeat, but the band of brothers continued to enjoy each other's company. The Fife Free Press of June 24th reported : "Last night the members of the Raith Rovers Football Club met together in a social capacity [in the hall of the Working Lads' institute] to do honour to one of their number, Mr William H. Mackay, the popular and well-known half-back." Mr Alex Strachan, one of the Honorary Presidents of the club, presided. Supper provided by Adam Smith of the National Hotel. Present was a writing desk, and a purse of sovereigns for his wife. Mackay "felt he had some years of hard play in him yet (loud applause). Songs were also given by members present, and a pleasant and enjoyable evening was spent."

Rovers opened 1893/94 season with a 4-2 victory over Clackmannan at Stark's Park, as reported in the Fife Free Press : "The football season of 1893-4 in the Kirkcaldy district was initiated on Saturday. The Raith Rovers set the ball in motion, and judging from the excitement attendant on the meeting of the local eleven and Clackmannan, who were their opponents, its is quite evident that the enthusiasm over the popular game is as strong as ever in the "Lang Toun ... many were anxious to see what the Rovers' team was to be .... the recent development in the constitution of football teams by the adoption of professionalism, was far from assuring."

Sandy Hall had returned from England, thus forming the half back line of Hall, Dall and Cowper that would trip off the tongues of 19th century football fans for many more years. Jock Eckford, Andrew Blyth and Jimmy Neilson joined the club, as Rovers built a strong side. Lambert came in at full back.

After a Saturday off due to the annual band contest at Raith, Neilston were beaten 3-0 in preparation for the first cup tie of the season, the 1st qualifying round of the Scottish Cup, at home to Dunfermline Athletic. "The weather was beautifully fine, and a large attendance of spectators lined the enclosure. Great interest was centred in the tussle, as it was generally believed that the Athletic had got together a strong team for the occasion, and that they fully anticipated giving the home team a hard run for victory."

It was a meeting of the only two professional sides in Fife, with Dunfermline rumoured to be on 5 shillings a week, and therefore grateful for their share of the £12 gate. Davie Walker and Alex Suttie helped themselves to hat-tricks as Rovers won 8-0. "Should the Rovers maintain the form shown by them on Saturday, more will certainly be heard of them in coming contests, as they will doubtless be ill to beat."

JACK COWPER

The left half lived in Thistle Street and was described in 1891 as "one of those players who seems to be in the right place at the right moment. An effective tackler, he kicks in a clean and easy manner."

The Fife Free Press reported, on December 24th 1892 : "On Saturday the Clackmannan were to have turned up and played the Rovers in their King Cup tie. They however failed to put in an appearance. Since then we understand that Clackmannan have written the Rovers intimating their intention of scratching to them, and wishing them all the success in their next tie with Bathgate.

League Champions Dumbarton beat Kirkcaldy & District 5-1, the team comprising players from both Rovers and Kirkcaldy. Two thousand watched Davie Walker give Rovers a first half lead over Renton at Stark's Park, but Murray equalised in the second half. Kirkcaldy kept their team to themselves (with no Rovers players) for their 6-2 defeat by Corinthians, and 1-0 reverse to Casuals.

Free scoring Rovers scored five goals for the third successive match, beating Alliance League champions Linthouse at Stark's Park in the April holiday fixture, followed by 4-2 and 7-1 home victories over Glasgow Battlefield and Fair City Athletic respectively. On the third Saturday in April, with the Links Market in full swing on Sands Road, Rovers beat Glasgow club Carrington 9-0.

BILL KAYE

Joined Rovers from Burntisland Thistle in 1891, and played at right back for six seasons, winning many medals.

The first two rounds of the King Cup were easily hurdled, both the Argyll & Sutherland Highlanders, and Broxburn Shamrock, beaten by the same scoreline, 8-1. Rovers won through to the fourth round of the Shield (where the latter team were beaten 2-0) with a little difficulty. Ferguson had opened the scoring for Clackmannan (who had arrived late and changed on the train) and Jimmy Walker equalised before half time. Rovers took the lead in the second half. "Almost immediately afterwards [Neilson's goal], and with fully twenty minutes to go, play was brought to an abrupt termination. The visitors' left back, W. Halley, who had been indulging in some very questionable play, and who had been previously warned during the game, was, at this stage, ordered off the field for deliberately charging J. Walker while about to play the ball. Halley refused at first to acquiesce, but eventually he went off, being accompanied by another of his club mates and the remainder of the team then left the field, leaving the scores at : Raith Rovers 2 Clackmannan 1."

1894 - Dunnikier school opened ; new Sheriff Court House in Whytescauseway opened in May

Lassodie certainly believed that a week later, swept away 7-0 in the first round of the Shield. A warning against complacency was given with a 4-0 defeat at St Bernards, although "apart from the forwards, there was little to choose between either team." Stirlingshire side Gairdoch journeyed to Kirkcaldy for the second qualifying round of the Scottish Cup, and won 3-2. "The boisterous nature of the weather was against a fine exhibition of the game. After criticising the players one is inclined to treat the referee the same way, but as nothing is to be gained from so doing, the best plan will probably be to "let sleeping dogs lie". Rovers' wretched form in the Scottish Cup therefore continued, but progress was made in the local cup competitions. Cowdenbeath were beaten 5-3 in the second round of the Shield, in front of the largest gate at Stark's Park for a match between Fife clubs.

In the run-up to the (economically) vital holiday friendly fixtures, the Fifeshire Advertiser's patience was tried on December 30th.

"The two local senior teams, or their committees, seem to be at loggerheads, and the motto, "Let brotherly love continue" seems to be an unknown quantity in their midst. To-day, both teams have matches at home ; last Saturday there was no match, and yet the two local elevens could not come to an arrangement to play a friendly in order to provide an afternoon's sport for our athletic loving community, and at the same time fill their (both) not overstocked coffers. This is surely far from a sportsmanlike manner of doing things. Who's to blame ? On behalf of the Rovers it is urged that arrangements could not be come to as to choice of ground. Kirkcaldy management, on the other hand, say they preferred to play on Newton Park, but would not object to meet at Stark's Park, and it was at one time practically an understood thing between the rival secretaries that the match would be played. However, it didn't come off. It is high time the "hatchet" was buried between the two teams. This sort of work will not raise the club responsible for it in the estimation of the public. "

Rovers advertised their main fixture as : "Grand Football Treat. New Years Day. Second visit of ex Champions of the world. 2pm, 6d/3d Ladies free." Two hours earlier, St Mirren made their first appearance in Fife, at Newton Park, where admission was 6d, with a seat in the grandstand an additional 6d. Three days later, London Casuals were due at Newton Park. Rovers had an important date on the evening of their match with Renton. "The Raith Rovers and a few friends are to meet in a social capacity in the National Hotel on Monday evening, when they are to present Mr A. Grieve, their much-esteemed goalkeeper, with a purse of sovereigns, on the occasion of his marriage."

Mr Strachan, President, referred to the recent death of Dr Campbell, a great loss to the club. Replies to toasts were given by Mr R Lambert and Mr H Ritchie. "At intervals during the evening, songs were given by the

following members of the company : Messrs W. McKay, A. Hall, D. Small, J. Thomson, A. Strachan, R Brown, A Elder, J Mitchell, R Lambert, D Louden, D Lambert, H Ritchie, A Grieve, A Hepburn, N McGhie, A Suttie, J.D. Gerrard, A cornet solo was also given by Mr A Watters, while Mr H Ritchie favoured the company with a recitation."

Rovers bade farewell to 1893 with a 5-0 home win over East Stirling, currently top of the Midland League, John Walker scoring four times. Ordinarily, the visit of Cowdenbeath to Newton Park would be a top attraction, but "owing to the counter-attraction at Stark's Park, the turn-out of spectators was very limited"

The visit of Leith Athletic in the semi final of the East of Scotland Shield was, rightly, billed as the "match of the season". Leith asked for goal-nets, but "the Rovers' committee fail to see the advisability of such needless expenditure on the part of a country club ..." Their modest status didn't stop them doubling the admission charge to 6d

"The holding capacity of Stark's Park has never before been so severely taxed as it was last Saturday .... A special train had been run from Leith .... and that alone brought 300 people .. In all there would be upwards of 3,000 people present, and the total money drawn at the gate amounted to fully £52. Leith travelled in a saloon carriage, and drove from the station to the field stripped and ready for the fray."

Rovers more than held their own against their exhalted visitors, and took the lead through Davie Walker two minutes after the interval. Leith equalised in controversial circumstances : "[goalkeeper] Grieve was so sorely bustled that in attempting to knock the ball out of danger he kicked it through his own goal, to the great chagrin of the team and its supporters. This seemed to take the heart out of the home team, as they fell away considerably after this." Leith won 3-1.

The following Saturday, the referee declared Cowdenbeath's pitch unplayable, and a friendly match of 2 x 40 minutes was played, which Rovers won 6-4. During the following week "….the Rovers' committee succeeded in making arrangements with the Railway Company to have the 5pm train from Dunfermline to Thornton, stopped at Cowdenbeath, thus allowing the supporters of the Kirkcaldy team to see the match, and get home again by the 6pm train. The facilities, we are glad to hear, were largely taken advantage of, and a large turn-out of football enthusiasts from the Lang Toun turned out at Cowdenbeath …" to see a 2-2 draw in the semi final of the Fife Cup. Rovers won the replay 6-0. "The Referee" sporting newspaper reported that : "Hall, of Raith Rovers, is the cleverest man in Fife. Played two seasons with Sheffield Wednesday ; is playing better than ever. Was offered place in Darwen recently, but refused." Burnley wanted to sign Jack Cowper, and for the second successive season, a bid from Leith Athletic for Jimmy Walker was declined. The professional era of Scottish football was moving rapidly into gear.

On 24th February, Rovers returned to Cowdenbeath for the semi final of the King Cup, but with three inches of snow lying, a friendly match of 2 x 35 minutes was played. It would appear that the Rovers players had anticipated the postponement. Two hundreds Rovers fans made the journey on a special train " … only to find that although the visitors took the field the majority of them were physically unfit to take part in a contest, and from start to finish the game was nothing but a laughable farce."

After ten minutes' play "it was apparent that there was more wrong with some of the Rovers than was at first supposed. Instead of being in their usual form the majority of them were simply incapable, and when they should have kicked the ball could only stand and look, or if they tried to kick, their efforts only created laughter. The exhibition they made was simply an insult to their reputation, and we would recommend their committee to investigate the matter and take steps to prevent such a thing happening again." Hall and Cowper both left the field before the end and Rovers lost 6-1.

A contemporary account spoke of more action off the field than on it. "As the team left the field at the close of the game the Cowdenbeath spectators lined up in the lane leading from the park to the North End Hotel, where the players changed, and as the Rovers fought their way through the crowd they had to run the gauntlet of severe kicking and punching. It was a discreditable exhibition on the part of Cowdenbeath people. Nor was that all. The Kirkcaldy supporters had to run for the station followed by a howling mob, and a force of police had to guard the station entrance to keep the miners outside the platform. The Rovers' team left Cowdenbeath in a hurry, and their departure was marked by a wild scene. As the brake drove through the streets it appeared to be empty – the only man to be seen being the driver ! The players were under the seats ! And the Cowdenbeath "enthusiasts" were chasing along behind the brake showering chunks of coal and road metal on the machine!"

There was worse to come when they returned to North End Park a week later ; a full strength Rovers team lost 4-0 (some reports have 4-1 with Davie Walker scoring the only goal of the second half). Cowdenbeath had gone to great lengths to get the pitch playable, pit ashes covering the goalmouths and before long the players were ankle deep in black mud. In the long and disreputable history of protests, Rovers' took some beating the following week. They protested against the lines being marked with sawdust in place of whiting ; the case was unsurprisingly dismissed. Cowdenbeath beat Kirkcaldy 6-2 in the King Cup Final, played at East End Park, Dunfermline.

Rovers' winless run was halted in spectacular style on the April holiday, when Second Division Champions Hibs journeyed to Stark's Park. The day started badly for the visitors ; they missed their train and kick off was delayed from 2pm to 3pm. Then a "heavy deluge of rain …. caused the spectators to seek refuge under the canvas …." Stark's Park at last being provided with some cover, albeit of a rudimentary and temporary nature.

Rovers won 7-0, and "too much cannot be said in praise of their splendid victory, which far eclipsed any previous exhibition given by them this season. "The "pill" will be a most bitter one for the Hibs to swallow, as it is by far the largest defeat they have sustained this season while out in such strong force as they were on Monday, and such a decided victory for a country club should advance the local team in the respect of other city clubs, and may in addition be the means of getting them a place in the Second League. The game must be classed as one of the finest ever seen in the district. The play throughout was on the fastest lines and by no means as one-sided as the score would seem to indicate."

The season ended on a winning note, Lochgelly United beaten 6-2 in the Final of the Fife Cup at East End Park, Dunfermline, which the Fife Free Press dismissed as " …. certainly not a place for playing off a final tie …."

The following week, the Evening News in Edinburgh did their best to attract support for the final Friendly match of the season : "The Heart of Midlothian have got a good guarantee from the Raith Rovers, and they visit Fife with a good reputation and a good team. The Rovers are showing wonderful enterprise, and this is one of the occasions on which the public should give them a handsome reward." Upwards of 2,000 spectators saw a 2-0 win for Rovers and it was "rumoured that after the game three of the Rovers' men were approached by the visitors with the view of securing their services for next season."

Rovers finished the season with a published record of 3 draws and 7 defeats from 35 matches, scoring 142 goals and conceding 59. The Annual General Meeting of the club was held in Burleigh Street Hall on 25th May, with Mr Lambert in the chair. "Mr Todd, treasurer, submitted the balance sheet for the past season, which showed a substantial balance in the hands of the club. The office bearers were appointed as follows : Honorary president., R.C. Munro Ferguson ; vice presidents Dr Curror and Mr A Strachan ; auditors : Messrs Samuel and J. Wyles. President D. Lambert, vice president William Elder, honorary secretary D. Todd, match secretary. R. Inglis ; treasurer J. Todd ; committee Messrs James Russell, David Mitchell, John Foster, W. Eckford, John Baxter, "D. Samuel", John Carr and John Miller"

The Fifeshire Advertiser in its edition of Saturday August 11th 1894 welcomed the "OPENING OF THE FOOTBALL SEASON. The great national game is upon us again. "The Gates Ajar" was proclaimed last Saturday throughout the country, but so far as

NEILSON (NEIL) DEUCHARS Lived in Hill Street and played for Rovers for five seasons, from 1890 to 1895.

A Friendly match with Burnbank Swifts was completed amid some difficulty. The visitors' train was late in arriving, and the match kicked off 15 minutes late, Rovers hurriedly changing to their reserve strip of white, the visitors arriving in dark blue. The referee stopped the match after 80 minutes (with Rovers 3-1 ahead) due to bad light. The following Saturday, the Fifeshire Advertiser reported : "It now turns out that Neilson's laziness in the second half is accounted for by his being quarrelled by Dall for not parting with the ball, the admonition taking the shape of "You would be better off the field". The "difference" between these two prominent members of the team is especially to be regretted at the present time when the club is in the midst of their most important cup ties. A great deal could be said on either side, but "the less said the soonest mended." Suffice it to say that neither of the players was in the right. Neilson showed a certain amount of "dourness" in acting as he did, while Dall, even although he is the captain of the club and is to a certain extent privileged, might have taken a more fitting place to give his "advice" than on the field, and before the large turnout of spectators." Jimmy Neilson went in the huff and refused to play in the next two matches, both cup ties which Rovers, fortuitously, safely negotiated.

JOHN LAMBERT

The match at North End Park, Cowdenbeath was drawn 2-2, starting a sequence of five successive matches between the teams. The Scottish Cup, third qualifying round tie at the same venue was drawn 3-3, the field being "a perfect quagmire". A good crowd was reported, despite the miners having been on strike for 16 weeks. More than 3,000 watched the Rovers, somewhat fortuitously, win the replay 2-1 at Stark's Park.

A thousand fewer saw the Shield replay at Stark's Park finish 0-0, and to Rovers' chagrin the second replay was played at North End Park. The East of Scotland Association, having watched the mounting acrimony between both clubs and their supporters, arranged for neutral linesmen. An 80th minute Eckford goal gave Rovers a 2-1 win, but the victory was tarnished by Rovers players being "very brutally treated" by Cowdenbeath supporters after the match. "Several free fights occurred outside the field, and at one time a melee of the wildest description was witnessed. Jack Eckford, his brother and an elderly man who came to his assistance, were kicked and struck on the way to the hotel. "When the team drove away from Cowdenbeath they were again subjected to the stone-throwing exercise by the miners, several of them being struck, and the brake being badly damaged."

Kirkcaldy and district is concerned, the season only commences today.
"The Rovers' committee have not been idle during the close season, and, we have no doubt, will place a team upon the field worthy of their opponent's steel. Stark's Park has also undergone much improvement since last season, having been drained and levelled, and a strong wood railing put up in place of the hold wire. All that is now required is a grand stand to make it complete"

There were pre-season concerns amongst the support as to the strength of the team. Sandy Hall had been lured to Hearts and John Cowper to Leith Athletic. John Lambert, Robert Robertson and John Eckford had moved up from Raith Athletic, Bill Kaye returned to the club, McLeod was recruited from Dunfermline Juniors and Alex Dawson from Cupar Athletic. Andrew Marshall, who had played with the club in its junior days, returned from the army. Alex Oag came in at left back.

The season started unpromisingly, at home to Leith Athletic. 4-2 behind, Alex Suttie dislocated his shoulder just before half time. Leith allowed Harry Simpson to replace him for the second half, possibly the first ever substitute in the club's history. The newcomer made little impact, Leith scoring four more without reply for an 8-2 victory.

Rovers' found their shooting boots in successive Thursday evening friendly matches against Kirkcaldy Cricket Club, a cricket match between the two clubs having been played earlier in the summer. Football on Saturday August 18th was out of the question. 25,000 converged on the grounds of Raith House for the annual band contest, which included the likes of Besses o' the' Barn, and Black Dyke Mills Bands.

More goals were scored against inferior opposition, with an 8-5 victory over Montrose, and successive 8-1 scorelines against Cartvale, and at Selkirk in the first round of the Scottish Cup where "the heavy rain, and consequent bad state of the ground, told seriously against good play." It undoubtedly helped that Selkirk had assembled a team specifically for the fixture, and without any training.
This drew the response from a Kirkcaldy FC official, when the Fife Free Press asked him about their prospects for the season : "After some positive things, he said "We have not as yet any shining light in the way of first league teams, nor do we want these so much. We wish to arrange to play with clubs that can play football and will play it ; not one or two big things, and the other teams to take goals off."

Predictably, this provoked a flurry of correspondence in the local papers. Kirkcaldy's supporters stated that their team retained their fixtures against familiar opponents in St Johnstone, Gordon Highlanders and Black Watch, "because these teams play football ; disdaining matches against league teams, as organised by Raith Rovers." In response came the accusation that the statements were made "not for the

purpose of giving the public useful information, but for no other purposes than to injure the Rovers in their creditable attempts to provide the Kirkcaldy public with the best football that can possibly be had."
"A. Rover" wrote : "Raith Rovers' goal register for last season cannot be tarnished by any slur cast from Newton Park, as no team in Fife ever rose to the eminence which they rose to last season, and I am quite confident they shall attain to still higher laurels, and shall this season, in their fixtures with those clubs who "cannot and do not play football" (League teams) give an excellent account of themselves, and still keep up the reputation of the "Lang Toun" in the football world."

Back came a reply : "There is only one thing I have to tell him, and that is, that the "Kirkcaldy heroes" as he sneeringly puts it, have all along had an honourable reputation, which they have as faithfully sustained. There are ups and downs in every club's life, and, if I may be allowed, I would say the Rovers should not whistle so loudly till they are out of the wood. The "Kirkcaldy heroes" are in no way disconcerted and are fully determined to maintain their reputation both as gentlemen and players of the dribbling code. Langtonian."

One correspondent may have got to the core of the debate when he stated that Kirkcaldy would not pay high guarantees due to their financial circumstances. They had certainly spent a great deal of money in building a cinder cycle track at Newton Park, and had continued to improve the impressive facilities at the ground. Their playing strength improved in unfortunate circumstances, many of the players of the recently dissolved Pathhead United joining Wanderers' Junior eleven.

Their financial woes were not alleviated by an early exit from the Scottish Cup, by Polton Vale after a replay, but the debate was continued where it counted, on the field of play, when the clubs met at Newton Park in the first round of the East of Scotland Shield.
"The kick off had been timed for 3.30, but large crowds began to arrive before three o'clock, and from then up till the time of starting a continual rush was kept up at both gates, with the result that the ticket sellers were not sufficient to cope with the demand made upon them. On account of this, the large gate which had been erected at the [Lady] Helen Street entrance, with the view of allowing for the easy exit of the spectators after the match was over, was thrown down as the time for starting drew near. In this way considerably over a hundred gained free admission, and a pound or two were lost to the funds of each club, but it is only fair to state that a number of those who gained admission in this way went and paid their money honourably to the officials.
"By half past three every available piece of ground round the ropes had been brought into requisition by the spectators, the railway embankment at the north end of the

pitch being also crowded with young folks, who made themselves heard after the match started, and the grand-stand was filled long before the teams made their appearance. Before the start, Mr A.A. Hay, Kirkcaldy's famous cyclist, rode round the track several times, but as it is not yet finished it was rather rough riding."

A few minutes after the advertised time, the Rovers, who had stripped at Stark's Park, stepped on to the field, and from the way in which they were greeted, it was evident that they were largely supported amongst the crowd" which the Fife Free Press put at 5,000.

Martin, a professional in an otherwise amateur side, and Weir put Kirkcaldy into a two goal lead, but Andrew Marshall and Davie Walker drew Rovers level by the interval. Both Walkers scored in the second half to win the tie 4-2, and give Rovers' fans bragging rights.   .

The team continued to make progress in cup competitions, and draw good crowds for attractive friendly matches (the October holiday visit of Dundee attracting more than 2,000). The East of Scotland Shield second round tie against Cowdenbeath was anticipated with relish, and in verse by "Caesar".

THE EVE OF BATTLE - GRIEVE'S ADDRESS TO HIS TEAM

Rovers wha hae hides clad red
Dribbled aft whaur Dall has led,
Raise your slogan, ye maun tread
    History's banefu' field.
Now's the time to mend your score,
Fear nae alien's battledore ;
Press them to the tune o' four -
    Lads who winna yield

Ye wha spoiled Edina's pride,
Stemmed the local eddying tide -
Heroes name will dare deride
    Show your latent powers.
Bang the leather 'tween the posts,
Show to a' ye are nae "frosts,"
Vain their shouts and peurile boasts
    Victory is yours.

By the cruel pangs o' fate,
Mem'ries o' your last defeat ;
Make your iron foemen sweat,
    Crush them now or aye.
Wrest from them the precious "Shield",
Forwards, mark ilk pawky chield,
Jink them like the vera diel,
    Ye shall win the day

The gruelling sequence of Raith v Cowdenbeath cup ties was interrupted on 20th October when Stark's Park hosted the 13th meeting between the East of Scotland FA and the Glasgow FA. The host association omitted all League club players, and fielded : Hynd (Cowdenbeath), Miller (Kirkcaldy), Kaye (captain, Raith Rovers), Bryce (Bathgate), Munro (Adventurers), Bauldie (Cowdenbeath) ; Walker (Raith Rovers), Stirling (Polton Vale), Allan (Bo'ness), Wilson (Lochgelly United), Reid (Adventurers)

Glasgow selected : Anderson (Battlefield), Crawford (Rangers), Dunbar (Celtic), Gibb (Partick Thistle), Robertson (Queen's Park), Bruce (Partick Thistle) ; Anderson (Battlefield), J. Proudfoot (Partick Thistle), Gray (Rangers), Clelland (Third Lanark), Lawrie (Cowlairs).

A 3-3 draw was played out over two x 35 minutes in a downpour, the "miserable weather" restricting the crowd to just over 1,000.

There was a feeling in the town that, at long last, this may be the season in which a local club could make progress in the Scottish Cup. "The draws for the first round of the final stage of the Scottish Cup competition has been causing a good deal of excitement in the Kirkcaldy district lately, and on Tuesday night there was great excitement amongst the large crowd which gathered outside the shop of Messrs J &D Young, who had a bill posted up intimating they would have the result, and when it became known that the Rovers were drawn with the 5th Kirkcudbright Rifle Volunteers at Stark's Park, great was the rejoicing."

The visitors from Dumfries were holders of the Churchill Cup, Southern Counties Cup and Southern Counties Charity Cup, and the 2pm kick off was ordered by the SFA "in order that the visitors may get home that night"

Rovers won 6-3, with Alex Suttie scoring a hat-trick, but they were about to fall foul of the rule book, which required goal-nets to be provided for matches in the later stages of the Scottish Cup. Although Rovers had telegraphed an order for this relatively new innovation, they had not arrived in time for the match.

"It is unfortunate that the goal-nets were not forthcoming, as this has proved the plea for hanging a protest. The circumstances attending the procuring of these nets were, however, such as to point to the fact that the Rovers did their best to fulfil the bye-laws of the game. One thing is certain that even supposing goal nets had been used it would in no way affected the result. Again, these articles were on the road since Tuesday. Whatever may be the upshot remains to be seen at the SFA meeting, but, from what we saw of the visitors, we believe they have too much of the sportsman in them to take advantage of such a technical defalcation."

The following Saturday, Rovers were at home to Cowdenbeath in the Fife Cup, and "the goal nets have arrived and will be in use." Their expense may, or may not, have been at cause of the following local difficulty, as reported in the Fifeshire Advertiser.

"Cowdenbeath were still owing the Rovers 7s 6d, a sum which has been due since the two teams played in the same tie last year, and as the Association had ordered Cowdenbeath to pay this money, the Rovers refused to open their gates and allow the spectators to come in, until the order was complied with. The crowd which had assembled to witness the game were, in

JOHN CAIRNS
First choice goalkeeper for four seasons, and occasional guest in seven more, between 1886 and 1898.
He lived in Cowan Street.

Predictably, there was a protest. Cowdenbeath insisted, at a Special General Meeting of the East of Scotland FA, that Eckford, one of Rovers regular professionals, had played this season and last for Raith Athletic. The Secretary of Raith Rovers wrote that Raith Athletic were merely the Second Eleven of Raith Rovers, therefore not another club. They had the same committee, though two secretaries. All Raith Athletic expenses were met by Raith Rovers. The protest was dismissed 10-2. Rovers were instructed to write a letter of apology following their letter requesting the SFA appoint a referee for the Shield tie "as Mr Williamson, who had refereed on a previous occasion, did not appear to know the rules of the game." In the course of a few remarks afterwards, Mr Williamson expressed the opinion that some of the officials of Raith Rovers were in the habit of betting on the result of ties. He condemned that practice, as these were the men who raised these protests."

In mid December 1894, it was announced that "a new covered in grand stand for Stark's Park has been started to this week, and is expected to be ready before the New Year."

A week later : "The Raith Rovers new stand is just about completed. It occupies a prominent position on the road side of the park. It is a splendid erection, and has been erected according to the plans of Mr Little, architect. A fine corrugated roof is placed over it.

The accommodation available will be sufficient for nearly 400 people. Messrs Scott & Co, joiners, Pathhead, who had the erection of the stand, have made a good job."

The stand was opened for a friendly match with League team St Bernards. "The Rovers new grand stand is to be opened by Mr A. Strachan, president of the club, before the start of the game, and the Trades' Band are to be in attendance and discourse music at intervals. These two items should tend to make the gate the largest which has been drawn at Stark's Park this season, providing the weather proves favourable."

1895 - Burgh School rebuilt on Wemyssfield thanks to a donation by Sir Michael Nairn; YMCA opened at the foot of Kirk Wynd, thanks to a donation by Provost Swan

Advert in the Fifeshire Advertiser, February 24th 1894.

"R. Black, Newsagent (successor to Isaac Robertson withith Football Edition of Glasgow Evening Times) begs to intimate that he delivers same from Whyte's Causeway to West End, Linktown, every Saturday Evening. Customers and the Public supplied at the earliest possible moment after the arrival of the train, thus avoiding the inconvenience of "waiting". Whyte's Causeway 9.50 ; West Bridge 10.20."

consequence, kept waiting outside, but out of respect for them, the home team ultimately agreed to play the match, but to claim the tie from the Association, as Cowdenbeath had refused to abide by their orders.

"About a quarter of an hour after the advertised time the gates were thrown open, and a general rush was made for admission, with the result that one of the gates was lifted off its hinges, and by the united efforts of the police and some of the members, it was kept in its place, and order was again restored. When the spectators got in they found the home team on the field stripped and ready for the fray, and the goal nets had been fixed up, presenting a rather novel appearances for Stark's Park." The match finished 2-2, Dawson of Rovers and Cairncross of Cowdenbeath being the first players to score in the new nets. Alex Dawson was described as a very clever youth from Buckhaven, although as a student his studies sometimes interfered with his football.

Rovers were ordered to replay their Scottish Cup tie, at Dumfries, by a 13-7 vote of the SFA Committee. "... the Rovers representative explained that the goal nets had been ordered early in the week, but had been delayed in transit by the Railway Company from England, and as a proof of his statement produced an invoice, which showed that the nets had been paid for in November."

The match, played at Palmerston, Maxwelltown, saw goal-nets being used for the first time in Dumfries, and Rovers took a 2-1 half time lead through Eckford and Walker. The Dumfries club then scored three times before Eckford scored to make it 4-3. Oag "scored" from a free kick but the goal was not allowed, and Walker hit the crossbar in the last minute, thereby starting a long and inglorious history of hard-luck stories to explain Rovers' annual exit from the Scottish Cup.

In Kirkcaldy, a large crowd had turned out in the High Street at Messrs J & D Young, booksellers, where the result was to be posted. Police had to clear a passageway. "... the largest which has yet turned out to learn the result of either a football match or a band contest, large as these have sometimes been. Disappointment was manifested in every countenance when it was intimated that the Rovers had lost by four goals to three."

Of course there was a protest, Rovers pointing to 1) the inefficiency of the goal nets ; 2) the ball was not properly inflated ; 3) there was an ineligible player (Somers) in KRV team. They were outvoted 11-5 – and Rovers were ordered to pay the expenses of Mr McDonald, the referee, for attending the meeting.

Despite losing four goals, Willie Dall, deputising for the unavailable custodian, played so grandly in the Rovers goal that he was retained there for some time, Andrew Grieve getting a rest. Towards the end of the season, Dall went to Manchester in search of work, and signed for Sheffield United.

Rovers lost all four friendly fixtures

over the New Year holiday period, which made great demands on the pockets of their supporters. Admission was increased to 6d for the Third Lanark and Sheffield United matches, the latter staged on a working day, and there was the additional opportunity of paying another 6d for a seat in the new covered stand. Unlike at Newton Park, Ladies were not admitted free.

An icy wind and snow showers meant a small attendance for the St Bernards match, and those who could attend the Sheffield United game saw the famed William "Fatty" Foulke in goal for the visitors.

Such reversals may have caused anxiety amongst Raith men when competitive football resumed, in the shape of a King Cup tie at Newton Park. There was more bad news on the selection front. The East of Scotland Association had declared that no player who had played in a Scottish League fixture could play in a King Cup tie, so Couper and Richardson (Leith Athletic and Hearts respectively) were excluded.

Following a frosty morning, the match was not declared "on" until 1.45pm, an hour before kick off, posters were hurriedly stuck around the town, and sandwichboardmen put out. In the circumstances, a crowd in excess of 2000 was most satisfactory. 4-0 up at the interval, Rovers added a fifth in the second half to confirm local supremacy.

They weren't getting things their own way in the corridors of power, however. Rovers claimed the drawn Fife Cup tie against Cowdenbeath as that club had not paid them the money they were due. Moreover, Rovers claimed that Bauldie of Cowdenbeath was ineligible. The Fifeshire Football Association found in Rovers favour, and ordered the replay to be at Stark's Park. Emboldened by the East of Scotland Association's ruling on eligible players, Cowdenbeath protested at Couper's involvement in Scottish League football with Leith Athletic. The Association found in favour of Cowdenbeath, and decreed that the replay should be at North End Park. Rovers put the matter in the hands of Mr Macbeth, solicitor, from Dunfermline. The replay took place at Stark's Park, but it cost Rovers £10 to persuade Cowdenbeath to switch.

Rovers continued to progress in the King Cup, winning 3-0 at Clackmannan, but only after a month's inactivity with the town in winter's grip. It gave D.J. McKinnon the opportunity to rework the words of "The Laird o' Cockpen".

SONG : RAITH ROVERS FOOTBALL CLUB

Air - "The Laird o' Cockpen"

Kirkcaldy may boast o' its fleetfooted sons
Poets and singers and lassies fu' braw
Curlers and bowlers, and kindred ones
But gie me the lads that play at fitba'
There's J. Walker and Blyth, just quite a treat,
And D. Walker in centre, O, lood may he craw,
wi' Sutie and Dawson, 'aye hard to beat

For they are the lads that play at fitba'

There's hardy Jock Cowper, skilful and bold,
and Richardson, lithe, sturdy and sure,
we' Jock Lambert, their glories are told
in pages that will for ever endure
And Oag and Kaye, the famous back line,
wi' Grieve in goal, the bulwark o' a'
Maintain a defence, perfect as time
and they are the lads that play at fitba'

Blithe Jamie Neilson, ance chief o' the clan
Leal is his heart, though he's noo awa
Aye lightsome he smiled when the goalie man
Baffled the foe and cleared man and ba
Success to ye Andrew, and may ye maintain
The powers displayed when the Hearts cam
tae fa
And a the great cracks that tae Stark's Park
came
To see how the Rovers played at fitba

Then hurrah for the lads in guid scottish blue,
Eckford, Neilson, Deuchars and Da(ll)
Brave are their hearts, sterling and true
And they are the lads that play at fitba
O, Kirkcaldy, richt prood may ye be
O the Raith Rovers and its noble train
Great are their glories won unto thee
To garland thy brow with laurels and fame

The replayed Fife Cup tie with
Cowdenbeath was drawn 1-1, and the
Association ruled that it should be played off
at Dunfermline, but "as the ground does not
belong to any club under the Association, the
Rovers have intimated an appeal" and instead
played the Rangers Swift's eleven at Stark's
Park. The Association then ruled that the
match should be played at Cowdenbeath.
"The Cowdenbeath having, however, had the
choice of ground when the teams met last, the
Rovers consider that this action of the
Association is against all common sense and
justice, and have agreed to withdraw from the
competition altogether." They also resigned
from the Association, resulting in a
forthcoming representative match to be
switched from Newton Park to Cowdenbeath,
as there were no longer any Kirkcaldy players
in the side.

The April holiday weekend involved
Rovers in two big fixtures. They were drawn
away to Edinburgh side Adventurers in the
semi final of the King Cup. They, being
ground-less, staged the match at Albert Street
Park, Norton's Old Ground, and the Fifeshire
Advertiser insisted that "without doubt, the
semi final of any cup was never played on a
worse ground. At first sight it presented the
appearance of an old quarry partially filled up.
There was not a particle of grass on the
ground, the whole being covered over with
ashes, which, on account of the heavy rains
that had fallen, afforded anything but a good
foothold. In inition to this, the playing ground
was in no way fenced in, while the touch lines
etc were simply marked off with sawdust. On
the ground of the pitch not being fenced, the
Rovers intimated a protest before the start of
the game." In the event they lost 2-1. A

further protest was lodged by Rovers, on the
ground of Allan having played League
matches with Leith Athletic.
Rangers brought a strong team to
Kirkcaldy on holiday Monday, induced by a
large guarantee, and were surprised to be
beaten 2-1, the student Dawson scoring both
goals. Two more League clubs followed in
quick succession, St Mirren (lost 1-2) and
Clyde (beaten 5-2, with Smith scoring four).
The Fife Free Press praised Rovers for their
enterprise in attracting teams of such a
standard to Kirkcaldy on a regular basis.
The Rangers match drew the
following recollections, some twenty years
later. "The international against England was
played on the following Saturday, and six of
the Rangers' players had been chosen to
represent Scotland. All the six played
against the Rovers and the only player
awanting from their full team, was their centre
forward. The Rovers played their usual side,
the forwards being Jimmy Walker, Andrew
Blyth, Davie Walker, Alex Suttie and Alex
Dawson. There was a great crowd of
spectators, who could scarcely credit the fact
that the elect – and elected – of Scotland's
best could be so well held in by an unknown
set of players like the Raith Rovers. But, as it
was, the unexpected happened. After getting
over the initial excitement and nervousness
consequent on meeting such giants of the
game, the Rovers' forwards literally took the
game in hands, and towards the finish were
simply walking round the Rangers' backs,
Nick Smith and Jock Drummond. The
Rangers' goalkeeper was beaten twice, while
the Rovers' goal only fell once. A feature of
the game was the easy manner in which
Jimmy Walker circumvented Neilly Gibson
and Smith and Drummond before crossing the
ball. Sandy Dawson, the Buckhaven student,
who scored the winning goal, was also a
dangerous player, and his shooting would
have beat a less capable keeper than
Haddow several times."
It took fully a month of deliberations
to settle the protested King Cup semi final.
The protest failed on a 4-5 vote, but there
were no fewer than 13 abstentions. Rovers
appealed, and the decision was overturned,
with the match to be replayed in Edinburgh.
Rovers eventually won 4-2, at the same
ground, thanks to a Suttie hat-trick. In the
meantime, both Kirkcaldy clubs had the sense
to avoid playing on Links Market Saturday,
although Stark's Park staged the final of the
East of Scotland 2nd Eleven Cup between
Bathgate and Lochgelly United.
On Saturday 11th May 1895, 2000
spectators converged on Bonnyrigg to see the
King Cup Final between Raith Rovers and
Loanhead team Polton Vale. Rovers
conceded goals on either side of half-time,
and although Lambert scored after 50
minutes, the final was lost by 2-1
They were still playing as late as 22nd
May, when Kirkcaldy were met at Stark's Park
in aid of Funds for the Cottage Hospital.
Admission was 4d, boys 2d, ladies free.
Covered stand 3d each. The Trades Band

ALEX SUTTIE
A prolific goalscorer between
1891 and 1897.
He lived in the High Street.

At long last Stark's Park had
protection against the
elements for a small
proportion of spectators.
The Robbie's Park pavilion
was moved to the south east
corner of the ground,
alongside the new stand.
Banking had yet to be
installed alongside the stand,
as the land tapered off to the
north east corner, nor was
there any embankment behind
either goal. The only
elevated spectating positions
were on land that did not
belong to Councillor Stark, the
railway embankment. Add a
small grandstand to Denfield
Park, home of the present day
Kirkcaldy YM Juniors, and you
will get some idea of the
limited facilities at Stark's Park
in 1894.

A friendly match with
Lochgelly United (which
Rovers won 6-1) was noted
for less savoury matters. "A
strong protest must be heard
against the foul language
heard round the ropes last
Saturday. It was disgusting.
It was noticeable that the
offenders were followers of
the United, and it is to be
hoped that the officials of the
Rovers will try and put a stop
to a repetition of this
reprehensible conduct today."

Season tickets, issued to members, were folded, covered cards which changed colour and texture each year. In 1895-96 the cover was in maroon patterned cloth, embossed in gold
The inside (see opposite page) had the member's details on the right hand page, with a blue club stamp. This Stand ticket cost 7/6d.

At the 1895 Rovers AGM, held at Burleigh Street Hall with Mr D Lambert in the Chair, the following office bearers were elected : Honorary Presidents R.M. Ferguson, MP ; A. Strachan, Dr Curror, John Oswald of Dunnikier. President Mr D. Lambert ; Vice President Mr Elder ; Secretary Mr J.M. Todd, Honorary Secretary Mr D. Todd, Treasurer Mr T. Keillor, Junior Secretary. Mr A. Elder. Committeee : Messrs. Lumsden, Stewart, Geddes, Eckford, Henderson, Mackie, Hardie, Anderson, Brown, Sharp, Taylor, Bogie, Morton, Elshender, Millar, Baxter. The meeting agreed to raise membership (ie season) tickets to 5/- (ground), stand 7/6d, with the junior ticket unchanged at 2/6d. Advertised around the same time was Raith Rovers' Grand eleven-a-side evening tournament for Juveniles, entry fee 3/6d a team ; winners prizes, handsome gold-centre badges, runners-up silver badges. Particulars from W.Eckford, 69 Links Street or T. Keeler, 27 Alexandra Street

played Selections on the Field "during the match". £20 was drawn at the gate, leaving £16 18/6d for the Hospital after expenses. "At the close of the game the band was suitably entertained by Provost Stocks at Osborne House."

The curtain came down on a long and trophy-less season on Friday 31st May, when Celtic drew 2,000 spectators to Stark's Park. The visitors arrived early "and were shown round Messrs Barry & Ostlere's Works during the afternoon, after which they adjourned to the Crown Hotel for tea." Two 35 minute halves were played, to allow Celtic to return by the last train, and the match was drawn 1-1. A fortnight later, Stark's Park hosted a British Ladies Football Club exhibition, a match lasting only 50 miniutes with 2,000 present.

Compared with the cost of a Raith Rovers membership in 1895, it was cheaper to buy a season ticket for Newton Park, where use of the covered and other stands cost 5/-. A ground ticket was 3/6d and "apprentice members" 2/-. Despite this, Kirkcaldy FC continued to plough money into their ground.

"Since the close of last season (Newton Park) has undergone great improvements, the centre of their field having been levelled, while the corners have been graduated off - which, we may say, is a much needed improvement. A new cycle track has been laid down, and also a foot track, which will be of great advantage to the team for training purposes ; and we are informed on good authority that baths are to be fitted up in the dressing rooms, and these indubitably will be highly recognised by both the local men and their guests. A new covered stand also graces the ground, and which, we can safely say, for comfort and appearance, is unsurpassed in the county district, and no doubt, this should prove a great boon to followers of the game at this enclosure." The cycle track, with a five foot banking, 5 laps to the mile, cost £250 to construct.

Rovers, meanwhile, were engulfed by selection problems. James Walker had signed for St Bernards during the close season, and Willie Dall, Andrew Marshall and Neil Deuchars had left the town to seek employment. Following some problems with summer five-a-side tournaments, the SFA suspended Alex Oag, William Kay, Robert Robertson, Jack Lambert, David Walker and Alexander Suttie for a month for "professional irregularities." Raith Athletic, holders of the Cowdenbeath Junior Cup, helped out with players. Charlie Moodie, the star of juvenile side Kirkcaldy Ramblers, had joined Raith Athletic, and was quickly promoted to the Rovers.

The second home friendly of the season, against Arbroath, was virtually a trial match for the following week's Scottish Qualifying Cup tie against Edinburgh Casuals.

As the Fife Free Press understated : "The severe stricture passed on the home club, at least so far as the majority of their playing members are concerned, has placed them in an unfortunate position. With the half of their playing eleven disqualified for a month, matters have opened anything but cheering for the committee."

Goalkeeper James Cairns and John Blyth were recruited from Kirkcaldy, and the Rugby players John Tod, Tom Lockhart and David Thomson (an ex Rovers player) were drafted into the team which narrowly beat the Edinburgh side 4-3.

As a thanks to the Rugby club for their assistance, Rovers cancelled the scheduled friendly match with Bo'ness and instead played "Scottish Corinthians", a team formed by Kirkcaldy Rugby club players, who included the three who played for Rovers the previous week, plus ex Rovers players Clunie in goal, Thomson at back and Blyth up front. The gate was to be shared, and it was a pity that the match attracted the smallest attendance at Stark's Park for some time

Suspensions over, Rovers' fielded a vastly different team for the second round of the Scottish Qualifying Cup, in which Dunipace were beaten 6-2. There was a shock the following week at School Park, Lochgelly, in an East of Scotland Shield tie. One-hundred and fifty Rovers fans made the trip, thanks to cheap fares from the North British Railway, and they helped swell a record attendance for Lochgelly. After a scoreless first half, Rovers collapsed to a 5-0 defeat.

Charlie Moodie came into the team in October, and stayed there for twelve years of sterling service. John Lambert moved from right half to fill the previously troubled centre half position. Jock Eckford replaced Jimmy Walker at outside right, Andrew Hunter came in at inside right.

Rovers bounced back to beat Montrose 3-1 in the third qualifying round of "the Scottish" and following a bye in round four, had the opportunity for revenge at Lochgelly, which they did not take, losing 2-1.

"Before starting their tie on Saturday the Raith Rovers protested against three of Lochgelly's players, on the ground that they played three men who had been guilty of professional irregularity. The men's names were Thomas Greenhorn, David Smith and Alexander Vail. It was stated by the Raith Rovers that these three men had taken part in a five-a-side competition at Strathmiglo Horticultural and Ornithological Society's Show (known as the 'Dog and Poultry Show') on July 20th, This protest came up for consideration at the Scottish Association's meeting on Tuesday evening, but as it was proved that Greenhorn and Vail were amateurs, the Association considered only the case of David Smith."

Mr Birrell and Mr Alexander, both of Kirkcaldy, gave evidence. Witnesses who saw the 5-a-sides were also called to identify Smith ; others spoke to say that he had been working in the pit that day, contradicted by another friendly (?) witness who said he had been with Smith on a cycle run to Stirling. Another admitted he was at Strathmiglo, but didn't play ! The SFA found in favour of the appeal, and agreed that the match would be replayed at Stark's Park. David Smith was suspended for a month.

Whyte (who was later sent off) opened the scoring for Lochgelly United, but Eckford equalised with one of the finest goals seen at the ground. Robb put through his own net for Rovers to win 2-1, in front of a crowd of 2,000.

The Fife Free Press reported that Lochgelly had lodged a protest "on the ground of some alleged professional infringement. The Rovers have also, it is understood, a good claim against United for some irrelgularity also." Lochgelly's protest was dismissed by the SFA, to the delighted of the great crowd who had amassed around Messrs Young's, booksellers, to whom the verdict was telegraphed.

Rovers were sent to Cowdenbeath in the first round of the King Cup and the Weekly News described the tie as "as lifeless as football could well be made." Despite that, Cowdenbeath won 5-0.

The largest crowd of the season, over 2,000, converged on Stark's Park for the Qualifying Cup semi final against King's Park, for whom Crawford scored a hat-trick in a 4-1 victory. Rovers' consolation was that their progression to this stage of the competition meant qualification for the Scottish Cup, the first time that Rovers would take part in the national trophy during the second half of the season.

Thus emboldened, Rovers won six and drew one of their next seven friendly fixtures. The last of that sequence was a New Year's Day match at home to Kirkcaldy, which the Fife Free Press regarded : "While for various reasons the day set apart for a trial of strength between the Raith Rovers and Kirkcaldy is ideal, it is sure to prove a big financial success." It was a time of great celebration for the young men of the town, as the YMCA building at the corner of Kirk Wynd and High Street was now completed, thank to Provost Swan's legacy.

The vagaries of the ballot bag saw Rovers and Lochgelly United meet for the second time that season in the Scottish Cup, this time in the competition proper. A sign of the changing hierarchy in Kirkcaldy football was that "Arrangements are being made to get half and full time results of Raith Rovers v Lochgelly match wired to Newton Park during progress of game," Kirkcaldy playing Armadale in a Friendly fixture.

Davie Walker opened the scoring at School Park, but Lochgelly won 2-1. Needless to say, a protest was lodged by Rovers, which the SFA upheld. Lochgelly had played David McLaren under the name of David Anderson, having previously played for Lochee United in the first round against Dundee Wanderers. Lochgelly were held to be ignorant of the situation, but the tie was ordered to be replayed at Newton Park,

reward for some assiduous sleuthing around Lochgelly and Lochee by Rovers president Mr A.W. Lumsden, although it was later recalled that "Mr Lumsden was cordially hated in Lochgelly for quite a long time afterwards."

"During the interval between the two portions of the game, the Rovers lodged a protest against the majority of the Lochgelly players, who they allege are illegible to take part in the Scotish Cup tie by their having taken part in a Consolation tie against Cowdenbeath in the close season It seems that such was the case, although the players were sanctioned by the East of Scotland Association, but did not apply to the SFA for re-instatement."

Several weeks later, the repercussions from the acrimonious tie rumbled on. "At a meeting of the Scottish Association Committee attention was again called to the conduct of the spectators in the tie between Lochgelly United and Raith Rovers, but on the report of referee Hendry, who was examined, the committee decided to do nothing in the matter. The remuneration to be allowed Kirkcaldy FC for the use of their park in the protested tie Raith Rovers v Lochgelly was under consideration. A letter read from Kirkcaldy stated that the "gate" amounted to £25 5d, stand to £1. 17s, and that 55 out of their 80 members had been admitted free. The committee awarded £5 and the stand drawings to Kirkcaldy FC"

Rovers did not need to call on their latest round of administrative sleuthing, as they won 5-2, watched by 3,000 spectators. A week later, it was to Easter Road for the second round tie. Willie Groves opened the scoring for the home side, but Walker equalised. John Lambert had to retire through injury during the second half, and Rovers conceded five goals in that period, their consolation being a share of the 3,500 gate.

There was speculation in the influential Scottish Referee newspaper that Fife may follow the example of other areas and form a senior League, perhaps to include Alloa and a re-constructed Dunfermline Athletic. Rovers, however, did not appear to be missing the regularity of League fixtures. Between the Hibs defeat and the end of the season, they played 15 friendly matches, winning all but two drawn and one lost. That was at Falkirk, the only occasion in that sequence of matches in which they ventured out of Kirkcaldy.

It was just as well that Rovers had not advanced to the latter stages of any of the cup competitions. At an SFA Committee meeting in April "On the complaint of the Raith Rovers, the Committee suspended John Blyth

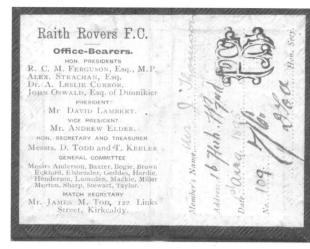

Members of the General Committee in 1895-96 included Messrs. Anderson, Baxter, Bogie, Brown, Eckford, Elshender, Geddes, Hardie, Henderson, Lumsden, Mackie, Miller, Morton, Sharp, Stewart and Taylor.
Match Secretary was Mr James M. Todd, 122 Links Street, and the President was Mr David Lambert.

Friendly matches were played no matter the conditions. On the Saturday between Christmas 1895 and New Year, Adventurers came over from Edinburgh, to find Stark's Park under three inches of snow, which was still falling. Despite that, 200 souls had paid for admission, and the game got underway. After 20 minutes of the second half, the referee called a halt with Rovers winning 7-0. The Fifeshire Advertiser reported that "It was impossible to propel the ball. The game was pretty much of a farce - the conditions rendering football impossible."

On April 4th, The Fifeshire Advertiser carried an advert on its front page for "Raith Rovers Football Club 11-a-side Juvenile evening football tournament. First prize ; 11 pairs of footbal boots or silver badges with gold centres. 2nd prize 11 superior football shirts or silver badges. Entry fee 3/6d per team, to W. Eckford, Links Street, or T. Keeler, 27 Alexandra Street." The competing teams were Institute, Overton Thistle, Ramblers, Scotia, Kinghorn Hearts, Blue Bell, West End, Our Boys, Renton, and Links Star.

An unsatisfactory 1896/97 season was rescued in the eyes of the locals by triumph in the new Nairn Charity Cup. Between 1500 and 2000, including the Trades Band and many councillors, saw a "fast and stubborn game" at Newton Park finish 0-0. The return match at Stark's Park earned the headline in the Kirkcaldy Times : "Disgraceful Scene at The Charity Cup Tie - Mobbing The Referee.

"During the progress of the game the decisions of the referee, Mr Williamson, President of the East of Scotland Association, were generally met with disapprobation by the larger portion of the crowd, whose manner of expressing their feeling was, to say the least, far from being in keeping with civilised beings.

"The Referee's conduct of the game did not seem to give general satisfaction amongst the spectators, and immediately on play being stopped a rush was made into the enclosure. The referee was surrounded by a howling mob, and came in for some rough handling from his cowardly assailants, which was also extended to several of the prominent members of both clubs and others who came to his assistance.

"The demonstration continued 'till he reached the pavilion, and he was afterwards followed to the Railway Station by a number of youthful tormentors."

The match, incidentally, finished 1-1 and a brave Charity Cup Committee drew lots for the venue of the third match, Newton Park winning. All eyes were on the referee, from Stirling. "Referee McArthur was perhaps impartial enough ; but he might with advantage have spared the whistle more."

Three thousand spectators, including the Provost, watched the first midweek match of the year, which Rovers won 2-1.

of the Kirkcaldy club for a month for playing for that club while a registered professional with another.   The Kirkcaldy Club, having acted in ignorance, was exonerated."

This seemed a spiteful act by Rovers, Blyth having apparently returned to play for Kirkcaldy once Rovers had lost interest in any cup competition.   The Scottish Referee was certainly getting exasperated over Rovers' over-reliance on the fine details of the rule book.

"When will this protesting have an end ? Raith Rovers were to the front once more, not this time over a dog and poultry show, but over a professional named Blyth. Mr Chapman, Kirkcaldy, a tall, smart and capable pleader, with a slight scarcity of locks, made out a good case for his club against Raith Rovers, he went into harmony - "Blythe, blythe, blythe was she, blythe was the but and ben." After hearing evidence, the Committee unanimously came to the conclusion that the Kirkcaldy Club had fully and completely proved they were not to blame in the matter, and exonerated that Club from all blame. Blyth, however, they suspended for a month."

In the new professional (and SFA-registration) era, it seemed that summer tournaments and sports were to be a thing of the past at Stark's Park. An advert appeared in the Kirkcaldy Times on 29th April : "STARK'S PARK, GRAZING TO LET for May, June, July, and August. Offers in writing to James M. Tod, Links Street, Kirkcaldy"

Rovers would have been better turning over their green sward to animal husbandry, according to the Fife Free Press's report of the match against Rangers Reserves, played on 2nd May. "The weather was delightful, and one would have expected, considering the weather conditions and importance of the game, to have seen an increased assemblage, but the truth seems to be the public are now tired of the season, giving a colouring to the desirability of adopting the argument to have the close season from the end of April."

Four days later, however, 2,000, paying £17, converged on Newton Park for the return friendly between the town's two senior clubs.   Rovers' New Year's Day victory was "discounted in some quarters, it was said, because of the festivities necessarily prevailing at such a time, and in consequence neither team being in any manner of means in "the pink of condition" (to use a familiar aphorism)." The next meeting would "prove the decider of championship honours". Rovers wore dark blue, Kirkcaldy in a striped ensemble, and the visitors were leading 4-0 (and had missed a penalty) when the match was finished 10 minutes early due to failing light

League football was back on the agenda in late June, according to the Fifeshire Advertiser of 20th June 1896.

"Following the lead of other parts of the country, attempts are being made to form a League of Fife and Perth clubs, and the following clubs have been asked to attend a meeting in Kirkcaldy to discuss the matter ;

Raith Rovers, Cowdenbeath, Lochgelly United., Fair City Athletic, St Johnstone, Dunfermline Athletic and Kirkcaldy.   As the difficulty of arranging first class friendly games in the provinces will be greater this season than ever, clubs should consider whether it is not more beneficial to encourage local leagues than risk guarantees to teams from a distance." The meeting took place at the People's Club and Institute in Kirkcaldy on July 4th. St Johnstone and Alloa sent their apologies, while Clackmannan joined those attending.

For one of the clubs involved, there was a reminder of the ticking timebomb that was their lease. "We hear that a proposal was recently made by a firm of local manufacturers for the purchase of Newton Park, which is at present held on lease by the Kirkcaldy FC. It is understood that the matter was brought under the attention of the factor of Raith Estate, but as the Cycle Track Company have laid out about £300 on the park, and there are still two years of the lease to run, it was felt that nothing could be done in the meantime, and the matter was left over till next meeting."

Rovers players returned to training from their close season break on Tuesday August 4th, and also trained two evenings later. "Both nights there was a good turn out of players."   Dunfermline Athletic left the junior ranks to join the new local League, and it was expected that another Dunfermline club would follow suit, to replace Raith Rovers "who have not as yet intimated whether they will support the new league or not."   Rovers were reluctant to lose their lucrative friendly fixtures against Scottish League clubs.

The Fife Free Press of 15th August had this to say of Rovers immediate prospects : FOOTBALL : RAITH ROVERS FC Preparations for the ensuing season are in a forward state at Stark's Park, and only the monster event in the Raith [the annual band contest] prevents the Raith Rovers making a start on the opening day. A beginning will be made, however, on Wednesday evening first, when the probable line-up of the Rovers will meet an eleven got together by Mr A.W. Lumsden, which should provide good practice for the opening match with Armadale next Saturday.   .... the prospect of a successful season at Stark's Park is no vain one, and to all appearance gives promise of being better than past years. Players : Beveridge (Methil Rovers), J, Cairns, P. Connell, J, Cowper, W. Dall, A. Dawson, Frew (Hearts of Beath), A, Grieve, A. Hunter, W. Kay, J. Lambert, J. Mathie, D. Menzies, C. Moodie, Russell (Hearts of Beath), A. Suttie, D. Walker. "Special attention will be given to the Junior eleven - Raith Athletic - which promises to be strengthened by the pick of last season's juveniles."

Unfortunately the opening friendly match, referred to above, did not proceed smoothly. "Only 8 men turned up for each side, the Combination being strengthened by two men from the crowd, who had no time to change into playing kit. It was fortunate that the crowd was so considerate, as, under ordinary circumstances, the management might have been reminded that they demanded value for money." Worse was to come in the second half ; the two Hearts of Beath men came off the park to catch their train, leaving it six men against ten.

Despite the close season speculation, Rovers stood aloof from League football, preferring to host prestigious friendly matches. Kirkcaldy, on the other hand, joined the Central League. There was an early upset in the East of Scotland Shield, Rovers losing 4-2 at Clackmannan in the first round. The inevitable protest was founded on one of Clackmannan's players having played during the close season, but it was dismissed by the East of Scotland Association, and the deposit money was retained.

The fourth round of the Scottish Qualifying Cup was reached, which ensured entry into the Scottish Cup proper, but results fluctuated widely. Dunfermline were beaten 8-1 on 19th December, but Rovers fell by the same score at Morton on 3rd October. A "huff" with the East of Scotland Association resulted in Rovers' withdrawing from the King Cup, resulting in two critical letters appearing in the local press. Both refer to Raith Rovers as "would be Second Leaguers." Rovers showed a "childish and unmanly spirit" in scratching.

The Scottish Referee was equally disdainful of Lochgelly United's walk over. "There is too much scratching going on. There may be an excuse for some clubs, owing to long journeys, but such an excuse is certainly not for the Rovers." Lochgelly fans accused Rovers of considering themselves above the likes of Lochgelly, with pretentions of League membership. In response, a poem from a Rovers supporter retorted that Rovers were tired of paying doctors' bills, and that an ambulance wagon formed no part of their accoutrements.

With Alex Oag gone, left back became a problem position, William Russell and John Cowper alternating. William Beveridge came in for Jock Eckford on the right wing, Dod Ramsay arrived, and Duncan Menzies and Smith shared left wing duties. With declining results, came falling crowds. The visit of Leith Athletic was typical. "The turnout of spectators was not so large as might have been expected, considering the prestige of the visiting team, who presently top the Second Division of the Scottish Football League, but this was no doubt attributable to the fact that sixpence was charged for admission."

A fortnight later, the season's first meeting of the two local teams attracted a crowd of 2,000. "Too seldom for their own benefit are the rivals pitted against each other in friendly encounters. Not only would more frequent meetings be appreciated by the football public, but they would be a means of replenishing the by no means over-stocked coffers of both clubs - a most essential point in present day football, for no such organisations can long subsist without a good

supply of hard cash." The match "a regular scorcher" finished 1-1.

In a major break with tradition, "The Newton Park club have not deemed it advisable to have a holiday match this year." It was speculated that Kirkcaldy did not relish the guarantee, which proved to be prescient as the town was covered in snow over the New Year holiday period, Rovers' activity being restricted to a 2-3 defeat by Kilmarnock, the Qualifying Cup holders.

The draw for the first round of the Scottish Cup was not kind to Rovers, Dumbarton away, and they lost 2-1, although a replay could have been gained had Rovers not missed a late penalty at "Fatal Boghead". The first round defeat "earned" Rovers a place in the Consolation Cup, in which they took two matches to dispose of Dunfermline Athletic, before losing 6-0 at Cowdenbeath.

With several trophy successes to follow in 1897/98, the previous season could be seen as a mere plateau in Rovers' inexorable ascent of the face of Scottish football. Kirkcaldy FC continued to toil in their shadow, remaining amateur, and relying on local players brought through Kirkcaldy Albion juniors and Bluebell juveniles to cut down on the expense of bringing players from a distance. In contrast, Rovers added Jack Cowper, back from Dumbarton, Edward Gillespie from Polton Vale, and Patrick Gallocher, formerly of Burnley, who was working in the town. "With such a galaxy of talent to pick from the future prospects of the Rovers are exceedingly bright." There was regret, however, that the two local senior sides had not amalgamated to form a stronger unit. "It was at one time anticipated that amalgamation would lead to one senior team, with a second eleven or junior string, being fixed up to uphold the reputation of Kirkcaldy, but this prospect is as far off being realised as ever, more's the pity."

Five hundred Rovers fans made their way to Lochgelly in a special train for the first round of the Qualifying Cup, and were rewarded with a 2-1 victory. Rovers won their first six cup ties of the season, and were unbeaten in friendly matches, but came unstuck at East Stirling in the fifth round of the Qualifying Cup, losing 1-0. Rovers started the game "under protest", insisting that McKie had "infringed professional regulations in June and July", but the key moment of the tie was the loss of Cowper through injury after only 17 minutes. The crowd of 6,000 at Merchiston Park, Bainsford, was estimated to include 600 from Fife.

Rovers lost their protest by one vote. "The result was anxiously awaited in the Lang Toun and a large crowd assembled in the vicinity of the Post Office to hear the verdict. When the information came that the Rovers had lost their protest, there were murmerings of discontent, and "hard lines" was the universal comment."

In the previous round, 300 had followed them to the Jute City for the 2-1 victory over Dundee Wanderers. The Fifeshire Advertiser reported : "Clepington

JIMMY NEILSON

A great servant to the club in the last decade of the 19th Century, and a regular goalscorer. He manufactured cycles, and later sold and repaired motor cars from his High Street garage

Having beaten Kirkcaldy 4-3 at Stark's Park in the first round of the King Cup (Alex Ramsay scoring all four goals), the meeting of both clubs at Newton Park in the first round of the Fife Cup a fortnight later was eagerly anticipated, and attracted a crowd of 2,500. Rovers were winning 2-1 when the match was stopped due to darkness 17 minutes from time - about the length of time the referee, Mr McArthur of Stirling, was late in turning up.
"The officially appointed referee intimated his coming in rather a novel manner. He waved his hand to the crowd from a passing train, and in a few minutes bounded breathlessly into the enclosure." The match was a poor exhibition "The Rovers were the better balanced team, but Kirkcaldy defied them with praiseworthy determination."

On 25th January 1897, Stark's Park hosted the fourth game in the Fife Junior Cup first round tie between Dunfermline and Dunfermline Athletic, Rovers having submitted the lower offer of rental of the two Kirkcaldy grounds.
1897 - The first self propelled vehicle arrived in Kirkcaldy

Park is by no means an ideal enclosure. It is almost entirely surrounded by gloomy mills and other high buildings and the spectators during the progress of the game are almost hovering on the touch-lines. The playing pitch seems to be short for a city ground and is a good bit off the spirit level. A covered stand along one side of the ground is capable of accomodating about 200 persons."

"One of the Rovers' enthusiasts, who emulated the great McGonogall, writes :

Cairns was the hero o' the day,
So was Cowper, an' so was Kay ;
Youngsters Moodie, Ramsay and Stocks,
They fairly knocked the Dundee folks.
Cocky Ramsay, he can shoot, -
Twa goals ca,' frae his wee foot.
Now that the Rovers at last have got
Fairley settled, they'll lift the pot !
Hooray

After the game, in Robertson's Restaurant, Wellgate, Mr D. Lambert presented to John Stocks "who has chosen to follow a 'life on the ocean wave' as an engineer" a beautiful briar pipe and tobacco pouch.

At a Meeting of the Central Football League held in Dunfermline in mid November, Alloa Athletic, Clackmannan, Cowdenbeath, Dunfermline Athletic, Hearts of Beath, Lochgelly United and Kirkcaldy agreed to re-start the League for another season, and resolved "to write to Raith Rovers asking them to become members, so that all local senior clubs might be included in the membership." Rovers had their eyes on other matters, namely a steady succession of cup ties.

Alex Oag returned at left back at Christmas, Edward Gillespie replaced William Russell at left half, John Eckford returned to the first team at outside left, and Alex Ramsay came in at inside left.

Rovers' first final of the season was at Newton Park, where Mossend Swifts awaited to contest the East of Scotland Qualifying Cup, a new competition and trophy. 3,000 paid £38 12s and saw Rovers win 4-0.

Once again, the draw for the first round proper of the Scottish Cup pitted Rovers against their conquerors in the Qualifying Cup. This time, East Stirling had to travel to Kirkcaldy. It was to be "a huge disappointment both on account of the game and the result. ... the home men simply courted failure from the start." The attendance of 4,000 was Rovers' highest to that point in their history, and they saw a 4-2 win for East Stirling. The biggest surprise was that no protest followed from Rovers.

More than 3,000 returned a week later for the semi final of the King Cup against Cowdenbeath. The match finished 0-0, but Rovers were once again in litigious mood and protested that Devine had played for Dunfermline Juniors in a Scottish tie at Arbroath. This was dismissed through insufficient evidence, but Rovers' deposit was returned, and the tie was ordered to be replayed. Rovers' claim for £3.10s expenses in the East of Scotland Qualifying Cup Fnal

was cut down to £2, the association declaring itself not liable for professional wages in finals.

Despite this minor set-back, Rovers' financial clout was shown by inducing St Bernards to give up ground rights for the first round tie of the Shield.   "It sounds rather odd that a team which is not considered good enough by those in authority to be included in the Second Division of the Scottish League, should make a team occupying a prominent position in the highest football circles play so hard to escape defeat."   Rovers did lose 5-3, however.

The Fife Free Press of 5th February reported that on the evening of the St Bernards match, "an interesting function was performed in the large warehouse of Messrs Tod, manufacturers, Links Street, by the members of the Raith Rovers Football Club. The occasion was the honouring of their much esteemed secretary, Mr James Tod, on the occasion of his wedding.

"Mr Lambert presented Mr Tod with a handsome gold watch and chain ; and a gold bracelet for his better half.   "He was a gentleman universally respected, and enjoyed the confidence of all the members as being thoroughly sincere and straightforward in all he did."   The Nairn Cup was duly filled, and the health of the donor toasted."

The following week, Rovers travelled to East End Park for the first round of the Consolation Cup.   The Fifeshire Advertiser advised : "About a couple of months ago the Athletic committee were compelled, through financial difficulties, to stop running their senior team, but for this occasion a special effort had been made to bring together as strong a combination as possible in order to try and redeem the fallen fortunes of the club." Rovers won 9-1, yet the star of the show was not on the scoresheet.   "George 'Dod' Ramsay "was responsible for several of the points. He improves every match."

Rovers won their second trophy of the season on 9th April, beating Alloa Athletic 3-1 at Newton Park in the Fife Cup Final. Over £30 was taken from 2,000 spectators. That evening, the teams and association officials had tea in Gibb's Rooms in the High Street, and the Cup was presented to Lambert, the Rovers' captain. "During the evening, the Cup was filled and "Success to the Rovers" pledged with enthusiasm. A number of excellent songs also enlivened the proceedings.

There was another new trophy to be contested, the Wemyss Cup, presented to the Fifeshire Football Association by R G E Wemyss, Esq, of Wemyss Castle, to be competed for by Fifeshire senior teams. Rovers suffered a rare defeat, at home to Cowdenbeath in the first round, but trotted out their "Devine" protest, which on this occasion was upheld.   The match was replayed at Stark's Park, as lively a game as had been seen there between bitter rivals.

Lambert, Kinnell and James Gibb were involved in a scuffle.   "The crowd broke in, but the field was soon cleared and the game proceeded. "Owing to the players clenching, no blows were struck, and the brawl consisted of a harmless tumble about on the turf." Mercer opened the scoring for Cowdenbeath, Eckford equalised after the interval, and an Oag free kick was scrambled between the posts in the last minute, for Rovers to win 2-1. Hearts of Beath were beaten in the semi final, and the Final, against Kirkcaldy, was held over to the following season.

Rovers' AGM elected the following officials for the next season. President Mr John Nicol, vice president Mr James M. Tod, honorary secretary Mr David Tod, honorary treasurer Mr David Mitchell ; match secretary Mr A.W. Lumsden. committee - Messrs R. Lambert, D. Lambert, H. Ritchie, T. Grierson, H. Page, D. Penny, H. Simpson, J. Millar, George Robertson, Thomson, T. Barrie. The honorary presidents were all re-elected - Mr RC Munro Ferguson, MP. Treasurer J. Kellock, Dr Leslie Curror, Mr D. Williamson, solicitor, Mr Alex Strachan. "The system of remuneration to the players was under discussion, and it was resolved to leave the matter in the hands of the committee."

Mr D. Tod, treasurer, reported an income of £585 3d 4 1/2d and expenditure of £ 501 8s 31/2d, leaving a balance of £ 83 15s 1d expected to be considerably augmented by the end of the season.

Alas, bad weather resulted in a low gate at the final of the East of Scotland Consolation Cup Final, staged at Vale Park, Loanhead. Rovers and Penicuik drew 1-1, drawings were £16 6s 1d and expenditure, including the badges, amounted to £12 2 6d. It was decided to replay at Newton Park, at a rental of £3. Penicuik were to be given £5 in travel expenses, Rovers, inexplicably, £3.

Rovers wore black arm bands for Mr Keillor, former treasurer of club, who had died in Edinburgh that morning. A strong wind spoiled the play, but Rovers won 2-1.

The Fifeshire Advertiser broke some bad news in reporting the match. "Previous to commencement of the game a triplet did some pacing to a local cyclist. General regret was expressed round the enclosure that very soon the splendid track which had been put down at no little cost will be swallowed up by the building fiend. The five years' lease granted by Mr Ferguson of Raith expires in November, and the Track Company has got notice to quit. It will be a pity indeed if the popular sport of cycling goes to the wall for want of a track."

The season finished with two matches to decide the Nairn Cottage Hospital Cup. The ties got off to a bad start. "Unfortunately the game was robbed of all interest about 20 minutes after the start when by the forcible (to say the least) play of Flanders, the Rovers left back, Gardiner, Kirkcaldy's outside right winger, was rendered hors de combat and had to be assisted off the field. It is a pity that the reputation of a class team like the Rovers should be endangered by such a player."

Councillors and Provost Hutchison

were in attendance at Newton Park for the second match. "During the progress of the game, Miss Nairn, of the Priory, the donor of the Cup, arrived, accompanied by Mrs Robert Wemyss, of St Michael's, and got a hearty reception as they took their seats." The Cup and gold badges were on display in the stand. Rovers won 6-0 and 8-0, completed their collection of trophies for the season, and disbursed a £3 bonus to each of the players. In the Fife Junior Cup Final, Raith Athletic beat Buckhaven United 2-1, meaning another trophy for the Stark's Park display case.

If 1897/98 was regarded as successful, it paled into insignificance compared with the following season, when Rovers won five trophies. They also, some would say belatedly, embraced League football, replacing East Stirling in the East of Scotland League, which also included Leith Athletic, Hearts, Dundee, St Bernards and Hibs.

The Fife Free Press looked forward to "Kirkcaldy Football Clubs' Prospects" in their issue of August 27th 1898 : "The Raith Rovers will be virtually the same team as last year. Not only is the club under able management, but financially they have never entered on a season under more favourable circumstances and with a bigger balance at their credit. Although the Raith Athletic may be weakened considerably by the first eleven drawing on the reserves, it should be as strong as ever, inasmuch as some excellent young players will be secured from the [Kirkcaldy] Renton [juveniles]."

"Kirkcaldy have this year gone in for professionalism. Of course, the club management are still in a dilemma as to the retention of their ground, but hopes are entertained that the lease will be renewed and everything end well."

The season opened with a home friendly against Fair City Athletic, which was won 5-1. Many questioned why the match was scheduled to compete with the Band Contest, but the fixture had originally been planned for Perth, and was switched due to a big cricket match. The following week, Dunipace called off at the last minute, and old rivals East Stirling won 3-2 in front of 3,500 spectators at Stark's Park a week later. "Mr Elder, referee, who had the teams under his charge, made a very fair referee, but at times his decisions did not meet with approval by the majority of the spectators, who shouted and called him "pretty" names. This state of matters is now getting very prevalent at football matches in Kirkcaldy."

Lochgelly had the measure of Rovers in the first rounds of the Scottish Qualifying Cup and East of Scotland Shield, but the first trophy of the season was captured with a 3-0 victory over Kirkcaldy at Newton Park in the final of the previous season's Wemyss Cup. One local paper estimated the crowd to be "upwards of 3,000", and "another part of the pailing broke down by the pressure of the crowd, and a grand stand was made of it by those who were fortunate enough to be in the vicinity." Embankments

JOHN THOMSON

The first in a long line of long-serving left backs, he made his debut for Rovers in 1888 and was still making occasional appearances in 1900. He lived in Forth Avenue, and ended his career as an amateur

On Friday May 27th, a smoking concert was held at the Masonic Hall. Mr Lambert presided, and there were presentations to Mr J. Lambert and Mr J. Kay on the occasions of their marriages. A handsome marble timepiece and a silver cake basket to Lambert, McKay got a gold watch and chain. "An excellent programme of songs was gone through ..... Mr Andrew Kinnear, of the Prince of Wales Tavern, purveyed to the satisfaction of all."
The Fife Free Press, on Saturday June 18th, printed a letter headed "Kirkcaldy Temperance Council and Football Telegrams". The Temperance Council hoped to be in a position to receive by wire football results in east, west and centre of town for the new season. "In the past these Saturday evening football telegrams have, in the truest sense of the term, been the "publican's" decoy, wherewith to trap the unwary bird." The letter suggested that rooms be acquired on the lines of the British workman's public house, and opened at convenient points along the high street "where our young men could meet on a Saturday night and discuss the leading football events of the day, crack their innocent jokes and in song and sentiment seek to create each other's enjoyment for a brief session, say at a nominal charge of one penny for admission."

ANDREW GRIEVE

A trip to Armadale in the semi final of the King Cup resulted in a 1-1 draw, and Rovers made no mistake in the replay with a 10-1 victory. A`week later, Cowdenbeath were beaten 1-0 at Stark's Park in the first round of the Consolation Cup, despite a hard pitch (that reliable indicator of playable pitches, the Beveridge Park pond, was frozen). "Five minutes before time was called Nisbet was ordered off the field. The game all through was of a very rough and tumble nature, but this time Nisbet deliberately lifted Stocks off his feet and threw him to the ground. Great feeling was manifested by the spectators when Nisbet refused to go. At one point the crowd broke into the ring, but the presence of a man in blue soon calmed them. After explanation Nisbet retired, and the game continued. As the Rovers omitted to hand in the names and addresses of their players, Cowdenbeath will probably protest."

Just before Christmas 1896, the Fife Free Press announced : "Many of our readers will learn with regret that Mr Thomas Keeler, the popular and esteemed treasurer of the Rovers, has just resigned his office in connection with the club. Circumstances necessitate his staying in Edinburgh this winter instead of travelling to and from there daily, and hence the reason of his resignation. Mr Keeler was a model official, and in the loss of him the Rovers have lost a painstaking and efficient treasurer."

had not yet been constructed around many football grounds, primarily because they were not needed when most attendances were below 2,000. In excess of this figure, spectating around the boundary fence or ropes became difficult on flat ground.

Rovers were getting into their stride, and lost just two of sixteen successive fixtures to the end of January. John Flanders, who had come into the team towards the end of the previous season, made the left back position his own. The wing half and inside forward positions were a bit of a moveable feast, with Jimmy Stocks, David Stewart, and John McQueen all being introduced to the team. A small attendance at the friendly against Vale of Leven on 26th November was attributed to the stormy weather. Those who took the trouble to attend had their patience tried before a ball had been kicked. "The game was to have started at 2.30, but it was after three before the ball was set a-rolling. The home team were being photographed down town, hence the delay."

Individual players, as well as the team, were gaining admirers. "Flanders, Raith Rovers, is the best back in the East just now. The Raith Rovers are looking round for a partner for him. Willie Kaye, the most gentlemanly back that ever played, is getting rusty."

In January, the Scottish Referee opined : "Raith Rovers are a team of many good parts which has never yet secured the place in Scottish football which they have won long ago. On their merits they ought to be members of the Second Division of the League, and next general meeting of this body, I hope, will endorse my opinion. Our other city clubs will find it just as difficult as Leith did on Saturday to beat them at Kirkcaldy. A club that is considered class enough to be included in the East of Scotland League, and which can draw with the Leith Athletic [in the opening League fixture], is surely good enough for Second League membership."

On the first Saturday in February a large Rovers support paid 1/- for a train trip to Edinburgh, to watch Rovers play Hearts in an East of Scotland League match at Tynecastle. Rovers lost 4-1, but "The losers are to be complimented upon the capital display they gave. Their forwards, headed by Neilson, the old St Bernards player, ran and passed cleverly, but displayed the usual provincial lack of finish."

Kirkcaldy were brushed aside 4-0 in the semi final of the Fife Cup. "A little more training on the part of Kirkcaldy would make these contests more interesting, as there would then be a chance of variety in the results," said the Fifeshire Advertiser.

That newspaper included a weekly contribution from an exiled Langtonian under the headline "Our Glasgow Letter". The sentiments of future generations of the Kirkcaldy diaspora were neatly summarised : "Perhaps in nothing does the earliest associations and leanings cling to one so much as in their relations to the realm of

sport. It is probably because of this that so wide an interest is felt here in the doings of the Raith Rovers since these were advanced to the higher sphere of Eastern Leaguers. Their success in that competition is viewed on all sides with feelings of the greatest satisfaction."

Six hundred followed Rovers to Hibs for an East of Scotland League fixture, "the Third Ward [Pathhead] contributing a large proportion of the travellers." The Fifeshire Advertiser was considerably more robust in its defence of the team than the Rovers rearguard (Hibs won 5-0) : "To hear some of the Edinburgh critics refer to several of the Rovers as "rough diamonds" was pardonable, but to hear of the reference to the doings of the "country club" was more than a Langtonian could bear. It is quite evident the geography of such "croaks" has been sadly neglected. Why, if Kirkcaldy increase at the same ratio she has been doing she will soon rival Edinburgh itself."

Rovers' first East of Scotland League victory came at the sixth attempt. Jimmy Neilson scored twice in the first half, but Dundee levelled through Methven and Millar before Neilson completed his hat-trick, for Rovers to win 3-2 in front of a delighted crowd of 3,000, including "D.R." who was moved to verse in the Fifeshire Advertiser :

Grieve was the hero of the day,
So was Gillespie and so was Kaye ;
The youngsters Moodie, Sinclair and "Cock"
Fairly bamboozled the Dundee folk.
Jocky Eckford, he can play,
So can McQueen and Dod Ramsay ;
Jamie Neilson he can shoot -
Three goals came from his wee foot.
How that they have got fairly settled,
They'll be near the top, horraye !   D.R.

The Final of the King Cup was scheduled for 25th March 1899, at Newton Park, but West Calder and 200 of their followers arrived in Kirkcaldy to find the ground under four inches of snow. No one from the East of Scotland Football Association thought to travel across on the morning of the match and advise the visitors of the conditions. West Calder were keen to play notwithstanding ; Rovers were not ; the Association wanted the teams to play a Friendly, but they could not agree. The match was played a month later, when Crawford gave West Calder a half time lead. John McQueen equalised, and Alex Ramsay scored the winner for Rovers.

"The visitors were all large heavily-built fellows, endowed with no concern for the limbs of opponents and a propensity for embracing the man who was taking the ball from them. ... In the second half, however, having got used to the outlanding tactics of their opponents, and with the wind at their backs, [Rovers] gave West Calder never a chance to add to their score." After the match, a social meeting was held in Mr Gibb's rooms where the Cup was presented to Raith Rovers. "…. at the end, on the suggestion of Mr Lambert, the cup as filled and emptied to the success of the winning team."

A new attendance record was set at Stark's Park for the April holiday fixture against Hearts in the East of Scotland League. Four thousand spectators paid £65 and saw Rovers lose 3-2. They also lost to Hearts of Beath in the semi final of the Wemyss Cup. Despite incessant Rovers' attacks, the visitors scored the only goal of the game. The Fifeshire Advertiser concluded : "The day was fine, and there was a very good gate, considering the comparative unimportance of the match. If the spectators did not see the best of football, they were treated to a farce which gave them about value for their money."

With two cups won, and three finals yet to play, the Annual General Meeting was a happy affair. The Treasurer's report showed a balance in favour of £202 18/7d, from Income of £700, and the following office bearers were elected. Honorary President : Mr R. C. Munro Ferguson, Drs Smith, Curror and Crichton, and Messrs Kellock, Strachan and D Williamson. President - Mr J. Nicol. Vice president Mr J. Blyth ; honorary secretary Mr D. Louden, treasurer Mr H. Ritchie (replacing Mr Mitchell), match secretary Mr A. W. Lumsden, 2nd XI secretary Mr Lowrie, committee - Messrs J. Millar, J. Thomson, W, Eckford, L. Simpson and J.M. Tod. "It was agreed to ask admission to the second division of the Scottish League. The meeting was then adjourned till some time in May after the close of the season."

The Nairn Charity Cup was won with 3-2 and 3-0 scorelines, while Rovers hosted the Fife Cup Final against Lochgelly United. "Play all through was fast, and the extraordinary tactics of the visitors added greatly to the charm of the game. But almost from the start it was evident that the Rovers were the superior team - as far as football was concerned, that is ; for in matters of tripping and horseplay the balance was all the other way."

The inevitable protest was tendered, on the grounds of the incompetence of the referee. The Fifeshire Association unanimously agreed to replay the tie, but Rovers' committee decided, "in justice to their players" not to entertain a replay.

The Kirkcaldy Times of 24th May advertised
GREAT FOOTBALL ATTRACTION
CHAMPIONSHIP OF FIFE
FIFESHIRE CHARITY ASSOCIATION CUP & BADGES
Raith Rovers (winners Fife, King and Kirkcaldy Hospital Cups) versus Cowdenbeath (winners of Consolation, Wemyss and Dunfermline Hospital Cups) at East End Park, Dunfermline on Saturday First, 27th May kick off 4.15 Admission 6d and 3d Referee Mr Wylie, Queen's Park
The Fifeshire Charity Association had been set up "for the purpose of helping charitable institutions in Kirkcaldy, Dunfermline and Cowdenbeath districts which

do not usually benefit by such means. Raith Rovers are very popular in Dunfermline, and a hearty welcome awaits them." The teams gave their services free, but were entertained to a "splendid tea" in the Commercial Temperance Hotel after the match.

A Charlie Moodie own goal gave Cowdenbeath the new trophy, and there was more bad news that afternoon from Buckhaven, where Raith Athletic lost 4-3 to Dunfermline Athletic Juniors in the final of the Fifeshire Junior Shield.

The Fifeshire Charity Association had been formed by two "gentlemen", one from Kirkcaldy and one from Dunfermline, who drafted elaborate rules, proposed, seconded and unanimously elected the necessary office-bearers (not one of whom ever was asked to a meeting) and solemnly and unblushingly sent a formal application to Mr McDowall, the secretary of the SFA, for permission to play a match at Dunfermline in aid of local charities a fortnight after the season had closed.

The necessary permission received, and East End Park hired for the match, a cup was purchased at a cost of £3 10/-, along with two sets of gold badges at 15/- each. Gate drawings amounted to a very respectable £38, but the cup and badges cost £21 10/- and the post-match "splendid tea" and other match expenses accounted for the remainder, save for 13/- which was handed over to the Dunfermline Cottage Hospital. The Fifeshire Charity Association had staged its first, and last, football fixture.

Back in Kirkcaldy, the reconvened AGM of Raith Rovers estimated that after paying two thirds of the bank balance to the players, the club would start the next season with "the very satisfactory balance of £90". All but Eckford of the players had been signed for next season.

"During the meeting a telegram was received intimating that the club had not been admitted to the second division of the League. This is disappointing ; but the Scottish qualifying finalists, Arthurlie and Dundee Wanderers, who were also applying for admission, never found a seconder, whereas the Rovers were supported by all the east clubs, and two of the west clubs. Another season like last should make their admission a certainty."

The voting was quite conclusive : Abercorn 35 Linthouse 32 Raith Rovers 12. Mr AW Lumsden pled the Rovers' case, citing easy railway facilities to visiting teams, a first class enclosure, and average gate drawings of £50. The Western vote was decisive. The Fife Free Press noted - "The influence of Mr Watt, Linthouse secretary, who is also secretary of the League, would probably have a bearing in the inclusion of these two western clubs The disappointment throughout the district at the Rovers being excluded is keen, but better luck may come their way next year."

The reserves at Raith Athletic kept themselves in trim over the summer months, according to the Fife Free Press of July 29th.

JOCK ECKFORD
A long-serving forward who was a prolific goalscorer, his Rovers' career stretched from 1892 to the club's first season in the Scottish League. He lived in Links Street.

On 15th October 1898 the referee (Mr McPherson) did not appear for the Fife Cup 1st round tie against Clackmannan. A friendly was played instead, and when the tie was staged three weeks later
"The Rovers did all the pressing, while during the last 20 minutes of the game Cairns stood with his hands in his pockets."
Rovers won 6-0.

On Wednesday 1st February 1899, at a meeting of the General Committee of the East of Scotland Association in the Exchange Hotel, Edinburgh, Cowdenbeath claimed the [Consolation Cup] tie. Mr Lumsden, Raith Rovers secretary, stated that "his club desired to 'scratch' from the competition, but also to keep faith with the public, so they adopted this method of doing so. Mr Williamson objected to such a proceeding, and asked how they were "keeping faith" with the public in allowing a match to go on as a cup-tie when they were not going to take any further part in the competition." A vote was taken, and Cowdenbeath were awarded the tie.

1898 - Whytehouse Mansions completed.
Dysart Golf club opened

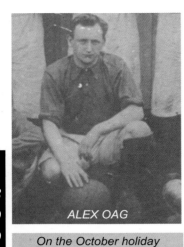

ALEX OAG

On the October holiday Monday 1899, 3,000 attended Stark's Park in "brilliant weather" to see the opening East of Scotland League match against Hibs, which finished 2-2. The match was best remembered for a Rovers goal, as recalled by one fan several years later.

"The greatest goal ever scored in Stark's Park – and that's surely saying a great deal – was scored by Alexander Mackie for Raith Rovers against the Hibernians. What rendered it all the more wonderful was by reason of it being scored against Internationalist Harry Rennie, then at the zenith of his ability and fame. At half-time the Hibs led by one goal to nothing. Immediately on re-starting, Mackie (who played centre forward) tipped the ball to Hector Macdonald, who slipped it back to the centre first time, and Mackie fastening on, let drive with terrific force from almost midfield, and beat the watchful Rennie all the way with an unsaveable shot into the far corner of the net. Needless to chronicle the great feat was hailed with deafening applause, the standites repeatedly rising to their feet and cheering vociferously. After the match Rennie acknowledged it was the only time he had been beaten by a ball shot in from forty yards out."

1899 - Adam Smith & Beveridge Halls opened by Andrew Carnegie on 11th October.

John Barry, Ostlere & Co merged with Shepherd & Beveridge and The Kirkcaldy Linoleum Co Ltd to form Barry, Ostlere & Shepherd Ltd

A SPLENDID ACHIEVEMENT. The Raith Athletic have been doing a "roarin' trade" in connection with 5-a-side football during the holidays, securing no fewer than three first prizes throughout the week. At the Highland Gathering at Kirkcaldy they beat Cowdenbeath, while at Methil on Pathhead Market Saturday they again disposed of the miners after three drawn games. The prizes awarded there were handsome English lever watches. At Springfield, on Saturday, they were again at the "top of the tree", travelling bags being the prizes obtained. This is surely a record to be proud of."

1899/1900 opened with some curmudgeonly remarks in the Fife Free Press: "Tuesday first will see the king of winter games - association football - once again in active operation. Athough the middle of August is, in the opinion of many, too early to commence the game, yet it is a fact that the Scottish people are eager to witness contests at any time of the year. To make a fresh start, the players are all to appear in new "togs"."

There was probably more interest in the proposal to merge John Barry, Ostlere & Co (Ltd), the Kirkcaldy Linoleum Company (Ltd), and Shepherd & Beveridge, to form Barry, Ostlere & Shepherd.

Rovers were short of bodies for the opening friendly against St Bernards, and fielded Bonthrone, Carmichael, Mackie and Gilmour of Raith Athletic, and Wyles of Buckhaven, "it being remarked that it was probably the youngest "senior" combination that had ever been played on a Scottish football field."

With between 27,000 and 30,000 attending the Band Contest at Raith, it was wise for Rovers to "sit out" the weekend. You had to look long and hard for newspaper references to Rovers' long-time local rivals, although one paper acknowledged : ".... it is refreshing to be made aware of the continued existence of the old Kirkcaldy Club. All right-thinking sportsmen would have regretted the demise of the black and white brigade who, though continually dogged by misfortune, have managed to plod carefully along."

Rovers had learned their lessons from previous seasons and organised several friendly matches before contesting the first round of the Qualifying Cup. One of them was against Cameronians, described as a "third class Glasgow club", the evidence being a 9-0 Rovers victory. Off the field, the club were ".... gradually making good progress in the ground improvements, and a splendid new temperance refreshment stall has just been erected between the pay-boxes and the pavilion."

Dunfermline Athletic, newly converted from juniors to seniors, were beaten 2-1 at East End Park in the first round of the Qualifying Cup. Rovers then guaranteed Clackmannan £12 to play the East of Scotland Cup tie at Stark's Park, which was duly won 5-1. The tricky trip to Burngrange Park, West Calder, in the second round of the Qualifying Cup was negotiated,

Gilmour scoring the only goal of the match.

The team was far from settled, however. Tom Lindsay and Andrew Grieve both had spells in goal ; John Scott came in at right back, to be replaced by James McLean later in the season, when Scott was suspended by the SFA for a month for a "misdemeanour". Peter Robertson shared the centre back position with John Lambert, and otherwise played at left half. John McQueen laid claim to the inside right position, George Drummond was centre forward, Alex Mackie inside left and James Gilmour the most regular left winger. Just about every player had a shot at outside right. Far too many players were fielded in the course of the season to achieve tangible success.

Two days before the "brilliant weather" of the October holiday fixture, the second round of the East of Scotland Cup at home to Lochgelly saw the other extreme of Kirkcaldy's climate. Owing to the stormy state of the weather, it was agreed to play the second half as a "friendly" and the game finished 1-1. At the start, Lochgelly said cup tie or no match, but changed their minds at the interval (when conditions were no worse). Ironically Lochgelly had the lead at the interval, although Rovers had missed a thrice-taken penalty. The Fife Free Press thought the enterprise was simply a money-making scam and believed the game should not have been played in such torrential rain. Rovers were without Blyth, who had "taken once more to the carrying code."

The match was replayed the following Saturday, and Rovers built a four goal lead. Then "Greenhorn handled ; Dorward and Neilson rushed on him, but the latter was swung round into the goal for his pains. A penalty, of course, resulted. Neilson was chosen to take the kick, but on the first attempt, the Lochgelly players refused to keep their places ; at the second attempt, Neilson was interfered with from behind. Once more the ball was placed, but on this occasion Kidd (Lochgelly) kicked the ball through his own goal, and the referee promptly ordered both teams to leave the field, saying he could not continue to referee a game when his orders were not obeyed. This decision happened when 17 minutes of the game remained to go, and, naturally, here was great excitement on the field as the teams slowly moved to the pavilion." On the Wednesday following, the East of Scotland Association suspended Greenhorn until next year (he called the referee a "notorious liar") and Kidd was suspended for a month.

In the third round of the Qualifying Cup, Rovers tried to induce Camelon to give up ground rights, but the Falkirk side declined. The attendance of 1,500 would have been more but for the Falkirk v Cowdenbeath tie being played just two miles away. Both teams changed in the school house adjoining the ground, and Rovers won 3-2 thanks to a 20 yard shot from Mackie.

The Qualifying Cup was being processed in a rush, with a 2-2 draw at

Bo'ness the following Saturday (while Stark's Park was hosting the second replay of the Arbroath v Dunblane tie) followed by a 3-1 victory in the replay at Stark's Park. Seven days after that, East Stirling were beaten 3-1 in Kirkcaldy.

The Fifeshire Advertiser reported : "4000 spectators were present at the start. The playing pitch was completely encircled, and the railway embankment was alive with onlookers. The improvised "grand stand" was patronised by several hundreds, while the covered in stand belonging to the club was crowded. Spectators from all parts of Fife were there, and it is safe to assert that there was never a larger attendance at Stark's Park." The gross takings of £82 would lend credence to that claim.

The supremacy of cup ties in the eyes of the footballing public was underlined by the following report in the Fifeshire Advertiser of Saturday October 28th, following Kirkcaldy's victory over Polton after a succession of defeats in the early rounds of several cup competitions. "It is a pleasure to be able to record a success - no matter how unimportant - for the black and white brigade. As in previous seasons, the improvement - if we may regard the form of Saturday in this light - comes too late, for there is now scarcely anything left worth fighting for. And friendly games nowadays are unfortunately looked upon with little concern ; it is now a cup-tie battle or nothing with the great British public."

Otherwise, it was black news for the town's oldest football club. "Near the top of Milton Road a new street is to be made to run eastwards and meet the new street emerging on Nicol Street called Beveridge Road. This street will cut through the Newton Park - the lease of which by the Wanderers Football Club expires next month - and will run straight on to Milton Road. Most of the ground on the line of the street has already been feued, while almost the whole of Newton Park has also been feued, and building operations will commence soon as the tenancy of the Club expires." Generations of football supporters attending Stark's Park in the ensuing 108 years, have parked their cars on Ava Street on the site of Newton Park.

No matter how well connected the club's officials, nor well appointed the facilities, nor impressive the history, a football club was nothing without a ground to call its own. Wanderers went the way of other local clubs would before them could not find a suitable replacement enclosure at a time of extensive development of the town's dwindling open spaces. The errors and omissions by others in this regard were well learned by Raith Rovers officials.

Successive Saturdays of Qualifying Cup ties were to be interrupted by an East of Scotland Cup tie against Selkirk, but a "blunder" by visiting officials meant that Rovers had to make do with First Eleven v Second Eleven. Eleven shillings was claimed from Selkirk for expenses of bill-posting the match that didn't take place.

Seven days later, some 500 Rovers fans took advantage of a special train to Arbroath for the Qualifying Cup semi final. It was to depart at 1.08 from Kirkcaldy and 1.12 from Sinclairtown (not stopping at Dysart) and a special deal negotiated by the Rovers committee meant that the ticket cost 2/6d – expensive considering the cost of admission to the match was just 4d. The train was delayed and the passengers missed the first 15 minutes of the match at Gayfield. There was worse to come ; Rovers lost 3-1. "Notes By A Roversite" in the following Saturday's newspaper wailed :

Oh, why left I my hame,
Why did I cross the Tay !
For I've never been the same
Since YON last Saturday !

"Defeated but not disgraced, though a draw would have been a decent development of the day's doings," was the general consensus, and the match referee, Tom Robertson of Glasgow, who was reckoned to be the best official in Britain, threw some light on Rovers' tactics. "Explaining the frequency of offside, he thought the Rovers backs played this game, which, he said, was now becoming quite prevalent in Scotland, the example being taken from the English teams. Until there was a sweeping alteration in the offside rule, his bugbear would always affect the game."

Rovers' preoccupation with the national cup competition meant that they were behind in the other cups, and on 2nd December they agreed to play two matches on the same afternoon. The first eleven won 2-1 at Polton Vale in the East of Scotland Cup semi final, while a reserve team beat Hearts of Beath 2-0 at Stark's Park in a King Cup tie. The biggest losers were Raith Athletic, who had to play their Scottish Junior Cup third round replay against Buckhaven United at Beveridge Park with a greatly weakened team.

As a result of these arrangements, the Fifeshire Advertiser thought a regular reserve team should be established, not so much for keeping the playing strength of the club, but to provide attractive fixtures when the first team were away from home.

There was trouble in the corridors of power, with the East of Scotland Association awarding the Cup semi final to Polton Vale. "It will be remembered the Raith Rovers wired Polton Vale that they could not see their way to playing the tie, but on further considering the matter they again wired the same night cancelling the first telegram The case came up before the Association, who ordered Polton Vale to play the tie at Loanhead, and, as stated above, the Rovers won. The Loanhead team now claim the tie, and have put the matter into their solicitors' hands. Surely there is something wrong with the committee of the ESFA when they reverse their decisions in this manner. The Rovers, however, do not intend to let the matter rest."

Rovers' involvement in the Scottish

JIMMY WALKER
His five seasons at Stark's Park brought plenty of goals before he signed for St Bernards. He lived in Hill Street

Rovers' complete ascendancy over Kirkcaldy was cemented with the visit to Stark's Park of Corinthians for the New Year Holiday fixture in 1900. The visitors, and their famous player G.O. Smith, were invited to a Grand Supper in the George Hotel, where Charlie Moodie, Rovers' popular captain, was given a marriage present, in the form of a bedroom suite, supplied by Matthew Spears, upholsterer, High Street. The match was played in heavy rain and a strong, gusty wind. Corinthians took a 4-0 lead and two of their players, Osborne and Foster left the field. With the ground a quagmire, the match was stopped twenty minutes early.

Rovers chose to enter the "Scottish County League", instead of playing friendly fixtures on those Saturdays not occupied by East of Scotland League matches. The opening match was at East Stirling on 27th January, and the Fifeshire Advertiser was far from welcoming. "Little or no enthusiasm was evinced over this match in the Kirkcaldy district. This may be accounted for by the re-action which sets in after the season is more than half-way through, when the doings of a club fail to interest in the same degree after they have passed the cup-tie stage."

ANDREW RAMSAY

March 24th 1900 saw Stark's Park used for a different ball game, Kirkcaldy playing Perthshire at Rugby in the semi final of the North of Scotland Cup, the Rugby club also severely inconvenienced by the loss of Newton Park. The previous week, Rovers had lost 3-2 at the new Dens Park, described by the Fifeshire Advertiser as "cramped, inaccessible and bumpy" although it did accommodate 3,000 spectators for the East of Scotland League fixture. Furthermore, the Fifeshire Advertiser was not impressed by the man in the middle at Dundee's new ground.
"A further word in regard to the refereeing. Passing over the many muttered imprecations from player and spectator alike, which his wonderful impartiality in making mistakes produced, it would be well if the referee on Saturday could tone down his anxiety to participate as a player in the game. The frequency of his coming into contact with the ball made one inclined to inquire which side he was playing for. If Mr Black is a first-class referee, the third-class men should obtain speedy promotion."
When Dundee played the return game at Stark's Park (billed by the press as "Marmalade v Linoleum") ".... with characteristic foresight, Mr A.W. Lumsden, the Rovers' secretary, has arranged for the receipt of telegrams every 15 minutes direct from Celtic Park, announcing the progress of the [Scotland v England] international. These will be made known at Stark's Park immediately on arrival."

Cup proper was once again of the shortest duration. They were drawn away to Third Lanark, at that club's first ground, also named Cathkin Park. Their second ground of that name was known in 1900 as the second Hampden Park, and occupied by Queen's Park, who did not open the present stadium (the third Hampden) until 1903.

Thirds were 2-0 ahead at half time and scored three more after the interval. Rovers' consolation goal came late in the game, from a free kick. The victors had four more "goals" disallowed, not always justifiably.

A sign of Rovers' new priorities came on Saturday April 21st, when they once again fulfilled two fixtures. A scratch team was put out at Dunfermline for the King Cup Final against Cowdenbeath, which the Miners won 5-1. The gate was £16, compared with the £64 taken at Newton Park for the equivalent fixture a year previously. Expenditure was £10 7/3d, and Rovers had asked for a guarantee of £4 10/-, arguing that they only got £5 from a large gate the previous year when they had sent their full first team. The committee voted to give Rovers £2 and Cowdenbeath £4.

Rovers' first team was deployed for a County League match, at home to Abercorn, which they won 2-0. There was a "good gate" at Stark's Park, on Links Market Saturday. The Fifeshire Advertiser connived a bad pun : "The proximity of the Fair and fair "music" had a kind of soothing effect on the game ; there was a complete absence of excitement, and the players did not exert themselves unduly. After all, it is nearing the close of the season, and the winter pastime is about nearing the stale period. The war absorbs more of the footballer's interest. Little wonder then that the game becomes boer-ing."

Towards the end of the season, Rovers made it known that they intended "making application for admission to the Second Division of the Scottish League and taking their performances throughout the season, they certainly deserve promotion to this body."

The annual meeting was held in Philp's School when John Nicol retired as president. Mr Lumsden retired as secretary, to be replaced by Mr. Harry Simpson. In contrast to the less successful results (due to the higher standard of opposition), financially the season was a huge success, with a record income of almost £1000 providing a handsome profit. It was reported that "The plans of the new ground at Clayholes were laid out before the meeting. The proposed enclosure, when laid out, will, we have no doubt, prove one of the best athletic grounds in the provinces."

The ground, on the site of the present Balwearie High School, came to nothing, as did Rovers application to join the Scottish League. Airdrie were re-elected, and East Stirling were chosen to replace Linthouse. The country's leading clubs were not yet prepared to venture into Fife in the quest for League points, having been happy

to make the journey for friendly fixtures (and generous gate guarantees) in the past. The (Glasgow) Evening Times noted on 17th May :

"For the third year in succession the Raith Rovers last night tried hard to gain entry into the Second Division of the Scottish League. They were defeated, however, by East Stirling, the only other candidate for the vacancy. The Kirkcaldy representative took his defeat in thoroughly sportsmanlike manner. Financially his club is in an enviable position – the East of Scotland competition is responsible for that – but their aim last night was to "gain promotion" as they called it. Better luck in the future."

The Fife Free Press was never to the front of the queue of people wishing for the start of a new football season. "The all too short close season is fast drawing to a conclusion, and this popular winter pastime will be again in full swing in a very short time. It is a pity that the Scottish Association could not manage to take a leaf out of the book of their brethern over the border, and extend their resting period until the beginning of September. Nevertheless, nine months - the regulation period for Scottish clubs - is sometimes too brief to carry through all the fixtures on hand."

"In connection with the proposed purchase of the new ground, belonging to Mr R C Munro Ferguson, known as "Clayholes", negotiations are still in progress. A sketch plan for the ground proposed to be acquired, which extends to 5.416 imperial acres, has been prepared by Mr Wm Dow, architect, Kirkcaldy, and should a satisfactory arrangement be come to between the parties the Rovers will be in possession of a pitch second to none in "Ye Kingdom.""

For Rovers, the season opened with a Wednesday evening friendly match at home to Cowdenbeath, played in "tropical" conditions. Rovers won 5-0. "Perhaps the new ball had something to do with it, the committee trying a new patent one, as used by the leading city clubs."

The visit to Cowdenbeath in the first round of the East of Scotland Shield attracted a crowd of 2,800, paying £47 17/-, Cowdenbeath's record gate. Rovers won 4-2, but it took three matches to dispose of the Miners in the Scottish Qualifying Cup.

Defeat came in the third round, at Merchiston Park, Bainsford, where East Stirling won 5-3. A delay in processing the transfer papers meant that new signing Harry Marshall did not play, "which caused much disappointment. At the last minute the Rovers were forced to alter their team owing to a protest against Harry Torrance and Hector McDonald, against whom professional irregularities were alleged." They took a chance on McDonald.

The team was much more settled. Jimmy Mackie came in as goalkeeper ; Peter Robertson and John Scott were the regular full backs, and new signings Jim Murphy and Harry Marshall added solidity to the half back line, Charlie Moodie moving to inside right. Hector McDonald was outside right, George

Drummond, Peter Douglas and John Rae shared the forward duties, particularly once Alex Mackie had left to work in Newcastle for the Customs department of the government. John Bell started the season at outside left.

As Rovers sought to compete at a higher, national, level of the game, so they had to extend the boundaries of their recruitment. The Fife Free Press complained : "In examining the Rovers team the effects of professionalism was painfully evident on Saturday, when , in a town of the size and importance of Kirkcaldy, only a couple of local players could be given a place. Of course, under the existing condition of things in football affairs, managers of country clubs have no other course left open for them to adopt."

A fixture against West Calder was once again problematic, although this time it was at Burngrange Park, in the East of Scotland Qualifying Cup semi final. With Rovers 3-1 ahead "The game was stopped by the referee about 5 minutes from time owing to darkness" The East of Scotland Association decided that the match should be replayed at Kirkcaldy, the delay to the kick off being caused by West Calder having to change their jerseys, due to a similarity with Rovers', who won the replay 4-2.

On 24th November, Rovers had a scheduled East of Scotland League fixture at Hearts, but the Fife Free Press reported that "A dispute has arisen between the local players and the committee, but, notwithstanding, a crack eleven has been got together, which should be able to give the Edinburgh men a hard game." David Fairbairn, formerly of Celtic and Partick Thistle, and William Tervit, ex`Southampton were among those drafted in, but Rovers lost 6-0.

Even competitions such as the East of Scotland Qualifying Cup were paling into insignificance compared with matches against Scottish League teams. The final was played at East End Park, Dunfermline, and attracted a crowd of just 1,800. Rovers beat Clackmannan 2-1 in "miserable weather" and on a "bad ground". Clackmannan lodged a protest that Harry Marshall had played a Combination [League] game for Alloa Athletic. The protest was withdrawn through lack of evidence, and replaced by an argument that the game should be replayed due to the state of the ground. The committee took no action.

Marshall was described by the Fifeshire Advertiser as "steady and reliable, although "Beefy" carried too much weight to be spry, and could stand a deal of toning down."

The night of 20th and 21st December 1900 saw a great storm batter Kirkcaldy, damaging a great deal of property. "Stark's Park came in for a share of the ravages of the storm, a considerable portion of the wooden pailing surrounding the football enclosure having been blown down. The large flagstaff at the entrance gate was also snapped in two. Happily the pavilion and grand stand remained intact."

The following day's Friendly match against Camelon proceeded as planned, causing the Fifeshire Advertiser to remark : "Stark's Park has withstood the incessant rain of the past two months well. Indeed, Stark's is one of the best drained parks in the East of Scotland, and always presents a decent surface even in the worst of weather. The fine stretch of firm turf was particularly welcome to the home team, after the sloughs of despond they have lately wallowed among."

Towards the end of December 1900, the country (correctly, unlike 99 years later) celebrated the end of the century, and the match against Corinthians on Monday December 31st was billed as the "last match of the century". Admission was Ground 6d, Grand-Stand [an additional] 6d, Reserved Stand by Ticket ; Ladies Free. "The grand-stand was gaily decorated with flags and streamers, and the reserved portion was fully occupied with a distinguished company."

The following day, while Rovers were playing at Arbroath, Stark's Park was occupied by Raith Athletic for a Scottish Junior Cup 4th round tie against Greenock Volunteers. The match was advertised as follows : "WELCOME TO THE VOLUNTEERS. WANTED, 10,000 PEOPLE to attend and test the accomodation of STARK'S PARK on NEW YEAR'S DAY at 12 o'clock, when the RAITH ATHLETIC will defend Fife against an attack by VOLUNTEERS from the West of Scotland."

A free Saturday on 5th January was hurriedly filled with a home friendly against Clackmannan. The Fife Free Press believed that ".... after their heavy week's work, the Rovers' players would have been none the worse of a rest." The fans too – only 500 turned up, to see a 2-0 home defeat.

"As miserable an exhibition of football as could well be imagined was the outcome of Saturday's meeting between Clackmannan and Raith Rovers. The Rovers Committee had a hard job to fix up a match for Saturday, and the pity was that they succeeded. It is to be hoped the committee will be more careful in future holiday occasions on the demands they make upon their players."

In early March, the Fifeshire Advertiser stated "It may be here mentioned that the Rovers aspire to become connected with the Second Division of the Scottish League next season, or alternately with the Northern League ..... It is certainly a pity that an important and populous centre like the county of Fife should not be represented, at least, in the Scottish League, and we may express the hope that next season Kirkca1dy may oust one of the laggards on the Second Division table. "

The annual election of office bearers brought the following results :
A W Lumsden president (telephone inspector) beat Andrew Buist (traveller)
Robert Ritchie (water inspector), beat William Eckford (floorcloth printer)
Mr H Simpson (meter inspector) beat Mr D

JIMMY MACKIE
The deaf and dumb goalkeeper made his debut for Rovers in 1900, and he was still playing the occasional match 15 years later. He was reserve goalkeeper when Rovers reached the Scottish Cup Final in 1913.

A friendly against West Calder on 17th November 1900 was scheduled to start at 4pm, but kicked off half an hour late. The Fife Free Press complained : "It was tea time before a start was effected. The visitors were, of course, to blame in consequence of their late arrival. On one occasion last year it will be remembered that the same club, when they visited Kirkcaldy, were about an hour late. West Calder is an awkward place to get out of, but arrangements should be made to leave by an earlier train."

Queen Victoria died on 22nd January 1901, and the following Saturday Rovers' friendly match against Cowdenbeath was played during the proclamation of King Edward VII at the Market Cross. "The referee, Mr Bailie, Edinburgh, declared the ground unplayable for the Fife Cup originally fixed upon, but Kirkcaldy's enthusiasm for football did not outrun their loyalty, and the attendance was, consequently, poor." There was no football the following week, on the day of the Queen's funeral.

1901 - Monday 26th May, General Post Office opened in Hunter street

ALEX GRIERSON

In an attempt to breathe life into the 1901 King Cup Final, the venue was chosen on the toss of a coin, Rovers beating Cowdenbeath 4-1 at Stark's Park before an impressive attendance of 3,000.

On 30th March 1901, at Cupar Sheriff Court, "William Deacon, floorcloth worker, Peter Gillespie and James Marr, all labourers, youths residing in Kirkcaldy, admitted breaking into the refreshment room at the clubhouse of the Raith Rovers Football Club and helping themselves to what they could lay hands on. They were sent to prison for seven days."

The 1901 census revealed the population of Kirkcaldy to be 33,973, up from 27,151 ten years earlier. It was now the 9th largest town in Scotland.

The Northern League started in 1891/92 and its first championship was shared by Dundee teams East End and Our Boys. Arbroath won outright in 1892/93, but the competition wasn't completed the following season, and not even started in 1894/95. It wasn't completed in 1911/12 and 1913/14, but Forfar won the last championship before the First World War in 1914/15

Whyte (law clerk) by 2 votes for Match Secretary

Mr D Mitchell (porter) having gained two votes fewer.

Successful for committee were Mr H. Ritchie, clerk, Mr A Simpson, joiner, Mr A Kinnear spirit merchant, Mr A. Buist, Mr J Nicol, grocer, Mr D Whyte, Mr R Russell. Raith Athletic officials, unopposed, were Match Secretary Mr Alexander Lowrie, Honorary Secretary Mr J Blyth, Honorary Treasurer, Mr D. Grant

The treasurer reported a small financial deficit for the season, due to matches being lost to bad weather. It was confirmed at the AGM that the club had been accepted into the Northern League, which was being extended to 12 clubs. The guarantee was £5, with the three Aberdeen teams to receive £10. A Dundee official had told his Raith counterpart that average gate drawings were £50 per match

There was considerable dispute over the vote for the position of Match Secretary, at a subsequent general meeting. Mitchell objected that there had been no clear majority for Mr Simpson, and proposed that there be another vote, this time with ballot papers sent to all members. Simpson withdrew, pointing out that only one quarter of the members were present. D. Whyte also withdrew. Mitchell was then selected by a small majority. Both Simpson and Mitchell attended the next committee meeting, assuming that they were secretary. Another meeting, and poll, was convened, with Mitchell gaining 74 votes and Simpson 50, a poor poll from a total membership of around 250.

A much more important vote took place at the Scottish League Annual General Meeting on 30th May. Partick Thistle were relegated from the First Division, and there were four contenders for the vacant twelfth place in the Second Division. Arthurlie topped the poll, ahead of Raith Rovers, Ayr Parkhouse and Ayr United.

1901/02

For season 1901/02, the Fife Free Press considered Rovers' prospects to be "very rosy. The committee, after a lot of hard work, have succeeded in getting a capable lot of players together, and only hope the public will rally round the club, and give it more support than it received last year. Amongst others who will sport the blue and white this season are : Oswald (Leith), Bonthron, McFarlane (Hibs), Moodie, Robertson (Cowdenbeath), Grierson (Raith Athletic), Mears (Leith Ivanhoe), Devine (St Bernards), Anderson (Dundee), Eckford (Middlesboro), Mackie, Macdonald and some good juniors."

It was indeed a fundamental strengthening of the squad, extending the policy of recruiting beyond Kirkcaldy and District.

The club's first ever full scale trial match opened the season, with the following teams :

Blue - Laing, Bonthron, McFarlane, Moodie, Laing, Grierson, Gourlay, Manning, Henderson, McLean, McCulloch

Stripes - Oswald, Brown, Dair, Smith, Robertson, Catton, Eckford, Devine, Weir, Anderson, McDonald

The competitive season opened with three successive Northern League fixtures (two draws and a victory). Dunfermline Athletic were drawn in the first round of the Qualifying Cup, and they were induced to give up ground rights with a guarantee of £20 and half the gate over £40. A 1-1 draw ensured that the tie would go to East End Park anyway, where there was a further 1-1 draw before Rovers won the second replay, at Stark's Park, 2-1.

The Fife Free Press reported : "Notwithstanding that it was "Lifeboat Saturday" in the town, there was a large crowd wending their way Stark's Park direction about 4 o'clock. Both clubs were out in plenty of time, but before commencing the game the Rovers players had to face the camera. The home team was photographed in its ordinary war-paint before starting, and then discarded the dark blue in favour of the colours of the Celtic."

Perennial late-comers West Calder were true to form for the second round tie. "West Calder were late in turning out. The Rovers' committee had a brake at the station awaiting their arrival, but the players said they would prefer to walk, in order to enable them to get their "legs stretched" after the long train journey." It was of little help, as Rovers won 6-1, but defeat came in the next round at Lochgelly United, where 3,000 witnessed Rovers' first visit to Lochgelly's new ground at Reid Park.

Perhaps Rovers had one eye on their glamorous October holiday fixture two days later, when £40 was taken at the gate to see Hearts, including the famous Bobby Walker, beaten 4-3. Rovers followed that with a 9-1 home win over Montrose in the Northern League. Defeats were few and far between – after a couple of seasons where the club's ambitions exceeded their playing prowess, the team was beginning to flourish.

Jim Oswald was in goal, Robert Bonthron and David Denholm at full back, Charlie Morris, Alex Grierson and the restored Charlie Moodie at half back, Jock Eckford returned on the wing with Hector McDonald on the opposite flank ; Alex Mackie and Jimmy Devine shared the inside duties with George Anderson, and Robert Weir started the season at centre forward.

The reluctance of associations to acknowledge the growing attraction of league competitions was illustrated once again on 7th December, when Rovers had a scheduled East of Scotland League match at Hibs. The East of Scotland Association insisted that they play Selkirk in the East Qualifying Cup on the same day. Rovers' dilemma was resolved by sending the first team to Easter Road, and having the reserves fulfil the cup tie. To ease their passage, "Selkirk have been induced by a judicious expenditure of filthy lucre to waive their claim to choice of ground ...." and on account of that significant expenditure, Rovers' members cards (season tickets) were

The Rovers team which played during the 1901-02 Northern League Championship winning season. Back row : D. Mitchell (Match Secretary) ; R. Ritchie (Vice President) ; R. Bonthron, J. Oswald, A. Lumsden (President), A. Mackie, D. Denholm, D. Arnot (Hon. Secetary), J. Blyth (Treasurer), J. Adams (Trainer). Middle row : C. Morris, G. Anderson, C. Moodie, J. Eckford, H. Macdonald In front : R. Weir, A. Grierson

The picture was taken in front of the old stand at Stark's Park, on the site of the present Main Stand.

The Northern League was one of several regional leagues which accommodated clubs excluded from the Scottish League, and the reserve elevens of First Division clubs. Kirkcaldy United won the Northern League in 1906/07.

suspended for the Selkirk match. The league game at Hibs was lost 1-0, but the reserves beat Selkirk 3-2 at Stark's Park in a "poor game, watched by a small crowd".

Rovers had arranged two attractive home fixtures for the New Year holiday period. "Kirkcaldy football enthusiasts will thus have a capital holiday programme at their command." They stayed away from the Northern League match against Orion on 28th December, however. The ground was in "deplorable state", being a sea of slush, and the "gate was all but invisible." More than 2,000 paid almost £40 to see St Bernards draw 2-2 in an East of Scotland League match on New Year's Day, following "brilliant forward play by the homesters".

The following afternoon, St Mirren were the visitors in a Friendly fixture and after Hector McDonald had put Rovers ahead, the visitors were awarded a penalty towards the end of the first half. "Moffat was entrusted with the kick, but just as he was lifting his foot Oswald flung his cap on the ground, which had the effect of putting Moffat off his guard, and the Rovers' goal was saved." Moffat did score in the second half, and the game ended 1-1

Rovers' next fixture was a Wemyss Cup tie at Dunfermline Athletic. They took a 2-1 lead into the interval, but when Hector McDonald scored in the second half, the Dunfermline goalkeeper had not made an effort to save the shot, presuming offside to have been signalled. The goal was given and Dunfermline's players surrounded the referee ; unfortunately, the crowd followed suit. No effort was made to clear the field and the match was abandoned after 70 minutes. "It is alleged that the referee received some rather nasty knocks from the infuriated enthusiasts."

The draw for the first round of the Fife Cup matched Rovers with new opponents, Kirkcaldy Amateurs. Formed out of the wreckage of home-less Kirkcaldy FC (previously Wanderers) and patronised by local GP and former Scotland internationalist

Dr John Smith, the Amateur club had found a pitch at Steedman's Park in Sinclairtown, and were seeking to re-establish themselves in Scottish football. They gave a decent account of themselves in the cup tie, losing 2-1 at Stark's Park. The tie was played over two legs, but as Steedman's Park was not properly barricaded, the return was also played at Stark's Park, for a financial consideration, where Rovers won 3-0 thanks to a Mackie hat-trick. It was observed that the local rivalry was not there, as before

Part of the reason may have been that most of the Amateurs team were Rovers veterans, including Andrew Grieve ; David Stewart, Peter Robertson Jimmy Neilson, John Lambert, Andrew Andrew Hunter, McQueen, John Cairns, and Alex Suttie.

A Charlie Moodie goal settled the East of Scotland Cup Final against Bathgate, played at Cowdenbeath. Even the Rovers fans in the small gate (drawings just £20 1/3d) at North End Park admitted it was a "lucky win for Raith." Bathgate intimated a protest, questioning the competency of the referee who had disallowed a goal, but that was later withdrawn. However, the Chairman of the Association, Mr Nisbet, refused to present the cup to the Rovers President, Mr Lumsden, who was under suspension by the Association until such time as he apologised to the secretary and the Association for remarks he made three years earlier when he spoke out against rules which had every match involving an Edinburgh club played in the city.

There were several meetings on the subject in the weeks that followed, with no headway made. "In outside circles the affair has caused no end of amusement, and but for petty jealousies of one kind and another the hatchet would have been buried long ago without anyone being regarded as having been forced to undergo the climbing down process."

Rovers' good form was attracting attention for their players. Bonthron and Morris were in the Northern League team

On 9th November 1901, Rovers had a wasted trip to Dundee, as reported in the Fife Free Press a month later.

"RAITH ROVERS CLAIM AGAINST LOCHEE. An important meeting of the Northern League Committee was held in the Central Dining Rooms, Arbroath, on Saturday - Mr John Davidson (Arbroath) president, in the chair. In connection with the match Lochee v Raith Rovers, which was declared off on account of the condition of the pitch, the Kirkcaldy club craved full points and expenses. Mr Mitchell (Raith Rovers) said his club withdrew the claim for points, but the other claim still held good. The Rovers had been at the expense of travelling to Lochee, and although other matches were played in town that day the referee declared the ground unplayable. He thought the Lochee were to blame for not having notified the club of the state of the pitch earlier in the day. The Commitee ordered both clubs to pool their expenses, which would then be divided equally."

1901 - The Station Hotel opened ; as did the Beveridge Library (in the Adam Smith & Beveridge Halls) ; and Dunnikier Church
1902 - Victoria Viaduct opened
Edward Ostlere died. He lived in Chapel House, now the Dean Park Hotel

CHARLIE MOODIE

On Thursday, April 24th 1902, Everton visited Stark's Park for a friendly fixture, kick off 6.30pm. Two thousand spectators paid £23, and a collection was taken for the recent Ibrox Disaster. The match finished 4-4, one of Everton's goals coming from the penalty spot (Oswald doffed his cap to no effect) and after the match the Rovers players and committee met in a social capacity and Mr Nisbet, President of the East of Scotland FA, handed over the ESFA Qualifying Cup "after which several songs were rendered, and toasts pledged and honoured."

The close season was broken on 21st June 1902 when Rangers sent a team to Stark's Park for a match played in aid of the Ibrox Disaster Fund. 1,500 paid £23, and the Trades Band gave their services free, to see the visitors win 3-1. "The game all through was of the farcical order, the players at no period showing like form." The teams were also far from representative. Rovers' goalkeeper Jimmy Mackie kept goal for Rangers, who fielded Stewart of Kilbarchan at right back and Kerr of Hearts at centre half. Their new centre forward, Alex Mackie, played against his old club. Rovers fielded six strangers, and there was some scepticism over the names some of them played under.

which played Dundee at Dens Park, while Alex Mackie was attracting attention from Glasgow and Edinburgh clubs, along with Everton, Stoke and Middlesbrough. He worked with HM Customs at Methil and could only play every other Saturday, but a Glasgow club was alleged to have offered to assist in a transfer to that city.

The Northern League match against Aberdeen at Pittodrie was (prematurely) regarded as a decider for the Championship and was won 2-0 by Rovers. A long and exhausting season was taking its toll as the fixtures extended into the middle of May. Rovers drew 3-3 with St Bernards in an East of Scotland League match at Stark's Park, but they started the match with just nine players. The game was played in stormy weather, which, combined with too many fixtures, resulted in a poor gate despite the attractive opposition.

Notwithstanding the exhaustion of the players, there was an exciting climax to the Northern League. Dundee's 'A' team had overtaken Rovers at the top of the table, but a 1-0 victory away to Dundee Wanderers, thanks to a Jim McDonald goal, saw Rovers draw level. The respective records were :
Rovers : Won 14 Lost 5 Drawn 3 Goals For 53 Against 25 Points 31
Dundee A : Won 13 Lost 4 Drawn 5 For 51 Against 26 Points 31

With no provision in the rules for this eventuality, a deciding match was played at Stark's Park on Thursday 15th May, in front of 2,000 paying £27 2/-. Fisher and Anderson scored in the first half to deny Dundee's reserves a second successive championship.

"The "curtain is now rung down" on the official football season and the Rovers are to be congratulated on their splendid record. They have only been defeated twice on their own ground, and never before have they occupied so high a position in the East of Scotland League table. Application has now been made for inclusion in the Scottish League, and they certainly deserve promotion on the season's work." Following previous disappointments, the local press were not optimistic of Rovers' prospects of election.

There were two vacancies for the Second Division, Port Glasgow Athletic and Partick Thistle having been elevated to an expanded First Division. On Monday May 19th, Raith Rovers, Falkirk, Albion Rovers and Ayr Parkhouse applied for admission, and Rovers and Falkirk were successful. Scottish League football would finally to come to Fife, and Kirkcaldy, in 1902/03 season.

Rovers retained membership of the East of Scotland League, giving them matches against Edinburgh's First Division clubs. Their membership came at a cost, however, as they had to give guarantees of £20 to the visiting clubs, while they received only £12. Emboldened by their new found status, they raised an objection.

The annual review of "Raith Rovers Prospects" in the local press was never so avidly, or nervously, read by supporters. The Fife Free Press ventured : "To run a

professional club in a provincial town is year by year becoming a more serious undertaking, for no sooner do the players give indication of developing into "stars" than they are attracted by the big offers wealthier city clubs can afford to make, and off they go to pastures new."

This may seem a strange, sobering emphasis, when the club was about to embark on a great adventure, but the reality is that the team whose success had earned the club election to the Scottish League, was dismantled by its players leaving for First Division clubs. Sam Robertson, Charlie Morris and Robert Bonthron all joined Dundee, Robert Weir went to Cowdenbeath, Hector McDonald to Leith Athletic, and the biggest loss of all, Alex Mackie, signed for Rangers.

The incarcerative retention of contract rules had not yet been introduced, and the transfer system for those few players signed during their contractual period, was in its infancy. Rovers received not a penny for the loss of more than half their team.

In their place came centre forward James Smith from Lochgelly Rangers, outside right Alex Hynd from Black Watch, Tom Cairns from Belfast Distillery ; James Orrock of Vale of Wemyss, Simpson Rankine from Edinburgh juniors, Tom Clark from Dundee juniors and Geordie Turner, right back, from St Johnstone. James "Dummie" Mackie, the deaf-and-dumb goalkeeper, returned from Lochgelly United.

Those who believed that the club's immediate prospects were bright, were infused with the notion that because the club has made such strides in recent year, they would continue to do so. At various times in the club's history, it has been forgotten that the sole reason for such progress was the quality of its players, which disappeared when they left the club. It was a harsh lesson first learned in 1902/03.

Despite their appearance on the national stage, local considerations still prevailed, and the opening League match against East Stirling on Saturday August 16th 1902 was switched to Bainsford, due to the Raith Band Contest in Kirkcaldy. Hynd scored Rovers' first goal in the Scottish League, from the penalty spot, but East Stirling scored four times to give Rovers a sobering start to their League career.

A sign of the problems which were to befall Rovers in that difficult, debut season was that they started their first ever home Scottish League match with nine men on the pitch. The two latecomers eventually appeared, having missed Mr Michael Nairn of Bendhue unfurl the Northern League championship flag, in doing so "expressing the hope that this would not be the last championship flag [Rovers] would have the honour of winning."

The number of players used, and the constant chopping and changing of the team, was testament to the poor results. Now in a national League, there was difficulty in persuading prospective local players to travel every other week. Against Abercorn in Paisley on 4th October, goalkeeper Mackie played outside left to make up the numbers.

A new left back in John Anderson of Musselburgh Fern was brought in just before Christmas, replacing David Denholm. Charlie Moodie and Grierson had spells of absence through the season, as did inside forwards Tom Cairns and George Anderson. The outside right position went from Hynd to John Rankine, then Eckford and back to Rankine, with cameo appearances from various players. John Green took over from Eckford on the left wing in mid season, while Jimmy Smith, John McGregor, David Wilson, and George Anderson were all tried at centre forward.

Rovers were bottom of the League by 14th December, failed to win any of their away matches (winning only three at home) and top scorer in the League was Eckford with just seven goals. The Cup was an even bigger disaster ; beaten 4-1 at Lochgelly in the first round of the Qualifying Cup on 6th September. Consideration was given to withdrawing from the East of Scotland League, but they fulfilled their fixtures, although the match against Leith Athletic at Logie Green, which was lost 2-3, brought the following understatement from the Kirkcaldy Times : "There appears to have been a good deal of feeling imparted into the game." Two Rovers players and one from the visitors were ordered off the field. The SFA found that Macauley and Charlie Moodie had "a kicking match" while ArchieTaylor was sent off for rough play. All three were suspended for one month.

At the same meeting, David Denholm asked the SFA to help him recover £4 18s in wages. Rovers`defence was that Denholm was suspended for misconduct. He was awarded £1 10s, being four weeks wages.

Fife Cup ties being played over two legs may have caused Rovers problems by way of fixture congestion, had they not lost home and away to Dunfermline Athletic in the first round.

On 31st January, a rare victory at home to East Stirling (by 1-0) saw Rovers forwards play "with great vigour". The Kirkcaldy Times extolled the new signing from Black Watch. "David Wilson, Rovers clever centre, is being tracked by a number of clubs, and is throught to have received a professional offer from Middlesbrough. He was spotted playing for Black Watch at Kirkcaldy Amateurs and is still playing with the Black Watch in the Army Cup. It is said that one of the Raith Rovers "occasional" playing members has put the English agents on the track of the centre, probably with the object of himself benefiting by the transaction to the loss of the club should Wilson accept the tempting bait. Such are the ways of the "professional" nowadays."

So desperate were results, and hapless the efforts of the management to correct them, that several more Black Watch soldiers were recruited, presumably to add

How the neigh- bourhood looked after 1903, when the trams came to Kirkcaldy. This is Links Street, looking west (towards Stark's Park), with School Wynd on the left. There were scores of shops on both sides of the street.

some "fight" to the team. Sadly, Wilson apart, their footballing abilities did not match their belligerence, and by the time the team hit rock bottom of the League, there were no "sodgers" left in the team. Rovers and Clyde shared bottom place in the Second Division, but as the First Division was increased to 14 teams, both had little difficulty in being re-elected at the Scottish League's Annual General Meeting. Raith Rovers (21 votes), Albion Rovers (21), Clyde (17) and Ayr Parkhouse (15) were to play in the Second Division the following season, Johnstone (with 14 votes) were not.

Many were unsurprised that the better players jumped ship during the summer months. Dave Wilson signed for Dundee, although Rovers were compensated financially. Jimmy Orrock and Simpson Rankine signed for Cowdenbeath, while Johnny Rankine played a trial for Rangers.

One who got away was Thomas Blackstock, who had played for the "reserve" team Raith Athletic, still playing in the Fife Junior League with home matches at Stark's Park, before signing for Leith Athletic. He signed for Cowdenbeath in May 1903, but was transferred to Manchester United without kicking a ball for Cowden. They received £50, and Leith also benefited handsomely. "The sum is practically found money to the Fifers" said a censorious Kirkcaldy Times. Blackstone's story had a tragic ending. Ten minutes into the Manchester United Reserves v St Helens match at Clayton on Monday 8th April 1907, the player collapsed, and was pronounced dead by a doctor. He was 25 years of age, and the third son of W.S. Blackstock, a Kirkcaldy headmaster.

Fife clubs had no direct representation on SFA committees, their interests supposedly looked after by their membership of the East of Scotland FA. To correct this historic anomaly, they resigned en masse, and formed a Fife League to supplement the fixture list, while resolving to make a determined effort to secure a seat at the SFA. The seceding teams were Rovers, Dunfermline Athletic, Hearts of Beath, Cowdenbeath, Lochgelly United, Kirkcaldy Amateurs and East Fife.

1903 - Gallatown school opened ; Electric lighting and tramways introduced on 23rd February following the opening of the Victoria Road Electricity Generating Station ; December, Police Headquarters opened on St Brycedale Avenue ; Victoria Road Church opened, the former premises taken over by the Boys Brigade.

The introduction of electric trams to the Links meant that the Links Market finally completed its gradual migration from Links Street to Sands Brae (now the Esplanade)

JOHN GRAY
Nicknamed "Dolly" after the popular song, whether he liked it or not. Gray was a goal-scoring inside left who provided excellent support to a number of centre forwards.

Mr David Whyte, a Rovers committee man and the Fifeshire Association's representative to the SFA, attracted some controversy when he cast a crucial vote in deciding the venue of the 1904 Scotland v England match. Celtic, the injured party, wrote to the SFA querying his eligibility to vote, due to the status of the new county association. Much more seriously, in the April holiday fixture against Cowdenbeath, Baxter, the Rovers' captain broke his leg. The teams met again a month later in a Benefit match for the injured (and hence unemployed) player.

Wednesday 20th April 1904, East Fife played West Fife at Stark's Park in a match to raise funds for the Fifeshire Football Association. Stewart, Grierson, Blackburn and Clarkson were the Rovers players selected.

1904 - Kirkcaldy Town Council took ownership of the harbour. On 14th November the King's Theatre opened at the East End of the High Street. Several names later, it became the ABC Cinema ; Kirkcaldy Golf Club Opened

The committee had learned their lesson, and recruitment for the second Scottish League season was much more purposeful that the year before. Goalkeeper James Don (Dundee Wanderers), left back William Leck (Lochgelly United), centre half Alex Philip (Lochee United) and forwards Robert Blackburn, Bernard Dillon, John Gray and Tommt Clarkson joined Robert Baxter, Alex Grierson and Simpson Rankine, virtually the sole remnants of the debut season. Before the campaign opened, however, Rovers' committee had to withstand further criticism, for a "poorly organised" Sports meeting in mid July.

Two wins in the first four matches was something of a false dawn. One of them was in the Qualifying Cup against Cowdenbeath, the 3,000 crowd paying more than £70. It took three games for Lochgelly to eject Rovers from the Qualifying Cup at the second round stage, although the Reid Park club were clearly the better team. By mid October, Rovers were bottom of the league and "making poor progress". Then came a heavy defeat (3-7) at Abercorn on a pitch that was practically flooded, but the team went on a seven game unbeaten run, which transformed the season.

George Stewart (Lochee United) and John Walker formed a new full back partnership, John McDonald came in at inside right from Strathclyde Juniors and the redoubtable Charlie Moodie, free from suspension, featured in various defensive positions. The final victory in the unbeaten sequence was a 4-0 defeat of Abercorn at Stark's Park, which brought this praise from the Kirkcaldy Times : "Their play was characterised by a judgement and understanding which were continuously absent in that of the Paisley team."

For clubs like Rovers, ejected early from the Scottish Cup, the short League programme came to an early conclusion. The last home League match of the season was played on 13th February, when Clyde were beaten 5-1. Two away matches brought a satisfactory ending to the League programme – and a notable improvement to fifth place. The season was completed with some friendlies, a variety of local cup ties, and of course Fife League fixtures.

Kirkcaldy United had been formed out of Kirkcaldy Amateurs, turned professional and joined the Eastern League and Fife League in which they drew 1-1 home and away with Rovers. The match at Overton Park, which they inherited from the Amateurs, drew a crowd of 2,000. Two hundred fewer attended the return at Stark's Park, possibly because of a counter attraction a short distance away. "Great crowds" attended a dead whale washed up on the beach.

Rovers ended the season with a trophy, the Central Counties Championship, described by the Kirkcaldy Times as "a competition inaugurated towards the end of the season to raise the wind at the fag end, and taken part in by a quartette of the leading clubs in the shires of Fife, Forfar, Perth and

Stirling." Rovers won 1-0 at Arbroath, and then beat East Stirling 5-0 at Stark's Park in the Final. The Wemyss Cup was also won, having survived a protest from Kirkcaldy United in the first round (George Stewart having played in the Qualifying Cup for Lochee United earlier that season) but Rovers did not compete for the Cottage Hospital Charity Cup, the matches being played between Kirkcaldy United and a Select XI.

There was less traffic in players over the summer of 1904. Anderson Inglis and John Maxwell (Kelty), John McDonald (Vale of Wemyss) and James Messer (Tayport) were the new signings. Once again, lessons were being learned : "Last year it will be remembered the whole of its players were complete strangers to each other, hence the bad start the club made with their Second League engagements."

Charlie Moodie faced competition from John Neilson (signed from Kirkcaldy United) at right half, and Messer was replaced by William Proctor, a Dundee junior, at inside right. James Bell was brought in at outside left, while Joe Wallace, who had joined the club towards the end of the previous season, formed a potent strike force with John Gray. Not potent enough in the Qualifying Cup, however, with another first round exit, to Cowdenbeath after a replay watched by 4,000 at Stark's Park. Early League results were disappointing, although matters improved after a 5-1 win at St Bernards in mid November. Third bottom was a step backwards, but nine League victories kept the fans impatience at bay.

With the benefit of historical perspective, the Kirkcaldy Times of 28th December 1904 contained an article, not in the sports columns, of greater significance to Raith Rovers than most of that season's match reports. As the traditional staple industry of the town, linen manufacture, slowly receded, Kirkcaldy became renowned for its manufacture of floor coverings, principally linoleum. Michael Nairn & Co, and Barry, Ostlere & Shepherd Ltd dominated the world-wide supply of an essential household product, in the days before fitted carpets. The wonder has always been as to why some of the former company's riches never found their way towards Stark's Park.

"Last night the annual treat to the Old Folks was given at the Corn Exchange. 500 were entertained. Sir Michael Nairn, Dysart House, presided, accompanied by Lady Nairn, the Misses Nairn and a number of local clergymen. Sir Michael, in his opening remarks, after referring to the entertainments provided at this season of the year as counter attractions to the public house, dealt with the question of football, and stated that he was approached the previous day for a subscription to assist a Football Club in Kirkcaldy.

"The club had got into debt to the extent of £150. When he received the application it fairly staggered him. He approved of football, and thought it was very good in its own way if kept within certain

limits, but in making enquiries into the application he found that this Football Club paid about £15 a week in wages to professional men. This was all humbug (hear, hear and applause). That was not sport at all, and he did not intend to give a penny to that club (hear, hear and applause). He was quite willing to give support to the recreation of young men, but he wished it to be made public that he would not support such a form of sport as this professional football. It was time, he added, that an end was put to such sport as that (applause)."

From time to time over the ensuing century, when the club's financial problems were threatening its existence, the call has gone out for outside help, from a local benefactor or the local council. The simple answer to these requests has always been ; you didn't need any help in getting into this mess. The attitude of Michael Nairn, who a month earlier had been created a baronet in the King's birthday honours list, may seem to be at variance with the wishes of a significant proportion of his workforce, who followed the club, but he was looking at it as a businessman, watching other businessmen run their business badly.

Once again, the League season finished early ; the last home match "one of the best games of the season" a 2-0 defeat by Hamilton Accies on 14th January, and the last away match three weeks later at Falkirk, in which Rovers were unfortunate in a 1-0 defeat.

The remainder of the season was once again filled with friendlies and local cup ties, the Fife Cup being contested in a League format. Judging by the events of the 4th March at Stark's Park, local rivalries were being resumed, now with Kirkcaldy United. Shaw of United hit Arthur Cumming, who was playing centre half for Rovers, in retaliation for tripping Duncan Menzies, and the referee sent him off. Brown left the field at the same time to have his injuries attended to, and a scuffle ensued. The Kirkcaldy Times reported "A ruck was made in the pavilion by the officials of the respective clubs, and matters assumed so alarming an aspect that the services of the police had to be requisitioned. Order was ultimately restored, and the game was resumed, but with no improvement." Amongst these "disgraceful scenes", Rovers won 1-0 thanks to a MacDonald penalty, and the 3,000 crowd paid £47.

There was a more structured form to the new signings for 1905/06 season. The core of the team was becoming established ; full backs Anderson Inglis and Arthur Cumming ; wing halves Charlie Moodie and Grierson ; Wallace and Gray up front and the extremely effective John McDonald on the left wing.

Added were Bill Dowie in goal, John Manning at centre half, outside right George Mitchell, while Jimmy Gourlay and George Dalrymple provided competition for the forward places. Local recruitment continued to be a problem. It was noted that Kirkcaldy's junior players seemed to prefer playing out of town, and as a consequence, the newly formed Raith Rovers Juniors (replacing Raith Athletic) fielded a younger side than was considered desirable.

On 2nd September, the Juniors played Cupar Athletic in a Fife Junior Cup tie immediately after Rovers' League match against Albion Rovers. The Kirkcaldy Times

*Rovers face the camera before the match against Cowdenbeath at Stark's Park on 14th October 1905
Back row : J. Adams (Trainer), Anderson Inglis, Bill Dowie, Arthur Cumming, A.G. Adamson (President)
Middle row : Robert Donaldson (Secretary), unidentified official, Charlie Moodie, John Manning, Alex Grierson, J. Nicol (Vice President)
Front row : James Strachan, James Wilkie, John McDonald, George Dalrymple, Jimmy Gourlay*

The format of the photograph was one that was in fashion at that time ; goalkeeper in between the full backs, in front of the half backs, with officials flanking the two back rows, and the attack at the front. Two of the regular forwards were missing through injury, centre forward Joe Wallace, and outside right George Mitchell. John McDonald moved from the left wing into the centre and James Strachan, in his second season at the club since signing from Arniston Rangers, played on the right wing ; one of only ten appearances in his two years at Stark's Park.

The origin of football ground names can be explained by a notice which appeared in the local press in early April 1887. Pitches were generally named after their owners, which could be confusing if one man owned more than one "park". It was announced that Sydney Galvayne, the celebrated Australian Horse-Tamer and Lecturer on Horse Dentition, would give an Introductory Lecture in his Marquee in "Mr Stark's Park", at the back of Messrs Barry, Ostlere & Co's Works, at the Railway Station" on Saturday 16th." Thus, Kirkcaldy had more than one "Stark's Park," the one we now know today being occupied by the Union Football Club.

Raith Athletic endured a stormy start to their 1899/1900 Fife Junior League season, during a match against Lochgelly Rangers at `School Park, Lochgelly. The Kirkcaldy Times reported : "As the game proceeded, things gradually grew from bad to worse, and, on the referee awarding a six yards' kick to the Raith - which the homesters alleged should have been a corner - a disgraceful scene occured. The outside left of the Lochgelly team caught hold of the referee - Mr Hodge, Dunfermline Juniors - and flung him violently to the ground. The player was ordered off the field .... Such brutal tactics as were adopted by several of the Lochgelly players on Saturday deserves to be severely dealt with by the Scottish Football Assocation, and Mr Hodge will be wanting in his duty if he does not lay the solid facts of Saturday's disgusting display before the parent body and see that justice is properly meted out." Mr Hodge, eight years later, became Raith Rovers' first secretary/manager.

In early May 1905, a Meeting of the Fifeshire Football Association accepted a gift of the Penman Cup, to be competed by clubs from Fife, Clackmannan, Stirlingshire, Linlithgowshire and Edinburgh, to maintain interest towards the end of each season. Initially, First League clubs were not to be entered.

reported : "Cupar could not raise a team, and only six took the field. It appears that several of the players of the Cupar club belong to Kirkcaldy, and through some cause or other they refused to take the field. The play only last for about half an hour and then they retired, the Juniors winning by 5 goals to nothing. It was more of a farce than a match."

At the other end of the age scale, Charlie Moodie was given a benefit game against Kirkcaldy United, when Rovers sported "a smart new outfit of dark blue jerseys and white knickers, supplied by Mr J Wingate & Co, shirtmaker and hosier."

Rovers' officials had to widen their net to sign promising young players, and in the days before transport networks were established, were often greatly inconvenienced in the process. Peter Napier's father was secretary of the club when they signed James Messer, the deed being accomplished by Mr Napier cycling from Kirkcaldy to Tayport, with a youthful Peter on the crossbar. "We sat on a dyke watching the match and eating a 'piece' and at the end my father signed Messer and cycled back to Kirkcaldy."

On the evening Anderson Inglis was signed, a deputation of committee men had made their way to his home at Oakfield, near Kelty. Negotiations, which ended with the player being given a sovereign, took longer than expected and after the last public transport left for Kirkcaldy. They were about to set out on foot when their new signing suggested that his father, who had a posting establishment, rig up a horse and four-seater and drive them home in style in the early hours of the morning.

Early results in the League were mixed, and the Qualifying Cup campaign was of the shortest duration once again, thanks to a 4-1 defeat at`East Stirling in the first round. Between 500 and 600 Rovers fans travelled to Merchiston Park (only 1000 attended a League match at Stark's Park a fortnight earlier), and Rovers were badly beaten. The problem appeared to be one of selection ; Inglis, Moodie, Grierson, Dalrymple and Wallace returned to the side for a League match at Vale of Leven the following week which Rovers won 2-1.

A largely settled team rescued the season in November and December, when eight League matches resulted in four wins and two draws. Eighth position in the League was an improvement, but not much, and it was apparent to everyone that Rovers had reached a turning point in their history. Gates were dropping in the wake of indifferent League form, and a surfeit of local cup ties. Friendlies were difficult to schedule, as clubs concentrated on League matches, and fans were becoming more discerning.

The highest attendance of the season was 3,500 who witnessed the New Year's Day League match against Hamilton Accies, the 1-1 draw "stubbornly contested". The following day, Kirkcaldy United were met for the third time that season (there were to be two more meetings) but the Kirkcaldy

Times thundered "Friendlies are a farce at holiday time – especially New Year – and this was demonstrated to the full yesterday." The sport was changing ; success in League and Cup competition was what fans now demanded.

"Onlooker", in a letter to the Kirkcaldy Times, highlighted a constant feature of football in the town : "For some cause or other, the members and supporters of the Raith Rovers senior club are giving little or no encouragement to help along, in a financial way, the Rovers junior team. The miserable turnout of spectators on Saturday at Stark's Park was not creditable by any means. For long the cry has been heard that local men should be reared to fill the vacancies that occur in the senior ranks. With that object in view the junior club sprang into existence this season. But, alas ! Instead of Stark's Park, the Beveridge Park, with its free admission, has become the centre of attention, with the regrettable result that the attendance at the Junior Rovers' football match, as witnessed on Saturday, was nothing short of a total failure. It's far from creditable on the part of members to give the juniors the cold shoulder."

The Fife Cup returned to a knock-out format, and Rovers won the trophy by beating Cowdenbeath 2-0 at Kirkcaldy United's new ground at Scott's Park on Beatty Crescent. A healthy crowd of 3,000 paid £70. It was decided to play the Wemyss Cup as a League competition, although the consequence was two matches a week being played until mid May. The resources of some clubs were stretched by this arrangement. Hearts of Beath agreed to switch their Wemyss League match from Crossgates to Stark's Park, in exchange for a guarantee. The match kicked off 20 minutes late, Hearts of Beath secretary Paterson played in goal, and Rovers won 5-0.

The practice remained for a big team to be lured to Stark's Park for the April holiday fixture, and a £25 guarantee brought Celtic to Kirkcaldy on the afternoon of Monday April 2nd. A large attendance was disappointed by the absence of Quinn, McLeod, Loney, Hay and Hamilton from the Celtic team, but they still won 4-1. The following week, St Bernards were the visitors for a friendly match, and despite fine weather, there was a "disappointing attendance".

In early April, centre forward Joe Wallace was transferred to Third Lanark, where shortly afterwards he suffered a double dislocation of his arm. At the end of the season, Dalrymple signed for Reading. There was a happier occasion for Rovers fans on Thursday April 26th, when a "Past Rovers XI" met the present team in a nostalgia match which was to be repeated on several occasions over the years. The present team won 3-2, but Rovers fans had the satisfaction of seeing Davie Walker and Dod Ramsay (from a penalty) once again find the net at Stark's Park.

Three cups were won during the season, Fife, Wemyss and Penman (the final of which attracted a crowd of 3,000 to

Cowdenbeath to see Rovers beat Alloa Athletic 3-1). Everyone was conscious that it was not enough to propel the club forward, and despite an indifferent record in the Second Division, Rovers submitted an application to be elected to the First Division of the Scottish League.

Amongst their attributes were cited good gate drawings and Kirkcaldy's excellent railway facilities, and the Fife Free Press considered that "Rovers make out a good case". It was not good enough to impress the First Division clubs, however, who preferred as little additional travelling as possible in their expanded League. Champions Leith were also overlooked, in favour of runners up Clyde, and fourth placed Hamilton Accies.

Complaints about the length of the season – and shrinking close season – are by no means a modern phenomenon. This is what the Kirkcaldy Times had to say about the impending 1906/07 season. "All too soon Association Football is again with us. Playing until 15th May and opening on 15th August, footballers encroach too dangerously on the dog days for the benefit of the pastime and its strenuous devotees, but the commercial trait – the game has begotten selfishness, with the result that other sports more suited to the prevailing climatic conditions suffer from the competition of the game of the masses. This season this particular feature is more prounouned than ever. On the earliest possible date – Wednesday first – in the League, now extended to 18 clubs, begins operations, and without a breathing space the pace is maintained throughout."

There was one significant addition to the squad for the new season – George McNicholl. Signed from Aberdeen as player-coach, he was only 27 when he signed for Rovers, a year younger than the team's 'veteran' Charlie Moodie. Barrell-chested, and not the quickest across the ground, as his height (5 ft 6 inches) and weight (13 stone) would suggest, he was nevertheless a natural footballer, and deadly within sight of goal.

Signed from Aberdeen, he made his debut in the Qualifying Cup first round tie at home to Kirkcaldy United. The £65 gate was satisfactory, but still short of the £95 banked by United for the visit of Partick Thistle in 1905, which attracted a crowd of 4,000 to an Overton Park which had been "banked with ashes around the ropes". More importantly, Rovers won, drew 3-3 with Lochgelly in front of 3,500 at Stark's Park in the next round, 1-1 in the replay and finally beat the Reid's Park club 1-0 in the second replay at Methil. McNicholl scored in each of the three games. There were disgraceful scenes at the finish of the deciding match, the referee, Mr Liddell, and Mr Young, Rovers' linesman, being attacked by the Lochgelly mob. Lochgelly got some minor revenge by winning the Fife Cup tie 3-0 at Stark's Park the following Saturday.

There was huge excitement in Fife in the run up to the fourth round tie against Cowdenbeath. "The Rovers are putting up additional pay boxes, and the enclosure in front of the grandstand has been fenced in and a charge will be made for admission." Ex Rover Davie Walker scored for Cowdenbeath and Jimmy Gourlay for Rovers, and a replay looked certain when George McNicoll scored late in the game to delight the majority of the 5,000 crowd. That was a new record for Stark's Park, with £100 6/6d taken at the gate and an additional £15 at the stand.

Rovers were drawn to play Clachnacuddin in Inverness, but the match was switched to Kirkcaldy with the promise of a large guarantee. Although the crowd amounted to just 2000, the expense was worth it ; Rovers comfortably won 4-0, with McNicoll scoring two more Qualifying Cup goals. Opponents in the semi final were a famous name from the early days of Scottish football history, Renton, self-proclaimed "Champions of the World" in 1888 when, as Scottish Cup holders, they beat FA Cup winners West Bromwich Albion in a "World Championship Decider".

It was a hard game at Tontine Park, "brim full of excitement" and won by a McNicoll penalty. George Mitchell was "wantonly and brutally kicked by a Tontine player when the ball was nowhere in the vicinity, and he was fortunate to be outwith the referee's vision." As Renton strove for the equaliser, in a real "hammer and tongs" cup tie, Rovers' young goalkeeper Dowie "was a veritable octopus in goal, and gave a marvellous display of fistic prowess, punching the ball clear in all directions and repeatedly over the bar." McNicoll and Inglis almost didn't play, arriving, somewhat breathless, just as two reserves were about to take the field in their place.

The Scottish Qualifying Cup Final at Tynecastle Park was the biggest game in Rovers' short history. Mr Donaldson, the club secretary, ensured a good following from Kirkcaldy by doing a deal with the North British Railway Company to provide 1/2d return train fairs. Three thousand took advantage, and a record crowd of 12,000 paid £225 12/3d, with £30 19/- more taken in the stands. McNicoll scored again in a 2-2 draw with St Bernards – Rovers were 2-0 ahead at half time, and retained that lead until 15 minutes from time. The replay was held at Easter Road the following Saturday when the return train fair was increased to 1/3d. A 13,000 crowd - a new record for the competition - paid £280, with Hibs keeping the £43 Stand takings.

The Trades Band accompanied the team to Edinburgh, and returned with them playing triumphant tunes, as Rovers`captured the Qualifying Cup with a 3-1 win. Who else but McNicoll was amongst the scorers.

GEORGE MITCHELL

1906 - James Shepherd. Linoleum manufacturer, died. Since 1873 he had lived in Rossend Castle in Burntisland

The origin of the club's name is, at the first level, quite straightforward - it was taken from the Raith Estate, from which the local land owner took his title.
How that word was arrived at is more challenging. There are similar words in Gaelic, the old Scots tongue and Celtic languages which have very different meanings.
The word raith in Scots Gaelic means quarter of a year, while reithe is a ram.
It has been suggested that the place name which is used throughout Scotland (areas of Cowdenbeath, and Auchenraith by Blantyre are just two examples) derives from the old Scots word Wread or Wreath, a small enclosure for confining cattle or for growing crops.
Alternatively, we can look to the Oxford English Dictionary for enlightenment. Raith is said to come from Rathe, an obsolete Scots word denoting rapidity in its performance or completion of an action ; quickly, rapidly, swiftly, without delay, promptly, soon.
If that seems inappropriate for some of the lumbering players who have graced Stark's Park with their bulk over the years, perhaps the O.E.D.'s definition of Rover is more suitable : without definite aim or object ; at random ; haphazard.
Even better, for life-time followers of the Rovers, is the definition "an inconstant lover"

JOE WALLACE

Rovers difficult start to life in the Scottish League was characterised by a difficulty in scoring goals. In their first season, 1902/03, their highest goalscorer in League matches was David Wilson, with four goals. It wasn't much better the following season, although outside left Tom Clarkson did manage to score eight times in the League, while John "Dolly" Gray scored two fewer. In January 1904, Joseph Wallace was signed from junior club Glasgow Perthshire, and immediately partnered Gray in attack, Simpson Rankine moving to centre half.

Wallace scored three times in six League matches and the following season both he and Gray each scored six times in nineteen League appearances.

Wallace was again joint top-scorer in 1905/06, along with John McDonald, both scoring seven times, with Wallace's coming in sixteen League matches.

He was transferred to Third Lanark in April 1906, and later played for Ayr Parkhouse and Hamilton Accies.

In 1906/07, Rovers at last got players into double figures for League goals, George McNicoll and George Dalrymple each scoring ten times, but a further year later, David Axford and Archie Devine could only muster nine apiece. Jimmy Gourlay beat his predecessors' records with fourteen goals in 1908/09.

It was John MacDonald's goal, however, which was best remembered. A slim, pale faced youth from Wemyss, he had struggled to find form on the right wing, but blossomed on the other flank. In the replay, he got possession of the ball in midfield, "beat half-back and full-back in clever fashion, and, although the latter clung to his heels for a good distance, "Jock" got in a low, long angular drive which fooled Ramsay, St Bernard's custodian. It was one of the finest goals ever seen scored."

Rovers won the match despite the cruel absence from the team of the stalwart forward Jimmy Gourlay, who had influenza, and they also lost George Dalymple, who had to be carried off during the match. They had to survive a scare late in the game, when St Bernards were awarded a penalty, however Bill Dowie saved both the kick and the rebound. What made the victory all the more satisfactory is that the team was largely made up of local lads. Bill Dowie, Arthur Cumming, Charlie Moodie, Alex Grierson, Jimmy Gourlay and George Mitchell were all from Kirkcaldy ; John McDonald and Jimmy Wilkie were from Wemyss, Johnny Manning from Burntisland and Anderson Inglis from Kelty.

The importance of the run to the final of the Qualifying Cup cannot be overstated. The revenue from the two final matches transformed the club's finances, which had been hitherto precarious, as they struggled to pay Scottish League wages to their players. A major problem was the structure of the Scottish Cup competition. The SFA, and the West of Scotland clubs which controlled its committees, insisted that the first two rounds of the Qualifying Cup competition be drawn within county boundaries. This meant that only one Fife team could qualify for the third round, and as the fourth round had to be reached to qualify for the Scottish Cup proper, the odds were stacked against the Kingdom's clubs. In many seasons prior to 1906, Raith Rovers truly survived on a hand-to-mouth basis.

On Friday 1st December, Dr John Smith presided over a Raith Rovers Concert at the Adam Smith & Beveridge Halls, at which Lady Helen Munro Ferguson presented the Qualifying Cup badges to the team. The vocalists were Miss Nettie Kellock (Kirkcaldy), Miss Esther Hood (Glasgow), Miss Clara Butt, contralto, Mr J.W. Bowie (Glasgow) tenor, Mr A. Rintoul (Kirkcaldy), Mr J.C. McLean (Edinburgh) comedian and "Jack Easy" (Glasgow) comedian. "Such an array of talent is sure to draw a crowded house" said the Kirkcaldy Times.

League fixtures, perhaps understandably, assumed secondary importance compared with the great cup run. A few of them hinted at the club's capabilities – a 4-0 win at Ayr Parkhouse, 3-1 at home to the old bogey team East Stirling, and a 5-0 home win over Vale of Leven on the last Saturday of 1906, when the biting wind swept the snow of the field, to expose a frost-bound playing surface.

January brought three heavy away defeats, the 4-1 reverse at Logie Green against Leith Athletic being particularly fraught. The afternoon started badly with the strips failing to arrive in time for kick off, Leith being kind enough to supply a set. Rovers finished with nine men, Cumming and McNicol retiring hurt.

The first round proper of the Scottish Cup, an unfamiliar concept to the Club, saw Aberdeen University defeated 5-0 at Stark's Park. Only 1,000 turned up. "The attendance was rather disappointing for a Scottish tie," said the Kirkcaldy Times" "but the cold afternoon may to some extent have affected the ardour of Raith's supporters, while the important Junior Scottish tie at Buckhaven had also an affect on the attendance." The 0-0 draw between Buckhaven United and Maryhill was attended by 3000, paying £25 on a 3d gate - £22 was taken at Stark's Park where 6d was charged.

The newspaper was unusually reluctant to mention two more telling factors ; that the fans didn't anticipate much of a contest, and there was disappointment at the transfer of John McDonald to Rangers the week before the tie.

One disconsolate fan was moved to write to his local paper. "The recent very mediocre displays given by our local team, Raith Rovers, are to be deplored. Now I learn that they have sold McDonald to the Glasgow Rangers for £100. This is a very underhand and shabby way of dealing with supporters who wish to see their team sport first class colours. To enter the First Division good players are wanted – not money – because once you have got good players you will get the £ s d. The policy now being adopted by the officials of letting their undoubted best players go is one of the most short-sighted they could adopt.

"The sooner the club is turned into a Limited Company the better it would be for both players and spectators. Sporting officials are wanted – men who know what sport really is – not simpletons who cannot keep good players once they have them. I trust that no more of the best players will be bartered away, but kept on to support the best game ever invented – football. "Observer, Kirkcaldy.""

Sadly, the sentiments, and the need to express them, have proved to be timeless.

Fatal Boghead lives up to its nickname with a 4-0 defeat in the League, and a realisation that Rovers were in danger of having to apply for re-election, being second bottom, albeit with games in hand due to their preoccupation with cup ties. To the delight of the supporters, and particularly "Observer", John McDonald was transferred back for the cup match against Ayr at Stark's Park, making use of the extremely flexible rule book for Cup registrations. Fourteen tons of sand were spread on the pitch to combat the winter weather which seemed always to descend on a Friday. The 3000 gate, including 400 from Ayr, paid £61 to see a surprisingly handsome victory for Rovers, by

4-0. Yes, of course McNicoll scored.

With a month between the second and third rounds, Rovers had the opportunity to move away from the bottom of the League, but a win, draw and defeat did little to help in that regard. The victory was hard-won, 4-3 at home to Ayr Parkhouse, with Dalrymple and Gourlay (broken jaw) lost to injury. Jimmy Stewart was signed from Pathhead United to bolster the League squad, but McDonald returned for the cup tie, as did Gourlay from injury. 15,000 witnessed arguably Rovers best result in their short history, a 2-2 draw at Tynecastle.

They were a goal behind at the interval, Thomson scoring direct from a free kick, when most spectators thought that Hearts should have had a penalty when Dowie upended Bobby Walker on the edge of the penalty area. Walker made up for that with "a really grand goal" early in the second half, but Rovers delighted their fans by battling back into the game. McNicoll scored in-off-the post, having had an early 'goal' chalked off despite spectators behind the goal insisting that the ball had crossed the goal-line. George Mitchell equalised not long afterwards with "the shot of his life". Rather than finish off a buckling Hearts team, Rovers were content to play out a draw. The match was refereed by Fred Heath of Birmingham, and took £339 12s 6d at the gate, plus £46 9s in the stands. By universal acclaim, John McDonald was the best player afield, his "display of scintillating brilliance which caused the Hearts' defenders to treat him in anything but a gentlemanly manner" doing much to hasten his permanent departure to Ibrox.

Hearts did not relish the replay at Stark's Park. They offered half the gate (including the stand), would pay all expenses and give free admission to Rovers' members (ie season ticket holders) to have the second

match at Tynecastle, but the lucrative offer was turned down, leaving Rovers with a lot of work to undertake in a fortnight. Additional pay boxes were erected, and "the work of banking up Stark's Park has been begun for the purpose of providing the extra accommodation that will be necessary for the great replay." The construction of the mounds behind both goals, which would eventually include substantial terracing, began with this fixture.

The committee offered the players the same generous bonus as for the first match ; £5 for a win and £3 for a draw. The Barry Ostlere & Shepherd Brass Band were in attendance, and Mr Heath returned from Birmingham to referee the replay. Post-match, the Kirkcaldy Times reported "Preparations on an elaborate scale were begun at Stark's Park, and carried through with great success, as the outcome of Saturday's game proved." The new railway embankment proved to be popular with the crowd, the grandstand and enclosure in front were full, as was the seated accommodation around the field of play." £310 was taken at the 17 payboxes, plus £60 from the Stand and Enclosure, by some distance a record for Fife, as an estimated 17000 watched a great contest, which Rovers were unfortunate to lose to a Bobby Walker goal. There was some controversy in Rovers' selection, "Wilkie was deposed by Dalrymple, a change which in no way strengthened the Rovers' attack."

Exhausted by their efforts, and deflated by defeat in the unchartered waters of the quarter final, Rovers completed their League campaign with three defeats and a draw. They finished in second bottom place, equal on points with East Stirling, and the Scottish Football League rules dictated that a play-off was required, the loser to apply for re-election. The match was scheduled for St

When Raith Rovers became incorporated in 1907, those wishing to buy shares could apply, inter alia, at A.G. Adamson's Chemist shop at the corner of Milton Road and Links Street. Andrew Adamson became one of the first Directors of the new Limited Company, and served in that capacity - with the occasional break for boardroom politics - for over twenty years.

The above photograph was taken in 1905. Most of the buildings in the photograph have been demolished, most recently in the early 1950s when the Links area was comprehensively redeveloped. It is possible that the gable end to the right of the photograph remains as part of "The Abbey" hotel (formerly the Abbotshall Hotel). In 1905 it was a manse. There has been considerable re-alignment of the major junction of Nicol Street, Links Street and Milton Road since the photograph was taken, and the present use of the site of Adamson's Chemist shop is the traffic island immediately to the north of the present Nicol Street at its junction with the High Street, next to the former Safeway car park.

1907 North school opened ; election of first Labour Party councillor, James Michie.

ARTHUR CUMMING

Signed from local juvenile club Dunnikier Athletic in July 1904, he made a handful of appearances in various defensive positions in his debut season, but in the last few weeks of the campaign, he settled into the left back position, partnering Anderson Inglis at full back.
For the next nine seasons, he was a fixture in the team, and participated in all of the club's successes during that spell. He won winners and runners-up medals in the Scottish Qualifying Cup in 1906 and 1907, a Second Division Championship medal in 1907/08, and numerous winners medals from local cup competitions.
He was in the Rovers team which entered the First Division in 1910/11, partnered by Tom Snoddy, then David Philip, as Inglis' career drew to a close. . Cumming played in the 1913 Scottish Cup Final.

Bernard's Gymnasium Ground on 4th May, but there was a "hitch in the arrangements" and the match was postponed, the large crowd which turned up having to be turned away. Leith Athletic's Logie Green enclosure staged the match a week later, which Rovers won 3-2, who else but McNicoll scoring the decisive goal from the penalty spot.

There were two more significant events for the club in May 1907. On 15th May, Raith Rovers Football & Athletic Club Limited was incorporated (see Appendix). The second event was another application for admission to the First Division, with little sense of irony from a club which narrowly escaped applying for re-election to the Second, but Mr D.A. Whyte, Club President, pointed out that "Fifeshire is the only important football county which is not represented in the First Division."

That remained so after the League AGM ; Clyde and Port Glasgow were re-elected to an unchanged First Division. Rovers had compiled a list of reasons for their elevation. The population of Kirkcaldy and surrounding areas, at over 40,000, compared favourably with any First League centre outside of the cities. That number would be at least doubled in the summer with the opening of Wemyss tramway, which would make Kirkcaldy easily and rapidly accessible from Levenmouth and the East Fife coal towns and villages.

The ground, a ten minute walk from the station, was "large and commodious – in fact from 10,000 to 12,000 spectators can easily at the present time be accommodated, and as there is terracing round the enclosure, all have a splendid view of the game. The ground can be made to accommodate anything between 15,000 to 20,000. The stand is large and covered in. The dressing rooms are at the rear of the stand, and all are fitted up with baths and all conveniences for the players. The entrance to the playing field from the pavilion is by a covered way under the stand, so that in going or coming from the field of play the players are entirely removed from the spectators."

Rovers cup exploits inevitably alerted the bigger teams to their players. The formidable centre half John Manning signed for Blackburn Rovers for £750, the highest fee paid to a Fife club, while Hearts took outside right George Mitchell, although centre forward Davie Axford and centre half George Chapman came to Rovers in part exchange. George McNicoll maintained his practice of spending only one year (and one successful Qualifying Cup campaign) at a club, and was replaced by Archie Devine. Jimmy Wilkie took over at right half from Charlie Moodie, who was restricted to cameo appearances, and Ben Sutherland and Gordon Bannerman shared outside right duties.

The backbone of the team was still in place, however, and 1907/08 proved to be the club's most successful season to date. Huge crowds attended the two matches in the first round of the Qualifying Cup against Lochgelly, Rovers handsomely winning the

Stark's Park replay 3-1 which drew £137, the second highest gate to be recorded in Fife. The crowd was one fewer after the interval, as recalled by the Kirkcaldy Times :

"During the retiral of the players to the pavilion for a much needed "breather" the Trades Band had a march around the field, the banners being again turned out evidently in an endeavour to cheer up the spirits of the Lochgelly supporters. The banner-bearers, however, got mixed with the bandsmen in front of the grandstand, and the drummer administered a well-deserved rebuke to one of the group by a couple of thumps on the back with his drumstick. He never missed the measured beat of his drum, but continued in good time. The Lochgelly man, evidently displeased at his back being used as a drum, made for the drummer, when he was collared by a "gentleman in blue" and escorted outside the field – the right place for him."

Rovers progressed through the Qualifying Cup as if to the manner born (and not just a recently acquired skill). East Stirling (4-0 at home after 'Shire had turned down a £70 guarantee to switch the venue of the first match, drawn 0-0), St Johnstone (3-1 in front of 5,000 at Perth), Dunblane (2-1 away, one of the hardest matches played that season, after Dunblane had turned down an offer to take the match to Kirkcaldy) and Dumfries in the semi final (5-0 at home) fell in the wake of the Kirkcaldy juggernaut, which came off its traction in the Tynecastle final. St Bernards exacted revenge on the previous season by winning 3-1. Three or four special trains left Kirkcaldy for Edinburgh, "efforts having been made to induce the employers to close their works at midday".

Rovers took the lead, Ramsay fumbling George Chapman's shot and Davie Axford scored from the rebound. At the other end, Chapman fouled Simpson in the penalty area and Buchanan scored from the spot. In the second half, Tennant put St Bernards ahead with a good shot, before Buchanan scored a second penalty, Chapman again conceding.

The two wingers had a real off day, their ineptitude that afternoon "throwing away all the good work of the inside men". The better team on the day won, St Bernards being all over Rovers (who were on a £5 bonus) in the second half. Outside left George Campbell was ill and should not have played, something recalled with deep regret a year later when he died following a prolonged illness.

The following two League games were lost, but Rovers found their step again and tasted defeat just four times in all competitions between 21st December and 30th April. William Mitchell took over from Sandy Grierson at left half, and first John Russell, then the cup-tied Harry Brown, displaced Ben Sutherland from the right wing, otherwise it was a settled and experienced first choice eleven, although John Ness took over from Bill Dowie in goal early in the spring.

In the Scottish Cup, Inverness Thistle gave a plucky show in "disagreeable weather" at 'Stark's Park, but the former Hearts duo of Chapman and Axford saw Rovers through 2-0. A special train carrying Rovers fans to Meadowside in Glasgow for the second round tie with Partick Thistle broke down en route and the fans did not arrive until half time. Their annoyance was eased with a tremendous performance by their favourites, who drew 1-1.

The replay attracted 12,500 to Stark's Park, although "on this occasion the railway embankment was not brought into requisition." Amid great excitement, Rovers won 2-1, Axford scoring both goals. There was frenzied activity at Stark's Park, which had seven days notice of the visit of Celtic in the third round. Additional banking was made up, and a capacity of 19,000 calculated without the railway embankment, and 23,000 with. It put Rovers' directors in a mind for permanent improvements, and there were thoughts of asking Archibald Leitch, the well-known civil engineer who had improved most of the leading football stadia on both sides of the border, for his views on the ground's prospects.

Unfortunately "wild weather" reduced the anticipated attendance from record proportions, and the elements spoiled the game. Fifteen minutes before the start, a sleet storm and strong winds forced the Trades Band to take shelter, and in the circumstances a gate of £242 (plus £40 from the stand and enclosure) was a "splendid return in view of the weather conditions." "Napoleon" McMenemy with two goals and Willie Kivlichan scored to give Celtic a 3-0 victory over a plucky Rovers' team.

The cup exploits resulted in a handsome profit of £213 2/9d for the period 5th April 1907 to 27th February 1908, although a 5% dividend reduced the retained element by more than £16. Some of the money was earmarked for Stark's Park : "The Raith Rovers management have resolved to proceed with the improvements on Stark's Park, including the levelling of the ground [pitch], immediately the season closes".

At the first Annual General Meeting of the new, Limited, company, held at Anthony's Temperance Hotel on 1st April 1908, the thorny subject of amalgamation was brought up. David Whyte, the Chairman, detailed the conditions that had been laid down by Kirkcaldy United ; that Rovers would settle United's debts, each member of United were to get one share in the company, the ground of the amalgamated club to be Scott's Park, and the name of the club to be Kirkcaldy. Mr Whyte considered the directors were quite justified in refusing to have anything to do with union on such conditions.

There was also a warning that, should the Rovers gain promotion to the First Division, existing and new shareholders would be asked to add to their shareholding, as Rovers would have to strengthen the team and improve the ground.

Rovers used their games in hand to overhaul their challengers for the League Championship, clinching the Second Division

title with a game in hand on 11th April ; McAinsh scored in a 1-0 win over Leith Athletic at Logie Green. As the season wound down, a friendly match was played at Stark's Park for the benefit of Kirkcaldy Cricket Club. "An additional attraction will be an exhibition of wrestling, etc., by the members of the Kirkcaldy Physical Club previous to the start of the game, and also at the interval".

The club's destiny was to be decided at the Annual General Meeting of the Scottish Football League on Monday 1st June 1908. In previous years, it could be said that Rovers' application for election to the First Division was optimistic, and somewhat opportunistic. However, with two Qualifying Cup Final appearances and a Second Division Championship from the previous two seasons, an expanded ground, sound finances and impressive attendances, they were doing rather more than knocking on the door of the elite division.

For the second successive season, Clyde and Port Glasgow Athletic had finished in the bottom two divisions, the Renfrewshire club preceding that with a second bottom place in the season before. That record, and Rovers' impressive credentials, would explain the extreme reaction to the result of the vote : Clyde 12, Port Glasgow Athletic 9, Raith Rovers 8, Dumbarton (Second Division runners up) 2, Abercorn 1, Ayr 0. Clyde and Port Glasgow therefore retained their places in the First Division.

The conspiracy theorists had a field-day. It was stated that Dumbarton had been put forward to split the vote, to ensure Rovers' failure. The Edinburgh Evening News thundered : "The Annual General Meeting of the Scottish Football League did very little to encourage football. By one vote it preferred the company of Port Glasgow Athletic to Raith Rovers, the Kirkcaldy team. In the Port Glasgow case it was an instance of possession being nine points of the law. This club has been long enough in the competition to show that the junior division would best suit their form and capabilities. A thriving club from Fife – one of the big industrial districts of Scotland, with the certainty of increasing – would have been a fresh source of strength to the League, just as Falkirk has been ; but there are a number of clubs who do not want strong rivals, who might endanger their own position. The League decidedly made a mistake in not promoting such an energetic, well managed team as Raith Rovers, centred in a fine sporting district."

Peter Hodge, Rovers' first secretary/manager, told the Kirkcaldy Times : "What made the disappointment all the heavier is that the club had the promise of support from 11 clubs, but when the vote was taken only 8 adhered to their promise [Aberdeen, Airdrie, Celtic, Dundee, Falkirk, Hearts, Hibs and Partick Thistle]. I may state that we are improving our ground as intended, the contractors having been on the game for a fortnight, in the hope that we may be fortunate

George McNicoll, pictured above with the Scottish Qualifying Cup, was no stranger to the trophy.
He signed for Rangers in April 1897 but was loaned to Port Glasgow Athletic, with whom he won the Qualifying Cup in December 1897, before signing for Partick Thistle in December 1898.
He won a Second Division Championship medal with Thistle in 1899/1900, but moved to Port Glasgow Athletic in April 1901. The Clune Park club were virtually permanent members of the First Division in those days, their location ensuring re-election when they finished at the bottom of the Division, which they did regularly.
In July 1904, McNicoll signed for Aberdeen, and scored both goals as they beat Renton in the Qualifying Cup Final at Dens Park in November 1904.
He joined Rovers in August 1906, and scored in every round as they won the Qualifying Cup.
At 13 stone and 5 foot 6 inches, he was no athlete, but he was a natural footballer.

1908 - Viewforth Secondary School opened ; The Kings Theatre was renamed The Hippodrome ; the Kirkcaldy and Wemyss tram service was extended to Leven ; Pathhead Baptist church opened ; St John's church opened ; and the East Pier was extended at the harbour.

LEAGUE HOPEFULS.

FIRST
LEAGUE
ENTRANCE

HERE YOU ARE
TRY YOUR LUCK!

RAITH
ROVERS   ABERCORN   DUMBARTON   AYR
UNITED   LEITH

"THE BIRD WILL PICK A CARD."

The "Scottish Sport" was a prestigious twice-weekly sports newspaper in the early years of the 20th century, and something of a house journal for the Scottish Football League. In previewing the 1910 League Annual General Meeting, the above cartoon signified the editorial frustration with the process by which new entrants to the First Division were chosen. Rovers, Abercorn, Dumbarton, Ayr United and Leith Athletic were depicted as potential new boys, awaiting the result of the lottery to pick which one would be promoted.

Kirkcaldy Times : 28th April 1909 "On Saturday, during the meal hour, the workers of the storing department of Barry, Ostlere & Shepherd's inlaid works, waited upon Mr David Axford and presented him with a dressing case on the occasion of his leaving the town."

The Kirkcaldy Times of 29th September 1909 reported a presentation to Arthur Cumming on the occasion of his marriage at Anthony's Temperance Hotel on Saturday evening. He received a handsome gold albert.

1910 St Brycedale Mission Hall in Coal Wynd was opened in June.

in our next application. But it is quite evident we cannot rely on every club's promise, even though it is most emphatically given, and it is no encouragement to either Directors or players of a Second Division team in a populous district like Kirkcaldy to win the Second Division Championship, and then be thrown over in the contemptible manner we were on Monday night." He admitted it was a bitter blow to the club.

The following week's local newspapers gave a more measured assessment, through scarcely less dismayed. Rangers, and particularly Queen's Park (faced with a choice of the good of the game or their own interests, Queen's had been expected to take the lead) were condemned in the Glasgow newspapers for the vote, and the "injustice" of omitting Rovers. It was claimed that many in the west did not want another "Falkirk" in their Division [runners up to Celtic that season, three years after election to the top division], and some commentators warned that the indefensible vote may precipitate the change that clubs fear most – automatic promotion and relegation. It is to the lasting shame of the leading clubs in Scottish football that this was not implemented until 1922, and only then after they were forced into it by clubs operating outwith the League signing Scottish internationals with impunity.

Notwithstanding the disappointment of having their ambitions cruelly curtailed, the club had undergone one of the biggest transformations in its history. Over a period of two seasons, 1906/07 and 1907/08, gates which had previously peaked at 4,000 now reached 17,000, and attendances at routine League matches that struggled to reach 1,500, had doubled in size. The reason for this was simple : a successful football team. Professional football had become a mass spectator sport, and, thanks to Raith Rovers, Kirkcaldy had a ringside seat.

It was possibly no bad thing that so many changes were made to the first eleven as Rovers tried to channel their outrage productively in 1908/09. There was a new goalkeeper in Jimmy Ewing from Newtongrange Star. Michael Donagher from Lochgelly joined Hugh Simpson of Bo'ness (who replaced George Chapman, transferred to Blackburn Rovers) and William Mitchell at half back. The season started with Richard Fraser from Dunfermline and John Walker from Motherwell in the forward line, although as time progressed, the only significant addition was William Wardrop, formerly with Third Lanark and Hamilton Accies, at inside

right, replacing Archie Devine, who had returned to Hearts.

On 15th August 1908, Lady Helen Munro Ferguson, in the absence of Provost Ferguson, unfurled the Championship flag before 4,000 spectators as Rovers opened their League season with a 1-1 draw against Dumbarton. Turnstiles were introduced at the gates for the first time, and the playing pitch had been relaid and "made level as a bowling green". As always with Rovers, there were thoughts of "what might have been"`had they been able to hang onto star players. That afternoon, Jock McDonald scored a hat-trick for Rangers.

If they had to come to terms with another season of Second Division football, there was a bigger shock in the Qualifying Cup. A single goal victory over East Fife (who included Charlie Moodie) in the first round was followed by the same scoreline, in reverse, at Broxburn. The victors' play was condemned as "robust and even rough", although Rovers were handicapped by the absence of Axford, who had an injured foot. Hugh Simpson was a controversial selection at centre forward in his place, the centre half found wanting in the forward line, and his replacement, wing half William Mitchell, floundered in defence. Every part of the team was therefore weakened by the inept handling of the forward's absence. The winning goal was scrambled home by Lawrie after Ewing had only parried a great drive by Willie McCartney, the former Hibs and Clyde player. A ground record attendance, paying £50, was of no consolation to Rovers, who had failed to persuade Broxburn to switch the fixture to Kirkcaldy. There would be no cup glory at Stark's Park that season.

The October holiday fixture was an underwhelming Wemyss League match against Dunfermline Athletic (won 4-0) with most attention in the town that afternoon focussed on Prime Minister Asquith receiving the Freedom of Kirkcaldy. The street named after him was built adjacent to the site of Newton Park.

Rovers had only the League on which to concentrate, and they had the unfamiliar early-season feeling of sitting atop after a 3-1 win at Arthurlie on 24th October. A fortnight later in Falkirk, Tommy McAinsh scored the only goal of the game three minutes from time. The crowd attempted to mob the referee at the end of the match, but three policemen and the East Stirling officials ushered him to the safety of the press box "and he remained there until the militant section of the crowd had dispersed."

On 21st November, Hill of Beath were at Stark's Park for a Penman Cup tie, but due to an accident on the railway, their players were delayed, and the match kicked off significantly late. On a cloudy afternoon, it started in semi darkness. The Kirkcaldy Times reported : "There were many ludicrous incidents. The game helped to keep the spectators in amusement, but all over it was a sorry spectacle, and hard lines for those who had paid 6d to see a football match. The referee called a halt to the farce about 15 minutes from time" with Rovers leading 5-0."

The middle goal in a fine 3-0 Scottish League victory over Leith Athletic at Logie Green was later recalled by a spectator. "The Leithites had been doing by far the major part of the pressing, and the equaliser seemed only a matter of time. However, Jimmy Gourlay, playing centre forward, received the ball at midfield, and deviating toward the right, he veered past half-backs and defenders until he found himself near the touch-line betwixt the penalty box and midfield. Suddenly he stumbled, but as he did so he shot, and with such force that the custodian never saw the sphere as it sped into the corner of the net. It was truly a magnificent goal."

All but four of the League fixtures had been fulfilled by 2nd January, but Rovers took just one point from the first three of the outstanding games, to hand the Championship to Abercorn, by three points. By the time the final game (against Ayr Parkhouse on 10th April) was won 3-0, the League title had gone to Paisley.

There was a more meaningful sadness at the news of the death of George Campbell, who had played for the club the previous season, at the age of 26 at home in Falkirk. He had been in indifferent health for a considerable time, and was forced to take to bed in his last week.

The season was completed with local cup ties, including the Stark Cup, presented some time before by Robert Stark, wine and spirit merchant, but not competed for the previous season. Kirkcaldy United were beaten 7-0 in Pathhead, but they won 2-1 on Pratt Street. There were difficulties at the Penman Cup semi final at home to East Stirling. "The 'Shire players took the Dunfermline portion of the train at Falkirk, and, failing to change at Dalmeny, were carried on to the "Grey City". In consequence the start was delayed until about 5.30. The original referee was unable to stay on and the clubs agreed to accept Mr J. Blyth, Kirkcaldy, as referee."

The Fife Cup, Penman Cup and Wemyss Cup (decided over a League format) joined the Stark Cup on the Stark's Park mantelpiece, but the club were condemned for their turnout at the benefit match of Bill Dorward`of Kirkcaldy United. The Kirkcaldy Times thundered : "The greatest fiasco of a football match ever witnessed in the district was the benefit game at Scott's Park on Monday Night for William Dorward." William Mitchell was in goal, the normal custodian Dowie was at centre half and George Mitchell was fielded at right back. "Clubs arranging for benefit games cannot expect to receive the support of the football public who are imposed upon in this way and Monday night's fiasco will have the effect of alienating support in future benefit matches".

Rovers applied for election to the First Division again, more in hope than anticipation. Morton and Partick Thistle retained their places, Raith Rovers and Dumbarton being unsuccessful. Hearts and Raith Rovers proposed automatic promotion "but the proposal received practically no support. The old method of leaving the matter in the hands of the committee would therefore be preserved."

It had been apparent for some time that Rovers were enjoying significantly higher home attendances than they met on their travels. "Raith Rovers proposed that ground clubs in the Second Division retain the whole gate but the motion was not accepted."

Once again and sensibly so, the core of the team remained intact for 1909/10 season, particularly the defence. John Wilson started the season at left half, but was replaced by Alex Grierson in October. Of the forwards, Gourlay, Wardrop and McAinsh remained, but the outside right position was shared by J.C. Bain and George Stark, while Tom Niblo and Archie McAuley became regulars.

Niblo was envisaged in the McNicoll role, a wise old head – and skilful footballer, who had played for Aston Villa, Nottingham Forest, Newcastle United, Aberdeen and Scotland. Rovers were invited to play in the Dunedin Cup, a pre-season competition staged by the Edinburgh clubs. Falkirk were beaten after a replay in the semi final, but Rovers lost to St Bernards at Tynecastle in the Final. Rovers won 1-0 at Cowdenbeath in the first round of the Qualifying Cup, the huge local interest in the tie resulting in a record crowd for North End Park, approaching 9000, but they met their match in Leith in the second round. Two thousand fans travelled from Kirkcaldy on special trains for the match at Logie Green. "During the interval the strains of the bagpipes were in evidence, while the continued yelping of the Powderhall whippets provided a novel accompaniment." It was a stirring match, with Leith on top in the first half and Rovers after the interval. The 1-1 draw was followed by a 2-2 draw in the replay, Bain equalising in the last minutes in another stirring tie in which both sides spurned numerous chances, but Rovers lost the second replay, at Easter Road, by the odd goal in three.

There was to be no national cup glory this season , although some consolation was derived from a share of the gate, 23,000 attending the three matches. Two days after the defeat by Leith, on the October holiday, English League Champions Newcastle visited Stark's Park, 5,000 seeing a powerful display in a 5-0 thrashing of Rovers.

The team did not lose a League

THE PROMOTION OF RAITH ROVERS.

THE KINGDOM

CROWNED AT LAST.

"Crowned at last" was the how "Scottish Sport" expressed its relief at the Kingdom of Fife, at last, achieving First Division representation following the Scottish Football League Annual General Meeting in 1910.

With elevation to the First Division, the club established a reserve team for the first time. They played their first fixture at home to Third Lanark, and the following team drew 1-1 : Hill, Inglis, Fyall, Moodie, Brown, Wilson, Mitchell, McLay, Seagur, Thomson and Thorburn. About 1700 paid £20 to watch Thomson score for Rovers in this Friendly fixture. The reserve team played a full programme of Friendly matches, and fulfilled many of the fixtures in the local cup competitions, including the Scottish Consolation Cup, in which they were beaten 2-1 by Cowdenbeath in the first round.

On Monday 24th April 1911, a match was played at Stark's Park to Benefit Kirkcaldy cricket club, who were based at nearby Beveridge Park. The match, between Past and Present Raith players, was drawn, 2-2.

1911 Kirkcaldy Town council took over the private gas system ; Trams were extended to Dysart

Most of the photographs of James Logan have him bespectacled, or wearing his distinctive tweed hat. Before he became Rovers manager in 1919, and before he had the need for spectacles, he was Rovers' centre half. He made rapid progress towards the rank of Captain on the Western Front during the First World War.

On Saturday March 12th 1910, the Fife Free Press carried the following story under the category "Local News"

DEATH OF A WELL-KNOWN VICTUALLER - The death took place on Saturday afternoon of Mr Robert Stark, licensed victualler, at his residence in Links Street, Kirkcaldy. Mr Stark had been in indifferent health for some time, but was able to be going about on Thursday in apparently good health, and his death was quite unlooked for. He was the proprietor of the "People's House" at the car terminus in Links Street, and was a great favourite with his patrons. For many years he was tenant of the football park occupied by Raith Rovers, which now bears his name. He also presented a handsome silver cup for annual competition between Raith Rovers and Kirkcaldy United. Mr Stark was pre-deceased by his wife two years ago, and is survived by a grown-up daughter and son, for whom much sympathy is felt in their sudden bereavement.

match until the eighth game, at Vale of Leven on 13th November, and then enjoyed another six matches unbeaten until a 4-1 defeat at Dumbarton on New Year's Day. They sat atop the Division for most of the season.

It took two games to dispose of Cowdenbeath in the first round of the Consolation Cup, then Hearts of Beath were defeated in the second round. Dunblane were put to the sword at Stark's Park in the next round, and despite failing to get on the scoresheet "McAulay was the outstanding player in the forward line, but inclined to overdo the gallery work." A 1-0 win at King's Park meant a trip to Perth for the semi final, where Rovers suffered an unexpected 1-0 defeat.

A more important defeat came the following week, losing 2-1 to St Bernards at The Gymnasium. Rovers now dropped below Leith Athletic into second place in the League. The team rallied with a 4-2 victory over Arthurlie at home, and a 2-1 win at East Stirling in their final League match. That left Rovers one point ahead of Leith, who had East Stirling to play in their final match.

A contemporary account recorded that "had the season not been at the 'national anthem' stage, the match must assuredly have been postponed. It had rained incessantly all forenoon, and the Shire's enclosure, funereal in aspect at any time, was in a most deplorable state on this occasion. For every visible blade of grass there was a gallon of water, and it was impossible to combine with any degree of accuracy. East Stirlingshire scored first and the Rovers had a severe struggle against the tide and their deficit. McAulay, however, ultimately equalised, and thus the score stood at the interval. During the second half the downpour had ceased, and it was possible to give an exhibition of something akin to football, I can recollect Willie Wardrop sending in a ball which indisputably crossed the line to be scooped out by Rab Bernard. The referee signalled "no goal" and the Rovers were robbed of another legitimate count. Eventually the same player scored a goal no referee could refuse, and the win enabled Raith to share the championship with Leith. But whew ! what a ground ! what a match !"

Leith and East Stirlingshire drew their final game, the teams were level on points, and the reasons for not having a play off match are lost in the mists of time. It was pointed out that had goal average been applicable in Scotland, as it was in England, Leith would have prevailed. The Second Division Championship title was, however, shared.

The club's third Annual General Meeting, held in Anthony's Hotel in late April, was attended by some controversy. "In connection with the election [of directors] some feeling was expressed over alleged canvassing." In reply to a question as to the Rovers' promotion to the first league, the chairman pointed out that the prospects were bright, and this year the club had been promised support by many of the leading

clubs.

This time, there was no disappointing outcome from the Scottish Football League Annual General Meeting The result of the voting was : Raith Rovers 13, Ayr United 2, Abercorn 1, Dumbarton 0.

Perhaps mindful of the botched attempt to improve the squad the last time the club entered a higher league, eight years earlier, several players were recruited for Rovers' debut season at the top level of Scottish football.

Goalkeeper Jimmy Ewing, left back Arthur Cumming, centre half Hugh Simpson and left half Alex Grierson remained in defence, although George Gilmour took over from Grierson in the second half of the season. David Philp was signed from Hearts and replaced that fine servant Anderson Inglis at right back. Sam Aitken came in at right half. Duncan McNeill replaced JC Bain at outside right, Harry Simpson started the season at inside right, but left after the 1-0 defeat at Dunfermline Athletic in the first round of the Qualifying Cup. He was replaced by Aaron Ramsay. Englishman Fred Gibson was signed from Sunderland to play on the left wing. Jimmy Gourlay and Archie McAulay continued to shoulder the goalscoring responsibilities.

The season opened with a Dunedin Cup tie at Tynecastle, Rovers losing 4-1 with McNeil scoring for the visitors. Two days later, the club made their debut in the First Division, but lost 1-0 at Morton. On Saturday, it was Pittodrie, and a 2-0 defeat. Stark's Park staged its first ever First Division match on Saturday 27th August 1910, and the glories and mysteries of top flight Scottish football were unveiled to the Kirkcaldy footballing public with a 10,000 attendance for the visit of Rangers. "In order to cope with the crowd, the grandstand was extended on either side, while the railway embankment, which has been leased by the management, was largely taken advantage of." The visitors won 2-0, but four days later, Rovers won their first match in the top league, 2-0 against Morton at Stark's Park, when Gourlay and Gibson scored.

Hibs visited Stark's Park for a League match on 24th September, and met a Rovers side which may not have played the part (beaten 1-3) but certainly looked it, as explained by the Kirkcaldy Times. "The Rovers are to turn out in their new rig out, which has been generously presented to the club by Mr Stewart, Draper, West End High Street. The jerseys are navy blue while, with the permission of Provost Munro Ferguson, the crest of our esteemed civic chief adorns the left breast. The jerseys, stockings, boots etc. are on view in one of Mr Stewart's windows. The gift is a most valuable and opportune one, for which Mr Stewart deserves thanks."

The October holiday fixture was a First Division match, and no ordinary one, Celtic being beaten 2-1 in front of 8,000 at Stark's Park. The result may have been a surprise, but it was no fluke. McAteer opened

the scoring for the visitors from "well out", but Gourlay equalised. One spectator later recalled :

"A feature of the match had been the manner in which Quinn didn't shine, the noted centre being unable to pierce the Aitken-Philip-Cumming triangle. Indeed, for the most part, Quinn was as stiff as a barber's pole, but not so outstanding. During the concluding spell, the game waged to and fro, and Raith's supporters would have been intensely pleased with a draw. Something better was in prospect, though, for Ramsay deceived Adams with a pretty speculator, and for the first time in their history the Rovers were leading Celtic. Gibson had been giving the opposing right half a sorry time of it, and he of the "sunny" disposition was not too particular how he stopped the pilgrim's progress. Raith defended with bull-dog tenacity during the remaining minutes, and Cumming was audacious enough to tell Quinn to "Buck up, as there wasn't long to go, Jimmy". Quinn immediately threw his arm around Arthur's neck, kissed him affectionately and called him an angel. Thus Rovers added one more item to the records of fame."

Another fine performance, although in a disappointing game, earned a 0-0 draw at Tynecastle, and Hamilton were beaten 4-0 in Kirkcaldy. Four single goal defeats followed, showing the narrow margin between success and failure in the higher division. One of them was against Clyde, whose winning goal was scored by Morrison described by one critic as "the best centre half seen at Stark's Park."

The team was boosted with the signature of George Gilmour, from Hearts, but one that got away was H.B. Seager, a noted cricketer and footballer, who had played with Queen's Park, Kirkcaldy United and, as a 17 year old, Corinthians. "It was thought that he would be secured for Raith Rovers" but he signed for Newcastle United instead.

Rovers were receiving plenty of plaudits for their spirited performances, but victories became elusive. There were eleven matches between two victories, and only three of them were drawn. The Kirkcaldy Times was sympathetic, describing the 3-0 defeat to Partick Thistle in these terms : "If ever the plucky Raith Rovers were overwhelmed by misfortune it was at Firhill Park. Very few of the large number of spectators will be bold enough to assert that the Partick Thistle were value for their three goal victory. "The Jags" will never again win by such a margin after having so little of the play."

There was no such attempt to put a good complexion on the 5-0 defeat at Parkhead on Hogmanay. Jimmy Quinn's great goal, from the edge of the penalty area (reportedly) literally burst the net.

Despite the results, team spirit remained buoyant, exemplified by a 3-3 draw at Airdrie, having been three goals down. The League season was saved with three wins and three draws in a six game spell starting on 11th February. The last of the sequence was a 1-0 win at Motherwell, where the home team arranged for some novel pre-match entertainment. "Throughout the day Motherwell had reported a "capture" in Consul, the almost human ape, who was given the privilege of setting the ball in motion, a feat which he did with the aptitude of a "player" of promise amid much merriment on the part of the 4,000 spectators." Rovers could have done with him in attack the following week at Kilmarnock, where the forwards were profligate, and the home side won 1-0 despite a great performance from Rovers' defence.

A final position of 15th (fourth bottom) was deemed a satisfactory debut season, the assessment made more palatable by joining

Rovers were photographed at Tynecastle on Monday 15th August 1910, two days before they made their debut in the Scottish League First Division. Back row : Goodfellow (Trainer), Alex Grierson, George McLay, Anderson Inglis, Jimmy Ewing, Edward Rathbone, Jimmy Gourlay, Michael Donagher, Sam Aitken.
Front row : Alex Thorburn, David Philip, John Wilson, Archie McAulay, Harry Simpson, Duncan McNeil, Fred Gibson, Arthur Cumming.

For the opening League match, Donagher replaced Wilson, Aitken played at centre half instead of Rathbone, and Gourlay was centre forward instead of McNeil.

There were several more changes to the team over the season as Rovers struggled to come to terms with higher League football. Several of the players in the picture, which the People's Journal published on 27th August 1910 under the title "Fife's First Scottish League Team", had the briefest of careers with Rovers. Rathbone (on a month's trial at his only senior club), Thorburn and Simpson between them appeared only 22 times for the club.

By the time of the next photograph, even more changes had been made to the team. Anderson Inglis had ended his long and distinguished first team career, and his right back position was taken by Tom Snoddy, who returned to Kirkcaldy in later years in a very different capacity - minister of Pathhead Church.

He is the last player to the right of the back row, next to trainer Clem Thomas. At the other end of that row are two more trainers, Jimmy Brown and Jimmy Goodfellow.

The postcard from which this photograph is taken is, unfortunately, uncaptioned, but it is thought that it was taken at the opening home League fixture against Airdrie on 26th August 1910.

The team was : McLeod (middle of back row) ; Snoddy, Cumming (front row far right) ; Aitken (with ball at feet), Simpson, Gilmour ; Ritchie, Thomson, Chalmers, Hastie, Gourlay (second player from left, front row).

The first three players in "civvies" at the back are Wilson, McLay and Philip.

The notice on the pavilion wall states : "Notice. No profane or obscene language allowed. By Order. The old pavilion sat behind the stand at the south west corner.

no less than Hearts on the 24 points total. As promised, Rovers had brought good gates to the top league, a phenomenon confirmed by the news that the 1911 census counted 39,600 inhabitants of the town, an increase of 5521 in ten years.

The 1911 close season was dominated by transfer news and speculation. It was reported that Rovers were trying to sign James Peggie (ex Hibs and Middlesbrough) and Arthur Metcalfe of Newcastle United but they were successful in signing a new goalkeeper in Robert McLeod, from Scottish Rifles, inside right William Thomson from Arthurlie, inside left John Hastie from Celtic and the former Hibs and Dumbarton winger Duncan Ritchie.

One player who did not arrive was Bobby Walker, the great Hearts and Scotland inside forward approaching the end of a long and distinguished career, who nevertheless promised Rovers that if he were to leave Tynecastle , and continue playing, it would be at Stark's Park.

The "Open to Transfer" list was an indefensible feature of the Scottish League rule book for many years. It allowed clubs to retain the registration of a player, without having to play or pay him, for as long as no-one paid the "transfer fee" demanded by the club. To the dismay of the Rovers faithful, Fred Gibson was "listed" at £75. The Kirkcaldy Times complained : "He is full of speed, very smart in rounding an opponent, and a class shot, and why a player of his standing should be placed upon the transfer list at such a high figure is a question which will puzzle the most staunch of Raith Rovers' supporters to answer."

What made this feudal system just about bearable for the player, was that he could sign for any club outwith the Scottish

League, and so Fred Gibson played for Dunfermline Athletic in 1911/12

Dave Philip and Cumming remained at full back, although Bill Collier replaced the redoubtable Arthur in the new year. The Reverend Thomas Snoddy, recruited from Vale of Clyde juniors, accompanied Sam Aitken in defence. George McLay took hold of the right half position, and the forward line settled to Duncan Ritchie, Duncan McNeill, Jimmy Gourlay, Tommy Brownlie and Jimmy Slack, with Ronald Orr, John Hastie and John Hunter featuring towards the end of the season. Brownlie came from Ashfield, and Slack from Petershill, at a time when Rovers found the Juniors to be a productive recruiting ground.

The first League victory took five fixtures to arrive, the opening one being a sobering 5-0 defeat at Ibrox. There was more bad news when it was announced in mid October that popular former captain, Willie Wardrop, had died of cholera in America. The mood of fans was not helped when, belatedly, a team was entered in the Reserve League. The Kirkcaldy Times explained : "On the ground that when the season tickets were sold, there was no Reserve XI, the management decided that members should pay for admission to these matches. Most of the members resented this, and rather than pay many of them preferred to remain outside."

On a happier note, playing fortunes improved from the 4-0 defeat of Third Lanark on 28th October, notably with two very late goals to beat Partick Thistle 3-2 at Stark's Park. The New Year, however, brought a collapse in form, which was unfortunate as this encompassed the Scottish Cup first round tie against Airdrie, which was lost at Broomfield in a replay. Rovers were up to their old tricks in immediately lodging a protest against Murphy and Rafferty of Airdrie, who alledgedly played for Cadzow St Annes v Inverkeithing Renton at Dunfermline on 3rd June in a Juvenile Cup semi final. Both players stated that they played for Royal Albert that afternoon in a 5-a-side tournament in Hamilton. The Rafferty case was dismissed by the SFA on a procedural technicality ; the Murphy protest was defeated 11-7 thanks mainly to a priest who stated that the player had refereed a Catholic Schoolboys match at Shettleston on that date. So much for the Royal Albert 5-a-sides ....

The natives were getting restless at the poor results, although the report in the Kirkcaldy Times headed "Mean Attack on Raith Rovers Players" had more to do with a local newspaper circulation war.

"Unwarranted attacks on Raith Rovers players have been made now and again in a certain quarter, but the meanest attempt to belittle the intelligence of the players is the statement made this week that the players can hardly write their own name. Some of the players would be ashamed to append their names to the silly drivel that appears from week to week in a contemporary, by an alleged "Sporting Editor" and billed as "the only correct and reliable football reports". It is safe to say that the members who presently comprise the Rovers' playing force are as intelligent and respectful a set of men as will be found anywhere. It is a consolation to know, however, that the publicity given to the contemptible statement will not be widespread."

Two draws and a victory in the last three League games (all away from home) hauled Rovers away from the bottom of the League and they once again finished in fourth bottom place. The season has not been without its difficulties. The coal strike was at its height in early spring, and both Queen's Park and Rangers had to supply their own coal to get their trains to travel to Kirkcaldy. On Monday, April 8th, the match at Parkhead was postponed due to heavy winds and before the game was replayed at the end of the month, Rovers embarked on a three-match Highland tour.

The following month, they gained moral kudos for their support of automatic promotion, to be voted on once again at the Scottish League's Annual General Meeting. The Daily Record stated : "Considering the difficulty they have had in steering clear of the bottom of the League table since entering the First Division, it says something for the sportsmanship of the Raith Rovers that they have been consistent supporters of automatic promotion. Mr T. Gray, Chairman of the Second Division, has received intimation of the Kirkcaldy club's intention to cast their vote again in favour of one club stepping up and another going down."

There was not the merest hint of a clue that Rovers were about to embark on one of the most successful seasons in their history when 1912/13 kicked off with three straight defeats in the League, followed by a sparkling 4-2 win over Hibs in which the Edinburgh club were outclassed. Then came three successive draws before Queen's Park were beaten 5-0 at Stark's Park, and a week later Celtic were defeated 2-1 watched by 10,000 spectators..

There were two new recruits in defence, the impressive opponent Bill Morrison from Clyde and James Logan signed from Bradford Park Avenue. Tom Cranston, Harry Graham and Harry Anderson joined Jimmy Gourlay and the happily restored Fred Gibson in the forward positions. Graham's transfer from Birmingham was confused and protracted. The English club claimed that they had transferred him to St Bernards, but the player had only signed a form for Raith Rovers. There was no Duncan Ritchie in the team, the inspirational winger having been transferred to Sheffield United during the summer.

In the wake of the disappointing start to the League season, the Kirkcaldy Times announced "RAITH ROVERS AND NEW TRAINING METHODS. The players of Raith Rovers must in future adopt the strenuous life, and on the instigation of the secretary (Mr Peter Hodge) more ball practice will be included in the programme of training. The new system, which has begun this week [commencing 9th September] includes shooting for goal, dribbling, squaring and trapping. This is an entirely new system, and Stark's Park is the only place in Scotland where it is being followed out at present. Willie Meredith, the great internationalist, is a strong devotee of ball practice, and often has two hours with the ball."

Successive generations of Rovers fans may have thought that their favourites at time looked like being strangers to a football, but that was certainly the case in the training of players in those days. Most of the work was physical conditioning, and the majority of football club trainers were not retired footballers, but sprinters and runners.

The change of training regime may have been inspired by Peter Hodge, but he did not stay to see its benefits come to fruition, nor did the trainer, James Aitken, who expressed trenchant opinions in an article which appeared in his name in the Edinburgh Evening Despatch. Hodge wrote to Aitken on 2nd October, censuring him for the tenor of his article, and the following day, Aitken replied in writing, and resigned. On 7th October, at a directors' meeting, Aitken's resignation was accepted.

There was a greater shock four weeks later. On 2nd November 1912, the Fife Free Press announced : "RAITH ROVERS SECRETARYSHIP. At a special meeting of the Directors of the Raith Rovers, it was unanimously resolved to make a change in the secretaryship of the club. It has been felt by the directors that the club has not made the progress anticipated with one devoting his whole time to the situation. We are officially informed that the sole reason of the directorate taking this step was with the view of the betterment of the club. A paper north

1913

61

BILL MORRISON

Rovers' right back in the 1913 Scottish Cup Final was Bill Morrison, a native of West Benhar, a mining village on the Lanarkshire - West Lothian border. He was signed by St Bernards from West Calder as a 23 year old in April 1902, and moved to Fulham for the start of the 1907/08 season. A year later, he signed for Glossop, and he returned to Scotland to sign for Clyde in May 1910. Two years later, he signed for Rovers, and his appearance in the 1913 Scottish Cup Final was his second in succession - he played for Clyde when Celtic beat them in the 1912 Final. Travelling problems from his Glasgow home to Kirkcaldy during the First World War resulted in his playing for Morton during the war years. He returned to Rovers as trainer in 1931, but left two years later. His son, Jimmy, played for Airdrie, Brechin City and East Fife, and signed for Rovers in May 1936

WILLIAM WINNING

1913 The Palace Cinema next to Sheriff Court was opened, and in the same year the Port Brae Cinema at the bottom of the High Street (south side) was also opened.
1914 On 18th February, Sir Ronald Munro Ferguson, KCNG and Lady Helen set out from Raith House to Australia, to take up duties as Governor General. There was a procession to the Adam Smith & Beveridge Halls, and then to the Station.

14th March 1914 at Stark's Park, the first match of Kirkcaldy Corinthians FC, a new amateur eleven, was played against N.B. Rovers. Johnny Leck, formerly with Rovers, will was one of the players of the short-lived Corinthians..

On 6th March, 1914, in a Reserve fixture at Riverside Park, Galston, where Rovers lost 1-0, James Thomson broke his leg.

HUGH SIMPSON

of the Forth publishes an article on the matter, the bulk of the statements in which are said by the officials to be unfounded."

On 11th November, Mr Charles Thomas, trainer of Kilmarnock FC for the previous five years, and before that St Bernards, was appointed trainer in place of Aitken. He was described as "a prominent figure on the running track".

A month after leaving his post, Hodge was presented with "a handsome gold watch and albert as a mark of esteem and respect by which he was held by his players". He had a spell in employment away from football, and then joined Stoke as manager in June 1914. There were six on the short leet for his old job ; A.S. Maley of Glasgow, Richardson of Petershill, Ronson and McCabe of Edinburgh, and two others who did not want to be identified.

The interviews did not lead to an appointment ; one of the directors, James Tod, assumed the tasks of Secretary, confirming the view of the directors that a full time appointment was unnecessary.

There were more good than bad results towards the end of the year. Two goals from Morrison earned a 2-2 draw at home to Rangers ; the double was achieved over Hibs with a 2-1 win at Easter Road, and Clyde were beaten 5-1 at Stark's Park on the Saturday before Christmas. The Rangers draw came at some cost, George McLay sustaining a severe injury.

The points gained in November and December were needed as the next six League matches brought just three draws, although Broxburn were swept aside, 5-0 at Stark's Park, in the second round of the Scottish Cup. The West Lothian club were induced to give up ground rights to the tie, in exchange for a guarantee of £60, half gate over £120, and a Friendly match in April.

In an otherwise settled team, centre forward was a problem position, with several players tried there, but none of them providing a long term solution. On 12th February 1913, Martin was signed from Sunderland. He failed to score in a 0-0 draw at home to Dundee, but opened the scoring in the Scottish Cup third round tie against Hibs at Stark's Park.

There was huge interest in the match, and careful preparations made for it. "In view of the importance of the game, it is expected there will be a record crowd, and every preparation is being made to provide comfort to the spectators, and prevent accidents. The conditions that have been made by the directors are that there will be no boys gate while there will be no pass out checks. Stands will be reserved for ticket stand holders up to 3pm (it was a 3.30 kick off). The admission to the stands will be 1/- each per person and 2/- for the reserved stand, for which tickets can be had from Mr A. G. Adamson, Chemist, Mr W.C. Richards, High Street, and Mr James Tod, at his office."

A record crowd converged on Stark's Park, blocking Pratt Street, with the turnstile operators struggling to cope. The receipts,

£356 and £35 in the stands, exceeded the previous record of £380 taken a month earlier when Hearts visited in the League. The Kirkcaldy Times reported : "It was the most stirring tie ever witnessed in Kirkcaldy. The game was full of incidents throughout and the interest never flagged from the start to the final kick." It ended 2-2, and Rovers won the replay a week later, Harry Graham scoring the only goal of the match watched by a new crowd record at Easter Road, 23,000, including 4,000 from Kirkcaldy.

The draw for the quarter final brought St Mirren to Kirkcaldy, and the Rovers management arranged for four additional turnstiles "to obviate congestion". Rovers won a keen encounter 2-1, the two Englishmen, Fred Martin and Fred Gibson, scoring in front of another large crowd. A "splendid win" over Motherwell was followed by a narrow defeat at Kilmarnock, by the odd goal in seven. On the Monday before the semi final, Rovers lost 1-4 at Parkhead, but were said to be "reserving their energies".

There was record railway traffic between Kirkcaldy and Edinburgh on Saturday 29th March, as Rovers and Clyde locked horns in the Scottish Cup semi final at Tynecastle. The match finished 1-1, watched by 28,000, Gourlay scoring for Rovers, and the teams returned the following week when Rovers won 1-0 thanks to a Martin goal.

The detailed organisation and relentless build-up to Cup Finals today would amuse our forebearers. In 1913, the Scottish Cup Final was played a week after Rovers qualified to play in it. Five days beforehand, Partick Thistle visited Stark's Park for a League match, and Rovers could be excused the 2-0 defeat, and the size of the home support, only 3,000, the rest presumably saving up for their trip to Celtic Park on the Saturday.

They were amongst 15,000 who saw Raith Rovers play in, to date, their one and only Scottish Cup Final. Falkirk proved to be the better team on the day, winning 2-0. Consolation was sought, and found, in the notion that had the excellent George McLay been fit, to complete the redoubtable half back line of McLay, Morrison and Anderson, the result may have been different. The Bairns, arguably a similarly resourced and supported club to Rovers, have subsequently played in two Scottish Cup finals. It is surely fair to say that for the Kirkcaldy club, the competition is jinxed.

The match was fast, open and attractive with wind advantage dictating the periods of ascendancy, Falkirk in the first half, Rovers in the second. In 21 minutes, McNaught rounded Arthur Cumming and passed to Croall, whose shot was beaten out by McLeod, but only into the path of Robertson who headed the opening goal. The scoreline remained at 1-0 until half time largely due to the Rovers defence which was ably marshalled by Bill Morrison. Falkirk centre half Tom Logan joined the attack six minutes into the second half and ran from the edge of the penalty area to score a second goal which dashed Rovers' hopes of getting back into the match. Despite plenty of possession, and a will to chase the game, Rovers were over-anxious in attack, the wingers shooting when they should have crossed, and the inside men shooting from too long a range.

The defeated team were far from disgraced, but could only regret the failure to raise their game – and find their scoring boots – on the day.

The League season was played out in fairly desultory fashion, three away games in four days bringing 1912/13 to a close without the usual glut of local cup ties. No-one took much notice of the fact that the team finished third bottom, all eyes had been on the Scottish Cup since January and for the first time in the club's history, no friendly matches had been required to fill the fixture list.

The vexed question of a full time manager/secretary was addressed by the directors during the close season. On 31st May it was reported that "Raith directors have had an interview with James Ashcroft in a player-manager connection, but no definite arrangement has been arrived at, and he crossed the border again on Saturday night." Ashcroft was an English international goalkeeper who had played for Woolwich Arsenal and Blackburn Rovers between 1900 and 1912. When the appointment was made, it was much closer to home, and much less glamorous. John Richardson, formerly Petershill manager, attended the Annual General Meeting at the end of June as "the new secretary"

There were significant changes to the team for 1913/14. Jock Neish and Willie Wallace shared the goalkeeping duties, with new full backs in Willie Winning and Bill Morrison, who stepped over from centre half, Arthur Cumming playing infrequently as his yeoman service to the club neared its end.

From October, the excellent wing halves Harry Anderson and James Logan had a new centre half for company in Willie Porter. Up front, Tom Cranston, Fred Martin and Fred Gibson were joined by Jock Rattray, John Waugh and latterly Jimmy Scott. Alex McCulloch, a former Leith Athletic inside forward, was signed from Coventry City but failed to make an impact, while Jimmy Gourlay, like Cumming, was nearing the end of an exceptional spell of service to the club.

The team got off to a dreadful start in the League, just two wins and three draws from the opening thirteen matches. The solution lay at the feet of the two Junior signings, Porter from Kirkintilloch Rob Roy, and Scott from Petershill. Scott scored in five out of six consecutive matches – the blank coming in a disappointing 3-0 defeat at home to Rangers, watched by 15,000. Against Aberdeen, Porter was moved from centre half to centre forward and scored a hat-trick in the 4-1 home win.

Disappointing results rarely make for

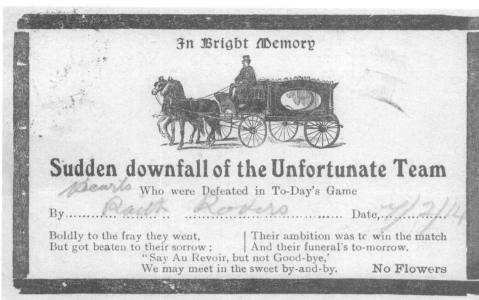

In Bright Memory

Sudden downfall of the Unfortunate Team

Hearts Who were Defeated in To-Day's Game

By...... *Raith Rovers* ...... Date,...7/2/14

Boldly to the fray they went, | Their ambition was to win the match
But got beaten to their sorrow; | And their funeral's to-morrow.
"Say Au Revoir, but not Good-bye,'
We may meet in the sweet by-and-by. No Flowers

harmonious Annual General Meetings, as proved by a letter to the local press by "Shareholder" following the meeting on 4th February 1914.

Rovers' Directors Criticised : What a Shareholder Thinks

Sir - As one of the shareholders of Raith Rovers Football and Athletic Club, Ltd, who attended the annual meeting in Y.M.C.A. Hall on Friday evening, I would suggest that, in view of the treatment we received at the hands of the chairman, the only way whereby we can show our disapproval of such methods is by returning a couple of new directors to the Board next January. They may not be any better, but if the action, or rather inaction, of the directors on Friday night is any criterion, they can't possibly be worse.

It was nothing short of an insult to the intelligence of the shareholders who attended the meeting to get such treatment. The chairman was asked by a shareholder to state the date of the appointment of the treasurer, who now enjoys a salary of £26 per annum. No satisfactory reply was obtained. Then when the question of the price of season tickets was brought up, the same thing occurred.

No valid reason was given for the increase – in fact, as one of the shareholders tersely put it, there was not reason for their attendance at all. The only way in which we are useful to the seven champions who control the destinies of the club is in January when there is a contest for seats on the board. Then we can see them tumbling over one another in their eagerness to solicit proxies or votes in their favour. After that operation is finished, as a gentleman remarked when leaving the hall, "we can all go to blazes !"

None of the directors present at the meeting had the courage to state their reason for increasing the price of ground and stand tickets by nearly 30 per cent.

The fact is, the annual meeting is a farce as it is the policy of the chairman to

RAITH ROVERS' PLAYERS JOINING THE EDINBURGH BATTALION

From an Edinburgh evening newspaper, October 1914

Two of the Raith Rovers' football team joined Sir George McCrae's Battalion last night, namely - McLay and Porter. McLay is seen writing his name, while Porter is behind. Richardson, the Raith Rovers' manager, is seen with Mr Furst, of the Hearts, on the right.

WILLIE BIRRELL
The casualties of the First World War are remembered by the names on War Memorials, but wars have more victims than just those who made the ultimate sacrifice. Willie Birrell was an extremely promising inside forward with Rovers at the outbreak of the war, but was taken Prisoner of War and denied the best years of his playing career.

have as little discussion as possible, and by means of the gentle art of snubbing to get the shareholders out again in Kirk Wynd in the shortest possible time, and with as little information of the doings of the club as they can extort.

When we take into consideration the fact that there was an income of over £6000 to be accounted for, that only on one night in the year have the shareholders any right to criticise its disposal, the replies of the chairman to the several very pertinent questions put to him by the shareholders was, to say the least, amazing. And, of course, it was always open to any of the directors to rise and explain matters ; but they endorsed his action by remaining silent.

I would suggest to the shareholders that an informal meeting be held in December every year to consider the affairs of the club and the election of directors in January.

Following the Rangers defeat, the next four matches were won in splendid fashion, followed by three straight defeats, a run halted on 27th December by a 4-1 home win over Dundee with the pitch covered in two inches of snow. Successive results in January brought conflicting emotions. Hibs were thrashed 3-0 at Easter Road, and a week later Rovers went down 1-0 at Douglas Park, Hamilton. The Freds, Gibson and Martin, were both ordered off, but at a subsequent meeting of the SFA Referees Committee, in merely censuring the players, it was decided that, as one local paper put it : "Gibson and Martin's offences were trivial to the extreme and it would have been an injustice to the club had they been forced to have dispensed with those two most valuable players in the forthcoming Scottish Cup with Hearts"

On the run up to the second round tie on 7th February, Kirkcaldy was once again gripped with cup tie fever. The Kirkcaldy Times reported : "The embankment has been added to considerably and crush barriers

have been erected round the enclosure with the object of adding comfort to the spectators ; in fact everything had been done possible to cope with the rush from the gates. A staff of 40 police from the Burgh and County have been requisitioned for duty at Stark's Park to regulate the traffic and look after the crowd generally. It might be as well to give a warning note to the public to look out for the "light fingered gentry" who are sure to be prowling around." Pickpockets had enjoyed rich pickings at the previous season's cup ties. The Trades Band would be entertaining the crowd an hour before kick off.

"The latest from headquarters is that the players are all in the best of condition, fit and ready for a hard 90 minutes. Systematic training, without over-exertion, is the rule. On Monday the day was spent at Burntisland over the golf course, while yesterday a visit was paid to Portobello, when the salt water bath was resorted to, and similar training will be resorted to during the remainder of the week."

The preparations were evidently flawless. Rovers won 2-0, both scored by the reprieved Martin, in front of 26,000 spectators. "Rovers played the game to win, and won. It was tactics that paid, and now that the worth of these has been learned at Stark's Park, they may be an abiding quality. Every man and mother's son of the Rovers worked for their £5 bonus and, well, it was a famous victory." The defence, in particular, held firm throughout.

The following week, there were only 5,000 at Stark's Park to see a disappointing 1-1 draw with Kilmarnock in the League but, after all, this was to be Rovers' year in the cup, wasn't it ? Meticulous preparations were made for the third round tie, away to Third Lanark. The team and club officials took the forenoon train to Glasgow, to be followed by 1,200 of their followers after they finished work at mid-day. The players relaxed at the Adelphi Hotel by playing billiards. "When the hotel party got out to Cathkin, they found the stand crowded, and the folks pouring into the field from all sides. The treasurer's face was wreathed in smiles."

The gate was just £27 short of Third Lanark's record, around 40,000, a testament to Rovers' drawing power, but the visitors were below their best and short of luck, and lost 4-1. The less generous of their followers pointed to a lack of experience in the team, and the fact that Bill Morrison, Arthur Cumming and George McLay "viewed the game from the steps of the pavilion enclosure instead of being in the proper places on the field." Morrison and Cumming had been irregular first team players that season, and an argument could be made for not including McLay, newly recovered from injury.

The following Saturday, Rovers lost 2-1 at Greenock, minus the services of left half Harry Anderson, who became the first Raith Rovers player to be capped for Scotland when he took the field against Wales at Celtic Park.

In the middle of the League table,

they had only respectability and pride to play for until the end of April, eventually finishing in 11th place, the highest achieved by a Raith Rovers team in Scottish League football.

There were some hefty victories in the home matches ; 3-0 at home to their cup conquerors ; 5-1 over St Mirren, and 5-2 over Hamilton Accies when two referees and three linesmen turned up for duty. The final home League match , against Queen's Park, was poorly attended. "The attendance", said the Kirkcaldy Times, "was indicative of the waning interest in the game." The public had their attention on more important matters, with storm clouds gathering over Europe.

The Rovers squad was kept largely intact as they planned for 1914/15 season. Gibson Todd from Musselburgh replaced Tom Cranston at outside right, and the Irishman Willie Lavery was the first choice left back, Morrison being used as cover for injuries. Fred Martin had a mixed start to the season, and shared the centre forward place with Fletcher Welsh, signed from Leith Athletic for £50, although Rovers had expected to pay half that.

The news that Grandstand season tickets were being raised from 12s 6d to 15s was followed by an announcement that at the Kirkcaldy Police Sports, to be held at Stark's Park on Thursday July 23rd, Fred Martin and Tom Law would sprint over 100 yards for a £20 prize. Marshall of Bradford City, the former Partick Thistle forward, heard of this and challenged Martin to a sprint over any distance from 100 to 220 yards, for any sum between £10 and £50." The professional sprint meetings participated in by many footballers over the summer months were both lucrative, and kept them in good trim.

Rovers got off to an auspicious start in the League with a 2-1 win at Motherwell, Gibson scoring both, from the penalty spot and "a rocket shot". Three days later, Rovers Reserves made their debut in the Scottish League Reserve Division, an encouraging attendance of 2000 paying £35 to see a 1-1 draw against Hearts Reserves.

For the first team, results were poor, with just two draws from the next six matches. The match at Hamilton on 5th September, a 1-1 draw, was watched by barely 2,000 spectators, the attendance "adversely affected by the present crisis." Three days later, Hugh Barr, latterly with Third Lanark, was appointed Rovers' trainer, to start the following Monday. On the same evening, the SFA decided that football was to continue, despite the declaration of war against Germany. A week later, a recruiting office was opened at the ground, and several young men were enlisted.

Everything clicked into place against Airdrie on 3rd October, Rovers winning 3-0 with goals from the new recruits Welsh (2) and Jimmy Todd. The Old Firm arrived in the space of five days, a 2-2 draw with Celtic on the October holiday Monday followed by a 2-1 defeat by Rangers, the 6,000 attendance indicative of the uncertain times. After a disappointing 2-2 draw at home to St Mirren,

Rovers travelled to Ibrox fearing the worst. The "glorious uncertainty of football" asserted itself once again, and goals by Harry Anderson and a Fred Gibson penalty gave Rovers an unexpected, but thoroughly merited, first ever victory at Rangers' ground.

After five of their players had enlisted in McCrae's Battalion (more of which later), "Raith Rovers directors have generously intimated to their players that any who enlist and are called into active service before the end of the football season will be paid half wages."

As the nights grew longer, and increasing numbers of young men embarked on troop ships bound for France and Belgium, football became a secondary consideration in the life of the town. The performances of the team did nothing to stir enthusiasm for the national game. After winning 3-0 at home to Kilmarnock on 14th November, Rovers won only one of the following twelve League fixtures (an improbable 5-1 thrashing of Aberdeen on 2nd January) through to the end of January. One of these was a home match against Third Lanark played at East End Park, Dunfermline, the SFA having closed Stark's Park from 14th to 28th December on account of an assault on the referee, Mr J. Kelso of Hamilton, at the end of the match against Dundee on 28th November

The Kirkcaldy Times asked : "The day has arrived when the management of Raith Rovers must realise how urgent is the necessity for the team being put on a winning basis. That the position is desperate is no denying when one reflects on all that was visible in the game against Hamilton Academical at Stark's Park on Saturday [beaten 3-1]".

Ironically, results perked up, with a draw and two victories in the next three games, but there appeared to be much discord behind the scenes at Stark's Park. In mid February, it was announced that two directors, James Todd and Andrew Dewar, had retired, their successors being John Kilpatrick and Thomas Smith. The same edition of the newspaper gave a thinly veiled account of rancour behind the scenes at Stark's Park, and a split boardroom.

Since forming the Limited Company in 1907, and having the directors elected by shareholders, where before committee men were elected by season ticket holders (members), few years had passed without changes to the composition of the Board of Directors. The change in status of the club's management seemed to bring out the worst example of "parish pump politics." The interesting aspect of this particular incident was that the man ousted, James Tod, had also acted as Secretary/Manager when the club reached the Scottish Cup final less than two years earlier, and had been active in the club's affairs since he was a boy.

The Kirkcaldy Times (17th February) had been told that had the two not resigned, the other five directors would have done so, and left the two men to run the club. "All that can be said on the matter is that it is to be

JOCK RATTRAY

The redoubtable Jimmy Gourlay (namesake of the future chairman) was top goalscorer for the second successive season in 1909/10, with 25 in all games, twelve in the League, twelve and three respectively ahead of Archie McAulay, who overtook his striking partner the following term with twelve goals, nine in the League.

Gourlay led the charts in 1911/12, scoring 16 goals, eight of them in the League, the same number as the consistent Duncan MacNeill.

When Rovers reached the Scottish Cup Final in 1912/13, top goalscorer, in League and all fixtures, was Fred Gibson with 17, five more than Harry Graham. The following season, Fred Martin was top scorer with 18, 14 in the League, Jimmy Scott scoring twelve League goals. Gibson and Scott each scored eleven League goals in 1914/15, although the former scored three goals in other first team matches, to Scott's single.

WILLIE PORTER

1915 Pathhead school opened Sir Michael Barker Nairn died on 28th November 1916 The Hippodrome (previously known as the King's Theatre) on the High Street became The Opera House, and latterly the ABC Cinema ; Dysart School opened

On 25th March 1916, the Raith Rovers v Queen's Park match was postponed due to a heavy snowfall. Only two League matches were played in Scotland that afternoon

David Whyte died on 10th October 1916. He had been the last President of the pre-incorporated Raith Rovers Football Club, in 1907, and was the only one of that club's office bearers to become a Director of the new company.

On Saturday 12th August 1916, Blues beat Reds 5-2 in the pre-season trial match. Amongst the trialists were O'Neill (with Blackburn Rovers the previous season), Forrest (Fulham), Duffy (Liverpool), Jock Rattray (Ayr United), Dunbar (Dumbarton Harp), Hayman (Ashfield), Stewart (Denbeath Star, who had been a Scotland junior internationalist the previous season), Thompson (Parkhead), Hutchison (Denbeath Star, the brother of Robert Hutchison, Rovers' inside right).

Season tickets for 1916/17 cost 6s 6d (32.5p) for the ground and 11s 6d (57.5p) for the ground plus grandstand. A reserved seat in the grandstand would cost 23 shillings for the season (£1.15) - all amounts inclusive of Entertainment Tax.

regretted that harmony has not existed on the management room of Raith Rovers. The official concerned is one who has for some years done much, and sacrificed a great deal on behalf of the club. In the past, he has been an invaluable member, and his place will be exceedingly difficult to fill."

For those who think that spin-doctoring is a modern phenomenon, Secretary John Richardson told the Fife Free Press that harmony was good, and the two directors who had resigned were watching Junior football on the club's behalf the previous Saturday. One of the directors denied that he had been at a Junior match.

There certainly wasn't much to cheer the population. There was to be no Links Market that year ("a disappointment for the bairns") and no Scottish Cup either. Results improved slightly, but there was a disconnected air surrounding the season's conclusion. The report of the Fife Cup tie against Kirkcaldy United on 20th March (which Rovers won 5-0) said "the dullness of the game was so patent at one point that the sound of the pipes from the roadway practically deprived the enclosure of spectators."

Following a 3-3 draw at Airdrie, goalkeeper Jock Neish was dropped for the first eleven match at Dens Park the following week, and asked to report for the Reserves match at Stark's Park. He refused to play, being "... dissatisfied with some remarks that were made anent his abilities during the Airdrieonians match by some person, and this it is stated is the cause of the dispute." Former goalkeeper Jimmy Mackie was pressed back into service. The season, in which Rovers finished second bottom of the First Division, could not end soon enough.

News of footballers, past and present, enlisting in the forces appeared in the newspapers on a weekly basis. Duncan Ritchie was a corporal in the 9th Battalion Black Watch, George Stoddart joined the Fife and Forfar Yeomanry, John McDonald, Jimmy Wilkie, Tommy Neish and Dave Chalmers all joined the Footballer's Battalion.

In late April, it was reported that Private William Collier of the Canadian Expeditionary Force, the youngest son of William Collier, March Street, had been posted to the front. He had played at left back for Rovers two seasons earlier, but a year earlier travelled to Canada to find work, joining up on the declaration of war. Collier, at least, was to return to gainful football employment after the war, and indeed win a Scotland cap whilst playing for Rovers.

Players enlisting were reported in the local press on a weekly basis, and, to an increasing extent, football news was dominated by non-playing exploits. The Kirkcaldy Times on 20th January 1915 reported : " Kirkcaldy Soldier Footballer Promoted. The many friends of Jimmy Logan, the popular Raith Rovers footballer, who recently enlisted in Sir George McCrae's Battalion Royal Scots, will be pleased to learn that he has been promoted from private to the

rank of corporal. Corporal Logan makes an excellent soldier, and ought to rise still higher in the ranks." In June, it was noted that having been promoted to sergent some month earlier, Logan was now a Sergeant Major. The reason for such rapid promotion (the slaughter of higher ranks) was never articulated. On 31st December 1915, he was promoted to Lieutenant, and in May 1916 played at right half for Scotland in the Military International at Goodison Park. Two months later, Mrs Logan, at her David Street home, was advised that her husband had been admitted to a London hospital suffering from deafness and shellshock following his involvement in the initial stages of the front offensive.

There was a more up-beat tone to the Kirkcaldy Times' coverage of Rovers' trial match on the eve of the 1915/16 season. "One was impressed with the good attendance at Stark's Park on Saturday. It was an indication that, despite the cry of carping critics that football is dead, the game still holds and will retain its hold on the public. The unfit for military service and those over army age want some relief from the agonising thoughts of the blood-red tragedy that is being enacted on the continent, and football is the one sport to supply this felt want."

A stirring and noble call ; which was not answered by the team, which failed to win a League match until Christmas Day. Those twenty-eight desperately disappointing matches yielded only seven goals, and never more than one per match, so it was not difficult to see where the problem lay. As early as 15th September, the Kirkcaldy Times said "wanted, a goalgetter" and in the weeks which followed came criticism of "unsatisfactory Rovers attack". "miserable failure of home forwards", "for sheer incompetency in attack Raith Rovers would be difficult to beat". The cause was certainly not financial – the SFA had decreed that every footballer was to be paid no more than £1 per match.

Following a heavy 3-0 defeat at Dens Park on 18th December, the Kirkcaldy Times boomed : "Position desperate – something must be done." Precisely what was difficult to suggest. The core of the club's playing strength was fighting for King and Country, Several promising players had been signed – goalkeeper Jimmy Brown, full back Bill Inglis, centre forward Willie Birrell, inside forward George Wilson, but they were young and lacked support. Crucially for the search for a winning team, the demands of military service meant a settled side was impossible.

A shuffling of the pack at Christmas and New Year had the desired effect ; the first win came with the 2-0 defeat of Clyde on Christmas Day, followed by a 1-0 win over Dumbarton on New Year's Day, Neil Turner scoring all the goals. Two days later, the team lost 2-0 at Kilmarnock, but 24 hours further on beat Hamilton Accies 2-0, Gibson scoring both goals. After a 1-0 defeat at Hibs, there were successive victories at

Motherwell (Turner hat-trick) and at home to Falkirk (Birrell hat-trick).

Rovers fans reading that day's Fife Free Press, on the evening of the victory over Motherwell, had their reverie quelled by the following report. "DEARER FISH SUPPERS. A meeting of the fish restauranteurs of Kirkcaldy was held in the Recreation Rooms on Monday afternoon, when they decided to form themselves into an association. It was also agreed to continue the supply of 1/2d worth of chips ; to increase fish suppers from 2d to 3d, and pudding suppers from 2d to 2 1/2d."

A 3-0 defeat at Ibrox, when Rovers gave Rangers a good game, was followed by a 6-0 reverse at Celtic Park a week later, on a day when Celtic fulfilled two league fixtures, winning 3-1 at Motherwell that evening. The last home match of the season was a splendid victory over Aberdeen, by 3-1, followed by a rather more typical 4-1 defeat at Hampden on the final day of the season. Rovers, predictably, finished bottom of the single division, the Second Division clubs having been left to their own devices for the duration of the war.

1916/17 was virtually a repeat of the preceding season. The first victory did not come until 16th December, a 2-0 win at home to Queen's Park. Only six goals were scored in the opening thirteen fixtures, until a Fletcher Welsh hat-trick won a point in a 3-3 draw at Easter Road.

There was radical surgery to the team after the first three matches (one point gained from a "well-merited" draw at Motherwell on the opening day. Centre half Charly Duffy, outside right Pat Monaghan and outside left Fred Gibson were dropped, replaced by Robert Pender, Jimmy Thompson and Sandy Archibald.

Another player was lost to the club after the 2-1 home defeat by Morton. The Kirkcaldy Times reported : "RAITH ROVERS' PLAYER APPREHENDED. At Kirkcaldy Police Court on Monday, Private W. Lavery, Royal Scots, was remanded pending the arrival of a military escort for being an absentee from his regiment. Lavery is the well known Raith Rovers right back. He took part in the Rovers v Morton game at Stark's Park on Saturday, at the close of which he was apprehended." It was noted that the military policemen took the opportunity of watching the game before doing their duty.

There were further, indeed constant, changes to the team as players were dropped, engaged in war-work, in the forces or simply couldn't get to games. A constant presence in the team were Sam Forrest, eventually at centre half, Jock Rattray at right half, who was one of several players to have a spell at centre forward (following a season with Ayr United), Harry Muir at left back, Sandy Archibald on the right wing and Alex Lindsay at inside right. Willie Winning and George Wilson played as often as they could. In the second half of the season Jimmy Abbott held down the inside left position, George Robson came in at full back , Walter Currie at left half and David Rougvie at centre forward.

As so often happens, the goals started flowing just as the local press could no longer withhold their criticism. Four days before Welsh's hat-trick, the Kirkcaldy Times wrote : "That forward line is really Raith's bugbear. But surely they can take a firmer grip of affairs and stop the vacillating policy which shuffles the lines in a most amateurish way, displaces properly placed men, and always ends in disaster."

Until an improbable and unexpected run of three successive wins early in the New Year, Rovers were bottom of the League. They finished second bottom, two points

McCrae's Battalion, the 16th Royal Scots, became known as the "Footballers Battalion" and here is its football team. Standing, right to left, are Sergeant C. Neill (trainer), Private J. Todd (Raith Rovers), Corporal A. Briggs (Hearts), Private P. Crossan (Hearts), Private Andrew Henderson (Falkirk), L.-Corporal Alex Henderson (Falkirk), Company Sergeant Major A.B. Ness (Hearts), Private G. McLay (Raith Rovers), Sergeant-Major F.A. Muir.

Seated - Private J. Boyd (Hearts), Private A. Wattie (Hearts), Captain J. Fowler, Colonel Sir George McCrae, Lieutenant R.C. Lodge, Private R.P. Wood (Falkirk), Private J. Scott (Raith Rovers).

On ground - Sergeant D. Currie (Hearts).

Of the twelve players pictured, three were from Rovers, three from Falkirk and six from Hearts. All three of the Rovers' players were killed in action.

Hearts are to be congratulated for continuing the tradition of ceremonially attending the memorial at Haymarket each year on Remembrance Sunday, but the contribution of Raith Rovers and Falkirk to the Footballers Battalion has never been recognised.

Dr John Smith moved to Kirkcaldy to be a General Practitioner in 1889, and quickly brought to the town the influential contacts he had in football circles. The interest which developed in the sport, in terms of playing and spectating, gathered momentum following the visits of famous clubs from England, and Queen's Park, to Newton Park, and later Stark's Park, thanks to the invitations extended by Dr Smith.
Born in Mauchline, Ayrshire, in 1855, he was educated at Mauchline Parish School and Ayr Academy before attending Edinburgh University, where he built a reputation as a scholar and all-round sportsman.
He played rugby for the University, and was considered for selection at full back for the Scotland team in 1876, denied only by the casting vote of the chairman. He returned to soccer, having played for Mauchline on his vacations, and formed the University football team in January 1879.
By then, he was an established internationalist, and indeed was one of the star players of the game in its earliest years.
His first game for Scotland was in the country's seventh international fixture, a 3-1 victory over England at Kennington Oval in March

above an Aberdeen team that was crippled by the drastically reduced transport system in the depths of the First World War. Even in war-time, bad results brought about a change of management. John Richardson, the former Petershill secretary/manager, left in mid November, to be replaced by the familiar figure of Peter Hodge, an appointment which saw goalkeeper Jock Neish return to the club. Two directors also resigned.

On Monday October 30th, James M Tod, until recently the dominant force in the Stark's Park boardroom, died, aged 42. The aerated water manufacturer lived in Balwearie Road, on the former site of one of the club's first playing pitches.

The following week, it was reported that "Willie Barr, Rovers' trainer, is a member of the new Pensions Committee. He's a busy man these days having many wounded Tommies under his care as a masseur." A fortnight later, he resigned to return to the west of Scotland to work in the hospitals there. A month later, he was replaced by Willie Smith of Musselburgh, who had lately been training a Junior team, and was once in charge of St Bernards.

To everyone's surprise, early in the New Year the reserve or 'A' team was resurrected, and was used to fulfil Loftus Cup, Fife League, Penman Cup and Wemyss Cup fixtures, the first eleven being busy enough trying to complete their League matches.

After a second successive victory, at Cathkin, the Kirkcaldy Times was in optimistic mode : "It must be very gratifying to Mr Hodge and the new trainer that success has attended the club almost since they took up their appointments, their record in that respect being remarkable." Willie Birrell featured in a 2-1 home win over Hibs. "On leave from the front, he asked for a game and his request was at once complied with."

As ever, there was a sobering postscript. "After tea in the evening the Raith directors and players made a presentation to Sergeant Ripley, who has done good work in the team this season, and who is returning to the front for the third time this week. Ripley is a North of England boy and a fine half-back, and he carries the best wishes of his Kirkcaldy colleagues with him in going to take part in the greater game."

A 2-1 home win over Hibs had Rovers fans dreaming of marching up the table, but it proved to be a false dawn. The next four games brought only one point, before Aberdeen were beaten 2-1 at Stark's Park. With Neish unavailable, Rovers had to borrow the Aberdeen reserve goalkeeper, and Falkirk's at Brockville the following week.

Spirits at Stark's Park were further depressed by the outcome of a meeting of the Scottish Football League in Glasgow on 15th March 1917, concerning the following season. "The opinion was expressed that owing to the difficulties in securing teams and the reduced travelling facilities, a splitting up of the competition has become a necessity. After a prolonged debate, it was officially intimated that the League had decided that "Dundee,

Aberdeen and Raith Rovers be asked to refrain from taking part in the competition next season, and that the average on-cost charges of these three clubs, from the last three years, be met by the clubs taking part in the competition next season. Should the restrictions continue at the opening of next season, a League may be formed to include Aberdeen, Dundee, Raith Rovers and the leading Fife clubs."

Peter Hodge expressed himself to be satisfied by the decision, stating that there are other things to be taken into account apart from the inconvenience to West of Scotland clubs ; such as the increasing urgency of the national work on which the bulk of players were engaged, and difficulty of getting them for away matches. The financial arrangements, he said, were entirely satisfactory.

The difficulties being experienced as 1916/17 drew to a close were exemplified by the efforts made to play an English trialist, Trotter, against Partick Thistle in the last home match of the season. He was to turn out the previous week against East Fife in the Fife Cup, but both he and Robson were "refused a railway ticket on account of the Easter rush." Willie Smith, the trainer, played at centre half in a 7-0 defeat at Greenock on 17th March.

A 3-1 defeat at Hamilton on 28th April 1917 proved to be Rovers last Scottish League fixture for more than two years, while every day brought reminders of why this had to be so. In mid May it was reported that Second Lieutenant David Philip of the Northumberland Fusiliers was reported wounded and missing on the Western Front. A Scottish Cup winner with Hearts, he later played for Leith Athletic and Rovers, before enlisting in McCrae's Battalion of the Royal Scots. Three weeks later, the Training and Reserve Battalion stationed in Kirkcaldy and District held their sports at Stark's Park.

Of the previous season's established first team, Robson, Robert Hutchison, Currie, Abbott and Muir returned to play in most of the Eastern League fixtures. The former Fulham player Sam Forrest, who had striven manfully in defence the previous season, despite his employment in the west, signed for Clydebank, who were drafted into the Scottish League to even up the numbers. Walter Kerr signed for St Bernards, and Inglis and Rattray "joined the colours".

The shortage of teams meant that four rounds of matches were played, against East Fife, Dunfermline Athletic, Armadale, Dundee, Cowdenbeath and Dundee Hibs. Aberdeen were left in splendid isolation and St Bernards, who were struggling to have their ground made ready, were refused a late admission. Lochgelly did not reply to the invitation, East Stirling were unable to take part, and Bathgate and Broxburn withdrew just before the start of the season. The inside forwards, Abbott and Wightman, on loan from Gillingham, bore the brunt of the goalscoring expectation, centre forward continuing to be a problem position. Despite the shortened programme - only 32 League and local cup ties being played - 28 different players were fielded. One of them, Lowther, played against his East Fife team-mates on 18th August, to make up the Rovers eleven.

With the team winning more than they lost, it was a more enjoyable season for Rovers fans, although war work and a punitive Entertainments Tax which increased the price of admission by a second 1d increment, to 8d, meant that crowds rarely reached 3,000. The team finished in third place, six points behind the joint winners Dundee and Cowdenbeath who had both managed to cross the Forth to play Armadale in the second half of the season (unlike Rovers) and therefore had played two more games.

The Club's 11th Annual General Meeting in July announced a loss for the year of almost £50, having received almost £370 from the Scottish Football League. The Directors reported that they were "… considering the situation for next season." At the A.G.M. "after serious discussion it was decided to suspend operations meantime. The reasons which led the directors to come to this conclusion were the last comb out of the mines, which would not only affect the "gate", but would also seriously interfere with the supply of young players, and so many players had been called up to the colours. The directors felt they would not be justified in incurring heavy financial liability meantime."

As the exhausted armies continued to slug it out in Western Europe, the people at home became increasing exhausted in the face of privation, and the unremitting effort to keep the war economy running in the absence of hundreds of thousands of able bodied men. On 31st July, only three clubs were represented at a meeting of the East of Scotland League in Kirkcaldy, and Raith Rovers were not among them. Rovers, Dundee and Armadale confirmed that they would be "sitting out" 1918/19.

The Daily Record of August 3rd noted : "In no part of the country has a heavier call been made on the young manhood for service with the forces than in Kirkcaldy and district. The town itself has furnished nearly 8000 men, or one-fifth of its total population, to the fighting forces, and the roll of Kirkcaldy men killed in action during the last four years is now approaching 800. The surrounding district, including Dysart, Kinghorn, Burntisland, Thornton, Markinch and Wemyss to Leven, has done equally well in the way of reinforcing the Army, and altogether something like 20,000 young men must have gone from the district from which the Rovers' supporters were drawn." The writer, "St Clair" concluded that "no one can question the wisdom of such a course."

At 3 o'clock on Sunday Morning, 19th October 1918, the guard of a passing train observed flames issuing from the grandstand at Stark's Park. The Burgh Fire Brigade and Peter Hodge were summoned, but the flames had taken hold and the fire burned for several hours. It died down when there was nothing

left to burn.

The dressing rooms, board room, press box etc., which occupied the whole of that side of the field next to Pratt Street, were destroyed, save for a few feet at the northern end. Turf was also charred and blackened to a considerable distance. Although Rovers had suspended play for the remainder of the war, both the playing pitch and the dressing rooms had been used by the military, and a match had been played on the Saturday afternoon.

The Armistice having been declared on 11th November, the first senior match of the season at Stark's Park was staged on 21st December, Dundee Hibs taking on a Fred Gibson XI in aid of the Distress Fund of the Discharged and Demobilised Sailors' and Soldiers' Federation. Most of Gibson's select came from the Highland Light Infantry Training Battallion which was stationed in Kirkcaldy, and four goals from Robbie and one from Gibson himself saw Dundee Hibs beaten 5-1, in front of a very impressive crowd of 5,000.

On 29th January 1919, the Kirkcaldy Times announced that "Raith Rovers are expected to resume operations on an early date. Mr Peter Hodge is again to take up the duties of secretary and manager, and it is likely that some important matches will be played during the present season. Sixteen of the club's players are available, or about to be demobilised."

Some reassuringly familiar names appeared at Stark's Park for the club's first match in a year, a 2-1 defeat to a Selected XI on 15th March. Nine games were played against local teams, spectators being charged League prices of 8d admission.

Two things happened in April to denote that Kirkcaldy was getting back to normality after five years of war. The Links Market was back, and the club and its directors were being criticised in the local press at their lack of preparedness for the forthcoming season. There were calls for a Public Meeting, such was the level of concern.

The Kirkcaldy Times did nothing to dispel such thoughts with their report of the 6-0 defeat at Dundee on 26th April, five of the goals being lost in the first half. "With the team which took the field at Dens Park against Dundee, Raith Rovers cannot hope for much success in First League circles. The first half display was lamentable."

There was one major institutional casualty of the First World War in the town's sporting circles – Kirkcaldy United were not mentioned in the list of teams said to be willing to play in the Eastern League the following season. The Pathhead club did not survive the war. Rovers directors, recognising that there would be no senior football for the town's enthusiasts when they were away from home, announced that an 'A' team would be entered in the Eastern League.

In late May, the Fifeshire Association met to disburse £50 to clubs in needy

1877. He played in the 2-0 victory in Scotland's first visit to Wales two days later, and scored in the 5-4 win over England at Kennington Oval in April 1879. He scored twice as Scotland won 3-0 at Wrexham two days later. His fifth cap came in the 5-4 victory over England at Hampden Park in March 1880, and scored a hat-trick in the return fixture in London a year later. He played twice more against both Wales and England, and was never in a beaten Scotland team. His 10 caps was the second highest total until 1900.

Smith played 18 times (scoring 7 goals) for Corinthians, including an 8-1 victory over English Cup holders Blackburn Rovers, and regularly played for Queen's Park. His playing career ended when the SFA decreed that he had breached his amateur status by playing for Corinthians against a professional club, Bolton Wanderers.

He toured Australia with the Scotland rugby team in 1888 and refereed the 1892 Scotland v England football match.

He lived, and conducted his medical practice, at Brycehall, now the offices of Charles Wood & Sons, Solicitors, in Kirk Wynd.

Dr John Smith died, still practicing as a GP, in November 1934.

The young men of the Links who combined to form Raith Rovers very quickly had to decide on a common colour of playing shirt, to distinguish them from their opponents. Most men possessed a blue shirt, the most common colour worn by manual workers, and that was the club colour which was adopted.

In 1887, it was remarked upon that the club had purchased a new set of jerseys, in blue and white halves (pictured on page 8). To celebrate the club's 125th anniversary, a similar style was adopted for 2008/09, albeit with the colours reversed, and the erroneous and misleading advice that this was the club's first ever strip.

The following year, it was back to blue jerseys, with white knickers (page 31). In 1890/91, the team were photographed in light blue and white striped jerseys and dark blue knickers (page 27).

In 1900, the reserve eleven, Raith Athletic, were photographed in dark (or navy) blue tops with white collars, worn with white knickers. However, the first team were still wearing medium blue in 1902 (page 45)

It would appear that navy blue was adopted when the club joined the Scottish League in 1902. The only variation in this strip, for several years, was in the collar, which was a white round-neck (page 48) and by 1905 was joined by a lighter blue (or grey) button panel (page 49). The white collar disappeared entirely during 1906/07 (page 55), but re-appeared in 1910 for the debut season in the First Division (page 59).

The club crest appeared on the jersey for the first time in 1910/11 (page 60).

The club started 1921/22 in dark blue (page 73) but by the end of that season, were wearing medium blue shirts with white collars, with the club crest embroidered on a navy blue shield (page 76). The lighter colour was used until midway through the Second World War. White cuffs were introduced in 1931, but were missing from the 1937/38 jersey (page 94).

circumstances, but Cowdenbeath and Raith Rovers did not wish to participate, and the money was divided between Dunfermline Athletic, Lochgelly United and East Fife.

Each year, on Remembrance Sunday, players, officials and supporters of Heart of Midlothian Football Club lead the annual Remembrance Service at the Memorial Clock outside Haymarket Station in Edinburgh. They remember the fallen in the 1914-18, and all subsequent, wars but principally the Hearts players who famously enlisted in the 16th Royal Scots, "The Footballer's Battalion" in December 1914.

Fourteen Hearts players joined the Battalion formed by Sir George McCrae, and so too did footballers of 74 other football clubs, including Kirkcaldy United, Wemyss Athletic, Crossgates Thistle, Cupar Violet, Hearts of Beath, Valleyfield Athletic, Inverkeithing United, Ladybank Violet, Leslie Hearts, Cowdenbeath, Dunfermline Athletic, East Fife and Raith Rovers.

Seven Tynecastle players made the ultimate sacrifice during the carnage of the First World War, and that Club's heroic contribution has been justly acknowledged, and remembered, over the ensuing decades. What has never been recognised is the sacrifice made by Raith Rovers during the First World War. Rovers' fortunes suffered to a far greater extent than Hearts, notwithstanding the awful waste of all of the young footballers' lives.

Prior to the introduction of conscription, Lord Kitchener's poster campaign encouraged Britain's young men to volunteer for duty in the autumn of 1914. A wave a patriotism swept the country, and considerable resentment grew at the continuation of organised professional football, which carried on as if nothing had happened.

Questions were being asked in the Houses of Parliament, and the government was on the point of stepping in to bring League football to a halt, when Sir George McCrae addressed an audience at the Usher Hall on 27th November 1914.

"This is not a night for titles : I stand before you humbly as a fellow Scot, nothing more and nothing less. You know I don't speak easily of crisis. But that is what confronts us. I have received permission from the War Office to raise a new battalion for active service. It is my intention that this unit will be characterised by such a spirit of simple excellence that the rest of Lord Kitchener's army will be judged by our standard. Furthermore, with the agreement of the authorities, I have undertaken to lead the battalion in the field. I would not – I could not – ask you to serve unless I share the danger at your side. In a moment I will walk down to Castle Street and set my name to the list of volunteers. Who will join me ?"

Hearts manager John McCartney, recognising the mood of the country, persuaded his Board of Directors to release players from their contracts to allow them to enlist. Around 500 supporters of the club

followed suit along with 150 Hibs' supporters. Other clubs in the East of Scotland quickly followed, and many of their players, along with other sportsmen, enlisted in Edinburgh in the 16th Battalion of the Royal Scots.

No fewer than seventeen Raith Rovers players enlisted, seven of them in "The Footballer's Battalion." Month by month, as season 1914/15 drew to a close, the effects were felt on the Club's results. After struggling to come to terms with the First Division status they won in 1910, an improvement to 11th position in 1913/14, and the continued strengthening of the team with a higher calibre of player, hopes were high of a successful period at Stark's Park.

From a mid table place at New Year 1915, results declined and the club finished second bottom. The sufferance of the club's directors and supporters at the decline, and then temporary loss, of their Football Club was nothing to the sacrifices made by the players who enlisted. The tragic waste of young lives which marked the gruesome carnage of the Western Front is illustrated by the stories of those who died fighting for King and Country.

Outside right James Todd, who had made his league debut for the club in August 1914, joined the Footballer's Battalion in December 1914 and died on 12th March 1916 in the front line near Fleurbaix. A 20 year old railway clerk from Easter Road, his death is described in Jack Alexander's book on McCrae's Battalion : "Todd took a large shell-fragment full in the chest ; he was carried to a dug-out and died before the guns had finished firing. Alfie Briggs, who attended the funeral at Erquinghem, wrote to McCartney : "Jimmy was in everything, a constant source of solace to us all with his good humour and cheerfulness. He is a sore loss."

Inside forward Jimmy Scott, a first team regular for two seasons, joined the Footballers' Battalion on 2nd December 1914 and died at Pozieres, on the Somme, on 1st July 1916. His remains are thought to have been buried in Gibson's Dump, an ammunition depot at the height of the battle which was transformed into a cemetery afterwards. Many stones are marked as an "Unknown Scottish Soldier."

George McLay joined The Footballers' Battalion on 1st December 1914 and was promoted to Sergeant. He died at Passchendaele on 22nd October 1917, posthumously winning the Military Medal for "conspicuous bravery". He had signed for the club from Glencraig Juniors in June 1910, and quickly became established as right half in the first eleven. He played a significant part in taking Rovers to the Scottish Cup Final in 1913, but was injured on 7th April, and he missed the Final the following week.

Private James B. Gibson MA, left half in the Scottish Cup Final team of 1913, died of his wounds at Dardenelles on 5th September 1915, aged 26 years. A former pupil of Kirkcaldy High School, where he played rugby, he served in the 6th Hauraki New Zealand Expeditionary Force. A teacher, he had moved to New Zealand in November 1913, as senior master at the Boys High School in Napier, New Zealand.

Former players were not spared the carnage. Anderson Inglis, the great full back of Rovers' early years in the Scottish League, served as a Private in the Army Vetinary Corps (due to his familiarity with horses) and then as a Lance Corporal in the East Lancs Regiment. He served in France from June 1915 and was killed at Passchendaele on 6th October 1917. He is commemorated on the large memorial at Tyne Cot Cemetery, on Kelty's war memorial, and on the family gravestone at Dunfermline Cemetery, overlooking East End Park.

The war wreaked its havoc not only on the battlefield. Private Kenneth Sutherland, Black Watch, died of appendicitis en route to the Military Hospital at Cromarty on 8th September 1917, aged 28 years. He lived at 32 Milton Road, Kirkcaldy. He had been a stock keeper with Michael Nairn & Co. Ltd, and had played for Rovers and Kirkcaldy United. He joined the army 10 weeks earlier, and died of appendicitis while training at Nigg.

Reserve team player John M. Melville joined Black Watch as a Trooper and died of dysentery in Cairo on 12th November 1917 aged 23. He lived at 19 Ava Street, Kirkcaldy.

The footballing careers of those who survived were often blighted by the war.

Fred Martin, centre forward in the 1913 Cup Final team, was injured while constructing an aeroplane in Coventry in July 1915, a propeller being set in motion while he was adjusting it. He severely lacerated his hand and his right foot was also badly cut.

Private Wiliam Birrell of the Black Watch, formerly on the office staff at Barry Ostlere & Shepherd, was taken prisoner in March after being wounded. In September 1918 it was reported that he was doing well in hospital in Germany, and had communicated with his parents who lived in Harriet Street. On recovering from his injuries, he resumed his playing career at Stark's Park, was sold to Middlesbrough, and then returned to manage Raith Rovers. He was manager of Chelsea from 1939 until 1952.

Centre half William Porter, who also joined the Footballers' Battalion on 1st December 1914, goalkeeper Willie Wallace, and young reserves Peter Lumsden, Alex Reekie and Alex Crichton, who all enlisted in the army, did not play again for Rovers. Rovers' first Scotland cap, Harry Anderson, left Stark's Park during the war years for a higher standard of football, while pre-war stalwarts such as Arthur Cumming, Bill Morrison and Fred Martin, who had all played in the 1913 Cup Final, and centre forward Fletcher Welsh, lost the best years of their playing careers between 1914 and 1919.

Some survived the horrors of the global conflict, and returned after the war to serve the club with great distinction.

James H. Logan, centre half in the 1913 Cup Final, joined the Footballers' Battalion on 2nd December 1914, was promoted to corporal in January 1915, sergeant in May 1915 and sergeant major late June 1915. He ended the war with the rank of Captain, and returned to Stark's Park as manager, where he led the club during a period of great success in the early 1920's

James M. Gourlay, a reserve team player and not to be confused with the prolific goalscorer of the same name, enlisted as a Trooper in the Fife & Forfar Yeomanry in December 1914, and returned to play a part in the formation of the Supporters Club, alongside his namesake. His significant mark on the club's history was as Chairman of the Football Club during their golden era of the late 1940s and early 1950s.

Jock Rattray joined the Footballer's Battalion on 2nd December 1914, but he was transferred to Dunfermline Athletic in August 1915. He returned to Stark's Park after the war, and was a member of the great team of the early 1920's.

George Stoddart enlisted as a Trooper in the Fife & Forfar Yeomanry on 13th April 1915 and when the fighting was over returned to Stark's Park for the first four games of 1920/21, before signing for Hull City.

The Club made several other, if less significant, contributions to the war effort, as described in the Kirkcaldy Times of 8th December 1915. "FOOTBALLS FOR OUR SOLDIERS. In order to provide funds for supplying footballs for our soldiers at the front, a collection will be taken at Raith Rovers v Hearts match on Saturday, and it is hoped that the response will be liberal. Up to date the Raith directors have forwarded thirty footballs to our soldiers."

Despite the on-going conflicts requiring military intervention throughout the world today, it is difficult to appreciate the devastation brought to a generation of young men by the First World War. To gain some measure of the cost in human lives, consider the Raith Rovers team on your next visit to Stark's Park. Nearly a century before, spectators at Stark's Park would be cheering on around half of the young men in the team for the last time, their footballing careers about to be consumed by the war that was supposed to end all wars.

On the eve of the 1919/20 season, the club's directors enunciated their hopes and aspirations. "Two factors that should help the 'gates' very considerably at Stark's Park in the coming season are that the bulk of the club's supporters are now demobilised, and that the Rosyth workers, of whom there are a very large number, are now having a half holiday on Saturday, a boon which they did not have in war-time. Altogether matters are looking very hopeful, and a most successful season is anticipated at Stark's Park."

Rovers returned to Scottish League fixtures with a bump, losing 4-1 at Falkirk, but they bounced back the following Saturday, beating Kilmarnock 5-1, Willie Birrell scoring four times. One point out of the next five matches shook confidence somewhat, by which time Frank Clark (a recruit from junior

ALEX LINDSAY

Alex Lindsay signed for Tottenham Hotspur in the summer of 1919 and, after a few years in the reserves at White Hart Lane, became an established first team player in the mid 1920s. He played for the Anglo Scots in an international trial in March 1923, and was at Spurs until 1930, playing 277 first team matches and scoring 67 goals. He moved to Thames, then a League club, and returned to Scotland with Dundee.

The club's dramatic decline as the First World War unfolded was illustrated in the goalscoring returns, Neil Turner scoring most in 1915/16, just eight, with young Willie Birrell next highest with five. It was no better the following season, Alex Lindsay scoring eight in the League plus one in the Fife League, with Fred Gibson next highest on six League goals. Predictably, the scoring rate picked up in the Eastern League in 1917/18, with Jimmy Abbott and David Weightman both scoring nine League goals, the former added six more in other fixtures to the latter's one.

On 22nd May 1919, Andrew Pratt died in Edinburgh. He was in his 75th year. A native of Markinch, he served his apprenticeship in the retail drapers shop of N. Lockhart & Sons. When they opened their power loom factory, he was transferred to its office, became a traveller, and then works manager. In 1884 he went into partnership with R.B. Heggie in Fergus Wynd. Fergus Wynd, and the various Fergus Places further inland, were named after Walter Fergus, an earlier linen manufacturer, who was four times Provost of Kirkcaldy between 1793 and 1826. The business of Messrs R.B. Heggie & Pratt was dissolved in 1905 on the death of Robert Heggie, and Pratt retired. He was for many years a councillor on Kirkcaldy Town Council, and Honorary Treasurer. A strong radical, he was a supporter of MP Sir Henry Dalziel for 20 years. Pratt Street was originally known as Gallochy Brae, and was renamed after Andrew Pratt. The origin of Gallochy is obscure, and it may originally have been Garrochie (in Aberdeenshire : Garrochie Brae was mentioned in a traditional Scots folk song). Heggie's Wynd in Linktown was named after Heggie's grandfather.

Some measure of the insanity of the registration system in Scottish football is that on Saturday February 28th 1920, in the Fife Cup semi final against Raith Rovers 'A' team at East End Park, Dunfermline fielded their Scottish internationalist Andy Wilson.

In the Eastern League v Western League match at Cowdenbeath on Saturday March 27th 1920, Rovers players Robert Hutchison (right back), Dick Berry (centre half) and Jimmy Christie played for the Eastern League.

1919 - Meikle's Carpet factory opened in Dysart ; A.H. McIntosh died in late September

The proceeds of the Public Trial on 11th August 1920 went to Victoria Nursing Association

club Denbeath Star) was replaced in goal by Alex McDonald, who in turn had been signed from juvenile Balgonie Scotia. George Robson returned to Stark's Park to replace Harry Muir at left back and John Dunn, signed from Leith Benburb, shared left wing duties with George Wilson.

Bill Inglis at right back, the half back line of Jock Rattray, Willie Porter and Harry Anderson, and forwards Willie Birrell, John 'Tokey' Duncan, Fletcher Welsh and Willie McLean, formed the core of the team. All but Anderson, Porter and Welsh of the 23-strong playing squad were Fifers.

Results improved slightly in the autumn, but the club had a major hurdle to overcome when Peter Hodge was appointed manager of Leicester City. He expressed "a reluctance to leave the Lang Toun", but there was no such reticence from potential replacements – there were no fewer than sixty applicants for his job.

The choice of the directors was a former player, Captain James Logan, given charge of the club at 33 years of age. Logan was one of six players to join McCrae's Battallion in late November 1914. Willie Porter was back at Stark's Park, Willie Lavery was with St Mirren, and three (George McLay, who won the Military Medal, Jimmy Scott and Jimmy Todd) had been killed.

At the time of his appointment, he was still in occupied Germany. "Showing unusual capability as an instructor, Logan was left behind when the battalion went into training quarters in England, to train the raw recruits who were coming in. He was later transferred to the 18th Battalion, in which he obtained his commission, going to France and seeing active service with another Battalion." The Kirkcaldy Times did not minimise his task at Stark's Park. "When he takes over the reins the new manager will find himself in the position of requiring to put a stout heart to a "stey brae."

At Cathkin Park on 27th September, Third Lanark and Rovers went "toe to toe" in a desperate battle for the points. Thirds won 4-3, and James Abbott broke his leg in only his third match of the season. Two months later, another trip to Glasgow finished in the same scoreline, with Fletcher Welsh scoring a hat-trick for the beaten team. Clyde had the luck on the day, at their temporary home of Celtic Park. Two "league tables" told conflicting stories ; Rovers were fourth bottom of the League, but Fletcher Welsh was joint top scorer.

The week after the Clyde match, Queen's Park visited Stark's Park, and despite Rovers having the bulk of the play, the visitors won 5-2, "Morton being especially lively". Seven days later at Dens Park, Rovers surpassed themselves in falling 4-5, Welsh scoring another hat-trick.

The natives were getting restless, and almost revolutionary. One wrote in the Kirkcaldy Times : "There is a certain town in England where the supporters of a club have formed what is called a "Supporters Club", which informs the management of the team

that if they do not try their best to run the club on a successful basis, they will withdraw their support. If something like that was formed here we may have a chance of something being done on the right lines."

"Supporter" wrote in another edition : "It is long past time that a wholesale change of the Board should be made, and men elected who can judge for themselves, and not listen over bars to judge men's capabilities."

The supporters appreciated the team's attacking prowess, and gates held up, despite very indifferent results. There was some return from the 'A' team, who enjoyed crowds of between 2,000 and 3,000 when the first team were on their travels. Around Christmas, right back Alex Sneddon, left back David Moyes from Cowdenbeath and the amateur inside left James Jessiman were all signed, and pitched straight into the first team. Results did not improve especially.

The struggles of the season were exemplified by the Scottish Cup campaign. Rovers had a cup run of six matches – fewer than they played in winning it in 1913 – but they featured in only two rounds. It took four games to dispose of East Stirling, the last two replays being staged at Tynecastle, and a 2-2 home draw against Morton in the next round was followed by a 3-0 defeat on a Wednesday afternoon in Greenock, a most unpleasant experience for Rovers and their players. "A rough crowd" threw stones at the Rovers`defence – a protest to the SFA was in vain – and Porter's frustration was vented at half time towards the referee, who sent him off for dissent. An appeal against the dismissal was deemed to be improperly lodged, and Porter was suspended, on 17th March, until May 15th "for making insinuations regarding the referee's honesty." He was probably fortunate that further remarks about his eyesight and parentage were not taken into consideration.

Towards the end of the season, James Bauldie became the latest in a series of centre forwards. Any lapses of concentration on his part could be explained by a report in the Kirkcaldy Times of 30th June 1920, headed "A Raith Rovers' Love Affair : Bowhill Lassie Gets £250 for Breach of Promise."

"A breach of promise action against James Bauldie, the Raith Rovers footballer, has been disposed of in Dunfermline Sheriff Court by the granting of decree against him of £250." The pursuer was Margaret Webster, 27 Scott Street, Bowhill. Bauldie resided at 37 Dundonald Den, Cardenden. She was 17, he 22. They started their romance on April 19th, and became engaged on October 19, to be married on February 20th. The wedding did not take place. "On 27th February, following up a claim by the pursuer against the defender for breach of promise and seduction, he undertook to pay the sum of £250 at the rate of £2 per week, so long as he was playing first class football ; otherwise £1 per week." Having failed to make any payment, the matter returned to court. The defender did not appear and was found against.

The club was still in "reconstruction mode" as they approached 1920/21 season, somewhat floridly reported by the Kirkcaldy Times on May 5th : "Already interesting specimens of the calligraphy of prominent footballers are in the hands of the management." After starting the season with the reserves, David Moyes established himself at left back. Harry Anderson's transfer to St Mirren was perceived as a blow, although the wily wing half was now classed as a veteran , but the loss of the club's first internationalist was compensated by the blossoming of its second, Bill Collier returning from the war as a commanding defender. The problem position of centre forward was filled by George Waitt, who together with inside left Jimmy McDonald arrived from Bradford City, and there was the significant addition of Aberdeen 's Bobby Archibald at outside left.

The Fife Free Press of May 22nd reported on a "New Training Policy. During their English visits the Raith directors were very favourably impressed by a system of training, which is described as being alien to Scottish clubs, and which is to be adopted at Stark's Park next season. The principle of training, without going into details, is ball practice of an unusual but very effective kind. Hitherto, ball practice has been an absentee from the training curriculum on the ground that being away from the ball for a week imparted eagerness on the Saturday. So now we know the reason for a lot of things that were obscure to us before. However, that's all to be remedied, and more than that there is to be no division, on the part of the players, between work and football, the conditions are to be such that no player will follow his ordinary occupation." Mercifully, later journalists could use the short-hand notation "full-time".

There was considerable optimism arising from the opening League match of 1920/21, a 1-0 win at Albion Rovers, in which the Raith defence played well. That was followed by four successive League defeats, prompting encouragement from an unorthodox quarter. "An additional incentive for Raith Rovers' forwards to score goals is contained in an announcement by the Fife Raincoat Company, Kirkcaldy, to the effect that they are prepared to award one of their coats to any Raith player who scores two

goals in any one match during the season."

Billy Birrell, John Duncan, George Waitt and Bobby Bauld were thus protected from spring showers by the season's end.

There was a much happier outcome from the next four games, which brought three victories, the last of which, against Kilmarnock, attracted a crowd of 10,000. The October holiday afternoon was filled by a League fixture against Queen's Park which Rovers won 5-1, with a hat trick from John Duncan, but centre half Willie Porter was absent from the team. His dispute over terms with the Directors led to him being placed on the transfer list, where he did not linger for long. The following day, Hearts gave Rovers £700, of which £200 went to Porter in recognition of his seven years of service to the club.

Another player in dispute with the club, George Stoddart, was transferred to Hull City on November 10th. Results were mixed, although there was much to console the fans in some plucky defeats, and there were some fine individuals playing for the club, so attendances kept up.

The five League matches from 11th December, to the vital (for prestige purposes in front of an enlarged crowd) New Year's holiday home game brought only two draws, and with the Scottish Cup looming, drastic action was taken. Porter's departure had been inadequately covered by the promotion of Berry, and later the bizarre switching of John Duncan to centre half. A permanent solution was found in Newtongrange Star's centre half, Dave Morris. Another junior recruit, from Hamilton club Cadzow St Anne's, was centre forward Tom Jennings, closely followed by Bobby Bauld, from closer to home, Glencraig Celtic. Goalkeeper Jimmy Brown returned from Airdrie.

The inclusion of the three juniors

The Raith Rovers side which finished third in the First Division in 1921-22, the club's highest ever League position.
Back row : Jimmy Brown, Jimmy Raeburn, David Moyes, Tom Jennings, Bill Collier, Jimmy Brown (assistant trainer and groundsman).
Front row : Tommy Duncan, John Duncan, Bill Inglis, Dave Morris, Bobby Archibald, Robert Bauld.
The photograph was taken at Celtic Park before the opening League match of the season, on Monday 15th August 1921. The choice of strip is jersey is interesting, navy blue with no badge or white trim.
The following season, the club reverted to lighter blue jerseys, but the badges in stock had navy blue backgrounds. The stockings remained navy blue

While the Duncan brothers moved on to supposedly greater things (in the English Second Division at Leicester City) the remainder of the 1921/22 team stayed at Stark's Park to form the backbone of the side which competed at the highest level of Scottish League football over the next three seasons. Alex James, Peter Bell and George Miller were introduced to the forward line.

The reserve team of 1922-23 line up in front of the new stand at Stark's Park. Back row : James C. Brown (trainer), George Barton, Jimmy Mathieson, Jimmy McClelland, Archie Morris, Mr L.K. Story.
Front row : John Campbell, John Thomson, Alex Gilmour, Fred T. Lindsay, John Boreland, Alex McBeath, John Gardiner.

1921 John Barry died, aged 75. He lived in Bennochy Park (now Abbeyfield)
1922 Viscount Novar become Secretary of State for Scotland
1923 Esplanade and sea wall completed by unemployed workmen (thrown out of work by the great trade depression which brought the economy to a halt in the early 1920s) who were then gainfully employed by the Town Council in transforming the eye-sore of a sea front for Kirkcaldy. There had been a reluctance to develop the area due to regular flooding at high tides and storms, but the stout walls built in 1923 have largely kept the sea at bay

Rovers director Andrew Adamson, a member of the SFA Selection Committee, was a linesman at the Scotland v England match at Villa Park in 1921/22

David Dawson and Fred Lindsay of the reserves were selected for the North team to play the West of the Scottish Alliance at Dens Park in 1921/22

was not enough to ensure success in the Scottish Cup. Tom Jennings scored on his senior debut at his hometown ground, but Hamilton Accies won 3-1 in the first round, their winning goals scored in the last few minutes, when a replay looked more likely. The loss of Cup ambitions meant that Rovers could not resist the £2,300 cheque offered by Middlesbrough for Billy Birrell, the fee exceeding the previous record sum received, £1,700 from Sheffield Wednesday for Fletcher Welsh. The injection of funds allowed the reserve team to be re-started, playing friendly matches to the end of the season under the tutelage of Jimmy McDonald, who had been signed as a player from Bradford City. A home match against Gala Fairydean attracted an attendance of 500. Those running the club recognised that improvement was required, and put in place the means of achieving this.

The losers were Abbotshall Juniors, who had stepped up from Juvenile status (when they played at West End Park) and used Stark's Park as their home ground. They completed the season by lodging at rivals' grounds, and reverted to the Kirkcaldy and District Juvenile League the following season, leaving Kirkcaldy to be represented by Dunnikier Colliery Juniors, and Dysart by Rosslyn, both in the East Division of the Fife County League.

Another junior, Jimmy Raeburn from Tranent, made his debut in a 1-0 defeat at Ibrox, Rangers' goal scored by Sandy Archibald. An unlucky 1-0 defeat at Ayr was followed by five matches without defeat, the new recruits rejuvenating both team and results. The visit of Celtic on 9th April was therefore anticipated with some relish, but the Kirkcaldy Times announced "No Nuisances Admitted".

"The Raith Rovers Management has decided that any person carrying flags, bugles or any other paraphernalia will be refused admission. The Rovers directors have evidently had enough of the flag waving and noise merchants, and the spectators I venture to think will not be averse to the decision."

Admission to the Celtic match was

1/-, 2/- for the old stand on Pratt Street and 1/6 for the new (railway) stand, and Rovers fans were rewarded with a 2-0 win, Tokey Duncan scoring both goals in front of 12,000 spectators

The league season finished with a visit by the other half of the Old Firm, for whom Tommy Muirhead scored the only goal of the game, although Rovers were clearly the better team on the day. They finished in 16th position in the 22 club lead, but the signs of improvement in the youthful team led to the conclusion that the season's progress had been satisfactory.

Few could have predicted the extent of the improvement in 1921/22, however. As has happened so frequently during the club's history, a season of great success arrived unexpectedly, following a recent history of struggle.

The painstaking and piecemeal acquisition of players during the previous two seasons bore fruit, without any additions during the summer of 1921. Perhaps the most significant signing was the trainer, Dave Willis, formerly a player with Newcastle United, Sunderland and Reading, and latterly player manager with Jarrow. The hope was that Willis, and manager Logan, would provide some stability, and ability, to the club. In the fourteen years since the Limited Company was formed, there had been four managers, Hodge (twice), Richardson and Logan, and no fewer than eight trainers, Janes, Goodfellow, Aitken, Thomas, Barr, Smith, Brown and Willis

Admittedly the First World War was a hugely unsettling factor in this period, but the first two post-war seasons had seen no fewer than four assistant trainers in Clark, Westwater, Butchart and Brown.

The Fife Free Press suggested that "There should be no question of Raith Rovers being chicken-hearted this season. On their new jerseys they carry a lion over the left breast."

Third place in the League, behind Celtic and Rangers, was unimaginable after just one point from the first three League games : a heavy defeat at Celtic Park, a narrow reverse at Motherwell, and a 1-1 draw at home to Celtic in which the champions-to-be were fully stretched. The first victory came at Hampden, two goals from Tom Jennings and a David Moyes penalty gaining a 3-1 victory. The young forwards were still trying to find their feet ; a 1-1 draw at Brockville was earned by staunch performances by the centre backs, and a 2-0 defeat in Coatbridge was largely due to weak finishing by the visitors. On that afternoon, the 'A' team entertained Falkirk at Stark's Park in a Second Eleven Cup tie, and attracted an attendance of 5,000. Kirkcaldy was willing, and able, to support an ambitious football club.

Clydebank were smashed 5-0 at

Stark's Park, and a draw at Paisley was followed by a 2-0 win at Airdrie. 15,300 turned up at Stark's Park to see Kilmarnock beaten 4-0. In the autumn, Rovers were unbeaten in 9 league matches, winning four of them. This run was brought to a surprise end on Christmas Eve at Stark's Park, Dunky Walker scoring a hat-trick for St Mirren in a 3-2 win. Rovers goals were scored by David Dawson, who was deputising for the injured Jennings.

Worries about the bubble bursting proved to be groundless ; Albion Rovers, Falkirk, Aberdeen and Hearts were all put to the sword in advance of a 1-0 victory at Ibrox, Jennings scoring on his return to the team. A 0-0 draw at home to Hibs was followed by a 2-2 home draw with Clyde in the first round of the Scottish Cup. Rovers were the better team on the day, but did not enjoy the best of fortune. The club were taking the expectation of a Cup run seriously, the team having prepared at Peebles during the previous week. The 1-0 defeat at Shawfield in the replay came as a considerable surprise. Neither team played well, but the deciding factor was the injuries sustained by a couple of defenders and by Tommy Duncan on the right wing.

The press were finding their independent voice as the country accustomed itself to peace. So incensed were Cowdenbeath by one report, that they sued the Daily Record for slander. At Stark's Park on 2nd January 1922, the players of Raith Rovers and Falkirk exacted their own revenge on the third estate, as described by the Kirkcaldy Times two days later.

"The press box is not by any means the safest place at Stark's Park, and this fact was exemplified on Monday when on one occasion the occupants had to withstand a shower of broken glass. After the incident it was a bit disconcerting to the reporters to see the ball coming in their direction so often, but their fears were justified, for in the closing minutes another pane of glass was smashed about them."

Rovers recovered well from their Cup defeat, beating Clydebank 3-0 at Clydeholm four days later, and losing just one of their next seven League matches, a 2-1 defeat at Easter Road in which Rovers put up a plucky fight despite being below their best. Collier was missing at Clydebank, winning a cap for Scotland against Wales at Wrexham. In March, Bill Inglis was named as a reserve

(to Scott of Falkirk) for the Scottish League v English League match at Ibrox. Dawson and Lindsay of the reserves were selected for the North team to play the West of the Scottish Alliance at Dens Park, and on 22nd March Inglis and Collier were selected for the Home Scots to play the Anglos in an International Trial match at Cathkin Park.

Rangers hit a "splendid" Rovers side with breakaway tactics in the League match played at Stark's Park on the April holiday, winning 3-0 despite the home team doing all the pressing. A crowd in excess of 20,000 watched a great game. That was followed by a 1-0 defeat at Third Lanark, and a similar scoreline at Dens Park, before Rovers rounded off their most successful League season ever with two 1-0 victories, Tom Jennings scoring against both Morton and Hamilton Accies.

The team finished in third place, two points ahead of both Dundee and Falkirk, although a distant 16 behind Champions Celtic, who had one more point that Rangers. Never before, or since, has a Raith Rovers team finished so high in Scottish League football. The team of 1921/22 therefore lays claim to the accolade of the club's best ever ; although many would argue that the 1956/57 side was their equal, if not better. Both seasons shared the same remarkable fact : the eleven that played in the first League match, was the same eleven that played in the last one. Proof positive that a settled team brings success. In 1921/22 it was Brown, Inglis, Moyes, Raeburn, Morris, Collier, T. Duncan, J. Duncan, Jennings, Bauld and Archibald.

As one of the leading clubs in Scotland, Rovers were initially invited on an eight match tour of Denmark and Germany, which was later condensed to three matches in Copenhagen. They left Kirkcaldy on 10th May 1922, travelled via London, Harwich and Esbjerg and arrived in Copenhagen on 13th May. They played the first of three games on

On the October holiday Monday, 1923, Peter Hodge returned to Stark's Park with his Leicester City team for Bill Collier's benefit match. Before the game, both teams and the respective officials lined up together to have the above photograph taken. Rovers team was : Brown, Inglis, Moyes, Barton, Morris, Collier, Bell, Miller, Hilley, James and Archibald. Leicester City fielded Hebden, Black, Osborne, Jones, O'Brien, Thomson, Tommy Duncan, Johnny Duncan, Chandler, Graham and Trotter. Adam Black was signed by Hodge from Bathgate, and went on to set the club record for appearances for Leicester. Mick O'Brien was an Irish internationalist and Willie Thomson was a former Clyde and Arthurlie wing half. There were four former Rovers players in the Leicester team ; Alex Trotter who had played twice in April 1917, Harry Graham who was inside right in the 1913 Scottish Cup Final team, and the Duncan brothers, Tommy and Johnny, who won a Scotland cap two years later. Centre forward was Arthur Chandler, a legendary scorer for City with 273 goals in 491 League and Cup appearances. He got on the scoresheet at Stark's Park - but so did George Miller, Con Hilley, Alex James, Bobby Archibald and a Black own goal as Rovers won 5-1.

The photograph which hangs on the wall of the Novar Bar in Nicol Street, wrongly attributed to the trip to the Canary Islands, was taken shortly after arrival in Denmark the year before. The above photograph was taken before one of the matches in Copenhagen.
Back row : Manager James H. Logan, Fred Lindsay, James Cowie, reserve goalkeeper Jimmy Mathieson, director David Hetherington and chairman Andrew G. Adamson.
Middle row : Trainer David Willis, Director William C. Ritchie, George Barton, Archie Morris, Jimmy Raeburn, Robert Bauld and director Robert Morrison.
Fron row : Dave Morris, Tom Jennings, Jimmy Brown, Bill Inglis, Bill Collier, John Slaven and Bobby Archibald.

Two instant clues as to the error made in the "Novar Bar" photograph is the absence of Alex James, who was not signed until later that year, and the presence of Bobby Archibald, who did not travel to the Canary Islands.
The photograph is reproduced on page 78 of Volume One of the pictorial history of the club, "Rovers Recalled".

Sunday May 14th – the club's first ever match on the Sabbath – and lost 3-1 in the Idraetsparken (the national football stadium) to B1903 Copenhagen (who merged with another club in 1992 to form the present FC Copenhagen).

A Danish newspaper reported that "Raith Rovers' play was disappointing, and showed that there exists a big gulf between the two leading Scottish teams, Celtic and Rangers, and other touring teams. The players were fast and strong, but they did not play the usual skilful ball-control, for which we admire the Scottish players. They played powerfully, perhaps too vigorously, and made the mistake – when defeat was in sight – to protest, by word and sign, against the referee's decisions.

"The passage across the North Sea had handicapped them physically, but this cannot excuse their unsportsman-like behaviour on the field of play. The halfbacks – Raeburn, D. Morris and Collier – were undoubtedly the backbone of the team. They are also reckoned as one of the best Scottish half-back lines. Collier is a Scottish internationalist, and he and Morris gave a very fine exhibition of head play.

"The defence, with robust tackling and long, clean kicking, was very strong and in the attack Archibald shone on the left wing, while Jennings dominated play on the other wing."

Another report, faithfully translated, said that "Raith Rovers didn't show their most brilliant side. They played very dirty, some of them. A. Morris and Collier were the worst. The latter was near to taking the life from Harry Hansen and should be been sent off." B1903 did not escape criticism, their persistent offside-trap making the game

boring, according to the reporter.

The Rovers party, which comprised fourteen players, four directors, manager and trainer, spent Monday sight-seeing, including the Stadium and the Circus. On Tuesday 16th, they beat a Copenhagen Select team 2-0 "with all effects of the voyage gone, Raith played a vastly improved game, and were applauded by the crowd for a smart victory." "The little Scot Archibald – an agile and strong guy with a set of crooked legs, who run in an enormous tempo …" was singled out as Rovers' danger man.

Two days later, however, they lost 3-1 to another Copenhagen select, all the goals coming in the second half. They arrived back at Liverpool Street Station in London on 22nd May.

Inevitably, Rovers success led to covetous glances from other clubs. The Duncan brothers were transferred to Leicester City during the summer of 1922, and there was a further blow after the first match of the season when Bill Inglis was injured and missed the first half of the campaign.

The losses were covered by the promotion of reserve right back Barton, Bobby Archibald moving from the left to the right wing, and Rutherglen Glencairn's Junior internationalist John Borland coming in at No.11. To replace the team's star player, John Duncan, George Miller and Eddie Brown were signed from Hearts. Miller, capped in a Victory international in 1919, proved to be a great success, but Brown was injured and had to retire at 21 years of age.

Much less heralded was the signature of several junior players, among them 19 year old Alex James who had played for north Glasgow junior side Ashfield between January and May 1922. With uncanny prescience he was described as "a veritable wizard on the ball," although he had a tendency for over indulgence at times. The Kirkcaldy Times on 4th October 1922, for example, reported : "James showed a tendency to over-do the trickery business against Motherwell and, on the whole, he non-plussed his own side as much as the visitors. His play was spectacular, but unprofitable."

Towards the end of September, it was announced that Rovers were introducing a gate for the unemployed, halving the normal admission price to 6d for the first team and 5d for the reserves. Tickets could be applied for from the local Labour Exchange.

Results were mixed during the early part of the season, although three successive League defeats in late October and early November brought about some overdue surgery to the team. James was brought in at inside right, having made half a dozen appearance at inside left earlier in the season, and been found wanting physically. Alex Gilmour, taller and sturdier, was signed from Roslyn Juniors and enjoyed an extended spell at inside left. Bobby Archibald was switched back to the left wing, and a succession of would-be right wingers were tried before Peter Bell was signed from Darlington (for the largest fee ever paid by Rovers, £1,100), his arrival coinciding with the return from injury of Bill Inglis.

The Kirkcaldy Times expressed many fans' sentiments when it wrote "Raith without Bill seems some how to be fundamentally wrong and lacks the necessary esprit de corps, which goes a long way towards success."

On 2nd December, the team's potential was displayed in a 4-0 win over the League leaders at Dens Park. On Saturday December 30th 1922, the new stand at Stark's Park was officially opened, and used for the first time, with Celtic the visitors in a League match. Despite Rovers having most of the play, they could not score, while Celtic scored every time they found the way to goal, somewhat fortuitously winning 3-0.

The new grandstand, built of brick, concrete and steel, transformed the appearance of Stark's Park, whose facilities were otherwise of a very rudimentary nature. The railway enclosure provided the only other cover, and a few hundred seats – everyone else had to stand, either round the pitch perimeter fence, or on the embankments behind both goals or on either side of the low structure below the railway. If it rained, most football fans stayed at home in front of the coal fire.

Two draws and a defeat (of Alloa Athletic), all at home, indicated an improvement in performance, which was underlined by a 1-0 win over the holders, Morton, at Stark's Park in the first round of the Scottish Cup. It was a well merited victory, with the half backs Raeburn, Morris and Collier outstanding. On 17th January, Moyes, Morris and Jennings played for the East of Scotland against the West in the International trial at Ibrox.

Raith Rovers andet Fodbold-Nederlag.

Det danske Hold sejrer. Skotterne har ikke spillet saa godt, som vi haabede.
En livlig anden Halvleg lastes med 4 Maal, deraf 3 i vor Favør.

SØNDAGENS SPORT

Fodboldkamp — Travløb

Den første dansk-skotske Fodboldkamp,

17,000 watched a poor game against Cowdenbeath in the second round, won 2-0, and after League victories over Hearts and Kilmarnock, the third round match at Second Division Dunfermline Athletic was won 3-0. The cup run came to an end in front of 31,000 at Celtic Park, Moyes putting the ball into his own net, although some newspapers credited McLean with the only goal of the game.

The following Saturday, Dave Morris missed the 2-1 defeat at Third Lanark as he was making his debut for Scotland in Belfast. He was back in his usual place the following Saturday when Rangers visited Stark's Park, Tom Jennings scoring twice without reply.

A final position of 9th in the First Division may have represented regression from the previous season, but there was a great deal to enjoy for Rovers fans, both from some splendid team performances and results, but more particularly from the high quality of the players on view every week.

The last six weeks of the season were dominated by local cup ties, and Rovers' capture of the Fife Cup was achieved in unusual circumstances. The semi final against East Fife at Stark's Park on Wednesday 11th April looked to be heading for a 0-0 draw when it was abandoned, in pitch darkness, with just six minutes remaining. The re-arranged game was also at Stark's Park, and Rovers won 4-0, in good light. The final at Cowdenbeath on 30th April was drawn 0-0, and the destination of the old trophy was decided by the number of corners won by the respective teams. A measure of the quality of the entertainment over the 120 minutes was that Rovers won by 1 corner to nil.

At the very end of the season, as if there hadn't been enough football for players and spectators alike, a Charity Cup competition was organised for Rovers and

Rovers were headline-makers in the Berlingske Tidende, then as now Denmark's leading newspaper, during their spell in the country. All three matches were the subject of lengthy match reports, illustrated by cartoons, two of which are reproduced below. The top one depicts Bobby Archibald and below that the "Skotske Trainer" is shown administering treatment to an injured player, in the rudimentary fashion of the day

Archibald laver Krumspring

PETER BELL

Duncan Menzies died at his home in Links Street (aged "well over 70") on January 27th 1923. He was the first President of the club. His son, David Menzies, became a regular in the left side forward positions of the Rovers team in 1895 and 1896. He played for Cowdenbeath and Kirkcaldy United before moving to Bradford City. After a six year spell as City trainer, he moved to Hull City and became their manager in 1916. In 1921 he started a five year spell as Bradford City manager, then had a long spell in charge of Doncaster Rovers. He was Hull City manager again for most of 1936, and died in service on 11th October 1936. Hull City and Bradford City were regular opponents for Rovers in Benefit matches, at home and in England, during Menzies' management of those clubs.

Kirkcaldy Times 9th August 1922 : "Previous to his departure for Leicester, "Tokey" Duncan, the ex-Raith forward, was married at Dunfermline. "Tokey" will be missed at Cowdenbeath, where he has shipped many winning whippets."

A Trialist outside right broke his leg in the Public Trial in 1922, and Rovers held collections at the first home matches of the season, raising £39 15/2 and £28 10/1d

East Fife to play home and away. Rovers won the first leg at Stark's Park by 2-0, but the Kirkcaldy Times was less charitable than the cause. "There was plenty of the "parlour" style in the play. While it amused the spectators at first, it latterly became stale. Towards the end it was very apparent that it takes a real hard contest to sustain the interest throughout." East Fife won 2-1 at Bayview. In a painful irony, McPherson of the home team broke his leg and ended up in the hospital which was the beneficiary of the match.

Following the success of the Danish tour of the previous summer, Rovers embarked on a trip to the Canary Islands on 28th June aboard the Highland Loch (7493 tons), which also carried a cargo of chilled meat along with other passengers bound for Buenos Aires. Having rounded Cape Finisterre in thick fog late on the evening of 30th June, the passengers were rudely wakened at 8am by the sound of the ship hitting a notorious rock, 'La Piedra de Amorosa.'

Subsequent accounts talk of heroism amongst the players in helping women and children abandon ship, but the truth is that the ship's boats were quickly and efficiently put into the shallow waters and then towed to the nearest ports by Spanish fishing boats. Captain Dave Morris recorded : "There was not the slightest sign of panic, and the rescuing of the passengers and crew was affected in less than a quarter of an hour, in spite of the vessel's very dangerous position."

Some of the boats made the four hour trip to Villagarcia, others to Correbedo. Those which landed at the former endured a most uncomfortable night in inhospitable accommodation, to the extent that many of the players preferred to roam the streets of the shanty town before continuing their journey on RMSP Darro, to Las Palmas, via Leixoes, Lisbon and Madeira. They did not reach Grand Canaria until 7th July. The Highland Loch, in the meantime, had been floated at high tide and limped into Vigo with Hold Number 2 flooded.

The following day, Rovers played mainland team Real Vigo at 5pm, who were also touring the islands, and beat them 3-1. Tom Jennings opened the scoring from the penalty spot in five minutes, followed by a goal from Alex James on the half hour. Vigo got a goal back from the penalty spot early in the second half, and an own goal by one of their full backs completed the scoring. Rovers players could hardly blame the referee – it was Bill Inglis, in the absence of a local official.

The main concern was the pitch, a converted bull ring which measured just 98 x 60 yards. It comprised soft, uneven sand and there was a pronounced slope. The locals, encouraged by fiercely partisan spectators, did not spare the boot.

Over the next fortnight, Rovers played – and won - five more games, beating Real Vigo by the only goal of the match, and then local teams Porteno 4-0, Gran Canaria

4-1, Victoria 2-0 and Marino 2-1.

On returning to Kirkcaldy on 31st July, manager James Logan made light of the newsworthy "shipwreck" and concentrated on the playing standards they found in the Canary Islands. "One thing in which they were deficient as regards equipment was the boots they played in. These were of the finest material, soft as a glove, and certainly they could not shoot with the same power as Rovers.

"As a matter of fact the shooting of Jennings simply electrified the spectators who were accustomed to seeing their home players endeavour to walk the ball into the net on every occasion." Jenning scored eleven goals on tour, including all five against Gran Canaria.

"They found it was impossible to part with the ball other than with the toe, which was their invariable custom. James they presented as 'Baby' on account of his diminutive stature but they went crazy over his cleverness on the ball. Another great favourite both on and off the field was James Brown, the goalkeeper. He was followed by crowds every other day and it was wonderful how he could make himself understood."

The players on tour were Brown, Inglis, McDougall, Barton, Morris, Collier, Hilley, Bell, Miller, Jennings, James, Ritchie and Cowie. Outside left Bobby Archibald was absent ; he was guesting with his former club Third Lanark, with whom he still trained, on a three-month tour of Argentina.

Alex Cowie, then a reserve player, made the trip in the absence of regular first team players Davie Moyes, who preferred to stay at home, Archibald and Jimmy Raeburn, who was a part-timer and could not get away from work. Writing sixty years after the incident, Cowie recalled :

"The pitch was on a par with the old Glasgow Junior grounds, baked earth, no grass and a single bar fence hugging the touchlines. The dressing room facility was poor so we changed in our hotel which backed onto the beach half way between the Port and town of Gran Canaria."

There was no raid on the Rovers squad over the summer of 1923, and little wonder. Large crowds meant that the players could be paid handsome wages, the equal of most at other Scots club and comparable with all but the First Division in England, where the "maximum wage" was in operation. It was therefore a familiar, and settled team, which opened the 1923/24 season by beating Dundee 3-0 in front of 18,000 at Stark's Park.

The defence was sound, the half backs resolute and the forwards at times irresistible. After fourteen League games, Rovers were one point (and a game in hand) behind second placed Airdrie, and five points behind leaders Rangers. A 14 days (two match) suspension handed out to Alex James by the SFA had little effect on results. James was ordered off in the 1-1 draw at Motherwell, having scored Rovers goal, and suffered the same fate a week later in the 3-0 home win over Falkirk at Stark's Park. He missed the 2-1 win at Kilmarnock and the 1-1 draw at home to Hearts, Con Hilley who had a year earlier been regarded as the likely replacement for John Duncan, proving to be an able deputy.

A couple of injuries disrupted the team towards the end of the year. Bill Collier was absent from early December, and played fitfully from late January to the end of the season. Jimmy Brown was injured during the second half of the League match at Airdrie on 29th December, finishing the game at outside left with Barton, himself deputising for the injured Inglis, going into goal. Jimmy Mathieson, the reserve goalkeeper, took over for the remaining League matches, although Brown was patched up for the cup ties.

In retrospect, the decision to abandon the reserve team, concentrating the finances on paying the full timers in the first team, proved to be a short term expedient. Stark's Park was occupied on alternate Saturdays by Dunnikier Colliery Juniors, Willie Reekie's Abbotshall team having one of its periodic spells in Juvenile football, for the want of a suitable ground.

Despite a 2-1 New Year's Day victory over Clyde, the next four league games brought just one point, and although Rovers remained highly placed in the League table, thoughts turned to Scottish Cup glory. Broxburn United were routinely beaten 3-0 at Stark's Park in the third round, and a battling 0-0 draw at Dens Park brought Dundee back to Stark's Park on the afternoon of Wednesday, 13th February. There was huge interest in the tie, won by a Peter Bell goal, and illustrated by a news report in the Kirkcaldy Times a fortnight later.

"Kirkcaldy School Management Committee meeting on Monday had brought to their attention that Abbotshall School had been closed at 2.30 on Wednesday 13th February [the match kicked off at 2.45]. Mr J.L. Hall, headmaster, wrote that the hours had been re-arranged during that day because of the football and "the likelihood of a big number of pupils absenting themselves in the afternoon. The result of the arrangement was that no pupil present in the morning was absent in the afternoon, so that the method taken had the object of preventing absenteeism …" the object he had in view. Other schools, in contrast, reported absentees that afternoon. The explanation tendered by the headmaster of Abbotshall School was accepted, and the matter was allowed to drop."

The draw for the third round brought St Bernards to Stark's Park. It also paired Rangers and Hibs ; Celtic had been beaten at Kilmarnock in the first round and of course Dundee had also been ousted. Rovers, sixth top of the First Division had only to overcome St Bernards, fifth bottom of the Second Division and 30 places below them in the League ladder, and they would be one of the highest placed teams in the quarter finals (in fact Rangers lost to Hibs at Ibrox). It wasn't so much the cup tie that was responsible for

stratospheric expectations in the town, but the prospect of greater glory thereafter. The fans truly believed that this would be the year that the Scottish Cup would come to Kirkcaldy.

They should have known better.

The 1-0 St Bernards victory was one of the biggest cup shocks of all time (Berwick Rangers, when they beat Rangers in 1967, were "only" 26 places below their visitors, for example). As has happened since, the conspiracy theorists had a field day in explaining the unexpected reversal, at the same time searching for a rational explanation for the dashing of huge expectations. On this occasion, the rumour was that no bonus was on offer to the players, such was the lowly status of their opponents. To compensate, the players arranged to bet on, and play for, a draw, and take care of St Bernards in the replay. An uncharacteristic slip by Morris let Young in to score for the visitors, which wasn't in the script. The forwards, mentally attuned to a 0-0 draw, couldn't conjure up an equaliser, and the match, progression in the cup and, allegedly, the bookies' money, was lost.

One common, characteristic of all these "rumours" over the decades, is that they feature the parsimony of the Rovers' management in offering no, or inadequate, bonuses to players ; another is that there is usually no substance to the rumours. The fickle fortunes of football are accepted by supporters only when they are favourable – when they are adverse, a logical explanation is required, and where non exists, it will be concocted from fevered imagination.

The "what might have been" regrets of players and supporters alike were magnified by the team winning five and drawing two of the next seven League matches, including a 2-1 win at Tynecastle (Alex James scoring twice), and 1-0 victories over both Old Firm teams on successive Saturdays in March, James scoring on both occasions. The five points dropped in the last three League matches of the season would have seen Celtic overtaken in third place, but still well short of champions Rangers, and a putative two behind runners up (and cup winners) Airdrie. Fourth place remained a marvellous achievement, but 1923/24 will always be remembered for what might have been, in the Scottish Cup.

Another legacy – and another myth – from that season was that Millwall, then a Third Division South team, had offered £50,000 for the entire Rovers forward line of Bell, Miller, Jennings, James and Archibald. In modern terms, taking a 1/- admission in 1924 and converting it to a £20 admission to a

Reserve team goalkeeper The Reverend John H. McKenzie chose the right day to make his only first team appearance of 1924/25, at home to Aberdeen on 6th December ; the team had its photograph taken that day.

Left back David Moyes, right half Jimmy Raeburn and centre forward Tom Jennings were all still at the club, but, like goakeeper Jimmy Mathieson, were absent for the visit of Aberdeen.

Gone from the club, however, were goalkeeper Jimmy Brown, Bill Inglis, Bill Collier and Bobby Bauld.

George Barton replaced Inglis at right back and proved to be a worthy successor, and a good servant to the club.

Outside left Alex Ritchie proved to be a more than useful replacement for Bobby Archibald, and formed a potent left wing partnership with the increasingly outstanding Alex James. Before the end of September 1925, however, James signed for Preston North End, and Ritchie moved into the inside forward positions, where he remained until the summer of 1928, when he signed for Blackpool. He later played for Reading, Watford, Bournemouth, Third Lanark, Hibs and Albion Rovers, and became manager of Third Lanark immediately after the Second World War.

The players photographed were : Back row, Dave Morris, Walter Marchbank, George Barton, John McKenzie, James Innes, George Chapman.

Front row : Peter Bell, Jimmy Neish, George Miller, Alex James, Alex Ritchie.

George Miller left for Hearts in January 1925 and within a year Morris had joined James at Deepdale

ALEX JAMES

The star player of the Arsenal team which dominated English football in the mid 1930s, it is scarcely an exaggeration to claim that Alex James was the world's greatest footballer at the peak of his remarkable career.
Born and brought up in very humble circumstances in Orbiston, in the heart of industrial Lanarkshire, his early prowess in junior football was spotted by Rovers' goalkeeper Jimmy Brown, who alerted director Bob Morrison.
He in turn championed the cause of the small, scrawny ragamuffin within the Stark's Park management, and took him under his wing when James moved to Kirkcaldy. This kindness was rewarded when James blossomed into an influential forward who stood out in First Division fixtures. He married the daughter of club trainer Dave Willis, and moved to Preston North End for a substantial fee in 1925. By the time Herbert Chapman signed him for Arsenal four years later, he was a Scottish internationalist (and one of the Wembley Wizards). At Arsenal, he won four League championship medals and two FA Cup winners medals, his performance against Huddersfield Town in the 1930 final being one of the best ever seen at Wembley.
He was truly one of the greatest footballers in the long history of the game.

Premier League match in 2008, the equivalent sum is £20 million, which renders that particular rumour as a gross exaggeration. In fact, when the five players came to be sold, piecemeal, over the next three years, the total sum raised was £7,350 or £3 million in 2008 terms.

The breakup of the great team of the early 1920s started in the summer of 1924, although the club's management could hardly be condemned for the sale of the first three players. The two Bills, Collier and Inglis, both left for Sheffield Wednesday for £500 and £250 respectively, and outside left Bobby Archibald, who lived in Glasgow and trained with Third Lanark, who signed him for £300. Two of the three were in, or nearing, the veteran class, at 34, 27 and 29 respectively, and the fairly modest fees received helped towards servicing the substantial debt taken on by the construction of the grandstand. In theory, their replacements were sound ; George Barton at right back, Con Hilley at left half, and Alex Ritchie on the wing. Jimmy Mathieson had supplanted the veteran Jimmy Brown in goal, but the core of the team remained ; Moyes at left back, Raeburn and Morris at half back, Bell and Miller on the right wing, and the two jewels in attack, Tom Jennings and Alex James.

David Moyes was described as "not a back of the showy type ; wholeheartedness and a tenacious tackler. He is a club man of high merit, and his resourcefulness has often saved Raith when in a tight corner. He is a man who does not believe in taking unnecessary risks, soundness and decisive clearing of his lines appealing to him more than display."

The Kirkcaldy Times anticipated matters thus : "Raith Rovers will be represented this season by a team which should be able to travel some, as the Yanks would say. All their heavy guns have been transferred. This, however, may be a disadvantage at times. There is not a Kirkcaldy man on the side now, by the way." Mathieson and Moyes were Fifers, however.

Anticipation in the town was nonetheless keen. "Raith's super supporter, who locates himself in the stand every Saturday, has been resting his voice all summer" … apparently to little avail after the first three League games of the 1924/25 season ; a 3-0 defeat at Ibrox, a 1-1 draw at home to Queen's Park and a 1-0 defeat at Hamilton. The team had sufficient quality to get back on track, although their best form was reserved for the second half of the season. Injuries were accommodated by judicious shuffling of the team, usually the inside forwards and wing half, the "spare man" being George Chapman, signed during the summer from Hearts, followed by Jimmy Miller (from Maryhill Juniors) later in the season.

On 6th December, Mathieson missed the match at home to Aberdeen through injury, and he was replaced by former Dunnikier Juniors' goalkeeper, the Reverend John H. McKenzie, who followed Tom

Snoddy's earlier example in swapping dog collar for dog house with his every mistake in the critical eyes of the supporters.

A 2-2 draw at home to Celtic on 27th December heralded an improvement in results, with just one defeat in the next eleven matches. That was at home to Hamilton on 3rd January, and it was Accies who ended Rovers' Scottish Cup hopes by winning 1-0 at Douglas Park in the third round. Once again, a good performance in a losing cup tie was fatally spoiled by a failure to take chances. There had been a scare in the previous round, Second Division Bo'ness drawing 0-0 at Stark's Park before a Tom Jennings hat-trick won the replay 3-1, and the first round hurdle of Clackmannan (beaten 3-0 at Stark's Park during which there was a solar eclipse) was negiotiated with more ease once the opponents had been induced to give up ground rights.

There was the by now customary tailing off of results towards the end of the season, but ninth place was nothing to be ashamed of, and irrespective of results, every Saturday brought the prospect of enjoying the play of Morris, James, and their stalwart team-mates.

Not Tom Jennings, however. He was sold to Leeds United for £3,000 in early March, quite a return on a £10 fee paid to his junior club. His departure was not unexpected. On 7th January the Kirkcaldy Times reported that "The centre forward has been rquested to find lodgings in Kirkcaldy in order to be training with his clubmates instead of doing his preparatory work elsewhere. Jennings does not relish the idea of residing in the Lang Toun." A month later, he was training at Celtic Park.

The Kirkcaldy Times reported little consolation for Rovers fans mourning the transfer of the remarkably prolific goalscorer. "If half the rumours that are flying around Kirkcaldy are true, it seems that Raith Rovers will soon be transferring half of their players."

Warning signs familiar to successive generations of Rovers fans were beginning to appear in the newspapers ; reports of the success of former players in English League football, and with major Scots clubs. George Miller was thriving at Hearts, and the Sheffield Wednesday v Leicester City match saw pre-match pleasantries exchanged by the respective captains who would be more than familiar to Rovers' fans, Bill Inglis and John Duncan. History has shown that the rising quantity and quality of ex-players plying their trade at a high level eventually tells on the standard of those who remain behind, and more pertinently those who inadequately replace the departed.

At least the reserve team had been re-formed, with Johnny Rattray re-signed in early November to be player coach in that side.

The major change in the summer of 1925 was not at Stark's Park, but in the football's legislative chambers. The offside law, which previously required three players between a forward and the goal to play him onside, was changed to two players, thereby releasing a player for deployment further upfield. There was an explosion in goal scoring as a consequence, but not, sadly, in the Rovers' "goals for" column.

There was no apparent cause for concern as the team, minus the temporarily injured Alex James, beat Dundee United 4-2 on the opening day of the new League season.

George Barton was injured before August was out, causing David Frame to move to full back with Willie Deuchars coming into the side. More significantly, Alex James was signed by Preston North End on 22nd September and the team was constantly reshuffled to cover for his loss. James followed his father-in-law out of Kirkcaldy ; Rovers trainer Dave Willis resigned on July 6th to take up a post at Nottingham Forest

Hard as it was to imagine, there was worse to come. Scotland captain Dave Morris joined James at Preston North End on 22nd December, the bank manager, if not the fans, consoled by a cheque for £4,800.

A perilous League position by the end of November provoked the signings of Hamilton Accies' experienced centre forward Allan Brown, outside right George Reay and inside left William Allison, both from Kettering Town (whose player manager was Bill Collier) and centre half Walter Marchbanks from Clydebank. As so often happens with clubs in decline, not only were the new recruits no match for those they replaced, but the club's recruitment system was increasingly considered to be incompetent. On October 10th 1925, the Fife Free Press remarked that "Wellesley [Juniors] have unearthed a champion goalkeeper in Thomson, from Bowhill. He is just a youngster yet, but should develop." Not with Rovers, sadly. To save money, the Reserve team was abandoned in October, Hibs taking over their fixtures in the Alliance League.

The breaks were also going against the club. Centre forward John Slavin had been "loaned" to Arbroath as he had been unable to dislodge Jennings from the first eleven. Rovers recalled him, and there was some delay while the SFA sorted out the registration technicalities to their satisfaction, during October. The Scottish Football League was not so accommodating. On December 2nd, Slavin was declared to be an Arbroath player until the end of the season, having been transferred by Rovers during the close season, despite the SFA regarding him a Raith Rovers player. The club was fined 25 guineas plus expenses, James Logan was fined 10 guineas and severely censured, and Mr R. McGlashan, the Arbroath secretary was fined 5 guineas and severely censured. At the end of the saga, Rovers were severely out of pocket, and Slavin was transferred by Arbroath, to join George Miller at Hearts, in late December.

Just to rub it in for the suffering Rovers fans, Alex James won his first Scotland cap in Cardiff less than two months after leaving for Preston. He was partnered in

attack by John Duncan. One was moved to write to the Kirkcaldy Times : "Having been associated with the Club as a supporter, member of committee and a director, I may say that one of the best members of committee and a director was a working man who admitted he had no knowledge of business, but I may say that his knowledge of football and football players from A to Z was amazing. I refer to the late respected John Cairns who was associated with the club. Men of his type are urgently required if we are not to have another second league team in Fife next season." D.S.

The message was clear, and has rung out over succeeding decades ; business acumen alone in the boardroom does not bring success to a football club. A knowledge of football, and footballers, is a more relevant attribute. The Kirkcaldy Times of 6th January reinforced the message, from a different angle. "Raith Rovers have made a good deal over the transfers, and their supporters are looking to them getting a strong side together again. It is certainly better to make money by drawing the crowds than by creating transferring "stars"."

The criticism was relentless. Every week there were accounts of former players and their great deeds with their new clubs. Jim McClelland had been transferred to Southend United in 1923 and was scoring goals aplenty for Middlesbrough, including five in a cup tie against Tom Jennings' Leeds United.

Inside right Alex Ritchie, who lost his place to Walter Grant in the Rovers first team, was transferred to Dunfermline Athletic in early March. On 24th March, the Kirkcaldy Times reported : "Ritchie has been a great success since he joined Dunfermline Athletic. It is curious how Raith players improve when they leave Stark's Park. McClelland Middlesbrough, Bauld Dundee United, Borland Hamilton Accies and Wright East Fife [sold to Cowdenbeath for £1000 in April] are among the forwards given free transfers by Raith Rovers in recent years. Couldn't they do with them all back now ?"

A week later and the Times noted : "It may be interesting to note that the Juvenile matches in the Beveridge Park are benefiting greatly through Raith's poor displays lately, and at a recent match the number of spectators was estimated at about 2,000."

Rovers' shock relegation at the end of 1925/26 was followed by an equalled unexpected immediate return to the top division, having finished second to champions Bo'ness.

At the end of the season, the Fife Free Press arranged to photograph the successful team, and published a very small and grainy photograph in their edition of 30th April 1927.

The quality of the photograph has not been improved by its further reproduction above, and the shadowy figures are :

Back row : Dave Clunie (Trainer), David McCaig, William Allison, Sidney Jarvis, James Muir, James Porter, Hugh Todd, George Barton and Director William Ferguson.

Middle row : Alex Ritchie, George Reay, John McNeil, John Pitcairn, Owen Dorrans, Tommy Turner and manager George Wilson.

In front, Jimmy Cowie and Tommy Batchelor.

Barton, Ritchie, Pitcairn, Dorrans and Turner all served the club for several seasons, but the remainder of the first team pool were not at Stark's Park for long, and there was a steady turnover of players of the next couple of seasons as the club sought to hang on to its cherished membership of the top division.

On 2nd November 1926, following the Denbeath Star v Wellesley junior match at Den Park, Celtic signed the Wellesley goalkeeper, 18 year old John Thomson. Rovers were also credited with an interest in the player, but took no action to sign him.

GEORGE MILLER

JOHN PITCAIRN

OWEN DORRAN S
A well-pixelated photo - no reflection on his personal habits - but photos of the wing half during his playing career have proved to be elusive

1925 Kirkcaldy War Memorial opened on 27th June, and in the same year the Museum and Art Gallery was opened ; Rialto Cinema opened ; automatic telephones were installed in Kirkcaldy 1926 Nairn's North factory at Den Road completed ; Tennis pavilion built in Beveridge Park

Rovers went into 1926 in joint second bottom position with Hibs, but the second half of the season brought only four victories, and one of those was in the Scottish Cup. The second round defeat at Greenock was not helped by centre forward Brown being sent off for disputing a refereeing decision.

Six successive defeats from early March included a 5-1 thumping at Hearts which summed up a dismal season, goalkeeper Mathieson being carried off the field midway through the first half with a suspected broken ankle. A fortuitous point at Aberdeen on the penultimate Saturday of the season gave Rovers a chance to escape relegation, provided they beat mid-table Queen's Park at home in the last match. Despite a goal from the ever-reliable captain David Moyes in a fighting performance, Rovers lost 2-1, and suffered the first relegation in their history. Although four points better off than bottom club Clydebank, they were two behind both Dundee United and St Johnstone, and safety.

There was further bad news for the football fraternity of the town in late May, when Abbotshall Juveniles lost the second replay of the final of the Scottish Juvenile Cup to Springburn.

In mid-May 1925, both manager Logan and trainer Willie Smith resigned from their posts. In the immediate aftermath of relegation, Logan was quoted as saying : "It is unspeakable. You can't do other than sympathise with the boys. Luck was dead against them. It certainly puts us in a bit of a hole, but we'll fight out of it, by hook or by crook !" On the showing of the defeat against Queen's Park, Rovers manager did not think that they were a team that deserved a fate such as relegation. "Misfortune has been the main cause over the season" proved to be his valediction. Four months later, it was announced that James H Logan had purchased the Airlie Arms Hotel in Kirriemuir. Smith became Reading's trainer.

Three weeks after Logan's departure George Wilson, the former Rovers, Hearts, Newcastle and Scotland outside left, and who had been a shopkeeper in Kirkcaldy High Street since returning from America, where he had managed the Falls River Club to successive American League championships, was appointed Raith Rovers manager.

There were wholesale changes to the team for Rovers' return to the Second Division after 17 years, the full timers quite naturally looking for another billet as the club reverted to part-time status . David Moyes was sold to Leicester for £500, and Walter Grant joined Con Hilley at Crystal Palace.

Only right back George Barton, right back Willie Deuchars, and forwards George Reay, Willie Allison, Owen Dorrans, Tommy Turner and Tommy Batchelor, remained. New signings included goalkeeper George Nisbet from Ayr United, full back Thomas Crickett from St Rochs, left half Hugh Todd from Falkirk and centre forward John Taylor from Bristol City.

The Kirkcaldy Times of 18th August reported that "six keen Roverites walked from Kirkcaldy to Stirling, a distance of 35 miles, on Saturday to see Raith's initiation into the Second Division. At Stirling they were spotted by the Rovers captain, who made a whip round, with the result that the valiant six were enabled to see the game, and follow it with a hearty tea, after which they were given a lift home in the charabanc." The tea would have consoled them in defeat, 3-2 to King's Park.

Jimmy Porter, the former Rosslyn Juniors and Dundee United defender, was signed and East Fife, Arbroath and St Bernards were defeated in succession, propelling Rovers to the top of the League. The 5,000 crowd for the St Bernards match (which was won 5-1) was very respectable, but they read in their Sunday newspapers the following day that there were no fewer than five ex Rovers players in the Middlesbrough v Preston match, James and Morris, Mathieson, McClelland and Birrell.

Rovers' finances were not helped by yet another fine imposed by the football authorities, this time in connection with the transfer of Peter Bell to Manchester City on 18th September. Bell had been placed on the transfer list at £500, and Rovers transgression by accepting more than that figure ; £325 more, to be precise, from Manchester City manager Peter Hodge. The intention was that Bell was to get the £325, but the League refused to give permission, and the money had not been paid to the player. The Scottish Football League fined Rovers £320, almost the excessive amount received by Rovers, which meant that the player received nothing from the deal, despite acknowledgement of several years of splendid service to Raith Rovers. Manchester City were also big losers ; it was quickly discovered that Bell no longer possessed the speed necessary for Second Divison football south of the border.

League results were not at all bad ; there were several sub-standard teams in the Division, and Rovers took full advantage of their deficiencies, beating Albion Rovers 7-1 and Queen of the South 7-2, and on successive Saturdays the home crowd saw Dumbarton beaten 4-2 and Stenhousemuir 4-0.

Memories of better players, and a higher league, were still fresh for supporters, and the local press. On 3rd November, the Kirkcaldy Times attacked on three fronts. "Fancy Raith Rovers giving a month's trial to Allan Brown ! Was he not well enough tried last year !" "While Raith Rovers are drawing poor gates at home, they are proving attractive visitors to most grounds." "The Raith Rovers directors have had to become stricter with some of their players who live out of Kirkcaldy, as some of them are showing lack of sufficient training."

After a great deal of discussion in the town, and in the letters pages of its newspapers, on 3rd November 1926 the inaugural meeting of the Raith Rovers Supporters Club was held at the Beveridge Halls. About 500 attended and Councillor

David Simpson, a former Director of the Football Club, presided. The Kirkcaldy Times reported : "Mr William Grieve, one of the originators of the club, stated that at no time was the Supporters Club more necessary than today." He pointed out that Supporters Clubs had been developed in England to question and challenge the Boards of Directors of Football Clubs. "With such an enthusiastic start the future of the Club is extremely bright, and if the same spirit is maintained much benefit should be derived from their meetings."

On 23rd November, the second meeting of the Supporters Club appointed a committee. Chairman was Councillor David Simpson, Vice Chairman William Grieve, Treasurer Andrew Heggie, Secretary Lindsay Morgan. The Committee included Alex Sunter, J. Sim, H. Heggie, David Deas, A. Terris and two well known former Rovers players of the same name, James A. Gourlay of Balfour Street, and James M. Gourlay of the Schoolhouse, Auchtertool. More of the last named later in this book !

In January, it was reported that "The Raith Rovers Supporters Club were not enamoured of the suggestion from the Rovers directorate with regard to the inauguration of a junior club with Stark's Park as its headquarters. This proposal was rejected, it being felt that the junior clubs in the district were none too well supported as it is, and that it would be better if they received home support. Senior football is the only type which pays in Kirkcaldy". This has certainly proved to be the case over the ensuing decades, and the reputation of the junior game was not helped the following May when the Fife Junior Cup Final between Wellesley and Rosslyn at Factory Park was abandoned after 85 minutes, with Wellesley leading 4-0 – because the ball burst.

There was certainly no lack of criticism of how the club was being run, nor lack of specific advice, such as that offered in the Kirkcaldy Times on 24th November. "Raith Rovers among other senior clubs were represented at the Scottish Junior Cup tie at Dunnikier Park. Willie Imrie, the powerful right half of Dunnikier, was the attraction, and he was the outstanding player on the field. Are Raith Rovers to allow this clever player to go somewhere else, or are they afraid of the White Form ?" Yes on both questions, unfortunately. Imrie signed for St Johnstone and later played for Scotland. It was also pointed out that since the war, 15 players had been transferred by Raith Rovers to English football.

Three away matches in December brought three defeats, followed by six successive victories in the League, a sequence interrupted by a very disappointing 4-2 defeat at Forfar in the first round of the Scottish Cup.

James Cowie had been signed from Keith in October and claimed the centre forward position. He was joined in attack in December by Miller of Hamilton Accies, and just before Christmas, Sidney Jarvis "a tall

RAITH ROVERS F.C. 1927-28.

and hefty youth" was yet another signing from Kettering Town. At 13 stone and 6' 1", he was an imposing figure at that time when cynical fans believed that Rovers' recruitment policy was confined to malnourished midgets.

Following the Cup defeat at Forfar, Rovers lost only one of their next 13 league matches, clinching promotion with a 6-3 victory over East Stirling at Stark's Park on 16th April, with two matches to spare. Bo'ness finished seven points ahead and were champions.

Despite the somewhat unexpected return to the top division, tensions remained high around the club's directorate. The local newspapers reported on a dispute with the Supporters Club at the end of May. The Football Club stated that they would not recognise the Supporters Club as long as Mr David Simpson (Chairman) and William Grieve (Vice Chairman) were in office. It was alleged that they had asked East Fife directors to stand against the Rovers Chairman, A.G. Adamson, for election to the SFA. The move to expel Grieve was defeated 38-17 at a Supporters Club meeting, but Simpson resigned, to be replaced by Mr J.A. Gourlay. Two months later, the other James Gourlay (the headmaster) was co-opted to the Raith Rovers Board of Directors. There was no doubting the growing strength and influence of the Supporters Club ; a matter of months after their foundation, they had a membership of 333 and a credit balance of over £212.

The season of Second Division football, albeit successful, cost Rovers £2404 as an operating loss. Manager Wilson was forced to strengthen his squad for the forthcoming challenge of the First Division, on the cheap.

The backbone of the team remained with the club ; goalkeeper Jimmy Muir, George Barton at right back, Deuchars, Pitcairn and Batchelor at half back, and up front George Reay, Owen Dorrans, Cowie, Allison and 'Tucker' Turner. The new signings did little to inflame the expectations of supporters ; Alex Bain from Fraserburgh, John Syme from West Calder, Arthur Pigg from Carlisle and Robert Crinean from Cambuslang Rangers. Centre forward Pigg

The Rovers team in 1927/28 was photographed and "presented free with the Compliments of the Brewers of Aitken's Championship Ales", who were a familiar advertiser in football club programmes in the late 1940s and early 1950s.

Rovers lined up : Back row, Johnny Beith, William Allison, James Muir, Alex Ritchie and Tommy Batchelor. Front row, George Barton, John Pitcairn, Willie Birrell, David McCaig, William Graham and Albert Pigg.

A late run propelled the team to safety from relegation and the significant player throughout the season was centre forward Albert Pigg, who scored 22 goals in 27 League matches. The next highest goalscorers (Willie Allison and Tommy Turner) scored six apiece.

The big Durham-born centre forward had been signed from Carlisle United, and after two seasons at Stark's Park he left for Barnsley

1927 Dunnikier Colliery closed 1927 Gladney House, birthplace of the famous architect Robert Adam in the Links,, was demolished

Fife Free Press 11th August 1927. "The Refreshment Bar at Stark's Park is now under new management. J & H Law will provide all refreshments at moderate prices."

1928 The Beveridge Library was transferred to the War Memorial complex.

ALEX RITCHIE

WILLIE DEUCHARS

TOMMY TURNER

was the only one to hold down a first team place, starting well with two goals in the 4-2 victory at Airdrie in the opening match of 1927/28.

It was a false dawn ; the next four League matches were lost.   Outside right Johnny Beath was signed from Anstruther Rangers in early October and went straight into the team.   A month later, Billy Birrell returned from Middlesbrough (as part of the deal which took left back Jarvis to Ayresome Park) and helped the side to a sequence of four unbeaten matches, including a 4-0 win at Dunfermline.   A week later, Rovers came back down to earth with a bump, losing 8-1 at Hampden, followed by a more understandable 3-2 defeat at Easter Road.

Manager George Wilson fell on his sword, resigning "on account of his health which he finds is unequal to the strain entailed by his duties", and was replaced by Billy Birrell, whose response was to draft in new players.   Bill McAllister had arrived from Queens Park Rangers, Jack Leckie was signed from Alloa to replace Muir in goal, David Hopewell of Cowdenbeath replaced Willie Graham, who had replaced Jarvis, at left back ; 20 year old Matt Hoggan was signed from Grange Rovers and made occasional appearances at centre half, and David Galloway from Wellesley Juniors was progressively introduced at inside left, burdened by the weight of expectation as 'the next Alex James'.

Part of the funding for these changes came from some enterprise on behalf of the Board, as announced in the Kirkcaldy Times on 9th November.   "Raith Rovers have for some time being doing their utmost to enlist the sympathies of local business men and it was officially announced that Messrs Barry, Ostlere & Shepherd had taken out a substantial hording in the grandstand."

A couple of draws gave encouragement in early January, as did an excellent 4-3 victory over Aberdeen at Stark's Park in the first round of the Scottish Cup.   A 2-2 draw at Motherwell in the second round had Rovers fans dreaming of Cup glory, but the replay was lost 2-1.   A 5-0 defeat at home to Hearts the following Saturday put Rovers in second bottom place, with Dunfermline a comforting distance below.   The next five games were lost, with only two goals scored, amid some desperate short-term signings in an attempt to stave off relegation.   Robert Kennedy of Falkirk, James Munro of St Johnstone and Jimmy Smith of Hearts were all brought in, although it was the youngsters Galloway and Turner who were the team's best players.

A home match against stranded Dunfermline on 24th March offered some solace, and an opportunity to make up the 5 point gap on the third bottom club.   Rovers grasped the life-line, winning 5-1 with Albert Pigg contributing a hat-trick.   He scored twice more to earn an unexpected 2-1 victory at Dens Park, and there was delight in holding Rangers to a 0-0 draw on the April holiday Monday.

The new manager's wholesale signings were having an effect, and two more victories, 1-0 at home to Queen's Park (Pigg again) and 3-0 at home to Hibs (Pigg 2 and Smith) hauled Rovers out of the relegation zone, but only one point ahead of Hamilton Accies and Bo'ness.   Safety was achieved by extending the unbeaten run to the end of the season, a hitherto unimaginable seven matches, with a 1-1 draw at Shawfield, and an improbable 3-0 victory at Celtic Park.   Rovers stayed up thanks to those last three points, concluding one of the greatest escape acts in the club's entire history.

On Monday May 28 before 2000 spectators at Stark's Park, a Barry, Ostere & Shepherd Select beat Nederlandsche Linoleum Fabriek 4-2 in a match refereed by Rovers manager Willie Birrell.   The return fixture in Kronmenje took place in July, but before that, serious matters were under discussion at the Rovers Annual General Meeting on 21st June 1928.

"Mr J. Bogie in his remarks before a fair muster of shareholders, took a rather serious view of the financial position of the club and expressed keen disappointment at the lack of financial support and assistance from the business people of the High Street – people who, he maintained benefited materially by the influx of football crowds, and people who had been appealed to for assistance and had failed to come forward., He maintained that it became a problem as to whether provincial clubs could continue to provide first League football without support in that direction.   He pointed out that the adverse financial position precluded the possibility of running an 'A' team next season, but hoped that that would only be a temporary measure."

The Rovers Directors could not be criticised for their fund-raising efforts.   In late March, the possibility of laying out a Greyhound Track at Stark's Park was advanced.   A deputation from a greyhound syndicate thought that the ground could be adapted for their purpose, and a club official was quoted as saying that the Raith Rovers could not carry on as they were doing, and although it was anticipated that objections would be taken in some quarters, the club must be conducted as a business proposition, and he was quite sanguine that the objections would be successfully overcome.   The plans came to nothing.

There were no funds available to significantly strengthen the team, although given the impressive finish to the preceding season, it was questioned in some quarters whether that was necessary – until the games started.   What was reckoned to be the club's smallest playing squad since they joined the First Division 18 years earlier, got off to a miserable start to the season.   A 0-0 draw at home to Third Lanark was the only point from the first eight games, and after the 7-1 defeat at Ibrox, the team sunk to bottom place.   There were a couple of wins in October to brighten the gloom, but a 2-0 defeat at Cowdenbeath later that month allowed the

Miners to leapfrog the Rovers at the bottom of the table.

Shortage of funds meant that the team could only be tinkered with. Jimmy McGorm, a juvenile signing from Cowdenbeath St Leonards, came in for Galloway at inside left, and Leslie Bruton was signed from Peterborough to partner Albert Pigg up front. The occasional victory kept them off the bottom, but by Christmas, third bottom place was four points distant.

Crowds were significantly down at a time of economic recession. In early October, the final of the East Fife Junior Cup was played at Stark's Park when Rovers were away from home, and attracted a crowd of less than 400, while 100 yards or so away a crowd of over 2,500 watched (free of charge) a first round Scottish Juvenile Cup tie in the Beveridge Park. On 8th December, while the team were being beaten 7-1 at Kilmarnock, the Supporters Club ran a bazaar to top up their own depleted funds.

Lawrence MacBain of St Johnstone, at inside right, and John Hutchison of Peterborough at right back, were introduced into the team early in the new year and while League results scarcely improved, there was a distracting, but nonetheless welcome, run in the Scottish Cup. Third Division Beith were overcome after a replay in the first round, Leslie Bruton scoring a hat-trick in the 4-1 win, and it also took two games to dispose of Bathgate, bottom of the Second Division, Bruton scoring all of the goals in the 5-2 replay at Stark's Park.

Another Second Division club, Dumbarton, were beaten 3-2 in the third round, and although Kilmarnock won 2-3 at Stark's Park in the quarter final, they were fully extended. The star-studded Rangers team which won 3-1 at Stark's Park were matched all the way by a battling Rovers team, who may have won the points had they taken their chances.

The reality of the League table was a constant reminder to Rovers fans of their club's predicament, and the ghosts of footballers past continued to haunt them. Included in the Anglo Scots team to play the Home Scots in an International trial match at Firhill on 13th March were Tokey Duncan, Tom Jennings and Alex James.

Successive home wins over Hibs and Falkirk at the end of March awakened hopes of another miracle revival to replicate that of the previous season, but they were followed by two away defeats in three days, at Clyde and St Mirren. A win and two draws in the final three matches was too little, too late to save Rovers from relegation ; they were five points from the safety of third bottom place.

Probably the most telling statistic was the attendance of 2,800 for the visit of Hibs on 23rd March. The Kirkcaldy footballing public, subsisting on low wages and uncertainty in the workplace, were not satisfied with the thin milk on offer at Stark's Park, when they had been used to cream for so many years.

As happens in times of economic constraint, the gap between the divisions in Scottish football grows wider. Promotion in 1926/27 was due more to the poor standard of the Second Division, than the quality of the Rovers team, as they found when they struggled to compete in the First Division. The encouraging form, and splendid results, of the last two months of 1927/28 could only be viewed, in retrospect, as an aberration. Although they dropped to the bottom of the League after 5th January 1929, and never left that position, they were always within touching distance of their fellow strugglers. What Rovers fans did not expect, as they viewed the prospect of Second Division football once again in the summer of 1929, was that they would be absent from the top table for nine years.

Understandably, the better players left. Albert Pigg went to Barnsley, Owen Dorrans to Morton, Bill McAllister signed for Hearts and Tommy Turner and Leslie Bruton were sold to Blackburn Rovers, the former having been selected in the Scotland squad for the continental internationals at the end of May. The Kirkcaldy Times commented : "While Raith's financial position will be eased a little by the deal, their prospects cannot be considered so bright". A month before, the rumour that Rovers were turning amateur was rubbished by directors.

Bruton's replacement was Fred Panther, who had scored 32 goals for Folkestone between Christmas and the end of the season. Tommy Batchelor moved from left half to right back, and Tommy Munro who had been freed after two years at Partick Thistle, came in at left back. Willie Campbell, Matt Hoggan and George Drain from Lochgelly Celtic, formed the half back line ; Beath, Galloway and Fred Panther were regulars in the forward line. The squad was

John "Tokey" Duncan was signed by Rovers in February 1918 from Lochgelly United and was one of the reasons who Rovers were so successful, so quickly, once First Division football resumed in 1919/20. He was as comfortable making goals from his inside forward position as he was in scoring them, and it was with some dismay that Rovers fans viewed his £1,500 sale to Leicester City in the summer of 1922.

He became the key player in a star-studded Leicester team, belatedly winning a Scotland cap in 1925. As he got older, he moved back to wing half, where he proved to be equally effective. In 1930, he wished to take over the running of the Turk's Head bar, not far from Filbert Street on Welford Road. The Leicester directors refused to sanction this, so Duncan hung up his boots. He returned to the club as manager in 1946, staying for three years before he returned to his pub.

A year after Duncan left Stark's Park, his place in the Rovers team was taken by Alex James, and although the two players did not share a club dressing room, they became firm friends, and good customers of the Turk's Head, as the above photograph would suggest.

Joe Cowan was one of the most prolific goalscorers in the club's history, for the short spell that he was at Stark's Park.

Born in Prestonpans on 25th February 1910, he was brought up in Methil and attended Aberhill School. He played for Markinch Rangers and then turned junior with Wellesley, that prolific nursery for senior clubs. After twelve goals in his first five appearances at that level, he was signed by Celtic. Wellesley manager Pat Duffy replaced him with Frank O'Donnell, and Celtic signed him too !

His two years at Celtic Park were unproductive - he made just one League appearance - and he signed for Rovers in July 1931. Back in Fife, the well built, compact (5' 7") centre found his scoring boots once again, and averaged precisely a goal-a-game in the Second Division in his first season - and he played in 34 League matches. He carried that form into other games, scoring seven times in seven cup ties.

1932/33 was even better ; 35 League goals in 27 appearances, with another 14 goals in a further 9 first team matches. Needless to say, such scoring form attracted the attention of other clubs, and Everton were said to be interested in signing him as an understudy to 'Dixie' Dean. Injury curtailed his activities in 1933/34, but he managed 15 goals in 18 League games. An unsatisfactory season led to him signing for East Fife in June 1934, although it took the intervention of the Scottish League Management Committee to provide him with a free transfer.

He continued to score goals freely at Bayview, with six in a match against King's Park in March 1936. Cowan was denied a place in the East Fife team which contested the later stages of the Scottish Cup (which they won) in 1938, as he was injured in early March. Always a part-timer, he was a foundry grinder and continued to play works football after he left Bayview at the end of their cup winning season. He died in Windygates in April 1991.

several players short, however, and the manager had to dust down his boots and return to the side in October. Outside left Jimmy Pryde was signed from Dundee early in December to bolster a threadbare attack.

After a dip in form in September and October, results improved, with Birrell making a difference in midfield. The Scottish Cup saw a marvellous cup tie at Stark's Park in the first round, two goals from Panther, a Birrell penalty and a great performance from Johnny Beath earning Rovers a 3-3 draw against First Division Aberdeen. The inconsistency which marked the team's performances during the League season was exemplified in the replay at Pittodrie, which Aberdeen won 7-0.

There were sufficient victories to keep the 2000 or so fans content, but there was no consistency of performance or results, nor the momentum necessary for a sustained promotion challenge. Fifth place in the League, fully 13 points behind the promotions places, could, however, be viewed as a platform on which to build.

There was indeed improvement the following season, to fourth position, just four points short of a promotion place, and there was no lack of entertainment for the Rovers fans. Ninety-three goals were scored in 38 League matches, 35 of them by new signing Jack Jarvis, formerly of Dunnikier Juniors, who was signed from Arbroath.

It was a season of remarkable scorelines ; a 5-6 home defeat by King's Park ; 5-2 home victory over Stenhousemuir and 6-3 at Ochilview ; 7-0 against Alloa, Jarvis scoring five ; 5-0 against Clydebank and 5-1 in the return game, and in the Fife Cup, a club record was set when St Andrews University were beaten 15-2, Jarvis helping himself to nine goals.

The team was largely unchanged from the previous season. Peter Henderson from Newtongrange Star was tried at centre half alongside Matt Hoggan ; George McLaren signed, like Hoggan, from Grange Rovers, became first choice at inside right, and Andrew Bell of Denbeath Star Juniors came in for Tom Munro at full back. Fred Panther, quick as well as robust in front of goal, was moved to outside right to accommodate Jarvis.

Hopes for promotion were hardly boosted by the appointment of Billy Birrell to the Secretary-Manager's job at Bournemouth & Boscombe FC on 3rd December. The following Monday, he was entertained by friends and well-wishers at the Rialto Tea-Room, chairman of proceedings being former Rovers player Mr P.G. Lumsden, captain of Kirkcaldy Cricket Club.

There were five names on the short-leet to replace him : Alexander Wright, manager of Queen of the South ; Jock McIntyre, former half back of Morton and Petershill ; Patrick Duffy, who had set up a conveyor belt of junior talent at Wellesley ; former manager James H. Logan, lately settled back in the town ; and James Cameron of Alva Albion Rangers. On Monday December 8th, James H. Logan was

appointed manager for the second time.

The Fife Free Press intoned : "Kirkcaldy people are no doubt getting tired of only seeing second rate teams at Stark's Park, and they will give manager Logan plenty of support if he can once again fill the breach and put Raith where they should be, that is in the First Division of Scottish football."

Notwithstanding his managerial prowess, Birrell was missed as a player. His replacement, a month later, was Alexander McKenzie who, with the best will in the world, was not in the same class. It took Morton three games to eject Rovers from the Scottish Cup, the second replay at Firhill (Rovers having lost the toss to decide between Edinburgh and Glasgow) being a rousing game which Rovers scarcely deserved to lose 2-0. One defeat in the next seven League matches propelled them up the League, the last match in that sequence, a 3-1 win over fellow promotion aspirants Third Lanark, being likened to a cup tie for its intensity. Matt Hoggan and Jimmy Blair were sent off, both subsequently fined £2 and severely censured.

As the season drew to a close, there was little room for error if Rovers were to make a late run into the promotion places. Some dubious tactical decisions, and an Alloa team in good form, resulted in a 3-2 defeat at Recreation Park, and Jarvis' brief absence through injury was felt at Volunteer Park Armadale, where the home team won 4-3, despite Rovers holding the lead until the last few minutes.

Five points from the last three matches represented a futile gesture of defiance, and a reminder of what might have been had such consistency been achieved earlier in the season. The fragility of the club's situation was illustrated by the crowd of 1000 (with promotion still theoretically possible) who saw a three goal lead squandered at home to Forfar Athletic, only for Jarvis to score the winner and complete his hat-trick. David Galloway was absent for the final match of the season, a 5-1 win at Clydebank in which Fred Panther scored four times – he had been sold to Aberdeen.

In early April, the prospect of Greyhound Racing at Stark's Park resurfaced. The Kirkcaldy Times reported : "Negotiations are at present in progress between Raith Rovers Football Club and a Glasgow firm, wherby greyhound racing is likely to be seen on the Kirkcaldy ground this summer. Manager Logan, when interviewed yesterday, said that while final arrangements had not yet been completed, there was every likelihood that this would be done, and greyhound racing inaugurated in Kirkcaldy. Measurements have already been taken of the ground with a view to considering its adaptability for the sport, and it is understood that with very little alteration it will prove quite satisfactory."

Later that month, Logan was quoted as saying that greyhound racing would start at the ground on 16th May. "It is expected that the alterations to the ground will be started

almost immediately. The barriers behind each goal will be removed and placed so as to allow a wide sweep for the racing. This will only slightly lessen the accommodation for the spectators." Nothing came of these plans, however, which was a blow to the directors, who, in the Annual Report published towards the end of June "viewed the financial position with no little concern, and an appeal was made to business men and the general public to rally round the club in the coming season."

Nothing more was heard of the matter, and on 15th December 1934 the purpose built Greyhound Stadium was built at Oriel Road.

Into the side for 1931/32 came goalkeeper Jock Wallace, provisionally signed from Wallyford Bluebell the previous season, and both the wingers of Denny Hibs, Joe McKay and outside left John Archibald. Michael McDonough took over from Alex McKenzie after the start of the season. The considerable blow of losing Jarvis to Arbroath (having refused terms and being placed on the transfer list until his move in November), was immediately compensated by the signing of Joe Cowan, who failed by only one to match his predecessor's 35 League goals. Once again, there was an improvement of one place in League position, to third, although the promotion places were more distant in terms of points, East Stirling and St Johnstone accruing nine more than Rovers.

The early part of the season was marked by the familiar lack of consistency, in both performance and results. A largely settled team brought about a significant improvement from mid October onwards, when only one of thirteen League matches was lost. There was an air of optimism around the club, shown by the decision to resurrect the Reserve team, who played their first match in the Edinburgh and District League (against Bathgate) on 3rd October.

League leaders East Stirling visited Stark's Park on 28th November, and Rovers won a rousing game 4-2, in front of a crowd of 4,000. A nagging doubt that it might not actually be Rovers season came from the realisation that the visitors were the better team, and many of Rovers' points were being earned by the excellent form of the Wallace in goal. A 2-1 victory at Armadale in a "strenuous game" brought the headline "Wallace the indefatigable". There was a more positive report from the 3-0 away win on Boxing Day : "Dunfermline outclassed", whereupon Rovers moved into second place in the League.

The first round of the Scottish Cup brought Inverness Thistle to Kirkcaldy, and an 8-1 victory for Rovers, Bobby Archibald who scored twice from outside right, considered a "success" on his debut, but the former Clydebank player lasted only three games. A fortnight later, Rangers arrived in the second round. The Kirkcaldy and District Amateur Association, and most Junior fixtures, were

Rovers had a remarkably settled team for the first half of 1932/33, and that was reflected in some good results, prompting hopes of a promotion challenge.

In goal was Jock Wallace, father of the future Rangers manager. Full backs were Bob Allan and George McGuire, a contrast between long and devoted service ahead, and a single season at the club. The wing halves were Johnny Beath, the ever-dependable Matt Hoggan, and William Dick. Outside right Davie Ovenstone was in the first of his three seasons at Stark's Park, with Davie Prentice inside. Joe Cowan was centre forward.

After the first few matches, George Bain was replaced at inside left by Sandy McKenzie, and at outside left was the latest in a steady stream of Archibalds to play for Raith Rovers, Jacky.

Back row : Dick, Hoggan, Beath, Wallace, Allan, McGuire
Front : Ovenstone, Prentice, Cowan, McKenzie, Archibald

TOMMY BATCHELOR

1929 Ravenscraig Park and Castle gifted to the town by Sir Michael Nairn on 29th June ; Technical school added to the High School buildings on St Brycedale Avenue ; Lady Blanche pit in Dysart closed

1930 Dysart incorporated in Kirkcaldy ; there was a two day "tropical storm" in the town in August

1931 Buses replaced trams in the town on 15th May ; the YWCA was opened on the Esplanade, and a couple of hundred yards further west, the Troxy Dance Hall was opened by Maciocia family. It was later known as the Burma Ballroom, and among its many later names and uses it became Jackie O's night club, who were the shirt sponsors of Rovers when they won the League Cup in 1994/95.

1932 On Sunday 3rd July, the memorial to John Thomson was unveiled at Cardenden Cemetary ; the Town Council opened their abattoir on Oriel Road ; and Sinclairtown Primary School was opened

On Tuesday March 13th, 1934 former Reserve team player James Barrie of 306 Links Street drowned while bathing at Seafield Tower. He also played for Abbotshall and Forth Amateurs.

1934 - Friday 16th November, saw the death of Dr John Smith of Brycehall after a long and serious illness

postponed to allow players and officials to witness the formidable team from Ibrox, who did not short-change the 19,800 spectators at Stark's Park in winning 5-0. Sam English scored a hat-trick, after Sandy Archibald had opened the scoring against his old club. English showed great courage in continuing to play at the highest level, with Rangers and Liverpool, but when he retired he admitted that, following the death of John Thomson in September 1931, he had endured seven years of "joyless sport".

Rovers quickly recovered from that heavy defeat, and won 1-0 at Easter Road the following Saturday, in somewhat fortuitous circumstances. Hibs missed two penalties (or more accurately both saved by Wallace) and scored Rovers goal for them. "Lucky Raith : home side by far the stronger" was the verdict, but Rovers returned home with both points and remained in joint second place with St Johnstone. A convincing 4-0 home win over Albion Rovers seemed to prime Rovers to push for promotion in the closing weeks, but a 6-1 defeat at Dumbarton came as a nasty jolt, from which Rovers failed to recover. Four defeats and three draws from the next seven League games saw valuable ground lost, culminating in a 5-1 debacle at East Stirling.

The League season finished early, on 16th April, with some youngsters drafted into the side showing up well in a 2-0 victory over Queen of the South at Stark's Park. Kirkcaldy and Dysart football fans looked for consolation from their favourites' failure to win promotion, in Rosslyn Juniors' progression to the semi finals of the Scottish Junior Cup. Their quarter final tie against Royal Albert had attracted a record 5000 attendance to Station Park, but they narrowly lost at Tynecastle to Glasgow Perthshire, by 1-0, in front of 7761 spectators.

The late season slump precipitated some radical surgery to the Rovers squad over the summer of 1932. Batchelor, McDonough, Pullar, Bobby Archibald, Chalmers and McKillop were all freed, and Bell, Mackay and McKenzie were placed on the transfer list.

Into the side came right back Bob Allan, signed from St Andrews United the previous season, left back George McGuire formerly of Clyde and Morton, left half William Dick from Hibs, and forwards David Ovenstone from Rosslyn, the ex-Celt David Prentice and George Bain, signed from Dundee United. Manager Logan insisted that the team was going "all out for promotion". The previous year, he had pinned his faith on youth, and the task proved to be beyond them. This season, he had signed some experienced players to overcome that hurdle. The cynics quickly had to eat their words ; King's Park were swamped 9-1 in the opening League game of the season at Stark's Park, Cowan scoring five times. Victories alternated with defeats until a 3-1 win at home to East Fife was followed by six wins and one draw.

The Directors were concerned at the falling off of the Boys Gate at Stark's Park, and were conscious of the popularity of amateur clubs at Beveridge and Ravenscraig Parks. The price of admission for under 14s was halved from 6d to 3d to encourage attendance, Ladies and Juveniles being expected to continue to pay the original tariff.

Following a scarcely deserved 2-1 defeat in a thrilling match at Easter Road, in which Hoggan was the best man afield, a disappointing performance at home to Forfar nevertheless secured both points. However, Rovers tactics were criticised in going down to St Bernards ; the close passing game deemed to be inappropriate for the conditions. A 5-1 victory at Armadale did not quell the criticism, the team being perceived as being reliant upon Wallace, Hoggan, and Cowan. The centre forward from Aberhill scored Rovers' goal against Hibs having married Miss Isobel Wilkie of Buckhaven in an Edinburgh Registry Office that morning, keeping the news secret from his colleagues until they met in the dressing room before the match.

The prophets of doom were proved to be correct with four successive defeats. In an attempt to regenerate the promotion push, inside right Andy Campbell was signed from Dundee, and George Innes from Clackmannan Juniors. In early February, Dumbarton's amateur internationalist half back John Parlane arrived. Fred Panther returned to the side, but momentum had been lost, as had revenue from the postponed New year holiday League match, on 3rd January, against Bo'ness, who had resigned from the League mid-season, unable to meet the guarantee to visiting teams. A friendly match was hastily arranged against a Scottish Junior Select. The previous day, Rovers had lost a "pulsating struggle" 2-1 at Methil. The Kirkcaldy Times reported : "Wallace was a queer mixture. His blunders cost Raith Rovers two goals and two points, yet his brilliance saved his side from disaster. I have never seen better goalkeeping than he provided in the second half."

There was a battling performance against First Division Falkirk in the Scottish Cup at Stark's Park, but the match was lost 2-1 and shortly afterwards former player Bill Morrison resigned as trainer. Successive high scoring victories at Edinburgh City (5-2) and at home to Arbroath rekindled hope of a late surge, but the next two matches were lost, and the two after that drawn. Rovers finished in sixth place, 13 points behind runners up Queen of the South.

At the Annual General Meeting in June, Chairman James Bogie admitted "None was more disappointed and sorry at the unfortunate outcome of their promotion hopes last season than the directors." They had a tremendously difficult task to fulfil, and he appealed to the sporting public of Kirkcaldy to give them due credit for the sacrifice they had made both in their leisure time and in a financial sense. Reporting a loss for the season of £813, the Chairman reminded shareholders that there had been no income from transfers because they had not encouraged offers, although they had received plenty. "That was not a policy we could carry on indefinitely, however, particularly if support was lacking."

He was true to his word, rather quicker than he imagined, and Johnny Beath was transferred to Albion Rovers before the start of 1933/34. Dick Hoggan joined his brother Matt in the team and started the season at left back, Bill Crichton from East Stirling was at left half and there were new forwards in Jim Black from East Stirling, Harry Oliphant from Arbroath and outside left Tommy Callaghan, formerly of Third Lanark.

The start to the season was wretched, a 5-0 home win over Montrose, in which Cowan monopolised the scoring, surrounded by five defeats. It was too much for James Logan, who resigned on 25th September, intending to devote his time to his High Street confectionery business. His own analysis of the team's failings did not make happy reading in the boardroom at Stark's Park.

"A month ago, on my initiative, I was given permission to pick the team. That's all, pick the team. The extent of the powers was to pick the team from the available talent. Anything beyond that my powers were just the same as before – limited to the specific approval of the directors. I had no free hand to bring in any trialists I liked or sign any players I liked."

The Chairman, Mr Bogie, who had recently been elected Treasurer of the S.F.A., responded : "The powers which Mr Logan had as manager were exactly those possessed and exercised by all football club managers. It apparently occurred to Mr Logan that he should, prior to his resignation, state his position for the purpose of justifying or excusing himself for the want of success being achieved by the club."

October brought better results, three wins and a draw, following the introduction of Kinnear on the left wing, Jimmy Penman a 17 year old from Dunnikier Juniors who replaced Cowan (who had a cartilage removed), right half Jimmy Scott from Newburgh West End - and the appointment of a new manager. The short leet was Hugh Shaw, a player with Hibs and East Fife, William Frame of Motherwell, Pat Duffy of Wellesley Juniors once again, and the successful applicant, former Airdrie, Hearts and Scotland player Bob Bennie who was appointed on 9th October but did not take up office until the expiry of Logan's period of notice on 22nd October. November, however, brought three more defeats, and the die was cast for the season despite obtaining Harry Smith's services from Dundee for the remainder of the campaign.

If Bob Bennie didn't realise the extent of his task on taking over the job, he certainly did on the Saturday before Christmas, when he had to dust off his football boots to make up the numbers in a 3-1 defeat at Alloa, a result which saw Rovers descend to sixth bottom of the Second Division. He was given some hope, however,

by two excellent performances – and results – over the holiday period. St Bernards were beaten 3-1 with young Penman scoring a hat-trick, followed three days later by a tremendous 6-2 win at Methil, Penman scoring four times. In typical fashion, those two victories were followed by a 0-0 draw at Brechin and a 1-0 home defeat to Arbroath. Then came a first round exit from the Scottish Cup, although Rovers took great credit from a 1-0 defeat at Aberdeen, described as a"gallant failure" In a titanic second half struggle, Wallace performed heroically in goal.

A 4-2 win over King's Park the following week was notable for "a grand goal by [David] Kinnear". "The winger raced half the length of the field, beating the right back twice before, from 18 yards, sending an unsaveable low shot which got the corner of the net. The crowd gave him the best cheer I have heard at Stark's Park for many a day." The young Kirkcaldy winger also excelled in a 6-0 home win over Edinburgh City, scoring a hat-trick. It came as no surprise when he signed for Rangers in early April, following out of Stark's Park Jock Wallace, who was transferred to Blackpool on St Valentine's Day for less than £2,000.

There were several moments to cheer Raith Rovers fans, therefore, but many more to infuriate them, primarily the inconsistency of their favourites. The team capable of beating top of the table Dunfermline Athletic 3-1 at East End Park, could lose 4-5 at Stenhousemuir a fortnight later (Cowan scoring all Rovers goals) and 2-5 at Dundee United the following week to bring the curtain down on a disappointing League season which ended in 9th position.

The Kirkcaldy Times reported on the Tannadice match in the following terms. "The team's weaknesses were thrown up on Saturday, and Bob Bennie and the directors will have to get busy collecting new talent if the club is to fulfil Mr Bogie's desire of stepping up at the end of next season. It has been a most unsatisfactory season so far as Raith are concerned. They made a poor start, and then, after what appeared at the time a determined effort to snatch promotion at the last possible moment, they faded away again, and have conducted their arrangements in a most uninspiring fashion. Surely a town of the size of Kirkcaldy should have a better-going side to support. The Langtonians are "fed up" with Second Division soccer, and are longing for the time when the Hearts, Rangers etc. once again journey to the Pratt Street enclosure."

It was reported that the players trained through the summer, the locals training twice a week, doing 12 laps of the pitch at Stark's Park followed by medicine ball practice, while the others trained in their own districts.

The "new talent" so desired by the Times' correspondent amounted to William Main, who had made two appearances at right half late in the previous season, and forwards Andrew Brown from Middlesbrough,

David Galloway came into the Rovers team towards the end of his first season at the club, 1927/28. From the start of the following season, and until he left the club, he was first choice inside left. A tricky, hardy player who could contribute his share of goals, he was playing at a level below his ability when Rovers were relegated to the Second Division.
Aberdeen recognised this and signed him towards the end of the 1930/31 season.
His career at Pittodrie was a lot shorter than expected, thanks to "The Great Mystery". To everyone's surprise, three long-standing first team stars, Hugh McLaren, Frank Hill and Benny Yorston, were dropped to the reserves in mid November 1931. There was no official explanation from manager Paddy Travers, but he admitted it was on account of "some domestic trouble". Galloway and Jimmy Black were soon added to the list of first team players consigned to the reserves, and after several weeks of silence and widespread rumours, it became apparent that none of the players would play for the Aberdeen first team again. Everyone involved took the secret to their respective graves, despite several requests to divulge the reasons for the abrupt end to their Pittodrie careers.
Yorston was sold to Sunderland for £2,000, Hill went to Arsenal, McLaren to Bradford City and David Galloway signed for Preston North End in July 1932. He later played for Port Vale, Carlisle and Clapton Orient.

JACK LECKIE

The resumption of League football in 1919/20 coincided with the emergence of Rovers' first substantial goalscorer for several years, Fletcher Welsh scoring 23. The next highest, Willie Birrell, scored seven.

"Tokey" Duncan and George Waite shared the honours with eleven goals each in 1920/21 before Tom Jennings dominated the scoring charts with 21 in the League the following season, then eight (out of 18 in all), 27 in 1923/24 following reform of the offside law and thirteen in 1924/25, two more than Alex James.

Allan Brown was top scorer with thirteen in the League in 1925/26, followed the next season by Alex Ritchie with 19 in the Second Division. Albert Pigg's 22 League goals went a long way to keeping Rovers in the First Division the following season, in contrast to Leslie Bruton's 14 in the 1928/28 relegation season. Pigg scored one fewer.

Fred Panther burst on the scene with 32 League goals, and nine in other first team games in 1929/30, but took second place to John Jarvis who scored 35 in 29 League games in 1930/31, plus another 14 in eight further matches. Joe Cowan average a goal a game in his 34 League appearances the following season, and beat that in 1932/33 with 35 goals in 27 League games, plus 14 more in other first team matches.

He was also top scorer in 1933/34 with 15 goals from 18 League matches, one more than teenager Davie Kinnear and Harry Oliphant.

Duncan Colquhoun from Millwall and Andrew Miller from Bowhill. The recruitment process didn't exactly inspire confidence amongst fans and critics alike, as described in the Kirkcaldy Times on August 8th 1934 :

"A rather novel step up into senior football is revealed in the signing, on Monday, by Manager Bob Bennie, of Alex Main, the young St Monance player. Main, who is a brother of the Rovers right half, deputised in the first trial [the previous Friday] for the Anglo Scot who was to have appeared in the inside berth. When it was learned that there was a last minute vacancy, Provost Gourlay, St Monance, the popular Raith director, said he might get someone on the spot to step into the breach.

"He approached Main, who had come to Stark's Park to see his brother play. Main played, and Provost Gourlay's faith in his capabilities was not let down. Amongst the newcomers, he was the best afield. He was asked at the conclusion of the game if he would consider signing, and now the Raith management have completed the deal."

In the pantheon of Raith Rovers' false dawns, 1934/35 looms large. The season opened with a 7-0 home thrashing of Brechin City, and two more home wins, over Edinburgh City and Leith Athletic. A 4-0 defeat at Dundee United was shrugged off with a 3-1 home win over Stenhousemuir. Maybe Joe Cowan, signed by East Fife having been granted a free transfer by the SFA, wouldn't be missed after all ? Eleven games without a win disabused that notion, by which time George Fulton had arrived from St Johnstone.

After a 3-2 defeat at Montrose, the Kirkcaldy Times asked "Are Raith Doomed ? Promotion Chances Fade. Half Backs Weak. Have the Raith directors given way to despair ? The team chosen to do battle against Forfar Athletic at Stark's Park was full of changes – a half back to play at full back [Matt Hoggan] ; a right half at centre half [William Main]; a trialist forward [Walker] to partner Colquhoun, and Andrew Miller switched over the inside left. Of course, it may be well said that some of the changes are not before time, but such a general upheaval at one stroke is hardly likely to bring the desired results all at once."

A fortnight later, Sandy Archibald was brought back to the club after 17 years of stellar service to Rangers, followed a week later by inside left George Denholm from Hearts of Beath. Archibald's wing play remained a delight, but while a couple of home wins came at the expense of Dumbarton and Alloa in early December, defeat was still the predominant result.

On 2nd November, Bob Bennie resigned, presumably in despair, and was immediately succeeded by Archibald, who initially could not inspire a change of fortunes. After a 2-1 defeat at King's Park, Rovers sunk to second bottom place, saved the ignominy of being the worst League team in Scotland by the eternal whipping boys Edinburgh City. Early in the new year, a new left back was

signed, James Sneddon, a 20 year old from Dunfermline United who played in a Wednesday afternoon league.

Just before the Scottish Cup first round tie against East Stirling, outside right James Wilson, a former colleague of Archibald's at Ibrox, was signed from St Mirren, and he helped Rovers to a 2-1 win in Bainsford. A thrilling 1-1 draw in the second round at Brechin was followed by an undeserved 4-2 defeat at Stark's Park in the replay, in front of a Wednesday afternoon crowd of 5,500.

A much changed team finished the season in uncharacteristic form, with a draw at Brechin, and then four successive victories, at home to Morton (6-0), St Bernards (3-0), King's Park (2-0) and a 4-3 win at Dumbarton to complete a strong finish to an otherwise desperately disappointing season in which Rovers finished 13th, which sounds much better than sixth bottom.

The Supporters Club added to their many enterprises with an Eleven-a-side tournament at Stark's Park, commencing Tuesday 14th May. There would be a match played every night until a winner emerged from the 30 entrants. The competition was completed in plenty of time for the start of pre-season training on 23rd July. It was announced that the normal pre-season trial match custom of 1st team attack v defence, with the rest of both teams made up of trialists, would be abandoned in favour of a 1st team v Junior XI fixture. The manager, who lived in Crossgates, may have been inspired by the opening of Crossgates Primrose's new ground, on the site of an old coal bing, on 27th July 1935. 1,500 attended the match on 1st August, in which Joyner of St Andrews United appeared at outside left.

At the monthly meeting of the Supporters Club (who had donated £90 to help the football club through the close season) at the Deaf & Dumb Institute on 2nd August, "Criticism of the condition of Stark's Park was made by Mr R. Herdman, Treasurer, who said that the condition of the ground was a disgrace to a senior club. He moved that they spend £10 on renovation. Mr R. Wilkie said he would rather suggest that they buy new jerseys for the players, and it was ultimately decided to spend £5 on jerseys and £5 on painter work."

Two wins and a draw from the opening seven League fixtures prompted the Kirkcaldy Times to report that "the difficulties of trying to run a successful football team with only 12 signed players are being realised by the Raith Rovers directors."

A new half back line was being tried in Michael McNeil, William Paterson of Arbroath and John Gilbert (Kirkford Juniors), while Hector Philip (Lochgelly Albert) and William Dobbie formed the left wing. The loss of the steady, reliable presence of Matt Hoggan at centre half was being felt. William Watson, signed from Renfrew Juniors, had a brief spell in that position in October, and returned to the side towards the end of the season, replacing John Philp from

Leicester City, who in turn moved to left back.

There was no escape from the conclusion that the policy of signing juveniles, amateurs and inexpensive juniors was relentlessly diluting the quality of the team, and there was no money available to reverse the policy. A 4-2 home win over the hapless Edinburgh City was the only victory in 12 League games stretching from 31st August to 16th November. Complete drubbings were mercifully few, aside from a 6-0 defeat by the League leaders at Love Street, and 6-2 at St Bernards, but that was thanks more to the mediocrity of the opposition, than any redeeming quality in a woebegone Rovers squad.

After the 2-1 home defeat by Alloa, the Kirkcaldy Times reported that "The players seem to have lost all confidence, and week after week they go out and get defeated by mediocre elevens. They are not very lion-hearted these days." One week, and another home defeat (to Leith Athletic) later, and it was "For weeks past there has been a cry for a new goalkeeper at Stark's Park. The cry is not unfounded, for Paterson has had ample opportunities of finding his feet. He has played a few really fine games for Raith, but in the majority he could hardly be written down as an asset. A new man is badly needed in that position."

Trialists came and went. John Lynas, formerly of Third Lanark, and Eddie McGoldrick of Dundee were released following short trials. "They were clever players, but without the dash and snap needed."

A 4-0 home win over Forfar was then followed by six successive League defeats, before Stenhousemuir were beaten 3-1. There was little surprise in a 4-2 home defeat by St Johnstone in the first round of the Scottish Cup, although the share of revenue from a 6500 crowd was a godsend to the empty coffers. Many believed the match should not have been played, such was the stormy weather, and one commentator said "never before have I seen the ground in such pitiable condition."

Everyone recognised that something had to be done to haul the town's football club from the mire into which it had sunk. A positive move was announced in the Fife Free Press of 30th November, with the launch of a 10,000 Shilling Fund, run by the newspaper, and its midweek sports and social edition the Kirkcaldy Times, and introduced by the editor in the following terms :

"I would remind Raith supporters that now is the time to send in their contributions. Sums from 1/- upwards will be most gratefully received, and the names of the contributors will be published in our columns each week. If you do not know any of the directors or members of the Supporters Club, hand in your contribution to the Fife Free Press Office, 35 Kirk Wynd, Kirkcaldy. We all want to see a successful Raith. Make this your good turn for the week."

The fund was launched with a 1500/- donation from the Directors and Supporters Club, and within a month 5439 ½ shillings had been donated. The £272 thus raised amounted to 7.5% of the previous season's turnover, the target therefore being 15%, a significant boost, but no root-and-branch restructuring of the club's finances. As disclosed in the annual accounts, the Shilling Fund contributed £419 16/9d by the end of April 1936. Michael Nairn & Co, incidentally, reported annual profits to 31st January 1935 of £252,088, roughly equivalent to £76 million in today's terms.

The examples shown by this generosity inspired others to offer more practical help to the club. The Dunfermline businessman, Mr J.A. Hill, proprietor of the Sinclairtown Laundry, offered to launder strips to the end of the season, a saving to the club of at least £10.

The new funds allowed some modest acquisitions. Richard Brownlie of Dundee St Joseph's Juniors at outside right, Alex Craigie from Morton at inside right, Pat McGill of Hearts at inside left all came into the team, but there was no magical transformation. A 4-2 defeat at East Stirling on 4th January consigned Rovers to the bottom place in the Scottish Football League, below even amateur side Edinburgh City, for the first time in its history. The Kirkcaldy Times recorded this dire milestone as follows : "Misfortunate has been their lot for several years past, but never before have they suffered such humiliation as at present. How a club's fortunes change ! Twelve years ago every football supporter north of the Tweed knew all about Raith, that Fife team which was challenging the mighty Celts and the supposed invincible Rangers."

A 3-2 victory at Edinburgh City hauled the club above Dumbarton on goal average, and a "sterling performance" in which McGill was the star, saw St Bernards beaten 4-1 at Stark's Park the following week, watched by only 500 spectators. Dumbarton and Montrose were also defeated before the season's end, but that only widened the gap from bottom club Dumbarton (and the requirement to apply for re-election) to five points. Rovers finished 1935/36 in second bottom place, the 37th best team in Scottish League football. The run in to the end of that miserable season involved a 6-0 defeat at Brockville and, on the final Saturday, 18th April, an 11-2 drubbing at Greenock when John Calder equalled a Second Division record by scoring eight goals.

"There are sore hearts at Stark's Park now", said the Kirkcaldy Times, "but perhaps the club officials will have learned a lesson, and now is certainly the time to make amends by adopting a progressive policy for next season."

Predictably, there was heated discussion on the club's predicament at the May Supporters Club meeting, presided over by Provost James Gourlay of St Monance, who was also on the Board of Directors. They wanted the Supporters Club to provide money to meet the running costs over the summer months, mostly raised from the

GEORGE FULTON

George Fulton took Cowan's mantle the following season and scored 25 times in 28 League appearances, with 19 from 31 the following season, and a goal a game from 28 League appearances in 1936/37.

Norrie Haywood set a new club record, which still stands, with 47 goals from 34 League games in the memorable 1937/38 season, and scored eight more in nine additional first team games. He scored just ten times in the First Division the following season, four less than Willie Dunn and eight less than Jock Whitelaw.

Davie Duncan was top goalscorer in 1939/40 with 17 in all first team games, but it was a guest player, George Whalley, who topped the list in 1941/42 with 13 goals. Willie Hurrell scored 16 the following season and Willie Penman started as he intended to go on with 17 goals in 1943/44, increasing that to 23 the following season.

WILLIAM CRICHTON

1935 Hunter hospital was opened, having been converted from Hunter House. John Hunter developed his father's cabinetmaking business in the mid 19th century and built many of the fine villas in central Kirkcaldy. He purchased St Brycedale House from Provost Swan and lived there until he died in 1916. He left funds to have the house turned into a hospital, but they were insufficient at the time, and were invested. By 1935, the fund was large enough to alter and extend the property ; Sinclairtown Library opened in Loughborough Road

1936 - The Lido, a privately owned indoor, heated swimming pool, was opened at Seafield on 21st July 1936. It's last use was as a sweetie factory for Alma Confectionery; The Employment Exchange was opened on Esplanade and, after a fire, the Burma Ballroom was opened.

Kirkcaldy Times 6th January 1937 : 19 year old David Kinnear of Rangers, 50 Kidd Street, Kirkcaldy was fined 7/6d or 10 days imprisonment for parking his car without lights in East March Street on 20th December.

1937 Burtons building opened at the corner of Whytescauseway and the High Street
1937 The Opera House became the Regal Cinema (later the ABC in the High Street ; the Rio opened in at the corner of St Clair Street and Millie Street, and the Carlton opened in Park Road

football tournament profits and the regular boxing tournaments promoted by the Supporters Club at the Adam Smith & Beveridge Halls.

Treasurer Herdman reminded the meeting that the Supporters Club had previously agreed to give money to the club only to pay for player transfers. "Mr Herdman said he was in favour of the Club giving Raith Rovers every shilling they had, but he wanted their money to benefit the Football Club's supporters. He was not in favour of them giving money that would go into the directors' pockets."

In stark contrast to what would happen many decades later, there was no hint of the manager taking responsibility for the club's plight. It was generally accepted that Sandy Archibald was doing the best he could with a poor set of players, which was all he could entice to the club from the meagre finances he had been allocated.

As often happens, out of the darkest tunnel comes a glimmer of light which shows the way forward to better fortune.   In mid May, David Baxter, the St Johnstone right half, was signed. A month later, Tom Crosskey, the Albion Rovers goalkeeper, and James McDonald, an inside right from Queen of the South, followed suit.

Later that summer, Bill Peattie, yet another from St Monance Swifts– rarely has that village produced such a stream of senior footballers, although none who signed for Rovers in the mid 1930s was of the calibre of their successor Charlie Cooke – centre half Jimmy Morrison of Brechin City, who replaced Dundee-bound Watson, Alex Glen from Forthill Juniors in Dundee, Tommy Gilmour of Albion Rovers and Charlie Whyte from Montrose, were all signed.   If the previous clubs of these (mostly) free transfers did not inspire confidence, at least the Rovers fans would not have to suffer the inadequacies of the previous season's squad.   Early in the new season, Peter Cabrelli arrived from Falkirk.

The Band Contest in the Raith grounds, in the natural amphitheatre between the main drive and the curling pond, which had been started in 1890, was revived on Saturday 8th August, catching the Scottish League fixture planners on the hop, as Rovers opened the season with a home match against Stenhousemuir.   Four successive opening victories put them top of the League by 5th September, when East Fife were the visitors to Stark's Park.

The Kirkcaldy Times reported : "It was quite like old times when the teams took the field. There were no bare patches in the terracing. Every vantage point had been secured and still the crowd came pouring in. No wonder the teams surpassed themselves. It is not often that they get such mass vocal support."   12,177 saw a thrilling 2-2 draw, and a 3-1 win at Edinburgh City the following Saturday put Rovers back on top of the League.   They left it late to beat Montrose 3-0 seven days later, but there was a festive air around Stark's Park as Bob Allan was

presented with a dressing case by the Supporters Club after six seasons of faithful service, the last two as captain. A club flag, donated by the Supporters Club, was flown for the first time.

Just as this tremendous start to the season (only one point dropped out of 14) was unexpected, so too was the collapse over the next three matches.   A robust Cowdenbeath side, indulged by a lenient referee, won 4-1 in front of 10,000 at Central Park, Forfar won 6-1 at Stark's Park and King's Park won 5-1 at Forthbank.   Former Dunfermline full back Fred Robson was brought in to replace the deperately missed Bob Allan, who had had taken up a teaching post in Birmingham, and Norman Fraser, Alex Glen's former team-mate at Forthill Athletic, was fielded at outside left.

The dramatic slide was halted by successive home wins over Dumbarton and Brechin, the latter thanks to a George Fulton hat-trick, but three successive defeats quelled any thoughts of promotion. Full back John Smith from Bo'ness Cadora was hastily called up, former Dundee United and Partick Thistle winger Peter Bain was brought in for three games, and inside forward John Steele was signed from Ayr United.

There was plenty of activity taking place in and around the club, but the team could not string together a sequence of results to match their start to the season, and get themselves back into the promotion chase.   On 21st November, the Supporters Club promoted one of their regular Boxing shows at the Adam Smith & Beveridge Halls, and attracted an audience of 1,200.   There were 3000 at Stark's Park a week later to see Musselburgh Athletic beat Lochgelly Albert 2-1 in a Scottish Junior Cup third round second replay.   Tempers became frayed, as so often happens at Junior Cup ties, and several crowd invasions of the playing field led to the police being called.

Some more faltering results in November and early December shattered the veneer of co-existence between the Football Club and the Supporters Club, who declared "We are dissatisfied with the directors' effort to regain promotion, and meantime members have decided not to hand over any money until some compromise is reached."

Perhaps coincidentally, the criticism seemed to galvanise the team, who found their scoring boots in beating Stenhousemuir 7-2 at Ochilview (Fulton scoring 5), East Stirling 5-0 at home and East Fife 4-3 at Methil on New Year's Day.   In a familiar pattern, the next five matches brought one draw and four defeats, one of these being a 5-0 home defeat to St Johnstone in the first round of the Scottish Cup, played on a Wednesday afternoon after the Saturday fixture had been postponed due to a snowstorm.

The Supporters Club had given the Football Club £60 to buy a player for the tie, but the directors claimed that they had tried, unsuccessfully. They were asked that the money be held over to purchase a player.

The season limped towards its conclusion, each victory succeeded by a defeat. The dismal weather, which caused several matches to be postponed during the winter, and the scourge of a flu epidemic, did not improve the mood, although there was much to enjoy in a 2-2 draw at home to Ayr United on 3rd April, Baxter's spectacular 30-yard shot being particularly memorable. Only 1,500 bothered to turn up to see Ayr win the point which secured the Second Division Championship. Rovers finished in 8th position – a significant improvement on the previous season, but 15 points short of a promotion place.

Early in the close season, the Supporters Club and Football Club published their respective annual accounts. The Football Club's total revenue was £5223, the Supporters Club's £1067, with £141 donated to Raith Rovers, and £3 to Dunnikier Juniors.

The Fife Free Press had reported, on 13th February : "Raith Supporters' Club have appointed a committee of three of their number to go talent spotting. Mr Herdsman (sic) honorary secretary, said that they had been helping Raith financially ; he thought they should assist them materially by bringing to the notice of the management suitable players." At the end of the season, Peter Napier argued against the continuation of this sub-committee, saying that it was a futile enterprise, as the management of the Football Club paid little attention to its recommendations.

There were four new signings for 1937/38, Eric McKay, a former Montrose goalkeeper who had been playing in Ireland, Norman Haywood from Queen of the South, Jock Whitelaw who returned to his native Fife via York City, and, following occasional trialist appearances over the previous two seasons, the teenage outside left Francis Joyner. Rovers fans wondered how the goals would come, as George Fulton had been transferred back to St Johnstone. Significantly, Bob Allan returned from Birmingham in late August. The opening League match of the season saw a narrow 4-3 win at Leith Athletic, followed by a 4-2 home win over Dundee United, which prompted the Kirkcaldy Times to write : "I think Raith have a stronger and more powerful set of forwards than they had a year ago. There is more weight in the attack than for many years, and weight, coupled with ability, is a good thing to have in the side." Never has such optimism been so inadequately expressed, given subsequent events.

The season started with six consecutive victories, including the previous season's Wemyss Cup semi final against Dunfermline. The new centre forward, Norrie Haywood, scored in them all, thirteen goals in all, including four in an 8-2 win at Brechin. The 5-3 win at East Fife was lyrically described by the Fife Free Press : "The game was one that will not readily be forgotten by those who saw it. Play began in a fever of excitement and the whole game was fought out with a speed and energy that

was little short of amazing in the warm autumn sunshine. If play quietened down a little in the last ten minutes it was not to be wondered at, for the players – like the spectators – had been unsparing in their expenditure of energy." The verdict was that Rovers had passed the test.

Victory at Methil induced 9,000 to turn up at Stark's Park for the visit of East Stirling, which was drawn 1-1. A fortunate 2-2 draw at Stenhousemuir the following week had the eternally pessimistic Rovers fans wondering if the bubble was about to burst, but Forfar were beaten 3-0 at Stark's Park (attendance down to 4,000), before three more points were dropped in the next two matches. Their bright start to the match at Cowdenbeath could not be sustained for 90 minutes, and despite a Gilmour hat-trick, Rovers lost 4-3. The draw at Dumbarton the following week was more unfortunate, Haywood having what looked like a sound goal disallowed.

A settled team roared back to form with eight successive victories, Rovers scoring six goals in four of them. The holiday period brought the second blip of the season ; a 4-4 draw at Tannadice followed by a 3-1 home defeat by an in-form East Fife team, watched by 19,500 on New Years Day. It was the first time neutral linesmen had been used in a Second Division match, and the gates at the Invertiel end were burst open by the force of the crowd trying to gain admission. Bill Peattie, who started a five match run in place of Jock Smith at left back, suffered a disappointing return to the side, and the finger was pointed with a change of goalkeeper for the remainder of the season, Davie Watson taking over from McKay. A hard-fought 3-2 win at Airdrie two days later got the team back on track, with ample revenge exacted against East Stirling who were beaten 8-1 at Firs Park. A 4-1 home win over Dunfermline set Rovers up for what should have been a routine Scottish Cup first round tie at home to Montrose, who had already lost 6-0 at Kirkcaldy that season. A Gilmour goal was all that separated the sides.

7-0 and 3-0 League victories, and a 9-2 demolition of Edinburgh City in the second round of the Cup, took the team up to their greatest test of the season, a Scottish Cup third round tie at First Division Partick Thistle. 32,497 witnessed goals from Haywood and Whitelaw outweigh a McKeenan penalty, awarded after Cabrelli handled. A combination of a nippy attack and a dour defence had overcome the team that would finish in 7th place in the First Division. Rovers fans gathered round their crystal sets on Monday afternoon to discover their quarter final opponents – East Fife !

Interest in the tie throughout the Kingdom, and beyond, was enormous. The 19,000 crowd set a record for Bayview, and the 2/- admission, double the norm, ensured record receipts. Along with the Falkirk v Rangers tie that afternoon, it was the first all-ticket match in Scotland, a new concept north of the border which was only contemplated

NORMAN FRASER

On 4th December 1937 the Directors increased the players' match bonus, providing proof to the sceptics that the club wanted promotion

Three reserve players in the 1937/38 season were signed during the previous season. Andy Meikleham, - Right half – (played in two League and one Scottish Cup tie in 1937/38) signed on a free transfer from Leith Athletic on 2nd September 1936. Born in Dysart, he played for Rosslyn Juniors, Bowhill Rovers, Alloa (in July 1930) St Johnstone and Leith Athletic. On his release from Rovers at the end of 1937/38, he signed for Dundee United, where he remained until August 1940.
John Gay – Inside left - Signed from Pittenweem Rovers during the summer of 1936, he was released at the end of the season. Played in one Friendly fixture in 1937/38.
Norman Fraser – Outside Left – signed from Forthill Athletic in October 1936, he was transferred to Montrose on 18th March 1938 and Brechin City five months later. He also played for Dundee United in the 1940 War Cup Final, and throughout the war years. He did not play for the first eleven in 1937/38.

1938 Raith Cinema opened on the site of Methven's Pottery on Links Street ; the Fire Station on Dunnikier Road opened

Pictured towards the end of the 1937/38 record-breaking season were : Back row, left to right : BILL PEATTIE – Full back – (7 League appearances that season plus one in the Scottish Cup)

one of a number of recruits from St Monance Swifts in the 1930s, he signed for Rovers in May 1936. Born in Anstruther Wester, he played in all three Scottish Amateur internationals in 1936 and remained a registered player with Rovers until 1946. He made eleven League appearances for Rovers in the First Division the following season and played a number of games for Dundee in the wartime league of 1939/40. Club linesmen were used in Second Division matches, and he is pictured above in that capacity.

BOB ALLAN – Right back – (32 Lge 4 SC, 1 Lge goal) signed from St Andrews United as an 18 year old in September 1931, he was a great servant to the club through the lean years of the 1930s. After graduating from Jordanhill College, he started a career as a PE teacher, which took him to Birmingham early in 1936/37 season. He returned to work in Scotland the following summer, and was restored to his accustomed position at Stark's Park. Typically, he was an ever-present in the First Division campaign of 1938/39, playing 38 times. He signed for Dundee in July 1939, but the Second World War ended his football career. He continued to play rugby, and enjoyed from a distinguished career in the Education Service in Edinburgh.

JOHN SMITH – Left Back – (30 Lge 5 SC, 1 Lge goal) signed from Bo'ness Cadora in October 1936 and remained a registered player with the club for ten years, eventually receiving a benefit of £600). He played 19 times for Rovers in the First Division in 1938/39.

DAVE WATSON – Goalkeeper – (14 Lge 5 SC) A former Ashfield junior, who played for Arsenal, Ayr United and Dundee United before signing for Rovers in October 1937. He was released in December of the following year after 11 League appearances and signed for East Stirling.

DAVE BAXTER – Right half – (30 Lge 4 SC, 2 Lge goals) signed as a 25 year old from St Johnstone in May 1936, he was from Lumphinnans and played for Bowhill Rovers. He was released in March 1940, having played 16 times for Rovers in the First Division in 1938/39. His father, Robert, played for the club in the early years of the century, and Dave's nephew also played for the club – Jim Baxter.

JIMMY MORRISON – Centre half – (34 Lge 5 SC – ever present) son of Bill Morrison, who was centre half in Rovers' Scottish Cup Final team in 1913. He had the same hair-style as his father and was nicknamed "Daddy". Signed from Brechin City in May 1936, having played for St Andrews United, Airdrie (from July 1929) and East Fife. He was released at the end of 1938/39 after 14 Division One appearances.

PETER CABRELLI – Left half - (34 Lge 5 SC – ever present) signed on a free transfer from Falkirk in August 1936, he left Dundee Osborne Juniors for Dundee in August 1929, and moved from Forfar Athletic (who he joined in August 1931) to Falkirk in December 1934. He spent three months on loan to King's Park in 1935/36. He played in 37 League matches for Rovers in the First Division in 1938/39. He was released by Rovers in September 1943, signed for Dundee United and was transferred to St Mirren three months later. He then had spells with King's Park, United again, and after the war Arbroath and Montrose. Next to him is trainer DAVE CLUNIE. Front row :

ALEX GLEN – Outside right – (34 Lge 5 SC – ever present – 5 Lge 1 SC goals) born in Dundee, he was signed from the junior club Forthill Athletic as a 20 year old in August 1936. Played in 24 League games in the First Division the following season, scoring 2 goals. While still a Rovers player, he played for Dundee United in the War Cup Final of 1940. He was freed by Rovers in August 1942.

TOMMY GILMOUR – Inside right – (34 Lge 5 SC – ever present – 35 League goals, 2 SC) signed from Albion Rovers (who he joined in December 1934) in July 1936, he was transferred to Rangers in April 1939 after 15 First Division appearances for Rovers, and 3 goals. During the war he guested for Dumbarton and Mansfield Town.

NORMAN HAYWOOD – Centre Forward – (34 Lge 5 SC – ever present – 47 Lge goals, still a club record, and 5 SC) born in Edinburgh, he was with Edinburgh City for the second half of 1932/33, and joined St Bernards the following season. He was transferred from Peebles Rovers to Queen of the South in December 1935, and arrived at Stark's Park on a free transfer as a 26 year old in May 1937. Scored 10 goals in 22 matches in the First Division the following season. He was temporarily transferred to St Bernards in April 1940, and freed to join Leith Athletic in June 1941.

JOHN WHITELAW – Inside left – (34 Lge 5 SC – ever present – 26 Lge 5 SC goals) started with Dunnikier Juniors, and joined Cowdenbeath in June 1934 from Inverkeithing Juniors. He joined York City, from whom Rovers signed him on a free transfer in May 1937. Top scorer for Rovers in the First Division the following season, with 18 goals in 35 League games. Initially freed in March 1940, he returned to the club briefly at the start of the 1941/42 season before leaving for St Bernards in September 1941. He emigrated to following the huge attendances (and large numbers locked out) for the Scottish Cup Final and Scotland v England match within a week of each other at Hampden the previous April. Rovers complained about receiving just 7500 tickets.

It was a great cup tie from beginning to end, with East Fife the smarter team. Haywood had an excellent game and kept the East Fife defence busy, but going into the last few minutes of the match, the home side led 2-1 with goals from Millar and a Jim Morrison own goal (Raith claiming that the centre half was fouled in the process). Francis Joyner, who had picked the wrong occasion to have an off-day, had scored direct from a corner kick. As East Fife pressed to close the tie, Rovers broke upfield with five minutes to play and won a penalty kick, which Jock Whitelaw converted.

The replay was four days later at Stark's Park, and the sole topic of conversation in Fife revolved round the match. 25,500 set a new record for the ground, although the receipts were over £500 less than the first match, thanks to normal League prices being charged. The Unemployed Gate was suspended, however. Admission prices were : A & B Stand 4/-, Ground 1/-, with the Railway Stand an additional 1/- and the enclosure an extra 6d.

With the kick off at 3.30pm on a Wednesday afternoon, there were logistical problems for many workers who wished to attend the match. Fife County Council had taken a dim view of absenteeism that afternoon, advising those members of staff who had attended the match that the council did not approve and that "recurrence of similar action would be treated as a serious offence."

As late as 31st May, the matter was still being discussed by the Council. "The attendance of Mr Gregor McGregor, Director of Education, at the Raith Rovers v East Fife cup tie was the subject of a long discussion."

Once again, East Fife played the better football, although Rovers fought harder. The attack could not achieve the fluency which had characterised its destruction of so many Second Division defences, and the team was reliant on some stirring displays in defence, notably from Bob Allan.

McCartney opened the scoring for the visitors in 15 minutes, but Norman Haywood equalised before half time. Herd put East Fife ahead from the penalty spot twelve minutes into the second half, and a rousing finish was guaranteed when Tait put through his own goal to level the match after 72 minutes.

Dave Baxter had failed a fitness test on an injury sustained in the first match, and from the small pool of reserves, who had been mostly glimpsed in local cup ties, Andy Meikleham was chosen to replace him. The only problem was that he had finished a night shift in the pit earlier that day. With two minutes to play, he was caught in possession, when a simple clearance was called for, and East Fife's attack was stopped only by Morrison handling on the goal-line. Herd

scored his second penalty of the match (the earlier one given after Cabrelli handled) to win the tie, deservedly, for East Fife.

The Methil men didn't squander their hard-won local derby victory ; they beat St Bernards in the semi final and Kilmarnock in the final, both after replays, to become the first, and so far only, team outwith the top division to lift the Scottish Cup.

There may have been deep disappointment in Rovers' ranks at their cup exit, but it did not show in their League results, although it took a last minute goal to win at Forfar three days after the cup tie, a battling performance which spoke volumes for the character and fighting qualities of the team. It was Rovers' first win at Station Park for eight years. The Championship was won the following Saturday, with four matches to spare, and in great style, Alloa beaten 8-3 at Recreation Park. In the third last match, at King's Park, Gilmour scored the club's 132nd League goal of the season, thus equalling the British record set by Falkirk two seasons earlier. His second of the game set a new record, which was extended to 142 by the end of the season. It has never been beaten.

The final six matches were all won, and Rovers returned to the First Division after nine long, hard seasons of exile, a huge 12 points ahead of third placed Airdrie. The club's depleted finances were also given a timely boost, not only from the cup run and some impressive League gates, but from the sale of teenage wing sensation Francis Joyner to Sheffield United for £1650 on 7th April. Scottish Amateur Internationalist Robert "Piper" McKay came seamlessly into the side to replace him.

The 1937-38 team which emerged without prior notice to thrill fans with its cup exploits, set a goalscoring record for British League football which will probably never be beaten, and restored Rovers to the First Division, showed how fickle football can be. The team was undoubtedly greater than the sum of its parts, and unlike the Rovers team which won the League Cup in 1994, none of them could point to significant playing achievements prior to 1937/38, nor did any of them aspire to great heights in the years which followed, although the impending World War robbed the younger players of the best part of their careers.

Nevertheless, their achievement was astounding, and their place in the club's history – and in the history of British football - deserves to be fully recorded.

On 29th April, thirteen hundred people attended a Victory Ball at the Burma Ballroom. The Fife Free Press reported "During the evening, The Masked Singer and the Two Whites entertained the dancers in pleasing fashion, while the dance music provided by Jack Cunningham and his band was most acceptable. The catering was efficiently carried through by the Rialto Tea Rooms, under the supervision of Miss Young."

Not unreasonably, Rovers fans were anticipating nothing less than a mid-table position in the First Division for 1938/39. The

Australia in 1954 where he died in February 1986, aged 73.

ROBERT "PIPER" MCKAY - Outside left – (6 Lge, 3 goals) Signed on 21st January 1938 from the Army, with whom he won three Scotland Amateur caps in 1934. Prior to serving in Egypt as an army piper, he had played for a Lochgelly club. He left Rovers at the end of 1938/39 season, having obtained a free transfer on appeal to the SFA, to sign for Stenhousemuir. He played 7 times for Rovers in the First Division.

McKay took over the outside left position for the closing matches, following the transfer to Sheffield United of ....

FRANCIS JOYNER (inset) – outside left – (28 Lge 5 SC, 21 Lge 2 SC goals) signed for St Andrews United on 17th July 1936 from Strathkinnes Amateurs, and in May 1937 he signed for Raith Rovers. He was transferred to Sheffield United on 8th April 1938 for £1650. An Army captain during the war, he guested for Rovers and Third Lanark amongst other clubs, and signed for Dundee on being demobbed. Rovers signed him again in August 1947, and in January 1950 he signed for Hamilton Accies. Until 1954/5 he had brief spells as Kettering Town, Falkirk, Forfar Athletic and Stirling Albion. He compiled the "Midnight Bureau" transfer news section of the Scottish Sunday Express for many years, concurrently with managing Third Lanark for a spell during their final season in existence (1966/67) and in October 1969 he started a short spell as manager of Stirling Albion.

ERIC MACKAY – Goalkeeper – (20 Lge). Signed in May 1937 following a month's trial. A junior with Ashfield, he signed for Dundee in March 1930 before spells with Dundee United, Cowdenbeath and Montrose. He had a spell in the Irish League prior to returning to Scotland to join Rovers.

NEIL P. ANDERSON, provisionally signed from Blairhall Colliery on 2nd December 1937 Played one League match and 1 Fife Cup tie in 1937/38. He was released in July 1939 and played for East Stirling until September 1940.

ERNIE TILL

1939 Braehead House opened as head quarters of Michael Nairn & Co ; 1939 Building of Town House started, and was suspended when war was declared ; the Burgh Boundary was extended to include Boreland

On 11th May 1940, a Fife XI beat an Army XI 8-4 at Stark's Park in aid of Red Cross Charities. The teams were : Fife : Gibson and Wilkie (East Fife), Rougvie (Raith Rovers), Russell (Sheffield Wednesday), Sneddon (East Fife), Brown (Dunfermline), Adams, McLeod and Watson (East Fife), Maule (Raitrh Rovers), Johnstone (Dunfermline). Watson (4), Adams (2), McLeod and Maule were the goalscorers. Army : Smith (Sheffield Wednesday), Nichol (Burntisland Shipyard), Jordan (Cowdenbeath), Cringan (Wolves), McLure (Albion Rovers), Page (Tottenham), Langley (York City), McWalter (Dundee), Veitch (Edinburgh City), Woodburn (Newcastle), Deakin (St Mirren). McWalter and Veitch each scored twice. £103 was raised

The club's hand-to-mouth existence was shown by the difficulty in raising the £15 transfer fee to Hall & Co FC for John Dutch, and his £10 signing on fee. Both were paid only thanks to the £25 donated by Raith Athletic for their use of Stark's Park in 1942/3

squad had been strengthened with Robert Campbell signed from Rangers, Alex Sharp from Falkirk, goalkeeper Richard McCreadie from East Stirling and former Scotland centre half Alex Low. Several youths and juniors were also signed as a reserve team was reformed to play in the newly created Scottish Reserve League (which replaced the Alliance).

The air of optimism around Stark's Park was palpable ; 400 ground season tickets were sold in ten days, and most of the 550 Stand season tickets were quickly sold. The A team beat the B team in "boiling temperatures" in the Public Trial match, and when the League season kicked off at Somerset Park, McCreadie was in goal and Low at centre half, alongside nine of the team who had rampaged to the Second Division Championship. Rovers were unlucky to lose 2-1, while the reserves were watched by 3,000 at Stark's Park as they beat their Ayr counterparts 6-2. The first eleven gained revenge in the return match 11 days later, winning 3-1 in front of 10,000 spectators, but only after a 4-2 home defeat to Partick Thistle, where 15,000 saw the Championship flag unfurled by Miss Bogie, sister of the Club Chairman. The flag stuck at half mast, and a wag in the crowd said that it was a bad omen for that day's game – and for the rest of the season as it turned out.

Once again, football's fickle nature chose to manifest itself at Stark's Park. Each occasional victory was heavily outweighted by several more defeats. The players who had taken the Second Division by storm the previous season found the step up in class difficult to negotiate, and the renowned fighting spirit slowly dissipated. The most convincing lower division Champions in Scottish League history were quickly mired in a relegation battle

"Piper" Mackay was an early victim of the early defeats, replaced by Eddie McArthur from Exeter City. Dave Watson returned for a spell in goal, only to be replaced once again by McCreadie. Campbell and Sharp played only cameo roles until more drastic surgery was enacted on the team in early October. Willie Dunn was signed from Southampton, replacing first of all Norman Haywood, and then Tommy Gilmour. Nineteen year old Ernie Till arrived from Crossgates Primrose and was thrown straight into the team at right half, in place of Baxter.

Till was outstanding in a 4-0 win at Arbroath – "pity it wasn't at home" thought the Kirkcaldy Times – and after an undeserved home defeat by Hibs, Hamilton Accies were beaten 2-1 at Stark's Park. The local press thought that this represented the "Turn of the Tide" ; Rovers were fourth bottom, but only two points ahead of backmarkers Albion Rovers. Unfortunately, the tide not so much turned as engulfed the listing ship. Of the next twelve League games, only one was won (3-2 at Shawfield), two were drawn (both at home in late December) and the rest lost.

There was no lack of fight in the team, few real drubbings, and several hard

luck stories. The match at home to Queen's Park on 19th November was played in arctic conditions, and a disputed goal gave Queen's the points in a thrilling hard-fought game which ended 5-4. The following week, 15,000 watched a "glorious struggle" against Hearts, but Rovers lost 2-1. At Aberdeen, a 6-3 defeat was made much worse by Smith having his leg broken in a tackle after 12 minutes.

The two drawn December games could easily have been won. Whitelaw missed a penalty against Albion Rovers, and a poor referee gave Rovers no favours against Third Lanark, the match proceeding only after the pitch had been cleared of snow. The hapless referee, Mr Thomson of Hamilton, was pelted with snowballs during and after the match, despite police intervention. All three bottom clubs were equal on points.

There was more recruitment ; a new goalkeeper in Ferguson, Dave Watson having been released ; Tim O'Keefe, borrowed from Hibs, at outside left, and Jim Kerr of Leith Athletic replacing Alex Glen on the opposite wing. Bill Peattie, and then Jim Morrison, took over from the unfortunate Smith at left back.

There was more than a glimmer of hope following successive victories in early January, with drama even before the Celtic match began at Stark's Park. Bill Peattie got in the road of a shot during the pre-match warm-up, and injured his leg. The team was hastily re-shuffled, and Jock Whitelaw, who had been dropped, was summoned from the grandstand and took the field after five minutes had been played. He scored twice, as did Ernie Till (with a memorable solo effort) and Norman Haywood, each goal better than its predecessor. Rovers fans in the 11,500 crowd enjoyed the game of the season, summarised as follows by The Sporting Post :

"Why is it that a team like Raith Rovers has not won a game, apart from to-day's smashing win, since November 12th ? This victory made Celtic look feeble, almost silly. Raith won by superior play in all departments. Forward, Haywood was a robust leader, and Whitelaw's wizardry and shooting was comparable with Tommy Walker's skill. All the forwards were grand at following up, and gave the Celtic defence a real shaking-up. Behind them Baxter blotted out Watters, and the home backs also did very well."

Whitelaw scored two at Motherwell a week later, as Rovers twice came from behind to win 4-2. The team played just as well the following week in the first round of the Scottish Cup, at home to Rangers, but an opportunist Alex Venters goal settled an incident-packed tie, watched by 21,747. Rovers, and 12,000 of their fans, were brought back down to earth seven days later when Arbroath won 3-1 at Stark's Park.

Back-to-back wins at Paisley and Hamilton kept Rovers abreast of those clubs in the safety positions, but five successive League defeats in March sealed their fate.

Rovers finished bottom of the League, seven points from safety. Missed chances, the lack of an experienced goalkeeper, and a bit of bad luck were offered as reasons for the briefest of stays back in the First Division. Neither manager nor players were blamed ; everyone tried their best and team spirit was good throughout. Till looked to be a real find, but at the end of the season Davie Baxter and Jimmy Morrison headed a list of six free transfers ; five more were placed on the Open to Transfer list, and Tim O'Keefe returned to Hibs. Tommy Gilmour was signed by Rangers.

With the threat of war hanging heavily over the country, there was a joyous occasion at the Rialto Restaurant on 2nd June when the Supporters Club made a presentation to Provost James Gourlay of St Monance, who retired after 12 years as Chairman. In that time £1500 had been gifted to the club, and much other work undertaken.

Hopes of a brief stay in the lower division suffered a set-back with the transfer of Bob Allan to Dundee on 25th July, and Rovers advertised for a new trainer (at £3 per week) to succeed Dave Clunie. It wasn't all bad news. Promising local players Davie Duncan and schoolboy internationalist Johnny Maule had been called up, along with Queen of the South centre forward Willie Smith, and the Rangers and Scotland full back Bob McAulay.

Rovers had a dreadful start to their return to the Second Division, losing 5-1 at Dundee, followed by a 2-0 home win over Brechin, a 2-1 defeat Hampden and a 3-1 loss at Stenhousemuir on Saturday 2nd September, further ignominy being heaped on a hapless Raith side by "Junior" scoring a hat-trick for the Warriors.

No-one paid much attention to the Rovers' woes the following day, when war was declared against Germany. Having learned their lesson from 1914, the football and government authorities put a stop to all organised football, although that was relaxed a fortnight later when it dawned on everyone that there would be no imminent invasion. Local cup ties were hastily arranged, against East Fife (home and away) and Dunfermline, and by mid October, following a further relaxation of restrictions on the realisation that the populace needed something to take their attention away from wartime deprivations, the Scottish League organised two regionalised League competitions.

All football contracts were cancelled, although registrations remained with the clubs, and with players joining the forces and taking employment in "reserved" occupations, the SFA and other national associations in the British Isles adopted a flexible approach to player movements.

Recent signings Dunn, Smith and McAulay found clubs closer to home, and were replaced by local boy Harry Brown from Reading, Willie Hume from Aberdeen, Jimmy Tulip from Alloa and John Murray from Plymouth Argyle. Haywood, Baxter,

Whitelaw and Low played when they could, infrequently. John Moodie was signed from Hearts to replace goalkeeper Robert Houston, who was injured in a gas explosion in Cupar. Moodie was absent for a month in November, and Rovers fans were astonished to discover his replacement was Jimmy Mathieson, last seen in the Rovers goal 13 years earlier, who had played the previous season for Queen of the South.

The biggest "transfer" shock was that of the manager, Sandy Archibald. Following the 2-0 home win over Dunfermline in the Fife Cup semi final on 14th October, Archibald left to take over as manager at East End Park. A week later, the club trainer, Willie Reekie, took over as manager. Well respected in local football circles as a player and manager of Dunnikier and Abbotshall Juniors, Reekie had been appointed reserve team trainer the previous season. A coal merchant, he agreed to manage the club's affairs for the duration of the war, and it is to his enormous credit that the club emerged from the conflict intact, and with a nucleus of first class footballers on their books.

Rovers debut in the North Eastern League was as undistinguished as their opening Scottish League result that season ; a 5-1 defeat at Pittodrie, and it was followed by a 5-1 home defeat by Hearts and a 5-0 drubbing at Stenhousemuir. That results provoked the Kirkcaldy Times to remark : "The Directors will have to do more serious thinking immediately if the doors are to remain open at Stark's Park for football, and not merely as the office of an ARP [Air Raid Precaution] post."

A 2-1 win over Dundee in a "grand match" the following Saturday was followed by two defeats, and then a remarkable 6-0 home win over Arbroath, the goals scored by the youngsters Maule, Till, Hume (2) and Duncan (2). After that it was gloomy fare for the dwindling crowds, with one draw and five defeats, that baleful sequence ended with an unexpected 6-0 home win over St Bernards, the hard-working Kinnear scoring a hat-trick. It was to be a month before they played again, due to heavy snowstorms.

In the meantime, on 11th December, James Gourlay was appointed headmaster of the North School, returning to work in Kirkcaldy, and on 2nd January 1943, he was appointed Chairman of the Board of Directors at Raith Rovers.

In the second half of the season, David Kinnear from Dunnikier Juniors, Alfie Pope from Hearts and Ralph Rougvie from Cowdenbeath took over from Peattie, Brown and Hume (who joined Hearts). Fulfilling fixtures was not an easy matter. There were only ten signed players available for the New Year's Day match at home to East Fife, and the junior Kinnear was fielded at centre forward, scoring both of Rovers' goals in a 2-5 defeat. The following day at Perth, Rovers were down to nine men. Kinnear played again, and Mackie of the home club lined up at left back against his team-mates. On 13th January at home to St Bernards, Rovers

ALEX LOW
A Scotland cap with Falkirk in 1934, he refused re-signing terms at Brockville and was on loan to Workington when Rovers signed him in 1938.
WILLIE HURRELL
Rovers received a significant transfer fee from Millwall just after the Second World War.

Photographed at the entrance to the pavilion at Tannadice on 15th August 1942. five of the players who appeared for Rovers during the war years. Left to right, Hickman, Walker, Phypers, Donald, Cairns. Looking on, in the far right of the photograph, is manager Willie Reekie.

Wing half Ernie Phypers was a Spurs player from June 1934 to June 1949, although he played mostly in the reserves. He made 33 League and Cup appearances for the first team. During the war he also guested for Clapton Orient, Doncaster Rovers, Southend United and West Ham. In 1949 he signed for Doncaster Rovers.

Cyril Walker cost Sheffield Wednesday £1150 from Gillingham in October 1937 but played only six first team matches before leaving for Chelmsford City. He also guested for Crystal Palace, Brighton, Watford and Norwich City during the war.

Full back John Cairns played for Leith Athletic and Dunfermline Athletic during the war, while John Donald was signed from Hall and Company, the Aberdeen junior club.

Jimmy Hickman was registered with Aston Villa, but the war deprived him of the best years of his football career. He was one of hundreds of players fielded by Rovers during the Second World War.

scored three goals between 41 and 44 minutes, in a 6-0 victory.

Results took a turn for the better, not least in the National Cup competition organised by the SFA and Scottish League for the 31 clubs in the two regional leagues (Cowdenbeath having resigned). The first round ties were played over two legs, Moodie saving a Murphy penalty kick to narrow the defeat to 4-2 at Celtic Park. To everyone's surprise, Rovers won the return match at Stark's Park 3-0, and gave a battling performance before losing 2-1 at Tynecastle in the second round. The competition was won by Rangers, who beat Dundee United 1-0 in the final, for whom Alex Glen – still a registered Rovers player – was at outside right. Kinnear joined the Air Force and at the end of the season the strike force from the memorable 1937/38 season, Whitelaw and Haywood, left for St Bernards.

The "Phoney War" over, the Scottish League abandoned operations in the summer of 1940, and clubs were left in limbo. Rovers decided against playing any fixtures, such were the uncertainties as Britain entered the first truly global "total war". Although matches continued to be played on Stark's Park, they were mostly between service units and local organisations, save for a fixture played in aid of the Sports Fund of the local Anti Aircraft Division. That was played on Saturday 14th December 1940, but such was the heavy wintry rain that the gate amounted to only £16 from an attendance of less than 800.

The teams were : SFA Select : Hall (Ayr United) ; Cowan (Rangers), Manderson (Airdrie). Thomson (Hamilton), Thomson and Brown (Rangers) ; Gilmartin (Hibs), Miller (Falkirk), McIntosh (Rangers), Brown (Hearts), Milne (Dumbarton).

Army XI : Rodger (Ayr United) ; Bob Allan (Dundee), Jones (Bradford City), Sharp (Albion Rovers), Mason (Falkirk), Wales (Motherwell) ; Degnan (Albion Rovers), Stevenson (Third Lanark), Younger (Partick Thistle), McCartney (East Fife), Louden (Albion Rovers).

Gilmartin, McIntosh, Brown (Hearts) and Milne scored for the SFA, who won 4-2, McCartney and Stevenson scoring for the

Army. The referee was J. Martin of Ladybank.

In June 1941, meetings were held in Dundee and then Kirkcaldy of clubs on the East Coast, from which it was decided to ask the SFA to administer a North Eastern League. With the majority of Rovers' signed players either abroad on active service or scattered throughout the UK, Willie Reekie had to assemble a squad of players. Davie Duncan was the only signed player to start the season. Rougvie and Murray returned, loaned by their respective clubs, and they were joined by John Abbie of St Bernards, Jimmy Fleming of Hibs, Robert Mauchline of Accrington Stanley and Francis Joyner of Sheffield United. George Whaley, formerly of Hearts was signed, and was joined by Jimmy Keogh of Thornton Hibs, Martin and Summers of Lochgelly Albert and two locally-based soldiers, Douglas Falconer and Willie McNaught.

Two League programmes were planned, split by a Cup competition. Rovers won 3, drew 1 and lost 10 of the first set of League matches and finished second bottom, above Leith Athletic who were homeless, and who borrowed Easter Road and then St Bernard's Royal Gymnasium ground. The scorelines reflected the chaotic organisation of the League, and its clubs, with the country in the depths of war. There were 8-1 and 7-1 defeats, and 9-5 and 9-3 victories. When Rovers were away from home, Stark's Park was used by the new Juvenile team Raith Athletic, a resurrection of an old name, under the watchful eye of Bert Herdman. Home and away defeats to East Fife resulted in the shortest possible participation in the North Eastern Cup, the trophy donated by William Mitchell, Chairman of Aberdeen, who beat Dundee United in the final, the victorious players being rewarded with three War Savings Certificates.

Rovers fared better in the second League series, losing only six matches. There was a novel amendment to the points system. In addition to two points for a win and one for a draw, the aggregate of the home and away matches against each team was taken, the winner gaining an extra point.

There was a huge turnover of players, with regulars such as left back Miller, left half Alex McDonnell, Alex Low at centre half, John Gould at outside right, Willie Hurrell at inside right and a young winger from Auchtermuchty called Jackie Stewart, being joined by a constant flow of visiting players.

Hearts and Hibs replaced Leith Athletic and St Bernards at the start of 1942/43, both clubs beginning to experience the difficulties which would lead to their demise. Doug Westland played in goal for Rovers in the first three matches, although Moodie, Gage and Keogh shared the position for the remainder of the season. Hickman, Cairns, Donald, Phyper, Smith and Wilkie joined Alex Low, Willie Hurrell and Davie Duncan as regulars at the start of the season. John Dutch (from Aberdeen junior side Hall &

Co), Bob Glassey and a prolific goalscorer with Raith Athletic, Willie Penman, were regulars after the New Year.

Nine of the first 14 League matches were lost and Rovers finished bottom, but progress was made in the North Eastern Cup, at the expense of East Fife. Aberdeen won the semi final 11-3 on aggregate, however, and went on to complete a League and Cup double   The last six League fixtures of the second series comprised five wins and one draw, despite the sale of Davie Duncan to Celtic just before Christmas. Rovers fared well in the end of season Mitchell Cup competition. Dundee United and East Fife were beaten on aggregate, and the first match of the final against Aberdeen was abandoned one minute into the second half.   In driving wind and rain, all the spectators were in the stands, with the terracing deserted, and the game was called off when Dyer, the Aberdeen right half, collapsed on the field.   The referee, Mr Godfrey of Stenhousemuir, collapsed on leaving the ground and was taken to hospital. He regained consciousness at 5am the following morning.   The match was played on 8th May.

A week later, the teams met again at Stark's Park and drew 1-1, in front of 9000 spectators.   14,000 saw Aberdeen win the second leg at Pittodrie 6-2, and the trophy.

There were further changes to the North Eastern League for 1943/44. Falkirk replaced Hibs, and in the second League series away wins would earn 3 points and an away draw 2 points.   Rovers reversed their usual pattern by faring better in the first half of the season, benefiting from a more settled team.   They finished three points ahead of Hearts at the top of the first League table. Willie Bruce from Banks o'Dee was in goal, Frank Shufflebottom and John Donald at full back, Dutch, Low and Alex Fletcher (an amateur from Ardeer) at half back, all being fielded in the majority of fixtures.   There was less certainty in the forward line, although Jackie Stewart and Willie Penman were the regular wingers.   Willie Hurrell was replaced by John Ventre from Carluke Rovers early in the new year, Ernie Waldron replaced Glassey, and there were brief appearances by Joe Payne, P.B.S. Lamb, Alex Hendry (Lewis United) and Norrie Haywood.

After a first round exit to Aberdeen in the North Eastern League Cup, Falkirk were beaten in the first round of the end of season Mitchell Cup.   After winning 4-2 at Brockville in the first leg, Falkirk fielded eight of their Southern League (first) team at Stark's Park. 3-0 down at half time, Jackie Stewart got a goal back from the penalty spot.   Dawson scored for Falkirk after 70 minutes, but Stewart scored again, ten minutes later, to put the match into extra time, where Willie Penman scored the winner with three minutes

to play.   In any case, Rovers were leading by 2 corners to 1 in extra time, the prescribed tie-breaking method.

After a 2-2 draw at Pittodrie, Aberdeen were beaten 2-1 at Stark's Park, watched by 5740.   All eyes were on the Rangers teamsheet for the first leg of the final, at Ibrox.   They fielded Woodburn, Waddell, Duncanson and McCormack, and won 3-2.   A slightly weaker Rangers team won the second leg at Stark's Park by the same scoreline, watched by 8944.

Having snubbed the North Eastern clubs in previous years, the Southern League teams relented and allowed their country cousins to enter the Summer Cup.   It was a brief excursion for Rovers, following a 2-1 home defeat by Morton in the first leg. Goals by Ventre and Haywood won the second leg at Cappielow by the same scoreline, and although Haywood beat Jimmy Cowan again in extra time, Morton scored twice more.

James C. Stewart, who had made a few appearances at the end of the previous season, formed the regular half back line for 1944/45 with Alex Low and Robert Kelly. William Montgomery of Ashfield was brought in at left half towards the end of the season ; Stewart and Penman remained fixtures on the wing, but there was a succession of inside forwards, including Alex Beattie, John Connor, Arthur Woon, who was Willie Penman's former strike partner at Raith Athletic, and the returning Bob Glassey.   Willie Hurrell and Johnny Maule played when service commitments allowed, and from February to the end of the season, a young Fifer on Celtic's books appeared at inside forward – Andy Young.   John Ventre was transferred to Falkirk in late August, Rovers earning £100 from their wartime enterprise, and commendably decided to share it amongst the players, offering £1 for an away win and 10/- for an away draw and a home win..   A sense that the war was nearing its final stages prompted the re-starting of Supporters Club meetings in November 1944.

The North Eastern League was

Not only did Rovers keep the flag of senior football flying in Kirkcaldy during the disruption of the Second World War, but Stark's Park also provided a focus for young footballers in the area.   The name Raith Athletic was resurrected for a team which was fielded in Juvenile football, a grade which was more active during the war than the amateurs and juniors.

Supporters Club treasurer Bert Herdman was the moving force behind Raith Athletic, who provided Rovers with a source of potential players. The best known graduate was Willie Penman, who is pictured above in the front row, far right.

Raith Athletic used Stark's Park for their home matches, and the club's kit.

There were no season tickets allowed for the North Eastern League, which Rovers rejoined in 1941/42, although Rangers were exempted as they intimated that their season tickets had been sold with North Eastern (Reserve team) League admission included

A levy was taken from each game (25%, with the home team keeping 55%), and the resulting pool at the end of the season amounted to £1401 6/11 which, with interest added, was distributed to each club as £175 10/4d.   For 1943/44, a guarantee to visiting clubs was introduced, the greater of £20 or 20%).

Rangers (second eleven) was accompanied on one of their visits to Stark's Park in the North Eastern League by former Scotland internationalist Alan Morton. He was pressed into service at half time to make an announcement to the crowd to encourage recruitment to the Forces. Watching him in the above photograph is Rovers director James Bogie.

There was a stormy outcome to the B Division Supplementary Cup tie replay between Rovers and Dundee United at Dens Park on 6th February 1946. At the end of 90 minutes, with the teams still tied on both goals (3-3) and corner kicks (4-4) the referee interpreted the instructions he had received from the Scottish League literally, and summoned both captains to the centre of the field to toss a coin to decide which team would win the tie. Willie McNaught chose correctly, but back in the pavilion, the Dundee United officials were incensed that there had been no consultation on the method of deciding the tie, such as another replay. Despite United's protests, supported by the Dundee-based press, the League backed the referee's decision.

expanded to ten clubs, with the addition of Dundee and Arbroath, King's Park being unsuccessful in their application.

Because of the additional League games, the North Eastern Cup was to be competed for by only the top four teams ; Rovers finished third in the first League series, but made an early cup exit at the hands of Dundee (who lost the Final to Aberdeen at Dens Park, in front of an attendance of 19,098) A poor start to the second series of League games was improved later on, allowing Rovers to finish in sixth position. Arbroath were beaten over two legs in the Mitchell Cup, but Aberdeen won the second round match at Pittodrie, played as late as 2nd June.

Although the modest crowds which continued to enter Stark's Park during the four seasons of war-time football would have insisted otherwise, results and trophies (of which there were none) were of secondary significance. The main purpose was to keep playing, thereby keeping the club alive, and for that Willie Reekie cannot be praised sufficiently. He was also able to bring through some young players who would, over the following decade, propel Rovers to great heights : Jackie Stewart, Willie Penman, Willie McNaught and Andy Young. Good professionals such as Willie Bruce and the full backs John Donald and John Dutch would help in Rovers transition to peace-time football, and pre-war registered players Johnny Maule and the veteran Alex Low were kept in touch with the club.

One need only look at other clubs to see how the lack of a guiding hand such as Reekie's set them back once normal football was resumed. Cowdenbeath and Alloa, both First Division clubs when war was declared, took decades to return to their previous level ; Dunfermline, who undoubtedly suffered from the shock of Sandy Archibald dying in 1946, were left trailing in Rovers' wake, while St Bernards and Kings Park did not survive the war. Rovers great success of 1948/49, with

McNaught and Young key players and Penman scoring profusely, both club and team funded by the huge proceeds of Stewart's sale to Birmingham City, was in no small part attributable to Willie Reekie's wartime service at Stark's Park.

Reekie and his (at times) frantically constructed teams also managed to provide entertainment for the duration of the war to the sporting public in Kirkcaldy and District. Apart from the bright young talent introduced to the club, and the cameo appearances of players returning for a brief spell of leave, there was the opportunity to see top quality players who guested for the club while stationed locally.

They included : Ernie Phypers of Tottenham Hotspur, Joe Payne of Chelsea (who had set an English League Third Division South record when he scored 55 goals in 39 games for Luton Town in 1936/37. The previous season, he set another record for that League, scoring 10 goals in one match against Bristol Rovers.), John Bonomy and Willie McFadyen of Motherwell, Alfie Pope of Hearts, Scottish internationalist Willie Imrie of St Johnstone, Jimmy Milburn of Leeds United (one of the Ashington clan), Irish Internationalist Willie Cook of Everton, John Harvey of Hearts, Ernie Waldron of Crystal Palace, Sammy Stewart and John Sneddon of East Fife (for one game only), George Gilmour of Hearts, Jimmy Briscoe Sheffield Wednesday, Benson of St Johnstone, former player Davie Kinnear of Rangers, Willie Aird of Morton, Jimmy Inglis of Falkirk and the spectacularly prolific goalscorer Vic Ruse of Carnoustie Panmure, and later Dundee.

There was also a fleeting glimpse of future Scottish Internationalists, with Alex Forbes (Dundee North End, later Arsenal) and George Aitken (Lochgelly Albert, later East Fife) playing for Rovers as youthful trialists.

With the end of the war in sight during the summer of 1945, it was proposed to form two Leagues, with the City and stronger provincial outfits (16 in all) in A Division, and the (13) "county" clubs in B Division, along with Dundee. A later meeting of the Scottish Football League clubs agreed to adopt that formula, with no mention being made of future arrangements. Some of the major clubs' chairmen were muttering about the wisdom of scrapping automatic promotion and relegation

Rovers therefore started 1945/46 season with a home B Division fixture against Arbroath, which they won 3-2. Fittingly, Willie Penman scored Rovers' first post-war goal in the 44th minute, although football historians continue to debate whether 1945/46 should be regarded as a war-time, or post-war, season.

There was certainly no Scottish Cup competition, the SFA instead promoting an end of season Victory Cup. A benign winter resulted in an early finish to the League programme, so the Scottish Football League continued with the format of the war-time Southern League Cup, involving round-robin qualifying competitions of four clubs, with knock out matches from the quarter finals onwards, and the 1945/46 competition is counted by some as the first League Cup competition (although, to add to the confusion, many simply saw it as a continuation of the war-time competition, and this was acknowledged for some years in official circles). While the Second Division clubs were waiting for the First Division sides to finish their slightly longer League programme, they started a B Division Supplementary Cup competition.

As players returned from the services, and their reserved occupations became less onerous, they returned to their registered clubs. Rovers, like most clubs, used a prodigious number of players in 1945/46, the still-elastic registration and playing regulations allowing trialists and guests to be fielded at will. To the war-time stalwarts such as Bruce, Donald, Dutch and Hurrell, were added pre-war returnees, Alex Low (who had played throughout the war), Johnny Maule and Ernie Till, who had spent several years posted abroad. There were recent signings who would not be long at the club ; Wotherspoon, Montgomery, Woon, and those who would dwell longer, Stewart, McNaught and Penman. Amid the confusion at other clubs, good players were plundered – Andy Young from Celtic and Malcolm McLure from Hearts. The second half of the season saw the arrival of right back Andrew Watson, centre half Robert Johnstone, inside right Hugh Colvan, centre half David Stark and an unlikely looking outside left from Chester, Harry Colville.

There was also a new manager. Willie Reekie announced during the summer that his task had been completed ; with the war about to end, his stewardship would also terminate. Perhaps influenced by the success of the coal merchant whose previous football involvement had been in the junior and juvenile grades, the directors turned to a French polisher who had piloted Raith Athletic to some success during the war – Bert Herdman.

The Fife Free Press of 4th August 1945 announced the new appointment in the following terms. "Mr Bert Herdman, treasurer of the Supporters Club, who has all along taken a great interest in the Rovers, and who is also well-known for his activities in connection with the successful juvenile formation, Raith Athletic, has been appointed temporarily. This appointment should be met with general satisfaction, as Bert is in touch with football affairs generally, and has a good idea of the talent available.

"The Directors offered Mr Herdman the post on a permanent basis, but he declined. He agreed to take over until a full time manager could be appointed." On 6th

October, having realised that he could not do the job justice in his spare time, Bert Herdman commenced full time employment at Stark's Park, an arrangement which continued until his sudden death 23 years later.

Home wins over Arbroath, Airdrie and Dunfermline in the early stages of the season, and a 7-0 win at Dundee United, distracted attention from too many defeats. In the nineteen League matches between a 5-0 defeat at home to Dundee on 29th September, and the final League fixture on 19th January, a 2-2 draw at Stenhousemuir, Rovers won only two more League games, both at home. One of the narrower defeats was a 1-0 victory for Albion Rovers at Stark's Park on 3rd November. The Kirkcaldy Times was moved to report : "Stein, the visitors' centre half, was the personality of the game. He put up a great display and played a big part in Albion Rovers' successes."

A month later, in the 4-1 home defeat by Dumbarton, Willie Penman collided with a goalpost and broke his leg. The club was ill-prepared for such serious injuries. There was no stretcher to hand, and Willie was lifted onto a door that someone had found lying in the groundsman's store, and was carted off to await an ambulance. Despite playing in just 17 of the club's 42 matches that season, only Jackie Stewart (with 17 from 38 games) and Penman's former Raith Athletic partner Woon with 10 from 13 games, exceeded his total of 8 goals (Andy Young matched that figure from 32 games).

Perhaps it is best to side with those historians who choose not to include this season in the record books ; Rovers finished joint bottom, with Arbroath. It was far from an auspicious start for the new manager.

It took three games, and the toss of a coin, to eliminate Dundee United from the B Division Supplementary Cup, before a 4-0 home defeat by Airdrie. Three wins and three defeats in the League Cup section was better than League form, but not enough to qualify for the knock out stages. To everyone's surprise, significant progress was made in the Victory Cup. Arbroath were

Another photograph of Raith Athletic, taken towards the end of the Second World War, when the players look a little bit older. Willie Penman is no longer a Raith Athletic player - he had signed for Raith Rovers - but the photograph includes Bert Herdman, to the far left.

Among the teams played by Raith Athletic were Leith Renton, Bowhill West End, Thornton Athletic, Leith Renton (who played at Easter Road), Bowhill Rovers, Dunnikier Athletic, Lochore, Old Boys Club (a rival Kirkcaldy team made up of former Boys Brigade members, and run inter alia by Rankin Grimshaw), Lochore, Bluebell, Kinglassie Boys Club, Dundonald Bluebell, Bayview Youth Club, Freuchie Our Boys and East Fife Juveniles.

In 1942/43 additional clubs in the Kirkcaldy and District League were Aircraft Sports Club, Balgonie Boys Club, Prinlaws United, Kennoway Hearts, Balgonie Scotia. Cup ties were played against Kelty Boys Club and Buckhaven Star.

The following season, Leslie Hearts, Denbeath Star, Rosslyn Juveniles, Bowhill St Ninians, Wemyss Athletic and Rose Street Rovers were on the fixture list.

In 1944/45 fixtures were played against Kelty Rangers, St Monance Swifts, Kirkcaldy Athletic, Kinghorn St Leonards, Markinch Victoria Rangers and Townhill.

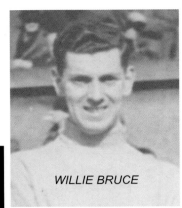

WILLIE BRUCE

For the second half of the 1941/42 season, boys and members of His Majesty's Forces were admitted at a 7d concession. Adults were charged 1/1d, including tax. Clubs were encouraged to allow free admission to "elementary schoolboys"

Despite the lack of funds, and offer from Hibs for Willie Hurrell was turned down on 1st February 1943.

On Saturday 23th June 1944, the Supporters Club organised an All in Wrestling show at Stark's Park

On 6th October 1945, the Royal Navy lost 8-2 to the RAF at Stark's Park, but only 1000 turned up, paying £94 19/5d towards Fife's £5,000 appeal for the YMCA War Service Fund. The Supporters Club made the figure up to £100. Rovers lost 5-3 at Perth in a B Division League match that afternoon, the day Bert Herdman became full time manager of the club.

1945 Dunnikier Park purchased by Kirkcaldy Town Council from the Oswald family ; 14th January 1945, death of Thomas McGilvray, 8 Lina Street, who took over (and renamed) the printing business on the retrial of John Cramb ; The Palace Cinema next to the Sheriff Court was destroyed by fire on 28th December

1946 Electricity generation in Kirkcaldy ceased with the closure of the Victoria Road works ; The Kirkcaldy Times of 4th September announced that the Ice Hockey Club was reforming ; St Columba's RC Church opened

beaten home and away, and Colvan and George Gilmour, recently signed from Hearts, scored the goals to beat A Division St Mirren at Stark's Park, the latter's described as "the prettiest" of goals.

The Kirkcaldy Times reported that "Raith owed their success to a steady, well balanced half-back line. Till was the mastermind once again, and his purveying was first rate. He seldom wasted a ball and gave grand service not only to the right wing pair but to the other forwards as well." A determined Rovers won a tousy game. Rovers were far from disgraced in losing 2-0 at Celtic Park in the third round, the verdict being that they expended too much nervous energy. In common with the pattern throughout Britain, crowds flocked back to Stark's Park, relieved that the war was over and some normality was returning to the way of life. In the context of the convulsion to everyone's lives over the preceding six years, the poor playing record of the local football club was of little consequence. There was also a glimmer of hope at the better form shown in the end of season cup tournaments, particularly as the eleven which beat St Mirren and lost honourably at Celtic, were all signed for 1946/47.

Proposals for a break-away "Scottish National League" were averted in the spring of 1946, at the expense of those clubs who had been in the First Division when war broke out in 1939, and now found themselves in B Division. The big city clubs got their way in retaining the 16 teams which formed A Division in 1945/46, but promotion and relegation was conceded. Interspersed with the opening League matches were fixtures in the B Division Supplementary Cup, played on midweek evenings. Rovers did well, beating Arbroath home and away in the first round, St Johnstone at Stark's Park in the second round, Alloa at home in the semi final despite Andy Young being ordered off 15 minutes from the end, and faced East Fife in the final. The local rivals proved to be too strong, and won both legs, but 18,000 saw the first match at Stark's Park, and an all-ticket 14,000 watched East Fife win the trophy at Methil. Rovers were given only 4,000 tickets, which sold out within an hour. On the day of the first leg, the Kirkcaldy Times reported that "the start of the game tonight has been delayed until 6.45 in order to allow the linoleum workers, who form a large percentage of the Raith support, time to be present at the kick off."

In the meantime, Rovers were unbeaten in their first six League fixtures, and a largely settled side was attracting admiring crowds to Stark's Park. War-time recruit Willie Bruce was in goal, Andrew Watson from Armadale Thistle at right back and Malcolm McLure at left back. Till, former Queen's Park and Partick Thistle Tony Johnstone and McNaught, moved from attack to defence, formed the half back line. Jackie Stewart, Colvan on loan from Hibs, Harry Muir from Lochore Welfare, Gilmour and Maule were the usual forwards, although Andy Young was

always in the team, showing his versatility by playing wherever the need arose.

Following the 3-0 home win over Cowdenbeath, watched by 14,000, it was reported that "Raith players had peaches at half time on Saturday. No wonder they had the pip for a bit in the second half. That's not all, earlier this season, they were given grapes at the interval. What about the "patient" supporters ?"

Poor results in the League Cup section carried onto a disappointing sequence of results up to Christmas. A couple of local forwards were tried in Elgin McIntyre and Jimmy Oatman, and results improved in January, following the introduction of Ron Henderson at centre half. Willie Penman returned to the first team, and was quickly and messily loaned to Brechin City, but he and Jackie Stewart scored twice in a splendid 4-3 victory at Dumfries in the first round of the Scottish Cup. McNaught was made captain for the match against his home town team, and gave an outstanding performance.

Penman and Stewart were also among Rovers four goalscorers in the next round at Arbroath, but the Red Lichties scored five times to end Rovers' cup ambitions for another season. A second Penman goal in 80 minutes was ruled offside, and resulted in a pitch invasion by some Rovers fans, who were evicted by the constabulary. Sixth position was a vast improvement on the previous season, but Rovers were 16 points shy of a promotion place, and the large number of players used throughout the season suggested that although half the side were settled in their positions, the other half were there to be replaced. Comprehensive home and away defeats by champions Dundee prompted the Kirkcaldy Times to opine : "Directors should heed the lesson – experience is needed for a promotion team." The team had done nothing to lift the gloom which enveloped the town (in common with the rest of the country). Post-war austerity was sorely felt, and the winter had been one of the most severe in living memory, causing the Home Secretary to ban all midweek football matches in Britain in February and March.

During the summer, there were rumours that manager Herdman, who had earlier in the season been described as "probably the most enthusiastic officer Raith have ever hand, for close on 20 years a very hard working official with the Supporters Club" was threatening to follow Sandy Archibald's example, and resign in disillusionment at the Board's lack of investment in the team.

While there was no loosening of the purse-strings in terms of paying transfer fees, or high wages to experienced players, at least the reserve team was re-formed for 1947/48, despite the £70 guarantee which applied in C Division.

There were instant dividends. Rovers opened the new season with four successive wins, in League and League Cup, and despite five games without a win, they won nine successive League matches in the run up to Christmas.   A 2-0 win at Dunfermline on the opening day inspired the Kirkcaldy Times to write : "With judicious moulding, Raith Rovers stand to enhance their reputation this season.   The basis is there – definitely."

There was a spectacular failure to qualify for the latter stages of the League Cup. The first five matches were won, and the final match was at Hamilton, who had won four of their previous games, losing only to Rovers (3-1 at Stark's Park). Devlin put Hamilton ahead after 34 minutes, but Francis Joyner equalised in 66 minutes. With 15 minutes to play, the 1-1 scoreline would have put Rovers into the quarter finals, but they lost no fewer than 5 goals in that time.   The post-mortem in the Kirkcaldy Times said that the game was lost in the boardroom. There had been too many changes to accommodate the absence of Andy Young, who injured his foot while working in a coalmine. Ned Weir, who was preferred to the unreliable Henderson at centre half, was dismissed as being "too old". He had been signed as player coach to the reserve team.   The team "collapsed like a pricked balloon in the last quarter of an hour." A 5-1 win over Dundee United on 29th November, watched by 8,500, propelled Rovers into the promotion places, and the second half was broadcast live on BBC Radio, with Peter Thompson commentating. A week later, a 6-2 home win over Stenhousemuir put Rovers top of the League, and all the fans had to worry about was the transfer speculation which swirled around Stewart and McNaught.

Athol McAra from Hearts started the season alongside McLure at left back, although he was replaced by Harry Muir after a couple of months. McNaught took over from Henderson at centre half, David Dalziel's signing from Newtongrange Star allowed Jackie Stewart to move inside, before moving back onto the right wing when Andrew Dolan, a summer signing from Alloa, returned to the side at inside right. Francis Joyner ("unorthodox but agile") returned to the club at outside left, and Penman switched to centre forward.   Perhaps the key signing, however, was former Hibs and Falkirk wing half Tommy Brady, who added the necessary guile and experience.   One retrograde step was the loss of goalkeeper Willie Bruce to Aberdeen, Brown, Harper and John Smith (from Preston Athletic) all being tried in his place.

The younger players looked to Brady for guidance and support, and thrived on it. He was not afraid to take responsibility either, even when it was beyond his normal remit. Assistant Trainer Alex Hamill recalled when Tommy put the team on an extra bonus, on his own initiative.

"The match was all square with twenty minutes to go, and a win was essential to keep the promotion push going. I was sitting on the touchline when I heard Tommy telling another player 'Get stuck in, we're on another £2". Two goals were scored, and the match was won. In the dressing-room afterwards, Brady told manager Herdman "I

put the boys on an extra £2 bonus." Bert, quite a character himself, threw his arms wide in a typical gesture and exclaimed "You'll get me executed." Just then, Mr James Gourlay, the chairman, came in and Tommy explained that things hadn't been going right and he had put the boys on an extra bonus. Everyone looked at the chairman, wondering what his reaction would be, but he just chuckled and congratulated Tommy, saying the team had done well to win."

McNaught at the back and Johnny Maule in midfield were naturally talented footballers, while Penman was a prodigious goalscorer. So, too, was Jackie Stewart. In the first 26 games of the season, he scored 22 goals, and it came as no surprise when Birmingham City signed him on 9th January.   What was a shock was the size of the fee. Normally, Rovers fans are surprised at how little their favourites fetch in the transfer market, but there could be no complaints about the £8000 received for Stewart's services. A year earlier, Leslie Johnstone had set the record between Scottish clubs when he joined Hibs from Clyde for £10,000, in the same month that Aston Villa paid Swansea Town a similar amount for the Welsh internationalist centre forward Trevor Ford.   Stewart became one of the most expensive players in British football when he left Stark's Park for Birmingham.

He was certainly missed in the second half of the season, despite a report that the Directors were prepared to spent "a thousand or two" from his fee to challenge for promotion.   Maule was moved to the right wing, but lacked Stewart's cutting edge and penetration.   His chosen replacement was former Rangers and Scotland internationalist Alex Venters, a big name signing, but clearly past his prime.   In mid February Pat McDonald and Joe Rae were signed on loan from Celtic.   An attempt was made to fill the troubled goalkeeping position, but terms could not be agreed with Jock Wallace, who was unhappy at Blackpool.   Another former player was approached, John Moodie, of Airdrie and Hearts, but he too slipped away.

Such was the frustration felt at Rovers' fall from the top of the Division, that the Kirkcaldy Times wrote the unthinkable : "Willie McNaught is losing the place as a pivot. Willie is so anxious for his own side to score goals, that he forgets that his main task is to prevent the opposition from scoring. His mistakes on Saturday [in a 5-2 defeat at Alloa] cost Rovers the points." McNaught, and Rovers recovered the following week to win 4-2 in a Scottish Cup tie in the mud at Stirling Albion, watched by an all-ticket crowd of 9,000 but a fortnight later they crashed out of the Cup, beaten 3-0 by a determined and focussed Airdrie team, who overpowered a Raith team which played pretty football with no penetration.

Only one win in the last six League

27th July 1946, Rosslyn Juniors 3 Markinch Victoria Rangers 3 at Station Park, Dysart, in front of 2,000 spectators – the first Fife Junior match since war broke out, in the new Fife Junior League competition.

28th September, Charity match at Stark's Park for the Kirkcaldy Branch of the RAF Benevolent Fund, Glasgow v Raith Rovers, Alex James was billed to play, but the team was : Leckie, Porter, Townley, McAllister, Hoggan, Batchelor, Beath, Johnstone, Colville, Cochrane, Turner.

The opening post-war reserve fixture, a C Division match against Montrose, was played on 9th August 1947, watched by 3,000 at Stark's Park. Peter Cabrelli played for Montrose, who won 3-1.   The large attendances didn't last, by November they were down to 300, some way short of the £70 guarantee.

Early in the season, the 9d gate for youths at Stark's Park was discontinued.   The press reported : "Too many "youths" were taking advantage of the concession. In fact, last Saturday, one of the "youths" who was waiting to get in for 9d was heard to remark that Raith had never had a decent team since the days of the £50,000 forward line, Bell, Miller, Jennings, James and Archibald.   Some memory, some youth !" Boys could still get in for a tanner (6d).

JACKIE STEWART

The £8,000 received by Rovers from Birmingham City for Jackie Stewart in 1948 transformed the club's finances, and also made the goalscoring winger the club's record sale for the next twelve years.
Using the Multiplier introduced in Appendix 3 of this book, it is possible to compare, on equal terms, the current value of the transfer fees received by the club over the decades.
Murray McDermott's £20,000 in 1981 is now worth £185,000, and Malcolm Robertson's £12,000 in 1975 would now amount to £290,000.
Willie Hurrell's £2,000 transfer to Millwall in 1946 is worth £320,000, and going right back to 1907, the £750 paid by Blackburn Rovers for John Manning would now cost £360,000.
Were Sheffield United to buy Francis Joyner in 2008, instead of 1938, the £1,650 fee would be almost £400,000, and Craig Brewster's £250,000 transfer free to Dundee United in 1993 would now cost £430,000.
Jock Wallace cost Blackpool £2,000 in 1934 (now worth £480,000), and Willie Birrell's £2,300 sale to Middlesbrough in 1921 is worth £552,000 today.
Rovers received £130,000 from Newcastle for Paul Sweeney in 1989 (£625,000) and Jimmy McEwan's £6,660 in 1959 would cost £640,000. £14,000 for Gordon Wallace in 1969 doesn't sound much, but it would cost Dundee almost

matches saw the promotion challenge fizzle out. The gap was being closed, however ; fourth place and only eight points short of a promotion place. It was with some justification that Rovers fans spent the summer dreaming "maybe this season ......" Before that, they had to endure the end of season local cup ties, the Kirkcaldy Times' verdict on the Fife Cup semi final against Cowdenbeath being : "The only bright interlude in a game that was devoid of all the essential qualities associated with football was the sun ...."

The transformation in the club engineered by the £8000 received from Birmingham City cannot be exaggerated. Both the Football Club Ltd., and the Grandstand Company Ltd., were wound up, the respective assets adopted by a single new company, which would be free of debt for the first time since 1923.

On 5th May, the Kirkcaldy Times reported. "At least we know the names of the directors of the "new" Raith Rovers, so these gentlemen will have to come into the limelight from now onwards and accept the plaudits and the criticisms. It will be a new role for Peter Napier, the ever-popular treasurer of the Supporters Club, to have to justify his team selection instead of tearing someone else's selection to ribbons. Perhaps, like Bert Herdman, he will discover it is easier to criticise than construct."

At the end of the season, former player Davie Duncan became the first B Division player to be selected for Scotland. It capped a memorable season for East Fife, who won the League Championship in a canter, the B Division Supplementary Cup, and the League Cup. The following season, the spotlight would be shone a little further west down the Fife Coast, but East Fife's success, and elevation to the top division, heaped more pressure on a Rovers team which had only flattered to deceive while their local rivals succeeded.

A number of players were signed over the summer, but most of them served only as reserves to a settled team, which was augmented by three significant signings. The imposing figure of Doug Westland arrived from Stoke City to fill the large gap between the goalposts, and the vastly experienced Allan Collins came in at inside right, to add guile and craft to the forward line. Jimmy Ellis deputised with Collins used sparingly. Johnny Maule was moved into his favoured midfield role, and outside right became the only unsettled position, Jimmy Menzies, Doug Stockdale from Lincoln City and George Carson all having brief spells in that position.

Terry Eden started the season at left back, but McNaught was moved there midway through September, and if he had looked a good player at centre half, he was outstanding at full back.

The season opened with a 3-1 home win over Queen's Park, the euphoria dampened the following Wednesday by a 2-1 defeat at Cowdenbeath. Starting with a 5-1 home win over East Stirling the following

Saturday, Rovers lost only one of their next 15 League and League Cup matches, and that was the meaningless last match of the qualifying section, which Rovers won for the first time (and their subsequent record wasn't terribly impressive either).

A draw at home to Cowdenbeath was followed by a 7-1 demolition of Stirling Albion at Annfield, the centre forward earning his "Six goal Penman" soubriquet. A 2-1 win over a strong Dunfermline team was a much tighter affair with Penman, and Rovers' strong half back line, the difference between two well-matched teams, but revenge was enacted against Cowdenbeath, by 6-0. Stirling Albion manager Tom Fergusson announced that he had formulated a plan to counteract Penman in the return match at Stark's Park. It worked – Willie scored just four times in Rovers' 6-2 victory, a performance "which should give the home supporters little doubt as to their team's capabilities."

The quarter final draw brought East Fife to Stark's Park, and there was massive interest in the tie. 26,000 tickets were sold for the match, and all the Boys Brigade and amateur matches at Beveridge Park were postponed. Bad weather reduced the actual attendance to 24,000, but most of them were captivated by an enthralling game in which Johnny Maule excelled. He opened the scoring from the penalty spot in 19 minutes, and Frank Joyner and Tommy Brady gave Rovers a 3-0 half-time lead which reflected how much they had subdued the A Division team.

Dave Morris scored for the visitors on the hour, but Penman restored Rovers' three goal lead. Morris scored twice in two minutes, but there was not enough time for Rovers and their fans to be nervous over a possible East Fife comeback, as a further minute later Joyner completed the scoring at 5-3. He and Penman had rampaged through the East Fife defence throughout the match, enabling Rovers to eliminate the cup holders.

The prospect of a national cup semi final saw no let up in Rovers' league endeavours, or goalscoring activities. A Joyner hat-trick was the feature of a 4-1 win at Tannadice, while Penman scored four times in a 6-0 home win over Ayr United.

Atrocious weather restricted the crowd for the League Cup semi final against Hamilton Accies at Celtic Park to just 16,000, and spoiled the spectacle. Rovers overcame the muddy conditions, with McNaught the best player afield. In 35 minutes Jimmy Ellis put Rovers ahead with a lovely low shot after Joyner had made the opening, and a minute into the second half, a long pass by Ellis set Joyner away. His cross was met by Willie Penman, who followed the ball into the goal-net. Rovers had qualified for their first national cup final since 1913.

There was a cup tie backlash, in the shape of a 2-0 defeat at Dunfermline, despite Rovers being the better team ; Dunfermline's defence stood solid. It was quite an afternoon in Fife, Rangers setting a new

ground record, 20,737, at Bayview.

Rovers bounced back to win 5-1 at Alloa, and two goals from the imperious Maule saw off a stern challenge by Kilmarnock at Stark's Park.   There could be few complaints about a 5-2 defeat at Stirling, however, and Cowdenbeath came to Stark's Park on Christmas Day with well defined tactics.   Rovers survived a mauling by the robust and ruthless visiting team and there was little Christmas spirit evident in a dour battle, which Rovers won 3-2.

That performance, owing more to character and determination than skill, put Rovers back on track.   At Firs Park on New Year's Day, Rovers play was as crisp as the snow-covered surface, and they won 5-1. Two days later at home to Hamilton, the surface was icy, but Tommy Brady, moved into attack, skated through the Accies defence and scored a hat-trick.   Brady's half back position was filled by the club's latest young recruit. "Leigh, playing his first game at left half before a home crowd, created a very favourable impression.   Fair-headed, this young player has height and speed as well as football skill. If he develops properly, he should prove a grand acquisition."

Both goalkeepers (Doug Westland and Ronnie Simpson) were outstanding in an open, entertaining match at Hampden, which ended 1-1, Penman scoring Rovers' equaliser, and he went two better the following week at home to Arbroath.

The draw for the first round of the Scottish Cup should have been favourable for Rovers, away to Leith Athletic, whose circumstances following the Second World War had consigned them to C Division.   The reality was altogether different.   A dour, unremitting cup tie was played on a heavy pitch, and the tie looked to be turning against Rovers in the first half.   Doug Westland had

been injured in a clash with Russell, and had to leave the field.   Willie Penman took over in goal, and before long had to face a penalty kick, awarded after a Rovers player handled . McCall's kick was full blooded, but Penman dived to his left to save, holding the ball at the second attempt.   The Kirkcaldy Times had this to say : "Though I live to be 100, I don't expect to see another story book incident to equal that.   It occurred at the most critical stage of the game, for Rovers, now a man short, were struggling, practically on their knees.   A goal for Leith at that moment and Rovers would, in all probability, have been out of the cup.   Bert Herdman told me on Monday that Brady wanted McLure to go in goal, but Bert told Penman to take over as the doctor considered that Westland would be able to return to the field in a short time.   It was a wise move."

Westland did indeed return before half time, and in the second half Tommy Brady scored the only goal of the match, in front of a record attendance at Meadowbank, 11,625.   Penman, McNaught and Till were the Rovers heroes against a Leith side which featured former Rovers Jock Wallace in goal, and Dalziel on the right wing.   Reserve Smith took over in goal for the visit to Stenhousemuir in the League the following Saturday, and did his career prospects no good in a 3-1 defeat.

The omens did not look good for Rovers' visit to Easter Road for the second round of the Scottish Cup, with Andy Young and Tommy Brady both absent through injury. Harry Colville was moved to centre half and was a revelation, the unexpected solidarity of the hastily assembled half back line earning Rovers a 1-1 draw.   Four days later, in a thrilling cup tie at Stark's Park, Rovers recovered from losing two goals in the first 23 minutes to take the lead against the reigning

Stand-in goalkeeper Willie Penman saves McCall's penalty kick in the Scottish Cup tie against Leith Athletic at Meadowbank in 1949, allowing Rovers to win 1-0.

£680,000 today, and Leeds United's £3,000 for Tom Jennings in 1925 is the equivalent of £720,000. The £80,000 paid by Luton for Andy Harrow in 1980 is worth £740,000, and Aberdeen's cheque for £6,500 for reserve centre half Jim Clunie in 1953 is worth £780,000 - as is Alex James' 1925 transfer fee of £3,250.

Ninth in the all-time transfer fee table is Pat Gardner in 1967, his £17,000 translating to £816,000, while the £109,000 received for Keith Wright in 1986 would now net £872,000.

Denis Mochan fetched £11,500 in 1962 and would cost £920,000 today, while Hearts' £10,000 for Willie Polland in 1960 would cost £960,000.

David Morris is at No.5 with £1.15 million, topped by Jackie Stewart in 1948 (£1.28 million), Stephen McAnespie in 1995 (£1.35 million), and Jim Baxter in 1960 (£1.5 million). Highest ever sale was Ian Porterfield, whose £45,000 fee in 1967 is now worth £2.16 million.

"Floor Soccer" was introduced at Kirkcaldy Ice Rink on Saturday 24th July 1948, and the trial match at Stark's Park on 7th August was conducted over 3 x 30 minute periods.

Unusually, there was no October holiday Monday game in 1949, Hearts would not agree to swap dates for the League game

The directors agreed on 13th December 1949 to award a £250 benefit payment to Willie McNaught. On 14th February 1950, he asked to be placed on the transfer list, as his wife had not settled in Kirkcaldy.

It was agreed to put the team up in Anthony's Hotel for three days over the New year holiday period, at a total cost to the club of £32 17/-

*1948 - The first motorcycle races took place in Beveridge Park
1949 - Abbotsrood Church in the High Street closed ; The Burgh boundary was extended to include Chapel Village.*

League champions, only for Sammy Kean to equalise in 82 minutes, and Colville to put through his own net two minutes later, to consign Rovers to a glorious 4-3 defeat. There was of, course one more cup tie to be fulfilled that season, the final of the League Cup, but before that Rovers suffered a real wobble in the League, losing three of the four League matches prior to the Final.   There were fears that the promotion chase would be lost, despite the club's early season form, prolific goalscoring, and cup heroics. Cruelly, Ernie Till missed the Cup Final through injury. His place was taken by Andy Leigh, in his ninth senior appearance.

The Kirkcaldy Times summed up Rovers' second ever national cup final with the headline : "To Raith The Glory – To Rangers The Cup."

In one of the best games seen in Glasgow that season, the two teams were well matched during an enthralling first half. Five minutes before the interval, Willie Penman breached the "Iron Curtain" defence to fire an unstoppable shot past Bobby Brown in the Rangers goal.   To a storm of boos, the referee took the word of his linesman and pronounced Penman to be offside.   It was a very relieved Rangers who heard the half-time whistle, with the score at 0-0.

Less than a minute after the interval, an unplayable Thornton cross was headed home by Torry Gillick, but Rovers fought back and Brady's shot slid past the upright, followed by a Penman header which scraped the cross-bar.   Just as Rovers looked like equalising, Thornton again prised open the Rovers defence with a neat past through to Paton, who made it 2-0.

If Penman's first half "goal" looked legitimate to many in the ground, there were few dissenters when he was brought down in

the penalty area by Brown, but the referee did not award a spot kick.   Rovers attacked until the final whistle, but could not breach the legendary Ibrox defence, which earned Rangers the first leg of the domestic trophy treble.   Bobby Brown was reckoned to be Rangers star player, which speaks volumes for the flow of play. This is what the Sunday Post correspondent had to say of the endeavours of the Raith team, who had worn a new set of strips ("billiard ball red" in the words of Andy Leigh) donated by the Supporters Club :

"Those B League boys were heroes all.   But especially there was Penman, McNaught and three great half-backs [Young, Colville and Leigh].   I don't know when last I've seen anybody cover as much ground as this chap Young.   He did the impossible by playing both sides of the field at once ! Queen's Park president, Mr Eddie Scott, handed over the trophy.   But between you and me I've a sneaking sympathy with the folk who shouted "Shame !"

It was back to the bread and butter of League football the following Saturday, and fresh life was breathed into Rovers promotion challenge by Willie Penman, who scored all the goals in a 5-0 defeat of Alloa at Stark's Park.   A robust Kilmarnock side brought them back down to earth a week later, with a 3-1 defeat at Rugby Park, although it was acknowledged that Rovers did not get the breaks. More worrying was a 0-0 draw at home to Stirling, with Brady briefly restored to the side in place of the injured Joyner, and Stockdale in the troubled outside right position.   In one of several attempts at filling the No. 7 shirt, Hugh Docherty was signed from Blackpool on 13th January.   Herdman, the master showman, paraded his new signing as "Stanley Matthews' deputy". Andy

Leigh had another description for him : "He was overweight, unfit and looked like a pub player."

Rovers lay fourth in the League, although they had games in hand. With four games to play, and their fellow challengers all in good form, there was little doubt that they had to win all four matches to have a chance of promotion – and even with that they would only match the points total of Stirling Albion, who had completed their fixtures.

Allan Collins scored the only goal of the match at Boghead, a close, hard fought victory. Fellow contenders Airdrie were beaten 3-0 at Broomfield, watched by 12,500. Both teams were well matched, but Rovers had more guile in attack, and Airdrie's defeat ensured Stirling Albion's promotion. Rovers could even afford the luxury of two missed penalties, by Maule and Brady.

A 1-0 win over St Johnstone at home was a nervous affair, but the stage was set for the final showdown at Stark's Park. Rovers had to win to leapfrog over Airdrie and Dunfermline into a promotion place ; Dunfermline simply needed a draw. 24,000 packed into Stark's Park expecting a titanic struggle, but the promotion race was as good as decided after 10 minutes when Dunfermline goalkeeper Michie was injured in a clash with Willie Penman. Willie Keith went into goal and had a great game, but 10-men Dunfermline were beaten 4-0, John Stirling (signed on a free transfer from his namesakes) and Allan Collins both scoring twice.

Rovers won the championship on goal average, thus completing a memorable season in which Willie Penman scored more goals than any Rovers player before or since, 58, although his 35 in the League fell short of Norman Haywood's record of 47 in 1937/38. The latter stages of the B Division Supplementary Cup ended the season, although in being beaten 2-1 at home by St Johnstone in the first leg of the final on 7th May, Rovers looked as if their minds were on the Civic Reception that evening at Anthony's Hotel, held in honour of their season's achievements.

A return to the First Division for the first time in ten years was relished by Rovers fans, who bought every season ticket available (Inland Revenue rules dictated that only 1000 could be sold, as they were not subject to Entertainment Tax, unlike turnstile admissions). Once again, there was expectation that the Second Division Champions and Cup heroes would survive in the top division, although even the most optimistic Rovers fan did not dare to imagine that this would stretch to 13 years.

Despite the handsome profits made the previous season, Rovers entrusted their First Division survival to the same squad which got them there, with a few peripheral additions such as inside right Ian Crawford from East Stirling, Young, McNaught and Colville were given full time contracts, followed by six of their team-mates, requiring the recruitment of a full time trainer, Willie Hunter of Blairhall Juniors being the successful candidate. Bert Smith, signed during the previous season from Dalkeith Thistle, was entrusted with the problem outside right position, McGregor was preferred to Westland in goal, and the only significant departure was senior pro Tommy Brady, who became player coach of Inverness Thistle.

On 5th August 1949 the Supporters Club organised a Victory Dance at the Burma Ballroom, at which the players were presented with mantelpiece clocks. The following evening, after the first Trial game, the players were presented with gold wrist watches and silver badges as finalists of the League Cup, by the Directors in Stuart's Café. Rovers got off to an appalling start to the season. The League Cup section brought five defeats and just one win, 6-2 at home to Stirling Albion. In the club's first top division League match in ten years, Eddie Turnbull

Pictured at the end of 1948/49 are : Back row : Malcolm McLure, Andy Young, Doug Westland, Harry Colville, Willie McNaught, Andy Leigh. Fron row : Doug Stockdale, Johnny Maule, Willie Penman, Allan Collins and Jimmy Stirling.

This was the eleven who played in the last three League matches of the season, and given the size of the crowd in the background, the photograph was probably taken before the final match of the season, at home to Dunfermline Athletic on 30th April 1949. Rovers what was effectively a promotion decider, 4-0, in front of a crowd of 24,150.

While the core of the team remained unchanged for several years, there was a succession of players to complete the first eleven, particularly wingers. Jimmy Stirling was signed from Stirling Albion in February 1949 but was mostly a reserve team player by the time he was freed at the end of the following season.

Doug Stockdale arrived from Lincoln City in the close season of 1948, and left for Ayr United in May 1951.

During the close season of 1950, the club made several attempts to sign Hearts players. £3000 was offered for the transfer of Urquhart and McSpadyen, who had been loaned to the club towards the end of the previous season. £3000 was then offered for Urquhart alone. The final offer to be rejected by Hearts was £5000 for Urquhart, McSpadyen and Currie. In mid June, a further attempt was made to sign Currie, and several weeks were spent in discussion with former Scotland internationalist Jimmy Simpson to obtain his permission to sign his son, Queen's Park goalkeeper Ronnie.

On 6th June 1950 it was agreed to pay Willie Penman a benefit of £250 net, £394 10/- gross

There were complaints about the cost of footballs, which cost a guinea pre war, and now cost £3 15/- "and they do not have the pre-war quality."

The Board Meeting of 7th November 1950 learned that Willie McNaught requested a transfer (a) to better himself financially, and (b) because his wife was not settling in Kirkcaldy. Three weeks later, it was agreed by the Board that if the player did not reconsider his request, Everton, Preston and Coventry were to be advised.

The following week, the Directors were told that Willie Penman had requested a transfer due to "discouraging remarks from the terracing."

During the winter months, indoor training was done at Rose Street Boys Club

1951 Alexanders build the bus station on the Esplanade

1952 Templehall Junior secondary opened, in advance of work commencing on the construction of the huge quantity of council houses in Templehall. Once completed, this solved the chronic housing shortage in Kirkcaldy.

gave Hibs a 19th minute lead at Stark's Park, but Rovers competed well during the first half. After the interval, however, a 20 minute spell of "power play" from Hibs blew Rovers apart, and the match ended 6-0 to the visitors. It did not take a genius to work out that the team needed strengthening for the higher grade of football, and immediately after the Hibs defeat, former Celtic inside forward Joe McLaughlin was signed from Aberdeen.

The flow of defeats was staunched by three successive draws, the 4-4 result at home to East Fife coming after Rovers fell three goals behind a minute into the second half.

There was no shortage of incident in the 2-2 draw at Celtic Park either. Played on a Home Internationals Saturday, Celtic were without five of their first team, and it took Willie Miller to save a Penman winner in the final minute of the match to keep a point at Parkhead. Penman was knocked out in the process, and stretchered off the field. In the dressing room, they brought him round with smelling salts, but in the shock, Penman sat up abruptly, and the noxious contents of the bottle were knocked into his mouth. To neutralise the chemicals, the trainer scraped plaster from the wall and got Willie to swill it around his mouth. He later recalled : "Skin peeled off the inside of my mouth for weeks afterwards." All that for a £1 draw bonus. There were more scenes better suited to the casualty ward during the 3-1 home defeat by Partick Thistle the following week. Goldie broke his nose, McLure (who with McNaught had been outstanding in defence) was concussed and collapsed on the field before the end of the match, and Andy Young broke his ankle.

The remaining twelve League fixtures of 1949 brought only three victories. To replace Young, Jim Woodcock was signed from Aberdeen junior football, and he added to the team's impressive endeavours, but did little to address the lack of craft and guile up front. The experiment of playing Harry Colville at centre forward was short lived (a 3-0 defeat at Pittodrie), and Tommy McSpadyen was signed on loan from Hearts to fill in for Malcolm McLure, who suffered a broken leg in the 2-1 defeat at Dundee.

There were sufficient draws, and the occasional sparkling victory, to prevent Rovers from being marooned at the bottom of the League. Clyde were beaten 7-1 at Stark's Park, and Rovers ensured their fans enjoyed Hogmanay with a 6-4 home win over Falkirk, seven of the goals being scored in a 37 minute spell. Goalkeeper McGregor was clearly at fault with some of the goals conceded, and after two more games – a 3-0 defeat at Methil and 1-1 draw against a physical Celtic team, George Johnstone was signed on a free transfer from Dunfermline. Jimmy Garth proved to be a loan acquisition from Clyde at inside left (£1,000 down payment and a further £2,500 if they wanted to keep him at the end of the season, which they didn't), but Rovers bade farewell to Francis Joyner, who was transferred to

Hamilton Accies on 6th January, to the dismay of many fans with memories of the Penman-Joyner partnership in attack. Willie was finding goals much harder to come by in A Division, not helped by an injury-enforced spell on the sidelines, in the company of Young, McLure and Woodcock, who fractured his thigh-bone.

A largely undeserved 3-0 win over Airdrie in the first round of the Scottish Cup heralded a bright spell of four successive victories. The heavier Rovers team won 2-1 at Stirling where there was hardly a blade of grass to be seen on the sanded, muddy playing surface. At the end of the match, the referee, Mr R.M. Mair of Glasgow, was knocked unconscious by a fan wielding a brick on the journey to the mansion house which contained the dressing rooms at Annfield.

Rovers beat Clyde 3-2 at home in the second round of the Cup, despite a Raith player failing to find the net, own goals being scored by Milligan who headed home a Penman cross, Mennie who booted in a Maule cross, and Campbell who side-footed a Garth shot past his own goalkeeper. As the scorers (if not the scoring) would suggest, Clyde were the better team. There was a much better performance the following Saturday in winning 1-0 at Third Lanark.

Successive defeats at Ibrox (where Rovers could have won a point with better finishing, Willie Penman - on the promise of a suit at Connell's - particularly at fault) and at home to Aberdeen plunged Rovers back into the relegation mire, but before that they had a Scottish Cup quarter final against Rangers.

A first half goal by Willie Findlay at Ibrox lulled Rangers into a false sense of security, and they allowed Rovers back into the match. In 65 minutes, Penman intercepted a Woodburn pass back to goalkeeper Brown, and all three players lay in a heap in the penalty area and watched the ball roll slowly over the goal-line. Four days later, a new ground record of 28,743 was set at Stark's Park for the 4 o'clock kick off, many of the town's factories re-arranging their shifts to allow their workers to attend the match. The same scoring pattern applied, Rangers' half time lead equalised, this time by Joe McLaughlin. Extra time failed to separate the teams, and the respective managers tossed a coin to decide the venue of the second replay. Legend has it that Bert Herdman won the toss – and chose Ibrox ! If true, he was amply rewarded by a share of the 63,000 gate, but Rangers had the game won by half-time, 2-0.

In the week of the Rangers replay, Johnny Urquhart was signed on loan from Hearts, and with the return of Andy Young to the team, Rovers set about securing their A Division place. Willie McNaught added to Rovers' catalogue of serious injuries, although the returning McLure partnered the steady, reliable McSpadyen at full back in McNaught's absence.

Urquhart scored on his debut to earn Rovers a point at Shawfield, although George Johnstone's heroics in goal were the significant factor. Most relegation fears were dispelled the following week when two late goals by Allan Collins consigned Hearts to defeat at Stark's Park. The League season was concluded with 4-1 and 2-0 home wins over Dundee and Queen of the South, leaving everyone to wonder what all the fuss had been about.

Through sheer will and determination, Rovers had overcome an horrendous season of injuries to finish above the relegation positions for the first time since 1927/28. Amid tremendous interest in the team (the average home attendance was in excess of 13,000) there was real appreciation of their achievements in adversity, although, being Kirkcaldy, something could be found to criticise.

The reserve team had cost the club £2000 over the season, and the Kirkcaldy Times complained : "The way the 'A' team has been run has made it a laughing stock this season. The majority of Raith supporters have purposely stayed away, because if they did go to a game they found the players being played out of position and even, on occasions, lads being asked at the last minute to strip and turn out for the Reserves. That is not good management."

The close season brought the usual batch of junior signings, and the experienced Willie Keith from Stirling Albion. 5,000 watched the first trial match, involving 26 players and two trialists, as the Reds and Blues drew 4-4. A last minute George Brander goal earned Rovers an opening day 3-2 win over Third Lanark in the League Cup, with the team wearing a new strip featuring two yellow bands on both jerseys and socks. Willie Penman scored the first goal of the season in Scottish football, in 65 seconds, against Ronnie Simpson, who was making his debut as a professional. Unfortunately the remaining five sectional matches brought two draws and three defeats, and there was a slow start to the League season, another home win over Third Lanark (4-0) the only victory in the opening four matches.

Two late goals by Joe McLaughlin against his former club earned a 3-2 victory at Parkhead, and that was followed by two wins and a draw from the next three matches. McNaught was missing from the side for the home draw with Morton on 21st October 1950, but there were few complaints as the left back was winning his first Scotland cap, the first Rovers player to be selected for his country for 25 years. Chairman Gourlay and manager Herdman travelled to Cardiff to see Willie play. The following week, with McNaught back in the side, Rovers won 3-2 at Brockville to go fifth in the League.

A 1-0 home defeat by Dundee illustrated that the team was not quite the finished article, prompting calls for the purse-strings to be loosened and the team to be strengthened, not with juniors but with "the finished article". The club retorted that they had tried to do this, but were being quoted ridiculous sums for reserve players.

McNaught followed his Scotland cap with selection for the Scottish League to play the English League, traditionally the second biggest representative match of the season and a true test of his abilities. Remarkably, it was the first time the Scottish League had selected a Rovers player. Unsurprisingly, given Rovers' record of selling their star players, several leading clubs south of the border were contemplating offers for McNaught. Sunderland's offer of over £11,000 was turned down, and it was pointed out that their £9 weekly wage was significantly below the £12 that Rovers were paying him.

In the fiercely competitive, and very high standard, A Division, Rovers were giving as good as they got, defeats being followed by splendid victories. The team was largely settled ; Johnstone, McLure and McNaught, McLaughlin, Colville and Leigh, Ernie Till being consigned to the reserves after losing his first team place through injury in September. Outside right continued to be a problem position, George Brander and Johnny McIlhatton, signed from Dundee, sharing with Johnny Maule. For the first half of the season. The tricky Maule was usually at inside right, partnering Kinghorn lad Les Murray. Andy Young showed his supreme versatility by playing most of the season at centre forward (scoring 18 League goals) with Willie Penman at outside left. Allan Collins made only cameo appearances.

Morton fans were denied the opportunity to see the peerless McNaught, as he was absent from the return game at Cappielow in January (which Rovers lost 2-0), in bed with the influenza which was sweeping the country. It caused him to miss another Scottish League cap, against the Irish League, but he returned to the Rovers team for the Scottish Cup first round tie at Firhill, and his uncharacteristic slip in the second half allowed Partick Thistle to equalise. A sign of the booming times in Scottish football was the comment by the Kirkcaldy Times : "The attendance at Firhill was rather disappointing on Saturday, for only 21,600 fans paid for admission." An Andy Young goal won the Wednesday afternoon replay at Stark's Park, and a couple of late goals put a flattering complexion on a 5-2 home win over a battling Brechin City team in the second round of the Scottish Cup.

It was something of a shock when bottom club Airdrie won 1-0 at Stark's Park in the League, causing some to rue the absence of Allan Collins' guile and intelligence in attack. The following Saturday, Rovers beat

Malcolm McLure in typical action, tackling Dundee's Scottish internationalist Billy Steel in front of the east terracing at Stark's Park

In early November 1951, Joe McLaughlin was appointed coach to the reserve team

Ernie Till was transferred to Arbroath on 14th November 1951 for a transfer fee of £300. The board agreed to pay the player a benefit of £315.

Harry Colville wanted to be placed on the Open to Transfer list in mid September, his fifth request in eighteen months. The board agreed that if a suitable offer was received, it would be considered.

In mid November 1951, there was a glimmer of hope that Hearts would transfer Johnny Urquhart to Rovers but they wanted Andy Leigh in exchange.

To celebrate their 25th anniversary, the Supporters Club donated a full strip to the club.

WHY RANGERS WORE RED : THE INSIDE STORY

Rangers created a bit of a surprise when they took the field on Saturday wearing Raith Rovers' red jerseys. The explanation was simple, but the story behind it is worthy of some publicity, writes "Novar".

When the Ibrox party arrived at Stark's Park it was discovered that they had brought only their light blue rig out – they didn't even have their equally famous "butchers" outfit with them [Rangers change strip had thin blue and white hoops].

Now Rangers have pulled this stunt before ; but Raith weren't falling for it this time, and immediately offered the Ibrox men the use of their red jerseys. Rangers weren't keen and suggested that Raith, who had often turned out in red before, should change. Manager Herdman firmly, but politely, refused, and even Assistant Manager Bob McPhail, with typical Ibrox diplomacy, could not get the adamant Raith manager to change his mind.

And so, Rangers appeared in red, and when it was all over I doubt very much if Raith minded footing a double laundry bill !

Billy Williamson of Rangers (in Rovers' change strip) challenged by Harry Colville

Rangers 3-1 at Stark's Park, the scoreline flattering the visitors, rather than the rampant home side. The Kirkcaldy Times said : "It was as decisive as any victory could be, for Raith not only defeated Rangers – they completely humiliated them." The same newspaper gave extended coverage to the first surprise which greeted the 24,000 crowd at Stark's Park (see side panel)

The Rangers result was no flash-in-the-pan, as Rovers won their next three matches, with Willie Penman to the fore, scoring in six successive games. There was a 2-1 win at Pittodrie, a resounding 4-1 defeat of Clyde at Stark's Park, and in between a tremendous 2-1 victory at Dens Park in the quarter finals of the Scottish Cup. Dundee, with Scotland inside forward Billy Steel foremost in a star-studded team, finished the season joint-second (with Rangers) in the League, but they suffered their first home defeat of the season to a Raith side in which Harry Colville was immense in a rock solid defence. The 41,600 attendance was a ground record.

The Clyde victory on 17th March was to be the Kirkcaldy public's last sight of the team that season. Groundsman Jock McIlravie's pitch was not only much admired, but also resistant to postponements, all of those being away fixtures. A 3-1 defeat at Tynecastle suggested Rovers had one eye on the following Saturday's Scottish Cup semi final at Hampden, where 84,640 formed the biggest crowd in Raith Rovers' history.

The match started in the worst possible way, Celtic scoring through Weir in just two minutes, but Rovers battled back into the game and equalised when Boden put through his own goal. McPhail restored Celtic's lead five minutes before half time, and with just ten minutes remaining, Penman rose to head home a Brander cross. A minute later, goalkeeper Johnstone appeared to be impeded by McPhail as he rose to clear a corner kick. The ball fell to Charlie Tully, who scored what proved to be the winner. Most agreed that Rovers were robbed of a replay, while conceding that Celtic were the better team on the day.

Perhaps understandably, the final four, away, League fixtures were lost, the first three without a goal being scored. Despite that, the team finished in a highly respectable 8th position, exactly mid-table in a top quality division.

In the run up to the Scottish Cup semi final, the Kirkcaldy Times profiled the players in the following terms :

George Johnstone : Exceptionally safe pair of hands, and displays remarkable agility for a veteran. Malcolm McLure : Excellent kicker of a ball with both feet and reveals an almost uncanny positional sense. Willie McNaught : There isn't a more polished defender in Scottish football today. Joe McLaughlin : Attacking wing half, the tactician in the side. Harry Colville : a model of consistency. Andy Leigh : strong in the tackle, a tireless worker. Johnny Maule : Clever in possession, his small stature makes him even

more elusive. Andy Young : Strong in defence, he is just as devastating in the target area. Willie Penman : appeared to lose scoring run, but [chairman] Gourlay wanted to move him back to centre forward where his faith has been repaid. Les Murray : wholehearted, a bit impetuous perhaps, but he displays extraordinary soccer intelligence at times, and is always up to snip a chance. George Brander : Strong and well built, he is a powerful runner who can shoot equally well with either foot. The fastest man in the side."

As a reward for their season's endeavours, Rovers players were taken on an end-of-season Highland tour, which McNaught left early to accompany Scotland on their continental tour, having a few weeks earlier been the reserve at Wembley.

Despite the season's successes, Bert Herdman sounded a note of caution at the cost of full time football. "With the average attendance of 12,000 spectators Raith Rovers cannot make ends meet unless they are fortunate enough to have a good run in one of the major cup competitions. If Rovers had not reached the semi final of the Scottish Cup last season, the club would have had a deficit of close on £3,000."

If Rovers fans were a little giddy at the success of their club in 1950/51, there was more of the same the following season, culminating in the club's third highest League position in their history. The close season of 1951 was unusually short, thanks to Glasgow Corporation's decision to mark the Festival of Britain by sponsoring two cup competitions. The Second Division clubs would compete for the St Mungo Quaich, while Rovers and their contemporaries in Division A would play for the St Mungo Cup.

Rovers paraded their two new wingers, Jimmy McEwan, purchased from Arbroath, and Jim McIntyre, from Irvine Meadow, on Saturday 14th July 1951 for the visit of Queen's Park in the first round. The 9000 crowd were certainly entertained by Rovers' free-flowing performance, if not the contest. The Amateurs were thrashed 9-0, Willie Penman scoring five times and both debutants joined him on the scoresheet.

From the second round (quarter finals) onwards all matches were played in Glasgow, which is why Rovers and Queen of the South found themselves at Celtic Park on Tuesday 17th July. The 2-2 draw was a decent result given that Rovers played for the last 25 minutes with Willie Penman in goal following an injury to George Johnstone. The replay was at the same venue the following evening, but not before Andy Young learned a painful lesson on how the club was run, or more particularly, who ran it.

"Bert Herdman was the Manager, but Jimmy Gourlay, the chairman picked the team," he recalled in later years. Unwittingly echoing Robert Graves' famous passage in I Claudius, "Augustus ruled the world but Olivia ruled Augustus", "Andy recalled the journey home from the first match at Parkhead. "The directors suggested that I stay the night in Kirkcaldy, but I wanted to go

home. My wife was on her own in the house and our first son was only a few weeks old. The team bus got to Crossgates and I asked that it take a slight detour to drop me off nearer my Lochgelly home. Mrs Gourlay would have none of it, insisting that, at that hour, the bus should carry on to Kirkcaldy. I was dropped off at Crossgates and, long after the last service bus, had to walk to Lochgelly. I didn't get home until 1 o'clock in the morning, after playing 90 minutes of football and walking for an hour, and had to play the following evening. I was furious, and wasn't going to play in the replay, but my wife's father talked me out of it and I played."

Andy's mettle was shown by his opening the scoring after five minutes of the replay and Jimmy McEwan scored in the second half to win the match 2-0. After the 3-1 defeat by Celtic in the semi final at Hampden on the Saturday, the Kirkcaldy Times asked of a disappointing display "Where was that fighting spirit ?" Probably on the midnight road from Crossgates to Lochgelly

The following week, the Public Trial saw plenty of goals, a 5-5 draw between Blues and Reds, but drew criticism from the Kirkcaldy Times. "I feel strongly inclined to remark that the first two periods [3 x 30 minute periods were played] were a greater trial to the three thousand-odd spectators than to some of the players. The introduction of juniors can be overdone, and I had the feeling

that this was the case at Stark's Park."

The League Cup section brought the usual outcome for Rovers, with four defeats and two victories. There was disappointment in the opening League match, Hibs winning 2-0 at Stark's Park, causing the Kirkcaldy Times to exclaim "This Raith team will not do" and there appeared to be some substance in that accusation as it took six more matches before the first League victory was registered, 4-1 at Greenock on 20th October. Despite the poor start to the season, which saw Rovers at the bottom of the League, if not detached, there was no sense of panic. Performances, if not results, were good, and the feeling was that the team was getting increasingly closer to point gathering form. Injuries interrupted the quest for a settled team. Malcolm McLure sat out the last three months of the year with a broken leg, replaced by the reserve right back, former Rosslyn Junior Alex Wilkie ; Willie Penman was out for the same period following a cartilage operation, while outside left McIntyre played only when his National Service commitments allowed.

The October holiday Monday fixture was a reserve match against Dundee, in which an 18 year old trialist inside forward put on a brilliant display, scoring two goals. After the match, the young miner (so no National Service committment) Bernard Kelly was signed from Muirkirk Juniors, an early dividend from the employment of Allan Collins

Lining up at Kingsmill Park, on 9th May 1951, before a friendly match against Inverness Thistle were, Back row : Manager Bert Herdman, Ernie Till, Malcolm McLure, George Johnstone, Jim Clunie, Andy Leigh, Harry Colville, Trainer Willie Hunter. Front row : Les Murray, Johnny Maule, Joe McLaughlin, Andy Young, George Brander

Charlie Drummond's signing was one of the legendary tales of Bert Herdman's long managerial career. Bert travelled to Falkirk to sign the Lochore Welfare goalkeeper on Sunday March 30th, to be told that he was at the pictures (Drummond lived in Carronshore). Bert asked the Cinema Manager to put a sign up on the screen, asking Drummond to report to his office, where he signed for Raith Rovers. Lochore Welfare were far from happy, and protested to the SFA that the signing was not valid under Junior rules, as it was done on a Sunday.

CHARLIE DRUMMOND

Kirkcaldy Corporation charged the club £28 4/11d to clear snow for the Hibs cup tie, and £5 3/- to haul in seats to place around the touchline. These boosted the capacity by several hundreds and were a feature of big games at Stark's Park during the period of huge attendances in the early 1950s.

On Wednesday 20th August 1952, the Reserve teams of Rovers and Third Lanark opened the new ground of Stoneyburn Juniors, Beechgrove Park. Rovers won 3-2, Peter Williamson of Thornton Hibs scoring a hat-trick. He was signed the following day.

On 14th February 1953, Fife Juniors drew 2-2 with Perthshire Juniors at Stark's Park. Willie Benvie of Lochore Welfarewas at inside right. He was later to serve the club briefly as a player, but for a far longer spell as trainer and coach.

1953 - Monday 6th July saw the opening of first phase of new Town House by Earl of Home, Minister of State for Scotland. In the same year, the Green Cockatoo restaurant at the east end of the High Street was opened ; the Lido swimming pool was closed ; as families began to move into Templehall in increasing numbers, the Valley Primary School was opened, and on Monday 1st June, Alex James died in the Royal Northern Hospital, London

as Ayrshire scout. To replace the injured Penman, Ernie Copeland was signed on loan from Dundee. Jimmy McEwan and Andy Leigh were named as reserves for the Scottish League v Irish League fixture, while McNaught was selected for the match against the English League at Hillsborough, but had to withdraw with a foot injury.

Copeland's arrival allowed Andy Young to drop back into his favoured right half position, and the benefits were shown in a comprehensive victory over Stirling Albion at Stark's Park. After a defeat at Dundee, and a last minute Copeland equaliser to get a home point against Airdrie, Rangers visited Stark's Park, this time remembering to pack their (white) change strip. A tremendous Rovers performance overpowered a stunned Rangers team, goals from Brander, Maule and McEwan earning a 3-1 victory. "It's only the name you are playing against nowadays" said a triumphant Bert Herdman.

A draw at Aberdeen, a win at Motherwell and a home win over Third Lanark propelled Rovers into a League position that better reflected the team's ability. There was much sympathy for an unlucky 4-2 defeat at Tynecastle, but a return trip of Auld Reekie the following Saturday was a humiliating experience, Rovers failing to force a single corner in the entire match as Hibs gave them a footballing lesson in a 5-0 defeat.

There were a few groans the following week when the draw for the first round of the Scottish Cup brought Hibs to Kirkcaldy. Although the club (optimistically) claimed that Stark's Park could now hold 36,000, the crowd was to be limited, by ticket, to 30,000, plus 1,000 season ticket holders

Rovers got back on track with an unbeaten run between the Hibs matches, including the first victory at Bayview in fourteen attempts, thanks mainly to George Johnstone in goal. A Bernie Kelly goal won the points against Celtic at Stark's Park, and a 2-0 home win over Morton installed Rovers in fifth top position – a far cry from late autumn when they were bottom, and full justification for the refusal to panic when results were going against them.

The visit of league leaders Hibs in the Cup was hugely anticipated. For the first time ever, all 30,000 tickets had been sold, but it started snowing on the Thursday night. The pitch was cleared of snow twice on Friday, and on Saturday morning another 3 inches lay, and the pitch was cleared again, in a blizzard. Rovers had by far the best of the 0-0 draw on the hard, slippery surface, with Tommy Younger in the Hibs goal credited with keeping his team in the Cup.

At Easter Road the following Wednesday the teams could not be separated after 120 minutes, largely due to a Rovers defence which had lost just two goals in 750 minutes since the 5-0 League debacle. The only change in personnel was, significantly, the return of Malcolm McLure at right back.

Following a 2-1 win at Stirling in farcical conditions (a snow and ice covered surface) it was back over to Edinburgh on

Monday February 4th for the second replay against Hibs, at Tynecastle. Rovers mastered the treacherous conditions and won 4-1. The Kirkcaldy Times reported : "Hibs lost the game because they tried to be Hibs – the polished football artists ! Artistry will not do when there is a mixture of sand, salt, water and ice as a playing surface. The quick turn was out – so was the player who attempted it. Raith thought quickly and shot quickly. That was their forward plan of campaign which proved a winner. Hibs tried a lot of the crossfield stuff which is lovely to watch – on a holding ground – but not when the players are taking a dive into the "briny" every second minute." Goals from Willie Penman in 2 and 57 minutes ensured that Rovers were always in control of the match.

A return trip to the same ground the following Saturday for the Second Round tie with Hearts was a poignant occasion. King George VI had died during the week, and the nation looked for every opportunity to pay tribute to the monarch who had led them through the Second World War. 47,000 packed into Tynecastle to see Hearts and Rovers line up in their tracksuits before the match and lead the crowd in two minute's silence, following by singing Abide With Me, and God Save the Queen. It was a memorable spectacle.

Hearts were the better team throughout, the Rovers' attack failing to function, and Willie Bauld scored the only goal with five minutes remaining. The Kirkcaldy Times summarised the campaign : "The Scottish Cup so far as Raith Rovers are concerned has provided them with close on £4,500 in money, has won the club an enviable reputation as courageous fighters, and on Saturday, a well deserved bouquet for being gallant losers, for they were first to congratulate their victors and wish them the best of luck in the succeeding rounds of the national tournament. Raith may not have achieved their ambition of winning the coveted trophy, a trophy on which they have yet to have their name inscribed, but they have created a lot of interest, recorded one unexpected and highly profitable win, and gone out without disgrace. Raith Rovers have gained in stature. After a very bad start, they have recovered in truly brilliant fashion to secure an honoured place in the League."

Celtic-mad Bernie Kelly scored the only goal at Parkhead to give Rovers their first ever League double over the Glasgow giants. A 2-1 win over Aberdeen gave Raith fans a highly favourable first look at a 19 year old signing from Stoneyburn Juniors. Like Kelly, "John" Williamson worked for the National Coal Board, and was thus exempt from National Service. Another new signing was the 6 ft 1 inch goalkeeper from Lochore Welfare, Charlie Drummond. The Kirkcaldy Times described the circumstances of his capture. "The player, who had arranged to visit Middlesbrough for an interview today [Wednesday] was at a cinema show in Stirling on Sunday when the following message was flashed on the screen : 'Will Charlie

Drummond of Carronshore go to the Manager's office at once ?' There he found Raith manager Bert Herdman." If 1951/52 found Rovers at the top of their game, so was their manager.

Rovers' first apearance on television was a 3-1 defeat at relegation-threatened Third Lanark, the day after BBC began broadcasting in Scotland. A week later, cup conquerors Hearts played as well as Rovers allowed them in being beaten 2-1 at Stark's Park. Their best League campaign in 28 years was rounded off with a 2-0 win over Motherwell.

Willie McNaught marked Tom Finney in Scotland's 2-1 defeat at Wembley ; he and Harry Colville were named as reserves for the Scotland v USA match at Hampden, and McNaught was in the Scotland party for their close season continental tour. Colville had turned down the opportunity of a trip to Wembley to run the line at the Kirkcaldy v Aberdeen schoolboys match at Stark's Park "a gesture that was thoroughly appreciated by officials of the Kirkcaldy Schools Football Association." In March, McNaught and Andy Leigh were chosen to play for a Scotland XI against The Army at Newcastle. To everyone's surprise, including the player's, Andy Young was consistently overlooked for representative honours.

Amid the euphoria of the club's exalted League position, and memories of stirring exploits in the Scottish Cup, there were two bits of bad news for Rovers fans during the summer. Admission to Stark's Park for the new season would cost 2/-, up by sixpence (a 33% increase) due to the punitive increase in Entertainment Tax from 1d to 4 1/2d, and Willie McNaught was considering emigrating to South Africa. The Kirkcaldy Times reported : "When I remarked that McNaught would be a difficult man to replace, the Raith manager reminded me 'We have lost players like Alex James, Dave Morris and Tom Jennings and still come out on top. We can do the same again.'" Thankfully, Bert Herdman's myopic interpretation of Rovers' history was not put to the test, and McNaught signed another contract.

This may be the appropriate juncture to examine the top division at a time of huge attendances in Scottish football. Those born too late to appreciate the sport in the early 1950's must wonder why so many fans, of so many clubs, called it the "golden age" of the game, and why a club like Rovers could go from fifth place in the League, to narrowly avoiding relegation the following season, and yet still their players are regarded as "all-time greats."

The explanation is in the even spread of talent throughout the League. In finishing fifth in 1951/52, Rovers were only 9 points better off than relegated Morton, who had a handful of Scottish internationalists in their team, including goalkeeper Jimmy Cowan, Tommy Orr and Alex Linwood. Below Rovers were teams packed with talent ; Partick Thistle with Jimmy Davidson, Jimmy McGowan, Tommy Ledgerwood, Willie Sharp

and Johnny McKenzie ; Motherwell had Andy Paton, Willie Redpath and full backs Kilmarnock and Shaw ; Billy Steel's Dundee boasted Doug Cowie and Bobby Flavell ; Celtic with Bobby Collins, Bertie Peacock, Bobby Evans and Charlie Tully ; Queen of the South with Billy Houliston, Jimmy Binning, Roy Henderson and Jackie Oakes ; Aberdeen had Baird, Yorston, Harris and Pearson ; Third Lanark with Jimmy Mason, Matt Balunas and Ally McLeod ; Airdrie had Ian McMillan, Jimmy Welsh and Willie Fraser, and St Mirren could field Willie Cunningham, Willie Telfer and Tommy Gemmell.

Above Rovers were Hibs of the Famous Five, Rangers, Hearts and their inside forwards Conn, Bauld and Wardhaugh, and the great East Fife team of Duncan, Fleming, Gardiner, Bonthrone, Finlay and Sammy Stewart. With only sixteen clubs in the top division, competition to remain above the two relegation places was fierce. The maximum wage in England meant that Scottish clubs could retain their better players by paying higher wages than they could obtain south of the border, and the big clubs in Glasgow and Edinburgh had their pick of youth and junior talent which meant that they rarely waved their cheque books at provincial clubs, thus leaving them with their best players. It was truly a golden period of Scottish League football, and a good time for Rovers to find themselves as members of the elite.

Despite the successes of the previous season, there were misgivings amongst Rovers fans as they approached 1952/53. Bernie Kelly missed the start of the season, having had a cartilage removed, and Copeland had returned to Dundee. The headline in the Kirkcaldy Times was : "Raith fans are worried. Need for new forwards. Problems for Management." The rise in admission prices had not gone down well, and season tickets had been slow to sell. "The football public is fickle and if Raith Rovers are not able to provide the goods – in this instance, the quality of entertainment demanded – the spectators will go elsewhere for their Saturday afternoon sport. They want stars, they want a winning team ! I sometimes wonder whether the Management really appreciate just how strongly the average fan thinks along these lines."

There was a marginal improvement in results in the League Cup section, but still no qualification for the knock out stages, and a dreadful start to the League season meant that the first victory did not come until the ninth game, by which time Copeland had returned from Dundee, this time permanently, and Kelly had been restored to the side. Management claimed that finances dictated that top quality players could not be purchased, and there was constant criticism that the steady stream of juniors signed by the club was not the way forward.

The first League victory, 2-1 at home to Aberdeen, came at a cost. Andy Leigh broke his arm above the elbow and he joined McLure, who tore knee ligaments, in hospital

JAMES W.M. GOURLAY Chairman of the Board of Directors from 1942 until 1964, most of that time spent in the top division.

At the Board Meeting of 16th September 1952, the Chairman reported on his findings regarding recurrent rumours of Complimentary tickets being sold to members of the public. The CID were asked to attend the complimentary ticket gate at the match against Celtic on 13th September, and questioned seven ticket holders, who advised that they had obtained them from two individuals. One of them, a compositor at the firm which printed the club's stationery, on being questioned by police and club officials, admitted that he had printed the tickets and distributed them. The other individual had been telling people that he had purchased the tickets from the Chairman and Manager, who were making money "on the side". He confirmed in writing that this was "without any foundation or facts." Because of the longstanding and close relationship between the club and the printers, no legal action was taken against the two individuals.

Season ticket sales up to 5th August 1952 were A Stand 362, B Stand 105 and Ground 477

Approval was granted at the board meeting of 22nd September 1952 for the Supporters Club to begin Hospital Broadcasts

IAN BAIN

An approach was made to Birmingham City in September 1952 to re-sign Jacky Stewart. In early November a swap was agreed with Aberdeen for Andy Leigh and Yorston, but it did not proceed. Six weeks later, enquiries were made about Ken Currie of Third Lanark (who Rovers had long admired while he was at Hearts) and Ernie Ewan of Aberdeen.
In October, it was proposed to swap Willie Penman for Archie Baird of Aberdeen

There was a dispute with Dundee over the terms of Ernie Copeland's transfer. Rovers expected to pay £1390 plus £1000 at the end of the season, while Dundee were looking for £2000 plus £1000 plus another £400 for the player.

Bernie Kelly's wages were stopped for a week after he missed the train, owing to fog, on the way to the home match against Hibs.

For the only time in the club's history, Rovers reached the Second Eleven Cup Final. They lost the first leg at Stark;s Park, Dundee winning 2-1 on 6th April 1953. Seven days later, they went further behind to a Turnbull goal after one minute of the second leg at Dens Park, but Albert Wood equalised on the night in 19 minutes. Irvine restored Dundee's advantage, and Wood scored a second with 18 minutes to play, but Rovers lost the Final 4-3 on aggregate.

that evening. For the last 20 minutes of the game, 9-man-Raith defended desperately. Young centre half Jim Clunie, deputising for Harry Colville, broke his leg in his third first team match during a 1-1 home draw with Motherwell. He finished the match limping on the left wing.

On 21st October, "by special request of the Chairman, captain and player William McNaught was asked to appear at the directors meeting, this to state his views on the team play, which has been very poor in recent weeks. Player McNaught stated there was complete harmony with the players on and off the field and thought that they would shortly give the form that justified them last season, when the holding grounds became available. He was asked his opinion on the forward formation, stated that he did not think McEwan and Maule made a good partnership on the right wing, he preferred Young at centre forward given the correct inside support. The meeting thanked player McNaught for his attendance, and before leaving he felt that some good purpose would be served if all the players met each other oftener, and it was agreed to meeting all players before lunch time and have a talk after lunch at Stuart's Restaurant, High Street, Kirkcaldy, every Saturday when available."

Over the next week, the Directors watched Rodger of Aberdeen and Copeland of Dundee, and enquired about Stott of Partick Thistle, concluding that it was imperative that the team be strengthened.

Jackie Williamson took Leigh's place in the team which went a further six matches before the next victory, unexpectedly at Parkhead, Copeland scoring the only goal of the game. That result proved to be the season's pivotal moment, and it was no coincidence that Copeland was the match winner, having scored in all eight of his appearances since returning to the club. "Copeland can't save Raith on his own" said the Kirkcaldy Times the previous week, when his equaliser won a point from the home match against Queen of the South, but Ernie was doing his best to disprove that assertion.

The Parkhead victory was described as "A ray of sunshine at last" and although Rovers were still three points adrift at the bottom of the table, and still deep in relegation trouble, they were given some hope, and perhaps a little faith. There was an air of grim reality around a club dogged by injuries, and operating under reduced finances, the lack of playing success and increased admission charges having had a marked impact on attendances.

After a 0-0 draw in the New Year's Day derby at Stark's Park, and an abortive trip to Paisley, when the match was called off due to thick fog thirty minutes before kick off, reigning League champions and League leaders Hibs were beaten 4-2 at Stark's Park. Ernie Copeland scored a hat-trick as Hibs were humbled, and supplanted at the top of the League by East Fife. The midfield was dominated by Bernie Kelly, who arrived at the ground from his Ayrshire home just 20

minutes before kick off.

A 3-2 win at Dens Park the following Saturday, with Copeland scoring two more, lifted Rovers off the bottom of the League for the first time that season. Ernie scored four in the 5-0 drubbing of Clachnacuddin in the first round of the Scottish Cup, and it was Penman's turn at home to Partick in the League, with both goals in a 2-2 draw. Rovers were the superior side at home to Hearts in the second round of the Scottish Cup, but Willie Bauld scored the only goal of the game to leave a huge Rovers support disappointed and disillusioned. A new record of 31,306 tickets were sold for the tie.

A tense bottom of the League battle at Third Lanark ended in favour of the home side, but an excellent performance, particularly in defence, earned a 2-0 win at Aberdeen, followed by an unlucky defeat at Motherwell. Nearly half of the League, seven clubs, were separated by just three points at the bottom of the Division following Rovers' 3-0 home win over Airdrie, Willie Penman scoring a hat-trick just two days before his wedding. He failed to find the net in a Wednesday evening match against Rangers, but Rovers won 3-1 with two goals from Andy Young and one from Bernie Kelly on the first occasion a white ball had been used at Stark's Park.

At Tynecastle three days later, Andy Leigh was injured after 20 minutes, but played on and Rovers won their third successive match, 2-1, thanks to a Kelly double. The season-long problem in attack manifested itself at home to Falkirk, when a 2-0 defeat dragged Rovers back into the relegation mire, but a fighting draw at Dumfries, earned by a resolute defence and Copeland's opportunist equaliser, was followed by a narrow 3-2 victory over Clyde, the two precious points being enough to guarantee Rovers' safety. Nothing was required from the final two games, at St Mirren and Hibs, which is just as well as both were lost.

Rovers finished with 26 points, just six less than the previous season, one ahead of relegated Motherwell. Falkirk and Airdrie shared Rovers points total, Aberdeen had one more and Queen of the South two more. Such was the closeness of the League that had Rovers won their final two matches, they would have finished in fourth place, locked with Hearts and Clyde.

The Rovers captain was outstanding throughout the troubled campaign, and drew the following praise from the Kirkcaldy Times. "Willie McNaught has shone throughout this season, not merely for his undoubted ability as a footballer, but because of his high sense of sportsmanship. He never allows himself to become ruffled and it is his sense of fair play as well as his delightful positional ability and clear-cut clearances, which have made him so universally admired throughout Scotland.

McNaught, who had captained the Scottish League against the Irish League in Belfast on 3rd September, was named Kirkcaldy's Sportman of the Year for the third successive year ; Andy Young made it a hat-

trick of second places.

There was a rare event at Stark's Park over the summer of 1953, a cheque being sent to a fellow Scottish League club to purchase a player. Right back Bobby Kirk was signed from Dunfermline for £1000, amid the annual draft of juniors and juveniles.

Three of the six League Cup section matches were won, not enough to secure qualification. The League season started in spectacular style, Hibs beaten 4-0 at Stark's Park in one of Rovers best performances in living memory. Four wins and two draws in the first eight matches put them in second place in a odd-looking League table, with Hibs bottom and Rangers second bottom. Queen of the South maintained their 100% record with a 5-1 thumping of Rovers on 31st October.

That started a catastrophic sequence of results comprising nine successive League defeats, a 1-1 draw at Methil on New Year's Day, followed by a home defeat by St Mirren – one point out of 22. Malcolm McLure returned at right back in preference to Kirk, while Jackie Williamson deputised for Andy Leigh, who was recovering from a broken hand. In attack, Willie Penman and Johnny Maule were replaced by Andy Young and Scott, but while time had caught up with the veteran duo, Penman's power and Maule's artistry had not been replaced.

There was a set-back of unusual circumstance towards the end of the season. Former East Fife manager Scot Symon, offered £10,000 to sign reserve centre half

Jim Clunie for Preston North End. The deal was agreed, and Rovers had lined up the signature of a couple of forwards in anticipation of the transfer fee, but Clunie did not want to leave. Early in the new year, however, Aberdeen signed him for £7,000. In came forwards Peter Rice from St Mirren and Scotland cap Davie Duncan, returning after 15 years, most of it spent productively on East Fife's left wing.

Back-to-back victories at Airdrie and at home to Celtic, with Charlie Drummond "inspirational" in goal, had the fans believing that the long-anticipated recovery was underway. It faltered on its path, however, the 5-3 defeat at Firhill being a far better performance than the 1-1 home draw with Stirling Albion. Drummond was less fortunate in the home match against St Mirren. With 10 minutes to play, and Rovers looking the likelier team to break the 1-1 deadlock, Blyth's cross came back off the crossbar and into the grateful arms of the Raith goalkeeper, who immediately threw the ball upfield. To the astonishment of the Raith players and supporters, the referee signalled a goal – St Mirren's winner.

The Scottish Cup brought some respite, and a record scoreline for Rovers in national competition. Coldstream were beaten 10-1 at Home Park, an uncovered public park pitch, rented for £5 from the Town Council. The 1115 spectators were thoroughly soaked, but Rovers handed back to their hosts £15 of their share of the £108 gate. The visit to B Division leaders

Pictured in their change strip of red shirts before the match at Dens Park on 12th September 1953, are :
Back row : Bobby Kirk, Andy Leigh, George Johnstone, Willie McNaught, Harry Colville, Jackie Williamson.
Front row : Jimmy McEwan, Andy Young, Ernie Copeland, Bernie Kelly, Willie Penman

For the start of the season 1953/54, there were new arrangements for the sale of match programmes, for which Bert Herdman received 30/- per match as organiser. The Lucky Programme Number was to be discontinued, although it re-appeared a few seasons later and remained in place until the early 1970s. Prizes over the years ranged from cinema tickets to cash.

Rovers owned a building, containing several flats, in Rosabelle Street, and in early November 1953 purchased a three-apartment house on Pratt Street for £600, which was promptly let to Andy Leigh. The Rosabelle Street property earned the club rental income.

DAVIE DUNCAN
Two spells at Raith Rovers,
with a marvellous career at
East Fife - and Scotland - in
between.

In August 1953, Jimmy Whittle of Hearts was being pursued by the Rovers management. In early December there was interest in Joe Hutton of Ayr United and George Hamilton of Aberdeen. In early December, Sunderland offered £10,000 for Willie McNaught, while Preston North End were quoted £8,000 for Jackie Williamson. In late December, £500 was offered to Rangers for Colin Liddle, a week after enquiries had been made about Tony Harris of Aberdeen and Alex Boden of Celtic.

Rovers and Falkirk agreed to play a Penman Cup tie under the Brockville floodlights in November 1953, but only friendly matches were permitted to be played under lights. Falkirk subsequently scratched from the competition, leaving Rovers to face Stenhousemuir in the semi final ; after a draw, Rovers also scratched.

Prior to the start of 1953/54 season, Bert Herdman used the impressive space devoted to club affairs in the Kirkcaldy Times to Review Rovers' Post War Record.

"Due to nobody's fault but to a six year war, [club officials] inherited a skeleton team and prospects as black as a a negro's countenance. The 1946/7 season sowed the seeds for a great Rovers

Motherwell in the second round was catastrophic. In the first minute, Drummond slipped and fumbled McNaught's pass back over his goal-line, and Motherwell capitalised on the goalkeeper's loss of confidence with two more goals in the opening quarter of an hour. Rovers fought back, but were profligate in front of goal, Copeland's 60th minute score being all they had to show for more than an hour's attacking play. Motherwell scored a fourth goal with five minutes remaining.

A home draw with Queen of the South put Rovers six points ahead of second bottom place, prompting the Kirkcaldy Times to comment "No wonder the Kirkcaldy supporters are saying : 'Thank goodness for Hamilton and Airdrie.'" There was neither cause, nor impulse, for panic on the part of the Directors. Bert Herdman later reflected : "The management, wisely, kept their heads during the exasperating period. They knew there was quality and plenty of it at Stark's Park. They retained faith in signings who have given us cause to cultivate that faith. There was no general raking-in of players from all over the shop as in season 1927-28, when Raith were similarly placed. Just a deft acquisition or two and a re-awakening of the old guard and solidity and success marched hand in hand."

Championship contenders Hearts were beaten 4-2 at Stark's Park in a thrilling match, Rovers going four ahead after 64 minutes, and this was followed by a point at Ibrox in a midweek fixture earned without McNaught immaculate presence - he was playing for the Scottish League in Dublin. It could easily have been two points, with Copeland missing two good chances to score in the dying minutes. A 5-0 thrashing of Hamilton Accies in Kirkcaldy confirmed the club's A Division status for another season, with three matches to spare. Rovers matched the previous season's points total, 26, but the difference in 1953/54 was that there were two teams marooned at the bottom of the table, and relegation was averted by the comfortable margin of 11 points. Ernie Copeland's 32 goals in League and Cup was bettered only by Charlie Fleming of East Fife (39) and Jimmy Wardhaugh of Hearts (34)

Full back Tom Weir, freed by East Fife, was the only close season signing of note in 1954, alongside the usual procession of juniors and juveniles. Bert Herdman was quoted in the Kirkcaldy Times of 7th July : "We know what we need and what we want in order to improve the team but finance is beating us. Rovers cannot pay high transfer fees – it is disappointing that only 700 of the permitted 1000 season tickets have been sold."

The twin brakes on Rovers progress, injuries and their failure to sign experienced players, conspired to produce another relegation-haunted season which started with the traditional failure to qualify from the League Cup section, despite the proferred bonus of a blazer and flannels in club colours.

The opening seven League matches brought victories over Dundee, St Mirren and

Stirling Albion, and a draw at Firhill, but seven of the next nine matches were lost. Kelly, McEwan (out for 12 weeks after a cartilage operation) and Copeland had all missed matches through injury, but worse was to come in a 6-0 home defeat by Hearts on 4th December. Willie McNaught was carried off after half an hour with badly torn ligaments in his left knee, and Charlie Drummond played three quarters of the match with a broken wrist. McNaught had been selected to play against Hungary (who had scored six and seven goals in successive matches against England) at Hampden in one of the most eagerly awaited Internationals for years, and had to withdraw. The prolonged absence of two players, Jimmy McEwan, who was recovering from a cartilege operation, and Bobby Buchan who had shown great promise after signing from Cowdenbeath, was felt over the winter months. Bernie Kelly and Jackie Williamson were available only when their National Service commitments would allow.

Rovers were outplayed in a 4-1 defeat at Dundee which caused the Kirkcaldy Times to admit that the "Relegation threat is real enough now". There was some respite with a well merited 4-1 home win over East Fife on New Year's Day, but that was followed by three successive defeats. In a desperate attempt to shore up the attack, veteran winger Eddie Rutherford was signed from Hearts, and Jackie Stewart was brought back from Birmingham, where he had been playing for the reserves for the previous year. A Kirkcaldy Times reader sought a higher remedy, following the 2-1 defeat at Stirling. "I am glad to see that Billy Graham is coming to Scotland, for I think he is the only person who can save Rovers now. " They were third bottom, one point ahead of East Fife.

The first away win of the season came at Cappielow in the 5th round of the re-structured Scottish Cup, thanks to a Copeland hat-trick, but Clyde had the better of a well contested cup tie in the next round. That left Rovers free to concentrate on their League position, but they continued to test their supporters' nerves with vastly contrasting performances. A 2-0 defeat at Dumfries had the prophets of doom at full voice, but it was followed by a 1-0 win over Rangers at Stark's Park, which was deserved if only for the resolution shown by the defence.

McNaught returned after injury, but it was at centre half, replacing Harry Colville, with Kirk and McLure the established full backs. Jimmy McEwan returned after an injury-strewn season, latterly a broken wrist, and Iain Bain came in at half back to allow Andy Young to venture further forward.

There was no lack of fighting spirit amongst the players, and in a fierce relegation battle results were ground-out rather than earned convincingly. Falkirk at home, and St Mirren away brought victories, a draw was prized out of Kilmarnock, and there were hard-luck stories in defeats at Tynecastle and Pittodrie, the latter ensuring that the club's fate would be decided on the last day of the League season, at home to

Hibs. Falkirk were virtually safe on 23 points ; Motherwell and Queen of the South had 22 ; Rovers were second bottom on 21, and Stirling were long since relegated with just six points. Even a victory might not be enough for Rovers, although Motherwell had to go to Ibrox, and Queen of the South were at home to East Fife.

15,000 watched Rovers get off to the best possible start, favoured by a strong wind. Bernie Kelly scored in 3 minutes and Andy Young in 14. Nerves, and having to face the wind, got the better of players and spectators alike in the second half, and Eddie Turnbull added to the agony with a goal for Hibs nineteen minutes from the end. The defence battled manfully to prevent further loss. East Fife did their fellow countrymen no favours in losing at Palmerston, but Motherwell lost 2-0 at Ibrox and finished below Rovers.

The Kirkcaldy Times described the relief. "This, without a doubt, was Stark's Park's most important game during the past six seasons. And it was, just as surely, the closest of all Raith's escapes from relegation. In acknowledging that, I offer the players my warmest congratulations on what has been a magnificent fighting recovery, a recovery which has taken them to a place of safety which did not seem possible a few weeks ago. But I also say this : let there be in this moment of triumph and jubilation a firm resolve on the part of everyone at Stark's Park that the like will not happen again."

As events unfolded in the corridors of power, the worry and panic was unnecessary. The 16 club A Division was transformed into an 18 club First Division, and neither Motherwell nor Stirling Albion were relegated. The Fir Park club have a remarkable record of avoiding relegation thanks to league reconstruction, and there is no guarantee that Rovers would have been saved by such means had they, and not the Steelmen, finished second bottom.

Financial worries were eased in the first week of May with the transfer of Bobby Kirk to Hearts for a fee in excess of £5000, a profit of almost £4,500. "The transfer will keep Raith Rovers solvent for another year", but Bert Herdman's response to the expanded First Division was that "relegation will mean financial suicide." There was a further windfall a month later, Falkirk paying £5000 for the services of Harry Colville, who had been a marvellous servant to Raith Rovers. A fortnight later, 19 year old Willie Polland was signed from Wallhouse Rose juveniles. Rovers put their faith in a youth policy, the wholesale signing up of young players who would be trained until they were ready for the first team. An arrangement was made with Nairn Thistle, the club subsidised by the town's biggest employers, for players to be farmed out to them and learn their trade in the rough tumble of the Fife Junior League.

Bert Herdman was in combative mood at the start of 1955/56, stating "Personally, I am convinced that most of the trouble was due to Raith's old enemy – Jinx.

Rovers have now spent six successive seasons in A Division and have never won a national honour. It would be ridiculous to assume that on that account we have not been a success in the top section." Success was not a word on the lips of the fans following just one win in six League Cup section matches, although the League season opened with a draw and two victories and after five matches Rovers sat atop the Division.

McLure and Weir started the season at full back, but Polland replaced the latter from October onwards. Ian Bain was at right half, allowing the club's most impressive player over the previous year, Andy Young, to play inside forward. Hamish McMillan, brother of Airdrie's Scottish Internationalist Ian, and the restored Scott were the wingers for the first half of the season as McEwan moved inside, and Thomson accompanied Copeland in attack. Bernie Kelly was not seen at full fitness until the second half of the season.

Hopes of a challenge for the championship were dispelled after a poor run from mid November until the end of the year, with three draws and five defeats. Herdman's early season optimism had been downgraded to a grimmer reality by the end of November, and in an article in the Kirkcaldy Times he spelled out Soccer Finance. The club needed an average gate of 14,000 to break even, and even in the heady days of 1921 to 1923, they only achieved 10,500. "Raith fans should be satisfied in having top section football at their door." High entertainment tax and insufficient regular support prevented provincial clubs from competing in the transfer market, while the development of young players was hindered by National Service, although one of them, Willie Polland, looked like an excellent capture. Ernie Copeland, in the meantime, was going through a barren patch in front of goal, and asked for a free transfer at the end of November. Instead, the Directors gave him a week off.

There was a transformation following a 3-0 defeat at Methil on Monday 2nd January. Kelly, who had earlier asked for a transfer, was restored to a permanent position, and George Stewart took over from Drummond in goal. Willie McNaught, who had been a beacon amidst the wreckage of the late autumn slump, found an even higher standard of performance at centre half. After a battling 1-1 draw at home against Celtic, the Kirkcaldy Times was moved to write : "McNaught was again outstanding at centre half – so outstanding that it makes me consider if we will ever see the like of him at Stark's Park again. The complete footballer and master tactician, he repulsed Celtic attack after Celtic attack with sheer skill and intelligence. He was the pivot around whom the whole defensive structure revolved, but he was so much more than that. By setting such a superb example, he was an inspiration to the whole team."

On the same afternoon, the

WILLIE POLLAND

revival, 1947/8 provided a good harvest and 1948/9 saw the bins overflowing with the corn of success – promotion won !"

Herdman singled out several players for special mention in this eight year spell. Ernie Till – "a man of mobile brain and dainty touches, he illuminated his side of the field with his dazzling presence. Beaten by the years, Ernie can look back on his long association with the club with the satisfaction sound and skilled service gives.

Francis Joyner – "whirlwind, dynamic personality. His pre and post war adventures with Raith Rovers were highly profitable."

Jackie Stewart – "The blood accelerates at the name ! This bunch of guts, ability and energy did much to make Raith re-adorn the football map.

Alan Collins – "Genial gentleman, scored vital goals (in the Scottish Cup against Hibs in 1949, scoring three against Ayr in 1948/49 after being 2-0 down at half time)."

Tom Brady – "Time-proof player. Yes, Tommy, although you didn't accompany the club into A Division you provides some of the slabs that paved the way."

Joe McLaughlin – "A pillar during our first A Division season. He had everything we desired, ability, experience, cool head, versatility and a net-finding right foot. His goals were often match winners."

In early December 1953, Preston North End offered £10,000 for Jim Clunie, three weeks before Rovers accepted £7000 from Aberdeen, with £500 of that going to the player.

In mid December, Bernie Kelly's request to be placed on the transfer list was turned down by the Board

A friendly match in England against Notts County on Saturday 30th January was postponed the day before the match due to a frozen pitch

On 8th September 1953, there was a fire in the boiler house, which was also used as a drying room for training and playing kit. The club's training kit was lost in the fire. The loss adjuster valued it at £78 10/-

1954 Work started on developing Seafield Colliery

A private trial match was staged at Stark's Park on 6th July 1954, involving juniors and juveniles. A special bus was run from Glasgow to transport the players

Johnny Maule, who had been signed by Stenhousemuir having been freed by Rovers, played only twice for his new club, then handed back his signing on fee of £50, explaining : "I would rather watch the Rovers than play for anyone else." Johnny was true to his word, attending virtually every home game until his death in January 1998. A month later, Willie Penman scored an 88th minute winner for Montrose in a C Division game against Rovers reserves.

Unsuccessful offers were made for Davie Laing of Hearts in early September 1954 ; and Jim Chalmers of Stirling Albion in late December

Stark's Park Youth Club, an attempt to resurrect a Juvenile team with close links to Rovers, was wound up during the 1954/55 season following a two year trial. The step up to the First Division was too much for juvenile players.

Reserves lost 7-1 at Brockville ; Charlie Drummond, married that morning, clearly had his mind elsewhere. The match prior to the Celtic game, a 3-1 home win over Queen of the South, was the start of a run of seven matches without defeat, and Rovers were finding their form at just the right time for a run in the Scottish Cup.

The much-postponed fifth round tie against Hibs was eventually played on Wednesday 8th February, at Easter Road – Rovers first match in Scotland under floodlights, although they had previously played several floodlit friendly matches in England. Jimmy McEwan put them ahead in 71 minutes, but Eddie Turnbull equalised with four minutes remaining of a thrilling Cup tie, in which Rovers were the superior side. The replay was five days later, on a Monday afternoon at Stark's Park, when Rovers built a three goal lead in 50 minutes, eventually winning 3-1.

Second Division promotion candidates Queen's Park proved to be a difficult hurdle to overcome in the next round, a 2-2 draw at Stark's Park followed by 1-1 at Hampden in the replay. The tie could have been settled in the final minute of the first match, but Andy Young missed from the penalty spot. Ernie Copeland scored two minutes before the end of extra time in the replay to give Rovers a home quarter final against Partick Thistle. 18,264 watched a monumental struggle, which lasted for 97 minutes with the trainers as busy as the players. The Kirkcaldy Times likened the second half to a battlefield, with players going down like ninepins. George Stewart in goal, McNaught and Copeland (who unusually was not amongst the scorers) were the architects a 2-1 Rovers victory, resulting in only the club's third appearance in the semi finals of the Scottish Cup.

58,488 packed into Easter Road to see Rovers tackle Hearts. Bert Herdman recalled : "The goal-less draw was fair to both contestants, but I felt that a thin slice of luck would have carried Raith Rovers into the final with a good chance of winning the Cup [against an ordinary Celtic side]. The replay was an anti-climax ; we shed our lustre and walked tamely out of the competition." A Jimmy Wardhaugh free kick in the first minute set the tone of the replay, but it took until his second goal in 73 minutes (Stewart dropping a Hamilton cross) before Hearts established their superiority over a ten-man Rovers team, McLure having departed with an ankle injury. Before that, Copeland suffered a cut on his eyebrow during a clash of heads. Crawford scored with four minutes remaining to make the final score 3-0.

Three days after the Cup defeat, Ernie Copeland scored four times in a 5-3 win at Pittodrie which banished any fears of involvement in the relegation dogfight. The final eight League matches brought five victories which propelled Rovers to 11th place in the 18 club League, a comfortable 11 points ahead of the relegation positions. Perhaps more importantly, the final touches were being

put to a very promising team. Ian Bain finished the season as Polland's partner at full back ; Drummond was restored to goal, the half back line of Young, McNaught and Leigh was settled, and Johnny Urquhart was signed from Hearts. Less heralded was Jackie Williamson completing his National Service in England.

The prospect rekindled Herdman's optimism. "The outlook has never been so good. In addition to the long-tried and ever true signatories, good acquisitions have been effected, and our list contains lads with innate talent who, I expect, will develop into outstanding A Division players."

1956/57 must surely be regarded as the most successful in the club's history. Fourth place in the First Division had been bettered once before, in 1921/22, and attained two years later, but the 1956/57 side also reached the Scottish Cup semi final. The 1948/49 team got to the League Cup Final and won a Championship, but it was the Second Division ; the 1994/95 side went won better and won the League Cup, but their Championship was, once again, of the lower League.

In terms of entertainment and the standard of players on show, the 1956/57 team must surely win the qualitative argument to win this one-club fantasy football league.

There were eleven full time players – plus Willie Penman, freed by Dundee United and on the look out for a club – when pre-season training started on 2nd July 1956 : McNaught, Young, Leigh, Bain, Drummond, McEwan, Copeland, Kelly, Urquhart, Williamson and Bennie Murney.

The League Cup section brought its usual outcome, failure to qualify, but there was a strong start to the League, with just one defeat in the opening nine fixtures, Airdrie winning a remarkable match 6-4 at Stark's Park. Two defeats in three games were followed by three successive home victories, 3-0 at home to Queen's Park, 4-0 at Brockville, and in between, a 5-1 victory over Rangers at Stark's Park.

Despite dominating the match from the first whistle, Rovers fell behind to a Simpson goal in 14 minutes, but Bernie Kelly equalised five minutes later. The destination of the points was determined by two goals in two minutes from Johnny Urquhart, just after the hour mark. The first came when he followed up to net a McEwan shot which rebounded off the underside of the crossbar. The Kirkcaldy Times described the second as follows : "Two minutes later came Urquhart's freakish second goal – a goal which left most of the 20,000 crowd gaping open-mouthed at the apparent incredulity of it all. It happened this way. Picking up a Williamson pass which the inside left laid right in his path, Urquhart cut menacingly into the penalty box. But he stumbled and fell as he shot for goal and the ball appeared to be going well over the bar until it suddenly dipped and landed in the net behind a bemused and bewildered Niven, who had emerged two or three yards to narrow the angle. Urquhart, who came to earth facing away from the goal, obviously didn't know he had scored until he heard the delayed roar of the crowd as the rest of the Raith players rushed to congratulate him."

Rangers enjoyed their best spell, as Rovers subconsciously fell back on their two goal lead, allowing the defence to share the plaudits with the attack. Two goals from Ernie Copeland in the final minute, the second with the last kick of the match, turned a comprehensive victory into a rout, in which Bain, Young, McNaught and Kelly were outstanding. The 5-1 victory allowed third placed Rovers to remain one point ahead of Rangers.

The team had confidence in their ability to bounce back from set-backs, a home defeat by Dundee on 29th December quickly forgotten by a 4-1 home win over East Fife in the New Year's Day derby, and a 3-0 home defeat by Partick Thistle three weeks later was followed by a long run of victories.

Hibs were beaten 4-1 at Easter Road on 26th January, the first of six successive victories, three in the League (Celtic 3-1 and St Mirren 7-0) and three in the Scottish Cup (Inverness Caledonian 3-2, Dundee United 7-0 and Dumbarton 4-0). After the narrow and controversial Cup semi final defeat, results tailed off a little, and had the last three, meaningless games of the season (played in four days, Friday, Saturday and Tuesday, to meet the 30th April deadline) not been lost, Kilmarnock would have been overhauled in third place.

Eighty-four goals were scored in the League, a total exceeded only by Champions Rangers. Bernie Kelly and Ernie Copeland both scored 24, and the left wing partnership of Jackie Williamson (13) and Johnny Urquhart (9) contributed a further 22. Kelly was selected for the Scotland B team which played at Birmingham in February, and along with Copeland was a reserve for the League International against the English at Ibrox, in which McNaught played at centre half.

The season's success was founded on a settled side, and no department was more solid than the half back line of Young, McNaught and Leigh, which was together for 38 of the 45 League and Cup ties. McLure and Bain were the full backs in 24 matches, and the forward line read McEwan, Kelly, Copeland, Williamson and Urquhart on 29 occasions.

The Scottish Cup campaign started with a tricky away tie at Inverness Caledonian. On a muddy pitch, Rovers took an early lead through their leading goalscorers, Copeland and Kelly, and when the latter scored the third from the penalty spot, their passage into the next round seemed assured. Caledonian fought their way back into the game and goals in 85 and 89 minutes left Rovers relieved to hear the final whistle.

The 7-0 scoreline against Dundee United in the sixth [second] round would be unimaginable today, but the black and white hooped Dundee team were then a struggling Second Division side. The rout was most

notable for Andy Leigh's first ever goal at Stark's Park, although he had scored two away goals in his previous nine seasons at the club. The following week, a second successive 7-0 win, over St Mirren took Rovers to second place in the League, although seven points distant from leaders Hearts. Bernie Kelly headed the country's goalscoring charts, with Copeland not far behind.

Another Second Division club, Dumbarton, were beaten 4-0 in the quarter final, the attendance of 18,001 setting a record for Boghead which was never beaten at Dumbarton's former home ground. Theoretically, the semi final draw was favourable to Rovers. Falkirk had got off to a dreadful start to the season and they and Ayr United were rooted at the foot of the table for much of it. Under new manager Reggie Smith however, they had shown signs of revival and their momentum had also carried them through to the Cup semi finals.

Rovers limbered up for the tie with only their second away League defeat of the season, 1-0 at Aberdeen in midweek, followed by a disappointing performance against the League leaders at Tynecastle, in which Rovers were flattered by the 2-1 defeat. They were also below par in a narrow 3-2 victory over Motherwell at Stark's Park on the Saturday before the Cup semi final. It was not the best time to be suffering a dip in form.

With the gates of Tynecastle shut on several hundred latecomers, 48,275 packed inside, Rovers appeared to be more afflicted by nerves than their opponents, who took the lead through Grierson in 17 minutes. Despite Falkirk playing a more determined, traditional cup tie style of football, Rovers' attempts to play measured, controlled football paid dividends when they went ahead by half time, with goals from Copeland and McEwan. Andy Leigh got in the way of a Moran cross and put into his own net in the first minute of the second half. Five minutes later, what seemed to be a perfectly good goal , a Copeland header from a Kelly cross, was chalked off for at best a marginal – more likely an incorrect – offside decision, but despite Rovers' fans cries of misfortune, Falkirk at least deserved a replay.

Willie McNaught inspects his Player of the Year Trophy, awarded by the Supporters Club, watched (on the left) by the kenspeckle figure of Jock McKay.

The blazer and flannels, promised if the team qualified for the League Cup quarter finals, were eventually purchased in February 1955. 15 blazers were purchased from James Bogie Ltd for £121, flannels were purchased from AK Melville & Son for £76 13/-, but the players would repay the club for these, and club ties were gifted by director Mr J Nicholl.

A private trial match was played at Burntisland on 9th July 1955. George Wright and Willie Knox were subsequently signed

The Scottish Football (Reserve) League was formed for 1955/56. C Division, in which Rovers Reserves played in the North-East section, was dissolved following a re-organisation of the Scottish Football League.

There was no ice hockey in Kirkcaldy in 1955/56.

Signing enquiries were made of Duncan Stanners of Rangers and Alex Wright of Bradford PA in mid August 1955, and Stirling Albion were approached for a swap with Bernie Kelly and John Smith, who was on Stirling's transfer list. Shortly afterwards, Kelly, who was unhappy with reserve team football, asked to be put on the transfer list.

Rovers failed to learn their lesson at the same venue four days later. Falkirk were quicker to the ball than a Rovers team which was guilty of over-elaboration, but there was much sympathy for the Kirkcaldy side as they attacked incessantly after the interval, chasing a 10th minute Falkirk lead. There was another disallowed goal, four goal-line clearances, and the refusal of a penalty when Alex Wright – a pre-season trialist for Rovers - appeared to play Kelly's shot with his arm. O'Hara broke away to score Falkirk's second goal with seven minutes remaining and it was the Bairns, not the Rovers, who went to Hampden for the Final (and beat Kilmarnock after a replay). Dreams of Scottish Cup glory for Rovers fans had to wait at least one more year (actually 51, and counting …..)

With league leaders Hearts, and championship contenders Rangers, over the horizon at the top of the League, and the Cup campaign over, it is perhaps understandable that results in the final six League matches left something to be desired, with just two victories. The regenerative powers of football never cease to amaze however. The April holiday Monday fixture was a reserve match against Rangers, and the Kirkcaldy Times report of the match included praise of Rovers' young centre half [Andrew] Thomson, who "… was well supported by the junior at left-half. The trialist, Jimmy Baxter, a 17-year-old Hill of Beath miner and left half of Crossgates Primrose, was afterwards signed by Manager Bert Herdman. He will remain with his junior side until the end of the present season. These two players were best of Raith's back six."

To everyone's surprise, Willie McNaught was overlooked for Scotland's end of season internationals, although Willie Bauld's withdrawal through injury meant that Ernie Copeland, at 34 years of age, was asked to travel on the Continental tour. On his selection, it was revealed by the SFA that Copeland had been one of the 22 players nominated to FIFA for World Cup qualification matches. He had also been one of the 22 nominated for the 1954 World Cup Finals, but was not included in the much smaller travelling party (which did not include any Rangers players ; they preferred to tour North America with their club). Despite all these near things, Ernie never played for his country, at any level.

In his end-of-season summary, Bert Herdman paid fitting tribute to one of the players given a free transfer. "I cannot close without paying tribute to Malcolm McLure, whom Father Time has spirited away from Stark's Park. He proved one of the most consistent, courageous and conscientious defenders Rovers ever had."

On the face of it, 1957/58 would appear to have been something of anti-climax. Rovers dropped to seventh in the League, and fell at the second hurdle in the Scottish Cup. Only two more League matches were lost than in the previous season, however, there were some sparkling victories, and the great team remained largely

intact throughout the season, so there was much to admire in individual, and collective, performances.

Understandably, Rovers were reluctant to break up this team, so there were no significant signings, but the players were one year older, and for a number of them that meant a downward trajectory in the bell diagram of their distinguished careers. The hope was that products of the youth policy would feed in as replacements, and this happened in the case of inside forward Jim Kerray, and to a lesser extent goalkeeper Jim Thorburn.

Most of the close season signing news revolved round the reluctance of Jackie Williamson and Bernie Kelly to re-sign. Both had been among a number of Rovers players to have received the permitted long-service, tax free bonuses, or 'benefits' at the end of the season ; but while those who had been full time for the previous five years received £750, Kelly and Williamson, who had been full time for only one year, received "just" £500. (It should be noted that such a sum would pay for a well appointed house in 1957. The existence of such tax-free lump sums, permissible every five years, also explains why so many star players in Scottish League teams were reluctant to move club, north or south of the border). Kelly and Williamson held out for the balance before they would re-sign, and both eventually relented, although a residue of resentment remained.

There was an improvement in League Cup results, four wins and two defeats, the second of these a thrilling 4-3 at Ibrox. Bernie Kelly scored all the goals in a outstanding personal performance in a 4-1 win at Firhill, and scored two more, as did Johnny Urquhart, in a 4-1 win over St Mirren. It was almost "winner takes all" in the final match of the section, Rangers at home, and while the four goals scored in the victory should have taken Rovers through on goal average, the three scored by Rangers allowed them to qualify by one fifth of a goal. Failure again, but it was exciting, and certainly entertaining.

The League season started brightly, with a 4-2 win over Third Lanark, and a 2-0 success at Dens Park, which had never been a fertile plain for Rovers. Bernie Kelly returned from playing for the Scottish League in Dublin and Rovers licked their lips in anticipation of a local derby against East Fife at Stark's Park – which was lost, 2-0, despite dominating much of the match.

It served only to shake the team from any complacency which may have encroached ; the next nine matches were without loss, including a draw at Celtic Park, a 4-1 home win over their Scottish Cup conquerors of the previous season, and a 5-0 home defeat of Clyde. A 2-0 win at Motherwell was scant reward for a masterful performance. That sparkling run took Rovers into second place, just a point behind leaders Hearts, with more than a third of the season played.

Perhaps it was the prospect of

becoming front runners in the race for the championship, but Rovers allowed anxiety to get the better of them in losing 1-0 to Aberdeen at Stark's Park. The forwards, in particular, had a wretched match. That spread to the defence when league leaders Hearts visited the following week, and won, comfortably, 3-0. Two more defeats, away from home, and then two draws, ended any pretence of a League championship challenge. Results, and performances, in January were a mixture of the very good and very bad. To some extent, the focus of attention was taken away from the disappointing loss in form by the Bucharest Dynamo saga.

The recently established European Cup had excited interest in club football on the continent and at home, and Rovers tried to tap into this new craze by arranging a friendly match with Bucharest Dynamo on 11th January 1958. When the League fixtures were announced, Rovers were down to play Queen of the South at home, but the fixture was brought forward to 19th October when both clubs' matches against that afternoon's League Cup finalists were postponed.

The Rumanians were to be paid a guarantee of £750, or half the gate, whichever was higher, and the match was made all ticket, admission being increased to 2/6d. 15,000 tickets had been sold, and arrangements were made to put on special trains to transport football fans from all over Fife. Rovers were to play in a new strip, made of silk for better visibility in the winter dusk, and with a thick white vertical band down the front of the navy shirt. The week before the match, the Rumanians withdrew, citing the death of the Minister of the Interior for their inability to travel.

That left Rovers with quite a dilemma – there were 15,000 tickets in people's hands, and the money realised from their sale had

been spent. The Belgian team Royal Antwerp were lined up as replacements, and the match was re-scheduled for 29th January (a Fife Cup tie against Cowdenbeath was played on the vacated 11th.) The special souvenir programme prepared for the Rumanians had been half printed, with several references to Bucharest Dynamo, and rather than incur the expense of scrapping that, it was used, with other half referring to the Belgian team. The final problem in this tangled tale was that Royal Antwerp didn't turn up, either. The Kirkcaldy Times, on the morning of the match, was taken in by the deception.

"Once again, the Raith management must be complimented on the enterprise and initiative they have shown in bringing a team of this calibre to Stark's Park, more especially after the disappointment they experienced at the hands of the Rumanians. The Royal Antwerp team, who play in Belgium under the name of Waterschei-Thor, but who use their royal nom-de-plume granted them by King Leopold in 1937, for travelling purposes ...."

They were in fact two different clubs. Royal Antwerp were the reigning Belgian champions and would have been attractive opponents for Rovers. Waterschei Thor were a Third Division amateur team, on a par with Rosslyn Juniors or Nairn Thistle, and that's who turned up at Stark's Park. Johnny Urquhart was told of the change of opponents as he climbed the steps to the players' entrance before the match ; Andy Leigh recalled "They looked and played like a pub team." The match was an embarrassment, watched by 12,000, and Rovers won a pedestrian affair 3-1, with the last two goals coming in the final ten minutes. On 17th March, Rovers were reprimanded by the SFA and were "advised to exercise greater care in future in trying to negotiate a game of this nature."

There was more sinister news for

Rovers line up to be photographed with their glamour Continental opponents on 29th January 1958, except it was Belgian amateur team Watershei-Thor who arrived in Kirkcaldy, rather than Bucharest Dynamo or Royal Antwerp. The Rovers players pictured, wearing the high-visibility silk playing kit donated by the Supporters Club, are :
Back row : Andy Leigh, Andy Young, goalkeeper Jim Thorburn and Jim Kerray.
Middle row : Ian McGregor, Willie Polland and Willie McNaught.
Front row : Jimmy McEwan, Bernie Kelly, Ernie Copeland, Jackie Williamson and Johnny Urquhart. Jim Kerray was listed as a substitute, coming on for Jackie Williamson at half time.

Centre half Ian McGregor was signed from Lochore Welfare in August 1957, and had the unenviable task of being deputy to Willie McNaught. He filled in for a number of injured defenders before being freed at the end of 1960/61, whereupon he joined Cowdenbeath.

1959 - Caledonian Mills in Prime Gilt Box Street closed ; St Andrews High School opened ; Fife's first crematorium was opened in Kirkcaldy.

Few individuals in the club's history served for so long, and with such distinction, and indeed in so many capacities, as Johnny Urquhart.

A prominent player in local schools and Boys Brigade circles, the outbreak of the Second World War curtailed his options when it came to junior or juvenile football. He maintained his links with the Boys Brigade, playing for Kirkcaldy Old Boys in the Juvenile League, and played trial matches for Rovers and East Fife during the war.

Towards the close of hostilities, he signed for Hearts, lured by the promise of regular football, as the Tynecastle club had a reserve team, whereas his local club did not.

An early place in the first team was conceded to a succession of big money signings, and towards the end of 1949/50 he spent a fruitful loan spell at Stark's Park, helping Rovers to retain their cherished A Division status.

For four years, from 1951, he was the established outside left to Hearts' legendary "Terrible Trio" of Conn, Bauld and Wardhaugh. In 1954 he played in the team which won the League Cup, breaking a long trophy drought for the Tynecastle Club, and he won a Scottish League cap in the same season.

In 1955/56 he lost his first team place, and in April 1956 he was transferred to Raith

Rovers the following week when 44 players were named for a World Cup trial match between Scotland and the Scottish League at Easter Road. Despite lying sixth in the First Division, not a single Raith Rovers player was named. It dawned on many supporters, in private thought, that the great team of the 1950's had past its peak.

East of Scotland League side Peebles Rovers were beaten in the first round of the Scottish Cup thanks to a well-taken hat-trick by Jimmy McEwan, but the team surrendered tamely in the second round at Dens Park, and lost 1-0. "Not good enough, not tough enough and did not fight hard enough" said the Kirkcaldy Times.

There was yet another exhibition of the traditional response to unexpected cup defeat, the appoortioning of blame to the management due to their parsimony towards the players. This happened after the St Bernards defeat in 1924, when Montrose came from four goals behind to win a two-legged League Cup tie in 1978, and when a handsome lead at the top of the League was squandered in 1980. In February 1958, the rumour mongers laid the blame on the change to the full time players' terms three months earlier. The Scottish League had introduced "Merit Payments", the top four clubs sharing in a levy on all League gates. Rovers reacted to this by increasing the full timers wages from £15 to £17, but paying bonuses only when the team were in the top four. Two points out of ten in December saw these payments cease.

Results were poor in the wake of the Cup defeat, a 3-1 home win over Queen's Park the only victory in six matches. Safe from relegation and out of the cup, the opportunity was taken to have a look at some of the reserves, and the young left back, John Lockerbie, signed from Peebles Rovers after his performance in the cup tie. At the other end of the age scale, East Fife enquired about Ernie Copeland, but nothing more was heard when Rovers quoted a fee of £600. Jim Baxter made his league debut, and opened the scoring (beating goalkeeper Jock Wallace, son of the pre-war Rovers player of the same name), in a 4-0 win over Airdrie on 12th April, as recorded in the Kirkcaldy Times :

"The scoring of the opening goal made it something of a dream debut for this young reserve player who was deputising at inside left for the injured Williamson. Not because of his goal, mark you, but because it set the seal on a performance that was full of promise and full of intelligence. Although he was less prominent in the second half, which was hardly surprising for an 18 year old in his first senior game, Baxter did enough in the first half, when he controlled and used the ball quickly and efficiently, to suggest that he is a young player with a future. And this in spite of the fact that he normally plays half back."

In mid April, Willie Polland was selected to play at left back for Scotland

Under 23s against Holland at Tynecastle ("out of position" remonstrated the Kirkcaldy Times, as Alec Parker of Falkirk was preferred at right back). Willie would have been Rovers' first player capped at this level, had he not owned up to the fact that he was a few days too old to qualify for the team, despite Bert Herdman advising him "don't let on – no-one will find out !"

Some better results as the weather warmed up halted the slide, and Rovers finished in a commendable seventh position, but few, if any, realised that this would be the last time in 50 years (and counting) that the club would finish in the top half of the top division in Scottish football.

Not only were some of the star players nearing the end of their careers, and therefore past their best, the Manager and Directors seemed to be losing their touch, too. The Kirkcaldy Times of 12th March reported that "Chairman James Gourlay and one of his directors were at the Alloa v Dunfermline game on Saturday, presumably to watch White, the home inside right, but so far there have been no developments." The Boardroom minutes disclosed that the Directors deliberated for several months over a move for Alloa's pale, slight midfield player, suggesting they drop their asking price, or throw in centre forward Denis Gillespie (who was an outstandingly consistent player for Dundee United throughout the 1960s) but it was Falkirk who met Alloa's valuation of £4,000, and then sold him to Tottenham Hotspur for five times that sum, eighteen months later. Imagine a Raith Rovers team with Jim Baxter and John White in midfield ....

There was a late end to the season as Fife and Penman Cup fixtures were fulfilled. On Wednesday 7th May, Dunfermline were beaten 3-2 at Stark's Park in the first leg of the Fife Cup final, but won the return at East End Park on the Saturday, 3-1 after extra time. On that same afternoon, Rovers sent a scratch team to Stirling for the Penman Cup Final, and lost 5-0.

The winds of change were blowing through Stark's Park. There were nine free transfers, the biggest clear-out at Stark's Park since the war, and Ernie Copeland, who had sat out much of the final two months of the season with an injury, announced his retirement. He and his family emigrated to Australia on 6th August. Willie McNaught applied for the East Fife Manager's vacancy, was interviewed, but the job went to Charlie McCaig, the Aberdeen trainer.

New signings were John Ward, an inside forward freed by Aberdeen, and Jackie Williamson's old partner at Stoneyburn Juniors, George Dobbie, who had performed well at centre forward with Third Lanark and Hearts. Jim French was the second recruit from Peebles Rovers ; Tommy White was one of several provisional signings from junior clubs and John's younger brother joined Ian McMillan's sibling, Hamish, at Stark's Park.

Attendances were in decline across Scottish football, and the solution of the authorities was to increase admission to 2/6d

Johnny Urquhart in action for Rovers against Rangers at Stark's Park. On this occasion, Rangers remembered to pack their change strip ; perversely, Rovers also wore theirs.

for the new season. The Kirkcaldy Times reminded everyone "…. Football is still the cheapest form of entertainment but there is no doubt that it will have to be more entertaining than it was last season if these increased prices are not to be cancelled out by a drop in attendances. And attendances will drop unless the standard of play improves and unless some players we could name are prepared to put more into the game."

Ten full timers restarted training on 7th July 1958 : Drummond, Polland, Young, McNaught, Leigh, McEwan, Williamson, Urquhart, Ward and Dobbie. Bernie Kelly had reverted to being a part-timer, and on 18th July, he preferred Leicester City to Nottingham Forest and left Stark's Park for a fee of £7,950 – almost half of the £15,000 that Leeds United offered in November 1957, turned down on a split vote by Rovers directors.

The Kirkcaldy Times paid him this tribute : "There have been better clubmen at Stark's Park than Bernie Kelly, but there have been few better entertainers. As a ball artist, he was supreme, and it is fair that we shall all remember him – and miss him."

Jim Thorburn started the season in goal, with Charlie Drummond on the open-to-transfer list, and Polland was partnered by Lockerbie at left back. Although Young, McNaught and Leigh formed the half back line for the opening day defeat at Third Lanark, Andy Leigh moved over to the right to accommodate Baxter, and Andy Young simply

played wherever he was needed in the team. The forward line in the early games was McEwan, Ward, Dobbie, Williamson and Urquhart, although Kerray soon replaced the disappointing Ward, and Jackie Williamson made way for a succession of makeshift inside lefts.

Four days after the League Cup defeat at Cathkin, Rangers were beaten 3-1 at Stark's Park in a thrilling match, but most talk afterwards was of the very public omission of Andy Young. He was selected to play in attack, but spoke to the Manager before the game. Herdman reported "He wasn't happy about playing his second game in five days in a position he had not occupied for three years, a position that was going to make even greater demands on his now limited pace and stamina." It was decided not to play him. It wasn't the happiest of Andy's seasons at Stark's Park. He was not an admirer of Willie McFarlane, the left back signed from Hibs, and when he questioned his selection with Herdman, he was told that McFarlane was the Chairman's choice.

There was further public discord early in the season when management and players finally reached a compromise on the payment of expenses, the club seeking to make economies in an area of significant expenditure. The biggest loser, Dundee-based Jimmy McEwan, made it known that he wanted a transfer. Hopes that a fitting replacement for Copeland had been found were raised when Dobbie scored a hat-trick

Rovers, where he enjoyed an Indian Summer to his playing career. He was a key component of what is arguably the club's greatest ever team in 1956/57, and he retained his first team place until midway through 1961/62. He became a coach, firstly with the reserves, and in that capacity he re-registered as a player in 1963/64. When he reluctantly hung up his boots, he was appointed to the Board of Directors, where he served, latterly as Chairman, until 1994, when he accepted the position of Club Chairman. His early years as a director were characterised by unpublicised, selfless work in scouting and assessing players, and nurturing the young reserves.

As chairman, he presided over some difficult years, and his legacy in that respect would have been very different but for the failed promotion bid in 1980. Very few men could match his service in Raith Rovers' 125 year history, and his surpasses all others in its longevity ; truly one of the club's 'Greats'.

A measure of the ability of Andy Young is that there was a significant portion of the Raith Rovers support who thought he was better than even McNaught.

There have been few more effective players in the club's history than the former miner from Oakley. He was comfortable in any position, such was his all-round ability, and outstanding in midfield or attack. He had no weakness and only the lack of genuine pace prevented him from dominating the international scene, as he did the domestic. To everyone's astonishment, he did not receive a representative honour ; one can only speculate how many caps he would receive in the present day, and he probably suffered from the belief amongst selectors than one Raith Rovers player in the team was sufficient.

A powerful header of the ball, with a blistering shot as a variation of a deft touch, he was a consistent goalscorer through his long and loyal service to the club as a player. Sadly, his post-playing abilities as a spotter and coach of young talent was not enjoyed at Stark's Park, where his outstanding performances as a player, over so many years, will never be forgotten.

against his former club, Third Lanark, but that was followed by a 6-0 drubbing at Ibrox, Rovers falling three behind after 15 minutes. Two wins out of four meant that, for the tenth successive season, there would be no place in the League Cup quarter finals.

The second League game of the season was at Dunfermline on 6th September, and after 15 minutes of play, with Rovers leading by a Jimmy McEwan penalty, horrendous thunder and lightening compelled referee Tom Wharton to take the players off the field for fifteen minutes. When the "frightening spectacle" subsided, the match was resumed, and Dunfermline equalised, but two minutes later the referee gave up the unequal struggle against the flooded pitch, and the match was abandoned.

Early League results were quite encouraging. Dundee were beaten 4-1 in an ill-tempered match at Stark's Park, Hibs were overcome 5-2 with Dobbie outstanding, despite not getting on the scoresheet, Rovers came from behind twice to draw 4-4 at Ibrox and following a 1-0 defeat of Kilmarnock, it was announced that Jim Baxter would be one of eleven young players (including Jimmy Gabriel and Davie Sneddon of Dundee, Willie Hunter and Ian St John of Motherwell, and Bertie Auld of Celtic) who would train with the Scotland squad before their match against Northern Ireland.

Many critics believed that the club badly needed an experienced inside forward, and Alfie Conn was signed from Hearts, but after three games in which he filled his playing kit to full capacity, he was injured and did not return to the team until the end of January.

A 5-0 mauling at Tynecastle was followed by two wins and two draws and, as winter arrived, the goals dried up dramatically, with just one draw from nine successive League fixtures. The team plummeted to fourth bottom of the division, but there was a defiant note in a Kirkcaldy Times article on 14th January 1959, headed "A Never Ending Struggle – but Raith will not be relegated ! Raith Rovers are obviously prepared to buy themselves out of trouble, and while this course may be regrettable because it emphasises the shortage of good, young players at Stark's Park, it does show that the management are determined to preserve the hard-won First Division status they have held for the past ten years. Apart from Dundee, Raith Rovers are the only club in Scotland who have won promotion since the war and

who have not since been relegated."

There was a spot of bother off the field too. The Minutes of the Board Meeting of 6th January 1959 recorded : "The Clerkess had forwarded a letter from her doctor stating she would be under medical treatment for the next three months. She would be leaving the office on Friday 9th January 1959. The meeting discussed the doctor's letter, and agreed to pay the clerkess for 3 months at the rate of 30/- per week. It was also agreed to engage a part time clerkess for three months." Such detail was not normally recorded in the minutes, but this was no ordinary period of incapacity. The clerkess was with child, and the father was one of the (married) players.

On top of the £1740 paid for McFarlane, and the £2250 for Conn, Ian Gardner was signed from Motherwell for £3000 in early January, but failed to score in his seven, injury-interrupted, League appearances that season. A fortnight, and two 4-2 defeats, after the rallying call, the Kirkcaldy Times adopted a new tone in reporting the "ominous display" at home to Third Lanark. "Real relegation football, played by a team bereft of ideas and fighting spirit and without faith in themselves and each other. Even the normally courageous McEwan threw in the sponge before the finish – and that is something I don't think we have ever seen at Stark's Park before."

Rovers were now third bottom, one point above Clyde, but there was a glimmer of hope in a fighting draw at home to Hibs in the first round of the Scottish Cup. The veteran half back line of Young, McNaught and Leigh was reformed, with Jim Baxter spared further punishment from his hapless team-mates. A fighting performance in the replay was not rewarded, and Hibs hung on to win 2-1.

In between the cup ties came a 3-1 League win at Partick Thistle, the club's first away points for more than a year, the result met with equal quantities of delight and relief. The new found confidence saw Rovers dominate the first half of a midweek home League match against Rangers, two goals by Jimmy McEwan giving them a 2-0 half time lead. Andy Matthew scored twice in the second half for Rangers, but Rovers pressed hard for the winner and had to settle for a 2-2 draw.

Luck deserted them at Tynecastle on 21st February. Not only were they unfortunate in losing 2-1, to a disputed penalty, with Alfie Conn scoring on his old stamping ground, but George Dobbie broke his leg after 70 minutes. It ended his playing career. Rovers fell into the relegation zone.

A well merited 3-0 home win over Airdrie eased a deal of tension, which returned after a 3-1 midweek defeat at Paisley. The mood of Rovers fans was not helped by the news of Jackie Williamson's transfer to relegation rivals Dunfermline Athletic for £1500. Clearly out of favour with the Rovers management, he had made it known for almost two seasons that he favoured a transfer, and he had been fielded everywhere but his preferred inside left position since the League Cup ties. Jock Stein had no such doubts, and built his rejuvenated Dunfermline team around the crafty inside forward.

Young, McNaught and Leigh rolled back the years to inspire a 3-0 win over third top Motherwell, lifting Rovers to fifth bottom, but still just two points above second bottom Clyde. One of the goalscorers was Jimmy McEwan, who received long-overdue representative recognition when he was selected for the Scottish League team to play Scotland in an International trial at Ibrox. Blackpool, seeking a replacement for Stanley Matthews, enquired about the Rovers winger.

On the morning of yet another midweek defeat, this time 1-0 at home to Aberdeen, the Kirkcaldy Times ruminated : "If Raith Rovers do escape relegation – and I am sure they will – they will obviously require to put their house in order for next season. The veteran players who will have saved them on this occasion can hardly be expected to do so again, which means that the management will have to do some worthwhile recruiting during the close season.

"To make this possible, something of a clearance will have to be made at the end of next month because it is becoming increasingly apparent that there are too many players at Stark's Park who have little or no hope of making the grade in the first team, while the natural ability of some of these young players has, for one reason or another, remainded undeveloped."

A tactical switch at half time at Dumfries earned a point from the team marooned at the bottom of the League, and Willie McNaught inspired a vital 1-0 home win over Clyde. "His intelligent reading of the game, his brilliant anticipation, and his amazing speed in recovery made him almost unbeatable – and reduced the Shawfield attack to almost complete impotency. I do not praise McNaught too highly. I merely give him the credit he deserved because, make no mistake, Raith would never have won this vital match without him." Johnny Urquhart scored the only goal of a frenetic game – McNaught excepted – after 72 minutes.

They still had work to do to secure their First Division status, and rose to the occasion in a well-merited victory over Celtic on the April holiday Monday. It was a successful climax to a long and bitter struggle, with subsequent results elsewhere rendering the final match of the season meaningless, as far as Rovers were concerned.

The game was at Falkirk, who had to win to stay up, provided that Dunfermline did not score a barrow-load of goals at home to Partick Thistle. Rovers had some interest in the outcome ; East Fife's relegation the previous season meant that a similar outcome for the Pars would leave Rovers without a lucrative local derby, and from the players' perspective, popular former team-mates Harry Colville, Ian Bain and Jackie Williamson were in the Dunfermline team. It was 1-1 at half-time at Brockville, but the half-time score from East End Park, 7-0 to Dunfermline, was met

with incredulity and despondency. Dunfermline, improbably, won 10-2, Rovers and Falkirk drew 2-2 and the Brockville club was relegated, two points behind Rovers.

Bert Herdman, with the benefit of hindsight, attributed the trials and tribulations of the second half of the season to "Ernest Copeland, one of our most successful players, had the misfortune to meet with an injury when playing against Celtic at Stark's Park in January. It was eleven weeks before Ernie was really fit. By that time general form had faded and our challenge was much weaker."

Rovers' last two matches of the season spoke volumes of the climax to the League campaign : a 1-1 draw at Dunfermline in the Penman Cup semi final, followed by an 8-2 Rovers win in the replay. The early summer news concentrated on benefit payments once again. Charlie Drummond was the only one of 21 retained players still to re-sign, unhappy with the level of his payment, parsimoniously calculated on the basis of his last season as a part-timer. McNaught, on the other hand, received his third benefit payment, and Leigh his second, "which proves that in this respect, Raith do not lag behind, perhaps even surpass, many of the bigger and wealthier clubs."

These hefty payments, and the cost of emergency transfers during the previous season, rendered the Stark's Park treasury bare, and the summer signings in 1959 were from youth and junior teams. Willie Hunter, who had spent two years with Hibs and one with Musselburgh Juniors, returned as masseur and physiotherapist, and would be in charge of training with coach Jackie Stewart.

A huge blow to football fans in the town was the announcement, on August 8th 1959, that the Kirkcaldy Times would no longer be published. A national printers strike had closed down all local papers from the end of June to early August, and the last and 4250th edition of the 2d midweek sports-and-entertainment newspaper, first published in September 1876, was on 17th June 1959 The surviving stablemate, the Fife Free Press, ventured the understatement : "No doubt many sportsmen in this area will regret the passing of the Times."

There was a mixture of new and old in the team which lined up for the League Cup qualifying section. Charlie Drummond was back in goal, Polland and McFarlane at full back, and Young, McNaught and Leigh at half

Ask any Raith Rovers player of the two decades from 1942, who was the best player they played alongside, and the answer is unanimous and instant : Willie McNaught. It was a national scandal that he played so infrequently for Scotland, but comparatively few fixtures, and the default selection of an Old Firm player, conspired against the former Dumfries builder.

He was simply a natural footballer, with god-given pitch awareness and an unerring eye for the passage of play. Moreover, he had a sublime left foot which could instantly control, and pass, a football. His left foot punched the ball, rather than struck through it, which meant that it arrived at its destination with pace and precision.

He had speed when he needed it, but the first five yards of a race were in McNaught's head, and his anticipation defused many opposition attacks before they required heroic tackles.

He may have regretted his decision to stay in Kirkcaldy throughout a playing career of prodigious length, but he was well rewarded in comparative terms with four lucrative (and tax free) loyalty benefits, and the distinction of being the club's greatest ever player.

All three players were halfway through their playing careers when the legendary half back line of Young, McNaught and Leigh was formed when Harry Colville left the club. Andy Leigh was regarded as the work-horse of the triumvirate, but he also possessed considerable footballing skills. He may not have been the most accurate passer of a football, nor, thanks to his largely defensive duties, a prolific goalscorer, but he was one of the better midfield players in the top division of Scottish football for all but a handful of his many seasons as a player.
There have been few better servants to the club on the field, and fewer still off it. After a brief spell coaching at Stark's Park, he became the organiser of the club's lucrative lottery. When a change of personal circumstances necessitated a job change, he and the club reacted to their mutual benefit and he became groundsman ; one of several roles he performed conscientiously at the club over nearly 50 years. Popular and personable, Andy kept in touch with former playing colleagues, the Kirkcaldy club's history and heritage sustained by the man from Rothesay.

back. Jim Kerray was moved to outside right, to replace Jimmy McEwan, who had been sold to Aston Villa for £6,640 after a decade of superb service at Stark's Park. The inside forwards were the veteran Conn, Tom White, called up from Bonnyrigg Rose, and another teenager, John McKinven from Bathgate Thistle. Johnny Urquhart remained at outside left.

The team were a revelation in the League Cup ties, winning five and losing only at Celtic Park (to a Willie McFarlane own goal). This splendid form continued into the opening League matches, a 2-1 win at Airdrie followed by 3-2 at home to Dunfermline and a 2-0 win at Dundee. The previous season's Penman Cup final was won 5-2 at home to East Stirling. This start was beyond supporters' wildest dreams – Rovers were joint top of the League with Rangers - and the unexpected 2-2 draw at home to newly promoted Arbroath in the first leg of the quarter finals was surely recoverable.

Despite Rovers being outplayed by a more determined, quick and robust Arbroath team in the second leg, they went ahead in 65 minutes through new signing Denis Mochan, a utility player signed for £2500 from East Fife with the intention of playing him at centre forward. The Red Lichties equalised after 74 minutes and took the game into extra time, after five minutes of which Brown scored his second goal. Rovers were desperately out of luck in their endeavours to equalise. They had a penalty claim turned down and hit the woodwork in the last minute, but could not force a third match.

The midweek exertions told on the old legs ; the confidence that the early season victories had engendered in the young players vanished ; and the wheels fell off Rovers' bandwagon, with five successive League defeats, in which only three goals were scored. Jim Baxter had been restored to the team in place of Andy Leigh, who eventually had surgery to remove a cyst from a cartilage, and who confided that he did not expect to oust the richly talented Baxter from the team in future. Denis Mochan was switched to left back, McFarlane failing to recover from the torrid night at Arbroath.

After a 4-0 defeat at Ayr the Fife Free Press insisted "something drastic will have to be done at Stark's Park if it is not to assume even more serious proportions." A week later, after a 2-1 home defeat by Partick Thistle, it was "new blood needed in attack",

which was heeded with the signatures of 26 year old Ian Spence from Stirling Albion, and 19 year old Willie Wallace from Stenhousemuir.

The new signings did the trick, and Rovers went racing back up the League with five successive wins, followed by a 1-1 home draw against Motherwell. Included in the sequence of victories was a 5-0 revenge over Arbroath, a 5-1 thumping of Aberdeen, 4-2 outplaying of Hibs, all at Stark's Park, and a thoroughly deserved 3-2 victory at Ibrox. Rangers went two goals ahead after 13 minutes through Scotland wingers Davie Wilson and Alex Scott, but Rovers hit back and equalised within five minutes with goals from Jim Kerray and the outstanding Jim Baxter, who beat three men and shot home from 20 yards. Kerray scored a deserved winner nine minutes into the second half. The half back line of Young, McNaught and Baxter was streets ahead of their counterparts, the increasingly impressive Mochan subdued Scott, and Kerray led the line to good effect. The first victory at Ibrox since Alex James scored the only goal of the game in 1924 put Rovers third in the League.

The only sobering note was Jim Baxter's request for a transfer, encouraged by reported interest from Blackpool, Birmingham, Everton and Aston Villa, although he later changed his mind, stating that he didn't want to go to England. "The fact is that Raith can't afford to let a player of Baxter's calibre and potentiality go for less than his true market price – a price that only English clubs are able and willing to pay." The comparison made was the £30,000 Spurs had given Hearts for Dave Mackay, although it was being asked "Will Baxter's transfer pay for the floodlights ?" which were budgeted to cost £14,000.

A £12,000 bid for Baxter was flatly refused by the Board, chairman Gourlay warning "I hope the public of Kirkcaldy will support us in this action," in other words turn up to matches to avoid a forced sale.

In a re-run of the oscillating form of early season, the next three League games were lost, but Dunfermline were beaten 2-0 in the New Year's Day derby, followed by a defeat at Celtic Park, Denis Mochan's brother Neil scoring the only goal of the game. Rovers fell behind to a Gerry Baker goal at home to St Mirren on 16th January 1960, but a hat-trick from Willie Wallace, two from Kerray and one by Conn, all in the second half, earned Rovers a 6-1 win.

Rovers failed to reach such heights over the remainder of the season. The 2-0 defeat at Hampden in the first round of the Scottish Cup was as unexpected as it was unwelcomed, and the loss of revenue of a cup run, and falling gates amid indifferent League form, was keenly felt at a time of huge capital expenditure for the club as floodlight towers changed the Kirkcaldy skyline.

An injury to Willie McNaught gave Willie Polland a short run at centre half, and then at right half as he filled in for Andy Young, while young Jim Stevenson was promoted from the reserves at right back.

Amid continuous speculation about Baxter's transfer, it was Jim Kerray who left, signed by Jock Stein for Dunfermline for a meagre £2000. Alfie Conn was replaced by Jim French, and three more youngsters were tried towards the end of the season, centre half McGregor and centre forwards Lawson and McDonald.

The Scottish Cup defeat cast a pall over the second half of the season, but after the near-thing of the previous year, Peter Napier, writing in the following season's Supporters Club Handbook, noted that "the management, with no fears of relegation, decided to give some of the younger players the chance to stake a place in the team. This meant that several of the players who had given the Club invaluable service had to give way to youth, although it proved costly in collecting League points, the team maintained a comfortable position in the middle of the League Table where they finished eleventh." In an 18 club League, that had to be considered satisfactory, and the introduction of several youngsters meant that the future, as well as the new floodlights, promised to be bright at Stark's Park. Inevitably, Jim Baxter did not appear in a Rovers jersey in 1960/61. His reluctance to play in England – and scandalous lack of international recognition while at Stark's Park, although he did win the club's one and only Under 23 honour – dissuaded any mega-money bids from south of the border, and Rovers' directors did their best in wrestling £16,000 from Rangers on 23rd June 1960. In view of Baxter's stellar talents, and his huge influence over the all-conquering Rangers team in his first five years at Ibrox, the fee was of course derisory, but it was the largest ever paid between two Scottish clubs until Rangers spent £26,500 on George McLean from St Mirren in January 1963.

To no-one's surprise, but resigned disgust in Kirkcaldy, Baxter was finally capped by Scotland on 9th November 1960, after just 19 games (and a League Cup winners medal) for Rangers.

Normality was resumed at the start of 1960/61 with failure to qualify from the League Cup section, the opening two results setting the tone for the first half of the season – a 5-0 defeat at Dens Park, followed by a 4-1 home win over Aberdeen. Jim Thorburn was now the first choice goalkeeper, and Stevenson and Mochan started the season at full back. Willie Polland opened at right half, stepping into the considerable boots of Andy Young, the first of the legendary half back line to retire from playing. Willie McNaught missed the first two months of the season through injury, Polland moving across to deputise, and Andy Leigh came back into the side following Jim Baxter's all-too-brief tenure of the No.6 jersey. Willie Wallace and the durable Johnny Urquhart started the season on the wings, with Ian Spence, Jim French, Arbroath's prolific centre forward Jim Easson and one Bernard Kelly disputing the inside forward positions.

Kelly's return was anticipated like the second coming, and his second debut for the club was greeted with messianic hysteria following a goal two minutes into the home match with Ayr United. Like Kelly' second stint at the club, further glory was not forthcoming – the match was drawn 1-1.

Three of the first four league matches were won, but for the next two months victories were confined to the three friendly matches arranged to make early use of the new floodlights. Israeli team Petach Tikva were beaten 4-1, the partially installed floodlights being used during the second half. Jimmy' McEwan's Aston Villa officially inaugurated the lights and were beaten 2-1, McEwan scoring in 85 minutes to everyone's delight, and Leeds United with a very young Billy Bremner, Norman Hunter, Jack Charlton and player manager Don Revie in the side, were beaten 4-1.

League results were patchy ; a 2-2 home draw with Celtic, followed by 1-0 at home to Clyde, before three successive defeats, followed by two draws and three victories, before five straight League defeats.

Following the visit of Jimmy McEwan's Aston Villa to officially open the Stark's Park floodlights in September 1960, Leeds United paid a visit a fortnight later. As with the Villa fixture, both teams lined up together for a photograph. Leeds had just suffered relegation from the First Division, and were to escape a further relegation by just five points, narrowing that safety margin to just three the following season. The potential for their recovery, and subsequent run of significant successes under Don Revie (pictured above as player-manager, next to Bert Herdman to the left of the middle row) was already apparent in the photograph, which includes Jack Charlton, Norman Hunter and Billy Bremner.

Revie, who later managed England, had strong connections with Rovers and Fife. He was signed for Leicester City by former Rovers player Johnny Duncan and married his manager's neice, the daughter of another former Rovers player, Tommy Duncan.

Andy Young lived along the road from the Duncan family in Lochgelly, and recalled Don, as a young footballer in the early 1950s, spending the summer months in the town working at his joinery trade on the house and shop the Duncan's owned in the Fife town.

The Revie's retired to Kinross.

JIM THORBURN

A room was rented at Central Chambers in late May 1959, and served as headquarters to the club's fundraising activities for several decades.

Enquiries were made during the close season of 1959 to sign John Buchanan and Gordon Smith from Hibs, and Jimmy Wardhaugh from Hearts.

Dundee United were quoted £1500 for Tom White in mid November 1959

Rangers started their pursuit of Jim Baxter in early December, offering £12,000, and in mid March Rovers were willing to accept £15,000 plus Andy Matthew and John Queen.

By 5th April 1960, John Lockerbie had not been seen at the club for three weeks and was suspended.

In 1960 there were close season enquiries about Matthew and Queen of Rangers, and an offer of £2,000 was made to Third Lanark for Joe McInnes. £2000 was offered to Leeds United for George Meek, formerly of Hamilton Accies. An attempt was made to buy Max Murray from Rangers in early December, and at the end of January interest was shown in re-signing Jim Kerray, then at Huddersfield Town, among other players.

There were teething problems with the new floodlights. The reserve team match on 10th December was abandoned after 78 minutes when the floodlights went out during a power cut, and the following week at the first team match against Airdrie the lights failed again and the interval lasted 25 minutes.

As the season wore on, the fans, and consequently the directors, became increasingly anxious over the team's ability to avoid relegation. In late November, it was announced that coach Andy Young would share responsibility for the first team with Bert Herdman, the decision taken following a Special Directors meeting on 15th November. This is what was minuted :

The Chairman requested the Manager to leave the Board Room as they wished to talk in private.

The Manager was recalled and the Chairman explained the business of the meeting

(1)   The Board of Management wishes more discipline with the players, including training hours and attendances.

(2)   The Manager's office hours were from 9.30am to 12.30pm, 2pm to 4pm.

(3)   The club's finances at the present time being at a low level, the Manager's increase of £3 weekly granted on August 9th be discontinued as from this date

(4)   The Manager and coach Andrew Young to choose both teams and place them before the Directors at each Tuesday meeting

(5)   The question of club scouts was discussed and it was agreed to meet them on a Sunday to be arranged.

The Manager agreed with the deliberations of the meeting, but referred to the office hours and said that the work in the office could not be done in those short hours.

The Manager left the Boardroom to allow Andrew Young to be interviewed in private. Afterwards both were in discussion with the full board. All points were discussed, and it was left with the Manager and Coach to choose the team selections for Saturday 19th November 1960.

Bert Herdman had more explaining to do to the Directors a week later, following an article by "Waverley" of the Daily Record on 23rd November 1960. The highly respected, and well connected, journalist made reference to the change of selection responsibilities from the board to Manager and Coach, and to Herdman's 16 years in charge being the longest spell of any manager in England or Scotland. He quoted Herdman as saying :

"During the past few seasons, I have thought it would not be a bad thing for us if we did land in the Second Division, believing at times it would be a good thing for our bank account. I speak strictly from the business point of view. At the end of season 1925/26 we were first relegated, and in the two

following years which we spent in the Second Division things were never so good for us. "With great enthusiasm the crowds rolled up in that lower circle and to shout the team onto victory. They wanted a return to the days when Rangers, Celtic, Hearts and other top-notchers were scheduled to play at Stark's Park.

"Our present sojourn in the First Division commenced in 1950 and during the intervening years there has been a steady decline in attendance figures. We have been unable to maintain a really profitable figure at our home games.

"Only when the 'big' teams came to Kirkcaldy have the turnstiles clicked in the desired fashion. For the majority of other fixtures there has been little enthusiasm. There has descended among the fans a complacency as we have gradually become recognised as a middle-of-the-table team, many of our supporters having decided that the only games worth seeing are those in which we are opposed to star elevens.

"Maybe a descent to the lower circle would shock the fans out of that complacency, leading to a return to tighter packed terracing. A year or two downstairs, it is conceivable, would do the football business in Kirkcaldy a tremendous lot of good. Even in our best-doing days in the First Division it has been a financial struggle, and I don't mind admitting that last season it was very serious. That is why we were forced to transfer Jimmy Baxter to Rangers."

The manager's protestations of being misquoted were a lot less reliable than his well-tuned football barometer which predicted the club's prospects. All momentum had been lost, and the old guard who had served the club so grandly in the past, were feeling weary.

The new team management partnership had to endure some bad luck. Dennis Mochan and Jim French were omitted from the team at Ayr, because they had not reported to the Kenilworth Hotel in Glasgow, as instructed, by 11am on the morning of the game. The match at Paisley on 7th January was postponed due to fog and frost, and re-arranged two days later. Jim Thorburn was carried off after half an hour, and the ambulance that was taking him to hospital was involved in a road smash. The following Saturday, Denis Mochan broke his leg after 13 minutes of the home match with Hibs.

A tricky Scottish Cup second round tie at Buckie Thistle was negotiated thanks to two Willie Wallace goals, but Celtic were too strong in the third round, and Rovers lost 4-1 at home. By then there had been huge changes in the team. Wilson and then McDonald came in at right back and Bobby Stein was introduced at wing half. In attack, Willie Wallace was moved to centre forward, with Cooper from Ardeer Thistle replacing him on the wing. Grant Malcolm and the veteran Andy Matthew, signed at last from Rangers, came in at inside forward.

The team's problems were felt to be in attack ; John Buchanan and Desmond Fox were bought from Hibs for a hefty combined fee of £5500 and Willie Benvie was signed from Dunfermline Athletic for £750. A Fox penalty gained both points on their debuts at Pittodrie. Results picked up a little after that boost to confidence, and relegation was averted with the luxury of two defeats in the last couple of League matches, and the transfer, in late April, of two of the better players in the team. Hearts were long-time suitors of Willie Polland, who in the previous year had added versatility in all defensive positions to his impressive talents as a football-playing right back. They would not meet the valuation of £15,000, with a further £10,000 to follow, but Rovers were desperate for the transfer fee, and clinched the deal by including top scorer Willie Wallace. "You're the spare pair of breeks, Willie" explained Bert Herdman to Wallace as both players were summoned off the golf course to unexpectedly sign for Hearts at Stark's Park. Rovers gratefully banked Hearts' cheque for £15,500.

A little bit of glamour in an otherwise forgettable season was introduced at the second leg of the final of the Fife Cup at East End Park, which, in the popular diversion of the time, was "kicked off" by television star Jeannie Carson.

It had been a wretched season for injuries, and too many youngsters were blooded, then rested, for anything resembling continuity of selection. The four point safety margin between third bottom Rovers and relegation should be seen in the context of Rovers winning seven of the eight points from fixtures against the two relegated teams, Clyde and Ayr United

The loss of Wallace and Polland did not enthuse Rovers fans as 1961/62 loomed. The Sports Editor of the Fife Free Press, writing in the following season's Supporters Club handbook, considered the transfer of two of the team's best players to be "a sad ending to a sad season – and an even sadder outlook for the future, a future which, at the moment of writing, seems fraught with anxiety and undertainty."

Few of the close season recruits allayed these fears. Wing half Mike Clinton from Clyde, centre forward or winger Bobby Adamson from Dundee and inside forward Jim Sharkey from Airdrie were the more experienced signings, amid a plethora of juniors and juveniles. The Directors could not be faulted for their efforts to strengthen the team. In May 1961 attempts were made to sign Andy Bowman of Hearts, Max Murray of Rangers, Neil Martin of Alloa and Eddie McCreadie of East Stirling, the last two going on to notable careers in the English First Division, and Scotland caps. There was certainly room for them ; after the paid and free transfers at the end of the season, Rovers employed just five full time players.

More significantly, Dennis Mochan and Tom White, freed from the shackles of National Service, returned to the first team, but Willie McNaught played his last competitive game for the club on 23rd August 1961, a League Cup tie at home to St

Johnstone, drawn 1-1 courtesy of a last minute Tom White equaliser. Willie missed the remainder of the season with an ankle injury, his place at centre half taken by Jock Forsyth, signed from Junior football. Sharkey broke his ankle in a reserve match at Love Street on 30th September, and did not play again for the first team.

When matters are not going smoothly on the field, one of the first accusations is a lack of fitness. At the Board meeting of 21st August 1961 : "Our trainer, W. Hunter was asked to review his training methods and after a very full discussion, the meeting was pleased on the points explained by the trainer. He was given full power to purchase any training gear he thought would be in the interest of players and club.

"The meeting discussed coaching methods for the young players who attended for training at Stark's Park, and with the trainer suggesting three nights for the young players instead of two nights, it was agreed to approach player John Urquhart with the view of assisting the trainer."

The first few months of the season saw a bewildering traffic in players, coming in and going out, but this hardly provided a smokescreen for the League table, with just one win in the opening ten League matches. On 16th October, the Directors advised Bert Herdman that they would be advertising for his replacement, ironically following a 7-0 victory over Cowdenbeath in the Fife Cup. There were 20 applicants for the post, and most Rovers fans accepted that the veteran Manager had run his course, and that a fresh, younger, face was needed in the manager's office. It was to general surprise, therefore, that his successor was announced as 65 year old Hugh Shaw, sacked a week earlier by Hibs, who was nine years older than his predecessor.

He had not officially taken over when Rovers made the trip to Dens Park on 18th November. Andy Leigh opened the scoring in 22 minutes, and it took a further 28 before high-flying Dundee equalised through Alan Gilzean. After that, both teams went goal crazy. Gilzean scored again in 52 minutes, Mike Clinton equalised six minutes later, then first season senior Ian Lourie restored Rovers lead in 60 minutes. Three minutes later, Bobby Adamson extended this lead, but six minutes after that Bobby Wishart got a goal back for Dundee. The game swung from one end to another until Bobby Seith equalised for Dundee in 86 minutes and, with two minutes to go, veteran winger Gordon Smith scored their winner – 5-4 for Dundee. The 15,000 spectators would never forget this thrilling, pulsating match.

A narrow 1-0 home defeat by Hearts

JIM KERRAY

DENIS MOCHAN

ALEX GRAY

WILLIAM WILSON

1960 - The Rialto cinema in the High Street was renamed The Gaumont, and the Carlton in Gallatown became a bingo hall.

On 5th April 1961 it was decided to decline the invitation to join the Dewar Shield Association.

Willie McFarlane was successful in his appeal to the Scottish League for a free transfer on 22nd September 1960

1961 - Torbain Primary School was opened ; work began on the Dunnikier housing estate. The town's population peaked at 53,700
1962 - The Gaumont was renamed the Odeon

1963 - Michael Nairn & Co. merged with Williamsons of Lancaster ; another High Street cinema changed its name, the Regal became ABC.
On 6th October 1963, The Beatles performed two shows at the Carlton ; Dysart Golf Club was closed, and Dunnikier Golf Club was opened

FRANK BURROWS

in Hugh Shaw's first match as manager was followed by a couple of wins in the League, on either side of a replay victory over Queen's Park in the Scottish Cup. With falling gates and a lack of Cup runs in recent seasons, there was no money available to lavish on transfer fees. Peter Price, previously a prolific centre forward for Ayr United, was signed on a free transfer, but his ten League appearances brought only one goal. By the time St Mirren arrived at Stark's Park in the third round of the Scottish Cup (Second Division Alloa having been beaten in the previous ground, with some difficulty), Rovers were fourth bottom of the League, but just one point above the relegation positions. There was no respite in the cup, the replay at Love Street lost 4-0.

Rovers' persistence was finally rewarded when Jim McFadzean agreed to sign from St Mirren, and former Falkirk, Third Lanark and Liverpool inside right Davie Kerr was signed from Inverness Thistle. Goals became more plentiful, but at both ends of the field. Bobby Gilfillan was signed from St Johnstone for £1,000, having failed to replicate his impressive goal scoring record at Cowdenbeath. Following one point from three games, the last five matches of the season were regarded with some trepidation. It was by then a settled team, however, and only a single point was dropped in those final five matches, although only one goal was scored in each of three of these games. Safety was clutched from the jaws of relegation with a run of results (if not performances) that was of championship proportions.

A blunder by Celtic's internationalist full back Jim Kennedy, in the penultimate match at Parkhead let Adamson in to score the only goal of the match in 76 minutes. This unexpected victory allowed Rovers to go into the last match of the season in pole position in one of the tightest relegation battles for some years. St Johnstone and Raith were on 25 points, Falkirk on 24, Airdrie and St Mirren on 23, and Stirling Albion had been relegated on 18 points.

Relaxed for the first time in many months, the team won a confident 3-1 victory over Aberdeen at Stark's Park on a memorable last Saturday of the season. Rovers finished as high as 13th, while Airdrie and St Mirren both won. Relegated were St Johnstone, who at 3 o'clock were level on points with Rovers. Both they and their visitors, Dundee, required just a point to achieve their respective ambitions, but Saints made the mistake of playing aggressively, and Dundee responded by winning the match, thus clinching the championship with points to spare, and relegating their hosts.

The Sports' Editor of "The Fife Free Press", writing in the following season's Supporters Club handbook, noted that "Raith's last minute spurt seemed to hinge on the signing of inside forwards Kerr, Gilfillan and McFadzean who, despite certain shortcomings, gave the attack a look of composure and confidence which had been

decidedly absent earlier in the season. I would go as far as to say that Raith would not have been faced with the constant fear of relegation had they begun the programme with the line-up which registered wins over Celtic, Hearts and Aberdeen during the closing stages.

"One other feature which must be recorded was the return to prominence of two of the "old brigade" – wing-half Andy Leigh and outside left Johnny Urquhart. At the start of the season it was expected they would spend the year helping to bring on the youngsters of the reserve string, but, as it turned out, they were regarded as automatic first team choices during the team's most difficult period."

Those excluded from the team in the remarkable end of season run were, in the main, freed, including Willie McNaught, who had a brief spell with Brechin City at the start of the following season, before injury retired him. His last appearance at Stark's Park was in a joint testimonial match with Johnny Urquhart, who was appointed youth coach during the summer. Some thought that the failure to mark McNaught's remarkable career with Rovers in a singular fashion, was mean spirited on the part of the club.

A feature of all commentaries on the club's fortunes over 1960/61 and 1961/62 was the sharp fall in attendances, at Stark's Park and indeed across the rest of Scottish football. It marked the end of the post-war boom in attendances ; thereafter, football clubs had to balance their books from non-turnstile income – player transfers or lotteries. The former usually precipitated a downward spiral as weakened teams attracted even fewer spectators.

During the summer, Dennis Mochan, desperate to leave a struggling side, was sold to Nottingham Forest for £11,500, Willie Wilson stepping up from the reserves to replace him. Felix McGrogan, from Pollok Juniors, took Urquhart's No. 11 jersey, and although the team was undoubtedly weakened by these two changes, on the same wing, there was the hope and belief that the end of season form would carry the team confidently into the 1962/63 season.

The League Cup section suggested that this optimism was not necessarily misplaced. Only two defeats was far better than usual return from the six matches, although there were three draws which meant that qualification was averted, as usual. Thereon in, it was arguably the worst season in the club's entire history.

The first League win did not arrive until 2nd January 1963, 2-1 at Love Street. Until then, there were only two draws, at home to Third Lanark and Clyde. Included in the unrelenting sequence of defeats were 6-0 at Dunfermline, 8-1 at Airdrie, 10-0 at Aberdeen, 8-1 at Dundee United and 5-1 at Dumfries (on the same afternoon that the reserves were beating Queens 8-1 at Stark's Park, Gilfillan scoring five). Tom White was sold to St Mirren for £1,000 in early October, although Rovers would have preferred Willie

Fernie in exchange. In his place came Joe Caven, signed from Brighton & Hove Albion for £1650 – unseen and unfit.

Compounding this misery for Rovers fans was one of the longest and most severe winters in British history. Rovers' 2-1 defeat at Third Lanark on 29th December was the only match played in Scotland in the wake of one of the worst snow storms ever seen in the country. Two Rovers' matches were postponed in January, and no game was played during the five weeks between 26th January and 2nd March, when Rovers lost 7-2 at home to Dundee United on a pitch described as resembling "underdone scrambled egg on overdone toast." There was a 3-2 win at Brockville, home draws against Rangers (improbably) and Queen of the South, and an away point at Dundee. In late March, the club's three scouts, Jimmy McDermid in Fife, Johnny Docherty in Edinburgh and Tommy Gallagher in Glasgow were suspended for three months to save some money.

Fourteen seasons of continuous membership of the top division ended on 18th May 1963, with an entirely characteristic 4-0 home defeat by Hibs. Only two League matches were won all season, both away from home, and five matches were drawn. The total of nine points gained was a record low in the modern game, only subsequently surpassed when Third Lanark, in their death throws, accumulated just seven points in 1964/65. 35 goals scored was the lowest in the Division ; 118 conceded the highest by a margin of 35. Rovers were 14 points short of safety, 12 behind the other relegated team, Clyde, and were relegated with six matches to play.

Pitched into this morass were promising young players such as Jack Bolton and Frank Burrows, who formed a decidedly callow centre back partnership towards the end of the season, Jock Forsyth's senior career having ended in some ignominy (he went on to pilot Glenrothes Juniors in their early, successful years, culminating in an appearance in the Scottish Junior Cup Final in 1968).

Full back Gordon Haig, a close season recruit from Ormiston Primrose, was thrown in towards the end of the season, and experience was drafted into the team during the campain in the shape of Tommy McDonald from Dunfermline, Joe Caven from Brighton, and former Hibs and Falkirk inside forward Andy Aitken. It was no way for Andy Leigh, appointed club captain at last, to finish his marvellous career at Stark's Park, although he was spared close witness of the unfolding shambles after his final appearance on 2nd March.

The carnage extended to the reserve team, who were missing five players against Airdrie on Monday April 30th. Maguire, Boner, Wood, Aitken and McPherson were involved in a "motor mishap" and reserve team coach Johnny Urquhart had to take the field along with three trialists. Astonishingly, Rovers' second string won 4-2 with Hutton of

Newburgh scoring twice.

In the Scottish Cup, bizarrely, Rovers reached the semi finals. Eyemouth United were beaten, with some difficulty, on a frost-bound pitch in the first round, followed a fortnight later by a thrilling, and battling 3-2 home win over Clyde, thanks to a fanastic save by Jim Thorburn in the last minute. A McNamee goal in 80 minutes won the third round tie at Third Lanark, to everyone's surprise, and few gave Rovers any hope against Aberdeen – who had won 10-0 in the League earlier in the season – in the quarter finals. Bobby Gilfillan put Rovers ahead in 15 minutes, and Cummings equalised twelve minutes later. Wilson missed a penalty for Rovers and Aberdeen paid for their complacency when Gilfillan scored the winner with two minutes remaining.

The semi final against Celtic at Ibrox was a step too far, and despite Tommy McDonald equalising an early Divers goal, and the match locked at 1-1 until seven minutes into the second half, Celtic won, comfortably, 5-2.

Most of the eleven players retained at the end of the season were youngsters ; all were or became part-time. Seventeen, plus Kerr and McFadzean released earlier, were freed. 67 year old Hugh Shaw resigned as manager at the end of the season, and was replaced on 21st May 1963 by Doug Cowie, 30 years his junior, who had been a marvellous wing half with Dundee and Scotland. Others on the short leet were Sammy Baird, Neil Mochan, Berwick manager Jim McIntosh, Jimmy Davidson and Willie Fernie. Willie Cunningham had earlier turned down the job.

Jim Thorburn and Jack Bolton were both sold to Ipswich Town during the summer, and Bobby Adamson was released from his full time contract to sign for Morton, effectively in a swap deal with the new manager. The vetertan former Celt Neil Mochan from Dundee United and ex Stirling Albion Jacky Thoms from Bath City were hardly earth-shattering replacements, and the signing of the less-than-tall Arbroath goalkeeper hardly quickened supporters' hearts, although Bobby Reid went on to become one of the club's greatest servants.

Rovers moved into uncharted waters in 1963/64. It was the first time since 1939 that they had to adjust from the top division to the lower, and no-one remembered how to do it. A new part-time squad had to be assembled, all the full time – and invariably better – players having been jettisoned, and a new, unproven, manager was entrusted with these formidable tasks.

Bravely, it was decided to continue with a reserve team, which played infrequently in the Combined Reserve League, and it was from its youthful ranks that part of the first team was reconstructed. The signing of experienced players at the tail end of distinguished careers was the other part of the strategy, as was the gamble of signing players in their mid-twenties who had been disposed of by other clubs. It was the

GEORGE LYALL

IAN PORTERFIELD

He stayed at the club after Lyall left for Preston North End, but was rewarded with a big money transfer to Sunderland towards the end of 1967

BOBBY EVANS

BOBBY STEIN

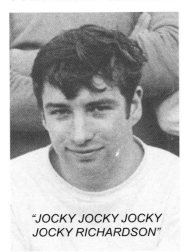

"JOCKY JOCKY JOCKY JOCKY RICHARDSON"

BOBBY REID

antithesis of the proven route to success of the previous decade ; a foundation of first class, well rewarded, long serving players, supplemented by the judicious signing of promising young players from other clubs, and the cream of junior talent.

The fans had something else to become accustomed ; a new strip. In 1960, Bert Herdman had introduced a new change strip of white shirts with two navy blue hoops, worn with navy shorts, which was donated by the Supporters Club. There were brief spells when this was preferred to the traditional navy shirt, but the latter had prevailed in recent seasons. In 1963/64, an all-white ensemble, with the two navy hoops, was installed as the first choice strip.

A 1-1 draw at home to East Fife in the opening League Cup tie gave no warning of the six defeats which followed, one in the club's first Second Division fixture in 14 years, a 2-1 defeat at Brechin. There were occasional victories to encourage both team and supporters, but these were outweighed by rather more defeats. The ups and downs could be quite severe. A 7-0 thrashing of Stirling Albion at Stark's Park was followed by an 8-1 defeat at Arbroath, and the week after a 5-1 win at Hamilton, Rovers lost 4-0 at Dumbarton. Each month seemed to bring a new low as the team plumbed greater depths of dismal performances. As a consequence, home attendances struggled to exceed 1,000.

Bobby Reid proved to be a useful acquisition in goal, and the full backs were Wilson and Haig, after young Alex Gray had been thrown in at the deep end at the start of the season. Frank Burrows and Bobby Stein, both promising young players, were the constants of the half back line. In late August, veteran centre half Willie Finlay – 15 years earlier one of the legendary East Fife half back line of Philp, Finlay and Aitken – was signed from Clyde, but he retired in November.

Ian Lourie and Felix McGrogan were purposeful wingers, but there was a constant shuffling of the inside forwards in an attempt to find a goalscoring combination. 19 year old Brian Menzies and Sandy McNiven played regularly ; Jackie Thoms from Bath City started the season but then left for Brechin City ; the veteran Neil Mochan at centre forward tried to team up with the fresh legs of 17 year old Jimmy Gilpin. Another experienced player, John Bell, was signed from St Johnstone in early November. He was second choice ; a fee of £500 had been agreed between the clubs for the transfer of another inside forward deemed surplus to requirements at Muirton Park, but Alex Ferguson refused to accept Rovers wages. Shortly afterwards there were signs that this disparate band were beginning to knit together. Five wins in seven matches held out some promise, but results turned again, including a dispiriting 4-0 defeat at Dumbarton in the first round of the Scottish Cup.

There was more than a hint that the club was "flying by the seat of its pants". Doug Cowie played for the reserves in

November in an attempt to give them an experienced guiding hand, and Johnny Urquhart followed his example in February. Neil Mochan, who had lost his first team place, returned to Celtic as assistant trainer in February.

Lessons about Second Division football were finally being learnt, and a big, lumbering centre forward in John Park was recruited from Stirling Albion.   The Scottish Cup exit was followed by a 6-1 home win over Montrose, which kicked off an eleven match unbeaten run.   That run propelled Rovers up to tenth place in the League, and they would have finished sixth had they not lost the final two fixtures, having spent most of the season in the bottom half of the Division.   The late season rally gave the dwindling band of supporters some hope that a promotion bid could be launched the following season.

There would be a new manager in charge, however. On Monday May 4th, Doug Cowie resigned, the day before his 38th birthday., "I enjoyed management, but I think coaching is more in my line" he admitted, as he returned to Morton, who had been runaway winners of the Second Division, as first team coach. He later served in the same position under Jerry Kerr and Jim McLean at Dundee United.   Trainer Willie Hunter also left, the club deciding they could not justify a full time position.

Rovers immediately turned to former player Andy Young, who had built a conveyor-belt of young footballing talent at Lochore Welfare, while also acting as Celtic's scout in Fife. He turned Rovers down, preferring to concentrate on his drapery business.   On Tuesday May 26th, 39 year old former Blackpool and Scotland goalkeeper George Farm was appointed manager, on a wage of £24 per week over a three year contract, and he had three months to move house to Kirkcaldy.   He had been player manager of Queen of the South in the First Division, but was fired as manager in January, although retained as a player.   His remaining months at Palmerston were acrimonious, and although he continued to keep goal as Queens fought, unsuccessfully, against relegation, he was not welcome on training nights.   Two days after his appointment, he made his first signing, 18 year old left half Ian Porterfield, one of Andy Young's bring young things at Lochore.   A fortnight later, 30 year old John Fraser, coach of St Andrews United, was appointed trainer.

Farm had little option but to continue with the three-pronged attempt at building a winning team ; promising youngsters, experienced pros, and a gamble on other clubs' rejects.

Former Scotland World Cup player Jim Murray, Bobby Wishart from Dundee's League Championship side and Alloa's Willie McLean all came into the middle category ; Airdrie's Pat Gardner, whom Farm had signed for Queen of the South and full back John Grant of Hibs fell into the latter.   It did not take the new manager long to sort out demarcation lines with his directors.   At the

Board Meeting of 4th August 1964 : "The Manager also brought up the matter of Directors approaching players before and during a game. The whole subject was discussed and it was agreed to respect the Manager's views on this."

Three wins and a draw from the first five League Cup matches inspired hopes of qualification, but the final match was lost, 3-2 at Dumfries. The first League match was won, 2-1 at home to Brechin, but the second victory did not arrive until the fifteenth match, by which time Rovers were in the bottom reaches of the League table. An 8-3 defeat at Montrose was, arguably, the club's lowest point since 1935/36.

A £3,000 bid for Frank Burrows from Falkirk was turned down in late July, but 21 year old outside left Felix McGrogan was sold to St Johnstone on October 1st, and Gordon Haig moved to Berwick Rangers later that month. At the Annual General Meeting in November, Jimmy Gourlay announced that he was standing down as chairman after 22 years, although remaining as a director, which he had been since 1927.

Radical surgery was performed on the failing team. John Park and Jim Murray were restored to the side, local youngster Henry Selfridge came in at left back, Ian Porterfield was given a run in the side, and stayed there, and Willie McLean was introduced to good effect in midfield. Results improved dramatically, with a seven match unbeaten run, followed by only one win in twelve matches. Included in the latest slump was a 2-1 defeat at Inverness Caledonian in the second preliminary round of the Scottish Cup. Rovers had played the prettier football ; but Caley played it as a cup tie.

Results improved a little as the season wound to a desultory end and thirteenth place in the nineteen club League table, a massive eighteen points short of a promotion place. To Rovers fans, it appeared that the club was destined for many more seasons in the Second Division, particularly when it was announced that 21 year old centre half Frank Burrows had been sold to Scunthorpe United on 4th May. There didn't appear to be much to enthuse over the list of retained players announced later that week, but in retrospect, Farm had cleared out a lot of the dead wood in the squad, principally the residue of players who had failed as First Division footballers and repeated that dubious distinction in the lower division. Retained were the likes of Reid, McLean, Gray, Stein and Gardner, and they had been joined by youngsters recruited from Fife youth and juniors clubs : Henry Selfridge, Ronnie Hutchison, George Lyall, Jocky Richardson and Ian Porterfield, the last two off Andy Young's conveyor belt of young talent at Lochore Welfare.

The impending success of this new mixture would not be known to Rovers fans who read of the appointment of their new Chairman, Rankin Grimshaw, as an International Selector on the SFA, and ruefully concluded that their man would not be subjected to a conflict of club interest in advising on the composition of the Scotland squad.

In the kind of perverse decision that constantly baffles observers of football, the youngest Rovers squad in living memory started 1965/66 at a club which had just disbanded its reserve team. This did ensure that there was less chopping and changing of the team, although a vast improvement in results may have led to that in any case.

Four wins and two draws in the League Cup section earned a quarter final place for only the third time in the competition's 20 year history, and following on were two wins and a draw in the opening League matches. The entire mood around the club, and attendances, rose. Bobby Reid in goal, young full backs McKeown and Gray, a half back line of Bobby Stein, Ian Porterfield and the one significant close season recruit, veteran centre half Bobby Evans, provided consistency and stability in defence. Up front, the youth of Ronnie Hutchison, Jocky Richardson and George Lyall blended with the vigour and craft of Pat Gardiner, and the older head of Willie McLean on the left wing.

The new combination had plenty of promise, but it was no match for Jock Stein's emerging Celtic side in the League Cup quarter finals. Joe McBride and John Hughes each scored a hat-trick, and Bobby Lennox and Jimmy Johnstone scored once apiece as Rovers lost 8-1 in the first leg at Stark's Park. Murdoch, Auld (with two) and Chalmers scored in a 4-0 home win at Parkhead in the second leg.

The team's confidence was dented, and the numbers in the "Lost" column began to mount, although there were several sparkling victories to encourage the fans. Hapless Third Lanark, close to extinction, were thumped 6-1, with George Lyall scoring four ; Queen's Park were beaten 5-1, Dumbarton 4-0 and Stranraer 5-0, all at home.

There was still the occasional lapse, such as an 8-0 thrashing at home to Airdrie which quickly sobered up the home crowd on 3rd January. It was revenge by the promotion chasing Diamonds for a 2-1 defeat at Broomfield during Rovers' early season unbeaten run. Inverness Caley were the opponents in the first preliminary round of the Scottish Cup, and the previous season's ignominy was averted, Ian Porterfield scoring the only goal of a game Rovers were fortunate to win, but Alloa won 1-0 at Stark's Park in the next round.

The presence of a bright young talent can often console fans who are disappointed with the pace of progress at a club, and the goalscoring exploits of George Lyall certainly lifted the mood at Stark's Park. The teenager was still at school, at Bell-Baxter High School in Cupar, when he was rattling in the goals at Stark's Park, and the story of his young life attracted the attention of the nation's sportwriters. Born in Wick, he attracted the attention of English League

WILLIE McLEAN

PAT GARDNER

Willie Butcher, who single handedly kept Crossgates Primrose juniors running over several decades, used to point to a picture on the pavilion wall at Humbug Park and tell newcomers or visitors : "I signed a man who played for the World."

The picture was of the FIFA selection who played England at Wembley in 1963 to celebrate the FA's centenary, and the player was Jim Baxter, who signed for Raith Rovers from Crossgates Primrose.

It was immediately obvious that the club had a rare talent in its midst. The slim, confident miner from Cowdenbeath developed into a sublime footballer . He glided across the pitch, his left foot caressing and dispatching the ball with unerring accuracy, disguised to wrong-foot the opposition defence. Baxter's playing career was tragically short. He lost his natural fitness after suffering a broken leg while playing for Rangers in a European Cup tie in Vienna in 1964, and did not have the self discipline in rehabilitation. He and the footballing world were denied what should have been the prime years of his career.

His skill and ability were of the type glimpsed possibly once in a generation, and he undoubtedly benefitted from his early tuition in League football at Stark's Park, surrounded by very good - and several outstanding - professionals.

Jim Baxter's football skills were made in heaven, and squandered on earth.

clubs when he was at school in Scarborough, and played for Sliema Wanderers when his father's Admiralty posting took the family to Malta. Young George won Malta's Junior Tennis championship, as well as playing football, rugby and cricket for his school, and become a champion diver. On his return to Scotland, he was spotted by a Rovers scout playing for Kingskettle Amateurs. Hearts wanted to sign Lyall and Porterfield, but their offer did not match Rovers' valuation of the teenage pair.

With no reserve team in which to view trialists, recruitment of new talent was a problem, and the manager gratefully, and gracefully, accepted the offer of Directors to spend their Saturday afternoons scouting at various matches. It was a throw-back to the 1950's, when the Board had the final say on signings at any level, having already viewed the prospective player in action.

There was an unaccustomed sight to Rovers fans of the 1960s, 70s, and 80s – a regular goalkeeper who was not called Reid or McDermott. Bobby Reid's work had taken him to England, and from mid February onwards he was replaced by Lanarkshire junior Tom Coates. Reid accepted a free transfer, although returned to the club when his job brought him back to Scotland. Earlier in the season, Rovers had made a second attempt (the first was in 1950) to sign Ronnie Simpson, then languishing in Celtic's reserve team.

Henry Selfridge replaced McKeown at right back for the latter part of the season, and Terry Christie took over from Ronnie Hutchison, who broke his leg at Forfar on 6th November, at outside right. There was an inevitability about George Lyall's transfer to Preston North End in March, and only his family's insistence that he complete his apprenticeship prevented Ian Porterfield following suit. McDonald was restored to a re-shuffled forward line to cover Lyall's absence. At the very end of the season, Rovers joined the modern era with a teen idol, Chris Spilarewicz, who sported a Beatle hair cut and carefree youthful exuberance somewhat incongruous from his genesis, Frances Colliery Juniors. He played in the final two matches and was instantly nicknamed "Ziggy" by the fans.

A nine match unbeaten run from 5th February raised hopes of Rovers gate-crashing the promotion chase, but they had started too far back and could not afford to drop any points, which they did in a tough encounter at East Fife, drawn 1-1, and an unexpected 1-0 defeat at Third Lanark. The season was probably summed up by the last three matches ; unbeaten, showing plenty of promise, but still short of a winning mentality, as all three were drawn. Fifth place was the outcome, seven points short of promotion. The club entered the new season with confidence, however. There were no free transfers, all 13 signed players retained, and the reserve team was reformed to play in the East of Scotland League.

Kirkcaldy boy Ian Lister, freed by

Aberdeen, started 1966/67 at outside right, and George Rennie filled the left half position, Porterfield being pushed, unproductively, into attack, for the League Cup ties which reverted to type – two wins, two draws, two defeats, no qualification. Unsuccessful attempts were made to sign centre forwards Stan Vincent from Hibs and Jim Murphy from Hearts, both deemed to be too expensive.

This disappointing form was not carried into League matches. After a 1-1 draw at home to Montrose in the opening match, the next six matches were won, with the loss of only five goals. A £5,000 offer from Clyde for Pat Gardner was turned down, but there was bad news from the reserve match against Spartans on September 24th, outside right Ronnie Hutchison suffering his second broken leg within a year. Rovers met their match at Morton, with a 1-0 defeat on 8th October, the goal scored by Jack Bolton although few present begrudged Rovers a point, and they proceeded to win eight and draw one of their next nine matches. Encouraged by this superb start to the season, sitting on top of the League, Bobby Gardiner was signed from Stirling Albion to bring experience to the forward line, but he only played in five matches before returning to Annfield. A much more far-sighted, and indeed inspired, capture was the Montrose striker Gordon Wallace, signed for £3,500 on October 14th.

The run came to an abrupt end at Gayfield Park on 10th December. Arbroath scored on either side of half-time, and then in 48 minutes before Pat Gardner could get on the scoresheet for Rovers, but two more goals for the home team led to an unexpectedly heavy 5-1 defeat. The response was to buy outside right Alan Miller from East Stirling, but for the next six weeks results were mixed.

There were defeats at Dumfries, in a great game which Rovers could have drawn, at Clydebank, where early dominance was thrown away, and another slightly fortunate 1-0 win for Morton, this time in front of 7,625 at Stark's Park. Only a few less had watched a Pat Gardner goal beat East Fife on New Year's Day, and Third Lanark were thrashed 6-1 on Rovers' last ever visit to Cathkin Park. Substitutes were introduced to Scottish football, leading to even more cramped conditions in the tiny trainers' dugouts which were located on either side of the players' tunnel, unhelpfully (for the occupants) situated some distance from the usual vantage point of the half way line. There were strict controls over their use – for injuries only – and the sight of a number 12 shirt remained a rarity. Ian Lourie was signed for a second time, from Airdrie, and Rovers fielded 14 year old Templehall High School pupil Graeme Ferguson in the reserve match against Eyemouth United on 21st January, possibly the youngest player to be fielded by the club in an official fixture.

The run of erratic results was followed by six successive victories, but only after bowing out of the Scottish Cup at the first hurdle, a last minute wind-assisted goal giving Queen's Park the verdict in a thrilling tie at Hampden.

Forfar and Brechin were both beaten 5-1, and East Stirling 6-1, all at Stark's Park, as the inside forward trio of Richardson, Wallace and Gardner began to fire on all cylinders. The experienced Tommy Mackle was brought in from Forfar at outside left, and to the delight and surprise of everyone, the business-end of the season could be faced with the considerable presence of Willie Polland in the team, signed on a free transfer granted by a grateful Hearts. Willie was therefore able to benefit from the £1000 signing on fee, after tax, a brave investment by the Board who had seen the overdraft double to £9,000 in the course of the season – secured by their personal guarantees

This delight turned to despair on his debut, a 2-0 defeat at Berwick, and after winning 4-0 at home against Queen's Park, and by the same scoreline at Cowdenbeath (courtesy of a Henry Mowbray own goal two minutes before the end, having being on the back foot for much of the game), there was huge disappointment in losing 1-0 at home to fellow promotion contenders Arbroath. From a position of being two points ahead of third placed East Fife, with two games in hand, at the turn of the year, Rovers were now three points behind Arbroath, with only one game in hand. Morton remained unassailable at the top.

With five games to go, there was little margin for further error, so the loss of a goal to Stenhousemuir after 90 seconds of a midweek home match meant a long, nervous game for Rovers fans, only partially eased by a Miller equaliser with nine minutes to go. There was no winner, however.

The following Saturday, the Warriors were beaten 4-0 at Ochilview, courtesy of a Gardner hat-trick, but much more importantly Arbroath were surprisingly beaten by bottom of the league East Stirling. A confident, well-merited 3-1 win at Hamilton was balanced by the loss of Alex Gray to an injury. Willie McLean was brought off the substitute's bench to deputise, the manager now settled on his preferred team, with Miller and Lister producing a potent supply on the right wing for the twin strikers of Wallace and Gardner.

Rovers took a big support up to Montrose in midweek, and a nervous first half performance was not helped by Livingstone opening the scoring for the home side on the stroke of half-time. Rovers found their form in the second half, but could make no impression on a well organised Montrose defence, and for their part the Gable Endies kept the Raith defence busy throughout the game. The match was well into injury time when Rovers launched one last, despairing attack. Bobby Stein advanced up the right wing and passed to Ian Lister. A shot was expected, but instead he struck a low cross to Pat Gardner, who turned and shot into the net via the upright.

The point was absolutely crucial ; it means that Rovers' fate was in their own hands, going into the last game of the season, at home to Queen of the South. There were few signs of the nerves of previous weeks when Gardner put Rovers ahead after 19 minutes, and although Lex Law equalised six minutes later, two goals from Gordon Wallace, in 32 and 36 minutes, gave Rovers a comfortable half-time lead which they increased to unassailable proportions with a Bobby Stein double on, and just after, the hour mark. McMurdo pulled one back for Queens, and the large crowd enjoyed the feast of goals. Wallace completed his hat-trick in 70 minutes, and Ian Lister finished the scoring with eight minutes to go. Rovers won 7-2, and were promoted, by one point. There was a good natured mass pitch invasion at the end, the players and manager George Farm, conspicuous in his trademark immaculate white shirt, being mobbed.

George Falconer, who had been Gordon Wallace's strike partner, and a thorn in the side of the Rovers' defence during the season, was signed from Montrose for the huge sum of £10,000, by some distance the club's record signing. This hefty expenditure restricted further recruitment to free transfers, although Jack Bolton's return to the club was welcomed. Bobby Kinloch from Hibs and the former Hearts player Jim Murphy were signed to add top division experience to the team, although the task of ensuring Rovers' survival was entrusted, at the beginning of the season, to those who had got them there.

Not the manager, however. On 12th July, George Farm was appointed Dunfermline Athletic manager and, a week later, his replacement was announced to rekindle memories of the last time the club replaced a manager who had piloted them to promotion. While Tommy Walker proved to be a better proposition than Hugh Shaw, his achievements in football management were firmly in the past, at the club he had graced as a player (Hearts) whom he had left in September 1966, subsequently taking up an administrative post at East End Park.

His first signing was Gordon Patterson, a 19 year old Fifer freed by Rangers, but he had a bigger task to fulfil in replacing Pat Gardner, whom George Farm signed for the third time. Rovers were playing a closed-door pre-season friendly at Bayview when Farm telephoned Stark's Park to say that he would increase his bid to £17,000 – a club record for Rovers. The board and manager left Bayview at half time to conclude the deal with Dunfermline, whose cheque funded a year's full time football at Kirkcaldy.

Seven-and-a-half thousand fans converged on Stark's Park for the pre-season friendly against Nottingham Forest on 5th August 1967. It proved to be a terrible day for the club. It was the first season in which Scottish clubs were permitted to play pre-season friendlies, and Rovers ambitiously invited the English League Champions, Manchester United, and then their City

APRIL 29

TV SATURDAY

From 12.45

GRANDSTAND

INTRODUCED BY DAVID COLEMAN

featuring

RUGBY LEAGUE . . .

RACING . . . TENNIS . . .

SWIMMING . . .

RACING
from Beverley

12.45
GRANDSTAND
TODAY'S TIMETABLE

12.55 Tennis	2.50 Racing
1.10 F.A. Cup news	3.5 Rugby
1.15 Tennis	3.20 Racing
1.50 Racing	3.35 Swimmi
2.5 Tennis	3.45 Rugby
2.20 Racing	4.25 Swimmi
2.35 Swimming	4.40 Results

These timings may be altered by

5.3
SPORTSREEL
from Scotland
News, film, and verdicts
from today's sport

1967

135

In the late 1970's, a popular footballing story was how a commentator, on learning of the club's promotion, announced to the nation that "They'll be dancing in the streets of Raith tonight".
Those with vague recollections of hearing the faux pas believed it took place on Grandstand, whose "teleprinter" announced the scores as they were received shortly after final whistles were blown across the country.
Rovers' two promotions in the late 1970s were clinched in midweek fixtures, so the likeliest date of the howler would have been Saturday April 29th 1967, when Queen of the South were beaten 7-2 at Stark's Park, enabling Rovers to return to the First Division.
The Radio Times for that week's viewing indicates that the presenter of Grandstand - and the commentator as results were being displayed on the teleprinter - was David Coleman.
Raith Rovers can therefore be added to the collection of Colemanballs.

JACK BOLTON

In February 1967, enquiries were made about Stirling Albion goalkeeper Bill Taylor and Andy Rolland of Cowdenbeath

On 28th March, the club resigned from the East of Scotland League, frustrated at the irregularity of fixtures.

Willie Benvie appointed Assistant Trainer on Boxing Day 1967 in succession to John Brown

Billy Mitchell was the club's first S signing in April 1968

1968 - Technical College tower opened

On 30th July 1968, an offer of £5000 was made to Cowdenbeath for Andy Kinnell

BRIAN COOPER

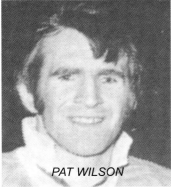

PAT WILSON

neighbours. Both declined, but Nottingham Forest, who were League runners up and FA Cup semi finalists, agreed to travel to Kirkcaldy, whereupon their team of internationalists utterly outclassed Rovers, winning 5-1 with Joe Baker scoring twice. Worse was the broken leg sustained by Willie Polland after only ten minutes.

After a dismal set of results in the League Cup section, with Bobby Kinloch partnering the veteran Evans in the centre of defence, the League campaign got under way with a 2-1 home defeat by Dunfermline – Rovers' spirited display probably meriting a draw – and a 3-0 defeat at Hibs. The skies brightened with a 7-1 home win over Stirling Albion, in which Gordon Wallace shone, scoring a hat-trick, with Ian Porterfield back on top form in midfield. While the team was finding life in the First Division difficult, their task wasn't deemed insurmountable. By late September nine players – Polland, Porterfield, Davie Sneddon (signed from Kilmarnock), Murphy, Smith, Wallace, Falconer, Lister and Gray joined trainer Fraser and manager Walker as full timers. Defeats at Perth and at home to Hearts were matched by a victory at Kilmarnock and a draw at home to Airdrie.

The win at Rugby Park was followed by 16 matches without a victory. This dismal run included a 6-2 defeat at Aberdeen, a 10-2 shocker at Ibrox followed by 4-0 at Dundee, and, arguably worst of all, a 6-0 thumping at Dunfermline on New Year's Day. There was continuous chopping and changing of the team in an attempt to halt the slide. Young players, not long out of junior football, were thrown in, such as Tommy Hislop at right back and Tom Davidson, replacing Bobby Evans who retired after 23 years in senior football, at the age of 40 . Willie Cunningham from Kirkcaldy Travel Club was thrown into the attack, as the entire playing pool took their turn of selection.

There were some bright spots amongst the gloom of poor results. The visit of the European Champions to Stark's Park on 25th November was keenly anticipated, and few who witnessed a gutsy Rovers performance were disappointed with the match. Rovers took the game to Celtic, and Jocky Richardson hit the post before Celtic scored. Bobby Reid saved a late Gemmell penalty, which would have made the scoreline even more unjust than the 2-0 in the record books. Rather than compel their illustrious visitors to change out of their famous hooped strip, Rovers hurriedly obtained a set of navy blue shirts, both teams taking the field without numbers on their backs [Celtic in those days having numbers only on their shorts].

The outstanding Bobby Reid broke his toe in training, and was replaced by reserve 'keeper Jim Gray, a Partick Thistle free transfer. He had an excellent debut in a 1-1 draw with Falkirk on a snow-covered, bone-hard surface, but then lost 10 and 4 at Ibrox and Dundee, and was replaced by 16 year old Oakley United goalkeeper Bobby Aitken, before Reid returned.

The defeat at Dens Park proved to

be Ian Porterfield's last appearance for Rovers. At the end of September, he was one of a number of Rovers players who played for the Fife Select against Sunderland at East End Park, in a match for the Michael Colliery Disaster Fund. Porterfield overshadowed Jim Baxter on the night, and Sunderland returned to Fife with their cheque book on Boxing Day. The £45,000 fee was a club record, but his absence precipitated four personnel changes and nine positional as Clyde visited a flu-ravaged team the following Saturday.

Mike Judge was signed on a free transfer from Dunfermline, but sat out a backs-to-the-wall 1-1 draw at Aberdeen in the first round of the Scottish Cup. Goalscorer Tommy Mackle had earlier hit the bar, and Davie Sneddon's 61st minute penalty found the same barrier, otherwise there would have been no need for the replay in gale force conditions at Stark's Park. The only goal of the game came in bizarre fashion, Bobby Reid's clearance caught by the wind and blown into his net. A 2-1 defeat at home to Kilmarnock, watched by only 2,500, left Rovers five points adrift of safety in second bottom place, albeit with two games in hand.

The turning point of the season came in mid February. Stirling Albion were beaten 7-0 at Annfield, recent signing Jim Gillespie, an outside left from East Stirling, helping himself to two goals. Tommy Hislop, playing his 14th League match, at long last discovered what a win bonus looked like on his payslip ! More of the Porterfield transfer fee was spent on two players from Aberdeen, a cultured midfielder in Dave Millar, and a sprightly winger in Pat Wilson. After a 3-0 defeat at Partick Thistle, Willie Polland returned to the team on 2nd March and Rovers beat Morton 3-1 at Stark's Park.

A settled team embarked on a run of results which was more Championship-chasing, than relegation-avoiding. Reid, Hislop and Gray at the back, with Stein and Polland in central defence, Miller and Sneddon in midfield, wingers Wilson and Gillespie, and in attack Wallace and Falconer. Davie Sneddon brought huge experience and pitch-craft to the midfield, as later recalled by Gordon Wallace : "He was a really good player and had a good knowledge of the game. He knew exactly what he was doing." The team had been radically changed to handle top division football, and with the imperious Polland at centre half, it found fresh purpose and confidence ; none more so than Gordon Wallace.

Following his two goals against Morton, he scored both in a 2-0 win in a re-arranged match at Tynecastle, two in a 3-1 home win over Aberdeen, and a magnificent hat-trick in a 3-3 draw at Dundee United. He was the star forward, but didn't score, in a 3-2 home win over St Johnstone in another re-arranged game. Celtic interrupted the sequence with a 5-0 win at Parkhead, but Rovers bounced back to beat Motherwell 3-1 at Stark's Park (another Wallace hat-trick) and Falkirk 2-0 at Brockville.

The victory over second-bottom Motherwell effectively assured the club's place in the First Division, an unlikely event just six weeks earlier. 19,038 packed into Stark's Park to see unbeaten championship chasing Rangers distinctly fortunate to win 3-2, and the following week a 2-0 defeat at home to Fairs Cup semi finalists Dundee was of no consequence, although Gordon Wallace, newly crowned Scottish Player of the Year – the first non Old Firm player to be recognised by Scotland's sportswriters - had an uncharacteristically quiet match under the scrutiny of Scotland manager Bobby Brown.

Three defeats in the final matches, the worst by far a 5-0 drubbing at the hands of a Harry Hood inspired Clyde at Shawfield, were of little consequence to Rovers fans who enjoyed the exhilarating run of results between 17th February and 6th April, and the 27 League goals scored by Gordon Wallace. They were almost half the club's total of 58 for the season, and a remarkable tally for a player of a club which finished third bottom of its Division.

Scotland's Player of the Year had this recollection of the season : "We had another good balance of experienced and younger players [following the team that got promoted], and from the turn of 1967/68 onwards we hit a fantastic run of form. I got the glory side of it, scoring 27 League goals, and had a real purple patch in February and March, and the transformation was unbelievable. I scored more than a dozen goals from about 20 shots at goal in that spell – everything I hit went in the back of the net. It was a wonderful season, and that year a load of us went full time for the first time, and it was only after the turn of the year that we started to benefit from being full time, and that's when the team took off."

It often happens that a spell of success towards the end of a season induces complacency in team building for the following season, and there were no significant signings over the summer months of 1968. Rovers thought they had signed Andy Kinnell from Cowdenbeath, but his exit from Central Park was entangled in contractual disputes, and his registration as a Raith player was not accepted.

Up-and-coming Queen's Park Rangers visited Stark's Park for a pre-season friendly, and their star player, Rodney Marsh, suffered the same fate as Willie Polland a year earlier. Two days later, at Wigan, Rovers gave Bobby Aitken a spell in goal towards the end of the match, Bobby Reid moving to outside right.

With Pat Wilson fully recovered from a late-season cartilage operation, it was the same Rovers team who started 1968/69, as finished the previous season, apart from a fully fit Jack Bolton replacing Bobby Stein. Early results weren't too bad, only two of the League Cup ties being lost (still no qualification, however), and there were League victories over Hibs, Abroath and Partick, all at home, and draws at St Mirren and Kilmarnock. The latter saw Rovers race

to a 4-0 half-time lead, which caused disbelief on half-time scoreboards across Scotland, but Tommy McLean inspired Kilmarnock to a second half comeback. Rovers were relieved to hear the final whistle with the score at 4-4.

Inevitably, Gordon Wallace received a lot more attention from wiser defenders following his goalscoring exploits the previous season, and he responded by playing a more withdrawn, supportive role, which allowed George Falconer to score more regularly. The intelligent, skilful Wallace proved himself to be much more than just a goalscorer, although Rovers could have done with his previous season's proliferation as they missed several chances in losing 2-1 at home to Dundee United.

The following week, the daunting task of playing at Celtic Park was made much harder when Bobby Reid was sent off after 12 minutes. Alex Gray took over in goal and broke his cheek bone in saving at a Celtic forward's feet three minutes later. The brave Rovers' captain played on, but was beaten twice by Bobby Murdoch. A week later, Falkirk were beaten 3-1 at Stark's Park, and Rovers lay in sixth bottom place, conscious of the relegation battle below them, but not overly concerned.

The next nine weeks shook that complacency. In a re-run of the winter slump of the previous season, Rovers failed to win a match between 23rd November and 1st February, when Falconer scored the only goal of the match at Arbroath, followed by four more games without a victory. Former Kilmarnock full back Ken McDonald replaced Tom Hislop, Willie Cunningham, Jock Richardson and former Aberdeen midfielder Willie Watt were given brief runs in the team, but Rovers couldn't buy a win. There was no respite in the Cup, Dunfermline winning a one-sided first round match at Stark's Park by 2-0.

The response was to change the pilot, and this is how it was recorded in the Board's Minutes. "Mr Grimshaw reported that Mr Uquhart and he had met Mr Walker earlier in the day and a most amicable discussion had ensued, the result of which Mr Walker had agreed to relinquish the post of Club Manager and to accept the post of Club Secretary alone.

"It was agreed, therefore, that a new Club Manager be appointed and so Mr A. Young, a former player of Raith Rovers FC, was offered the situation which he accepted. Mr Young joined the Board Meeting and was welcomed on behalf of the Directors by Mr Grimshaw. Mr Walker preferred his congratulations and good wishes.

"Mr Young retired to make a telephone call and upon returning to the Board Meeting intimated that he was in "two

GORDON WALLACE

KENNY LINDSAY

... and another goalscorer named GORDON WALLACE

BENNY McGUIRE

On Monday September 25 1967, a match was played in aid of the Michael Colliery Disaster Fund at East End Park.

The result was Fife Select 4 (Edwards 31, Porterfield 55, Dewar 60, Rolland 70), Sunderland 2 (Hughes 5, Barry own goal 44). Attendance 7,000, receipts £2,000.

Fife Select : McGann (sub Reid half time), Callaghan, Rolland, Barry, Gilchrist, Porterfield, Edwards, Burns, Dewar, Murphy (sub Jack half time), Wallace

Sunderland : Foster, Irwin, Parke, Todd, Kinnell, Baxter, Hughes, Suggett, Martin, Heslop, Gauden.

1969 - Kirkcaldy Swimming Pool was opened

On 7th August 1969, it was agreed to wind up Raith Juveniles, which had been run by David Robb for the previous two seasons.

On Monday February 9th 1970, Billy Mitchell scored for the Scottish Professional Youth team in a 2-1 defeat by Falkirk Reserves. Also playing was Jimmy Brown (then of Dunfermline Athletic)

The death of Mrs Gourley recorded in the board minute of 17th February 1970.

Following an incident at the Station Hotel on 11th, 12th March 1970, seven players were each fined £5 by the club.

minds" and requested that Mr Grimshaw and Mr Urquhart might call at his home around 8pm – 8.30pm tonight for further discussions with Mr Young's wife before he finally made up his mind to accept the post.   Mr Grimshaw and Mr Urquhart agreed to attend at Mr Young's home tonight at the time stated."

The following week's Minutes confirmed that "Mr Young upon further consideration had declined to accept the post as Manager of this Club."   He remained in charge of Dunfermline's youth scheme and in his stead, former Rangers and Dundee United forward Jimmy Miller hung up his boots to take over as team manager on 9th February. His last match as a professional footballer had been against Rovers in a Second Eleven Cup tie, when he scored a late equaliser.   He found a team short of confidence – and luck – and second bottom of the League.

His first victory was absolutely crucial, a 3-1 win over third bottom Falkirk at Brockville, with Alan Millar restored to the team at outside right.   That was followed by a midweek home win over Aberdeen, thanks in the main to three blunders by Ernie McGarr in the visiting goal.   Dave Miller missed a penalty at home to St Johnstone, although it scarcely mattered in a 5-1 defeat, and a fighting draw at Dundee showed that Rovers were up for the battle against relegation.

Two bad performances plunged Rovers back into deep trouble, 3-0 at home to Hearts and 2-0 at Airdrie, but with Falkirk also toiling, and Arbroath doomed, relegation was avoided with a 4-0 home win over a disinterested Dundee team in the final match of the season.   Three of the goals were scored by the striking partnership of Wallace and Falconer, who between them accounted for 29 of the team's 45 League goals.

Unlike the previous season, the team selection was quite settled throughout the campaign, prompting concern that the players at the new manager's disposal would be good enough for a third successive season in the top division.   There was also some question over harmony within the club : the proposed close season tour of the Highlands was called off when the players would not accept the additional money offered for them to take part.

The cost of maintaining full time players told on the transfer budget, which was restricted to signings from junior football, albeit of the calibre of centre forward Colin Sinclair from Linlithgow Rose, and midfielder Kenny Lindsay from Penicuik Athletic.   The former displaced the previous season's top scorer George Falconer, the latter eventually took Alex Gray's left back position.

All eyes were on Stark's Park for the opening League Cup tie, against Rangers and Jim Baxter, who had returned to the club on a free transfer from Nottingham Forest.   This was far from the Slim Jim who last graced the ground with his sublime footballing talents. Rovers gave a good account of themselves, and despite a thunderbolt shot from Sinclair in 88 minutes, lost 3-2.   In the return match, Gordon Wallace scored twice and Sinclair once in a 3-3 draw.   Celtic scored five in both

matches, and with Rovers reduced to sharing the crumbs with Airdrie, it was no surprise that the dismal League Cup qualification record lived on.

There was more than a hint of the "old pals act" when 30 year old Ralph Brand was signed on a free transfer from Sunderland, joining his partner in the renowned Rangers strike force of five years earlier.   Brand made his debut at Greenock the week after Rovers opened the League season with a 1-0 home win over Airdrie on 30th August, missed the 1-0 win at home over St Johnstone on 8th November through unjury, and therefore had to wait until 20th December, when he scored in the 2-1 home win over Morton, for his first win bonus.

Rovers' struggles were not helped by the sale of Gordon Wallace to Dundee for £14,000 on 16th September, thus ending prolonged speculation about when, and how, the team's best player would leave.   The veteran Brand proved to be no substitute, and not even the re-introduction of Willie Watt (briefly), Jack Bolton in defence, former Manchester United youth David Weir at left back and Mike Judge in attack, could alter the team's downward trajectory.   Scottish youth cap Brian Cooper was introduced to good effect in midfield, and Benny McGuire, signed from East Stirling, was a clever player, but neither could transform the flow of results.

There were some encouraging signs ; League leaders Dunfermline held 1-1 at Stark's Park by an otherwise young Rovers team, with veterans Reid and Polland outstanding in defence, but that was followed by a 7-1 defeat by a rampant Celtic.   In most other games, Rovers matched their opponents until it came to the putting the ball in the net.   Colin Sinclair looked the part up front, but he enjoyed little support.

The bloated playing squad came under close scrutiny.   Willie Watt was released, former Hibs forward Stan Vincent arrived on a month's loan, and Rovers tried to sign Tommy Traynor from Hearts, who would not accept Falconer in exchange.   There was a mini rally in early December, with a 1-1 home draw with Clyde followed by the win over Morton.   It could have been better had the intervening match at Airdrie not been abandoned at half time, after both teams had scored on the hard, rutted pitch pockmarked with pools of surface water.

Even in those (comparatively) better times, there was the air of inevitable catastrophy about to engulf the club.   Jim Gillespie had been freed at the beginning of December, and continued training at Stark's Park until Christmas Eve, whereupon he signed for Dunfermline.   Chairman Victor Beattie told the press that he should have been sold, not freed ; he had missed the Board Meeting at which the decision had been made, and was shocked to hear of it. On January 1st, Gillespie made his debut for Dunfermline, against Rovers at East End Park, and rounded off an excellent performance with two goals in a 3-0 victory. Former Valleyfield Colliery centre half Alex

Buchanan, deputising for the injured Polland, and his defensive colleagues, were no match for a rampant Pars side.

There was arguably worse misery in the next local derby, a 3-0 defeat to Second Division East Fife in the first round of the Scottish Cup. At Shawfield on 7th February Willie Polland had to go off after 30 minutes with a gashed shin which required 17 stitches. Diminutive midfielder Davie Sneddon moved back to play as sweeper and marshalled the defence superbly to earn a 1-1 draw, courtesy of a Ralph Brand equaliser with two minutes remaining.

Pat Wilson returned to the team after a prolonged absence – poisoned ankle, pulled muscle and twisted knee among the succession of injuries – but Alex Gray was in and out of plaster with a chipped bone in his ankle. There was a re-run of the Watershei Thor fiasco ; a visit from the touring Russian side Kharkov Metallist was postponed at a late stage. They had agreed to play four matches in Britain, but an agent had arranged six games, and they objected to playing at Stirling, Kirkcaldy and Dumfries on successive nights.

At Love Street, Rovers raced to a 3-0 half time lead, but collapsed in the second half and had to settle for a draw, which was also the outcome of the meeting of the bottom two teams at Stark's Park, only 1,500 watching the match against Partick Thistle. "Only a miracle would save Rovers" was the considered opinion of most, but they had reason to reconsider when Rangers were beaten 2-1 at Stark's Park in a midweek re-arranged match.

Alan Miller put Rovers ahead in 18 minutes and Andy Penman equalised eight minutes later. Three minutes from half time, Brian Cooper scored Rovers' second, and the whole team battled manfully to prevent Rangers from equalising. Cooper's domination of John Greig in midfield was a feature of a famous victory, which he followed up with both goals in a 2-1 win at Motherwell.

With the teams above them consistently picking up points, only a 100% record from the remaining four matches would have given Rovers the merest glimmer of a chance of escaping relegation, and with Alan Miller and Cooper missing through injury, a 3-0 defeat at home to Hearts effectively consigned Rovers to the Second Division. A last minute Falconer penalty earned a draw at Perth, but relegation was confirmed when another late goal, by Ralph Brand, could win only a point at home to Ayr United.

The following week, it was decided to cut the playing staff from 26, 17 of them full time, and revert to part-time football, albeit with Tommy Walker and Jimmy Miller remaining full time. The painful lessons of seven years earlier had not been learned. Full time football is financial suicide unless the players are carefully selected and are of sufficient quality to justify compensating them for not having to work at another job to earn a living.

In the early 1950's, a small core of players were thus singled out ; Young, McNaught and Leigh, McEwan and Copeland, the goalkeeper. When the scheme was extended to include the whole of the first team, in 1956, the squad had sufficient talent in depth to justify it. The downturn, in both playing and financial terms, came when those players were replaced by inferior talents, on their betters' full time terms. That could not be used as an excuse between 1967 and 1969, by which time you would be hard pushed to find seven suitable candidates for full time football at Stark's Park, let alone seventeen. It takes an unusually strong board of directors, and manager, to prevent full time football becoming an end in itself, as opposed to a selectively used means to an end. The financial mayhem which engulfed the club after 1997 arrived by wandering into the same trap.

For the final League game at Tannadice on 18th April 1970, Scottish Youth internationalist Billy Mitchell was restored to the team at centre forward, and youngsters Ken Brown and Jimmy Wilson were also selected. Willie Polland had announced his retirement, part time training being incompatible with his public house commitments in Armadale, but he and Bobby Reid marshalled the teenage defence in the 4-2 defeat. None of the Rovers fans in the 5,000 crowd could imagine that it would be 23 years before they would again see their team play in the top flight of Scottish football.

Whiteside, Polland, Weir, Davidson, Alan Miller, Brand, Judge and McManus – all full timers – were freed, along with Alex Buchanan. Record signing George Falconer was placed on the transfer list ; all retained players were to be part-time, in the Second Division.

While no-one relished the return to the outposts of Scottish football on a fortnightly basis, there was justifiable optimism at the team's prospects of a quick return to the top division. The back three of Bobby Reid, Alex Gray and Kenny Lindsay were surely among the best in the lower division ; David Miller, the veteran Davie Sneddon, Benny McGuire and Pat Wilson combined experience with talent. Colin

TOMMY HISLOP

Described by team-mates as "Rangers daft", which explains his nickname of "Kai", after Kai Johansen, Rangers' Danish full back in the mid 1960s, Tommy Hislop was a fine servant to Raith Rovers.

Kilmarnock enquired about David Miller during 1969/70, and were quoted £15,000, then £8,500, then £8,000

1970 - Tay Road Bridge opened ; Capshard Primary School opened

On 7th July 1970, the Penman Football Association was wound up

In a closed door friendly match on Tuesday 9th February 1971, Broxburn Athletic were beaten 7-1, Sinclair (3), georgeson (2), Wallace and Mitchell the scorers.

Professional sprinter Stuart Hogg was coaching the players in sprinting, and local weightlifter Phil Caira also assisted in training.

1971 - Fire damaged McIntosh's factory on Victoria Road

RODDY GEORGESON

Tommy Walker, full time Secretary of the club, was asked to find another job during a round of economies towards the end of 1971. He left Stark's Park on 15th January, and two days later started a new job, his first ever outside football. As part of the same cost-saving exercise, the club resigned from the Combined Reserve League in October.

Stark's Park hosted an "It's A Knock Out" tournament on 26th May 1971, reflecting the interest generated by the television programme of the same name, and its European extension "Jeux Sans Frontieres".

1972 - Balwearie High School extended ; the former Carlton cinema in Park Road was destroyed in a fire.

BILLY BROWN

Sinclair and Brian Cooper had enjoyed very encouraging debut seasons, the late season debutants Billy Mitchell, Kenny Brown and Jimmy Wilson showed promise and there were the unknown quantities of the two new signings from Penicuik Athletic, Murray McDermott and another centre forward called Gordon Wallace.

The transition from full time to part time, First Division to Second Division, football proved to be very difficult. The season opened brightly with a 1-0 (Sinclair) home win over Montrose in the League Cup section, in front of 2,500. One more win (2-1 over East Stirling) and four defeats later, the opening home League match was watched by half that number, and drawn with Arbroath. The fourth match without a win was a humbling 5-1 defeat at Bayview. Rovers had gone 2-1 behind after 31 minutes against East Fife when Bobby Reid was alleged to have struck the goalscorer Finlayson, and was sent off. A penalty was given, which Bertie Miller scored against Alex Gray, and the home side completed the scoring through a Brian Cooper own goal two minutes into the second half. Benny McGuire was also sent off late in the game for taking his frustrations out on Miller who, not for the first, or last time, gave the Rovers defence a torrid time. It was a long journey home from Methil for the Rovers faithful that evening, and it was followed by a 3-0 defeat at Clydebank.

Sinclair scored all four against Stenhousemuir in a Stark's Park victory, but that was followed by two draws and a 4-0 defeat at Arbroath. 1,500 saw a 2-0 win over Brechin City at Stark's Park on 26th September, and two days later Jimmy Miller resigned after 18 months as manager. Ray Cormack, freed by Dundee, had been introduced at outside left, and former Hibs centre half Ian Wilkinson, to little effect ; Roddy Georgeson was signed on a free transfer from Dundee, and Murray McDermott achieved what no other goalkeeper had done in eight years, and displaced Bobby Reid. Jack Bolton was sold to Dumbarton for £5,000 in September without donning a first team jersey that season. George Falconer had played in the two pre season matches against Hartlepool, but walked out of Stark's Park after being asked to sit on the bench for the opening League Cup tie, and wasn't seen again. He was sold to Dundee for £5,000 on 2nd October.

The Rovers board had got the message by now ; Andy Young was not asked for a third time to become Manager, but Willie Polland was, and he too declined, preferring to enjoy his retirement from football and concentrate on his pub. There were 51 applicants, and on October 20th, Bill Baxter moved from table topping East Fife to become Rovers manager. Two days later, he completed the pre-arranged signing of Bathgate Thistle's gangling centre half, George Innes, and a week later made his first capture when 19 year old full back Bill Beveridge was signed from Clackmannan.

Baxter's first match in charge was a

2-2 draw at home to Albion Rovers, thanks to a last minute Pat Wilson equaliser, followed by a hard-luck backs-to-the-wall story at Firhill, where they lost 1-0. Thereafter, results improved appreciably, but a lot of ground had to be made up, without arguably the team's best player. David Miller was transferred to St Mirren for £10,000 on November 12th.

He therefore missed the 6-4 home win over Queen's Park, in which Rovers galloped to a four goal lead after 55 minutes before complacency – and a shambolic offside-trap – set in, allowing the visitors to score three times. It was 4-3 with six minutes to play, and Roddy Georgeson's 86th minute goal was cancelled out two minutes later, before Billy Mitchell put a false sense of security on the scoreline by netting on the final whistle.

The new found purpose and confidence in the team was epitomised by the 2-1 home win over league leaders East Fife on New Year's Day, in front of a crowd of 8,000. That game marked the debut of former Hearts centre half Arthur Thomson, who certainly added solidity to the defence, but his last minute slip at Stenhousemuir the following day cost Rovers a point from a 3-3 draw. No one dwelt on that costly mistake in the days that followed in the aftermath of the Ibrox Disaster, which happened at the precise moment of Stenhousemuir's equaliser.

Successive wins over Forfar at home (3-2, after being 3-0 up in 50 minutes) and Brechin City away (4-1, this time Rovers scoring three in the last twenty minutes) saw the team elevated to fourth position, and very much in contention for promotion. Few gave Rovers much hope at Perth in the Third Round of the Scottish Cup. St Johnstone were not flattered by their third place in the First Division (above Rangers) and Rovers were without Benny McGuire, who followed up his two weeks suspension earlier in the season for the Methil sending off, by a 28 day ban for accumulating four cautions.

Jim Pearson and Kenny Aird put Willie Ormond's team deservedly 2-0 ahead after 51 minutes, and the tie looked over, but Saints were profligate in front of goal and allowed Rovers to equalise with goals from George Innes and substitute Brian Cooper. The replay at Stark's Park three days later was a pulsating cup tie in the great traditions of the competition. Roddy Georgeson delighted the majority of the 8,438 crowd by putting Rovers ahead in 8 minutes, only for Benny Rooney to equalise six minutes later. Transfer listed Colin Sinclair, restored to a re-shuffled team in McGuire's absence, put Rovers ahead again two minutes later. John Connelly equalised on the stroke of half-time. In a frantic second half, Sinclair completed his hat-trick in 50 and 63 minutes, and a Henry Hall goal nine minutes from time ensured a thrilling finish, but Rovers hung on to reward great performances, both collectively and individually, with a 4-3 win. The Daily Record headline the following morning summed it up perfectly : "Super Sinclair is

Raith Hero".

The gargantuan efforts against St Johnstone were felt the following Saturday, when the 3,700 home crowd were dismayed to see Stirling Albion win 2-1. Worse was to come at East Stirling the following week, a 4-2 defeat leaving Rovers adrift of the promotion race. Clyde visited Stark's Park in the next round of the cup, and the two teams managed barely half a dozen attempts at goal between them in a damp squib of a game, which finished 1-1. Legend has it that McGuire, restored to the team on the completion of his SFA suspension, enjoyed himself rather too much over the weekend and had to be extricated from police custody prior to the replay at Shawfield, where Rovers gave a marvellous performance to claim another First Division scalp. Georgeson and Sinclair were again the scorers, restricting themselves to one apiece in a 2-0 win, the Daily Record showing a lack of originality with "Super Sinclair Smashes Clyde". On the same evening, Celtic won at East End Park, to set up a quarter final tie with Rovers at Parkhead.

A poor Dumbarton performance was punished 3-0 at Stark's Park, but Rovers' faint promotion hopes were finally extinguished with a 2-0 defeat at Albion Rovers. They fared no better at Celtic Park, outclassed 7-1 (4-0 down at half time), the only consolation being a share of the 32,000 gate. The cheque was barely cleared by the time Jim Dempsey was signed from Hamilton Accies for £4,000. The season meandered, aimlessly, to a close. Benny McGuire asked for a transfer after being dropped, 34 year old Davie Sneddon was, optimistically, put on the transfer list, and a £3500 bid for Colin Sinclair from Walsall was turned down. Brian Cooper, who missed the drubbing at Parkhead, had a cartilage and cyst removed from his knee, but had more difficulty resisting attempts by Bill Baxter to sell him to East Fife, where his brother was one of the directors. A swap deal for Jamieson and Finlayson was agreed by the manager, but the Board wanted an additional £2,000, and Cooper remained at Stark's Park, until the next attempt to transfer him to Methil.

At the end of the season, eight players were freed from the bloated squad, four (including Sinclair and McGuire) were open to transfer, and Donald Urquhart was among five S signings who were retained. Before the end of season trip to Lloret de Mar, where matches were scheduled against Lloret and Gerona, full back Alex Jamieson was signed on a free transfer from East Fife.

There was more movement of players in June and July. In came centre half Dick Staite, freed by Clyde, veteran wing half Jimmy Thomson from Dunfermline, and former Hibs, Arsenal and Scotland winger Johnny McLeod, who had been playing in Belgium. Several youngsters were also signed, but Billy Mitchell was signed for Celtic by Jock Stein, amid great publicity, for £1000, and Colin Sinclair was sold to Darlington for £5000. There was a further blow when Alex Gray emigrated to Australia. The last signing

of the summer was unquestionably the best, Scottish junior international winger Malcolm Robertson, from Penicuik Athletic.

The new formation failed to gell. Up front, Wallace and Georgeson, though clever players, lacked the height and bulk of the departed Sinclair and Mitchell. Brian Cooper was not restored to full fitness until September, and the team looked decidedly pedestrian at times with Staite, Thomson and McLeod struggling with the bagatelle style of play in the Second Division.

Results, and performances, were disappointing, verging on dire. After a promising 2-1 opening day victory over East Fife in the League Cup, only two of the next fourteen games were won. Ian Lister, freed by St Mirren, was brought back to the club, and Bobby Reid and Arthur Thomson were restored to the side. One of the victories was an unexpected 6-1 victory over Dumbarton at Stark's Park, but it was followed by a defeat and a draw, before three wins in four games gave the dwindling band of supporters something to shout about. Brian Cooper moved back to replace Jim Thomson as sweeper, where he would excel for several seasons.

After two more defeats, Brechin were beaten 4-0 at Glebe Park, but Stirling Albion won 5-2 in Kirkcaldy on 27th November. The following day, manager Bill Baxter was summoned to a meeting with the Chairman, where he tendered his resignation.

He told the Fife Free Press : "If I got the chance again, I would be a bit harder with some of the players. I feel that some players let themselves and the club down. They set themselves a standard with cup wins last season against St Johnstone and Clyde but they didn't maintain this standard. They were not prepared to work at it."

After Bert Herdman's sixteen years in charge, Rovers had gone through six managers in ten years, and the seventh was no stranger to the hot seat at Stark's Park. Two days after Baxter left, George Farm returned to Raith Rovers to work with the odd collection of veterans and promising youths, and an empty bank account.

Playing much the same eleven as Baxter's latter selections, Rovers won three and drew one of their next four matches. January proved to be more problematic, a draw on New Year's Day at Cowdenbeath, defeat at Albion Rovers two days later, and a home draw with Queen's Park, before an unconvincing 2-1 win over Brechin City in the second round of the Scottish Cup.

George Farm identified the cause of the poor start to the New Year. He criticised the modern player for "over indulgence" during the festivities, believing that "he seems to find it more and more difficult to remember his obligations to his club and supporters at this time of year."

A 2-0 defeat at St Mirren gave little hope for the visit of Farm's former employers, Dunfermline Athletic, in the third round of the Cup, but the latent promise of Malcolm Robertson burst to fruition and he rounded off

TOM BROWN
A skinny, angular forward with a awkward running style, he nevertheless had a quick turn of pace, good ball control and had an eye for goal. He may have been unfashionable, but he was very effective, and a good servant to the club.

1971

141

East Fife wanted to sign Murray McDermott, who was on the open to transfer list at start of 1972/73, but they could not agree terms with the goalkeeper.

At the end of October 1972, four players were under consideration for signing : Alex Gray in Australia, Colin Sinclair at Darlington, ex Dunfermline player Bert Paton and Ernie Hannigan of Queen of the South. A month later, an attempt was made to bring Bobby Stein (East Stirling) back as centre half, but he declined to return to Stark's Park. Other centre halves mentioned were Jackie McGrory of Kilmarnock, Drew Rogerson of St Mirren, Jim Craig of Celtic and Ian Campbell of Ayr United

On 6th November 1972, it was resolved at a Board Meeting that there were to be no women on the team bus.

George Farm was fined £50 by the SFA on 28th December 1972 for an article in the match programme of 11th November.

*1973 - Greyhound track at Oriel Road closed
1974 - West Mill closed ; the Odeon cinema in the High Street was destroyed in a fire on Boxing Day, and the Rio Cinema in St Clair street closed.*

JIM DEMPSEY
The hard-working, hard-tackling midfield player was no mean footballer, and in a manner replicated by Donald Urquhart in later years, when he was on form, the team invariably played well.

During the power restrictions which crippled many clubs in the winter months of season 1973/74, Rovers were at least able to do some training, thanks to a generator installed before the floodlights were erected in 1960. That wasn't powerful enough for the full floodlights, but coped admirably with the training lights on the roof of the stand and the railway enclosure. These lights had not been used for 13 years when they were tried out in November 1973, and after replacing a few worn-out bulbs, they were used for evening training sessions – until the supply of fuel for the generator ran out, again due to strike action and government restrictions. Nevertheless, Rovers were not as badly hit as many other clubs by the industrial trouble which crippled the country - but the bad weather more than made up for that.

A Second Division Reserve League had been formed, but the midweek, floodlit fixtures had no sooner commenced than floodlit football was banned due to the Fuel Emergency.

At the end of the season, it was decided to support Ballingry Juveniles as a nursery club, but five months later the arrangement was moved to Leven Royals.

a superb individual performance with the second goal of a well merited 2-0 win.

There was better to come in the fourth round. Dumbarton had not looked back following their 6-1 defeat in the League at Stark's Park in September, and were sitting atop the Division. Boghead once again lived up to its name, but Robertson's performance transcended the conditions, and the rest of the team were not far behind as they won 3-0. Kilmarnock were drawn to visit Stark's Park in the quarter finals, and many optimists in the 10,815 crowd were relishing the prospect of a semi final appearance, but the First Division team was too strong, individually and collectively, for a battling Rovers team. Dick Staite's tap-in goal (which made it 2-1) proved to be merely a consolation in a 3-1 defeat.

As happened the year before, the remaining League fixtures were fulfilled in desultory fashion and Rovers finished the season three places lower, in 11th position in the 19 club Division. The cup run had provided George Farm with some working capital, however, and he spent it on signing on fees and wages as he married the better parts of the team he inherited, with some astute signings. Unfortunately, Kenny Lindsay was lost to the club when he emigrated to Australia.

The strong tackling Billy McLaren was signed from East Fife, and the skilful Ron Selway came from Dundee. The national press seemed more excited than the fans about 31 year old Joe Baker signing for Rovers, his brief return to the scene of his former glories at Hibs having brought only disappointment. They changed their mind when they saw him play. To balance this experience, Donald Urquhart was brought in at full back, and Tom Brown made a seamless transition from Fife Junior football at outside right.

A change of format in the League Cup meant that two Second Division clubs were grouped with two First Division sides, and Rovers opened with four successive defeats, followed by four straight wins, which included the opening two League games. There would be a valid claim for saying the fates conspired against Rovers in the League Cup. Joe Baker missed the first two games thanks to a SFA suspension incurred during his spell at Easter Road, and he lasted just 15 minutes of his competitive debut at Falkirk before going off with a badly gashed leg. Warming up for that match, Bobby Reid dislocated his finger and was replaced by Murray McDermott.

The defence knitted into a better unit, anchored by the muscular presence of Jim Dempsey in midfield. Baker quickly found his scoring touch, and revelled in the service he was given from midfield players who could pass a ball, two conventional wingers, and a quick, mobile strike partner in Gordon Wallace.

The man who was in England's extended World Cup squad just six years earlier displayed a natural footballer's ability that had not been seen at Stark's Park since

Jim Baxter left for Rangers ; and boy, could he score ! A hat-trick in a 3-2 win at home to Forfar, five in an 8-1 home win over Berwick, four in a 6-4 win at Brechin, and singles and doubles aplenty.

Mid October brought a reminder that the team weren't quite the finished article. Fellow promotion candidates Clyde and Dunfermline defeated Rovers on successive Saturdays, and while results and performances remained good, and occasionally brilliant, lapses such as a 2-0 defeat at home to Stenhousemuir, and a 1-0 defeat at Forfar on New Year's Day, imposed a regular dose of reality.

In search of the final, elusive piece of the jigsaw, Farm brought in experienced midfield players Ernie Hannigan, Gordon Whitelaw and Ian McPhee for brief trial periods. Former Morton and Dundee United centre half Billy Gray was brought in to replace Dick Staite, who had retired abruptly, and Peter Donaldson stepped up from Haddington Athletic to share full back duties with the dependable Tommy Hislop, and young Donald Urquhart.

There was no distraction from the Cup this year. Stenhousemuir were surmounted with some difficulty, and a replay, in the second round, and a valiant effort at First Division Motherwell was not enough to improve on a 2-1 defeat. Much more important was the failure to beat Clyde at Stark's Park the following Saturday, the League leaders content with a 0-0 draw.

The next five League matches were won, with Baker and Georgeson sharing out most of the goals between them, and Rovers fans were dreaming of a late run into one of the two promotion places. The fifth victory proved to be pyrrhic, however. Eric Smith had transformed the fortunes of perennial strugglers Hamilton Accies since taking over as manager, and they were in no mood to surrender their own unbeaten run. Their robust tactics had early success ; an over-the-ball tackle saw Joe Baker carried off after just 18 minutes. It proved to be the undoing of both teams ; Baker was out for the rest of the season, and Tom Brown moved into the centre and scored both goals in a battling 2-0 victory, ably assisted by a storming performance on the right wing by substitute Donald Urquhart.

Without Baker, and with McLaren and Wallace also picking up injuries, only one point was gained from the next three matches. Clyde and Dunfermline kept on gathering points and although Rovers finished in third place, they were five points short of promotion.

The team lacked a vital, elusive ingredient, and most of all a large dose of good fortune, which would have bridged the gap and given them what they deserved, individually and collectively – promotion to the top division. Farm admitted as much at the end of the season as he searched for a dominant centre half, midfield playmaker and a big centre forward to play off Joe Baker. Despite the disappointment of failure, it was a hugely enjoyable season of free flowing, attacking football, and an rare opportunity to see a master footballer at work in Joe Baker.

If the manager had shown a sure touch in team building before the start of 1972/73, his approach to 1973/74 was much less convincing. There could be no complaints about his analysis : the addition of a centre half, a midfield player and a centre forward could provide promotion. The chosen recruits, Drew Rogerson, Wilson Wood and Jimmy Jack respectively, did not improve the team, however.

Tom Brown was somewhat unjustly dropped in preference to a youngster signed from juvenile football in Dundee, Alex Rice, who certainly looked the part, but his early form fizzled out before the end of August. There was some back luck too ; Malcolm Robertson astonished everyone by announcing that he was having a cartilage operation during the summer, and didn't start a League game until late September. Jim Dempsey's season lasted just 50 minutes before he broke his leg in a League Cup tie at Dumfries.

Farm's biggest blunder was the free transfer handed to Roddy Georgeson. The blond striker would have struggled in the top division, and he had an infuriating habit of wandering into offside positions, but he worked hard and contributed double-digit goals every season. For several years thereafter, he came back to haunt Rovers in the jerseys of Montrose, Dunfermline and Meadowbank.

His replacement was Jimmy Jack, a prolific scorer and strong leader of the line for many years with Arbroath, but he failed to forge a partnership with Baker, who preferred an equally deft and mobile partner rather than a target man, and after thirteen appearances (which, in fairness, brought seven goals) he was freed to join Bath City.

Bert Graham, freed by Rangers, and Bobby Clelland from Stirling Albion, brought little improvement to the team, and Wilson Wood, who required the SFA to adjudicate on which of the two contracts he had signed would take effect, the Raith Rovers one or the Hamilton Accies one, proved to be a disappointing replacement for another premature free transfer, Billy McLaren. The combative midfielder paid the price for indifferent form in his debut season as he struggled to regain fitness after a series of injuries, but went on to have a long career in Scottish football, including spells in the top division.

Very much on the plus side was the introduction of Billy Brown at full back, and winger Ronnie Duncan, although it did mean that the fans saw little of Donald Urquhart, and had to wait until Jack left before Tom Brown was restored to the forward line.

Misfortunes, misjudgement and malfunctions meant that the season got off to a disappointing start, although there was the unaccustomed luxury of qualification from the League Cup section, thanks to a change of rules which allowed two teams to advance.

Rovers gave a tremendous performance in the first leg at Easter Road, a goal three minutes from time separating the teams in a thrilling 3-2 defeat. To the delight of everyone in the 10,693 crowd, Joe Baker put Rovers 2-1 ahead in 50 minutes, only for Pat Stanton to equalise ten minutes later. Eddie Turnbull's marvellous Hibs side won 2-0 in the second leg at Stark's Park.

Before the home League match with St Mirren on 29th September, Chairman Rankin Grimshaw addressed the players on their poor start to the season. They the lost 2-4. Rovers were well off the promotion pace before they clicked into gear towards the end of October, a 1-1 draw at Kilmarnock followed by four successive victories. New Year proved to be a sobering experience, however, with a 4-0 defeat at League leaders Airdrie on 29th December, and a 2-1 reverse at home to Cowdenbeath on New Year's Day, when only 2,500 turned up.

The three-day week, imposed by Edward Heath's Government as they battled with striking unions, and a cold snap meant that Rovers played no League matches for four weeks during January. Stark's Park's first ever Sunday fixture was in the third round of the Scottish Cup, when Rovers took a 2-0 lead over Morton within the first 20 minutes. The First Division team fought back, however, and equalised with five minutes to go. Two days later, a 1.30 kick off on a Tuesday afternoon at Cappielow (the use of floodlights being banned during the Fuel crisis) ended goal-less after 120 minutes, Dempsey and Mitchell being sent off during extra time. The second replay was arranged for neutral Tynecastle the following Sunday afternoon, 24 hours after both clubs fulfilled scheduled League matches. With fixtures already lost to the weather, and the uncertain prospect of midweek floodlit football being re-established, the clubs and authorities wanted no more postponements.

After a 2-2 draw at home to Montrose on the Saturday (attendance just 1037, with many fans having to work as part of their three-day-week), Rovers had the best of the third match against Morton at Hearts' ground. An uncharacteristic slip by Brian Cooper led to the only goal of the game, a minute before half time.

Unlike previous seasons, Rovers' exit from the Scottish Cup was followed by excellent form in the League, with just one defeat in the final sixteen matches of the season. The run coincided with Jim Dempsey's return from injury, the true value of the much criticised defensive midfielder only realised in his absence. Dempsey's return was to some extent diluted by the retirement, through injury, of Ron Selway. Billy Mitchell had been brought back to the club, and there were brief appearances from winger Archie Lindsay, striker John Simpson, and, in the closing weeks of the season, former

MALCOLM ROBERTSON

At the Board Meeting of 16th September 1974, Brian Cooper was suspended following incidents at Stranraer five days earlier.

A Second Division Select played their Italian counterparts in an 'international' match in Pescara on December 30th 1974. Rovers' only representative in the pool of 28 players for a trial match at Brockville on 9th December was Malcolm Robertson. Unfortunately, Malcolm was then under SFA suspension, was not permitted to play in the trail, and therefore was not included in the 18 man squad which travelled to Italy

The Second Division Reserve League was again arranged, and Rovers finished second bottom of the first round of seven matches. After three matches were played of the second round (reduced to six games due to the resignation of Cowdenbeath) Rovers followed their example.

In late November, Hamilton Accies offered Neil Hood in exchange for Jim Dempsey, turned down because Hood lived in Ayrshire. In January, Dempsey was offered to Cowdenbeath in exchange for Evan Stewart and David Cairns, and in early February Dempsey plus £1000 went to Stirling Albion in exchange for Gus McMillan.

FOOTBALLER OF THE YEAR
SUNDAY MAIL
Presentation of REX STATUETTE

To Willie McNAUGHT
CAPTAIN RAITH ROVERS F.C. & SCOTTISH INTERNATIONALIST

❋❋❋❋❋❋❋❋❋

RIO CINEMA KIRKCALDY
SUNDAY, 17th FEBRUARY, 1957
PROGRAMME . . . . . . PRICE 6d.

Two Raith Rovers players have received the considerable acolade of being named Scottish Footballer of the Year.
In response to the introduction of the English Player of the Year Award, by the Football Writers' Association south of the border, R.E. Kingsley, 'Rex' of the Sunday Mail, chose a Scottish Player of the Year at the end of every calendar year.
The first recipient, in 1951, was Gordon Smith of Hibs, followed by Willie Thornton (Rangers), Bobby Evans (Celtic), Jimmy McGowan of Partick Thistle in 1954 and George Young, the Rangers and Scotland captain.
In 1956, the choice was Willie McNaught.
'Rex' described the Rovers captain as the "most graceful kicker of a ball in Scotland. In his fifteen years as a professional footballer Willie McNaught has never once been cautioned or reprimanded by a referee. His will control is equalled only by his ball control.
No footballer I have ever seen can play that ball with more elegance and easy grace - especially in a defensive position. He has been honoured his his country on 11 occasions. But you and I know very well that had he been playing with one of the more fashionable clubs in the West, this would have been more than doubled. For the setting can enhance even the purest gem.
There are no dramatics about the Rovers' captain. But great humanity ... and sportsmanship.

Cowdenbeath and Stirling winger Bobby Lyall. Joe Baker, very much a marked man in his second season, was not so prolific, scoring 15 goals (12 less than his debut season at significant personal cost, as he was on an extra bonus with every goal he scored), but Malcolm Robertson scored a commendable 21 League goals, and the under-rated Tom Brown contributed another 11. It is a measure of how indifferent was the injury afflicted early season form that the splendid run in the last third of the season merely lifted Rovers to fifth place in the League, a distant 13 points from promotion.

Murray McDermott ascribed the disappointment of failing to improve on the previous season, to the beginning of the end of a managerial career. "We had a good team in 1972/73, and finished third, but the extra push didn't come the following season and we finished fifth, a bit flat. Maybe George Far, was beginning to lose his effect on players – his style of management and motivation perhaps only had a short term impact on players. Jim Dempsey broke his leg early in the season and we lost our way a little bit. Jim was a good guy, a real enthusiast, a real one-hundred percenter, and not a bad player."

By no means for the first time in the club's history, a late run of good results at the end of one season proved to be a false dawn of optimism once the new season got under way. Understandably, George Farm made few changes over the summer. Donald Urquhart was restored to the team, in midfield, full back Jimmy Brown was signed on a free transfer from Dunfermline, and John Hislop stepped up from Tranent Juniors in attack. To the dismay of supporters, he was a replacement, rather than a partner, for Joe Baker, who retired on a point of principle following a disagreement over terms with the manager. His last match was a 60 minute appearance in the pre-season friendly against Preston North End at Stark's Park on 7th August, in which his former England colleague Bobby Charlton, Preston's new player-manager, graced the Stark's Park turf and scored the last of Preston's four first half goals.

Results in the League Cup section were, once again, depressingly disappointing, unbeaten at home (wins against Berwick and Hamilton, and a draw with Queen of the South) and three away defeats. The encouragement of a 2-0 win at Cowdenbeath in the opening League match was followed by a home defeat by East Fife, and two away, goal-less, draws. A midweek win over Stranraer was followed by four defeats and a draw, leaving Rovers in 16th position by mid October. For once, it was not essential to finish in the top two positions in the League. League reconstruction into three divisions (which Rovers had voted against) meant that a top six finish would be sufficient to qualify for the middle division ; below that, and Rovers would be spending (at least) a season amongst the real minnows of Scottish football.

George Farm had put his faith in improving the squad of 19 part-time

footballers in an enlarged coaching staff which comprised Bert Paton, Willie Benvie and Bill McTavish, and physiotherapist Bob Methven. The manager advocated "a sophisticated scouting system to ensure a continuous flow of younger players into the club is essential for a part-time club like ourselves."

Paton, who had made such an impact on his arrival as coach at Stark's Park midway through the previous season, left to manage Cowdenbeath at the end of September, and took McTavish with him. He succeeded Andy Matthew at Central Park, who resigned after being "sick and disillusioned with modern football and footballers."

Defeats at Forfar (the hapless Angus club's only victory of the season), Berwick and Hamilton were followed by a home draw with Queen's Park, when the crowd dipped below 1000. On Thursday, October 17th, Farm tendered his resignation. Never short of a quotable comment, he let rip after leaving Stark's Park for the second time.

"I should feel miserable," he said, "but I just feel relieved. Football has problems at every level, but the attitude and behaviour of players both on and off the field has finally convinced me that there is no long-term future for club managers. The game itself is in grave danger as a spectator sport." Farm referred to a "nucleus of players" on the Raith staff who had not shown the required interest on the field. "There has been a dramatic change among players in the last two or three years," he said, "I could see the signs when I was at Dunfermline. The customers are not interested about what goes on behind scenes. They want to be entertained by players and the final responsibility must be taken by teams. Unfortunately, some players don't have the talent or the inclination."

Directors Bobby Reid and Johnny Urquhart took charge of the team for the match at Stirling Albion (which was lost 2-1) and signed experienced centre half Jim Taylor from Forfar Athletic. They also asked club captain Brian Cooper to return to Stark's Park – he walked out following a bitter argument with Farm – and both played with distinction for the remainder of the season.

To Cowdenbeath's chagrin, Farm's replacement was his former coach, Bert Paton, who left Central Park after a month in charge following which he could boast that he was the only unbeaten manager in that club's history. Bill McTavish once again followed Paton, and Cowdenbeath replaced them with Dan McLindon, who appointed as his assistant one Francis Connor.

Paton's appointment did not prove to be a happy one for any of the parties involved. Results improved, but not by much, and certainly not enough to make up the leeway from the bad start to the season. The team was far from settled as the manager sought to improve it by replacing the players he inherited (and had previously coached). Tom Brown, Donald Urquhart and recent signing Bobby Conn from Hearts were dropped, Willie Brown was injured and Wilson Wood eased out.

Several players came in for short spells, without making an impact. One of them was Gus McMillan, a striker from Stirling Albion, who failed to score in five appearances, the last at centre half. Much more significantly, he arrived at Stark's Park on a swap deal with Jim Dempsey, who went on to give many years of sterling service to Stirling, and then Hamilton Accies.

League newcomers Meadowbank Thistle beat Rovers 1-0 at the Commonwealth Stadium on 11th January for a rare victory, and a fortnight later Queen of the South put Rovers out of the Scottish Cup. The following week, high-flying Hamilton Accies were beaten at Stark's Park, proving that the players were capable of better performances. The next seven League matches brought two draws and only one win, and a Board Meeting on 24th March confronted the looming reality of a season in the third division, and a mounting overdraft.

Bill McTavish was dismissed on a "last in, first out" basis. Paton demanded McTavish's reinstatement and on the directors' refusal, he resigned "over a matter of principle". He later said, "I was left with no alternative but to quit as the directors went over my head and made a decision to sack one of the members of the staff. They said the reason was finance, but that doesn't matter, it was the way they did it without even asking me. If I had let the directors get away with that they would have walked all over me in future. I appreciate they are under pressure because of the club's debt but they could have gone about it differently. I am shocked and disillusioned and the whole affair leaves a very bad taste. [McTavish found out about his dismissal when he opened his wage packet and found his National Insurance Card inside.]

"The Board approached me for the job and I was promised complete control, but this has not been the case. I had to suffer constant interference at all levels and the ridiculous sacking of Bill McTavish was the last straw. I was employed to run the team. I was told to appoint the staff I wanted and get rid of the staff I didn't want. The playing staff, coaching and scouting were all to be my responsibility. It should have been as simple as that, but after 15 years in professional football the directors tried to tell me my job. I would not have dreamed of telling them how to run their known particular businesses. Also, on Monday as well as the sacking of Bill McTavish, I was told by the directors that the club would not be running a reserve team. I realise the lack of money is the cause, but I could have been involved in the discussion and the decision. And the Board then submitted to me a list of the players they wanted freed. I could not tolerate such a set-up and just had to get out."

Chairman Rankin Grimshaw responded by saying "I am not complaining about the way everything has turned out. Things have not been going well for the club and we can hardly get any worse. We are in debt but Mr Paton spent something like £7,000 on players in five months and we have nothing to show for the money." The Rovers Chairman was a very visible target for media commentators. He was President of the S.F.A. and had been critical of Willie Ormond's performance as Scotland manager. He and the ever-quotable George Farm exchanged insults in the press – with the major loser the image of the club.

Unsurprisingly, results did not improve to the end of the season, but on Tuesday April 22nd, Rovers' third manager of the season was appointed, Andy Matthew completing the merry-go-round of managerial movements between Cowdenbeath and Kirkcaldy. Born and bred in the town, Matthew said "The directors have assured me that I will be in complete control and I am looking forward to the challenge, having got back my appetitie for the game after being out of the scene for a few months now. Raith are in a false position at the moment as some of the teams above us are not as good as we can be. But that's all in the past. We must now plan for next season, and promotion to the First Division."

That promotion campaign started with the traditional failure to progress in the League Cup, and was followed by draws in the opening two League matches, but some enterprising play was matched by a refusal to accept defeat, and it quickly became apparent that things were on the move (upwards) at Stark's Park.

The slimmed-down playing staff did not encourage tinkering with team selections, and the settled eleven were assisted by a relatively injury-free season. The defence was experienced and solid, Murray McDermott in goal, full backs Jim and Billy Brown, with Jim Taylor and Brian Cooper in the centre. Tom Brown and Donald Urquhart complimented each other in midfield, the former being replaced midway through the season by Davie Hunter, recuited from Kirkcaldy YM Juniors. Malcolm Robertson and Ronnie Duncan on the wing provided the ammunition for Gordon Wallace and Bert Graham.

All of these players were at the club during the disasterous 1974-75 season – perhaps it was consistency of management that was required, rather than from the players. In early December, Malcolm Robertson was sold to Ayr United for £12,000, John Hislop taking his place in the team, and shortly afterwards Tom McFarlane, a skilful midfield player from Comrie Colliery Juniors, was added to the pool.

Concerns about the effect Robertson's departure would have on the team were ill-founded ; the next nine matches were all won, including a tricky away tie at Peterhead in the first round of the Scottish Cup, the visit of League leaders Clydebank in the second round, and First Division Arbroath in the third. Ironically, Robertson's transfer improved the team, who could not longer rely on just "giving the ball to Malcolm" in the hope

These words came from the programme produced for the presentation ceremony, held at the Rio Cinema in St Clair Street on Sunday 17th February 1957.

Subsequent winners included Alex Parker (Falkirk), Dave Mackay (Hearts), Harry Haddock (Clyde), Willie Toner (Kilmarnock) and John Cumming (Hearts).

The Scottish Football Writers' Association presented their first award to Billy McNeill of Celtic in 1965, followed by John Greig (Rangers) and Ronnie Simpson (Celtic). The first non-Old Firm player to win the award was Gordon Wallace, following his goalscoring exploits in 1967/68. He received the trophy at the Football Writers' Annual Dinner in Glasgow on Sunday 28th April 1968.

The following year, the award went to Bobby Murdoch of Celtic, before Pat Stanton became only the second winner from outwith the Old Firm in 1970.
He was followed by Martin Buchan (Aberdeen), Dave Smith (Rangers), George Connelly (Celtic), the Scotland World Cup Squad in 1974, Sandy Jardine and John Greig (Rangers), Danny McGrain (Celtic), Derek Johnstone (Rangers)

BERT GRAHAM

Manager Andy Matthew missed pre-season training and the first friendly match of 1975/76, as he was on a three week holiday with his family. This had been booked following his departure from Cowdenbeath, with no expectation of such an early return to football management.

After a week's training at Bramall Lane, Ronnie Duncan was the subject of a transfer bid from Sheffield United in mid May 1976. Having been told by Rovers that their initial £15,000 bid was too low, United doubled it – only to be told that it was still too low.

The fourth round draw for the Scottish Cup was held in the boardroom at Stark's Park, immediately after the third round match against Arbroath. 14 year old Stewart Reid, son of Director Bobby, and 13 year old Brian Leigh, son of former player and Development Club organiser Andy, drew the numbered balls which saw Rovers travel to Montrose in the fourth round, when Stewart's dad came out of retirement to play in goal.

Jock Grimshaw retired after 15 years as groundsman at Stark's Park during 1976/77. He had previously taken care of the "Big Green" at Kirkcaldy Bowling Club.

On 21st April 1977, the Board agreed to pay 50% of the cost of goalkeeper Murray McDermott's contact lenses

that his dribble would end in a goal, or a penalty. The close passing game which developed, post-Robertson, proved to be very successful for the remainder of the season.

The fans responded to this run – unbeaten in League and Scottish Cup – and 6,626 watched Gordon Wallace score the only goal of the Arbroath cup tie, a far cry from the 475 who saw Andy Matthew's first match as manager at the end of the previous season.

"Football Focus" on national BBC television caught on to the last unbeaten League run in Britain and sent a camera unit to the home match against Queen's Park on 31st January, with the inevitable consequence, a 2-0 defeat, the first in the League. It is often the reaction to a defeat which matters more than the loss itself, and despite losing an early goal at Stranraer the following Saturday, Rovers put in a solid, professional performance to win 3-1.

Billy Brown later recalled the fate-tempting publicity surrounding the Queen's Park match : "The television camera was in the dressing room before the game, and it was definitely a feeling of impending disaster. We were 1-0 down within about eight minutes of the kick off and we never got going at any stage of the game. That's sod's law in football, as soon as you open your mouth you tend to put your foot in it. We got back on the rails afterwards, and we had a good team at the time, playing good football."

High-flying First Division team Montrose were at home in the fourth round of the cup, and Rovers hopes of another "giant killing" were dealt a blow when Murray McDermott succumbed to the influenza epidemic which caused the postponement of the previous Saturday's League match against Stirling Albion. With no reserve goalkeeper on the books, director Bobby Reid dusted off his boots and let no one down at Links Park, but a below par Rovers team were beaten 2-1.

Clydebank and Alloa had kept pace with Rovers at the top of the Second Division throughout the season. As the shortened League programme reached its early finish, there was little margin for error, and that was expended in a 0-0 home draw with lowly East Stirling, Jim Brown missing a twice-taken penalty. It was the last falter on the journey to promotion, however. Gordon Wallace scored the only goal of the match at Stirling, and Berwick Rangers were beaten 3-0 in a midweek match at Stark's Park to set up a "winner takes all" match at Alloa. The fixture suffered a late postponement due to a flooded pitch, but the following week, on 31st March, Rovers fans made up the majority of the 3400 crowd which saw a 64th minute Davie Hunter goal win both points, and promotion.

It was a remarkable transformation, from the same set of players who had so signally failed the previous season, and a thoroughly enjoyable campaign of freeflowing, attacking football, built on the foundation of a sound defence.

The final League matches were played in the middle of a qualifying section for the Spring Cup, a hurriedly-arranged tournament for First and Second Division clubs to give them fixtures in March and April after the completion of just 26 League games. Rovers extended their winning ways into their Spring Cup section, and gave a good account of themselves in drawing 2-2 with First Division Dumbarton at Stark's Park in the first leg of the knockout stage – a rare home fixture on a Links Market Saturday. Two days later, the effects of an intense end of season caught up with the team, and they finished the season with an uncharacteristic 4-0 defeat at Boghead.

The simple football philosophy which worked so well for Rovers in the Second Division, was ill equipped for the far more organised opposition in the First Division. Andy Matthew told one newspaper : "I have always felt there was too much nonsense talked by people involved in football. Too many people at club and international level are putting too many airy fairy ideas into the game. They lay down tactics for practically every player, forecast what their opponents will do – and end up giving their own men very little chance to express themselves on the field.

"Of course a certain amount of planning is required. I see my job as finding the right blend, getting craftsmen into certain positions, grafters into others. But once I have picked the side I just give them their heads and the freedom to get to grips with the game the way it happens and not as we think it might happen.

"We have no time for blackboards or deep tactics here – that is what is killing the appeal of the modern game for the fans. Here, I pick a boy for a certain job because I know that is what he is good at and apart from the broad outline of strategy I then just send them all out to play the game in their own way."

Unfortunately for those laudable sentiments, Rovers were about to join what was arguably the strongest secondary Division in the history of the the Scottish League   Although Clydebank had pipped Rovers for the Championship, they had been beaten four times, and the other match drawn, but the Bankies upped their game, and their tactics, in the higher division, and thrived at the opposite end of the league table from their serial conquerors of the previous season.

Two experienced signings were added to the squad for the new season, former Rangers full back Willie Mathieson, at last signing for his home town club on a free transfer from Arbroath ; and Stewart Wheatley, a defensive midfield player freed by Falkirk.

The all-important momentum that was necessary for a successful season was never built as the team struggled from the outset. The only victory of the League Cup section was against Queen's Park ; Airdrie won 4-1 at Stark's Park, and Derek Whiteford ran rampage at Broomfield, scoring a hat-trick in a 7-1 demolition of a shell-shocked Rovers side. The opening twelve League matches

brought just one win, Brian Cooper scoring a late goal to beat Arbroath at Stark's Park.

The team, so confident and free-flowing the previous season in cup ties against several of the teams from the higher division, looked short of confidence, inspiration and fitness. Willie Brown returned from a long period of injury to displace Mathieson, who retired. The promising young Cowdenbeath centre forward Andy Harrow was purchased for £5,000, and the team was re-shuffled with Wheatley eased out of the team. Bert Graham and John Hislop took turns to partner Harrow up front.

Eventually, results took a slight turn for the better. East Fife were beaten 1-0 at Stark's Park, Davie Hunter's goal interrupting an afternoon of seven bookings and a sending off, and Falkirk were overcome 2-1 at Brockville, followed by a draw at Perth. The next five matches brought only one point, however, and Rovers were rooted in the relegation zone going into the Scottish Cup tie against Albion Rovers. They were the victims of a change of rules, which saw the promoted teams – rather than the relegated teams – included in the first two rounds, and a trip to Coatbridge was the consequence, having received a bye in the first round ballot. Gordon Wallace put the Kirkcaldy Rovers ahead in 34 minutes, but John Brogan started a career-long habit of scoring against them by equalising midway through the second half. Eleven minutes later, Jimmy Cant, a stalwart Arbroath player for many years who had been exchanged with Tom Brown (going to Montrose) in an attempt to add experience to the side, was caught in possession and the Coatbridge Rovers scored the winning goal.

With the exception of Harrow, the same team as the previous season found reserves of strength and resolve, and drew

the next two away games, then beat Dumbarton 3-1 at Stark's Park. A couple of defeats, including a 4-0 reverse at Dundee, slowed the revival, but results improved as winter turned to spring. Tom Houston came into the side at right back, adding to the youthful endeavour of the team,, but the fixture list worked against Rovers at the 'business end' of the season.

Rovers' last five matches were against St Mirren and Clydebank, both home and away, and a resurgent Morton, in third place. The first two clubs were disputing the championship, and in the circumstances Rovers probably did well to get two points (from a home win over Clydebank) from these four fixtures. The better results in March gave Rovers a chance of survival going into the final Saturday of the season ; they had to beat Morton at Stark's Park, and hope that either East Fife or St Johnstone would fail to win their fixtures. East Fife drew 3-3 at Dumbarton, and St Johnstone had an incredible 4-1 win at Dumfries. Despite the results elsewhere, Rovers would have stayed up had they beaten Morton, and hopes were high when Willie Brown opened the scoring from the penalty spot in 10 minutes. A very competent Morton team took a 3-1 lead by the 78th minute, but in a pulsating last five minutes Gordon Wallace scored for Rovers, McGhee for Morton, and, in the last minute, John Hislop completed the scoring. Rovers had battled valiantly, but the 4-3 defeat consigned them to a swift return to the basement division.

At various stages of Rovers' rally towards the end of 1976/77, glimpses were shown of some young players emerging from the restored reserve side. Tom Houston, Lennie McComb, Gordon Pettie and Chris Candlish would become first team regulars in

Pictured before the start of 1977/78 is the squad who, with a couple of notable additions, would win promotion to the First Division. The second half of the season would be overseen by another manager, in Willie McLean, however.

Back row, left to right : Chris Candlish, Jim Taylor, Scott Ferguson, Calum Frame, Murray McDermott, Gordon Pettie, Lennie McComb, Tom Houston and coach Jim Gillespie.

Middle row : Coach Willie Benvie, Davie Hunter, Gordon Wallace, Andy Harrow, Tom McFarlane, Donald Urquhart, John Hislop, Davie Thomson, coach Alex Kinninmonth and physiotherapist Bob Methven.

Front tow : Derek Steel, Brian McDonough, Adam Moffat, Graham McKay, manager Andy Matthew, Ian Wildridge, George Purvis, Ronnie Duncan and Jimmy Brown.

1975 - Nairn & Williamson taken over by Unilever ; Barnet & Morton's department store in the High Street became House of Fraser ; Kirkcaldy Town Council ceased to exist after several centuries, to be replaced by Kirkcaldy District Council, which took in a larger area of Fife, including Glenrothes

IAN STEEN

A broken leg cut short Willie Penman's 1945/46 season, when Jackie Stewart led the scoring charts with 17 goals in all first team games, although Arthur Woon was the top League goalscorer with ten.

Andy Young scored 17 in all games in 1946/47 before Penman returned with 22 League goals in 1947/48. At one point during 1948/49, Norrie Haywood's record looked in jeopardy, but Willie Penman had to settle for 35 goals in 29 League games, although his season's return of 58 (from 47 games) was three better than Haywood's total, thanks to 17 goals in nine League Cup ties as Rovers reached their second national final.

Goals were harder to come by in A Division, and nine were scored by both Penman and Allan Collins, before Andy Young took over again in 1950/51 with 18 League goals. No one reached double figures in 1951/52, Ernie Copeland scoring eight in the League plus one in the Penman Cup, but that started his domination of the goalscoring charts. He had 17 League goals in 1952/53, followed by 24, 11 (plus 9 more in 1954/55) and 17. In 1956/57, both Copeland and Bernie Kelly scored 24 League goals, the latter adding 13 more to Ernie's 9. Kelly also topped the list the following season with 14 League goals and eleven in other fixtures.

the Second Division, and central defender David Thomson was pressed into immediate service at the start of 1977/78, Brian Cooper walking out in protest over the cut in the weekly wage from £18 to £12. Murray McDermott and Gordon Wallace also refused to re-sign, although they later recanted.

Murray McDermott later explained why, every two years, he and Cooper appeared to be in dispute with the club. "One of the bones of contention that Brian and I had was that we had played many years for the club, and contributed quite a lot, or so we both thought. We used to see players come and go and get a lot of money, and do very little for the club. That was always at the back of our minds. Most pre-seasons, there would be one or two new players there who had been given good signing-on money. That was probably at the back of my mind, and I'm sure it was at the back of Brian's too, because he was a very good servant to Raith Rovers, and one of the most consistent players I played with. I can't remember him having a bad game."

Willie Brown suffered badly from a long-term injury, and the left back position was occupied by Davie Hunter, then another young reserve in Brian McDonough, and finally by Chris Candlish. It was already a young team, and getting younger, which perhaps explains why games were drawn which should have been won, and while the young defence conceded few goals, they were hard to find at the other end of the park.

The first half of the season will not be recalled by many as being a particularly successful period in the club's history, but only two of the opening 20 League matches were lost, at the unlikely venues of Forfar (on the opening day) and Brechin. The annual ignominy of the League Cup section was avoided, thanks to the competition being restructured into a two-legged, knock-out format. Rovers lost home and away to Arbroath in the first round, but an Andy Harrow goal won the Scottish Cup first round tie against Stenhousemuir. Gordon Wallace, who had endured an unhappy start to the season, joined his namesake at Dundee United with Rovers receiving £12,000.

Uncharacteristically, the festive period brought a dreadful sequence of results. Promotion challengers Dunfermline inflicted a 1-0 defeat at Stark's Park on Christmas Eve (goalscorer Roddy Georgeson) followed by a 2-1 home defeat by Forfar, Alex Brash scoring the winning goal – the ghosts of Christmas Past and Future haunting Rovers during the Carol season. A 2-1 win at Stenhousemuir on 2nd January provided some respite, but in the second round of the Cup, Rovers lost 6-0 at Berwick. They had played worse and won, but missed several chances at crucial points of the game, and enjoyed no luck on the day.

Andy Matthew did the honourable thing and resigned. Directors Bobby Reid and Johnny Urquhart completed the signing of Gordon Forrest from Alloa Athletic for £3,000, and he scored a hat-trick in a 7-1 win in the following Saturday – against Berwick

Rangers. Despite the scoreline, and the remarkable transformation in results within seven days, the match will be remembered by the 1489 spectators for Rovers' third goal, scored by Gordon Pettie.

His mazy run has been extended, and the number of players beaten increased, with each retelling over the succeeding years, but this is how the Fife Free Press described it : "In the 61st minute he collected a throw from McDermott, ran the entire length of the field, avoiding and shrugging off numerous tackles, and finally slipped the ball past Lyle."

Having failed to persuade Jim McLean to release Gordon Wallace from Dundee United to become player/manager at Stark's Park, the Board's second choice as replacement for Andy Matthew came as a mild surprise, but with a track record of achievement in the top division with Motherwell, there were few dissenting voices when Jim's brother Willie McLean was appointed on 26th January .

The element of organisation that was missing under the laissez-faire style of Andy Matthew was immediately imposed on the team, helped by the recruitment of the two experienced players who everyone acknowledged were badly needed by the eager, but youthful, team. And what two players ! Gordon Wallace, only recently excused first team duties at Dundee United after a distinguished spell across the road at Dens Park and a purposeful spell at Tannadice, was signed on February 9th He made an immediate impact, scoring twice in a 4-0 home win over Meadowbank as Rovers, and McLean, built an unbeaten run of nine matches. He looked like a player that had recently been playing two divisions higher ; skilful, intelligent and a natural finisher. His release from Dundee United came as a surprise to those who read Jim McLean's comments in the Daily Express on 23rd January, when he explained why Wallace would not be Rovers' new player manager : "We don't like to stand in the way of any player making a move like this, but we cannot afford to let Gordon go. He must figure in our plans for at least the rest of the season."

A measure of Wallace's class is that the difficulties he found in adjusting from full time team-mates in the Premier Division to part-time colleagues two divisions lower, did not show in his play. "It is always difficult for a full time player to go down a League, especially when one of my earlier games back was Meadowbank away at the Stadium. I had never played there and I must admit I thought I was playing on the moon ! There was nobody there, and I found it really difficult from playing in the Premier League before full grounds. I was very lucky in playing with Andy Harrow, who was my legs."

A month later, the vastly experienced midfield player Tommy Murray was signed, and he scored on his full debut in a 3-1 home win over Brechin. That was followed by a 1-1 draw at Falkirk in midweek, then a 1-0 reverse at Stranraer, the one and only defeat suffered by McLean that season. Two goals from

Gordon Wallace put Rovers ahead at Brockville in another midweek game, but the Bairns equalised on the final whistle, and wiped out Rovers' margin for error.

It wasn't needed. Forfar and Albion Rovers were both beaten 2-0 at Stark's Park, followed by narrow wins over Berwick (2-1 away) and Brechin, 1-0 at home, thanks to a Tommy Murray goal. In a delicious quirk of the fixture list, Rovers' destiny would be decided in the final two League matches of the season, away to both of their promotion challengers.

Victory at Shawfield on Wednesday, 26th April 1978, would put Rovers out of Dunfermline's reach. It was a tight, nervous game (at least on the terraces), but Wallace and Murray piloted their young charges through a tough fixture against the League leaders in which McDermott was outstanding behind a hard-pressed defence. In 32 minutes, Murray played a classic pass inside the full back for Ronnie Duncan to run onto. His cross was perfect for Andy Harrow, running into the penalty area, to rise majestically to bullet a horizontal header into the Clyde goal. It was a dramatic, flowing, classic goal fit to clinch promotion.

A win on Saturday at Dunfermline (which was achieved 2-0) and Clyde dropping a point at home to Stranraer (which they didn't) would have added the Championship, but no-one was complaining about losing the flag on goal difference ; Rovers were moving up again.

The euphoria which entranced Raith Rovers and their supporters following the promotion campaign slowly dissipated during a low-key preparation for 1978-79. Willie McLean kept reminding everyone of the hard task ahead as Rovers sought to establish themselves in the First Division.

The team took a while to get into its stride. The only significant signing of the close season was centre half Alan Forsyth, who set a new club record when he was signed from Dundee United for £15,000. He initially looked uncomfortable in his new surroundings and carried a suspension over into the first two League matches. Gordon Wallace did not return from his summer season in the United States until mid August, Tom McFarlane and Tommy Murray were on holiday and Murray McDermott had his bi-annual signing dispute with the club ; all of which contributed to the Anglo Scottish Cup tie being lost, home and away, to Morton.

The opening League match brought a 3-1 defeat at Shawfield, Jacky Myles kicking off a playing career which would last almost 30 years (much of it in Lothian Junior circles) by scoring for both sides. Indeed, his career would long outlive Clyde's former home, but the memories of his 40 yard back-pass which sailed over McDermott and into the net in just 14 minutes have also endured. The absentees were back a week later, and Rovers swept Clydebank aside, going 4-0 up in 37 minutes, before allowing the visitors back into the game by conceding two goals. The opening spell produced attacking football of a quality that had not been seen from a Rovers team for many years, sublimely orchestrated by the veterans Wallace and Murray.

A two goal first leg lead was squandered in the League Cup tie against Queen's Park, and Rovers were fortunate to progress on penalty kicks. That was followed by an incredible tie against Montrose. Rovers played well in winning 3-0 at home, and extended their lead when Gordon Wallace scored after 5 minutes of the second leg at Links Park. Thereafter, the home side dominated the game, inspired by a magnificent performance by Bertie Miller on the wing. In the 79th minute, Montrose levelled the tie, and with Rovers desperately hanging on, they scored the winner two minutes later. It was a stunning turn around in fortunes, and as the supporters searched for a reason for the dramatic collapse, the usual rumours of bonus disputes were resurrected.

In the League, results, and performances, were inconsistent, superb displays of attacking football (a 5-0 win at Arbroath, 4-0 at home to Queen of the South and Montrose), balanced by several defeats, some of them undeserved. Rovers played superbly at Dumfries, with Murray and Duncan on the left wing forcing a virtuoso performance from the veteran Queens' goalkeeper Alan Ball, but Rovers lost 2-1.

The steady midfielder Robin Thomson, signed from Stirling Albion, make his debut in a 0-0 draw at Montrose just before a heavy and enduring frost effectively shut down Scottish football for a month. When Rovers resumed, they beat Queen of the South 3-0 at Stark's Park, which set them up nicely for the visit of Hearts the following week in the Scottish Cup.

There was an angry mood amongst the visiting support, who made up the majority of the 9640, all-ticket crowd. Their star player, Eamon Bannon, had just been sold to Chelsea, and their team was at the bottom of the Premier League. The rock hard, slippery pitch determined the course of the game. Malcolm Robertson revelled in the conditions, as did Tommy Murray who was an early substitute for the injured Donald Urquhart. Despite playing most of the good football on view, and testing Dunlop in the Hearts goal on a number of occasions, Rovers succumbed to the dazzling skills and balance of Robertson, whose two goals underlined his match-winning ability ; indeed he was the difference between the two teams.

As the Scottish Cup was lost at the first hurdle, so was the Manager ; Willie McLean left to take charge at Ayr United in the Premier Division. More bad weather meant that player-coach Gordon Wallace had to wait a full month for his semi-managerial baptism, at League leaders Kilmarnock, where Rovers gave a good account of themselves despite losing 2-1. Allan Forsyth, having been dropped in November, was beginning to look the part in defence.

The weather intervened again four

Anyone conducting a poll to select an all-time-greatest-team would be wasting their time asking a Raith Rovers supporter of the 1970s to pick the best goalkeeper they have ever seen. Most would select Murray McDermott, leaving the researcher to wonder why a part-time goalkeeper, who spend almost all of his career outwith the top division, would be in anyone's best-ever selection.

Those who saw the Edinburgh civil servant in action would know why. Content to be part-time, he was not a showy goalkeeper. A natural eye for the ball and pitch awareness meant that his footwork made difficult saves look easy. His unfussy, routine gathering of a cross-ball - the litmus test of any goalkeeper - was similarly undemonstrative. When he had to, Murray could fling himself around the goal, but his was a calm, reassuring presence, touched with the occasional ball-stopping brilliance.

Naturally fit and, after losing his "puppy fat" slim and lithe, he could have kept goal for Rovers for another ten years, shattering every appearance record, but the club was reluctant to recognise Murray's worth, and suffered the consequences of letting him go midway through his long playing career.

Rovers fans of the era are still touched by sadness at the mention of his name, as he died young, aged 53, in 2003. Those of us who watched him every week have not seen a better goalkeeper, at Stark's Park or anywhere else.

BOBBY FORD

The winter of 1978/79 was so severe that the first team friendly at Stark's Park against Dundee United on 9th January was played behind closed doors. Conditions were too bad to ask the public to pay for admission. Rovers lost 3-1.

Gordon Wallace was one of the four players nominated for the First Division Player of the Year Award by the Scottish Professional Players' Union for 1978/79. The others were Brian McLaughlin (Ayr United), John Bourke and Ian Gibson (Kilmarnock). On this occasion, Gordon was unsuccessful, McLaughlin winning the award.

Part of the Directors strategy to improve the financial situation at the club was to sell season tickets to local businessmen. The minute of the Board meeting held on 3rd September 1979 admits to a poor response to the scheme. "It was noted with disappointment that only one season ticket had been purchased from the exercise of this offer made to the Industrialists of Kirkcaldy and surrounding district." Despite this, £15,000 was placed at the manager's disposal to purchase players.

days later, the match at Dumbarton being abandoned after an hour following a heavy snow storm. The team was not playing badly, but it was not winning matches either, and it slid into the relegation positions after a 1-0 home defeat to Hamilton. The club needed firm direction, which was given two days later when Gordon Wallace was confirmed as Player-Manager, and a further two days on, he ensured that his old boss did not enjoy an early return to Stark's Park when Ayr United were beaten 2-0.

After bad weather descended again, veteran midfield player Bobby Ford was signed from Montrose, and made his debut in the replayed match at Boghead, which Rovers lost 3-0, to a John Whiteford hat-trick. A battling performance at Shawfield, with McDermott and Forsyth outstanding in defence, earned a draw, followed by a 1-0 win at Airdrie, Bobby Ford taking charge of the midfield in the second half.

A bright young St Johnstone eleven swept Rovers aside at Muirton Park, and few could deny that Dundee deserved the points at Stark's Park. Much worse was the 2-1 home defeat by Arbroath. Wallace had dropped himself, and the out-of-touch Donald Urquhart, but performances did not improve. The teams met again at Stark's Park four days later – such was the disruption to the fixture list caused by the severe winter – and in a tense, nervous match, a Wallace penalty with three minutes to go gave Rovers two priceless points.

Hard-fought draws at Montrose and at home to St Johnstone meant that Rovers went into the home match against Hamilton knowing that a win would guarantee another season in the First Division. Rovers delighted their fans with an excellent display of uninhibited, skilful football, with the old-heads Ford and Wallace superb on the right wing. Late goals from Ford and Harrow had the fans wondering why they had not seen such effervescence from the team in the preceding months.

The final two fixtures saw Rovers involved in the promotion fight, rather than the relegation struggle which had haunted the spring months. Clydebank needed to win by eleven clear goals at Stark's Park to pip Kilmarnock for promotion – they had to settle for one, in a 2-1 win, and six days later Dundee had to win at Dens Park to clinch promotion, which they did, unconvincingly.

It was a strange season, oddly satisfying despite the real threat of relegation at one point. McDermott was excellent in goal, right backs Tom Houston and Brian McDonough were solid, and Chris Candlish oozed class and composure. Tommy Murray, at the tail end of a distinguished career, offered only reminders of his skill and influence, and Donald Urquhart started well then faded, in contrast to Allan Forsyth's

season. Thomson, McFarlane and young Lennie McComb were good players in a good team, but no help in a struggle. Up front, when Gordon Wallace played well, so did his willing runners in Andy Harrow and Gordon Forrest, but Wallace's concerns as a manager when results turned against him impacted on his performances. Ronnie Duncan had a fitful season on the wing.

The hope going into the new season was that the defence would remain solid, and that punch would be added to the attack. There seemed little prospect of the latter when the close season signings were restricted to midfielder Ian Steen, freed by Dundee United, and the veteran winger, and League Cup nemesis, Bertie Miller.

Once the competitive matches got underway in season 1979/80, it was quite obvious where the strength of the team lay. Rovers drew their first four League matches 0-0, and beat East Fife 1-0 and 2-0 in the League Cup. Not only were no goals conceded in the opening six matches, there was never a prospect of a goal being lost. On the rare occasions the defence was breached, Murray McDermott was unbeatable.

The fifth successive League draw (this time 2-2, at Perth) was a veritable game of two halves. The goal-barrier having been breached at last, what followed was a feast of goal-scoring football. Hearts, absent from the top flight for the first time in their history, were favourites for promotion and attracted 4,632 to Stark's Park for a midweek fixture. They witnessed a true classic of a football match. Rovers got off to a slow start with Malcolm Robertson giving Tom Houston a torrid time. The former Rovers winger crossed for O'Connor to head the opening goal in 6 minutes, but Rovers steadily battled back into the match and thoroughly deserved their equaliser when Andy Harrow rammed home an unstoppable shot from 30 yards, five minutes before half time. Rovers' delight was short-lived ; Robertson crossed for O'Connor to head Hearts back into the lead three minutes later.

Rovers got a standing ovation from their fans as they left the field at half-time, and responded by finding another gear in the second half. In rampant form and inspired by Bobby Ford and several other top-class performances throughout the team, Bertie Miller equalised in 67 minutes and Ford hit the winner with six minutes to go amid scenes of uninhibited delight amongst Rovers fans. It was a superb match, but there was an encore four days later at home to the other relegated team, Motherwell, managed by former Scotland boss Ally McLeod.

Rovers were 2-0 up when Wallace's penalty was saved, otherwise the result would have been a lot more emphatic than 5-2. It was a highly satisfactory display against a star-studded (and expensively assembled) team, with Bobby Ford excellent in midfield and the player-manager a class apart in attack. The good form continued four days later with an excellent performance in winning

3-1 at Hamilton. The two points came at a cost, however, Chris Candlish sustaining an injury late in the match which hampered his form for several months.

The first defeat of the season, in the eleventh fixture, at home to Clydebank, was largely self inflicted. The purse strings were opened and Pat Carroll was signed from Hibs for £10,000, his introduction to the team (in place of 'Tosh' McFarlane) coinciding with a slump in League form, although St Johnstone were beaten 3-1 at Muirton Park in an excellent performance in the second leg of the League Cup tie, the first game at Kirkcaldy having finished 1-1. A packed defence ensured a 0-0 draw at Tannadice in the first leg of the quarter final, and a hard-tackling, defensive performance at home deserved more than the narrow 1-0 defeat. With six minutes remaining, Ronnie Duncan looked to have cancelled out Hegarty's 70th minute goal, but the equaliser was mysteriously disallowed.

The cup run – Rovers' best in the competition since 1949 - with some healthy attendances, and £2,500 in sponsorship money, helped pay for striker Ian Ballantyne, signed for £12,500 from Dundee United. He was badly needed ; Rovers had gone from third top to third bottom in the space of eight League fixtures.

There was an instant dividend, the debutant scoring in 12 minutes at Motherwell, and there was a great deal of encouragement from the performances which earned the 2-1 win, not the least from Pat Carroll in midfield. The 3-0 defeat at Ayr was not nearly as bad as the scoreline suggested, but a 1-1 draw against Arbroath saw Rovers slide into the relegation positions. In losing 1-0 at home to Dumbarton, Rovers hit the woodwork three times, leaving the fans to wonder if fate was against their team, but a signal that better times were ahead came at Airdrie, when the second bottom club beat the second top side 3-0, Ian Ballantyne scoring a hat-trick.

The signing of Ballantyne allowed the player manager to enact his pre-season plan of dropping the first part of his job description. He finished a marvellous playing career with his high standards maintained to the end, his enduring qualities appreciated by those who had the privilege of playing alongside him. Andy Harrow recalled : "'Stubby' was a tremendous help to me in my career, in fact I would say that he was the one who made me into a player. He gave me tremendous help on the field, and was brilliant with the advice he gave me when I was transferred from the club. He could put the ball on a sixpence (or a new fivepence !) and the amount of goals he made for me with his shielding and running off the ball was terrific. He must be one of Rovers greatest ever players. He had a great brain, and was usually a couple of moves ahead of everyone else. I was a youngster when I played with him, and probably didn't take everything in, but looking back on my career, he was a really good player."

His replacement (Ballantyne) scored the only goal of the match in the New Year's Day derby against Dunfermline, but failed to find the net as Rovers lost 1-0 at home to a resurgent Motherwell, followed by a hard fought draw at Hamilton. Rovers remained in a relegation placing, but it looked to be a false position, as the second half of the season proved.

The draw for the third round of the Scottish Cup meant a trip to Celtic Park, against the European Cup quarter finalists. The record books show a narrow 2-1 win for Celtic, and everyone at the game remembers Ronnie Duncan's failure to capitalise on a chance to equalise late in the match, but the reality was that only the woodwork and a superlative performance by Murray McDermott kept the scoreline respectable.

The team took some encouragement from the experience, however, and posted four successive League victories, to catapult them up the League. The manager, at last, had a settled team ; the peerless McDermott in goal, a back four of Houston, Forsyth, Thomson and Candlish. In midfield the increasingly influential Pat Carroll, and the age-defying Bobby Ford were anchored by the dependable Donald Urquhart. Up front, Harrow's mobility caused defences no end of bother, while Ballantyne lurked in the penalty area to snap up chances, many of them created by Bertie Miller, who was enjoying an Indian summer on the wing.

The sixteen League fixtures which followed the home defeat by Motherwell contained just one further loss, at Clydebank. Rovers returned to Kilbowie eleven days later, and the 3-0 victory from a superb performance was much more representative of the second half of the season. Candlish (who scored twice), Carroll and Miller (who scored the other goal) were an irresistible combination down the left wing, and the Houston, Ford pairing on the right wing wasn't bad either.

The final match of the season was at Berwick, who opened the scoring in four minutes. Rovers then played their hosts off the park, scoring three times before half-time. Assumptions that the season was over were premature ; Berwick took advantage of Rovers' complacency to equalise, and the point dropped meant that they had to settle for fifth place, rather than third. Notwithstanding that minor disappointment, it had been an astonishing recovery from a relegation position at the turn of the year, and the free-flowing, attacking football, buttressed by a mean defence, was a delight to watch.

Rovers fans were much too experienced to let their imaginations run wild with anticipation over the summer of 1980, but those who allowed their optimism to get the better of memories of previous disappointments were not disappointed in the second half of the year.

Once again, there were no significant additions to the playing squad over the close season. The team had evolved over several years, with piecemeal additions rather than wholesale changes engendering

IAN BALLANTYNE

Early season signing speculation in the summer of 1979 assumed an exotic dimension with the story that Rovers were interested in signing a student at Kirkcaldy Technical College who had been capped 20 times for Zambia. Nothing came of it, however.

The club's first ever open day, sponsored by kit suppliers Bukta, was held on Sunday October 14th. Scotland manager Jock Stein was principal guest.

In May and June 1980, Chris Candlish played in all three games for the Scotland semi professional team in the tournament in Holland. Scotland won the trophy, ahead of Holland, Italy and England.

CHRIS CANDLISH

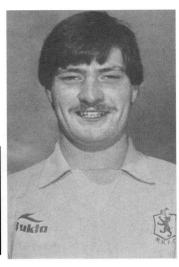

TOMMY WALKER

The Board Minute of 5th November 1979 recorded :

"Mr Wallace intimated he had finally decided to give up the playing side of the game. He felt it was now imperative for him to concentrate on the managerial side. Commenting on the team's recent League performances he was of the opinion that their overall ability had reached its limitation. To improve would mean the purchasing of at least one, possibly two experienced players. While the reserve side were leading the East of Scotland First Division Reserve League, the players were too immature to regularly participate in the first team. The Board agreed to make money available to Mr Wallace to sign a replacement for himself and consider the position thereafter. The Chairman thanked Mr Wallace for his frank report. He considered the Manager's decision to stop playing would have an adverse effect on the team's performance. It must however be understood that the Club were very fortunate to have a Manager who had been prepared to play and lay himself open to spectator criticism at two levels."

At the Board Meeting of 26th May 1980, it was agreed to give the manager a three year contract

1980 - Meikle's Carpet factory in Prime Gilt Box Street closed for business

team spirit and continuity of selection. Micky Lawson, freed by St Johnstone, took Ronnie Duncan's No. 11 jersey, and the team performed well in pre-season matches, beating Chelsea 3-2 at Stark's Park.

There was a stern test in the opening League fixture against Hibs, experiencing lower League football for the first time in almost 50 years, at Easter Road. Rovers gave a determined, intelligent and highly skilled display with Lawson, Ford and especially Forsyth outstanding. Despite being under sustained pressure at times, the 1-0 win was well merited, Ian Ballantyne scoring in the final minute. They were brought back to earth with a bump the following Saturday, Clydebank feasting on a Rovers off-day and winning 4-0 at Stark's Park.

After beating Falkirk home and away in the first round of the League Cup, Dunfermline were beaten 2-0 in the League, with some ease, at East End Park, before extra time was required to eliminate Dumbarton from the League Cup. Dreams of a Cup run were dashed on the rocks of Clydebank, who won 1-0, home and away. By 24th September, Rovers had lost just six times in 1980 ; once to Celtic, once to Motherwell, and four times to Clydebank.

With Derek Steel in defence in place of David Thomson, Falkirk were beaten 2-1 at Stark's Park to move up to fourth place, despite failing to hit the heights of performance seen in the second half of the previous season. A distinctly fortunate point at Motherwell, and two goals from the in-form Harrow to win the points at Stirling, moved Rovers into second place, their highest position in Scottish football for two decades.

Everything clicked into place on 20th September, when Dumbarton were demolished by 4 goals to 1 at Stark's Park. The Railway enclosure had seen many thrilling games, and countless great footballers, in its 60 years, and it was fitting that the Raith players served up such a show for the antique structure's last public use before demolition. Superlatives would not do justice to this Raith performance, with Harrow and Lawson devastating up front and Urquhart crowning a dominating display with the best goal seen for many seasons.

Rovers lined up at Hamilton the following week minus Andy Harrow, who had been sold to Luton Town for £90,000. Forsyth and Urquhart were suspended and the team looked disorganised in losing 2-1. Derek Frye, an habitual scorer against Rovers, scored the only goal of a match at Ayr which Rovers did not deserve to lose on 1st October, but fears that the bubble had burst were ill-founded ; it was to be the last defeat for three months.

Substitute Colin Harris added the necessary firepower to beat East Stirling at Stark's Park ; an under-performing Dundee team were held 0-0 and bottom of the League Berwick beaten 4-1 to restore Rovers to second place. Ballantyne scored twice to beat Motherwell at home, and opened the scoring which set Rovers on their way to a 3-0

win at Perth. At home to Stirling, Ford and Miller were outstanding in an attacking, clinical dismantling of an inferior side. Ballantyne (two) and Harris shared the goals, reflecting their developing partnership – and Rovers were top of the League.

The entertainment continued in a closely contested 2-2 draw at Dumbarton, and Harris scored the only goal of another hard match at home to Hamilton, with Urquhart the best player afield. For three weeks, Rovers lay dormant, the weather cancelling one fixture, and Dundee's preoccupation with the League Cup final accounting for another. They picked up the pieces at home to Berwick on December 13th with a 3-0 win, Bertie Miller shining and Ballantyne and Harris again sharing the goals. Some old fashioned grit and determination were needed to see off the challenge of promotion rivals Ayr United, the 2-1 win stretching the unbeaten run to 10 games.

That run was extended by one more game, the New Year's Day match at home to Dunfermline. The first half was a dour battle, with Dunfermline looking lively under new boss Pat Stanton, and not allowing Rovers to settle. A late rally culminated in a Ballantyne penalty goal in 85 minutes, but it was scarcely vintage stuff for the 4000 crowd who had to wait 10 minutes for the game to start due to the queues on Pratt Street.

Rovers journeyed to Falkirk on January 3rd, having picked up points, but not their play, in recent weeks. A lifeless performance was duly rewarded with a 1-0 defeat, and Gordon Wallace expressed relief that the pressures of the 11 game unbeaten run had been lifted, believing that the players would go on to finish the promotion job successfully.

His comments looked to have some substance when League leaders Hibs came to Stark's Park determined to overturn the result from the opening game of the season. They also attracted the biggest crowd seen at the old ground for many years, in excess of 10,000, with temporary entrance gates having to be opened and the start delayed for 10 minutes. Long queues in Pratt Street made it seem like old times – and so did the result.

The match proved to the cynics, and to the players themselves, that Rovers had what it took to gain promotion. Certainly, Hibs hit the woodwork twice and McDermott gave an inspired, flawless performance, but team work and combination play was excellent, and they deserved the points in a tense game. Steen and Forsyth (penalty) scored the goals in the 2-0 win.

There were words of warning, however, in the Fife Free Press match report. "Raith Rovers proved conclusively that they have the ability and the temperament to achieve their golden dream of promotion to the Premier League. Whether these qualities alone would ensure survival in the white-hot cauldron of the top league is debatable. Strength in depth is essential, and one or two injuries could spell disaster."

Hard on the heels of the Hibs came

an all-ticket Scottish Cup tie against Alex Ferguson's Aberdeen, the third successive season Rovers had been drawn against the reigning League Champions in the third round. Another 10,000 queued to get into Stark's Park to see a determined Raith side take on a youthful Aberdeen team depleted by injuries to key international players. Rovers gave an excellent account of themselves and worried Aberdeen on a number of occasions. The game developed into an exciting, open cup tie after Drew Jarvie capitalised on hesitation in the home defence to open the scoring in 10 minutes.

Rovers fought back and deservedly equalised in 62 minutes through Colin Harris. For six minutes, the ground was abuzz with the distinct possibility of a major cup shock, but failure to clear a loose ball in the penalty area allowed man of the match Mark McGhee to score the winner. Despite the disappointment of yet another early cup exit, there was consolation in the knowledge that this Rovers team could compete with any team in Scotland.

A defensive line-up the following week earned a point from a scoreless match at Motherwell, and a last minute own goal gave Rovers a scarcely deserved home win over Dumbarton, in atrocious playing conditions (driving wind and rain). A Colin Harris goal mid way through the first half at home to lowly Berwick Rangers induced a severe attack of nerves, and Berwick equalised with six minutes remaining.

Rovers' excellent position, second in the League with games in hand over Hibs above, and the chasing pack below, was improved by victory at Stirling Albion, thanks to a last minute goal from Allan Forsyth. The worrying aspect, apart from the team's loss of form, was the shortage of home fixtures still to be played, and the thought that Rovers had used up more than their share of good fortune to that point of the season.

A 0-0 draw at home to East Stirling reinforced the view that midfield and attack had ceased to function effectively. McDermott and Forsyth in particular, and the rest of the defence in general, were holding things together, but the team clicked back into gear at Hamilton, rounding off a sparkling performance with a 2-0 win. Ten League games remained, and the mathematicians amongst the support calculated that 12 out of 20 points, taking the total to 55, would secure promotion. What should have been a straightforward proposition assumed more daunting proportions when Donald Urquhart started a five match suspension.

The match at Dundee on 14th March was a vital game for the home side ; a defeat would end their promotion challenge. If there was a turning point of the season for Rovers, a three minute spell in the middle of the second half would qualify. Up until the hour mark, Rovers looked good, containing the Dundee attack and contributing the major part of what good football was on show. In 62 minutes, a freak cross-come-shot from Geddes confused McDermott, who could only

help the effort into the net. Not a minute later, Scrimgeour scored again before Rovers could recover. In 65 minutes, Ian Ballantyne was sent off following a needless off-the-ball incident with Mackie. The game was lost, the top scorer faced a spell of suspension, and Geddes added a third before Bertie Miller scored a late consolation goal. Miller and Ford were excellent, but McDermott, hero and mainstay on so many occasions, had an ill-timed off-day.

The outlook improved ten days later when new signing Bobby Russell scored the only goal of the game at Firs Park, and a 1-1 draw at home to Ayr United, on the fringe of the promotion race, was a good result in view of the injury and suspension-weakened team. Bobby Ford, who had been injured in training, was particularly missed. A point at home to Falkirk was a disappointing return against mediocre opposition, a fierce Brian McDonough shot coming back off the bar in 75 minutes, but Rovers were at least keeping to their point-a-game schedule.

Dens Park proved to be an unhappy hunting ground once more, a close match settled 2-1 in the home team's favour, with Rovers' stars exclusively in defence. Seven points were needed from the final five matches, and the last of the home games was on April 4th, when bogey-team Clydebank were the visitors. Rovers gave a much better performance than of late, showing more purpose and better form, but the breaks did not go their way as Clydebank thanked the woodwork and made several goal-line clearances. Bankies had opened the scoring, and debutant winger John Mitchell's equaliser did have a touch of good fortune about it.

St Johnstone (away) was a key fixture for both clubs, chasing promotion, and despite at least an equal share of the play, Rovers lost 2-0 ; the booking of Allan Forsyth meant that he would be suspended for the final three fixtures. The fixture list was exhibiting a cruel face, and Rovers journeyed to Easter Road with two points essential to breathe life back into their faltering promotion bid. A Hibs win would add the Championship trophy to the promotion they had already achieved. A lack of incision up front cost Rovers dear when they lost goals on either side of half time, and the match was effectively over by the 48th minute. Rovers dropped out of the top two positions for the first time in six months.

Although mathematically possible, promotion was now generally conceded, and that was confirmed after a 3-0 defeat at Clydebank on a night when nothing went right, culminating in Urquhart being sent off in 71 minutes for remarks to a linesman, made no doubt in frustration. What could have been a gala occasion, the last League match of the season at Dunfermline, became a fixture to be painfully fulfilled. In 23 minutes, a reckless challenge by Grant Jenkins saw McDermott and McDonough share an ambulance to hospital, both with head injuries.

ALLAN FORSYTH

Bobby Ford was one of the four nominations for the Scottish Players' Union First Division player of the Year award at the close of 1980/81 season.

As a new craze swept the sport in England, a floodlit cricket match was played at Stark's Park on Thursday 24th September 1981. Only 700 attended the match between Kirkcaldy Cricket Club and Lords Taverners.

Rovers entered an Under 15 team in the Eastercraigs Easter tournament in Glasgow for the first time in 1982

The Club finally took their leave of the property market in June 1982, when 59 Pratt Street was sold for £6525.

1982 - Extension built on Sheriff Court (hardly in keeping with the original Scots baronial design). Kirkcaldy's Jocky Wilson became World Darts Champion

Paul Sweeney played for Scotland Under 18s in the 1-1 draw at Ibrox against Wales on 15th February 1983

Director Mario Caira's horse, Robbie's Park, named after the club's first enclosure, was a winner at Perth Races during the season.

1981 - It was all change on the Esplanade, with the closure of the county bus station, and the demolition of the gas holder.

COLIN HARRIS

Harsh critics of the Board of Directors who criticised them for having no strategy to halt the club's decline were wrong. There was a plan, albeit one that was neither water-tight nor injury-free. The Board Minute of 28th September 1981 articulated the cunning plan. "Owing to the disappointing league results a lengthy discussion took place on how the team could be strengthened. A possible transfer of player C. Candlish could open the way for acquiring new players, which the Manager considered essential to help the team to score goals. The Board approved Mr Wallace should pursue this course without delay."

BERTIE MILLER

Ian Ballantyne took over in goal and Rovers played with 10 men until the interval, when it was learned that McDermott would not be returning to the ground. In a final show of defiance, Rovers dug-in at the back, the midfield worked hard and combined well, with Ford an inspiration, and in 49 minutes Bobby Russell scored the only goal of the game. It was an inspiring, brave end to a season which promised so much but delivered only dreadful disappointment.

Indeed, it was arguably the most disappointing season in the club's history. A ten year absence from the top flight of Scottish football – made more exclusive in 1975 when it was reduced to just ten clubs – promised for so long to be ended. For a spell between October and January, Rovers had played some of the best football ever seen in the five years of the middle division, and the best at the club for much longer, and yet they stumbled and fell with the finishing post in sight. What went wrong ?

The knee-jerk reaction from some supporters was that the Board of Directors did not want promotion, a traditional response that did not square with the signature of Russell and Mitchell late in the campaign, and the preferred bonus of £1,000 per man and a "holiday in the sun". The bad breaks came at the wrong time, particularly at Dundee and in the fixture sequence towards the end of the season. There was a lack of depth in the player pool, particularly when key players – Urquhart, Forsyth and Houston – were suspended, while Colin Harris was too young and inexperienced to adequately replace the transferred Harrow. Had Bobby Russell been signed immediately after Harrow left, it might have been different ; had Urquhart not missed the first match at Dundee throught suspension ; had Murray McDermott not precipitated a catastrophic five minutes by making his first significant error of the season …. it ended up as a season of "what if's."

The Manager, Gordon Wallace, reasoned that the side was experienced in the situations they found themselves in, but could not handle the psychological pressures of being in the firing line as the season's climax neared. There were plenty of old heads amongst the youngsters, however, and perhaps Gordon's later reflections on the season, made several years later, were more measured.

"One of the problems was that the teams played each other three times and we got the backlash of the fixtures. We were away to Dundee, Ayr United, St Johnstone and Hibs, all twice. We had done really well in the first round, but we had to go to all these places twice.

"Anyone will tell you that you don't win things playing football in the latter stages of the season. Grit and determination and working your way through it wins things, and we didn't do it. We tried everything, and I look back on that at myself and criticise myself and think that, as a young manager, my man management could have been better or slightly different. I look at the players and ask

if they could have done better, but at the end of the day we didn't have enough people that knew what winning was about.

"If you look at their subsequent careers, very few of them went on to play in the Premier League, so it wasn't as if it was a team that was overloaded with talent – and I'm not being critical of the players when I say this, but they were all good First Division players - that team going into the Premier League would have really struggled."

The optimists hoped that the experience would stand the team in good stead, and that a renewed promotion challenge would be launched the following season. The realists, however, feared that the long-suffering Kirkcaldy footballing public, cynically aware of the continued failure of successive Raith Rovers sides to bring their promises to fruition, and critical of the perceived lack of ambition, or ability, or resources, would simply turn their backs on the club.

Those worse fears were to come to fruition. The team did not bounce back from their disappointment, and indeed became more concerned with relegation battles than promotion campaigns in the years that followed. The veterans Bobby Ford and Bertie Miller played fewer games, more youngsters were thrown into the first team, some purchases proved to be disappointing, and for the first time in living memory, there was a problem with the goalkeeping position.

Murray McDermott's stellar service deserved a better finale than being stretchered off after 23 minutes at East End Park. His bi-annual dispute over terms boiled over into a terminal row with the manager, and when the new Berwick Rangers manager, Frank Connor, offered £ 20,000, the latest, and arguably the best, of a long line of competent goalkeepers left Raith Rovers.

His departure shaped the club's future for the next five years, an outcome foreseen by the elder statesman in the Boardroom, former Chairman Rankin Grimshaw, who asked that his dissent to the sale of the inspirational goalkeeper be minuted. Compounding the folly was the decision to promote the young reserve team goalkeeper, Tom Walker, who was subjected to a baptism of fire in the League Cup, briefly restored to its old format of early season qualifying sections. Rovers were drawn with Dundee, Morton and Rangers, and the promise of the opening day victory at Dundee – a result that was so desperately needed four months earlier – was displaced by the reality of a 5-2 defeat at home to Morton, and an 8-1 thrashing at Ibrox, when the defence looked all at sea, as the result would suggest.

Former Scotland internationalist Bobby Robinson was signed to cover for Bobby Ford in midfield, but otherwise it was the same squad who had stuttered over the last three months of the previous season. Early season results were poor. The first League win did not come until the sixth fixture, at home to East Stirling, when Bobby Robinson scored the only goal of a game watched by less than 1,000. That was followed by five successive defeats, before Ballantyne scored twice in the last three minutes to earn an improbable win at home to Queen of the South.

That sparked a mini revival ; Lloyd Irvine, signed on a free transfer from Stirling Albion, scored a 60th minute equaliser to earn a draw at Kilmarnock, Ian Ballantyne notched the winner at Falkirk and Willie Gibson and Bobby Ford got the goals which beat Hamilton Accies 2-0 at Stark's Park. Gibson had been an excellent centre forward for Hearts for several years, but had been sold to Partick Thistle for £35,000 earlier that year. Gordon Wallace broke the club's record transfer fee by reimbursing Thistle £30,000 to sign him on 9th October.

Unbeknown to the cheery Fifer, there was a phenomenon at Stark's Park known as "the curse of the record signing", in which a long line of increasingly expensive players failed to hit the promised heights. He did score nine goals in the remaining two-thirds of the season, most of them points winners, and in that respect there was some return from the high expenditure. Gibson's signing was followed, a fortnight later, by that of fomer Dundee goalkeeper Ally Donaldson, signed from Hibs for a "nominal fee".

Two League defeats followed, and a Scottish Cup third round exit at Dundee despite a battling rearguard action which deserved a draw, before four successive League victories prevented the team from being stranded at the foot of the division. Ballantyne and Gibson got amongst the goals, but the inconsistency which characterised this deeply disappointing season manifested itself in four defeats out of five, the exception being a 1-0 win at East Stirling, Gibson scoring with two minutes to play.

Home form was particularly disappointing, but that looked to have been addressed when first half goals from Ballantyne (2) and Gibson gave Rovers a 3-1 lead over Kilmarnock. The visitors scored on the stroke of half time, and equalised with 14 minutes to play. Charlie Spence, a 19 year old signed from Whitburn Juniors earlier in the season, showed promise on the left wing, and Craig Robertson came into the side at right back, with Tom Houston moving to central defence. There seemed to be plenty of youthful talent coming through the ranks, but the first team was low on confidence, and a settled side was elusive.

The point from the Kilmarnock match, following a 2-0 win from a workmanlike performance at Dumbarton, guaranteed safety from relegation, which was just as well as the closing seven League matches earned just one win and one draw. Only 950 watched the final, dismal match of a bad season, a 1-0 defeat at home to St Johnstone, with the scoreline kept down thanks to an excellent display by Tommy Walker, restored to the goalkeeping position.

In the summer of 1982, Bobby Ford followed Bertie Miller (who had signed for Cowdenbeath in February) out of Stark's Park

and in their place came several youth signings, and Colin More, a centre half freed by Hearts. 1982/83 largely followed the pattern of its predecessor ; mostly defeats interspersed with a couple of sequences of wins which perversely showed what the playing squad was capable of, but so rarely delivered. As before, the League Cup section warned of the struggles to follow, two draws and four defeats against Falkirk, St Johnstone and Dundee United.

Two defeats and a draw in the opening three League matches were followed by a 2-1 win at Dunfermline (Colin Harris scoring both goals) and a 3-1 win at home to Queen's Park. Two more away defeats were followed by a run of six successive wins, which had the fans dreaming of a push for promotion, but ultimately contributed a bank of points which prevented relegation.

Unsurprisingly, this run was put together by a settled team, which had been augmented by the signing of goalscoring midfielder Jim Kerr from Airdrie. Tommy Walker was looking more assured in goal, Houston and McDonough were steady full backs (Chris Candlish being absent with an ankle injury), Colin More and the restored David Thomson at centre back, Donald Urquhart, Bobby Robinson and Kerr in midfield, and in attack Bobby Russell, Colin Harris and Charlie Spence.

The star man was Colin Harris, bringing to fruition his undoubted promise as he matured physically and gained confidence and experience. Including the defeats at Partick Thistle on 25th September and St Johnstone on 13th November, he scored in eight successive League matches. Many of his goals were spectacular ; one was a penalty (at home to Falkirk) and one was a shot from Jim Kerr which looked to be heading for the corner flag before it hit the recoiling Harris's back and rebounded into the Ayr United net. The team played with confidence and purpose, and gave the long suffering fans something to shout about after two years of disappointment.

To the dismay of the supporters, the confidence and form dissipated as unexpectedly as it had arrived. A run of two draws and four defeats towards the turn of the year saw the team slide down the League table. Jim Marshall, signed from Cowdenbeath in exchange for Willie Gibson plus a balancing payment, made his debut in a 2-1 win at Airdrie. Five days later, in the New Year's Day match, Bobby Russell opened the scoring within the first minute, and Rovers went on to thrash Dunfermline 6-0. It was sweet revenge for the manager, who was on the receiving end of an identical scoreline, as a Rovers player, fifteen years earlier.

It proved to be yet another false dawn, however. The next five matches were lost, including the third round Scottish Cup tie at East Fife, when Robin Thomson returned to haunt his former club by scoring the only goal of the match. In the face of dwindling crowds, the financial boost of a good cup run had been desperately needed, and the

WILLIE GIBSON

The minutes of the Board Meeting of 18th October 1982 reported : "The manager gave a brief report which included the team's three successive wins which were a source of great satisfaction to all connected with the club. While having a playing staff of 29, 26 players were required every week to fulfil first and reserve team fixtures, but there was a possibility of getting some experienced players transferred to make way for the introduction of younger players at a less cost to the club. It was felt that certain players had reached their zenith with the Club and a change would benefit both player and Club."

Colin Harris was selected in the Scotland Semi Professional squad which played in the Four Nation Tournament in England in May 1983. He scored in the 2-1 defeat by England

Iain Livingstone, a Schoolboy-form signing, was in the Scotland Under 16 pool for the UEFA Championship match against Iceland on 19th June 1983. He played for Scotland Under 16s v England at Motherwell on 19th October 1983, in the UEFA Championship

The club's Centenary Dinner was held at the Ambassadeur Hotel on 20th October 1983

Paul Smith was selected for the Scotland Semi Professional squad for the Four Nations Championship in Italy in May 1984.

A badge first appeared on Raith Rovers jerseys in 1910, but it took more than 40 years for the chosen insignia to appear as the club's crest on official documents.

Prior to 1910, the club badge was a sketch of a contemporary football, surrounded by the words "Raith Rovers".

The 1910 insignia was said to be derived from that of the Laird of Raith, and that crest was the only one to appear on jerseys until the practice fell out of fashion in the late 1950s.

The Sporting Post in September 1956 asked Bert Herdman for the derivation of the badge. The Rovers manager stated that it was from the "old estate of Raith", and featured the "shield of the Covenanters. The decoration at the bottom is their staff. The 13 points on the lion's mane represent the deaths of the 13 martyrs of the Covenant."

The original owners of the crest, the Melvilles of Raith, were certainly involved in the Covenanting hostilities, but it is believed that the shield is actually a buckle, which is a not uncommon heraldic device. There are several romantic tales regarding the choice of the buckle, including repairs to a monarch's carriage and to the girth belt of the horse carrying Mary, Queen of Scots.

A more prosaic explanation is that a buckle in heraldry signifies self-defence and protection, as well as victorious fidelity in authority, which is why it appears quite often in heraldry, often in an oval.

response was to embark on a cost cutting exercise, precipitating a downward spiral which would have only one consequence.

The occasional victory kept the spectre of relegation at bay, and reminded the despairing support of what the players could achieve. With Paul Smith, signed on a free transfer from Dundee, introduced to the attack in place of Spence, the team won 5-0 at Hamilton, followed ten days later by a marvellous 4-2 home win in a tremendous match against promotion-chasing Hearts at Stark's Park. How could the same set of players achieve such results, from such sparking performances, and yet lose to teams who had, on paper, inferior players ?

The fans gave their own verdict in time-honoured fashion. The final League match of the season, a 2-2 draw at home to Queen's Park, was watched by 700.

Among the economies introduced after the Scottish Cup exit at Methil was a decision not to renew Gordon Wallace's three year contract when it expired at the end of the season. This did not amount to a dismissal, simply that he would not have the comfort and security of a contract (nor a rise in salary). The former striker was a coach of no little ability, could spot and develop players, and was an able tactician, but he perhaps lacked the drive, and force of personality to turn the club's fortunes around, or motivate a board of directors to gamble on success. There was a resigned acceptance, therefore, when he took up the offer of a coaching position at his former club, Dundee United.

On the face of it, the choice of his successor was imaginative and held much promise. Former Dundee full back Bobby Wilson had made a great success in managing Lossiemouth, and in particular Keith, in the Highland League, and was eager to return to his native Fife to make his name as a manager in the Scottish League. Rovers fans viewed the appointment with some optimism, and it coincided with the club's Centenary Season, which normally helped to lift the mood of a celebrating club. Unfortunately, Rovers chose to mark their 100th birthday by being relegated to the lowest level in Scottish League football.

The season got off to a shambolic start. Gordon Wallace left at the end of July, although he had given plenty of notice, and it took until the end of the first month of the new season to secure his replacement. Alex Kinninmonth had resigned as coach at the end of the previous season (although he was to return as Reserve Team coach in early October) and for the first month of the season the team was under the care of the new coach, 29 year old Dick Campbell, who had recently retired as a player with East Stirling.

Only youngsters were signed over the summer, and the playing squad was stretched beyond its lower limit as the new season started. With Tommy Walker recovering from injury, Hill of Beath Hawthorn goalkeeper David Westwood played in the pre-season friendlies, followed by Andy Graham, signed on loan from Dundee United.

Bobby Russell walked out of the club after the friendly matches, and began a protracted process of being loaned to various clubs before finally signing for Falkirk. Mike Galloway, an 18 year old freed by Berwick Rangers, was fielded in the pre-season tournament at Keith, but not pursued (he went on to sign for Hearts, then Celtic with whom we won a Scotland cap, and he played against Rovers in the 1994 League Cup Final)

Tom Houston and Chris Candlish joined Walker in Bob Methven's treatment room for several months, so Cowdenbeath's Keith Ferguson was borrowed for the first six competitive games of the season, and the team for the opening League match (a 1-1 draw at Brechin) was made up by two trialists, former Rangers and Hearts striker Chris Robertson and, as an unused substitute, Billy Blackie. The paper-thin squad and injured list meant that young players Paul Sweeney, Keith Wright and Jocky Hill were thrown into first team action. In the long run, it did their future careers no harm (Hill's being restricted to junior football) but they, understandably, struggled to come to terms with First Division football.

Jim Kerr, uncharacteristically, missed a penalty at Pittodrie against the European Cup Winners Cup holders in the first round of the League Cup, restored to a knock-out format. It made no difference to the result – Rovers were beaten 9-0, and while they performed much better in the second leg at Stark's Park, the tie was lost 12-0 on aggregate.

It was little wonder that the first win did not come until 8th October, when Clyde were beaten 2-1 at home, followed by a similar scoreline at Alloa and a 0-0 draw at home to Airdrie on the day the club celebrated its Centenary. From then until 29th February, when Kilmarnock were beaten 2-1 at Kirkcaldy in a re-arranged fixture, Rovers won only against Meadowbank Thistle, home and away. The occasional draw meant that they did not become detached at the bottom of the League, but it was a grim struggle all season.

With Tommy Walker restored to health (if not athletic fitness), Andy Graham returned to Dundee United, and in February Walker was replaced by veteran ex Hibs goalkeeper Jim McArthur. Tom Houston returned to the side at the turn of the year, but Candlish missed most of the season following belated surgery to a mis-diagnosed ankle injury. Allan Forsyth left for Dunfermline in October, and David Thomson retired from playing shortly afterwards. Centre forward Paul Ramsay was signed from Musselburgh Athletic, but his call-up was delayed by their involvement in the Scottish Junior Cup ended.

Brian Ritchie, from Dundonald Bluebell, joined him in the first team, and Iain Philip was signed from Dundee United while still recovering from a broken leg. His first taste of action did not come until mid March, when Rovers launched their bid for survival. A four match unbeaten run comprising three wins (at home to Partick Thistle, at

Kilmarnock and an incongruous 5-0 home win over Ayr United) and a draw at home to Clyde, gave everyone hope that a late run would save the club from what had seemed, for most of the season, to be an inevitable fate.

Three successive defeats were far more typical, but in the penultimate match, four goals from Jim Kerr (two from the penalty spot) were the feature of a 6-0 home win over Brechin City. Relegation would be decided on the last day of the season. Rovers had to win at Meadowbank, and hope that Ayr United would not beat promoted Dumbarton at Boghead. Prospects looked bright after 3 minutes when Kerr rifled home the opening goal, but two minutes later former trialist Chris Robertson equalised. With seven minutes to go, Jim Marshall scored a deserved winner, but word got round that Ayr United had gained a scarcely credible 3-0 win at Dumbarton, and Rovers were relegated.

In many respects it was a logical progression from the struggles of the previous two seasons, and the absence of any money to strengthen the team as a consequence of falling attendances. The hope was that the new manager would have turned things round, but he had to work with severely constrained resources, and although the margin of failure was narrow, a last day escape would probably have been only a stay of execution.

There was only one significant change to the first team as 1984/85 got underway, former reserve goalkeeper Alan Blair returning to fill the troubled goalkeeping position. A disappointing start to the season saw defeats in each of the opening three League matches, including a 5-1 thumping at Cowdenbeath. In between was a surprising 2-0 win over Clydebank in the second round of the League Cup, Paul Smith scoring both goals, and the reward was a third round match at Ibrox. Rovers were not disgraced in the 4-0 defeat, but there was disappointment in the size of the 'gate' from the 7,000 crowd.

An extra defender was fielded in the tie, and the man dropped was the previous season's top scorer Jim Kerr, who promptly asked for a transfer. A month later he was on his way to Brechin City, in exchange for Charlie Elvin, and Mitch Bavidge was signed from the manager's former club, Keith. Bobby Wilson told the board "get me Elvin and Bavidge and I will get you promotion", but it was an individual supporter who contributed the modest funds to sign the players, such was the emptiness of the cupboard at Stark's Park.

Results improved, as the young players began to find their feet in League football, supported by the experience of Colin More and Iain Philip in defence, and Donald Urquhart and Charlie Elvin in midfield. Billy Herd deputised for the injured Tom Houston, Paul Sweeney developed into a splendid left back as Chris Candlish continued his struggle for fitness, Craig Robertson moved into midfield to good effect, and up front Keith Wright and Paul Smith began to score with regularity.

The team lacked consistency, however, with too many draws and defeats. Queen's Park, Montrose, Stranraer, Cowdenbeath, Alloa, Stenhousemuir and Stirling Albion all won at Stark's Park, provoking disenchantment among the supporters which was only partially lifted by a stirring 2-1 win at Dunfermline on 2nd January and a 5-3 victory at Dumfries.

The disappointment of inconsistent results in the League was alleviated by a mini cup run. After a draw at Hampden, Queen's Park were beaten by a Paul Smith goal in the replay. A last minute equaliser by Craig Robertson earned a draw against First Division Clyde (managed by future Scotland manager Craig Brown) and the same two players, Smith and Robertson, scored in a tremendous 2-1 win in the replay at Shawfield.

The reward was a home match against Alex Ferguson's Aberdeen in the third round, and Rovers gave a very good account of themselves in losing 2-1, although there was never any danger of them winning the tie. To bolster the midfield, and add more experience to the team, Gordon Leitch was signed from Forfar Athletic, and once he had settled in, the team embarked on a run of nine successive victories. One of them, a thrilling 3-2 win at East End Park, arguably cost Dunfermline promotion. The run was badly needed ; Rovers were third bottom of the basement division when it started.

The late-season football was entertaining and productive, with Wright and Smith engaged in an enthralling contest to decide who was leading goalscorer (Wright's 22 League goals beat Smith's 19, but the latter could add 4 in the Scottish Cup and 2 in the League Cup). At Coatbridge on a Tuesday evening, 2nd April, they shared the goals equally in the 6-0 win. Wright scored a hat-trick when Rovers returned to Cliftonhill 25 days later, and Smith retaliated with two, to Wright's single, when Berwick Rangers were beaten 3-0 at Stark's Park in the penultimate game of the season.

The problem was that this excellent run of nine victories came in the last ten matches of the season, far too late to feature in the promotion race. Montrose showed them what might have been on the last day of the season when, already promoted, they won 3-1 at Stark's Park.

Given the stirring exploits of the last two months of the season, there seemed little reason to contemplate changes for 1985/86, although Donald Urquhart announced his retirement at the early age of thirty. Wearied by carrying struggling Rovers teams on his broad shoulders for so many years, he was no fan of the easy-going regime run by the manager, nor the parsimonius manner in which the club was being run, and gave up the unequal struggle.

In later years, one of the club's all-time great servants reflected : "We would go for a meal and on a bus when I was 15 playing in the reserves, then to go to [first

The crest did not appear on club notepaper until after the Second World War. Before that, an ornate design involving the club initials and "Kirkcaldy" was surrounded by the corporate title, "The Raith Rovers Football & Athletic Club Limited." Inexplicably, the crest ceased to be used in the mid 1960s, and a new badge was introduced, featuring a lion rampant with an old fashioned football atop a shield. A decade later, an attempt to restore the old badge was made, but it was a crude repesentation, with the lion now rampant, facing outward, and holding a shield which contained the club initials and a panelled football. The theory is that someone described the old crest to a supplier in a telephone conversation, and this was what resulted. This was usually printed with the crest in white on a navy background, sometimes in a square, sometimes a circle and sometimes a shield shaped. This became the official badge until 1996, when a new commercial manager, bemused by the several crests on view in the pavilion at Stark's Park, undertook some research. The 1910 crest was reintroduced and registered with the Lord Lyon King of Arms, hopefully settling for ever on the insignia of the Melvilles of Raith as the badge of Raith Rovers Football Club.

STEVIE SIMPSON

1984/1985 was the second year of the club's first shirt sponsorship, Mazda's involvement introduced by Murray Grubb whose motor dealership had that franchise.

At the end of the season, Paul Smith replaced Ken Eadie of Brechin City in the Scotland squad for the four nations Semi Professional tournament in Holland

In June 1985, an offer of £8000 by Forfar Athletic for Craig Robertson was declined.

1985 - The Swiss company Forbo purchased Nairns from Unilever ; Frances Colliery closed

The Fife Cup was played as a four-team tournament on the weekend of 2nd and 3rd August 1986 at Stark's Park, the first time this format was used. The competition was sponsored for the first, and last, time by Alex Penman (Builders) Ltd. Each of the four teams received £1000.

Gary Voy's promising football career was brought to an end through injuries he received in a car crash on 13th February 1987. A product of Rovers' youth system under Gordon Wallace, he left to play full time for Dundee United, but returned to Stark's Park and was fielded as a central defender in the first team by Bobby Wilson. Frank Connor moved him to right back in his final playing season.

team] games in cars was totally unprofessional.   When we were away from home, say in Edinburgh, we would have to be at Stark's Park for 1 o'clock and we would jump in a car and arrive at the ground for two. Then we had an hour to get a warm up and do whatever we had to before the game. I must admit it was the worst spell at the club for me and it killed me because I loved Raith Rovers."

Ronnie McLafferty, who had come into the team towards the end of the previous season after being signed from Newtongrange Star, proved to be a competent first choice goalkeeper, and Gary Voy, a young defender freed by Dundee United having been developed by Rovers' youth system, was introduced to a three-man central defence.

Contrary to expectations, the team got off to another poor start, losing at home to St Johnstone in the opening League match, and at Stranraer in the first away game. Absent at Stair Park, for the only time that season, was goalkeeper Ronnie McLafferty, who was being married that afternoon.   His replacement was Dundee United's third choice goalkeeper, Scott Thomson, who made a more indelible mark on the club's history nine years later. After beating East Stirling 3-1 in the first round of the League Cup, Clydebank were held 1-1 at half-time in the second round, but the roof fell in during the second half and Bankies won 7-2.

Three successive draws did little to improve the League position, although the third came in a thrilling 3-3 draw at Dunfermline, two goals being scored by Billy Gavine, recently signed from St Johnstone, who contributed little after his brace at East End Park.   Three days later, the first League win of the season was at the expense of Queen's Park, at Stark's Park, but three defeats in the next four games kept the team in the wrong half of the League table.

The week after a 2-0 win at East Stirling, Stenhousemuir arrived at Stark's Park and were two goals down within eight minutes, and trailed 5-0 after 36.   The visitors got a goal back just after half-time, but Rovers built a 9-1 lead with just 65 minutes played. Paul Smith had scored a hat-trick, Keith Wright went two better, and Jim Marshall scored once.   Rovers fans were left frustrated as the team could not contrive another goal, to get into double figures, in the last 25 minutes and it was Stenhousemuir who scored the final goal of the game.

A bewildered Raith support, which numbered less than 700, were left to contemplate the poor results previously achieved by this team who could win 9-2. Their confusion was compounded a week later.   Rovers travelled to Meadowbank Stadium and probably had the edge in a scoreless first half, but in a catastrophic second half they lost 6-0, seven days after a 9-2 win.

Bobby Wilson's misery was completed by being reported to the SFA, allegedly for swearing at the referee. He

denied the charge, clarifying what he had said: "I hope you're as disappointed with your performance as I am with my ****** team's." A week later, following a 2-1 defeat at home to Dunfermline on 16th November, the manager admitted that his team would not be promoted. "Experience goes a long way in this league, and we have too many youngsters in the team.   Even recognised first team regulars like Paul Sweeney and Keith Wright are only 20 years old.   We do not have the strength in depth to take us up."

The next eight games resulted in two draws and six defeats, including a 2-0 capitulation at Dunfermline in the first round of the Scottish Cup.   With at least one more season in the Second Division a foregone conclusion, and no cup run, the directors' response was to make further cuts. Bobby Wilson was given a month's notice that his position would become part-time. Coach Dick Campbell resigned on 9th January, and four days after his part-time status took effect, following a 2-0 defeat at Dumfries, Wilson was sacked.   He did not go quietly : "I thought I was improving myself by coming to Stark's Park, but accepting the manager's job was the biggest mistake of my life.   My former club Keith was run a lot more professionally than Raith Rovers who are heading down a one-way street."

A blank Saturday while the third Round Scottish Cup ties were being played was probably a blessing in disguise, for a week later another 2-0 defeat was suffered at Stenhousemuir.   Three days after that, Albion Rovers came to Kirkcaldy in a re-arranged league game, and the only goal of the game, scored by Paul Smith after five minutes, watched by just 369 spectators, prevented Rovers from sinking to the very bottom of the Scottish League.

Alex Kinninmonth, recently Reserve team coach, was rapidly promoted, twice, and presided over an upturn in results. A 3-3 draw against promotion contenders Dunfermline was followed by convincing victories at home to Berwick and Stranraer, and away to Meadowbank and St Johnstone, while the Board of Directors considered their next appointment, acutely aware that they couldn't afford to get it wrong again.

The last match under the control of the quietly spoken, competent Kinninmonth was a 2-1 defeat at Arbroath, and on the eve of the visit of Cowdenbeath the following Saturday, it was announced that the new manager would be Frank Connor, recently sacked as assistant manager by Celtic.   He had made his name as a charismatic coach at several clubs under Dan McLindon, and then earned a good reputation, although with little tangible success, as manager of Cowdenbeath and Berwick Rangers, before teaming up with Davie Hay to manage the club he played for as a goalkeeper, Celtic.

Connor had watched Rovers' games in the prolonged period between being approached by the Raith board, and his negotiating a settlement with his former employers, and had asked around others who

had a knowledge of contemporary Second Division football. "I was told they had half a team", he said, referring to the likes of Paul Sweeney, Paul Smith, Craig Robertson and Keith Wright, and the promising Billy Herd, comprising half of the side languishing near the bottom of the Second Division.

Connor's first signing was arguably his most important, and the most significant given the reconstruction of the club over the next few years. Alistair McIlroy, who had worked for the club under Gordon Wallace, and for Connor at Cowdenbeath, returned as chief scout.

His first game as manager was a 2-1 win over Cowdenbeath at Stark's Park, but he realised the extent of his job the following week, when East Stirling pulvarised Rovers at Stark's Park in winning 4-1, and a dismal performance at Berwick ended in a 1-0 defeat. The extent of his task in enticing the fans back through the turnstiles at Stark's Park was quantified on the evening of Tuesday April 22nd 1986, when two goals apiece from Paul Smith and Billy McNeill beat Stranraer 4-1, watched by a record low League crowd of 254.

The meaningless closing weeks of the season gave Connor an opportunity to decide which positions most needed strengthening, and the the last three matches, all at home, were won, with Wright and Smith amongst the goals.

Unlike his successors, Connor would not take 'no' for an answer when it came to extracting money from the Board of Directors for signing on fees and wages to obtain a better standard of player. As a coach and tactician, he was no better than Gordon Wallace or Bobby Wilson, but as a handler of directors, he was beyond compare.

Frank Connor's personality ensured that the players he wanted to keep would be happy to re-sign, although Paul Smith was

sold to Motherwell for £12,000, with Andy Harrow returning to Stark's Park in part-exchange. For the first time in several years, there was an infusion of playing talent and, as in the signing of Harrow, the experienced players came from higher divisions. Dundee United's iconic goalkeeper Hamish McAlpine, Forfar's resolute centre half Alex Brash, Dunfermline's steady midfielder Ian Gordon and Harrow joined the cream of Fife junior football, identified and signed by Alastair McIlroy. They included Billy Spence from Jubilee Athletic, Bobby Wilson and Eric Archibald from Hill of Beath Hawthorn and two players who took the Second Division by storm, winger Stevie Simpson from Oakley United and sweeper Glenn Kerr from St Andrews United.

'Bingo' Simpson, an orthodox right winger who was strong, brave and very skilful, became an instant hit with the fans during the pre season friendlies and Fife Cup ties, which were all won. He scored Scotland's first goal of the season, in 25 seconds, in the opening League match at Stranraer, and while most Rovers fans were content with a 1-1 draw from one of the most difficult fixtures in the calendar – not least for geographical reasons – Frank Connor made it known after the match that the performance was not of the required standard.

There was worse to come in 2-1 defeat at Arbroath in the first round of the League Cup in midweek, which prompted Alex Brash to admit to his wife, on his return home that night, that he may have made a mistake in signing for Rovers. It was a different story on the following Saturday in the opening home match. An Andy Harrow hat-trick was the highlight of a comprehensive 5-0 win over promotion favourites Ayr United. Just as important was the 1-0 win at Meadowbank the following week, with Keith

Hopes were high for a push for promotion when this squad photograph was taken before the start of 1985/86. Alas, those hopes had been dashed before the turn of the year, and within a month manager Bobby Wilson had been sacked, to be replaced some weeks later by Frank Connor. Promotion had to wait yet another year.
Back row, left to right : Billy Herd, Colin More, Alan Walker, Gary Voy, Iain Phillip, Jimmy Marshall.
Middle row : Dick Campbell (coach), Paul Smith, Chris Candlish, Ronnie McLafferty, Craig Robertson, Keith Wright, John Campbell (assistant physiotherapist), Gordon Miller (coach).
Front row : Alex Kinninmonth (coach), Ian Livingstone, Billy McNeill, Charlie Elvin, Bobby Wilson (manager), Gordon Leitch, Paul Sweeney, Tommy Falls and Bob Methven (physiotherapist).

Within a few years, Paul Smith, Craig Robertson and Keith Wright would all be playing in the Premier Division, the last named winning a Scotland cap. Paul Sweeney was the last of the talented quartet to leave Stark's Park, in a six-figure transfer to Newcastle United.

HAMISH McALPINE

On 24th January 1987 Rovers were drawing 0-0 at half time at home to East Stirling when Frank Connor administered a memorable tongue lashing to his team, in the course of which he gave the forwards a demonstration of how to make their physical presence felt. Unfortunately coach Alex Kinninmouth was standing too close to the gesticulating manager, and suffered a bloody nose. The players, supposedly chastened by their irate manager, struggled to suppress their laughter.

In April 1987, provisional signings Scott McGregor and Gary Dackers played for Scotland Juvenile Under 18s against Northern Ireland.

The Supporters Club football team retained the Newlands Trophy by beating Rangers 5-3 in the Final at Stark's Park in April 1987. They later added another trophy to complete a successful season.

Craig Robertson scored the only goal of a trial match at East End Park on 12th May 1987 for the Scotland squad to contest the Semi Professional Tournament , and played in the matches staged at Stark's Park and East End Park

Colin Harris was nominated for the SPFA Second Division Player of the Year award, which was won by Ayr United's John Sludden.

Wright scoring, and Rovers went on to built an unbeaten run of 14 League matches, in the course of which they attained top spot in the League, before a very good Meadowbank team won 3-2 at Stark's Park on 22nd November. The concerns of Mr & Mrs Brash had been unnecessary.

A draw at Hampden the following week was achieved with two goals from Colin Harris, brought back to the club by Connor in his first player purchase (aside from the juniors) in anticipation of the sale of the team's prize asset, Keith Wright, who played his last match at Hampden prior to joining Dundee.

Two more draws and another defeat at Arbroath cast some doubt on the wisdom of Wright's sale, as the flow of goals momentarily dried up, but Harris and Harrow scored in a 2-0 home win over Albion Rovers which kicked off another seven match unbeaten run. Included were a comprehensive 4-0 win over Vale of Leithen in a much-postponed Scottish Cup tie, and a 1-0 win over First Division Queen of the South in the next round, thanks to a superb performance by Colin Harris on a barely playable pitch.

It wasn't just the manager's infectious enthusiasm and motivational powers which helped resurrect the club. He brought discipline and organisation to Stark's Park, best exemplified by the case of Jim Marshall. Formerly a carpenter in "The Dubbie" (Frances Colliery), when the pit was shut down Jim started an insurance round, which was not always compatible with training on two evenings a week. More often than not, once a week, Bobby Wilson would receive a telephone call half an hour before training was due to start, with some excuse from the midfield player. He was an honest and hard-working player, and naturally fit, but Jim's place in the team was taken for granted by all and sundry, irrespective of his attendance record on training nights.

Not so with Frank Connor. The first time he tried it with the new manager, he was left out the team, and sat in the stand at Central Park on 13th September 1986, looking quite stunned at his omission from the side which won 2-1. Connor barked at the programme editor as he enquired, privately, after the match as to the reason for Marshall's absence : "I would have selected you before picking him this afternoon. No train, no place in the team on Saturday." Jim didn't miss another training session, and the rest of the team learned from his example.

With Meadowbank, Stirling Albion and Ayr United locked with Rovers in the promotion chase, a 1-0 defeat in a midweek match at Berwick was a set-back, as was the loss of Gary Voy who sustained severe injuries in a car crash a couple of days later, thus ending a promising playing career. Other injuries were limiting the mobility and ability of key players, notably the team's principal source of goals, Harris, and midfielder Ian Gordon, whose intermittent presence always improved the team.

The visit of Highland League club Peterhead in the fourth round of the Cup should not have caused too many problems, but Rovers were beginning to look bashed and battered. Alex Brash equalised an early Peterhead goal, and as the match meandered to a close, a rare goal from Chris Candlish - the day before his Testimonial dinner - looked like being the winner but slack defending immediately after a McAlpine penalty save allowed Peterhead to equalise with seven minutes remaining. A replay was the last thing Rovers needed as Connor battled to keep spirits up, and players fit to play, as the promotion chase reached a critical stage. Rovers went 3-1 ahead after half an hour at Peterhead's old ground, but the home side deservedly scored twice in the last 13 minutes, and it was the Scottish League team who were relieved to reach the sanctuary of extra time. Colin Harris was patched up to play in a third match at neutral Gayfield, where Rovers at last showed their class in a comprehensive 3-0 win to qualify for the quarter finals for the first time in 15 years.

To bolster the squad, Connor signed Gordon Dalziel, a great prospect when he burst into the Rangers team as a teenager, but whose career went off track after lucrative moves to Manchester City and Partick Thistle, followed by monthly contracts at East Stirling. He scored on his debut to earn a point at home to Stirling. In 12 games that season, palpably unfit and low in confidence, he did little to enthuse the Raith support, but he did score seven goals, including a last minute equaliser at Cowdenbeath which had Connor dancing up the touchline in a mixture of delight and relief ; both goals in a 2-2 draw at Arbroath, the winner at Albion Rovers and the opening two goals in the last, crucial, match of the season. Dalziel started as he was to continue at Stark's Park – scoring vital goals, and in abundance.

As the promotion push spluttered on, there was a quarter final tie to be played at Stark's Park. St Mirren got the draw that the other six clubs were dreading, but it was a weakened Rovers side who went behind to an 18th minute goal. New signing from Falkirk Bryan Purdie was ineligible, Alex Brash and Billy Herd were suspended, and Colin Harris lasted until half time, when he was replaced by John Wright, a lifelong Rovers fan who had come to prominence at Kirkcaldy YM Juniors and had shone in the midweek Reserve team matches. Jim Marshall lasted just twenty minutes more, and Gordon Dalziel and Ian Gordon were carrying injuries.. Rovers gave a good account of themselves in front of an old fashioned crowd of almost 8500, and St Mirren's second goal, in the last minute, was a cruel twist of the knife ; but only a fully fit Rovers team firing on all cylinders would have beaten the team from two divisions higher, who went on to lift the trophy.

Perpetual substitute Billy McNeill, an honest, hard-working midfield player, scored the winner in a 3-2 home win over Berwick Rangers, but that was followed by three, nervous, anxious draws before a visibly slowing Andy Harrow scored the only goal of a home match over Stenhousemuir. A 2-1 win at Albion Rovers and two more tentative draws were ground out, the one at Ayr proving to be crucial, although it meant that, with two games to play, Rovers' fate rested with the other promotion candidates. A leg-weary end to the match at Perth saw St Johnstone equalise with three minutes to play.

There was almost an air of resignation as the official party, and no more than one hundred supporters, made the long trip back to Stranraer, where the weary journey had begun nine months earlier. Promotion was out of Rovers' hands, but they were one of three clubs who still had a chance of accompanying convincing champions Meadowbank Thistle into the First Division.

Alex Kinninmonth had been convinced for several months that the season would 'go to the last kick of the ball'. Publicly, Frank Connor was defiant : "If ever a team deserved to be promoted it is Raith Rovers. The breaks have gone against us all season, and we are due a bit of luck on our side" he insisted, but privately he was admitting to the very real possibility of disappointment. Ayr United required only a draw at home to Stirling Albion to deprive their opponents, and Rovers, of the remaining promotion place.

Rovers endured a very nervous first half hour which made a nonsense of the confident noises being made before the start. Right winger Creaney gave Billy Herd all manner of problems and scored in only four minutes. Failure to win at Stranraer would mean that Ayr (win or draw) or Stirling (win) would be promoted. Gordon Dalziel latched onto a McAlpine clearance and levelled the score in 32 minutes. It was an opportunist goal and settled the early nerves, but many who had grown old in experiencing disappointment from their team feared nothing better than a draw, and at half time that looked the likeliest outcome given Rovers' stuttering performance.

There was good news from Ayr at the interval, however. Stirling were 2-0 up, having scored in 4 and 21 minutes. It was a different Raith team in the second half. They scented promotion and tore the Stranraer defence apart in a blistering spell of seven minutes, scoring three times and missing several more. Thereafter, the match at Stair Park was meaningless. On the field, the 22 players went throught the motions, with more interest being shown by the Raith players in what was happening 30 miles up the road at Somerset Park.

On top of the visitors dug-out, Rovers' travelling reserves had commandeered a powerful radio from a local supporter, and were listening to a live commentary of the Ayr v Stirling game on West Sound. The first bad news came nine minutes into the second half – Ayr had been awarded a penalty. Wilson's shot was saved by Andy Graham, who had played a number of games on loan to Rovers a few seasons earlier.

The joy of the increasing crowd of anxious Raith fans and officials huddled round the radio was unconfined when Stirling scored a third goal in 64 minutes. A goal for Ayr (making it 1-3) four minutes later was shrugged off, but a second goal, in 76 minutes, began to spread anxiety amongst the crowd. Fourteen minutes to go at Ayr and Stranraer, and Ayr United needed only one more goal to pip Rovers, and Stirling, for promotion.

The news from the radio was hardly soothing. Ayr were attacking relentlessly ; they hit the post ; they hit the bar ; Andy Graham and his defenders were performing heroics. Twice in the last few minutes an Ayr man was through with only Graham to beat, and twice the goalkeeper parried the ball to safety. On both occasions, commentator Jim Sherry (a former Ayr player) started to say "GOAL" only to be cut short by Graham's heroics.

Some 30 seconds before the end of the Stranraer v Rovers match, the final whistle blew at Somerset Park. Stirling had won 3-2 and, incredibly, Raith Rovers had been promoted. Of all the permutations of results that these two fixtures could have thrown up, the only two that would promote Rovers – a win at Stranraer and a Stirling victory at Ayr – had come to pass. The joyous shouts of the Rovers fans, officials and reserves round the radio was the signal for unrestrained rejoicing, on the terracing, in the stand, on the Rovers bench and on the field. Referee Williamson played his part by ending the game promptly on the 90th minute. A season which started for Rovers at Stranraer after 25 seconds of the first match, was not settled until about 25 seconds before the end of the last game, at the same, distant venue. Alex Kinninmonth got it just about right – it went to the last kick of the ball, but not in the match in which Raith Rovers played.

It could be argued that Rovers used up several years' worth of good fortune, given the events at Somerset Park, but that would diminish the huge amount of work undertaken during the season by everyone at the club, as they were carried along by the manager's drive and enthusiasm. Chris Candlish, who was freed after 13 years at the club, believed that Connor "talked us up", but it was a close call. Many supporters, continually perplexed by the apparent eagerness with which the club sold its best players, thought that the sale of Keith Wright could have cost the club promotion. Connor himself admitted "it nearly did", but argued that the club's debt had to be addressed (modest as it was by later standards). It was a rare lapse in the manager's single-minded pursuit of improvement on the field, but in this instance he rode his luck and deserved his success.

The long desired return to the First Division was accompanied by some strengthening of the squad. John McStay, who had been a young reserve at Motherwell when Frank Connor was Jock Wallace's assistant manager, was signed on a free transfer, as was the former St Johnstone

ALEX BRASH

1987

161

Jimmy Joyce, who for several decades was kit-man and boot-boy at Stark's Park. Jimmy died at Cameron Hospital in September 1998, in his early 80's, following a year of failing health. He was a faithful worker for the Rovers, available at all hours to lay out kit, take in laundry, clean boots and run the baths. He was a familiar figure at the tunnel mouth, and an accurate weather vane. If it was summer, Jimmy could be seen in his sleeve-less jersey. If it was winter, he wore a muffler. The bunnet was pan-seasonal. He famously tussled with Alex McDonald, then player manager of Hearts, as the latter passed down the tunnel on the way to an early bath. Jimmy spent every Sunday at Stark's Park cleaning up after the previous day's game, and his sole "reward" was a lunch on the left-overs from Saturday's pavilion catering. He ate particularly well one day - much to the chagrin of the then-Chairman, whose packed lunch had been confused with Saturday's leftovers. His devoted service was recognised by the Club at its Centenary Dinner, when he received an inscribed salver. Jimmy Joyce was a real Rovers man.

CAMMY FRASER

IAN GIBSON

ANDY HARROW

player manager Ian Gibson, and Alastair McLeod, Murdo's younger, under-achieving brother, who had failed to justify Kilmarnock's large transfer fee to Dumbarton. Craig Robertson was transferred to Dunfermline for £25,000.

The squad, which had been stretched to breaking point by the late-season demands a few months earlier, was further strengthened by the graduation of some of the young players brought to the club by Alastair McIlroy. Throughout the previous season, and for several years to come, the Monday evening Reserve fixtures were a delightful bonus for the keenest supporters. The individual and collective displays of a stream of promising young talent were a joy to watch. At the start of 1987/88, Alan Strachan and Ian Ferguson joined the previous season's recruits George Fairgrieve and John Wright, in the first team squad. There was also the equivalent of a new signing, as the manager had spent many hours of the close season personally restoring Dalziel to full fitness.

The first match back in the First Division was a very sobering experience, Kenny McDonald scoring a hat-trick for Forfar Athletic in a 4-1 win at Stark's Park. Two goals from Colin Harris and one from Jim Marshall at Dumfries, and a battling 0-0 draw at Firhill, got things on an even keel, but three straight defeats in the League, and a plucky 2-1 defeat at home to Dundee United in the League Cup (having beaten Clydebank by the same score in the previous round) underlined the reality of life in a higher division.

The turning point came at Rugby Park on 12th September 1987. Rovers went two down after eleven minutes, but battled back to take the lead in 57 minutes, before Kilmarnock equalised four minutes later. In 79 minutes, Hamish McAlpine gathered a passback and launched a clearance which seemed to gather momentum as it flew through the air. It bounced once on the edge of the penalty area and looped over the startled Kilmarnock goalkeeper for the winning goal. Meadowbank, Clydebank, Airdrie, and Dumbarton were beaten in quick succession, and another heavy defeat (3-0) at Forfar was followed by victories over Queen of the South and Hamilton Accies as Rovers moved up the League to the unanticipated fringes of the promotion race.

The lively striker, and man of many clubs, David Lloyd had been signed from St Johnstone, and after a couple of defeats, at home to Kilmarnock and a 3-4 goal-feast at Meadowbank, former Rangers midfielder and Kirkcaldy resident Cammy Fraser came out of injury-enforced retirement to replace Glenn Kerr as sweeper.

It was a controversial change in the eyes of Rovers fans. Kerr had been outstanding in the promoted team of the previous season, and did not appear to be out of his depth in the higher division, but in post-match pleasantries with opposing manager, Frank Connor was discovering that clubs were identifying the former junior as a weak spot in Rovers' defence. The manager's critics were almost proved right on Fraser's debut. Rovers went 4-0 ahead in assured fashion at home to Partick Thistle, with doubles from McStay and Dalziel. Thistle scored in 59, 65 and 82 minutes, and looked like adding to their comeback every time they attacked, right up until the referee blew the final whistle, Rovers' mightily relieved to hang on to win 4-3.

It did not take Fraser long to win over the doubters, however, as he showed the pitch craft and skill which brought him to the fore at Hearts and Dundee, and earned him the admiration of Graeme Souness at Ibrox. By the end of the season, veteran supporters were declaring him the best player seen in a Rovers jersey since Willie McNaught. He found little to trouble him during the local derby at home to East Fife on November 7th. The final scoreline was 7-1, but it could have been double that in one of the most one-sided games ever seen at Stark's Park. The 1-0 half time scoreline was scant reward for their domination, thanks in part to East Fife's centre half being sent off before half an hour had been played, and after the interval Colin Harris (with two goals) and Gordon Dalziel (with a hat-trick) spearheaded a relentless barrage of attacks. Many home fans felt sorry for the visitors, such was the brutality of their defeat.

That was the start of a sequence of nine matches which included just one defeat, a 5-1 win at Dumfries and a 4-0 home win over Meadowbank. The dice was rolling in Rovers' favour, even in the ballot bag, as Rangers were the opponents, at home, in the Scottish Cup. The match was twice postponed and finally played on Monday February 8th – two days after Rovers were beaten 5-0 at Firhill. Bolstered by another of the manager's old protégés (at Celtic), Ronnie Coyle, who had been signed from Clyde, the team matched Souness's collection of internationalists from England and Scotland, and thoroughly merited a 0-0 draw. Rovers survived what looked to be a valid penalty claim when McCoist appeared to be fouled, but it took the intervention of Rangers player-manager to calm their nerves in the closing stages of the match as Rovers sensed the possibility of an astonishing victory. Rangers played out the final minutes of the match passing the ball sideways and backwards in their own half, prompting Colin Harris to mock their caution by sitting on the ball on the half way line, with nine Rangers players between him and their goal.

The all-ticket 10,000 crowd was a far cry from the 254 of 21 months earlier, as was the 35,144 who watched the replay two days later at Ibrox. Ian Durrant put Rangers ahead from the penalty spot in 15 minutes and five minutes into the second half David Lloyd delighted the Rovers support by equalising with an elegant header. It was backs to the wall stuff for the remainder of the match, however, and Rangers scored three times in the last ten minutes to win 4-1.

Rovers were by no means disgraced by their Cup exit ; the coffers were boosted and players and supporters alike were emboldened by the realisation that the club had been raised above the level of the lowest division. They were exciting times at every level of the club, as it woke from a lengthy torpor, and embraced the changing face of Scottish football. New commercial manager Alex Kilgour was an enthusiastic promoter of the club's image, and helped launch a lottery which was a worthy, if belated, successor to the lucrative ventures of the Stark's Park Development Association under Bert Herdman in the early 1960s, and Andy Leigh and Bob Bell in the late 1970s.

There was meaningful investment in the youth policy, with a squad taken abroad to play in the Vieux Conde Tournament in Northern France. Having beaten Olympique Marseille 4-1 in the semi final, the Raith Rovers team lost to the Polish national team in the final. At younger age levels, four teams were formed under the banner of Raith Rovers Boys Club, and the gap between youth and first teams was bridged by most of the young reserve players playing for Lochgelly Albert in the Fife Junior League on Saturday afternoons. All three initiatives produced a stream of young talent which provided the nucleus of a future first team which would eventually reach the Premier League and win the League Cup. Some of those who did not stay for that journey were sold for significant transfer fees, which paid for (more experienced) replacements. The foundations of the future success of the club may have been excavated with promotion in 1986/87, but they were well and truly cemented-in the following season.

Safe from relegation, there were only three wins in the final 12 League matches as a very satisfying season meandered to its over-long end. There was more interest in the exploits of the reserve team, who, apart from entertaining the faithful fans on Monday evenings, beat Hearts 3-1, Dundee 2-1 and Celtic 1-0 at Parkhead to reach the semi final of the 2nd Eleven Cup, which they narrowly lost 2-1 at home to Rangers in front of a crowd which approached the 899 who saw the final home first team League match of the season, in which Queen of the South were beaten 4-2.

That attendance was a reminder that fans were returning to Stark's Park at a slower rate than they had deserted the stands and terraces in disgust seven years earlier. Frank Connor, who had a keen appreciation of the club and its environment, could never understand why attendances, in a town of Kirkcaldy's size, were not much larger. It has been a thoroughly satisfactory season, but the road back to top flight football for Rovers was to involve a long, and hard-fought

journey.

The vastly experienced former Dumbarton and Stirling Albion goalkeeper Gordon Arthur was signed during the close season, to replace Hamish McAlpine, who had retired, rather abruptly, after being largely responsible for Kilmarnock's goals in a 2-2 draw at Stark's Park on 5th March. Colin Harris had gone too, the week after McAlpine. If his majestic performance at Dumfries in the previous season's cup tie was the best by a Raith Rovers player in recent memory, his last appearance was arguably the worst witnessed by a Rovers crowd. Two-down at half time at Meadowbank, Harris was hauled off at half time after an apalling performance. That evening, Frank Connor telephoned Hamilton Accies manager John Lambie, who had enquired earlier about the availability of the richly talented striker, and Harris was promptly transferred, still at the peak of his powers.

Experienced players were signed from Premier League clubs, full back Derek Murray from Dundee United, centre forward Eric Ferguson from Dunfermline Athletic ("I signed his twin," sighed Connor as the former Rangers striker failed to make any kind of impact) and Alan Logan, a tricky forward from Partick Thistle.

A sell-out, all ticket crowd at the opening pre-season friendly against Rangers saw an impressive debut from teenager Shaun Dennis, who covered for the injured Alex Brash, in the last season of a long and distinguished career. Cammy Fraser joined his defensive partner in the treatment room after pulling a hamstring in a short lived resurrection of the public trial match. Before a ball had been kicked in anger, the pattern for an injury-strewn season had been set.

All the pre-season games were lost, albeit against tough opponents, and Rovers were well beaten in the opening League match at Perth. Defeat in the League Cup was most unfortunate, the team having the best of the ninety minutes plus extra time at Brockville. The penalty kick contest was getting to the fascinating stage, at 8-9 to Falkirk, when substitute Billy Spence missed from the spot – with a couple of more experienced players delaying their involvement in the contest.

A 2-1 home win over Queen of the South was followed by two draws and four defeats, and the manager decided that drastic action had to be taken to avoid the "second season syndrome" which often brings problems to promoted teams. The spectacularly inconsistent Stuart Romaines was signed from Falkirk to add some power to the forward midfield positions, and Cammy Fraser returned from injury to bolster a largely defensive formation which included full backs McStay and Murray, centre backs Brash and Coyle, and Ian Gibson in the "Donald Urquhart" role in midfield. Fraser volunteered for midfield duty, a noble act given his injury record. Although the reserve side was full of promising young talent, they were only seen in the first team near the end of the season,

IAN FERGUSON

Two Rovers S signings, Scott Wright and Robert Raeside, played for Scotland Under 18s against Northern Ireland at Dumfries on 11th March 1989

There was controversy before the 1988/89 season started when Rovers' new playing strip featured royal blue shirts. Many fans were upset at the move away from the traditional navy blue colours.

1987 - The Green Cockatoo restaurant in the High Street closed
1988 - Seafield Colliery closed and the last cycle races were held in Beveridge Park
1989 - Seafield Colliery towers were demolished ; Jocky Wilson became World Darts Champion once again.

GORDON ARTHUR

DEREK MURRAY

ALAN LOGAN

PAUL SWEENEY

when the team's league position was secured.

Better results were ground out, but it was not always a pretty sight. From the start of the season to a 3-1 win at Meadowbank on 11th February, more than one goal was scored on only three occasions, the aforementioned 2-1 win over Queen of the South, a similar victory over Forfar at home on 26th November, and a completely uncharacteristic 5-3 win over Partick Thistle on Guy Fawkes' Day. Single goals were scored on no fewer than 19 occasions ; there were three 0-0 draws and only two scoreless defeats.

The prospect of another Scottish Cup tie at home to Rangers, and the need for more points to ensure safety, prompted the signing of veteran centre half Bobby Glennie from Dundee, who took over from Brash at centre half, with Shaun Dennis sent back to the reserves. A capacity crowd thought they may be witnessing a real cup upset when Gordon Dalziel opened the scoring against star-studded Rangers in the 53rd minute of the cup tie at Stark's Park, but a slack pass by Ronnie Coyle 14 minutes later was cruelly punished by a 30 yard pile-driver from Ian Ferguson, and it was the reigning Scottish champions who were relieved to take the tie to a replay at Ibrox, where they won 3-0.

Encouraged by their excellent performance in the first match against Rangers, the team embarked on an eight game unbeaten run in the League, and began to find the net more frequently. Queen of the South were beaten 4-1 at home on 4th March, Alex Brash ending his Rovers career on a high note with two of the goals, but the most memorable match of an otherwise artless season came the following week, at Dunfermline.

The great rivals were striving for a quick return to the Premier League, but were completely outplayed by a Raith team in which everything clicked into place. The fans, too, were in fine voice on a memorable afternoon. The scoreline was utterly misleading – Dunfermline were thumped 1-0. Cammy Fraser was outstanding at sweeper, memorably breaking up a Dunfermline attack with an audacious over-head pass-back to Gordon Arthur, and just as impressive was the player of the season, Paul Sweeney, who capped a flawless performance by crossing for Gordon Dalziel to head the only goal of the game five minutes from time, rounding off a perfect afternoon for the vocal travelling support.

Ten days later, Sweeney was transferred to Newcastle United in the club's first six-figure deal, a portion of which was used to sign the highly skilled Hamilton Accies winger Martin Nelson. Three wins, three defeats and a draw rounded off a season which reinforced Rovers' position in the First Division, but which provided just 55 League goals from 39 matches. Dalziel was the top scorer with 11, most of them points winners.

A slightly more expansive policy was adopted for 1989/90, encouraged by three wins from the first three League matches.

Ian Ferguson, tall, powerful and a product of the youth system, partnered Dalziel up front, and there was much more evidence of the fruits of the youth policy, including a continuation of the Monday evening entertainment from the Reserve team.

Another experienced defender, Ian McLeod, was signed from Falkirk, although he proved to be a powerful force going forward. Ian Gibson left to be player-manager at Arbroath in August, and Bobby Glennie followed suit, to Forfar, a month later. Connor, who had signed a three year contract, his first at the club, diverged from his usual policy of recruiting older players from higher divisions by signing the widely admired Stuart Sorbie from Alloa, but reverted to type in replacing Glennie with another experienced defender from Dundee in George McGeachie.

The purse-strings were prised open in October when forward Kenny McDonald was bought for £80,000 from Airdrie, a new club record. He may have maintained the "curse of the record signing" with a disappointing year at the club, but he scored 10 League goals and, more significantly, motivated Gordon Dalziel to double his scoring tally to 20, thus setting a pattern for the club's record league goalscorer in the years which followed.

Dunfermline gained revenge for their humiliation five months earlier when they dumped Rovers out of the League Cup at the first time of asking, 3-0 at East End Park, and the largely satisfactory League form was not carried into the Scottish Cup. A two goal lead was surrendered at Greenock in the third round tie, and Rovers lost 3-1 in the fiery replay. With Rovers chasing an equaliser, Morton settled the match with a controversial goal in the last minute. The referee was faced by a larger-than-usual baying mob hanging over the enclosure wall to harangue the officials as they made their way down the players' tunnel at the end of the match. One of them knocked the ball from the referee's grasp, was promptly arrested for assault, and following a court case had the distinction of being the first – and so far only – supporter to be banned sine die by the S.F.A. The ban proved to be as effective as the Rovers' defence that night, and the fan has continued to attend matches, at home and abroad, over the ensuing two decades.

Despite the disappointment of an early cup exit, only one of the subsequent 14 league games to the end of the season was lost. Meadowbank were beaten 3-0, Ayr United 5-2 and Alloa 4-0 as the team welded into an efficient, compact and entertaining unit. McStay, Dennis, Coyle, Fraser and Murray formed a formidable back line, in front of a competent goalkeeper in Gordon Arthur. In midfield McLeod and Romaines provided support for the skills of Nelson and young Phil Burn, while up front any combination of Logan, Ferguson, Dalziel and McDonald knew the way to goal.

Frank Connor was sufficiently satisfied with the team's progress that he felt it was time to take the club onto "the next step" on the path to the Premier Division. Full time football was out of the question – home attendances remained obdurately below 1500 – but he failed to persuade the directors to increase the players' wages to introduce a third night of training.

Despite the manager's disappointment at the lack of ambition in the Boardroom, the same squad assembled for duty in 1990/91, with no significant additions, all the new faces coming from the rich flow of talent out of the reserve team. The team continued where they had left off at the end of the previous season, with the only defeat in the opening nine League and League Cup ties coming in the now annual visit to Ibrox.

A 2-1 win in the opening round of the League Cup at Forfar came courtesy of a last minute Dalziel goal, but a splendid performance saw Premier League Hibs beaten in at Stark's Park, George McGeachie scoring the only goal of the game. The least said about the 6-2 defeat at Ibrox the better.

The only other defeat in the first sixteen competitive fixtures was 2-0 at Ayr, which was followed by a run of League and Cup results (in the new competition for clubs outwith the Premier League to mark the Scottish League's Centenary) which culminated in a 5-1 win at Airdrie. Two excellent Centenary Cup results, 3-0 at Falkirk and 3-2 at home to Hamilton Accies, were followed by an undeserved defeat after extra time at home to Dundee, the eventual winners of the trophy.

A 0-0 draw at home to Partick Thistle was the lull before the storm of a bizarre match at Falkirk. Although play was evenly shared throughout the 90 minutes, there was an air of "something not quite right" about Rovers, particularly in defence, and they suffered by far the worst defeat of the Connor era, 7-1. The explanation emerged over the next few days. The manager had arrived late, and distracted, at Brockville. Former Scotland striker Joe Jordan had just been appointed manager of Hearts and, in need of some inside knowledge of Scottish League football, he asked his former coach at Bristol City, Jimmy Lumsden, who he could recommend as an assistant. Lumsden, who coached Celtic's Reserves and Youths alongside Frank Connor several years earlier, unhesitatingly recommended the Rovers manager, and he met with Jordan and Hearts officials on the morning of the Falkirk game.

His acceptance of the opportunity to return to the Premier League, and full time football, left Rovers in need of a manager, but there was much for his successor to work with. The team sat in third place in the League, level on points with Hamilton Accies and only three points behind leaders Airdrie. The squad was settled, an excellent mixture of experience and youth, with several more promising young players in the pipeline. As the Raith board argued in their negotiations for compensation with Wallace Mercer, they had lost not just a manager, but the "heartbeat of the club". The consolation was that he had left a club utterly transformed from the near-comatose outfit he had inherited four and a half years earlier ; solvent, solid, bristling with potential, and providing a platform for the unimaginable heights that would be scaled over the next five years.

One of Connor's many achievements was that the 'r' word, relegation, was banished from the Stark's Park vocabulary for many years to come.

As Murray Cheyne took temporary charge of the first team, the manager's job was advertised and after several weeks of deliberation, the Chairman, Johnny Urquhart convinced his fellow directors that Willie McLean should return to Stark's Park, but he would not uproot his family from Ayr and turned down the offer of the job. The choice was then between two contrasting men. Two of the directors favoured Jim Leishman, who had left Dunfermline Athletic in acrimonious circumstances four months earlier. The majority, however, preferred the bright, energetic Dunfermline Athletic player, Jimmy Nicholl, who had been encouraged to apply primarily as it would give him experience of the interview process. He had no expectations of being successful, but on 20th November 1990 he was unveiled as the new player manager.

He arrived carrying an injury, and did not appear as a player until February 2nd, when a Craig Brewster-inspired Forfar beat Rovers 3-1 at Station Park. It was the last of a sequence of six matches without a win, which included a third round defeat in the Scottish Cup at home to Hamilton, George McCluskey scoring the only goal of the match five minutes from time.

The difficult start to Nicholl's managerial career could have been anticipated. He took over a team, and a set up, which bore the unmistakeable stamp of his successor, and he had to familiarise himself with the routines, habits and limitations of part-time football for the first time in his career. With money to spend, he began looking for players in his native Ireland, north and south of the border, and signed Damien Dunleavy from Sligo Rovers for £20,000.

There was little Nicholl could achieve in his first half season. The team had a solid foundation, with a back three of Gordon Arthur, John McStay and Ian McLeod ; Shaun Dennis and George McGeachie at centre back ; Ronnie Coyle, David Sinclair and Nicholl himself in midfield, and the prolific Gordon Dalziel, the increasingly impressive Ian Ferguson, and highly skilled Martin Nelson up front.

Cammy Fraser was surprisingly freed by his former Rangers team-mate on 14th March, and Logan, Simpson, Romaines and Murray were put on the transfer list. They were being replaced by youngsters such

Gordon Dalziel had a spell with South Melbourne Hellas in Australia during the summer months of 1889, playing a couple of games for them.

The Cowdenbeath v Dunfermline Scottish Cup tie was played at Stark's Park on 24th February 1990

Stark's Park has been remarkably immune from vandalism or graffiti, but on 22nd July 1990, floodlight lamps purchased by Rovers and intended to be used for evening training were stolen from Beveridge Park.

Young midfield player Phil Burn fractured his pelvis in a car crash in late October 1990.

During a period of suspension, Shaun Dennis spent a few days training at Southampton.

1991 - Kirkcaldy High Street was pedestrianised ; the rugby club stand built in Beveridge Park

Full time training started on 4th July 1991 for the first time since April 1970.

Gordon Dalziel was voted First Division Player of the Year by the Scottish Professional Footballers Association at the end of 1991/92.

MARTIN NELSON

In the unaccustomed surroundings of the Second Division, Felix McGrogan and Jimmy Gilpin each scored 14 League goals, with Gilpin winning 20-17 overall. John Park scored twelve goals in just 15 League appearances in 1964/65 before Jocky Richardson scored 21 to George Lyall's 15 the following season. Richardson scored 21 League goals in the 1966/67 promotion season, but Pat Gardner scored 29, with eight more in other games. Gordon Wallace weighed in with 18 in the League, and was unrivalled with 27 from 34 League matches as he helped Rovers escape from relegation in 1967/68.

George Falconer scored three more League goals (with 16) than his striking partner the following season and the relegation season in 1969/70 saw Ralph Brand and Mike Judge score most League goals, just five each, although Colin Sinclair scored ten in total. Gordon Wallace topped the list in 1970/71, but it was another of that name who scored 14 League goals in his debut senior season, and he scored 19 the following season before Joe Baker arrived in 1972/73 to score 25 times in 24 League matches.

Malcolm Robertson was top the following season with 21, and scored ten in all games, along with Gordon Wallace and John Hislop in 1974/75, the latter scoring most League goals, nine.

as full back David Young and a very promising centre back Robbie Raeside. The team wasn't going to be relegated, and it wouldn't be promoted, so while there was a feeling of aimless drifting as 1990/91 meandered to a close, it gave the manager valuable learning time.

At the end of the season, he admitted to the Fife Free Press : "It took time to get used to dealing with players and they took time to change. Looking back, I probably gave them too much allowance. I lowered my standards instead of trying to raise their's. A lot of the guys worked hard during the day and came in for training, and I didn't clamp down hard enough. I should have.

"At our first training session I planned to have a short, sharp 5-a-side game of 30 minutes each way. They couldn't do it, so I cut it back to 20, and then 15, and then 10. I adjusted to suit them because I was new – but next year we will be back to 30 and I will be demanding a lot more."

The manager had made the same complaint to the Board of Directors, reminding them of the promises that were made at his interview about introducing full time football, an unfulfilled ambition of his predecessor. He had also been frustrated in his attempts to sign Paul O'Brien from Dunfermline and Steve McBride from Portadown earlier in the year, both players unimpressed by the part-time status on offer. The debate which ensued exposed a schism amongst the directors, the majority of whom were resisting the offer of substantial investment (but majority control) from one of their colleagues.

Having agreed in early May to introduce full time training, there was a change of mind on Monday May 6th, and another about-turn the following day, when it was announced that 18 players would be full time the following season : Dennis, Burn, Ferguson, Dunleavy, Raeside and Sinclair, six young reserves and 6 youth players from the club's schoolboy signings.

Chairman John Urquhart told the Fife Free Press : "This is a major development for Raith. It is a big step forward. We have stretched ourselves to go full time, although it is difficult to put a final figure on it [the cost was quoted at £100,000 per season]. It should help the younger players, and give them a chance to improve at a quicker rate, and establish themselves in the first team. That is the way forward, and it has been successful at other clubs." Thus ended 21 years as a part-time club, the longest spell since the club joined the Scottish League. It started a period of 14 years as a full time club, itself the longest in the club's history.

Although the club's spectacular, if brief, period of success did not begin until 1992/93, the final pieces of the jigsaw were laid the previous season. Craig Brewster was signed during the close season, a transfer tribunal eventually setting the fee at £57,000. Winger Trevor Williamson was purchased from Portadown, and centre forward Alan McKenzie from Cowdenbeath,

although he sustained an ill-timed injury just two months after being signed.

The funds for those purchases came to Rovers by a circuitous route. Keith Wright's transfer to Dundee more than four years earlier had realised a paltry £35,000, but Rovers were to receive 20% of any future transfer fee over that amount. It was with some delight that they learned of Hibs' £450,000 purchase of the player in early August. Even more money came Rovers' way in early October when Ian Ferguson was sold to Hearts for £100,000

Part of that particular fee was spent very wisely. Peter Hetherston was signed from Falkirk for £20,000, arriving with a troublesome reputation, but showed none of that as he settled into Rovers midfield. What he did display was a very clever football brain and abundant skill. Brewster moved further forward to support Gordon Dalziel, and as the season progressed, there was the feeling that the club was moving forward once again, following the hiatus which followed Connor's departure.

Jock McStay later reflected on that period in the club's history, when a change of manager could have been fraught with unpleasant consequences. "The team was doing well when Frank left, and it was Jimmy's first job. He had always been a full time player and he didn't really understand the part-time set up. He tried to change it all, and the team slipped back a bit, but it was a learning process for Jimmy as well, and he learned the hard way, learned from his mistakes, and it worked out well for him. He brought the experienced players like myself and Daz, Ian McLeod and George McGeachie back into the team, and he signed Peter Hetherston which was the start of the upsurge."

The early part of the season had the usual highs and lows of a team in development. A 5-0 defeat at Partick Thistle and a 3-1 defeat at home to Hamilton Accies failed to dispel the memories of a superb performance in the second round of the League Cup at home to Scottish Cup holders Motherwell. Alan McKenzie opened the scoring in 7 minutes, and despite Rovers being on top, Motherwell equalised through Stevie Kirk 45 minutes later. Six minutes after that, Martin Nelson scored a memorable goal. Rather like Gordon Pettie's goal, the distance of Nelson's sublime chip gains yards with every telling but it was almost 35 yards, from close to the touchline, and found the top corner of the goal.

Brewster scored twice for a rampant Raith team in the closing 15 minutes to seal a memorable 4-1 victory over the Premier Division club whose manager, Tommy McLean, described the game as "a holocaust". Rovers were simply brilliant. The reward was a trip to Parkhead, where Rovers were not disgraced in losing 3-1.

Those were isolated moments of encouragement, however. The fundamental changes being made by the new manager were taking time to come to fruition. The disappointing end to the previous season was met with stoicism from a dwindling number of spectators at Stark's Park, but several poor performances, and defeats, in the opening League matches of 1991/92 caused a more vocal backlash, mostly against the board of directors. [During one particularly acrimonious defeat, it was announced over the Public Address system that the fans chanting for the board's removal should put their objections in writing !] Perhaps more importantly, home attendances continued to drop. There wasn't complete harmony within the squad, which was an awkward mixture of full time and part time. Jock McStay was put on the transfer list in September, and Alan Logan was free to join another club.

Another home defeat in October prompted to Fife Free Press to report : "Forget promotion – on Saturday's evidence, Raith might yet end up battling against relegation. The Kirkcaldy side's tale of woe plumbed new depths with a ghastly 3-1 defeat at the hands of Hamilton … out played, out thought and out-witted on their own back yard." The attendance was 1007.

The cup for First and Second Division clubs, then under the sponsorship of B&Q, had never been a happy hunting ground for Rovers, but they reached the penultimate stage, winning on penalties at Clydebank after a 1-1 draw and extra time and 3-2 at Morton (Dalziel hat-trick, which he repeated at Stirling in the League four days later). There was disappointment in the semi final at Hamilton, however. With Nelson absent through injury, the team lacked width and were rarely seen as an attacking force. Gordon Dalziel put Rovers ahead from the penalty spot in 58 minutes, but it was an undeserved lead, and Hamilton scored in 71 and 80 minutes to qualify for the final.

With the manager acting as assistant to Billy Bingham with the Northern Ireland international squad, another Ulsterman, Martin Harvey, was brought to Kirkcaldy as Rovers assistant manager in November. Shaun Dennis, who had been called into the Scotland Under 21 squad the previous year, became the first Raith Rovers player to win a cap at that level when he played against Switzerland on 10th September 1991.

In the Scottish Cup, there was hope of an upset with the visit of mid-table Premier League St Johnstone, but they demonstrated that Rovers remained a promising "work in progress" by winning 2-0. Despite that disappointment, significantly better League results during the winter months meant that Rovers remained on the fringe of the promotion race until a 0-0 draw with Partick Thistle on 11th April, and the last month of the season was used to strengthen the foundations of a largely settled team, with some more young players graduation from the prolific youth system. Jason Dair made four appearances as a substitute in the closing weeks of the season, Stevie Crawford appeared in a Fife Cup tie, and the diminutive Colin Cameron was sent across to Sligo Rovers in Ireland for experience of first team

football, one of a number of players loaned to Irish clubs.

The supporters, who were now enjoying the football on offer, and the individual skills of many of the players, did not realise it at the time, but the last seven League matches of 1991/92, all unbeaten, served notice of what was to come the following season. More importantly, the players were beginning to realise that Connor's oft-repeated "the next step" was a real possibility. In the Fife Free Press of 8th May 1992, Jimmy Nicholl described his ambition for the following season : "What I am looking for is a different approach from the entire team. At the start of the season, I don't think the players believed they were capable of winning promotion. Now they do – and saw how close we came to going up – but we suffered because of our early results."

The only significant pre-season signing was Ian Thomson, a sturdy left sided attacking midfielder whose £20,000 fee from Queen of the South was decided by a transfer tribunal. Former Rangers and Motherwell midfielder Bobby Russell had also been signed, but after a few days' pre-season training concluded that the condition of one of his knees pointed only to retirement. Goalkeeper Tom Carson replaced Gordon Arthur for the winter months, but it was a predictable, settled side which lined up against newly relegated St Mirren for the opening League match, at Stark's Park on 1st August 1992. McStay and McLeod at full back, Dennis and Coyle between them, Sinclair, Hetherston and Nicholl in midfield, and Dalziel, Brewster and Dair up front.

The match started off as a fairly even contest, up to the point of Rovers' third goal, with just over half an hour played. Thereafter, it turned into a rout, Dalziel completing his hat-trick in a 7-0 trouncing of the bookies' favourites for promotion. Those who tried to place a bet on Rovers after the match in the previously generous "handicap league" found that no bets were being taken on the opening day League leaders.

It was "after the Lord Mayor's Show" on Tuesday evening, when Stirling went home with a point from a score-less draw, but the 1-1 draw at Kilmarnock the following Saturday was deemed satisfactory. In the League Cup, Rovers made an early exit, out-gunned 4-1 at Hibs, but that merely inspired a run of seven successive League wins. Indeed it would be a total of 17 League games before Rovers tasted defeat again, their first in the League.

The first five wins in the opening run were by a single goal. George McGeachie replaced Davie Sinclair, and Alan McKenzie came in for Jason Dair, in a tighter formation which saw Thomson, Dalziel and Brewster share in the goals, the first named scoring the only goal of the match at Dunfermline. Dalziel scored a hat-trick at Cowdenbeath, and he and McKenzie scored in a 2-0 win at Meadowbank, before a run of four successive draws, which ended with a 4-1 home win over Dumbarton, Dalziel scoring in 32 seconds and

ALLY GRAHAM

Wallace was again to the fore with 21 in all first team games the following season, and eleven in 1976/77 as Rovers suffered relegation once again.

Andy Harrow and Ronnie Duncan both scored eleven League goals in 1977/78, Andy's Scottish Cup goal edging him in front, and Gordon Wallace (mark I) topped the list the following season with 14 League goals. In 1979/80, Ian Ballantyne scored one more League goal than Andy Harrow (with 12), but the latter's five other goals put him on top, two ahead of Ballantyne, whose twelve League goals topped the list in 1980/81, with twelve more to follow in 1981/82.

Colin Harris scored 18 League goals the following season and Jim Kerr scored 16 from midfield as Rovers suffered relegation in their Centenary season. 1984/85 saw a battle between Keith Wright (22 League goals) and Paul Smith (19), although 15 more for Smith in other matches took him nine ahead of Wright. The following season saw a dead-heat in the League, with 21 apiece, and 7-6 to Wright in other fixtures.

SCOTT THOMSON

With interest in the team growing on the back of the successful start to 1992/93, local musicians Crooked Jack produced a cassette tape of Rovers players singing in October.

Jimmy Nicholl was named Scottish Brewers Manager of the Month for October 1992

The Reserve League Cup tie at Stark's Park against Stirling Albion on 14th December 1992 did not kick off until 8.15. Match officials had not been appointed, and Cowdenbeath-based referee Jim Renton, and a couple of linesmen, were hurriedly summoned to Stark's Park. The match went into extra time, finished 1-1 and Rovers won 4-1 on penalties. It was almost eleven o'clock before the handful of spectators left Stark's Park that evening, the latest finish in the ground's long history.

Gordon Dalziel and Craig Brewster were nominated for the SPFA 1st Division Player of the Year Award, which Gordon Dalziel retained.

1992 - Kirkcaldy Cricket Club left their ground at Bennochy Road, playing for a short while back at Beveridge Park before folding.

88 minutes, with McStay and Nicholl netting in between. One of the draws was at Paisley, St Mirren having recovered from their awful start of the season, and a tight, determined performance which overcame the sendings off of Dennis on the hour, and McStay twenty minutes later, was evidence that Rovers had the full repertoire of attributes to sustain a challenge of promotion.

Thanks to that remarkable start to the season, Rovers were never out of the two promotion places, which was to be the focus of attention all season. There was no distraction from the B&Q Cup ; a weakened team (for which the club were fined by the Scottish League) losing on penalties to Meadowbank Thistle, after 120 scoreless minutes at Stark's Park..

Thanks to the emerging youngsters from the reserve and youth teams, the pool had sufficient depth to handle injuries and suspensions. Shaun Dennis was out for three months, and Raeside (briefly), McGeachie, Coyle and Sinclair covered. When Ian Thomson moved to left back to cover for another unsung hero, Ian McLeod, Stevie Crawford came into the attack.

Three excellent results in November kept Rovers' noses in front ; Crawford scoring the only goal of the home local derby against Dunfermline, Dalziel scoring two late goals in a 3-0 win at home to Cowdenbeath, with another two in a thrilling 4-3 win at Greenock. The first League defeat of the season came in a midweek game at Clydebank, but the 3-0 scoreline did not reflect Rovers domination of the match. It was just one of those nights, and a 5-0 win over Meadowbank, followed by 3-1 at home to St Mirren, confirmed Rovers credentials at the top of the League.

On a frosted pitch at Ochilview, a 3-0 win over Stirling Albion was very satisfactory, as was a 0-0 draw at Dunfermline on 2nd January. The Scottish Cup would provide no distractions from the promotion push, although that was probably not in the master plan. Rovers were already one goal down when Tom Carson was injured after 20 minutes of the third round match at Kilmarnock. Davie Sinclair took over in goal, joining Andy Young in the distinction of having worn every jersey for the club, and lost another goal 9 minutes later. An uncharacteristically dispirited Rovers side lost three more in the second half, and had to dwell on the 5-0 scoreline as bad weather closed in, with the next, cathartic match 17 days later. Revenge was exacted on Clydebank in a 4-2 victory at Stark's Park, but four days later Kilmarnock gave notice of their challenge at the top of the League by winning 3-0 on another unhappy return to Rugby Park.

That was the last meaningful defeat of the season. Results were steady rather than spectacular, but the settled, confident team had strength in all the necessary areas, and a determination that this was to be their year. March brought three challenging fixtures in succession. The awkward trip to Paisley was negotiated with a 1-1 draw in midweek. Kilmarnock came to Stark's Park hoping to cut the gap at the top, but goals from Brewster and Dalziel capped a dominant performance. The following week, Jimmy Nicholl scored both goals against his former club Dunfermline, in front of a 7,000 crowd at Stark's Park. Almost there.

A 0-0 draw at Ayr was followed by a thrilling game at Hamilton, on a day when results elsewhere, and a Rovers win, could have sealed promotion. Accies were intent on spoiling the party and opened the scoring in 9 minutes. Dalziel equalised in 58, but Hamilton restored parity a minute later. Rovers' cause was never lost with Brewster in the side, however, and with 7 minutes to go, he fired in an equaliser from 30 yards.

Fittingly, promotion was clinched at home the following week, Brewster scoring twice against Dumbarton, and results elsewhere meant that the Championship was also confirmed, with five games remaining. The 17 years since the Premier League was formed – plus the five before that - was by far the longest spell in their history that Rovers had remained outwith the top division in Scotland. Fans had watched other, notionally smaller, clubs reached that promised land – Clydebank, Dumbarton, Hamilton Accies, Ayr United, and particularly Dunfermline Athletic. There were a few tears shed at Stark's Park on 10th April 1993 when Rovers, at long last, returned to their place in the sun.

The constant tinkering with the numbers in the various Scottish Leagues, part of a prolonged process which would culminate in the top clubs breaking away in 1998, meant that 44 League games were played in the First Division, and it seemed to take forever to fulfil the remaining, meaningless fixtures which, understandably, included two more defeats in the final three matches, doubling the total for the season. These tail end games provided an opportunity for some youngsters, with Colin Cameron in particular enjoying a run of appearances.

Notwithstanding the spectacular success of two years later, 1992/93 remains for many Rovers followers (too young to remember the mid 1950s) the best season they have ever seen at Stark's Park. There were youngsters of great promise and real talent ; several first class professional players, and a handful of match-winning goalscorers. One of Bill Shankly's great sayings was that a successful football team is like moving a piano ; it takes eight men to carry it, and three to play it.

McStay, McLeod, Coyle, Sinclair, McGeachie and Thomson were the bedrock of the team, performing dilligently and professionally throughout the season. At opposite ends of their careers were centre

half Shaun Dennis and Jimmy Nicholl, the player manager frequently showing why he had won 73 caps for Northern Ireland. The virtuoso performances were from that remarkable goalscorer Gordon Dalziel, who scored a career best 33 in the League ; the smoothly powerful match-winner Craig Brewster, who scored 22, and the slightly built wizard in midfield, Peter Hetherston.

Brewster later pointed to the impact of his fellow luminaries : "Peter Hetherston was a great acquisition for the club. He came in halfway through the previous season and as soon as he came in, that was when we began to pick up. A lot of the credit has to go to the whole team, but you have to look at certain individuals who gave that extra something. Gordon Dalziel's goals spoke for themselves. He was a fantastic goalscorer. We complimented each other very well, and helped each other. He was a penalty box striker whereas I was not."

Hopes that Nicholl would follow Bert Herdman's example and establish the club in the top division for a lengthy period (hardly fanciful when one considers that Kilmarnock, promoted in second place no fewer than eleven points behind Rovers – with only two points for a win – have never been relegated since) had to be considered against some conveniently ignored fault-lines which lurked beneath Stark's Park.

Those who had argued against full time football had been proved wrong on the pitch, but correct on the balance sheet. Rovers were losing money at an alarming rate. The League table did not lie when it comes to football prowess, but nor did

attendance figures in the bank manager's estimation, and there was an ominous reminder of that when only 1961 turned up for the last home League match of the season.

For two years, the club had been a happy place, in the dressing room and around the pavilion. Good humour and harmony had been fostered and was well rewarded with success on the pitch, but it was at the expense of difficult decisions being swept under the carpet, and the manager's ambitions, personally and for the club, being indulged at every turn with no thought as to how they would be funded in the long term.

Rovers fans, however, had no cause for such gloomy thoughts over the summer of 1993 as they relished the prospect of Premier Division football for the first time at Stark's Park.

The club was severely handicapped before the season started. The latest round of League reorganisation had seen the top division teams attempt to reduce the number in their League from 12 to 10. The process by which this would be achieved was contentious, and the vote at the Scottish League AGM on Thursday May 27th 1993 was extremely close, and effectively settled by the vote cast by the Raith Rovers representative, Bob Paxton.

He was placed in the awkward position of insisting to fellow Rovers directors that he vote in concert with his colleagues on the League Management Committee, who wished to appease the big clubs by agreeing to three out of the twelve Premier clubs being relegated, with only the First Division champions promoted, to bring the top league

Champions in waiting - lining up, in their change strip, before the start of 1992/93.
Back row : David Young, David Sinclair, Peter Hetherston, Gordon Arthur, Craig Brewster (also pictured below), Trevor Williamson, Shaun Strang.
Middle row : Ian Thomson, John McStay, Ian McLeod, Shaun Dennis, Robert Raeside, Ronnie Coyle, George McGeachie, Philip Burn.
Front row : John Valente, Alan McKenzie, Gerry Docherty, Jimmy Nicholl, Martin Harvey, Gordon Dalziel, Joe Small.

DANNY
LENNON

The team was restored to its former navy blue coloured jerseys by 1945/46, white fold over collars and cuffs being introduced to that colour for the first time (pictured on page 107).

Clothing remained under ration for several years after the end of the war, and in 1949/50 the team wore navy blue jerseys with Scotland-style lion rampant badges, the kit presumably borrowed or purchased second hand to circumvent the obstacles in obtaining a newly manufactured set.

During 1950/51, two gold-coloured hoops were added to the navy blue jerseys, still with white fold over collars, but with no cuffs (page 111). The following season, however, the hoops disappeared, only to re-appear in 1952/53. Both varieties, with and without hoops, were worn in 1953/54. By 1954/55, the hoops had disappeared again.

In 1957/58, in recognition of the increasing incidence of floodlit matches, a "high visibility" strip was donated by the Supporters Club. This had a thick white vertical stripe down the front, and round white colours and cuffs. The shorts were of a shiny fabric, designed to reflect the floodlighting (page 121). Change strips had varied from red to white and back again,

down to 10 clubs for the following season. Rovers' daunting task of staying in the Premier League would be rendered much more difficult, if not impossible ; third bottom would not represent safety, but for one season only, relegation.

Rovers' board botched the situation badly. The Chairman, Peter Campsie, had left an unofficial meeting of similarly concerned clubs admitting that he did not relish the task of telling Paxton that he had to vote against the proposal. An awkward, indecisive board meeting on 10th May failed to even decide on voting on the matter. The minute recorded : "How to vote at the League AGM re League reconstruction re Status Quo or 4 leagues of 10 was discussed but no final decision taken."

The Fife Free Press, published on the same day of the League AGM, carried a story, headlined "Rovers posed to reject plans" in which Campsie was quoted as saying "The status quo suits us fine. The four leagues of 10 proposal will be voted down. Now that the threat of the Super League is almost dead, teams will opt for the status quo."

Contrary to that statement, Paxton voted in favour of the change and was photographed in the following day's papers as "the man who saved Scottish football." He admitted : "Perhaps in the short term I have done Raith a disservice – but I've done the best thing for the club in the long run. If some form of reconstruction had not gone through, there would have been a lot of disquiet among other clubs and there could well have been threats of a breakaway. My views were known to the board. They were informed that if I was the only representative of the club at the meeting then they knew how I would vote."

It was an uncomfortable dilemma for all involved, and was handled extraordinarily badly. Inevitably, everyone lost in the end ; Rovers were relegated, Paxton resigned from the Board and consequently the League Management Committee, and the top clubs broke away anyway three years later. Badly handled, too, were the contract negotiations with Craig Brewster, who declined the club's offer and was transferred to Dundee United for a staged payment of £ 250,000.

The bank overdraft long since exceeded, and some hurried re-terracing of both ends of Stark's Park being undertaken to make the ground fit for Premier Division crowds, there was no money spent on the squad for the start of the season. Two left backs were signed on free transfers, Julian Broddle from St Mirren and Jason Rowbotham from Plymouth Argyle, and Rovers embarked on Premier League life with the squad which had got them promoted, minus 22-goal Brewster.

The introduction to Premier Division football was a gentle as it could be, a home match against St Johnstone, which was drawn 1-1, Shaun Dennis in 37 minutes equalising a Paul Wright goal scored 8

minutes earlier. A 2-1 defeat at home to Arbroath in the League Cup was a sobering experience, and while away defeats at Hearts and Motherwell (the latter by a hefty 4-1) might have been expected, there was disappointment at only taking a point apiece from the visits by Partick Thistle and Dundee United.

There were routine skelpings at Celtic and Aberdeen, but Hetherston scored the only goal of the game for the club's first victory, at Dundee, and there was much to be admired in the grit and determination shown in a 1-1 home draw with Rangers. By then, the purse-strings had been opened and two players signed, goalkeeper Scott Thomson from Forfar Athletic for £45,000 plus Gordon Arthur, and centre forward Ally Graham, for £100,000. The big striker had a brief debut, taken off injured after 21 minutes of the Rangers game, but he was fit to play 90 minutes the following week.

Hetherston repeated his match-winning feat at Dundee with the only goal of the home game against Hearts, which came in the midst of three draws. A heavy home defeat by Motherwell was followed by two excellent away points, on a Tuesday night at Dundee United, Jason Dair and Stevie Crawford scoring in the second half to turn round a 2-0 half time deficit, and at the unlikely venue of Ibrox, where Ally Graham made the score 2-2 with ten minutes to go.

Following a 2-0 defeat at Celtic Park, Gordon Dalziel scored twice to beat bottom club Dundee 2-1 at Stark's Park. Peter Hetherston was substituted after 52 minutes, his pelvic problem deteriorating to the stage where it had to be treated. He was to be absent for the next ten weeks, and on top of the loss of Brewster, the prospects of survival were not bright. The double was done over Hearts, thanks to a Davie Sinclair goal which should have beeen added to by Stevie Crawford, who broke from the halfway line to run, unchallenged, on the Hearts goal, only for the ball to slide narrowly past a post.

The club's fortunes changed dramatically after that match at Tynecastle, played two days after a stormy Annual General Meeting on 16th December. The Board of Directors were under severe pressure from the bank to reduce the overdraft, which had grown beyond control, and more money still had to be found for the continuing repair work on the terracing. The weather intervened to ensure that no games were played for a month ; the income from vital home holiday fixtures was therefore lost, and the Chairman resigned, to be followed shortly afterwards by two of his colleagues.

Peter Campsie told the Fife Free Press "Due to the present financial position of the club and due to the present position of the team in the Premier Division, I have stood down as chairman, director and honorary club secretary. As chairman I was under great pressure to redevelop the stadium to meet Lord Justice Taylor's requirements and this has put a heavy burden on the club's finances. I hope my action will bring closer my desire for a new share issue, which is well overdue."

Jimmy Nicholl, whom the avuncular Campsie had indulged throughout their working relationship, paid tribute to his part in re-introducing full time football at the club. Unfortunately, he could not find a way of paying for it.

Although the supporters were oblivious to – and properly disinterested in – the board room machinations, the meaningful action for the remaining months of the season was not on the pitch. When play resumed on 12th January, Rovers endured a depressingly poor set of results. There were home defeats by Partick Thistle and Dundee United, a 1-1 home draw with St Johnstone, and a 2-2 draw at Dundee – all fixtures which, realistically, had to be won if the team were to finish safe in fourth bottom position, above some of these teams.

The first victory of the new year came over Brechin City in the third round of the Cup, but the next round was lost, 1-0, at Aberdeen, an improvement on the 4-0 League defeat at the same venue a week earlier. There were better performances against the Old Firm, with a 0-0 home draw against Celtic, and a narrow 2-1 defeat to Rangers three weeks later. Stephen McAnespie, a young right back who had spent a short spell in Sweden after being freed by Aberdeen, was signed, although the manager preferred to select the more experienced John McStay in that position.

On transfer deadline day, Hibs' midfielder Danny Lennon was signed for £30,000, due to unorthodox logic in the boardroom. Attempts to inject additional funds by opening up the share capital were not going well ; a number of former directors were resisting the plans. The Lennon transfer was sanctioned on the basis that if, by some miracle at that stage, the share issue went ahead, finances would not be a problem. If it didn't, the club was in such debt that another £30,000 would make little difference in the likely financial meltdown.

Hetherston returned from injury and scored the winner in a 3-2 home win over Kilmarnock but the next victory came 11 games later, on the last day of the season, by which time relegation had long been a foregone conclusion.

The weekend starting Friday 15th April 1994 threw up a couple of apocalyptic incidents. On that date, the final few, crucial shareholders agreed to back the extension of the share capital (see financial appendix) and plans could be formulated to attempt a swift return to the Premier League. The following day, only one person amongst the 42,600 people in Ibrox failed to see Rangers' centre forward Duncan Ferguson head-butt Jock McStay. That person was the match referee.

Unfortunately for everyone concerned, Ferguson was nursing a suspended jail sentence and because the referee did not send him off (and allow football justice to prevail), the Procurator Fiscal asked the police to get involved. The

Raith player, who was very much the innocent party, attracted unwanted attention from fans and media alike, principally because he happened to be the cousin of the Celtic captain. The club tried to protect him from the ferocious media interest in the case, but the SFA, acting on the referee supervisor's report (their rules did not allow them to act on television pictures of the incident) took no account of McStay's welfare.

The club decided not to attend the public circus of the SFA Committee meeting in Glasgow and for its impertinence was suspended from Scottish football until they bowed the knee. Stevie Crawford was selected for an Under 21 international abroad, and the squad announcement press release indicated that he would travel only if his club's suspension was lifted.

Although firmly minded otherwise, the directors decided that less damage would be done by attending the reconvened hearing, in order that McStay confirm what the referee's supervisor and countless cameras had witnessed. Ferguson and Rangers' lawyers argued that because of police involvement, the SFA could not act on a matter which was sub judice. By the time he served a football suspension for the incident, and indeed his suspended jail sentence, Duncan Ferguson was an Everton player. The last word went to the SFA, actually 46 and 61 of them, the number of words in successive sentences in a rant against the Rovers in their annual report.

More importantly from a Raith Rovers perspective, it was an inappropriate way for Jock McStay to end his seven years at Stark's Park. He was a hard-working, diligent defender who was rarely injured or suspended, and adapted and contributed to every advance made by the team during his long service to the club. After sharing the right back spot with Stevie McAnespie in the pre-season matches, he was released. He made one more telling contribution to the club's cause ; as part of the Falkirk squad which beat Rangers in the League Cup the following season, helping pave the way for Rovers to win the trophy.

Against historical precedent, it was a settled side which suffered relegation. Shaun Dennis missed just one League match, Ronnie Coyle three, and Jock McStay, Jason Dair, Peter Hetherston, Colin Camerson, Jason Rowbotham, Jimmy Nicholl, Scott Thomson and Ally Graham all played in more than three quarters of the League programme. This was more by necessity than design, as the club could only afford the bare minimum of first team (full time) players. The team missed Brewster badly, Hetherston was absent for eleven consecutive League games, only one of which was won, and Dalziel started 20 of the 44 League games, although he still managed to top the club's goalscoring list.

Despite the shortest possible stay in the top division, there was much to console the supporters. The Manager set the team out to play attacking, attractive football at

DAVID KIRKWOOD

with a thick medium blue band used on white jerseys from 1937 until during the Second World War (page 101). Until 1958/59, the change strip was red, but during that season, the Supporters Club donated a set of white shirts with two navy blue bands, and navy collars. It was worn with navy shorts (page 122).
In 1959/60, in recognition of the changing fashions in football shirts, a white V neck was introduced to the first choice navy shirts, with white cuffs.
The following season, several shirts were worn. The white-with-two-blue-bands was used with a ligher blue fold-over collar ; the V-navy ensemble remained in use, and a new V-necked shirt was introduced, with two thin white trims, also used at the cuffs (page 129).
All three were in use in 1961/62, the two-blue-hoops now having white fold-over collars.
For the next two seasons, that strip, and the double-trim V neck on navy alternated, but by 1964/65, the club settled on an all white strip, with two navy hoops, and modern round collar-less necks.
On the backs, were small navy numbers, above the hoops, but on the club's return to the First Division in 1967/68, large red numbers were stitched over the hoops (page 139).
In 1969/70, navy shorts were reintroduced, but it was back to white for the next two seasons, and small numbers on the back.

JULIAN BRODDLE

There was a significant change in 1972/73 with the introduction of an all-royal-blue strip, with two white hoops on the socks and the club's initials in the badge area (which had been badge-less since 1958).
White shorts were reintroduced in 1975/76, along with plain red socks.
The changing face of football kit was reflected in the Raith Rovers strip in 1977/78 with the introduction of a manufacturer's logo (Bukta) to both the right breast, and between two stripes which ran down each sleeve. A modern white V-and-collar combination was also introduced (pictured on page 147). The following season, the contemporary version of the club badge was introduced, and blue socks re-appeared in 1979/80.
The first change for several years came in 1984/85, when the double-trim V neck came back in fashion (after 24 years) and a pin-stripe was introduced.
That season, and the one before, saw the first shirt-sponsorship at the club, Mazda cars.
There was another major change in 1985/86, with the return of navy blue (pinstripe) with white sleeves (page 159), and a change of sponsor to Barnetts, then Laidlaws the following season (the shirt sponsorship largely dependent upon who supplied the manager's car or club mini

every opportunity, and as a consequence the quality of entertainment was very high throughout the season. In contrast, fans of fellow newcomers Kilmarnock endured a season of dull, defensive football, although their team did escape relegation on the final day. The lack of available funds meant that the three young players, Jason Dair, Stevie Crawford and Colin Cameron, had to be thrown in as first team regulars. At times they looked out of their depth, but they gained valuable experience which stood them in good stead the following, and subsequent seasons.

There was an underlying feeling around the ground, however, that the club (as distinct from the team) didn't believe that they were of Premier Division calibre. Ronnie Coyle was later asked if the club was set up for Premier Division football, and he replied : "It was as if they were playing at it, although we always believed that we were good enough against teams like Motherwell. We went up to Aberdeen, gave them a doing in the first 20 minutes, and got beat 4-1. There was a lot of naivety, and I don't think we were geared up off the field to make as much as we could have done out of the whole experience. But the players enjoyed it, although we lost heavily to the bigger teams, we always knew that we were better than most of the teams in the division, although we didn't get the results."

It was a far-from gloomy outlook, therefore, and the last two games of the season rather summed it all up. Motherwell came to Stark's Park and threatened to run amok in the first 20 minutes. Paul Lambert scored after a minute, but Rovers fought back to take the lead, Graham scoring in 23 and Dalziel three minutes later. Stevie Kirk equalised five minutes before half time, and Lambert scored his second seven minutes after the interval as Motherwell re-asserted their superiority. Towards the end of the game, Rovers showed great spirit in staging another come-back, and the excellent Hetherston, who had looked every inch a Premier division player since returning from injury, equalised in the final minute. His appreciative gestures to the crowd at the end of the final home game of the season indicated that he was unlikely to be seen in a Rovers jersey the following season.

Newly released from their SFA suspension, the club visited Tannadice to play the Scottish Cup finalists, with both senior goalkeepers, Scott Thomson and Tom Carson, injured. Youth team goalkeeper Brian Potter was promoted, and had an assured game as Rovers built a three-goal lead by half time, Jason Dair capping an outstanding performance with two spectacular goals. United scored twice in the last four minutes, but Rovers ended their first spell of Premier League football with a rare victory. Seven days later, United won the Scottish Cup for the first time, the only goal of the Final scored by – Craig Brewster.

` Another reason for optimism at Stark's Park was the news that, thanks to the

expanded share capital and the purchase of the majority of these shares by the new Chairman, the club had the funds to get the bank off their backs, remain full-time the following season, re-sign those players the manager wanted to keep (in particular the promising youngsters Dair, Crawford and Cameron) and continue to pay Jimmy Nicholl a competitive salary. The financial situation was further improved by the transfer of Peter Hetherston to Aberdeen for £212,500. It put the bank account in the black for the first time since 1968.

The only significant signing of the close season was midfielder David Kirkwood from Airdrie, a transfer tribunal ruling that Rovers had to pay £75,000. He spent most of the season injured. The major transfer speculation in the early months of the season surrounded the Manager.

Having been interviewed for the Dundee United and Northern Ireland managers' positions during the previous season, it was obvious that Jimmy Nicholl saw Raith Rovers as a stepping stone for his managerial ambitions, and he did not relish a move out of the Premier League spotlight. Kilmarnock had lost their manager, Tommy Burns, to Celtic, and pursued that illegal approach through the football 'courts' in high indignation, which did not stop them from refusing to take 'no' for an answer when they asked the Rovers board to speak to Jimmy Nicholl.

The manager was not at all happy at the Board's insistence that he honour the new contract he had signed, following relegation, three months earlier. "I signed the wrong contact with the wrong people," he told a Board Meeting on 27th July and, correctly anticipating the response, continued ".... and don't say you are doing it for the supporters. There are too few of them to count." He then announced that he wished to have no further dialogue with the Board and would communicate only with the Chairman, when necessary.

He didn't realise how close he came to being allowed to go. On Kilmarnock's third attempt at obtain permission to speak with Nicholl, a board meeting was hurriedly convened early one midweek afternoon. Two directors were against permission being granted ; one was in favour, and the fourth had no difficulty in invoking the contract, but was conscious of the corrosive effects of having an embittered manager. He asked for suggestions about who would be appointed were Nicholl to go, and cast his vote with the majority view when he heard the names of the obvious candidates.

The manager's unhappiness was reflected in the opening League results, a 1-1 draw at home to St Johnstone for the second successive season, the same result at home to Hamilton Accies, a 1-0 defeat at Dunfermline, another 1-1 draw, at home to Clydebank, and a particularly pallid 0-0 draw at Stranraer which provoked rumbles of discontent from the travelling supporters.

The only victories had come in the

League Cup. The first round was at League newcomers Ross County, where Bobby Wilson had done a marvellous job, winning several Highland trophies, piloting them to victories over League teams during Scottish Cup runs, and now into the Scottish League, thanks to the Paxton-facilitated reorganisation. They had no answer to Rovers' fitness and experience. Once Colin Cameron had put them ahead in 55 minutes, resistence wilted, with Ally Graham heading three goals in the six yard box on the way to a 5-0 win. It might have been different had Scott Thomson not made a splendid save midway through a scoreless first half.

There was another hat-trick in the next round, this time for the outstanding Colin Cameron in a thrilling, and slightly fortunate, 3-2 home win over Kilmarnock, under their new manager Alex Totten who, as East Fife manager, would have been the obvious choice to succeed Nicholl at Stark's Park, had Nicholl got Totten's new job (I hope you're following this !)

There was another dose of good luck in the draw for the quarter final, fellow First Division side St Johnstone, at Perth. By then the squad had been strengthened by the signing of former Dundee United players Ian Redford and David Narey, the latter particularly required as Ronnie Coyle would be out of action for several months through an ill-timed injury.

Rovers qualified for their first League Cup semi final for 45 years with an excellent performance at McDiarmid Park, thoroughly meriting their 3-1 victory in a pulsating cup tie. At long last fans were glimpsing the team's capabilities, and it was followed by the first League win of the season, at the sixth attempt, recovering from losing a goal at Paisley in 90 seconds to win 2-1. Ally Graham scored the winner seven minutes from time. A comprehensive 3-0 home win over Ayr United was balanced by the loss of further, vital League points from two draws followed by a 3-1 defeat at Perth.

Three days later, Rovers returned to that venue for the third time in a month, where Airdrie awaited in the semi final of the League Cup. Early nerves were settled when Ally Graham opened the scoring in 39 minutes, but the close contest against the always-combative, and habitually competent Airdrieonians took a turn for the worse in 69 minutes. Goalkeeper Scott Thomson was harshly sent off for handling outside the penalty area, similar offences in the intervening years being punished by no more than a caution. With reserve goalkeeper Raymond Allan cup-tied (having played for Motherwell in the competition earlier that season) teenager Brian Potter was the substitute goalkeeper and was pitched into action, Davie Kirkwood being the outfield player sacrificed.

Potter was blameless when Steve Cooper equalised five minutes later, and thereafter dealt comfortably with everything that got through the resolute defence in front of him. His nine colleagues battled tirelessly

to shepherd the match to a conclusion after extra time, with no further goals. A place in the final would be decided by penalty kicks. Rovers had scored their five (through Shaun Dennis, Stevie McAnespie, Colin Cameron, Stevie Crawford and Danny Lennon), and Airdrie their first four when Potter dived to save Alan Lawrence's penalty. First Division Rovers were in the third final in their entire history, and kit man John Valente won the sprint from the bench to congratulate the teenage hero of the hour.

Scott Thomson, whose own moment of glory was only a month away, later recalled : "Bill Crombie, who was the ref who made the decision, was in charge of a match around Christmas time, and he had a quiet word with me and told me with hindsight that the sending off was harsh. I believe it was the way it was meant to be. If I had stayed on, maybe we wouldn't have won. It was to be Brian Potter's night. Fate."

The fans' euphoria was somewhat moderated four days later when Dunfermline visited Stark's Park on League business. With Scott Thomson automatically suspended, Raymond Allan made his debut in goal, the McDiarmid Park hero retaining his place on the substitute's bench. Raymond was a superb servant to Cowdenbeath over 17 seasons, breaking Rovers' fans' hearts in several derby matches down the years. He did it again on October 29th 1994, with an uncharacteristically poor performance in a 5-2 defeat. There may have been a League Cup Final to look forward to, but the League table made gloomy reading after 11 matches :

1	Dunfermline	23 points
2	Airdrieonians	21
3	Dundee	21
4	Clydebank	16
5	St Johnstone	14
6	Raith Rovers	12
7	Hamilton Accies	11
8	Ayr United	10
9	St Mirren	9
10	Stranraer	5

A small part of the leeway was made up with three successive wins, by 3-0, 4-2 and 3-0 showing that the team had found their shooting boots. With Final places at stake, they had every incentive to impress the manager. David Sinclair had contrived a booking in an earlier match to make sure that his two match suspension did not include Sunday 27th November 1994.

Jason Dair was restored to the starting eleven in an attack-minded team selection, which was vindicated in 18 minutes Rovers opened the scoring. From a Dair corner on the left, Ally Graham helped Stevie Crawford win possession on the edge of the Celtic penalty area. Crawford wriggled past a defender before firing a low shot into the Celtic net. It capped a confident, assured opening by the Rovers' team, who exhibited fewer nerves than their supporters, understandably unaccustomed to such occasions.

JASON DAIR

bus). The new manufacturer was Spall.
Accompanied by vocal protests from some supporters, royal blue was reintroduced in 1988/89, the second year of shirt sponsorship by The Mercat Shopping Centre. This had a diagonal shadow-stripe, white V neck and white shoulder yoke.
The shirt remained unchanged the following season, but for a change of sponsorship to Kingsway Entertainments, who were also in place in 1990/91, but on a new design of blue shadow-stripe.
Navy blue re-appeared for 1991/92, with white trim, and John Grubb as shirts sponsors for this, and the following (promotion) season.
The club's debut in the Premier League saw the introduction of a new navy blue and white top, supplied by Diadora, and sponsored by Kelly's Copiers. This style was also worn as the club won the League Cup in 1994/95, with Jackie O's on the front.
Third-choice strips were permitted for the first time, and Rovers' was a very popular Barcelona-style red-and-royal blue stripe (which was actually the previous season's Grimsby Town change strip). Kelly's Copiers re-appeared in 1995/96, on a new style of navy shirt, with shadow stripe and white trim round the collar-less neck and cuffs. Suppliers were the "Rovers Collection" (page 170)

TONY ROUGIER

A new third choice strip had a tartan design, but it was not worn again after the League Cup defeat at Airdrie in August 1996.
Back in the First Division in 1997/98, there was a new navy top, with red and white (especially below the shoulder) trim, although the manager preferred the all-yellow change strip for a few months, before the authorities pointed out that the club's registered first choice was navy. Sponsor was Fife College.
In 1998/99, there was a further change, of manufacturer (Xara), sponsor (Kelly's Copiers for the third time) and shirt design, a simpler navy shadow-stripe with white trim.
Changes were now being made on an annual basis, with FiFab (Fife Fabrications) as shirt sponsors in 1999/2000, and a new shirt style with white trim and V necks (page 171). TFG took over as manufacturers in 2000/1, so there was a variation in design, with a collar-and-V neck and two shoulder stripes.
The perennial hope of traditionalists that the old stripes would make a re-appearance was partially satisfied in 2001/2, when the V-necked navy jersey had two white stripes (page 186).
The following year, the navy tops had white piping and a round collar, and a new sponsor in Bar Itza (page 188)
In 2003/4, V necks came

Celtic began to find their feet and equalised after 32 minutes, Boyd's cross from the left was headed back across goal by Galloway to the unmarked Andy Walker in the goal area, who dived to head the ball past Scott Thomson. The next fifty minutes of play were distinctly uncomfortable for Rovers, as Celtic pressed relentlessly. As in the later stages of the semi final, every Rovers player performed heroically, the forwards tracking back when necessary, while trying to keep the Celtic defence as busy as possible ; the defence battled manfully to repel constant Celtic attacks. The veteran Narey rolled back the years to give an outstanding performance, and his colleagues were not far behind.

With six minutes to go, the pressure finally told. John Collins advanced from midfield, played the ball to Charlie Nicholas on the edge of the penalty area and he flicked it on to Andy Walker, who turned and shot against the post. Nicholas reacted quicker than Julian Broddle to the rebound and left footed the ball into the net from close range.

The Glasgow giants then made the fatal mistake of thinking that the match was over. From the re-start, Rovers enjoyed practically constant possession, and just four minutes after the body blow of Celtic's late goal, Jason Dair received the ball on the right wing, midway inside the Celtic half. He moved forward, beat one player and shot with his left foot from 30 yards. Gordon Marshall was caught off guard and, rather than catch or beat it clear, parried the ball downwards, and it bounced up invitingly in the centre of the goal area. If there was one man in Scottish football who would be waiting to pounce on a loose ball in front of goal, it was Gordon Dalziel, and the club's record goalscorer added to his tally with the most important goal of his long career, nodding the ball over the line.

The Rovers fans who filled the Govan Stand at Ibrox were delirious with joy, and the team found fresh legs and new belief from the unexpected reprieve. Celtic couldn't believe that the green and white beribboned cup had been snatched from their grasp, and could not recreate their earlier momentum in extra time, during which Rovers were the better team. After 120 minutes play, it was to be penalty kicks again, and this time the League Cup was at stake ; history to be made, and with it a place in Europe.

Julian Broddle and Gordon Dalziel having been substituted in extra time, the other experienced players in the team, knowing the implications of what was to follow, stood back when the penalty kickers were nominated. Rovers' Youth coach Jimmy Thomson later reflected : "In games I've been involved in before when it has gone to penalties, it is sometimes very difficult to get players to take them. But that day I think the whole lot of them would have taken a penalty. There was no fear in them at all. It's possible that having the penalties in the semi final also helped." As in the semi final, it was the team's youngsters who stepped up to the

penalty mark.

Shaun Dennis shot right as Marshall dived the other way ; Willie Falconer did the same as Thomson guessed wrongly ; Jason Dair shot right, but rather close to the goalkeeper, and it went under him, a close call ; John Collins shot left with Thomson going the other way ; Colin Cameron's shot into the left corner was too strong and accurate for the goalkeeper to save it ; Andy Walker shot left with Thomson diving right ; Stevie Crawford reprised Dair's effort, Marshall's unhappy afternoon continuing as the ball went under him ; Paul Byrne shot left with Thomson diving right ; Stevie McAnespie and Marshall did the same. The last of the mandatory ten penalties was the closest to being missed, Mike Galloway's shot to right touched by Scott Thomson as it deflected over the line.

Jason Rowbotham, no veteran at 25 years of age, scored the first of the "sudden death" penalties, sending Marshall the wrong way as he hit it to the right. His opposite number was Paul McStay, who approached the penalty spot to the groans of Rovers fans who saw little prospect of the Scottish internationalist failing. Those watching on television at home heard the commentator say "Surely it is unthinkable that the Celtic captain will miss." One or two perceptive optimists, however, wondered why the gifted footballer was only No.6 on his team's penalty-taking roster.

"We had the feeling that McStay was going to miss his penalty," remembered Jimmy Thomson. "He kept going back to the ball and touching it – I think he touched it three times, and we're all looking at each other saying "he's in trouble here, he's not sure of this." That's not taking anything away from our goalkeeper, who had to save it, but it was a nice height for him."
There wasn't much wrong with McStay's crisp, low shot, but Scott Thomson guessed its direction, dived to his right and palmed the ball clear. He started in the direction of his exultant colleagues in the centre circle, looked round to make sure that the referee was happy that the match had been settled, and joined in the joyous mayhem. Tears were shed by players and fans alike as Gordon Dalziel received one of the three great trophies of Scottish football, the first Raith Rovers player to do so. In its 111th year, the club were winners at long last.

Once the celebrations were over, the post-match pictures taken with the trophy, and everyone got their voices back, there was the far from trifling matter of promotion to be addressed. The first three League results post-Ibrox did not encourage hope of ultimate success. Ayr United applauded the new Cup holders onto the Somerset Park pitch six days later, and proceeded to dominate the 1-1 draw, a last minute "winner" acrobatically cleared by Davie Sinclair from a couple of feet over the goal-line.

The Cup was paraded round Stark's Park before the match against St Mirren postponed on 26th November, but it took a

Dalziel penalty to equalise an early John Hewitt goal, and two more points were dropped in an unconvincing performance. Worse was to follow at Dundee four days later, with a 2-1 defeat.

The manager set his team a specific target of of nine points from the next three matches. They did much better than that, winning the next eight League games in a sustained run which at last showed the form of which they were capable. The return to the team from injury of the Player Manager helped greatly, and the purposeful running of Barry Wilson, signed from Ross County (where his father was manager) in September but cup tied, freshened up the attack.

Captain Danny Lennon, cruelly injured in training a fortnight before the Cup Final, returned to the side, as did Ronnie Coyle, allowing David Narey a well deserved break.

There were some stirring performances in the run of victories. The first one, 3-2 at home to Airdrie on Boxing Day, settled by a glorious strike from Davie Sinclair in the last minute, was as good a game as has been seen at the old ground. Ally Graham epitomised the best season of his career with the only goal of the game in 82 minutes on a frozen East End Park, which had the combined effect of denying promotion rivals three points, while reducing Rovers' deficit.

A match at Stranraer should have been followed by a ferry trip to Ireland for a friendly game, but that was cancelled after the original fixture fell to a flooded pitch. Rovers made the long journey back three days later, to win 4-2. 2-1 at Paisley, with Crawford scoring both, was no mean result.

Added to that run were two victories in the Scottish Cup, at home to Ayr and a superb second half performance at Dundee to win 2-1. Two points were dropped at home to the same team in a 0-0 draw a week later, but the promotion push continued with an excellent 2-1 win at the unforgiving (temporary) home of Airdrieonians.

For the third successive round of the Cup, Rovers had to face the same opponents on successive Saturdays in League and Cup. The Scottish Cup quarter final at Stark's Park was the third cup clash of the season against the Diamonds (who had won a B&Q Cup second round tie after extra time and penalties), and revenge was exacted for the League Cup semi final. Airdrie, who were 2-0 ahead at the interval, were convincing winners by 4-1.

The dip in form continued with a 1-1 draw at home to Stranraer, but three single-goal wins continued the march on the top of the table. What little margin for error existed – only one team would gain promotion from the 10 club League – went with another home defeat by Airdrie, this time much less

deserved, and marred by the unjust sending off of Ally Graham for an inoccuous challenge.

As the injury-blighted season reached its climax, it should be noted that while goalkeeper Scott Thomson missed just one of 36 games, only McAnespie, Cameron and Dennis had League appearance totals into the 30s, and Broddie, Dennis, Dalziel, Graham, Crawford and Narey in the mid 20s.

With Ronnie Coyle injured and Shaun Dennis suspended for three matches, the assured presence of David Narey was restored to the team. Rarely, if ever, has a player made such a telling contribution to a club's history in just 21 appearances. A measure of this very impressive man is that every one of them was for the full 90 minutes. The pre-transfer deadline signing of Trinidad & Tobago international Tony Rougier, was with future seasons in mind, as he played only fleetingly in the last two months of the season.

Another strong performance at faltering Dundee earned a 2-0 win, and Rovers used up every last ounce of good fortune in winning 2-1 at Perth. St Johnstone deservedly went ahead in 59 minutes and were stunned four minutes later when Allan Preston spectacularly volleyed a speculative cross into his own net. Just before the final whistle, Stevie Crawford kept his composure to advance on goal and score an unlikely, and undeserved, winner.

It was a crucial victory which meant that the odds of finishing top of the League tilted very much in Rovers favour. They could afford to draw their last two matches and win the championship, because the first match was against closest challengers Dunfermline. Rovers had the better of the first half exchanges in front of a 9300 crowd at Stark's Park, and after the interval retreated into defence to preserve the precious point from a 0-0 draw. A huge travelling support made their way to Hamilton Accies' temporary home at Firhill for the final match of the season.

STEVIE CRAWFORD, celebrating a player of the month award in 1994/95, alongside the Manager of the Month, and a couple of glasses of the sponsor's product

back, as did white sleeves (and Xara as manufacturers), and the biggest surprise the following season was that there was no change (page 185). In 2005/06, there was a variation on the same theme, navy shirts, round necks and white sleeves which extended over the shoulders.

Navy shorts were added in 2006/07, there was yet another variation in the white sleeve-and-shoulder design, and the round neck had a pointed white trim. There was also a new sponsor, Coolforce (page 189).

It was all change for 2007/08, although the navy shorts remained.

A new variation of white trims was used on the navy top, supplied now by Puma, and the shirt sponsors were Fife Autocentre.

The convention of coinciding manufacturing, sponsorship and design contracts over two seasons has not been achieved for several years, to the chagrin of parents faced with the demands of offspring who want to wear up-to-date replica tops ; a far cry from the working shirts chosen by the club's founders in 1883.

David Sinclair, who captained Raith Rovers in the Olympic Stadium in Munich, reflected on the UEFA Cup experience in an interview in the Stark's Bark fanzine.

You don't know what way to turn when you've been freed [by Dunfermline Athletic] as a young boy ; you have no qualifications, no other career. I didn't even dream of playing in Europe. The match against the Faroes team was fairly straightforward, but the match against Akranes, the Icelandic champions, was another matter. They had a few good players, one of whom, Siggi Jonson, later played with Dundee United ; and the Gunnlaugson brothers, who were both signed by Feyenoord at the time. I spoke to Siggi about it when we were both at United, he said "we destroyed you" and I said that we played them at their own game, and defended well. Tommo pulled off some of the best saves you'll ever see in Iceland. Siggi told me that they came over to Stark's Park expecting to beat us, because they thought they had more quality in their side, so they were gutted when we went into the big round, and not them. We couldn't believe the draw we got, they don't come much bigger than Bayern Munich.

The first leg at Easter Road was hard, and we let ourselves down by the way we started. We started off sloppy, and if you play like that against quality teams they'll punish you, and they did. Klinsmann scored after something like 9 minutes, and we struggled and they scored a second goal, but we started to get some belief in the second half and their goalkeeper made a great save from a Mickey Cameron header. Shaun and I played well at centre back, but we were playing some of the best players in Europe in Papin and Klinsmann. I got Papin's top after the second leg, so I have a great souvenir to go with the memories.

Just before the second leg Jimmy Nicholl says to me "Sinky, you're the captain" and

Despite the presence of the manager in midfield, the first half performance was riddled with nerves. Thankfully, Accies had nothing to play for, and looked as if they would rather be on the beach. In the second half, Colin Cameron moved onto the right wing and began to retain possession, restoring some semblance of order to the team's untidy play. Robbie Raeside had an outstanding match at the back, and the only moment of genuine anxiety was when Accies' forward Peter Duffield failed to make contact with a low cross into the goal area.

The 90 minutes felt like 190, but at last the referee blew his final whistle, and Rovers added the First Division Championship trophy to the League Cup on the Stark's Park boardroom. It was a close run thing, far from the spectacle of two years before, but a testament to the resolution and professionalism of the players, and the organisational and persuasive abilities of the manager and his coaches. Rovers were back in the Premier Division, and this time could also look forward to the UEFA Cup.

The former Dundee United team-mates Redford and Narey having retired, experience was drafted into the side in the shape of two more former Tannadice stalwarts, Alex Taylor and Jim McInally, whose £150,000 transfer fee from United set a new record for Raith Rovers. Tony Rougier started the season as a first team regular, and a busy close season programme prepared the growing squad for an early start in the UEFA Cup. The draw for the preliminary round was kind to Rovers : the Champions of the Faroe Islands, Goto Itrottarfelag, who were routinely beaten 4-0 at Stark's Park on Tuesday August 8th 1995, watched by 5,082. Jason Dair had the honour of scoring Rovers' first European goal, in the 21st minute. Steven McAnespie struck a low pass down the right wing, where Stevie Crawford flicked it into the path of Tony Rougier. He appeared to have run the ball over the Invertiel-end goal-line, but hooked his leg round a defender to surprise the goalkeeper with a low ball which went under his body. The unmarked Dair at the far post stretched to poke the ball into the net.

The second leg at Toftir, the Faroe Islands national stadium, was more notable for the sense of occasion witnessed by the fifty or so travelling Rovers fans, than the match itself, which meandered to a 2-2 draw. The most memorable aspect of the play was a miss by Tony Rougier from a range of between one and two feet, when he managed to scoop the ball over the crossbar.

For Rovers fans who had witnessed miserable performances and dire results at some of the outposts of Scottish football over the preceding decades, there was something special about being present at the club's first match in Europe, an unimaginable prospect for most of our lives. The location added to the sense of occasion. Those who travelled by ferry – a round trip of almost a week – performed a feat of some endurance. The air travellers, on a chartered former Aer Lingus

plane complete with wing struts, took off at Aberdeen, topped up the fuel tank at Wick, and descended down a fjord into the Faroes airport, then had the pleasure of hopping across the islands alternately by ferry and causeway. It rained every ten minutes.

The party mood was moderated somewhat when it was discovered that the overnight accommodation was in a Seaman's Mission, and therefore alcohol-free. The supermarket across the road reluctantly sold them a crate of the local brew, but refused to supply a bottle opener. Gull's Ale tasted as if it had been extracted from the eponymous creature. The summer of 1995 in Scotland was one of the hottest on record, with several weeks of unbroken sunshine. The heatwave was not shared by the Faroe Islands however, and the match took place in a howling gale. The local fans came to the match dressed for a midweek match at Broadwood in January, and were bemused by the t-shirted visitors. Everyone got wet and cold, but no-one cared. Rovers had graduated to European football.

Those dreaming of sunnier climes in the first round proper were defied by the draw – IA Akranes, champions of Iceland – even closer to the North Pole ! Before that, some domestic matters had to be attended to, and the fixture compiler rewarded the newly promoted club with an opening match against Celtic at Stark's Park, followed by a trip to Ibrox.

Rovers gave a decent account of themselves against Celtic, losing to a solitary Pierre van Hooijdonk goal, but Rangers inflicted a heavy defeat. In the League Cup, the ballot bag was as unforgiving as the League fixture computer. The second round was seeded on the basis of League position, and the holders Raith Rovers were drawn away to – Celtic.

The re-run of the previous season's final, this time at Celtic Park, saw one of Rovers' finest performances in recent memory. They matched, and frequently bettered, a much improved Celtic team throughout the 120 minutes. Man of the match was Tony Rougier, who gave Rudi Vata a torrid time, and who equalised Van Hooijdonk's opening goal. The tie looked to be heading to a penalty decider for the second successive season when, in the final minute of extra time, an exhausted Julian Broddle failed to get distance on a clearance to touch. From the throw-in, Celtic scored an undeserved winner.

In the UEFA Cup, Rovers were once again at home in the first leg, and were extremely flattered by the 3-1 victory over the very accomplished Icelandic champions, for whom the outstanding Gunlaugsson twins provided a constant threat. Rovers deserved credit for taking their chances, twice by Danny Lennon and once by Barry Wilson, but there was little doubt of the task that would confront them in Iceland.

Rather more fans travelled by plane to Iceland than to the Faroes, and while better clad, were surprised by the chilly temperature which met them, on 26th September. There was nothing subtle about Rovers' tactics ; defence and midfield were packed with Stevie Crawford a loan figure on the half-way line. A superlative performance by Scott Thomson in goal and heroic defending by his colleagues restricted Akranes to a single goal.

The euphoric Rovers fans mingled with the team as they awaited their respective (delayed) flights home at Keflavik airport, although many noted that Jim McInally sat apart. In a match which should have suited his experience and combative style, the manager preferred to select those who had served him so well in recent seasons, and the club's record signing was used only as a time-wasting substitute three minutes from the final whistle.

The draw for the next round brought a dream tie – German giants Bayern Munich, but before that Rovers had to devote some attention to their quest for another 'first' for the club – survival in the Premier League. They also had to find a new right back. Once the Old Firm fixtures were consigned to the record books, there were two excellent home wins over the sort of clubs that Rovers were going to have to beat if relegation was to be avoided – Kilmarnock and Partick Thistle.

On their return from Iceland, Rovers received an offer for Stevie McAnespie that they could not refuse. Bolton, who had sold Jason McAteer to Liverpool for £4 million, offered £900,000 ; not a bad return on someone signed for nothing barely 16 months earlier, and who had played 376 minutes of top division football in Scotland. It didn't feel like much of a bargain when Rovers suffered a heavy 3-0 defeat at Aberdeen, but on the Wednesday evening at Stark's Park Hibs were swept aside by a superb Rovers performance of attacking football. The outstanding Colin Cameron scored twice and Davie Sinclair once in a 3-0 win, arguably their best at home under Jimmy Nicholl.

An equally merited 2-0 win at another established Premier League club, Motherwell, followed on the Saturday, Sinclair scoring again in the midst of the best form of his career. Understandably, attention was then diverted to Bayern Munich, the first leg sandwiched by a 4-2 defeat at Hearts and a 1-0 defeat at home to Falkirk in a bad-tempered match.

To the dismay of traditionalists, the first leg was switched to Easter Road, having already been reversed (Bayern were drawn at home in the first leg) to suit German TV coverage. UEFA, encouraged by the bureaucrats at Park Gardens, designated the match as 'high risk', for which no standing would be permitted. Faced with the threat of limiting the Stark's Park capacity to a ludicrous 2,500, Rovers opted for the nearest UEFA-approved stadium, 45 minutes drive across the Forth Road Bridge.

The bemusement was compounded by the experience of those Rovers fans who attended the three European away matches. Toftir resembled Kilbowie Park without the covered enclosures ; there were better appointed Fife Junior grounds than the grass-embanked ground of the Icelandic champions ; and the approach to the Olympic Stadium in Munich was through a beer garden. Inside that imposing stadium, most of the crowd was standing, and there was no segregation. Those of a romantic disposition still believe that Rovers' unbeaten home record in Europe would have been preserved the moment the German's team coach turned into Pratt Street, had the game been played on home soil.

The star studded German team won 2-0 in Edinburgh, Jurgen Klinsmann scoring both goals. At times, they sliced through the Rovers team at will, but there were also passages of play in which Rovers gave as good as they got. It took an instinctive save from Oliver Kahn to keep out a close-range Colin Cameron header.

The Saturday before the second leg, Rovers earned a good point at home to Rangers from a 2-2 draw in which Tony Rougier once again showed his strength and skill, compelling Rangers to try three different markers in the course of the game. There was some surprise when the Rovers team was announced before kick off ; Shaun Dennis was inexplicably dropped, with first team debuts for young defenders Mark Buist and Ian McMillan.

The lack of expectation of the thousand-or-so Rovers fans who travelled to Munich by road and air added to their enjoyment of the occasion. The Olympic Stadium had seen many great football matches and other sporting occasions, and the travellers from Fife were to witness another on Hallow'en 1995. After 43 minutes in which Bayern looked content to nurse their two goal lead from the first leg, Danny Lennon scored from a free kick, the only goal scored by a British players in any European competition that week. The half time scoreboard showing FC Bayern 0 Raith Rovers FC 1 was captured by hundreds of Kirkcaldy's cameras. In the second half, some sloppy defending allowed Klinsmann and Babbel to give Bayern the one goal margin of victory that one felt they would have done enough to achieve no matter how well Rovers played, but the players had done themselves, and their supporters, proud.

It wasn't just the fans who were nursing monumental hang-overs on their return to Scotland ; Saturday's league match was lost at Kilmarnock, by 5-1. Two draws and two victories came from the next four matches, however, and after a 2-1 defeat at Falkirk, a very satisfactory year was rounded off with a draw at home to Hearts and a win at Easter Road.

Thanks to the windfalls of the McAnespie transfer and the £500,000 television contract with German TV (which stipulated exclusive rights to Rovers' home European ties against German opposition for the 10 years, starting with the 6pm kick off at Easter Road), the plans to reconstruct Stark's Park were well funded, and there was money to spare to strengthen the team.

In an unusual role reversal, it was the board of directors who were nagging the

I felt for Shaun at the time because he was the skipper. I don't know why, he must have had his reasons, but it was a real pleasure to lead the team out into the Olympic Stadium. It was great to come out and look behind the goals to see all the Rovers fans, with their banners out, and it was good for me because my family were over at the match. A lot of the fans had dug deep to get over to the match, and it was great to see such a large support. It was really heart warming to see a lot of friends there.

In contrast to the first leg, we started the second leg well, mind you if you can't play in a setting like that you shouldn't be in the game. We took the match by the scruff of the neck and wee Danny's free kick put us one up at half time - so what if it was deflected, Danny said it was going in anyway ! At half time we said that if we started the second half the same way we would have a chance, and I remember pinging a long cross in and Tony Rougier just needed to hit the target to make it 2-0, but he hit the side netting. We kept on plugging away, but they got stronger and came back into the game, with Ronnie slipping up. At 1-1 we had our backs to the wall, and the 2-1 defeat was hard to take after dominating the early part of the game, but we let ourselves down in the first game, didn't take our chances and defended sloppily.

SACHA OPINEL

Colin Harris returned in 1986/87 to score 22 League goals. Gordon Dalziel scored seven in eleven games, the only time he did not finish the season as top scorer at the club. Twenty five, eleven, twenty, 25, 26, 33 (with Craig Brewster scoring 22 in 1992/93), eight, and fifteen were his annual returns as he surpassed Willie Penman's record for total peace-time League goals scored.

Post-Dalziel, Colin Cameron scored nine League goals in 1995/96, and the following season Peter Duffield and Danny Lennon scored five apiece in the League, Duffield winning by a nose with two goals in friendly matches, to match Tony Rougier's total in all first team games.

Keith Wright returned to score ten in 1997/98, and Craig Dargo scored eight League goals the following season, then twelve in 1999/2000. Rovers had their first continental top goalscorer the following season, Nacho Novo scoring 19 times in the League. Karl Hawley, on loan from Walsall, was top League scorer with seven goals in 2002/03, and John Sutton with thirteen topped the list the following season. The 2004/5 relegation season saw three players score four League goals, Sacko Hamed, John Martin and Pat Clarke, with Hamed scoring ten in all first team games, including friendlies.

In 2005/6 Paul McManus scored 15 League goals, then seven the following season, and Graham Weir topped the list with eleven League goals in 2007/08.

manager to sign players, of a higher calibre than the two who were recruited, former Aberdeen reserve full back Mark Humphries, freed by Bristol City, and Neil McKilligan, freed by Ayr United. They were less than enthused at the manager's plans to swap Jim McInally for Peter Hetherston. Unwisely, a relieved McInally was pictured with an Aberdeen strip at Pittodrie, the day before the deal collapsed after Hetherston's long-term pelvic injury failed a medical in Kirkcaldy.

None of this helped the mood of the manager, nor his relationship with the Board of Directors which had been, at best, uneasy for the previous 18 months, and now deteriorated into rancour. Rather like Neville Chamberlain, Nicholl's career was on a downward trajectory after Munich. The Board were becoming concerned at the declining form of the team – an overdue win over Falkirk the only League victory in two months. There was little evidence of the previous battling qualities of the team in a 2-0 defeat at Tynecastle, four days before a wintry midweek trip to Aberdeen.

Listening to radio reports on the journey north, Rovers fans were warned to anticipate the fixture being the last with Jimmy Nicholl in charge of the team. Sure enough, the following day he announced he was leaving, although his destination was a surprise to many commentators who had predicted a glittering future for Rovers' talented young Manager. Millwall, dropping down the English Second Division at an alarming rate, was not an obvious career move.

The undeserved 1-0 defeat at Pittodrie proved to be a milestone in the club's history, although Munich was the pivotal moment. The lustre of the Nicholl years had begun to fade in the preceding weeks and months, but from 8th February 1996 the over-achieving orchestra would be without their inspirational conductor. Moreover, his parting shot was to provide the media with a catalogue of petty grievances which set the tone of a full decade of colourful reports seeping out of Stark's Park, none of which enhanced the image of the club.

Nicholl's main target was Chairman and majority shareholder Alex Penman, whose singular manner had upset a number of people who had worked for, and alongside him, at Stark's Park. While those he had crossed derived some pleasure from his discomfiture, on this occasion he did not deserve the criticism levelled by his manager, whom he had indulged beyond all previous limits of his patience. Perhaps more importantly, two years earlier, when the club was desperately in need of an injection of funds to preserve full time football and thus retain the services of its stalwart players, promising youngsters, and bright young manager, Penman was the only man to open his cheque book, a fact ignored by the handsomely remunerated manager who unfairly excoriated him in the media.

The priority, post Nicholl, was to preserve the club's coveted Premier League

place. To steady the ship, Rovers turned to the youth team coach, Jimmy Thomson (assistant Martin Harvey, along with physiotherapist Gerry Docherty, having left for Millwall with Nicholl). As a short-term solution, it worked well, but everyone in football who knew the affable, hard-working Thomson recognised that he was simply not cut out for top level management ; everyone, that is, apart from the Rovers' board. Jim McInally was to be his assistant.

There was an ugly mood amongst the support at the home game against Hibs two days after Nicholl's departure, thanks to the one-sided press coverage, but much relief after a narrow 1-0 victory, as vital for psychological reasons as for the three points. The new manager was charged, and funded, with the task of recruiting new players.

Goalkeeper Bobby Geddes was signed from Kilmarnock (Scott Thomson having broken a thumb), full back Greg McCulloch and winger Scott Thomson from Aberdeen, veterans Steve Kirk, swapped from Falkirk for Ally Graham, and Miodrag Krivokapic from Motherwell ; and, for very large fees, striker Peter Duffield and full back Paul Bonar from Airdrie. McCulloch and Thomson were initially to arrive at Stark's Park in exchange for Stevie Crawford plus £500,000, but Crawford and Roy Aitken were at odds on which position the former would play.

Results improved slightly, but the Premier League is an unforgiving place for a team in transition. Partick Thistle (3-0 away win) can often be followed in the fixture list by Rangers. Rovers lost 2-4 at home defeat having looked set for victory when a Davie Kirkwood penalty put them 2-1 ahead after 68 minutes, only for Rangers to find at least two more gears in the final 10 minutes of a pulsating match. For every unexpected point (a 2-2 home draw with Aberdeen), there were unscheduled defeats at Kilmarnock and at home to Hearts.

The match at Brockville on 6th April was a crucial game. Relegation-haunted Falkirk had to win to close the gap with Rovers and the handful of teams between them, while a Raith win would virtually secure safety. Tony Rougier equalised in 25 minutes, but Falkirk took the lead again six minutes later. The turning point of the match came in 58 minutes when Ally Graham won a penalty against his former colleagues. Maurice Johnston's shot was saved by Bobby Geddes, and Rovers went on to win 3-2, Robbie Raeside who did well in deputising for the injured Shaun Dennis, scoring a rare goal.

The season closed with a 4-1 defeat at Celtic Park, where a Scottish Cup tie was lost three months earlier, but there was belief that the new signings would be good enough for the challenge of retaining Premier Division football at Stark's Park the following season.

In both 1993 and 1995, Rovers gained promotion to the top division with a set of players who many fans believed could lay the foundations of a long period of top level football, in much the same way as Young,

McNaught, Leigh, Penman, Maule and Co. did in 1949. Then, as in 1995, the club enjoyed the luxury of concentrating on the field of play ; money in the bank meant that financial and economic concerns did not impinge on the prime purpose of the organisation.

The keynote of the Herdman-Gourlay era was that everything necessary was done to keep the keystone players at the club. Flair players such as McEwan and Kelly could be sold for large fees, but the bedrock of the team remained to bring through their replacements. The lynchpin of the 1995/96 team was Colin Cameron, who was transferred to Hearts on deadline day 1996 for £ 250,000 plus John Miller. The directors insisted that Cameron was intent on leaving, and with rumours of the abolition of transfer fees swirling around the protracted legal process of Jean Marc Bosman's dispute with the French FA, they banked Hearts' cheque. Cameron's departure was scarcely felt in the closing weeks of the season, but the hard-working, skilful, goal-scoring midfielder who went on to win 28 Scotland caps was never replaced, and he was most certainly missed the following season.

Delusions of adequacy were strengthened by the first six pre-season friendlies being won without a goal conceded. Little heed was taken of the poor standard of the opposition. Further money was spent in strengthening the team. Paul Harvey, who had often shone in midfield against Rovers, became the third six-figure signing that year from Airdrieonians. The £212,000 fee brought with it the "curse of the record signing" passed on from Jim McInally. Paul Browne, an Aston Villa reserve centre back who, with a little more patience and guile, could have been obtained on a free transfer, was signed for £120,000 following a transfer tribunal ruling. Kevin Twaddle was purchased from St Johnstone for £82,000 and David Craig arrived on a free transfer from Hamilton Accies.

The newcomers replaced Stevie Crawford, Davie Sinclair and Jason Dair, who rejoined Jimmy Nicholl at Millwall for a combined fee of £900,000, despite his debut season having ended with relegation to the Third Division. The transfers were the culmination of months of unseemly exchanges between the clubs, not least Millwall's sudden interest in signing Paul Hartley from Hamilton Accies despite Rovers' prolonged pursuit of his signature.

The successful team of the previous seasons had therefore been dismantled, and many questioned Jimmy Thomson's credentials for the forthcoming fight, but there was a third reason for 1996/97 getting off to a season-defining terrible start – plain bad luck. The construction of two-and-half new grandstands at Stark's Park caused Rovers to ask for successive away matches at the start of the season, and the Scottish League obliged them with visits to Ibrox and Parkhead. In between was a tricky League Cup tie at Airdrie.

Tony Rougier scored twice, and missed several easier chances in a match which Rovers should have won by some margin. Instead, Peter Hetherston returned to haunt them with a 76th minute equaliser, and veteran Ken Eadie scored the winner four minutes before the end of extra time. It was a team devoid of confidence which welcomed Motherwell to Stark's Park on 24th August, and which promptly lost two goals in the opening half hour. Two minutes later, Danny Lennon had the opportunity to get the Rovers back into the match, but he missed from the penalty spot. The 3-0 home defeat cost Jimmy Thomson his job.

Rovers' luck appeared to change with the recruitment of Tommy McLean as his replacement. Appointed on Tuesday 3rd September, for the remainder of that week he was embroiled in a court case against previous employers Hearts. His only sight of his new charges, prior to the visit of Aberdeen on 7th September, was a closed door evening match at Livingston.

Three-one down after 26 minutes against Aberdeen, McLean hauled off Paul Browne at half time and the second half damage was limited to a fourth Aberdeen goal. Swift action was required to stem the losses, and the new manager was not slow in his diagnosis, but a week after his appointment he resigned. His brother Jim, Dundee United's chairman, had sacked Billy Kirkwood at the weekend and wanted Tommy to replace him. Rovers were bought off with £60,000, but the Board did not know where to turn for his replacement.

Ian Porterfield was given too little time to confirm his interest in the position, and McLean's agent, Jock Brown, suggested Iain Munro, whom St Mirren were about to appoint as their new manager. Rovers directors took his advice, and Munro was confirmed as the club's fourth manager in seven months on 16th September. The Courier proved to be a better judge than the Directors : "'The Premier League is the place to be,' said the man who will have done wonders if Raith Rovers are still there at the end of the season." Five days later, Tommy McLean returned to face the approbrium of the Rovers' crowd, and was rewarded with a 3-2 defeat, but for Rovers it proved to be the last, defiant glimmer of resistance in a dismal season.

Football is an unforgiving mistress, and when things start going against a club, they do so cumulatively. Little went right that season ; there was a huge turnover of players following constant transfer speculation ; the manager proved to be incapable of reversing the team's fortunes, often appearing unfocused. Even the weather conspired against Rovers - every home match Saturday was dreich, wet and windy.

The season was probably best summed up by the home match against Dunfermline on 16th November. Played in heavy rain, the start was delayed by a power failure in the new stands (an inevitable occurrence at every new ground, despite a history of warnings as to inadequate power

SCOTT THOMSON

1996

179

GREG McCULLOCH

CRAIG McEWAN

CARSTEN HALLUM

SOREN ANDERSEN

JAY STEIN

management), John Miller scored an own goal in 12 minutes and Hamish French doubled Dunfermline's lead 12 minutes later. A minute from half time, Shaun Dennis, the last man remaining from those who had seen the club grow from a struggling Second Division outfit to cup winners and membership of the Premier Division, had suffered enough of the mayhem around him. He launched a tackle on Gerry Britton which owed more to kung fu than the SFA coaching course at Largs, and left the field to the cheers of the Rovers fans whose frustrations he had accurately reflected in a rare moment of decisive action in a drifting season.

John Miller, who arrived from Hearts as part of the much lamented Colin Cameron's transfer, contributed to the lack of a sense of purpose at the club, as later described by Jimmy Thomson :

"I used to watch him playing for Hearts, scoring goals from late runs into the box, but he seemed to want to play a different game for us. I spoke to him about this and he thought he should have been more of a playmaker at Raith Rovers, but I wanted him to do the good things he had done at Hearts. I had difficulty getting this through to him."

There was a succession of administrative faux pas, culminating in a fine of £10,000 for fielding three trialists in that catastrophic Dunfermline match. One of them, Odd Areld, who was replaced by Peter Duffield after 72 minutes, looked as if he was playing his first ever football match.

Amongst the signings made by Iain Munro were Graham Mitchell, freed by Bradford City, David Lorimer, freed by Hamilton Accies, and from the same club Derek McGill, whose £2,500 transfer fee was decided by a transfer tribunal (Hamilton had asked for £60,000, Rovers' valuation was nil). None of those signings inspired, although two of the Scandinavians who were drafted in helped stage a mini-revival with three wins and a draw in four matches in late November and early December. Vetle Andersen stayed until the end of the season, but the purposeful winger Kent Bergerson could not be persuaded to stay beyond six matches.

Three more Scandinavians arrived early in the new year, Soren Andersen, Carsten Hallum and Janne Makela. They all looked as if they were on their holidays, rarely breaking sweat as they played through the close season months of their native countries. These players were demonstrably more competent than many of their new colleagues, but the "native" players were resentful at their presence in the team.

Paul Harvey later reflected on being replaced by Vetle Andersen : "Some of the other boys were in the same position as myself. Iain Munro kept on bringing in players, Scandinavians and the likes, and it was only disrupting the squad. There had been a good atmosphere at the start of the season, good harmony in the squad, we were starting to get to know one another, but that went as the season progressed and players came and went."

Goalkeeper Scott Thomson did not restrict his analysis to the foreign players. "There were so many changes in the team. Too many players were allowed to leave at the same time and there was no time given for the team to gel. It took until Christmas before there was a real belief that we could stay up. That's when he got back into the challenge with the teams above us." There was further gloom for the fans as Shaun Dennis was sold to Hibs for £125,000 plus Andy Millen.

Bayern Munich returned to Scotland to play Celtic in Peter Grant's Testimonial match, and, the previous evening, fulfilled a promise made a year earlier to play at Stark's Park. Rovers fans took the opportunity to cast their judgement on how the club was being run by shunning the over-priced tickets, and it took a late announcement of a £3 discount or refund to boost the crowd to 4780. Peter Duffield scored the only goal of the match.

In the League, it was a case of "thank goodness for Kilmarnock". In between a 1-0 win at Rugby Park on 11th January and a 2-1 win against them on 5th March, Rovers lost four League matches and drew two. They did, however, win 4-1 at Airdrie in the Scottish Cup, and safely negotiated a tricky fourth round tie at Brechin.

Desperate times bring desperate measures, which accurately describes the appointment of Jimmy Nicholl as Munro's assistant on 27th March. Sacked by Millwall's Administrator on 10th February, he admitted to Richard Gordon in an interview on Radio Scotland that Stark's Park was probably the last place he wished to be. The Scottish Cup quarter final at First Division Falkirk looked winnable, but Rovers were set up for a draw, allowing Falkirk to dominate the first half and open the scoring two minutes before the interval. The second half improvement was too little, too late, and Falkirk won 2-0, beat Celtic after a replay in the semi final and lost to Kilmarnock in the Final.

The die was long since cast for the season prior to League defeats by Dunfermline and Dundee United and an unexpected 1-1 home draw with Celtic preceded a 5-0 drubbing at Motherwell. After 51 minutes, and 2-0 down, the manager decided on a double substitution, taking off Alex Taylor and Paul Harvey. The replacements were the expensively disappointing Paul Bonar and, instead of promising young striker Craig Dargo, veteran midfielder Steve Kirk. The fans, stupefied for several months by the chaos that had unfolded before their glazed eyes, finally gave vent to their frustrations.

At the end of the match, the Manager unwisely exchanged words with the Chairman as they boarded the team bus, and Munro found a sympathetic ear from the media when he recounted the manner in which he was effectively sacked. The media unleashed a torrent of abuse on Penman for so ill-treating one of their most assiduous courtiers, but there was not even a hint of demur from the Rovers' support. If they had criticism of the Board, it was that the manager should have been on his way several weeks earlier. Jimmy Nicholl was asked to take charge until the end of the season, but he expressed his solidarity with the departed manager and left the club.

Three days later, Rovers fans had to endure a 6-0 trouncing by Champions elect Rangers at Stark's Park in a match brought forward from the Saturday – yet another administrative cock up, a League match against Rangers scheduled for Links Market Saturday. A 2-0 defeat at Aberdeen was followed by a 1-1 home draw with Hibs on Saturday May 10th 1997. Peter Duffield scored Rovers last goal in the Premier League for 11 years …. and counting.

Whoever on high had it in for the Rovers hadn't finished with them in 1997. There were front page headlines as it was alleged that the Chairman had assaulted a press photographer outside the ground, although he was acquitted in court in September, the sheriff ruling that there was no corroborative evidence. Penman had had enough and looked for a buyer for his shares, one of several prospective buyers proving to be a serial con-man (more press headlines). Weeks of press reports and speculation at least improved the supporters' vocabulary – the "consortium" became the most frequently used word in a football context around the town.

The two remaining directors had set about the task of identifying a new manager. Tommy Burns, newly-sacked by Celtic, turned up two hours late for an interview, which was not taken further to the relief of both parties, and Gordon Dalziel was keen to leave Somerset Park for Stark's Park. In the absence of a single bidder, a plan had been put to the Chairman to facilitate his withdrawal, but with no sign of positive action, the directors resigned in frustration and four days later Alex Penman appointed a new manager – Jimmy Nicholl. A week later, Penman sold his shares to Alan Kelly, whose photocopier supply company had previously sponsored the jerseys.

If 1996/97 was bad, what followed was catastrophic, although in the short term there was certainly an improvement in the quality of football on offer. The previous board, in their last meaningful action, chose not to offer new contracts to those players whose (Premier Division) contracts had expired. Into that category came goalkeepers Scott Thomson and Bobby Geddes, Miodrag Krivokapic, David Kirkwood, Alex Taylor, two young reserves and eight YTS players. The rationale was that the club had to reduce the wage bill faced with the certainty of a huge drop in income.

That policy was swept aside by the incoming owner. Guido Van De Kamp was signed to replace Thomson, on a higher salary. Keith Wright and Ian Cameron were signed from Hibs in exchange for Tony Rougier ; Kevin Fotheringham from Hamilton

Accies and Lee Dair from Rangers. David Kirkwood was re-signed. There was to be no return to the club for Martin Harvey, instead Nicholl chose Alex Smith as his assistant manager, and on his recommendation, a six figure sum was spent on Scotland Under 21 full back Craig McEwan, from Smith's former club Clyde. In due course, Terry Butcher and John Brownlie were added to the full-time coaching staff. If there was a financial strategy at all (which is doubtful) it was a gamble on an immediate return to the Premier League.

Things looked rosy at the start of the season, following another unbeaten pre-season programme, this time in Ireland and at Stranraer. Forfar Athletic were thumped 5-0 in the opening League Cup tie, with Duffield scoring a hat-trick and Ian Cameron rounding off an outstanding match with a goal. In the Challenge Cup, there was a comfortable 4-2 win at Clyde, but the opening two League matches proved to be tougher, and were drawn.

The third round of the League Cup saw Hearts visit Stark's Park, and the 2-1 defeat flattered Rovers. Hearts winner was scored after Craig McEwan simply bounced off Stephane Adam as the Hearts forward gathered the ball on the edge of the penalty area before advancing on goal and shooting past Van de Kamp. That was the start of a dreadful run of four defeats and two draws, which included a Challenge Cup defeat at Stranraer, where Paul Hartley made his debut.

Millwall had gone into administration, and faced with having to settle all football debts, were more than happy to commute the balance due on the Sinclair / Dair and Crawford transfer, in exchange for transferring Hartley (valued at £200,000) and Jason Dair. Results improved markedly, with four successive victories, but they were followed by two defeats, at Airdrie and, crucially, at home to Dundee. The Dens Parkers were the surprise package in the First Division, racing to the top under the management of Jocky Scott, and with Jim McInally outstanding in midfield. Their victory at Stark's Park on 8th November in the twelfth game of the season put them nine points ahead of Rovers. The emergence of a runaway leader of the division was not in Rovers' grand plan, as only the top team would be promoted.

There were more good results than bad, and the quality of entertainment could not be faulted. Van de Kamp proved to be an excellent goalkeeper, Scott Thomson had

GUIDO VAN DE KAMP
His spell at the club coincided with problems off the park, which unjustly taints the memories of one of the best goalkeepers to play for Rovers

It was announced that 24 year old Bosnian internationalist Dino Valentic had signed for Rovers on 30th August 1995, but on 30th November it was disclosed that he had failed to get a work permit. He had played in a reserve match without obtaining international clearance, and after Paddy Atkinson was also fielded in an another reserve match without clearance being obtained, Rovers were fined £100 by the Scottish League on 22nd December.

Jimmy Nicholl received the Scottish Professional Sports Photographers Association Personality of the Year award on 4th December 1995.

Training kit and boots were stolen from Stark's Park on 18th February 1996, providing problems for the following day's training.

PAUL BROWNE

On 29th October 1996, it was announced that Ian Munro had abandoned plans to bring two Vasalunds players on trial from Sweden, following tabloid revelations that one of them, Moses Nsebuga, had appeared in a pornographic film three years earlier. The other was Goran Marklund.

Kevin Nicol played for Scotland Under 15 schools against Poland on 14th October 1997

Alan Kelly not only shaped the club's future by running up loses of over £1 million in 1997/98, he was also party to the break up of the Scottish Football League. The ten Premier Division clubs required the help of additional clubs to tip the balance of the weighted voting as they sought to break away. On 12th January, it was disclosed that Raith Rovers, Dundee, Airdrie and St Mirren would vote with the ten Premier Division clubs, thus paving the way for the formation of the SPL.

Past and present Rovers monopolised the January 1998 Manager of the month awards. Jimmy Nicholl in the First Division, Steve Kirk of East Fife in the second and Paul Smith of Berwick Rangers in the third received that month's awards.

been converted into an effective overlapping full back, Fotheringham was an unexpected bonus as a partner to Paul Browne in defence and there was plenty of experience in midfield with Danny Lennon, John Miller and the increasingly impressive Hartley. Up front, Keith Wright, Craig Dargo and Jason Dair always carried a goal threat.

Two things were necessary to launch a meaningful promotion challenge ; a long run of victories, and a Dundee collapse. Neither happened, nor was there a Scottish Cup run, despite an excellent performance in the third round to win 2-1 at Easter Road over Premier League opponents. Falkirk repeated their treatment of the previous season, this time at Stark's Park in the fourth round.

That was followed by a 3-1 defeat at Morton, and a 1-1 draw at home to Airdrie, McEwan putting through his own goal two minutes from time. That effectively ended faint hopes of promotion. Marvin Andrews was signed in early March and struggled to acclimatise to Scottish League football, while Andy Walker was inexplicably signed on loan from Sheffield United at the cost of £1,000 per week.

The final twist of the knife came in the fifth last match of the season, when Dundee arrived at Stark's Park needing a point to clinch promotion, which they achieved with a 1-1 draw. A decade before, third place in the First Division would have been viewed as a successful season, but the level of expectation had been raised, as had the financial imperative. Rovers were ten points behind Champions Dundee, and five behind Falkirk, who rather wasted the play-off position, as Brockville was deemed not to be Premier League compliant (which would not have been a problem for Stark's Park).

Unbeknown to all but a few Rovers fans, irreparable damage had been done, which became apparent only when the financial accounts for the season were published in December 1998, showing a loss of £1,076,000.

That single season of profligate spending, and ultimate failure on the pitch, ensured that Raith Rovers would never be the same again. The club's borrowing ability was impaired, possibly for ever, culminating in the loss of ownership of Stark's Park.

Despite the inevitability of a drastic cut in the playing budget, there were two additions to the first team pool over the summer of 1998, with Dave Bowman hoping to succeed where his former Dundee United midfield colleague, Jim McInally had failed. A younger midfielder, local boy Steve Tosh, had been signed from St Johnstone on transfer deadline day. Pre-season friendlies were in the Highlands, rather than in Ireland, but when the serious work got underway, Rovers lost two and drew one of the opening three League matches. A win at Airdrie gave everyone a boost, although team and supporters alike did not enjoy listening to the post-match radio interview in which Jimmy Nicholl effectively advertised for sale the goalscorer, and Rovers outstanding player,

Paul Hartley.

Three draws and two defeats saw the team sink to ninth place. Few realistically expected Rovers to win the Championship, and with it the only promotion slot, given the inadequacies shown by the squad over the previous season and its subsequent weakening, and in 1998/99 there was no surprise package – Hibs' were everyone's favourite for the top spot. A dismal start, in which goals proved to be hard to find, had fans more concerned with the bottom two positions, and relegation.

The return from injury of Craig Dargo and Danny Lennon did not lead to an immediate improvement in results, while Marvin Andrews' return from injury proved to be premature. Gerry Britton was brought in on loan from Dunfermline, replacing Keith Wright, who left for Morton for £20,000 , and that coincided with something of a revival, starting with a 1-1 draw at Falkirk, followed by a 2-0 home win over basement club Stranraer, a draw against Clydebank at their new "digs" at Boghead, a home draw against Hamilton, and an unexpected 2-0 win at Ayr.

By far the most impressive performer in that vital spell – nine points gathered, three less and they would have been relegated – was Paul Hartley, and it came as little surprise when he was sold to Hibs for £200,000 four days before Christmas. Guido van de Kamp and Kevin Fotheringham (when he wasn't suspended) battled manfully in defence, but their team-mates looked dispirited in the face of relentless cuts in expenditure and, in early February wages were cut and payments of bonuses were deferred until the end of the season. The financial writing (in deepest red) had been on the wall for some months. Kelly had turned off the tap of his investment, and increasingly desperate measures were taken to raise working capital. On 7th August, Rovers' season ticket holders were given the opportunity to buy a lifetime's ticket to Stark's Park, provided they handed over £1000 plus VAT and it was admitted on 19th November that players would have to be sold. A week later, "The Courier" carried a front page headline "Cash Crisis Threat to Raith Rovers", followed a day later by a director, who had resigned two days prior to that, insisting that the club's problems had been exaggerated.

Having increased the price of season tickets by 35% in the summer, then offered a £20 discount once it became apparent that there were few takers, admission prices were halved for the match against Stranraer on 21st November, probably adding about 500 to the gate and giving a overdue lesson in football economics to the novices running the club. The financial situation was not helped by Ian Munro successfully suing the club for £45,000 plus his costs, in compensation for his sacking.

Alan Kelly had practically washed his hands of the day-to-day running of the club, ceding responsibility for keeping the creditors at bay to a firm of Dundee accountants, and sanctioning a revolving door of directors who at least made some effort to motivate supporters into realising the seriousness of the club's financial position. What they couldn't do was improve performances and results on the field of play.

There was no succour for supporters or bank manager in the cup competitions. In the League Cup at the start of the season, after a 2-0 home win over Clydebank, Rovers played well in losing to Hearts at Tynecastle only after extra time. 2-0 down after 23 minutes, they got back into the tie with a goal from teenage debutant Paul Shields four minutes before the interval. Paul Hartley scored a deserved equaliser in 87 minutes.

Prayers for a big money draw in the Scottish Cup were not answered, but there was worse to come when Second Division Clyde arrived at Stark's Park. Laden with debt after an expensive, failed attempt to break into the Premier League, their solution was to turn to the management team of Maryhill Juniors. A team filled with players from that level beat Rovers 4-0.

A 2-1 win over Clydebank the following week was followed by five League matches without a win. The focus of attention was on paying bills, rather than winning points and there was more than a hint of desperation about the sale of Jason Dair to Dunfermline for just £20,000. Fund-raising friendlies were arranged against Hearts, Aberdeen and Rangers, while in the business of staying in the First Division, the only wins to the end of the season were against the bottom two clubs, Hamilton Accies and Stranraer. Rovers survived simply because two clubs were having an even worse season that they were.

The team at the end of the season was unrecognisable from that at the start. Derek Holmes was signed on loan from Hearts, former Hamilton Accies player John McQuade was signed because he agreed to play as an amateur, and there was a succession of debuts for young players from the reserves. On and off the field, things were falling apart, and what appeared to be salvation came from an unexpected, and unspecified, source during the summer.

Peter Hetherston had, a year earlier, been dismissed as assistant manager of Partick Thistle, along with manager John McVeigh, following their relegation to the Second Division on the last day of the season. Hetherston suggested to some friends that they may wish to invest in Rovers, who had a Premier League compliant stadium with 10,000 seats (a rarity outwith the top division at that time), and the proven potential for returning to the top flight.

They purchased Kelly's majority shareholding, installed a Managing Director, and appointed McVeigh as manager and Hetherston as his assistant on 14th June. The departing manager had another field day in the press. He found out about his impending dismissal from one of the young reserves, who had heard it from a director's daughter in a nightclub. The fans had no appetite for such mascinations, but the

episode epitomised the manner in which the club was being run in the decade following the League Cup win.

Money appeared to be no object as a succession of new players were signed, Steve Hamilton, Kevin Gaughan, player coach Kenny Black, Paul Agnew, Jamie McKenzie, Paul Tosh, Alex Burns and Brian Hetherston, brother of Peter and recently a Scotland Under 21 internationalist with St Mirren.

An air of enthusiasm swirled around the ground. McVeigh favoured the Frank Connor style of management, which did not concern those still at the club who remembered the legacy of the latter, and early results were encouraging, with the notable blip of an awful 6-0 home defeat by St Mirren. In the League Cup, there was an unlucky defeat on penalties to Premier League Motherwell, and on 28th August Didier Agathe made his debut in a League match at Airdrie. He scored a hat-trick, and looked a class apart. That was followed by a 5-1 home win over Ayr United the following Saturday.

Marvin Andrews was showing excellent form at centre half, adding awareness and craft to his impressive physical presence ; Jay Stein and Agathe were penetrating wingers and the best of the pre-season intake, Alex Burns, was sharing the goals with Craig Dargo (when the latter was fit). The team wasn't quite the finished article, but it looked capable of sustaining a promotion bid, and certainly seemed to have the moral fibre for the challenge. A flat display at Morton was punished by a 2-0 defeat (Keith Wright scoring against his former team), but that was followed by a 2-2 home draw against newly relegated Dunfermline, a 2-0 win at Inverness and a 2-1 home win over Falkirk.

A last minute defeat at Paisley was followed by three wins and two draws, but to the astonishment of everyone, John McVeigh was sacked on 1st December. There was an immediate backlash from fans and media alike, and belatedly, it was announced that he had been dismissed for bullying young players. That, too, came as a surprise to everyone in and around the club.

The truth was that McVeigh had incurred the displeasure of one of the new directors, who, backed by the owner, insisted to the rest of the board that the manager had to go. In an attempt to legitimise this unjustifiable action, they blackened his reputation and left him with no option but to take legal action to clear his name. The subsequent protracted court action simply drew attention to the manner in which the club was being run, and owned, and kicked off three years of a constant stream of unsavoury publicity in the nation's newspapers.

The only unsurprising aspect of this bizarre sequence of events was that Hetherston was installed as manager. In fairness to him, there followed more good results than bad, and a semblance of a promotion challenge was sustained until the closing weeks of the season. The source of Agathe was tapped for more French players,

CRAIG DARGO

Rovers' assistant manager Alex Smith was appointed part-time manager of Scotland's Under 21 squad during 1998/99, in succession to Newcastle's Tommy Craig.

Kevin Nicol was included in the Scotland Under 16 squad to play to matches v Sweden in March. He played in the 2-1 win at Broadwood on 23rd March 1999. He was in the Scotland Under 17 squad for a tournament in Portugal in May

When John McVeigh was appointed manager, he was committed to making a film with Robert Duvall and Ally McCoist entitled "The Cup". Duvall made a number of visits to Stark's Park during the period of filming in various locations across Scotland.

In mid August 1999, Paul Shields was included in the Scotland Under 18 squad, and Kevin Nicol in the Under 17s.

Rovers reached the Reserve League Cup Final, which they lost 2-1 to Dunfermline at Stark's Park on 10th May 2000. Nish and Templeman scored for the visitors with Paul Shields scoring for Rovers, who fielded : Coyle, Maughan, Ellis (sub Hampshire), Kirkwood, Hamilton, Black, Fotheringham (sub Rushford), Steve Tosh, Shields, Craig and Stein. Unused substitute was Nicol.

THE LIVINGSTON THREE
From the top, Alex Burns,
Marvin Andrews and Steve
Tosh, together sold to
Livingston for a total of
£22,500.
All three would go on to play
in the Premier League, in
Andrews case with Rangers
(as pictured) while Rovers slid
down the League.

with mixed results. Antoine Preguet was a very classy left back who knew his worth – which was more than Rovers could afford to pay him – so he played just two games, while Yanis Beggue made little impact. Combative left back Sacha Opinel was signed, as was former World Youth Cup winner Jean Phillipe Javary, a hard tackling midfield player. In a season of surprises, one of the biggest was the sale of Paul Shields to Celtic for £100,000. Eighteen of his twenty-six first team competitive appearances had been as substitute, he had scored just three goals, and he had not played a full ninety minutes for the club.

Among several excellent results were home and away victories over promotion challengers Dunfermline Athletic, preserving an unbeaten record against one of the two teams promoted to form the new 12 club SPL. In a rousing New Year Derby, goals from Burns, Paul Browne and Steve Tosh, stretching from the first to the 89th minutes, earned a merited 3-0 victory. At East End Park on 18th March, Rovers fans were still celebrating Paul Browne's opening goal when Craig Dargo rattled home a long-range shot less than a minute later. That was followed by three more victories, but hopes of a late run to secure promotion required the victories to be continued into the final four fixtures, and a listless performance at Brockville on 15th April resulted in a 1-0 defeat.

Fifth place, twelve points shy of promotion, was a disappointing conclusion to a season which had more highs than lows, on the pitch at least. Concerns about the running the club were conveniently ignored as long as players of the calibre of Andrews, Burns, Agathe and Dargo were being fielded each week. Perhaps the promised promotion would be achieved the following season ?

Since the unforgettable 7-0 defeat of St Mirren in 1992, Rovers had failed to win their opening League match, and that record continued with a 2-1 home defeat at the hands of Alloa, thanks in part to Sasha Opinel being sent off for a reckless challenge in 58 minutes. The next four League matches brought three wins and a draw, however, and victories at East Fife and at home to Arbroath in the League Cup brought a big pay day – and a 4-0 defeat – at Celtic. The cup conquerors had signed Didier Agathe, following a short spell at Hibs whom he joined on freedom of contract which meant no compensation for Rovers, although they were the recipients of a very generous cheque from Brentford for the signature of Javary. Dargo had been sold to Kilmarnock for £60,000 during the close season.

Their replacements were distinctly underwhelming ; Ivan Mballa, and former Celtic player Gerry Creaney, who had palpably lost his fitness. None the less, goals were flowing freely and the defence was looking solid.

Rovers were outstanding in winning 4-0 at Livingston on 16th September, Marvin Andrews capping a monumental performance with two goals and Alex Burns and Paul Tosh

combining to good effect up front to complete the scoring. Unfortunately, this was followed by a 1-0 home defeat by Morton the following week, and in a re-run of the previous December's inexplicable and unexpected decision to sack the manager, two days later the team's three best players were sold to Livingston. At one stroke, ambitions for promotion were ended.

The fans were furious, particularly when it was discovered that the total transfer fee received for Marvin Andrews, Alex Burns and Stevie Tosh was £22,500. The directors claimed that £100,000 was being raised, but that dubious figure was arrived at by adding in the players' wages to the end of the season. What they didn't calculate was the loss of 500 admissions at every home match, which was (at least) the consequence of their actions. The club's owners, who were upfront at the outset that their interest in the club was to make money, had discovered that the very opposite was the reality of life in the Scottish League First Division, particularly for a full time club, and that increasing amounts of their money were required to keep the wages, and the other bills, paid. Their response was the age-old, error-strewn road in football – to cut costs. The warning signs had been there some months earlier. The company who provided the matchday stewarding at Stark's Park petitioned the Court of Session for the appointment of a provisional liquidator on 19th May 2000 as they sought to have their bill for 1998/99 season settled. Four days later, it was paid thanks to an early pay-out from the Scottish League.

In an attempt to quell the uproar, the fans were asked along to a meeting at Stark's Park on 2nd October. Long before the appointed time, it was apparent that the Lounge of the 200 Club would be far too small for the several hundreds who turned up. The meeting was hurriedly relocated to the seats of the main stand, and for disinterested observers it must have been hugely entertaining. For those fearful for the club's future, its shambolic conduct was ominous.

Peter Hetherston, who was as shocked as the fans at the news that his star trio were being transferred, brought in a succession of former team-mates to shore up the team. Shaun Dennis, who had lost his first team place at Hibs, spent three months on loan, and Marc Miller, Ray McKinnon, John Inglis and Andy Smith joined Mark Jones, Paddy Kelly and several foreigners in arriving at Stark's Park.

On 24th October it was announced that all employees of the club would accept a reduction of 25% in their wages, but it later emerged that the players had not been consulted. Four days later, the Sunday Mail linked the owners of the club to one of Scotland's most prominent gangsters. The financial situation was eased a little on 21st December when Dene Shields, who had started only one League match for the club, was sold to Sunderland for £60,000.

Following a 2-1 win at troubled Morton on 11th November, Rovers won only one of their next fourteen League matches, and that was at home to bottom of the League Alloa. Bottom of the Second Division Stirling Albion put Rovers out of the Scottish Cup at the first hurdle, which was Guido Van De Kamp's last match for the club. He was offered a free transfer to reduce the wage bill. Bizarre team selections, notably Paul Tosh at left back, added to the shambolic air surrounding the club.

The third last match of the season proved to be crucial, away to fellow relegation strugglers Alloa. Goals from Andy Smith (who made a significant contribution after being freed by Kilmarnock) and Paul Tosh earned Rovers a 2-1 win, followed by a 5-0 defeat of another struggling club, Airdrieonians, the following Saturday. Those six points saved Rovers from relegation, Morton (who descended with Alloa) finishing just three points behind. An unsung hero all season was veteran midfielder Kenny Black, whose stoic performances rolled back the years of a distinguished career, and shored up a faltering side.

There was an enormous upheaval in the playing squad over the summer of 2001, and for the first two months of the season, it seemed that the club would not be troubled with relegation worries for the second successive season. A draw and two defeats from the opening three League fixtures were followed by three wins, a draw and a defeat. New Spanish winger Nacho Novo proved to be a real goal threat, and his goal-making talents were eagerly finished off by the veteran Scott Crabbe. Montrose and Falkirk were beaten in the League Cup before Craig Brewster returned to his old stamping ground and scored both goals in Hibs' 2-0 victory.

The promise quickly evaporated, however, although closer examination of the team revealed the reality of the squad. Goalkeeper Monin was capable of great saves, but prone to expensive errors. Greg McCulloch and Paul Browne had not improved in their long years at the club, and while Shaun Dennis (signed permanently on being freed by Hibs) and Andy Smith provided a solid backbone to the side, neither were getting quicker or more mobile, nor was the veteran man-of-many clubs Darren Henderson.

An influx of more foreign players over the winter, and the return of Mark Jones from Chesterfield, failed to halt the slide. The club was fined £20,000 (half of it suspended for two years) for irregularities surrounding his loan from the English club during the previous season. Rovers did not win a match between 25th September and 2nd February, and the Scottish Cup run was of the briefest duration following a 1-0 defeat at Second Division Hamilton Accies. By then, Peter Hetherston had gone, resigning on 11th December. Former Dundee and Aberdeen manager Jocky Scott was appointed in his place eight days later, after Queen's Park coach John McCormack had been offered the job and declined it.

Third in the League after beating St Mirren 3-0 at Stark's Park on 22nd September, Rovers were bottom after a 5-1 defeat at Inverness on 10th November. The introduction of some more short-term signings in January raised hopes of salvation, and there were four wins and a draw from six League matches between January 19th and February 23rd, when Falkirk were beaten 5-1 at Stark's Park to lift the team out of the bottom two places ; but the next six matches, brought just three draws, and Rovers sank to the bottom, where they stayed. The dismal season proved, once again, that star players alone cannot bring success to a team, if they are not assisted by competent team-mates. Novo, as his subsequent career with Dundee and Rangers proved, was an outstanding forward, Paquito as skilful a midfield player as had been seen at the club for some years, and some of the other foreigners, such as full backs Zoco and Tejero, were competent. Jay Stein had stayed too long at the club, however, and his early promise was not fulfilled, while the remainder of the team were either ill-suited for the top half of Scottish football, or simply past their best.

The last two matches of the season were lost, 1-0 at Partick Thistle and by same scoreline at home to Ross County, the goal being scored six minutes from time with Rovers looking incapable of scoring. Four more points would have meant another season in the First Division, as a rash of insolvency-induced relegations and resignations meant that only one club was relegated, and that was bottom of the League Raith Rovers.

Having precipitated the club's relegation by severe cost cutting, the owners embarked on the exact opposite strategy, and invested heavily in the team and a new management regime in 2002/3. Jocky Scott was dismissed, and his replacement was former Airdrie player Antonio Calderon, a Spaniard who was asked to bring a revolutionary "continental approach" to the club. He had initially arrived in Scottish football as one of Steve Archibald's Spanish imports at Airdrie, in a short lived and ill-fated attempt to stave off that club's bankruptcy.

Former Livingston and Stirling Albion manager Raymond Stewart, Tayport's junior cup winning boss Dave Baikie, and Cowdenbeath manager Keith Wright had all been interviewed for the vacancy at Stark's Park, and Wright was offered the job but declined when it was explained that he could not bring his assistant manager. That had to be Paquito, a very skilful, elegant Spaniard, who moved from right back to midfield, and was number two to Calderon, who continued as a player.

Assistant Manager PAQUITO

Paquito was one of the players nominated for the SPFA Second Division Player of the Year in 2002/03. It was won by Chris Templeman of Brechin City.

Antonio Calderon and Dick Campbell shared the Bells Second Division Manager of the Year award. Calderon had won it for three successive months during the season,.

KEVIN FOTHERINGHAM

SHAUN DENNIS

There was a limit to how secretive the closed door trial match at Hamilton on 13th July 2003 could be, as its main purpose was for players to try to impress the watching scouts, agents, coaches and managers.
A team sheet was distributed to the invited guests, bearing the following names :
Yellow team : Jean Paul ; John Fritter, Mark Crouther, Alan McDermott, Paul O'Neill, Paul McGlinchey, Tano Patrice, Marlin Walters, John Sutton, Ross O'Donahue and Greig Watson. Substitutes : Johan Briquez, Loffi Requalme, Joel Bevis, Frank McEwan, Harding, Mohammed Aquarme, Ryan Maxwell.
Blue team : Chura Samir, Gordon Sims, Jean Alexandre, Nicosia Alain, Reclaine Djelool, Vincent Talo, Tom Jones, Ian Dawes, Kevin Storrie, Franco, Craig Downie. Substitutes : Dominique Jean Zephen, Romaud Bova, Michael Martin, Daniel Addo, Scott Mulligan, Ryan Mahon, Murray Watson.

On 15th December 2003 Rovers travelled to Spain for a three day training trip. The following day, Tuesday 16th December, they played Spanish Second Division club in a friendly match and drew 3-3, the goals scored by Ryan Blackadder (2) and John Sutton

There was another convulsive turnover of players. Remaining from the previous season were young full back Laurie Ellis, Shaun Dennis who played his first Second Division match fourteen years after first joining the club, French midfielder Wilfred Nanou, Paul Hampshire and veteran striker Andy Smith.

Among the foreign imports were Martin Prest, a potentially match-winning, but temperamental winger, goalkeeper Raul and full back Cristian Patino. Former Clyde forward Brian Carrigan was signed from Stockport County , and among the players on loan were Darren Brady from Livingston, Colin Boylan from Dundee, and muscular centre forward Karl Hawley from Walsall.

It took the new manager a few games to find his feet and assess the players at his disposal, so early season results were mixed, with just two wins in the opening six League matches. There were early, and expensive, departures from the League and Challenge Cups, at home to Alloa and away to Airdrie United respectively.

The situation was transformed by a surprisingly comfortable 4-0 win at Hamilton on 21st September, which was followed by two wins, a defeat, a draw, then a twelve match unbeaten run to 18th January, which included victories in the first two rounds of the Scottish Cup.

A measure of the liberal financial situation at the club was a venture into the transfer market, diminutive striker Paul McManus signed from East Fife with the £15,000 determined by a transfer tribunal. As autumn turned to winter, he began to share the scoring duties with the somewhat bulkier and less mobile Smith and Hawley. That splendid sequence of results, mostly earned by some excellent, flowing football in which Calderon and Paquito suggested that they were playing at several levels below their natural class of football, propelled Rovers to the top of the League, where they remained for the rest of the season.

Hopes of a Scottish Cup run were dashed with a 2-0 defeat at a strengthening Inverness Caledonian Thistle, and that was followed by two draws and a defeat in the League. The team was strengthened by three more signings, Graeme Fyfe, Ray McKinnon and the return of Dene Shields in an attempt to get the promotion run back on track, and that strategy worked, for promotion would not have been secured without the nine points won from three matches in eight days in early March, all at Stark's Park. The team had lost its early fluency and resolve, and won only two of its last ten matches of the season.

The Second Division Championship was secured by four points from Brechin City, with Airdrie United a further point behind. What promised to be a glorious romp to the title deteriorated into a grim struggle to hang on at the top of the League, but Calderon and his players achieved what successors have so far failed to do, and lifted Rovers out of the Second Division. The fans were pleased, some of them delighted, the rest ruefully

reflecting that seven years earlier they had been watching their favourites, not at Brechin, Berwick, Cowdenbeath, Forfar and Stenhousemuir, but in Toftir, Akranes, Munich, and in the Premier Division.

Promotion proved to be a costly exercise, however. That year's accounts, when they were eventually published (unaudited), revealed a loss of almost £75,000. The owners were clearly unwilling to commit a similar sum in the First Division, and the consequence was another grim battle against relegation.

Yet another reversal of financial strategy was obvious before the season started. It was made known that the club were organising a closed door trial match, but unlike those events which were routine pre-season fixtures up until friendlies became the norm in the mid 1960s, the match would not involve signed players, but free agents looking for a club. Moreover, the match on Sunday 13th July would not be played at Stark's Park, but at New Douglas Park, Hamilton, in which some of the club's owners had a financial interest.

Unorthodox and inpecunious it may have appeared, but it did result in the club signing John Sutton, younger brother of Celtic's Chris, and the ponderous, but skilful centre forward scored 13 of the club's 37 League goals, which did much to save them from relegation. A month earlier, in late June, there was a bizarre episode involving Arbroath centre half Eddie Forrest, who appeared to have been "hoaxed" into thinking that he had received the offer of a full time contract from Raith Rovers.

Other newcomers to the squad at the start of the season were loan signings Craig Stanley, a midfielder from Walsall, Steven Robb of Dundee and Livingston's Richard Brittain. A seemingly endless stream of trialists, foreign players, juniors and youths appeared for a handful of matches, as the manager sought to find a team to compete at a noticeably higher level of football. He was assisted in his recruitment by a Director of Football, former Lochee United manager David Martin. To the surprise of many, Paul McManus and Andy Smith were released to join Albion Rovers and Clyde respectively.

Early results were encouraging, with three Challenge Cup ties won to advance to the semi finals of a tournament in which Rovers had historically failed. Despite dominating the first round League Cup tie at Second Division Arbroath, niave defending allowed the home side to score the only goal of the match, from the penalty spot, in the final minute. The scorer was one-time Rovers youth player John Cusick. In the semi final of the Challenge Cup, Rovers lost 4-0 at home to Caledonian Thistle.

Only one of the first six League matches was lost, and an excellent 1-0 win at St Johnstone, with the player manager scoring the only goal of the game, put Rovers in second place. The following week, however, the same selection lost 7-1 at home to Ross County, and followed that with a run of 11 League games which brought only one victory, 2-1 at home to Brechin. Rovers saw in the New Year in eighth position in the League, hovering perilously close to the relegation positions.

The response was to throw even more players into the squad. Karl Hawley was brought back for another spell on loan, Jamie Langfield replaced the flamboyant but error-prone Spanish goalkeeper Gonzalez and the Novo-like Beto Carranza had a brief spell in attack. The last two had been sacked by Dundee's administrator, and to pay their wages at Stark's Park, £2 was added to the admission price for the League match against St Johnstone on 29th November. The one consistent and competent recruit was the Macedonian Goran Stanik at left back.

A 2-0 win at home to Falkirk on 3rd January 2004 raised hopes of a happier new year (Rovers had won just 10 League matches in the calendar year 2003). It was a false dawn, however, and a 3-1 home defeat in the third round of the Scottish Cup by Kilmarnock was followed by two draws and four defeats in the League.

More players were thrown into the mix ; Pereira, Nieto, Capin and Ferrero from the continent, Jonathan Smart from Dundee amateur football, and winger Lloyd Young from Tayport juniors. As happened a year before, a short spell in March rescued the season. On 6th March St Mirren were beaten 2-0 Stark's Park, with goals from Ferrero and Pereira. Calderon scored in a 1-1 draw at Brechin four days later, followed by two goals from Pereira to beat Ayr United at Stark's Park. Ten days later, Queen of the South were beaten 3-1 at Stark's Park with goals from Pereira, Paquito and (a Scots name on the scoresheet at last) a Thomson own goal. Ten points from four successive matches should be seen in the context of the three point margin at the end of the season between Rovers and relegated Ayr United. None of the final nine League fixtures was won.

Rovers fans were well used to bizarre news – and lurid rumours – emanating from Stark's Park, but what was to follow truly surpassed even the worst of the crazy deeds of the previous five years. It was announced that Antonio Calderon was to be replaced as manager by Anelka – no, not Nicholas, the France, Arsenal, Real Madrid etc. forward, but his brother Claude. In return for injecting a six-figure sum, the diminutive Anekla would be given complete control of playing matters at Stark's Park. There had been rumours of all sorts of illegal activities swirling around the club, but most fans regarded this as nothing less than the prostitution of the club's playing activities. When it all, predictably, turned sour within a couple of months, several directors protested that they had been against the scheme, but there had been no resignations, but instead silence from those quarters, when it was proposed and announced.

One fan took the process a stage further and announced, in the Novar Bar, that he was going along to the club with a cheque for £500, on the proviso that he played in one match. It didn't happen, but his logic seemed to be consistent with club policy, and that supporter would at least have reduced the debt by a fraction, unlike Nsinba Lusamba. The 20 year old, born in Zaire and a French speaker, had telephoned Rangers to ask for a trial (he had played briefly with Ilkeston Town the previous season). Someone at Ibrox, helpfully, told him to contact Raith Rovers, where he might find the prevailing culture more familiar. After a few days training, he lined up for Rovers in a First Division match at Hamilton on 7th August 2004. He was replaced by Jonathan Smart at half time. Rovers lost 2-0.

Sky, who obviously recognised a disaster waiting to unfold, approached the club with an offer to make a 'fly on the wall' documentary. Mercifully, this particular financial blandishment was declined. They filmed Ron Atkinson imploding at Peterborough United instead.

Only Brady, the saintly Paquito and novices Smart and Young remained from the previous season. In came thirteen foreign players, and several Dundee juniors, recruited by the club's Director of Football, Dave Martin, who persuaded former player and manager Gordon Wallace, between jobs, to help with the coaching. Gordon recalled : "These guys may have looked alright in training, but as soon as I saw them in a match, I thought 'Oh oh, we've got a problem here.'" The matches he was referring to were a 3-3 draw with Highland League Huntly, and a 3-1 defeat at Berwick. A third pre-season friendly was won, 3-2 at East Fife, but only after most of the foreign players had been substituted by youth team players at half time.

When the serious stuff started, it was an unmitigated disaster. Apart from a 1-1 draw at Airdrie United on 21st August, every one of the opening nine League matches was lost, as were the first round ties in the League Cup (at Stranraer) and the Challenge Cup (at home to Albion Rovers). The club were the laughing stock of Scottish football, but the noise from the stands at Stark's Park was certainly not laughter. Anelka recognised the inevitability of the entire folly, and returned to France, writing off his substantial investment. Less amusing was the investigation by the Scottish Football League into a bet made on Rovers to lose the last game of the previous season, at Ayr. On the advice of the League's lawyers, no further action was taken when the Director in question insisted that it was his son who had placed the bet, albeit using his father's credit card. The club seemed to be finding fresh depths of mud in which to bury its name, on a weekly basis.

Rovers turned to former goalscoring hero Gordon Dalziel as Anelka's replacement. He had been managing Glenafton Athletic for a few months after being sacked by Ayr United, having achieved some success, if no lasting legacy, with the help of Chairman Bill Barr's financial backing. A 2-2 draw at home to Hamilton Accies was followed by a 2-1 win

DARREN BRADY

COME ALL THE FAITHFUL

If Raith Rovers now could only be like
How I remember when
They played the Hearts with Conn and Bauld
and Wardhaugh : I was ten

The crowds four deep down Pratt Street stretched
Way round past Starkie's Bar
Jostling in friendly banter rare
It was a sight by far

To give the Rangers, Celts and Hibs
A taste of things to come
From twenty, thirty thousand strong
Supporters' clamour sung

We sang the praises of our heroes
Girt in the navy blue
Immaculate Wullie staunch at the rear
Wi' Young and Andy Leigh too

There in the vanguard going for goals
Bold Ernie and our Benny
Frae Jimmy Mac's pinpoint cross
The ba's speed netbound plenty

But sair's the fecht, Raith's loyal fans ken
Fur e'en with Baxter's genius
We had to wait till '94
Till Nicholl silverware gi'en us

But we've again oor Premier goal
To strive fur Euro glory
We stunned the "Munchen" at half-time
Next year a fairy-tale story ?

James Bogie, September 1996

PAUL McMANUS

Gordon Dalziel was sent to the stand by the match referee on two occasions during 2005/06, at home to Ayr United on 17th September, and on Boxing Day at Greenock during a mad two minutes in which Willie Lyle was sent off for his second bookable offence, to be followed to the showers by Chris McLeod, who had come on as a substitute barely 15 seconds earlier. He left the field without kicking the ball.

On 26th March 2006, it became illegal to smoke in an enclosed space, which included the stands at Stark's Park. Smokers in the South stand had no-where to go for a fag at half-time, and on the first occasion, they were allowed onto the track at half time.

Sunday 27th May 2007, Under 17 League Cup Final Raith Rovers 2 Alloa Athletic 2 at Stark's Park, Rovers won 4-3 on penalties.
The following year, on 11th May 2008, Rovers won the Under 19 League Cup Final, beating Stenhousemuir 3-1 in the Final at Stark's Park. Bryce, Halley and Whatley scored for Rovers, Love equalising for the visitors on the hour.
Rovers' team : Amos, Pirret, Scott, Adamson, Darlington (sub Beveridge), Wedderburn, Main, Whatley, Graham, Halley (sub Mackie) Bryce, Thomson (subs Woods).

at home to St Johnstone, and Shaun Dennis provided stability at the back when Dalziel brought him back to the club once again.

The relief of having a conventional manager in charge led to better performances, but such was the poverty of the squad which remained – most of Anelka's signings having followed him home to France – that results scarcely improved. The St Johnstone victory was followed by two defeats, then a 1-1 draw at Ross County and 0-0 at home to Partick Thistle, before six successive League defeats. Second Division Alloa won 2-0 in the third round of the Scottish Cup at Stark's Park, and the final fourteen League fixtures brought just two victories. With little or no finance at his disposal, Dalziel could do nothing to stave of an ignominious relegation. By the season's end, Rovers were a massive 30 points from safety.

The one good thing to come from the debacle of 2004/5 was that the club's owners had had enough. They encouraged a well publicised campaign to have the club bought "by the community". No wonder they backed it, for it meant that they got all their money back, the only device with which that could be achieved. The reality was not quite so clearcut, as will be explored in an appendix to this book.

In his first full season in charge at Stark's Park, Gordon Dalziel enjoyed a relatively injury-free run, allowing him to field a fairly settled team. After the usual comings and goings in the January transfer window, he pronounced himself satisfied with his squad for the second half of the season. With the introduction of play-offs to decide promotion and relegation between the three lower divisions, only four clubs in the Second Division would be guaranteed continuing membership by the end of 36 fixtures. Unfortunately, Rovers were one of them. There were occasions during the season when involvement in the promotion chase looked likely, but there were other times when there were nervous glances at the two relegation positions.

In goal was Alastair Brown, a Scotland Under 21 squad player on loan from Hibs. Willie Lyle, signed from the manager's old club Ayr United, and Laurie Ellis (returned from St Mirren on a free transfer) were the usual full backs, and between them were Todd Lumsden, signed from Hamilton, and

Chris McLeod (from Arbroath). Mark Campbell was signed on the January transfer deadline, on a free transfer from St Johnstone, and was thereafter preferred to McLeod.

In midfield, Chris Silvestro (freed by Albion Rovers) and Ian Davidson were the regulars, and were joined by former Rangers and Scotland veteran Derek Ferguson for the first part of the season, Neil Jablonski and Emilio Jaconelli. Veteran strikers Scott Crabbe and Eddie Annand (freed by Dumbarton) took it in turn to partner Paul McManus (re-signed from Stranraer) up front, with Fairbairn or Crilly on the wing.

The previous clubs of the new players (and the veteran status of some of them) should have provided some warning of the potential for failure to return to the First Division at the first time of asking, but such negativity was swept aside with a bright start to the season, in which progress was made in the League Cup and Challenge Cup. Alongside the three cup ties won were five of the opening nine League matches, but between October 22nd, when 2446 watched the home match against Morton, and 26th November, when half that number watched Peterhead at Stark's Park, only one point out of eighteen was won.

By the time the Second Round of the Scottish Cup came around (the first round having been negotiated thanks to a bye) a good cup run was imperative for financial reasons. The previous week, only 1060 had watched the League match against Dumbarton, and there were full time wages to be paid to some members of the squad. Rovers reserved one of their worst performances of the season for the Cup tie at Hampden on 10th December, Queen's Park winning 2-0.

Two draws and two wins from late January to mid February were followed by five games without a win, and a season of no achievement meandered to its end.

A welcome distraction from the failure of the team to get the club back into the top half of Scottish League football was the high profile "Reclaim the Rovers" campaign, heavily publicised by the Fife Free Press. The hard work of many individuals raised £100,000, which went towards buying out the West of Scotland-based owners on 30th December. They had made it known that they would no longer provide additional funds for the club and, in stark contrast to the emollient words used when the ground had been sold, threatened eviction (see appendix). The scare tactics worked, and they received their money. Unfortunately, none remained to improve the team, and the fans reacted in time-honoured fashion, by refusing to turn up to watch sub-standard football. A Gala Day on 14th January to celebrate the takeover involved a parade of former players, a pipe band and kids admitted for £1, and attracted an attendance of 2,236, but Stirling Albion won the match.

Gordon Dalziel's task was not made any easier when his already inadequate

budget was further cut over the close season. There were to be no more full time players signed, and the new policy was to reduce the numbers of those who remained on full time contracts. Jablonski, Ellis, Lyle, Jaconelli and Clarke were all released, and goalkeeper Ally Brown's loan period ended. YTS goalkeeper Stuart Hall was also freed. They were replaced by goalkeepers Michael Brown, freed by Forfar Athletic, and Chris Fahey, freed by Stenhousemuir. Other newcomers were Amand One from Cowdenbeath, Sean Kilgannon from Partick Thistle, Kevin Fotheringham from St Johnstone, Neil Janczyk on loan from St Johnstone, Stephen Manson from Berwick Rangers and former Division One Player of the Year Ian Harty, who had been in dispute with Hamilton Accies and had hardly played the previous season.

Despite the disastrous experience of the Anelka episode, Rovers still found it difficult to refuse what appeared to be a free gift. It was announced that there would be a tie up with the youth division of the Italian Football Federation, but The Non League Paper in England, where clubs had proved to be more discerning, exposed a scam, and Rovers were left with just red faces. Ominously, it appeared that the lessons of even recent history had not been learned at Stark's Park.

The season that followed was one of unprecedented ups and down, with fans' emotions plumbing the depths of despair, soaring to delight and high expectation, only to end in ultimate disappointment.   There have been good seasons and bad seasons in following the club, but rarely have the highs and lows been so pronounced and recurring as they were in 2006/07.

The team got off to a dismal start, losing the opening games in the League,

League Cup and Challenge Cup, before picking up the first point in a 0-0 draw at home to Forfar.   A 1-0 win at Peterhead was followed by an awful performance in losing 3-1 at Cowdenbeath, and on Thursday 31st August, Gordon Dalziel was sacked.   Both sides maintained a respectful silence as the club's greatest League goalscorer was the latest to discover that returning to a club where success had been achieved usually resulted in tarnishing a cherished reputation.

Those who analysed his time as manager at Stark's Park, with the perfect vision of hindsight, contrasted his previous success in charge of Ayr United as being heavily funded by his chairman's personal wealth.   The opposite was the case at Stark's Park, as it was for his mentor Frank Connor, but despite their close association over many years, Dalziel did not have Connor's unique skills of extracting blood out of a stony-broke boardroom.

There was surprised delight at the appointment of Craig Levein as the new manager. He came with the pedigree of significant achievement in the Premier League, and was still in his prime. It was stated at the outset that he would not be under contract, and would be free to leave if a Premier Division club approached him. It did not take long for this loose arrangement to be tested, and after just 52 days Levein left to go through the revolving manager's door at Dundee United.

In terms of results, Levein's brief record at Stark's Park was poor, one win (at Stranraer in his first match) three draws and three defeats. He did identify many of the fundamental problems at the club – poor training facilities for the largely part-time squad on dark nights, poor organisation on and off the pitch and inadequate players, and

Craig Levein had just about time during his brief spell as manager of Raith Rovers in 2006/07, to organise a squad photograph.
Back row : Brian Marr (kitman), Neil Janczyk, Chris Silvestro, Stephen Tulloch, Amand One, Michael Brown, Mark Campbell, Chris Fahey, Marvin Andrews, Iain Davidson, Colin Leiper, Brian Fairbairn, Physiotherapist Paul Cameron
Front row : Ian Harty, Stephen Manson, Kevin Fotheringham, Paul McManus, Assistant Manager Gary Kirk, Manager Craig Levein, Todd Lumsden, Steven Bonar, Sean Kilgannon, Hjalmer Thorarisson

Photo courtesy D.C. Thomson

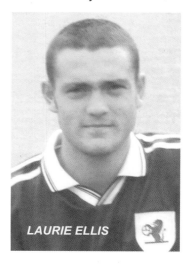

LAURIE ELLIS

CHRIS SILVESTRO

TOD LUMSDEN

he did recommend his successor, his former youth coach at Hearts, John McGlynn.

Levein also signed two players who helped turn the season around. Full back Craig Wilson, signed on loan from Dunfermline Athletic, was voted the Players' Player of the Year, and to general surprise, Marvin Andrews returned. Released by Rangers at the end of the previous season, the Trinidad and Tobago internationalist attributed his return to Stark's Park on a three year contract to God's will, although the highest wages in the Second Division (by some distance) may also have helped, as did former Chairman Alex Penman's generous contribution towards funding them. Amongst the short term signings were Icelander Hjalmar Thorarinsson, lent by Hearts.

The process to select McGlynn from a short list of six was prolonged and his first match was a 1-1 home draw with Stranraer, which did little to lift Rovers out of the relegation play-off (second bottom) place. A 2-1 win at Alloa boosted morale, but a dreadful performance the following week saw Third Division Dumbarton win 1-0 at Stark's Park to eject Rovers from the Scottish Cup. Only 1,186 turned up a week later for the home match against Ayr United, to discover that Marvin Andrews had been dropped by the new manager. The decision was justified with the club's first home win of the season – on December 16th, and that was followed a fortnight later by a 5-2 win over Peterhead.

The January transfer window saw a flurry of activity with players coming and going. Ian Harty made an early return, appearing as a trialist for Stirling Albion at Stark's Park a matter of days after his release. Derek Carcary was signed on a free transfer from Rangers, and Steven Hislop, son of former Rovers favourite John, arrived from Livingston. The lumbering Armand One, surely the largest player to play for the club, eventually left to join his former Cowdenbeath manager, Mixu Paatelainen, at TPS Turku in Finland.

After losing 2-1 at home to Cowdenbeath in the New Year fixture, Rovers embarked on one of the best runs in the entire history of the club. Seven wins and a draw from the next eight fixtures propelled the club out of the relegation zone, and into the play off positions. The 1-0 home defeat by Stirling Albion on 10th March was brushed off as a rare lapse, as five wins and a draw from the last seven League games saw Rovers approach the play-offs in high confidence.

The manager had worked wonders on the team. Fahey, who had replaced Mark Brown who dislocated his shoulder during the Alloa victory in December, achieved six successive clean sheets, Wilson and either Fotheringham and Pelosi were sound full backs, and Campbell and the restored (and fit) Andrews were superb in central defence. Hislop added a touch of class, and Carcary genuine pace, to the attack, and the team was firing on all cylinders.

John McGlynn attributed part of the transformation to improved fitness, principally because the number of full time players rose from three to nine. The Board of Directors insisted that the club was living within its means, despite this U-turn in policy.

Having built up the fans' enthusiasm and expectations, there was a further oscillation in emotions with failure in the play offs. Stirling Albion, playing neat, quick, along-the-grass football, were the better team in the first leg at Stark's Park, which ended 0-0. They continued their domination at Forthbank, and were well worth their 3-1 victory. They went on to beat the second bottom team of the First Division, Airdrie United, over two legs in the Play Off Final, and earned promotion with champions Morton. The Greenock club had clinched automatic promotion, and the title, at Stark's Park on 14th April, despite losing 2-0 in front of 2,000 of their fans in the 4,327 crowd ; Stirling's defeat at Ayr United that afternoon meant that Morton could not be caught.

Despite the promise, and subsequent expectation, of the second half of the season, there was to be no such glory for Rovers. Surely the desperately desired escape from the Second Division would be achieved the following season ?

Pre-season preparations got off to a bad start, for team and fans alike. Back-to-back matches were arranged at Southport and Chester, but both games fell victim to torrential rain. A match against Southport was hurriedly arranged on Vauxhall Motors' training pitch at Ellesmere Port, but the Astroturf pitch was deemed unsuitable for Marvin Andrews and Andy Tod. Southport had their own selection problems for the 11.30 kick off, and borrowed two of Rovers' reserves one of whom, Jamie Mackie, scored their final goal in a 3-1 victory. Not all of the fans who had arranged a weekend in Lancashire / Cheshire knew of the match, and those who did were poorly rewarded for their dedicated support.

There were also problems closer to home. Kevin Fotheringham received an offer from East Fife which would double his wages. Unsurprisingly, Rovers chose not to match the largesse of the Third Division club, who also signed Paul McManus, opportunistically, when it emerged that there had been a technical problem with the paperwork for his new contract at Stark's Park. Once again, more money was being offered at New Bayview, far in excess of what Rovers, on crowds of twice the size of East Fife's, could reasonably afford.

New arrivals for 2007/8 were former youth team player Craig Winter and Ryan Borrus, both freed by Dumbarton, former Hearts players Graham Weir, recently with Queen of the South, and Robert Sloan from Alloa, veteran Dunfermline striker Andy Tod, Marco Pelosu on loan from Hearts and East Stirling goalkeeper Keiron Renton.

The close and pre-season difficulties were shrugged aside as the season opened with three successive wins, the 1-0 victory at Airdrie being the club's first opening day success since the thrashing of St Mirren in

1992. Clyde were swept aside in the first round of the League Cup, thanks mainly to a superb performance by Derek Carcary, and the team was most unfortunate to lose the first round Challenge Cup tie at Perth, on penalties after holding the First Division promotion contenders to a 1-1 draw after extra time. Similarly, there was much to admire in a 3-1 defeat at Premier League Motherwell in the second round of the League Cup.

The occasional defeat, such as a 1-0 defeat at Cowdenbeath and a 3-2 home defeat by Ayr United, denied Rovers top spot in the League, but they were on the shoulders of early leaders Queen's Park, and then newly relegated Ross County, who ominously won 2-0 at Stark's Park on 15th September. Victories outnumbered dropped points, however, and the attack was significantly strengthend with the signing, on loan from Dundee United, of David Goodwillie in early November.

There was a degree of stability in the team, although the forwards were liable to rotation and substitution. In contrast to the settled team, there were constant changes in the assistant manager's position. Gary Kirk belatedly left to rejoin Craig Levein at Dundee United, and the vastly experienced Donald Park replaced him, only to move quickly to Hibs. Former player Paul Smith took over a position which had, in recent seasons and various labels, been occupied by Shaun Dennis, Gordon Wallace, Dave Martin, George Gemmell, Frank Connor, Paquito and John Hollins.

The potential banana-skin of a trip to Castle Douglas to play Threave Rovers in the third round of the reconstructed Scottish Cup was successfully negotiated with a 5-0 scoreline, although there were a few nervous moments before the third goal was scored. The following week, a battling performance at Dingwall earned a 3-2 victory over Ross County, and fans were daring to believe that automatic promotion could be achieved. A home draw with Brechin prompted some reappraisal, but it was followed by a 3-0 win at Ayr, and although there was once again disappointment in dropping two home points to Peterhead on December 22nd, the point that was won took Rovers above Ross County, to the top of the table.

Rovers then suffered an attack of vertigo, with a deserved defeat at bottom of the table Berwick Rangers. They bounced back to survive a spirited fight back from Alloa at Stark's Park, and took advantage of some good fortune in a 4-1 win at Cowdenbeath. There were signs of cracks appearing in the team which had looked so impressive in the earlier stages of the season. Clean sheets were now few and far between, with Marvin Andrews struggling to accommodate his long-standing knee injury. There was more variety in personnel than improvisation in tactics in attack, where Andy Tod was beginning to look every one of his 36 years. David Templeton was signed on loan from Hearts, and Northern Irish Youth International Nial Henderson arrived from Gretna, via a loan spell at Dumbarton.

Supporters drew little comfort in the thought "well, it was coming" when Ross County won 1-0 in Kirkcaldy on 5th January, and there was a marked contrast between the narrow Challenge Cup defeat earlier in the season, and the comprehensive 3-1 St Johnstone victory in the fourth round of the Scottish Cup. The slide was delayed by victories over Queen's Park and Berwick Rangers, but they were followed by four successive defeats, which allowed Ross County to build an impregnable lead at the top of the table. All utterances, public and private, were concentrated on the play offs, and Marvin Andrews bowed to the inevitable and at last underwent surgery to his troublesome knee.

It was noted that there was none of the momentum, anticipation and optimism which had accompanied the run to the play offs at the end of the previous season, with home form particularly unsatisfactory, exemplified by a defeat by Queen's Park and a draw against Brechin as the season neared its conclusion. The half-time score, 2-1 behind, at relegated Berwick caused more alarm, although the team rallied to win 5-2, but the warning signs re-appeared in the final league match of the season, which Peterhead won 5-2 at Stark's Park.

Rovers did not play particularly badly in the first leg of the play-off semi final against Airdrie United, but two moments of indecision by goalkeeper Chris Fahey resulted in the loss of two goals, to which the home team rarely looked like responding. Airdrie were in command throughout the second leg at the Excelsior Stadium, a last minute equaliser from Graeme Weir putting a veneer of respectability on the score for Rovers. It was an expensive aggregate defeat ; although Airdrie United lost to First Division Clyde in the Play Off Final, they were promoted to the First Division following the demotion of Gretna.

The final chapter of the playing fortunes over a century and a quarter of Raith Rovers' history could, selectively, sum up the club's history : flashes of brilliance, longer spells of competence but, in the end, disappointment for long-suffering supporters. After three years of trying to escape, there would be at least one more season in the bottom half of Scottish league football The end of the club's 125th season certainly provoked the thought that has sustained several generations of Kirkcaldy's footballing public, and which had kept alive the flames, flickering embers or isolated spark in the Stark's Park grate – there is always next season !

IAN DAVIDSON

One of the hardest parts of completing this book was the choice of an appropriate title. Matthew Elder, Sports Editor of the Fife Free Press, kindly ran a competition in the newspaper for supporters to suggest a title, and there was a very good response.

The vast majority of the suggestions were quite suitable, but they had already been considered by the author, and had any of them been chosen, it would have defeated the object of the exercise. Several included the word "Dancing", and they were given serious consideration.

The winner was chosen from a short list of six. "A Roar From the Past" was suggested by A. Thorpe of Cupar ; "Raith Faith" by Ian Finlayson of Canmore Gardens, and "Raith Rovertime 125" by Tom Murray of Dysart.

The most original was "Haud Yer Braith, Here Comes Raith" from D. Wallace of Balmoral Drive, and the runner-up was "Raith Against Time" by George Sinclair of Duddingston Drive.

The chosen title, "Always Next Season" was submitted by the pseudonymous Geordie Munro who gave his or her address as Stark's Park, Kirkcaldy. By coincidence, he or she chose the last three words of the book.

PETER HODGE

*20th May 1907 to 12th November 1912 ;
and October 1916 to 9th September 1919*

On the incorporation of Raith Rovers Football and Athletic Company Limited, Peter Hodge was appointed the club's first salaried Secretary / Manager. He had been secretary of a Juvenile team in Dunfermline in 1890, then became secretary of Dunfermline Juniors and was a referee for ten years, officiating at Scottish League Second Division matches between 1897 and 1906. Prior to joining Rovers he was honorary secretary of Dunfermline Athletic.

In his first season at Stark's Park the team reached the final of the Scottish Qualifying Cup, but failed to match their success of the previous year's final. However they did win the Second Division Championship, followed that with second place, then in 1909-10 were joint Champions with Leith Athletic. This at last opened the door to the First Division, following several unsuccessful attempts to be elected.

Rovers occupied the lower reaches of the First Division in their early years of membership, but Hodge slowly assembled a squad of useful players, a trait he was to repeat throughout his long managerial career.

Following a shift in power and influence in the Boardroom, he was dismissed in November 1912 and in June 1914 he took over at Stoke City for one season, leading them to the Championship of the Southern League. They were then elected to the Football League, displacing Glossop.
In October 1916 he returned to Fife to co-ordinate recruitment to the armed forces, and he was reinstated as Rovers manager for the difficult remaining years of the First World War.
Leicester City, newly re-constructed out of Leicester Fosse, persuaded Hodge to become their first secretary-manager in September 1919. He signed many great players for Leicester, not least from his native Scotland, and his best signing was reckoned to be Johnny Duncan, from Rovers, in July 1922. Leicester missed out on promotion on goal average in 1922/23, but were Second Division champions in 1925, Duncan scoring 30 goals. Hodge frequently returned to Stark's Park for players, among them Duncan's brother Tommy, George Waite and Harry Graham.

He unexpectedly left to manage Manchester City, newly relegated to the Second Division, in May 1926. They missed out on promotion in his first season, by a tiny fraction of goal average, but won the Championship in 1927/28 and were third in the top division the following year. Hodge was tempted back to Leicester by a five year contract in March 1932. He found the club in decline, but they did reach an FA Cup semi final in 1934. On 30th July 1934, while visiting his sister in Perth, he fell ill, was admitted to Perth Royal Infirmary and died shortly afterwards.

JAMES MICHAEL TOD

12th November 1912 to June 1913

Along with his brother, he featured in the earliest part of Rovers' history, being among the band of Links youths who formed the club. His father owned a factory which wove heavy-duty items, such as girths for horses. The family was also involved in aerated water manufacture (lemonade) and had a factory in Glasswork Street for many years.

James Tod was elected to Rovers' board on 22nd March 1911 and in November 1912 he appeared to be the leading player in the move to dismiss Peter Hodge, whereupon Tod took over secretarial duties at the club. In his season in charge, the club reached the Scottish Cup final but finished third bottom of the First Division.

He was ousted from the board by his fellow directors in February 1915 and following several months of ill health, died on 30th October 1916, in his 43rd year.
The Reverend James Dickson of the West End Congregational Church, on the Sunday after Tod's death, told the congregation : "His qualities were not of the showy order, but of sterling worth ; he was quiet and unassuming, steady, upright, faithful and reliable. He had a kindly heart and a manly disposition, which won the esteem of all who knew him."

JOHN RICHARDSON

June 1913 to October 1916

A former official of the Scottish Junior Football Association, he was treasurer of Petershill prior to his appointment at Stark's Park. In his only peacetime season at the club, Rovers finished mid-table in the First Division, and the remaining years of his tenure were blighted by the constraints of the First World War. When Peter Hodge returned to work in Fife, Richardson was dismissed.

He was unsuccessful in seeking election to the Rovers Board in March 1920. He was appointed Third Lanark manager in May 1925, following their relegation to the Second Division. They finished in sixth position in 1925/26, fourth in 1926/27, and won promotion in second place in 1927/28, by which time Richardson had left to become Falkirk manager, on 23rd November 1927. For the first two years of his spell at Brockville the team finished comfortably in the middle of the First Division, and improved to seventh place in 1929/30. They fell down the League the following season, and in 1931/32 finished third bottom, prompting Mr Richardson's resignation.

He was appointed Rovers manager for the second time on 8th December 1930

The club narrowly failed to win promotion at the end of 1930/31, and although they finished third the following season, promotion was even more distant in terms of points. There was a decline to sixth place in 1932/33 and following a poor start to the following season, Logan resigned in October 1933.

Logan's relationship with the board, which was traditionally responsible for player recruitment and selection but ceded that responsibility to the manager when promotion was not instantly achieved, was troubled latterly. He was appointed manager of Wrexham on 29th January 1934, having a year before been interviewed by Lincoln City, and his record at the Racecourse Ground was not bad ; they reached the Third Round of the FA Cup, finished eighth in their Division in 1936/37, and tenth the following season.   He resigned at the end of 1937/38

JAMES HENRY LOGAN

9th September 1919 to 14th May 1926
8th December 1930 to 22nd October 1933

Born in Dunbar on 11th October 1885, he moved from Juvenile football to St Bernards, then joined Edinburgh Myrtle, with whom he became a Scottish Junior Internationalist.   He played five times for Bradford City in 1905, and then enjoyed three successful seasons at Chesterfield, before returning to Bradford, this time to the Park Avenue club, in 1909. He joined Rovers in May 1912 and was one of three six-footers who formed the half back line as they made their way to the Scottish Cup Final.   He enlisted as a Private with the Royal Scots at the start of the First World War and was a Captain when he returned to Rovers in 1919, at 33 years of age, to be manager.

After two seasons in the lower reaches of the single-division Scottish League, Rovers reached their highest ever League position in 1921/22, finishing third behind Celtic and Rangers. After falling to ninth, they finished fourth in 1923/24, before an ageing team, and the repeated sale of the club's better players following the expensive construction of the main stand at Stark's Park, resulted in relegation in 1926.

Apart from the exalted league positions, Logan's first spell in charge at Stark's Park is notable for the succession of great players who were brought to the club ; internationalists Johnny Duncan, Dave Morris and Alex James, and other accomplished players such as Tom Jennings, George Miller, Peter Bell, Bill Collier and David Moyes.

Following his resignation as Rovers manager in May 1926, he purchased the Airlie Arms Hotel in Kirriemuir in September of that year and later returned to Kirkcaldy to run a tobacconist's shop in the High Street.

GEORGE WILLIAMSON WILSON

4th June 1926 to 16th December 1927.

Born in Lochgelly in 1884, as a 15 year old miner he played for Thomson Rovers juveniles, Lochgelly Rangers and, along with his three older brothers who had just fallen out with the committee at Lochgelly United, Buckhaven United prior to joining Cowdenbeath in 1902. In May 1903 he joined Hearts, for whom he scored the only goal of the 1906 Scottish Cup Final. They were twice runners up in the First Division during his spell at Tynecastle.   Short and heavily built, he was nonetheless very fast, extremely skilful and was much coveted by leading English clubs for his match-winning ability.

Along with his brother David (who had a notable career with Everton and Hearts) he cost Everton £800 in May 1906.   Having refused to re-sign for the following season, he was dropped from the Cup Final team and signed for Irish club Distillery in the close season of 1907, costing Newcastle United a record fee of £1600 in November 1907.   Known, ironically, as "Smiler" because of his dour demeanour, the diminutive goal scoring left winger won League Championship and FA Cup winners medals at St James' Park.   He won 6 Scotland caps between 1904 and 1909, one cap for the Scottish League in 1906, and one cap for the Irish League during his brief spell in Belfast.

He returned to his native Fife during the First World War and signed for Raith Rovers in September 1915.   Five years later he left for East Fife, helping them win the Scottish Qualifying Cup in 1920/21, when he scored the opening goal in the final.   While living in David Street in Kirkcaldy, he ran a hairdresser's and tobacconist's establishment in the High Street, but on 24th May 1923 he sailed to Vancouver to join several family members who had previously emigrated. He played with the local club St Andrews for a few years and later managed Falls River in the American Soccer League.

Wilson returned to Kirkcaldy and was appointed Rovers manager in May 1926, leading the club back into the First Division at the first attempt.   1927/28 started badly, however. Wilson recognised that he was ill-suited to the task of rebuilding the club, and he resigned, later returning to Canada, where he died on 2nd June 1960

WILLIAM BIRRELL

19th December 1927 to 3rd December 1930

Born in Cellardyke on 13th March 1897 his family moved to Kirkcaldy and he was a clerk in Barry Ostler & Shepherd's when he was signed by Raith Rovers from Inverkeithing United (having started with St Andrews Juniors) in December 1915. Birrell served with the Black Watch in the First World War and was a prisoner of war in Russian Poland. On returning to Kirkcaldy at the end of the war, part of his convalescence was, with permission from Sir Michael Nairn, to swim in the lake in the Three Trees Park (now Ravenscraig Park) which formed the grounds of Dysart House.

He recovered to shine as an inside forward with Rovers in the First Division, and he was transferred to Middlesbrough for £2300 in January 1921, soon becoming an influential and inspirational midfield general at Ayresome Park. A war wound limited his appearances as the club surrendered its First Division status but he returned to form and captained the side during the 1926/27 promotion campaign. He returned to Stark's Park in November 1927, and barely a month later was appointed player-manager following the resignation of George Wilson.

As player manager, he engineered a dramatic escape from relegation, but Rovers were relegated again in 1929, and failed to feature in the promotion race the following season. In December 1930 he left to manage Bournemouth, but struggled to lift them from the lower reaches of the Third Division South. The club were kept afloat thanks to a "Shilling Fund" set up by the local press, and even a £4,000 share issue failed to lift the club. In 1934 they had to seek re-election, having conceded 100 League goals.
In 1935 he became manager of Queen's Park Rangers, and improved their position every season, just missing out on promotion to the Second Division.

In April 1939 he was appointed manager of Chelsea, whom he piloted through the difficult years of the Second World War. He led them to the FA Cup semi finals in 1950, when they lost to Arsenal after a replay, but required 0.044 of a goal to escape relegation the following season, winning their last three matches to stay in the First Division. In 1952 they once again lost to Arsenal in an FA Cup semi final replay, and shortly afterwards he announced his retirement. Chelsea's highest league position under his management was thirteenth, but his scouting network and youth policy were said to be the envy of every other club and when Ted Drake took over from him, the foundations of the 1954-55 Championship winning side were in place. Birrell worked as a clerk in Kenton, where his son was a solicitor. He died in November 1968.

ROBERT HUNTER BROWN BENNIE

22nd October 1933 to 2nd November 1934

Born in Slamannan on 27th March 1900, he graduated from schools football in Airdrie to Parkhead Juniors, and signed for Third Lanark in 1917. He was transferred to Airdrieonians in December 1920, and was a skilful left half in the star-studded team which won the Scottish Cup in 1924, and which was runner-up in the League Championship for four successive years from 1923. He won three Scotland caps in 1925 and 1926, the first two alongside Dave Morris. In May 1928 he moved to Hearts for the considerable transfer fee of £2,300 and the following season won his only Scottish League cap.

Bennie retired from playing at the end of 1932/33 and was appointed Rovers manager on 9th October 1933, starting work a fortnight later. The poor squad he found at Stark's Park prompted him to register as a player in December 1933. Following a disappointing mid-table finish, and no prospect of improvement the following season, he resigned in November 1934. He died on 27th July 1972

ALEXANDER ARCHIBALD

5th November 1934 to 14th October 1939

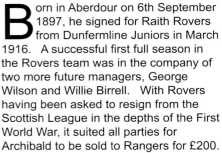

Born in Aberdour on 6th September 1897, he signed for Raith Rovers from Dunfermline Juniors in March 1916. A successful first full season in the Rovers team was in the company of two more future managers, George Wilson and Willie Birrell. With Rovers having been asked to resign from the Scottish League in the depths of the First World War, it suited all parties for Archibald to be sold to Rangers for £200.

As a miner, he was spared military duties, and he was ever-present as Rangers won the Scottish League in 1917/18. It was the first of no fewer than twelve Championship medals; he won three Scottish Cups, and was in two losing finals, eight Glasgow Cup winners and six Glasgow Merchants' Charity Cup winners medals. His 514 League appearances for Rangers are a club record, and he played another 152 first team matches, scoring a total of 162 goals. Of medium height (5ft 8 ½") he was well built, weighing 11st 12lbs and was an extremely powerful and aggressive runner with a powerful shot. Speed and clever ball skills made him the complete winger, which Rangers recognised in fielding him for 17 years. He won eight Scotland caps between February 1921 and 1932, and twelve Scottish League caps.

Archibald returned to Stark's Park in November 1934 and within a fortnight was appointed manager following Bob Bennie's resignation. He retired as a player at the end of that season, but not before impressing his players with his accurate crosses from the wing, delivered without the benefit of his former pace. His playing career, at the very highest level, persuaded the directors to give him unprecedented control over player recruitment and selection.

He has the distinction of managing Rovers to their lowest league position (second bottom in 1935/36), and two seasons later to one of the high points of their history, when they set the British League goalscoring record (142 goals in 34 matches) in winning the Second Division Championship. Severely constrained by the club's debt, he could not prevent relegation the following season.

He resigned on 12th October 1939 to move to Dunfermline Athletic, which he described at the time as "improving my position". He worked at Rosyth Dockyard during the war, and managed Dunfermline in the North Eastern League for £4 a week, part time. In 1945/46 he reverted to full time, his salary rising to £8 per week plus 5% of any transfer deal, of which there were several. He died, unexpectedly, at home in Crossgates on 29th November 1946, aged 49, his death attributed to the stresses of two jobs and rationed food throughout the war.

The Kirkcaldy Times paid this tribute : "With a pawky sense of humour, he was a cheery soul who could always see the silver lining no matter how overcast the sky. He tackled the job of Rovers manager with enthusiasm and determination, and told the directors, on his appointment, that given a free hand, he would put Raith back in the First Division." The Funeral was at Dunfermline Cemetery on Monday 2nd December.

WILLIAM REEKIE

21st October 1939 to 24th July 1945

Willie Reekie died at his home at 2 Asquith Street, on the morning of 11th December 1956, three days after his beloved Raith Rovers had beaten Rangers 5-1 at Stark's Park. He was 60 years of age and had been in poor health over the previous 18 months.

He was trainer under Sandy Archibald at the outbreak of war, and took over the running of the team when Archibald left to manage Dunfermline Athletic. Once it became obvious that Rovers' playing activities had to be scaled back as the war progressed, he was asked to run the club on a 'care and maintenance' basis for the duration of the war.

In the Kirkcaldy Times obituary, it was noted that "These were dark days for Scottish football, but with the aid of guest stars from the Services, Mr Reekie always managed to put a Raith team on the field. His greatest capture was Willie McNaught, who was spotted playing in an Army game at Kinghorn, but Mr Reekie was also responsible for bringing players like Andy Young and Jackie Stewart to Stark's Park.

"When hostilities ceased in 1945, Mr Reekie handed over the managerial duties to his brother-in-law, Mr Bert Herdman, but he continued to take an active interest in the affairs of the club and attended matches right up to the end. He saw Raith defeat Queen's Park two weeks ago.

"After resigning from the managership at Stark's Park, Mr Reekie devoted most of his time to the coal merchant's business which was set up by his father before the First World War, and which he entered as a partner when he returned from that conflict after serving with the Black

Watch. As a young man, Mr Reekie himself was a prominent footballer. He played for Abbotshall Juveniles, for whom he scored a record number of goals from the centre-forward position, and from there he went on to play for Rosslyn Juniors and Dunnikier Juniors. He actually spent a season as a Raith Rovers' player, leading the reserve attack in season 1923-24.

"In later years he showed his prowess on the bowling green where he was a dexterous exponent with the "woods". A former president of the West End Club, he won every competition open to him as a member. During the war, he raised a large sum of money for the Red Cross when he sponsored a bowling tournament amongst all the Fife clubs.

"Mr Reekie is survived by his wife, a daughter and two sons, the younger of whom will succeed his father in business." The funeral took place in Kirkcaldy Cemetery on 13th December 1956.

Willie Reekie is perhaps the greatest unsung hero of the club's history. A real "football man" who played for and managed Juvenile and Junior teams in the town for many years, he accepted the post as Rovers manager with one proviso : it was only for the duration of the war, and his task was to keep the club alive, and maintain the fabric of Stark's Park, during that period. Not only did Reekie achieve that, but when he resigned with the declaration of peace imminent in July 1945, he left the club with players of the calibre of Willie McNaught, Willie Penman, Jackie Stewart and (on loan from Celtic) Andy Young ; and retaining the services of the promising young players of the distant pre-war years, Ernie Till and Johnny Maule. His modesty extended to his remuneration at the club, but he could look back on the achievements of the 1950s with great pride, as he had laid the foundations for its subsequent success during the club's (and the country's) darkest years.

ROBERT RODGER HERDMAN

25th July 1945 to 19th October 1961

Bert Herdman joined the three-year old Supporters Club in 1929 and served on their committee as Treasurer between 1930 and 1945, forming a close working partnership with Chairman Jimmy Gourlay and Secretary Peter Napier which continued after the war when both of these gentlemen served on the board of directors of the Football Club. Along with his colleagues on the committee, he took full part in organising fund raising activities, which included whist drives, dances, sales of work, boxing competitions at Stark's Park and in the Adam Smith Hall, football tournaments and the usual services to members such as buses to away matches and to international matches at Hampden and Wembley.

In the early years of the Second World War, he was one of the founders of the Secondary Juvenile Club Raith Athletic, which became a prolific source of young players for Raith Rovers during the 1940s, not least of whom was Willie Penman.

When Willie Reekie stood down towards the end of the war, Herdman was appointed part time Manager on 24th July 1945 at £2 10/- per week, and on 25th September agreed to go full time on £6 per week including expenses, once he had discovered that the job could not be done on a part-time basis.

Writing in the Supporters Club Silver Jubilee Handbook in 1951, he said : "I am pleased and proud that during my managership the club reached the League Cup Final and the Scottish Cup semi final, broke records in home, away and neutral ground attendances, had a player several times capped and other men duly noted by the selectors. As Manager, too, I saw a £10,000 bank overdraft wiped out, a new Company formed, the club receiving and paying their highest-ever transfer fees. The fight has been hard and prolonged but I have never quailed nor faltered in my desire to serve club and supporters to the limit of my strength and ability."

He was to do so for another ten years, which brought two more Scottish Cup semi finals, high finishes in the First Division, and arguably the club's greatest-ever team in 1956/57.

In 1951, the Kirkcaldy Times had this to say about the Manager : "Of a volatile disposition, a piercing eye and a ready tongue, he also has the happy knack of picking up players and if they failed to find their best form in their original berth, juggles with them until he has made them stars."

The week after being told he was being replaced (16th October 1961) he was offered the Assistant Secretary's job at £14 per week, but instead he continued to work for the club as organiser of the Stark's Park Development Club, which, through raffles and Bingo Tickets, raised a prodigious sum of money throughout the 1960s. He was also involved in the construction of the 200 Club in the Main Stand at Stark's Park. He died of a heart attack on 22nd August 1968 at his home at 36 Lady Helen Street, fittingly on a midweek (Thursday) evening, at 7.30pm. At his funeral service at Kirkcaldy Crematorium, one of his former players was heard to remark to another, "If Bert knew that this many were going to turn up, he'd have made it all ticket !"

His death certificate gave his date of birth as 2nd April 1904, as did his marriage certificate (he married Jean Booth Blyth at Whytehouse Avenue on 29th March 1929), but Bert was actually a year younger than he thought – and his surname wasn't Herdman.

He was born on 2nd April 1905 at 101 West High Street, Buckhaven, to Isabella Simon, a housekeeper. No father's name was on the birth certificate, and the infant's name was recorded as Robert Simon. In later years, Isabella Simon married George Rodger, a Bill Poster, but it is believed that Robert was then adopted by Mr & Mrs Herdman, in Kirkcaldy. Jock McKay, whose strident tones reverberated around Stark's Park on matchdays for several decades, grew up in the same street as Herdman and recalled that every year, on his birthday, an impressive limousine would arrive in the street, and Bert would be summoned in to his house. Nothing was ever said about this annual occurrence, but Jock reasoned that Bert's natural father was a man of some substance.

Robert Simon became Robert Simon Rodger, who then became Robert Rodger Herdman, appropriately abbreviated to R.R. Herdman, which was entirely appropriate given his unqualified devotion to the other R.R., Raith Rovers. A French polisher by trade, he lived at 19 Maryhall Street for much of his married life.

He was an unlikely candidate as manager of a top class Football Club (which Raith Rovers was throughout the 1950s). His playing career did not progress from the playground or the street. Andy Young recalled : "He had nothing to say about football, but occasionally lifted our spirits by saying something that made us laugh. We played in a big match, and were on a big bonus - £25 and a barathea blazer. At half time we were 2-0 down, and Bert addressed us in the dressing room. "Well boys, you're no' doing so well today. 2-0 down, you ken that's two sleeves of that barathea blazer away already." We won 3-2. Bert was alright to get on with. He didn't know much about football, but he got good players to sign for Rovers, and you have to give him credit for that."

Andy Leigh remembered when Bert's frustration at the team's inept first half performance prompted him to demonstrate how to kick a football, in the dressing room at half time. "The ball richochetted off his foot and broke a dressing room window !" Willie Penman, when asked to assess Bert's technical knowledge, chuckled and mimicked him : "Keep the high baws low."

A lifetime's spectating and his war years running Raith Athletic gave him an eye for a player, and their best position. Above all else, his love of the club and unlimited dedication to its cause overwhelmed any limitations he may have (including a stutter and an inability, or unwillingness, to drive a motor car). He was an exemplary advert for Scottish elementary education, being highly literate, efficient and organised in his conduct of the club's administration and finances.

Most of the stories about Bert – and there are enough of them to fill another book of this size – revolve round his parsimony with the club's money, which he spent as if it were his own. His players had a grudging admiration for him, rather than affection or gratitude. It was his job to husband the club's limited resources to best effect, and that meant paying the players as little as he could get away with. He did not court their popularity, simply the long-term welfare of his beloved club.

Decades after hanging up their boots, his former players would chuckle at the mention of his name, and concede "well, I suppose he was doing his job" before recalling another humourous Herdman-ism. Johnny Urquhart's favourite was "I've signed many a bad player, but never a bad eater" and Jim Baxter continued the culinary theme when he recalled the aftermath of a spectacular victory in Glasgow (probably the 3-2 win at Ibrox in 1959). The players were nagging Herdman for an enhanced bonus, and he went off, reluctantly, to consult his directors as the official party sat down to a post-match meal in a Glasgow restaurant. He returned, looking pleased with himself. "B-b-b-boys, I've spoken to the chairman about your

The club has never had a better servant, and there is a strong argument that it has never had a better manager. R.R. Herdman was the greatest Raith Rover of them all.

HUGH SHAW

20th October 1961 to 15th May 1963

Signed for Hibs from Clydebank Juniors in August 1918, he left for Rangers in July 1926. In August 1927 he signed for Hearts, and in September 1930 moved to East Fife, where he remained until November 1932. A month at Leith Athletic and a spell at Elgin City concluded his playing career. He became Hibs assistant trainer

in 1934, and head trainer in 1936. Shaw was appointed manager in January 1948 on the death of Willie McCartney. Hibs won the League Championship in 1948/9, 1950/1 and 1951/2, and he led them into the inaugural European Cup competition, where they reached the semi finals. They were twice finalists in the Scottish Cup and once in the League Cup. He was dismissed as Hibs manager in October 1961 and within a matter of days was appointed as Bert Herdman's successor, despite being nine years his senior at 65.

A spirited late revival, due principally to the introduction of several new players, saw the team climb clear of the relegation positions, which had been a forlorn hope for much of the season. The least said about 1962/63 the better, although Rovers did reach the semi final of the Scottish Cup. On leaving Rovers Hugh Shaw ran a newsagents in Edinburgh's Marchmont area. He died in February 1976 in an Edinburgh hospital, aged 80.

DOUGLAS COWIE

21st May 1963 to 8th May 1964

Born on 1st May 1926 in Aberdeen, he was signed by Dundee from Aberdeen St Clements juniors in September 1945. Midway through 1947/48 he established himself in the first team at Dens Park, and he remained there until 1960/61. A League Cup winner in 1951/52 and

bonus, and you can eat A La Carte instead of Table d'Hote !" The players were underwhelmed, but couldn't help but smile.

He was a familiar figure about the town, always properly attired in a three piece suit, and a fedora hat in all but the summer months. In the early sixties, the Kirkcaldy Cine Camera Club made a film about life in the town, and a random shot of the High Street captured Bert walking between appointments, a familiar and entirely appropriate sight, particularly when fund raising became his full time occupation at Stark's Park.

The town's independent shop keepers used to dive into the back shop at the sight of Bert approaching their doorway, looking for some of their goods to be donated for one of the highly profitable seasonal Prize Draws, which featured an impressive list of prizes. When the 200 Club was being built inside the Main Stand, Bert visited McIntosh's Furniture factory "on the scrounge" for timber and wood panelling. "You can have anything marked with chalk, they're our rejects" said the store foreman. Herdman made sure he had a stick of chalk in his pocket on his next visit.

He may appear to be an anachronism as a football manager, but he was decades ahead of his time as a commercial manager, raising huge sums of money from off-field activities which subsidised full-time football, and paid for the inordinately expensive floodlights. The vanity of most men would have seen them leave the club after losing the manager's job, but Herdman uncomplainingly moved into full-time fundraising, and the Development Club's High Street offices in Central Chambers meant that he would not be a unwelcomed spectre for his successors in the pavilion at Stark's Park.

1952/53, he played in the Dundee team which lost the Scottish Cup Final in 1952. In March 1953 he won a Scotland B cap against England, followed a month later with the first of 20 Scotland caps. His last Scotland cap came in the 1958 World Cup Finals, and he also played in the 1954 World Cup Finals, the only Scot to play in both. He won three Scottish League caps. He was a splendid wing half, a good all-round footballer and an inspirational competitor. His quality is shown by the number of caps won at a time of comparatively few internationals, and in the face of fierce competition from Old Firm players.

He moved to Morton in 1961/62 and played there for two seasons, before joining Rovers as manager on an annual salary of £1,500. On 29th November 1963 he registered as a player and played in the occasional reserve match.

Having failed to win the club instant promotion, he resigned, admitting that he was not really cut out for management, much preferring to coach players. He returned to Morton in that capacity, and from May 1966 spent several years as coach at Dundee United under Jerry Kerr and Jim McLean. As the younger generation of coaches arrived, he switched to scouting duties in November 1971.

GEORGE NEIL FARM

26th May 1964 to 12th July 1967
29th November 1971 to 17th October 1974

Born in Slateford, Edinburgh on 13th July 1924, he first played football at Longstone Village Primary School, Tynecastle Secondary and Hutcheson Vale and was in the Royal Navy during the war. Provisionally signed by Hibs from Armadale Thistle in October 1946, he made the first of just seven League appearances for Hibs in 1947/48. In September 1948, he was transferred to Blackpool for £2,700. He was on the losing side in the 1951 FA Cup Final but, despite being culpable for at least two of Bolton's goals, won a winner's medal in the Matthews Final two years later. He set the club appearances record (461 in the League alone) which has subsequently been surpassed only by Jimmy Armfield.

Against Preston on 29th October 1955, he was injured during the game and returned to the field to play outfield, heading a consolation goal in a 6-2 defeat. That season, Blackpool finished as runners-up in the First Division, the highest ever place in their history.

While at Blackpool, he won 7 Scotland caps between October 1952 and April 1954, and was surprisingly recalled for the three match continental tour in May 1959. In February 1960, he joined Queen of the South for £2,000, having for some time intimated that he and his wife wished to return to live in their native Edinbrugh. In his third season at Palmerston he helped win promotion to the First Division, by which time he was player-manager. He helped Queens avoid relegation in

1962/63, and played in half the League matches as they were relegated the following season. Throughout his playing career he had a unique way of catching the ball, with one hand above and one below.

He was sacked as Queen's manager in January 1964, but bizarrely retained as a player (and told to train away from Dumfries) and in the summer of 1964 he was appointed Raith Rovers manager. It took him a season to "assess the damage" and begin to turnover players ; a season to build a team which blended youth and experience ; and a season to deliver, culminating in a return to the First Division in April 1967. He succeeded Willie Cunningham as manager of Dunfermline in July 1967 and at the end of that season they won the Scottish Cup Final. A year later they reached the semi final of the European Cup Winners Cup, but after a poor start to 1970/71, he was sacked in October 1970.

After a year out of the game, he returned to Stark's Park and led the team to the quarter finals of the Scottish Cup. He built an excellent team in 1972/73, which featured Joe Baker, but the vital, final ingredient was elusive and Rovers could not overhaul two strong teams – Clyde and Dunfermline – at the top of the table. The following season was one of disappointment, and with no further improvement in prospect for 1974/75, he resigned in mid October.

On leaving Stark's Park for the second time (with a £750 pay off), he spent Saturday afternoons with Kirkcaldy native Richard Park, presenting an innovative football programme on Scotland's first commercial radio station, Radio Clyde. When Radio Forth went on air, he became their sports presenter, and afterwards had short spells as a lighthouse keeper and a school janitor. He died just one day after his 80th birthday in 2004.

He was one of the most distinctive, and strongest, personalities to inhabit the Manager's office at Stark's Park. Always immaculately dressed and groomed, he possessed a versatile repertoire of invective, and was never slow to use it. Bert Paton tells the tale of Geo (as he always signed his forename) reading his newspaper by the living room window of his house in the town's exclusive and very prim and proper Raith Estate. All the front gardens were open-plan, and one of the neighbours was exercising their dog. Geo opened the window, and bellowed : "Get your ******* dog off my ******* lawn, and pick up his ******* **** while you're at it !"

Billy Brown recalled : "George thought he was big time and tried to make the Rovers like that as well, but he was a full-time manager of a part-time club and that made it very difficult and there were certain things that maybe he couldn't accept because of where he had been before."

In his first spell at the club, he brought in good players, young and old, and succeeded in his task of returning the club to the top flight. In his second spell, there was perhaps more promise than delivery, but his teams were worth watching. Murray McDermott considered that "George had a lot of ability, mind you I don't know what it was. He knew the game, although he wasn't a great tactician. He was very organised ; his team-talks were well structured, but not in a tactical sense. I think he fancied himself as a special motivator – kicking boys up the arse was his speciality. He wasn't a bad manager. Bertie Paton was his assistant at one stage, and that was a good double act because Bertie was a good coach, a good trainer and knew the game very well, and he was tactically very astute. They were a good pairing."

TOMMY WALKER

20th July 1967 to 29th January 1969

Born in the village of Livingston Station on 26th May 1915, he played football at Livingston Primary School, Bathgate Public School, Livingston Juveniles and Berryburn Rangers. After a season with Linlithgow Rose, whom he joined from Broxburn Rangers, he signed for Hearts in May 1932.

He won his first Scotland cap against Wales at Aberdeen in November 1934, and toured North America with Scotland the following summer. He won 19 more caps before the outbreak of the Second World War, which interrupted his studies for the Ministry in the Church of Scotland, and made five appearances for the Scottish League. He was one of the best inside forwards in Europe in the late thirties, with consummate ball skills and impressive passing ability, and a "natural footballer's" pitch awareness.

He played 10 times for Scotland during the Second World War, famously lending his collection of Scotland International jerseys so that the team could have a complete strip for one of those fixtures. His last two international appearances were in 1945/46.

In September 1946 he joined Chelsea, but returned to Tynecastle at the end of that season (probably setting a record for the number of League appearances in a single season, 39 for Chelsea and 9 for Hearts). He made one appearance in 1948/9, before hanging up his boots the following season, having been made assistant manager in December 1948. He took over from David McLean as manager in February 1951.

Hearts seemed to be rooted in fourth place in the First Division in the early 1950s, but they were runners up to Celtic in 1953/54, and ended a long, trophy-less drought when they won the League Cup in October 1954. They followed that with a Scottish Cup victory the following season, and in 1956/57 were only two points behind Rangers at the top of the League. In 1957/58, Hearts set a new First Division League goalscoring record with 132 in winning the Championship by 13 points. They were runners up the following season, but won it again in 1959/60 and won the League Cup in 1958, 1959 and 1962,

losing the 1961 final to Rangers after a replay. On 22nd November 1960 he was presented with an OBE at Buckingham Palace, the first Scottish footballer to be decorated.

Having sold Dave Mackay and Alex Young to English clubs, Hearts slipped a few places down the League, but in 1964-65 a 1-0 or goal-scoring defeat (or better) at home to Kilmarnock in the final game of the season would have won another Championship. After a disappointing final full season at Tynecastle, Walker resigned in late September 1966. He joined Dunfermline as administrator in December of that year, and was appointed Manager of Rovers when George Farm made the opposite journey. Rovers avoided relegation in his only full season as manager, but they were deep in trouble again when he demitted the manager's part of his duties at Rovers on 29th January 1969. Knowledgeable about football and footballers, he showed no signs of transforming the playing fortunes of the club. After two years as full-time Secretary of the club, he was made redundant, and worked as an office manager in Edinburgh until he retired. He was made a director of Hearts in October 1974, becoming vice chairman in 1979. He died in Edinburgh on 11th January 1993.

JIMMY MILLAR

9th February 1969 to 28th September 1970

Born in Edinburgh on 20th November 1934, he was a wing half with Merchiston Thistle when he signed for Dunfermline Athletic in August 1952 and in his third season at East End Park, scored 19 goals in as many League games when he was moved into attack. Rangers signed him for £5,000 in January 1955, but it took a further two years before he broke into the first team at Ibrox, and in 1958/59 his

appearances were restricted by National Service, when his NCO at Glencorse Barracks was Willie Polland. From 1959 to 1965 he was first choice in Rangers attack, latterly paired with Ralph Brand as the Ibrox club carried all before them in domestic football.

Despite his lack of inches (he was 5 ft 6") he was remarkably good in the air, and proved to be a natural goalscorer as well as a willing worker. He

certainly fitted in well to a Rangers team that was an irresistible blend of players of all shapes and sizes, plus Jim Baxter.

He won Championship winning medals in 1960/1, 1962/3 and 1963/4, League Cup winners medals in 1960/1, 19962/3 and 1964/5 and Scottish Cup winners medals in 1959/60, 1961/2, 1962/3. 1963/4 and 1965/6. Included in his 33 European appearances was the 1960/61 European Cup Winners Cup Final, when Rangers lost to Fiorentina. Capped four times for the Scottish League between 1961 and 1962, he won two Scotland caps in 1962/63.

In July 1967 he moved to Dundee United, where he played 24 times before accepting the manager's job at Stark's Park. His last match as a player was a 2nd Eleven Cup tie against Rovers at Tannadice when he scored a late equaliser.

Millar's arrival at Stark's Park provided the impetus for a second successive escape from relegation, but he could not prevent a third, and despite introducing a promising stream of juvenile and junior signings, he decided that part-time football was neither to his liking nor capabilities, and he resigned to concentrate full time on his public house in Leith. Murray McDermott thought it was a lot more fundamental : "I believe he didn't like being a football manager, it just wasn't his cup of tea."

BILL BAXTER

20th October 1970 to 28th November 1971

Born in Leven on 21st September 1924, he was on the groundstaff at Wolves as a 14 year old, having played for Wemyss schoolboys. He was in the navy during the war, and captained the Wolves second team to three successive Central League championships. He was at Molineux from March 1945 to November 1953, and made 43 League appearances in that spell, when Wolves were one of the strongest teams in England.

He played 98 times for Aston Villa until 1956/7, when he coached the youth team, then the second team. He returned to his native Fife when his wife died, and was coach under Jimmy Bonthrone as East Fife finished third in the Second Division for two successive seasons. When Bonthrone moved to Aberdeen, Baxter took over as manager at the start of 1970/1, and with coach Pat Quinn orchestrating events in midfield, East Fife built a commanding lead at the top of the Second Division. That was presumably what prompted the Rovers board to appoint him manager in October 1970, and although they reached the quarter finals of the Scottish Cup, little progress was made in the League. After a disappointing start to 1971/72, he was dismissed at the end of November. He returned to England to live, and had no further involvement in football apart from watching his sons Stuart and Michael play professionally. Tragically, Michael died during a match when he played for Preston North End.

BERT PATON

22nd October 1974 to 24th March 1975

Born in High Valleyfield on 29th April 1942, he was signed by Dunfermline Athletic from Leeds United in July 1961, becoming established in the Dunfermline team in 1965/6, when they were one of the top teams in Scotland. A goalscoring midfield player, he was a key player as they reached the quarter finals of the Fairs Cup in 1965/66, and the semi finals of the Cup Winners Cup Final in 1968/69, and he played in Dunfermline's Scottish Cup winning team in 1968. A broken leg suffered soon after the start of 1969/70 effectively ended his playing career. He made only 8 more appearances for Dunfermline before joining his former team-mate Harry Melrose for a month at Berwick Rangers in 1972/73.

After coaching Lochgelly Albert, George Farm appointed him Rovers' coach on 29th November 1973. He left on 24th September 1974 to manage Cowdenbeath and returned as Rovers manager on 22nd October 1974. He tried to radically change a faltering team, but did not make the best use of the modest resources he was given. Having not been consulted on a round of cuts to the playing and coaching budget, he resigned on 24th March 1975.

He coached Hearts under Willie Ormond until October 1978, and after building up a thriving public house in Rosyth (having earlier run a grocer's shop there) his next involvement in the game was as assistant to Alex Totten at Dumbarton. They piloted the Sons into promotion contention in the First Division in 1986/87 and then dropped down into the Second Division with St Johnstone. They won promotion to the First Division the following season, and then into the Premier League in 1990. He was unexpectedly, and unjustly, fired in the close season of 1992, and returned to management at Dunfermline in 1993/94, succeeding Jocky Scott.

After two second place finishes, they won the First Division Championship in 1995/96 but in January 1999, with the Pars bottom of the Premier League, he resigned, to be succeeded by his assistant, Dick Campbell.

The roles were reversed in May 2000 when Campbell became manager of Brechin City, and Paton eventually joined him as assistant manager. He stayed with Brechin when Campbell left to manage Partick Thistle, but when Dick's twin Ian was dismissed as manager in March 2006, Paton also left.

A shrewd football brain and pawky, west Fife good humour made him popular in the dressing room. Billy Brown concurred : "Bert Paton was one of the best managers that I have worked with. He was a smashing fella'. Because of the Leagues changing, he had to do everything in a hurry. I think he tried to do too much in a hurry because of that and things just didn't work out. I think he ruffled a few feathers, people who had been there for years, and they didn't like it. I liked Bert, I thought he was enthusiastic and he had a lot of good ideas. He knew the game, he was a hardy bloke who looked after himself in a lot of different ways, and it was an enjoyable time working for him. Murray McDermott agreed : "I had a lot of time for Bert, but I think he made a few bad signings."

ANDY MATTHEW

22nd April 1975 to 10th January 1978

Born in Kirkcaldy in 1932, he attended Viewforth Secondary School and won four caps for Scotland in Boys Club internationals while with Rose Street Boys Club. Signed in December 1949 by East Fife from Bayview Youth Club with whom he won the Under 17 Secondary Youth Cup, he became the established first team outside right in 1953/54, when he won a League Cup winners medal. The following season, East Fife reached the semi final of the same competition. In July 1958 he was transferred to Rangers for £4,500, and played twice in the European Cup the following season. After several attempts over a number of years, Raith Rovers finally signed him in September 1960, paying £2000, and eleven months later he joined Dunfermline for £750. In August 1962, he became one of the few players to play for all four Fife senior teams when he joined Cowdenbeath, where he played regularly until 1966/67. He spent a year as trainer, and was appointed manager early in 1968. His final appearance was as a substitute during 1968/9. He took Cowdenbeath to promotion in 1970 and to the League Cup semi final the following season. He resigned on 14th September 1974, admitting that he was finding it difficult to relate to modern players, but he was appointed Rovers manager on 22nd April 1975.

His benign style of management fitted perfectly with a happy "band of brothers" who won promotion the following season, losing only one League game in the process. They came close to escaping relegation in a high quality First Division in 1976/77, but little had been done to improve the team, either tactically or in its components. He resigned on 10th January 1978, but left enough for Willie McLean to work with and, with the addition of two key signings, win promotion at the end of the season. He was appointed to the Raith Rovers board on 7th December 1978 and resigned on 27th December 1983. Andy Matthew died on 4th October 1992 while playing golf in Kinross.

Billy Brown considered

that "Andy Matthew wasn't what you would call a "hands on" manager, we never saw him with a tracksuit on, but he brought some stability. He didn't change the team very often ; 2, 3, and 4 for about twenty consecutive games were Brown, Brown and Brown ! It was certainly a really enjoyable time."

Murray McDermott thought "He was a nice man with a different approach. He certainly wasn't a tactician – Andy's only tactic was doubling the bonus at half time if we were doing badly, which was quite successful. He was good at reading a game, watching a player and fitting a team together – he knew about football, not in terms of moving players around like chess pieces, but he knew players and he knew the game. There was a wee bit of that about George Farm. Andy was just a nice man ; he was a canny individual who never raised his voice. He gave us as much financial rewards as were going at that level, and he got the players on his side."

WILLIE McLEAN

30th January 1978 to 28th January 1979

He made his Scottish League debut for Hamilton Accies as a trialist from Stonehouse Violet juniors in 1955/56, but it was from Larkhall Thistle that he joined Airdrie in February 1957. He lost his first team place in 1958/9 and, on being freed, was signed by Sheffield Wednesday. In August 1960 he returned to the Scottish League with Alloa Athletic, where he scored 18 times in 34 Second Division matches in one season. He played 30 times at outside left for Queen of the South as they won promotion to the First Division in 1961/2, and played in around half their matches the following season. A season at Clyde was successful, with another promotion campaign, before a return to Alloa in June 1964. Rovers signed him for £100 four months later and he played a significant role in the promotion campaign of 1966/67, deputising for the injured Alex Gray at left back in the final, vital matches of the season. After a handful of appearances at the start of 1967/68, he hung up his boots. He had a brief spell as Rovers' Lanarkshire scout between 23/4/68 and 11/7/68. He had a spell as full time Secretary of the Players Union, the SPFA, coached at Dunfermline, St Mirren and became full time Queen of the South Manager in March 1973, lifting them from 11th to 4th in the Second Division.

In September 1974 he

became manager of Motherwell in the First Division, where Craig Brown was his assistant. Motherwell won the last place in the Premier League for 1975/76, and despite keeping them in a comfortable mid-table position, and taking them to two Scottish Cup semi final appearances, Motherwell were looking for more, and McLean was sacked in December 1977.

Within two months he was back in management, at Stark's Park, where he brought organisation, and Gordon Wallace and Tommy Murray, to a competent team which went on a late run to win promotion.   After a good first half to 1978/79, he left for Ayr United, who missed out on promotion to the Premier League on goal difference.   After three seasons at Somerset Park, he had a brief spell as manager of Morton, where he succeeded his brother, but he could not prevent their relegation from the Premier League in 1984/85. He spent a couple of years managing in Cyprus and then worked for Motherwell as a coach until he retired in 2000.

"He was a wee astute guy who knew his football," according to Murray McDermott. "He was a dour wee McLean, but I found him alright. He was good on the technical side, a good coach, good trainer, and he got us organised. He signed good players, like Gordon Wallace and Tommy Murray."

GEORGE GORDON WALLACE

30th January 1979 (confirmed 10th March 1979) to 31st July 1983

Born in Dundee on 20th June 1943, he was signed by Dundee from Dundee North End in 1959 having come to prominence in Dundee Schools football with Rockwell Secondary School, then Lawside Rangers (and had a trial with Leeds United as a 16 year old).   He could not break into the first team squad as Dundee were developing into League Champions, and he returned to the junior grade with Alyth United. Montrose signed him in December 1962, starting a long and distinguished senior playing career which made him one of the most prolific goalscorers in the history of Scottish football.

He joined Rovers in October 1966 at a cost of £3,500, helped them to promotion, and almost single handedly kept them up the following term with an astonishing scoring sequence in the second half of the season.   His 27 goals in 34 League games, for a team which had looked relegated at the turn of the year, prompted the Scottish Football Writers to vote him Scotland's Player of the Year for 1967/68, the first player from outwith the Old Firm to be so honoured.   He benefitted from full time training, having left his trade as a fitter with Bonar Long. In September 1969 he returned to Dens Park for £14,000, where the goalscoring continued at the upper reaches of Scottish football.   He played seven times in the UEFA Cup, scoring three times, and in December 1973 he scored the only goal of the League Cup Final against Celtic.

Following Dundee's surprise relegation from the

inaugural Premier League, he was freed in April 1976, and after a summer playing in the star-studded North American Soccer League with Seattle Sounders, he was signed by Jim McLean for Dundee United, where his experience helped develop the young players who won so many honours with United over the next decade. He played twice more in the UEFA Cup, and in February 1978 returned to Stark's Park for £2000 to inspire a late run to promotion. He enjoyed an Indian Summer to his playing career before hanging up his boots after a few months of the 1979/80 season.

Wallace was appointed first team coach with selection responsibilities on 30th January 1979 and was confirmed as player-manager at a meeting at the Dunnikier House Hotel on 10th March 1979. Initially, the wind was at his back, inheriting a solid squad which included a number of the country's best part-time players, and he had some money to spend on the team thanks to a very profitable lottery and the windfall transfer fee received for Andy Harrow.   The first two years of his management were characterised by a winning, entertaining team.   After failure was snatched from the jaws of promotion in 1981, it became an uphill battle to rebuild the team, in the face of falling revenue.

It was probably to the satisfaction of all parties that he left at the end of July 1983 to become coach at Dundee United, in which capacity he shared in that club's subsequent successes at home and abroad.   He became Dundee manager on 20th February 1989 but they were relegated the following season, and failed by one point to return immediately to the Premier League at the end of 1990/91.   He was replaced by Iain Munro, and Dundee went on to win the First Division Championship, while Wallace went to Dunfermline on 7th October 1991 to be assistant to his former Dundee colleague Jocky Scott.   Dunfermline finished bottom of the Premier League, and were a distant third to Rovers in 1992/93, which cost the management team their jobs on 19th May 1993. After a spell scouting for his former Seattle Sounders colleague Harry Redknapp, he returned to Tannadice as a coach.

On 4th September 1998, he left along with Tommy McLean, and spent a number of years as Youth Team Coach at Forfar and Arbroath.   He had a few spells helping out with coaching at Stark's Park, before he returned to Dens Park towards the end of 2004, where he has filled a number of roles, including Youth organiser, first team coach and General Manager.

Murray McDermott thought "Gordon Wallace handled the transition from player to manager very well. He did a very good job, and I remember sitting in the dressing room admiring how he was handling the player-manager's role. He had to go out on the park, play up front, and come in and try to sort things out in the dressing room. It wasn't easy, and at that time I was really impressed. I thought he was a great player, and as a player-manager, with all the problems he had to deal with, I thought he was different class.   Later on, when results turned, I think he tried to act like Jim McLean, and that wasn't really in his nature."

ROBERT A. WILSON

11th September 1983 to 22nd January 1986

Born in Windygates on 23rd July 1943, he began as a prolific centre forward with Windygates Thistle, moved to left back and shortly afterwards was signed by Dundonald Bluebell. After playing a trial match for Dunfermline, he was signed by Cowdenbeath in December 1961 and quickly developed into one of the best young full backs in the Second Division, benefiting from the coaching skills of manager Archie Robertson, who recognised that attacking, overlapping full backs were about to come into fashion. Dundee signed him for £5,000 in March 1966 and he was a fixture in their team until his final season, 1975/76. In that time he played in the 1967/68 League Cup Final and won a winner's medal in the same competition in 1973/74. Dundee were regular semi finalists in both national competitions, and Wilson played 20 times in the Fairs and UEFA Cup competitions, helping Dundee reach the semi finals in 1967/68. In that season, he won a Scottish League Cap.

He made his mark as player manager of Lossiemouth in 1976/7 and 1977/8, and in May 1978 he joined Keith, where he won an impressive haul of Highland League titles and cups, and enjoyed several high profile runs in the Scottish Cup. They won three successive Highland League championships in 1978/9, 1979/80 and 1980/81 and the Aberdeenshire Cup in 1979/80

Keen to progress into the Scottish League, he was appointed Rovers manager on 29th August 1983 and took charge on 11th September, the delay being due to Keith playing in the Highland League Cup Final (which they won). Having initially received notice that his job was changing to part-time, he was dismissed on 22nd January 1986.

Wilson had a brief spell as one of Jim Leishman's assistants at Dunfermline Athletic after he left Raith Rovers, and was appointed Chief Scout on 6th March 1986, but his best work was at Ross County, whom he joined when they were at a very low ebb in their fortunes. At Dingwall, he won further titles and cups in the Highland League, and was manager when they won election to the Scottish League in 1994. After leaving Victoria Park in 1996, he was content to travel round the country watching his elder son Barry play for a succession of clubs, latterly in the Premier League.

Even with the benefit of hindsight, Bobby Wilson's appointment as manager could hardly be criticised. He was a proven winner as manager, extremely personable and

technically competent. What he lacked was a ruthless edge, and the extra drive and ambition which would persuade a club and its directors to extend themselves. He could not look to his directors at Stark's Park for any kind of momentum, and it was not in the nature of the modest and contented man to enforce radical change.

The brutal truth is that a club of Rovers' potential was beyond his range as a manager, and everyone who knew him at Stark's Park was delighted for him when he enjoyed great success with Ross County.

FRANK CONNOR

21st March 1986 to 5th November 1990

Born in Airdrie on 13th February 1936, despite his short stature he was a goalkeeper in schools, boys guild and amateur football before spells in junior football with Polkemmet and Armadale Thistle. Signed by Celtic from Blantyre Celtic in March 1960 following the completion of his National Service, he played in all six League Cup qualifying section matches at the start of 1961/2, but made just two League appearances, and was freed at the end of the season, having won a Reserve League Cup winners medal. He spent a season and a half in the Irish League with Portadown before joining St Mirren in November 1963, without making a first team appearance. He played three times for Third Lanark as they were relegated in 1964/5, and returned to Ireland, this time with Derry City, where he won an Irish League Championship, and the Gold Cup. He played in the European Cup for Derry, having appeared in the Cup Winners Cup with Portadown. Albion Rovers signed him in August 1968, but a dislocated shoulder ended his playing career.

He became a coach with Albion Rovers, Alloa (1973/74 to October 1974), Hamilton and Cowdenbeath, usually in tandem with manager Dan McLindon and in February 1976 he donned the goalkeeping gloves again for a single match for the Miners. When McLindon left Central Park in mid February 1976, Frank took over as Manager, and was asked by Jock Stein to return to Celtic Park as coach to provisional and schoolboy signings in September 1977. This fitted in well with his full time job, initially as a sheet metal worker in Glasgow, and latterly as an inspector at Honeywell at Newhouse. He became reserve team coach when Billy McNeill took over, and developed a succession of future international players.

Two seasons as manager of Berwick Rangers from November 1980 brought disappointment, as they were relegated and then failed to win promotion, and he joined

Motherwell as assistant to Jock Wallace before returning to Celtic as assistant to manager Davie Hay in July 1983. He was surprisingly sacked midway through a season which ended with Celtic as champions, and eight weeks later accepted the manager's job at Stark's Park, starting on 21st March 1986. He later reflected "It was a job I take a great deal of pleasure in looking back on. The club was on a down and had been for a few years but with help from the people there we got the place buzzing again and the only sad thing about my time there is that I never got them into the Premier League."

During his three-and-a-half years at Stark's Park, he turned down opportunities to manage Airdrie and Partick Thistle, but on 5th November1990, he was appointed assistant to Joe Jordan at Hearts, who paid Rovers £32,500 compensation.

Hearts were consistently "the best of the rest" (after the Old Firm), but Jordan was sacked in May 1993, and Connor returned to Celtic Park as a coach in various capacities, and under a succession of managers (Liam Brady, Lou Macari and Tommy Burns) including a spell as caretaker manager in which Celtic were unbeaten in October 1993. They won three matches (one against Sporting Lisbon and one at Ibrox) and drew the fourth game.   Assistant manager to Billy Stark at Morton from October 1997, he resigned in mid December 1999. He had a brief spell helping Murray Cheyne at Pencaitland in 2000/1, and later that season joined Gordon Dalziel at Ayr United.   His final active involvement in football was a couple of short-term part-time stints at Stark's Park.

Ronnie Coyle, who played for him at Celtic and Rovers, said : "Frank was a great man manager, tremendous at motivating players. He left the training side of things to coaches who were better at it, but he knew what he was good at and he knew how to blend a team together.   He was a hard wee b****** as well, he would come down on you like a ton of bricks, and apart from Cammy Fraser, I doubt if there was anyone who wasn't scared of him at some point or another."

Connor's years in Kirkcaldy may have been trophy-less, but in terms of transforming the club's fortunes, he must be regarded as amongst the very best in the club's history. He inherited "half a team", and he used the transfer fees received from the sale of Keith Wright, Paul Smith, Paul Sweeney and Craig Robertson to progressively improve the side, and lift the entire club from its torpor. He introduced a comprehensive and meaningful youth system, from which his successor reaped rich benefits.

Painstakingly, he raised the standards of every aspect of the club, increasing turnover and payroll and transfer budgets, but not the level of debt ; he had worked for some of the poorest clubs in the Scottish League, and recognised the reality of football finance. Moreover, this Lanarkshire man, steeped in the culture of industrial west-central Scotland, found an empathy and understanding with Kirkcaldy and its football

people. He left with his task – a place in the Premier Division – unfulfilled but he recognised that persuading the board of directors to reintroduce full time football – the necessary platform for "the next step" – was one battle that he would not win.

He didn't do it alone, and has always acknowledged and appreciated the help he got from others, so the final analysis of his impact on the club is not quite accurate or literally true, but it will serve as a deserved and succinct summary : Frank Connor single-handedly rebuilt the club from the depths of the lowest Division, to the threshold of the Premier Division and unimagined success.

JAMES MICHAEL NICHOLL

20th November 1990 to 8th February 1996
20th June 1997 to 14th June 1999

Born to Irish parents in Hamilton, Ontario in 28th December 1956, the family returned to Northern Ireland and Nicholl played football at Whitehouse Primary School then Rathcoole Secondary School. He then played Boys Brigade football in Newtownabbey, for Glymower Wolves Boys' Club, and attracted the attention of Manchester United.   He was signed as an apprentice in 1971 and made his first team debut in April 1975, thriving under managers Dave Sexton and Tommy Docherty, under whom he won an FA Cup winners medal in 1979. When Ron Atkinson was appointed manager he made it known that he preferred John Gidman, who he signed from Everton, and the Northern Ireland internationalist spent the next three years at Old Trafford struggling to return to the first team.

After a short spell on loan at Sunderland in 1981/82, he joined the summer exodus of experienced professional players to the North American Soccer League, with Toronto Blizzard, returned to play 29 matches for Sunderland in 1982/83, and went back to Toronto for the summer of 1983.   At the end of their season he signed for Rangers, in October 1983, and won a League Cup winners medal.   He spent two seasons at West Brom, and returned to Ibrox in August 1986, where he won two more League Cup winners medals, in 1986/7 and 1987/8, and a League Championship medal in 1986/7.

He played five European Cup and six UEFA Cup ties for Rangers in three seasons.   Latterly he was reserve team coach at Ibrox.   In July 1989 he joined Dunfermline Athletic, where he played nine times before being appointed player manager of Rovers in November 1990.   His last appearance as a player was as a substitute in 1995/96.   He represented Northern Ireland in two World Cup Finals and won 73 caps.

He was appointed Rovers manager on 20th November

1990 and assistant manager of Northern Ireland in mid January 1992. He wanted to succeed Billy Bingham as Northern Ireland manager but his application in February 1994 foundered on his salary expectations. He had been considered for the Dundee United manager's job during the previous year. On signing a two year contract in April 1994, he was also appointed to the Rovers board, but resigned as a director three months later when he was refused permission to talk to Kilmarnock about succeeding Tommy Burns. He was interviewed for the Norwich City job in June 1995 and finally left, for Millwall in February 1996.

He found that club in freefall, and they were relegated from the Second Division a few months after he took over. With prospects of immediate promotion evaporating when the club was put into Administration, he was made redundant midway through 1996/97. The following Saturday, he made a high profile appearance as a player for Bath City, and was sent off. He returned to Stark's Park as assistant to Iain Munro, becoming his replacement as manager in June 1997.

After leaving Stark's Park when new owners took over in June 1999, Dick Campbell gave him a coaching job at Dunfermline Athletic (filling the vacancy left by John McVeigh, who had become Rovers manager), and Nicholl was retained by new manager Jimmy Calderwood in November 1999. Both moved to Aberdeen in the summer of 2004.

In terms of tangible trophies, Jimmy Nicholl was the club's most successful manager, winning its only national Cup and two League Championships, taking Raith Rovers - twice - into the new elite of Scottish football, the Premier Division.

He, and Raith Rovers, benefitted mutually from the fate that drew them together at exactly the right time. The qualities which the young player-manager brought to the club in 1990 were precisely those required to build on the remarkable work done by his predecessor.

He was acutely aware of the importance of a happy dressing room, and worked hard to achieve that. Goalkeeper Scott Thomson recalled "…. coming back on the team bus after we won the Championship against Hamilton at Firhill, and having a long chat with Julian Broddle. He mentioned that he had been in the game for a lot of years, starting in first team football at 16, and he had never known a team spirit like we had at the Rovers. The players would fight for each other in matches, and had a real "togetherness" built up, I suppose, over a number of years as the team was being pieced together. It was interesting to hear that particular aspect picked out by a player who had played for a number of clubs on both sides of the border, over a long number of years."

Ronnie Coyle concurred : "The whole unit was bonded together and it was a great squad to be in at the time. There was no bitching and no arguing and everyone had a good night out every few weeks. It was the best social life I have ever experienced, and that's how we thrived because we knew how to enjoy ourselves off the field and we went onto the park to enjoy ourselves too. We never changed our tactics to long ball or defensive, we always played the same game. I think Jimmy Nicholl could have changed the tactics to go defensive and grab a point here or there, but what's the point of that ? We were never organised enough to stay in the Premier League [in 1993/94] but it was a great experience to get all the plaudits for playing good football and then go and win the First Division again. I don't think there will be many teams who will do that."

Craig Brewster said : "It was the best two years of my life football-wise. The whole atmosphere at the club was tremendous, there was a great group of guys and I'll always remember my time at Raith with a great deal of affection."

It is rare to find one of his former players with a bad word for him. Goalkeeper Scott Thomson explained "Jimmy Nicholl was a great 'man' manager, always gave you the belief that you could do anything, individually and as a team." Ronnie Coyle summed him up as "Great knowledge of football, great training coach, brilliant on the training field and as a player-manager.

Nicholl led by example, as recalled by his youth coach, and successor as manager, Jimmy Thomson : "There was a buzz about him ; he used to come to work in the morning with these wee short steps as if he was running, and everything was lifted up with his mannerisms, it was infectious and that's what used to spread about the club. It was great, the whole place got a lift from it."

The marriage of bright young manager and up-and-coming club was made in heaven, but it was never going to be long-lasting. Jimmy Nicholl had ambitions beyond Stark's Park, as the succession of job interviews between 1993 and 1996 would suggest. Similarly, there was no long-term strategy on his ill-advised return to the club in 1997, when he was given, and spent, a transfer and wages budget which became the ruination of the club.

His second spell, in which he failed to win a third First Division championship to return the club to the imagined riches of the Premier League, tainted the legacy of his golden first period, proving the old adage "never go back." If consolation could be found in the financial carnage which followed, it was that future managers would no longer have the albatross of Nicholl's early success around their necks, in the way that Alex Ferguson has proved impossible to follow at Aberdeen.

In the eleven years since he left Stark's Park for the second time, Jimmy Nicholl has been an assistant manager, well-remunerated, and operating in the Premier League, so what seemed, in the early 1990s, to be a promising managerial career has hardly been a failure. There have been no more winners medals, however, and the sublime irony is that the highlights of his career in football management were achieved at Raith Rovers, whom, at the time, he did not consider big enough to satisfy his ambitions.

Such hubris should not detract from his achievements in his first spell at Stark's Park, which took the club to unimagined heights, and for that he deserves to be considered amongst the club's greatest managers.

JIMMY THOMSON

9th February 1996 (confirmed on 23rd February) to 27th August 1996

Born on 25th March 1945, signed by Alloa from Newtongrange Star towards the end of 1967/68 season, he was a regular midfield player at Recreation Park until Frank Connor signed him for Cowdenbeath in May 1977. He spent two seasons at Central Park, and became coach under Pat Stanton. The pair moved on to Dunfermline Athletic, and then to Hibs, when Thomson, a part-timer, became reserve team coach.

He returned to Alloa as coach to Willie Garner at the start of 1983/84, and was appointed manager in February 1984, but failed to stave off relegation from the First Division. He took them straight back, in second place, the following season, but they were bottom of the First Division when he left in April 1986. He returned to Dunfermline as Reserve and Youth team coach and in November 1987 became manager of Berwick Rangers, but they finished joint bottom of the Second Division, and were in bottom position when he left in September 1988. It was back to Dunfermline as youth team coach and after a short spell out of the game, he had just taken over as manager of Gala Fairydean when Jimmy Nicholl asked him to be Rovers Youth coach at the end of September 1993.

When Nicholl and Martin Harvey left in February 1996, Thomson was the only remaining full time member of the coaching staff. Popular and experienced, he was a wise choice as a caretaker manager, but his past experience showed that the personable Thomson simply didn't have the qualities to succeed in the cut-throat business of football management. His appointment as a Premier League manager was doomed to failure, compounded by a succession of bad breaks at the start of the 1996/97 season.

After leaving Rovers, he was Berwick Rangers manager from November 1996, but they finished bottom of the Second Division and he left in August 1997, to be replaced by former Rovers player Paul Smith.

Greig at Rangers, but League success eluded the Ibrox club, and after he and Greig left the club, he became manager of Morton on 25th November 1983, guiding them to the First Division Championship. He repeated that feat the following season with Motherwell, and a long period of sustained improvement at Fir Park culminated in a Scottish Cup win in 1991. He managed to fall out with an excellent Chairman at Fir Park and left them –third in the Premier League - in June 1994. Shortly afterwards he joined Hearts, but they could finish no higher than sixth the following season (Motherwell were runners up to Rangers) and on 21st July 1995 he left Tynecastle.

On 3rd September 1996 he was appointed manager of Raith Rovers, but lasted only seven days. The day after his only match in charge, a defeat by Aberdeen, Dundee United sacked Billy Kirkwood and Jim McLean wanted his brother as their new manager.

He had initial success at Tannadice, taking them to third in the Premier Division and a League Cup Final in his first season, but they fell to seventh the following season, and after a disappointing start to 1998/99, he negotiated a settlement and left "by mutual consent" on 4th September 1998. He was in charge of Rangers' Youth system for a few years, and has latterly been employed by the SFA and SPL in scouting and coaching capacities.

ALEXANDER IAIN FORDYCE MUNRO

16th September 1996 to 14th April 1997

Born in Uddingston on 24th August 1951, he signed for St Mirren from Drumchapel Amateurs in December 1969, suffered relegation to the Second Division at the end of his first full season in the first team, and after two seasons in the Second Division, he signed for Hibs in May 1973. He played in the losing team in the 1974/5 League Cup final, having won a Drybrough Cup winners medal at the start of the previous season. In April 1976 he was transferred to Rangers but played only eleven first team matches at Ibrox before returning to St Mirren in November 1977. He found his best form at Love Street as St Mirren established themselves in the Premier League, and he won both winners and runners up medals in the Anglo Scottish Cup.

In October 1980 he was transferred to Stoke City, and ten months later moved to Sunderland. In March 1984 he returned to Scotland to sign for Dundee United, playing seventeen times before returning to Hibs in March 1985. He won another League Cup runners up medal the following season, and played his last match in September 1986. He was capped seven times for Scotland during his second spell at St Mirren, in 1978/9 and 1979/90, and made one appearance for the Scottish League.

He was appointed coach at Dunfermline Athletic, and was caught up in the controversy which surrounded Jim Leishman's elevation to General Manager in the summer of 1990. He kept Dunfermline in the Premier League the following season, but was sacked on 17th September 1991. On 7th October 1991

TOMMY McLEAN

3rd September 1996 to 10th September 1996

Born in Ashgill, Lanarkshire, on 2nd June 1947, he was the youngest of the three McLean brothers (typically the most successful manager of the three, Dundee United's Jim, was the only one not to manage Rovers !). He signed for Kilmarnock from Birkenshaw Amateurs in October 1962 and won a League Championship medal in his debut first team season, then starred in their European Cup matches in 1965/6. The following season, they reached the semi final of the Fairs Cup. He was transferred to Rangers in June 1971 where he remained a first team player for ten years. In that time he won Championship medals in 1974/5, 1975/6 and 1977/8 ; League Cup winners in 1975/6, 1977/8 and 1978/9 and Scottish Cup winners in 1972/3, 1976/7, 1977/8, 1978/9 and was a beaten finalist in 1976/7, 1979/0 and 1981/2. He played in 54 European club matches for Rangers and Kilmarnock and won a European Cup winners Cup final in Barcelona in 1972.

He played twice for Scotland Under 23s and six times on Scotland's World tour in the summer of 1967. He was selected seven times for the Scottish League and made his full Scotland debut in 1968, winning five more caps ; unusually, all while a Kilmarnock player - he was not selected for Scotland in his ten years at Ibrox.

He became first team coach, and then assistant manager under John

he succeeded Gordon Wallace as manager of Dundee, but resigned on 21st February 1992.   In June of that year, he was appointed manager of Hamilton Accies, and was on the verge of being appointed St Mirren manager, when Rovers brought him back to Premier Division management.   He failed to save the club from relegation in 1996/97 and was sacked on 14th April.   He has coached abroad since then.

The Rovers directors, shell shocked at the turn of events which saw them lose Tommy McLean after a week, were almost panicked into appointing Munro, whose early promise as a top flight manager had long since dissipated.   Throughout his seven months at Stark's Park there was always a semi-detached relationship between manager and club, and there were no complaints from the fans when he was sacked once the fight against relegation was conceded.

third the season after, missing out on promotion by two points. At the end of April 2002 he moved to Stenhousemuir and did well to keep the club in the Second Division in his first full season, but they struggled in 2003/4 and McVeigh resigned on 22nd January 2004. Since then, he has been out of football, working as a rehabilitation officer in prisons.

A manager from the old school ; loud, straight-talking, excitable, his CV resembled Frank Connor's, and there were hopes that a prolonged spell would allow McVeigh to rebuild the club as that other Monklands man had.   Unwittingly, McVeigh had joined a far from stable ship, and he very quickly fell out with the new owners.   Their attempts to justify their surprise sacking of the manager who had lifted the club to third place in the League blackened his name, and he felt compelled to clear it in court.   His five months in charge resulted in two years of unseemly reports of the subsequent case in Kirkcaldy Sheriff Court.

JOHN McVEIGH

14th June 1999 to 1st December 1999

Born in Coatbridge on 25th January 1957, he signed professional forms for Airdrie in June 1975, having been reared by Airdrie Boys Club, and he became a regular first team player in 1976/77.   After helping Airdrie to promotion to the Premier League in 1980, he struggled to command a first team place the following season, emigrated to Australia and played for Brisbane City.   He returned to Scotland in October 1982 and signed for Clyde where he played for four seasons before joining Hamilton Accies, newly promoted to the Premier League in 1986.   In December of that year he moved to Kilmarnock, and in October 1987 to Falkirk, who were relegated from the Premier Division at the end of the season.

He served as a coach and reserve team manager under several managers at Falkirk, and had a spell in charge of Musselburgh Athletic when Falkirk used them as a nursery team.   Alex McDonald asked him to return to Airdrie as assistant manager shortly after the start of 1991/92, and he was at Broomfield when they reached two Scottish Cup Finals, four League Cup semi finals, won the B&Q Cup and spent two seasons in the Premier League.   In the summer of 1997 he became manager at Partick Thistle, but the planned sale of the club to the Steedmans did not happen, and Thistle were relegated to the Second Division on the last day of the season, whereupon he and his assistant, Peter Hetherston, were sacked.

A year as coach under Dick Campbell at Dunfermline followed, before he was appointed Rovers manager in the summer of 1999.   Shortly after being sacked by Rovers, he was appointed the first full time manager of Albion Rovers in March 2000, when he found them at the bottom of the Third Division.   They improved to seventh the following season and

PETER HETHERSTON

1st December 1999 to 11th December 2001

Born in Bellshill on 6th November 1964, he signed for Falkirk from Bargeddie United in December 1984 and within two years was a first team regular, by which time the Bairns were in the Premier League.   He was transferred to Watford in July 1987, and then to Sheffield United in February 1988, returning to Brockville in July of that year.   He won a first Division Championship medal in 1990/91, but had fallen out of favour at Brockville when Rovers signed him for £15,000 in October 1991. He was one of the star players in the Rovers team over the next three seasons, winning a Championship medal in 1992/93.   In the summer of 1994 he became the club's record sale when he joined Aberdeen, for whom he came on as a substitute in the 1995/96 League Cup final, which they won.   After 43 first team appearances for Aberdeen, including one in the UEFA Cup, he signed for Airdrie in March 1996, where injuries restricted his appearances to thirteen.   After seven appearances for Partick Thistle in 1997/8 he stopped playing, and became assistant to manager John McVeigh.

The pair were dismissed after Partick's last day relegation at the end of 1997/98, and after a year out of the game, he returned to Stark's Park as assistant manager, before taking over as manager on 1st December 1999.

In his first half season in charge, he built on the foundations left by McVeigh and kept the club in contention for promotion until the final weeks of the season. There was promise of the same, or better, at the start of the following season, but he was fatally undermined when his three best players, Alex Burns, Marvin Andrews and Steve Tosh, were sold to Livingston.   Thereafter, neither the club nor its emasculated manager would

progress, and it became a grim process of attrition until Hetherston finally had enough in December 2001. He returned to management with Albion Rovers, ironically as John McVeigh's replacement, in May 2002, and took them to within a point of promotion at the end of his first season. They slid back down the League, however, and Hetherston resigned on 1st December 2003, before he could appear before an SFA committee for comments made about a female assistant referee. Less than impressed by her performance at an Albion Rovers match, and at the introduction of female officials in general, he opined "She should have been at home making her man's tea."

JOHN ALEXANDER SCOTT

19th December 2001 to 30th April 2002

Born in Aberdeen on 14th January 1948, a schoolboy signing for Chelsea from Aberdeen Grammar School in June 1963, he returned to Scotland to sign for Dundee in August 1964. Within two years he was a first team regular, and helped them reach the semi final of the Fairs Cup, and the final of the League Cup, in 1967/68. Along with two other future Rovers managers, Bobby Wilson and Gordon Wallace, he won a League Cup winners medal in December 1973. He won two Scotland caps in June 1971, and a Scottish League cap in March 1973.

In August 1975 he was transferred to Aberdeen, where he won a League Cup winners medal in 1976/77. After spending the summer of 1977 in the North American Soccer League, he signed for Dundee in November 1977. His last appearances for Dundee were in 1980/1, although he remained registered as a player until 1983/4. He was coach at Dens Park before becoming manager in June 1986. Two years later, on 1st June 1988, he resigned to become co-manager of Aberdeen, with Alex Smith. In September 1991, he became manager of Dunfermline Athletic but was sacked on 19th May 1993 having failed to win promotion back to the Premier League. In January 1994 he

became manager of part-time Arbroath but resigned on 13th April 1994. He managed Hibs for a few months towards the end of 1996, before joining the coaching staff of Dundee United on 29th September 1997. In February 1998, he replaced John McCormack, who had taken Dundee to the top of the First Division, and in June 2000 he lost his job in equally controversial circumstances when Ivano Bonetti was appointed. Shortly afterwards, he became manager of Notts County, but was sacked on 11th October 2001 after a disappointing start to the season in the English Second Division. The club chairman commented : "Unfortunately, his straightforward management style and temperament increasingly conflicted with a more open relationship with others, from supporters and the media to the staff and board." Following his five months at Stark's Park, he had a spell in charge of Sunderland's reserve team and was assistant to Bobby Williamson at Plymouth Argyle, taking charge for four matches after Williamson was sacked in September 2005.

The vastly experienced Scott was ill-prepared for the poor quality he found on arrival at Stark's Park, and was unable to make the necessary changes, in morale, tactics or selection, to reverse the inexorable slide towards relegation. The decision not to offer him the job beyond the end of the season was probably a relief to all parties.

ANTONIO CALDERON

1st July 2002 to 19th May 2004

Born in Cadiz on 2nd June 1967, he played in La Liga in Spain for Real Mallorca and Rayo Vallecano (under Jose Antonio Comacho, the former national team manager) and by the end of the 1990s he was captain at Lleida in the First Division. Brought to Airdrie by Steve Archibald in August 2000 he quickly showed his midfield skills as the Spanish influence illuminated the First Division. He won a Challenge Cup winners medal before the lack of meaningful finance meant that Archibald's Spanish revolution hit the buffers, and he was transferred to Kilmarnock in March 2001, where he played 24 times in the Premier League and made two appearances in the UEFA Cup.

Calderon joined Rovers in July 2002 and guided them, on and off the pitch, to the Second Division championship. He found both tasks much tougher in the First Division the following season, and returned to Spain in May 2004. He was in charge of the Reserve team at his home club of Cadiz until 11th October 2007, when he became first team manager/coach of the Spanish Second Division club. He was sacked on 6thy April 2008 after a poor run of results, and the club were relegated at the end of the season.

The intention behind his appointment at Stark's Park was to bring continental practices and habits to the playing squad, but there were too many ordinary Scots making up the numbers, and the lack of coherent strategy from the boardroom meant that such changes were never properly implemented.

CLAUD ANELKA

7th June 2004 to 8th October 2004

His football credentials appeared to amount to being the brother, and sometime agent, of Nicholas Anelka, a French internationalist who had played for Arsenal, Liverpool and Real Madrid et al. He had approached a number of other clubs with a proposal to inject several hundreds of thousands of pounds, in exchange for complete control of playing matters ; only the Rovers bit the bait. The players he brought to the club, principally from France, may have been highly skilled on the ball, but they had not played at any sort of professional level, and were woefully short of the pitch craft and tactical awareness necessary to survive in the Scottish First Division.

GORDON DALZIEL

11th October 2004 to 31st August 2006

Born in Motherwell on 16th March 1962, he was signed by Rangers from Bonkle Youth Club in September 1977 and became a teenage sensation in the Rangers first team in 1981/2, winning the League Cup and losing in the Scottish Cup Final, repeating the latter the following season. Taking advantage of the new freedom of contract regulations, he signed for Manchester City in December 1983 and returned to Scotland to sign for Partick Thistle in September 1984, where he scored seven goals in 26 first team appearances in his first season. Remarkably, he failed to score a single goal in 19 first team appearances the following season and he was released at the end of 1985/6. He scored twice in ten appearances in the Second Division during a three month spell with East Stirling, from December 1986 to February 1987, and Frank Connor signed him for Rovers on 25th February 1987, his faith rewarded with seven vital goals in twelve League and Cup matches as Rovers won promotion.

A marvellous career at Stark's Park was crowned by captaining Rovers to the League Cup final win in November 1994, fittingly scoring a typical equaliser to take the match into extra time. His 170 League goals for Rovers is a

club record, and in 1991/2 and 1992/3 his fellow professionals voted him First Division Player of the Year. In the summer of 1989 he had a short spell with South Melbourne Hellas and was granted a Testimonial in 1992/3. When asked in 1997 who was the biggest influence on his career, he replied : "Frank Connor. I was down and out at Partick Thistle and Frank got me by the scruff of the neck and worked me hard at Raith. He really believed in me. Even now he'll come on the phone and give me great advice, or a clip round the ear. He's been a father figure to me."

He joined Ayr United in August 1995, but scored just four times in 24 appearances and after one substitute appearance in 1996/97, he hung up his boots. He took over as manager at Somerset Park in 1996, and at the end of his first full season, they won the Second Division Championship ; by 1998/99 they were third in the First Division. They went one better two seasons later, but finished seven points short of the championship, and a place in the Premier League. Despite finishing in third place in 2001/02, a poor start to the following season, and a worsening financial situation as Chairman Bill Barr's generous funding dried up, he was dismissed on 20th November 2002. He managed in Ayrshire Junior football before returning to Stark's Park in October 2004. After leaving Rovers, he returned to that grade, and was manager of Glenafton Athletic when they were beaten at Thornton Hibs in the quarter finals of the Scottish Junior Cup in 2007/8.

Although there have been several instances of former players returning to Stark's Park to become successful managers, Gordon Dalziel, like Jimmy Nicholl, should have heeded the advice "never go back". The turmoil behind the scenes, and recognition of his marvellous service as a remarkably prolific goalscorer, muted criticism of his failure to lift the club out of the Second Division, or avoid relegation in his first part-season. Those who criticised his appointment, pointing to his achievements at Ayr United being largely attributable to generous funding, may have been right. Moreover, the daily commute from Prestwick cast doubts on his total commitment to the task at hand.

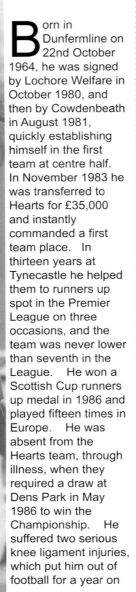

CRAIG LEVEIN

5th September 2006 to 30th October 2006

Born in Dunfermline on 22nd October 1964, he was signed by Lochore Welfare in October 1980, and then by Cowdenbeath in August 1981, quickly establishing himself in the first team at centre half. In November 1983 he was transferred to Hearts for £35,000 and instantly commanded a first team place. In thirteen years at Tynecastle he helped them to runners up spot in the Premier League on three occasions, and the team was never lower than seventh in the League. He won a Scottish Cup runners up medal in 1986 and played fifteen times in Europe. He was absent from the Hearts team, through illness, when they required a draw at Dens Park in May 1986 to win the Championship. He suffered two serious knee ligament injuries, which put him out of football for a year on both occasions.

Levein won two Scotland Under 21 caps in 1984/85, and was voted SPFA Young Player of the Year that season, and the following. He won the first of sixteen Scotland caps against Argentina in March 1990, and played in that year's World Cup finals. His final cap came in November 1994. In March 1993, he captained Scotland in a friendly match against Germany. Following a short spell as coach with Livingston, he returned to Central Park as manager in November 1997,

and after two and a half seasons near the bottom of the Third Division, he built the team which was promoted at the end of 2000/2001. He left mid season, however, becoming Hearts manager on December 1st. He led Hearts to two successive third places in the Premier League behind the Old Firm, and consequently UEFA Cup football, before leaving for newly-relegated Leicester City in November 2004. He failed to take the Foxes back into the Premiership, however, and was sacked on Burns Night in 2006. On the face of things, his appointment as Rovers manager was quite a coup for the club, but it was on the understanding that it was only until a better job arose, and he left for Dundee United a month later. Since then, he has fared better than his predecessors, post Jim McLean. He was not at Stark's Park for long enough to make any sort of impact, suggesting that the Directors were naïve to leave themselves exposed to such a one-sided, open-ended arrangement.

JOHN McGLYNN

Appointed 21st November 2006

Born in Musselburgh on 16th December 1961, he was a schoolboy signing for Dundee United in October 1976 while with St David's High School in Dalkeith. He signed for Bolton Wanderers on leaving school in October 1979, having played for Musselburgh Windsor juveniles. In December 1980 he returned to Scotland to play for Berwick Rangers, but could not help them avoid relegation to the Second Division, where he played for the next two seasons. In the summer of 1983 he joined junior club Musselburgh Atheltic, and was reinstated amateur in October 1984, joining Whitehill Welfare in the East of Scotland League where the hard-tackling midfielder played for three years.

He coached Lothian United from Under 13 to Under 18 level from 1987 onwards, and was co-manager at Easthouses Lily and Musselburgh Athletic. His old colleague at Musselburgh, Billy Brown, asked him to coach Hearts' under 16 side on a part-time basis in 1996 and in 1998 he became full time, working his way through the coaching ranks at Tynecastle. He assisted Peter Houston's youth team as they won the Youth Cup Final in 1998 and was youth coach when his team beat Rangers in the 2000 Final. He guided Hearts to the Youth League title in 2001 and then moved up to coach the reserves under Craig Levein. He had three spells as caretaker manager to the first team as the club installed a revolving door to the manager's office, following the departures of Craig Levein, John Robertson and George Burley. Although notionally an assistant

to a succession of foreign head coaches, he assumed more responsibility than the same position would require at other clubs.

He transformed the club's fortunes in the second half of his first season at Stark's Park, but fell at the final hurdle of the play-offs. It was much the same the following season, a bright opening spell which saw Rovers lead the League in early winter, turned to disappointment and ultimate failure in the play-offs. Hopes for his success in his third year at the club rest on a greatly reduced budget.

Appendix 2 - Stark's Park

In its earliest days, Raith Rovers played on Sands Road (now the Esplanade) behind Peter Purvis's school, and on the sands when the tide was out. Their first grass pitch was in the vicinity of the present Kirkcaldy Golf Club, from where they moved to the old (pottery) clay hole where now stand the houses on Balwearie Road and the playing pitch of Balwearie High School.

They first played on a flat, grassed part of Robbie's Park on 29th March 1884. Robbie's Park had its locus in the north-eastern part of the area covered by the Beveridge Park, and extended, in its length, from Raith Gate to Southerton Farm. On 11th November 1886, the club took possession of a permanent area of Robbie's Park, rented from the Laird of Raith. Their first match on their first, proper home pitch, was two days later.

The new ground was positioned in what is now Beveridge Park, on the site now occupied by the Park gardener's house and a portion of the ornamental gardens, near the corner of Boglily Road and Southerton Road. A wooden pavilion was erected in the summer of 1887. In late November 1888, it was reported that "The Raith Rovers ground has been greatly altered during the past week. Another piece of ground has been taken in, so that two pitches have now been made. The first eleven pitch has been shifted west, while the second string is to play on the side next to the road. With such a splendid ground, the Rovers should get on, What will the next thing be ? A pavilion for the second eleven ?"

A few weeks later, the praise and expectation was qualified. "The Rovers' new pitch is broader than the last one, while the fencing is of a much stronger description. Canvas has been put up at the end of the ground to prevent the view from the road, and is a decided improvement on the ground. The pitch is not so good as the old one, but may become better after being played on for some time."

Several years earlier, in the spring of 1881, the town's first football club, and its senior side, Kirkcaldy Wanderers moved into Robert Stark's grazing park on Callochy Brae. Stark's Park saw its first building constructed in 1884, when Mr Heggie, secretary of Kirkcaldy Golf Club, whose headquarters then were at Robbie's Park, offered Kirkcaldy Wanderers that club's golf house for £10 [in modern terms, in excess of £5,000]. Terms of payment were agreed, and on 28th January 1884, the club met in their new pavilion for the first time, Mr H. Westwood acting as toastmaster to the club's future success.

Wanderers played there for the next season and a half, before moving to Newton Park. Thereafter, home matches were played at Stark's Park by Kirkcaldy Rangers (1885/86), Union (1886/87 and 1887/88), and Links Fern (1888/89).

The Fife Free Press of June 17th 1887 reported : "On Monday evening the members of the Union Football Club met in a social capacity in Mr R. Stark's, West Bridge, and presented Mr Stark, jnr. with a handsome alabaster gilt clock, on the occasion of his marriage. Mr Stark, senior, made a few remarks, and said he would always do his best for the club, and that the park would be at their service whenever they required it." In 1888/89, the new tenants, Links Fern, had been on the receiving end of a protest from their opponents earlier in the season that their new pitch was "not a private ground".

In 1889/90 and 1890/91, no single club had exclusive use of the pitch, which compared unfavourably with the pitches at Robbie's Park and Newton Park for flatness and drainage. There was also less demand, with a huge reduction in the number of Junior teams in the town.

Rovers' ground at Robbie's Park, lost to the Park gardener's house and a portion of the ornamental gardens in the summer of 1891, had been widely admired, and the architectural lines and stout construction of the pavilion made it one of the best in provincial football. It had a little porch in front, with the two steps up, and over the doorway the "R.R.F.C." monogram carved by Alex Leitch, a former player who was a carver with McIntosh's furniture manufacturers. The club were keen to retain the structure (in the absence of any building at their new ground), so it was sawn in half and both parts transported by horse and cart down Abbotshall Road and Pratt Street, to be erected at the club's new ground, where it would stay for almost 30 years, although latterly swamped in size by the adjacent grandstand.

The removal of the pavilion was a major exercise for the Rovers' officials, and took a great deal of planning. Jim Tod, a future secretary, manager and director of the club, steadied the load as it slowly made its way towards the foot of Pratt Street, accompanied by club members and players on foot. They had forgotten about the railway bridge ; Tod had to make a swift descent to avoid being knocked off, and the only casualty was one of the turned ornaments that adorned the roof of the pavilion.

A press box was built on the Railway side of the ground in October 1891, and in 1893/94 there was mention of a canvas cover at the ground. In the summer of 1894, " a strong wood railing was put up in place of the hold wire" and the pitch was drained and levelled

In December 1894, a covered grandstand was erected at Stark's Park. Prior to this, the pavilion (formerly at Robbie's Park) was placed at the Beveridge Park end of the ground, on the spot where the half-time scores were later displayed. This necessitated the players to force their way through the spectators at the beginning and end of the game. On completion of the stand, however, the pavilion was moved to

The Robbie's Park pavilion, subsequently moved to Stark"s Park and photographed in 1889

The main stand at Stark's Park was destroyed in a fire in 1918.

the back of it, where it remained until the new stand was built in 1922.

The grandstand had six rows of seats and a pitched roof. The local press reported in mid December 1894 : "The Raith Rovers new stand is just about completed. It occupies a prominent position on the road side of the park. It is a splendid erection, and has been erected according to the plans of Mr Little, architect. A fine corrugated roof is placed over it. The accommodation available will be sufficient for nearly 400 people. Messrs Scott & Co, joiners, Pathhead, who had the erection of the stand, have made a good job." It was first used in the match against St Bernards on 29th December 1894.

In the close season of 1899 "a splendid new temperance refreshment stall" was erected between the pay-boxes and the pavilion and a flag pole stood by the pay boxes. The unhelpful location of Stark's Park was recognised, and in 1900 plans were drawn for a new ground at Clayholes, but finances dictated that nothing came of this plan.

The enclosure in front of stand was fenced in for the Qualifying Cup tie against Cowdenbeath on 20th October 1906, when extra pay boxes were installed, and banking was added to the flat ground and gentle slopes around the ground for the Hearts Scottish Cup tie on 23rd March 1907.

For the Scottish Cup tie against Celtic on 22nd February 1908, additional banking was made up, and a capacity of was 19,000 calculated without the railway embankment, and 23,000 with ; sixteen pay-gates were opened. The pitch was measured at 116 yards x 65 yards. Prior to the rebuilding of the ground in 1995 it was 113 yards x 69 yards, and post reconstruction it was 113 yards x 70 yards.

In the close season of 1908 turnstiles were introduced at the gates for the first time, and the playing pitch was relaid and "made level as a bowling green". Those improvements cost £216 12/6d [equivalent today to £104,000].

On 28th June 1910, there was a special meeting of the Kirkcaldy Dean of Guild Court held in the Town Hall, to consider Rovers' ambitious proposals for a new grandstand. There had been a visit to Firhill where a bigger stand of the same design (by the same architect) had been erected. Rovers' stand doubled the number of exits and it was recommended that the urinal provision should be improved. It was 200 feet in length, 24 feet wide and had seating accommodation for 1,400.

Beneath were to be dressing rooms for home team and visitors, referee, board room and press box. The press box was at the back of the stand, enclosed with glass, with an entrance by special stair and room for 12 reporters. "It is

proposed to introduce the telephone so that half-time results of other matches may be obtained. Another feature is a section of reserved seats, to which access can be obtained while the game is in progress. The stand is to be constructed in steel, with a corrugated iron roof." The Architect was William Reid of Glasgow. The location was to be on the Pratt Street side, with the south gable a yard or so up from the edge of the penalty area, extending northwards to the north gable which was several yards short of the opposite penalty area. It was almost, but not quite, centred on the half-way line. He plans were passed, but the stand was never constructed.

For the first visit of Rangers in the Scottish League on 27th August 1910, "In order to cope with the crowd, the grandstand was extended on either side, while the railway embankment, which has been leased by the management, was largely taken advantage of." Hitherto, spectators stood at the foot of the railway embankment, which was fenced off. The south extension of the stand was 75 feet long, the north 60 feet long, and each had a paybox and exit at the rear, and two stairways to the front. The roof sloped backwards, there were wind shutters at the back, and a cross-spar fence at the front. At either corner of the ground on Pratt Street, there were new sliding exit gates. The cost of the extension was £432 13/5d, [£208,000] with a further £228 7/5d [£110,000] spent the following year on increasing the banking round the ground, not least on the railway side, the rental being on a rolling annual basis.

In the summer of 1912 a brick foundation was installed to the centre of the grandstand and four additional turnstiles were opened for the Scottish Cup quarter final against St Mirren Cup on 8th march 1913, the cost of those improvements amounting to £156 2/11d [£75,000]

The Turnstile Block at the Beveridge Park End had two single and three double turnstiles with roller exit doors on either side. The Boundary wall was constructed at the same time. The house on the corner (later known as Bill Collier's house) was described as Mr Anderson's property (completed on 30th October 1894), and the present car park was Mrs Bowman's Feu, with stables (constructed in June 1906) at the bottom corner. A short way along the lane to the stables was the small wooden Secretary's office.

It was by no means unusual to see builders at work in Pratt Street around that time. Invertiel Manse was built in 1885, the tenement houses were constructed between February 1895 and October 1901. St Peter's Episcopal Mission Church was constructed in January 1906, and was later called St

September 1922, the hastily constructed replacement main stand and pavilion, shortly before their demolition

Columba's. Milton Terrace was built from January 1903.

For the Scottish Cup tie against Hearts on 7th February 1914, "The embankment has been added to considerably and crush barriers have been erected round the enclosure with the object of adding comfort to the spectators." The cost was £261 8/3d [£125,000].

On Sunday 19th October 1918 a fire destroyed the wooden grandstand. £750 [£300,000] was received in insurance, and the replacement cost £726 to construct. This was 78 feet long and had seven rows of seats, and it was built on the site of the present main stand, towards the south end of the ground.

By the end of December 1920, the new (Railway) stand at Stark's Park was nearing completion. Seating 2000, it was described as "patchwork", but its construction provided seating on both touchlines at the ground, amounting to between 2500 and 3000. The cost was £978 16/5d [£235,000].

In early January 1921, there was a good deal of discussion in the Fife Free Press about improving the ground. There was a large amount of waste ground behind the pavilion at the south east corner, and the south west corner was to be banked up to match the south terracing. "Some use could also be made of the ground to the North East of the pitch, which is presently unused."

The Kirkcaldy Times reported on January 11th 1922 : "Lord Novar has made an offer on favourable terms to sell Stark's Park to Raith Rovers. It is understood that it is in the intention of the club to accept the offer and, when they acquire the ground, they will construct a large stand, making provision for 35,000 to 40,000 spectators" - 10,000 more than before. A

fortnight later, it was reported that a 20 year lease was bought for £1500 (£200 being generously knocked off by Viscount Novar of Raith). The total cost to the club was capitalised as £1712 5/7d, [£410,000] and £1000 of that was taken out in a mortgage. This was paid off in £200 instalments, in 1923/24, 1924/25, 1925/26, 1926/27 and finally in 1946/47.

Planned improvements were to include "the erection of a new and commodious stand on the Pratt Street side of the ground, to run from one side of the playing pitch to the other. The club offices and stripping quarters will probably be situated under the proposed stand after the fashion of some of the larger grounds."

On Tuesday April 25th 1922, plans were approved for the new grandstand, to cost £10,000 [£2.4 million]. There would be seating for 2,500, with 5,000 standing in the enclosure in front. The architects were William Williamson and George B Deas, Kirkcaldy.

The old stand was on the balance sheet at a value of £874 9/8d [£210,000], and the structure, fixtures and fittings and press box realised £96 1/- [£23,000] at a roup conducted by Mr John Rough, auctioneer . The net loss in the Balance sheet of £778 8/8d was replaced by the same notional value given to 2000 Ordinary shares at £1 each, received from the Grand Stand Company.

The Kirkcaldy Times announced on Wednesday 13th September 1922. "Raith Rovers Football Club have been granted authority to erect entrance gates at Stark's Park on condition that the petitioners will give a guarantee to take down the entrances and put them back to the distance required by the Town Council should Pratt Street at any time be widened."

This grainy newspaper photograph shows Bill Inglis scoring from the penalty spot against Cowdenbeath in January 1923. A and B Stands are in use, but C Stand was still being constructed and the roof panels were not installed.

Shortly after completion of the main stand in 1923 ; terrace-free embankments, wooden crush barriers, factory chimneys in the background, a wooden fence round the perimeter, and advertisements painted on the stand roof.

There were four double and one single turnstiles and 8 foot and 15 foot exit doors at the south corner.

The main section of the new grandstand was opened on Saturday 30th December 1922 [the angled section behind the goal-line had not been completed, with the unclad steel beams of the roof clearly visible in an action photograph taken from behind the opposite goal].

Present at the opening were the Presidents of the SFA, Scottish League, Viscount Novar who was the Secretary of State for Scotland and Major-General Sir Robert Hutchison MP, who had played for the club in 1902. "On behalf of the contractors Mr Fraser presented Lord Novar with a gold key." The huge expense of purchasing the ground and erecting the grandstand (which, in fairness, has outlived the vast majority of its contemporaries) precluded further expenditure on the ground for the next thirty years.   Until the early 1950s, therefore, the Main Grandstand on Pratt Street was at appears today, although the red brickwork was unpainted.   In front and alongside running north was banking for standing spectators. There was steeper banking behind both goals. The Railway Stand was as it appeared until it was demolished in 1981, but included seating, and at the Inverteil end there was banking for standing spectators ; the equivalent at the Beveridge Park end was largely flat.   The only terracing was in the enclosure in front of the Main Stand, and it was wooden planks which shuttered the ash infill.   A small number of wooden crush barriers were dotted around the ground.

In the first week of November 1945, loudspeakers were erected to announce the team before kick off and in late October 1946, the Kirkcaldy Times announced : "At Stark's Park an effort is to be made to install arc lamps around the field, so that players do get a chance of a kick about on training nights.". The problem for reserve players, not playing on a Saturday, was that they never get to kick a ball during the winter months.

Six weeks later : "The old Railway Stand, which has been made into a covered enclosure [i.e. the seats were removed], has certainly proved a god send to the "faithful" this season. If the advertisement on the front was removed, at least another couple of hundred spectators could use the enclosure and see the game." It was the only covering for standing spectators.

The Kirkcaldy Times reported on 2nd April 1947 that the new corrugated iron fence at the old Mill End was nearing completion. "It provides grand protection for the spectators from the west winds. It is hoped that when funds are sufficient, to put a roof over this portion of the terracing."

All of those improvements were funded by the Supporters' Club, and their costs did not appear on the Football Club balance sheet.

The minutes of a board meeting on 29th March 1950 noted : "Letter received from British Railways intimating that if the club wished to continue with the lease of the Railway Embankment, the annual rent would now be £50 [£8,000] . The meeting agreed to pay the increased rent, as they contemplated erecting a renewal to the covered enclosure." At the board meeting of 30th May 1950, it was agreed to form a Supporters

Harry Colville helps out George Johnstone in a Fife Cup tie in 1953, with the uncovered Beveridge Park end terracing in the background, complete with half-time scoreboard at the back.

A packed Stark's Park for the visit of Dundee in the early 1950's, with the Evening Dispatch advert on the roof the stand prominent, below the air raid siren.

Club Office by partitioning a part of the Checkers' room.

Even if the club had wanted to, significant ground improvements in the years immediately after the Second World War would have been difficult to enact. Ministry of Works officials told the club on 17th April 1951 they could not erect a covered enclosure at the West Mill end. "There is a shortage of labour and available labour is required for essential work. Men could not be spared to do the work entailed by the erection of such a covered-in enclosure."

Never short of a pithy retort, Bert Herdman's reaction was that if the spectators in the terracing got wet it was possible they might be off work the following week and there would be a shortage of labour, whereas if the covered enclosure was erected the spectators would be able to see the games in comfort. The Kirkcaldy Times reported : "The argument, admitted the official, was original, but not sufficiently impressive to cause a change of decision."

At the board meeting of 30th April 1951, "it was agreed to complete, by terracing, the flat piece of ground at the West End of the covered enclosure, this to be done by casual labour and using 400 [at a cost of £100, £16,000 today] railway sleepers. The half-dozen or so full-time players earned extra

money during the months of the close season by constructing this terrace, under the supervision of Willie McNaught, who had previously been a builder.

At the board meeting of 3rd June 1951, it was also agreed to build concrete steps at the entrance leading to the pavilion ; build a ladies lavatory in the building presently occupied by the checkers ; build a gents lavatory in the Gents urinal at the bottom terracing, and a wall or railing was to be erected at the rear of stand, this for public safety. The terracing of the enclosure was concreted during the summer of 1951.

The Kirkcaldy Times reported on 29th August 1951 : "Added comfort for fans in A Stand at Stark's Park is now provided by the safety glass panel which has been erected at the north end of the stand. More money for the window cleaner." The cost of the improvements in 1951/2 was £1532 [£245,000], of which the Supporters Club donated £1410 [£226,000].

The Kirkcaldy Times reported on 11th June 1952 that there were plans to extend the Railway enclosure from corner flag to corner flag, in stages, to provide cover there for 4000 spectators. Bert Herdman said "The day has passed when fans will stand in pouring rain to watch a match."

Harry Colville heads clear, watched by Willie McNaught and Jimmy Mason, during the visit of Third Lanark in September 1950. Schoolboys sit by the touchline in front of the railway stand, with the long-standing advert for the Edinburgh Evening News, which retained its place until the structure's demolition.

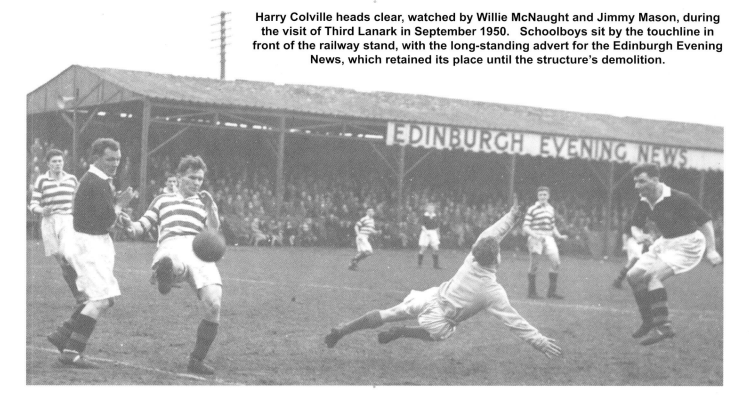

The Beveridge Park end cover being constructed in August 1954, with the railway sleeper terracing clearly shown.

Those intentions were short-lived however, and it was decided instead to erect a new enclosure at the bottom [Inverteil] end, as the lease on the railway embankment only ran to May 1960. In any case, the Ministry of Works had refused permission to replace the Railway Stand in September 1952.

In late April 1953, however, a warrant was issued by the Ministry of Works for a covered enclosure behind the Mill Street goal, to accommodate 2,000, taking the total under cover at the ground to 7,000.

The cost was £1408 [£170,000], of which the Supporters Club contributed £620 [£75,000]. Architects were Whyte & Nicol, 31 North Frederick Street, Glasgow. There were four sections of 25 feet between pillars, a depth of 25 feet, pitched roof, with a "future extension" of 10 feet behind. In June 1953, it was agreed to put a roof over the dugouts.

By the last week of August 1954, the covered enclosure at the Beveridge Park end was completed at a cost of £2500 [£300,000], with £1700 [£204,000] donated by the Supporters Club. The initial estimate from the builders, Barnet and Morton (received in May) had been £1859, plus £333 in other costs. It was constructed in short time, between 2nd and 21st August.

Early in October 1955, work began in fitting out the gym at Stark's Park, which was completed by the end of November, with the Supporters Club contributing to the cost. In the summer of 1956, the interior of the Pavilion was refurbished, with terrazzo concrete on the floors.

Three years after first announcing the intention, on 23rd October 1958 it was agreed to engage Oliver Melville's and Barnet and Morton to erect training lights on the stand roof. On 21st December 1958, two poles were erected in front of the Railway Enclosure for training lights, further restricting the view from within that structure. Once again, the Supporters' Club stumped up for the cost.

In early August 1959 a Stark's Park Development Club was formed to raise funds for floodlights and the Supporters Club donated £1000 [approximately £100,000] at the Football Club's Annual General Meeting in late September. Work started following planning permission being granted in mid December. On 3rd May 1960, the Board learned of residents' complaining about TV interference once the pylons were erected. A full test of the floodlights, in the presence of police and railway officials, was on 25th August 1960.

The total cost of the floodlighting, as capitalised and including £390 to the East of Scotland Electricity Board, was £11227 14/7d [nearly £1 million]. This entire sum was donated by the Supporters Club (£2,250) and the Starks Park Development Club (£8978), and was not funded by the sale of Jim Baxter, as popular myth has it.

The floodlights were installed by Miller and Stables Ltd., Electrical and Civil Engineers, 15 Duncan Street, Edinburgh 9. The towers were 91 feet in height, with a 17 foot head for holding the lights.

In the summer of 1962 the remainder of the Pratt Street side terracing was concreted, and trackside advertising was introduced for the first time. This was by no means the first advertising seen at the ground. As soon as the Main Stand was built in 1922, adverts were painted on the roof, to be seen by standing spectators and, perhaps more importantly, rail passengers. Long after the rental had ceased to be collected, the outline of a Youma malted loaf could still be seen on wet days, and before that the advert for the Evening Dispatch underneath the training lights.

An advert for Nelson cigarettes was painted on the roof of the Inverteil-end cover, and at the opposite end Players' Please (for John Players cigarettes) was displayed for many years. At the south-west corner, a free-standing advertising hoarding for King George IV whisky was a prominent landmark, and the fascia of the railway stand was covered by an advert for the Evening Dispatch, and then the Evening News when the former ceased publication.

The 200 Club was formed in September 1964, and the premises were opened in the summer of 1966. The construction of the small lounge inside C stand, and the upstairs office at the rear of A stand, obtained planning consent in February 1967.

The lower parts of the terracing behind both goals was concreted in the close seasons of 1965 and 1966, and the summer of 1968 new steps were constructed to the main stand. The first test of the ground's capacity for several years was the League Cup tie against Rangers in August 1969. 22,000 ground and enclosure tickets were printed for the match. In the hope of a replay against Celtic in the Scottish Cup quarter final in 1971, 16500 ground tickets were printed, 3500 enclosure, 2039 stand, making a total 22039.

It was decided to build new dugouts in late September

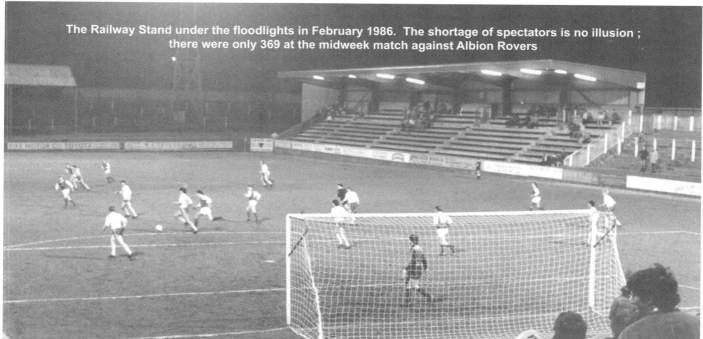

The Railway Stand under the floodlights in February 1986. The shortage of spectators is no illusion; there were only 369 at the midweek match against Albion Rovers

1969, by which time a new grass mower shed had been erected alongside the track-side half time scoreboard at the Inverteil end.   The dugouts were eventually constructed in the summer of 1972, replacing the small, side-glazed sunken constructions on either side of the players' tunnel.   In January 1970 glass bricks were fitted in the Boardroom, replacing the previous windows which looked onto the enclosure.

In late January 1972, Stark's Park was professionally valued at £28,000 [£1.7 million].   After several years of complaining about the poor illumination, new halogen bulbs were fitted in the floodlights in September 1973, at a cost of the modern-day equivalent of more than £100,000.
On 7th January 1980, the board turned down the Supporters' Club's request for a Souvenir Shop at the ground.

After three decades of talking about it, in late March 1981, Rovers received planning permission from Kirkcaldy District Council to start work at the end of the season on a new covered railway enclosure, costing between £150,000 and £200,000.   Ninety feet long, it would be capable of being

converted into a seated stand.   Work commenced on Monday 18th May 1981, but the project was beset by a sequence of problems and delays, and the Railway Stand was finally opened for the last two home matched of 1981/82, several months late .   The cost was £209,744 [£2 million] of which £115,607 was grant-aided by the Football Grounds Improvement Trust, set up in the aftermath of the 1971 Ibrox Disaster.

The cover extended from the south west corner flag to the half-way line.   There were 1,080 seats, unfortunately of the base-only plastic moulded variety (with no backs) but the view from the stand was elevated and uninterrupted.   From the north gable to the north west corner flag, steep concrete terracing was constructed, which afforded an excellent view for standing spectators.   There were two turnstiles at the south west gable, and a refreshment bar at the back of the stand.

New floodlighting was installed on the existing pylons in the close season 1985 at a cost of £19,378 [£200,000] of which £16,000 was received in grants.   On 30th September 1985, the Railway Embankment was purchased from British

Gordon Dalziel and Paul Sweeney in attack against Kilmarnock in October 1987, with the Nelson cigarettes advert still visible on the roof of the Invertiel end cover

Stevie Simpson shoots against Dumbarton in February 1988, with the sparse visiting support taking shelter under the Beveridge Park end cover

Rail for £2250 plus £100 in fees [£23,500].

In mid April 1987, work started on the refurbishment of the concrete walls and brickwork of the main stand, the first structural repairs to have been undertaken since the stand was built, and necessary to repair the ravages of the salty atmosphere in which it had stood for 63 years. The estimated cost was £75,000 [£500,000] of which around half was received in grants.

At the end of August 1989, the capacity of Stark's Park was reduced by 15% to 8460, by the local authority. Standing capacity was reduced to 5441, and the movement of supporters at half time (from behind one goal to another) was to be severely curtailed in the aftermath of increasing terracing violence elsewhere in the country. A fortnight later, the segregation arrangements were reversed with Rovers fans sent to the Beveridge Park end.

In mid June 1991, it was disclosed that Rovers and East Fife had been in secret talks to share a new ground on the

outskirts of the town. Two years later, East Fife were keen to involve Rovers in a project to build a new ground in Glenrothes. On October 3rd 1991, Fife Council reduced the capacity of Stark's Park from 8516 to 8231. The main stand was reduced from 2073 to 2058, North terracing 2898 to 2630, and the South terracing increased from 3545 to 3592. A week later, the total was confirmed as 8280. In mid July, segregation arrangements were once again reversed, and the home fans were back at the Invertiel end.

In the summer of 1992 new steps were constructed for the Players Entrance to the ground, and a new gym and treatment area was built in the pavilion. A great deal of work was required to the ground to make it passably suitable for Premier League football. In the close season of 1993 two new turnstiles were constructed at the home end (south east corner), bought from Stirling Albion's old ground at Annfield. Crush barriers were installed on the east terrace ; the home end was concreted ; the 200 club refurbished with a view towards

The distinctive turnstile block at the south east corner of the ground.

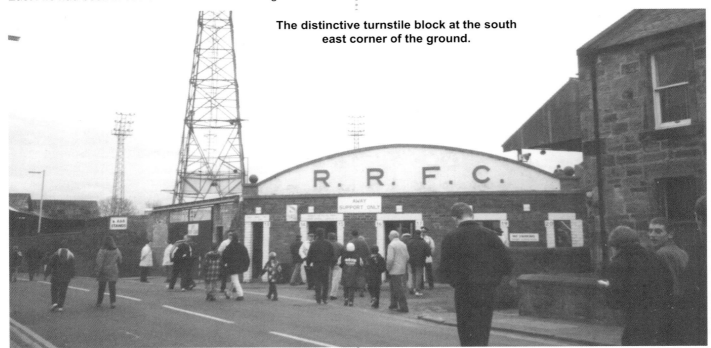

The Beveridge Park end after the construction of concrete terracing in 1993/94.

providing pre-match meals, and a snack bar was built in C stand. Towards the end of 1993/94 a television platform was constructed on the terracing beside the Railway Stand.

The concreting of both end terraces was an expensive and disruptive process, which cost £300,000 [£500,000] of which half was received in grants. On 1st September 1995 it was announced that plans to build a new stadium at Randolph had fallen through, and on 19th December 1995, planning permission was granted by Kirkcaldy District Council for the redevelopment of Stark's Park.

On 1st April 1996, work started on demolishing the Beveridge Park end terracing (reconstructed three years earlier), followed by the dismantling of the Inverteil end covering. Over the summer months the Railway Stand was extended northwards to the corner flag (providing 627 seats), and two enormous stands were built behind both goals by Barr Construction of Ayr, each accommodating 3,368 spectators. A narrow road went behind the South stand and the Railway Stands. Sadly, the distinctive and pleasing turnstile block at the north east corner was demolished, and the two turnstiles in the Pratt Street wall which gave entrance to A and B Stands were blocked off. Access to the Main Stand was by a newly constructed sloping roadway, and a particularly ugly fence-and-turnstile arrangement in front of the Stand. The old underpass to the terracing beneath C stand was converted into offices.

The pitch was levelled and moved slightly south-ward, rendering the enclosure largely unusable. This, and the north-east terracing beside it were the only remnants of terracing, and were redundant in the new era of all-seated accommodation.

A capacity of 10,271 seats – just over the criterion for future membership of the top division – was therefore achieved, at a cost of £2.7 million, of which £1,573,000 was offset by grants. The balance was funded by the sale of Stephen McAnespie to Bolton Wanderers for £900,000, and the broadcasting fee received from Germany for the Bayern Munich UEFA Cup tie at Easter Road.

The new stands were officially opened at the League match against Hearts on 12th October 1996, with Tom Wharton and Bert Sturgeon of the Football Trust and Dr Lewis Moonie and Jim Farry in attendance. The highest attendance at the reconstructed ground was 9,745, in the penultimate home match in the Premier Division, against Rangers on 15th April 1997.

The roof of the Main Stand, which was becoming increasingly porous, began to receive some attention in April and May 1998, and on 11th June it was admitted that more

drastic action was required. No season tickets were sold for the stand, which was out of bounds for spectators for long parts of the following season.

On 21st September 1999 a £200,000 upgrade of the main stand was announced, including the installation of individual plastic seats, replacing the raised wooden bench seating in B and C stands. On 10th March 2000, during high winds, a floodlight gantry slipped at an angle and the pylon had to be removed, necessitating the closure of Pratt Street and evacuation of local householders. Fife Council temporarily suspended the safety certificate, and the match against Airdrie on 25th March kicked off at 2pm.

The new part of the Railway Stand was last used on 10th May 1997, the final Premier Division match against Hibs (total attendance 6,274), and over the next couple of seasons, the seats gradually disappeared, until none was left. In an attempt to save stewarding costs, the older part of the Railway Stand was closed from 2000/1, and in the ensuing years has shown progressive signs of a lack of maintenance.

On 17th September 2003, it was revealed that, on 5th August 2003, the Board of Directors had sold Stark's Park to West City Developments Ltd., and leased it back from them at a rent of £72,000 per annum for the first five years, and £79,200 for the following five years.

The current capacity of the ground is given as 8,473 seats.

Appendix 3 - Legal & Financial

Raith Rovers was formed as a loose coalition of Linktown youths but once they joined the Kirkcaldy Junior Football Association in 1884, the cost of purchasing kit and footballs, and renting a pitch, had to be met by charging admission and levying subscriptions. It says much for the calibre of the individuals, and the quality of their elementary education, that teenagers could organise such matters, and over the next few years, Raith Rovers Football Club became a well-run members club. Annual subscriptions entitled members to free admission to home matches, being effectively season tickets. The unprecedented revenues earned from the Scottish Qualifying Cup success of the autumn of 1906 reinforced the belief that the way ahead for the growing, and ambitious, club was incorporation.

The potential for raising share capital, and the limited liability of the owners would enable the club to raise and borrow funds to improve the facilities at Stark's Park, and invest in the team to achieve their ambition of election to the First Division.

The old members club went out on a high note. At its final meeting (the 24th) members learned that the revenue for the year to 5th April 1907 was £2211 [2008 equivalent £1.06 million], a record for a provincial club. The visit of Hearts in the Scottish Cup alone earned the club £370 [£172,800]. There was a profit of £400 [£192,000], and the meeting agreed to sell the club's assets to the new Limited company.

Raith Rovers Football and Athletic Club Limited was incorporated on 15th May 1907, with a nominal share capital of £2000 [£960,000], made up of 8000 5/- (25p) shares, payable at 2/6d [£60] per share initially.

The prospectus, dated 20th May 1907, stated that "The Company will take over the assets and all engagements of the Raith Rovers' Club, as at 5th April 1907, under burden of the liabilities, which are practically nil.

"The assets consist of (1) the Club's interest in Stark's Park, Kirkcaldy – a fully equipped football enclosure, a lease of which has been obtained from Mr Munro Ferguson for a period of ten years, as from 15th May, 1907, (2) Covered Grand Stand, Pavilion, Offices and Payboxes erected in said park, (3) Claims on 38 signed on league players, (4) stock of football outfits and appurtenances, and (5) Cash in bank and in the hands of the Treasurer of the Club (£184 7/3d) [£90,000].

"The purchase price paid by the Company to the Trustees of the Club is the extremely low one of £260 [£124,800], payment of which amount is to be accepted in shares distributed amongst the present members of the club.

"Applications for shares should be …. lodged with any of the following : (1) the Company's Bankers [The Commercial Bank of Scotland, Limited, Kirkcaldy], (2) Mr A.G. Adamson, Chemist, West End, High Street, Kirkcaldy,. (3) Mr John Nicoll, Grocer, Links Street, Kirkcaldy ; (4) Mr Jas. W. Duncan, Printer, High Street, Kirkcaldy ; (5) Mr Alexander H. Forrester, Chemist, 142 St Clair Street, Kirkcaldy."

The club's solicitors were Messrs Beveridge & Aitken, Kirkcaldy, the auditor was W.D. Wallace, High Street, Kirkcaldy.

Most of the club's first directors had fairly brief periods of office. Andrew G. Adamson, Chemist, of 6 James Grove, was off the board by March 1912, and re-appeared for a few months during 1913/14, then returned for a long spell on the board in the early 1920s, during which time he was a regular linesman in Scotland's international matches.

James W. Duncan, Printer, 26 Lady Helen Street, stepped down within two years. James D. Gerrard, Grocer, of William Street and then Bridgeton, resigned within three years, as did Robert McCartney, Engineer, of 13, then 26, Whytehouse Mansions. John Nicoll, a Fruit Merchant and Grocer of 221 Links Street, then 4 Milton Road, was off the board by March

1912, while James W. Urwin, Brewer, Milton Road, did not last a year.

A Secretary/Manager was appointed for the first time, Peter Hodge of 4 Links Street.

The longest continuous servant of the original directors proved to be David Alexander Whyte, the former President of the old club, a Cashier, of 30 David Street, who died in office, on 11th November 1916.

There was no place on the board for Andrew Kirk Buist and Robert Donaldson, Treasurer and Secretary respectively of the old club, but they were among the 84 members who each received 12 full paid up, 5/- [£120] shares in the new company (Listed on opposite page)

The share allotment was far from a resounding success. Only 914 of the 6960 available shares were sold, realising just £228 10/- [£110,000].

The first annual general meeting of the club was held at Anthony's Temperance Hotel, West End, Kirkcaldy on 1st April 1908, at 8pm. Members learned that for the period from 5th April 1907 to 29th February 1908, the club had made a profit of £213 2/3d [£103,000]. The second AGM reported a loss of £384 2/2d [£185,000] : "The early dismissal of the team from the Scottish Cup Competitions, and the bad weather, have been the principal causes of this unlooked for result."

Annual meetings were held at a number of venues before falling numbers in attendance allowed them to be conducted in the Boardroom at Stark's Park. As well as Anthony's Hotel (which was not the later-named establishment in West Albert Road, but the Whyte House, between Whytescauseway and Whytehouse Avenue, which was finally demolished in 2008) meetings were held at Oswald's Wynd Hall and the YMCA (Swan Memorial Hall) in Kirk Wynd,

The year to 30th April 1913 (the financial year end had been changed the previous year) disclosed a profit of £920 [£441,000], which cleared all accumulated debt. The Directors Report stated : "The financial success attained for the past year has been mainly due to the team's achievements in the Scottish Cup ties. The honour of figuring in the final of the Scottish Cup is not an every day occurrence." Perhaps the understatement of the century ?

To pay for the new grandstand that was to be erected at Stark's Park, The Raith Rovers Grand Stand Company Limited was formed on 8th June 1922, with capital of 2000 Ordinary shares at £1 [£240], and 8000 £1 Preference shares paying a 6% dividend.. The dividend would be paid out of the profits of operating the stand, the premium charged for a seat less operating, repairing and financing costs.

The building rights were purchased from the Football Club for £2,000 [£480,000], the consideration being the entire Ordinary shares. The initial subscription sold 5679 shares, which had increased to £7092 [£1.7 million] by the end of 1928. Between then and the dissolution of the company in 1948, only 150 more shares were purchased – hardly surprising since the last dividend paid was in 1929, and a third of the 6% dividend at that.

The total cost of building and improving the stand was £11272 9/9d, plus £295 14/8 in preliminary costs, including the formation of the company [£2.8 million]. There was therefore a shortfall of £4326 [£1 million], which by 1947 was largely funded by an overdraft of £3552 [£600,000].

Major shareholders in the Grandstand company were : Barry Ostlere & Shepherd Ltd £500 [£120,000] ; James Bogie, Archibald Bryce, Alex Fraser, Alex Hutchison, R.C. Lockhart, Eliza Morgan and G.L. Aitken, each with £200 [£48,000].

The original directors were Andrew Grieve Adamson, Altmohr, Milton Road ; John Sidney Harris, Victoria Bar, High

ORIGINAL SHAREHOLDERS IN RAITH ROVERS FOOTBALL & ATHLETIC CLUB LIMITED, IN 1907

R. McCartney, Whytehouse Mansions
John Nicol, Grocer, Nicol Street
George Dow, 280 Links Street
John Inglis, 114 Commercial Street
Thomas Aitken, High Street
William Eckford, Nicol Street
John Cairns, Mid Street
Andrew Dewar, 6 Milton Road
William Grierson, 153 Links Street
Henry Heggie, 28 Ava Street
Andrew Macbain, 20 Bridgeton
John Warrender, 43 Aitken Street
William Kay, 25 Octavia Street
William Innes, 24 Rosabelle Street
John Speed, High Street, Dysart
John Miller, 17 Quality Street
George Brown, 37 Aitken Street
Henry Francis, 63 Sutherland Street
Robert Page, 198 St Clair Street
James Brown, 153 Links Street
Andrew McNaught, 17 Mill Street
D. Simpson, 2 West Albert Road
James Lawson, Maryhall Street
Andrew Bell, 93 Harcourt Road
J. Paul, 35 High Street
George Reekie, 61 Loughborough Road
Robert Duncan, 26b Rosslyn Street
William Keir, Dunnikier School
George Arnott, 236 St Clair Street
William Peggie, Links Street
David Kerr, 193 St Clair Street
John Campbell, Heggies Wynd
John Aitken, Normand Road, Dysart
Henry Napier, Forth Avenue
Thomas Grierson, Links Street
Robert Crombie, 81 Victoria Road
D. Thomson, Harcourt Road
Andrew Lambert, 204 Links Street
William Peggie jnr., 34 Roslyn Street
D. Barclay, Nether Street
D. Neilson, 2 Bell Wynd
William Ramsay, 22 Rose Street
John Cran, 31 Octavia Street
Thomas Blyth, Post Office, High Street
Andrew Hood, 43 Pratt Street
Robert Roberts, 80 Balfour Street
D. Innes, Kings Buildings
Alex Ramsay, 32 Cowan Street
John McIlrady, 18 Mill Street
James Alexander, 2 Gas Houses
R. Simpson, Bandon Avenue
Alex Arnot, 6 Nicol Street
James Dingwall, Braehead Cottages
William Wright, Rosslyn Street
Andrew Methven, 178 New Road

George Macbain, Viceroy Street
John Dickie, High Street
John Doig, 38 Harcourt Road
D. Eadie, 7 Pottery Street
A.K. Buist, Sang Road
D.A. Whyte, David Street
D. Urquhart, 56 Pratt Street
W. McAlonie, 11 Millie Street
Peter Weepers, 165 Park Road
W. Macbain, 200 Links Street
John Reid, 25 Victoria Road
A.R. Blewes, James Groves
D. McLaren, 5 Pratt Street
James Wyles, 86 Pratt Street
Robert Peebles, 9 Dunnikier Place
George Irvine, Quality Street, Dysart
A. Wyness, 37 Loughborough Road
A. Inglis, High Street
A. Forrester, Chemist, St Clair Street
A.G. Adamson, Chemist, 1 Links Street
James Walker, 229 Links Street
R. Donaldson, 6 Regent Place
Robert Williamson, 39 East Smeaton Street
Henry Baillie, Henrys Wynd
John Cuthill, Ann Place
D.A. Whyte, 30 David Street
Andrew Gibb, Confectioner, Kirkcaldy
A. Galloway, 4 Battery Place
Andrew Halliday, 11 Lina Street
James Arthur, 25 Kirk Wynd
R. Richards, 46 Maryhall Street
George Rae, 485 High Street
James Ramsay, 8 Nelson Street
George Suttie, Rose Street
David Small, 40 Nelson Street
Alex Scott, 5 Glebe Park
David Boak, 48 Harcourt Road
Thomas Barrie, Ramsay Road
James Gerrard, Bridgeton
David Napier, 15 Union Street
A. Cunningham, 59 Edward Street, Borland
William Slidder, Factory Road
James Elder, 29 Ava Street
David Fernie, 17 Glasswork Street
R. Kirkpatrick, 81 Pratt Street
Robert Brown, 52 Links Street
William Thomson, 9 Caises Square
James Peebles, 9 Dunnikier Road
William Wilson, West Smeaton Street
P. Galloway, 13 Oswalds Wynd
E. Anderson, 184 Links Street
John Nelson, 77 Links Street
G. Brown jnr., Aitken Streey
H. Lambert, 76 Balfour Street
Andrew Barrie, 1 Ann Place
John Crombie, Hill Street
Thomas Hunter, Loughborough Road
J. Chrystal, 39 Victoria Street, Borland

Street, Dysart ; David Hetherington, Solicitor, Torwood, 27 Beveridge Road ; George Kilpatrick, Commercial Traveller, 340 High Street ; Robert Jack Morrison, Public Works Contractor, 60 Dunnikier Road, William Chalmers Ritchie, Spirit Merchant, 54 Victoria Road, and Thomas Smith, Manager D. Hill Pipe Works Co. Ltd., Manuel Cottage, 121 Dunnikier Road

A Special General Meeting of the Football Club on 14th July 1924 amended the Memorandum of Association to permit greater borrowing, in view of the struggle the directors were experiencing in running a full time first team and a reserve team during a trade depression (and hence lower gates).

Shares in the Football and Athletic Club Ltd continued to be sold in a dribble, with some larger sales in successful seasons, £247 [£60,000] in 1919/20, £200 [£48,000] in 1927/28 and £50 [£12,000] in 1937/38. The total share capital issued at the end of the company's life in 1948 was £1201 15/-, around £800 short of the full authorised value.

On 16th March 1948, Bert Herdman, Company Secretary, wrote to the shareholders of both companies :

"For some time past the activities of both Raith Rovers Football Club and Raith Rovers Grand Stand Companies have been embarrassed by the existence of the two Companies as separate entities and this has seriously handicapped the efficiency of both concerns. The welfare of both Companies depends on the ability of the Football Club to field a successful team and this in turn depends to a large extent on suitable financial facilities being available. The constitutions of the two Companies preclude them from affording to each other the mutual help which is essential. The Directors of both Companies have therefore unanimously agreed to recommend that the two Companies should be amalgamated under a single new Company, which will take over the assets of both Company."

Shareholdings would be preserved in the new company, but shareholders in the Grand Stand Company would (in theory) receive only 4% interest in their new Preference shares, as opposed to 6% in the old company. "While therefore, these shareholders will require to write off the arrears of Preference dividend they will thus have a better security for their shares than they hold at present. Further, the directors consider that there is a better prospect of maintaining a Preference dividend of 4% than the old rate of 6% which could not be met."

At Extraordinary General Meetings on 8th April 1948, the members approved a motion to wind up both companies voluntarily, with Thomas Andrew Menzies, 154 High Street, Kirkcaldy, appointed liquidator. The catalyst for this significant tidying up exercise was the sale of Jackie Stewart to Birmingham City, for a sum of money - £8,000 [almost £1.3 million] - which cleared both companies' debts ; £3,740 in

ORIGINAL SHAREHOLDERS IN RAITH ROVERS FOOTBALL CLUB LIMITED IN 1948

Adamson, Andrew G, Altmohr, Milton Road – Chemist

Adie, David, 6 Pottery Street – Pottery worker

Aitken, Thomas, Aitken & Co, St Monance – Clerk

Airtken, John, Normand Road, Dysart – Clerk

Alexander, James, 2 Gas Houses – Labourer

Anderson, Edward, Andrew Street, Dysart – Restauranteur

Anderson, George S, 14 West Albert Road – Shipping Agent

Anthony, James, West Albert Road – Hotel Proprietor

Anthony, John, Anthony's Hotel – Gardener

Arthur, James, Kirk Wynd - Boilermaker

Burns, Thomas, 166 Institution Street – Linoleum worker

Barclay, David, Overton Road – Joiner

Barclay, James, Kingskettle – Spirit Merchant

Baird, David, High Street – Spirit Merchant

Barn, Michael, High Street – Saddler

Barr, Hugh B, 21 Sang Road – Law clerk

Barrie, Thomas, Ramsay Road – School teacher

Barrie, Andrew, 1 Ann Road – Labourer

Bell, Andrew, 24 Den Road – Cabinet maker

Bell, George, Sang Place – Mechanic

Beveridge, Alexander, 14 Seafield Road – Labourer

Binning, George, Nicol Street – Factory worker

Blair, Thomas S, 113 Balfour Street – Warehouseman

Blewes, David, Abbotshall Road – Painter

Blyth, Thomas, High Street – Newsagent

Boak, David, 126 Dunnikier Road – Lithographer

Bogie, James, Swan Road – Hatter

Brown, Charles, Loughborough Road – Doctor

Brown, James, Alison Street – Kilnman

Brown, Robert, Cowan Street – Labourer

Brinton, William, 88 Abbotshall Road, Glasgow – Yarn Dresser

Buchanan, John, High Street – Boat merchant

Buist, Andrew – Forth Temperance Street – Traveller

Buynan, James, 7 Balfour Street – Traveller

Calderwood, John, High Street or Bandon Avenue – Piano Tuner

Campbell, David, Victoria Gardens – Waste Merchant

Campbell, James L, David Street – Waste Merchant

Cargil, James, Dunnikier Road – Tobacconist

Chalmers, James, 26 Whins Road, Alloa – Gas Stoker

Chisholm David, North of Scotland Bank, Kirkcaldy – Accountant

Chrystal, James, 63 Frances Road, Borland – Miner

Clark, Francis, Ice Breezer, Dysart- Colliery Manager

Clark, John, Laurel Bank, Dysart – Colliery Manager

Clunie, George, 46 George Street, Edinburgh – C.A.

Cran, John, 276 Links Street – Joiner

Crombie, John, Redburn Wynd – Floorcloth worker

Crombie, Robert, 83 Victoria Road – Miner

Cunningham, Robert, 59 Edward Street, Borland – Miner

Currell, James, Seaview, Dysart – Doctor

Currie, Robert L, Meldrum Road – Dancing Master

Curror, Alex L, Nicol Street – Doctor

Deas, Alex, Rosebank, Victoria Road – Chauffeur

Deas, David, 5 Viewforth Terrace – Clark

Deuchars, Lawrence, 5 Novar Crescent – Wood carver

Diack, James L, 63 Dunnikier Road – Grocer

Dickie, John Law, Ayr – Watchmaker

Dingwall, James, Braehead Cottages – Lino worker

Doig, John, 38 Harcourt Road – Joiner

Donaldson, Robert, 30 Booth Street, Manchester – Block cutter

Douglas, Robert, Lochrie Bank – Aerated Water Manufacturer

Dow, Alex, Galafoot, Galashiels – Gas Manager

Dow, George, 83 Links Street – Traveller

Dow, William, Pottery Road – Traveller

Drennan, William, Townsend Place – Mantler

Drummond, William, Town hall Inverkeithing – Baker

Drysdale, Alex, 26 High Street, Dysart – Blacksmith

Dryburgh, Richard S, 333 High Street – Grocer

Duncan, James, East End Printing Work -Printer

Duncan, Robert, 26 Roslyn Street – Printer

Eckford, William, Hendry Wynd – Floorcloth worker

Ecklington, William, Alexander Street – Spirit Merchant

Elder, James, 29 Ann Street – Floorcloth worker

Ferguson Munro, R.C., Raith House

Fernie, David, 17 Glasswork Street – Labourer

Ferguson, William, 79 Nicol Street – Dairyman

Fisher, Harry, High Street, Cowdenbeath – Newsagent

Forrester, Alex, St Clair Street – Chemist

Forrester, Thomas, St Catherine Street, Cupar – Chemist

Foster, George, Ivy Lane, Dysart – Miner

Francis, Henry, 63 Sutherland Street – Baker

Fraser, Alex, Millie Street – Builder

Fyfe, David, 1 Nicol Street – Stationer

Fyfe, James, 1 Nicol Street – Picture Framer

Galloway, Allan, 4 Rattray Place – Baker

Galloway, Peter, 13 Oswald Wynd – Machineman

Gerrard, James, William Street – Grocer

Gibb, Andrew, High Street – Confectioner

Gourlay, James W.M., Milton Road – Schoolmaster

Greig, John N, High Street – Watchmaker

Grierson, Henry, St Marys Terrace – Carter, Labourer

Grierson, William, 153 Links Street - Carter

Griffiths, James, 6 Berwick Place – Miner

Halliday, Andrew, 11 Lina Street – Cabinetmaker

Heggie, Henry, 23 Ava Street – Clerk

Hetherington, David, Balwearie Road – Lawyer

Hood, Andrew, Masserene Road – Lino Worker

Hutchison, Thomas, Kinloch Street, Ladybank – Bottler

Hutchison, Thomas, Somerton Road – Bottler

Inglis, John, Commercial Street – Mechanic

Innes, David, Rosslyn Street – Blockcutter

Innes, William, 24 Rosabelle Street – Labourer

Irvine, George, Quality Street, Dysart – Factory worker

Irvine, William, Balyriggie, Dysart – Fish Merchant

Jameson, William, 36 Alexandra Street, Dysart – Plasterer

Kay, William, Rutland Hotel, Matlock Bath – Carver

Kaye, Thomas, Milton Road – Clerk

Keir, William, 133 Mid Street – Cabinet maker

Kerr, David, 193 St Clair Street – Tailor

Kilpatrick, Andrew, 81 Pratt Street – Tailor

Kilpatrick, George, 340 High Street – Traveller

Kincaid, James, West Fergus Place – Gas Manager

Kinninmonth, Douglas, Lathries Bank – Aerated Water Manufacturer

Lambert, Andrew, 95 Pratt Street – Linesman

Lambert, Henry, 9 East Smeaton Street – Linesman

Leckie, Robert, Co-op Society, Ldeith – Manager

Linton, Harry, 52 Pottery Street, Gallatown – Miner

Linton, Robert, 52 Pottery Street, Gallatown – Miner

Logan, James, 27 David Street – Confectioner

McBain, Andrew, 78 Strathkinnes Road – Labourer

McBain, William, Milton Road – Grocer

Martin, John T, Royal Bank of Canada, Montreal – Banker

May, George, Hill Street – Banker

Mayer, William, West Mills – Insurance Agent

Meldrum, James, Hunter Street – Electrician

Melville, A.K., Milton Road – Hatter

Methven, Andrew, 100 Roslyn Street – Cabinet Maker

Methven, William, Normand Road, Dysart – Mechanic

£
S
D

222

Millar, John, 1 Quality Street, Floorcloth worker
Mitchell, James, 20 Alexander Street – Labourer
Morgan, Andrew, 21 Balfour Street – Labourer
Morgan, Lindsay, Gow Crescent – Electrician
Monaghan, John, 41 Relief Street, Dysart – Miner
Moodie, Charles, 43 Harcourt Road – Lino worker
Morrison, Robert, Balwearie Road – Contractor
Munro, David, School Lane – Coachbuilder
McCrae, Thomas, 13 East Port, Dysart – Miner
McGlashin, Archibald, 169 Balsusney Road – Doctor
McGregor, Alexander, Links Street – Grain Merchant
McIntosh, Phinias, Park Road, London
McIlravie, John, 87 Pratt Street – Labourer
McLaren, David, Bell Wynd – Labourer
McNaught, Andrew, 17 Mill Street – Labourer
McKay, Thomas, Abbotshall Road – Manager
McKay, Andrew, Links Street – Spirit Merchant
McLeod, James, Normand Road, Dysart – Saddler
McMaster, Angus, 129 Dunnikier Road – Spirit Merchant
Napier, David, 248 St Clair Street – Labourer
Napier, Peter, Strathkinnes Road – Labourer
Nelson, Dougal, 128 St Clair Street – Lathsplatter
Nelson, James, Links Street – Fruiterer
Nicol, David, Towers, Dysart – Contractor
Nicol, John, Milton Road – Fruiterer
Norrie, Robert, Hunter Street – Saddler
Page, Robert, 150a Mid Street – Slater
Paton, David, 84 High Street – Warehouseman
Paul, James, 35 High Street – Mechanic
Paxton, Walter, 88 Alexander Street – Grocer
Peebles, Robert, 9 Dunnikier Road – Craneman
Peebles, James, 8 Dunnikier Road – Moulder
Peggie, Wiliam, 34 Roslyn Street – Factory Worker
Penman, Thomas, Bridgeton – Spirit Merchant
Philip, Henry, 59 Nicol Street – Tailor
Provan, William, The Hotel, Kirkliston – Hotel Keeper
Rae, George, 391 High Street – Lino worker
Raith Rovers Supporters Club
Ramsay, George, 6 Commercial Street – Spirit Merchant
Ramsay, James, 9 Nelson Street – Lino worker
Ramsay, William, 243 St Clair Street – Lino worker
Reekie, George, 61 Loughborough Road – Manager
Richards, Robert, 46 Maryhall Street – Lino Worker
Ritchie, William, Townsend Place – retired
Reid, John, 41 Hillside, Cowdenbeath – Clerk
Roberts, James, Station Hotel – Spirit Merchant
Roberts, Robert, 44 Forth Avenue – Engineer
Robertson, Richard, 335 High Street – Joiner
Ross, William, High Street, Dysart – Bricklayer
Rodgers, William, 41 Maria Street – Cabinet maker
Ritchie, Robert, 28 Lady Helen Street – Water Engineer
Sandilands, George, Merchiston, Fergus Place – Master of Works
Scott, Alexander, 50 Gt Junction Street, Leith – Boiler Maker
Scott, John, Milton Terrace – Contractor
Sim, James, 28 Patterson Street – Labourer
Simpson, David, 2 Albert Road – Joiner
Simpson, Murdoch, 19 High Street – Joiner
Simpson, Robert, 9 Bandon Avenue – Joiner's traveller
Simpson, William, 258 High Street – Joiner's traveller
Skinner, Dominic, Elgin Street – Postman
Skinner, Thomas, 65 Sutherland Street – Labourer
Slidder, William, Factory Road – Labourer
Small, David, 40 Nelson Street – Lino Worker
Smith, William, 5 Dalkeith Road, Edinburgh
Smith, William, 121 Dunnikier Road – Dyer

the Grandstand Company and £598 in the Football Club as at 15th May 1947.

The closing shareholding of the Grand Stand Company (2000 Ordinary at £1 ; £ 7242 Preference) was converted to £9192 (£1.5 million) in new company shares, with £50-worth not taken up.
£1201 15/- [£200,000] in Football and Athletic Club shares was converted into the same number of shares in the Football Club. It should be noted that there were no new funds subscribed, and the final £1,606 of shares were not sold until 1980 [£20,000].   The ground, buildings and furnishings at 15th May 1948 were capitalised at £10323 9/1d [£1.6 million].

There were eight directors of the new company, the six from the Grandstand Company, Robert Wilkie who was a director of the Football and Athletic Club, and a new director in Peter Napier. They were :
William Ferguson, Farmer, Bankhead, Raith, Kirkcaldy
Alexander Fraser, Builder, 22 Boglily Road, Kirkcaldy
George Sandilands, 5 West Fergus Place, Kirkcaldy
James William Main Gourlay, Headmaster, Inverie, Milton Road, Kirkcaldy
James Stein, 19 Abbotshall Road, Kirkcaldy
John Nicoll, Fruit Salesman, 38 Milton Road, Kirkcaldy
Robert Wilkie, Block Cutter, 52 Balsusney Road, Kirkcaldy
Peter Sharp Napier, Post Office Porter, 18 Massereene Road, Kirkcaldy
Secretary was Robert Rodger Herdman, 19 Maryhall Street, Kirkcaldy.

There is one notable, common characteristic of all the directors listed above : they all lived and conducted their business in Kirkcaldy.   In later years, the parochial constitution of football boardrooms was generally derided as the "Pork Butcher Syndrome", the choice of that particular trade inspired by Bob Lord, who presided over Burnley FC, and the Football League, for many years.

Apart from encouraging fellow local businessmen to support the club commercially, and just as importantly donate or discount their goods and services, there was a powerful motivational benefit arising from such local management.   The

Speed, John, High Street, Dysart – Builder
Stark, Robert, Links Street – Spirit Merchant
Stewart, John, 33 Abbotshall Road – Secretary
Sunter, Alexander, Elm Street, Dundee – Clerk
Suttie, George, Rose Street – Brush maker
Suttie, Mitchell, 51 Market Street
Spence, John C, Lomond View, Durham Square, Portobello – Traveller
Spence, William, Lomond View, Durham Square, Portobello – Cashier
Thomson, Alex, Harbourhead Hotel – Spirit Merchant
Thomson, David, Harcourt Road – Cabinet maker
Thomson, William, Casse Square – Labourer
Tod, James, Beveridge Road, Aerater Water Worker
Urquhart, David, 21 Horse Wynd – Tailor
Walker, George, High Street, Dysart – Spirit Merchant
Walker, James, 224 Links Street – Turner
Wallace, Robert K, 25 Countess Street, Saltcoats – Pawnshop Manager
Wallace, William D, 48 Loughborough Road – Accountant
Wallace, William T.D., Balwearie Road – Doctor
Warrender, John, 43 Aitken Street – Traveller
Wedderspoon, William, Park Road – Painter
Weeper, Peter, 128 Institution Street – Mechanic
Whyte, David, 30 David Street
Williamson, James, 81 Nicol Street – Lino Worker
Williamson, William, Royal Hotel, Dysart – Spirit Merchant
Wilkie, John, Hill Street, Dysart – Engineman
Wilson, John, 5 Terrace Street, Dysart – Engineman
Wilson, John, Mill Street, Dysart – Engineman
Wilson, William, 66 East Smeaton Street – Miner
Wight, William, Rosslyn Srreet – Draper

directors were constantly accountable for their husbandry of the club's affairs ; at work, at leisure, in the High Street on Saturday morning and in the Kirk on Sunday.   The team's failure made for an uncomfortable existence in the town for the directors, and fear of that potential criticism concentrated their minds and redoubled their efforts.

One of the first "outsiders" on the Raith Rovers board was an Edinburgh merchant banker, Iain Watt.   He suggested that the club increase its share capital by utilising a new scheme promoted by the government to encourage investment in young, growing companies.   Raith Rovers was neither, but it did qualify for the Business Expansion Scheme.   Provided the investors were existing shareholders, they could recover income tax from the government at their marginal rate of tax, which at the time could be as high as 60%.   In other words, £10,000 worth of shares would cost the investor £4,000, and the government £6,000.

In 1983/84, Rovers raised £38,000 [£350,000] by this method, increasing the share capital to £50,000, which was further increased by £30,000 [£240,000] three years later. This was heaven-sent money for Rovers, but it introduced a new dimension to the club's ownership ; holders of significant shareholdings who began to take a proprietorial, rather than pastoral, outlook.   The new blocks of shares were concentrated in only a few hands, and they could easily combine to force through, or block, major changes.   The consensus of a widespread number of small shareholders was replaced by an oligarchy whose actions and decisions could potentially be influenced by consideration for their own investment.

That was the background to two decades of boardroom turmoil at Stark's Park. When the club were at last promoted to the Premier Division in 1993, it was obvious that it was seriously undercapitalised.   Local builder Alex Penman had tried, and failed, on a number of occasions, to persuade the board to allow him to invest hundreds of thousands of pounds in the club, but there was personal antipathy, and the consequent dilution of their shareholdings would mean that some of the other directors would lose their joint control of the club.

This off-field battle was of annoyance or irrelevance to the majority of fans whose concern was what was happening on the pitch, but at least it was fought out in the open, with shareholders and the general public (via the local newspapers) kept informed of the full details.

When Penman returned to the boardroom for the third time, a final attempt was made to increase the share capital of the Football Club, but at a Special General Meeting in February 1994, the shareholdings of Watt, local businessman William Robertson and Lochgelly publican Bob Paxton combined to defeat the motion ; together, they had more than 25% of the shareholding, and the proposed amendment to the Articles of Association required a 75% majority.

It was explained to one supporter, sceptical of the chances of success against such implacable opposition, that to get to the other side of a mountain, one did not necessarily have to scale it ; it could be walked round.   It was noted by recently elected director and Company Secretary Charlie Cant, that the vote in favour of the resolution at the E.G.M. was very close to 50% of the entire shareholding.   The chosen strategy was to form a Holding Company, which, provided it could acquire more than half of the shares of the existing company, would then issue a greatly expanded share capital.

Interim Chairman Bill Shedden and his fellow directors spent the next two months tracking down, coaxing and cajoling shareholders holding slightly more than half of the shares to transfer them to the new company, in return receiving shares in that company.   The alternative was to allow the bank to appoint a Receiver.   In that connection, a Chartered Surveyor was asked to value Stark's Park, which he did on Friday February 26th 1994.   The following day, Rangers were at Stark's Park, and their two substitutes, Duncan Ferguson and Alexei

Mikhailichenko, had between them cost Rangers 20 times the value of the stadium they were visiting.

Raith Rovers F.C. Holdings Ltd., incorporated as Orangelily Ltd. a month earlier, with a share capital of £550,000 [£950,000], took control on 15th April 1994.   It's first A.G.M., on 15th June 1995, learned that 322215 £1 shares had been issued, £281375 [£482,000] in exchange for cash, and the balance to former shareholders (50.87%) of the Football Club. Alex Penman's Building company bought £250,000 [£430,000] of the new shares.   The beauty of this particular takeover was that every penny raised went to the club ; no money was spent on buying out existing shareholders.

That cash injection, and the transfer fee received from Aberdeen for Peter Hetherston (slightly more than £200,000), paid off the entire accumulated debt and allowed full time football to be sustained at Stark's Park.   Shortly afterwards, the League Cup was won, followed by promotion back to the Premier League, and the UEFA Cup run.   The events of 1994, on and off the field, changed the Club for ever, but there was an inevitable unintended consequence.

The club was now owned by one person, and that person could sell his shares to another person and that's what happened, twice, with disastrous consequences.   The last year of Alex Penman's ownership was marked by growing acrimony, and he sold his shares in July 1997 to Alan Kelly, whose photocopier supply company had sponsored the club in 1993/94.   Despite huge sums of money spent in signing and paying players (and coaches), Rovers failed to return to the Premier League in Kelly's two years of ownership, and in that time losses amounted to more than £1.6 million, a figure that a club of Rovers' size could never realistically hope to repay.

In July 1999, Kelly sold his shares to Danny Smith, who was acting on behalf of his brother-in-law, Glasgow property developer Alex Short.   They stated at the outset that they hoped to make money from running the club.   An account of the events of the next six years would alone fill a book of this size.

In the unfolding circus, Companies Acts requirements were regularly breached.   Corporate governance appeared to go out of the window ; annual meetings for five consecutive years were between three and nine months late, culminating in the accounts to 30th June 2006 being put before shareholders almost two years later.   From June 2002 onwards, the accounts have been unaudited.   In May 2008, shareholders received their first communication for two years, with proposals to legitimise the neglect of the previous decade by removing the requirement to publish accounts and hold annual meetings. Prior year adjustments and Extraordinary items for significant amounts appeared regularly in the accounts, which became increasingly abbreviated and of no use to shareholders in forming a view as to how their club was being administered.

The blame for this chaos was placed on the West-of-Scotland based owners, but they could not have done it on their own.   They were enthusiastically supported by longer-term followers of the Raith Rovers who should have known better.

On 5th August 2003, the club sold Stark's Park to West City Developments Ltd., and leased it back from them at a rent of £72,000 per annum for the first five years, rising to £79,200 for the following five years.   The reduction in debt for the consolidated Football Club and Holding Company, from the balance sheet at 30th June 2003, to that made up to 30th June 2004 (both unaudited), was £971,000.   At 30th June 2003, Bank borrowings had been £702,500, with an interest charge for the previous year of £52,800.

West City Developments Ltd was incorporated on 14th January 2002 with two shareholders, Colin McGowan, owner of a Paisley carpet firm, and Turnbull Hutton, a Fifer based in Edinburgh who was a former director of United Distillers.   The Directors report for the period to 31st January 2003 stated "The principal activity of the Company is of Builders and Property Developers. During the period the company purchased land in

Kirkcaldy which is the subject of planning application for house building," not, it must be stressed, Stark's Park !

The sale of Stark's Park was announced at the Annual General Meetings held on 17th September 2003 (convened nine months late). There was no mention of the transaction in the Directors' Report which accompanied the papers calling the meetings, nor in the accounts (which were the last to be audited). The following year's accounts showed that McGowan and Hutton had resigned as directors of both the Football Club and Holding Company on 29th July 2003, presumably to avoid a conflict of interest. Their resignations had not been publicly announced, although their names were quietly dropped from the list of Directors in the club programme after the issue dated 12th August.

Writing in the match programme on 27th September 2003, "Boardroom Insider" was effusive in his praise of the deal, which was "in the club's best long-term interests". There was "no hidden agenda" in the device of a third company, West City Developments. In the match programme of 29th November 2003, the deal was described as "a stroke of genius".

What it did provide was an exit strategy for the owners, who had been forced to lend significant sums of money in the gamble to get back into the Premier League. Sure enough, in late 2005, Colin McGowan was threatening to evict the club from Stark's Park as they couldn't pay the rent, contradicting the messages given out 27 months earlier (the Courier had been told on 17th September 2003 "There is no question of this club ever being thrown out of Stark' Park.")

Danny Smith resigned as Managing Director on 31st December 2003, following a row with the club's financial backers over their future investment plans. On 7th January 2004, his controlling interest in the Holding Company was transferred to Mario Caira, making him, on the face of things, the club's owner.

On 22nd January 2005, his shares were transferred to West City Developments Ltd., who thus became the owners of the enterprise. Caira, however, only had a 25% interest in that company. At the same time, Turnbull Hutton transferred his remaining 19950 shares in the Holding Company into West City Developments. Despite resigning as a director of both Football Club and Holding Company on 29th July 2003, and not being re-appointed until 30th June 2004, Hutton was named as Smith's successor as Chairman on 7th January 2004 !

In the Holding Company's accounts to 31st January 2004, additional assets of £725,035 were acquired, presumably Stark's Park. This was funded by an additional Bank Loan of £453,000, and additional investors' loans of £295,000. Mortgages with AIB Group (UK) Plc [Allied Irish Bank] were recorded in 2002 and 2003.

On 30th June 2004, Mario Caira and Alexander Short became directors, with equal shares to McGowan and Hutton. The Company had a turnover of £722,000 and after tax, made a profit for the year of £65,458. At 31/1/2005, the investors' loan had been reduced from £525,000 to £217,000, and bank borrowings were reduced from £594,166 to £411,179

The company made net profits of £7500 and £2700 for the next two years, with its balance sheet little changed over that period, as far as can be discerned from abbreviated accounts. On 13th September 2007 the company's name was changed to Stark's Park Properties Ltd.

In that timeframe, McGowan and Short relinquished their shareholding (resigning as directors on 30/12/05), and the shares of Hutton and Caira both reduced to 11%. 27% were taken by New Raith Rovers Limited, and 51% by NRR Investments Ltd.

Both of these companies had been formed in late 2005 as a vehicle to buy out Alex Short and his fellow creditors. The club's future was cast in doubt via some lurid reports in the press, fronted by McGowan on behalf of the owners and "investors" who were desperate to get their money out, and those who were keen to remain in office, or assume office, once they had gone.

The Fife Free Press in particular campaigned for supporters to raise funds to buy out the ultimate owners, and many fans worked long and hard, and donated their own hard-earned money, towards that end, raising approximately £100,000.

At one point, it appeared that the principal replacement investor would be former Chairman Alex Penman, but he withdrew at the eleventh hour, confiding that he was uneasy at the bulk of his cash injection going into the pockets those responsible for some of the debt in the first place.

NRR Investments Ltd has as its registered office the Edinburgh address of Duncan Young & Co. Ltd., who are the Company Secretaries. It has one director, John Geddes Sim of Bangkok. A previous director was David Sinton, from 30th November 2005 to 22nd November 2006, when he resigned, at the same time stepping down as Chairman of the Football Club. New Raith Rovers Limited was formed in November 2005 with an authorised share capital of £1 million. Between 11th November 2005 and 3th January 2006, £705,001 shares were issued, as follows :

David B Sinton £5001
Raith Rovers Independent Supporters' Society £100,000
James Goudie QC of London, £5000
Turnbull Hutton, Edinburgh £175000
Mario Caira, Kirkcaldy £175000
NRR Investments Ltd £180000
Val McDermid, Alnmouth, £5000
Ian Rankin, Edinburgh £5000
Lord Thomas Murray Elder, Glasgow £5000
Dr William Campbell, Edinburgh £5000
Nick Hornby, London £5000
Richard Park, London £5000
Rt Hon Gordon Brown MP £5000
Caroline Pike, London £5000
Tom Morgan, Perth £25000

In round terms, the money was spent as follows :

£421,500 to purchase 57 % of the shareholding of the Holding Company (£363,000), and the balance, approx £58500, to purchase 27% of the £217000 of "Investors Loans" shown in the balance sheet of Starks Park Properties (formerly West City Developments) at 31st January 2006
£14,000 in the bank
and
£269,500, being a loan of £349,500, presumably to the Football Club, net of £80,000 due for payment.

By consolidating the net liquid liabilities of the two companies at 30th June 2005, and the three companies (Football Club, Holding Company and New Raith Rovers) at 30th June 2006, there was a reduction of debt by £537,000. Approximately £200,000 of that was due to the net profit for the trading year. It would appear that some £300,000 of debt was repaid, presumably to the departing shareholders who had lent the enterprise working capital over the previous years

Sadly, those good people who put their hands in their pockets could point to little effective difference from their endeavours, apart from the departure of (presumably grateful) former owner(s). The consolidated debt at the end of June 2006 (restated in the following year's accounts) was about £250,000, and with Stark's Park owned by a separate company, albeit one with common shareholders, but in the effective control of majority shareholder John Sim's wholly owned company, there was no collateral to borrow against. In the year to 30th June 2007, the club made a further loss of £131,000, although on 20th October 2006, Penman Kirkcaldy Ltd subscribed to £100,000 of shares in New Raith Rovers Limited. Despite that, the club remains skint.

Season	07/08	08/09	09/10	10/11	11/12	12/13	13/14	14/15	15/16	16/17	17/18	18/19	19/20	20/21	21/22	22/23	23/24	24/25	25/26	26/27	27/28	28/29	29/30	31/32	32/33	33/34	34/35	35/36	36/37	37/38	38/39	39/40	40/41	41/42	42/43
Admission (£)	0.025	0.025	0.025	0.025	0.025	0.025	0.025	0.025	0.025	0.0292	0.0292	0.0338	0.05	0.05	0.05	0.05	0.05	0.05	0.05	0.05	0.05	0.05	0.05	0.05	0.05	0.05	0.05	0.05	0.05	0.05	0.05	0.05	0.05	0.0542	0.0542
Multiplier	480	480	480	480	480	480	480	480	480	411	411	355	240	240	240	240	240	240	240	240	240	240	240	240	240	240	240	240	240	240	240	240	240	221.5	221.5
Gate Drawings	0	0	0	1197	1486	1577	1687	931	634	617	258	0	2308	2499	2830	2177	2306	2400	1798	1071	1766	1550	970	1094	726	455	545	473	862	2183	2570	495	0	374	654
less share	0	0	0	-541	-689	-727	-796	-551	-301	-252	-49	0	-832	-1042	-1032	-839	-906	-912	-835	-426	-750	-654	-312	-453	-337	-256	-271	-239	-316	-691	-947	-237	0	-115	-193
Season Tickets	0	0	0	89	89	105	139	94	24	21	4	0	32	95	126	108	83	96	71	45	115	139	90	89	80	71	60	70	71	48	170	103	0	0	0
Away Matches	0	0	0	597	828	1162	926	635	465	392	44	0	749	843	1038	1087	868	960	772	339	719	622	272	290	308	289	247	223	296	640	763	339	0	42	88
Entertainment Tax	0	0	0	0	0	0	0	0	0	-110	-60	0	-540	-616	-660	-533	-579	-417	-309	-174	-303	-278	-160	-192	-148	-90	-107	-76	-136	-297	-400	-76	0	-82	-205
Transfer Fees	0	0	0	0	190	55	127	34	12	0	108	0	540	504	0	432	24	908	2070	701	0	354	1422	18	0	486	0	0	0	396	0	76	0	0	82
Donations	0	0	0	0	0	0	0	0	0	0	0	0	0	0	0	0	0	0	0	0	16	36	6	30	17	32	27	130	38	25	24	9	0	5	0
Football Authorities	0	0	0	0	0	0	0	0	0	0	152	0	0	0	0	0	0	0	0	0	0	0	0	0	0	0	0	0	0	0	0	0	0	80	90
Interest	0	0	0	1	3	13	11	0	0	0	0	0	0	0	0	0	0	0	0	0	0	0	0	0	0	0	0	0	0	0	0	0	0	0	0
Grandstand Company	0	0	0	0	0	0	0	0	0	0	0	0	0	0	0	78	245	0	299	5	68	-97	-17	65	45	35	45	53	82	0	0	0	0	0	0
Sundry Income	0	0	0	7	22	26	10	14	11	8	3	0	4	8	12	13	10	23	30	22	27	36	28	37	25	25	25	26	31	40	29	34	34	34	39
Wages etc	0	0	0	896	1520	1237	1373	1352	561	486	316	0	1490	1536	1760	1670	1545	1582	1499	1293	1625	1287	734	513	451	395	459	428	493	710	1393	302	4	137	219
Transfer Fees	0	0	0	173	185	171	298	54	120	15	0	0	293	0	14	304	2	86	1282	347	235	227	252	9	6	65	25	38	18	0	231	0	0	2	4
Interest (inc G'stand Co. Div's)	0	0	0	0	8	17	2	20	61	31	58	0	16	8	9	16	48	161	168	151	190	320	210	175	173	140	140	140	140	72	46	105	57	54	55
Sundry expenditure	0	0	0	259	329	344	332	274	249	213	107	0	337	465	662	685	502	699	593	448	409	433	371	312	300	282	289	248	267	347	559	363	55	159	235
Trading Profit net Depn	94	-184	61	21	-113	442	99	-542	-146	-69	-21	7	125	282	-129	-151	-48	420	304	-576	-1097	-528	721	-55	-195	211	-305	-151	10	1060	-212	318	-57	35	78
Fixed assets additions	0	104	0	208	109	75	125	0	16	1	5	131	86	235	0	0	0	2705	0	0	0	0	0	0	0	0	0	0	0	0	0	0	0	0	0
Grants received	0	0	0	0	0	0	0	0	0	0	0	0	0	0	0	0	0	0	0	0	0	0	0	0	0	0	0	0	0	0	0	0	0	0	0
Share capital increase	0	0	0	0	15	36	2	9	2	0	0	0	59	10	4	0	1363	0	1	0	387	0	36	0	0	0	0	0	0	12	0	0	0	0	0
Sundry Debtors	0	0	7	0	0	0	0	0	0	0	29	47	0	0	0	68	96	311	316	0	680	584	579	523	521	521	521	521	521	634	834	852	644	622	593
Bank	0	14	0	0	74	31	0	0	14	0	0	184	0	5	0	0	0	0	0	0	0	0	0	0	0	0	0	0	0	901	0	0	0	0	0
Sundry Creditors	0	102	27	168	459	0	69	551	780	708	775	738	26	178	108	529	624	475	516	0	639	549	544	585	669	602	682	662	651	721	893	922	685	626	590
Bank Overdraft	0	0	3	4	0	0	19	71	0	43	21	0	203	0	191	156	188	381	62	1079	2743	3040	2218	2491	2599	2336	2559	2730	1780	2491	1632	1594	1732	1604	1571
Mortgage	0	0	0	0	0	0	0	0	0	0	0	0	0	0	0	240	192	144	96	48	0	0	0	0	0	0	0	0	0	0	0	0	0	0	0
Net Liquid Assets (Liabilities)	0	-88	-24	-172	-384	31	-88	-622	-766	-751	-767	-507	-230	-173	-299	-858	-909	-690	-358	-1127	-2701	-3005	-2183	-2552	-2747	-2418	-2720	-2872	-1911	-1678	-1691	-1664	-1773	-1608	-1569

Season	43/44	44/45	45/46	46/47	47/48	48/49	49/50	50/51	51/52	52/53	53/54	54/55	55/56	56/57	57/58	58/59	59/60	60/61	61/62	62/63	63/64	64/65	65/66	66/67	67/68	68/69	69/70	70/71	71/72	72/73	73/74	74/75	75/76	76/77	77/78
Admission (£)	0.0625	0.0625	0.075	0.075	0.075	0.075	0.075	0.075	0.075	0.1	0.1	0.1	0.1	0.1	0.1	0.125	0.125	0.125	0.15	0.15	0.125	0.15	0.15	0.15	0.25	0.25	0.25	0.2	0.2	0.2	0.25	0.3	0.5	0.6	0.5
Multiplier	192	192	160	160	160	160	160	160	160	120	120	120	120	120	120	96	96	96	80	80	96	80	80	80	48	48	48	60	60	60	48	40	24	20	24
Gate Drawings	646	597	1148	1685	0	0	3752	3460	3071	2790	2561	2066	2617	2506	2660	1901	1896	1906	1187	980	338	271	551	681	1306	1367	1250	713	824	602	548	323	435	457	385
less share	-199	-170	-313	-664	0	0	-1733	-1631	-1441	-1160	-1086	-946	-1212	-1089	-1396	-1004	-1005	-1084	-681	-939	-328	-271	-385	-391	-729	-757	-748	-361	-390	-320	-279	-175	-217	-248	-166
Season Tickets	0	0	0	55	0	0	406	523	539	447	451	413	324	370	372	259	215	188	150	131	61	54	45	56	126	126	144	68	80	80	76	67	45	98	48
Away Matches	154	139	295	582	0	0	2313	2320	2905	1226	1384	1283	1984	1945	1569	1647	1426	1087	1178	1185	363	283	331	324	783	880	1226	529	274	306	318	177	178	267	144
Entertainment Tax	-187	-176	-419	-228	0	0	-280	-275	-268	-603	-583	-427	-508	-500	0	0	0	0	0	0	0	0	0	0	0	0	0	0	0	0	0	0	0	0	0
Transfer Fees	24	19	320	net	0	0	net	net	net	net	604	183	net	net	net	185	256	1692	675	196	330	386	630	net	1500	160	303	491	39	net	net	net	195	net	229
Donations	0	0	3	18	0	0	8	0	0	0	0	0	0	268	114	195	0	5	226	663	1008	650	558	487	291	369	987	1686	1781	1868	1393	1191	1230	1149	1251
Football Authorities	77	79	55	47	0	0	0	0	0	0	0	0	0	0	0	0	147	58	60	18	118	205	275	482	132	91	86	234	347	580	745	548	470	179	416
Interest	0	0	0	0	0	0	0	0	0	0	0	0	0	0	0	0	0	20	5	0	0	0	0	0	7	10	2	0	0	0	0	0	0	0	0
Grandstand Company	0	0	0	0	0	0	0	0	0	0	0	0	0	0	0	0	0	0	0	0	0	0	0	0	0	0	0	0	0	0	0	0	0	0	0
Sundry Income	36	28	39	16	0	0	15	8	27	23	51	31	33	51	107	64	98	60	92	87	68	57	51	37	55	82	56	54	74	74	59	32	38	30	52
Wages etc	225	274	476	746	0	0	2666	3314	3350	1999	2361	2200	2253	2605	2749	2457	2333	2975	2339	2367	1574	1253	1145	1595	2281	2420	2621	2009	1623	1563	1643	1455	1015	978	1377
Transfer Fees	17	8	102	51	0	0	797	264	350	182	0	net	248	33	7	net	net	net	net	net	net	net	net	403	0	net	net	net	net	90	45	159	net	182	net
Interest (inc G'stand Co. Div's)	45	43	32	26	0	0	0	0	0	0	1	0	0	0	0	0	0	0	0	0	0	0	0	17	4	1	7	43	47	77	76	95	66	10	23
Sundry expenditure	243	233	372	436	0	0	809	827	1030	559	529	549	619	873	750	595	639	744	483	515	517	407	413	419	484	614	782	1103	1315	1261	946	996	760	942	1038
Trading Profit net Depn	56	0	129	154	24	247	156	-43	56	-51	451	-190	75	0	-120	160	29	121	0	-629	-209	-86	442	-815	666	-764	-164	192	-9	150	105	-588	500	-203	-126
Fixed assets additions	0	0	0	0	0	0	0	0	237	6	169	223	0	0	0	0	385	693	0	0	1	0	6	0	10	42	65	72	99	0	155	260	0	0	138
Grants received	0	0	0	0	0	0	0	0	156	43	9	274	5	0	0	0	384	456	198	0	0	0	0	0	0	0	0	0	0	0	0	0	0	0	0
Share capital increase	0	0	2	2	0	0	0	0	0	0	0	0	0	0	0	0	0	0	0	0	0	0	0	0	0	0	0	0	0	0	0	0	0	0	0
Sundry Debtors	497	437	226	213	0	366	9	204	29	10	29	230	43	54	69	40	292	169	962	158	79	43	105	15	75	75	72	113	54	0	50	0	14	0	126
Bank	0	0	0	101	0	88	477	553	239	217	427	231	334	401	305	477	198	965	2	86	3	2	247	0	723	15	7	9	6	0	6	0	22	0	8
Sundry Creditors	485	468	276	241	0	19	543	528	108	125	211	278	227	196	256	353	302	626	225	389	130	32	137	309	408	365	328	250	168	131	178	175	175	206	245
Bank Overdraft	1322	1300	756	568	0	233	0	0	0	0	0	0	0	0	0	0	0	367	304	0	258	291	0	208	0	189	428	521	560	431	262	985	0	117	411
Mortgage	0	0	0	0	0	0	0	0	0	0	0	0	0	0	0	0	0	0	0	0	0	0	0	0	0	0	0	0	0	0	0	0	0	0	0
Net Liquid Assets (Liabilities)	-1309	-1331	-806	-495	0	203	-57	229	160	102	245	183	150	259	119	164	189	140	434	-145	-307	-279	216	-502	389	-463	-677	-649	-668	-562	-383	-1160	-139	-323	-521

Season	78/79	79/80	80/81	81/82	82/83	83/84	84/85	85/86	86/87	87/88	88/89	89/90	90/91	91/92	92/93	93/94	94/95	95/96	96/97	97/98	98/99	99/00	00/01	01/02	02/03	03/04	04/05	05/06	06/07
Admission (£)	0.8	1	1.3	1.3	1.3	1.3	1	1.2	1.5	2	2.5	3	3.5	4	5	7	6	8	10	10	12	11	12	12	10	12	12	12	12
Multiplier	15	12	9.23	9.23	9.23	9.23	12	10	8	6	4.8	4	3.43	3	2.4	1.7145	2	1.5	1.2	1.2	1	1.091	1	1	1.2	1	1	1	1
Gate Drawings	541	556	678	347	248	196	402	165	421	593	569	299	434	422	508	709	1193	803	728	294	313	430	389	293	245	314	0	0	0
less share	-254	-235	-277	-53	-17	-21	-115	-3	-88	-89	-85	-25	-11	-59	-3	-17	-61	-53	0	0	0	0	0	0	0	0	0	0	0
Season Tickets	74	69	56	85	34	26	21	31	31	52	65	61	63	77	46	256	132	328	204	118	84	0	0	0	0	0	0	0	0
Away Matches	200	281	235	124	43	50	78	27	55	194	234	36	187	126	53	59	65	418	52	150	8	0	0	0	0	0	0	0	0
Entertainment Tax	0	0	0	0	0	0	0	0	0	0	0	0	0	0	0	0	0	0	0	0	0	0	0	0	0	0	0	0	0
Transfer Fees	net	net	net	194	584	191	53	140	620	131	498	193	386	542	188	471	425	1841	1200	392	235	151	214	120	150	45	0	0	0
Donations	1133	760	691	567	206	458	281	358	156	222	236	192	142	120	83	124	235	40	16	28	132	96	0	0	0	104	0	275	0
Football Authorities	165	243	270	199	206	223	387	305	371	288	261	412	324	352	167	130	297	885	312	146	206	121	132	129	104	0	0	0	0
Interest	0	0	0	0	0	0	0	0	0	0	0	0	0	0	0	0	0	0	0	0	1	0	0	0	0	0	0	0	0
Grandstand Company	0	0	0	4	0	0	0	0	0	0	0	0	0	0	0	0	4	40	5	0	0	0	0	1	5	0	0	0	0
Sundry Income	27	29	24	13	65	93	104	123	86	149	166	187	156	136	105	273	493	438	170	126	236	273	173	121	201	266	335	0	0
Wages etc	843	934	869	826	803	606	715	643	760	802	731	671	749	1300	1401	1256	1945	1945	1227	1609	1052	856	543	531	471	349	0	0	0
Transfer Fees	267	253	net	360	0	67	143	81	305	356	357	633	373	329	49	302	255	803	432	343	0	0	0	0	18	357	0	0	0
Interest (inc G'stand Co. Div's)	41	49	22	22	34	96	85	93	58	35	35	40	29	46	44	40	26	46	19	19	61	54	49	61	5	1	1	0	0
Sundry expenditure	733	666	571	622	544	477	596	338	325	394	366	303	310	229	275	342	513	714	462	493	550	365	213	272	262	528	0	0	0
Trading Profit net Depn	-71	-217	751	-453	-351	-102	-416	-88	133	-127	386	-351	126	-227	-651	-2	-25	1233	497	-1291	-562	-124	92	-213	-85	39	-313	90	-131
Fixed assets additions	0	0	271	1649	16	0	4	217	396	406	53	141	22	115	82	495	27	1061	2019	37	33	0	0	0	2	5	0	0	4
Grants received	0	0	0	0	26	7	0	160	291	169	0	84	22	86	40	260	0	0	1573	0	0	0	0	0	0	72	0	0	0
Share capital increase	0	19	0	0	0	351	0	0	240	0	0	0	0	0	0	0	644	21	1	3	32	59	68	19	38	0	0	0	0
Sundry Debtors	105	53	422	75	38	95	117	89	331	36	278	45	33	130	52	50	61	393	492	82	108	510	536	94	94	84	152	157	175
Bank	5	2	8	0	0	2	1	0	0	0	0	0	0	0	0	0	592	1067	315	373	303	2	6	8	10	6	7	18	15
Sundry Creditors	91	74	179	241	281	153	433	554	221	187	185	107	92	132	648	194	246	728	396	326	870	1545	1287	1305	927	554	863	616	863
Bank Overdraft	469	375	42	594	731	568	565	333	407	352	94	301	89	346	347	699	830	782	361	1297	1011	738	704	889	944	0	0	0	0
Mortgage	0	0	0	0	0	0	0	0	0	0	0	0	0	0	0	0	0	0	0	0	0	0	0	0	0	0	0	0	0
Net Liquid Assets (Liabilities)	-450	-394	209	-759	-974	-624	-879	-798	-297	-503	-363	-149	126	-348	-943	-842	-422	-49	50	-1167	-1470	-1771	-1465	-1650	-1767	-464	-704	-441	-673

This, and the previous page contain extracts from the annual accounts published by the Football Club between 1908 and 2007. The information on these reports has been distilled to provide summary totals of key elements of the club's finances ; categories of income and expenditure, and balance sheet items to indicate capital expenditure (mostly on the ground and its structures), and liquid assets and debts, to provide a picture of the club's pressing indebtedness (or, rather less frequently) the extent of its surplus funds.

This exercise has been undertaken to provide comparisons across succeeding periods of the club's history. To make this meaningful, the published figures have been translated into 2008 values. This has been done by taking the ground admission charge for each season (eg 6d, or £0.025 in 1907/09) and applying a multiplier to bring each contemporary admission up to £12. In other words, there are 480 (old) sixpences in £12, so the figures in the 1907/08 accounts have been multiplied by 480, while those in 2006/7 have been multiplied by 1.

Regrettably, the information is not complete. The first two sets of accounts published by the club following incorporation, in 1908 and 1909, contained few details. In 1947/8, final accounts were the responsibility of the liquidator of the two companies, and were not published. The first set of accounts of Raith Rovers Football Club Limited, in 1949, did not provide details. Those last two omissions are particularly regretted, as they were seasons of huge income for the club.

Some details have been routinely omitted from 1996 onwards, and many more from 1999. Latterly, published figures have been unaudited.

From 1924 until 1947, the figures are an amalgamation of two companies, the Football Club and the Grandstand Company. From 1994 to date, they are an amalgamation of another two companies, the Football Club and the Holding Company, with the addition in 2006 and 2007 of a third company, the former West City Developments.

Gate drawings are shown gross until 1957, therefore including Entertainment Tax, which is then shown as a deduction from income. From 1973, all figures do not include VAT.

Until 1981, League gates were shared with visiting clubs (subject to a guaranteed amount being paid). This allows comparison of the totals paid to visiting clubs, and the sum received by Raith Rovers from visiting other grounds. In every case these totals include cup ties, exclusively so from 1982 onwards.

For a number of years, transfers were reported in net terms. That word appears in either expenditure or income, showing that the opposite was the net effect that season.

Donations is largely income from supposed third party fundraising activities (Stark's Park Development Association, lotteries, bingo tickets etc.).

Grants received, shown beneath fixed asset expenditure, include specific donations (from the Development Association, Supporters Club etc.) to meet capital projects, and later the Football Grounds Improvement Trust.

For those with no interest in the club's fluctuating financial fortunes, the exercise at least provides a multiplier, which allows transfer fees (for instance) to be compared in current terms on an equal basis with modern-day sums of money.

Appendix 4 - Internationals

REPRESENTATIVE MATCHES AT STARK'S PARK

1930/31 Scottish Juvenile Cup Final, Blairhall 2 Thornton Hibs 1, Saturday 13th June 1931

1937/38 Schools International, Scotland under 14s 7 Ireland 0, Saturday 30th April 1938, attendance 9471

1937/38 Juvenile International, Scotland 5 Ireland 0, Saturday 7th May 1938

1950/51 Schools International, Scotland Under 15s 1 Wales 1, Saturday 21st April 1951, attendance 8000. David Sneddon (Ayrshire) played

1952/53 Police International, Belgium v Switzerland, Thursday 4th August 1952

1958/59 Amateur Youth International, Scotland v Wales, Saturday 18th April 1959.   Alex Ferguson (Queen's Park) played. Gate takings were £229 17/-

1958/59 Scottish Amateur (Under 16s) Cup Final, Drumchapel Amateurs 1 Smeaton Boys Club 0, Saturday 16th May 1959

1959/60 Scottish Junior Cup semi final, St Andrews United v Thornton Hibs 16th April 1960, and replay on 23rd April 1960

1966/67 Police International : April

1968/69 Schools International, Scotland Under 15s 3 Wales 1, Saturday 17th May 1969

1969/70 Youth International, Belgium 2 Turkey 0, part of the UEFA Youth Tournament held in Scotland, Wednesday May 20th 1970, attendance 500

1974/75 Police International : Scotland 0 England 1, Monday April 7th

1974/75 Schools International, Scotland Under 18s 1 England 1, 10th May 1975

1977/78 Schools International (Under 18s, celebrating 75th anniversary of Scottish Schools FA). Scotland 2 England 1, Saturday 13th May 1978, attendance 6000

1981/82 Schools International (Under 15s), Scotland 3, England 0, 24th April 1982, attendance 6000

1986/87 Womens International, Scotland 1 England 3, Sunday 12th October 1986, attendance 300

1986/87 Schools International, Scotland 9 Faroe Islands 0, Friday April 17th 1987. Rovers only S signing, David Sword of Leven Royals, played

1986/87 Four Nations Tournament, Scotland 1 Netherlands 0, Monday May 18th 1987
Four Nations Tournament, England 4 Netherlands 0, Wednesday May 20th 1987
Four Nations Tournament, Italy (winners) 0 Netherland 0, Friday May 22nd 1987

1987/88 Schools International ; Scotland Under 16s 1 Netherlands 1

1987/88 Scottish Womens FA Cup Final, Inveralmond Thistle v Whitehill Ladies, Sunday 1st May 1988

1988/89 Schools International : Scotland Under 15s 2 Netherlands 2, Saturday 8th April 1989

1988/89 Womens International, Scotland v England, Sunday 30th April 1989

1990/91 Schools International, Scotland Under 18s v Ireland on 5th March 1991

1991/92 Schools International, Scotland Under 15s 2 France 2, 8th May 1992

1997/98 Under 21 International, Scotland 1 Finland 1, 21st April 1998. Kick off 2pm, attendance 1113

1999/00 Youth International, Lithuania v Bosnia Herzegovina, Thursday September 16th 1999

2000/01 Schools international, Scotland Under 15s 0 Northern Ireland 0, Thursday 9th November 2000

2003/04 Scottish Junior Cup semi final, Tayport 1 Glenrothes 0, Friday 30th April 2004, attendance 3080

2007/08 Under 17 International, Scotland 0 Slovakia 4, Wednesday 19th September 2007, attendance 586

2007/08 Under 17 International, Slovakia 5 (section winners) Leichtenstein 0, Monday 24th September 2007

RAITH ROVERS PLAYERS WHO HAVE WON REPRESENTATIVE HONOURS

On pages 230 and 231 is a list of all the players who have been chosen for their country while playing for Raith Rovers. Five players have played for the full Scotland team, but the club's most capped player, and the next highest cap-winner, are from Trinidad & Tobago.   Both Marvin Andrews and Tony Rougier played for their country on many more occasions than either Dave Morris or Willie McNaught did for Scotland, but the question of which played most times, and how many, is extremely difficult to answer.

The lack of certainty is due to the poor record keeping by football statisticians in the Caribbean, and the huge number of games played by countries in that area, many of them friendlies and regional cup competitions.   Close examination of the record books does identify which of the two players was capped most often whilst at Stark's Park, but a precise figure is impossible to establish.

Tony Rougier signed for Raith Rovers from United Pretrotrin, on 13th March 1995, and was a highly effective winger for Rovers until Hibs signed him on 17th July 1997. In his 28 months at Stark's Park, Trinidad & Tobago played 42 international matches.   Rougier definitely played in eight of these games, and probably in one other.   He scored at least one goal (in an 8-0 win over the Dominican Republic in a World Cup qualifying match in June 1996) and in one match, against the USA on 25th November 1996, he was replaced at half time by Marvin Andrews, then playing for San Juan Jabloteh.

It is possible that Rougier could have played in 10 more matches, as the Trinidad & Tobago teams in the Caribana Cup (August 1995), Copa Caribbean (May and June 1996) and a friendly against Jamaica (May 1997) have not been recorded.   Due to the timing of his appearances with Raith Rovers, it is unlikely that he played in the other 23 matches.   The best conclusion that may be drawn is that Tony Rougier was capped at least 8 times, up to a maximum of 19, whilst a Raith Rovers player.

Marvin Andrews was signed from Carib FC on 11th February 1998, and played centre half for Rovers until he, Alex Burns and Stevie Tosh together were sold for £22,500 to Livingston on 5th October 2000.   In his 32 months at Stark's Park, Trinidad & Tobago played 40 international matches. Andrews definitely played in 22 of them, which exceeds the maximum figure achievable by Rougier (19).   It can be stated, with little fear of contradiction, that Marvin Andrews is the club's most capped player. But how many ?

He may have played in 8 more Friendly and Copa Caribbean (June and July 1999) matches, and either did not play, or is unlikely to have played, in the remaining ten matches. Marvin therefore won at least 22 caps whilst a Raith Rovers player, with the possibility of eight more, making a maximum of 30.

AMONG THE ONES THAT GOT AWAY ......

Only five players have represented Scotland while registered as Raith Rovers players. Many more former internationalists played for the club as their careers drew to a close ; quite a number made their senior debuts for Rovers, and went on to win many caps for subsequent clubs.

In that latter category are such luminaries as Jim Baxter and Alex James, and in recent years Colin Cameron. Most of the other future internationalists won only a handful of caps, but there is one player who was a very prominent Scottish Internationalist in the early years of the 20th Century, but who is seldom remembered today. John Walker is Rovers' Forgotten Internationalist.

Born in the Ayrshire town of Beith on 8th October 1882, John Walker first played football for Eastern Burnside, and then turned Junior with Cambuslang Rangers. He enjoyed a spell with Burnbank Athletic, the Hamilton junior club, but it was from Maryhill Juniors that he joined Raith Rovers on 11th November 1903. He started his Junior football career as an outside left, but converted to left back after first playing in that position in a lunchtime match while working in a factory.

He made his debut three days later at Hamilton, in a Second Division match which Raith won 4-1. He did not play the following week, at home to Leith Athletic, but returned to the first team, at left back, for the next nine matches, the last of which was a 3-1 defeat at Arthurlie in a Second Division fixture on 9th January. He was absent from the first team until mid March, when he returned for the end-of-season local cup ties and friendlies in which he played firstly at right back, then reverted to left back.

In these matches, he won winners medals in the Wemyss Cup and Central Counties Championship. In total that season, he played 7 League matches, 5 games in the Fife League, 4 Friendly appearances, three times in the Wemyss Cup and once in the Central Counties Championship Final.

Writing in a Raith Rovers match programme in 1949, a club official recalled "This fair haired, majestic lithe lad played his first match early in season 1903-04 at Douglas Park, Hamilton. He was born to the berth. Resolute, fearless, an expert tackler with a powerful punt, he was the ideal defender, with deference to Bill Inglis and other high-grade backs, Walker must be classified as the best full back Raith ever signed from juniordom."

His appearances for Rovers were curtailed by a leg injury, and it is said that he consulted the Celtic trainer for a second opinion. Rovers were not amused by this, and in the ensuing fall out, Walker vowed never to play for the club again. He walked out and in 1904/05 season played for his home town club Beith, a non league side.

In 1905/06, he signed for Rangers, making his debut at right back in a Benefit match at Dundee on 30th August. He made his League debut at left back in a 4-1 win at Port Glasgow Athletic on 7th October, and missed only four matches until early January, playing in both full back positions. He was absent from the first team from 13th January until 24th March, when he returned for the last two League games of the season, both at outside left. His final game for Rangers was on May 1st, in a 3-0 win at Queen's Park in a Glasgow League fixture.

He signed for Cowdenbeath for the 1906/07 season, returning to Stark's Park for a Qualifying Cup tie on 20th October 1906. Strangely, for an out-and-out defender who did not score a goal for any of his other clubs in a long and distinguished career, he

was fielded at centre forward and opened the scoring for "The Miners". Rovers won 2-1, and indeed went on to win the prestigious trophy.

On 2nd September 1907 "Jock" Walker was transferred to Swindon Town, then a Southern League team. It was there that he blossomed as a player, gaining the reputation of being the Southern League's finest full back. He was "capped" four times by that League, and in 1911 he was part of the Swindon team which won the Southern League Championship. In his spell at the club, they were runners up in the League three times, and finished 4th and 5th in the other two seasons. They reached the semi finals of the FA Cup in 1910, losing to Newcastle United and 1912, losing 1-0 to Barnsley in a replay.

On reporter wrote that he was "Consistent with clean clearances, and quick thinking in resuming his position and intercepting passes.". Another said that he was "A dashing and powerful tackler ; has nothing to learn as to how to stop a man." He stayed with Swindon until September 1913, when he was transferred, for the then-considerable sum of £1,100, to Middlesbrough, after 214 Southern League appearances and a further 34 first class cup ties.

It was at Swindon that he won the commendable total of 9 Scotland caps - at a time when only three Internationals were played each season. On 6th March 1911, he made his Scotland debut at Ninian Park, Cardiff, in a 2-2 draw. Among his team-mates were goalkeeper Jimmy Brownlie (Third Lanark), Peter McWilliam (Newcastle), Alex Bennett (Rangers) and Jimmy McMenemy (Celtic).

He played in the 2-0 victory over Ireland at Celtic Park on 18th March 1911, and in the 1-1 draw with England at Goodison Park on 1st April. The following March, he retained his position when the Home International championships resumed with a 1-0 win over Wales at Tynecastle, although his full back partner changed from Donald Coleman (Aberdeen) to Alex McNair (Celtic). He played in the 4-1 win in Belfast a fortnight later, and on 23rd March played in the 1-1 draw with England at Hampden, watched by 127,307.

The last three caps in his nine consecutive appearances came with three different partners ; Bobby Orrock of Falkirk in the 0-0 draw with Wales at Wrexham on 3rd March 1913 ; Donald Coleman in the 2-1 win over Ireland in Dublin on 15th March, and Alex McNair in the 1-0 defeat by England at Stamford Bridge on 5th April 1913. By then, he had played his last game for Swindon Town. He was 5 ft 8 inches tall, and his weight at the peak of his career was 12 stones.

The Middlesbrough history book recalls that "he was initially played at right back on his arrival from Swindon, but switched to the left as a highest ever league placing of third was achieved in his first season at Ayresome Park (in which he played 37 League matches and 1 Cup tie). He was unfortunate to have the war interrupt his career and lost his place to the emerging Walter Holmes when peace returned." In his second season with Middlesbrough, 1914/15, he played 33 League games and 1 Cup tie, and in 1919/20 he played 34 League games and 1 Cup tie. In his last season at Ayresome Park, he played just two League games.

During the war years, he returned to Swindon as a guest player, but when he left Middlesbrough it was to sign for Reading, in May 1921. He played a total of 58 League games for Reading, and 2 FA Cup ties, over two seasons, although there was some criticism when he was re-signed for the second season, as he was approaching 40 years of age. However, he was made captain and his experience and positional play made up for his ageing legs.

His last League game was against Queens Park Rangers in March 1923, when he was 40 years and 5 months old, making him Reading's oldest League player. He was never happy playing against his beloved Swindon Town, and it was reported that he requested to play for the reserves rather than play against their first team at the County Ground.

Once he finished playing, he ran a fish shop near Swindon Town's ground, and he died in the Wiltshire town on 16th December 1968.

HARRY ANDERSON
Rovers' first internationalist

Season	Honour	Details
1911/12	Full trial	Duncan Ritchie played outside right (and scored) for the Home Scots against the Anglo Scots in the International Trial at Firhill on 11th March 1912
1913/14	Full cap	Harry Anderson played left half for Scotland in a 0-0 draw with Wales at Celtic Park on 28th February 1914
1915/16	Military Cap	James Logan played right half for Scotland in a 4-3 defeat to England at Goodison Park on 13th May 1916 in aid of the Lord Mayor of Liverpool's War Scroll Fund
1921/22	Full cap	Bill Collier played left half for Scotland in a 2-1 defeat against Wales at Wrexham on 4th February 1922
1921/22	League Reserve	Bill Inglis named as reserve (to Scott of Falkirk) for Scottish League v English League match at Ibrox on 18th March 1922
1921/22	Full trial	Bill Inglis played right back for the Home Scots against the Anglo Scots in the International Trial at Catkhin Park on 22nd March 1922
1921/22	Full trial	Bill Collier played left half for the Home Scots against the Anglo Scots in the International Trial at Cathkin Park on 22nd March 1922 (Sandy Archibald of Rangers was in the same side, and Willie Birrell of Middlesbrough played for the Anglo Scots)
1922/23	Full cap	David Morris played centre half for Scotland in a 1-0 win over Ireland in Belfast on 3rd March 1923
1922/23	Full trial	David Moyes played left back for East of Scotland against West of Scotland in the International Trial at Ibrox
1922/23	Full trial	David Morris played centre half for East of Scotland against West of Scotland in the International Trial at Ibrox
1922/23	Full trial	Tom Jennings played centre forward for East of Scotland against West of Scotland in the International Trial at Ibrox
1922/23	Full trial	Bill Collier played left half for the Home Scots against the Anglo Scots in the International Trial at Cathkin Park on 20th March 1923 (Sandy Archibald of Rangers was in the same side, and Willie Birrell of Middlesbrough played for the Anglo Scots)
1923/24	League cap	David Morris played centre half for the Scottish League in a 1-0 win over the Irish League in Belfast on 31st October 1923
1923/24	Full trial	David Morris played centre half for Scotland A in the International Trial at Catkhin Park on 1st April 1924
1923/24	Full cap	David Morris played centre half for Scotland in a 2-0 win over Ireland at Celtic Park on 1st March 1924, scoring the second goal in 88 minutes
1923/24	Full cap	David Morris played centre half for Scotland in a 1-1 draw with England at Wembley on 12th April 1924 - Scotland's first appearance at the one-year-old stadium
1924/25	Full cap	David Morris played centre half, and captain, for Scotland in 3-1 win over Wales at Tynecastle on 14th February 1925. Bob Bennie of Airdrie played at left half
1924/25	Full cap	David Morris played centre half, and captain, for Scotland in a 3-0 win over Ireland in Belfast on 28th February 1925. Bob Bennie of Airdrie played at left half
1924/25	Full trial	David Morris played centre half for Scotland A against Scotland B in the International Trial at Shawfield on 17th March 1925. John Duncan (Leicester City) was in the same team
1924/25	Full trial	Alex James played inside left for Scotland A against Scotland B in the International Trial at Shawfield on 17th March 1925.
1924/25	Full cap	David Morris played centre half, and captain, for Scotland in a 2-0 win over England at Hampden on 4th April 1925 ; Scotland thus winning the Home International championship under Morris's captaincy
1927/28	Full trial	There were three former Rovers players in the Anglo Scots side which played the Home Scots at Firhill in the International Trial on 13th March 1928 ; John Duncan (Leicester City), Tom Jennings (Leeds United) and Alex James (Preston North End)
1932/33	Amateur cap	John Parlane played left half for Scotland Amateurs in the 1-0 defeat to England at Dulwich on 25th March 1933
1932/33	Amateur cap	John Parlane played left half for Scotland Amateurs in the 1-0 win over Wales at Bangor on 8th April 1933
1939/40	Wartime cap	Ernie Till played right half for Scotland against an Empire Army team at Tynecastle on 24th April 1940
1950/51	League Reserve	Willie McNaught was reserve left back (to Sammy Cox of Rangers) for the Scottish League match against the Irish League in Belfast on 27th September 1950
1950/51	Full cap	Willie McNaught played left back for Scotland in the 3-1 win over Wales at Cardiff on 21st October 1950
1950/51	Full cap	Willie McNaught played left back for Scotland in the 6-1 win over Northern Ireland at Hampden on 1st November 1950
1950/51	League cap	Willie McNaught played left back for the Scottish League in the 1-0 victory over the English League at Ibrox on 29th November 1950
1950/51	Full cap	Willie McNaught played left back for Scotland in the 1-0 defeat by Austria at Hampden on 13th December 1950 - Scotland's first home defeat to a foreign country
1951/52	League Reserve	Andy Leigh was reserve left half (to Joe Baillie of Celtic) for the Scottish League v Irish League match at Ibrox on 26th September 1951
1951/52	League Reserve	Jimmy McEwan was reserve outside right (to Bobby Collins of Celtic) for the Scottish League v Irish League match at Ibrox on 26th September 1951
1951/52	League selection	Willie McNaught was selected at left back for the Scottish League against Football League at Hillsborough on 31st October 1951, but withdrew due to an inflamed tendon on his left foot. His placed was taken by Sammy Cox of Rangers
1951/52	B cap	Willie McNaught played at left back for Scotland against The Army at Newcastle on 3rd March 1952
1951/52	B cap	Andy Leigh played at left half for Scotland against The Army at Newcastle on 3rd March 1952
1951/52	League cap	Willie McNaught played left back for the Scottish League in the 2-0 win over League of Ireland in Dublin on 17th March 1952
1951/52	Full cap	Willie McNaught played left back for Scotland in the 2-1 defeat by England at Hampden on 5th April 1952
1951/52	Full reserve	Willie McNaught was in the Scotland travelling party for the May 1952 internationals in Denmark and Sweden, but Sammy Cox of Rangers played in both matches.
1952/53	League cap	Willie McNaught played left back, and was captain, for the Scottish League in the 5-1 win over Irish League at Belfast on 3rd September 1952
1952/53	League Reserve	Jimmy McEwan was reserve outside right (to Jacky Stewart of East Fife) for the Scottish League match against Irish League at Belfast on 3rd September 1952
1953/54	League cap	Willie McNaught played left back for the Scottish League in the 4-0 win over Irish League at Ibrox on 9th September 1953. Doug Cowie of Dundee was centre half
1953/54	League cap	Willie McNaught played left back for the Scottish League in the 3-1 win over League of Ireland in Dublin on 17th March 1954
1953/54	League Reserve	Andy Young was reserve right half (to Bobby Evans of Celtic) for the Scottish League against League of Ireland in Dublin on 17th March 1954
1954/55	Full cap	Willie McNaught played left back for Scotland in the 2-2 draw with Northern Ireland at Hampden on 3rd November 1954. Bobby Evans (Celtic) and Doug Cowie (Dundee) were the wing halves
1956/57	B cap	Bernie Kelly played inside right for Scotland B in the 4-1 defeat to England B at St Andrews, Birmingham on 7th February 1957
1956/57	League cap	Willie McNaught played centre half for the Scottish League in the 3-2 win over the Football League at Ibrox on 13th March 1957
1956/57	League Reserve	Bernie Kelly was reserve inside right (to Willie Fernie of Celtic) for the Scottish League v Football League match at Ibrox on 13th March 1957
1956/57	League Reserve	Ernie Copeland was reserve centre forward (to Willie Bauld of Hearts) for the Scottish League v Football League match at Ibrox on 13th March 1957.
1957/58	League cap	Bernie Kelly played, and scored, for the Scottish League in the 5-1 win over League of Ireland in Dublin on 18th September 1957.
1958/59	Under 23 cap	Jim Baxter played left half for Scotland Under 23s in their 1-0 defeat to Wales at Tynecastle on 10th December 1958.
1958/59	Full trial	Jimmy McEwan played outside right for the Scottish League against a Scotland XI in the International trial at Ibrox on 16th March 1959
1959/60	Full trial	Jim Baxter left half played for the Scottish League against a Scotland XI in an International trial at Ibrox on 1st February 1960
1969/70	Youth trial	Billy Mitchell scored for the Scottish Professional Youth team in a 2-1 defeat by Falkirk Reserves. Also playing was Jimmy Brown (then of Dunfermline Athletic)
1974/75	C trial	Malcolm Robertson selected for Second Division Select Trial at Falkirk on 9th December 1974, but he was under SFA suspension and was not allowed to play
1978/79	Youth cap	Tom Walker played for Scotland Youth in their 4-1 win over Yugoslavia in an International Youth Tournament in Italy.
1979/80	C cap	Chris Candlish played in all three games for Scotland semi professionals, against Holland, Italy and England, in a Four Nations Tournament in Holland in May and June 1980
1982/83	Youth cap	Paul Sweeney played for Scotland Under 18s in a 1-1 draw with Wales at Ibrox on 15th February 1983
1982/83	C cap	Colin Harris played for Scotland semi professionals in the Four Nations Tournament in England in May 1983, scoring in the 2-1 defeat by England
1983/84	C cap	Paul Smith played left half for Scotland semi professionals in the Four Nations Tournament in Italy in May 1984
1984/85	C cap	Paul Smith played for Scotland semi professionals in the Four Nations Tournament in Holland in May 1985
1986/87	Juvenile cap	Scott McGregor, a provisional signing, played for Scotland Juvenile Under 18s against Northern Ireland
1986/87	Juvenile cap	Gary Dackers, a provisional signing, played for Scotland Juvenile Under 18s against Northern Ireland
1986/87	C cap	Craig Robertson played for Scotland semi professionals in the Four Nations Tournament staged at Stark's Park and East End Park
1989/90	Youth squad	Robert Raeside in Scotland Under 18 squad v Sweden in September 1989
1990/91	Under 21 squad	Shaun Dennis selected in Scotland Under 21 squad v Rumania at Easter Road on 11th September 1990
1990/91	Under 21 squad	Shaun Dennis selected in Scotland Under 21 squad v Switzerland on 16th October 1990, but was withdrawn to play in the B&Q Cup tie against Hamilton Accies
1990/91	Under 21 cap	Shaun Dennis an unused substitute for Scotland Under 21s in Bulgaria on 13th November 1990
1990/91	Under 19 cap	Robert Raeside played for Scotland Under 19s in a friendly against Eire at McDiarmid Park on 18th March 1991, match abandoned due to flooding after an hour
1990/91	Under 21 squad	Shaun Dennis selected in Scotland Under 21 squad v Bulgaria at Kilmarnock on 26th March 1991
1991/92	Under 21 squad	Shaun Dennis selected in Scotland Under 21s v Switzerland in Bulle on 10th September 1991
1991/92	Under 21 squad	Robert Raeside in Scotland Under 21 squad v Denmark at Easter Road on 18th February 1992
1991/92	Under 21 squad	Shaun Dennis an unused substitute for Scotland Under 21s v Germany in Bochum on 10th March 1992

Season	Honour	Detail
1993/94	Under 21 squad	Jason Dair in Scotland Under 21 squad in Malta on 16th November 1993
1993/94	Under 21 squad	Stephen Crawford in Scotland Under 21 squad in Malta on 16th November 1993
1993/94	Under 21 cap	Stephen Crawford played the first 65 minutes for Scotland Under 21s in Austria on 19th April 1994
1993/94	Under 21 cap	Stephen Crawford played for Scotland Under 21s v Egypt in the Toulon Tournament on 30th May 1994
1993/94	Under 21 cap	Stephen Crawford played for Scotland Under 21s v Portugal in the Toulon Tournament on 1st June 1994
1993/94	Under 21 cap	Stephen Crawford played for Scotland Under 21s v Belgium in the Toulon Tournament on 3rd June 1994
1994/95	Under 21 cap	Stephen Crawford played the first 66 minutes for Scotland Under 21s in Finland on 6th September 1994
1994/95	Under 21 squad	Jason Dair in Scotland Under 21 squad in Finland on 6th September 1994
1994/95	Under 21 cap	Stephen Crawford played, and scored, for Scotland Under 21s against Russia at Cumbernauld on 15th November 1994
1994/95	Under 21 cap	Stephen Crawford played, and scored twice, for Scotland Under 21s in Greece on 17th December 1994
1994/95	B cap	Colin Cameron replaced Paul Lambert at half time for Scotland B v Northern Ireland B at Easter Road on 21st February 1995
1994/95	B cap	Danny Lennon played for Northern Ireland B v Scotland B at Easter Road on 21st February 1995
1994/95	Under 21 cap	Stephen Crawford played for Scotland Under 21s in Russia on 28th March 1995
1994/95	Under 21 cap	Stephen Crawford played for Scotland Under 21s in San Marino on 25th April 1995
1994/95	Full cap	Stephen Crawford came on as a substitute for Darren Jackson in 62 minutes in Scotland's Kirin Cup match against Equador in Japan on 24th May 1995, and scored the winning goal in Scotland's 2-1 win in the 83rd minute
1994/95	Under 21 cap	Stephen Crawford played for Scotland Under 21s against Mexico in the Toulon Tournament on 5th June 1995
1994/95	Under 21 cap	Stephen Crawford replaced Duncan Jupp in 61 minutes for Scotland Under 21s against France in the Toulon Tournament on 7th June 1995
1994/95	Under 21 cap	Stephen Crawford replaced Duncan Jupp in 79 minutes for Scotland Under 21s against South Korea in the Toulon Tournament on 9th June 1995
1994/95	Under 21 cap	Stephen Crawford replaced Stuart Gray at half time for Scotland Under 21s against Brazil in the Toulon Tournament on 12th June 1995
1995/96	Under 21 cap	Stephen Crawford played for the first 62 minutes of Scotland Under 21's 3-0 win over Greece at Kilmarnock on 15th August 1995. He was replaced by Simon Donnelly of Celtic
1995/96	Under 21 cap	Stephen Crawford replaced Kevin Harper after 65 minutes of Scotland Under 21's 5-0 win over Finland at Broadwood Stadium on 5th September 1995
1995/96	B cap	Colin Cameron came on as a substitute for Alex Rae of Millwall in 65 minutes in Scotland B's 2-1 win in Sweden on 10th October 1995
1995/96	Under 21 squad	Stephen Crawford in the Scotland Under 21s squad for the match against San Marino at Firhill on 14th November 1995
1995/96	Under 21 cap	Stephen Crawford played for the first 72 minutes of Scotland Under 21's 2-1 defeat in Hungary on 12th March 1996. He was replaced by Jamie Fullarton of St Mirren
1995/96	B cap	Danny Lennon played for Northern Ireland B v Norway B in Coleraine on March 26th 1996
1995/96	Youth squad	Graham Bogie selected in the Scotland Under 16 squad for the European Youth Championships
1995/96	Under 21 cap	Stephen Crawford replaced Christian Dailly after 72 minutes of Scotland Under 21's 3-1 victory over Hungary at east Road on 26th March 1996
1995/96	Under 21 cap	Stephen Crawford replaced Andy Liddell after 72 minutes of Scotland Under 21s 2-1 defeat by Spain in the semi finals of the European Championship in Barcelona on 28th May 1996
1995/96	Under 21 cap	Stephen Crawford replaced Christian Dailly after 66 minutes of Scotland Under 21s 1-0 defeat by France in Barcelona for the 3rd/4th place play off of the European Championships on 31st May 1996
1996/97	Under 21 cap	Paul Browne played for Scotland Under 21s 4-0 defeat in Austria on 30th September 1996
1996/97	Under 21 cap	Paul Bonar played for Scotland Under 21s 4-0 defeat in Austria on 30th September 1996
1996/97	Under 21 cap	Paul Bonar played for the first half for Scotland Under 21s in the 0-0 draw v Latvia on 6th October 1996. He was replaced by Marc Anthony of Celtic
1996/97	Under 21 cap	Paul Bonar replaced Charlie Miller of Rangers after 39 minutes of Scotland Under 21s 1-0 win in Estonia on 8th October 1996
1996/97	Under 21 cap	Paul Bonar played for the first hour of Scotland Under 21s 4-1 defeat by Sweden at Tannadice on 9th October 1996
1996/97	Full squad	Janne Makela recalled to the Finland squad for the international played on 29th March 1997
1996/97	B cap	Danny Lennon in the Northern Ireland B squad on 29th March 1997 - in total he made six appearances for Northern Ireland at that level.
1997/98	Under 21 cap	Craig McEwan played for Scotland Under 21s in the 3-0 defeat by Belarus at McDiarmid Park on 5th September 1997. He was replaced by Andy Seaton after 62 minutes
1997/98	Under 21 cap	Craig McEwan played for Scotland Under 21s in the 4-2 defeat by Latvia at Livingston on 10th October 1997. He was replaced by Russell Anderson after 52 minutes
1997/98	Youth squad	Jay Stein was in the Scotland under 18 squad for the UEFA Youth Championships qualifying group in France in mid October
1997/98	B cap	Danny Lennon played for the first hour of Northern Ireland B v Eire B in Dublin on 11th February 1998
1997/98	Under 21 cap	Craig McEwan played for Scotland Under 21 in the 2-1 defeat by Denmark at Stirling on 24th March 1998
1997/98	Under 21 squad	Craig Dargo selected for the Scotland Under 21 squad for the match against Denmark at Stirling on 24th March 1998, but withdrew through injury
1997/98	Under 21 cap	Craig McEwan played for Scotland Under 21s in the 1-1 draw with Finland at Stark's Park on 21st April 1998
1997/98	Under 21 cap	Craig Dargo played for Scotland Under 21s in the 1-1 draw with Finland at Stark's Park on 21st April 1998, being substituted by Graham after 64 minutes
1997/98	Under 21 cap	Craig McEwan played for Scotland Under 21s in the 3-0 defeat in Eire on 18th May 1998
1997/98	Under 21 cap	Craig Dargo played for Scotland Under 21s in the 3-0 defeat in Eire on 18th May 1998
1997/98	Under 21 cap	Craig McEwan played for Scotland Under 21s in the 1-1 draw with Northern Ireland in the Triangular Tournament in Eire on 20th May 1998
1997/98	Under 21 cap	Craig Dargo came on as a substitute for Campbell for Scotland Under 21s in the 1-1 ddraw with Northern Ireland in the Triangular Tournament in Eire on 20th May 1998
1997/98	Under 21 cap	Craig McEwan played for Scotland Under 21s in the 4-0 defeat in Italy on 23rd May 1998
1997/98	Under 21 cap	Craig Dargo played for Scotland Under 21s in the 4-0 defeat in Italy on 23rd May 1998
1998/99	Under 21 cap	Craig McEwan played for Scotland Under 21s in the 0-0 draw in Lithuania on 4th September 1998
1998/99	Youth squad	Paul Shields named in the Scotland Under 17 squad for a tournament in Belgium also involving Holland and Denmark
1998/99	Under 21 cap	Craig Dargo played for Scotland Under 21s in the 2-0 win over Estonia at Airdrie on 9th October 1998, being substituted by Alex Notman. Dargo scored after 6 minutes
1998/99	Under 21 cap	Craig McEwan came on as a substitute for Russell Anderson after 30 minutes in Scotland Under 21s 2-0 win over Estonia at Airdrie on 9th October 1998
1998/99	Under 21 cap	Craig Dargo played for Scotland Under 21s in the 2-0 defeat in Belgium on 14th October 1998
1998/99	Under 21 cap	Craig Dargo came on as a substitute for Campbell after 83 minutes in Scotland Under 21s 2-0 defeat in Belgium on 14th October 1998
1998/99	Under 21 cap	Craig McEwan played for Scotland Under 21s in the 2-2 draw with Belgium at Love Street on 18th November 1998
1998/99	Under 21 cap	Craig Dargo played, and scored two goals, for Scotland Under 21s in the 2-2 draw with Belgium at Love Street on 18th November 1998
1998/99	Under 21 cap	Craig McEwan played for Scotland Under 21s in the 1-0 defeat by Czechoslovakia at Motherwell on 30th March 1999, being substituted by Gary Teale after 86 minutes
1998/99	Under 21 cap	Craig Dargo came on as a substitute for Lee McCulloch after 76 minutes in Scotland Under 21s 1-2 defeat by Czechoslovakia at Motherwell on 30th March 1999
1998/99	Under 21 cap	Craig Dargo played for Scotland Under 21s in the 2-1 defeat in Germany on 27th April 1999, and was substituted by Ian Anderson after 58 minutes
1998/99	Under 21 cap	Craig McEwan came on as a substitute for Jamie Buchan after 83 minutes in Scotland Under 21s 2-1 defeat in Germany on 27th April 1999
1998/99	Under 21 cap	Craig Dargo came on as a substitute for Mark Burchill after 86 minutes in Scotland Under 21s draw with Northern Ireland in the Triangular Tournament at Inverness on 4th June 1999
1998/99	Youth squad	Kevin Nicol in the Scotland Under 17 squad for a tournament in Portugal in May
1998/99	Under 21 squad	Craig Dargo was an unused substitute for Scotland Under 21s 3-2 defeat in the Czech Republic on 8th June 1999
1998/99	Under 21 squad	Craig McEwan was in the squad for Scotland Under 21s 3-2 defeat in the Czech Republic on 9th June 1999
1999/00	Youth squad	Paul Shields selected for Scotland Under 18s squad for August internationals
1999/00	Youth squad	Kevin Nicol selected for Scotland Under 17s squad for August internationals
2005/06	Under 21 squad	Alistair Brown, on loan from Hibs, included in Scotland Under 21 squads in September and October 2005
2006/07	Under 20 squad	Neil Henderson included in Northern Ireland Under 20s squad for a three team tournament in Portugal in April 2007, but withdrew through injury

Key : Round reached in Scottish (SC), League (SLC) and League Challenge Cups (LCC) is shown, Q = Qualifying Cup / round / group. P = Preliminary round (ie before top League clubs enter the Scottish Cup) ; 16 = last 16

Scottish League record, example : 1935/1936, Scottish League Division 2, 17th position out of 18 in that Division, 37th out of 38 in the whole of the Scottish League. 34 League games played, 6 won at home, 3 drawn at home, 8 lost at home, 36 goals scored at home, 35 goals conceded at home, 3 wins away from home, no draws away from home, 14 defeats away from home, 24 goals scored away from home, 61 goals conceded away from home, 21 points won.

Season	Trophies won	Scottish Cup (round reached)	League Cup (ditto)	Trophies won
1884-1885		SC		
1885-1886				
1886-1887	Kirkcaldy Junior Cup			
1887-1888	Kirkcaldy Junior Cup			
1888-1889	Kirkcaldy Junior Cup			
1889-1890		1		
1890-1891	King Cup ; Fife Charity Cup	1		
1891-1892	Midland League Champions ; Fife Cup	1		
1892-1893		1		
1893-1894	Fife Cup	Q		
1894-1895		1		
1895-1896		2		
1896-1897	Nairn Cup	1		
1897-1898	East of Scotland Qualifying Cup ; Fife Cup ;	1	East of Scotland Consolation Cup ; Nairn Cup ; Wemyss Cup	
1898-1899	King Cup ; Nairn Cup ; Fife Cup	Q		
1899-1900		1		
1900-1901	East of Scotland Qualifying Cup ; King Cup ; Wemyss Cup	Q		
1901-1902	Northern League Champions ;	Q	East of Scotland Qualifying Cup	

Season	Position Nationally	Home P W D L F A	Away W D L F A	Pts	SC	SLC	Trophies won
1902-1903	SLD2 11/12 23/24	22 3 3 5 20 21	0 2 9 14 34	11	Q		Nairn Cup
1903-1904	SLD2 5/12 19/26	22 4 4 3 24 16	4 1 6 16 22	21	Q		Central Counties Championship ; Wemyss Cup
1904-1905	SLD2 10/12 24/26	22 7 0 4 18 11	2 1 8 12 23	19	Q		Wemyss Cup
1905-1906	SLD2 8/12 24/28	22 5 4 2 27 19	1 3 7 11 23	19	Q		Penman Cup ; Fife Cup ; Wemyss Cup / League
1906-1907	Play-off 1		1 0 0 3 2				Neutral venue
1906-1907	SLD2 10/12 28/30	22 5 2 4 25 18	1 2 8 14 30	16	1		Scottish Qualifying Cup
1907-1908	SLD2 1/12 19/30	22 9 1 1 25 7	5 1 5 12 16	30	qf		Scottish Qualifying Cup Finalists
1908-1909	SLD2 2/12 20/30	22 8 3 0 31 8	3 3 5 15 14	28	Q		Penman Cup ; Fife Cup / League / Stark Cup
1909-1910	SLD2 2/12 20/30	22 9 2 0 21 7	5 3 3 14 13	33	Q		
1910-1911	SLD1 15/18 15/30	34 6 6 5 26 22	1 4 12 10 33	24	Q		
1911-1912	SLD1 15/18 15/30	34 6 6 5 25 22	3 3 11 14 37	27	1		Penman Cup
1912-1913	SLD1 16/18 16/32	34 5 7 5 33 28	3 3 11 13 32	26	F		Scottish Cup Finalists
1913-1914	SLD1 11/20 11/32	38 9 4 6 38 22	4 2 13 18 35	32	16		
1914-1915	SLD1 19/20 19/34	38 5 8 6 31 27	4 2 13 22 41	28			Fife Cup ; Wemyss Cup
1915-1916	SFL 20/20 20/20	38 8 3 8 21 24	1 2 16 9 41	23			
1916-1917	SFL 19/20 19/20	38 6 2 11 22 41	2 5 12 20 50	23			
1919-1920	SFL 19/22 19/22	42 10 3 8 33 29	1 7 13 28 54	32	16		
1920-1921	SFL 16/22 16/22	42 14 0 7 38 21	2 5 14 16 37	37	1		Wemyss Cup ; Fife Cup
1921-1922	SLD1 3/22 3/42	42 12 7 2 41 16	7 6 8 25 27	51	1		Fife Cup
1922-1923	SLD1 9/20 9/42	38 9 8 2 18 14	4 5 10 13 29	39	qf		Fife Cup
1923-1924	SLD1 4/20 4/56	38 13 3 3 40 12	5 4 10 16 26	43	16		Penman Cup ; Dunedin Cup
1924-1925	SLD1 9/20 9/56	38 11 4 4 34 22	3 4 12 19 39	36	16		Fife Cup ; Penman Cup
1925-1926	SLD1 19/20 19/56	38 9 2 8 30 30	2 2 15 16 51	26	2		
1926-1927	SLD2 2/20 22/40	38 15 2 2 65 22	6 5 8 27 30	49	1		
1927-1928	SLD1 17/20 17/40	38 7 5 7 35 32	4 2 13 25 57	29	2		
1928-1929	SLD1 20/20 20/40	38 7 5 7 34 39	2 1 16 18 66	24	qf		
1929-1930	SLD2 5/20 25/40	38 11 2 6 61 29	7 6 6 33 38	44	1		Fife Cup
1930-1931	SLD2 4/20 24/40	38 15 3 1 60 25	5 3 11 33 47	46	1		
1931-1932	SLD2 3/20 23/40	38 12 3 4 49 26	8 3 8 34 39	46	2		
1932-1933	SLD2 6/20 26/40	34 12 3 2 55 24	4 1 12 28 43	36	1		
1932-1933	SLD2	1 0 0 0 0 0	1 0 0 5 1	2			Armadale record expunged
1932-1933	SLD2	1 0 0 0 0 0	1 0 0 2 1	2			Bo'ness record expunged
1933-1934	SLD2 8/18 28/38	34 11 3 3 46 16	4 2 11 25 39	35	1		
1934-1935	SLD2 13/18 33/38	34 11 1 5 48 29	2 2 13 26 53	29	2		
1935-1936	SLD2 17/18 37/38	34 6 3 8 36 35	3 0 14 24 61	21	1		
1936-1937	SLD2 8/18 28/38	34 9 3 5 38 26	7 1 9 34 40	36	1		Penman Cup ; Wemyss Cup
1937-1938	SLD2 1/18 21/38	34 15 1 1 68 20	12 4 1 74 34	59	qf		
1938-1939	SLD1 20/20 20/38	38 4 2 13 33 44	6 0 13 32 55	22	1		Wemyss Cup
1939-1940	SLD2	4 1 0 1 3 3	0 0 2 2 7	2			
1945-1946	SLDB 13/14 29/30	26 5 0 8 27 30	1 2 10 21 50	14	qf*		* in Victory Cup
1946-1947	SLDB 6/14 22/30	26 7 3 3 25 17	3 3 7 20 35	26	2	Q	B Division Supplementary Cup Finalists
1947-1948	SLDB 4/16 20/32	30 9 1 5 48 29	5 5 5 35 37	34	1	Q	Penman Cup ; Fife Cup
1948-1949	SLDB 1/16 17/32	30 12 1 2 44 16	8 1 6 36 28	42	2	F	League Cup Finalists ; B Division Supplementary Cup Finalists
1949-1950	SLDA 9/16 9/32	30 7 3 5 34 29	2 5 8 11 25	26	qf	Q	
1950-1951	SLDA 8/16 8/32	30 8 2 5 30 16	5 0 10 22 36	28	sf	Q	
1951-1952	SLDA 5/16 5/32	30 9 2 4 23 14	5 3 7 20 28	33	2	Q	
1952-1953	SLDA 12/16 12/32	30 5 7 3 25 20	4 1 10 22 33	26	2	Q	Fife Cup
1953-1954	SLDA 12/16 12/32	30 7 3 5 37 21	3 3 9 19 39	26	16	Q	Fife Cup (shared)
1954-1955	SLDA 14/16 14/32	30 9 1 5 34 23	1 2 12 15 34	23	16	Q	Fife Cup (shared)
1955-1956	SLD1 11/18 11/37	34 6 7 4 30 30	6 2 9 28 45	33	sf	Q	Fife Cup
1956-1957	SLD1 4/18 4/37	34 10 2 5 52 32	6 5 6 32 26	39	sf	Q	Fife Cup
1957-1958	SLD1 7/18 7/37	34 10 2 5 37 20	4 5 8 29 36	35	2	Q	Penman Cup
1958-1959	SLD1 14/18 14/37	34 9 3 5 33 25	1 6 10 27 45	29	1	Q	
1959-1960	SLD1 11/18 11/37	34 7 3 7 38 29	7 0 10 26 35	31	1	qf	Fife Cup (shared)
1960-1961	SLD1 16/18 16/37	34 5 4 8 26 34	5 3 9 20 33	27	16	Q	
1961-1962	SLD1 13/18 13/37	34 5 5 7 24 29	5 2 10 27 44	27	16	Q	Fife Cup

1962-1963	SLD1	18/18	18/37	34	0	4	13	16	48	2	1	14	19	70	9	sf	Q	
1963-1964	SLD2	10/19	28/37	36	9	2	7	40	24	6	3	9	30	37	35	1	Q	
1964-1965	SLD2	13/19	31/37	36	5	6	7	23	24	4	8	6	31	37	32	P	Q	
1965-1966	SLD2	5/19	23/37	36	10	3	5	43	23	6	8	4	28	20	43	P	qf	Fife Cup (shared)
1966-1967	SLD2	2/20	20/38	38	15	2	2	55	17	12	2	5	40	27	58	1	Q	Fife Cup
1967-1968	SLD2	16/18	16/37	34	5	4	8	32	30	4	3	10	26	56	25	1	Q	Fife Cup
1968-1969	SLD1	16/18	16/37	34	6	2	9	23	29	2	3	12	22	38	21	1	Q	Fife Cup
1969-1970	SLD1	17/18	17/37	34	4	6	7	15	24	1	5	11	17	43	21	1	Q	
1970-1971	SLD2	8/19	26/37	36	8	7	3	35	23	7	2	9	27	39	39	qf	Q	
1971-1972	SLD2	11/19	29/37	36	9	5	4	39	22	4	3	11	17	34	34	qf	Q	Fife Cup
1972-1973	SLD2	4/19	22/37	36	11	5	2	42	16	8	4	6	31	26	47	1	Q	
1973-1974	SLD2	6/19	24/37	36	10	4	4	42	28	8	5	5	27	20	45	1	16	
1974-1975	SLD2	13/20	31/38	38	11	3	5	33	22	3	6	10	15	22	37	1	Q	
1975-1976	SLD2	2/14	26/38	26	6	6	1	21	14	9	4	0	24	8	40	16	Q	Fife Cup
1976-1977	SLD1	13/14	23/38	39	7	7	6	29	27	1	4	14	16	41	27	P	Q	
1977-1978	SLD2	2/14	26/38	39	10	7	2	36	15	9	8	3	27	19	53	P	1	
1978-1979	SLD1	11/14	21/38	39	8	3	8	29	21	4	5	11	18	34	32	1	16	
1979-1980	SLD1	5/14	15/38	39	8	7	5	30	22	6	8	5	29	24	43	1	qf	
1980-1981	SLD1	4/14	14/38	39	12	7	1	27	11	8	3	8	22	21	50	1	16	Fife Cup
1981-1982	SLD1	12/14	22/38	39	5	2	13	13	32	6	5	8	18	27	29	1	Q	
1982-1983	SLD1	9/14	19/38	39	8	3	8	32	29	5	5	10	32	34	34	1	Q	
1983-1984	SLD1	13/14	23/38	39	6	6	8	33	30	4	5	10	20	32	31	1	1	
1984-1985	SLD2	7/14	31/38	39	9	1	9	30	25	9	5	6	39	32	42	1	16	
1985-1986	SLD2	9/14	33/38	39	11	3	6	41	27	4	4	11	26	38	37	P	2	
1986-1987	SLD2	2/14	26/38	39	8	10	1	34	19	8	10	2	39	25	52	qf	1	Fife Cup
1987-1988	SLD1	5/12	17/38	44	10	4	8	45	33	9	3	10	36	43	45	1	16	
1988-1989	SLD1	7/14	17/38	39	8	6	6	29	25	7	4	8	21	27	40	1	1	
1989-1990	SLD1	5/14	15/38	39	10	4	5	30	22	5	8	7	27	28	42	1	1	Fife Cup
1990-1991	SLD1	7/14	17/38	39	7	5	8	22	26	7	4	8	32	38	37	1	qf	LCC qf
1991-1992	SLD1	5/12	17/38	44	11	7	4	33	16	10	4	8	26	26	53	1	16	LCC sf
1992-1993	SLD1	1/12	13/38	44	17	5	0	54	14	8	10	4	31	27	65	1	1	LCC 1
1993-1994	SLPD	11/12	11/38	44	3	12	7	25	35	3	7	12	21	45	31	16	1	
1994-1995	SLD1	1/10	11/40	36	8	8	2	27	18	11	4	3	27	14	69	qf	W	LCC 16
1995-1996	SLPD	6/10	6/40	36	7	5	6	23	21	5	2	11	18	36	43	1	1	
1996-1997	SLPD	10/10	10/40	36	3	5	10	18	39	3	2	13	11	34	25	qf	1	
1997-1998	SLD1	3/10	13/40	36	9	5	4	25	12	8	4	6	26	21	60	16	16	LCC 16
1998-1999	SLD1	8/10	18/40	36	5	5	8	19	27	3	6	9	18	30	35	1	16	
1999-2000	SLD1	5/10	15/40	36	11	3	4	35	21	6	5	7	20	19	59	1	1	LCC qf
2000-2001	SLD1	7/10	19/40	36	5	4	9	24	26	5	4	9	17	29	38	1	16	LCC 1
2001-2002	SLD1	10/10	22/40	36	7	5	6	31	25	1	6	11	19	37	35	1	16	LCC 16
2002-2003	SLD2	1/10	23/42	36	10	4	4	28	14	6	7	5	25	22	59	1	1	LCC 1
2003-2004	SLD1	8/10	20/42	36	5	8	18	28		3	5	10	19	29	34	1	1	LCC sf
2004-2005	SLD1	10/10	22/42	36	3	4	11	19	33	0	3	15	7	34	16	1	1	LCC 1
2005-2006	SLD2	7/10	29/42	36	5	5	8	25	28	6	4	8	19	26	42	P	2	LCC qf
2006-2007	Play offs		2	0	1	0	0	0	0	1	3							
2006-2007	SLD2	3/10	25/42	36	7	5	6	22	18	11	3	4	28	15	62	P	1	LCC 1
2007-2008	Play offs		2	0	0	1	0	2	0	1	0	2	2					
2007-2008	SLD2	3/10	25/42	36	8	3	7	28	27	11	0	7	32	23	60	1	16	LCC 1

HONOURS

233

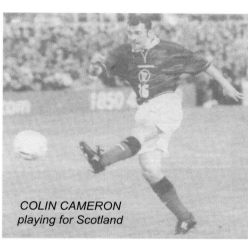

COLIN CAMERON
playing for Scotland

MATCH BY MATCH STATISTICS - Key to the next 118 pages.

Day = day of the week
Note = further details of fixture detailed in panel beneath statistics
Venue = Home, Away or Neutral venue
Comp = Competition, see list below   Att - Attendance

ASC 1-1	Anglo Scottish Cup [1st round 1st leg]
B	Benefit / Testimonial match
BDSC F-1	B Division Supplementary Cup [Final 1st leg]
C	Charity Match
CC 2r	Cowdenbeath [Junior] Cup [2nd round replay]
CCC	Central Counties Championship
CL	Scottish Counties League
DC F2R	Dunedin Cup [Final 2nd replay]
DrC	Drybrough Cup
EL	Eastern League
ESL	East of Scotland League
ESQC 1r2	East of Scotland Qualifying Cup [1st round 2nd replay]
ESS SF	East of Scotland Shield [semi final]
F	Friendly match
FC Fr	Fife Cup [Final replay]
FCC F	Fifeshire Charity Cup [Final]
FL	Fife League
KC 3	King Cup [3rd round]
KJC 1	Kirkcaldy Junior Cup [1st round]
L1	Scottish League [top division]
L2	Scottish League [2nd highest division]
L3	Scottish League [3rd highest division]
L3 PO-1	Scottish League [3rd highest division, Play Off 1st leg]
LC S	Scottish League Cup [qualifying section]
LCC QF	Scottish League Challenge Cup [quarter final]
LoC	Loftus Cup
MC SFr	Mitchell Cup [semi final replay]
ML	Midland League
NC	Nairn Charity Cup

NEC SF-1	North Eastern Cup [semi final 1st leg]
NEL 1	North Eastern League [1st competition of season]
NESC SF-1	North Eastern League Cup [semi final 1st leg]
NL PO	Northern League [play off]
PC 2r2	Penman Cup [2nd round 2nd replay]
RC	Rosebery Cup
SC 1P	Scottish Cup [1st Preliminary Round]
SCC Fr	Scottish Consolation Cup [Final replay]
SJC 3	Scottish Junior Cup [3rd round]
SM 2r	St Mungo Cup [2nd round replay]
SmC 1-1	Summer Cup [1st round 1st leg]
SpC S	Spring Cup [qualifying section]
SQC 4r	Scottish Qualifying Cup [4th round replay]
StC	Stark Cup
T SF	Pre Season Tournament [semi final]
UC Pr-2	UEFA Cup [preliminary round 2nd leg]
VC 1-2	Victory Cup [1st round 2nd leg]
WC 1r	Wemyss Cup [1st round replay]
WL	Wemyss League

Against players names :
r = replaced by substitute (and time)
b = booked/cautioned
X = sent off (and time)
m = missed penalty (and time)
s = saved penalty (and time)
1,2,3 etc. = number of goals scored
p = penalty
u = used substitute (and time, or *** key to player replaced)
substitutes listed without 'u' did not leave the bench
og = own goal
25, 12, 47 etc = Raith Rovers goal times, scored by the players as listed from left to right

Substitutes, own goals, goal times and opponents' scorers

Notes

Crossbars were made compulsory in 1882, tape having been introduced in 1865 ; in 1882 the two handed throw-in was introduced ; in 1883 the four home counties' FA's codified the laws

1884/1985   (1) First round of Kirkcaldy Wanderers Badge competition ; at Stark's Park   (2) Walked off after 7/17 minutes   (3) abandoned after 65 minutes   (4) abandoned after 31 minutes

1885/1886   (5) Leith Rovers were billed to play Rovers at Robbie's Park on 3rd October, but the port side did not make the journey over the Forth, as the following week's newspaper reported that the 1st Eleven played the 2nd Eleven and won 7-0.   (s) at Stark's Park   (w) at Newtown Park

1886/1887   (1) Rovers were to have played Caledonia from the West of Scotland, but the visitors couldn't travel. Instead, a scratch Rovers team drew 3-3 at home to Leith Albion. The 1d admission for football was cheap in comparison to other public entertainment. For example, admission to the pantomime at Theatre Royal, Kirk Wynd cost 6d for the pit and 3d in the gallery   (2) Benefit match   (3) lost 3-1 on corners   (4) Benefit for Jimmy Taylor   (s) at Stark's Park   (w) at Newtown Park

Day	Date	Opponents	Note	Venue	Comp	Res	1	2	3	4	5	6	7	8	9	10	11	Opponents' scorers
	1883-84																	
s	14-Dec	West End Rangers		A	F	0-5												
s	16-Feb	West End Rangers		A	F	2-1												
s	29-Mar	Whitebank		H	F	2-0												
	1884-85																	
s	25-Oct	Thistle	1	A	KJC 1	1-2												
s	15-Nov	Kirkcaldy Rangers		A	F	0-3												
s	22-Nov	Kirkcaldy Albion		H	F	4-0												
s	06-Dec	Kirkcaldy Wanderers 3rd		H	F	4-3												
s	13-Dec	Townsend Swifts		H	F	4-1												
s	03-Jan	2nd Blues, Wemyss		H	F	4-1												
s	17-Jan	Randolph Rangers, Gallatown		H	F	3-2												
s	31-Jan	Denburn		A	F	5-0												
s	14-Feb	Rose, Burntisland		H	F	2-1												
s	21-Feb	Randolph Blues		H	F	4-1												
s	07-Mar	Union		H	F	2-1												
	1885-86																	
s	19-Sep	Royal Albert, Dunfermline		A	F	1-0	Lyall	Clark,W	Clark,W	Norval	Jarvis,W	Russell	Nelson	Litster 1	Chalmers	Holburn	Jarvis,D	
s	26-Sep	Thistle		H	F	2-1	Lyall	Jarvis,D	Jarvis,D	Norval	Jarvis,W	Russell	Nelson	Chalmers	Litster 1	Holburn 1	Clark,D	
s	03-Oct	Second Eleven	5	H	F	7-0	Lyall	Clark,W	Russell	Norval	Jarvis,W	Russell 1	Nelson 1	Chalmers 2	Litster 2	Holburn 2	Clark,D 2	
s	10-Oct	Star	s	A	F	7-1	Lyall	Clark,W	Russell	Norval 1	Jarvis,W	Russell 1	Nelson	Chalmers	Litster 3	Holburn	Clark,D	
s	24-Oct	Wellwood, Dunfermline		H	F	0-0	Lyall	Jarvis,W	Russell	Norval	Jarvis,W	Russell	Nelson	Chalmers	Litster	Holburn	Clark,D	
s	31-Oct	Kirkcaldy Albion		H	F	4-2	Lyall	Jarvis,D	Clark,W	Norval	Jarvis,W	Russell	Nelson 2	Chalmers	Litster	Holburn 1	Clark,D	
s	07-Nov	Union		A	F	1-0	Lyall	Jarvis,D	Clark,W	Norval	Jarvis,W	Russell	Nelson	Chalmers	Litster	Holburn	Clark,D	
s	21-Nov	Thistle	2	A	F	3-2	Lyall	Jarvis,D	Clark,W	Norval	Jarvis,W	Russell	Nelson	Chalmers 1	Litster 2	Holburn 1	Clark,D	
s	12-Dec	Star		H	F	0-0	Lyall	Jarvis,D	Clark,W	Norval	Jarvis,W	Russell	Nelson	Chalmers	Litster	Holburn	Clark,D	
s	19-Dec	Kirkcaldy Rangers		H	F	1-1	Chapman	Clark,W	Russell	Norval	Jarvis,W	Hazells	Nelson	Jarvis,D	Litster	Holburn 1	Clark,D	Lessells
s	26-Dec	Kirkcaldy		A	F	1-4	Chapman	Clark,W	Russell	Norval	Jarvis,W	Hazells	Nelson	Jarvis,D 1	Litster	Holburn	Clark,D	Myles, Napier, an other
s	09-Jan	Kirkcaldy 2nds		H	F	1-2	Chapman	Clark,W	Russell	Norval	Jarvis,W	Hazells	Nelson	Jarvis,D 1	Litster	Holburn	Clark,D	
s	16-Jan	Kirkcaldy Albion	3	H	B	1-1	Chapman	Clark,W	Russell	Norval 1	Jarvis,W	Hazells	Nelson	Jarvis,D 1	Litster 1	Holburn	Clark,D	Bailie, an other
s	30-Jan	Kirkcaldy Rangers		A	F	1-3	Lyall	Clark,W	Russell	Norval	Jarvis,W 1	Hazells	Nelson 1	Litster	Jarvis,D	Holburn 1	Chalmers	
s	06-Feb	Vale of Eden, Cupar		A	F	4-0	Lyall	Clark,W	Russell	Norval	Jarvis,W	Hazells	Nelson 1	Elder	Jarvis,D	Donaldson 1	Clark,D 1	
s	13-Feb	Thistle		H	F	3-3	Chapman	Jarvis,W	Russell	Norval	Jarvis,W	Russell	Nelson 2	Litster	Chalmers	Clark,D 1	Chalmers	
s	20-Feb	Abden		H	KJC 1	7-0	Chapman	Clark,W	Russell	Norval 1	Jarvis,W	Russell	Nelson	Litster 2	Chalmers 3	Clark,D	Donaldson	
s	27-Feb	Loughborough Swifts	4	A	KJC 2	4-1	Chapman	Jarvis,D	Russell	Norval	Jarvis,W	Russell	Nelson	Litster	Chalmers 2	Clark,D 2	Donaldson	
s	13-Mar	Kirkcaldy Rangers	s	A	F	1-4	Lyall	Jarvis,D	Russell	Norval	Jarvis,W	Russell	Nelson	Litster	Chalmers	Clark,D	Donaldson	
s	20-Mar	Kirkcaldy	w	A	F	2-6	Chapman	Clark,W	Russell	Hazells	Norval	Jarvis,W	Nelson	Holburn 1	Litster	Chalmers	Clark,D	Doig (2), Cook, Herd, an others
W	27-Mar	Kirkcaldy Albion	w	N	KJC SF	0-5	Chapman	Clark,W	Jarvis,D 1	Russell	Norval	Jarvis,W	Nelson	Holburn	Elder	Clark,D	Chalmers	Ramsay Gosling Ritchie Hunter Deuchars
s	07-Apr	Kirkcaldy		H	F	2-2	Chapman	Clark,W	Clark,W	Russell	Hazells	Jarvis,W	Litster	Holburn 1	Elder	Clark,D	Chalmers	
W	10-Apr	Kirkcaldy Albion	w	N	KJC SF	0-1	Chapman	Jarvis,D	Russell	Hazells	Halliday	Jarvis,W	Norval	Holburn 1	Elder	Clark,D	Chalmers	
s	01-May	Wellwood, Dunfermline		A	F	0-5	Chapman	Jarvis,D	Russell	Hazells	Halliday	Jarvis,W	Norval	Litster	Nelson	Clark,D	Chalmers	
	1886-87																	
s	11-Sep	Union	s	A	F	4-1	Lyall	Clark,W	Clark,W	Russell	Hazells	Hepburn	Nelson 2	Holburn	Ramsay 1	Clark,D	Chalmers 1	
s	18-Sep	Burntisland Thistle 2nds		A	F	2-2	Lyall	Jarvis,D	Clark,W	Russell	Hazells	Hepburn	Nelson	Holburn	Ramsay	Clark,D 2	Chalmers	
s	02-Oct	Dunnikier		A	F	4-1	Lyall	Jarvis,D	Clark,W	Russell 1	Hazells	Hepburn	Nelson 1	Holburn 1	Ramsay 2	Clark,D 1	Chalmers 2	
s	09-Oct	Novar		A	F	6-0	Lyall	Jarvis,D	Clark,W	Russell	Hazells	Hepburn	Nelson	Holburn 1	Ramsay 3	Clark,D 1	Chalmers	
s	23-Oct	Dunnikier		A	F	5-0	Lyall	Jarvis,D	Clark,W	Russell	Hazells	Jarvis,W	Nelson 2	Burt 1	Ramsay 2	Clark,D 1	Chalmers	
s	30-Oct	Blackburn		A	F	6-0	Lyall	Jarvis,D	Clark,W	Russell	Hazells 1	Jarvis,W	Nelson	Holburn 3	Nelson 3	Clark,D 1	Chalmers	
s	06-Nov	Caroline, Granton		A	F	2-2	Lyall	Jarvis,D	Clark,W	Russell	Hazells	Jarvis,W	Nelson	Holburn 1	Ramsay	Clark,D 1	Chalmers	
s	13-Nov	Kirkcaldy Albion	2	H	B	5-2	Lyall	Jarvis,D	Clark,W	Russell 1	Hazells	Jarvis,W 1	Nelson	Litster 3	Litster 2	Clark,D 1	Chalmers 1	
s	20-Nov	Claremont Park		A	F	3-0	Lyall	Jarvis,D	Clark,W	Russell	Hazells	Jarvis,W 1	Nelson	Holburn	Litster	Clark,D	Chalmers 1	
s	27-Nov	Thistle		H	KJC 1	11-0	Lyall	Jarvis,D	Clark,W	Russell 1	Hazells 1	Jarvis,W 1	Nelson 4	Holburn 4	Ramsay 2	Clark,D 2	Chalmers 3	
M	04-Dec	St Clair, Edinburgh		H	SJC 1	9-1	Lyall	Jarvis,D	Clark,W	Russell 1	Hazells 1	Jarvis,W 1	Nelson	Holburn 1	Ramsay 1	Clark,D	Chalmers 1	
s	03-Jan	Leith Athletic	1	H	F	3-3	Cairns	Jarvis,D	Holburn	Russell	Hazells	Jarvis,D	Nelson	Litster 3	Ramsay	Clark,D	Chalmers	
Tu	04-Jan	Cowdenbeath		H	F	3-4	Lyall	Jarvis,D	Hepburn	Hazells	Hazells	Jarvis,D	Nelson 2	Litster 2	Nelson 3	Clark,D	Chalmers 1	
s	08-Jan	Parkhead United		A	KJC 2	7-2	Ramsay	Jarvis,D	Clark,W	Russell	Russell	Jarvis,W	Lyall	Litster 3	Nelson 3	Holburn	Chalmers	
s	15-Jan	Woodburn, Edinburgh		H	SJC 2	0-7	Lyall	Jarvis,D	Clark,W	Hazells	Russell	Jarvis,W	Arthur	Litster	Ramsay	Clark,D	Chalmers	
s	22-Jan	Burntisland Thistle 2nds		H	F	1-2	Ramsay	Jarvis,D	Clark,W	Hazells	Hepburn	Jarvis,W	Nelson	Holburn	Ramsay 1	Holburn	Chalmers	
Th	12-Feb	Vale of Eden, Cupar		A	F	9-0	Ramsay	Jarvis,D	Clark,W	Hazells	Russell	Jarvis,W 1	Nelson	Holburn	Litster 2	Holburn 2	Chalmers	
s	19-Feb	Union	s	A	KJC SF	2-1	Cairns	Jarvis,D	Clark,W	Hazells	Russell	Jarvis,W	Nelson	Holburn	Litster 1	Clark,D 1	Chalmers	
s	26-Feb	Thistle		H	F	7-1	Lyall	Jarvis,D	Clark,W	Russell 1	Russell 1	Jarvis,W	Nelson	Holburn	Litster 2	Clark,D 3	Chalmers 3	
s	05-Mar	Union		H	KJC SF	1-1	Cairns	Jarvis,D	Clark,W	Hazells	Russell 1	Jarvis,W	Nelson	Holburn	Litster	Clark,D	Chalmers 2	
s	19-Mar	Heathertbell, Edinburgh		H	F	3-4	Lyall	Jarvis,D	Clark,W	Hazells	Russell 1	Jarvis,W	Arthur	Holburn	Litster 1	Clark,D 1	Chalmers 1	
s	26-Mar	Kirkcaldy Albion	w	N	KJC F	3-3	Lyall	Jarvis,D	Clark,W	Hazells	Russell	Jarvis,W	Nelson	Holburn	Litster 2	Clark,D 1	Chalmers 1	Deuchars Barker Sinclair
s	02-Apr	Kirkcaldy Albion	w	N	KJC Fr	4-0	Ramsay	Jarvis,D	Clark,W	Hazells	Russell	Jarvis,W	Nelson 3	Holburn	Litster	Clark,D	Chalmers	
s	16-Apr	Kirkcaldy Albion	3	H	B	1-1	Ramsay	Jarvis,D	Clark,W	Hazells	Russell	Jarvis,W	Nelson	Holburn 2	Ramsay 1	Clark,D	Chalmers	
s	21-Apr	St Vincent		H	F	2-2	Ramsay	Jarvis,D	Clark,W	Holburn	Nelson	Jarvis,W	Russell	Doig	Litster	Clark,D	Chalmers	
Tu	23-Apr	Dalry Albert		H	F	1-2	Cairns	Jarvis,D	Clark,W	Hazells	Nelson	Jarvis,W	Russell	Doig 2	Litster 1	Clark,D	Chalmers	
s	26-Apr	National Swifts		H	F	3-1	Ramsay	Jarvis,D	Clark,W	Hazells	Russell	Jarvis,W	Nelson 1	Doig	Litster 2	Clark,D	Chalmers	McBean og 1 Connelly (2)
s	30-Apr	Kirkcaldy Wanderers	4	H	B	4-2	Ramsay	Jarvis,D	Clark,W	Hazells	Russell 1	Jarvis,W	Nelson 1	Doig	Litster	Clark,D	Chalmers	
s	07-May	St Leonards		A	F	0-7	Ramsay	Jarvis,D	Clark,W	Hazells	Russell	Jarvis,W	Nelson	Doig	Litster	Clark,D	Chalmers	
s	14-May	Norton Park		H	F	2-2	Ramsay	Jarvis,D	Clark,W	Hazells	Russell	Jarvis,W	Nelson	Doig 1	Litster 1	Clark,D	Chalmers	
s	21-May	Campbellfield		A	F	1-3	Ramsay	Clark,W	Clark,W	Hazells	Russell	Jarvis,W	Nelson 1	Doig	Litster	Clark,D	Chalmers	Downes, T. (2)

Substitutes, own goals, goal times and opponents' scorers

1887/88

Three half backs were adopted in Scotland, one of the six forwards moving back

(1) Benefit for W Mackie, played at Stark's Park

(2) Benefit for McPhee

(3) Benefit for Jimmy Taylor

(4) Played at Kirkcaldy Albion's pitch at Robbie's Park

1888/1889

Last season as Juniors

(1) Benefit for J. Oliphant

(2) at Elders Park, Pathhead

(3) Two halves of 30 minutes played

(w) at Newtown Park

Day	Date	Opponents	Note	Venue	Comp	Res	1	2	3	4	5	6	7	8	9	10	11	Subs / scorers
S	16-Jul	Kirkcaldy Rangers	1	A	B	6-2	Ramsay	Adamson	Clark,W	Jarvis,W	Russell	Hazells	Nelson 1	Brown	Litster 2	Clark,D	Chalmers 3	
S	20-Aug	St Bernards 2nds		H	F	2-6	Ramsay	Adamson	Clark,W	Jarvis,W	Russell	Hazells	Nelson	Brown	Litster	Clark,D 2	Chalmers	
S	27-Aug	Pathhead United		H	F	3-1	Ramsay	Adamson	Clark,W	Jarvis,W 2	Russell	Hazells	Nelson 1	Brown	Litster	Clark,D 1	Chalmers	
S	03-Sep	Adventurers		H	F	2-3	Ramsay	Adamson	Jeffreys	Jeffreys	Addison	Hazells	Nelson 1	Jarvis,D 1	Litster	Holburn	Chalmers	
S	10-Sep	St Leonards		H	F	3-3	Ramsay	Clark,D	Clark,W	Jarvis,W	Russell	Hazells	Nelson 1	Holburn	Litster	Nelson	Chalmers	
S	17-Sep	Hearts A		H	F	2-3	Ramsay	Adamson	Clark,W	Jarvis,W 1	Russell	Hazells	Litster	Holburn	Nelson 1	Holburn	Chalmers	
S	24-Sep	Blackford, Edinburgh		H	F	4-1	Ramsay	Adamson	Clark,W	Jarvis,W	Russell	Hazells	Nelson 1	Litster 1	Henderson 1	Chalmers	Chalmers	
S	01-Oct	Dysart		A	F	14-0	Ramsay	Clark,W	Adamson	Jarvis,W 1	Russell	Hazells	Nelson 3	Litster 3	Henderson 1	Chalmers 1	Clark,D	
S	08-Oct	Union		H	F	5-1	Ramsay	Clark,W	Adamson	Jarvis,W	Russell	Hazells	Nelson 1	Litster 3	Henderson 2	Chalmers 3	Clark,D 2	Wilson
S	15-Oct	Wellwood, Dunfermline		H	F	4-1	Ramsay	Adamson	Clark,W	Jarvis,W	Russell	Hazells	Nelson	Litster	Henderson	Chalmers 1	Clark,D 1	
S	22-Oct	Dalry Albert		H	F	2-2	Ramsay	Clark,W	Adamson	Jarvis,W	Russell	Hazells	Jeffreys	Litster 2	Henderson 1	Chalmers	Clark,D 1	Dalrymple og 1
S	29-Oct	St Leonards		H	SJC 1	5-3	Ramsay	Clark,W	Adamson	Jarvis,W	Russell	Hazells	Nelson	Litster 1	Henderson	Chalmers 3	Clark,D	Colthard + another
S	05-Nov	Dunfermline Athletic 2nds		H	F	2-6	Russell,J2	Hazells	Adamson	Hepburn	Hazells	Jarvis,W	Nelson 2	Litster 1	Henderson	Chalmers 1	Clark,D	
S	12-Nov	Leith Athletic 2nds		H	F	3-1	Russell,J2	Hazells	Clark,W	Hepburn	Hazells	Jarvis,W	Hepburn,A	Litster 1	Henderson 1	Jarvis,D 2	Webster	
S	26-Nov	2nd Athenians		H	F	3-1	Ramsay	Clark,W	Jarvis,D	Jarvis,W	Russell	Jarvis,W 1	Nelson	Litster	Webster	Chalmers	Clark,D 2	
S	03-Dec	North Western Edinburgh		H	SJC 2	2-1	Ramsay	Adamson	Clark,W	Hazells	Russell	Jarvis,W	Nelson 1	Litster	Galloway	Chalmers	Clark,D 1	Ward / Anderson
S	10-Dec	Dysart		H	KJC 1	9-0	Ramsay	Ramage	Adamson	Hazells	Russell	Jarvis,W	Nelson 1	Litster 2	Galloway	Chalmers 3	Clark,D 3	
S	17-Dec	Leith Albion		H	F	5-0	Ramsay	Ramage	Adamson	Hazells	Russell	Jarvis,W	Nelson	Litster	Jarvis,D 3	Chalmers	Clark,D	
S	23-Dec	Kirkcaldy Albion		A	F	2-0	Ramsay	Ramage	Adamson	Hazells	Russell	Jarvis,W	Webster	Litster	Jarvis,D 2	Chalmers 1	Clark,D	
S	30-Dec	Claremont Park		H	F	3-0	Ramsay	Clark,W	Adamson	Hazells	Russell	Jarvis,W	Nelson 1	Litster	Jarvis,D 2	Chalmers 1	Clark,D 2	
M	01-Jan	Elderslie, Govan		H	F	1-6	Ramsay	Clark,W	Adamson	Hazells	Russell	Jarvis,W	Nelson 1	Litster 1	Jarvis,D 1	Chalmers	Clark,D 1	Sinclair
Tu	02-Jan	Rosevale, Glasgow		H	F	4-6	Ramsay	Adamson	Clark,W	Hazells	Russell	Galloway	Webster	Lyall	Norval	Norval	Jeffreys	
S	07-Jan	Wishaw Thistle		H	SJC 3	3-4	Ramsay	Clark,W	Adamson	Hazells	Russell	Jarvis,W	Nelson 1	Litster	Jarvis,D 3	Chalmers 1	Jeffreys	
S	14-Jan	Kirkcaldy Albion		A	F	1-1	Ramsay	Clark,W	Adamson	Hepburn	Russell	Jarvis,W	Nelson 1	Miller	Jarvis,D 1	Chalmers	Jeffreys	
S	21-Jan	Dalry Albert		H	F	1-2	Ramsay	Clark,W	Adamson	Hazells	Russell	Jarvis,W 1	Nelson 1	Litster	Jarvis,D 1	Jarvis,D	Clark,D	
S	28-Jan	Dunfermline Albion		A	F	4-3	Ramsay	Clark,W	Adamson	Hazells	Russell	Jarvis,W	Webster	Litster 1	Jarvis,D	Jarvis,D	Clark,D 1	
S	04-Feb	Union		A	F	5-0	Ramsay	Clark,W	Adamson	Hazells	Russell	Jarvis,W	Nelson	Litster 2	Nelson 3	Nelson 2	Clark,D 1	
S	11-Feb	Woodburn, Edinburgh		H	F	0-2	Ramsay	Clark,W	Adamson	Hazells	Russell	Jarvis,W	Nelson	Jarvis,D 2	Nelson	Nelson 3	Clark,D	
S	25-Feb	St Bernards 2nds		H	F	2-4	Ramsay	Clark,W	Adamson	Hazells	Russell	Jarvis,W	Jarvis,W	Jarvis,D 2	Henderson	Chalmers	Clark,D	own goal 1
S	03-Mar	Arbroath Nomads		H	F	2-2	Ramsay	Clark,W	Adamson	Hazells	Russell	Jarvis,W	Whannell	Jarvis,D 1	Henderson	Chalmers	Hepburn,D	Watson 30 Bruce 31
S	17-Mar	Kirkcaldy Wanderers		A	F	3-6	Ramsay	Clark,W	Adamson	Hazells	Russell	Jarvis,W	Whannell 2	Jarvis,D 2	Henderson 2	Litster	Clark,D 1	Mathie Hughes Millar Lawson Doig Napier
S	24-Mar	Pathhead United		A	KJC SF	1-1	Ramsay	Clark,W	Adamson	Hazells	Russell	Jarvis,W	Whannell	Henderson	Henderson 1	Chalmers 1	Clark,D 1	Burnet
S	07-Apr	Pathhead United		H	KJC SFr	4-1	Ramsay	Clark,W	Adamson	Hazells	Russell	Jarvis,W	Whannell 1	Henderson	Henderson	Chalmers	Clark,D	Philp
S	14-Apr	Fern	4	N	KJC F	1-5	Ramsay	Clark,W	Wilson	Hazells	Webster	Hayles	Whannell	Webster	Henderson 1	Chalmers 1	Clark,D	Skae (3) + 2 others
S	21-Apr	Arbroath Nomads		A	F	7-0	Ramsay	Adamson	Clark,W	Hazells	Russell	Jarvis,W	Nelson	Nelson	Henderson 2	Chalmers 1	Clark,D 1	
S	28-Apr	Murhouse Rovers	2	H	B	7-0	Ramsay	Clark,W	Clark,W	Hazells	Russell	Jarvis,W	Nelson 1	Nelson	Henderson 1	Chalmers 1	Clark,D	
S	05-May	Crusaders, Edinburgh	3	H	B	2-2	Ramsay	Clark,W	Clark,W	Hazells	Russell	Calderwood	Henderson 1	Nelson	Henderson 1	Litster	Clark,D	Cannon Young
S	12-May	Adventurers		H	F	4-0	Ramsay	Clark,W	Clark,W	Hepburn,D	Russell	Jarvis,W	Chalmers	Nelson	Henderson	Chalmers 1	Clark,D	
		1888-89																	
S	18-Aug	St Leonards		A	F	3-5	Ramsay	Thomson	Jarvis,W	Hepburn,D	Nelson	Russell	Chalmers	Dall 2	Whannell	Jarvis,D 1	Litster	Calder Young
S	01-Sep	Woodburn, Edinburgh		H	F	3-2	Ramsay	Thomson	Adamson	Hazells	Hazells	Jarvis,W	Chalmers 1	Webster	Dall 2	Marshall	Jarvis,D	
S	08-Sep	Dalry Albert		A	F	3-4	Ramsay	Thomson	Adamson	Hazells	Hepburn,D	Hazells	Chalmers 1	Dall	Dall	Dall	Jarvis,D 2	
S	15-Sep	Pathhead United		H	F	5-0	Ramsay	Thomson	Adamson	Russell	Nelson 1	Jarvis,W	Chalmers 1	Dall 1	Henderson,W	Webster	Jarvis,D 2	
S	22-Sep	North Western Edinburgh		H	F	2-1	Ramsay	Thomson	Adamson	Hepburn,D	Nelson	Jarvis,W	Chalmers	Dall	Henderson,W 2	Marshall	Jarvis,D	
S	29-Sep	Hibernian 2nds		H	F	3-0	Ramsay	Thomson	Adamson	Russell 1	Nelson	Jarvis,W	Chalmers 2	Dall	Henderson,W 2	Barns	Jarvis,D	
S	06-Oct	Bainfield, Edinburgh		A	F	8-1	Ramsay	Thomson	Adamson	Russell 1	Nelson	Jarvis,W	Chalmers 2	Dall 3	Barns	Jarvis,D	Marshall	
S	13-Oct	Cowdenbeath North End		A	CC 1	9-0	Ramsay	Thomson	Adamson	Jarvis,D	Nelson,D	Hepburn,D	Chalmers 2	Dall 1	Jarvis,D	Marshall 2	Jarvis,D	
S	27-Oct	Pathhead United		A	SJC 1	1-3	Ramsay	Thomson	Adamson	Russell 1	Nelson 1	Jarvis,W	Chalmers 1	Russell 1	Henderson,W 3	Marshall	Jarvis,D	Burnett Elder Bogie
S	10-Nov	Albany		H	F	6-0	Ramsay	Thomson	Adamson	Russell	Nelson	Jarvis,W	Chalmers 2	Dall 1	Henderson,W	Hepburn,A	Jarvis,D	
S	17-Nov	Kirkcaldy Albion		H	F	2-2	Ramsay	Thomson	Adamson	Russell	Nelson	Jarvis,W	Chalmers 1	Dall 2	Henderson,W 1	Marshall	Jarvis,D	Deuchars (2)
S	24-Nov	Our Boys, Leslie		A	F	3-0	Ramsay	Thomson	Adamson	Hepburn,D	Nelson	Jarvis,W	Chalmers	Dall 1	Henderson,W 2	Marshall,A2	Jarvis,D	
S	08-Dec	Burntisland Thistle		H	F	2-1	Ramsay	Thomson	Adamson	Russell	Nelson	Jarvis,W	Chalmers 1	Dall 2	Henderson,W 1	Marshall,A2	Jarvis,D 2	Foster
S	15-Dec	Pathhead United		H	KJC 1	4-0	Ramsay	Thomson	Adamson	Russell	Nelson	Jarvis,W	Chalmers 2	Dall 1	Henderson,W	Marshall,A2	Jarvis,D 1	
S	22-Dec	Norton Park Reserves	3	H	F	3-0	Ramsay	Thomson	Adamson	Hazells	Duff	Marshall	Myles	Dall	Henderson	Henderson	Henderson	
S	29-Dec	Lochgelly Athletic Juniors		A	CC 2	3-2	Ramsay	Thomson	Adamson	Nelson	Russell	Jarvis,W	Chalmers	Dall 1	Jarvis,D	Marshall,A2	Jarvis,D 2	
Tu	01-Jan	Adventurers	w	N	F	2-2	Jarvis,W	Thomson	Adamson	Nelson	Russell	Jarvis,W	Henderson	Dall 1	Jarvis,D 1	Marshall,A2 1	Cook 2	
S	19-Jan	Kirkcaldy Albion	w	N	KJC F	2-0	Ramsay	Thomson	Adamson	Hepburn,D	Russell	Jarvis,W 2	Chalmers	Dall 1	Jarvis,D	Marshall,A2 1	Henderson 2	
S	26-Jan	Dalry Albert		H	F	3-2	Ramsay	Thomson	Hepburn,D	Russell	Russell	Jarvis,W	Henderson	Dall 1	Henderson 1	Marshall,A2 1	Henderson	White Begbie
S	09-Feb	Pathhead United	1	A	B	3-5	Ramsay	Thomson	Adamson	Russell	Nelson 1	Jarvis,W	Jarvis,D	Dall	Henderson 3	Dall 2	Henderson	Burnett (2) Baxter Elder + og
S	23-Feb	Lochgelly Athletic Juniors		A	CC 2r	7-2	Ramsay	Thomson 1	Adamson	Russell	Nelson	Williamson	Henderson	Henderson 1	Norval 3	Dall 3	Chalmers 1	
S	09-Mar	Norton Park		H	F	3-2	Muir	Thomson	Buchanan	Nelson	Russell	Williamson	Henderson	Ross	Norval 2	Dall	Chalmers	
S	16-Mar	St Leonards	2	N	F	2-3	Currie	Thomson	Adamson	Nelson	Cameron	Williamson	Chalmers	Ross	Norval 1	Dall	Chalmers	Hughes (2) Penman
S	30-Mar	Woodburn, Edinburgh		H	F	2-3	Ramsay	Thomson 1	Adamson	Nelson	Russell	Williamson	Henderson 1	Cameron	Norval 2	Marshall,A2	Ramsay	Paton Fee + another
S	06-Apr	Kirkcaldy Albion	w	N	CC SF	3-4	Cairns	Thomson 1	Adamson	Nelson	Russell	Williamson	Henderson	Marshall,A2	Norval 2	Dall	Chalmers	2 others + Ritchie Deuchars 89
S	20-Apr	Bellstane Birds		H	F	1-3	Currie	Thomson	Nelson	Hepburn,D	Russell	Williamson	Chalmers	Marshall,A2	Marshall,A2	Marshall,A2	Dall	

236

1889-90

Day	Date	Opponents	Note	Venue	Comp	Res.	Att.	1	2	3	4	5	6	7	8	9	10	11		Substitutes, own goals, goal times and opponents' scorers
S	24-Aug	Dundee Wanderers		H	F	0-3		Cairns	Nelson	Thomson	Adamson	Sturrock	Henderson,J	Clark	Dall	Stewart	Cook	Chalmers		Shepherd + another
S	31-Aug	Fifeshire Hibernian	1	H	F	5-2		Cairns	Nelson	Thomson	Henderson,J	Main	Hall	Leitch 1	Cameron 1	Chalmers	Dall 1	Cook 1	own goal 1	
S	07-Sep	Dunfermline Athletic		H	SC 1	1-2		Cairns	Nelson	Thomson	Chalmers	Main	Hall	Dall	Cameron	Barker	Cook 1	Webster		Bruce (2)
S	14-Sep	Kirkcaldy Wanderers	2	A	ESS 1	0-4	1500	Cairns	Nelson	Thomson	Hall	Main	Henderson,J	Cameron	Dall	Barker	Cook	Chalmers		Davie Jarvis, D (2) Smith
S	28-Sep	Norton Park		A	F	1-5		Cairns	Nelson	Thomson	Hall	Main	Henderson,J	Cameron	Dall 1	Barker	Cook	Chalmers		
M	07-Oct	Kirkcaldy Albion		H	F	2-3		Lyall	Nelson	Morton	Hall	Buchanan	Hazells	Dall	Cameron	Wilson 1	Henderson,J	Webster 1		Bogie Deuchars
S	12-Oct	Cowdenbeath		H	FC 1	2-8		Ramsay	Nelson	Morton	Hall	Buchanan	Hazells	Dall	Cameron	Wilson	Henderson,J 2	Webster		Thomson Hughes Graham + 5 others
S	19-Oct	Townhill		H	F	8-1		Ramsay	Nelson	Morton	Hall	Buchanan	Hazells	Dall 3	Henderson,J 1	Tynie 1	Webster 1	Cameron 2		
S	26-Oct	Burntisland Thistle		A	F	1-1		Ramsay	Nelson	Thomson	Hall	Buchanan	Hazells	Dall	Henderson,J	Tynie 1	Webster	Urquhart		
S	02-Nov	Kirkcaldy Albion		A	F	2-3		Morton	Nelson	Thomson	Hall	Buchanan	Robertson	Dall 1	Henderson,J	Tynie 1	Chalmers	Urquhart		Brown Bogie Deuchars
S	09-Nov	St Andrews University		H	F	10-1		Morton	Nelson	Thomson	Buchanan	Chalmers	Henderson,J 1	Hall 1	Cameron 2	Henderson,A	Dall 3	Urquhart 3		
S	16-Nov	Celtic Reserves		H	F	4-5		Morton	Nelson	Thomson	Chalmers	Buchanan 1	Henderson,J	Hall 1	Urquhart 1	Dall	Henderson,A 1	Cameron		Murray Collins (2) + 2 others
S	23-Nov	St Johnstone		H	F	4-4		Morton	Nelson	Graham	Chalmers	Buchanan	Henderson,J	Thomson	Urquhart	Dall 2	Henderson,A 2	Cameron		
S	30-Nov	Pathhead United		H	F	3-3		Clunie	Nelson	Thomson	Wishart	Morton	Chalmers	Webster 1	Cameron	Dall 1	Henderson,A	Hall 1		Bogie Harley (2)
S	07-Dec	Cowdenbeath		A	KC 2	2-6		Morton	Nelson	Thomson	Cameron	Henderson,J	Chalmers	Webster 2	Urquhart	Dall	Henderson,A	Hall		
S	14-Dec	Penicuik Athletic		H	F	7-1		Morton	Nelson	Thomson	Buchanan 1	Cameron	Henderson,J	Leitch 4	Urquhart	Dall 1	Hall 1	Chalmers		
S	21-Dec	Dunfermline Athletic		A	F	3-7		Morton	Nelson	Thomson	Buchanan 1	Cameron	Henderson,J 1	Leitch	Urquhart	Dall	Hall	Chalmers	McLean og 1	Wilson Hamilton Murray (2) Hutchison ????
S	28-Dec	Kirkcaldy Wanderers		H	F	6-2		Morton	Nelson	Thomson	Chalmers	Buchanan	Hall 2	Leitch 1	Urquhart 1	Dall 2	Cameron	Henderson,A		Myles + another
W	01-Jan	Rangers		H	F	0-4		Morton	Nelson	Thomson	Williamson	Buchanan	Hall	Leitch	Urquhart	Dall	Cameron	Norval		Gibb another, scrimmage Gossland (2)
S	01-Feb	Cameron Highlanders		H	F	6-3		Morton	Nelson	Thomson	Urquhart	Henderson,J	Chalmers	Webster	Leitch 3	Dall 2	Henderson,A	Hall 1		
S	08-Feb	Bellstane Birds		H	F	7-4		Morton	Nelson	Thomson	Chalmers	Henderson,J	Buchanan	Hall	Urquhart 2	Dall 2	Cameron 1	Leitch 2		
S	15-Feb	Adventurers		A	SCC	1-2		Ramsay	Morton	Thomson	Buchanan	Chalmers	Henderson,J	Henderson,A	Wilson 1	Dall	Cameron	Hall		
S	01-Mar	Adventurers		H	F	6-2		Morton	Nelson	Thomson	Buchanan 1	Chalmers 1	Henderson,J 2	Hall	Cameron	Dall	Urquhart	Leitch 2		
S	08-Mar	Norton Park		H	F	7-2		Morton	Nelson	Thomson	Buchanan	Chalmers	Henderson,J	Leitch 2	Urquhart 2	Dall 3	Cameron	Hall		
S	22-Mar	Cowdenbeath	3	H	B	4-2	1600	Morton	Nelson	Thomson	Buchanan	Chalmers	Henderson,J	Leitch 2	Urquhart 1	Dall	Hall	Cameron 1		Hughes (2)
S	29-Mar	Black Watch, Perth		H	F	2-0		Morton	Nelson	Thomson	Buchanan	Chalmers	Henderson,J	Leitch 1	Urquhart	Dall 1	Hall	Cameron		
S	12-Apr	Leith Athletic 2nds		H	F	1-1		Morton	Nelson	Thomson	Buchanan	Chalmers	Henderson,J	Leitch	Urquhart	Dall 1	Hall	Cameron		
S	26-Apr	Burntisland Thistle		H	F	2-1		Morton	Nelson	Thomson	Buchanan	Chalmers	Baxter 1	Leitch	Urquhart	Thomson,G 1	Hall	Cameron		Cowan 43
W	21-May	Kirkcaldy Albion		A	F	2-3		Clunie	Russell	Millar	Duffus	Henderson,J	Hall 2	Dall	Leitch	Cummings	Urquhart	Cameron		
		1890-91																		
S	09-Aug	St Bernards		H	F	4-2		Gourlay	Nelson	Thomson	Hall	Millar	Henderson,J	Dall 1	Leitch 1	Mackay 1	Cameron	Hughes 1		Hall Clements NS
S	23-Aug	Fairfield, Glasgow		H	F	9-6		Ramsay	Nelson	Addison	Hall	Henderson,J	Thomson,G	Bogie 3	Deuchars 1	Mackay 3	Dall 1	Miller 1		
S	30-Aug	Partick Thistle		H	F	4-5		Ramsay	Nelson	Thomson	Hall	Henderson,J	Baxter	Cameron 1	Dall 1	Mackay 2	Bogie	Deuchars		Gilchrist Clark (3) McLeod
S	06-Sep	Hearts		A	SC 1	2-7		Ramsay	Nelson	Thomson	Hall	Baxter	Henderson,J	Dall	Cameron 1	Mackay 1	Bogie	Deuchars		Somerville Baird (2) Taylor (2) McPherson (2)
S	20-Sep	Edinburgh Teachers	1	H	ESS 1	8-1		Ramsay	Nelson	Thomson	Hall	Baxter	Henderson,J	Dall 3	Leitch 2	Mackay	Bogie 2	Deuchars 1		
S	27-Sep	Lassodie		H	F	8-2		Clunie	Nelson	Thomson 1	Hall 1	Baxter	Cameron 1	Dall 2	Leitch	Mackay 2	Bogie 1	Deuchars		
S	04-Oct	Lochgelly United		A	FC 1	1-1		Clunie	Nelson	Thomson	Hall	Henderson,J	Cameron	Dall	Leitch 1	Mackay	Bogie	Deuchars		
M	06-Oct	Edinburgh Exhibition		A	F	7-0		Clunie	Nelson	Thomson 1	Hall	Henderson,J	Cameron	Dall 3	Leitch	Mackay 2	Bogie	Deuchars 1		
S	11-Oct	Kirkcaldy Wanderers		A	F	0-3		Clunie	Nelson	Thomson	Hall	Baxter	Henderson,J	Dall	Leitch	Mackay	Bogie	Deuchars		Dunnough (2) Urquhart
S	25-Oct	Lochgelly United		A	FC 1r	7-2		Clunie	Nelson	Thomson	Hall	Mackay	Neilson 1	Dall 2	Cowan 2	Leitch	Bogie 2	Deuchars		
S	01-Nov	Dunfermline Athletic		A	F	6-3		Clunie	Nelson	Thomson	Hall 1	Mackay	Webster	Dall 1	Leitch	Wilson	Bogie 3	Deuchars 1		
S	08-Nov	Alloa Athletic		A	KC 1	2-2		Clunie	Nelson	Thomson	Hall	Mackay	Webster	Dall	Leitch	Cowan 2	Bogie	Deuchars		Hendry McLauchlan
S	15-Nov	Alloa Athletic		H	KC 1r	3-1		Clunie	Nelson	Thomson	Hall	Mackay	Webster	Dall 1	Leitch	Cowan 1	Bogie 1	Deuchars		Laing ?
S	22-Nov	Burntisland Thistle	2	H	F	0-0		Clunie	Nelson	Thomson	Hall	Mackay	Webster	Dall	Leitch	Cowan	Bogie	Deuchars		
S	29-Nov	Champfleurie		A	KC 2	6-3		Clunie	Nelson	Thomson	Hall	Mackay	Webster	Dall	Leitch 2	Cowan 2	Bogie 2	Deuchars		
S	06-Dec	Pathhead United		A	F	4-1		Clunie	Nelson	Thomson	Hall	Mackay	Webster	Dall 1	Leitch	Cowan	Bogie 2	Deuchars 1		Cumming
S	13-Dec	4th V.B.R.S.		H	KC 3	10-0		Clunie	Nelson	Thomson	Hall 1	Mann 1	Webster	Dall 2	Leitch 1	Cowan 2	Bogie 3	Deuchars		
S	20-Dec	Lassodie		A	FC SF	1-5		Clunie	Nelson	Thomson	Hall	Mackay	Webster	Dall	Leitch	Cowan 1	Bogie	Deuchars		
S	10-Jan	Kirkcaldy Albion		A	F	5-0		Clunie	Nelson	Neilson 1	Hall	Mackay	Webster	Dall 2	Leitch 1	Cameron	Bogie 1	Deuchars		
S	17-Jan	Cameron Highlanders		H	F	5-2		Clunie	Nelson	Thomson	Hall	Mackay	Webster	Cameron	Neilson 1	Cowan 2	Bogie 2	Deuchars		
S	31-Jan	Bathgate Rovers	3	H	KC SF	0-0		Clunie	Nelson	Thomson	Hall	Mackay	Webster	Dall	Leitch	Cowan	Bogie	Deuchars		
S	07-Feb	Lassodie		H	SCC 2	10-1		Clunie	Nelson	Thomson	Hall	Mackay	Webster	Dall 1	Leitch 2	Cowan 1	Bogie 4	Deuchars 2		
S	14-Feb	Bathgate Rovers		H	KC SF	8-2		Clunie	Nelson	Thomson	Hall 1	Mackay 1	Webster	Dall	Leitch	Cowan 3	Bogie 3	Deuchars		another + Murnin
S	21-Feb	Burntisland Thistle		A	F	7-2		Clunie	Nelson	Thomson	Hall	Mackay 3	Webster	Dall	Leitch 2	Cowan 2	Bogie	Deuchars		
S	28-Feb	Armadale	4	N	KC F	3-1		Clunie	Nelson	Thomson	Hall	Mackay	Webster	Dall	Leitch 1	Cowan 1	Bogie 1	Deuchars		Chalmers
S	14-Mar	Broughty Ferry		H	F	5-3		Clunie	Nelson	Thomson	Hall	Mackay	Coupar	Dall 2	Leitch 1	Cowan	Bogie 1	Deuchars 1		
Th	19-Mar	Montrose		A	F	4-1		Clunie	Nelson	Thomson	Hall 1	Mackay	Coupar	Dall	Leitch	Cowan	Bogie 3	Deuchars 1		
S	28-Mar	Johnston Wanderers		H	F	5-0		Clunie	Nelson	Thomson	Hall	Mackay	Coupar	Dall	Leitch 1	Cowan 1	Bogie 2	Neilson 1		
S	04-Apr	Leith Athletic	5	N	RC	2-4	1000	Clunie	Nelson	Thomson	Hall	Mackay	Murnin	Dall 1	Leitch	Cowan	Bogie 1	Deuchars		Clements McQueen, H Mathieson (2)
S	18-Apr	Dundee Harp		H	F	8-2		Clunie	Nelson	Thomson	Hall	Mackay 2	Henderson,J	Dall 1	Leitch 1	Wilson	Bogie 2	Deuchars 2		McCann McReadie
S	25-Apr	Dunfermline Athletic		A	F	5-3		Clunie	Nelson	Thomson	Hall	Mackay 1	Neilson	Dall	Leitch	Cowan 1	Bogie 2	Deuchars 1		
S	02-May	Hearts A		A	F	1-8		Clunie	Nelson	Thomson	Hall	Mackay	Neilson	Dall	Leitch	Cowan 1	Bogie	Deuchars		Shand Gordon (3) Fairbairn (2) Baird scrimmage
S	09-May	Johnston Wanderers		A	F	1-2		Clunie	Nelson	Thomson	Hall	Mackay 1	Neilson	Dall	Leitch	Cowan	Bogie	Deuchars		
S	23-May	Dunfermline Athletic	6	A	C	3-2		Clunie	Nelson	Thomson	Hall	Mackay	Cameron 1	Dall 2	Leitch	Cowan	Bogie	Deuchars		another + Gillespie
S	06-Jun	Dunfermline Athletic	w1	N	C	5-2		Clunie	Nelson	Thomson	Hall	Mackay	Cameron	Dall	Leitch 1	Cowan 1	Bogie 3	Deuchars		Campbell + another

1889/1890
First season as seniors
(1) Fifeshire Hibs were a new team from Lochgelly
(2) Takings were £11, admission was 2d and 1d
(3) Benefit for James Russell ; takings £20

1890/1891
Last season at Robbie's Park
Penalty kick introduced
(1) Abandoned during second half
(2) abandoned after 55 minutes
(3) abandoned after 15 minutes due to a storm
(4) at Logie Green
(5) at Tynecastle
(6) Charity Cup Final
(w1) Charity Cup Final Replay ; at Newton Park

Substitutes, own goals, goal times and opponents' scorers

Day	Date	Opponents	Note	Venue	Comp	Res.	Att.	1	2	3	4	5	6	7	8	9	10	11	Substitutes, own goals, goal times and opponents' scorers
S	15-Aug	Grangemouth		H	ML	2-1		Clunie	Nelson	Thomson	Cameron	Hall	Mackay	Dall 1	Leitch	Deuchars	Bogie	Cowan 1	McFarlane
S	22-Aug	Alloa Athletic		A	ML	2-1		Clunie	Couper	Thomson	Cameron	Hall	Mackay	Wishart 1	Dall	Mann	Deuchars	[man short]	Hendry
S	29-Aug	Bridge of Allan		H	ML	9-3		Clunie	Kay	Thomson	Mackay 1	Nicholson 1	Couper	Hall 2	Dall	Cameron 2	Bogie 3	Cowan	
S	05-Sep	Broxburn		A	SC 1	1-2		Clunie	Kay	Thomson	Cameron	Mackay	Couper	Nicholson	Dall 1	Cowan	Deuchars	Bogie	Chalmers (2)
S	12-Sep	Dunblane		H	ML	4-3		Clunie	Kay	Thomson	Hall	Mackay	Couper	Nicholson	Dall 2	Cowan	Deuchars	Bogie 2	Ramage Weir Ramsay
S	19-Sep	Lochgelly United		H	ESS 1	5-1		Clunie	Kay	Thomson	Hall	Mackay	Couper	Dall 2	Nicholson 1	Bogie 2	Deuchars	Cowan.	Cowper og
S	26-Sep	Adventurers		H	F	5-1		Clunie	Kay	Thomson	Hall	Mackay	Couper	Dall	Nicholson	Cowan 2	Bogie 1	Deuchars 2	Baxter
S	03-Oct	Alva		A	ML	6-5		Clunie	Kay	Thomson	Hall	Mackay	Couper	Dall	Nicholson	Cowan 1	Bogie	Deuchars 3	Morton Davidson + 3 others
S	10-Oct	Burntisland Thistle		A	ESS 2	6-0		Clunie	Kay	Thomson	Hall	Mackay	Couper	Dall 4	Nicholson	Cowan 2	Bogie	Deuchars	
S	17-Oct	Dunfermline Athletic		A	F	2-1		Clunie	Kay	Thomson	Hall	Mackay	Couper	Dall 1	Nicholson	Cowan 1	Bogie	Deuchars	
S	24-Oct	Clackmannan		H	ML	9-1		Clunie	Thomson	Thomson	Hall 1	Mackay	Couper 2	Cameron 2	Leitch	Dall 1	Wishart 3	Deuchars	Ferguson
S	31-Oct	Pollton Vale		H	F	6-0		Clunie	Thomson	Kay	Nicholson	Couper 1	Dall 2	Cameron	Leitch	Wishart 2	Deuchars	Cowan	McKechnie (2)
S	07-Nov	Burntisland Thistle		A	KC 1	4-1		Clunie	Thomson	Kay	Nicholson	Mackay	Dall 2	Cameron	Leitch	Wishart	Deuchars	Cowan 2	
S	14-Nov	Camelon		A	ML	1-2		Clunie	Thomson	Kay	Nicholson	Couper	Dall	Cameron	Leitch	Wishart	Deuchars	Cowan 1	
S	21-Nov	Adventurers		H	ESS 4	3-2		Clunie	Kay	Thomson	Nicholson	Nelson	Leitch	Cameron 1	Dall 1	Cowan	Leitch	Deuchars 1	Baxter, T. 30 Stewart, T. 20
S	05-Dec	Dunfermline Athletic		H	KC 2	5-3		Clunie	Kay	Thomson	Nicholson	Mackay	Couper	Cowan 2	Leitch	Wishart 1	Deuchars	Dall 2	Bruce + 2 others
S	12-Dec	St Bernards		A	ESS 5	2-3		Clunie	Kay	Thomson	Nicholson	Couper	Mackay	Cowan 1	Leitch	Couper	Deuchars 1	Walker	Stuart Clark + another
S	19-Dec	Dunfermline Athletic		H	F	3-1		Clunie	Kay	Thomson	Couper	Nicholson 1	Leitch	Wishart	Deuchars	Cowan 1	Mackay	Walker 1	
S	26-Dec	Dunfermline Athletic		H	KC 2	5-1		Clunie	Kay	Thomson	Couper	Nicholson	Mackay 1	Wishart	Dall 1	Leitch	Deuchars 1	Cowan 2	Bruce
S	09-Jan	Northern, Glasgow		H	F	2-3		Clunie	Kay	Thomson	Nicholson	Mackay	Couper 1	Wishart	Deuchars	Cowan	Dall 1	Leitch	Fraser Thomson og scrimmage
S	23-Jan	Our Boys, Dundee		H	F	4-6		Clunie	Kay	Thomson	Nicholson	Mackay 1	Couper	Wishart	Deuchars	Cowan 1	Dall 2	Leitch	Dagrie Gregory Dundas pen Peters + 2 others
S	30-Jan	Victoria United		A	F	2-1		Clunie	Kay	Thomson	Deuchars	Couper	Leitch	Dall	Leitch	Cowan	Wishart 1	Nicholson 1	
S	13-Feb	Bathgate Rovers		A	KC 3	1-3		Clunie	Kay	Thomson	Nicholson	Nelson	Couper	Leitch	Dall 1	Mackay	Wishart	Nicholson	Deuchars (og) Dunlop Kennedy
S	20-Feb	Camelon		H	ML	5-5		Clunie	Nelson 2	Thomson	Nicholson	Deuchars	Couper	Dall 1	Wishart 1	Cowan 1	Walker	Neilson	McGregor Drummond Spears + 2 others
S	27-Feb	Clackmannan	1	A	ML	1-3		Cairns	Kay	Thomson	Deuchars	Mackay	Couper	Walker	Dall 1	Cowan 1	Deuchars	Cameron	Whyte Halley (2) Forsyth
S	12-Mar	Lochgelly United		H	FC SF	4-0		Cairns	Kay	Thomson	Couper	Mackay	Couper	Leitch	Walker 2	Cowan 1	Deuchars	Neilson	
S	19-Mar	Dunfermline Athletic		H	ML	7-1		Cairns	Kay	Thomson	Couper	Mackay	Deuchars	Walker 1	Wishart	Cowan 4	Neilson 3	Dall	Neives
S	26-Mar	Bridge of Allan		A	ML	1-1		Cairns	Kay	Thomson	Couper	Mackay	Deuchars	Walker 1	Wishart	Cowan	Neilson	Dall	
S	02-Apr	Kirkcaldy		H	F	2-1		Cairns	Kay	Thomson	Deuchars	Mackay	Couper	Neilson 1	Dall	Leitch 1	Wishart	Walker	
M	04-Apr	Northern, Glasgow		H	F	1-1		Cairns	Kay	Thomson	Couper	Mackay	Deuchars	Walker	Wishart	Cowan 2	Neilson	Dall	McNaughton
M	09-Apr	Dunfermline Athletic		H	ML	3-1		Clunie	Kay	Thomson	Nelson	Cameron	Couper	Walker 1	Wishart	Cowan 2	Leitch	Neilson	Cannon
S	16-Apr	Lochee United		H	F	5-0		Cairns	Nelson	Thomson	Deuchars	Couper	Mackay	Neilson 1	Walker 1	Cowan 2	Dall 1	Wishart	Nicol
S	23-Apr	Cowdenbeath	2	N	FC F	3-1	2500	Cairns	Kay	Thomson	Deuchars	Mackay	Couper	Walker	Neilson 2	Cowan 1	Dall	Neilson 2	Drummond
S	30-Apr	Dunblane		A	ML	1-2		Cairns	Kay	Thomson	Deuchars	Mackay	Couper	Walker 1	Wishart	Cowan	Dall	Cameron	
S	14-May	Alva		H	ML	7-0		Cairns	Kay	Thomson	Mackay	Neilson 1	Couper	Walker 4	Wishart 1	Dall 1	Deuchars	Cowan	
S	21-May	Grangemouth		A	ML	5-0		Cairns	Kay	Thomson	Couper	Mackay	Deuchars	Walker 2	Wishart 1	Cowan 1	Dall	Neilson 1	
M	23-May	Pathhead United	3	A	F	1-1		Cairns	Hood	Barclay	Deuchars	Hunter	Couper	Walker	Cameron	Lambert 1	Dall	Neilson 1	Smith
S	28-May	Dunfermline Athletic		A	ML	2-3		Cairns	Hood	Barclay	Deuchars	Hunter	Couper	Walker	Cameron	Lambert 1	Dall	Neilson 1	
M	30-May	Pathhead United		A	F	4-1		Cairns	Hood	Barclay	Deuchars	Hunter	Couper	Walker	Cameron 1	Lambert 1	Dall 1	Neilson 1	Harley
Tu	31-May	Kirkcaldy Wanderers		A	F	3-1		Cairns	Hood	Thomson	Deuchars	Dall	Dall	Wishart	Walker	Lambert	Suttie 1	Neilson 1	Shaw og 1 / Sinclair

First season at Stark's Park
Linesmen replaced umpires
(1) an Alloa newspaper had the score as 4-1
(2) at East End Park
(3) two 30 minutes played

The Fife Free Press of Saturday May 4th 1889 included a portrait & sketch of Mr Thomas Nelson, Captain Raith Rovers

"Among our junior footballers the name of Thomas Nelson is well known. He first came into prominence as a football player in the ranks of the Thistle during the season of the Wanderers' badges. The Thistle, it may be remembered, met the Albion on three different occasions for the possession of the badges, but eventually they had to succumb to the latter club. At the end of the season Tom joined the Rovers, and the example was shortly afterwards followed by most of the Thistle players. Since then Nelson has figured prominently in the Rovers. His place was right wing, but a short time ago he was put at half-back, a position he has sustained with honour to himself and his club. As a football player he may be termed a good, all-round man, his style being clean and effective. Tom now captains the team with much acceptance."

Day	Date	Opponents	Note	Venue	Comp	Res.	Att.	1	2	3	4	5	6	7	8	9	10	11	Substitutes, own goals, goal times and opponents' scorers
S	07-Aug	Cowdenbeath		A	F	5-4		Grieve	Barclay	Bonnella	Cameron	Deuchars	Mackay	Walker,J	Neilson 1	Walker,D 2	Suttie 2	Lambert	Syme (2) Young
S	03-Sep	Grangemouth		H	F	2-3		Grieve	Couper	Thomson	Cameron	Mackay	Dall	Walker,J	Cowan	Lambert	Neilson 1	Suttie 1	
S	10-Sep	Broxburn		H	F	3-1		Grieve	Kennedy	Thomson	Duffus	Mackay 1	Couper	Walker,J 1	Campbell	Walker,D 1	Suttie	Wishart	
S	17-Sep	Lassodie		H	ESS 1	14-0		Grieve	Kennedy	Thomson	Duffus	Mackay 2	Couper 1	Walker,J 3	Tod 1	Walker,D 2	Dall 2	Neilson 3	
S	24-Sep	Smithston Hibernians		H	SC 2	1-3		Grieve	Kennedy	Thomson	Duffus	Mackay	Couper	Walker,J	Suttie	Cowan 1	Dall	Neilson	
S	01-Oct	Victoria United		A	F	0-0		Grieve	Kennedy jnr	Thomson	Duffus	Mackay	Couper	Dall	Walker,J	Walker,D	Suttie	Neilson	
M	03-Oct	Coupar Angus	1	H	F	7-0		Grieve	Barclay	Crichton	Dall 3	Mackay	Tod	Walker,J	Lambert	Walker,D 2	Neilson	Suttie 2	
S	08-Oct	Kirkcaldy		H	ESS 2	6-0		Grieve	Kennedy jnr	Thomson	Crichton	Mackay	Couper	Walker,J	Lambert	Walker,D 2	Suttie 2	Neilson	Mack Alexander
S	15-Oct	Cambuslang		H	F	3-1		Grieve	Kennedy jnr	Thomson	Crichton	Mackay	Couper	Walker,J 1	Dall 1	Walker,D 2	Suttie	Neilson 1	Jagger
S	22-Oct	Adventurers		H	F	5-2		Grieve	Kennedy jnr	Thomson	Crichton	Mackay 1	Tod	Walker,J 1	Lambert	Walker,D 2	Suttie 1	Neilson 2	Spowart Frew
S	29-Oct	Edinburgh University	2	H	ESS 3	9-1		Grieve	Nelson	Thomson	Deuchars	Mackay	Couper	Walker,J 2	Dall 1	Walker,D 2	Suttie 3	Neilson 1	
S	05-Nov	Dunfermline Athletic		A	KC 1	3-2		Grieve	Nelson	Thomson	Deuchars	Mackay	Couper	Walker,J	Dall 1	Walker,D 2	Suttie	Neilson 2	Ross og 1
S	19-Nov	Grangemouth		A	F	2-1		Grieve	Nelson	Thomson	Deuchars	Mackay	Couper	Walker,J	Dall 1	Walker,D 1	Suttie	Neilson	
S	26-Nov	Rangers A		H	F	6-2		Grieve	Nelson	Thomson	Deuchars	Mackay 1	Couper	Walker,J 1	Dall 1	Walker,D 1	Suttie 2	Neilson 1	Robb (2)
S	03-Dec	Kirkcaldy		A	FC 2	4-1		Grieve	Nelson	Thomson	Deuchars	Mackay	Couper	Walker,J	Dall	Walker,D 1	Suttie 2	Neilson 1	Dall og
S	10-Dec	Lochgelly United		H	F	2-2		Grieve	Deuchars	Thomson	Wishart	Mackay	Couper 1	Walker,J	Dall	Walker,D 1	Suttie 1	Neilson 1	Smith (2)
S	24-Dec	Lochgelly United		H	ESS 4	8-2		Grieve	Nelson	Thomson	Deuchars	Mackay	Couper 1	Walker,J 3	Dall 1	Walker,D 1	Suttie 2	Neilson	Vale, T Lion
M	02-Jan	Renton		H	F	1-1	2000	Grieve	Bird	Thomson	Deuchars	Mackay	Tod	Walker,J	Dall	Walker,D 1	Suttie	Neilson	Murray
S	14-Jan	Kirkcaldy	1	H	F	4-0		Grieve	Nelson	Barclay	Deuchars	Mackay	Tod	Walker,J	Dall	Walker,D 1	Suttie	Neilson 2	Arnott og 1
S	21-Jan	Kirkcaldy		H	FC 2	7-2		Grieve	Nelson	Thomson	Crichton	Mackay	Deuchars	Walker,J 3	Wishart	Walker,D 1	Suttie 1	Neilson 2	Anderson Hughes
S	28-Jan	Bathgate		A	KC 3	1-1		Grieve	Nelson	Barclay	Crichton	Mackay	Deuchars	Walker,J	Tod	Walker,D 1	Suttie	Neilson	Thomson Murnin, J
S	04-Feb	Bathgate		H	KC 3r	1-2		Grieve	Nelson	Thomson	Crichton	Mackay	Couper	Walker,J	Dall	Walker,D 1	Suttie	Neilson	Phemister
S	11-Feb	Cowdenbeath		H	F	3-1		Grieve	Nelson	Millar	Crichton	Mackay	Couper	Walker,J 1	Dall 1	Walker,D	Suttie 1	Neilson 1	Scott Mackie Crossan
S	18-Feb	St Bernards		H	ESS SF	1-3		Grieve	Nelson	Coupar	Deuchars	Thomson,D	Crichton	Walker,J 1	Dall	Walker,D	Dall 1	Dall 1	
S	25-Feb	Cowdenbeath	3	A	B	4-4		Grieve	Nelson	Thomson	Brown	Mackay	Couper	Walker,J 2	Tod	Dall 1	Suttie 2	Neilson	
S	11-Mar	Edinburgh University		H	F	4-2	2500	Grieve	Nelson	Thomson	Lambert	Mackay	Couper	Walker,J	Dall 1	Walker,D 1	Suttie 2	Neilson	Murison Benzie
S	18-Mar	Victoria United		A	F	5-0		Grieve	Nelson	Thomson	Lambert	Mackay	Couper	Walker,J 1	Dall 2	Walker,D 2	Suttie 1	Neilson	
S	25-Mar	Wishaw Thistle		H	FC SF	5-3		Grieve	Nelson	Thomson	Deuchars	Mackay	Couper	Walker,J	Dall 2	Walker,D 2	Suttie 1	Neilson 1	Smith (2) + another
S	01-Apr	Lochgelly United		H	F	5-3		Grieve	Nelson	Thomson	Crichton	Mackay 1	Couper	Walker,J	Dall 1	Walker,D 1	Suttie	Neilson 2	Smith Steel (2)
M	03-Apr	Linthouse		H	F	4-2		Grieve	Nelson	Thomson	Lambert	Mackay 1	Tod	Tod	Walker,J	Tod 1	Suttie 1	Stewart 1	
S	08-Apr	Battlefield		H	F	7-1		Clunie	Nelson	Thomson	Deuchars	Mackay 1	Lambert	Thomson,D	Tod	Dall 2	Suttie 2	Neilson 1	Henderson Kilgour
S	15-Apr	Fair City Athletic		H	F	9-0		Grieve	Nelson	Thomson	Deuchars	Mackay 1	Couper	Walker,J 1	Dall 2	Walker,D 1	Suttie 2	Neilson 1	Gray
S	22-Apr	Carrington, Glasgow		H	F	2-2		Grieve	Nelson	Thomson	Deuchars	Mackay	Couper	Walker,J 2	Thomson,D 1	Walker,D 1	Suttie 1	Neilson	own goal 1
S	06-May	Cowdenbeath	w	N	FC F	2-2		Grieve	Nelson	Thomson	Deuchars	Mackay	Couper	Walker,J 1	Dall	Walker,D 1	Suttie	Neilson 1	Hendry Law
S	20-May	Strathmore, Dundee		A	F	7-2		Grieve	Nelson	Thomson	Deuchars	Mackay	Couper	Stewart	Eckford	Walker,D 3	Suttie 1	Neilson 3	
S	24-May	Kinghorn	1	H	F	4-1		Grieve	Nelson	Thomson	Deuchars	Mackay	Couper	Stewart	Eckford	Walker,D 2	Suttie 1	Neilson 1	
S	27-May	Cowdenbeath		N	FC Fr	1-2		Grieve	Nelson	Thomson	Deuchars	Mackay	Couper	Walker,J	Lambert	Walker,D 1	Suttie	Neilson	Drummond 50 scrimmage 85

Penalty kicker could not play the ball twice, and time could be added on for a penalty to be taken at the end of a match

(1) two x 30 minutes played

(2) The Edinburgh University team included Robert Hutchison of Braehead.

(3) Benefit match for R Law of Cowdenbeath, who broke his leg in a Fife Cup tie against Dunfermline Athletic

(4) at East End Park

(w) at Newtown Park

The Fifeshire Advertiser, during 1889/90, includes a Portrait of William Jarvis, Kirkcaldy Wanderers

"He first played in 1884-85 for Raith Rovers when they were knocked out of the Kirkcaldy Wanderers junior badge contest by the now defunct Thistle. He continued to play for Raith Rovers until well on in last season until some differences arose between him and the committee, when he and his brother joined Kirkcaldy Wanderers. A half back, Mr Jarvis is an anxious player, and if the finer points of the game are at time awanting in his play, he makes up for it by genuine hard work. He can always be depended upon, no matter what sort of match has to be played, and it would be a good thing for our local clubs if they had more men of his stamp in their teams."

"The greatest of all the Kirkcaldy Ramblers, was Willie Dall, who played inside left in the heavy defeat by Pathhead United. A week later, he was signed by Raith Rovers and rapidly developed into a great player, reckoned to one of the best all-round footballers ever reared in the Lang Toun. Not tall, but sturdily built, and versatile, he played in every position for Rovers, including goalkeeper. Moreover, he excelled in every position. He was probably at the height of his considerable powers when he was centre half in the famous Rovers half back line of Hall, Dall and Cowper, after the Rovers turned senior in 1889/90."

Day	Date	Opponents	Note	Venue	Comp	Res	Att	1	2	3	4	5	6	7	8	9	10	11	Substitutes, own goals, goal times and opponents' scorers
S	12-Aug	Neilston		H	F	4-2		Grieve	Couper	Hood	Dall	Lambert	Hall	Blyth 1	Neilson	Walker,D 2	Suttie	Eckford 1	Halley White
S	26-Aug	Clackmannan		H	F	3-0		Cairns	Deuchars	Lambert	Hall	Dall	Couper	Neilson	Walker,J 2	Walker,D 2	Suttie 1	Eckford	
S	02-Sep	Dunfermline Athletic	1	H	SQC 1	8-0	700	Grieve	Bird	Lambert	Hall	Dall 1	Couper	Walker,J	Neilson	Walker,D 3	Suttie 3	Wilson 1	
S	09-Sep	Lassodie		H	ESS 1	7-0		Grieve	Bird	Lambert	Hall	Dall	Couper	Leitch	Walker,J 3	Walker,D 3	Suttie 1	Wilson 3	
S	16-Sep	St Bernards		A	F	0-4		Grieve	Bird	Lambert	Hall	Deuchars	Couper	Leitch	Neilson	Walker,D	Suttie	Suttie	
S	23-Sep	Gairdoch		H	SQC 2	2-3		Grieve	Bird	Lambert	Hall	Dall 1	Couper	Neilson	Neilson	Walker,D	Dall	Wilson 2	Kemp (2) Shaw
M	02-Oct	Dunfermline		A	F	3-1		Grieve	Bird	Lambert	Hall	Dall	Couper	Walker,J	Wilson	Walker,D 2	Suttie	Neilson	
S	07-Oct	Cowdenbeath		H	ESS 2	5-3		Grieve	Lambert	Thomson,J	Hall	Dall	Couper	Walker,J 1	Wilson	Walker,D 3	Suttie 1	Neilson 1	Vale Scott + another
S	14-Oct	Broxburn Shamrock		H	F	6-3		Grieve	Bird	Thomson,J	Hall	Dall	Lambert	Walker,J	Wilson	Walker,D 3	Suttie 1	Neilson 1	
S	21-Oct	Vale of Leven		H	F	4-1		Grieve	Lambert	Lambert	Hall	Dall	Lambert	Bird	Eckford 1	Walker,D 1	Suttie	Neilson	Logan
S	04-Nov	Aberdeen		A	F	4-3	2000	Grieve	Bird	Lambert	Hall 2	Dall	Couper	Walker,J 2	Wilson	Walker,D	Suttie 2	Neilson	
S	11-Nov	Argyll & Sutherland Highlanders		H	KC 1	8-1		Grieve	Bird	Lambert	Hall 2	Thomson,J	Couper 1	Walker,J 2	Wilson	Walker,D 3	Suttie	Suttie	Ferguson
S	18-Nov	Clackmannan		H	ESS 3	2-1		Grieve	Bird	Lambert	Hall	Dall	Couper	Walker,J 1	Blyth	Walker,D	Neilson 1	Suttie	Campbell
S	25-Nov	Burnbank Swifts	2	H	F	3-1		Grieve	Bird	Lambert	Hall	Dall 1	Couper	Walker,J 1	Blyth	Walker,D 4	Neilson	Suttie	O'Neil
S	02-Dec	Broxburn Shamrock		H	KC 2	8-1		Grieve	Lambert	Thomson,J	Hall	Dall	Couper 1	Walker,J	Wishart 2	Walker,D	Suttie	Blyth 1	
S	09-Dec	Broxburn Shamrock		H	ESS 4	2-0		Grieve	Lambert	Thomson,J	Hall	Deuchars	Couper	Walker,J 1	Wishart	Walker,D 3	Suttie 1	Blyth	
S	16-Dec	Lochee United		H	F	9-0		Grieve	Lambert	Thomson,J	Hall	Simpson	Couper	Walker,J 3	Blyth 1	Walker,D	Neilson 1	Suttie 1	
S	30-Dec	East Stirling		H	F	5-0		Grieve	Lambert	Thomson,J	Hall	Simpson	Couper	Walker,J 4	Blyth	Walker,D 1	Neilson 2	Suttie 1	Gilfillan 30 secs McNee
M	01-Jan	Renton		H	F	4-2		Grieve	Lambert	Thomson,J	Hall	Simpson	Couper	Walker,J 1	Blyth	Walker,D 1	Suttie 1	Suttie 1	
S	13-Jan	Bathgate		H	F	5-0		Grieve	Lambert	Thomson,J	Hall	Dall 1	Couper	Walker,J 2	Blyth	Walker,D 1	Suttie 1	Neilson	Grieve og Scott Hislop
S	20-Jan	Leith Athletic	3	H	ESS SF	1-3	3000	Grieve	Lambert	Thomson,J	Hall	Dall	Couper	Walker,J	Blyth 1	Walker,D 1	Suttie	Neilson 1	McQuire Collins (2) Lambert og
S	27-Jan	Cowdenbeath		A	F	6-4		Grieve	Lambert	Thomson,J	Hall	Dall 1	Couper	Walker,J	Blyth 1	Walker,D 2	Ross	Neilson 1	
S	03-Feb	Cowdenbeath		A	FC SF	2-2		Grieve	Lambert	Thomson,J	Hall	Dall	Couper	Walker,J 2	Blyth	Walker,D	Suttie	Neilson	
S	10-Feb	Cowdenbeath		H	FC SF	6-0		Grieve	Lambert	Thomson,J	Hall	Dall	Couper	Walker,J	Blyth	Walker,D 2	Suttie 4	Neilson	
S	17-Feb	Battlefield	4	H	F	4-2		Grieve	Deuchars	Thomson,J	Hall	Dall 3	Couper	Hunter	Blyth 1	Bryce	Suttie	Wishart	Anderson Neil
S	24-Feb	Cowdenbeath	5	A	F	1-6		Grieve	Deuchars	Thomson,J	Hall	Dall	Couper	Tod	Blyth	Walker,D 1	Walker,D 1	Neilson	Drummond Scott Beveridge + 3 others
S	03-Mar	Cowdenbeath		A	KC SF	0-4		Grieve	Deuchars	Thomson,J	Hall	Dall	Couper	Tod	Blyth	Walker,D	Walker,D	Neilson	Scott Collins Beveridge (2)
S	17-Mar	Cambuslang		H	F	2-2		Grieve	Deuchars	Thomson,J	Hall	Lambert	Couper	Walker,J	Dall 1	Dall 1	Suttie 1	Neilson 1	Smith Russell
S	24-Mar	Cowlairs		H	F	2-4		Grieve	Lambert	Thomson,J	Hall	Dall	Couper	Walker,J	Blyth	Walker,D	Suttie 1	Neilson 1	
S	31-Mar	Carluke		H	F	1-1		Grieve	Lambert	Thomson,J	Hall	Simpson	Couper	Collier	Simpson	Walker,D	Suttie	Neilson 1	Edgar (2) Scott + another
M	02-Apr	Hibernian		H	F	7-0	2000	Grieve	Lambert	Thomson,J	Hall	Dall	Couper	Walker,J 1	Blyth 3	Walker,D 3	Suttie 2	Neilson 1	Robertson, J
S	14-Apr	Northern, Glasgow		H	F	3-0		Grieve	Lambert	Thomson,J	Hall	Dall 1p	Couper	Eckford	Blyth	Walker,D 1	Suttie 1	Neilson 1	
S	21-Apr	Adventurers		H	F	4-0		Grieve	Lambert	Thomson,J	Hall	Simpson	Simpson	Walker,J	Blyth 1	Walker,D 2	Suttie	Neilson 1	
S	28-Apr	Lochgelly United	6	N	FC F	6-2		Grieve	Lambert	Thomson,J	Hall	Dall 2	Couper	Walker,J 1	Blyth 2	Walker,D 1	Suttie 1	Hunter 1	
S	05-May	Hearts		H	F	2-0	2000	Grieve	Cassells	Thomson,J	Lambert	Dall	Couper	Walker,J 1	Blyth	Walker,D	Suttie	Neilson 1	White, J Cairns
S	19-May	Kirkcaldy	7	H	B	2-3	1500	Grieve	Cassells	Thomson,J	Hall	Dall	Lambert 1	Walker,J	Hunter	Walker,D 1	Suttie	Neilson	Cairns Stewart Gardiner

Professionalism permitted in Scotland from May 1893 (in England it was on 20th July 1885)

(1) *£12 receipts at 6d adult admission*

(2) *Abandoned 80 minutes, bad light*

(3) *£52 receipts*

(4) *"Blyth created considerable laughter by knocking off the helmet of a constable who was walking sentry behind the posts at the time."*

(5) *two 35 minutes played*

(6) *at East End Park*

(7) *Benefit for Trades Band*

In their series of "Football Favourites", the Kirkcaldy Times of September 2nd 1896 features William Cowan of Kirkcaldy FC

"His connection with Kirkcaldy football may be said to have extended back to 1889. At present he is one of the most prominent of the Kirkcaldy quintette. He is a native of Paisley, but coming to Binend Oil Works in 1887, it is there we find him first coming to prominence as a football player. He became associated with Binend Rangers, and showed such prominence that he was ultimately secured by Kirkcaldy Albion, which were then in their prime. In 1889 junior football in Kirkcaldy was in a flourishing condition, the great rivals of the time being the Raith Rovers and the Albion. Ultimately, Cowan was found in the ranks of the Raith Rovers, where he played centre. The two seasons he was associated with this club they won the King Cup, Fife Cup, Midland League Championship, and the Fife Charity Cup. For the last three years he has been associated with the Kirkcaldy club. Cowan is still as enthusiastic as ever. He is a splendid player, possessing weight and stamina - two very essential qualities in a good footballer, and it may be here noted that he has played in every position but back and goalkeeper. His parents reside at Westmarch at the present time. The sketch is from a photo by R.G. Rettie, Kirkcaldy."

Substitutes, own goals, goal times and opponents' scorers

Day	Date	Opponents	Venue	Comp	Res	Att	1	2	3	4	5	6	7	8	9	10	11	Substitutes, own goals, goal times and opponents' scorers
S	11-Aug	Leith Athletic	H	F	2-8	2000	Grieve	Kaye	Thomson	Lambert	Robertson	McLeod	Dawson	Marshall	Walker,D	Suttie 1 r45	Eckford	Simpson u45 — Lithgow (2) Patterson, J (2) Fraser Walker McFarlane (2)
Th	16-Aug	Kirkcaldy Cricket Club	H	F	3-0		Dall	Kaye	Thomson	Lambert	Robertson	McLeod	Dawson 1	Marshall 1	Hunter	Blyth 1	Eckford	
Th	23-Aug	Kirkcaldy Cricket Club	H	F	6-2		Dall	Kaye	Thomson	Lambert	Robertson	McLeod	Dawson 2	Marshall	Hunter 2	Blyth	Eckford 2	
S	25-Aug	Montrose	H	F	8-5		Grieve	Fair	Robertson	Lambert 1	Baxter	Deuchars 1	Eckford 2	Blyth 1	Walker,D	Marshall 1	Dawson 3	Dunn Millar (2)
S	01-Sep	Selkirk	A	SC 1Q	8-1		Grieve	Kaye	Robertson	Lambert 1	Baxter	Deuchars 1	Thomson	Blyth 1	Walker,D 3	Marshall 1	Dawson 1	Allen og 1
S	08-Sep	Cartvale	H	F	8-1		Grieve	Kaye	Dall	Lambert	Deuchars	Baxter 1	Eckford 3	Walker,D	Marshall 2	Hunter 1	Dawson 1	Kay
S	15-Sep	Kirkcaldy	A	ESS 1	4-2	5000	Grieve	Kaye	Deuchars	Lambert	Mackay	Duffus	Walker,J 2,1p	Blyth	Walker,D 2	Marshall 1	Neilson	Martin Weir
S	22-Sep	Uphall	A	SC 2Q	4-2		Grieve	Kaye	Deuchars	Lambert	Mackay	Duffus	Walker,J 1	Blyth	Walker,D	Marshall 2	Baxter	
S	29-Sep	Mossend Swifts	H	F	3-0		Grieve	Oag	Robertson	Lambert	Mackay	Duffus	Walker,J 1	Blyth	Deuchars 2	Baxter	Thomson	another + Sawers Fleming
M	01-Oct	Dundee	H	F	1-3	2000	Grieve	Kaye	Robertson	Lambert	Marshall	Duffus	Walker,J	Blyth	Walker,D 1	Suttie	Eckford	
S	06-Oct	Cowdenbeath	A	ESS 2	2-2		Grieve	Kaye	Deuchars	Lambert	Mackay	Duffus	Walker,J 2	Blyth	Walker,D	Marshall	Eckford	Cairncross Drummond Deuchars og
S	13-Oct	Cowdenbeath	A	SC 3Q	3-3		Grieve	Kaye	Oag	Lambert	Richardson 1	Duffus	Walker,J	Blyth	Walker,D 1	Marshall	Eckford 1	Cairncross 25
S	27-Oct	Cowdenbeath	H	SC 3Qr	2-1	3000	Grieve	Kaye	Oag	Lambert	Richardson	Duffus	Walker,J	Blyth	Walker,D 1	Marshall	Eckford	
S	03-Nov	Cowdenbeath	H	ESS 2r	0-0	2000	Grieve	Kaye	Oag	Lambert	Richardson	Duffus	Walker,J	Blyth	Walker,D	Suttie	Eckford	Frew, J
S	10-Nov	Cowdenbeath	A	ESS 2r2	2-1		Grieve	Kaye	Oag	Lambert	Richardson 1	Couper	Walker,J	Eckford 1	Marshall 1	Suttie	Neilson	McLean Vale Wilson 42
S	17-Nov	Lochgelly United	H	ESS 3	2-3		Grieve	Kaye	Oag	Lambert	Marshall	Couper	Blyth	Blyth	Marshall 1	Suttie	Neilson	Oag og Robertson (2)
S	24-Nov	5th KRV Dumfries	H	SC 1	6-3		Grieve	Kaye	Oag	Lambert	Blyth	Couper	Richardson	Walker,D	Richardson 1	Suttie 3	Dawson 2	Cairncross Collins
S	01-Dec	Cowdenbeath	H	FC 1	2-2		Grieve	Kaye	Oag	Lambert	Richardson	Couper	Eckford 2	Blyth	Walker,D	Suttie 1p	Dawson 1	Sharp Aitken Henderson Morley
S	08-Dec	5th KRV Dumfries	A	SC 1	3-4	2000	Dall	Kaye	Deuchars	Lambert	Deuchars	Couper	Walker,J 3	Blyth	Walker,D 1	Suttie 1	Neilson	Dawson McDuff
S	15-Dec	St Andrews University	H	KC 1	8-3		Dall	Kaye	Oag	Lambert	Blyth	Dawson 2	Walker,J 2	Tod	Walker,D 2	Suttie 1	Dawson	
S	22-Dec	Adventurers	H	F	7-0		Dall	Kaye	Oag	Lambert	Richardson 1	Couper 1	Walker,J	Blyth	Walker,D	Suttie 1	Dawson 2	Clelland (2) Oswald (2)
S	29-Dec	St Bernards	H	F	2-4		Dall	Deuchars	Simpson	Lambert	Richardson	Couper	Walker,J	Dawson 2	Walker,D	Marshall	Dawson 1	Gardiner (2) Fyfe (2)
Tu	01-Jan	Third Lanark	H	F	1-4		Dall	Kaye	Dall	Lambert	Richardson	Dawson	Simpson	Couper 1	Walker,D	Marshall	Neilson 1	Hutton Docherty Watson Davis
Th	03-Jan	Sheffield United	H	F	2-4		Grieve	Kaye	Oag	Deuchars	Dall	Neilson	Dall	Blyth	Walker,D 1	Eckford	Dawson 1	Ford, W Ford, J McGlashan Hayes
S	05-Jan	Arbroath	H	F	1-4		Grieve	Kaye	Oag	Lambert	Deuchars	Marshall	Richardson	Blyth	Walker,D	Eckford	Dawson	
S	12-Jan	Kirkcaldy	A	KC 2	5-0	2000	Grieve	Kaye	Oag	Lambert	Dall	Neilson	Oag	Blyth	Walker,D 1	Suttie 2	Dawson 1	
S	19-Jan	Edinburgh Casuals	H	F	2-0		Grieve	Lambert	Oag	Lambert	Dall	Dall	Blyth	Gillespie 1	Walker,D 2	Suttie	Dawson	
S	23-Feb	Clackmannan	A	KC 3	3-0		Grieve	Kaye	Oag	Lambert	Marshall	Marshall	Neilson 2	Blyth	Walker,D	Suttie 2	Dawson 1	Alexander
S	02-Mar	Battlefield	H	FC 2	7-1	2000	Grieve	Kaye	Oag	Marshall	Marshall	Couper	Dall	Dall	Walker,D 4	Suttie	Eckford	scrimmage 30
S	09-Mar	Cowdenbeath	H	F	1-1		Grieve	Kaye	Oag	Marshall	Nicholson	Deuchars	Neilson	Couper	Walker,D	Suttie	Dawson 2	Paterson Macdonald, J
S	16-Mar	Hearts A	H	F	3-2		Grieve	Robertson	Oag	Lambert	Marshall	Deuchars	Eckford	Blyth	Walker,D 1	Suttie	Dawson	Gibb
S	23-Mar	Rangers Swifts	H	F	2-1		Grieve	Robertson	Oag	Lambert	Lambert	Couper	Walker,J 1	Blyth	Walker,D 1	Suttie	Dawson 1	
S	30-Mar	Adventurers	A	KC SF	1-2		Grieve	Kaye	Oag	Neilson	Lambert	Marshall	Walker,J	Blyth	Walker,D 1	Dawson 1	Dawson	Cowan
M	01-Apr	St Mirren	H	F	2-1		Grieve	Kaye	Oag	Marshall	Lambert	Couper	Walker,J	Couper	Walker,D	Smith 4	Dawson	Taylor Mullen
S	06-Apr	Clyde	H	F	1-2	2000	Grieve	Kaye	Oag	Deuchars	Lambert	Couper	Walker,J 1	Couper	Walker,D 1	Smith 1	Dawson 1	Cochrane Stevenson
S	13-Apr	Lochgelly	H	F	5-2		Grieve	Kaye	Oag	Corstorphine 1	Lambert	Couper	Walker,J	Couper	Walker,D 1	Suttie 3	Eckford 2	Wilson
S	27-Apr	Adventurers	A	KC SFr	6-1		Grieve	Kaye	Oag	Marshall	Lambert	Suttie	Deuchars 2	Blyth	Walker,D	Menzies	Dawson 1	
S	04-May	Scottish Corinthians	H	F	6-4	2000	Grieve	Robertson	Oag	Couper 1	Lambert	Neilson	Walker,J	Blyth	Walker,D 1	Suttie	Eckford 2 1	Lockhart, T Neilson Thomson (2)
W	08-May	Lochgelly United	H	F	2-5		Grieve	Kaye	Oag	Marshall	Lambert 1	Neilson	Walker,J	Blyth 3	Walker,D 3	Suttie	Eckford	
M	06-May	Potton Vale	A	F	1-2		Grieve	Kaye	Oag	Marshall	Marshall	Smith 1	Walker,J 1	Blyth	Walker,D 1	Suttie	Dawson	Baxter, T Smith 46
S	11-May	Victoria United	A	KC F	1-1		Grieve	Kaye	Oag	Marshall	Marshall	Couper	Walker,J	Blyth	Walker,D	Menzies	Dawson	Clark
S	18-May	Kirkcaldy	H	NC	2-2		Grieve	Kaye	Oag	Robertson	Lambert	Couper	Walker,J 1	Blyth	Walker,D	Eckford	Eckford 1	Davidson Stewart
F	22-May	Celtic	H	F	1-1	2000	Grieve	Kaye	Oag	Suttie	Lambert	Couper	Walker,J 1	Blyth	Walker,D	Eckford	Neilson	McMahon

Referee could made decisions without teams having to appeal ; restrictions on charging goalkeepers were introduced

Substitutes, own goals, goal times and opponents' scorers

Day	Date	Opponents	Note	Venue	Comp	Res.	Att.	1	2	3	4	5	6	7	8	9	10	11	Substitutes, own goals, goal times and opponents' scorers
S	10-Aug	Clyde		H	F	2-3		Grieve	Kaye	Oag	Gillespie 2	Lamber	Suttie	Eckford	Lees	Walker,D	Menzies	Birrell	Goldie (3)
S	24-Aug	Arbroath		H	F	1-4		Cairns	Grieve	Lindsay	Nelson	Cairns	Couper	Lockhart	Douglas 1	Lees	McLeary	Eckford	Keir (3) 1pen Ford
S	31-Aug	Edinburgh Casuals		H	SQC 1	4-3		Cairns	Tod	Blyth,J	Simpson	Douglas	Couper	Lockhart	Walker, D 1	Thomson 1	Eckford 2	Dawson	Mackay (2) + another
S	07-Sep	Scottish Corinthians		H	F	4-2		Grieve	Couper	Hood	Blyth,J	Douglas	Couper	Weir	Hunter 1	Simpson 1	Eckford 2	Torbet	R. Black og 1 Blyth Black, J
S	14-Sep	Dunipace		H	SQC 2	6-2		Grieve	Kaye	Oag	Blyth,J	Lambert	Lambert	McAuley	Blyth,A 1	Walker,D 2	Suttie 2	Eckford	Oag og Hamilton
S	21-Sep	Lochgelly United		A	ESS 1	0-5		Grieve	Kaye	Oag	Blyth,J	Lambert	Couper	McAuley	Weir	Walker,D 1	Suttie	Eckford	Smith Nisbet Oag og + 2 others
S	28-Sep	Montrose		H	SQC 3	3-1		Grieve	Kaye	Oag	Blyth,J	Lambert	Couper	McLeary	Douglas	Moodie	Suttie	Eckford 2	Thornton
S	05-Oct	Hearts A		H	F	1-5		Cairns	Kaye	Oag	Blyth,J	Lambert	Couper 1	Blyth,A	Hunter	Gillies	Suttie 1	Eckford	McCartney og 1 Taylor Cairns og McKee (3)
M	07-Oct	Hibernian		H	F	5-5		Grieve	Kaye	Oag	Blyth,J	Smith 1	Couper 1	Blyth,A	Lambert	Moodie	Suttie 1	Eckford 2	Breslin Tullis Kennedy Robertson (2)
S	12-Oct	Cambuslang		H	F	6-2		Cairns	Kaye	Oag	Blyth,J 1	Lambert 2 1p	Couper	Allister 1	Smith	Gillies	Suttie 2	Eckford	Cochrane Neill
S	26-Oct	Lochgelly United		A	SQC 5	2-3		Cairns	Kaye	Oag	Blyth,J	Lambert	Couper	Eckford 2	Smith	Walker,D	Suttie	Torbet	
S	02-Nov	Lochgelly United		H	SQC 5	2-1	2000	Cairns	Kaye	Oag	Blyth,J	Lambert	Blyth,J	Nelson	Eckford 1	Suttie	Smith	Wright	Robb og 1
S	09-Nov	Cowdenbeath		A	KC 5	0-5		Cairns	Kaye	Oag	Blyth,J	Lambert	Couper	Eckford	Smith	Suttie	Smith	Wright	Whyte
S	16-Nov	King's Park		H	SQC SF	1-4	2000	Grieve	Kaye	Blyth,J	Moodie	Lambert	Suttie	Nelson	Blyth,A	Walker,D	Eckford	Dawson 1	Fotheringham Crawford (3)
S	23-Nov	Cowdenbeath		H	F	3-2		Cairns	Kaye	Robertson	Moodie	Lambert 1	Blyth,J	Simpson	Hunter	Walker,D	Suttie 2	Nelson	another + Gibb pen
S	30-Nov	Mossend Swifts		H	F	3-1		Cairns	Kaye	Oag	Moodie	Lambert	Blyth,J	Eckford	Hunter	Walker,D 1	Suttie 2	Nelson	Neilson McConnell, T
S	07-Dec	Falkirk		H	F	2-0		Cairns	Kaye	Oag	Moodie	Lambert	Blyth,J	Oag	Hunter	Walker,D	Suttie	Nelson	
S	14-Dec	Dunfermline/Ath.Juniors		A	F	1-1		Cairns	Kaye	Oag	Blyth,J	Lambert	Couper	Eckford	Walker,D	Walker,D	Suttie 1	Moodie	Beveridge
S	21-Dec	Dundee		H	F	3-1		Cairns	Kaye	Oag	Moodie	Lambert	Couper	Eckford 1	Hunter	Walker,D	Suttie 2	Nelson	Keillor
S	28-Dec	Adventurers	1	H	F	7-0		Cairns	Robertson	Oag	Moodie	Lambert 1	Couper	Eckford 1	Hunter	Walker,D 3	Suttie 3	Robertson,A	
W	01-Jan	Kirkcaldy		H	F	3-1	2000	Cairns	Robertson	Blyth,J	Moodie	Simpson	Couper	Eckford 1	Hunter	Walker,D	Suttie	Nelson 2	Davidson
S	11-Jan	Lochgelly United		A	SC 1	1-2		Cairns	Kaye	Oag	Moodie	Lambert	Couper	Eckford	Collier 1	Walker,D	Suttie	Nelson	Nisbet Kinnell
S	18-Jan	Bathgate		H	F	5-0		Cairns	Kaye	Robertson	Moodie	Lambert	Couper	Eckford 3	Hunter 1	Walker,D	Suttie	Torbet	
S	01-Feb	Lochgelly United	w	N	SC 1r	5-2	3000	Cairns	Kaye	Robertson	Moodie	Lambert 1	Couper	Hunter	Eckford 2	Walker,D 1	Suttie 2	Nelson	Adie (2)
S	08-Feb	Hibernian		A	SC 2	1-6	3500	Cairns	Kaye	Robertson	Moodie	Lambert	Couper 1	Eckford 1	Hunter	Walker,D 1	Suttie	Nelson	Groves Smith (3) Neill Murdoch
S	15-Feb	Stenhousemuir		H	F	5-0		Cairns	Kaye	Blyth,J	Moodie	Lambert	Couper 1	Eckford 1	Blyth,J	Walker,D 2	Suttie 2	Allan 1	
S	22-Feb	Battlefield		H	F	3-2		Cairns	Kaye	Blyth,J	Moodie	Lambert	Couper 1	Hunter	Eckford 1	Traill	Suttie	Allan 1	Smith og 1 Anderson Christie
S	29-Feb	East Stirling		H	F	1-0		Cairns	Kaye	Robb	Moodie	Lambert	Simpson	Eckford	Hunter	Walker,D	Suttie 1	Nelson	
S	07-Mar	Linthouse		H	F	2-1		Cairns	Kaye	Mathie	Moodie	Lambert	Couper	Eckford 1	Menzies	Walker,D	Menzies	Nelson 1	Cameron
S	14-Mar	Polton Vale		H	F	2-1		Cairns	Kaye	Mathie	Moodie	Lambert	Suttie	Collier 1	Blyth,A	Walker,D 1	Blyth,A	Nelson	Smith
S	21-Mar	Scottish Corinthians		H	F	4-1		Grieve	Kaye	Mathie	Moodie	Lambert 1	Couper	Eckford	Hunter	Walker,D 1	Suttie	Dall 2	Connell
S	28-Mar	Falkirk		A	F	1-2		Cairns	Kaye	Mathie	Moodie	Lambert 1	Couper	Eckford	Connell	Walker,D	Suttie	Dall	
S	04-Apr	Hearts A		A	F	1-1		Cairns	Kaye	Robb	Moodie	Lambert	Couper	Walker,D	Hunter	Connell	Suttie 1	Dall	White
M	06-Apr	Annbank		H	F	1-0		Cairns	Kaye	Robb	Moodie	Lambert	Menzies	Hunter	Walker,D	Connell	Suttie	Dall 1	
S	11-Apr	Clackmannan		H	F	3-0		Cairns	Kaye	Robb	Moodie	Lambert	Couper	Hunter 1	Walker,D	Connell	Dall 1	Menzies 1	
S	25-Apr	Arbroath Wanderers		H	F	6-1		Cairns	Kaye	Mathie	Nelson 2	Lambert 1	Moodie	Walker,D 1	Hunter	Dall 1	Menzies 1	McLeary	Young
S	02-May	Rangers A		H	F	2-2		Cairns	Kaye	Robb	Moodie	Simpson	Paton	Hunter	Walker,D 1	Connell 1	Dall	Menzies	Boyd (2)
W	06-May	Kirkcaldy		A	F	4-0	2000	Cairns	Kaye	Robb	Moodie	Lambert	Couper	Beveridge	Dall 1	Hunter 1	Hunter 1	Menzies 1	
S	09-May	Alloa Athletic		H	F	6-0		Cairns	Kaye	Robb	Paton	Lambert	Moodie	Dall 2	Connell	Walker,D 2	Menzies 2	Hunter	
Th	14-May	Cowdenbeath		H	F	5-2		Cairns	Kaye	Mathie	Paton	Lambert	Moodie	Dall	Connell	Walker,D 3	Menzies 2	Hunter	Johnston Drummond

Posts and crossbars must not exceed 5 inches in width

(1) Abandoned, snow, 65 minutes

(w) at Newtown Park

1896-97

Day	Date	Opponents	Note	Venue	Comp	Res.	Att.	1	2	3	4	5	6	7	8	9	10	11	Substitutes, own goals, goal times and opponents' scorers
W	18-Aug	Scottish Combination	1	H	F	1-2		Cairns	Kaye	Urquhart	Moodie	Lambert	Couper	Hunter	Dall	Walker,D	Frew	Russell	Neilson (2)
S	22-Aug	Armadale		H	F	3-1		Cairns	Kaye	Couper	Moodie	Lambert	Russell	Hunter	Dall	Walker,D 1	Ramsay,D 2	Menzies	Holt
S	29-Aug	Mossend Swifts		A	SQC 1	2-1		Cairns	Kaye	Couper	Moodie	Lambert	Russell	Beveridge	Connell	Frew 1	Walker,D 1	Menzies 1	McLay Henderson Forsyth + another
S	05-Sep	Clackmannan		A	ESS 1	2-4		Cairns	Kaye	Dall	Moodie	Lambert 1	Russell	Beveridge	Hunter	Frew 1	Suttie 1	Menzies 1	Wood
S	12-Sep	Cowdenbeath		H	SQC 2	2-1		Cairns	Kaye	Couper	Moodie	Lambert	Russell	Beveridge	Connell	Walker,D	Walker,D	Menzies 1	another + Scott Sharpe Baird
S	19-Sep	Hearts A		H	F	1-4		Cairns	Kaye	Couper	Moodie	Lambert	Russell	Dall	Connell	Frew	Walker,D	Menzies 1	
S	26-Sep	Vale of Leven		H	SQC 3	1-0		Cairns	Kaye	Couper	Moodie	Lambert	Russell	Beveridge	Walker,D 1	Frew		Menzies	Chalmers Skene + 6 others
M	03-Oct	Morton		A	F	1-8		Cairns	Kaye 1	Couper	Moodie	Dall	Russell	Lambert	Beveridge	Walker,D	Frew	Menzies	Gilhooley Dougall Berry
S	05-Oct	Hibernian		H	F	1-3		Cairns	Kaye	Couper	Moodie	Cairns	Russell	Dall	Lambert	Walker,D	Frew	Hunter	Rae Tennant Francis Burt
S	17-Oct	Falkirk		H	F	4-4	1000	Cairns	Kaye	Couper	Moodie 2	Lambert 2,1p	Russell	Beveridge	Hunter	Walker,D	Menzies	Frew	
S	24-Oct	King's Park		A	SQC 4	2-3		Cairns	Kaye	Couper	Menzies	Lambert	Russell	Beveridge 1	Ramsay,G 1	Walker,D	Menzies	Frew	Brand (2) 1 pen McInnes
S	31-Oct	Dunfermline Athletic		H	KC 1	1-2		Cairns	Kaye	Couper	Moodie 1	Lambert	Russell	Beveridge 1	Ramsay,G 2	Walker,D 1	Suttie	Frew	Bruce Beattie
S	07-Nov	Battlefield		H	F	7-1		Cairns	Kaye	Russell	Menzies	Lambert 1	Menzies	Beveridge 1	Ramsay,G 2	Frew	Blyth,A 1	Smith 1	Henderson
S	14-Nov	Leith Athletic	2	H	F	1-1		Cairns	Kaye	Russell	Moodie	Lambert	Menzies	Beveridge	Ramsay,G	Frew	Walker,D	Smith 1	scrimmage
S	21-Nov	Adventurers		H	F	5-0		Dall 1	Kaye	Russell	Moodie	Lambert	Menzies	Beveridge 1	Ramsay,G	Walker,D 1	Hunter 1	Smith 1	
S	28-Nov	Kirkcaldy		A	F	1-1		Cairns 1	Kaye	Russell	Moodie	Lambert	Couper	Beveridge	Ramsay,G	Walker,D	Menzies	Smith	Otto
S	12-Dec	Polton Vale		H	F	3-3		Cairns	Kaye	Russell	Moodie	Lambert 1	Couper	Beveridge 1	Ramsay,G	Walker,D 1	Hunter	Smith	Jack (2) Amos
S	19-Dec	Dunfermline Athletic		H	F	8-1		Cairns	Kaye	Russell	Moodie	Lambert 2,1p	Couper	Beveridge 3	Dall	Walker,D 1	Blyth,A	Smith 2	
S	26-Dec	St Bernards 2nd		H	F	3-2		Cairns	Kaye	Russell	Moodie	Lambert 1	Robertson	Beveridge	Irvine	Walker,D 1	Smith 1	Ramsay,G	another + Barber
F	01-Jan	Kilmarnock		H	F	1-3	1000	Cairns	Mathie	Russell	Moodie	Lambert	Couper	Frew	Walker,D	Smith 1	Robertson	Ramsay,G	McEvoy McLean Campbell
S	09-Jan	Dumbarton		A	SC 1	1-2		Cairns	Kaye	Russell	Moodie	Lambert	Couper	Beveridge	Dall	Walker,D	Ramsay,G 1	Frew	Mair (2)
S	23-Jan	Dunfermline Athletic		H	SCC 1	4-4		Cairns	Kaye 1	Russell	Moodie	Dall	Couper	Beveridge	Hunter	Walker,D 3	Ramsay,G	Eckford	Marshall (2) Beveridge Moultrie
S	06-Feb	Dunfermline Athletic		A	F	0-3		Cairns	Kaye	Russell	Moodie	Lambert	Stocks	Beveridge	Suttie	Walker,D	Hunter	Ramsay,G	Moultrie Beveridge scrimmage
S	13-Feb	Kirkcaldy		H	F	5-1	2000	Cairns	Kaye	Couper	Moodie	Birrell	Russell	Beveridge 1	Ramsay,G 1	Dall 1	Suttie 1	Smith 1	Thomson pen
S	20-Feb	Dunfermline Athletic		A	SCC 1r	3-1		Cairns	Kaye	Mitchell	Moodie	Stocks	Russell	Ramsay,G	Dall 1	Walker,D	Walker,D	Beveridge 1	Hynd
S	27-Feb	Hearts A		A	F	1-4		Cairns	Kaye	Muir	Moodie	Stocks	Dall	Ramsay,G 1	Smith	Walker,D	Walker,D	Beveridge	White (2) Sharp Livingston
S	13-Mar	Lochgelly United		H	F	4-2		Cairns	Kaye	Russell	Moodie	Stocks	Robertson	Ramsay,G 1	Dall	Walker,D 1	Ramsay,A 1	Smith 1	McLaren Wilson
S	20-Mar	Cameronians (Glasgow)		H	F	5-1		Cairns	Kaye	Lambert	Moodie	Stocks	Robertson	Hunter 1	Dall	Ramsay,A 1	Suttie 1	Smith 2	Martin
S	27-Mar	St Bernards		A	F	4-0		Cairns	Kaye	Flanders	Moodie	Stocks	Ramsay,G	Beveridge 2	Hunter 1	Walker,D	Ramsay,A 1	Smith	
S	03-Apr	Kirkcaldy		A	NC	0-0	2000	Cairns	Kaye	Flanders	Moodie	Stocks	Ramsay,G	Beveridge	Dall	Walker,D	Ramsay,A 1	Smith	
M	05-Apr	Cowdenbeath	*	H	F	3-0		Cairns	Kaye	Flanders	Sinclair	Moodie	Ramsay,G	Fisher 1	Hunter	Walker,D 1	Ramsay,A	Beveridge 1	3 others + Hutton Gibb Miller
S	17-Apr	Cowdenbeath		A	SCC 2	0-6		Cairns	Kaye	Flanders	Sinclair	Moodie	Ramsay,G	Fisher	Hunter	Walker,D	Ramsay,A	Beveridge	
S	24-Apr	Dunfermline Athletic		A	F	2-1		Cairns	Kaye	Flanders	Moodie 1	Lambert	Stocks	Beveridge	Eckford	Walker,D	Ramsay,A 1	Smith	Martin, J
S	01-May	Kirkcaldy		H	NC	1-1	2200	Cairns	Kaye	Flanders	Moodie	Lambert	Stocks	Beveridge	Eckford	Walker,D	Ramsay,A 1	Smith 1	Cowan
Th	06-May	Kirkcaldy		A	NC	2-1	3000	Cairns	Kaye	Flanders	Moodie	Stocks	Ramsay,G	Mackay 1	Dall	Walker,D 1	Ramsay,A	Smith	Downie
S	08-May	Blantyre		H	F	5-1		Cairns	Kaye	Flanders	Moodie	Suttie	Ramsay,G	Eckford	Beveridge	Walker,D 1	Hunter 2	Smith 2	

First season as professionals
(1) Both teams had only 8 players
(2) Abandoned 70 minutes, bad light

Day	Date	Opponents	Note	Venue	Comp	Res	Att.	1	2	3	4	5	6	7	8	9	10	11	Substitutes, own goals, goal times and opponents' scorers
S	04-Sep	Adventurers		H	F	3-0		Cairns	Kaye	Couper	Moodie	Thomson	Gillespie	Ramsay,G 2	Carrocher	Walker,D	Eckford	Ramsay,A	
S	11-Sep	Lochgelly United		A	SQC 1	2-1		Cairns	Kaye	Couper	Moodie	Stocks	Gillespie	Ramsay,G	Carrocher	Walker,D	Ramsay,A 1	Eckford	
S	18-Sep	Alloa Athletic		A	ESQC 1	1-0		Cairns	Kaye	Couper	White	Stocks	Moodie	Ramsay,G	Wilson	Walker,D	Eckford 1	Ramsay,A	
S	25-Sep	Dunfermline Athletic		A	SQC 2	2-1		Cairns	Kaye	Couper	Moodie	Stocks	Gillespie	Ramsay,G	Carrocher	Walker,D 1	Ramsay,A	Eckford	Moultrie
S	02-Oct	Stenhousemuir		H	F	3-3	600	Cairns	Kaye	Couper	Moodie	Stocks	Couper	Beveridge	Carrocher	Walker,D 1	Ramsay,A 2	Eckford	Glen Glegg Tonnar
M	04-Oct	Hearts of Beath		H	F	3-3		Cairns	Kaye	Flanders	Moodie	Stocks	Couper	Beveridge	Carrocher	Walker,D 1	Ramsay,A 1	Eckford	Brown Barclay Frew 88
S	09-Oct	Alloa Athletic		A	SQC 3	1-0		Cairns	Kaye	Couper	Moodie	Stocks	Gillespie	Beveridge	Carrocher	Walker,D	Ramsay,A	Eckford	
S	16-Oct	Lochgelly United		H	ESQC 2	5-1	2000	Cairns	Kaye	Couper	Moodie 1	Lambert	Gillespie	Beveridge 1	Ramsay,G	Walker,D 2	Ramsay,A 2	Neilson	Vale, P
S	23-Oct	Dundee Wanderers		A	SQC 4	2-1	3000	Cairns	Kaye	Couper	Moodie	Stocks	Ramsay,G	Beveridge	Ramsay,G	Walker,D	Ramsay,A 2	Eckford 1	McNamara + another pen
S	30-Oct	Penicuik		A	ESQC 3	3-2		Cairns	Kaye	Couper	Moodie	Lambert	Gillespie	Findlay	Neilson	Ramsay,A 4	Ramsay,A 1	Eckford	
S	06-Nov	Armadale		H	ESQC SF	5-1	2500	Cairns	Kaye	Gillespie	Moodie	Lambert	Neilson	Findlay 2	Neilson	Ramsay,A	Hunter 1	Eckford 1	Russell
S	13-Nov	East Stirling		A	SQC 5	0-1	6000	Cairns	Kaye	Couper	Moodie	Lambert	Gillespie	Findlay	Carrocher 1	Ramsay,A 1	Ramsay,A	Eckford	McKie
S	20-Nov	Kirkcaldy		H	KC 1	4-3	2000	Cairns	Kaye	Moodie	Lambert	Carrocher	Moodie	Findlay	Neilson	Neilson 2	Walker,D	Eckford	Stewart (3)
S	27-Nov	Clackmannan		H	KC 2	4-1		Cairns	Kaye	Gillespie	Moodie	Lambert	Ramsay	Ramsay	Carrocher	Neilson 1	Walker,D 2	Eckford	Harrower pen
S	04-Dec	Kirkcaldy	1	A	FC 1	2-1	2500	Cairns	Kaye	Cowe	Moodie	Carrocher	Gillespie	Neilson	Neilson	Walker,D	Walker,D	Eckford	Otto
S	11-Dec	Mossend Swifts	w	N	ESS F	4-0	3000	Cairns	Kaye	Cowe	Moodie	Lambert	Gillespie	Findlay 1	Ramsay,G	Hunter	Hunter	Eckford	
S	18-Dec	King's Park		H	F	1-1		Cairns	Kaye	Couper	Moodie	Carrocher	Gillespie	Findlay 2	Ramsay,G	Neilson 3	Walker,D 4	Eckford	Cowan
S	25-Dec	Vale of Leven		H	F	3-0		Cairns	Kaye	Oag	Moodie	Lambert	Neilson	Findlay	Hunter	Neilson 2	Walker,D	Eckford	
S	01-Jan	Renton		H	F	9-1		Morton	Lambert	Oag	Moodie	Carrocher 1	Cairns	Neilson	Walker,D	Neilson	Walker,D 1	Ramsay,G 3	McIntyre
M	03-Jan	Montrose		A	F	4-3		Cairns	Kaye	Oag	Moodie	Carrocher 1	Gillespie	Cowan	Ramsay,G 1	Walker,D	Ramsay,A	Ramsay,A
Tu	04-Jan	Locked Out Engineers	2	N	B	3-1		Cairns	Kaye	Oag	Moodie	Carrocher	Gillespie	Cowan	Ramsay,G 1	Ramsay,A 2	Walker,D	Ramsay,A 2	
S	08-Jan	East Stirling		H	SC 1	2-4	4000	Cairns	Kaye	Oag	Moodie	Wilkie	Gillespie	Cowan 1	Carrocher	Ramsay,A 1	Neilson 1	Eckford 1	McQueen Jardine Alexander Murray
S	15-Jan	Cowdenbeath		H	KC SF	0-0	3000	Cairns	Kaye	Oag	Moodie	Carrocher	Gillespie	Findlay	Blyth	Walker,D 3	Neilson 1	Neilson	
S	22-Jan	Kirkcaldy		A	FC 1	4-0	2000	Cairns	Kaye	Oag	Moodie	Lambert	Gillespie	Eckford	Ramsay,G	Neilson	Ramsay,G	Walker,D	
S	29-Jan	St Bernards		H	ESS 1	3-5	3000	Cairns	Kaye	Oag 1	Neilson	Lambert	Gillespie	Eckford 1	Ramsay,G	Ramsay,A	Walker,D 2	Findlay 2	McInnes Lee (2) Robertson Ritchie
S	05-Feb	Dunfermline Athletic		A	SCC 1	1-2		Cairns	Kaye	Oag	Moodie	Lambert	Gillespie	Eckford 1	Ramsay,G	Walker,D 1	Ramsay,A 2	Eckford	Findlay
S	12-Feb	Cowdenbeath		H	WC 1	6-0		Cairns	Kaye	Oag	Moodie	Lambert	Gillespie	Eckford 2	Walker,D 3	Findlay	Ramsay,A 1	Eckford 2	Gibb Paton
S	19-Feb	Alloa Athletic		H	SCC 2	3-3		Cairns	Kaye	Lambert	Moodie	Wilson	Gillespie	Findlay	Ramsay,G	Neilson	Ramsay,A	Eckford 4	Henderson + 2 others
S	26-Feb	Clackmannan		A	FC SF	2-1		Cairns	Kaye	Oag	Moodie	Lambert	Wilson	Ramsay,G	Ramsay,G	Walker,D 3	Ramsay,A	Eckford	Forsyth
S	05-Mar	Clackmannan		H	FC SFr	5-1	2000	Cairns	Kaye	Oag	Moodie	Lambert	Gillespie	Findlay	Ramsay,G	Walker,D	Ramsay,A 1	Eckford	
S	12-Mar	Royal Albert		H	F	5-0		Cairns	Kaye	Flanders	Moodie	Lambert	Couper	Neilson	Ramsay,G 1	Walker,D	Walker,D	Neilson 2	
S	19-Mar	Scottish Amateurs		H	F	2-4	1500	Cairns	Kaye	Flanders	Moodie	Gillespie	Couper r	Hunter	Ramsay,A 3	Walker,D	Ramsay,A	Eckford 1	Lambert u; Samson McFarlane (2) Duncan
S	26-Mar	Victoria United		A	F	2-1		Cairns	Kaye	Flanders	Moodie	Lambert	Robertson	Hunter	Ramsay,G 1	Walker,D	Ramsay,A	Eckford 2	MacPherson
S	02-Apr	Selkirk		A	SCC SF	4-2		Cairns	Kaye	Flanders	Moodie	Lambert	Gillespie	Neilson	Ramsay,G	Walker,D	Ramsay,A 1	Eckford 3	
S	09-Apr	Alloa Athletic	w	N	FC F	3-1	2000	Cairns	Kaye	Oag	Moodie	Lambert	Gillespie	Findlay	Ramsay,G 1	Walker,D	Walker,D	Eckford	Miller
W	16-Apr	Cowdenbeath		H	WC 1	2-1		Cairns	Kaye	Oag 1	Moodie	Lambert	Gillespie	Neilson	Ramsay,G	Walker,D 3	Ramsay,A 2	Eckford 1	Mercer
S	20-Apr	Hearts of Beath		H	WC SF	2-1		Cairns	Kaye	Oag	Moodie	Lambert	Ramsay,G	Ramsay,G	Blyth	Walker,D 1	Ramsay,A	Eckford	Scott
S	23-Apr	Penicuik	3	N	SCC F	1-1	1000	Cairns	Kaye	Oag	Moodie	Lambert	Gillespie	Findlay	Blyth	Walker,D	Ramsay,A 1	Eckford	McNamara 90
M	25-Apr	Hearts of Beath		H	WC SFr	7-1		Cairns	Kaye	Oag	Moodie	Lambert	Gillespie	Neilson	Blyth	Walker,D 3	Walker,D 3	Eckford 3	
S	30-Apr	Penicuik	w	N	SCC Fr	2-1	2000	Cairns	Kaye	Flanders	Moodie	Lambert	Ramsay,G	Ramsay,G	Ramsay,G	Walker,D 1	Ramsay,A	Eckford	Russell
S	07-May	Kirkcaldy		H	NC	6-0		Cairns	Kaye	Flanders	Moodie	Lambert	Ramsay,G	Neilson 1	Blyth	Walker,D	Ramsay,A 2	Eckford 3	
S	14-May	Kirkcaldy		A	NC	8-0		Cairns	Kaye	Flanders	Moodie	Lambert	Ramsay,G	Neilson 1	Blyth 2	Walker,D 3	Ramsay,A	Eckford 2	Hamilton, A

Handling now had to be intentional to be penalised

(1) Match abandoned after 73 minutes

(2) Benefit match for "Locked Out Engineers" played at Easter Road

(3) at Loanhead

(w) at Newtown Park

Day	Date	Opponents	Note	Venue	Comp	Res.	Att.	1	2	3	4	5	6	7	8	9	10	11	Substitutes, own goals, goal times and opponents' scorers
S	20-Aug	Fair City Athletic		H	F	5-1		Cairns	Sinclair	Flanders	Moodie	Lambert	Stocks	Ramsay,G	Stewart	Bain 3	Ramsay,A 1	Eckford 1	Arnott
S	03-Sep	East Stirling		H	F	2-3	3500	Cairns	Kaye	Flanders	Moodie	Lambert	Stocks	Eckford	Ramsay,G	Bain 1	Stewart	Torbet 1	Mackie Kaye og Hailstanes pen
S	10-Sep	Lochgelly		A	SQC 1	0-1	2000	Cairns	Kaye	Flanders	Moodie	Lambert	Sinclair	Ramsay,G	Stewart	Walker,D	Ramsay,A	Eckford	Turner
S	17-Sep	Hearts of Beath		A	ESQC 1	3-0		Cairns	Kaye	Flanders	Moodie	Stocks	Sinclair	McQueen	Ramsay,G 1	Walker,D	Ramsay,A 1	Eckford 1	
S	24-Sep	Kirkcaldy	1	A	WC F	3-0	3000	Cairns	Kaye	Flanders	Moodie	Stocks	Sinclair	Neilson	Ramsay,G	Stewart 2	Ramsay,A	Eckford 1	Peattie 10 pen Eadie
S	01-Oct	Lochgelly		A	ESS 1	0-2	2000	Cairns	Kaye	Flanders	Moodie	Stocks	Gillespie	Gillespie	Ramsay,G	Stewart	Ramsay,A	Eckford	Smith Gray + 2 others
M	03-Oct	Clyde		H	F	1-4		Cairns	Lambert	Flanders	Moodie	Stocks	Gillespie	Eckford 1	Ramsay,G	Stewart	Ramsay,A	Torbet	Kerr
S	08-Oct	Mossend Swifts	2	H	F	7-1		Cairns	Kaye	Gillespie	Moodie	Lambert	Sinclair 1	McQueen	Ramsay,G	Walker,D 2	Ramsay,A 2	Eckford 1	White og 1
S	15-Oct	Clackmannan		H	F	1-0		Cairns	Kaye	Flanders	Moodie	Stocks	Sinclair	McQueen	Ramsay,G	Walker,D	Ramsay,A 1	Eckford	
S	22-Oct	Orion		A	F	1-5		Cairns	Kaye	Flanders	Moodie	Lambert	Sinclair	Fisher	Ramsay,G	Walker,D	Ramsay,A	Eckford	4 others + Webster
S	29-Oct	Hearts of Beath		A	KC 1	2-1		Cairns	Kaye	Flanders	Moodie	Stocks 1	Sinclair	Ramsay,G	Stocks 1	Walker,D	Ramsay,A 1	Eckford	
S	05-Nov	Clackmannan		H	FC 1	6-0		Cairns	Kaye	Flanders	Moodie	Lambert	Sinclair	Ramsay,G 1	Stocks 2	Neilson 2	Ramsay,A	Eckford 1	
S	12-Nov	Kirkcaldy		A	KC 2	6-0		Cairns	Kaye	Flanders	Moodie	Lambert	Sinclair	McQueen 1	Stocks 3	Neilson 1p	Ramsay,A 1	Eckford 1	
S	19-Nov	Scottish Amateurs		H	F	3-1		Cairns	Kaye	Flanders	Stewart	Lambert	Sinclair	McQueen 1	Ramsay,G	Neilson 1	Ramsay,A 1	Eckford	Henry
S	26-Nov	Vale of Leven		H	F	4-2		Cairns	Kaye	Flanders	Moodie	Lambert	Stewart	McQueen	Milne	Stocks 2	Ramsay,A	Neilson 2	Rodgers Ryan
S	10-Dec	St Mirren		H	F	1-2		Cairns	Kaye	Flanders	Moodie	Lambert	Stewart	McQueen	Ramsay,G	Neilson	Ramsay,A	Eckford 1	McNeilly (2)
S	24-Dec	Armadale		A	F	4-3		Cairns	Kaye	Flanders	Sinclair	Stewart	Stewart	McQueen	Ramsay,G 1	Stocks 1	Ramsay,A 1	Neilson	Henderson Kaye og Whyte
S	31-Dec	Stenhousemuir		H	F	11-5		Dall	Strang	Flanders	Moodie	Taylor 1	Sinclair	Ramsay,G 3	Stocks	Neilson 4	Bell,W	Bell,J 3	Shearer Bennett (2) Halliday Brown, J
M	02-Jan	Arthurlie		H	F	5-1		Lambert	Kaye	Flanders	Moodie 1	Taylor	Sinclair	Ramsay,G 1	Stocks	Mackie	Taylor	Eckford 3	McMillan
S	07-Jan	Leith Athletic		H	ESL	2-2		Cairns	Kaye	Flanders	Moodie	Lambert	Sinclair	McQueen	Ramsay,G	Neilson	Stocks 1	Eckford 1	scrimmage Dryburgh
S	14-Jan	Armadale		A	KC SF	1-1		Addison	Kaye	Flanders	Moodie	Lambert	Sinclair	Ramsay,G	Stocks	Walker,D 1	Stocks	Neilson	Henderson
S	21-Jan	Armadale		H	KC SFr	10-1		Addison	Kaye	Flanders	Moodie	Lambert	Stewart 1	McQueen	Stocks 2	Neilson 2	Ramsay,A 1	Eckford 3.1p	Livingstone (2) 1 pen Walker, R + another
S	28-Jan	Cowdenbeath		H	SCC 1	1-0		Addison	Kaye	Flanders	Moodie	Lambert	Stewart	McQueen	Stocks	Neilson	Stocks	Eckford 1p	
S	04-Feb	Hearts		A	ESL	1-4		Addison	Sinclair	Flanders	Moodie	Lambert	Stewart 1	Ramsay,G 1	Ramsay,A 1	Walker,D	Stocks	Eckford 1p	Methven (2) Clark
S	11-Feb	Dundee		A	FC SF	4-0		Addison	Kaye	Flanders	Moodie	Lambert	Stewart	McQueen	Stocks	Neilson	Stocks 1	Eckford 1	Houston Ritchie Cameron Godsman
S	18-Feb	Dundee		A	ESL	0-3		Addison	Sinclair	Flanders	Moodie	Lambert	Stewart	McQueen	Stocks	Walker,D	Stocks	Eckford	
S	25-Feb	St Bernards		H	ESL	4-4		Addison	Kaye	Flanders	Moodie	Lambert	Stewart	Ramsay,G 1	Stocks	Neilson 1	Ramsay,A 1	Eckford 1	McGerigan Porter Murray Callaghan (2)
S	04-Mar	Hibernian		A	ESL	0-5		Addison	Flanders	Nisbet	Moodie	Stocks	Stewart	Ramsay,G	Milne	Walker,D	Ramsay,A	Eckford 1	Methven Millar
S	11-Mar	Dundee		H	ESL	3-2	3000	Grieve	Kaye	Flanders	Moodie	Lambert	Sinclair	Ramsay,G	McQueen	Neilson 3	Ramsay,A 1	Eckford	Anderson
S	18-Mar	Leith Athletic		A	ESL	1-1		Grieve	Gillespie	Gillespie	Moodie	Neilson,John	Sinclair	Ramsay,G 1	McQueen	Stewart 1	Ramsay,A 1	Eckford	Hunter Ritchie (3) Houston Turner + another
S	01-Apr	St Bernards		A	ESL	1-7	4200	Addison	Kaye	Flanders	Moodie	Neilson,John	Sinclair	Ramsay,G 1	McQueen	Neilson,John	Ramsay,A 1	Eckford	Taylor (2) + another pen
M	03-Apr	Hearts		H	WC SF	2-3		Grieve	Kaye	Stewart	Moodie	Lambert	Sinclair	Ramsay,G	Blyth	Neilson	Ramsay,A 1	Blyth	Stirling
S	08-Apr	Hearts of Beath		H	ESL	0-1		Grieve	Lambert	Stewart	Moodie	Lambert	Sinclair	Ramsay,G	Walker,D	Neilson	Ramsay,A	Eckford	Brodigan
S	15-Apr	Hibernian		H	ESL	2-1	2000	Grieve	Kaye	Stewart	Moodie	Stocks	Neilson,John	McQueen 1	Blyth	Neilson	Ramsay,A 1	Eckford 1	Crawford
S	22-Apr	West Calder	w	N	KC F	2-1	3000	Grieve	Kaye	Stewart	Moodie	Lambert	Ramsay,G	McQueen 1	Blyth	Neilson	Ramsay,A 1	Eckford 1	Houston Hunter
S	29-Apr	Kirkcaldy		H	NC	3-2		Addison	Sinclair	Stewart	Moodie	Lambert	Ramsay,G	Neilson	McQueen	Blyth	Ramsay,A 1	Eckford 2,1p	
W	06-May	Lochgelly United		H	FC F	2-0	2000	Grieve	Kaye	Stewart	Moodie	Lambert	Ramsay,G	Neilson	McQueen	Blyth	Ramsay,A 1	Eckford 1	
S	06-May	Kirkcaldy		A	NC	3-0		Grieve	Kaye	Stewart	Moodie	Lambert	Ramsay,G	Neilson	McQueen	Blyth 1	Ramsay,A	Eckford 2	
S	13-May	Leith Athletic		H	F	3-3		Grieve	Grant	Stewart	Moodie	Neilson,John	Ramsay,G	Neilson 1	McQueen	Blyth 1	Ramsay,A	Eckford 1	Fotheringham Lowe Gardiner
S	27-May	Cowdenbeath	3	N	FCC	0-1	2000	Grieve	Grant	Stewart	Moodie	Lambert	Ramsay,G	Sinclair	Neilson,John	Blyth	Ramsay,A	Philip	Moodie og

(1) 1897/98 Final
(2) Apparently three of Mossend's best players missed the train. The Fifeshire Advertiser reported "Considering the strong counter attraction of the Lifeboat Demonstration, the crowd that witnessed the match was a large one."
(3) at Dunfermline
(w) at Newtown Park

Day	Date	Opponents	Note	Venue	Comp	Res.	Att.	1	2	3	4	5	6	7	8	9	10	11	Substitutes, own goals, goal times and opponents' scorers
								Grieve	Bonthron	Carmichael	Sinclair	Lambert	Wilson	Wyles	Blyth	Mackie,A	Gilmour	Ramsay	
Tu	15-Aug	St Bernards		H	F	1-3	1000	Grieve	Moodie	Sinclair	Paton	Lambert	Ramsay 1	Wyles 1	Blyth	Mackie,A	Gilmour	Ramsay	Bell Wallace Cameron
S	19-Aug	Bo'ness		A	F	4-4		Harley	Moodie	Robertson	Paton	Robertson	Ramsay	Dorward	Fyfe	Drummond 1	Mackie,A	Gilmour 2	Callaghan Cairns
S	26-Aug	West Calder		H	F	7-2		Lindsay	Moodie	Stewart	Moodie	Lambert	Ramsay	McQueen	Fyfe 1	Drummond 1	Mackie,A	Gilmour 5	
S	02-Sep	Cameronians		H	F	9-0		Lindsay	Scott	Stewart	Moodie	Robertson 1	Ramsay	Fyfe	McQueen 3	Drummond 1	Mackie,A 1p	Gilmour 3	
S	09-Sep	Dunfermline Athletic		A	SQC 1	2-1	1800	Grieve	Scott	Stewart	Paton 2	Robertson	Ramsay	Dorward 1	McQueen	Drummond 1	Mackie,A 1	Gilmour	Hutchison
S	16-Sep	Clackmannan		H	ESQC 1	5-1		Sinclair	Sinclair	Stewart	Neilson,John	Robertson	Ramsay	Dorward	McQueen	Drummond 1	Mackie,A 1	Gilmour	Wilson
S	23-Sep	West Calder		A	SQC 2	1-0	800	Lindsay	Moodie	Stewart	Paton	Robertson	Ramsay	Dorward	Neilson,John	Drummond	Mackie,A	Gilmour 1	
S	30-Sep	Lochgelly		H	F	1-1		Grieve	Moodie	Stewart	Paton	Lambert	Robertson	Dorward	Blyth 1	Drummond	Mackie,A	Gilmour	Prior
M	02-Oct	Hibernian		H	ESL	2-2	3000	Grieve	Moodie	Stewart	Moodie	Robertson 1	Ramsay	Dorward 1	Blyth	Drummond	Mackie,A 1	Gilmour	McGuigan Breslin
S	07-Oct	Lochgelly	1	H	ESQC 3	4-0	3000	Grieve	Moodie	Stewart	Moodie	Robertson	Ramsay	Dorward	Blyth	Drummond 1	Mackie,A 1	Gilmour	
S	14-Oct	Camelon		A	SQC 3	3-2	1500	Lindsay	Scott	Scott	Paton	Robertson	Moodie	Dorward	Neilson,John	Drummond 1	Mackie,A 1	Gilmour 2	another + Gillespie
S	21-Oct	Bo'ness		A	SQC 4	2-2		Lindsay	Moodie	Bruce	Paton	Robertson	Ramsay	Neilson,John	Neilson,John	Drummond	Mackie,A 2	Gilmour	Campbell og 1
S	28-Oct	Bo'ness		H	SQC 4r	3-1	2500	Lindsay	Scott	Moodie	Paton	Robertson	Robertson	Neilson,John	McQueen	Drummond	Mackie,A 1	Barclay 2	Gallacher
S	04-Nov	East Stirling		A	SQC 5	3-1	4300	Lindsay	Scott	Flanders	Moodie	Lambert	Robertson	Ritchie	McQueen	Drummond	Mackie,A 2	Barclay	McKie
S	18-Nov	Arbroath		A	SQC SF	1-3	4500	Lindsay	Scott	Flanders	Moodie	Lambert	Robertson	Ritchie	McQueen	Drummond 1	Mackie,A 1	Ramsay	Leuchars (2) Middleton
S	25-Nov	Leith Athletic		H	ESL	4-0	1000	Lindsay	Scott	Flanders	Paton	Lambert	Ramsay	Mackie,A 2	McQueen 1	Drummond	Stewart	Neilson 1	
S	02-Dec	Polton Vale		A	ESQC SF	2-1	500	Lindsay	Scott	Flanders	Moodie	Robertson	Robertson	Barclay 1	McQueen 1	Drummond	Ritchie	Neilson,John	
S	02-Dec	Hearts of Beath		H	KC 1	2-0	1000	Lindsay	Bruce	Stewart	Moodie	Lambert	Cook	Dorward	Blyth,A	Mackie,A	Mackie,A	Gilmour	
S	09-Dec	Lochgelly United		H	KC 2	4-2	1500	Lindsay	Scott	Flanders	Moodie	Robertson	Paton	Mackie,A 1	Neilson,John	Neilson,John 2	Drummond	Ramsay 2	Hutton (2)
S	30-Dec	Peebles		H	KC SF	3-1		Grieve	Cook	Flanders	Paton 1	Lambert	Robertson	Ramsay	Neilson,John	Drummond	Stewart 1	Neilson	
S	30-Dec	Camelon		A	KC SF	6-0		Lindsay	Scott	Flanders	Moodie	Robertson	Sinclair	Mackie,A 1	Neilson,John	Barclay	Gilmour 2	Neilson	
M	02-Jan	Corinthians		H	F	0-4		Grieve	Scott	Flanders	Moodie	Lambert	Paton	Ramsay	Neilson,John	Drummond 1	Bell,W 1	Hutchison 1	
S	06-Jan	Hearts		A	ESL	0-7		Grieve	Scott	Flanders	Moodie	Lambert	Robertson	Ramsay	Neilson,John	Drummond	Mackie,A	Neilson	Foster (2) Dunn Blacer
S	13-Jan	Third Lanark		A	SC 1	1-5	1000	Lindsay	Scott	Flanders	Moodie	Robertson	Paton	Ritchie	McQueen	Drummond 1	Mackie,A	Neilson	Michael (4) McLean Sharp ???? scrimmage
S	20-Jan	St Bernards		H	ESL	1-1	1000	Grieve	Scott	Flanders	Moodie	Robertson 1	Ramsay	Neilson	McQueen	Drummond 1	Mackie,A	Ramsay	
S	27-Jan	East Stirling		A	CL	1-3		Grieve	Scott	Flanders	Paton	Lambert	Robertson	Neilson	McQueen	Drummond 1	Mackie,A	Gilmour	Turner
S	17-Feb	Hearts of Beath		H	WC 1	3-0	1000	Lindsay	Bruce	Stewart	Moodie	Robertson	Ramsay	Dorward 1	McQueen	Drummond	Mackie,A 2	Gilmour	
S	24-Feb	East Stirling		H	CL	4-2	1500	Grieve	Stewart	Bruce	Moodie	Robertson	Ramsay	Dorward 1	McQueen	Drummond	Mackie,A 3	Gilmour	
S	03-Mar	Ayr		A	CL	2-2		Grieve	Bruce	Barclay	Moodie	Robertson	Ramsay	Dorward	McQueen	Barclay	Mackie,A 2	Gilmour	Heron Clark
S	10-Mar	St Bernards		A	ESL	1-6		Lindsay	Barclay	Scott	Moodie	Lambert	Ramsay	Dorward 1	McQueen	Robertson	Mackie,A	Gilmour	Calder Kelt
S	17-Mar	Dundee		A	ESL	2-3	3000	Lindsay	Scott	Scott	Moodie	Robertson	Robertson	Dorward 1	McQueen	Drummond 2	Mackie,A 1	Gilmour	McDonald Robertson (2) 1 pen
S	24-Mar	Motherwell		A	ESL	2-2	1500	Grieve	McLean	Scott	Moodie	Robertson	Robertson	Dorward	McQueen	Drummond	Mackie,A	Gilmour	
S	31-Mar	Leith Athletic		A	CL	0-3	700	Lindsay	McLean	Scott	Moodie	Lambert	Robertson	Dorward	McQueen	Drummond	Mackie,A	Gilmour 1	Wood Duffy (2)
M	02-Apr	Hearts		H	ESL	1-3	3000	Grieve	McLean	Scott	Moodie	Lambert	Robertson	Dorward 1	McQueen	Drummond	Mackie,A	Gilmour 1	Livingstone Porteous Michael 89
S	07-Apr	Dundee		H	ESL	2-0		Grieve	McLean	Black	Paton	Lambert	Robertson	Dorward 1	Ramsay	Dryburgh	Mackie,A	Gilmour 1	
S	14-Apr	Dunfermline Athletic		A	WC 2	3-6		Mackie,J	Sinclair	Bruce	Paton	Lockhart	Cook	Barclay 2	Neilson,John	Thomson	Stewart	Ramsay	
S	14-Apr	Ayr		A	CL	1-3		Grieve	Scott	Scott	Moodie	Lambert	Robertson	Dorward	Blyth 1	Drummond	Mackie,A 1	Gilmour	
S	21-Apr	Abercorn		H	CL	2-0	1000	Mackie,J	McLean	Scott	Moodie	Lambert	Ramsay	Dorward 1	Fisher	Drummond	Mackie,A	Gilmour	
S	21-Apr	Cowdenbeath	2	N	KC F	1-5	800	Clunie	Sinclair	Bruce	Black	Paton	Cook	Neilson	McQueen 1	Thomson	Lockhart	Stewart 1	
S	28-Apr	Hamilton Academical		H	CL	4-3		Mackie,J	McLean	Scott	Moodie	Lambert	Ramsay	Dorward	McQueen	Drummond 2,1p	Mackie,A	Gilmour 2	McDonald Rooney Keir
W	02-May	Hibernian		H	ESL	4-3	1500	Grieve	Scott	McLean	Moodie	Lambert	Robertson	Dorward	Ramsay	Drummond 1	Mackie,A 3	Gilmour	Douglas McCartney Murray
S	05-May	Cowdenbeath		H	F	4-3		Grieve	Scott	McLean	Moodie	Robertson	Hutchison	Dorward	McQueen	Drummond 1	Mackie,A 2	Gilmour 1	Walker Mercer Gibb, John
S	12-May	Motherwell		H	CL	0-1	1200	Stanners	Scott	McLean	Paton	Robertson	Hutchison	Dorward	Ramsay	Mackie,A	Gilmour	Bell,J	
Tu	15-May	St Bernards		H	ESL	1-0	800	Stanners	Bonthron	Bruce	Paton	Robertson	Ramsay	McGaffney	Gardner	Temple	Drummond	Mackie,A 1	

(1) match unfinished
(2) at Dunfermline

The Fife Free Press during 1899/1900 included a photograph and profile of Charlie Moodie, noting that he had played two seasons in Boys Brigade football, juvenile with Ramblers for four seasons, three as captain, and seven weeks with Raith Athletic before Raith Rovers called him up for the cup tie v Lochgely United in 1894/5, when he was 17. He missed only four matches in four seasons, and possesses twelve gold, one gold centre and two silver medals. He was 5' 6.5", and 10.5 stone.

Substitutes, own goals, goal times and opponents' scorers

Day	Date	Opponents	Note	Venue	Comp	Res	Att	1	2	3	4	5	6	7	8	9	10	11	Substitutes, own goals, goal times and opponents' scorers
W	15-Aug	Cowdenbeath		H	F	5-0		Mackie.J	Bonthron	Scott	Moodie	Lambert 1	Robertson	McDonald	Brown 1	Drummond 1	Bell 2	Gilmour 1	Smith Tenant
S	18-Aug	Dunfermline Athletic		A	F	3-1		Mackie.J	Bonthron	Scott	Moodie	Lambert	Ramsay,G	McDonald 1	Brown 1	Drummond 1	Bell 1	Gilmour	Cairns (2) Nangle
S	25-Aug	Arthurlie		H	F	4-2		Mackie.J	Bonthron	Scott	Moodie	Lambert 2	Ramsay,G	McDonald	Brown 1	Drummond 1	Bell	Gilmour	Clements
S	01-Sep	West Calder		H	F	5-3		Mackie.J	Bonthron	Torrance	Moodie 1	Lambert	Ramsay,G 1	McDonald	Brown	Drummond 1	Bell	Mackie.A	Walker, D Moodie og
S	08-Sep	Hearts of Beath		H	SQC 1	4-1		Mackie.J	Scott	Torrance	Moodie 2	Robertson	Ramsay,G	McDonald 1	Brown	Mackie.A 1	Rae	Bell 1	Kidd Mercer, W Walker
S	15-Sep	Cowdenbeath		A	ESQC 1	4-2	2800	Mackie.J	Scott	Torrance 1	Moodie	Robertson	Ramsay,G	McDonald	Brown 2,1p	Mackie.A	Rae	Bell	Nicol Turner
S	22-Sep	Cowdenbeath		A	SQC 2	3-3	3000	Mackie.J	Scott	Torrance 1	Moodie	Robertson	Ramsay,G	McDonald	Brown 1p	Mackie.A 2	Rae	Bell	McGinnes Murray Douglas
S	29-Sep	Cowdenbeath		A	SQC 2r	2-2		Mackie.J	Scott	Torrance	Moodie	Lambert	Robertson	McDonald	Brown	Drummond 2	Mackie.A	Bell	
M	01-Oct	Hibernian		H	ESL	0-3	2000	Mackie.J	Scott	Torrance	Ramsay,G	Lambert	Robertson	McDonald	Brown	Drummond	Mackie.A	Bell	
S	06-Oct	Cowdenbeath	1	N	SQC 2r2	2-1		Mackie.J	Bonthron	Torrance	Moodie	Lambert	Robertson	McDonald 1	Rae 1	Drummond 1	Mackie.A	Bell	Gillespie (2) Reid Laidlaw + another
S	13-Oct	East Stirling		A	SQC 3	3-5		Mackie.J	Bonthron	Scott	Murphy	Marshall	Robertson	McDonald 1	Brown	Drummond 2	Mackie.A 1	Bell	Bauldie + another
S	20-Oct	Dunfermline Athletic		A	ESQC 2	3-2		Mackie.J	Bonthron	Scott	Murphy	Marshall	Robertson 1	McDonald	Brown	Drummond 2	Rae	Bell	
S	27-Oct	Leith Athletic		H	ESL	2-0	1600	Mackie.J	Bonthron	Scott	Murphy	Marshall 1p	Robertson	McDonald	Brown	Drummond	Rae	Bell 1	
S	03-Nov	West Calder	2	A	ESQC SF	3-1		Mackie.J	Bonthron 1	Scott	Murphy	Marshall	Robertson	McDonald	Bell 1	Drummond	Rae 1	Gilmour	Handling McCartney Raisbeck
S	10-Nov	Hibernian		A	ESL	2-3		Mackie.J	Bonthron	Scott	Murphy	Marshall	Robertson 1	Bell	Drummond	Moodie	Mackie.A	Gilmour	White Russell
S	17-Nov	West Calder		H	ESQC SFr	4-2		Lambert	Bonthron	Scott	Murphy 1	Marshall m	Robertson	Bell	Drummond	Moodie 1	Mackie.A 2	Gilmour	Houston (3) McLachlan + 2 others
S	24-Nov	Hearts		A	ESL	0-6	1500	Mackie.J	Marshall,?	Torrance	Murphy	Marshall	Robertson	Fairbairn	Moodie	Tervit	Gilmour	Bell	Lorne
S	01-Dec	Clackmannan	1	N	ESQC F	2-1	1800	Mackie.J	Lambert	Scott	Murphy	Marshall	Robertson	McDonald	Moodie	Douglas 2	Drummond 2	Ramsay,G	
S	08-Dec	Lochgelly United		A	KC 1	5-0		Mackie.J	Bonthron	Scott	Murphy	Marshall	Robertson	McDonald 1	Moodie	Douglas 2	Drummond 2	Rae	
S	15-Dec	Camelon		H	F	4-0		Mackie.J	Bonthron	Torrance	Murphy 1	Marshall	Robertson	Moodie 1	Nicol	Douglas	Ramsay,G 1	Rae 1	
S	29-Dec	Lochgelly		H	F	3-0		Mackie.J	Bonthron	Scott	Murphy	Marshall	Robertson	McDonald	Moodie 2,1p	Douglas 1	Drummond	Rae	
M	31-Dec	Corinthians		H	F	1-1	2500	Mackie.J	Bonthron	Scott	Murphy	Marshall	Robertson	McDonald	Moodie	Douglas	Drummond	Bell 1	Stanborough
Tu	01-Jan	Arbroath		A	F	4-2		Mackie.J	Bonthron	Scott	Murphy	Marshall	Robertson	McDonald	Moodie 2,1p	Douglas	Drummond	Bell 2	Middleton (2)
W	02-Jan	Victoria United		A	F	3-5	500	Lambert	Bonthron	Scott	Lambert	Marshall	Robertson	McDonald 2	Moodie	Douglas 1	Rae	Gilmour	Slater Watson Burnett (3)
S	05-Jan	Clackmannan		H	F	0-2		Mackie.J	Bonthron	Scott	Murphy	Robertson	Ramsay,G	McDonald	Moodie	Douglas	Drummond	Gilmour	Lorne Ferguson
S	12-Jan	West Calder		H	KC SF	5-2		Mackie.J	Bonthron	Scott	Ramsay,G	Lambert	Robertson	McDonald 2	Drummond 1	Douglas	Rae	Bell 2	Terry Cairns
S	19-Jan	Leith Athletic		A	ESL	0-3		Mackie.J	Bonthron	Scott	Murphy	Robertson	Ramsay,G	McDonald	Drummond	Douglas	Gilmour	Rae	Mitchell Taylor Wood
S	26-Jan	Cowdenbeath		H	F	2-4		Mackie.J	Bonthron	Scott	Murphy	Marshall 1	Robertson	McDonald 1	Moodie	Douglas 1	Rae	Drummond	Walker (2) Mercer + another
S	09-Feb	Hibernian		H	F	2-2	1000	Mackie.J	Bonthron	Scott	Murphy	Marshall	Robertson	McDonald 1	Moodie 1	Douglas	Gilmour	Stewart	Handling Murray
S	23-Feb	Clackmannan		H	ESS	3-1	1000	Mackie.J	Bonthron	Scott	Murphy	Marshall	Robertson 1	McDonald	Moodie 2	Douglas	Rae	Stewart	Lorne
S	02-Mar	Dundee		A	ESL	2-3	2000	Mackie.J	Bonthron	Scott	Murphy	Marshall	Robertson	McDonald 1	Moodie	Drummond 1	Douglas 1	Stewart	Robertson (2) Tarbet
S	09-Mar	Cowdenbeath		H	KC F	4-1	3000	Mackie.J	Bonthron	Scott	Murphy	Marshall	Robertson	McDonald	Moodie 1p	Drummond 1	Drummond 1	Stewart 1	Kellock
S	16-Mar	Cowdenbeath		A	FC 1	1-0		Mackie.J	Bonthron	Scott	Murphy	Marshall	Robertson	McDonald 1	Moodie	Douglas 1	Drummond	Bell	
S	23-Mar	Dundee		H	ESL	0-1	1800	Mackie.J	Murphy	Leck	Hutchison	Marshall	Robertson	McDonald 1	Moodie	Drummond 1	Drummond	Bell	Reid
S	30-Mar	St Bernards		H	ESL	3-3		Mackie.J	Bonthron	Scott	Murphy	Marshall	Robertson 1	McDonald	Moodie	Stewart	Drummond 1	Mercer	Annan og 1
S	06-Apr	Dunfermline Athletic		A	WC SF	2-0		Mackie.J	Bonthron	Scott	Murphy	Marshall	Robertson	McDonald 2	Moodie	Drummond	Rae	Bell	
S	13-Apr	Cowdenbeath		H	FC SF	1-0		Mackie.J	Bonthron	Scott	Murphy	Marshall	Robertson	McDonald	Stewart	Drummond 1	Rae	Bell	
S	20-Apr	East Stirling		H	F	2-1		Mackie.J	Murphy	Leck	Hutchison	Marshall	Robertson	McDonald 1	Fisher	Drummond 1	Gilmour	Mercer	Mackay
W	24-Apr	St Bernards	3	H	ESL	2-2		Mackie.J	Blackstock	Leck	Murphy	Marshall	Gilmour	Johnston 1	Johnston 1	Fisher 1	Gardiner	Mercer	Lee Prior (2)
S	27-Apr	Dundee		H	F	2-2		Mackie.J	Bonthron	Leck	Murphy	Marshall	Grierson	McDonald 1	Lambert	Johnston 1	McCusker	Bell	Leck og McKay
W	01-May	Cowdenbeath	4	N	WC F	2-1	1000	Mackie.J	Bonthron	Stewart	Murphy	Marshall	Robertson	McDonald 1	Stewart 1	Drummond	Gilmour	Bell	McIlvenny Prior
S	04-May	Cowdenbeath	4	N	ESS	0-0		Mackie.J	Bonthron	Scott	Murphy	Marshall	Robertson	McDonald	Moodie	Drummond	Rae	Bell	Walker, D
S	11-May	Leith Athletic	5	N	ESS	0-1	1500	Mackie.J	Bonthron	Scott	Murphy	Marshall	Robertson	McDonald	Moodie	Drummond	Rae	Gilmour	Fotheringham

(1) match unfinished
(2) at Dunfermline
(1) at Dunfermline
(2) abandoned 85 minutes
(3) Away fixture, switched to Stark's Park
(4) at Tynecastle
(5) at Easter Road

Substitutes, own goals , goal times and opponents' scorers

Day	Date	Opponents	Note	Venue	Comp	Res	Att	1	2	3	4	5	6	7	8	9	10	11	Substitutes, own goals, goal times and opponents' scorers
Th	15-Aug	Lochgelly United	1	H	F	2-1		Oswald	Bonthron	McFarlane	Moodie	Lang	Grierson	Eckford	Devine 1	Weir 1	Manning	Smith	Wilson
S	17-Aug	Orion		A	NL	1-1		Oswald	Bonthron	McFarlane	Moodie	Lang	Grierson	Eckford 1	Devine	Weir	Anderson	Mearns	Grant
S	24-Aug	Aberdeen		H	NL	2-2	2000	Lang	Bonthron	McFarlane	Moodie	Robertson	Grierson	Manning	Devine 1	Weir	Anderson 1	Eckford	Mackie, C Brash
S	31-Aug	Dundee A		H	NL	2-0		Oswald	Bonthron	Denholm	Moodie	Morris	Grierson	Eckford	Devine 1	Weir	Anderson	Mackie,A 2	Anderson
S	07-Sep	Dunfermline Athletic		H	SQC 1	1-1		Oswald	Bonthron	Denholm	Moodie	Morris	Grierson	Eckford	Devine	Weir	Anderson	Eckford	Ryan pen
S	14-Sep	Dunfermline Athletic		A	SQC 1r	1-1		Oswald	Bonthron	Denholm	Moodie	Morris	Grierson	Eckford	Devine	Lang	Anderson	Mackie,A 1p	Masterton
S	21-Sep	Dunfermline Athletic		H	SQC 1r2	2-1	2100	Oswald	Bonthron	Denholm	Moodie	Morris	Grierson	MacDonald,H	Mackie,A 2	Weir	Anderson	Eckford	Grant
S	28-Sep	West Calder		H	SQC 2	6-1		Oswald	Bonthron	Denholm	Moodie	Morris 1	Grierson	Eckford 2	MacDonald,W	Weir 2	Anderson 1	MacDonald,H	
S	05-Oct	Lochgelly United		A	SQC 3	2-3	3000	Oswald	Bonthron	Denholm	Moodie	Morris	Grierson	Eckford	MacDonald,A 2	Weir	Anderson	MacDonald,H	scrimmage Vail Martin
M	07-Oct	Hearts		A	ESL	4-3	2500	Lang	Bonthron	Denholm	Moodie 1	Morris	Grierson	MacDonald,H	MacDonald,A 2	Anderson 1	Mackie,A 2	McCulloch	Buick Thomson (2)
S	12-Oct	Montrose		H	NL	9-1		Oswald	Bonthron	Denholm	Moodie 1	Morris	Robertson	MacDonald,H 1	Devine 2	Weir	Anderson 2	Grierson 3	Bowman, C
S	19-Oct	Lochee United		H	NL	3-1	1000	Oswald	Bonthron	Denholm	Moodie	Morris	Robertson	Eckford	Devine 2,1p	Weir	Anderson 1	MacDonald,H	Sturrock
S	26-Oct	Cowdenbeath		A	ESQC 1	0-4		Oswald	Bonthron	Denholm	Robertson	Morris	Grierson	MacDonald,H 1	Devine	Mackie,A	Mackie,A	Anderson	Moir (2) + 2 others
S	02-Nov	St Johnstone		A	NL	3-1		McFarlane	Scott	Denholm	Lang 1	Robertson	Robertson	MacDonald,H	Devine 1	Weir	Mackie,A 1	Eckford	Johnston og 1
S	16-Nov	Dundee Wanderers		H	NL	3-1		Oswald	Bonthron	Denholm	Moodie	Morris	Robertson	MacDonald,H	Devine	Weir	Mackie,A 1	Bell,J	
S	23-Nov	Cowdenbeath		H	ESQC 1r2	1-1	1800	Oswald	Bonthron	Denholm	Moodie	Morris	Grierson	MacDonald,H	Mackie,A 1	Weir 1	Anderson	Eckford 1	Moir
S	30-Nov	Cowdenbeath		H	ESQC 1r2	3-2		Oswald	Bonthron	Denholm	Moodie	Morris	Grierson	Mearns	Robertson	Weir 2	Anderson	Eckford 1	Drummond, G
S	07-Dec	Selkirk	2	A	ESQC 2	3-2		McFarlane	Scott	Blyth	Lang	Robertson	Cook	Mearns	Devine 1	Maxwell	MacDonald,W 1	Anderson	Drummond, G Ramsay
S	07-Dec	Hibernian		A	ESL	0-1	1200	Oswald	Bonthron	Denholm	Moodie	Morris	Grierson	MacDonald,H	Mackie,A	Weir	Anderson	Eckford 1	Douglas Melrose
S	21-Dec	Dunfermline Athletic		H	ESQC 3	2-0		Oswald	Bonthron	Denholm	Moodie	Morris	Grierson	Devine 1	Mackie,A 1	Weir 1	Anderson	Eckford 1	McCall
S	28-Dec	Orion		H	NL	6-0		Oswald	Bonthron	Denholm	Moodie	Morris	Grierson	Devine	Mackie,A 2	Weir 2	Anderson	Eckford 1	
S	01-Jan	St Bernards		H	ESL	2-2	2200	Oswald	Bonthron	Denholm	Moodie	Morris	Grierson	MacDonald,H 1	Devine	Weir	Anderson	Eckford 1	Moffat
Th	02-Jan	St Mirren		H	F	1-1	1700	Oswald	Bonthron	Robertson	Moodie	Morris	Grierson	MacDonald,H 1	MacDonald,W	Weir	Anderson	Bell,J	
S	04-Jan	Dunfermline Athletic	3	A	WC 1	3-1		Oswald	Bonthron	Robertson	Moodie	Morris	Grierson 1p	MacDonald,H 1	Mackie,A	Weir	Anderson	Eckford 1	Ryan pen
S	11-Jan	Dundee A		A	NL	0-2		Oswald	Bonthron	Denholm	Robertson	Morris	Grierson	MacDonald,H	Mackie,A	Weir	Mackie,A	Eckford 1	Gowans Cowie
S	18-Jan	Kirkcaldy Amateurs		H	FC 1	1-0	1200	Oswald	Robertson	Denholm	Moodie	Morris	Grierson	MacDonald,H	MacDonald,J	Mackie,A 2	Anderson	Eckford 1	Forrester
S	25-Jan	Bathgate	4	N	ESQC F	1-0		Oswald	Robertson	Flanders	Moodie	Morris	Robertson	MacDonald,H 1	MacDonald,J	Robertson 1	Anderson	Eckford 1	
S	01-Feb	Hibernian		A	ESS	0-6		Oswald	Bonthron	Denholm	Moodie 1	Morris	Grierson	MacDonald,H	MacDonald,J	Mackie,A 3	Anderson	Eckford 1	McGeachan (2) Robertson Atherton Callaghan McCartney
S	08-Feb	Forfar Athletic		H	NL	5-0		Oswald	Bonthron	Denholm	Robertson	Morris	Grierson	MacDonald,H 1	MacDonald,J	Weir 2	Anderson	Eckford 1	
S	15-Feb	Victoria United		H	NL	1-0		Oswald	Bonthron	Denholm	Moodie	Morris	Grierson	MacDonald,H	MacDonald,J	Mackie,A 1	Anderson	Eckford 1	
S	22-Feb	Kirkcaldy Amateurs		H	FC 1r	3-0		Oswald	Bonthron	Bonthron	Moodie	Robertson	Robertson	MacDonald,H	MacDonald,J	Weir	Anderson	Eckford	
S	01-Mar	Montrose		A	NL	2-1		Oswald	Bonthron	Denholm	Moodie	Robertson	Robertson	MacDonald,H	MacDonald,J	Weir 2	Anderson	Eckford	
S	08-Mar	Dundee A		H	ESL	1-1	2000	Oswald	Bonthron	Denholm	Moodie	Morris	Grierson	MacDonald,H	MacDonald,J	Mackie,A 1	Anderson	Bell,J	Lloyd
S	15-Mar	Leith Athletic		H	ESL	1-0		Oswald	Bonthron	Denholm	Moodie	Morris	Grierson	MacDonald,H	MacDonald,J	Weir	Eckford 1	McCulloch	
S	22-Mar	Victoria United		A	NL	2-1	1700	Oswald	Robertson	Denholm	Moodie	Robertson	Robertson	MacDonald,H	MacDonald,J	Mackie,A 1	Eckford 1	McCulloch	Thom
S	29-Mar	Arbroath		H	NL	2-1		Oswald	Bonthron	Denholm	Moodie	Morris	Robertson	MacDonald,H	Eckford 1	Weir 1	Anderson	Grierson	Hay 4
S	05-Apr	Arbroath		A	NL	7-3		Oswald	Bonthron	Denholm	Moodie	Morris	Robertson 1	MacDonald,H 2	Weir 1	Mackie,A 2	Anderson	Eckford 1	Willocks (2) Black
M	12-Apr	Hibernian		H	ESL	1-1	2000	Oswald	Bonthron	Denholm	Moodie	Morris	Robertson	Eckford	McFarlane	Mackie,A 1	Johnstone	Anderson	Hunter 5
S	12-Apr	Lochee United		A	NL	1-1		Oswald	Bonthron	Denholm	Moodie 1p	Morris	Grierson	MacDonald,H	McFarlane	Robertson	Johnstone	Eckford	Gilligan og 1; Fleming
S	19-Apr	Forfar Athletic		A	NL	1-1		Oswald	Robertson	Denholm	Moodie	Morris	Grierson	MacDonald,J	McFarlane	Eckford 1	Johnstone	Simpson	Young
Th	24-Apr	Everton		H	F	4-4	2000	Oswald	Ness	Denholm	Orrock	Morris	Grierson	MacDonald,J	Carroll 1	Mackie,A 2	Eckford 2,1p	Haxton	scrimmage Bell Settle pen Proudfoot
S	26-Apr	Aberdeen		A	NL	2-0	2000	Oswald	Robertson	Denholm	Moodie	Morris	Grierson	MacDonald,H	Carroll	Mackie,A 1	Anderson	Eckford	
W	30-Apr	Cowdenbeath		H	NL	0-1		Oswald	Robertson	Denholm	Moodie	Morris	Grierson	MacDonald,H	Carroll	Mackie,A	Anderson	Simpson	Doig Buchan pen 89
S	03-May	St Johnstone		A	NL	0-2		Oswald	Robertson	Denholm	Moodie	Morris	Grierson	MacDonald,H	McCulloch	Weir	Anderson	Eckford	
M	05-May	St Bernards		H	ESL	3-3		Oswald	Ness	Denholm	Orrock	Brown	Grierson	Eckford	McCulloch 1	MacDonald,J 3	Speedie	Simpson	Lyall (2) Brown
W	07-May	Cowdenbeath		A	NL	2-3	2000	Oswald	Robertson	Denholm	Moodie	Morris	Grierson	MacDonald,J	McCulloch 1	Mackie,A	Eckford	Fotheringham 1	Horne (2) Mercer
S	10-May	Dundee Wanderers		A	NL	1-0		Anderson	Pitblado	Robertson	Moodie	Morris	Moodie	MacDonald,H	MacDonald,J 1	Mackie,A	Anderson 1	Haxton	
M	12-May	Dundee		A	ESL	2-0		Oswald	Robertson	Denholm	Orrock	Orrock	Clark	Rankine	Fisher 1	Speedie	Anderson 1	Simpson	
Th	15-May	Dundee A	5	H	NL PO	2-1	2000	Oswald	Denholm	Denholm	Orrock	Morris	Moodie	MacDonald,H	MacDonald,J 1	Mackie,A 1	Burton	Eckford	Cowie

(1) two x 30 minutes played
(2) fixture fulfilled by Reserve eleven
(3) abandoned after 70 minutes
(4) at Cowdenbeath
(5) Championship play-off

1902-03

Day	Date	Opponents	Note	Venue	Comp	Res	Att	1	2	3	4	5	6	7	8	9	10	11	Substitutes, own goals, goal times and opponents' scorers
S	21-Jun	Rangers	1	H	B	1-3	1500	Hamilton	Pitblado	Stevenson	Orrock	Morris	Grierson	Ritchie 1p	McEwan	Denholm	Cairns	Eckford	Bow (3)
S	16-Aug	East Stirling		A	L2	1-4	2500	Mackie	Taylor	Denholm	Orrock	Rankine,S	Clark	Hynd 1p	MacDonald,J	Smith	Cairns	Eckford	Dobbie Pollock Baird Campbell
S	23-Aug	Clyde		H	L2	1-1	1500	Mackie	Taylor	Turner	Moodie	Rankine,S	Clark	Hynd	MacDonald,J	Smith	Cairns	Eckford 1	Gray
S	30-Aug	Ayr		A	L2	0-5	1700	Keir	Taylor	Turner	Moodie	Rankine,S	Orrock	Hynd	MacDonald,J	Smith	Cairns	Grierson	Drain (2) White Young Mackie og
S	06-Sep	Lochgelly United		A	SQC 1	1-4		Simpson	Taylor	Turner	Orrock	Rankine,S	Grierson	Hynd	Moodie	Smith	Cairns	Eckford	Neasham Turner og Haxton Nicoll
S	13-Sep	Selkirk		H	ESQC 1	11-0		Simpson	Taylor	Denholm	Moodie	Rankine,S 1	Grierson	Hynd 1	Cairns 2	Smith 5	Anderson,G 1	Eckford 1	
S	20-Sep	Arthurlie		H	L2	7-1	1500	Simpson	Taylor	Denholm	Moodie	Rankine,S	Grierson	Hynd 2	Cairns	Smith 2	Anderson,G	Eckford 3	Maley Arthur Irvine
S	27-Sep	Scottish Amateurs		H	F	1-0		Simpson	Taylor	Denholm	Moodie	Rankine,S	Grierson	Hynd	MacDonald,J	Smith 1	Anderson,G	Scott 1	
S	04-Oct	Abercorn		A	L2	1-3	1500	Simpson	Taylor	Denholm	Moodie	Rankine,S	Grierson	Hynd	Cairns	Smith 1	Anderson,G	Mackie	McGeachan
M	06-Oct	Hibernian		H	ESL	1-1	2000	Mackie	Taylor	Denholm	Moodie	Rankine,S	Grierson	Hynd	Green	Smith 1	Anderson,G	Eckford	Bolton McLaughlan
S	11-Oct	Port Glasgow		H	F	2-2		Mackie	Taylor	Denholm	Orrock	Grierson	Clark	McGregor	Green 1	Scott 1	Newman	Hynd	Thomson
S	18-Oct	Airdrie		H	L2	0-1	3000	Mackie	Taylor	Denholm	Orrock	Rankine,S	Grierson	Hynd	McGregor	Smith	Anderson,G	Eckford	McLean Rooney McIlvenny
S	25-Oct	Hamilton Academical		H	L2	1-3	1500	Mackie	Taylor	Denholm	Moodie	Rankine,S	Grierson	Hynd	Cairns	McGregor	Anderson,G	Eckford	Miller
S	01-Nov	St Bernards		A	L2	1-1	1400	Mackie	Taylor	Denholm	Moodie	Rankine,S	Grierson 1	Hynd	Cairns	McGregor	Anderson,G	Eckford	
S	08-Nov	Arthurlie		A	L2	3-3	1700	Mackie	Taylor	Denholm	Orrock	Rankine,S	Grierson	Green	Cairns	McGregor	Anderson,G 1	Moodie 2	Fotheringham pen McAulay Gordon (2)
S	15-Nov	Broxburn		A	ESQC 2	0-4		Mackie	Moodie	Denholm	Orrock	Rankine,S	Grierson	McGregor	Cairns	MacDonald,J	Anderson,G	Green	White Young Gillespie
S	22-Nov	Leith Athletic		A	L2	0-3	1900	Mackie	Taylor	Grierson	Orrock	Rankine,S	Baxter	Rankine,J	Cairns	McGregor	Anderson,G	Hynd	Henderson, J Henderson, W
S	29-Nov	Ayr		H	L2	1-2	1500	Mackie	Taylor	Denholm	Orrock	Rankine,S	Moodie	McGregor	Eardley	McGregor	Anderson,G	Eckford	Pelan Thomson (2) Rombach pen
S	13-Dec	St Bernards		H	L2	3-4	1400	Mackie	Taylor	Denholm	Orrock	Rankine,S	Grierson	Rankine,J	Eardley	Wilson 1	Anderson,G	Kane	Smith (2)
S	20-Dec	Airdrie		A	L2	2-2	2000	Mackie	Taylor	Anderson,J	Moodie	Rankine,S	Baxter	Wilson,R 2	Eardley 1	Wilson 1	Anderson,G	Kane	Pringle Goudie
S	27-Dec	Leith Athletic		H	L2	2-2	3000	Mackie	Taylor	Anderson,J	Moodie	Rankine,S 1	Baxter	Wilson,R	Cairns	Wilson 1p	Anderson,G	Green 1	Curran McIlvenney
Th	01-Jan	Falkirk		A	L2	0-2	3000	Mackie	Taylor	Anderson,J	Moodie	Rankine,S	Baxter	Rankine,J	Cairns	Wilson	Anderson,G	Green	Gilchrist Leslie
S	03-Jan	Hamilton Academical		A	L2	1-2	1300	Mackie	Taylor	Anderson,J	Moodie	Rankine,S	Anderson,G	Anderson,G	Eardley	Wilson	Mackay	Green	
S	24-Jan	Clyde		H	L2	1-0	2000	Mackie	Taylor	Anderson,J	Moodie	Rankine,S	Grierson	Eardley	Eardley	Cairns	Anderson,G	Green	Leishman McLaughlin
S	31-Jan	East Stirling		H	L2	1-2	2500	Mackie	Taylor	Anderson,J	Baxter	Rankine,S	Grierson	Rankine,J	Bain	Wilson 1p	Anderson,G	Eckford 1	McLeod (2)
S	07-Feb	Falkirk	2	A	L2	0-2		Mackie	Taylor	Anderson,J	Baxter	Rankine,S	Robertson	Rankine,J	Bain	Wilson	Anderson,G	Eckford	Carmichael (2) McLaughlin Gregg
S	14-Feb	Dunfermline Athletic		H	FC 1	2-4	4500	Simpson	Baxter	Anderson,J	Moodie	Rankine,S	Grierson 1	Rankine,J	Cairns	Cairns	Anderson,G	Eardley	
S	21-Feb	Falkirk		A	FC	0-1		Mackie	Taylor	Anderson,J	Moodie	Rankine,S	Grierson	Rankine,J	Cairns	Wilson	Anderson,G	Eardley 1p	Sharp Crainey
S	28-Feb	Dunfermline Athletic		A	L2	1-2	3000	Mackie	Taylor	Anderson,J	Moodie	Rankine,S	Grierson	Rankine,J	Cairns	Anderson,G 1	Anderson,G	Eckford	Young, J
S	07-Mar	Motherwell		H	L2	3-1	1500	Mackie	Taylor	Anderson,J	Moodie	Rankine,S	Grierson	Rankine,J	Cairns	Anderson,G 1	Eckford	Green 1	Lynn Hamilton (3) Sharp pen
S	14-Mar	Abercorn		H	L2	2-5	2000	Mackie	Taylor	Anderson,J	Moodie	Rankine,S	Grierson	Rankine,J 1	Cairns 1	Anderson,G	Eckford	Eckford 1	Walker Gordon Anderson
S	21-Mar	Motherwell		A	ESL	2-3	1900	Mackie	Orrock	Taylor x	Moodie x	Rankine,S	Grierson	Rankine,J	Wilson,R	Wilson 1	Green 1	Green 1	
S	28-Mar	Leith Athletic		A	ESL	4-0	2000	Mackie	Taylor	Anderson,J	Moodie x	Rankine,S	Grierson	Rankine,J 1	Cairns	Anderson,G 1	Anderson,G	Green	Thomson (3) Dalrymple
S	04-Apr	Kirkcaldy Amateurs		A	WC SF	0-4		Mackie	Taylor	Anderson,J	Baxter	Rankine,S	Grierson	Rankine,J 1	Cairns	Moodie	Eckford	Green	Walker
M	06-Apr	Hearts		H	ESL	1-1	1500	Dorward	Taylor	Scott	Baxter	Bromwell	Baxter	Eckford	Cairns	Wilson 1	Anderson,G	Green	Brewster
S	11-Apr	Leith Athletic		H	ESL	5-1		Mackie	Mackie	Anderson,G	Orrock	Rankine,S	Baxter 1	Wilson,R	Cairns	Wilson 2,1p	Eckford	Green	McFarlane (2) White (2) Gilligan Moore
S	18-Apr	Dunfermline Athletic		A	ESL	1-6	4000	Mackie	Crawford	Anderson,G	Orrock	Rankine,S	Baxter	Eckford	Cairns	Wilson 1	Stalker 2	Mackay	Fisher pen
S	25-Apr	Dundee		H	F	1-1		Dorward	Crawford	Anderson,G	Baxter	Campbell	Grierson	Eckford	Orrock	Cairns	Stalker	Eckford	Burton
S	02-May	Kirkcaldy Amateurs		H	F	2-1		Dorward	Crawford 1	Anderson,J	Moodie 1	Baxter	Grierson	Rankine,J 1	Cairns	Rankine,S 1	Johnstone	Eckford	Bell Walker (2) Hunter
S	09-May	Lochgelly United		A	ESL	1-4	900	Dorward	Taylor	Anderson,J	Orrock	Baxter	Grierson	Rankine,J	Cairns	Foster	Anderson,G	Eckford	Kerr
M	11-May	Hearts		A	ESL	0-1		Dorward	Taylor	McNeil	Orrock	Baxter	Grierson	Cairns	Cairns	Foster	Manning	Green	
W	13-May	Dundee		H	F	2-0	1200	Dorward	Taylor	McNeil	Orrock	Baxter	Grierson	Rankine,J 1	Cairns	Manning	Manning	Eckford	
S	23-May	Kirkcaldy United		A	NC	2-0	600	Don	Anderson,J	Leck	Baxter	Philip	Grierson	Rankine,J 1	Moodie	Rankine,S 1	Mackay	Black	Rae Fisher
S	30-May	Kirkcaldy United		H	NC	4-2		Don	Anderson,J	Leck	Baxter	Philip	Grierson	Rankine,J	Aitken	Rankine,S 2	MacDonald,J 1	Black 1	

(1) Match in aid of the Ibrox Disaster Fund
(2) Match abandoned after 50 minutes ; Rovers were losing 1-2

Substitutes, own goals, goal times and opponents' scorers

Day	Date	Opponents	Note	Venue	Comp	Res	Att	1	2	3	4	5	6	7	8	9	10	11	Substitutes, own goals, goal times and opponents' scorers
S	15-Aug	East Stirling		H	L2	1-2	1500	Don	Owens	Leck	Baxter	Philip	Grierson	Blackburn	Dillon 1	Rankine	Gray	Black	Baird Dobbie
S	22-Aug	Clyde		A	L2	1-0	2000	Don	Owens	Leck	Baxter	Philip	Grierson	Blackburn	Dillon	Rankine 1	Gray	Clarkson	
S	29-Aug	Ayr Parkhouse		H	L2	2-3	1800	Don	Owens	Leck	Baxter	Philip	Grierson	Blackburn	Dillon	Boyle	Gray 1	Clarkson 1	Garven Muir Cameron
S	05-Sep	Cowdenbeath		H	SQC 1	1-0	3000	Don	Philip	Leck	Baxter	Rankine	Grierson	Blackburn	Dillon	Boyle 1	Gray	Clarkson	
S	12-Sep	Cowdenbeath		A	FL	1-2		Don	Philip	Leck	Baxter	Rankine	Grierson	Blackburn	Dillon	Boyle 1	Gray	Clarkson	
S	19-Sep	Lochgelly		H	SQC 2	2-2	4000	Don	Philip	Leck	Baxter	Rankine	Grierson	Blackburn	Dillon 1	Boyle	Gray	Clarkson 1	Devine Haxton
S	26-Sep	Lochgelly		A	SQC 2r	1-1		Don	Owens	Anderson	Moodie	Philip	Grierson	Blackburn	Clarkson	Dillon	Gray	Black	Prior
M	03-Oct	Lochgelly	1	N	SQC 2r2	0-1	4000	Don	Owens	Anderson	Moodie	Philip	Grierson	Blackburn	Clarkson	Dillon	Gray	Black	Gildea
S	05-Oct	Lochgelly		H	FL	0-1		Don	Anderson	Leck	Moodie	Owens	Grierson	Mackie	Dillon	Rankine	George	Black	
M	10-Oct	St Bernards		H	L2	1-2	1500	Mackie	Philip	Owens	Moodie	Philip	Grierson	Blackburn	Dillon	Bell 1	Gray	Clarkson 1	Joyce Lyall
S	17-Oct	St Bernards		A	L2	2-1	1400	Don	Owens	Leck	Owens	Owens	Baxter	Blackburn	Dillon	Bell	Gray	Clarkson 1	Scott
S	24-Oct	Abercorn		A	L2	3-7	1500	Don	Owens	Leck	Moodie	Rankine	Baxter	Blackburn 1	Dillon	Bell	Gray	Clarkson 1	Turnbull (2) Irvine (3) Owen og Smith pen
S	31-Oct	Falkirk		H	L2	3-1	2000	Don	Moodie	Walker	Moodie	Philip 1	Grierson	Blackburn 1	Dillon	Rankine 1	Gray	Clarkson 1	Laird
S	07-Nov	Albion Rovers		H	L2	2-2	1500	Don	Moodie	Moodie	Moodie	Bell	Grierson	Blackburn 2	Dillon	Rankine 1	Gray 1	Clarkson m	O'Rourke (2)
S	14-Nov	Hamilton Academical		A	L2	4-1	2000	Mackie	Moodie	Moodie	Baxter	Philip	Grierson 1p	Blackburn	MacDonald.J	Rankine	Gray 1	Clarkson	McGuire
S	21-Nov	Leith Athletic		H	L2	1-1	2000	Don	Owens	Stewart	Owens	Philip	Grierson	Blackburn 1	Dillon	Rankine 1	Gray 2	Dillon 1	Fotheringham pen
S	28-Nov	Kirkcaldy United	2	A	F	4-1		Don	Stewart	Stewart	Baxter	Philip	Grierson	Blackburn	MacDonald.J	Rankine	Gray	Clarkson	Rankine
S	05-Dec	Hamilton Academical		H	L2	1-1	2500	Don	Stewart	Stewart	Baxter	Philip	Grierson	Blackburn	MacDonald.J	Rankine	Gray 3	Dillon 1	McLean pen
S	12-Dec	Abercorn		H	L2	4-0	1000	Don	Stewart	Walker	Baxter	Philip	Grierson	Blackburn	MacDonald.J 1	Rankine 2	Gray 1	Dillon 1	
S	19-Dec	Ayr		H	L2	2-2	2000	Don	Stewart	Walker	Baxter	Philip	Grierson	Moodie	MacDonald.J	Rankine	Gray 1	Dillon 1	Aitken Hamilton
S	26-Dec	East Stirling		A	L2	0-3	1000	Don	Stewart	Walker	Baxter	Philip	Grierson	Moodie	MacDonald.J	Rankine	Gray	Dillon 1	Reid pen Laurie (2)
F	01-Jan	East Fife		H	FL	3-0		Leck	Stewart	Walker	Moodie	Rankine	Grierson	Dillon 1	MacDonald.J	Owens 1	Gray	Dillon	
S	02-Jan	Falkirk		A	L2	0-2	2000	Mackie	Stewart	Stewart	Rankine	Philip	Grierson	Blackburn	Clarkson	Gray	MacDonald.J	Clarkson	Miller pen Campbell
M	04-Jan	Beith		H	F	2-2		Mackie	Leck	Stewart	Moodie	Philip	Baxter	Dillon	Burns	Wallace 1	MacDonald.J	Clarkson	Colligan og 1
S	09-Jan	Arthurlie		A	L2	1-3	1000	Mackie	Stewart	Stewart	Owens	Philip	Grierson	Blackburn	Moodie 1	Rankine	Gray	Dillon	Coyle Gelvin pen
S	16-Jan	Ayr Parkhouse		A	L2	0-0	1800	Mackie	Moodie	Stewart	Baxter	Rankine	Grierson	Rankine	Thomson	Wallace	Gray	Dillon	
S	23-Jan	Arthurlie		H	L2	2-1	1500	Mackie	Stewart	Stewart	Baxter	Rankine	Grierson 1	Blackburn	Rankine	Wallace	Gray	Thomson 1	Eason Logan (2)
S	30-Jan	Kirkcaldy United		A	FL	1-1	2000	Mackie	Moodie	Stewart	Baxter	Rankine	Grierson	Blackburn 1	Clarkson	Wallace 1	Gray	Dillon	Logan
S	06-Feb	Albion Rovers		A	L2	2-3	1800	Don	Moodie	Stewart	Baxter	Philip	Grierson	Blackburn	Dillon 1	Wallace	Gray	Clarkson 1	Fisher
S	13-Feb	Clyde		H	L2	5-1	1500	Don	Moodie	Stewart	Baxter	Philip	Grierson	Blackburn	Dillon 1	Wallace	Gray 1	Clarkson 2	Scott 40 Main 50 McGill
S	20-Feb	Kirkcaldy United		H	FL	1-1	1800	Don	Moodie	Rankine	Rankine	Philip	Grierson	Blackburn 1	Dillon	Wallace	Gray	Clarkson	Walker
S	27-Feb	Dykehead		H	F	3-0		Don	Moodie	Stewart	Baxter	Rankine	Grierson	Blackburn	Clarkson	Nicholson 1	Gray 1	Thomson 1	
S	05-Mar	Leith Athletic		A	L2	2-0	1900	Don	Moodie	Stewart	Baxter	Rankine	Grierson	Blackburn	Dillon	Wallace 1	Gray	Clarkson 1	
S	12-Mar	Ayr		A	L2	1-2	1500	Mackie	Walker	Stewart	Moodie	Philip	Grierson	Blackburn	Dillon	Wallace 1	Gray 1	Clarkson	Wylie og 1
S	19-Mar	Stenhousemuir		H	F	3-0		Mackie	Walker	Stewart	Moodie	Rankine	Grierson	MacDonald.J 1	Dillon	Wallace 2	Gray 2	Clarkson	
S	26-Mar	Kirkcaldy United		A	WC 1	3-0	2200	Don	Walker	Stewart	Baxter	Rankine	Grierson	Blackburn	Clarkson	Wallace	Gray	Clarkson 3	
M	02-Apr	Dunfermline Athletic		H	FL	2-0		Don	Walker	Moodie	Baxter	Rankine	Grierson	Clarkson	Dillon	Wallace	Gray 1p	Thomson 1	
S	04-Apr	Lochgelly		A	FL	1-2		Don	Walker	Stewart	Baxter	Rankine	Grierson	Dillon	Moodie	Wallace	Leck 1	Clarkson	Ramsay
S	09-Apr	Arbroath		A	CCC	0-2		Mackie	Stewart	Stewart	Moodie	Rankine	Grierson	Dillon	Moodie	Wallace	Gray	Clarkson	
S	16-Apr	East Fife		A	CCC	1-0		Don	Leck	Stewart	Moodie	Philip	Grierson	Dillon	Rankine 1	Wallace	Gray	Clarkson	
S	23-Apr	East Fife		A	FL	1-1		Don	Leck	Walker	Moodie	Philip	Grierson	Rankine 1	Rankine	Wallace 1	Gray	Clarkson 1	
W	27-Apr	Queen's Park		H	FL	0-2		Mackie	Leck	Walker	Moodie	Philip	Grierson	Rankine	Proctor	Rankine	Gray	Clarkson	Johnstone
S	30-Apr	Hearts of Beath		H	FL	2-0		Don	Walker	Walker	Moodie	Philip	Grierson	Proctor	Dillon	Wallace	Gray	Clarkson 1	Richmond Taylor
W	04-May	Cowdenbeath	3	H	B	2-0		Mackie	Inglis	Oswald	Moodie	Neilson	Grierson	Messer	Proctor	Thomson 1	Maxwell	Clarkson 1	
S	07-May	Kirkcaldy United		H	F	3-3		Don	Leck	Walker	Walker	Philip 2	Grierson	Clarkson	Rankine	Wallace 1	Gray	Newman	Thomson Penman
W	11-May	East Fife		H	WC SF	4-0		Mackie	Moodie	Moodie	Neilson	Philip 1	Grierson	Dillon	Rankine	Wallace 3	Gray	Clarkson	Gildea Haxton
F	13-May	Cowdenbeath		H	WC F	2-1		Mackie	Walker	Walker	Neilson	Philip	Grierson	Dillon	Rankine	Wallace 1	Gray	Clarkson 1	Fisher Manson Shaw
S	14-May	East Stirling		H	CCC F	5-0		Mackie	Stewart	Walker	Neilson	Philip 1	Grierson	Dillon	Rankine 2	Wallace 1	Gray 1	Clarkson	Robertson pen

(1) at Dunfermline

(2) Should have been a Fife League fixture, but the pitch was so bad that a friendly was played.

(3) Benefit match for Baxter, the Rovers captain, who broke his leg in the match between the clubs on the April holiday Monday.

Day	Date	Opponents	Note	Venue	Comp	Res.	Att.	1	2	3	4	5	6	7	8	9	10	11	Substitutes, own goals, goal times and opponents' scorers
M	15-Aug	Kelly Rangers	1	A	B	1-1													
Th	18-Aug	Lochgelly		H	F	1-0		Mackie	Inglis	Stewart	Moodie,C	Cumming	Grierson	MacDonald,J	Messer	Wallace 1	Maxwell	Wilson	Duncanson Irvine Abbies
S	20-Aug	Abercorn		A	L2	1-3	1500	Don	Inglis	Stewart	Moodie,C	Neilson	Grierson	MacDonald,J	Wilson	Wallace	Gray 1	Clarkson	Rankine, J (2)
W	24-Aug	Kirkcaldy United		H	F	2-2		Don	Inglis	Stewart	Moodie,C	Cumming	Grierson	Fyfe	Messer 1	Gray 1	Maxwell	Bell	McCulloch
S	27-Aug	East Stirling		H	L2	4-1	1500	Don	Inglis	Stewart	Moodie,C	Philip	Grierson	Clarkson 2.1p	Wilson	Wallace 1	Gray	Bell 1	Gilden
S	03-Sep	Cowdenbeath		A	SQC 1	1-1	3500	Don	Inglis	Stewart	Moodie,C	Philip	Grierson	Clarkson 1p	Wilson	Wallace	Gray	Bell 1	Gilden (2)
S	10-Sep	Cowdenbeath		H	SQC 1r	1-2	4000	Don	Inglis	Stewart	Moodie,C	Philip	Grierson	Clarkson	Wilson	Messer	Gray	Bell	
S	17-Sep	Albion Rovers		A	L2	1-1	2000	Don	Inglis	Cumming	Neilson	Philip	Stewart	MacDonald,J	Messer	Moodie,C 1	Maxwell	Bell	Penman (4)
S	24-Sep	Leith Athletic		A	L2	1-4	1000	Don	Inglis	Cumming	Moodie,C	Philip	Neilson	MacDonald,J 1	Messer	Wallace	Maxwell	Bell	
S	01-Oct	Albion Rovers		H	L2	1-0	1500	Don	Inglis	Stewart	Neilson	Philip	Grierson	MacDonald,J	Messer	Wallace	Gray	Bell 1	Neilson
M	03-Oct	Third Lanark		H	F	2-1	2000	Mackie	Inglis	Stewart	Neilson	Messer	Grierson	MacDonald,J	Proctor	Wallace 2	Gray	Lee	Dow
S	08-Oct	Leith Athletic		H	L2	0-1	2000	Mackie	Moodie,C	Stewart	Neilson	Messer	Grierson	MacDonald,J	Proctor	Wallace	Messer	Clarkson	Connolly Lyon Queen
S	15-Oct	Falkirk		H	L2	1-3	2000	Mackie	Inglis	Stewart	Neilson	Philip	Grierson	MacDonald,J	Proctor	Wallace 1	Gray	Clarkson	Mackie Stewart og McNicol
S	22-Oct	Aberdeen		A	L2	1-3	4000	Don	Inglis	Stewart	Neilson	Messer	Grierson	MacDonald,J	Moodie,C	Wallace 1	Gray	Bell	Hunter Wemyss
S	29-Oct	St Bernards		H	L2	1-2	800	Don	Cumming	Stewart	Moodie,C	Philip	Messer	MacDonald,J	Neilson	Janes 1	Gray	Wallace	Brown, S (2) White Stewart og
S	05-Nov	Ayr		A	L2	0-4	1000	Don	Inglis	Stewart	Neilson	Philip	Grierson	Messer	Proctor	Wallace	Gray 1	Clarkson	Anderson
S	12-Nov	St Bernards		A	L2	5-1	1400	Don	Inglis	Stewart	Neilson 1	Philip	Grierson	MacDonald,J 1	Proctor	Wallace 2	Gray 1	Clarkson	Curran
S	19-Nov	Hamilton Academical		A	L2	0-1	600	Don	Inglis	Stewart	Neilson	Philip	Grierson	MacDonald,J	Proctor	Wallace	Gray	Clarkson	Anderson
S	26-Nov	Abercorn		H	L2	2-1	1000	Mackie	Inglis	Stewart	Neilson	Philip	Grierson	MacDonald,J	Proctor	Wallace	Gray 2	Bell	Anderson
S	03-Dec	Ayr		H	L2	3-0	600	Mackie	Inglis	Stewart	Moodie,C	Philip	Grierson	MacDonald,J 1p	Proctor	Moir 1	Gray 1	Bell	Anderson
S	10-Dec	Clyde		A	L2	0-1	2000	Mackie	Inglis	Stewart	Neilson	Philip	Grierson	MacDonald,J	Proctor	Wallace	Gray	Bell	Logan
S	17-Dec	Arthurlie		H	L2	4-1	1000	Mackie	Inglis	Stewart	Neilson	Philip 1	Grierson	MacDonald,J 1	Proctor 1	Wallace	Gray	Bell 1	Murray
S	24-Dec	East Stirling		A	L2	3-1	1300	Mackie	Inglis	Stewart	Neilson	Philip	Grierson	MacDonald,J 1	Proctor	Wallace 1	Gray 1	Bell	Menzies, A. (2), 1 pen Boyle
S	31-Dec	Arthurlie		A	L2	0-3	900	Mackie	Inglis	Stewart	Neilson	Philip	Grierson	MacDonald,J	Proctor	Wallace	Gray	Bell 1	
M	02-Jan	Clyde		H	L2	1-0	2000	Mackie	Inglis	Cumming	Moodie,C	Philip	Moodie,T	Mitchell	MacDonald,J	Niblo 1	Gray	Bell	Shaw
Tu	03-Jan	Kirkcaldy United		A	F	1-1		Don	Inglis	Stewart	Neilson	Philip	Grierson	Cumming	Proctor 1	Wallace	MacDonald,J	Bell	Dewar (2) Kinnell
W	04-Jan	Dunfermline Athletic		A	FL	2-3		Don	Inglis	Stewart	Neilson	James	James	MacDonald,J	Philip	Wallace 1	Gray 1	Bell	Proudfoot (2)
S	07-Jan	Aberdeen		H	L2	1-0	1500	Mackie	Inglis	Stewart	Neilson	Philip	Grierson	MacDonald,J 1	Proctor	Wallace	Gray	Bell	
S	14-Jan	Hamilton Academical		H	L2	0-2	1200	Mackie	Inglis	Stewart	Neilson	Philip	Grierson	MacDonald,J	Proctor	Wallace	Gray	Bell	
S	21-Jan	Lochgelly United		A	FL	2-0		Mackie	Inglis	Stewart	Neilson	Philip	Grierson	MacDonald,J 1p	MacDougall	Wallace 1	Gray	Bell	Clements pen
S	28-Jan	Hearts of Beath		H	WC 1	2-1	1000	Mackie	Inglis	Stewart	Neilson	Philip 1p	Grierson	MacDonald,J 1	Proctor	Wallace	Gray	Bell	Miller pen
S	04-Feb	Falkirk		A	L2	0-1	2000	Mackie	Inglis	Stewart	Neilson	Cumming	Grierson	MacDonald,J	Proctor	Wallace	Gray	Bell	Thomson
S	11-Feb	East fife		H	FL	5-1	2000	Mackie	Inglis	Stewart	Neilson	Neilson	Grierson	MacDonald,J	Moodie,C 2	Wallace 1	Gray 1	Bell 1	Pitblado pen
S	25-Feb	Dunfermline Athletic		H	FL	3-1	2000	Mackie	Inglis	Stewart	Moodie,C	Philip	Grierson	MacDonald,J	MacDougall	Wallace 1	Gray	Bell 1	Pitblado pen; Pitblado og 1
S	04-Mar	Kirkcaldy United		H	FL	1-0	3000	Mackie	Inglis	Stewart	Moodie,C	Cumming	Grierson	Neilson	Proctor	Wallace	Thomson	MacDonald,J 1p	
S	18-Mar	Cowdenbeath		H	FL	1-3	2100	Mackie	Inglis	Stewart	Neilson	Philip	Grierson	MacDonald,J 1p	MacDougall	Proctor	Thomson	Wallace	Horne Mercer (2)
S	25-Mar	Lochgelly		H	FL	2-0	1800	Mackie	Moodie,C	Stewart	Neilson	Philip	Grierson	Proctor	MacDougall	Wallace	Gray	MacDonald,J	
S	01-Apr	Kirkcaldy United		A	FL	2-0	1800	Mackie	Inglis	Cumming	Neilson	James	Grierson	Proctor	MacDougall	Wallace	Gray 2	MacDonald,J	Walker, J McColl
M	03-Apr	Rangers		H	F	0-2	3200	Mackie	Inglis	Cumming	Neilson	Winning	Grierson	Strachan	MacDougall	Wallace	Gray	MacDonald,J	Coogan
S	08-Apr	Clyde		H	F	2-1	2000	Mackie	Inglis	Cumming	Neilson	James	Grierson 1	Strachan	MacDougall	Wallace	Gray 1	MacDonald,J	
S	15-Apr	Cowdenbeath		A	FL	5-1		Mackie	Inglis	Cumming	Neilson	Grierson 1	Moodie,C	Moodie,C	MacDougall	Wallace 1	Gray 1	MacDonald,J 2	Moir + 2 others
S	22-Apr	East Stirling		H	F	3-0		Mackie	Inglis	Cumming	Lang	Stewart	Marr	Livingstone	Jones	Wallace 1	Gray 2	MacDonald,J	
F	28-Apr	Sunderland		H	F	3-3		Mitchell	Inglis	Cumming	Moodie,C	Stewart	Marr	Newman	Lawson 1	Proctor 1	Gray 1	Moodie,C	Bridgett Gemmell Howie
S	29-Apr	Hearts of Beath		H	FL	2-1		Mackie	Inglis	Cumming	Neilson	Stewart	Grierson	McDougall	Proctor	Wallace 2	Gray	MacDonald,J	Clements pen
S	06-May	East Fife		A	FL	1-1		Mackie	Inglis	Cumming	Moodie,C	Stewart	Grierson	Moodie,C	McDougall	Wallace 1	Gray	MacDonald,J	Robertson, W.
W	10-May	Cowdenbeath		H	WC SF	3-1		Mackie	Inglis	Cumming	Neilson	Stewart	Stewart	Proctor 1	McDougall	Wallace	Gray	MacDonald,J 2	
F	12-May	Kirkcaldy United		A	B	0-2													
S	13-May	Vale of Wemyss		A	B	0-1													
M	15-May	Dunfermline Athletic		H	WC F	5-0		Mackie	Inglis	Cumming	Moodie,C	Grierson	Stewart	McDougall	Proctor 2	Wallace	Gray 2	MacDonald,J	

(1) In aid of fundraising for the Junior club's new pavilion

Day	Date	Opponents	Note	Venue	Comp	Res.	Att.	1	2	3	4	5	6	7	8	9	10	11	Substitutes, own goals, goal times and opponents' scorers
Tu	15-Aug	Kirkcaldy United	1	H	B	2-2		Dowie	Inglis	Cumming	Manning	Grierson	Moodie,T	Mitchell 2	Wilkie	Dalrymple	Anderson	MacDonald,J	Gourlay Hartley
Th	17-Aug	East Fife		H	WC	1-0		Thomson	Cumming	Stewart	Manning	Grierson	Moodie,T	Strachan	Dalrymple	Wallace	Wilkie	Mitchell	
S	19-Aug	Abercorn		A	L2	2-2	1500	Thomson	Cumming	Stewart	Moodie,C	Manning	Moodie,T 1	Strachan	Dalrymple	Wilkie	Gray 1	Wilkie	Hope Dillon
S	26-Aug	Clyde		A	L2	2-2	2200	Thomson	Cumming	Stewart	Moodie,T	Manning	Grierson	Mitchell	Dalrymple	Wilkie 2	Gray	MacDonald,J	Walker Philip
Tu	29-Aug	Hearts of Beath		H	WC	3-1		Dowie	Moodie,C	Stewart	Manning	Inglis 1	Grierson	Mitchell	Dalrymple	Wilkie 1	Gray	MacDonald,J	Clement; Dair og 1
S	02-Sep	Albion Rovers		H	L2	2-3	1000	Thomson	Cumming	Stewart	Neilson	Inglis	Grierson	Mitchell	Dalrymple	Wallace 1	Gray	MacDonald,J 1	White (2) Donald
S	09-Sep	East Stirling		H	L2	2-2	1500	Thomson	Cumming	Stewart	Neilson	Moodie,T	Grierson	Strachan	Wilkie 1	Gourlay	Gray	MacDonald,J 1	Murray Whyte
S	16-Sep	East Stirling		A	SQC	1-4		Thomson	Cumming	Stewart	Neilson	Manning	Moodie,T	Strachan	Wilkie	Gourlay	Gray	MacDonald,J 1p	Strang Hotchkiss McLeod Murray
S	23-Sep	Vale of Leven		A	L2	2-1	2000	Dowie	Inglis	Cumming	Moodie,C	Manning	Grierson	MacDonald,J	Wilkie 1	Gourlay	Dalrymple	Gourlay	Stewart
S	30-Sep	Vale of Carrick		H	F	7-0		Dowie	Inglis	Cumming	Moodie,C	Manning	Grierson	MacDonald,J	Wilkie 1	Wallace 1	MacDonald,J 5,1p	Moodie,T	
M	02-Oct	Airdrie		H	F	2-3		Dowie	Inglis	Cumming	Neilson	Marshall	Grierson	Mitchell 1	Wilkie	MacDonald,J 1	Dalrymple	Moodie,T	Gildea (2), 1 pen Millar
S	07-Oct	Kirkcaldy United		A	FC 1	2-0	2000	Dowie	Inglis	Cumming	Moodie,C	Manning	Grierson	Mitchell	Wilkie 1	MacDonald,J 1	Dalrymple	Gourlay	
S	14-Oct	Cowdenbeath		H	L2	0-1	3000	Dowie	Inglis	Cumming	Moodie,C	Manning	Grierson	Strachan	Wilkie	MacDonald,J	Dalrymple	Gourlay	Mercer
S	21-Oct	Albion Rovers		A	L2	1-3	1800	Dowie	Inglis	Cumming	Moodie,C	Manning	Moodie,T	Mitchell 1	Wilkie	MacDonald,J	Gourlay	Gourlay	McLean Donald Quinn
S	28-Oct	Ayr		H	L2	5-2	1500	Dowie	Inglis	Cumming	Moodie,C	Manning	Grierson	Mitchell 1	Wilkie	Wallace 2	Gray 1	MacDonald,J	Garry (2)
S	04-Nov	Dunfermline Athletic		A	FC SF	2-2	1500	Dowie	Inglis	Cumming	Moodie,C	Manning	Grierson	Mitchell	Wilkie 1	Wallace 1	Gray	MacDonald,J	Pitblado Ferguson
S	11-Nov	Dunfermline Athletic		H	FC SFr	2-0	2000	Dowie	Inglis	Cumming	Moodie,C	Manning	Grierson	Mitchell 1	Wilkie	Wallace	Gray	MacDonald,J 1	
S	18-Nov	Leith Athletic		A	L2	0-1	1800	Dowie	Inglis	Cumming	Moodie,C	Manning	Grierson	Mitchell	Wilkie	Wallace	Gray	MacDonald,J	Henderson
S	25-Nov	Vale of Leven		H	L2	3-2	1000	Dowie	Moodie,C	Inglis	Moodie,T	Manning	Grierson	Mitchell	Dalrymple 1	Wallace 1	Gray 1	Gourlay	McCulloch Stewart pen
S	02-Dec	Abercorn		H	L2	5-1	1100	Dowie	Inglis	Cumming	Moodie,C	Manning	Grierson	Mitchell 1	Dalrymple 1	Wallace 1	Gray 1	MacDonald,J 2p	Darroch
S	09-Dec	Hamilton Academical		A	L2	0-3	1000	Dowie	Inglis	Cumming	Moodie,C	Manning	Grierson	Mitchell	Dalrymple	Wallace	Gray	MacDonald,J 1	McIlvenny McLean Caldwell
S	16-Dec	East Stirling		A	L2	1-1	700	Dowie	Inglis	Cumming	Wilkie	Manning	Grierson	Mitchell	Dalrymple	Wilkie	Gray	Wilkie	Whyte
S	23-Dec	St Bernards		H	L2	4-3	1200	Dowie	Inglis	Stewart	Moodie,C	Manning	Grierson	Mitchell	Dalrymple	Wallace	Gray	MacDonald,J 3,2p	McGettigan Guthrie (2)
S	30-Dec	Leith Athletic		H	L2	2-1	1500	Dowie	Cumming	Borthwick	Moodie,C	Manning	Grierson	Strachan	Dalrymple 1	Wallace	Gray	MacDonald,J	Cameron
M	01-Jan	Hamilton Academical		H	F	1-1	3500	Thomson	Cumming	Cumming	Gibson	Howieson	Grierson 1	Mitchell 1	Wilkie	Quinn	Dalrymple	Grierson	Scholes
Tu	02-Jan	Kirkcaldy United		H	F	1-0	3200	Thomson	Moodie,C	Moodie,C	Moodie,C	Manning	Moodie,T	Mitchell	Dalrymple	Dowie	Rae	MacDonald,J	
W	03-Jan	Beith		H	F	0-1	2000	Thomson	Scott	Leck	Janes	Gibson	Grierson	Strachan	Rae,J	Montgomery	Gray	MacDonald,J	Chalmers
S	06-Jan	Arthurlie		A	L2	0-2	1700	Dowie	Inglis	Cumming	Moodie,C	Manning	Grierson	Dalrymple	Dalrymple	Wallace	Gray	MacDonald,J	Smith Dobbie
S	13-Jan	Ayr		A	L2	1-2	1700	Thomson	Moodie,C	Stewart	Moodie,T	Manning	Grierson 1	Mitchell	Wilkie	Wilkie	Gray 1	Strachan	Garry pen McBean
S	20-Jan	St Bernards		A	L2	2-5	1400	Thomson	Cumming	Cumming	Stewart	Manning	Grierson	Mitchell	Dalrymple 1	Wallace	Gray	Dowie	Beveridge (2) Gray (2) McDonald
S	27-Jan	Cowdenbeath		A	L2	1-2	1800	Dowie	Inglis	Cumming	Moodie,C	Manning	Grierson	MacDonald,J	Dalrymple 1	Wallace	Gray	Gourlay 1	Mercer (2) 1 pen
S	03-Feb	Clyde		A	L2	1-1	2000	Dowie	Inglis	Cumming	Moodie,C	Manning	Grierson	MacDonald,J	Wilkie	Wallace	Gray	Gourlay	Clark pen
S	10-Feb	Queen's Park Strollers		H	F	5-3		Skene	Moodie,T	Cumming	Wilkie	Manning	Grierson	MacDonald,J 1	Dalrymple 2	Wallace 1	Gray 1	Gourlay	Sim Thomas (2)
S	17-Feb	Hearts of Beath		H	WL	5-0		Dowie	Inglis	Cumming	Moodie,C	Manning	Grierson	Dalrymple 2	Dalrymple 2	Wilkie	Gray	Gourlay 1	
S	24-Feb	Arthurlie		H	L2	1-1	1500	Dowie	Inglis	Cumming	Moodie,C	Manning	Grierson	MacDonald,J 1	Wilkie 2	Dalrymple	Gray	Gourlay	Logan
S	03-Mar	Cowdenbeath	2	N	FC F	2-0	3000	Dowie	Inglis	Cumming	Moodie,C	Manning	Grierson	MacDonald,J 1	Wilkie	Dalrymple 1	Gray	Gourlay 1	
S	10-Mar	Kirkcaldy United		A	WL	3-1		Dowie	Inglis	Cumming	Moodie,C	Manning	Grierson	MacDonald,J	Wilkie	Dalrymple 1	Gray 2	Gourlay	Fairley
S	17-Mar	Bathgate		A	PC 1	2-1	1000	Dowie	Inglis	Cumming	Moodie,C	Manning	Grierson	MacDonald,J	Wilkie 1	Dalrymple 1	Gray	Gourlay	Sharp
S	31-Mar	St Bernards		H	F	1-1		Dowie	Inglis	Cumming	Moodie,T	Manning	Grierson	MacDonald,J	Wilkie 1	Dalrymple	Gray	Gourlay	Smith pen
M	02-Apr	Celtic		H	F	1-4		Dowie	Inglis	Inglis	Wilkie	Manning	Grierson	MacDonald,J	Wilkie	Peggie 1	Gray	Fraser	Thomson Orr pen McNair Bennett
S	07-Apr	East Fife		A	WL	2-0		Dowie	Inglis	Cumming	Moodie,C	Manning	Grierson	MacDonald,J	Wilkie	Dalrymple 1	Gray	Gourlay 1	
S	14-Apr	Stenhousemuir		A	PC 2	2-2		Dowie	Inglis	Cumming	Moodie,C	Manning	Grierson	MacDonald,J	Wilkie	Dalrymple 1	Gray	Gourlay 1	Logan (2)
W	18-Apr	Lochgelly		H	WL	2-0		Dowie	Moodie,C	Cumming	Moodie,T	Manning	Grierson	Mitchell	Wilkie	Gourlay 2	Gray 1	MacDonald,J	
S	21-Apr	Stenhousemuir		H	PC 2r	1-1		Dowie	Inglis	Cumming	Moodie,C	Manning	Grierson	MacDonald,J	Wilkie	MacDonald,J	MacDonald,J	Gourlay	Murray
W	25-Apr	Lochgelly		A	WL	2-0		Dowie	Inglis	Cumming	Moodie,C	Manning	Grierson	Mitchell	MacDonald,J 1p	Wilkie	Gray	Gourlay	
Th	26-Apr	Raith Rovers Past XI		H	F	3-2		Brown,J	Dick	Moodie,C	Gow	Grierson 2	Moodie,T	Mitchell	Wilkie	Roughhead	Peggie 1	Fraser	Walker, D. Ramsay, G. pen
S	28-Apr	Stenhousemuir		H	PC 2r2	3-1	3000	Dowie	Inglis	Cumming	Moodie,C	Manning	Grierson 1	MacDonald,J 1p	Wilkie	Dalrymple 1p	Gray	Gourlay	Black
Th	03-May	Cowdenbeath		H	WL	4-1		Dowie	Moodie,C	Cumming	Moodie,T	Manning	Grierson	MacDonald,J 1p	Wilkie 1p	Dalrymple 1p	Mitchell 1	Gourlay	Miller
S	05-May	Lochgelly		A	PC SF	2-1		Dowie	Inglis	Cumming	Moodie,T	Manning	Grierson	MacDonald,J	Wilkie	Dalrymple 2	Gray	Gourlay	McCartney
Th	10-May	Dunfermline Athletic		H	WL	3-1		Dowie	Inglis	Cumming	Moodie,C	Grierson 1	Moodie,T	MacDonald,J	Wilkie 1	Blyth	Mitchell	MacDonald,J 1	Low pen
S	12-May	Alloa Athletic	3	N	PC F	3-1	3000	Dowie	Inglis	Cumming	Moodie,C	Grierson 1	Grierson	Grierson 1	Wilkie	Wilkie 1	Gray	Gourlay 1	Fleming
M	14-May	Cowdenbeath		A	WL	2-3		Dowie	Inglis	Cumming	Moodie,C	Manning	Grierson	MacDonald,J 1	Wilkie	Dalrymple	Gray	Gourlay 1	own goal 1
Tu	15-May	Kirkcaldy United		H	WL	2-0		Dowie	Inglis	Cumming	Moodie,T	Manning	Grierson	MacDonald,J	Wilkie	Dalrymple 1	Gray	Gourlay	

(1) Benefit for Charlie Moodie
(2) at Scott's Park
(3) at Cowdenbeath

Substitutes, own goals, goal times and opponents' scorers

Day	Date	Opponents	Note	Venue	Comp	Res.	Att.	1	2	3	4	5	6	7	8	9	10	11	Substitutes, own goals, goal times and opponents' scorers
W	15-Aug	Kirkcaldy United		A	F	1-0		Dowie	Smart	Cumming	Moodie,C	Manning 1	Grierson	MacDonald,J	Wilkie	Miller	Brannigan	Gourlay	Haggerty McCulloch
S	18-Aug	Vale of Leven		A	L2	0-2	3000	Young	Moodie,C	Cumming	Moodie,T	Manning	Grierson	MacDonald,J	Wilkie	Miller	Brannigan	Gourlay	Donaldson
W	22-Aug	East Fife		H	F	3-1		Dowie	Moodie,T	Moodie,T	Moodie,C	Manning	Grierson	Gourlay 1	Young 2	Mitchell 1p	Fraser	Fraser	Miller McMahon
S	25-Aug	Cowdenbeath		H	L2	1-2	1400	Dowie	Inglis	Cumming	Moodie,C	Manning 1	Grierson	MacDonald,J	Wilkie	McNicoll	Brannigan	Gourlay	Lyon
S	01-Sep	Kirkcaldy United	1	H	SQC 1	2-1	3000	Dowie	Inglis	Cumming	Moodie,C	Manning 1	Grierson	MacDonald,J	Wilkie 1	McNicoll	Mitchell	Gourlay	Menzies
S	08-Sep	Albion Rovers		H	L2	0-1	1400	Dowie	Inglis	Cumming	Moodie,C	Manning	Grierson	Mitchell	Gourlay	McNicoll	Brannigan	Fraser	Paterson Devine Gray
S	15-Sep	Lochgelly		H	SQC 2	3-3	3500	Dowie	Inglis	Cumming	Moodie,C	Manning 1	Grierson 1	Mitchell	Wilkie	McNicoll 1	Gourlay	MacDonald,J	Scott
S	22-Sep	Lochgelly		A	SQC 2r2	1-1	4300	Dowie	Inglis	Cumming	Moodie,C	Manning	Grierson	Mitchell	Brannigan	McNicoll 1	Gourlay	MacDonald,J	
S	29-Sep	Lochgelly	2	N	SQC 2r2	1-0	4400	Dowie	Inglis	Cumming	Moodie,C	Manning	Grierson	Mitchell	Brannigan	McNicoll 1	Gourlay	MacDonald,J	
M	01-Oct	Hibernian		H	F	0-1		Young	Nairn	Cumming	Moodie,T	Dick	Grierson	Mitchell	Dowie	Brannigan	Fraser	MacDonald,J	McCann
S	06-Oct	Lochgelly		H	FC 1	0-3		Dowie	Cumming	Cumming	Moodie,C	Manning	Grierson	Mitchell	Brannigan	McNicoll	Gourlay	MacDonald,J	Peggie (2) McCartney
S	13-Oct	Ayr Parkhouse		A	L2	4-0	1300	Dowie	Inglis	Cumming	Gourlay	Manning	Grierson	Mitchell 1	Wilkie	McNicoll 1	Gourlay 1	Fraser	
S	20-Oct	Cowdenbeath	3	H	SQC 4	2-1	5000	Dowie	Inglis	Cumming	Moodie,C	Manning	Grierson	Mitchell	Dalrymple 1	McNicoll 1	Wilkie	MacDonald,J	Walker
S	27-Oct	Clachnacuddin	4	H	SQC 5	4-0	2000	Dowie	Inglis	Cumming	Moodie,C	Manning	Grierson	Mitchell	McNicoll 2	McNicoll 2	Gourlay	MacDonald,J 1	
S	03-Nov	Abercorn		A	L2	1-1	1000	Dowie	Inglis	Cumming	Moodie,C	Brannigan	Grierson	Mitchell	Brannigan	Dalrymple 1	Gourlay	MacDonald,J 1	Caig
S	10-Nov	Renton	5	A	SQC SF	3-1	3500	Dowie	Nairn	Cumming	Wilkie	Manning	Grierson	Mitchell 1	Dalrymple	McNicoll 1p	Gourlay	MacDonald,J	
S	17-Nov	East Stirling		H	L2	3-1	1400	Dowie	Inglis	Cumming	Moodie,C	Manning	Grierson	Mitchell 1	Dalrymple 2	McNicoll 1	Gourlay	MacDonald,J	Henderson
S	24-Nov	St Bernards	6	N	SQC F	2-2	12000	Dowie	Inglis	Cumming	Moodie,C	Manning	Grierson	Mitchell	Dalrymple	McNicoll 1	Gourlay	MacDonald,J 1	Tait Beveridge; Sloggie og 1
S	01-Dec	St Bernards	7	N	SQC Fr	3-1	13000	Dowie	Moodie,C	Cumming	Moodie,C	Manning	Grierson	Mitchell	Wilkie	McNicoll 1	Dalrymple	MacDonald,J	Findlay; Reid og 1
S	08-Dec	Ayr		H	L2	3-1	1000	Dowie	Nairn	Cumming	Moodie,T	Manning	Grierson	Mitchell	Wilkie	McNicoll 1	Dalrymple 2	MacDonald,J	Rodgers
S	15-Dec	Dumbarton		H	L2	0-4	1400	Dowie	Inglis	Cumming	Moodie,C	Manning	Grierson	Mitchell	Dalrymple	McNicoll	Dalrymple	MacDonald,J	Hill McCormick Teasdale Brander
S	22-Dec	Leith Athletic		A	L2	3-3	1400	Dowie	Inglis	Cumming	Moodie,C	Manning	Grierson	Mitchell	Brannigan 1	McNicoll 2	Dalrymple 2	MacDonald,J 1	Noon Moffatt (2), 1 pen
Th	25-Dec	Hibernian		A	F	0-2	500	Dowie	Denholm	Denholm	Smith	Gray	Denholm	Mitchell	Wilkie	Dalrymple	Stewart	Gourlay	Ray McCallum
S	29-Dec	Vale of Leven		H	L2	5-0	1300	Dowie	Moodie,C	Moodie,C	Moodie,T	Johnston	Grierson	Mitchell	Wilkie 1	McNicoll 1	Brannigan 1	Gourlay	
M	31-Dec	Falkirk		A	F	2-2		Dowie	Nairn	Nairn	Moodie,T	Mitchell	Moodie,C	Mitchell	Brannigan	Brannigan 1	Gourlay 1	Gourlay	McDougall Laird
W	02-Jan	Kirkcaldy United		H	F	1-4		Mackie	Moodie,C	Borthwick	Mitchell	Sloan	Grierson	Dowie	Dalrymple	Brannigan 1	McLean	Grierson	McNulty Thomson Burnett Messer
S	05-Jan	Leith Athletic		A	L2	1-4	1700	Dowie	Moodie,C	Cumming	Moodie,T	Manning	Grierson	Gourlay	Wilkie	McNicoll 1p	Dalrymple	MacDonald,J	Moffat (3) Walker
S	12-Jan	Albion Rovers		A	L2	1-4	1100	Dowie	Hamilton	Cumming	Moodie,C	Manning	Grierson	Gourlay	Brannigan	McNicoll 1	Brannigan	MacDonald,J 1	McNab (2) Menzies pen Main
S	19-Jan	Ayr		A	L2	1-3	1800	Dowie	Hamilton	Cumming	Moodie,C	Manning	Grierson	Mitchell	Dalrymple 1	McNicoll	Dalrymple 1	MacDonald,J	Main (2) Rodger
S	26-Jan	Aberdeen University	8	H	SC 1	5-1	1000	Dowie	Hamilton	Cumming	Moodie,C	Manning 1	Grierson	Mitchell	Dalrymple 2	McNicoll 1	Gourlay	MacDonald,J 1	Wilson
S	02-Feb	Dumbarton		A	L2	0-4	1500	Dowie	Hamilton	Cumming	Moodie,C	Manning	Grierson	Mitchell	Wilkie	McNicoll 1	Dalrymple	Gourlay	Hill (3) Stevenson
S	09-Feb	Ayr		H	SC 2	4-0	3000	Dowie	Inglis	Cumming	Moodie,C	Manning	Grierson	Mitchell 1	Dalrymple 1	McNicoll 1	Gourlay	MacDonald,J 1	
S	16-Feb	Ayr Parkhouse		H	L2	4-3	1400	Dowie	Inglis	Cumming	Moodie,C	Manning	Grierson	Mitchell 2	Wilkie 1	Dalrymple 1	Gourlay	Moodie,T	McColl Waugh Williamson
S	23-Feb	Arthurlie		A	L2	1-3	900	Dowie	Nairn	Cumming	Moodie,C	Manning	Grierson	Mitchell	Wilkie 1	McNicoll	Gourlay	Moodie,T	Clark Allan (2), 1 pen
S	02-Mar	East Stirling		A	L2	3-3	1100	Dowie	Inglis	Cumming	Moodie,C	Hamilton	Grierson	Moodie,T 2	Wilkie	McNicoll 1	Brannigan 1	Stewart	Baird Morris pen McNair
S	09-Mar	Hearts		A	SC 3	2-2	15000	Dowie	Inglis	Cumming	Moodie,C	Manning	Grierson	Mitchell 1	Wilkie	McNicoll 1	Manning	MacDonald,J	Thomson Walker
S	16-Mar	Abercorn		H	L2	4-0	1400	Dowie	Nairn	Cumming	Moodie,C	Manning	Grierson 1	Mitchell	Gourlay 1	McNicoll 1	Gourlay 1	Stewart 1	
S	23-Mar	Hearts		A	SC 3r	0-1	17000	Dowie	Inglis	Cumming	Moodie,C	Manning	Grierson	Mitchell	McNicoll	McNicoll 1	Gourlay	MacDonald,J	Walker
M	30-Mar	Arthurlie	9	H	L2	1-2	1400	Dowie	Inglis	Cumming	Wilkie	Dalrymple	Moodie,T	Mitchell 1p	Dalrymple	Mitchell 1p	Gourlay	Stewart	Stirling Miller
M	01-Apr	St Bernards		H	L2	1-1	2000	Dowie	Inglis	Cumming	Wilkie	Manning	Grierson	Mitchell	Brannigan	McNicoll 1	Gourlay	Gourlay	Hall
S	06-Apr	Cowdenbeath		A	L2	0-3	2500	Dowie	Moodie,C	Cumming	Moodie,C	Manning	Grierson	Mitchell 1	Wilkie	Dalrymple	Gourlay	Stewart	Ramsay pen Wood Brown
S	13-Apr	St Bernards		A	L2	2-3	500	Dowie	Moodie,T	Cumming	Wilkie	Manning	Grierson	Mitchell	Brannigan	McNicoll 1	Dalrymple	Gourlay	Hall (2) Tait
S	20-Apr	East Fife		A	WC	4-2		Dowie	Hamilton	Cumming	Manning	Grierson 1	Mitchell	Dalrymple 1	Brannigan 1	Gourlay 1	Stewart	Moodie,T	Marr Middlemas pen
S	27-Apr	Kirkcaldy United		A	F	0-2		Dowie	Hamilton	Cumming	Moodie,T	Jones	Grierson	Mitchell	Wilkie	McNicoll	Brannigan	Gourlay	Lyon Neilson pen
W	01-May	East Fife		H	WC	1-1		Dowie	Nairn	Cumming	Moodie,C	Grierson	Moodie,T	Mitchell	Wilkie 1	McNicoll	Dalrymple	Stewart	Stalker
W	08-May	Rangers		H	F	2-2		Dowie	Johnston	Innes	Wilkie	Innes	Nairn	Rae	Stewart	Black 2	McFarlane	Gourlay	May Kyle
S	11-May	East Stirling	10	N	L2 PO	3-2		Dowie	Nairn	Cumming	Wilkie	Manning	Grierson 1	Mitchell	Dalrymple 1	McNicoll 1p	Brannigan	Gourlay	Chalk McMillan

(1) Rovers received £63 in share of gate

(2) at Bayview ; Rovers received £292 as their share of the gate for the three matches

(3) Rovers received £100 in share of gate

(4) Rovers received £56 in share of gate

(5) Rovers received £63 in share of gate

(6) at Tynecastle

(7) at Easter Road

(8) Rovers earned £15 in share of gate

(9) Rovers earned £644 from the two Scottish Cup ties against Hearts

(10) League re-election deciding match, at Logie Green

Day	Date	Opponents	Note	Venue	Comp	Res.	Att.	1	2	3	4	5	6	7	8	9	10	11	Substitutes, own goals, goal times and opponents' scorers
Th	15-Aug	Kirkcaldy United		A	F	1-0		Dowie	Wilkie,A	Borthwick	Wilkie,J	Chapman	Grierson	Mitchell,G	Devine 1	Axford	Gourlay	Wylie	
S	17-Aug	Cowdenbeath	1	H	B	1-0	3000	Dowie	Wilkie,A	Cumming	Wilkie,J	Chapman	Grierson	Mitchell,G	Devine	Axford 1	Gourlay	Wylie	
W	21-Aug	Kirkcaldy United	1	H	B	2-2		Mackie	Wilkie,A	Anderson	Wilkie,J	Chapman	Grierson	Newman	Gourlay	Axford 2	Smith	Campbell	Lyon (2)
S	24-Aug	Vale of Leven		A	L2	3-0	1600	Dowie	Wilkie,A	Cumming	Wilkie,J	Chapman	Grierson	Mitchell,G	Devine 2	Axford	Gourlay 1	Campbell	
S	31-Aug	Ayr		A	L2	0-2	2000	Dowie	Inglis	Cumming	Wilkie,J	Chapman	Grierson	Smith	Devine	Axford	Gourlay	Wylie	Main Montgomery pen
S	07-Sep	Lochgelly		A	SQC 1	0-0	5000	Dowie	Inglis	Cumming	Wilkie,J	Chapman	Grierson	Sutherland	Devine	Smith 1	Gourlay	Campbell	
S	14-Sep	Lochgelly	2	H	SQC 1r	3-1	6800	Dowie	Inglis	Wilkie,A	Wilkie,J	Chapman	Grierson	Sutherland 1	Devine	Smith	Gourlay	Campbell	Haxton
S	21-Sep	Leith Athletic	3	H	SQC 2	1-0	4000	Dowie	Inglis	Wilkie,A	Wilkie,J	Chapman	Grierson	Sutherland 1	Smith	Mitchell,G	Gourlay	Campbell	
S	28-Sep	Abercorn		A	L2	0-2	2700	Dowie	Inglis	Wilkie,A	Wilkie,J	Chapman	Grierson	Sutherland	Devine	Devine	Gourlay	Campbell	Curran Craig
S	05-Oct	East Stirling		A	SQC 3	0-0	3200	Dowie	Inglis	Wilkie,A	Moodie,C	Chapman	Grierson	Sutherland	Devine	Phillips	Gourlay	Campbell	
M	07-Oct	Dundee		H	F	1-4	1000	Dowie	Inglis	Wilkie,A	Wilkie,J	Chapman	Grierson	Sutherland	Devine	Phillips	Gourlay	Wylie 1	Dainty pen McDermott Hunter + og
S	12-Oct	East Stirling	4	H	SQC 3r	4-0	6000	Dowie	Inglis	Cumming	Wilkie,J	Chapman 1p	Grierson	Sutherland	Devine	Axford 1	Gourlay 1	Campbell	
S	19-Oct	St Johnstone		A	SQC 4	3-1	5000	Dowie	Inglis	Cumming	Wilkie,J	Chapman	Grierson	Sutherland 1	Devine	Axford 1	Gourlay 1	Campbell	Cameron
S	26-Oct	Hearts of Beath		H	FC 1	5-0		Dowie	Inglis	Cumming	Wilkie,J	Mitchell,W	Grierson 2,1p	Sutherland	Gourlay 1	Axford 1	Devine 1	Stewart	
S	02-Nov	Dunblane		A	SQC 5	2-1	2200	Dowie	Inglis	Cumming	Wilkie,J	Chapman 1p	Grierson	Sutherland	Devine	Axford 1	Stewart	Stewart	Murdoch
S	09-Nov	Cowdenbeath		H	L2	2-0	1600	Dowie	Inglis	Cumming	Wilkie,J	Chapman 1	Mitchell,G	Sutherland	Devine 2	Axford 2	Russell	Russell	McLaren og 1
S	16-Nov	Dumfries		H	SQC SF	5-0	6200	Dowie	Inglis	Cumming	Wilkie,J	Chapman 1	Grierson	Sutherland	Devine	Axford 1	Russell	Russell	
S	23-Nov	Arthurlie		H	L2	4-2	1600	Dowie	Inglis	Cumming	Wilkie,J	Chapman	Grierson	Sutherland	Devine	Axford 1	Gourlay 2	Russell	Easson Clark
S	30-Nov	St Bernards	5	N	SQC F	1-3	18000	Dowie	Inglis	Cumming	Wilkie,J	Chapman	Grierson	Sutherland	Devine	Axford 1	Gourlay	Campbell	Buchanan (2) 2 pens Tennant
S	07-Dec	Albion Rovers		H	L2	1-2	1600	Dowie	Wilkie,A	Cumming	Wilkie,J	Chapman	Grierson	Mitchell,G	Devine	Axford 1	Gourlay	Russell	Main McKenzie
S	14-Dec	Arthurlie		A	L2	1-3	700	Dowie	Inglis	Cumming	Mitchell,W	Mitchell,W	Wilkie,A	Sutherland	Gourlay 1	Axford	Devine	Russell 1	Stirling Easson (2)
S	21-Dec	St Bernards		H	L2	2-0	1400	Dowie	Inglis	Cumming	Mitchell,W	Chapman	Grierson	Sinclair	Gourlay 1	Axford 1	Devine	Brown	
S	28-Dec	Ayr		H	L2	4-0	1800	Dowie	Inglis	Cumming	Mitchell,W	Chapman	Grierson	Bannerman	Gourlay 1	Axford 1	Devine 2	Brown 1	
W	01-Jan	Benwick Rangers		A	F	3-1		Dowie	Inglis	Cumming	Wilkie,A	Chapman	Grierson	Bannerman	Gourlay 1	Axford 1	Devine 1	Brown 1	
Th	02-Jan	Kirkcaldy United		H	PC 1	1-1	3500	Dowie	Inglis	Cumming	Mitchell,W	Chapman 1	Mitchell,W	Bannerman	Gourlay	Axford	Devine 1	Brown	Gray
S	04-Jan	Dumbarton	6	H	L2	2-1	3200	Dowie	Inglis	Cumming	Mitchell,W	Chapman	Grierson	Bannerman	Gourlay 1	Axford	Devine	Grierson	Stewart
S	11-Jan	Ayr Parkhouse		A	L2	2-3	1300	Dowie	Inglis	Cumming	Mitchell,W	Chapman 1	Grierson	Bannerman	Gourlay 1	Axford 1	Devine	Brown	Skillen (2), 1 pen Wilson
S	18-Jan	Abercorn		H	L2	1-0	2400	Dowie	Inglis	Cumming	Wilkie,A	Chapman 1	Grierson	Bannerman 1	Gourlay 1	Axford 2	Devine 1	Brown	
S	25-Jan	Inverness Thistle		H	SC 1	1-0	1200	Dowie	Inglis	Cumming	Wilkie,J 1	Chapman	Mitchell,W	Bannerman	Gourlay	Axford	Devine	Brown	
S	01-Feb	Albion Rovers		A	L2	1-0	800	Dowie	Wilkie,A	Cumming	Wilkie,A	Chapman 1	Mitchell,W	Bannerman	Gourlay	Axford 1	Devine	Russell	
S	08-Feb	Partick Thistle	7	A	SC 2	1-1	4000	Dowie	Inglis	Cumming	Wilkie,J	Chapman	Mitchell,W	Bannerman	Gourlay	Axford 1	Devine	Brown	McGregor
S	15-Feb	Partick Thistle		H	SC 2r	2-1	12500	Dowie	Inglis	Cumming	Wilkie,J	Chapman	Mitchell,W	Bannerman	Gourlay	Axford 2	Devine	Brown	Kennedy
S	22-Feb	Celtic	8	H	SC 3	0-3	14000	Dowie	Inglis	Cumming	Wilkie,J	Chapman	Mitchell,W	Sutherland	Gourlay	Axford	Devine	McAinsh	Kivilchan McMenemy (2)
S	29-Feb	St Bernards		A	L2	3-2	2000	Ness	Inglis	Cumming	Wilkie,J	Chapman	Mitchell,W	Gourlay	Gourlay 1	Axford 1	Devine 1	McAinsh	Simpson, J. Simpson, H
S	07-Mar	Ayr Parkhouse		H	L2	2-0	3000	Ness	Inglis	Cumming	Wilkie,J	Chapman	Mitchell,W	Sutherland	Gourlay	Axford 1	Devine 1	McAinsh	
S	14-Mar	Dumbarton		A	L2	1-3	2500	Dowie	Inglis	Cumming	Wilkie,J	Chapman 1	Mitchell,W	Sutherland	Gourlay 1	Axford	Devine 1	Brown 1	Brander Nesbit (2)
S	21-Mar	Vale of Leven		H	L2	1-1	2000	Ness	Inglis	Cumming	Wilkie,J	Chapman	Mitchell,W	Bannerman	Bannerman	Axford	Devine	Brown	McIntosh
S	28-Mar	Leith Athletic		H	L2	2-2	900	Ness	Inglis	Cumming	Cumming	Chapman	Mitchell,W	Gourlay	Stewart	Axford	Devine 1	McAinsh	Dewar Rose
S	04-Apr	Kirkcaldy United		A	PC 1r	1-0		Ness	Cumming	Wilkie,A	Wilkie,J 1p	Mitchell,W	Grierson	Bannerman	Phillips	Axford	Phillips	McAinsh 1	
M	06-Apr	East Stirling		H	L2	2-0	1600	Ness	Inglis	Cumming	Wilkie,J	Chapman	Mitchell,W	Sutherland	Phillips	Axford 1	Devine 1	Brown	
S	11-Apr	Leith Athletic		A	L2	1-0	2000	Ness	Inglis	Cumming	Wilkie,J	Mitchell,W	Brown	Brown	Gourlay	Axford	Devine	McAinsh 1	
W	15-Apr	Leith Athletic		H	PC 2	1-0	2000	Ness	Chapman	Cumming	Wilkie,J	Chapman	Mitchell,W	Sutherland	Gourlay	Axford	Devine 1	McAinsh 1	
S	18-Apr	Falkirk		H	F	2-1	3000	Ness	Inglis	Wilkie,A	Wilkie,A	Mitchell,W	Grierson	Donald	Gourlay	Axford	Devine	McAinsh 1	Simpson
W	22-Apr	Woolwich Arsenal		H	F	1-0		Ewing	Inglis	Wilkie,A	Wilkie,J	Chapman	Mitchell,W	Sutherland	Andrews	Axford 1	Devine	McAinsh 1	
S	25-Apr	St Bernards		H	L2	1-2	3000	Ewing	Inglis	Wilkie,A	Wilkie,J	Chapman	Mitchell,W	Donald	Gourlay	Axford	Gourlay	Brown	Logan Simpson, J
M	27-Apr	East Fife		A	F	0-0		Ness	Day	Wilkie,A	Moodie,C	Roberts	Day	Sutherland	Gourlay	Axford	Devine	McAinsh 1	
W	29-Apr	Amateur Eleven	9	H	B	2-1		Williams	Newman	Newman	Newman	Newman	Donald	Donald	Bannerman	Bruce	Bannerman 1	Stewart	
S	30-Apr	East Stirling		A	L2	1-0	1000	Ness	Inglis	Cumming	Wilkie,J	Chapman	Mitchell,W	Brown	Gourlay	Axford	Devine 1	McAinsh	

Manager : Peter Hodge

(1) Benefit for Alex Grierson
(2) Rovers earned £240 over the two matches
(3) Rovers received £95 as share of the gate
(4) Rovers earned £160 from the two matches
(5) at Tynecastle ; Rovers received £392 as share of the gate
(6) Receipts £56
(7) Rovers received £282 as share of the gate
(8) Rovers earned £240 from the match
(9) Benefit for Cricket Club

Substitutes, own goals, goal times and opponents' scorers

Day	Date	Opponents	Note	Venue	Comp	Res.	Att.	1	2	3	4	5	6	7	8	9	10	11	Substitutes, own goals, goal times and opponents' scorers
S	15-Aug	Dumbarton		H	L2	1-1	4000	Ewing	Inglis	Cumming	Donagher	Simpson	Mitchell,W	Mitchell,G	Gourlay	Axford 1	Walker	McAinsh	Hill
W	19-Aug	East Fife		H	WL	6-0		Ewing	Wilkie,A	Cumming	Donagher	Simpson	Mitchell,W	Mitchell,G 1p	Kemp 2	Axford 3	Gourlay	Fraser	
S	22-Aug	Cowdenbeath		A	L2	0-0	4000	Ewing	Inglis	Wilkie,A	Donagher	Simpson	Mitchell,W	Mitchell,G	Kemp	Axford	Walker	McAinsh	Pitcairn
W	26-Aug	Dunfermline Athletic		A	WL	0-1		Dowie	Inglis	Cumming	Donagher	Simpson	Grierson	Mitchell,G	Fraser	Seath	Fraser	Alexander	
S	29-Aug	Ayr		H	L2	4-0	3000	Ewing	Inglis	Cumming	Donagher	Simpson	Mitchell,W	Mitchell,G	Walker	Axford 2	Walker 1	McAinsh 1	
S	05-Sep	East Fife	1	H	SQC 1	1-0	3100	Ewing	Inglis	Cumming	Donagher	Simpson	Mitchell,W	Mitchell,G 1p	Walker	Axford	Fraser	McAinsh	Watson
S	12-Sep	Albion Rovers		A	L2	0-1	3400	Ewing	Inglis	Cumming	Donagher	Simpson	Grierson	Mitchell,G	Gourlay	Axford	Mitchell,W	McAinsh	Lawrie
S	19-Sep	Broxburn		A	SQC 2	0-1	2500	Ewing	Inglis	Cumming	Donagher	Simpson	Grierson	Mitchell,G	Gourlay	Simpson	Wardrop	McAinsh	McCallum Kidd
S	26-Sep	Vale of Leven		H	L2	4-2	2000	Ewing	Inglis	Wilkie,A	Donagher	Simpson	Grierson	Mitchell,G 1	Gourlay 1	Wardrop 1	Walker	McAinsh	Torrance
S	03-Oct	Abercorn		A	L2	0-1	1800	Ewing	Inglis	Cumming	Donagher	Simpson	Grierson	Seath	Wardrop	Axford	Gourlay	McAinsh	
M	05-Oct	Dunfermline Athletic		H	WL	4-0		Ewing	Wilkie,A	Cumming	Donagher	Mitchell,W	Grierson	Mitchell,G 2,1p	Wardrop	Alexander 1	Gourlay 1	Fraser	
S	10-Oct	Albion Rovers		H	L2	3-1	1900	Ewing	Inglis	Cumming	Donagher	Simpson	Mitchell,W	Mitchell,G 1	Wardrop 1	Axford 1	Gourlay 1	McAinsh	Neilson pen
S	17-Oct	Abercorn		H	L2	0-0	1900	Ewing	Wilkie,A	Cumming	Donagher	Simpson	Mitchell,W	Mitchell,G	Wardrop	Axford	Gourlay	McAinsh	
S	24-Oct	Arthurlie		A	L2	3-1	1100	Ewing	Inglis	Cumming	Donagher	Simpson	Mitchell,W	Mitchell,G 1	Wardrop 1	Axford 1	Gourlay	McAinsh	Crawford pen
S	31-Oct	St Bernards		H	L2	4-1	3000	Ewing	Inglis	Cumming	Donagher	Simpson	Mitchell,W	Fraser	Wardrop 1	Gourlay 2	Axford	McAinsh 1	Hyde
S	07-Nov	East Stirling		A	L2	1-0	1000	Ewing	Inglis	Cumming	Wilkie,A	Simpson	Mitchell,W	Fraser	Wardrop	Donagher	Axford	McAinsh 1	
S	14-Nov	St Bernards		A	L2	3-3	800	Ewing	Inglis	Cumming	Donagher	Simpson	Grierson	Mitchell,G	Wardrop 1	Gourlay 1	Axford	McAinsh 1	Findlay Hyde (2)
S	21-Nov	Hill of Beath	1	H	PC 1	5-0	800	Ewing	Inglis	Cumming	Donagher 1	Simpson 1	Grierson	Mitchell,G	Wardrop 1	Gourlay 1	Axford 2	McAinsh 1	
S	28-Nov	Ayr Parkhouse		A	L2	2-2	1800	Ewing	Inglis	Cumming	Donagher	Simpson 1	Grierson	Mitchell,G	Wardrop	Gourlay 2	Axford	McAinsh	Cameron (2)
S	05-Dec	Cowdenbeath		A	L2	4-1	2300	Ewing	Inglis	Cumming	Donagher 1	Simpson	Grierson	Mitchell,G	Wardrop	Gourlay 1	Axford	McAinsh 1	Forrest
S	12-Dec	Leith Athletic		A	L2	5-0	1600	Ewing	Inglis	Cumming	Donagher	Simpson 1	Mitchell,W	Mitchell,G	Wardrop	Gourlay 2	Axford 3	McAinsh 1	
S	19-Dec	Arthurlie		H	L2	2-2	1900	Ewing	Wilkie,A	Cumming	Donagher	Simpson	Grierson	Mitchell,G	Wardrop	Gourlay	Axford 1	McAinsh 1	Logan Paterson
S	26-Dec	Dumbarton		H	L2	4-1	3000	Ewing	Inglis	Cumming	Donagher	Simpson	Grierson	Fraser	Wardrop	Gourlay 2	Axford	McAinsh	Hill (2)
S	02-Jan	East Stirling		H	L2	6-2	2100	Ewing	Wilkie,A	Cumming	Andrews	Davidson	Walters	Seath 1	Dowie 2	Sutherland 1	Walker	Fraser	Niblo Wilkie
M	04-Jan	Hearts of Beath	2	A	B	1-2	500	Dowie	Wilkie,A	Anderson	Mitchell,W	Simpson	Wilkie,A	Muir	Wardrop	Gourlay 1	Axford 1	McAinsh 1	Main (2) McMillan Black
Tu	05-Jan	Kirkcaldy United		A	L2	2-0	1500	Ewing	Donagher	Cumming	Donagher	Simpson 1	Grierson	Pearson	Allan	Gourlay 1	Axford	McAinsh 1	
W	06-Jan	Falkirk		A	B	4-0	1700	Dowie	Inglis	Cumming	Donagher	Simpson	Grierson	Mitchell,G	Wardrop	Gourlay 1	Axford 1	McAinsh	
S	09-Jan	Ayr		A	L2	2-2		Ewing	Inglis	Cumming	Donagher	Simpson	Grierson	Mitchell,G	Wardrop 1	Gourlay 1	Walker	McAinsh	Wills pen Graham
S	23-Jan	Broxburn Athletic		H	PC SF	1-4	2600	Ewing	Inglis	Cumming	Mitchell,W	Simpson 1	Grierson	Mitchell,G	Wardrop	Gourlay	Axford	McAinsh	Law
S	30-Jan	Dunfermline Athletic		H	FC SF	1-2	2000	Ewing	Inglis	Cumming	Donagher	Simpson	Grierson	Mitchell,G	Wardrop 1	Gourlay	Axford	McAinsh	Findlay pen Howatt
S	06-Feb	Dunfermline Athletic		A	FC SFr	3-0		Ewing	Mitchell,W	Cumming	Donagher	Mitchell,W	Grierson	Seath	Wardrop 3,1p	Seath	Axford	McAinsh	
S	13-Feb	Leith Athletic		H	L2	0-0	2000	Ewing	Mitchell,W	Cumming	Mitchell,W	Simpson	Grierson	Seath	Wardrop	Seath	Walker	McAinsh	
S	20-Feb	Vale of Leven		A	L2	3-0		Ewing	Inglis 1	Cumming	Donagher	Simpson 1	Sutherland	Mitchell,W	Wardrop 1	Gourlay	Walker	McAinsh	
S	27-Feb	Ayr Parkhouse		A	WL	4-3		Ewing	Inglis	Wilkie,A	Donagher	Simpson 1p	Sutherland	Stark	Wardrop 1	Gourlay 2	Axford	McAinsh	Henderson Holland Wilkie pen
S	06-Mar	Bo'ness		H	F	1-2	2200	Dowie	Inglis	Cumming	Donagher	Simpson	Mitchell,W	Bain,JC	Wardrop	Gourlay 2	Axford 1	McAinsh	Thomson (2) Lochhead
S	13-Mar	Lochgelly		A	WL	2-3	2000	Ewing	Mitchell,W	Cumming	Donagher	Simpson	Wilkie,A	Bain,JC	Wardrop 1	Gourlay 1	Axford	McAinsh	Brown (3)
S	20-Mar	Kirkcaldy United		H	StC	4-3	2000	Ewing	Mitchell,W	Cumming	Donagher	Simpson	Grierson	Bain,JC	Wardrop	Gourlay 2	Axford	McAinsh 1	Hay Brown
S	27-Mar	East Stirling		H	WL	7-0	1700	Ewing	Mitchell,W	Mitchell,W	Donagher 1	Simpson 1	Sutherland	Mitchell,G 1	Wardrop 2	Gourlay 2	Sutherland 1	McAinsh 1	
S	03-Apr	Kirkcaldy United		A	StC	2-3		Ewing	Inglis	Cumming	Donagher	Simpson 1	Mitchell,W	Stark	Wardrop 1	Gourlay	Walker	McAinsh	McCartney pen Kirwan Chalmers
M	05-Apr	Clyde		H	F	2-3	2900	Ewing	Inglis	Cumming	Donagher 1	Mitchell,W	Sutherland	Stark	Wardrop 1	Gourlay	Walker	McAinsh	
S	10-Apr	Ayr Parkhouse		H	L2	3-0		Ewing	Inglis	Cumming	Donagher 1	Simpson	Mitchell,W	Mitchell,G 1p	Wardrop	Gourlay 1	Axford 1	McAinsh	
S	17-Apr	East Stirling		H	PC F	1-0		Dowie	Inglis	Cumming	Donagher	Simpson	Grierson	Mitchell,G	Wardrop	Gourlay 1	Axford 2	McAinsh	
W	21-Apr	Lochgelly		A	WL	1-0		Dowie	Inglis	Wilkie,A	Gibson	Mitchell,W	Sutherland	Stark	Mitchell,G 1	Brown	Henry	Fraser	
S	24-Apr	East Fife	3	N	FCF	3-0	2900	Dowie	Inglis	Cumming	Donagher	Simpson	Grierson	Mitchell,G	Wardrop	Gourlay	Axford 1	McAinsh 1	Niblo Low Brown
M	26-Apr	Kirkcaldy United	4	A	B	0-3		Mitchell,W	Mitchell,G	Newman	Newman	Dowie	Newman	Newman	Newman	Newman	Newman	Newman	Croall
W	28-Apr	Alloa Athletic	3	N	FCF	3-1		Dowie	Inglis	Cumming	Donagher	Simpson	Grierson	Mitchell,G	Wardrop	Gourlay 2	Axford	McAinsh 1	

Manager : Peter Hodge
(1) Abandoned after 75 minutes
(2) Benefit for George Campbell
(3) at Cowdenbeath
(4) Benefit for Bill Dorward (United goalkeeper)

Substitutes, own goals, goal times and opponents' scorers

Day	Date	Opponents	Note	Venue	Comp	Res.	Att.	1	2	3	4	5	6	7	8	9	10	11	Subs, own goals, goal times and opponents' scorers
M	16-Aug	Hearts		H	DC	1-0	4500	Ewing	Inglis	Mitchell,W	Donagher	Simpson	Wilson	Bain,JC	McAuley	Gourlay 1	Wardrop	McAinsh	
S	21-Aug	Abercorn		H	L2	2-0	3000	Ewing	Inglis	Cumming	Donagher	Simpson	Wilson	Bain,JC 1	Niblo	Gourlay	Wardrop	McAinsh	Logan Brown
M	23-Aug	Falkirk		H	DC SF	2-2	3000	Ewing	Inglis	Cumming	Donagher	Simpson 1p	Wilson	Wardrop	Wardrop	Niblo	Niblo	McAinsh	Hay
W	25-Aug	Dunfermline Athletic	1	H	WC	0-1		Mackie	Rennie	Borthwick	Paterson	Mitchell,W	Grierson	Stark	McAuley	Innes	Harley	Shand	Brander
S	28-Aug	Dumbarton		H	L2	2-1	3000	Ewing	Inglis	Cumming	Donagher	Simpson	Wilson	Bain,JC 1	Wardrop	Gourlay 1	Niblo	Niblo	
M	30-Aug	Falkirk		A	DC SFr	2-0		Ewing	Inglis	Cumming	Donagher	Simpson	Wilson	Bain,JC 1	Wardrop	Niblo	McAuley	McAinsh	Graham
W	01-Sep	St Bernards		A	DC Fr	0-1		Ewing	Inglis	Cumming	Donagher	Simpson	Wilson	Gourlay	Gourlay	Gourlay	Wardrop	McAinsh	
S	04-Sep	Cowdenbeath	2	N	SOC 1	1-0	8800	McLuskie	Rennie	Cumming	Donagher	Simpson	Wilson	Bain,JC 1	McAuley	Gourlay	Wardrop	McAinsh	
S	11-Sep	Albion Rovers		A	L2	1-0	1300	Ewing	Inglis	Cumming	Donagher	Simpson	Wilson	Bain,JC	McAuley	Gourlay	Wardrop	McAinsh	
W	15-Sep	Lochgelly	3	A	B	0-4		McLuskie	Rennie	Borthwick	Paterson	Mitchell,W	Grierson	Stark	Innes	Innes	Harley	Shand	Brown Frail (2) Gildea
S	18-Sep	Leith Athletic		A	SOC 2	1-1	7000	Ewing	Inglis	Cumming	Donagher	Simpson	Wilson	Bain,JC	McAuley	Gourlay 1	Wardrop	McAinsh	Lindsay
S	25-Sep	Leith Athletic		H	SOC 2r	2-2	6000	Ewing	Inglis	Cumming	Donagher	Simpson 1	Wilson	Bain,JC 1	McAuley	Gourlay	Wardrop	McAinsh	Lindsay pen Paterson
S	02-Oct	Leith Athletic	4	N	SOC 2r2	1-2	8000	Ewing	Inglis 1p	Cumming	Donagher	Simpson	Wilson	Bain,JC	Bain,JC	Gourlay	Wardrop	McAinsh	Stewart pen Lindsay
M	04-Oct	Newcastle United		H	F	0-5	5000	Ewing	Inglis	Dick	Mitchell,W	Donagher	Wilson	Stark	Donagher	Gourlay	McAuley	Niblo	Whitson Anderson Howie Metcalfe (2)
S	09-Oct	Cowdenbeath		H	FC	2-3	3000	Ewing	Inglis	Cumming	Donagher	Simpson	Wilson	Stark	McAuley	Bain,JC 1	Gourlay 1	Niblo 1	Thomson (3)
S	16-Oct	East Stirling		H	L2	1-0	2000	Ewing	Inglis	Cumming	Mitchell,W	Simpson	Wilson	Stark	McAuley	Bain,JC	Gourlay 1	Niblo	
S	23-Oct	Cowdenbeath		A	L2	1-0	1800	Ewing	Inglis 1p	Cumming	Donagher	Mitchell,W	Grierson	Stark	McAuley	Bain,JC	McAuley 1	Niblo	
S	30-Oct	Albion Rovers		H	L2	3-0	1900	Ewing	Inglis	Cumming	Donagher	Donagher	Grierson	Stark	McAuley 1	Gourlay 1	McAinsh	Niblo	
S	06-Nov	Ayr Parkhouse		A	L2	2-0	900	Ewing	Inglis 1	Smith	Wilson	Donagher	Grierson	Bain,JC	McAuley	Gourlay 1	McAinsh	Niblo	
S	13-Nov	Vale of Leven		A	L2	1-2	2500	Ewing	Inglis	Cumming	Wilson	Donagher	Grierson	Stark	McAuley	Gourlay	McAuley 1	Niblo	Browning Robertson pen
S	20-Nov	Cowdenbeath		H	L2	3-2	3000	Ewing	Inglis 2p	Cumming	Wilson	Donagher	Grierson	Stark	McAuley	Gourlay	McAuley 1	Niblo	Thomson Dewar
S	27-Nov	Vale of Leven		H	L2	0-0	1900	Ewing	Inglis	Cumming	Wilson	Donagher	Grierson	Bain,JC	McAuley	Gourlay	McAuley	Niblo	
S	04-Dec	Ayr		A	L2	3-2	1600	Ewing	Inglis	Cumming	Wilson	Donagher	Grierson	Bain,JC	Wardrop 1	Gourlay	McAuley 1	Niblo 1	McLean (2)
S	11-Dec	Abercorn		A	L2	1-1	200	Ewing	Inglis	Cumming	Smith	Donagher	Grierson	Bain,JC	Wardrop	Gourlay	McAuley 1	Niblo	Curran
S	18-Dec	St Bernards		H	L2	2-1	1000	Ewing	Inglis	Cumming	Mitchell,W	Donagher	Grierson	Stark	Wardrop	Gourlay 2	McAuley 1	Niblo	Gracie
S	25-Dec	St Bernards		A	L2	2-1	2000	Ewing	Inglis 1p	Cumming	Simpson 1	Donagher	Grierson	Stark	McAuley 1	Gourlay 2	McAuley	Niblo	Wilkie
S	01-Jan	Dumbarton		A	L2	1-4	2500	Ewing	Inglis	Cumming	Simpson	Donagher	Grierson	Stark	Wardrop	Gourlay	McAuley	Niblo 1p	Brander Hill (2) Speedie
M	03-Jan	East Stirling		H	PC 1	1-2	3000	Ewing	Inglis 1p	Cumming	McAinsh	Simpson	Grierson	Bain,JC	Wardrop	Gourlay	McAuley	Niblo	McNeillage (2) 1 pen
Tu	04-Jan	Dundee Hibernian		A	F	1-1		Ewing	Inglis	Dick	Donagher	Simpson	Mitchell,W	Stark	McAuley 1	Niblo	Gourlay	McAinsh	
W	05-Jan	Falkirk	5	H	B	3-0		Ewing	Mitchell,W	Dick	Donagher	Donagher	Mitchell,W	McAuley 1	McAuley 1	Niblo 1	Gourlay 1	McAinsh	
S	08-Jan	Cowdenbeath		A	SCC 1	1-1		Ewing	Inglis	Cumming	Simpson	Donagher	Grierson	Bain,JC 1	McAuley	Gourlay 1	McAuley	Niblo	Thomson
S	15-Jan	Cowdenbeath		H	SCC 1r	2-0		Ewing	Inglis	Cumming	Smith 1	Simpson	Grierson	Stark	McAuley	Gourlay	McAinsh	Niblo	
S	22-Jan	Hearts of Beath		H	SCC 2	3-1		Ewing	Inglis	Cumming	Donagher	Simpson	Grierson	Bain,JC	McAuley 1	Gourlay 2	McAinsh	Niblo	Anderson
S	05-Feb	Leith Athletic		A	L2	0-0	4400	Ewing	Inglis	Cumming	Donagher	Donagher	Grierson	Bain,JC	McAuley 1	Gourlay 2	McAinsh	Niblo	
S	12-Feb	Dunblane		H	SCC 3	4-0		Ewing	Inglis	Cumming	Donagher	Simpson	Grierson	Bain,JC 1	McAuley	Gourlay 2	Wilson	McAinsh 1	
S	19-Feb	King's Park		A	SCC 4	1-0		Ewing	Inglis	Cumming	Donagher	Donagher	Wilson	Bain,JC 1	McAuley	Gourlay 1	Wardrop	McAinsh 1	
S	26-Feb	Ayr		H	L2	2-0	2300	Ewing	Inglis	Cumming	Donagher	Simpson	Grierson	Bain,JC	Wardrop	Gourlay 1	McAuley 1	Niblo	
S	05-Mar	Leith Athletic		H	L2	1-1	4200	Ewing	Inglis	Cumming	Donagher	Donagher	Grierson	Bain,JC	Wardrop	Gourlay 1	McAuley	McAuley	Paterson
S	12-Mar	Ayr Parkhouse		H	L2	1-0	2200	Ewing	Inglis	Cumming	Donagher	Wilson	Grierson	Bain,JC	Wilson	Gourlay 1	McAuley	McAinsh	
S	19-Mar	Kirkcaldy United		H	WL	0-0		Ewing	Inglis	Cumming	Wilson	Donagher	Grierson	Bain,JC	Simpson	Gourlay	McAuley	McAinsh	
S	26-Mar	St Johnstone		A	SCC SF	0-1	6000	Ewing	Inglis	Cumming	Donagher	Simpson	Grierson	Bain,JC	Wardrop	Gourlay	McAuley	Niblo	Phillips
S	02-Apr	St Bernards		H	L2	1-2	1700	Ewing	Harley	Cumming	Simpson	Donagher	Grierson	Mitchell,G	Wardrop	Gourlay	McAuley	Niblo	Graham Fleming pen
M	04-Apr	Sunderland		H	F	3-5		Ewing	Inglis	Cumming	Donagher	Wilson	Wilson	Burns 1	Wardrop	Gourlay 1	McAuley	Niblo 1	Low (2) Mordue Hall Tait
S	09-Apr	Arthurlie		H	L2	4-2	1900	Ewing	Inglis	Cumming	Wilson	Simpson	Grierson	McAuley 2	McAuley 1	Gourlay 1	Wardrop 1	McAinsh	Gracie (2)
S	16-Apr	East Stirling		A	L2	2-1	900	Ewing	Inglis	Cumming	Wilson	Donagher	Grierson	McAuley 1	McAuley 1	Gourlay 1	Wardrop 1	McAinsh	Inglis og
W	20-Apr	West of Fife Juniors		H	F	1-1		Ewing	Wilkie	Cumming	Donagher	Simpson	McIntyre	Bain,JC	McAuley	Gourlay 1	Wardrop	McAinsh 1	
S	23-Apr	Partick Thistle		A	F	0-3	2000	McLuskie	Wilkie	Cumming	Donagher	Donagher	McIntyre	Bain,JC	McAuley	Gourlay	Wardrop	McAinsh	Branscombe Lowrie Raisbeck pen
W	27-Apr	Dunfermline Athletic		A	WL	0-0		McLuskie	Inglis	Cumming	Wilson	Donagher	Grierson	Law	McAuley	Roberts	Wardrop	Niblo	
S	30-Apr	Kirkcaldy United	6	A	StC	1-1		Ewing	Inglis	Cumming	Donagher	Simpson	McIntyre	Bain,JC	McAuley 1	Niblo	Wardrop	Harley	Gray

Manager : Peter Hodge

(1) 1908/09 Deciding match
(2) at Tynecastle
(3) Benefit for John McLean, who contracted a severe illness playing for Lochgelly last season and had been in hospital until a short time beforehand.
(4) at Easter Road
(5) Benefit for Anderson Inglis
(6) The fixture doubled up as a Stark Cup match and a Wemyss Cup tie

Day	Date	Opponents	Note	Venue	Comp	Res.	Att.	1	2	3	4	5	6	7	8	9	10	11	Substitutes, own goals, goal times and opponents' scorers
M	15-Aug	Hearts		A	DC 1	1-4	7700	Ewing	Inglis	Cumming	Wilson	Rathbone	Philip	Thorburn	McAuley	McNeil 1	Simpson,Harry	Gibson	Harker (2) Walker, R. McLaren pen
W	17-Aug	Morton		A	L 1	0-1	5200	Ewing	Inglis	Cumming	Donagher	Aitken	Philip	Thorburn	McAuley	Gourlay	Simpson,Harry	Gibson	Gracie
S	20-Aug	Aberdeen		A	L 1	0-2	8000	Ewing	Inglis	Cumming	Donagher	Aitken	Philip	Thorburn	Simpson,Harry	McNeil	Gourlay	Morgan	McIntosh Lennie
M	22-Aug	Kirkcaldy United	N3	A	B	1-4		McCluskie	Moodie,C	Philip	Donagher	Rathbone	Grierson	Thomson	McLay		McLay	Morgan	Seager (2) Fotheringham Gray
S	27-Aug	Rangers		H	L 1	0-2	10000	Ewing	Philip	Cumming	Wilson	Aitken	Grierson	Thorburn	Simpson,Harry	Gourlay 1	Simpson,Harry 1	Gibson	Gordon Smith
W	31-Aug	Morton		H	L 1	2-0	4300	Ewing	Philip	Cumming	Wilson	Aitken	Grierson	Thorburn	Simpson,Harry	Thorburn	McAuley	Gibson 1	
S	03-Sep	Dunfermline Athletic		A	SQC 1	0-1	6500	Ewing	Inglis	Cumming	Wilson	Aitken	Grierson	Mitchell	Simpson,Harry x	McNeil	McAuley	Gibson	Croall
S	10-Sep	Hearts		H	NEC 1	1-3	4000	Ewing	Inglis 1p	Cumming	Philip	Aitken	Grierson	McNeil	McLay 1	Thorburn	Thorburn	Thorburn	McLaren pen Buchanan Harker
S	17-Sep	Lochgelly United	1	A	WL	1-0	2500	Ewing	Inglis 1p	Cumming	Philip	Donagher	Grierson	McNeil	Ramsay	McNeil	McLay 1	McNeil	
S	24-Sep	Hibernian		H	L 1	1-3	6000	Ewing	Philip	Cumming	Donagher	Aitken	Grierson	McAuley	Ramsay	Thorburn 1	McLay	Gibson	Rae Anderson, D Peggie
M	01-Oct	Abercorn		A	F	3-1	1000	Ewing	Philip	Cumming	Aitken	Simpson,Hugh	Wilson	McNeil	Ramsay	McAuley	McAuley	Gibson	Horne
S	03-Oct	Celtic		H	L 1	2-1	8000	Ewing	Philip	Cumming	Aitken	Simpson,Hugh	Grierson	McNeil	Ramsay 1	Gourlay 2	McAuley 1	Gibson	McAteer
S	08-Oct	Hearts		A	L 1	0-0	10000	Ewing	Philip	Cumming	Aitken	Simpson,Hugh	Grierson	McNeil	Ramsay	Gourlay 1	McAuley	Gibson	
S	15-Oct	Hamilton Academical		H	L 1	2-0	4000	Ewing	Philip	Cumming	Aitken	Simpson,Hugh	Grierson	McNeil 1	Ramsay 1	Gourlay	McAuley	Gibson	
S	22-Oct	St Mirren		A	L 1	1-2	6000	Ewing	Philip	Cumming	Aitken	Simpson,Hugh	Grierson	McNeil	Ramsay	Gourlay	McAuley	Gibson	Cunningham Husband
S	29-Oct	Clyde		H	L 1	1-2	7500	Ewing	Philip	Cumming 1p	Aitken	Simpson,Hugh	Grierson	McNeil	Ramsay 1	Gourlay	McAuley	Gibson	Morrison Collins
S	05-Nov	Queen's Park		A	L 1	1-2	7000	Ewing	Philip	Cumming	Aitken	Simpson,Hugh	Grierson	McNeil	Ramsay	Gourlay	McAuley	Gibson 1	Bowie Craigie
S	12-Nov	Motherwell		H	L 1	0-1	5000	Ewing	Philip	Cumming	Aitken	Simpson,Hugh	Grierson	McNeil	Ramsay	Gourlay	McAuley	Gibson	Robertson
S	19-Nov	Falkirk		A	L 1	0-0	5000	Ewing	Philip	Cumming	Aitken	Simpson,Hugh	Grierson	McNeil	Ramsay	Gourlay	McAuley	Gibson	
S	26-Nov	Aberdeen		H	L 1	0-1	3500	Ewing	Philip	Cumming	Aitken	Simpson,Hugh	Donagher	Thorburn	Ramsay	Gilmour	Gourlay	Gibson	Travers
S	03-Dec	Partick Thistle		A	L 1	0-3	8000	Ewing	Philip	Cumming	Donagher	Simpson,Hugh	Leslie	Thorburn	Gilmour	Gourlay	Gilmour	Gibson	Elmore Gardiner, N. Branscombe
S	10-Dec	Kilmarnock		H	L 1	1-1	4300	Ewing	Philip	Cumming	Aitken	Simpson,Hugh	Grierson	Mitchell	McAuley	McAuley	McAuley 1	Gibson 1	Allan
S	17-Dec	Hamilton Academical		A	L 1	1-3	1000	Ewing	Philip	Cumming	Aitken	Simpson,Hugh	Grierson	Mitchell	Ramsay	Gourlay	McAuley 1	Gibson 1	McLaughlin (2) Davie
S	24-Dec	Falkirk		H	L 1	2-2	3000	Ewing	Philip	Cumming 1p	Aitken	Aitken	Grierson	Thorburn	Ramsay	Gourlay	Gilmour	Thorburn	Agnew pen Rattray
S	31-Dec	Celtic		A	L 1	0-5	7000	Ewing	Philip	Cumming	Aitken	Aitken	Grierson	Thorburn	Wilson	Gourlay	Gilmour	Thorburn	McAteer McMenemy (2) Quinn Hastie
M	02-Jan	Alloa Athletic		A	PC 1	3-1	3600	Ewing	Inglis	Fyall	Aitken	Donagher 1	Gilmour	McNeil	Ramsay	Gourlay 1	McAuley	Gibson 1	Hannah
Tu	03-Jan	Kirkcaldy United		N	FC 1	3-1	2500	Ewing	Inglis	Fyall	Moodie	Wilson	Grierson	Thorburn 1	Ramsay	McAulay 2	McLay	Gibson	Cooper
W	04-Jan	Dunfermline Athletic	N4	H	B	1-1	5500	Hunter	Simpson	Cumming	Kinnear	Grierson	Kinnell	McLay	Meek	Johnstone 1	Whittet	Gourlay	Hamilton
S	07-Jan	Dundee		A	L 1	2-1	3500	Ewing	Philip	Cumming	Aitken	Simpson,Hugh	Gilmour	McNeil 1	Ramsay	McLay	Gourlay 1	Gibson	Hamilton
S	14-Jan	Airdrie		A	L 1	3-3	10000	Ewing	Philip	Cumming	Aitken	Simpson,Hugh 1	Gilmour	McNeil	Ramsay	McAuley 1	Gourlay 1	Gibson	Thomson Young, S. Neilson pen
S	21-Jan	Dundee	N1	N	FC F	1-3	3400	Ewing	Philip	Cumming	Aitken	Simpson,Hugh	Gilmour	McNeil	Ramsay	Gourlay 1	Gourlay 1	Gibson	Walker (2) Fraser
S	28-Jan	Dunfermline Athletic		A	WL	2-2		Hunter	Snoddy	Cumming 1	Aitken	Aitken	Wilson	McNeil	Bain,JC	McAuley	Johnstone	Gourlay	Livingstone Mackenzie
S	28-Jan	Falkirk	N5	H	WL	1-1		Ewing	Inglis	Fyall	Moodie	Donagher	Reekie	Mitchell	Ramsay	Thorburn 1	McLay	Ednie	Henderson
S	04-Feb	Rangers		H	L 1	1-4	9000	Hunter	Snoddy	Cumming	Aitken	Simpson,Hugh	Gilmour	McNeil	Ramsay	McAuley 1	Gourlay	Gibson	Bogie Gordon Reid (2)
S	11-Feb	Third Lanark		H	L 1	2-2	7000	Hunter	Snoddy	Cumming	Aitken	Simpson,Hugh	Gilmour	McNeil 1	Ramsay	McNeil 1	Gourlay	Gourlay	Rankine Chalmers
S	18-Feb	Hearts		H	L 1	3-2	4000	Ewing	Snoddy	Cumming	Wilson	Simpson,Hugh	Gilmour	McNeil 1	Ramsay	McAuley 2	McLay	Gourlay	Snoddy og Harker
S	18-Feb	East Fife		N	FC SF	2-0		Hunter	Inglis	Fyall	Moodie	Donagher	Grierson	Thorburn	Reekie	Thorburn	Johnstone 2	Gibson	
S	25-Feb	Airdrie		H	L 1	1-1	6500	Ewing	Snoddy	Cumming	Aitken	Simpson,Hugh	Gilmour	McNeil 1	Ramsay	McAuley 1	McLay	Gibson	Young, S.
S	04-Mar	St Mirren		H	L 1	4-0	6000	Hunter	Snoddy	Cumming	Aitken 1	Simpson,Hugh	Gilmour	McNeil 1	Mitchell	McAuley 1	McLay	Gourlay 1	
S	04-Mar	Dunfermline Athletic	N1	N	FC F	0-0	2500	Hunter	Inglos	Cumming 1p	Moodie	Donagher	Grierson	Thorburn	Mitchell 1	Johnstone	Wilson	Gourlay 1	Raisbeck pen Gardiner
S	11-Mar	Partick Thistle		H	L 1	2-2	6500	Ewing	Snoddy	Cumming	Moodie	Simpson,Hugh	Gilmour	Thorburn	Ramsay	McAuley 1	Gourlay 1	Gibson	
S	18-Mar	Motherwell	2	A	L 1	1-0	4000	Hunter	Snoddy	Cumming	Moodie	Donagher	Gilmour	McLay	Ramsay	McAuley	McLay	Gourlay	
S	18-Mar	Clackmannan		N	PC 3	4-0		Ewing	Inglis	Fyall	Moodie	Donagher	Grierson	Thorburn	Mitchell 1	Johnstone 1	Wilson 2	Gourlay	Howie
S	25-Mar	Kilmarnock		A	L 1	0-1	4000	Hunter	Snoddy	Cumming	Aitken	Donagher	Gilmour	McNeil 1	Ramsay	McAuley	McLay	Gourlay	Livingstone, Izatt
S	25-Mar	Dunfermline Athletic	N2	N	FC Fr	1-2		Hunter	Inglis 1	Cumming	Moodie	Donagher	Grierson	Thorburn	Mitchell	Wilson	Johnstone	Johnstone	Young, S (2) Struthers Murphy Williams
S	01-Apr	Airdrie		A	F	3-5		Ewing	Philip	Cumming	Moodie	Wilson	Grierson	McLay	Reekie	McNeil 3	McLay	Gourlay	Colombo, Hay
S	01-Apr	Kirkcaldy United	N3	H	WL	2-2	3200	Hunter	Snoddy	Cumming	Philip	Simpson,Hugh	Grierson	Thorburn	Ramsay	Main 1	McAulay 1	Gibson	McFie
S	08-Apr	Queen's Park		H	L 1	1-1		Ewing	Inglis	Cumming	Moodie	Simpson,Hugh	Gilmour	McNeil 1	Ramsay	McAuley	McLay 1	Gourlay	Columbo
M	10-Apr	Kirkcaldy United	3	A	WL	1-2	2300	Hunter	Snoddy	Cumming	Moodie	Donagher	Gilmour	Thorburn	McLay	Gourlay	McAuley	Gibson 1	Hosie McConnell
S	15-Apr	Third Lanark		H	L 1	2-3		Ewing	Snoddy	Cumming	Moodie	Simpson,Hugh	Grierson	McNeil 1	Ramsay	McNeil 1	McLay 1	Gibson	
S	15-Apr	Lochgelly		N	WL	2-0		Ewing	Inglis	Cumming	Fyall	Simpson,Hugh	Philip	Thorburn 1	Ramsay	Thorburn 1	McLay 1	Reekie	
M	17-Apr	Clyde		A	L 1	0-0	2500	Ewing	Snoddy	Cumming	Wilson	Simpson,Hugh	Gilmour	McNeil	Ramsay	McNeil	McAuley	Gibson	Dixon Smith
S	22-Apr	Hibernian		H	L 1	0-2	6000	Hunter	Snoddy	Cumming	Aitken	Simpson,Hugh	Grierson	McNeil	Ramsay 1	Gourlay	McLay	Gibson	Hamilton Ratt Newlands (2)
S	29-Apr	Dunfermline Athletic		H	PC SF	3-4		Ewing	Snoddy	Cumming	Aitken	Simpson,Hugh	Gilmour	McNeil	McAuley 2	McAuley 2	McLay	Gourlay	Hendron (2), Curle
S	29-Apr	Cowdenbeath		N	WL	1-3		Hunter	Philip	Fyall	Moodie	Donagher	Grierson	Thorburn	Kinnear	Johnstone 1	Gibson,J	Gibson,F	

Manager : Peter Hodge

(1) Wemyss Cup played in a League format this season
(2) Butler sent off
(3) Fixture doubled up as a Stark Cup match and a Wemyss League fixture
(N) Not included in statistics
(N1) Fulfilled by reserve team, played at Lochgelly
(N2) Fulfilled by reserve team, played at Scott's Park
(N3) Benefit for Tom Paton, 2 x 35s played ; fulfilled by reserve team
(N4) Arthur Cumming Benefit
(N5) Second Wemyss League match played on the same afternoon, fulfilled by reserve team

Day	Date	Opponents	Note	Venue	Comp	Res	Att	1	2	3	4	5	6	7	8	9	10	11	Substitutes, own goals, goal times and opponents' scorers
W	16-Aug	Rangers		A	L1	0-5	12000	McLeod	Snoddy	Cumming	Aitken	Simpson	Gilmour	McNeil	Thomson	Chalmers	Hastie	Ritchie	Galt Hogg Reid (2) Bennett
S	19-Aug	Aberdeen		A	L1	1-3	11000	McLeod	Snoddy	Cumming	Philip	Simpson	Gilmour	McNeil	Thomson	Chalmers	Hastie 1	Ritchie	Wyllie pen McIntosh Main
W	23-Aug	Falkirk		H	DC SF	3-2	3500	McLeod	Snoddy	Cumming	Aitken	Wilson	Gilmour	Ritchie 1	Thomson	Chalmers 1	Hastie	Gourlay 1	Robertson (2)
S	26-Aug	Airdrie		H	L1	1-1	5000	McLeod	Snoddy	Cumming	Aitken	Simpson	Gilmour	Ritchie	Thomson	Chalmers	Hastie	Gourlay 1	Williams
W	30-Aug	Hearts		A	DC F	1-1	7200	McLeod	Philip	Cumming	Aitken	Wilson	Snoddy	Ritchie	McLay	Chalmers	McNeil	Gourlay 1	Abrams pen
S	02-Sep	Morton		H	L1	1-1	3000	McLeod	Philip	Cumming	Aitken	Wilson	Snoddy	Ritchie 1	McLay	Chalmers	McNeil	Gilmour	Turnbull
W	06-Sep	Hearts	1	A	DC Fr	1-1	4250	McLeod	Snoddy	Cumming	Aitken	Simpson	Wilson	McNeil	McLay	Chalmers	McNeil 1	Hastie	Abrams
S	09-Sep	Falkirk		H	NEC 1	0-2	5000	McLeod	Snoddy	Cumming	Aitken	Simpson	Wilson	McNeil	McLay	Chalmers	Thomson	Ritchie	McDonald Logan
M	11-Sep	Hearts		A	DC F2R	0-1	4500	McLeod	Philip	Cumming	Aitken	Simpson	Wilson	McNeil	Thomson	Gilmour	Thomson	Chalmers	Smith
S	16-Sep	Hamilton Academical	4	A	L1	1-0	4000	McLeod	Simpson	Cumming	Wilson	Aitken	Gilmour	Ritchie	McNeil	Snoddy 1	Brownlie	Slack	Rodgerson Anderson, A (2)
S	23-Sep	Hibernian		A	L1	0-3	4500	McLeod	Simpson	Cumming m	Wilson	Aitken	Snoddy 1	Ritchie	McNeil	Chalmers	Brownlie	Slack	
S	30-Sep	Falkirk		H	L1	1-0	3000	McLeod	Philip	Cumming	Aitken	Simpson	Snoddy	Ritchie 1	Hastie	Gourlay	Brownlie	Slack	
M	02-Oct	Celtic		H	L1	1-2	8000	McLeod	Philip	Cumming	Aitken	Aitken	Snoddy	Ritchie	Hastie	Gourlay	Brownlie	Slack	McMenemy Nichol
S	07-Oct	Kilmarnock		A	L1	1-3	5000	McLeod	Inglis	Cumming	Aitken	Aitken	Snoddy	Ritchie 1	Hastie	Gourlay	Brownlie	Slack 1	Armour, A Cunningham, J Cunningham, A
S	14-Oct	Dundee		H	L1	1-1	7500	McLeod	Philip	Cumming	Aitken	Simpson	Snoddy	Ritchie	Hastie	Gourlay	Brownlie	Slack 1	Hamilton
S	21-Oct	Clyde		A	L1	0-2	6000	McLeod	Philip	Cumming	Aitken	Simpson	Snoddy	Ritchie	Hastie	McNeil	Brownlie	Slack	Todd Jackson
S	28-Oct	Third Lanark		H	L1	4-0	4000	McLeod	Philip	Cumming	Gilmour	Aitken	Snoddy	Ritchie	McNeil 2	Gourlay 2	Brownlie	Slack	Dawson Mercer
S	04-Nov	Hearts		A	L1	0-2	8000	McLeod	Philip	Cumming	Gilmour	Wilson	Snoddy	Ritchie	McLay	Gourlay	McNeil	Slack	Kirkwood Clark
S	11-Nov	Kilmarnock		H	L1	3-2	4000	McLeod	Philip	Cumming	Gilmour	Aitken 1	Snoddy	Ritchie	McNeil 1	Gourlay 2	Chalmers	Slack	Lennie
S	18-Nov	Aberdeen		H	L1	1-1	5000	McLeod	Philip	Cumming	Gilmour	Aitken	Snoddy	Ritchie	McNeil	Gourlay	Chalmers	Slack	
S	25-Nov	Partick Thistle		H	L1	3-2	5000	McLeod	Philip	Cumming	Gilmour	Aitken	Snoddy 1	Ritchie	McNeil 1	Gourlay 1	Chalmers 2	Slack	Marshall Snoddy og
S	02-Dec	Queen's Park		A	L1	1-2	3500	McLeod	Philip	Cumming	Gilmour	Aitken	Snoddy	Ritchie	McNeil	Gourlay 1	Brownlie	Slack	Ramsay Forsyth
S	09-Dec	Morton		A	L1	1-0	7000	McLeod	Philip	Cumming	McLay	Aitken	Gilmour	Ritchie	McNeil	Gourlay	Brownlie	Slack 1	
S	16-Dec	Motherwell		H	L1	3-0	5000	McLeod	Philip	Cumming	McLay	Aitken	Gilmour	Ritchie	McNeil 1	Gourlay 1	Brownlie	Slack 1	
S	23-Dec	St Mirren		A	L1	0-2	3500	McLeod	Cumming	Cumming	McLay	Aitken	Simpson	Ritchie	McNeil	Gourlay 1	Brownlie	Slack	Duff Callaghan
S	30-Dec	Hibernian		H	L1	2-2	6000	McLeod	Cumming	Cumming	McLay	Aitken	Simpson	Ritchie	McNeil 1	Gourlay	Brownlie 1	Slack	Patterson Lamb
M	01-Jan	Kirkcaldy United		H	WL	2-1		McLeod	Philip	Collier	Leitch 1	McLay	Wilson	Ritchie	Brownlie	Chalmers 1	Hastie	Slack	Hay
Tu	02-Jan	Cowdenbeath	2	H	B	1-2	4000	Ewing	Inglis	Cumming	Chalmers	Aitken	Snoddy	Gibson	McNeil	Gourlay 1	Black	Hunter	Thomson McKenzie
S	06-Jan	Clyde		H	L1	0-5	5000	McLeod	Philip	Collier	Cumming	Aitken	Brownlie	Ritchie	McNeil	Gourlay	Chalmers	Slack	Walker Hamilton Cameron Carmichael Morrison
S	13-Jan	Third Lanark		A	L1	0-2	4500	McLeod	Philip	Collier	McLay	Aitken	Gilmour	Ritchie	McNeil	Gourlay	Brownlie	Slack	Maindo Whittle
S	20-Jan	Hamilton Academical		H	L1	1-2	10000	Ewing	Collier	Snoddy	McLay	Aitken	Gilmour	Ritchie 1	Brownlie	Snoddy 1	Orr	Slack	McLaughlin, J.H. Millar, P.
S	27-Jan	Airdrie		H	SC 1	0-0	8000	McLeod	Philip	Snoddy	McLay	Aitken	Wilson	Ritchie	McNeil 1	Chalmers	Chalmers	Gourlay 1	
S	03-Feb	Airdrie		A	SC 1r	1-3	5000	McLeod	Philip	Davie	McLay	Aitken	Wilson	Ritchie	McNeil	Chalmers	Orr	Gourlay 1	Templeman (2) Young, S
S	10-Feb	Dundee		A	L1	2-2	6500	McLeod	Philip	Collier	McLay	Aitken	Wilson	Ritchie 1	McNeil 1	Snoddy 1	Orr	Gourlay	Bellamy Comrie
S	17-Feb	Hearts		H	L1	3-1	4000	McLeod	Philip	Cumming	McLay	Aitken	Wilson	Ritchie	McNeil	Snoddy 1	Orr 1	Gourlay	Hegarty pen
S	24-Feb	St Mirren		H	L1	1-1	5000	McLeod	Philip	Collier	McLay	Chalmers	Wilson	Ritchie	McNeil	Snoddy	Hastie 2	Hastie	Migner
S	02-Mar	Airdrie		H	L1	1-5	3000	McLeod	Snoddy	Snoddy	McLay	Simpson	Wilson	Ritchie 1p	McNeil	Gourlay	Orr	Gourlay	Thomson (2) Hunter (2) Cole
S	09-Mar	Motherwell		A	L1	0-0		McLeod	Snoddy	Snoddy	McLay	Aitken	McLay	Ritchie	Brownlie	Gourlay	Hastie	Slack	
S	16-Mar	Motherwell		H	L1	0-3	6500	McLeod	Snoddy	Snoddy	Aitken	Aitken	Wilson	Ritchie	McNeil	Gourlay	Hastie	Hunter	Robertson (3)
S	23-Mar	Rangers		H	L1	0-1	5000	McLeod	Philip	Snoddy	McLay	Aitken	Wilson	Ritchie	McNeil 1	Gourlay	Hastie	Hunter	Gordwin
S	30-Mar	Partick Thistle		A	L1	0-1	1500	McLeod	Philip	Gibson	McLay	Aitken	Wilson	Ritchie	Brownlie	Morgan 1	Hastie	Hunter 1	King Coham
M	01-Apr	Kirkcaldy United	3	H	WL	2-2	5000	McLeod	Philip	King	McLay	Baird	Hastie	Ritchie	Orr	Brownlie	Hastie	Slack 1	
S	06-Apr	Dumbarton		A	F	2-0	2000	McLeod	Philip	Snoddy	Gilmour	Simpson	Wilson	Gilmour	Brownlie	Thomson	Thomson	Slack	
S	13-Apr	Falkirk		A	L1	0-3	4000	McLeod	Philip	Snoddy	Gibson	Aitken	Wilson	Gilmour	McNeil 1	Gourlay 2	Hastie	Hunter	Hamill Speedie (2)
M	15-Apr	Elgin City		A	F	3-0		McLeod	Philip	Snoddy	McLay	Aitken	Leitch	Gilmour	McNeil	Gourlay	Hastie	Keay	
Tu	16-Apr	Buckie Thistle		A	F	0-1		Cassidy	Philip	Collier	McLay	Aitken	Wilson	Gilmour 1	McNeil 1	Gourlay 2	Taylor 2	Hunter	
W	17-Apr	Inverness Caledonian		S	F	3-3	4000	McLeod	Philip	Snoddy	McLay	Aitken	Wilson	Gilmour	Thomson	Gourlay	Hastie	Hunter 1	Simpson Stewart J. (2)
S	20-Apr	Celtic		A	L1	2-0		Chalmers	Philip	Snoddy	McLay	Gibson	Leitch	Gilmour	Thomson 1	Gourlay	Hastie	Hunter 1	
W	24-Apr	East Fife		H	WL	1-1		McLeod	Philip	Collier	McLay	Leitch	Wilson	Gilmour	Hope	Hastie	Hastie	Keay	
S	27-Apr	Hibernian		H	F	1-2	1000	McLeod	Philip	Snoddy	McLay	McLay	Wilson	Gilmour	Brownlie 1	Gourlay 2	Hastie	Hunter	McMenemy
M	29-Apr	Kirkcaldy Cricket Club		H	B	3-3		Mackie	Chalmers	Newman	Brownlie	Newman	Newman	Newman	Hope	Newman 3	Newman	Newman	Gray (2)
Tu	30-Apr	Dunfermline Athletic		A	WL	3-1		Chalmers	Philip	Collier	McLay	Gibson	Leitch	Gilmour	Newman	Newman 2	Hastie 1	Keay	Smith

Manager : Peter Hodge

(1) receipts £170

(2) Jimmy Gourlay's benefit match started 30 minutes late – five of the Rovers players missed their train connection in Edinburgh

(3) Fixture doubled up as a Stark Cup match and a Wemyss League fixture

(4) Paterson missed penalty

Day	Date	Opponents	Note	Venue	Comp	Res	Att	1	2	3	4	5	6	7	8	9	10	11	Substitutes, own goals, goal times and opponents' scorers
S	17-Aug	Aberdeen		A	L1	0-2	8500	McLeod	Philip	Cumming	McLay	Morrison	Logan	Cranston	Hope	Anderson	Stewart	Hunter	Wilson Sage
M	19-Aug	Hibernian		A	DC SF	1-4	4500	McLeod	Philip	Cumming	Wilson	McLay	Logan 1	Cranston	Hope	Anderson	Stewart	Hunter	Grosset Fleming Hendren Callaghan
S	24-Aug	Falkirk		H	L1	0-1	8000	McLeod	Philip	Cumming	McLay	Gibson,J	Logan	Cranston	Graham	Anderson	Anderson	Gibson,F	McMillan
S	31-Aug	Clyde		A	L1	0-1	8000	McLeod	Philip	Cumming	McLay	Gibson,J	Logan	Cranston	Graham	Anderson	Anderson	Gibson,F	Allan
W	04-Sep	Cowdenbeath	1	H	PC SF	4-2		McLeod	Gibson,J	Cumming	McLay	Gibson,J	Logan	Cranston 1	Graham 1	Gourlay 1	Anderson	Gibson,F 1	Lancaster Currie
S	07-Sep	Hibernian		H	L1	4-2	7000	McLeod	Philip	Cumming	McLay	Gibson,J	Wilson	Cranston	Graham	Gourlay 2	Anderson	Gibson,F 2	Patterson Bell
S	14-Sep	Falkirk		A	NEC 1	2-6	6500	McLeod	Philip	Cumming	McLay 1	Morrison	Logan	Cranston	Graham	Gourlay	Anderson	Gibson,F 1p	Croall (3) Robertson (2) Logan
S	21-Sep	Motherwell		A	L1	1-1	5000	Mackie	Philip	Morrison	McLay	Logan	Gibson,J	Cranston	Graham	Gourlay	Anderson 1	Gibson,F	Bellamy
S	28-Sep	Kilmarnock		H	L1	0-0	3000	McLeod	Morrison	Cumming	McLay	Logan	Gibson,J	Cranston	Graham	Gourlay	Gibson,J	Gibson,F	
S	05-Oct	St Mirren		H	L1	2-2	3000	Mackie	Morrison	Morrison	McLay	Logan	Gibson,J	Cranston	Graham	Gourlay 1	Anderson 1	Gibson,F	Cole Megner
M	07-Oct	East Fife	1	H	PC F	0-0		Mackie	Philip	Cumming	Wilson	Morrison	Wilson	Hunter	Graham	Hope	Stewart	Gibson,F	
S	12-Oct	Queen's Park		H	L1	5-0	3500	McLeod	Philip	Cumming	McLay	Morrison	Gibson,J	Hunter	Graham	Gourlay	Gourlay	Gibson,F 2,1p	Drever og 1
W	16-Oct	Edinburgh & Dist Wrestg Lge		H	F	10-1		Mackie	McLay	Cook	Gillespie	Logan 1	Lowther	Cranston 2	Hope 1	Stewart 4	Anderson 2	Gibson,F 1	Monteith
S	19-Oct	Celtic		A	L1	2-1	10000	McLeod	Philip	Cumming	McLay	Logan	Anderson	Cranston 1	Graham	Morrison 1	Gourlay	Gibson,F 1	Dodds pen
S	26-Oct	Partick Thistle		A	L1	0-2	8000	McLeod	Philip	Cumming	McLay	Logan	Anderson	Cranston	Graham	Morrison	Gourlay	Gibson,F	Branscombe (2)
S	02-Nov	Hamilton Academical		H	L1	3-5	3000	McLeod	Philip	Cumming	McLay 2,1p	Wilson	Anderson	Cranston	Graham 1	Morrison	Gourlay	Gibson,F	Rippon (3) Waugh McNeil
S	09-Nov	Dundee		A	L1	0-1	6000	McLeod	Philip	Cumming	McLay	Logan	Anderson	Cranston 1	Graham	Stewart	Stewart	Gibson,F	Walker
S	16-Nov	Airdrie		A	L1	1-0	4000	McLeod	Philip	Cumming	McLay	Morrison	Anderson	Cranston	Graham	Logan	Hope 1	Gibson,F 1p	
S	23-Nov	Morton		A	L1	2-2	4000	McLeod	Philip	Cumming	McLay	Morrison	Anderson	Cranston	Graham	Logan	Hope 1	Gibson,F	Brown (2)
S	30-Nov	Hearts		A	L1	0-2	9000	McLeod	Philip	Cumming	McLay	Morrison	Anderson	Cranston	Hope	Stewart	Stewart	Gibson,F	Dawson Wilson pen
S	07-Dec	Rangers		H	L1	2-2	10000	McLeod	Philip	Cumming	McLay	Morrison 2	Logan	Cranston	Logan	Logan	Stewart	Gibson,F	Reid Smith
S	14-Dec	Hibernian		A	L1	2-1	5000	McLeod	Philip	Cumming	Logan	Morrison	Anderson	Cranston	Graham	Anderson	Graham	Gibson,F	Hendren
S	21-Dec	Clyde		H	L1	5-1	4000	McLeod	Philip	Cumming	Logan	Morrison 1	Anderson	Cranston	Graham 3	Gibson,J 1	Graham	Gibson,F	Jackson
S	28-Dec	Hamilton Academical		A	L1	0-4	5000	McLeod	Philip	Cumming	Logan	Morrison	Anderson	Cranston	Hope	Gibson,J	Graham 3	Gibson,F	McBride (2) Rippon (2)
W	01-Jan	East Fife	1	H	PC F	4-1		McLeod	Gibson,J	Cumming	Logan	Morrison	Anderson	Cranston	Hope 1	Stewart 1	Graham 1	Gibson,F 2p	Hay
S	04-Jan	Aberdeen		H	L1	0-0	9000	McLeod	Philip	Cumming	Logan	Morrison	Anderson	Cranston	Hope	Gibson,J	Graham	Gibson,F	
S	11-Jan	Third Lanark		A	L1	0-0	2000	McLeod	Gibson,J	Cumming	Logan	Morrison	Anderson	Cranston	Graham	Stewart	Hope	Gourlay	
S	18-Jan	Hearts		H	L1	3-3	9000	McLeod	Philip	Cumming	Logan	Morrison	Anderson	Cranston 1	Graham	Stewart 2	Gourlay	Hunter	Dawson (3)
S	25-Jan	Third Lanark		H	L1	1-3	5000	McLeod	Philip	Cumming	Logan	Morrison	Anderson	Cranston	Graham 1	Stewart	Gourlay	Hunter	Rankine Spiers pen Brown
S	01-Feb	Rangers		A	L1	0-4	8000	McLeod	Morrison	Cumming	Wilson	Logan	Anderson	Cranston	Graham	Stewart	Hope	Gibson,F	Reid (2) Goodwin (2)
S	08-Feb	Broxburn		H	SC 2	5-0	7500	McLeod	Philip	Cumming	Logan	Morrison	Anderson	Cranston	Hope	Stewart 2	Graham 3	Gibson,F	
S	15-Feb	Dundee		H	L1	0-0	5000	McLeod	Philip	Cumming	Logan	Morrison	Anderson	Cranston	Hope	Martin 1	Graham	Gibson,F	
S	22-Feb	Hibernian		H	SC 3	2-2	16600	McLeod	Philip	Cumming	Logan	Morrison	Anderson	Cranston	Hope	Martin	Graham	Gibson,F 1	Rae Fleming
S	01-Mar	Hibernian		A	SC 3r	1-0	23000	McLeod	Morrison	Cumming	Logan	Morrison	Anderson	Cranston 1	Graham	Martin	Gourlay	Gibson,F 1	
S	08-Mar	St Mirren		H	SC 4	1-0	15500	McLeod	Morrison	Cumming	McLay	Logan	Anderson	Cranston 1	Graham	Stewart	Gourlay	Gibson,F 1	Elmore
S	15-Mar	Kilmarnock		A	L1	3-4	4000	McLeod	Morrison	Cumming	McLay	Gibson,J	Anderson 1	Cranston 1	Graham	Martin 1	Gourlay 1	Gibson,F 1p	Dickie (2) Cunningham, A. Culley
S	22-Mar	Motherwell		H	L1	2-0	5000	McLeod	Philip	Cumming	McLay	Logan	Anderson	Cranston	Graham	Martin	Gourlay 1	Gibson,F	Quinn (3) Gallagher
S	29-Mar	Celtic		A	L1	1-4	8000	McLeod	Morrison	Morrison	McLay	Morrison	Anderson	Cranston	Graham	Stewart	Gourlay	Gibson,F 1	Reid
S	05-Apr	Clyde		H	L1	1-1	28000	McLeod	Morrison	Cumming	McLay	Logan	Anderson	Cranston	Graham	Martin 1	Gourlay 1	Gibson,F 1	
M	07-Apr	Partick Thistle	2	N	SC SF	1-0	19000	McLeod	Philip	Cumming	McLay	Logan	Anderson	Cranston	Hope	Martin	Gourlay	Gibson,F 1	Branscombe (2)
W	12-Apr	Falkirk	3	N	SC F	0-2	40000	McLeod	Morrison	Cumming	Logan	Logan	Anderson	Cranston	Graham	Martin	Gourlay	Gibson,F	Logan Robertson
S	16-Apr	Broxburn		A	B	4-1		Mackie	Philip	Morrison	Anderson	Gibson,J	Cranston	Newman	Hope	Hope	Stewart 2	Stewart 2	Clark
W	19-Apr	Morton		A	L1	0-1	5000	McLeod	Morrison	Cumming	Gibson,J	Gibson,J	Cranston	Cranston	Graham	Gourlay	Gourlay	Gibson,F	Stevenson
W	23-Apr	Airdrie	1	H	PC F	2-4	2000	McLeod	Morrison	Cumming	Gibson,J	Gibson,J	Cranston	Cranston	Hope 1	Logan	Gourlay	Gibson,F 1	Templeman (2) Reid (2)
S	26-Apr	St Mirren		A	L1	4-4	3000	McLeod	Morrison	Cumming	Gibson,J	Logan	Cranston	Cranston	Graham 1	Martin 1	Gourlay 1	Gibson,F 2	Magner (3) Sowerby
M	28-Apr	Falkirk		A	L1	1-0	3000	McLeod	Philip	Cumming	Gibson,J	Logan	Anderson	Cranston	Graham	Martin	Gourlay	Gibson,F	
W	30-Apr	Queen's Park		A	L1	0-1	3000	McLeod	Philip	Cumming	Wilson	Logan	Anderson	Hope	Graham	Martin	Gourlay	Gibson,F	Walker

Manager : Peter Hodge to 12th November ; James Tod from 12th November

The Stark Cup was played for on Saturday 20th April at Stark's Park, when the reserve team beat Kirkcaldy United 2-1 (Gillespie and Hope : McIntosh)

(1) 1911/12 competition

(2) at Tynecastle

(3) at Celtic Park

Day	Date	Opponents	Note	Venue	Comp	Res	Att	1	2	3	4	5	6	7	8	9	10	11	Substitutes, own goals, goal times and opponents scorers
S	16-Aug	Morton		H	L1	1-2	4500	Wallace	Morrison	Winning	McLay	Logan	Anderson	Cranston	McCulloch	Rattray	Gourlay	Gibson,F 1p	Gourlay Stevenson
M	18-Aug	Falkirk		H	DC 1	2-2	4000	Wallace	Philip	Winning	McLay	Morrison	Anderson 1	Cranston	Rattray	Rattray 1	Gourlay	Gibson,F	McCulloch Ferris
W	20-Aug	Falkirk		A	DC 1 R	2-5		Wallace	Philip	Winning	McLay	Morrison	Anderson	Cranston	Rattray	Martin 1	McCulloch	Gibson,F 1	McNeasht Robertson (2) Croal (2)
S	23-Aug	Airdrie		A	L1	2-5	9000	Neish	Philip	Winning	McLay	McLay	Davidson	Cranston 1	McCulloch	Martin	Rattray	Gibson,F 1	Reid (3) Thomson Winning pen
W	27-Aug	Cowdenbeath		A	FC 1	1-2		Wallace	Philip	Winning	Davidson	Anderson	Anderson	Cranston	McCulloch	Martin	Rattray	Gibson,F 1p	Brownlie Cunningham
S	30-Aug	Hibernian		H	L1	1-1	5000	Neish	Morrison	Winning	McCulloch	McLay	Anderson	Cranston	Waugh	Rattray 1	Gourlay	Gibson,F	Adam
M	01-Sep	Broxburn		A	B	1-1		Wallace	Morrison	Winning	Marr	Anderson	McGlone	Cranston	Henretta	Martin 1	Traill 1	Scott	Curran
S	06-Sep	Clyde		H	L1	1-0	12000	Neish	Winning	Cumming	Logan	Morrison	Anderson	Cranston	Waugh	Martin 1	Rattray	Gibson,F	
S	13-Sep	Motherwell		H	L1	0-3	4000	Neish	Winning	Winning	McCulloch	McCulloch	Anderson	Cranston	Waugh	Martin	Rattray	Gibson,F	Kelly, H (2) McStay
S	20-Sep	Queen's Park		A	L1	0-2	10000	Neish	Winning	Cumming	McLay	Logan	Anderson	Cranston	Waugh	Martin	Anderson	Gibson,F	Morton, R Paul
S	27-Sep	Falkirk		H	L1	0-1	6000	Neish	Winning	Winning	McLay	Morrison	Davidson	Cranston	Waugh	Rattray	McCulloch	Gibson,F	Robertson
S	04-Oct	Hearts		H	L1	0-0	10000	Neish	Winning	Morrison	McLay	Porter	Anderson	Cranston	Waugh	Rattray	McCulloch	Scott	
M	06-Oct	Airdrie		H	L1	1-1	6000	Neish	Winning	Morrison	McLay	Porter	Anderson	Cranston	Gourlay	Martin	Waugh	Scott	Reid
S	11-Oct	Kilmarnock		H	L1	1-3	5000	Neish	Winning	Morrison	McLay	Porter	Anderson	Cranston	Waugh	Martin 1	Scott 1	Gibson,F	Waddell Dickie Neil
S	18-Oct	Aberdeen		H	L1	4-1	5000	Neish	Winning	Morrison	McLay	Logan	Anderson	Cranston	Rattray	Porter 3	Waugh	Scott 1	McLeod
S	25-Oct	Dundee		A	L1	1-2	12000	Neish	Winning	Morrison	McLay	Logan	Anderson	Cranston	Rattray	Porter	Waugh	Scott 1	Hogg Kelso pen
S	01-Nov	Rangers		H	L1	0-3	15000	Neish	Winning	Morrison	McLay	Logan	Anderson	Cranston	Rattray	Porter	Waugh	Scott	Duncan Reid Bennett
S	08-Nov	St Mirren		A	L1	1-0	8100	Neish	Winning	Morrison	Logan	McLay	Anderson	Cranston	Porter	Porter	Waugh	Gibson,F	
S	15-Nov	Ayr United		H	L1	5-1	6000	Wallace	Winning	Morrison	Logan	Porter	Anderson	Cranston 1	Scott 1	Martin 2	Waugh	Gibson,F	Gray
S	22-Nov	Third Lanark		A	L1	2-0	10000	Wallace	Winning	Morrison	Logan	Porter	Anderson	Rattray	Scott 2	Martin 1	Waugh	Gibson,F	
S	29-Nov	Partick Thistle		H	L1	3-0	5000	Wallace	Winning	Davidson	Davidson	Porter	Anderson 1	Rattray	Scott	Martin 2	Waugh	Gibson,F	Armstrong og 1
S	06-Dec	Falkirk		A	L1	0-4	6000	Wallace	Winning	Morrison	Philip	Porter	Anderson	Rattray	Scott	Martin	Davidson	Gibson,F	
S	13-Dec	Celtic		H	L1	1-2	12000	Wallace	Winning	Morrison	Logan	Porter	Anderson	Rattray	Scott 1	Martin	Waugh	Gibson,F	Robertson (2) Gibbons Croall
S	20-Dec	Partick Thistle		A	L1	1-2	10000	Wallace	Winning	Morrison	Logan	Porter	Anderson	Rattray	Scott 1	Martin 1	Waugh	Gibson,F	Owers Browning
S	27-Dec	Dundee		H	L1	4-1	3000	Wallace	Winning	Cumming	Rattray	Porter	Anderson	Cranston	Scott 1	Martin 2	Waugh	Gibson,F 1p	Eardman Hamilton
Th	01-Jan	Dumbarton		H	L1	0-1	8000	Wallace	Winning	Cumming	Rattray	Porter	Anderson	Cranston	Martin 1	Porter	McEwan	Gibson,F	Skene
S	03-Jan	Aberdeen		A	L1	0-1	10600	Wallace	Winning	Cumming	Rattray	Porter	Anderson	Cranston	Scott	Porter	Waugh	Gibson,F	Rowan Lawrie
M	05-Jan	Hearts		A	NEC	1-2	2000	Wallace	Winning	Morrison	Rattray	Logan	Porter	Cranston 1	Martin 1	McEwan	Waugh 1	Gibson,F	Wyllie
S	10-Jan	Hibernian		A	L1	3-0	5000	Wallace	Winning	Morrison	Rattray	Porter	Anderson	Rattray	Scott	McEwan 1	Waugh	Gibson,F	Abrams Dawson
S	17-Jan	Hamilton Academical		A	L1	0-1	6000	Wallace	Winning	Cumming	Logan	Porter	Anderson	Cranston	Martin x	McEwan	Martin	Gibson,F x	
S	24-Jan	Clyde		H	L1	2-0	4500	Wallace	Morrison	Cumming	Logan	Porter	Anderson	Rattray	Scott 1	Martin	Martin	Gibson,F 1	Bain pen
S	31-Jan	Rangers		A	L1	0-4	10000	Wallace	Winning	Lavery	Logan	Porter	Anderson	Cranston	Scott	Martin	Waugh	Gibson,F	
S	07-Feb	Hearts	(1)	H	SC 2	2-0	26000	Wallace	Winning	Lavery	Logan	Porter	Anderson	Rattray	Scott	Martin 2	Waugh	Gibson,F	
S	14-Feb	Kilmarnock		H	L1	1-1	5000	Wallace	Winning	Lavery 1	Logan	Porter	Anderson	Rattray	Scott 1	Morrison	Waugh	Gibson,F	Reid (2) Stewart (2)
S	21-Feb	Third Lanark		A	SC 3	1-4	40000	Wallace	Winning	Lavery	Logan	Porter 2	Anderson	Rattray	Scott	Martin 1	Waugh	Gibson,F	
S	28-Feb	Morton		A	L1	1-2	7000	Neish	Winning	Winning	Rattray	McLay	Porter	Cranston	McEwan	Martin 1	Waugh	Gibson,F	Neil
S	07-Mar	Hamilton Academical		H	L1	5-2	4000	Wallace	Winning	Lavery	Logan 1	McLay	Porter	Cranston	Scott 2	Rattray 2	Waugh	Gibson,F	Ramsay (2) McFie Mountford
S	14-Mar	Motherwell		A	L1	2-3	3000	Wallace	Winning	Winning	Rattray	McLay	Porter 1	Scott	McEwan	Martin	Waugh	Gibson,F 1	Gourlay Cullen
S	21-Mar	Ayr United		A	L1	0-0	6000	Wallace	Winning	Morrison	Logan	McLay	Porter	Scott	McEwan	McEwan	Anderson	Gibson,F	Bain Kyle
W	25-Mar	Third Lanark		H	L1	3-0	4000	Neish	Winning	Morrison	Logan	Porter	McEwan	McEwan	Scott	Rattray 2	Waugh 1	Gibson,F	Whitehead (3)
S	28-Mar	East Fife		A	WC	0-1		Neish	Winning	Cumming	McLay	Porter	Davidson	McEwan	Scott	Martin	Waugh	Gibson,F	
S	04-Apr	St Mirren		H	L1	5-1	4000	Neish	Winning	Morrison	Logan	McLay	Porter	Rattray 1	Waugh 1	Martin 2	Anderson 1	Anderson 1	Bernard pen
M	06-Apr	Dumbarton		A	L1	2-2	2000	Wallace	Winning	Morrison	Logan	McLay	Porter	McLay	Waugh	Rattray 1	Anderson	Gibson,F 1	Elmore
S	11-Apr	Kirkcaldy United		H	F	6-1		Neish	Lavery	Morrison	McLay 1	McLay	Davidson	Scott	Hough 1	Haldane	McKenzie	Gibson,F 2	Gilden Sheedie
S	18-Apr	Hearts	(2)	A	L1	0-2	7000	Wallace	Winning	Morrison	Logan	Logan	Porter	Scott	Waugh	Rattray	Anderson	Gibson,F	Gourlay
W	22-Apr	Dunfermline Athletic	(3)	H	B	2-2	1000	Wallace	Philip	McLeod	Taylor	Porter	Davidson	Todd 1	Hough	McEwan 1	Scott	Gibson,F	Wattie Mercer
S	25-Apr	Queen's Park		A	L1	1-0	4000	Wallace	Winning	Morrison	Logan	McLay	Porter	Rattray	Scott	McEwan	Anderson	Gibson,F 1p	Conner Hall
W	29-Apr	Celtic		A	L1	1-2	4000	Wallace	Winning	Winning	Logan	McLay 1	Porter	Scott	Waugh	Rattray	Anderson	Gibson,F	Gallagher (2)

Manager : John Richardson

From the start of this season, goalkeepers were not permitted to handle the ball outside the penalty area

(1) Record crowd at time
(2) at Easter Road
(3) Arthur Cumming Benefit

Day	Date	Opponents	Note	Venue	Comp	Res.	Att.	1	2	3	4	5	6	7	8	9	10	11	Substitutes, own goals, goal times and opponents' scorers
S	15-Aug	Motherwell		A	L1	2-1	6000	Wallace	Cumming	Lavery	Rattray	McLay	Porter	Turner	Scott	Martin	Anderson	Gibson 2,1p	Waugh
W	19-Aug	Hibernian		A	DC	0-3	2700	Wallace	Cumming	Lavery	Rattray	McLay	Porter	Turner	Scott	Martin	Anderson	Gibson	Hendren (3)
S	22-Aug	Hearts		H	L1	1-3	8000	Wallace	Cumming	Lavery	Logan	McLay	Anderson	Turner	Scott 1	Rattray	Anderson	Gibson	Graham (2) Wilson
W	26-Aug	Dunfermline Athletic	1	A	B	6-1		Wallace	Cumming	Lavery	Rattray	Porter	Anderson	Todd	Scott	Welsh 4	Gourlay,JM 1	Gibson 1	Fleming
S	29-Aug	Clyde		A	L1	0-1	7000	Wallace	Morrison	Lavery	McLay	Porter	Anderson	Todd	Rattray 1	Welsh	Martin	Gibson	Hanlon
S	05-Sep	Hamilton Academical		A	L1	1-1	2000	Wallace	Morrison	Lavery	McLay	Porter	Anderson	Todd	Rattray	Martin	Welsh	Gibson	Lennie
S	12-Sep	Hibernian		H	L1	1-1	5000	Wallace	Cumming	Lavery	McLay	Porter	Anderson	Todd	Rattray	Martin	Welsh	Gibson 1	Walker Cresswell
S	19-Sep	Queen's Park		A	L1	1-2	4000	Wallace	Cumming	Lavery	McLay	Porter	Dunbar	Todd	Rattray	Martin	Scott 1	Gibson	Smith, J. (2) Brown
S	26-Sep	Third Lanark		A	L1	0-3	4000	Wallace	Morrison	Lavery	Logan	Porter	Anderson	Todd	Rattray	Welsh 2	Scott	Gibson	
S	03-Oct	Airdrie		H	L1	3-0	3000	Wallace	Morrison	Lavery	Logan	Porter	Anderson	Todd 1	Rattray	Welsh 1	Scott	Gibson	Morrison og Gallacher
M	05-Oct	Celtic		H	L1	2-2	5000	Wallace	Morrison	Lavery	Logan	Porter 1	Anderson	Todd	Rattray	Welsh	Scott	Gibson 1p	Bennett Gordon
S	10-Oct	Rangers		H	L1	1-2	6000	Wallace	Morrison	Lavery	McLay	Porter	Anderson	Todd	Rattray	Welsh	Scott	Gibson	Brown (2)
S	17-Oct	St Mirren		H	L1	2-2	3500	Wallace	Morrison	Lavery	McLay	Porter	Anderson	Todd 1	Rattray	Martin m	Welsh 1	Scott	Cairns
S	24-Oct	Rangers		A	L1	2-1	14000	Neish	Cumming	Lavery	McLay	Porter	Anderson	Todd	Scott	Welsh	Turner	Gibson 1p	Morrison Thomson, G Glancey
S	31-Oct	Falkirk		H	L1	1-3	2000	Neish	Morrison	Lavery	McLay	Porter	Anderson 1	Todd	Scott 1	Welsh	Turner	Gibson	Main
S	07-Nov	Aberdeen		A	L1	3-1	5000	Neish	Morrison	Morrison	Rattray	Porter	Anderson	Todd	Scott 2	Welsh 1	Turner 1	Gibson	
S	14-Nov	Kilmarnock		H	L1	3-0	4000	Neish	Morrison	Morrison	Logan	Porter	Anderson	Todd	Rattray 1	Welsh 1	Scott	Gibson 1p	
S	21-Nov	Morton		A	L1	0-1	5000	Neish	Cumming	Lavery	Rattray	Porter	Anderson	Todd	Scott	Welsh	Turner	Gibson	Buchanan
S	28-Nov	Dundee	2	H	L1	1-1	3000	Neish	Cumming	Lavery	Logan	Porter	Anderson	Todd	Rattray	Martin	Scott 1	Gibson	Brown
S	05-Dec	Ayr United		A	L1	0-3	3000	Neish	Cumming	Lavery	Logan	Porter	Anderson	Todd	Rattray	Martin	Scott	Gibson	McLaughlin pen Mackenzie Richardson
S	12-Dec	Dumbarton		H	L1	1-2	1000	Neish	Morrison	Morrison	Rattray	Porter	Anderson	Todd	Scott	Martin	Turner	Gibson 1p	Gettins Brown
S	19-Dec	Third Lanark	3	H	L1	1-1	3000	Neish	Morrison	Morrison	Logan	Porter	Anderson	Todd	Todd	Welsh 1	Martin	Gibson	Smith J.W.
S	26-Dec	Hearts		A	L1	0-4	8000	Neish	Morrison	Lavery	Logan	Porter	Anderson	Todd	Scott	Welsh	Scott	Gibson	Wattie (2) Gracie (2)
F	01-Jan	Dumbarton		A	L1	1-3	2000	Neish	Lavery	Cumming	Logan	Thomson	Anderson	Gourlay	Rattray	Martin 1	Thomson	Gibson	Steel Travers McGregor
S	02-Jan	Aberdeen		H	L1	5-1	3000	Neish	Lavery	Cumming	Logan	Morrison	Anderson	Gourlay	Martin 1	Rattray 3	Thomson 1	Gibson	Cail
Tu	05-Jan	Partick Thistle		A	L1	1-2	5000	Neish	Lavery	Cumming	Logan	Morrison	Anderson	Scott	Martin 1	Rattray	Thomson	Gibson 1	N Harris Gardner
S	09-Jan	Kilmarnock		A	L1	1-3	3000	Neish	Lavery	Cumming	McLay	McLay	Anderson	Todd	Martin	McLay	Thomson	Gibson	Cunningham, A Culley (2)
S	16-Jan	Hamilton Academical		H	L1	1-3	1500	Neish	Morrison	Morrison	McLay	Porter	Anderson	Todd	Martin	Martin	Thomson	Gibson	Miller, I Kelly Husband
S	23-Jan	Partick Thistle		H	L1	2-2	2500	Wallace	Lavery	Cumming	Logan	Porter	Anderson	Rattray	Scott	Martin 2	Thomson	Gibson	Whittle Branscombe
S	30-Jan	Queen's Park		H	L1	3-1	3000	Neish	Lavery	Cumming	Logan	Porter	Anderson	Rattray	Turner	Martin	Turner 1	Gibson 2	Morton, J.
S	06-Feb	Motherwell		H	L1	2-1	2000	Neish	Lavery	Cumming	Logan	Porter	Anderson	Todd	Scott	Martin 1	Turner 1	Gibson m	Waugh
S	13-Feb	Hibernian		A	L1	1-2	5000	Neish	Cumming	Lavery	Logan	Porter	Anderson	Rattray	Scott 1	Turner 1	Turner	Gibson	Fleming (2)
S	20-Feb	Morton		H	L1	1-1	3000	Neish	Cumming	Lavery	Logan	Porter	Anderson	Rattray	Scott 1	Martin	Turner 1	Gibson	Stevenson, J.
S	27-Feb	Falkirk		A	L1	1-3	1500	Neish	Cumming	Lavery	Logan	Porter	Anderson	Rattray	Scott	Martin	Turner	Gibson 1p	McNaught Ramsay Glancy
S	06-Mar	Clyde		H	L1	2-0	3000	Wallace	Lavery	Cumming	Logan	Porter	Anderson	Turner	Rattray 1	Martin	Scott 1	Gibson	
S	13-Mar	St Mirren		A	L1	2-3	5000	Neish	Lavery	Cumming	Logan	Porter	Anderson 1	Turner	Rattray 1	Martin 1	Scott	Gibson	Brannick Clark Page
S	20-Mar	Kirkcaldy United		H	FC 1	5-0		Neish	Cumming	Lavery	Logan	Porter	Anderson	Rattray	Scott 1	Martin 1	Turner 1	Gibson	
S	27-Mar	Celtic		A	L1	1-3	6000	Neish	Cumming	Lavery	Morrison	Morrison	Anderson	Rattray	Scott 1	Martin 2	Turner	Gibson 1	McColl (3)
S	03-Apr	Ayr United		H	L1	0-0	3500	Neish	Cumming	Lavery	Logan	Logan	Anderson	Todd	Scott	Martin	Turner	Gibson	
M	05-Apr	Lochgelly United		H	WC SF	3-2	1500	Neish	Cumming	Morrison	Inglis	Logan	Porter	Todd	Stoddart	Martin 2	Turner	Gibson 1	Ramsay Scott
S	10-Apr	Airdrie		A	L1	3-3	2000	Neish	Cumming	Lavery	Logan	Porter	Dunbar	Rattray	Scott 2	Martin 1	Turner	Gibson	Dunbar og Reid (2)
S	17-Apr	Dundee		A	L1	0-3	6000	Wallace	Cumming	Lavery	Logan	Porter	Wilson	Rattray	Scott	Martin	Turner	Gibson	Stevens Hogg
Th	22-Apr	Denbeath Star		A	B	2-1		Mackie	Cumming	Lavery	Inglis	Porter	Collier	Birrell	Todd	Rattray 2	Scott	Gibson	
S	24-Apr	East Fife		A	F	3-1		Mackie	Cumming	Lavery	Logan	Porter	Wilson	Harper	Todd 1	Rattray 2	Scott	Gibson	McMahon
W	28-Apr	East Fife		H	FC F	4-0	1500	Wallace	Cumming	Lavery	Logan	Porter	Inglis	Turner	Rattray	Welsh 2	Scott	Gibson 1p	
F	30-Apr	Cowdenbeath	4	A	WC F	0-0		Wallace	Cumming	Lavery	Logan	Porter	Inglis	Turner	Rattray	Welsh	Scott	Gibson	Cumming og 1

Manager : John Richardson
Ten yard rule introduced for free kicks
Rovers scratched from Penman Cup

(1) J Brown benefit
(2) Team wore black armbands following the death of Bill Morrison's wife. He had missed the match at Greenock the previous week while he tended her in her illness
(3) played at East End Park ; Stark's Park closed by SFA
(4) after extra time, won 1-0 on corners

Day	Date	Opponents	Note	Venue	Comp	Res.	Att.	1	2	3	4	5	6	7	8	9	10	11	*Substitutes, own goals, goal times and opponents' scorers*
S	21-Aug	Airdrie		H	L1	1-1	2500	Patterson	Inglis	Lavery	Henderson	McKerley	Foster	Monaghan	Hutchison	Porter 1	Turner	Butler	Thomson
S	28-Aug	Clyde		A	L1	0-1	4000	Patterson	Inglis	Lavery	Henderson	McKerley	Foster	Monaghan	Hutchison	Porter	Turner	Butler	Scouller
S	04-Sep	Queen's Park		H	L1	0-3	4500	Patterson	Inglis	Lavery	Henderson	McKerley	Foster	Monaghan	Hutchison	Welsh	Turner	Butler	Keith (3)
S	11-Sep	St Mirren		H	L1	0-1	4000	Patterson	Inglis	Lavery	Henderson	McKerley	Foster	Monaghan	Hutchison	McTavish	Wilson,G	Butler	Bruce
S	18-Sep	Hamilton Academical		A	L1	0-2	5000	Patterson	McKerley	Lavery	Henderson	McKerley	Porter	Monaghan	Hutchison	McTavish 1	Wilson,G	Butler	Kelly (2)
S	25-Sep	Hibernian		H	L1	1-1	2000	Patterson	McKerley	Lavery	Henderson	Scott	Porter	Monaghan	Hutchison	McTavish	Wilson,G	Butler	Taylor
S	02-Oct	Ayr United		A	L1	1-1	4000	Patterson	McKerley	Lavery	Henderson	Scott	Porter	Monaghan 1	Hutchison	McTavish	Wilson,G	Gibson	Richardson
S	09-Oct	Third Lanark		A	L1	0-1	4000	Patterson	Inglis	Lavery	Henderson	Scott	Porter	Monaghan	Hutchison	McTavish	Wilson,G	Gibson	Orr
S	16-Oct	Falkirk		A	L1	0-0	4000	Patterson	McKerley	Inglis	Scott	Carter	Porter	Monaghan	Hutchison	Turner 1	Hutchison	Turner	
S	23-Oct	Rangers		H	L1	1-3	3000	Patterson	Inglis	Inglis	McKerley	Porter	Foster	Monaghan	Hutchison	Turner	Hutchison	Butler	Hendry Reid (2)
S	30-Oct	Morton		A	L1	0-4	4000	Brown	Scott	Inglis	Henderson	McKerley	Porter	Monaghan	Hutchison	Turner	McTavish	Wilson,G	Buchanan (3) Stevenson
S	06-Nov	Kilmarnock		H	L1	1-1	3000	Brown	Scott	Inglis	McKerley	Porter	Foster	Monaghan	Hutchison	Turner	Wilson,G	Gibson 1	Culley
S	13-Nov	Aberdeen		A	L1	1-2	5500	Brown	Scott	Inglis	McKerley	Scott	Wilson,R	Monaghan	McTavish 1	Lavery	Wilson,G	Gibson	Inglis og Archibald
S	20-Nov	Partick Thistle		A	L1	0-2	4000	Brown	Scott	Inglis	McKerley	Scott	Wilson,R	Monaghan	Hutchison	Henderson	Turner	Turner	McTavish Leitch
S	27-Nov	Celtic		H	L1	0-2	5000	Brown	Scott	Lavery	McKerley	Scott	Inglis	Turner	Hutchison	Hutchison	Wilson,G	Gibson	Gallagher McColl
S	04-Dec	Dumbarton		A	L1	0-1	3000	Brown	Inglis	Inglis	Foster	Scott	Foster	Turner	McTavish	Turner	Wilson,G	Gibson	Ritchie
S	11-Dec	Hearts		H	L1	1-2	1000	Brown	Scott	Robson	McKerley	Scott	Inglis	Monaghan	Hutchison 1	Turner	Wilson,G	Cobban	Miller (2)
S	18-Dec	Dundee		A	L1	0-3	5000	Brown	Scott	Robson	McKerley	Scott	Inglis	Monaghan	Hutchison	McTavish	Wilson,G	Cobban	McCulloch (2) Stirling
S	25-Dec	Clyde		H	L1	2-0	2000	Brown	Scott	Robson	Henderson	Scott	Porter	Monaghan	Hutchison	Turner 2	Wilson,G	Cobban	
S	01-Jan	Dumbarton		H	L1	1-0	4000	Brown	Inglis	Inglis	McKerley	Scott	McTavish	Birrell	Hutchison	Turner 1	Wilson,G	Cobban	
M	03-Jan	Kilmarnock		A	L1	0-2	4000	Brown	Inglis	Robson	McKerley	McKerley	Porter	Birrell	McTavish	Turner	Wilson,G	Gibson	McKnight Culley
Tu	04-Jan	Hamilton Academical		H	L1	2-0	3000	Mackie	McKerley	Robson	Henderson	Wilson,R	Foster	Birrell	Abbott	McTavish	Wilson,G	Gibson 2	
S	08-Jan	Hibernian		A	L1	0-1	5000	Brown	Inglis	Inglis	Hutchison	McKerley	Foster	Monaghan	Abbott	Porter	McTavish	Cobban	Kilpatrick
S	15-Jan	Motherwell		A	L1	4-1	3000	Brown	Inglis	Robson	Hutchison	Wilson,R	Porter	Monaghan	Abbott	Turner	McTavish	Cobban	Waugh
S	22-Jan	Falkirk		H	L1	3-1	3000	Brown	Inglis	Robson	Hutchison	Wilson,R	Foster	Monaghan	Abbott	Birrell 1	Turner 3	Cobban	Robertson
S	29-Jan	Hearts		A	L1	1-2	8500	Brown	Inglis	Robson	Hutchison	Wilson,R	Foster	Monaghan	Abbott	Birrell 3	Turner	Cobban	Welsh Graham, H
S	05-Feb	Partick Thistle		H	L1	2-0	4000	Brown	Inglis	Robson	Hutchison	Wilson,R	Foster	Monaghan	Abbott	Birrell 1	Turner 1	Cobban 1	
S	12-Feb	Third Lanark		A	L1	0-2	4000	Mackie	McKerley	Inglis	Hutchison	Walker	Foster	Monaghan	Abbott	Birrell	Turner	Cobban	McLean (2)
S	19-Feb	Ayr United		A	L1	0-4	4000	Brown	Inglis	Robson	Hutchison	Walker	Foster	Monaghan	Turner	Birrell	Wilson,G	Gibson	Ingram (2) McKenzie Gray
S	26-Feb	St Mirren		A	L1	0-2	5000	Brown	Inglis	Robson	Hutchison	Wilson,R	Foster	Monaghan	Abbott	Turner	Turner	Duncan	Bruce Loverby
S	04-Mar	Morton		H	L1	2-1	3000	Brown	Inglis	Robson	Hutchison	Wilson,R	Foster	Monaghan 1	Wilson,G 1	Wilson,G	Turner	Cobban	Grant
S	11-Mar	Airdrie		A	L1	1-2	4000	Brown	Inglis	Robson	Hutchison	Wilson,R	Foster	Monaghan	Wilson,G 1	Birrell	Turner	Cobban	Anderson Mair
S	18-Mar	Motherwell		H	L1	1-0	3000	Brown	Robson	Robson	Hutchison 1	Wilson,R	Henderson	Archibald	Abbott	Birrell	Turner	Cobban	
S	01-Apr	Dundee		A	FC SF	0-2	4000	Mackie	Inglis	Robson	Henderson	Wilson,R	Foster	Archibald	Wilson,G	Abbott	Abbott	Cobban	Duffus McCulloch
M	03-Apr	East Fife		A	L1	1-0	10000	Brown	Lavery	Robson	Hutchison	Wilson,R 1	Foster	Archibald	Wilson,G	Hutchison	Turner	Gibson	
S	08-Apr	Rangers		A	L1	0-3	10000	Brown	Robson	Robson	Hutchison	McKerley	Inglis	Archibald	Wilson,G	Newbigging	Turner	Gibson	Gordon, J. (2) Paterson
S	15-Apr	Celtic		A	WC SF	0-6	3000	Brown	Robson	Robson	Hutchison	McKerley	Foster	Archibald	Abbott	Newbigging	Turner	Gibson	Dodds Gallacher (3) O'Kane
W	19-Apr	Cowdenbeath		H	L1	1-3		Brown	Crichton	Robson	Inglis	McKerley	Monaghan	Monaghan	Abbott	Inglis 1	Hutchison	Wilson,R	Paterson (2) Tait
S	22-Apr	Aberdeen		A	FC F	3-1	3000	Brown	Lavery	Robson	Hutchison	McKerley	Foster	Monaghan	Abbott 1	Newbigging 2	Hutchison	Gibson	Main
W	26-Apr	Cowdenbeath		A	L1	0-2		Brown	Inglis	Robson	Henderson	McKerley	Foster	Monaghan	Abbott	Newbigging	Hutchison	Gibson	
S	29-Apr	Queen's Park		A	F	1-4	4000	Mackie	Inglis	Robson	Hutchison	McKerley	Foster	Monaghan 1	Abbott	Newbigging	Turner	Duncan	Morton, R (3) Morton, A
S	20-May	Scotland Junior XI	1	H	F	1-1	4000	McLeod	Lavery	McLeod	Henderson	McKerley	Inglis	Monaghan	Abbott	Blyth	Turner 1	Kelly	Frame

Manager : John Richardson
Ten yard rule introduced for corner kicks
(1) in aid of War Funds

Substitutes, own goals, goal times and opponents' scorers

Day	Date	Opponents	Note	Venue	Comp	Res	Att	1	2	3	4	5	6	7	8	9	10	11	Scorers
S	19-Aug	Motherwell		A	L1	2-2	4000	Brown	Winning	Inglis	O'Neil	Duffy	Forrest	Monaghan	Hutchison	Welsh	Turner 1	Gibson 1	Ferguson (2)
S	26-Aug	Falkirk		H	L1	0-6	2000	Brown	Lavery	Inglis	O'Neil	Duffy	Forrest	Monaghan	Hutchison	Welsh	Turner	Gibson	Comrie.D. (2) Watson Gibbons McLauchlan Shearer
S	02-Sep	Queen's Park		A	L1	1-3	4000	Brown	Inglis	Lavery	O'Neil	Duffy	Forrest	Monaghan	Rattray	Welsh 1	Turner	Gibson	Sibbald McMillan Morton, RM
S	09-Sep	Morton		H	L1	1-2	4000	Brown	Lavery	Muir	O'Neil	Duffy	Forrest	Rattray	Abbott	Welsh	Turner	Thomson 1	Gourlay McNeil
S	16-Sep	Clyde		A	L1	0-2	4000	Brown	Winning	Muir	O'Neil	Forrest	Forrest	Rattray	Hutchison	Welsh	Turner	Thomson	McGowan Jackson
S	23-Sep	Ayr United		H	L1	1-3	3000	Brown	Winning	Muir	Rattray	Forrest	Dunbar	Archibald	Kilpatrick	Sloan 1	Pender	Thomson	Cringan Crossbie Marshall
S	30-Sep	Hamilton Academical		H	L1	0-1	3000	Brown	Winning	Muir	Hutchison	Forrest	Dunbar	Archibald	Kilpatrick	Welsh	Pender	Thomson	Stewart
S	07-Oct	Hearts		A	L1	1-2	8000	Brown	Winning	Muir	Rattray	Forrest	Pender	Archibald	Kilpatrick 1	Kilpatrick	Turner	Thomson	Keirnan Mercer
S	14-Oct	Dumbarton		H	L1	0-3	1500	Brown	Winning	Muir	Rattray	Forrest	Pender	Archibald	Lindsay	Kilpatrick	Turner	Gibson	Lister (2) Semple
S	21-Oct	St Mirren		A	L1	0-0	3000	Brown	Winning	Muir	Rattray	Forrest	Pender	Archibald	Lindsay	Kilpatrick	Turner	Gibson	
S	28-Oct	Partick Thistle		A	L1	0-2	6000	Brown	Hutchison	Winning	Rattray	Forrest	Pender	Archibald	Lindsay	Kilpatrick	Wilson,G	Gibson	Brinscombe Bowie
S	04-Nov	Kilmarnock		H	L1	0-4	2000	Brown	Winning	Muir	Ripley	Hutchison	Pender	Turner	Lindsay	Welsh	Wilson,G	Gibson	Fulton (2) Armstrong (2)
S	11-Nov	Airdrie		A	L1	0-2	2000	Neish	Winning	Muir	Ripley	Forrest	Pender	Archibald	Hope	Welsh	Wilson,G	Gibson	Rankin Yarnell
S	18-Nov	Hibernian		A	L1	3-3	3000	Neish	Winning	Muir	Ripley	Forrest	Pender	Archibald	Hope	Welsh 3	Wilson,G	Gibson	Fleming Miller (2)
S	25-Nov	Rangers		H	L1	1-4	3000	Brown	Winning	Winning	Abbott	Forrest	Pender	Archibald 1	Lindsay	Rattray	Wilson,G	Gibson	Riddell Bennett Archibald (2)
S	02-Dec	Celtic		H	L1	1-4	3000	Mackie	Hutchison	Muir	Ripley	Forrest	Ripley	Archibald	Lindsay 2	Rattray 1	Wilson,G	Gibson	McColl (3) Browning
S	09-Dec	Dundee		A	L1	2-6	3000	Inglis	Winning	Robson	Inglis	Forrest	Pender	Archibald	Lindsay 1	Rattray	Wilson,G	Gibson	Brown (6)
S	16-Dec	Queen's Park		H	L1	2-0	2000	Neish	Winning	Robson	Rattray	Forrest 1	Ripley	Archibald	Lindsay 1	Rattray	Wilson,G	Gibson	
S	23-Dec	Kilmarnock		A	L1	0-3	2000	Brown	Winning	Robson	Ripley	Forrest	Currie	Monaghan	Lindsay	Archibald	Abbott	Thomson	Culley (2) Rutherford
S	30-Dec	Clyde		H	L1	1-1	3000	Neish	Inglis	Robson	Ripley	Forrest	Currie	Archibald	Lindsay	Rattray	Wilson,G	Gibson 1	Lindsay
M	01-Jan	Dumbarton		H	L1	2-2	2000	Brown	Robson	Inglis	Hutchison	Forrest	Pender	Archibald	Lindsay 1	Rattray	Abbott 1	Gibson	Thom (2)
Tu	02-Jan	Aberdeen		A	L1	3-0	2000	Neish	Winning	Robson	Ripley	Forrest	Currie 1	Archibald	Lindsay 1	Rattray	Abbott	Gibson 1	
S	06-Jan	Third Lanark		H	L1	1-0	4000	Neish	Robson	Muir	Ripley	Forrest	Currie	Archibald 1	Lindsay	Inglis	Abbott	Thomson	
S	13-Jan	Hibernian		A	L1	2-1	2000	Neish	Robson	Muir	Hutchison	Forrest	Currie	Archibald	Lindsay	Birrell	Abbott	Gibson 2	Lennie
S	20-Jan	Hearts		H	L1	1-4	4000	Neish	Robson	Muir	Rattray	Inglis	Abbott	Archibald	Lindsay	Rattray	Wilson,G 1	Gibson	Gibson Denyer Cartmell (2)
S	27-Jan	St Mirren		H	L1	1-1	3000	Brown	Winning	Muir	Rattray	Forrest	Currie	Archibald	Lindsay	Rattray	Abbott	Gibson	Lindsay
S	03-Feb	Celtic		A	L1	0-5	15000	Neish	Robson	Muir	Rattray	Forrest	Currie	Archibald	Lindsay	Rougvie 1	Abbott	Gibson	Gallagher (2) McColl (2) McAtee
S	10-Feb	Airdrie		H	L1	0-2	3000	Greig	Robson	Muir	Inglis	Inglis 1	Currie	Archibald	Lindsay	Rougvie	Abbott	Gibson	Yarnell (2)
S	17-Feb	Aberdeen		A	L1	2-1	4000	Stewart	Winning	Winning	Rattray	Inglis	Currie	Archibald	Lindsay 1	Rougvie	Abbott	Wilson,G	Walker
S	24-Feb	Falkirk		A	L1	1-1	4000	Neish	Robson	Robson	Ingiis	Forrest	Currie	Archibald	Lindsay	Rougvie	Abbott 1	Wilson,G	Gibbons
S	03-Mar	Dundee		H	L1	3-2	3000	Neish	Robson	Muir	Rattray	Forrest	Currie 1	Archibald	Lindsay	Rougvie	Abbott 1	Cobban 1	McCulloch Steven
S	10-Mar	Third Lanark		H	L1	0-1	3000	Neish	Robson	Muir	Rattray	Forrest	Currie	Archibald	Lindsay	Rougvie	Abbott	Cobban	Bissett
S	17-Mar	Morton		A	L1	0-7	5000	Neish	Rougvie	Winning	Pender	Smith	Currie	Archibald 1	Lindsay	Monaghan	Abbott	Cobban	Paterson (3) Gourlay McNab McIntyre Seymour
S	24-Mar	Rangers		A	L1	3-4	5000	Neish	Winning	Robson	Rattray	Inglis	Currie	Archibald 1	Lindsay	Rougvie 1	Abbott	Cobban 1	Cairns Livingstone (3)
S	31-Mar	Motherwell		H	L1	2-1	3000	Neish	Robson	Muir	Rattray	Inglis	Currie	Archibald	Lindsay	Cobban	Abbott 2	Wilson,G	Morgan
M	02-Apr	Cowdenbeath		H	FL	4-2	3000	Chapman	Robson	Muir	Ross	Gilhooley	Whiteford	Archibald	Lindsay 1	Ramsay 1	Abbott	Wilson,G 2	Paterson (2)
S	07-Apr	East Fife	1	A	FC	0-1	3000	Neish	Robson	Muir	Rattray	Inglis	Currie	Archibald	Lindsay 1	Gibson	Abbott	Wilson,G	Law
S	14-Apr	Partick Thistle		H	L1	3-1	3000	Neish	Robson	Muir	Rattray	Inglis	Currie	Archibald	Lindsay 1	Trotter 1	Abbott	Gibson 1	Reid
S	21-Apr	Ayr United		A	L1	1-2	2000	White	Winning	Robson	Rattray	Forrest	Currie	Archibald 1	Lindsay	Trotter	Abbott	Gibson	Waddell (2)
S	28-Apr	Hamilton Academical		A	L1	1-3	4000	Bruce	Winning	Muir	Rattray	Forrest	Currie	Archibald	Lindsay 1	Rougvie	Abbott	Gibson	Murphy Wilson Kyle

Manager : John Richardson to October ; Peter Hodge from October
(1) after extra time

Day	Date	Opponents	Note	Venue	Comp	Res.	Att.	1	2	3	4	5	6	7	8	9	10	11	Substitutes, own goals, goal times and opponents' scorers
S	18-Aug	East Fife		A	EL	1-0	2000	Kerr	Stewart	Robson	Hutchison	Grieve	Currie	Rougvie 1	Abbott	Wightman	McKinnon	Lowther	
S	25-Aug	Dunfermline Athletic		H	EL	4-0	2000	Kerr	Stewart	Robson	Hutchison	Grieve	Currie	Rougvie 1	Abbott 2	Wightman 1	McKinnon	Young	O'Brien Steele
S	01-Sep	Armadale		A	EL	1-2	3000	Kerr	Stewart	Robson	Hutchison	Grieve	Currie	Rougvie 1	Abbott	Wightman	McKinnon	Young	
S	08-Sep	Dundee		H	EL	0-0	3000	Kerr	Stewart	Muir	Hutchison	Lowther	Currie	Rougvie	Abbott	Wightman	McKinnon	Young	
S	15-Sep	Cowdenbeath		A	EL	0-2	3500	Kerr	Stewart	Muir	Hutchison	Lowther	Currie	Rougvie	McDonald	Wightman	Abbott	Young	Muir + another
S	22-Sep	K.O.S.B.		H	F	8-2		Kerr	Lowther	Muir	Hutchison	Stewart	Currie	Wightman	McDonald	Rougvie 3	Abbott 5	McKinnon	
S	29-Sep	East Fife		H	EL	2-0	1800	Kerr	Stewart 1p	Muir	Hutchison	Grieve	Currie	Aitken	McLean	Robson	Abbott	Young 1	
S	06-Oct	Cowdenbeath		H	FC	1-0	2500	Kerr	Robson	Muir	Hutchison	Grieve	Currie	Aitken	McLean	Wightman 1	Abbott	McKinnon	
S	13-Oct	Dundee Hibernian		A	EL	1-1	3500	Kerr	Stewart	Muir	Hutchison	Grieve	Currie	Young	Smith	Wightman 1	Abbott	McKinnon	
S	20-Oct	Dundee Hibernian		H	EL	5-2	2000	Kerr	Stuart	Muir	Hutchison	Stewart	Currie	Young 1	McLean	Wightman 3	Abbott 1	McKinnon	
S	27-Oct	Armadale		H	EL	5-0	1500	Kerr	Stuart	Muir	Hutchison	Grieve	Currie	Young 1	McLean 2	Wightman 1	Rougvie 1	McKinnon	McGuire Ferrier
S	03-Nov	Dundee		A	EL	0-4	2000	Kerr	Stewart	Muir	Hutchison	Grieve	Currie	Young	Smith	Wightman	Abbott	McKinnon	Moyes Taylor Lamb Murray
S	17-Nov	Dunfermline Athletic		A	EL	4-2	2000	Kerr	Stewart	Muir	Hutchison	Grieve	Currie	Young 2	Abbott	Wightman 2	McLean	McKinnon	Duncan Smith
S	24-Nov	Cowdenbeath		H	EL	0-3		Kerr	Stewart	Muir	Hutchison	Grieve	Currie	Young	Abbott	Wightman	McLean	McKinnon	Gow Gibbons McKay
S	08-Dec	Armadale	1	H	PC	0-0	1500	Kerr	Robson	Muir	Hutchison	Stewart	Currie	Young	Abbott	Wightman	McLean	McKinnon	
S	15-Dec	Dundee		A	EL	5-2	3000	Kerr	Stewart	Robson	Lowther	Inglis 1	Currie	Young 1	Abbott 3	Wightman	Birrell	McKinnon	Taylor Murray
S	22-Dec	Dunfermline Athletic		H	EL	1-2	1500	Kerr	Stewart	Muir	Lowther	Grieve	Currie	Young 1	Abbott	Rougvie	Wightman	McKinnon	Alexander Fisher, N
F	01-Jan	Dunfermline Athletic		A	LoC	2-1		Kerr	Stuart 1p	Muir	Milliken	Wilson.R	Currie	Young	McLean	Shand 1	Gilmour,N	McKinnon	
S	26-Jan	Cowdenbeath		A	EL	0-0	2000	Kerr	Stewart	Robson	Hutchison	Inglis	Currie	Young	Abbott	Shand	Wightman	McKinnon	
S	02-Feb	Dundee		H	EL	1-2	2000	Kerr	Stewart	Robson	Hutchison	Muir	Currie	Young	McLean	Duncan 1	Wightman	McKinnon	Taylor (2)
S	09-Feb	East Fife		A	EL	0-0		Kerr	Stewart	Robson	Hutchison	Muir	Currie	Shand	Abbott	Shand	Wightman	McKinnon	
S	16-Feb	Cowdenbeath		H	EL	2-0	2000	Kerr	Stewart	Robson	Hutchison	Muir	Currie	Wightman	Abbott 1	Wightman	McLean 1	McKinnon	
S	23-Feb	Armadale		A	PC	0-2		Kerr	Stewart	Robson	Hutchison	Muir	Currie	Lowther	Abbott	Wightman	McLean	McKinnon	Sneddon (2)
S	02-Mar	Hibernian		A	DC	0-1	5000	Kerr	Stewart	Robson	Hutchison	Muir	Currie	Duncan	McLean	Shand	McLean	McKinnon	Bennett
S	09-Mar	Dundee Hibernian		A	EL	1-1	1500	Kerr	Stuart	Muir	Hutchison	Inglis	Currie	Duncan	McLean	Shand 1	Wightman	McKinnon	McCabe
S	16-Mar	Dundee Hibernian		H	EL	3-0	2000	Kerr	Stuart	Muir	Hutchison	Inglis	Currie	Duncan 1	Abbott 1	Shand 1	Wightman	McKinnon	
S	23-Mar	East Fife		H	EL	2-0	2000	Kerr	Stewart	Muir	Hutchison	Currie	Grieve	Duncan 1	Abbott	Shand	McLean 1	McKinnon	
S	30-Mar	Dunfermline Athletic		A	EL	2-1		Kerr	Stuart 1	Muir	Inglis	Currie	Grieve	Duncan	Abbott 1	Shand	Wightman	McKinnon	Jackson
S	06-Apr	Dunfermline Athletic	1	N	FC F	1-1		Kerr	Stuart	Muir	Hutchison	Currie	Grieve	Duncan	Abbott 1	Shand	Wightman	McKinnon	Brown
S	13-Apr	Cowdenbeath		H	WC SF	2-1	1000	Kerr	Stuart	Muir	Hutchison	Currie	Bacon	Lowther	Abbott 1	Shand 1	Wightman	McKinnon	McCulloch
S	20-Apr	Dunfermline Athletic		H	FC Fr	0-1	2000	Kerr	Stuart	Muir	Bacon	Currie	Robson	Duncan	Abbott	Shand	Wightman	McKinnon	Baillie
S	27-Apr	East Fife		A	WC	0-2	2000	Kerr	Stewart	Muir	Aitken	Currie	Lowther	Wilson,G	Abbott	Duncan	Wightman	McKinnon	Allan, A. (2)

1918-1919

Day	Date	Opponents	Note	Venue	Comp	Res.	Att.	1	2	3	4	5	6	7	8	9	10	11	Substitutes, own goals, goal times and opponents' scorers
S	15-Mar	East Scotland Select XI		H	F	1-2		Kerr	Stuart	Muir	Rattray	Inglis	Currie	Thorburn	McLean,T	Welsh 1	Gourlay	McKinnon	Rodger Traill
S	22-Mar	East Scotland Select		H	F	3-1		McDonald	Todd	Muir	Hutchison	Herd	Currie 1	Anderson	McLean,T 1	Shand 1	Traill	Brown 1	Veitch
Th	27-Mar	East Fife		H	F	5-1	2000	Kerr	Inglis	Robertson	Rattray	McLean,W	Collier	Anderson 1	McLean,T 1	Welsh 2	Traill	Brown 1	McMahon
S	05-Apr	Cowdenbeath		A	F	2-1		Kerr	Robertson	Muir	McLean,W	Currie 1	Collier	Anderson	McLean,T	Alexander	Traill	McKinnon	McLean, J.
M	07-Apr	Dundee		H	F	4-4	2500	Kerr	Todd	Stuart	Rattray	Currie	Collier 1	Gourlay	Stoddart	Welsh 4	Welsh 2	McKinnon	Paterson (3) Phillips
S	12-Apr	Cowdenbeath		H	F	5-2		Kerr	Inglis	Muir	Rattray	McLean,W	Collier	Rodger	McLean,T	Welsh 4	Traill 1	Wilson,G	Brown (2)
S	19-Apr	East Fife		A	F	2-1		Kerr	Todd	Stuart	Rattray	Currie	Collier	Gourlay	Stoddart	Welsh 1	Traill 1	Wilson,G	
S	26-Apr	Dundee		A	F	0-6		Kerr	Inglis	Muir	McLean,W	Currie	Rattray	Rodger	Wilson,G	Welsh	McLean.T	Brown	
S	10-May	East Fife		A	F	0-1		Kerr	Inglis	Muir	Rattray	Currie	McLean,W	Gourlay	Stoddart	Welsh	Traill	McKinnon	Chalmers

Manager : Peter Hodge
Loftus Cup, Fife League, Penman Cup and Wemyss Cup fixtures completed by Reserve team
(1) at Cowdenbeath

Substitutes, own goals, goal times and opponents' scorers

Day	Date	Opponents	Note	Venue	Comp	Res	Att.	1	2	3	4	5	6	7	8	9	10	11	OG	Subs / opponents' scorers
S	16-Aug	Falkirk		A	L1	1-4	4500	Clark	Inglis	Muir	McLean	Porter	Anderson	Birrell	Duncan,J	Welsh	Traill 1	Wilson		Harvie pen Wood McDougall (2)
S	23-Aug	Kilmarnock		H	L1	5-1	8000	Clark	Inglis	Muir	Rattray	McLean	Anderson	Duncan,J 1	Christie	Birrell 4	Traill	Wilson		McLean
M	25-Aug	St.Johnstone		N	F	2-2		McDonald	Todd	Campbell	Collier	Renfrew	Berry	Hutcheson	McFarlane 1	Abbott	Brown 1	Patterson		McQueen Taylor
Tu	26-Aug	Partick Thistle		A	L1	0-3	8000	Clark	Inglis	Muir	Rattray	McLean	Anderson	Duncan,J	Christie	Birrell	Traill	Dunn		Harris (2) Mitchell
S	30-Aug	Celtic		A	L1	0-3	10000	Clark	Inglis	Muir	Rattray	McLean x	Anderson	Duncan,J	Traill	Birrell	Christie	Dunn		McInally (2) Gallagher
W	03-Sep	Ayr United		A	L1	1-1	3000	McDonald,A	Inglis	Robson	Rattray	McLean	Currie	Traill	Porter	Birrell 1	Christie	Duncan,J		Crosbie, J
S	06-Sep	Hearts		H	L1	0-1	12000	McDonald,A	Inglis	Robson	Rattray	Porter	Anderson	Duncan,J	Welsh	Birrell	Currie	McDonald,J		Miller
Tu	09-Sep	Rangers		A	L1	2-3	8000	McDonald,A	Inglis	Robson	Rattray	Porter	Anderson	Duncan,J	Welsh	Birrell	Abbott	McDonald,J		Archibald Cunningham Patterson
S	13-Sep	Motherwell		A	L1	1-4	10000	McDonald,A	Inglis	Robson	Rattray	Porter	Anderson	Birrell	Traill 1	Welsh 2	Abbott	Currie		Ferguson (2) Rankin Ferrier
S	20-Sep	St.Mirren		H	L1	3-0	6000	McDonald,A	Inglis	Robson	Rattray	Porter	Anderson	Birrell 1	Traill	Welsh 2	Abbott	Duncan,J		
S	27-Sep	Third Lanark		A	L1	3-4	5000	McDonald,A	Inglis	Robson	Rattray	Porter	Anderson	Birrell	Duncan,J 1	Welsh 2	Porter 3	Wilson		Orr (2) Allan Inglis og
S	04-Oct	Hamilton Academical		A	L1	5-5	4000	McDonald,A	Inglis	Robson	Rattray	McLean	Anderson	Birrell	Duncan,J	Welsh 2	Duncan,J	Wilson		Thornley (5)
S	04-Oct	East Fife	N	A	FC 1	1-0		Laverock	Campbell	Muir	Hutcheson	Berry	Currie	Brown	Christie	Baldie	Collier	Dunn	Fisher og 1	
M	06-Oct	Clyde		H	L1	3-1	6000	McDonald,A	Inglis	Robson	Rattray	McLean	Anderson	Birrell	Duncan,J	Welsh 2,1p	Porter	Dunn 1		Aitken
S	11-Oct	Rangers		H	L1	1-2	16000	McDonald,A	Inglis	Robson	Rattray	McLean	Anderson	Duncan,J	Birrell	Welsh 1	Porter	Wilson		Gordon Archibald
S	18-Oct	Airdrie		H	L1	3-2	7000	McDonald,A	Inglis	Robson	Rattray	Porter 1	Anderson	Birrell	McLean	Welsh 2	Duncan,J	Dunn		Duff (2)
S	25-Oct	Dumbarton		A	L1	1-1	4000	McDonald,A	Inglis	Robson	Rattray	Porter	Anderson	Duncan,J	McLean	Birrell	Wilson 1	Dunn		McDearmid
S	01-Nov	Partick Thistle		H	L1	2-0	9000	McDonald,A	Inglis	Robson	Rattray	Porter	Anderson	McDonald,J	McLean	Birrell 1	Duncan,J 1	Dunn		Wood (2)
S	08-Nov	Hibernian		A	L1	0-2	15000	McDonald,A	Inglis	Robson	Rattray	Porter	Anderson	McDonald,J	McLean	Birrell	Duncan,J 1	Dunn		Bell (2) Rawlings
S	15-Nov	Dundee		H	L1	1-3	8000	McDonald,A	Inglis	Robson	Rattray	Porter	Anderson	Birrell	McLean	Welsh 1	Duncan,J 1	Dunn		Archibald Hutton
S	22-Nov	Aberdeen		H	L1	2-2	8000	McDonald,A	Robson	Muir	Inglis	Porter	Anderson	Birrell	McLean 1	Welsh 1	Duncan,J	Dunn		McGowan (2) Quinn Morris
S	29-Nov	Clyde	1	A	L1	3-4	2000	McDonald,A	Campbell	Muir	Rattray	Porter	Anderson	Birrell	McLean 1	Welsh 3	Duncan,J	Dunn		Cameron Bell (3) Morton
S	06-Dec	Queen's Park		H	L1	2-5	5000	McDonald,A	Robson	Muir	Rattray	Porter	Anderson	Birrell	McLean 1	Welsh 3	McLean 1	Wilson		McLaughlin Bell (3) Shade (2)
S	13-Dec	Dundee		A	L1	4-5	10000	Brown	Campbell	Muir	Rattray	Porter	Porter	Duncan,J	Birrell	Welsh 3	McLean 1	Wilson		Middleton
W	20-Dec	Ayr United		H	L1	2-1	6000	Brown	Inglis	Muir	Rattray	Berry	Anderson	Duncan,J	McLean	Welsh 1	Anderson 1	Wilson		Walker Fulton Anderson Paton
S	27-Dec	Clydebank		H	L1	1-4	3000	Brown	Inglis	Muir	Rattray	Porter	Anderson	Duncan,J	McLean	Welsh 1	Christie	Wilson		
Th	01-Jan	Falkirk		H	L1	0-0	9000	Dickson	Inglis	Muir	Rattray	Porter	Anderson	Duncan,J	Birrell	Welsh	McLean	Wilson		McAtee McInally Cassidy
S	03-Jan	Celtic		H	L1	0-3	16000	Dickson	Sneddon	Inglis	Porter	McLean	Anderson	Duncan,J	Jessiman	Welsh	McLean	Dunn		McKenzie
S	10-Jan	Queen's Park		A	L1	2-1	7000	Dickson	Sneddon	Inglis	Duncan,J	Porter	Anderson	Birrell	McLean	Baldie 1	Jessiman 1	Dunn		
S	17-Jan	Hamilton Academical		H	L1	1-0	8000	Dickson	Sneddon	Inglis	Duncan,J	Porter	Anderson	Birrell	McLean	Baldie	Jessiman	Wilson	Little og 1	Smith, J Culley
S	24-Jan	Kilmarnock		A	L1	0-2	5000	Dickson	Sneddon	Moyes	Duncan,J	Porter	Anderson	Birrell	McLean	Baldie	Jessiman	Neilson		Thomson
S	31-Jan	St.Mirren		A	L1	1-1	5000	Dickson	Inglis	Moyes	Inglis	Porter	Anderson	Birrell	Traill	Baldie 1	Jessiman	Wilson		
S	07-Feb	East Stirling		A	SC 2	2-0	6000	Dickson	Inglis	Moyes	Sneddon	Porter	Anderson	Birrell	McLean	Baldie 1	Jessiman	Wilson		Sime
S	14-Feb	East Stirling		H	SC 2r	1-1	12000	Dickson	Inglis	Muir	Sneddon	Porter 1	Anderson	Duncan,J	Dunn	Birrell	Dunn	Wilson		
W	18-Feb	Dunfermline Athletic	N H	FC SF	1-2	10000		McDonald	Brown	Muir	Rattray	Porter	Duncan,J	Birrell	McLean	Cant	Anderson	Christie		Wilson, Neave
Th	19-Feb	East Stirling	2 N	SC 2r2	4-0	5000		Brown	Inglis	Muir	Rattray	Porter	Duncan,J	Birrell 1	McLean	Baldie 2	Anderson	Dunn 1		
S	21-Feb	Morton	3 N	SC 2r3	2-2	15000		Brown	Inglis	Muir	Rattray	Porter	Duncan,J	Birrell 1p	McLean	Baldie 1	Anderson	Wilson		
W	25-Feb	Clydebank		A	SC 3r	0-3	8000	Black	Inglis	Muir	Rattray	Porter x	Anderson	Duncan,J	McLean	Baldie	Anderson	Wilson		Connor (3)
S	28-Feb	Hearts		A	L1	1-1	14000	Brown	Moyes	Sneddon	Duncan,J	Porter	Anderson	Birrell	McLean	Millar 1	Jessiman	Wilson		Murphy
W	28-Feb	Dunfermline Athletic	N1	A	B	1-2		McDonald	Brown	Moyes	Hutcheson	Berry	Collier	Trail	Dunsire	Cant	Christie	Neilson		
S	06-Mar	Dumbarton		H	L1	2-0	8000	Brown	Inglis	Muir	Rattray	Porter	Duncan,J	Birrell	Rattray 1	Millar	Anderson 1	Wilson		Wilson
S	13-Mar	Aberdeen		A	L1	1-3	10000	Brown	Inglis	Muir	Rattray	Berry	Collier	Birrell	McLean	Millar	Anderson 1	Dunn		
S	20-Mar	Albion Rovers		H	L1	3-0	8000	Brown	Inglis	Muir	Duncan,J	Porter	Anderson	Birrell	Cant 1	Baldie 2	Jessiman	Wilson		Connor (3)
S	27-Mar	Motherwell		A	L1	0-2	8000	Brown	Inglis	Moyes	Rattray	Duncan,J	Anderson	Birrell	Cant	Baldie	Millar	Wilson		Gardiner (2)
S	03-Apr	Clydebank		H	L1	1-3	7000	Dickson	Inglis	Moyes	Rattray 1	McLean	Duncan,J	Birrell	Jessiman	Cant	Anderson	Dunn		Fulton Paton (2)
M	05-Apr	Lochgelly		H	WC	0-1		Dickson	Sneddon	Moyes	Duncan,J	Berry	Collier	Trail	Dunsire	Baldie	Christie	Dunn		Russell
S	10-Apr	Airdrie		A	L1	1-3	4000	Brown	Inglis	Moyes	Rattray	Berry	Duncan,J	Birrell	Jessiman 1	Cant	Anderson	Wilson		Weir Reid, J Aird
W	14-Apr	Cowdenbeath	N1 A	B	2-0			Dickson	Todd	Moyes	T.Duncan	J.Duncan	Berry 1	Rae	Watters	Trail 1	Bruce	Neilson		
S	17-Apr	Hibernian		H	L1	1-0	6000	Brown	Inglis	Muir	Duncan,J	Berry	Collier	Wilson	Rattray	Millar	Jessiman 1	Wilson		
S	24-Apr	Morton		A	L1	0-0	8000	Brown	Inglis	Muir	Rattray	Berry	Collier	Trail	McLean	Trail	Jessiman	Dunn		
M	26-Apr	Albion Rovers		A	L1	3-0	3000	Brown	Inglis	Moyes	Duncan,J	McLean	Anderson	Duncan,J	Duncan,T	Cant	Jessiman	Wilson		French
W	28-Apr	Morton		H	L1	1-1	6000	Brown	Inglis	Moyes	Rattray	Berry	Collier	Trail	Cant	Cant	Dunsire	Dunn		
S	01-May	Third Lanark		H	L1	0-2	9000	Brown	Inglis	Muir	Duncan,J	Berry	Collier	Trail	Watters	Millar	Jessiman	Dunn		Benvie Walker, F
S	08-May	Fifeshire Select		H	F	1-1		Dickson	Birrell	Birrell	Rattray	Duncan,T	Collier	Duncan,T	Duncan,T	Robertson	Roberts	Archibald		Baldie

Manager : Peter Hodge to 9th September ; James Logan from 9th September

Penman Cup tie on 6th December 1919, Dundee A 3 Raith Rovers A 1 ; The Loftus Cup was also fulfilled by reserve team

(1) at Celtic Park   (2) after extra time, at Tynecastle, receipts £392   (3) at Tynecastle, receipts £200

(4) £200 raised ; fixture fulfilled by reserve eleven, not included in summary statistics

(N) fixture fulfilled by reserve team

(N1) Benefit for McPheat, fulfilled by reserve team

Day	Date	Opponents	Note	Venue	Comp	Res.	Att.	1	2	3	4	5	6	7	8	9	10	11	Substitutes, own goals, goal times and opponents' scorers
M	16-Aug	Albion Rovers		A	L1	1-0	7500	Dickson	Inglis	McInnes	Rattray	Porter	Duncan,J	Birrell	Stoddart	Waitt	McDonald	Archibald 1	Scott pen Hamilton Meldrum
S	21-Aug	Falkirk		H	L1	1-3	12000	Dickson	Inglis	McInnes	Rattray	Porter	Duncan,J	Birrell	Stoddart	Waitt 1	McDonald	Archibald	McPhail
W	25-Aug	Kilmarnock		A	L1	0-1	4000	Dickson	Inglis	McInnes	Rattray	Berry	McDonald	Birrell	Stoddart	Waitt	Duncan,J	Archibald	Kinloch Kerr (2)
S	28-Aug	Partick Thistle		A	L1	1-3	22000	Dickson	Inglis	McInnes	Duncan,J	Porter	McDonald	Archibald	Watters	Waitt 1	Watters	Archibald	Maxwell (2) Forbes
W	01-Sep	Hearts/Hibs XI	1	H	B	2-3	6000	Porter	Inglis	McInnes	Duncan,J	Porter	Collier	Birrell	Watters	Waitt 1	Duncan,T	Dunn	Stewart Ferguson
S	04-Sep	Motherwell		H	L1	1-2	8000	Dickson	Inglis	McInnes	Duncan,J	Collier	Collier	Birrell	Berry	Waitt	Duncan,T	Archibald	
W	08-Sep	Partick Thistle		H	L1	1-0	8000	Dickson	Inglis	Moyes	Duncan,J	Collier	Collier	Birrell	Berry	Waitt 1	Duncan,T	Archibald	
S	11-Sep	Third Lanark		A	L1	0-3	7000	Dickson	Inglis	McInnes	Rattray	Collier	Collier	Birrell	Berry	Waitt	Duncan,T	Archibald	Allan Bennie Cullen
W	15-Sep	Kilmarnock		A	L1	3-1	7000	Dickson	Inglis	Moyes	Rattray	Porter	Collier	Birrell	Birrell 1	Waitt 1	Berry	Archibald	French
S	18-Sep	Dunfermline Athletic		H	L1	2-0	10000	Dickson	Inglis	Moyes	Rattray	Porter	Collier	Archibald	Birrell 1	Waitt 1	McDonald 1	Dunn 1	
M	20-Sep	Hearts		A	PC	0-1		Brown	Inglis	Moyes	McInnes	Berry	Collier	Archibald	Duncan,J	Duncan,J	Watters	Dunn	Wilson pen
S	25-Sep	Hearts		H	L1	0-2	20000	Dickson	Inglis	Moyes	Rattray	Porter	Duncan,J	Archibald	Birrell	Waitt	McDonald	Dunn	Murphy Miller
S	02-Oct	Dundee		H	L1	1-2	12000	Brown	Inglis	McInnes	Rattray	Porter	Collier	Archibald	Birrell 1p	McDonald	McDonald	Dunn	McLean Bell
M	04-Oct	Queen's Park		H	L1	5-0	8000	Dickson	Inglis	McInnes	Rattray	Berry	Collier 1	Birrell	Duncan,J 3	Waitt 1	McDonald	Archibald	
S	09-Oct	Airdrie		A	L1	1-3	7000	Dickson	Inglis	Moyes	Rattray	Berry	Collier	Birrell	Duncan,J	Waitt 1	Watters	Archibald	Henderson (3)
S	16-Oct	Dumbarton		H	L1	3-1	8000	Dickson	Inglis	Moyes	Rattray	Berry	Collier	Birrell 2	Duncan,J	Waitt 1	Watters	Archibald	Raeside
S	23-Oct	Aberdeen		A	L1	0-1	15000	Dickson	Inglis	Moyes	Rattray	Berry	Collier	Birrell	Duncan,J	Waitt	Watters	Archibald	Connon
S	30-Oct	Hibernian		A	L1	2-4	8000	Dickson	Inglis	Moyes	Rattray	Berry	Collier	Birrell	Duncan,J	Waitt	McDonald	Archibald	
S	06-Nov	St Mirren		A	L1	2-2	8000	Dickson	Inglis	Moyes	Rattray	McInnes	Collier	Duncan,J	Duncan,J 2	Waitt 2,1p	McDonald	Archibald	Love (2) Thomson
S	13-Nov	Clyde		H	L1	2-3	6000	Brown	Inglis	Moyes	Rattray	Berry	Collier	Birrell	Duncan,J	Waitt	McDonald	Archibald	Rae
S	20-Nov	Morton		H	L1	0-1	7000	Brown	Inglis	Moyes	Rattray	Berry	Collier	Birrell	Duncan,J	Waitt	Watters	Dunn 1	
S	27-Nov	Celtic		A	L1	0-5	10000	Dickson	Inglis	Moyes	Rattray	Duncan,J	Collier	Archibald	Birrell	Waitt	Watters	Dunn	Cringan McAtee Gallagher Longmuir (2)
S	04-Dec	Hamilton Academical		H	L1	1-0	7000	Dickson	Inglis	Moyes	Rattray	Duncan,J	Collier	Archibald	Birrell	Bell	McDonald	Dunn	
S	11-Dec	Clydebank		A	L1	1-1	5000	Dickson	Inglis	Moyes	Rattray	Duncan,J	Collier	Archibald	Birrell	Bell	McDonald	Dunn 1	Marchbanks
S	18-Dec	Queen's Park		A	L1	2-3	10000	Dickson	Inglis	Moyes	Rattray	Duncan,J	Collier	Archibald	Archibald	Bell 1	McDonald 1	Dunn	Fyfe Pirie McAlpine
S	25-Dec	Albion Rovers		H	L1	2-4	7000	Brown	Inglis	Moyes	Rattray	Duncan,J	Collier	Birrell	Birrell	Bell	Duncan,T	Archibald 1	Bennett Reid Blue Craig
S	01-Jan	Falkirk		A	L1	2-2	6000	Brown	Inglis	Moyes	Rattray	Morris	Collier	Duncan,J	Birrell 1	Bell 1	McDonald	Archibald 1	Townsley Moore
M	03-Jan	Third Lanark	2	H	B	1-2	12000	Dickson	Inglis	Moyes	Rattray	Morris	Duncan,T	Duncan,J	Duncan,J	Bell 1	Bauld	Archibald	Welsh Orr
Tu	04-Jan	Fifeshire Select		H	B	2-1	7200	Dickson	Inglis	Moyes	Renton	Berry	Collier	Rattray	McDonald 1	Dawson	Dawson	Cant	Patterson
S	08-Jan	Dundee		H	L1	1-0	8500	Brown	Inglis	Moyes	Rattray	Collier	Collier	Duncan,J	Bell	Bell	Bauld	Archibald	
S	15-Jan	Dumbarton		A	L1	0-2	3000	Brown	Inglis	Moyes	Rattray	Morris	Collier	Duncan,J	Birrell	Bell	Duncan,J	Archibald	Walker Browning
S	22-Jan	Hamilton Academical		A	SC 1	1-3	7000	Brown	Inglis	Moyes	Rattray	Morris	Collier	Archibald	Archibald	Jennings 1	Duncan,J	Bauld	Cullen Little McMillan
S	29-Jan	St Mirren		A	L1	3-1	8000	Brown	McInnes	Moyes	Rattray	Morris	Collier 1	Archibald	Birrell	Jennings 1	Bauld	Bauld 2	Pringle pen
W	09-Feb	Rangers		A	L1	0-1	10000	Brown	Inglis	Moyes	Raeburn	Morris	Collier	Rattray	Duncan,J	Jennings	Bauld	Archibald	Archibald
S	12-Feb	Ayr United		A	L1	0-1	5000	Brown	Inglis	Moyes	Raeburn	Morris	Collier	Rattray	Duncan,J	Jennings	Bauld	Archibald	Quinn
S	19-Feb	Lochgelly		H	LoC	0-1	5000	Brown	Inglis	Moyes	Raeburn	Morris	Duncan,T	Reekie	Duncan,J	Jennings	Bauld	Robb	Galloway
S	23-Feb	Hearts		H	L1	2-1	8000	Brown	Inglis	Moyes 1	Raeburn	Morris	Collier	Rattray	Duncan,J 1	Jennings 1	Bauld	Archibald	Murphy
S	26-Feb	Dundee		A	L1	0-0	12000	Brown	Inglis	Moyes	Raeburn	Morris	Collier	Rattray	Duncan,J	Jennings	Bauld	Archibald	
S	05-Mar	Clydebank		A	DC SF	3-0	5000	Brown	Inglis	Moyes	Raeburn	Morris	Collier 1	Rattray 1	Bell	Jennings 1	Bauld 1	Archibald	
S	12-Mar	Hamilton Academical	3	H	L1	0-0	6000	Brown	Inglis	Moyes	Raeburn	Morris	Collier	Duncan,J	Duncan,J	Jennings	Bauld	Archibald	
Th	17-Mar	East Fife	4	A	B	1-2		Dickson	Inglis	McInnes	Johnstone	Berry	McDonald	McDonald	Duncan,J 1	Bell	McDonald	Archibald 1	
S	19-Mar	Airdrie		H	L1	3-2	7000	Brown	Inglis	Moyes	Raeburn	Morris	Collier	Duncan,T	Bauld	Jennings 1	Bauld	Archibald	McNamee Henderson
W	23-Mar	East Fife		H	WC	1-0	1000	Brown	Inglis	Moyes	Raeburn	Morris	Collier	Duncan,T 2	Watters	Jennings 1	Bauld	Archibald 1	
S	26-Mar	Motherwell		A	L1	1-2	5000	Brown	Inglis	Moyes	Raeburn	Morris	Collier	Duncan,T	Duncan,J 1	Jennings 1	Bauld	Archibald	Ferguson (2)
S	02-Apr	Ayr United		H	L1	2-1	10000	Brown	Inglis	Moyes	Raeburn	Berry	Collier	Duncan,T	Duncan,J	Jennings 1	Bauld	Archibald	Stevenson
M	04-Apr	Middlesbrough		H	F	3-0	8000	Brown	Inglis	Moyes	Raeburn	Morris	Collier 1	Duncan,T	Bell 2	Bell	Bauld	Gibson	
W	06-Apr	Cowdenbeath		H	FC 1	2-0	6000	Brown	Inglis	Moyes	Raeburn	Morris	Collier	Duncan,T	Black	Jennings	Bauld	Archibald	
S	09-Apr	Celtic		H	L1	2-0	12000	Brown	Inglis	Moyes	Raeburn	Morris	Collier	Duncan,T 2	Duncan,J 2	Bell	Bauld	Archibald	
Tu	12-Apr	Dunfermline Athletic		H	WC SF	1-0	8000	Brown	Inglis	Moyes	Raeburn	Morris	Collier	Duncan,T	Duncan,J 1	Jennings 1	Bauld	Archibald	
S	16-Apr	Hibernian		A	L1	1-1	7000	Brown	Inglis	Moyes	Raeburn	Morris	Collier 1	Duncan,T	Duncan,J	Jennings	Bauld 1	Archibald	Ritchie
M	18-Apr	Hearts		A	DC SF	0-3	10000	Brown	Inglis	Moyes	Raeburn	Morris	Collier	Duncan,T	Duncan,J	Jennings	Bauld	Archibald	Forbes (2) Wilson, W.
W	20-Apr	Lochgelly		H	FC SF	3-1	5000	Brown	Inglis	Moyes	Raeburn	Berry	Collier	Rattray	Duncan,J 1	Bell 1	McDonald	Archibald 1	Tonner pen
S	23-Apr	Clyde		A	L1	1-2	3000	Dickson	Inglis	Moyes	Raeburn	Morris	Collier	Duncan,T	Duncan,J 1	Jennings 1	Bauld	Archibald	Fleming (2)
W	27-Apr	Hull City	5	H	B	3-1	8000	Brown	Inglis	Moyes	Rattray	Morris	Collier	Duncan,T	Duncan,J 1	Bell 1	McDonald	Archibald 1	McInie
S	30-Apr	Rangers		H	L1	0-1	12000	Brown	Inglis	Moyes	Raeburn	Morris	Collier	Duncan,T 1	Duncan,J	Jennings	Dawson	Archibald	Muirhead
W	04-May	Dunfermline Athletic	6	A	FC F	3-2		Brown	Inglis	Moyes	Raeburn	Morris	Collier	Duncan,T 1	Duncan,J 1	Jennings 1	Bauld	Archibald	Croal Wilson
F	06-May	Cowdenbeath	7	H	C	4-0		Brown	Inglis	Moyes	Raeburn	Morris	Collier	Duncan,T 1	Duncan,J 1	Jennings	Dawson 1	Archibald	
S	07-May	Fife Select		H	WC F	4-0	12000	Brown	Inglis	Moyes	Raeburn	Morris	Collier	Duncan,T 1	Duncan,J 1	Jennings 2	Bauld 1	Archibald	
S	14-May	Fife Select	8	A	C	0-2		Brown	Inglis	Moyes	Raeburn	Morris	Collier	Duncan,T	Duncan,J 1	Jennings 1	Dawson	Archibald	Currie Tonner

Manager : James Logan.   No offside from throw ins.   (1) Willie Porter Benefit   (2) Jock Rattray Benefit   (3) General Election Day   (4) Archie Main Benefi   (5) Bill Inglis Benefit (6) after extra time, full time score was 1-1   (7) to raise funds for Kirkcaldy War Memorial   (8) in aid of West Fife hospitals
Monday 2nd August 1920 Raith Rovers 3 Kirkcaldy Cricketers 1   (the cricket match was played on 29th July)

Day	Date	Opponents	Note	Venue	Comp	Res	Att	1	2	3	4	5	6	7	8	9	10	11	Substitutes, own goals, goal times and opponents' scorers
M	15-Aug	Celtic		A	L1	0-4	12000	Brown	Inglis	Moyes	Raeburn	Morris,D	Collier	Duncan,T	Duncan,J	Jennings	Bauld	Archibald	McAtee Longmuir (2) Cassidy
S	20-Aug	Motherwell		A	L1	1-2	8000	Brown	Inglis	Moyes	Rattray	Morris,D	Collier	Duncan,T	Duncan,J	Jennings	Bauld 1	Archibald	Ferguson (2)
S	27-Aug	Celtic		H	L1	1-1	20000	Brown	Inglis	Moyes	Raeburn	Morris,D	Collier	Duncan,T 1	Duncan,J	Jennings	Bauld	Archibald	McLean
W	31-Aug	Queen's Park		A	L1	3-1	5000	Brown	Inglis	Moyes 1p	Rattray	Morris,D	Collier	Duncan,T	Duncan,J	Jennings 2	Bauld	Archibald	Scott
S	03-Sep	Falkirk		A	L1	1-1	8000	Brown	Barton	Moyes	Rattray	Morris,D	Collier	Duncan,T	Duncan,J	Jennings 1	Bauld	Archibald	McLeary
M	05-Sep	Albion Rovers		A	L1	0-2	6000	Brown	Barton	Moyes	Raeburn	Morris,D	Collier	Duncan,T	Duncan,J	Jennings	Bauld	Archibald	Greenshields Reid
S	10-Sep	Clydebank		H	L1	5-0	10000	Brown	Inglis	Moyes	Raeburn	Morris,D	Collier	Duncan,T	Duncan,J 1	Jennings 3	Bauld 1	Archibald 1	
S	17-Sep	St Mirren		A	L1	1-1	12000	Brown	Inglis	Moyes	Barton	Morris,D	Collier	Duncan,T	Duncan,J	Jennings 1	Bauld	Archibald	Thomson
M	19-Sep	Airdrie		A	L1	2-0	3000	Brown	Inglis	Moyes	Barton	Morris,D	Collier	Duncan,T	Duncan,J	Jennings	Bauld 1	Archibald	
S	24-Sep	Kilmarnock		H	L1	4-0	15300	Brown	Inglis	Moyes	Barton	Morris,D	Collier	Duncan,T	Duncan,J 2	Jennings	Bauld 1	Archibald 1	
W	28-Sep	Airdrie	1	H	B	0-0	5000	Brown	Inglis	Moyes	Rattray	Morris,D	Collier	Duncan,T	Duncan,J	Jennings	Bauld	Archibald	
S	01-Oct	Partick Thistle		A	L1	1-2	10000	Brown	Inglis	Moyes	Barton	Morris,D	Collier	Duncan,T	Duncan,J 1	Jennings	Bauld 1	Archibald	Blair (2)
M	03-Oct	Bradford City		H	F	3-1		Brown	Inglis	Moyes	Rattray	Morris,D	Collier	Duncan,T	Duncan,J 1	Jennings 2	Bauld	Archibald	Wright
S	08-Oct	Aberdeen		H	L1	2-1	8000	Brown	Inglis	Moyes	Rattray	Morris,D	Collier	Duncan,T	Duncan,J	Jennings 2	Bauld	Archibald	French (3)
S	15-Oct	Morton		A	L1	1-3	8000	Brown	Barton	Moyes	Raeburn	Morris,D	Collier	Duncan,T	Duncan,J 1	Jennings 1	Bauld	Archibald	
S	22-Oct	Airdrie		H	L1	1-0	5000	Brown	Inglis	Moyes	Raeburn	Morris,D	Collier	Duncan,T	Duncan,J	Jennings 1	Bauld	Archibald	Allan
S	29-Oct	Clyde		H	L1	1-1	12000	Brown	Inglis	Moyes	Raeburn	Morris,D	Collier	Duncan,T 1	Duncan,J	Jennings	Bauld	Archibald	Wood
S	05-Nov	Dumbarton		A	L1	2-1	3500	Brown	Inglis	Moyes	Raeburn	Morris,D	Collier	Duncan,T	Duncan,J	Jennings 1	Bauld 1	Archibald	Miller, T.
S	12-Nov	Ayr United		H	L1	5-0	7000	Brown	Inglis	Moyes	Raeburn	Morris,D	Collier 1	Duncan,T	Duncan,J	Jennings 2	Bauld 1	Archibald	
S	19-Nov	Hearts		A	L1	1-1	20000	Brown	Inglis	Moyes	Raeburn	Morris,D	Collier	Duncan,T	Duncan,J	Jennings 1	Bauld 1	Archibald	Hillhouse Reid
S	26-Nov	Third Lanark		H	L1	2-2	6000	Brown	Inglis	Moyes	Raeburn	Morris,D	Collier	Duncan,T 1	Duncan,J	Jennings 1	Bauld	Archibald	Nall
S	03-Dec	Hamilton Academical		A	L1	2-1	6000	Brown	Inglis	Moyes	Raeburn	Morris,D	Collier	Duncan,T 2	Duncan,J	Jennings	Bauld	Archibald	
S	10-Dec	Dundee		H	L1	0-0	15000	Black	Inglis	Moyes	Raeburn	Morris,D	Collier	Duncan,T	Duncan,J	Jennings	Bauld	Archibald	
S	17-Dec	Kilmarnock		A	L1	2-2	5000	Brown	Inglis	Moyes	Raeburn	Morris,D	Collier	Duncan,T 1	Duncan,J	Dawson	Bauld 1	Archibald	Gibson Watson
S	24-Dec	St Mirren		H	L1	2-3	6000	Brown	Inglis	Moyes	Raeburn	Morris,D	Collier	Duncan,T 1	Duncan,J	Dawson 2	Bauld	Archibald	Walker (3)
S	31-Dec	Albion Rovers		A	L1	3-0	7000	Brown	Inglis 1	Moyes	Raeburn	Morris,D	Collier	Duncan,T	Duncan,J	Rattray	Bauld 1	Archibald	
M	02-Jan	Falkirk		H	L1	2-1	12000	Brown	Inglis	Moyes	Raeburn	Morris,D 1	Collier	Duncan,T	Duncan,J	Dawson 1	Bauld	Archibald	Goudie
Tu	03-Jan	Aberdeen		A	L1	2-1	8000	Brown	Inglis	Moyes	Raeburn	Morris,D	Collier	Duncan,T	Duncan,J	Dawson 1	Bauld 1	Archibald	Thomson
S	07-Jan	Hearts		A	L1	3-1	10000	Brown	Inglis	Moyes	Raeburn	Morris,D	Collier	Duncan,T	Duncan,J	Dawson 1	Bauld 1	Archibald 1	Miller, G.
S	14-Jan	Rangers		A	L1	1-0	20000	Black	Inglis	Moyes	Raeburn	Morris,D	McBeath	Duncan,T	Duncan,J	Jennings 1	Bauld	Archibald	
S	21-Jan	Hibernian		H	L1	0-0	8000	Brown	Inglis	Morris,A	Raeburn	Morris,D	Collier	Duncan,T	Duncan,J	Jennings	Bauld	Archibald	
S	28-Jan	Clyde		H	SC 1	2-2	12000	Brown	Inglis 1p	Morris,A	Raeburn	Morris,D 1	Collier	Duncan,T	Duncan,J	Jennings	Bauld 1	Archibald	Fleming Duncan
W	04-Feb	Clyde	2	A	SC 1r	3-0	25000	Brown	Inglis	Morris,A	Raeburn	Morris,D	Collier	Duncan,T	Duncan,J	Jennings 1	Bauld 1	Archibald	Thompson
S	04-Feb	Clydebank	3	A	L1	1-1	2000	Brown	Inglis	Morris,A	Raeburn	Morris,D	McBeath	Wilson	Duncan,J	Jennings	Bauld 1	Archibald	
S	11-Feb	Dumbarton		H	L1	2-0	2000	Brown	Inglis	Morris,A	Raeburn	Morris,D	Collier	Wilson	Duncan,J	Jennings	Bauld 1	Archibald 1	
S	18-Feb	Hibernian		A	WC 1	0-2	3000	Brown	Inglis	Morris,A	Raeburn	Morris,D	Collier	Wilson	Duncan,J	Jennings	Bauld	Archibald	Wood pen
W	22-Feb	Queen's Park		A	L1	1-1	5000	Brown	Inglis 1	Morris,A	Raeburn	Morris,D	Collier	Wilson	Dawson	Jennings	Bell	Archibald	Young (2)
S	25-Feb	Ayr United		A	FC SF	2-1	4000	Brown	Inglis	Morris,A	Raeburn	Morris,D	Collier	Duncan,T	Dawson 1	Jennings	Bell 1	Archibald	Dickson
M	04-Mar	Motherwell		H	L1	0-3	20000	Steele	Inglis	Moyes	Rattray	Morris,D	Collier	Duncan,T	Duncan,J	Jennings	Bauld	Archibald	Lennie
S	11-Mar	Hibernian		H	PC 2	2-1		Brown	Inglis	Morris,A	Raeburn	Morris,D	Collier	Duncan,T 1	Wilson	Slaven 1	Dawson	Archibald 1	Walker
S	18-Mar	Partick Thistle		A	L1	0-1	8000	Brown	Inglis	Morris,A	Raeburn	Morris,D	Collier	Duncan,T	Slaven	Jennings	Bauld	Archibald	Cant (2)
Th	23-Mar	East Fife	4	A	DC SF	0-0	6000	Brown	Inglis	Morris,A	Rattray	Morris,D	Collier	Duncan,T	Slaven	Dawson	Bauld	Archibald	Brown
S	25-Mar	Clyde	5	A	PC SF	1-1	3500	Steele	Inglis	Morris,A	Raeburn	Morris,D	McBeath	Duncan,T	Slaven	Jennings	Bauld	Archibald	Little
W	29-Mar	Cowdenbeath		H	F	1-1		Brown	Inglis	Morris,A	Raeburn	Morris,D	Collier	Duncan,T	Slaven	Jennings 1	Bauld 1	Archibald	Archibald Henderson (2)
M	03-Apr	Rangers		H	L1	2-1	15000	Brown	Inglis	Moyes 1p	Raeburn	Morris,D	McBeath	Duncan,T	Slaven	Jennings 1	Bauld	Archibald	Reid
S	08-Apr	Dundee Hibernian	6	A	B	0-0		Brown	Morris,A	Miller	Raeburn	Morris,D	Wilson	Duncan,T	Slaven	Jennings	Dawson	Archibald	
M	10-Apr	Third Lanark		A	L1	0-1	12000	Brown	Inglis	Moyes	Raeburn	Morris,D	McBeath	Newman	Bell	Slaven	Archibald	Jordan	Crilley
Th	13-Apr	Alloa Athletic		H	L1	1-0	10000	Steele	Inglis	Morris,A	Raeburn	Morris,D	Collier	Duncan,T	Duncan,J	Jennings 1	Bauld	Archibald	Smith
S	15-Apr	Scottish Junior XI		H	F	1-1	3000	Brown	Inglis	Moyes	Rattray	Morris,D	McBeath	Duncan,T	Duncan,J	Jennings 1	Bauld	Archibald	
M	17-Apr	East of Scotland XI		H	F	1-0	7000	Steele	Barton	Morris,A	Raeburn	McBeath	Raeburn	Duncan,T	Bell	Hunter	McConnachie	Jordan	Cowan
W	19-Apr	Dundee		A	L1	0-1	12000	Brown	Inglis	Moyes	Raeburn	Morris,D	McBeath	Duncan,T	Jennings	Slaven	Archibald	McConnachie	
S	22-Apr	Morton		H	L1	1-0	10000	Brown	Inglis	Morris,A	Raeburn	Morris,D	Collier	Duncan,T	Duncan,J	Jennings 1	Bauld	Archibald	
W	26-Apr	Alloa Athletic		H	PC SF	1-0	3000	Brown	Inglis	Morris,A	Rattray	Morris,D	McBeath	Duncan,T	Slaven	Jennings 2	Bauld	Archibald	Gunn
S	29-Apr	Hamilton Academical		H	L1	1-0	7000	Brown	Inglis	Moyes	Raeburn	Morris,D	Collier	Duncan,T	Duncan,J	Jennings 1	Bauld	Archibald	
Sn	14-May	B 1903 Copenhagen		A	F	1-3	10000	Brown	Morris,A	Inglis	Collier	Morris,D	Raeburn	Barton	Jennings	Slaven	Bauld 1	Archibald	25 ...Nilson 37 Steen 72 Jorgenson 87
Tu	16-May	Copenhagen Select	7	A	F	2-0	8000	Brown	Barton	Morris,A	Raeburn	Morris,D	McBeath	Archibald	Inglis	Jennings 1	Collier 1	Bauld	4, 74
Th	18-May	Copenhagen Select		A	F	1-3	6500	Brown	Barton	Morris,A	Lindsay	Morris,D	Collier	Jennings j45	Raeburn	Slaven	McBeath	Archibald	Inglis u45 1 ... Nilson (2) 49, 70 Jorgensen 80

(4) Lost 14-2 on corners   (5) after extra time   (7) Opponents selected from AB, B1903 and Frem

Manager : James Logan   *(1) Jimmy Brown Benefit*   *(2) Gate receipts £805 excluding tax*   *(3) Bill Collier playing for Scotland at Wrexham*   *(5) after extra time*
(6) Peter Hyde benefit, at Chancelot Park, Leith.   Select team came from Musselburgh, Leith Athletic, Falkirk, Leith Amateurs, Kings Park and Hearts

1922/23 (opposite page) *Manager : James Logan*   *(1) 1921/22 competition*   *(2) Jack Baird Benefit*   *(3) Takings £945 excluding stand and tax*   *(4) match abandoned after 84 minutes due to darkness*
(5) at Tynecastle   *(6) after extra time, won 1-0 on corners*   *(7) Charity Match*   *(8) Wemyss Memorial Hospital match*

Day	Date	Opponents	Note	Venue	Comp	Res.	Att.	1	2	3	4	5	6	7	8	9	10	11	Substitutes, own goals, goal times and opponents' scorers
W	16-Aug	Dundee	1	A	PC F	1-3	15000	Brown	Inglis	Moyes	Raeburn	Morris,D	Collier	Brown,	Miller	Jennings 1	Bauld	Borland	Turner Cowan Troup
S	19-Aug	Falkirk	1	A	L1	1-1	12000	Brown	Barton	Moyes	Raeburn	Morris,D	Collier	Brown,	Miller	Jennings 1	Bauld	Borland	Thomson
W	23-Aug	East Fife	1	H	FC F	2-0		Brown	Barton	Moyes	Raeburn	Morris,D	Collier	Archibald	Miller 1	Jennings 1	McGibbon	Borland	
S	26-Aug	Aberdeen		A	L1	0-1	16000	Brown	Barton	Moyes	Raeburn	Morris,D	Collier	Archibald	Miller	Jennings	Bauld	Borland	Miller
W	30-Aug	Airdrie		A	L1	0-4	6000	Brown	Barton	Moyes	Raeburn	Morris,D	Collier	Archibald	Miller	Jennings	Bauld	Borland	Morris og Reid, A Howieson (2,1p)
S	02-Sep	St Mirren		H	L1	2-1	15000	Brown	Barton	Moyes	Raeburn 1	Morris,D	Collier	Brown,	Miller	Jennings 1	James	Borland	Stevenson
W	06-Sep	Dunfermline Athletic		H	FC 1	4-2	5000	Brown	Barton	Moyes	Raeburn	Morris,D	McBeath	Archibald	Miller 1	Jennings 3	James	Borland	Brown
S	09-Sep	Celtic		A	L1	0-3	15000	Brown	Barton	Morris,A	Raeburn	Morris,D	McBeath	Archibald	Miller	Jennings	James	Borland	Gilchrist Crilley McLean
W	13-Sep	St Andrews University		H	WC 2	7-0		Steele	Barton	Morris,A	Lindsay	Campbell	Collier	Thomson 1	Miller 3	Slaven	James 1	Borland 2	
S	16-Sep	Airdrie		H	L1	0-0	6000	Brown	Barton	Moyes	Raeburn	Morris,D	Collier	Brown,	Miller	Jennings	James	Archibald	
W	20-Sep	Dundee Hibernian		H	PC 2	2-1		Steele	Barton	Morris,A	Lindsay	Campbell	McBeath	Johnstone 1	McGibbon	Slaven	Bauld 1	Borland	Balloch
S	23-Sep	Kilmarnock		A	L1	2-1	7000	Brown	Barton	Moyes	Raeburn	Morris,D	Collier	Archibald	Miller	Jennings	James 1	Borland 1	Brown
W	27-Sep	Dunfermline Athletic	2	A	B	0-1	2900	Steele	Lindsay	Moyes	Campell	Morris,A	McBeath	Thomson	Miller	Slaven	McGibbon	Borland	Clarke
S	30-Sep	Motherwell		H	L1	1-1	7000	Brown	Barton	Moyes 1p	Raeburn	Morris,D	Collier	Archibald	Miller	Jennings	James	Borland	Brown
S	07-Oct	Hearts		A	L1	0-0	25000	Brown	Barton	Moyes	Raeburn	Morris,D	Collier	Archibald	Miller	Jennings	Bauld	Borland	
S	14-Oct	Clyde		H	L1	1-0	8000	Brown	Barton	Moyes	Raeburn	Morris,D	Collier	Archibald	Miller	Jennings 1	Bauld	Borland	Ritchie McColl
S	21-Oct	Hibernian		A	L1	0-2	10000	Brown	Barton	Moyes	Raeburn	Morris,D	Collier	Archibald	Miller	Jennings	Bauld	Borland	Cowan McLean (2)
S	28-Oct	Dundee		A	L1	0-3	8000	Brown	Barton	Moyes	Raeburn	Morris,D	Collier	Thomson	Miller	Jennings	Bauld	Borland	Brown, A. (2) Gourlay McNab
S	04-Nov	Morton		A	L1	0-4	6000	Brown	McDougall	Moyes	Raeburn	Morris,D	Collier	Jennings	Miller	Borland	Bauld	Archibald	Johnstone
S	11-Nov	Third Lanark		H	L1	1-0	6000	Brown	Barton	Moyes	Raeburn	Morris,D	McBeath	Jennings	James 1	Borland	Gilmour	Archibald	
S	18-Nov	Rangers		A	L1	0-1	15000	Brown	Barton	Moyes	Slaven	Morris,D	McBeath	Borland	Raeburn	Jennings	Gilmour	Archibald	
S	25-Nov	Hamilton Academical		A	L1	4-0	5000	Brown	Barton	Moyes	Raeburn	Morris,D	Collier	Thomson	Miller 1	Jennings	Gilmour	Borland	Walls
S	02-Dec	Dundee		A	L1	0-0	18000	Brown	Barton	Moyes	Raeburn	Morris,D	Collier	Thomson	James	Jennings	Gilmour	Archibald	
S	09-Dec	Ayr United		H	L1	2-1	4000	Brown	Barton	Moyes	Raeburn	Morris,D	Collier	Thomson	James	Jennings	Gilmour	Archibald	Walls
S	16-Dec	Albion Rovers		A	L1	0-3	12000	Brown	Barton	Moyes	Raeburn	Morris,D	Collier	Miller	James	McClelland	Gilmour	Archibald	Gibson Kinloch Lambie
S	23-Dec	Partick Thistle		A	L1	0-3	5000	Brown	Barton	Moyes	Raeburn	Morris,D	Collier	Thomson	James	Jennings	Gilmour	Archibald	Cassidy (2) Gilchrist
S	30-Dec	Celtic		H	L1	0-0	15000	Brown	Barton	Moyes	Raeburn	Morris,D	Collier	McKechnie	James	Jennings	Gilmour	Archibald	
M	01-Jan	Falkirk		H	L1	1-1	4600	Brown	Barton	Moyes	Raeburn	Morris,D	Collier	McKechnie	James	Inglis 1	Gilmour	Archibald	Smith
Tu	02-Jan	Aberdeen		H	L1	1-1	8000	Brown	Inglis	Moyes	Raeburn	Morris,D	Collier	Jennings	James	Bauld	Gilmour 1	Archibald	
S	06-Jan	Hibernian		A	L1	1-0	10000	Brown	Inglis	Moyes	Raeburn	Morris,D	Collier	Bell	James	Bauld	Gilmour	Archibald	
S	13-Jan	Morton		H	SC 1	1-0	8000	Brown	Inglis	Moyes	Raeburn	Morris,D	Collier	Bell	James	Gilmour	Bauld 1	Archibald	
S	20-Jan	Clyde		A	L1	0-0	11000	Brown	Inglis	Moyes	Raeburn	Morris,D	Collier	McKechnie	James	Gilmour	Bauld	Borland	
S	27-Jan	Cowdenbeath		H	SC 2	2-0	4000	Brown	Inglis 1p	Moyes	Raeburn	Morris,D	Collier	Bell	James	Bauld 1	Gilmour	Archibald	
S	03-Feb	Hearts		H	L1	2-1	10000	Brown	Inglis	Moyes	Raeburn	Morris,D	Collier	Bell	James	Bauld	Gilmour	Archibald	
W	07-Feb	Kilmarnock		H	L1	1-0	6000	Brown	Inglis	Moyes	Raeburn	Morris,D	Collier	Bell	James	James 1	Gilmour	Archibald	
S	10-Feb	Dunfermline Athletic		A	SC 3	3-0	12900	Brown	Inglis	Moyes	Raeburn	Morris,D	Collier	Bell	McDougall	Bauld	Gilmour 1	Archibald	
W	14-Feb	Ayr United		A	L1	0-2	3000	Brown	Barton	Moyes	Raeburn	Morris,D	Collier	Bell	James	Gilmour	Gilmour	Archibald	Williamson
S	17-Feb	Albion Rovers		H	L1	1-1	5000	Brown	Inglis	Moyes	Raeburn	McBeath	Collier	Bell	James	Gilmour	Gilmour	Archibald	
S	24-Feb	Celtic	3	A	SC 4	0-1	31000	Brown	Inglis	Moyes	Raeburn	Morris,D	Collier	Bell	James	Bauld	Gilmour	Archibald	
W	27-Feb	Alloa Athletic		A	L1	1-0	4600	Brown	McDougall	Moyes	Raeburn	Lindsay	Collier	Bell	Miller	Jennings 1	Gilmour	Archibald	Cunningham McKenzie
S	03-Mar	Third Lanark		A	L1	1-2	8000	Brown	McDougall	Morris,A	Raeburn	Morris,D	Collier	Bell	Miller	Jennings	James 1	Archibald	Christie
S	10-Mar	Rangers		H	L1	2-0	10000	Brown	Inglis	Moyes	Raeburn	Morris,D	Collier	Bell	Miller 1	Jennings	James	Archibald	Moyes og
S	17-Mar	Hamilton Academical		A	L1	1-1	4000	Brown	Inglis	Moyes	Raeburn	Morris,D	Collier	Bell	Miller	Jennings 1	James 1	Archibald	
S	24-Mar	Motherwell		A	L1	0-2	4000	Brown	Inglis	Moyes	Raeburn	Morris,D	Collier	Bell	Miller	Jennings	James	Borland	Walker, F Hillhouse
M	02-Apr	Hibernian		H	L1	2-2	4000	Brown	Inglis	Moyes	Raeburn	Morris,D	McBeath	Bell	Miller	Jennings 1	James 1	Borland	
S	07-Apr	St Mirren		H	L1	1-1	9000	Brown	Barton	Moyes	Raeburn	Morris,D	Collier 1	Bell	Miller	Jennings	James 1	Bauld	Kirkwood
W	11-Apr	East Fife		A	L1	0-0		Brown	Inglis	Moyes	Raeburn	Morris,D	Collier	James	Miller	Jennings	Gilmour	Archibald	Ferguson (2)
S	14-Apr	Partick Thistle	4	H	FC SF	1-0	6000	Brown	Inglis	Moyes	Raeburn	Morris,D	Collier	Bell 1	Miller	Jennings	James	Archibald	Ritchie Dunn
M	16-Apr	Hibernian		H	L1	2-0		Brown	Barton	Moyes	Barton	Morris,D	Collier	Bell	Miller	Jennings	James	Archibald	Walker
W	18-Apr	Falkirk		A	DC SF	0-1		Brown	Inglis	Moyes	Inglis	Morris,D	Collier	Bell	Miller	Jennings	James	Archibald	
S	21-Apr	Cowdenbeath	5	N	DC F	0-5		Brown	Inglis	Morris,A	Lindsay	Morris,D	McBeath	Bell	Miller	Jennings	Bauld	Archibald	
W	25-Apr	East Fife		A	WC SF	4-0		Brown	Barton	Moyes	McBeath	Morris,D	Collier 1	Bell	Miller 1	Slaven	James 1	Archibald	Hunter, John
S	28-Apr	Morton		H	FC SF	1-1		Brown	Barton	Moyes	McBeath	Morris,D	Collier	Bell	Miller 1	Jennings 1	James	Archibald	Devine (2) Leonard Sinclair Birrell
M	30-Apr	Cowdenbeath	6	A	FC F	0-0		Brown	Barton	Moyes	McBeath	Morris,D	McBeath	Bell	Miller	Jennings 1	James	Archibald	French
S	05-May	East Fife	7	H	F	2-0	4000	Mathieson	Barton	Moyes	Slaven	Morris,D	Collier	Jennings	Miller 2	Slaven	James	Archibald	
S	12-May	East Fife	8	A	F	1-2		Mathieson	Barton	Moyes	Slaven	Morris,D	Collier	Jennings 1	Miller	Newman	James	Archibald	Weir (2)

Substitutes, own goals, goal times and opponents' scorers

own goal 1 *pen*

Day	Date	Opponents	Note	Venue	Comp	Res.	Att.	1	2	3	4	5	6	7	8	9	10	11	Scorers
Sn	08-Jul	Real Vigo	1	A	F	3-1		Brown	Barton	McDougall	Cowie	Morris	Collier	Bell	Miller	Jennings 1p	James 1	Hilley	
W	11-Jul	Real Vigo	1	A	F	1-0		Brown	Inglis	McDougall	Barton	Morris	Collier	Bell 1	Ritchie	Jennings	James 1	Hilley x	
Sn	15-Jul	CD Porteno	1	A	F	4-0		Brown	Inglis	McDougall	Barton	Morris 1	Collier	Ritchie	Miller	Jennings 2	James 1	Hilley	
W	18-Jul	Gran Canaria	1	A	F	5-1		Brown	Barton	McDougall	Cowie	Morris	Collier	Ritchie	Miller	Jennings 5	James 1	Bell	
F	20-Jul	C Victoria O	1	A	F	2-0		Brown	Inglis	McDougall	Cowie	Morris	Collier	Bell	Ritchie	Jennings 1	James 1	Hilley	
Sn	22-Jul	Marino	1	A	F	2-1		Brown	Inglis	McDougall	Barton	Morris	Collier	Bell	Miller 1	Jennings 1	James 1	Hilley	
S	18-Aug	Dundee		H	L1	3-0	18000	Brown	Inglis 1p	Moyes	Raeburn	Morris	Collier	Bell	Miller	Jennings 1	James	Archibald	McLure Johnstone
W	22-Aug	Rosslyn Juniors	2	H	F	2-0		Brown	Lumsden	Moyes	Raeburn	McBeath	Todd	Bell	Miller 1	Burns	James	Hilley	
S	25-Aug	Clyde		A	L1	1-2	5000	Mathieson	Inglis	Moyes	Raeburn	McBeath	Collier	Bell	Newman 1	Miller	James	Archibald	
W	29-Aug	Dunfermline Athletic		A	WC 1	2-0	3500	Mathieson	Barton	Moyes	Raeburn	McBeath	Collier	Jennings	Miller	Slaven	James 2	Archibald	
S	01-Sep	Clydebank		H	L1	1-0	6000	Brown	Inglis	Moyes	Raeburn	Morris	Collier	Bell	Miller	Jennings 1	James	Archibald	
S	08-Sep	Hamilton Academical		A	L1	2-0	5000	Brown	Barton	Moyes	Raeburn	Morris	Collier	Bell	Miller	Jennings 2	James	Archibald	
W	12-Sep	Cowdenbeath		A	PC SF	1-0	4000	Brown	Inglis	Moyes	Raeburn	Morris	Collier	Bell	Miller	Jennings 1	James 1	Hilley	
S	15-Sep	Queen's Park		A	L1	1-2	10000	Brown	Inglis	Moyes	Raeburn	Morris	Collier	Bell	Miller 1	Jennings	James 1	Archibald	McAlpine (2)
S	22-Sep	Partick Thistle		H	L1	4-1	10000	Brown	Barton	Moyes	Raeburn 1	Morris	Collier	Bell	Miller 1	Jennings 2	James 1	Archibald	Lambie
S	29-Sep	Morton		A	L1	4-0	7000	Brown	Barton	Moyes	Raeburn	Morris	Collier 2	Bell	Miller 1	Jennings 2	James	Archibald	
M	01-Oct	Leicester City		H	B	5-1	6000	Brown	Inglis	Moyes	Barton	Morris	Collier	Bell	Miller 1	Hilley 1	James 1	Archibald 2	Chandler
S	06-Oct	Hibernian		A	L1	0-4	16000	Brown	Inglis	Moyes	Raeburn	Morris	Collier	Bell	Miller	Jennings	James	Archibald	McColl (2) Halligan Ritchie
S	13-Oct	Third Lanark		H	L1	6-1	7000	Brown	Inglis	Moyes	Raeburn	Morris	Collier	Bell	Miller 1	Jennings 4	James 1	Archibald 1	Reid
S	20-Oct	Celtic		A	L1	0-0	10000	Brown	Barton	Moyes	Raeburn	Morris	Collier	Bell	Miller	Jennings	James 1	Archibald	
S	27-Oct	Ayr United		H	L1	4-1	7000	Brown	Inglis	Moyes	Raeburn	Morris	Collier	Bell	Miller 1	Jennings 2	James 1	Archibald	Cunningham
S	03-Nov	St Mirren		A	L1	1-1	7000	Brown	Inglis	Moyes	Raeburn	McBeath	Collier	Bell	Miller 1	Jennings 1	James 1	Archibald	Merrie
S	10-Nov	Falkirk		H	L1	3-0	7000	Brown	Inglis 1p	Moyes	Raeburn	Morris	Collier	Bell	Miller 1	Jennings 1	James x 1	Archibald	Smith
S	17-Nov	Kilmarnock		A	L1	2-1	5000	Brown	Inglis 1p	Moyes	Raeburn	Morris	Collier	Bell	Miller	Jennings 1	Hilley	Archibald	McLean
S	24-Nov	Hearts		H	L1	1-1	15000	Brown	Inglis	Moyes	Raeburn	Morris	Collier	Bell	Miller 1	Jennings	Hilley	Archibald	Rankine
S	01-Dec	Aberdeen		A	L1	0-1	11000	Brown	Inglis	Moyes	Raeburn	Morris	Collier	Bell	Miller	Jennings	James	Archibald	
S	08-Dec	Airdrie		H	L1	2-0	17000	Brown	Inglis	Moyes	Raeburn	Morris	McBeath	Bell	Miller	Jennings 2	James	Archibald	Henderson
S	15-Dec	Rangers		H	L1	0-1	20000	Brown	Inglis	Moyes	Raeburn	Morris	McBeath	Bell	Miller	Jennings	James	Archibald 1	Ferguson
S	22-Dec	Motherwell		A	L1	3-1	6000	Brown	Inglis	Moyes	Raeburn	Morris	Slaven	Bell	Miller	Jennings 2	James 1	Archibald 1	Purves (2) Wilson Mathieson og
Tu	25-Dec	Berwick Rangers		A	F	3-4	2000	Mathieson	Barton	Moyes	Raeburn	Morris	McBeath	Ritchie 1	Miller	Slaven	James	Archibald	Russell
S	29-Dec	Airdrie		A	L1	0-1	6000	Mathieson	Inglis	Moyes	Raeburn	Morris	McBeath	Bell	Miller	Jennings	James	Archibald	Thomson
Tu	01-Jan	Clyde		H	L1	2-1	5000	Brown	Inglis	Moyes	Raeburn	Morris	McBeath	Bell	Miller	Jennings 2	James 1	Ritchie	Anderson (2)
W	02-Jan	Clydebank		A	L1	1-2	4000	Brown	Inglis	Moyes	Raeburn	Morris	Collier	Bell	Miller	Jennings 1	James	Archibald	Duncan
S	05-Jan	Dundee		A	L1	1-1	18000	Brown	Inglis	Moyes	Raeburn	Morris	Collier	Slaven	Miller	Jennings 1	James	Archibald	Ritchie McColl
S	12-Jan	Hibernian		H	L1	0-2	10000	Mathieson	Inglis	Moyes	Raeburn	Morris	McBeath	Bell	Miller	Jennings	James	Archibald	Gibson Hair
S	19-Jan	Partick Thistle		A	L1	0-2	8000	Mathieson	Inglis	Moyes	Raeburn	Morris	Collier	Bell	Miller	Jennings	James	Archibald	
S	26-Jan	Broxburn United		H	SC 1	3-0	6000	Mathieson	Barton	Barton	Raeburn	Morris	Collier	Bell	Miller 2	Jennings 1	Hilley	Archibald	Thomson
S	02-Feb	Hamilton Academical		H	L1	0-1	8000	Mathieson	Inglis	Moyes	Raeburn	Morris	McBeath	Bell	Miller	Jennings	James	Archibald	
S	09-Feb	Dundee		A	SC 2	0-0	27200	Brown	Inglis	Moyes	Raeburn	Morris	Hilley	Bell	Miller	Jennings	James	Archibald	
W	13-Feb	Dundee		H	SC 2r	1-0	15000	Brown	Inglis	Moyes	Raeburn	Morris	Hilley	Bell 1	Miller	Jennings	James 1	Archibald	
S	16-Feb	Aberdeen		H	L1	0-3	8000	Mathieson	Inglis	Moyes	Raeburn	Morris	Collier	Bell	Miller	Slaven	James	Archibald	Puddefoot Hunter Bryce
W	20-Feb	Falkirk		A	L1	0-3	4000	Mathieson	Barton	Moyes	Raeburn	Morris	Collier	ER	Miller	Jennings	James 1	Archibald	Young
S	23-Feb	St Bernards		H	SC 3	1-1	5500	Brown	Inglis	Barton	Raeburn	Morris	Hilley	Bell	Miller	Slaven	James	Archibald	Ferguson
W	27-Feb	Motherwell		H	L1	1-1	5000	Brown	Barton	McBeath	Raeburn	Slaven	Collier	Bell	Miller	Jennings	James	Ritchie	Green
S	01-Mar	Hearts	8	A	L1	1-1	16000	Mathieson	Barton	Moyes	Raeburn	Slaven	McBeath	Bell	Miller	Jennings 2	James 1	Archibald 1	McKenna
S	08-Mar	Third Lanark		A	L1	1-1	4000	Mathieson	Barton	Moyes	Raeburn	Morris	Slaven	Bell	Miller	Jennings 1	James 1	Archibald	
S	15-Mar	Queen's Park		H	L1	2-0	5000	Mathieson	Barton	Moyes	Raeburn	Morris 1	Slaven	Bell	Miller	Morris 1	James 1	Ritchie	
S	22-Mar	Celtic		H	L1	1-0	5000	Mathieson	Barton	Moyes	Raeburn	Morris	Collier	Bell	Miller	Jennings 1	James	Archibald	
S	29-Mar	Rangers		A	L1	3-0	10000	Mathieson	Barton	Moyes	Raeburn	Morris	Slaven	Bell	Miller	Jennings 1	Hilley	Archibald	
W	02-Apr	Dunfermline Athletic		A	FC 1	1-0		Mathieson	Barton	Moyes	Raeburn	Morris	Slaven	Bell	Miller 2	Jennings 1	James	Archibald	
S	05-Apr	Kilmarnock		H	L1	4-1	7000	Mathieson	Barton	Moyes 1p	Raeburn	Morris	Slaven	Bell	Miller 2	Hilley	James 1	Ritchie	Gray
M	07-Apr	Dundee		H	PC F	1-0		Mathieson	Barton	Moyes	Raeburn	Morris	Slaven	Bell	Hilley	Hilley	James 1	Archibald	
Th	10-Apr	East Fife	5	A	B	1-0		Mathieson	Inglis	Inglis	Harper	Hilley	Collier	Bell	Newton	Miller 1	James	Cowan	
W	12-Apr	Ayr United		A	L1	0-1	2000	Mathieson	Slaven	Moyes	Raeburn	Morris	Collier	Ritchie	Bell	Roberts 1	James	Archibald	Cunningham
W	16-Apr	Lochgelly United		H	FC SF	0-1		Brown	Inglis	Hilley	Raeburn	Morris	Slaven	Bell	Miller	Slaven	Hilley	Ritchie	
S	19-Apr	Morton		A	L1	0-2	4000	Mathieson	Barton	Hilley	Raeburn	Morris	Slaven	Bell	Hilley	Slaven	Hilley	Ritchie	Blair Brown
M	21-Apr	St Rochs	6	A	F	4-2		Mathieson	Inglis	Hilley	Raeburn	Williams	Collier 1	Bell	Wright	Ritchie 1	James 1	Ritchie 1	
W	23-Apr	Cowdenbeath		A	FC F	1-1		Mathieson	Barton	Barton	Raeburn	Slaven	Collier	Bell	Hilley	Miller	James 1	Miller	Wilson
S	26-Apr	St Mirren		H	L1	1-1	6000	Mathieson	Inglis	Moyes	Raeburn	Morris 1	Slaven	Bell	Miller	Jennings	James 1	Turner	Wood
M	28-Apr	Hearts		A	DC SF	2-1	5000	Mathieson	Barton	Moyes	Raeburn	Morris 1	Slaven	Bell	Miller	Jennings 1	James	Archibald	Green
W	30-Apr	Hibernian		A	DC F	1-0	4000	Mathieson	Inglis	Hilley	Raeburn	Morris 1	Slaven	Bell	Miller 1	Jennings 1	James	Archibald	
S	03-May	East Fife	7	N	FCC SF	7-2		Mathieson	Barton	Barton	Raeburn	Morris	Hilley 2	Bell 2	Miller 1	Jennings 1	James 1	Turner	Cahill Edgar
W				H	FCC SF	1-0		Mathieson	Inglis	Barton	Raeburn	Morris 1	Slaven	Bell 1	Miller 1	Jennings 1	James 1	Ritchie	
S	10-May	Cowdenbeath		A	FCC F	0-2		Mathieson	Barton	Hilley	Raeburn	Morris	Caldwell	Ritchie	Miller	Jennings 1	James	Turner	Leonard Devlin

Column header (rotated): *Substitutes, own goals, goal times and opponents' scorers*

Day	Date	Opponents	Note	Venue	Comp	Res.	Att.	1	2	3	4	5	6	7	8	9	10	11	Substitutes, own goals, goal times and opponents' scorers
S	16-Aug	Rangers	1	A	L1	0-3	15000	Mathieson	Barton	Moyes	Raeburn	Morris	Slaven	Bell	Miller	Jennings	James	Ritchie	Henderson (3)
M	18-Aug	Newtongrange Star		A	F	5-1		Mathieson	Barton	McBride	Raeburn	Morris	Chapman	Bell 1	Miller	Jennings 3	James	Hilley 1	Elliott
W	20-Aug	Dunfermline Athletic		A	PC1	4-0		Mathieson	McBride	Moyes	Cowie	Morris	Chapman	Bell	Miller 3	Jennings 1	Hilley	Turner	
S	23-Aug	Queen's Park		H	L1	1-1	10000	Mathieson	Barton	Moyes	Raeburn	Morris	Slaven	Bell	Miller 1	Jennings	James	Ritchie	Russell
W	27-Aug	Cowdenbeath	2	A	FCF	1-3		Mathieson	McBride	Moyes	Raeburn	Morris	Slaven	Bell	Miller	Jennings	James	Hilley 1p	Dorrans Devlin (2)
S	30-Aug	Hamilton Academical		A	L1	0-1	14000	Mathieson	McBride	Moyes	Raeburn	Morris	Slaven	Bell	Miller	Jennings	James	Hilley	Brown
W	03-Sep	Dundee		H	PC SF	2-0	5000	Mathieson	Barton	Moyes 1p	Raeburn	Morris	Hilley	Ritchie	Miller	Jennings 1	James	Bell	
S	06-Sep	Falkirk		H	L1	2-0	9000	Mathieson	Barton	Moyes	Raeburn	Morris	Hilley	Ritchie	Miller	Jennings 2	James	Bell	
S	13-Sep	Partick Thistle		A	L1	0-0	14000	Mathieson	Barton	Moyes	Raeburn	Morris	Hilley	Ritchie	Miller	Jennings	James	Bell	
W	17-Sep	St Johnstone		H	PC F	3-2	3000	Mathieson	Barton	Moyes	Raeburn	Morris	Chapman	Ritchie	Miller 1	Jennings 1	James 1	Bell	Fleming (2)
S	20-Sep	Hibernian		H	L1	1-3	14000	Mathieson	Barton	Moyes	Raeburn	Morris	Hilley	Ritchie	Miller	Jennings 1	James	Bell	Dunn McColl Halligan
W	24-Sep	Darlington	3	A	B	4-6		Mathieson	Barton	Moyes	Newbould 1	Morris	Hilley	Bell 1	Deuchars	Jennings 1	James 1	Turner	
S	27-Sep	Third Lanark		A	L1	4-2	5000	Mathieson	Barton	Moyes	Raeburn 1	Morris	Hilley	Bell	Miller 1	Jennings	James 1	Ritchie 1	McInally Walker
M	29-Sep	Ashfield		A	F	4-1	2000	Mathieson	McBride	Moyes	Chaplin	Morris	Hilley	Ritchie	Russell 4	Jennings	James	Turner	
S	04-Oct	Ayr United		H	L1	2-1	8000	Mathieson	Barton	Moyes	Raeburn	Morris	Hilley	Ritchie	Miller 1	Jennings	James 1	Bell	Cunningham
M	06-Oct	Cowdenbeath		H	WC1	1-1	4000	Mathieson	McBride	Moyes	Cowie	Morris	Chapman	Ritchie	Hilley	Jennings	James	Bell 1	Pullar
S	11-Oct	Airdrie		A	L1	0-1	6000	Mathieson	Barton	Moyes	Raeburn	Morris	Chapman	Ritchie	Hilley	Slaven	James	Bell	McPhail
S	18-Oct	Cowdenbeath		H	L1	3-1	15000	Mathieson	Barton	Moyes	Raeburn	Morris	Hilley	Ritchie	Miller 1	Jennings 1	James 1	Bell	Leonard
S	25-Oct	St Johnstone		A	L1	2-4	10000	Mathieson	Barton	Moyes	Raeburn	Morris 1	Slaven	Bell	Miller	Jennings 1	James	Turner	Walker Hart Howieson (2)
S	01-Nov	Hearts		H	L1	0-1	10000	Mathieson	Barton	Moyes	Raeburn	Morris	Slaven	Bell	Miller	Jennings	James	Turner	
S	08-Nov	St Mirren		A	L1	0-3	9000	Mathieson	Barton	Moyes	Raeburn	Morris	Slaven	Bell	Deuchars	Jennings	James	Ritchie	McCrae Gillies Thomson
S	15-Nov	Kilmarnock		H	L1	3-1	7000	Mathieson	Barton	Moyes	Raeburn	Morris 1	Hilley	Taylor	Miller	Jennings	James 2	Ritchie	Brown
S	22-Nov	Morton		H	L1	2-0	3000	Mathieson	Barton	Moyes	Raeburn	Morris	Taylor	Bell	Miller	Jennings 2	James	Ritchie	
S	29-Nov	Dundee		A	L1	0-2	10000	Mathieson	Barton	Moyes	Cowie	Morris	Hilley	Bell	Miller	Jennings	James	Ritchie	Halliday McDonald
S	06-Dec	Aberdeen		H	L1	2-2	8000	Mathieson	Innes	Moyes	Raeburn	Morris 1	Hilley	Bell	Miller	Jennings	James 1	Ritchie	Cosgrove Jackson, W.
S	13-Dec	Motherwell		A	L1	1-2	4000	McKenzie	Barton	Moyes	Marchbanks	Morris	Chapman	Bell	Neish	Miller 1	James	Ritchie	Ferguson Ferrier
S	20-Dec	Kilmarnock		A	L1	0-3	7000	Mathieson	Innes	Moyes	Marchbanks	Morris	Chapman	Bell	Neish	Miller	James	Ritchie	Smith Lindsay (2)
Th	25-Dec	Berwick Rangers		A	F	6-1		Mathieson	Innes	Moyes	Cowie	Marchbanks	Slaven	Taylor	Miller 1	Chapman 2	James	Hilley 3	Borthwick
S	27-Dec	Celtic		H	L1	2-2	8000	Mathieson	Barton	Moyes	Raeburn	Morris	Chapman	Bell	Taylor	Slaven	James 1	Turner 1	Fleming (2)
Th	01-Jan	Cowdenbeath		A	L1	1-1	6000	Mathieson	Barton	Moyes	Raeburn	Morris	Chapman	Bell	Hilley	Miller 1	James	Turner	Wilson
S	03-Jan	Hamilton Academical		A	L1	0-1	6000	Mathieson	Barton	Moyes	Raeburn	Morris	Chapman	Bell	Hilley	Miller	James	Turner	Brown
S	05-Jan	Dundee		H	L1	4-3	4000	Mathieson	Barton	Moyes	Hilley	Marchbanks	Chapman	Bell	Neish	Miller 2	James 1	Ritchie 1	McLean Hunter McDonald
S	10-Jan	Hearts		A	L1	2-2	12000	Mathieson	Barton	Moyes	Hilley	Morris	Chapman	Bell	Neish 1	Miller	James 1	Ritchie	McMillan (2)
S	17-Jan	St Johnstone		H	L1	0-0	8000	Mathieson	Barton	Moyes	Hilley	Marchbanks	Chapman	Bell	Neish	Jennings	James	Turner	
S	24-Jan	Clackmannan	4	H	SC1	3-0	5600	Mathieson	Barton	Moyes	Slaven	Morris	Chapman 1	Bell	Neish 1	Jennings	James 1	Turner	
S	31-Jan	Falkirk		A	L1	1-1	8000	Mathieson	Barton	Moyes	Slaven	Morris	Chapman	Bell	Neish	Jennings 1	James	Ritchie	Puddefoot
S	07-Feb	Bo'ness		H	SC2	0-0	10000	Mathieson	Barton	Moyes	Raeburn	Marchbanks	Chapman	Bell	Hilley	Jennings	James	Ritchie	
W	11-Feb	Bo'ness		A	SC2r	3-1	6000	Mathieson	Barton	Moyes	Raeburn	Morris	Hilley	Bell	Deuchars	Jennings 2	James 1	Turner	Kelly
S	14-Feb	Motherwell	5	H	L1	1-0	4000	Mathieson	Barton	Moyes	Marchbanks	Morris	Chapman	Bell 1	Ritchie	Jennings	James	Marshall	
S	18-Feb	St Mirren		H	L1	2-0	3000	Mathieson	Barton	Moyes	Raeburn	Morris	Hilley	Bell	Ritchie	Jennings 1	James 1	Marshall	
S	21-Feb	Hamilton Academical	6	A	SC3	0-1	14500	Mathieson	Barton	Moyes	Raeburn	Morris	Miller J	Bell	Ritchie	Jennings	James	Turner	Moffat
W	25-Feb	Hibernian		A	L1	0-3	8000	Mathieson	Barton	Moyes	Raeburn	Morris	Hilley	Bell	Ritchie	Jennings	James	Marshall	Dunn (2) McColl
S	28-Feb	Aberdeen		A	L1	3-2	6000	Mathieson	Barton	Moyes	Chapman	Morris	Miller J 1	Bell	Ritchie 1	Jennings 1	Deuchars	Marshall	Jackson, W. Perie
S	07-Mar	Third Lanark		H	L1	2-0	8000	Mathieson	Barton	Moyes	Raeburn	Morris	Miller J	Bell	Ritchie 1	Chapman	James 1	Marshall	
S	14-Mar	Ayr United		A	L1	1-3	4000	Mathieson	Barton	Moyes	Raeburn	Morris	Miller J	Bell	Ritchie 1	Jennings	James	Marshall	Tolland McKenzie Brae
S	21-Mar	Partick Thistle		H	L1	5-1	5000	Mathieson	Barton 1	Moyes 1p	Raeburn	Morris	Miller J 1	Bell	Ritchie	Deuchars	James 1	Marshall 1	Grove
W	25-Mar	Rangers		A	L1	0-4	10000	Mathieson	Barton	Moyes	Raeburn	Morris	Miller J	Bell	Ritchie	Deuchars	James	Marshall	Archibald Henderson (3)
S	28-Mar	Celtic		A	L1	0-2	6000	Mathieson	Barton	Moyes	Raeburn	Morris	Miller J	Bell	Ritchie	Deuchars	James	Turner	McGrory Thomson
M	06-Apr	Darlington	7	H	B	3-0		Mathieson	Innes	Moyes	Hilley 1	Morris	Miller J	Cowie 1	Ritchie 1	James	Neish	Turner	
W	08-Apr	Cowdenbeath		A	WC1r	0-2		Mathieson	Barton	Moyes	Raeburn	Morris	Miller J	Bell	Ritchie	Neish	James	Turner	Pullar Devlin
S	11-Apr	Cowdenbeath		H	L1	0-2	6000	Mathieson	Innes	Moyes	Raeburn	Morris	Miller J	Bell	Ritchie	Neish	James	Marshall	McPhail Gallacher
W	15-Apr	Cowdenbeath	8	H	FC SF	0-0		Mathieson	Barton	Moyes	Raeburn	Morris	Miller J	Bell	Cowie	Deuchars	James	Neish	
S	18-Apr	Morton		A	L1	3-2	3000	Mathieson	Barton	Moyes	Raeburn	Morris	Miller J	Ritchie	Neish	Slaven 1	James	Marshall 2	Brown Orr
M	20-Apr	Hearts		H	L1	0-1	7000	Mathieson	Innes	Moyes	Raeburn	Morris	Miller J	Taylor	Neish	Slaven	James	Marshall	McMillan
Th	23-Apr	East Fife		A	DC SF	0-1	3000	Mathieson	McDougall	Moyes	Raeburn	Pitcairn	Chapman	Taylor	Ritchie	Slaven	James	Neish	
S	25-Apr	Queen's Park		H	FC F	0-2	12000	Mathieson	Barton	Moyes	Raeburn	Marchbanks	Miller J	Ritchie	Neish	Scott	James	Marshall	Crawford Nicholson
Th	30-Apr	Carlisle United		A	B	3-1		Mathieson	Barton	Moyes	Neish	Pitcairn	Miller J	Ritchie	Harris 1	Slaven 1	James	Bell 1	
S	02-May	East Fife	9	H	C	1-3		Mathieson	McDougall	Moyes	Neish	Pitcairn	Miller J	Ritchie	Scott	Slaven	James	Turner 1	Weir (2) Barrett

1923/1924 (previous page). Manager : James Logan. (1) in Gran Canaria (2) Benefit match for Rosslyn Juniors (3) Bill Collier Benefit (4) takings more than £70 (5) McPherson Benefit (6) Benefit for Langbank Home (7) at Tynecastle ; receipts £125 (8) David Moyes playing for Scotland v Ireland

1924/1925 (this page) Manager : James Logan. Goals could be scored direct from corner kicks ; the offside law changed, with one less defender required to keep a player onside. (1) Opening of Victoria Park (2) 1923/24 final (3) Benefit for Hugh Dickson (4) Receipts £230 (5) Dave Morris playing for Scotland v Wales (6) Receipts £600 (7) Benefit for David Moyes (8) won 3-2 on corners (9) West Fife Charity Cup semi final

Day	Date	Opponents	Note	Venue	Comp	Res	Att	1	2	3	4	5	6	7	8	9	10	11	Substitutes, own goals, goal times and opponents' scorers
S	15-Aug	Dundee United		H	L1	4-2	12000	Mathieson	Barton	Moyes	Frame	Morris 1	Miller	Buchanan	Ritchie 2	Scott 1	Dorrans	Bell	Howieson (2)
W	19-Aug	Rosslyn Juniors		A	F	2-1	800	Brown	Neish	McDonald	Cairney	Pitcairn	Cairns	Grant	Deuchars 1	Watson	Dunsire 1	Turner	Kay
S	22-Aug	Queens Park		A	L1	0-4	9000	Mathieson	Barton	Moyes	Pitcairn	Morris	Miller	Buchanan	Ritchie	Scott	James	Bell	Barr (2) McAlpine (2)
W	28-Aug	Cowdenbeath		A	FC SF	2-4	1500	Mathieson	Frame	Miller	Deuchars	Pitcairn	Cairns	Bell	Ritchie	Dorrans	James	Grant 1	Leonard Letham Smith Rankine, A
S	29-Aug	Partick Thistle		H	L1	1-1	6000	Mathieson	Miller	Moyes	Frame	Morris	Miller	Bell	Ritchie	Scott 1	James	Grant	Hair
W	02-Sep	East Fife		A	WC	4-3	2000	Mathieson	Miller	Moyes	Deuchars 1	Pitcairn	Cairns	Bell	Ritchie 1	Buchanan 2	Dorrans	Grant 1	Giblin Wilson (2)
S	05-Sep	Hamilton Academical		A	L1	1-3	6000	Mathieson	Frame	Moyes	Deuchars	Morris	Cairns	Bell	Ritchie 1	Scott	Dorrans	Grant	Thomson (2) Gibson
S	12-Sep	Airdrie		H	L1	2-1	9000	Mathieson	Frame	Moyes	Deuchars	Morris	Miller	Ritchie 1	Dorrans	Scott 1	James	Bell	McPhail
S	19-Sep	Falkirk		A	L1	0-3	10000	Mathieson	Frame	Moyes	Deuchars	Morris	Miller	Ritchie	Dorrans	Scott	James	Bell	Mulhall Hunter Paterson
S	26-Sep	Hibernian		H	L1	1-0	8000	Mathieson	Frame	Moyes 1p	Deuchars	Morris	Miller	Grant	Ritchie	Scott	Dorrans	Bell	
W	30-Sep	Lochgelly		H	PC 1	0-2	1500	Mathieson	Neish	Cairns	Deuchars	Pitcairn	Miller X88	Buchanan	Grant	Scott	Dunsire	Turner	Miller McNeil, Jas
S	03-Oct	Morton		A	L1	0-1	5000	Mathieson	Slater	McDougall	Deuchars	Morris	Miller	Bell	Dorrans	Scott	Ritchie	Turner	Graham
M	05-Oct	Newcastle United	1	H	B	1-6	3000	Mathieson	Frame	Moyes	Deuchars	Morris	Cairns	Bell	Ritchie	Neish 1	Dorrans	Dunsire	Clark (3) Cowan McDonald Mitchell
S	10-Oct	Dundee		H	L1	1-0	6000	Mathieson	Frame	Moyes	Deuchars	Morris	Miller	Bell	Dorrans 1	Scott	Miller	Ritchie	
S	17-Oct	Cowdenbeath		A	L1	1-2	8000	Mathieson	Frame	Moyes	Grant	Morris	Miller	Bell	Dorrans 1	Deuchars	Ritchie	Cairns	Devlin Letham
S	24-Oct	Clydebank		A	L1	3-2	5000	Mathieson	Frame	Moyes	Deuchars	Morris	Miller	Bell	Dorrans 1	Neish 2	Ritchie	Cairns	Fleming Smith
S	31-Oct	Rangers		H	L1	1-0	10000	Mathieson	Frame	Moyes	Deuchars	Morris	Miller	Bell	Dorrans	Neish 1	Ritchie	Cairns	
S	07-Nov	Motherwell		A	L1	0-5	4000	Mathieson	Frame	Moyes	Deuchars	Morris	Miller	Bell	Dorrans	Neish	Ritchie	Cairns	McGrath McFadyen (2) Ferrier (2)
S	14-Nov	Celtic		H	L1	1-2	10000	Mathieson	Frame	Moyes	Deuchars	Morris	Miller	Bell	Dorrans	Grant 1	Curley	Ritchie	McGrory (2)
S	21-Nov	Kilmarnock		A	L1	0-3	3000	Mathieson	Frame	Moyes	Miller	Morris	Cairns	Bell	Neish	Grant	Curley	Ritchie	Smith Weir (2)
S	28-Nov	Aberdeen		H	L1	0-1	6000	Mathieson	Curley	Moyes	Grant	Morris	Miller	Bell	Ritchie	Brown	Dorrans	Turner	Bruce. R.
S	05-Dec	St Johnstone		A	L1	1-3	5000	Mathieson	Frame	Moyes	Deuchars	Morris	Miller	Ritchie	Deuchars	Brown	Curley	Turner	Swallow og 1 / Swallow McLean Black
S	12-Dec	Motherwell		H	L1	2-1	4000	Mathieson	Frame	Moyes	Grant	Morris	Cairns	Bell	Dorrans	Brown 2	Curley	Ritchie	McFadyen
S	19-Dec	Partick Thistle		A	L1	1-2	6000	Mathieson	Frame	Moyes	Deuchars	Morris	Cairns	Bell	Dorrans	Brown 2	Curley	Turner	Ness Grove
S	26-Dec	Kilmarnock		H	L1	4-5	3000	Mathieson	Frame	Moyes 1p	Deuchars	Marchbanks	Miller	Reay	Ritchie 1	Brown 1	Allison 2	Bell	Weir (2) Smith Walker Cunningham
F	01-Jan	Cowdenbeath		H	L1	2-1	10000	Mathieson	Frame	Moyes	Deuchars	Marchbanks 1	Miller	Reay	Ritchie 1	Brown 1	Allison	Bell	Devlin
S	02-Jan	Dundee		A	L1	1-1	12000	Mathieson	Frame	Moyes	Deuchars	Marchbanks	Cairns	Reay	Dorrans	Brown 1	Allison	Bell	Campbell
M	04-Jan	Hearts		H	L1	1-3	10000	Mathieson	Frame	Moyes	Deuchars	Marchbanks	Miller	Reay	Curley	Brown 1	Allison	Bell	Slaven Dand Murray
S	09-Jan	Celtic		A	L1	0-1	10000	Mathieson	Frame	Miller	Deuchars	Marchbanks	Cairns	Reay	Deuchars	Deuchars	Allison	Bell	McStay, W.pen
S	16-Jan	Morton		H	L1	3-0	5000	Mathieson	Frame	Moyes	Deuchars	Marchbanks	Miller	Reay	Grant	Brown 2	Allison 2	Bell	
S	23-Jan	Ayr United		H	SC 1	3-1	5200	Mathieson	Frame	Moyes	Deuchars	Marchbanks	Miller	Reay	Grant	Brown 2	Allison 1	Bell	Kilpatrick
S	30-Jan	St Mirren		A	L1	3-0	8000	Mathieson	Frame	Moyes	Deuchars	Marchbanks	Miller	Reay	Grant	Brown 3	Allison	Bell	
S	06-Feb	Morton	2	A	SC 2	1-3	5000	Mathieson	Frame	Moyes	Deuchars	Marchbanks	Miller	Reay	Grant 1	Brown x 1	Allison 1	Bell	Hamilton, J. pen Cunningham Fleming (2)
W	10-Feb	St Johnstone		H	L1	2-2	5000	King	Frame	Moyes	Deuchars	Pitcairn	Miller 1	Reay	Grant	Brown	Allison	Bell	Hart Black
S	13-Feb	Rangers		A	L1	2-4	15000	Mathieson	Frame	Moyes 1p	Deuchars	Marchbanks	Miller	Reay	Grant	Ritchie	Allison	Bell	Hamilton, J. pen Cunningham Fleming (2)
W	24-Feb	Airdrie		A	L1	0-6	4000	Mathieson	Frame	Moyes	Deuchars	Marchbanks	Miller	Reay	Grant	Brown 1	Ritchie	Bell	McPhail (5) Raich
S	27-Feb	Clydebank		H	L1	2-3	2000	Mathieson	Frame	Moyes	Deuchars	Marchbanks	Miller	Reay 1	Brown 1	Brown 1	Dorrans	Bell	Bauld Welsh Finlay
S	13-Mar	St Mirren		A	L1	1-3	5000	Mathieson	Frame	Moyes	Deuchars	Marchbanks	Miller	Reay	Dorrans 1	Brown	Curley	Bell	Gebbie (2) McCrae
S	20-Mar	Hibernian		A	L1	0-2	7000	Mathieson	Frame	Moyes	Grant	Marchbanks	King	Reay	Deuchars	Barton	Bell	Turner	Murray (2)
S	27-Mar	Falkirk		H	L1	1-4	5000	Mathieson	Barton	Moyes	King	King	Cairns	Bell 1	Grant	Brown	Brown	Turner	Gowdy (3) Todd
S	03-Apr	Hearts	3	A	L1	1-5	12000	Mathieson	Frame	Moyes	Deuchars	King	Miller	Bell	Dorrans	Brown 1	Allison	Turner	Smith White, J. McNeil Miller Edgar
S	10-Apr	Hamilton Academical		A	L1	0-2	4000	Mathieson	Frame	Moyes	Deuchars	King	Miller	Bell	Dorrans	Brown	Allison	Turner	Williamson Kelly
M	12-Apr	Dunfermline Athletic	4	A	WC F	1-1	5000	King	Frame	Miller	Barton	Pitcairn	Cairns	Reay 1	Grant	Batchelor	Curley	Turner	Wilson
S	17-Apr	Aberdeen		A	L1	1-1	8000	Mathieson	Frame	Moyes	Deuchars	Pitcairn	King	Bell	Dorrans	Grant	Allison 1	Turner	Carroll
M	19-Apr	Hibernian		A	DC	1-4	2000	Mathieson	Barton	Miller	Deuchars	Pitcairn	King	Bell 1	Brown	Curley	Batchelor	Turner	McColl (2) Walker Kerr
S	24-Apr	Queens Park		H	L1	1-2	10000	Mathieson	Frame	Moyes 1	Deuchars	Pitcairn	King	Reay	Dorrans	Grant	Allison	Turner	McDonald Nicholson
S	01-May	East Fife	5	A	C	0-2	2000	Mathieson	Frame	Moyes	Deuchars	Pitcairn	Miller	Barton	Batchelor	Curley	Allison	Turner	Mackie Wood

Manager : James Logan

(1) Dave Morris Benefit

(2) Receipts £205

(3) goalkeeper Jimmy Mathieson broke his ankle midway through the first half

(4) lost 10-2 on corners

(5) Hospital Charity Match ; Receipts £130

Day	Date	Opponents	Note	Venue	Comp	Res	Att	1	2	3	4	5	6	7	8	9	10	11	Substitutes, own goals, goal times and opponents' scorers
S	14-Aug	King's Park		H	L2	2-3	5000	Nisbet	Crickett	Miller	Deuchars	Pitcairn	Todd	Reay	Dorrans	Taylor	Allison 1	Turner	Robertson Walker Love
S	21-Aug	East Fife		H	L2	4-2	5000	Nisbet	Crickett	Porter	Deuchars	Pitcairn	Todd	Reay 1p	Dorrans	Taylor	Allison 2	Turner	Weir Ward
W	25-Aug	Dunfermline Athletic		A	FC 1	3-3		Muir	Barton	McDougall	Deuchars	Porter 1	Cairns	Ritchie	Reay	Batchelor 1	Allison 1	Turner	Sutton Bayne Wilson pen
S	28-Aug	Arbroath		A	L2	3-1	2500	Muir	Porter	Porter	Deuchars	Pitcairn	Todd	Reay	Dorrans	Batchelor 1	Allison 1	Turner	Bell
W	01-Sep	Lochgelly United		H	WC 2	3-5		Muir	Crickett	McDougall	Deuchars	Porter	Miller	Taylor	Dorrans	Ritchie 1	Curley	Cairns 1	Don Campbell Paterson Moffat Archibald
S	04-Sep	St Bernards		H	L2	5-1	5000	Muir	Porter	Cairns	Deuchars	Pitcairn	Todd	Reay 1	Dorrans	Ritchie 1p	Allison 2	Turner 1	Duke
S	11-Sep	Bathgate		A	L2	3-1	1700	Muir	Barton	Porter	Deuchars	Pitcairn	Todd	Reay	Dorrans	Ritchie 2	Allison 1	Turner	Cullen
S	18-Sep	Nithsdale Wanderers		H	L2	1-0	3500	Muir	Barton	Porter	Deuchars 1	Pitcairn	Todd	Reay	Dorrans	Ritchie	Allison	Turner	
W	22-Sep	Nithsdale Wanderers		H	FC 1r	3-3		Muir	Crickett	Porter	Deuchars	Pitcairn	Todd	Reay 1	Dorrans	Ritchie 1	Batchelor	Turner 1	Hutchison Stein (2)
S	25-Sep	Bo'ness		A	L2	0-2	3000	Muir	Barton	Porter	Deuchars	Pitcairn	Todd	Reay	Dorrans	Ritchie	Allison	Turner	Martin (2)
S	02-Oct	Arthurlie		H	L2	1-2	3300	Muir	Barton	Porter	Deuchars	Pitcairn	Todd	Reay 1	Dorrans	Ritchie	Allison	Turner	Armstrong Clark
M	04-Oct	East Fife		H	PC 1	4-1		Muir	Barton	Cricket	Deuchars	Porter 1p	Cairns	Reay 1	Dorrans	Ritchie 3	Todd	Turner	Ward, J
S	09-Oct	Clydebank		A	L2	0-2	2000	Muir	Barton	McDougall	Batchelor	Porter	Cairns	Reay	Dorrans	Ritchie	Allison	Turner	Evans Fleming
S	16-Oct	Albion Rovers		H	L2	7-1	4000	Muir	Barton	Porter 1	Deuchars	Todd	Cairns	Reay 1	Dorrans 2	Brown,A 1	Batchelor 1	Ritchie 1	Dick
S	23-Oct	Armadale		A	L2	0-2	1500	Muir	Barton	Porter	Deuchars	Pitcairn	Todd	Reay	Dorrans	Brown,A	Batchelor	Ritchie	McMillan Morgan
S	30-Oct	Queen of the South		H	L2	7-2	4000	Muir	Barton	Porter	Deuchars	Pitcairn	Todd	Reay	Dorrans 1	Cowie 2	Allison 2	Ritchie 2	Gilmour Niven
S	06-Nov	Third Lanark		H	L2	3-0	4000	Muir	Barton	Porter	Deuchars	Pitcairn	Todd	Reay	Dorrans	Cowie	Allison 3	Ritchie	
S	13-Nov	Forfar Athletic	1	A	L2	2-2	1600	Muir	Barton	Porter	Deuchars	Pitcairn	Todd X	Reay 1	Dorrans	Cowie	Allison	Ritchie 1	Hill McLean
S	20-Nov	Dumbarton		H	L2	4-2	3500	Muir	Barton	Porter	Deuchars	Pitcairn	Todd	Reay 1	Dorrans 1	Cowie 1	Allison 1	Ritchie 1	Davis pen Mitchell
W	27-Nov	Stenhousemuir		A	L2	4-0	4000	Muir	McAvoy	Porter	McCaig	Pitcairn	Batchelor 1	Reay	Dorrans 1	Cowie 1	Allison	Ritchie 1	
S	04-Dec	East Stirling	2	A	L2	0-3	4000	Muir	Barton	McAvoy	Deuchars	Pitcairn	Batchelor	Reay	Dorrans	Cowie	Allison	Ritchie	Russell Cotter Stoddart
S	11-Dec	Ayr United		A	L2	1-2	3000	Muir	Barton	McAvoy	Deuchars	Pitcairn	Porter	Reay	Dorrans	Cowie	Todd	Ritchie	Tolland Brae
S	18-Dec	Alloa Athletic		A	L2	2-3	3000	Muir	Barton	Jarvis	Deuchars	Pitcairn	Todd	Reay	Miller	Cowie 1	Allison 1	Turner	Swanson (2) Lindsay
S	25-Dec	King's Park		H	L2	2-0	2700	Muir	Barton	Jarvis	Deuchars	Pitcairn	Todd	Reay	Miller 1	Cowie 1	Allison	Ritchie	
S	01-Jan	East Fife		A	L2	1-0	7000	Muir	Barton	Jarvis	Deuchars	Pitcairn	Batchelor	Reay 1	Miller	Cowie	Dorrans	Turner 1	
M	03-Jan	Arbroath		H	L2	4-2	2900	Muir	Barton	Jarvis	Deuchars	Pitcairn 1	Batchelor	Reay 1	Miller	Cowie 2	Dorrans	Turner	Hardie Farquhar
S	08-Jan	St Bernards		A	L2	2-1	1700	Muir s	Barton	Jarvis	Deuchars	Pitcairn	Batchelor	Reay 1	Miller 1	Ritchie	Dorrans 1	Turner	Allison pen
S	15-Jan	Bathgate		H	L2	1-0	3000	Muir	Barton	Jarvis	Deuchars	Pitcairn	Batchelor	Reay	Miller	McNeil 1	Dorrans 1	Turner	
S	22-Jan	Forfar Athletic	3	A	SC 1	2-4	2500	Muir	Barton	Jarvis	Todd	Batchelor	Todd	Ritchie	Miller	McNeil 1	Dorrans 1	Turner	Black (2) Hill (2)
S	29-Jan	Nithsdale Wanderers		A	L2	4-2	1200	Muir	Barton	Jarvis	Deuchars	Pitcairn	Batchelor	Reay 1	Dorrans 1	Ritchie 1	Ritchie 1	Turner 1	Ballantyne (2)
W	12-Feb	Arthurlie		A	L2	2-3	1700	Muir	Barton	Jarvis	Deuchars	Pitcairn	Batchelor	Reay	Dorrans	McNeil	Miller 2	Cowie	Elliot Clark Jessiman
S	19-Feb	Clydebank		H	L2	0-0	3000	Muir	Barton	Jarvis	Deuchars	Batchelor	Todd	Reay	Dorrans	Miller	Miller	Ritchie	
S	26-Feb	Albion Rovers		A	L2	1-1	3000	Muir	Barton	Jarvis	Deuchars	Pitcairn	Batchelor	Reay	Dorrans	Miller	Ritchie	Ritchie	Hamil
S	05-Mar	Armadale		H	L2	3-0	2900	Newman	Barton	Porter	Deuchars	Pitcairn	Batchelor	Ritchie 1	Dorrans	Cowie 2	Allison	Turner	
S	12-Mar	Queen of the South		A	L2	1-1	2600	Muir	Jarvis	Jarvis	Deuchars	Pitcairn	Batchelor	Ritchie	Dorrans	Cowie	Allison	Turner 1	McCall
S	19-Mar	Third Lanark		A	L2	0-0	4000	Muir	Jarvis	Jarvis	Deuchars	Pitcairn	Batchelor	Reay	Dorrans	Cowie	Allison	Turner 1	
S	26-Mar	Forfar Athletic		H	L2	5-0	3000	Muir	Barton	Jarvis	Deuchars	Pitcairn	Todd	Reay 1	Dorrans	Cowie	Dorrans 1	Turner 1	
S	02-Apr	Dumbarton		A	L2	3-1	1300	Muir	Porter	Porter	Deuchars	Pitcairn	Todd	Reay 1	Ritchie 2.1p	Cowie	Dorrans	Dorrans	Harvie
S	04-Apr	Bo'ness		H	L2	3-3	7000	Muir	Barton	Jarvis	Deuchars 1	Pitcairn	Todd	Reay 1	Ritchie	McNeil 2	Dorrans	Turner	Cottingham (2) Martin
M	09-Apr	Stenhousemuir		H	L2	0-0	1200	Muir	Barton	Porter	Deuchars	Pitcairn	Todd	Reay 1	Ritchie 2.1p	McNeil	Dorrans	Turner	
M	11-Apr	Hearts		A	DC	1-7	4000	Muir	Crickett	Jarvis	McCaig	McCaig	Todd	Cowie	Batchelor	Dougall	Allison	Turner 1	Morgan (4) Smith McMillan Murray
S	16-Apr	East Stirling		H	L2	6-3	3500	Muir	Barton	Jarvis	Deuchars	Batchelor	Todd 1	Reay	Ritchie 2	McNeil 1	Dorrans 1	Turner 1	Docherty (2) Stoddart
W	20-Apr	Dunfermline Athletic	4	A	FC 1r2	1-1		Muir	Barton	Jarvis	Deuchars	McCaig	Batchelor	Reay	Dorrans	Reay	Allison	Turner	Nixon og 1 Skinner
S	23-Apr	Ayr United		H	L2	3-1	2500	Muir	Barton	Porter	McCaig	Pitcairn	Todd	Reay 2	Dorrans	McNeil 1	Allison	Turner	Nisbet
W	27-Apr	Ex Raith Rovers	5	H	B	1-2	1500	Newman	Barton	Newman	Deuchars	Pitcairn	Todd	Reay	Dorrans	Newman 1	Allison	Turner	Cowie Jennings
S	30-Apr	Alloa Athletic		A	L2	2-3	2000	Muir	Jarvis	Newman	McCaig	Pitcairn	Todd	Reay	Miller 1	Cowie	Dorrans	Turner 1	McMillan (3)
S	07-May	East Fife	6	A	CSF	3-3		Muir s	Jarvis	Batchelor	McCaig	Pitcairn	Deuchars	Ritchie 1	Dorrans	Cowie	Allison	Turner 2	Wood, J (2) Nairn

Manager : George Wilson

(1) McLean sent off

(2) Sports Dispatch : "The players did not leave the field at half time. A mist, which began to creep across the ground threatened darkness."

(3) receipts £108

(4) lost 1-2 on corners

(5) George Barton Benefit

(6) Fife Charity Cup ; Lost 5-7 on corners

Day	Date	Opponents	Note	Venue	Comp	Res	Att.	1	2	3	4	5	6	7	8	9	10	11	Substitutes, own goals, goal times and opponents' scorers
S	13-Aug	Airdrie		A	L1	4-2	7000	Muir	Barton	Jarvis 1	Deuchars	Pitcairn	Batchelor	Ritchie	Dorrans 1	Pigg 2	Allison	Turner	Muir Neil pen.
S	20-Aug	Aberdeen		H	L1	2-3	9000	Muir	Barton	Jarvis	Deuchars	Pitcairn	Batchelor	Reay	Dorrans	Pigg 1	Allison 1	Turner	Cheyne Yorston McDermid
S	27-Aug	St Johnstone		A	L1	1-2	7000	Muir	Barton	Bain	Deuchars	Jarvis	Batchelor	Ritchie	Dorrans	Pigg 1	Allison	Turner	Munro (2)
W	31-Aug	Cowdenbeath		H	FC 2	2-4		McFarlane	Jarvis	Conaty	Conaty	McCaig 1	Batchelor	Ritchie	Goulden	Pigg	Cowie	Turner	Lindsay (3) Wilton
S	03-Sep	Celtic		H	L1	0-3	14000	McKinlay	Barton	Jarvis	Conaty	McCaig	Batchelor	Reay	Dorrans	Pigg	Allison	Ritchie	McGrory (2) McInally
W	07-Sep	Dunnikier Juniors		A	B	2-1		Muir	Bain	Graham	McCaig	Pitcairn	Batchelor	Reay	Nicol	Pigg 2	Goulden	Ritchie	Smith
S	10-Sep	St Mirren		A	L1	3-4	7000	Muir	Barton	Jarvis	Deuchars	Pitcairn	Batchelor	Reay	Ritchie	Pigg 2	Dorrans	Cowie 1	McDonald McCrae (2) Sutherland
S	17-Sep	Partick Thistle		H	L1	4-2	3000	Muir	Barton	Jarvis	Deuchars	McCaig	Batchelor	Ritchie	Dorrans 2	Pigg 1	Allison 1	Turner	Kinloch Gibson
S	24-Sep	Hearts		A	L1	0-2	18000	Muir	Barton	Jarvis	McCaig	Pitcairn	Batchelor	Reay	Dorrans	Pigg	Allison	Turner	McMillan Murray
S	01-Oct	Motherwell		H	L1	2-4	5000	Muir	Barton	Jarvis	Goulden	McCaig	Batchelor	Reay	Dorrans	Pigg 1	Allison 1	Turner	Cameron Stevenson (2) Ferrier
M	03-Oct	Cowdenbeath		H	WC 2	3-1		Muir	Barton	Batchelor	McCaig	Jarvis	Cowie	Reay	Smith	Pigg	Dorrans 2	Turner 1	Wilson
S	08-Oct	Cowdenbeath		A	L1	1-3	8000	Thomson	Barton	Jarvis	Ritchie	McCaig	Batchelor	Beath	Dorrans	Pigg	Allison	Turner 1	Lindsay (2) Chambers
S	15-Oct	Bo'ness		H	L1	3-2	3000	Thomson	Barton	Graham	McCaig	Pitcairn	Batchelor	Beath	Ritchie 1	Pigg 1	Allison	Turner	Martin Oswald
S	22-Oct	Rangers		A	L1	0-7	10000	Thomson	Barton	Graham	McCaig	Pitcairn	Batchelor	Ritchie	Dorrans	Cowie	Allison	Turner	McMillan (2) Fleming (3) Morton Pitcairn og
S	29-Oct	Kilmarnock		H	L1	1-3	4000	Thomson	Barton	Jarvis	McCaig	Pitcairn	Goulden	Beath	Dorrans	Pigg	Allison 1	Ritchie	Weir Thomson (2)
S	05-Nov	Hamilton Academical		A	L1	3-3	2000	Thomson	Barton	Jarvis	McCaig	Pitcairn	Batchelor	Ritchie 1	Pigg 1	Beath 1	Allison	Turner	Moffat Dick Howe
S	12-Nov	Falkirk		H	L1	2-2	4000	Muir	Barton	Graham	McCaig	Pitcairn	Batchelor	Beath	Birrell 1	Pigg	Allison 1	Turner	Kennedy, P Paterson
S	19-Nov	Dunfermline Athletic		A	L1	4-0	4000	Muir	Barton	Graham	McAllister	Pitcairn	Batchelor	Beath 1	Birrell 1	Pigg	Allison	Turner	Wilson og 1 Cameron og 1
S	26-Nov	Dundee		H	L1	1-1	8000	Muir	Barton	Graham	McAllister	Pitcairn	Batchelor	Beath	Birrell	Pigg 1	Allison	Turner	O'Hare
S	03-Dec	Queen's Park		A	L1	1-8	10000	Leckie	Barton	Graham	McAllister	Pitcairn	Batchelor	Beath	Birrell	Pigg	Allison	Turner 1	Crawford Chalmers McLelland (3) McAlpine (3)
S	10-Dec	Hibernian		A	L1	2-3	9000	Leckie	Barton	Graham	McAllister	Pitcairn	Batchelor	Ritchie	Birrell	Beath	Allison 1	Turner 1	Haggerty Halligan Stark
S	17-Dec	Clyde		H	L1	2-0	4000	Leckie	Barton	Graham	McAllister	Pitcairn	Batchelor	Beath	Birrell	Pigg 1	Allison 1	Turner	
S	24-Dec	Airdrie		H	L1	5-0	5000	Muir	Barton	Hopewell	Deuchars	Hoggan	Batchelor	Beath	Birrell 2	Smith 2	Galloway	Turner	Smiles og 1
M	26-Dec	Berwick Rangers		H	F	6-1		Muir	McCaig	Batchelor	McCaig	McCaig 1	Batchelor	Beath 1	Birrell 1	Pigg 1	Galloway	Ritchie 1	Piercy
Tu	27-Dec	Carlisle United		A	B	2-2		Leckie	Barton	Hopewell	McAllister	Pitcairn 1	Batchelor	Cowie	Beath 1	Ritchie	Allison	Turner	Jackson Graham
M	02-Jan	Bo'ness		A	L1	1-1	4000	Leckie	Barton	Hopewell	McAllister	Hoggan	Batchelor	Ritchie	Birrell 1	Ritchie	Allison	Turner	Heeps
Tu	03-Jan	St Mirren		H	L1	1-2	6000	Leckie	Barton	Hopewell	McAllister	Hoggan	Batchelor	Beath	Birrell	Ritchie	Allison	Turner 1	McCrae (2)
S	07-Jan	St Johnstone		H	L1	0-0	5000	Leckie	Pitcairn	Hopewell	McAllister	Hoggan	Batchelor	Beath	Birrell	Pigg	Allison	Turner	
S	14-Jan	Partick Thistle		A	L1	0-5	8000	Leckie	Barton	Hopewell	McAllister	Hoggan	Batchelor	Beath	Dorrans	Pigg	Allison	Turner	Gibson (2) McDougall Salisbury
S	21-Jan	Aberdeen	1	H	SC 1	4-3	8000	Leckie	Barton	Hopewell	McAllister	Pitcairn	Batchelor	Beath	Birrell 1p	Pigg	Galloway	Turner 1	Bruce (3)
S	28-Jan	Cowdenbeath		H	L1	0-1	5000	Leckie	Barton	Hopewell	McAllister	Hoggan	Batchelor	Beath	Birrell	Allison	Galloway	Turner	Lindsay
S	04-Feb	Motherwell	2	A	SC 2	2-2	7000	Leckie	Barton	Hopewell	McAllister	Hoggan	Batchelor	Ritchie 1	Birrell	Allison 1	Galloway	Turner	Cameron Stevenson
W	08-Feb	Motherwell	3	H	SC 2r	0-5	8000	Leckie	Barton	Hopewell	McAllister	Hoggan	Batchelor	Ritchie	Birrell	Allison	Galloway	Turner	Kiernan Cameron
S	11-Feb	Motherwell		H	L1	0-5	10000	Leckie	Barton	Hopewell	McAllister	Hoggan	Batchelor	Beath	Birrell	Kennedy	Allison	Turner	Rogers Miller Devlin McMillan Lindsay
W	15-Feb	Motherwell		A	L1	0-6	2000	Leckie	McCaig	Hopewell	McAllister	Hoggan	Goulden	Beath	Birrell	Munro	Galloway	Turner	McMurtrie Douglas Tenant, T Stevenson Ferrier (2)
W	29-Feb	Kilmarnock		H	L1	0-1	3000	Page	Barton	Hopewell	McAllister	Hoggan	Batchelor	Reay	Dorrans	Munro	Allison	Galloway	Cunningham
S	03-Mar	Aberdeen		A	L1	0-3	10000	Page	Pitcairn	Hopewell	Deuchars	Hoggan	Batchelor	Kennedy	Birrell	Munro	Kennedy	Turner	Cheyne (2) Yorston
S	10-Mar	Hamilton Academical		H	L1	1-4	4000	Page	Pitcairn	Hopewell	Pitcairn	Hoggan	Batchelor	Ritchie	McAllister	Kennedy	Galloway	Turner	Weir (2) McKay McCormack
S	17-Mar	Falkirk		A	L1	1-4	4000	Page	Barton	Hopewell	Pitcairn	Hoggan	Batchelor	Birrell	Birrell	Smith 1	Galloway 1	Turner	Morrison (4)
W	21-Mar	Armadale		H	PC SF	4-0		Muir	Barton	Hopewell	McAllister	Hoggan	Batchelor	Ritchie	Birrell	Pigg 3	Allison 2	Turner	
S	24-Mar	Dunfermline Athletic		H	L1	5-1	4000	Page	Barton	Hopewell	McAllister	Hoggan	Batchelor	Smith 1	Ritchie 1	Pigg 2	Galloway 1	Turner	Carruthers
S	31-Mar	Dundee		A	L1	2-1	3000	Page	Barton	Hopewell	McAllister	Hoggan	Batchelor	Smith	Dorrans 1	Pigg	Galloway 1	Ritchie	Smith
M	02-Apr	Rangers		H	L1	0-0	9000	Page	Pitcairn	Hopewell	McAllister	Hoggan	Batchelor	Beath	Dorrans	Pigg	Galloway	Richmond 2	
S	07-Apr	Queen's Park		H	L1	1-0	7000	Muir	Pitcairn	McDougall	McAllister	Hoggan	Batchelor	Smith 1	Dorrans	Pigg	Galloway	Turner	
S	14-Apr	Hibernian		A	L1	3-0	4000	Muir	Pitcairn	Hopewell	McAllister	Hoggan	Batchelor	Smith	Dorrans	Pigg	Galloway	Turner 1	
M	16-Apr	Hearts		A	DC	1-0	1800	Leckie	Porter	Graham	Deuchars	McCaig	Goulden	Smith,J 1	Smith,R	Smith,R	Allison	Turner	
W	18-Apr	Hearts	4	A	DC F	2-2		Muir	Pitcairn	Hopewell	McAllister	Graham	Batchelor	Reay	Kennedy	Smith,R 1	Galloway 1	Turner	McMillan Murray
S	21-Apr	Clyde		A	L1	1-1	8000	Muir	Pitcairn	Hopewell	McAllister	Hoggan	Batchelor	Smith	Smith	Pigg 1	Galloway	Turner	Simpson
M	23-Apr	Celtic		A	L1	3-0	1000	Muir	Pitcairn	McDougall	McAllister	Hoggan	Batchelor	Beath 1	Dorrans	Pigg 1	Galloway	Ritchie 1	
Tu	24-Apr	Clachnacuddin		A	F	3-2		Pearson	Pitcairn	Hopewell	McCaig	Hoggan	Batchelor	McCaig	Dorrans	Smith,R 1	Ritchie 2	Turner	Robertson Chisholm
W	25-Apr	Fraserburgh		A	F	1-5		Pearson	Pitcairn	McDougall	McAllister	Hoggan	McAllister	Beath	Smith,R	Ritchie 1	Ritchie	Turner	Birnie (2) Bain, G (2) Turner
Th	26-Apr	Peterhead	5	A	F	2-4		Muir	Pitcairn	Graham	McCaig	Hoggan	Batchelor r45	McCaig	Birrell	Ritchie	Dorrans	Ritchie 1	Shewan (2) Wyness (2)
S	28-Apr	Dunfermline Athletic		A	WC F	0-2		Pearson	Pitcairn	Graham	McAllister	Hoggan	Batchelor	Ritchie	Dorrans	Pigg	Galloway	Turner	Dickson, T.W. (2)

Manager : George Wilson to 16th December.   Willie Birrell from 19th December

(1) Receipts £317
(2) Receipts £228
(3) Receipts £315
(4) Lost 2-9 on corners
(5) Attendance "record gate"

Day	Date	Opponents	Note	Venue	Comp	Att.	Res.	1	2	3	4	5	6	7	8	9	10	11	Substitutes, own goals, goal times and opponents' scorers
S	11-Aug	Partick Thistle		H	L1	5000	2-4	Leckie	Pitcairn	Hopewell	McAllister	Hoggan	Batchelor	Bain	Dorrans	Pigg	Galloway 2	Turner	Gibson (3) Fraser
S	18-Aug	Motherwell		A	L1	5000	1-3	Leckie	Pitcairn	Hopewell	McAllister	Hoggan	Batchelor	Smith	Dorrans 1	Pigg	Galloway	Turner	Ferrier (3)
W	22-Aug	Alloa Athletic	1	H	PC F		0-2	Rankine	Pitcairn	Hopewell	McAllister	Hoggan	Batchelor	Walker	Smith	Pigg	Galloway	Turner	McNeil, J Hill
S	25-Aug	Third Lanark		H	L1	7000	0-0	Leckie	Pitcairn	Hopewell	McAllister	Good	Good	Smith	Smith	Pigg	Batchelor	Turner	
W	29-Aug	East Fife		A	WC 1		1-1	Leckie	McDougall	Hopewell	McAllister	Good	Dorrans	Smith	Galloway	Pigg 1	Batchelor	Turner	Weir
S	01-Sep	St Johnstone		A	L1	9000	1-3	Leckie	Pitcairn	Hopewell	McAllister	Good	Batchelor	Walker	Dorrans	Payne	Galloway	Turner	McBean Munro Webb
S	08-Sep	Hearts		H	L1	12000	0-2	Leckie	Pitcairn	Hopewell	McAllister	Hoggan	Batchelor	Smith	Dorrans	Payne	Galloway	Turner	Battles (2), one pen
S	15-Sep	Queen's Park		A	L1	12000	0-5	Leckie	Pitcairn	Hopewell	McAllister	Good	Good	Payne	Dorrans	Pigg	Batchelor	Turner	McLellan (3) Scott Nicholson
S	22-Sep	Rangers		A	L1	15000	1-7	Leckie	Pitcairn	Hopewell	McAllister	Hoggan	Good	Payne	Dorrans	Pigg 1	Galloway	Turner	McMillan Fleming (3) McPhail (2) Morton
S	29-Sep	Aberdeen		A	L1	12000	1-3	Leckie	McDougall	Hopewell	Pitcairn	Hoggan	McAllister	Galloway	Smith	Pigg 1	Dorrans	Turner 1	Cheyne Mellie (2)
M	01-Oct	Ayr United		H	L1	4300	4-2	Leckie	McDougall	Hopewell	Pitcairn	Hoggan	McAllister	Galloway	Smith 1	Pigg 1	Dorrans 1	Turner 1	Smith Brae
S	06-Oct	Dundee		H	L1	8000	0-3	Leckie	McDougall	Hopewell	Pitcairn	Hoggan	McAllister	Bloxham	Smith	Pigg	Galloway	Turner	Smith (2) McNab
S	13-Oct	Hamilton Academical		H	L1	5000	3-1	Leckie	McDougall	Hoggan	McAllister	Pitcairn	Hopewell	Bloxham	Meagar	Pigg 2	Dorrans 1	Turner 1	Jack
S	20-Oct	Cowdenbeath		A	L1	3000	0-2	Leckie	McDougall	Batchelor	McAllister	Pitcairn	Hopewell	Bloxham	Meagar	Pigg	Dorrans	Turner	Pullar Lindsay
S	27-Oct	St Mirren		H	L1	4000	1-5	Leckie	McDougall	Batchelor	McAllister	Good	Hopewell	Beath	Dorrans	Pigg 1	McGorm	Turner	McCrae (2) McDonald, J. Rankine
S	03-Nov	Celtic		A	L1	7000	1-3	Leckie	Pitcairn	Hoggan	McAllister	Good	Hopewell	Beath	Galloway	Pigg	McGorm	Turner	Thomson, A. McGrory (2)
S	10-Nov	Airdrie		A	L1	4000	3-2	Leckie	Pitcairn	Hoggan	McAllister	Good	Hopewell	Beath 1	Galloway	Pigg 2	McGorm	Turner	Paterson McDonald
S	17-Nov	Hibernian		A	L1	7000	0-2	Leckie	Pitcairn	Hoggan	McAllister x	Good	Hopewell	Beath	Dorrans	Pigg	Galloway	Turner	Wilkinson Bradley
S	24-Nov	Falkirk		A	L1	5000	1-4	Leckie	McDougall	Hoggan	McAllister	Pitcairn	Hopewell	Beath	Smith	Pigg 1	Dorrans	Turner	Morrison (4)
S	01-Dec	Clyde		H	L1	3500	3-0	Leckie	Pitcairn	Hopewell	McAllister	Good	Batchelor	Beath	Dorrans	Pigg 1	Bruton 2	Galloway	
S	08-Dec	Kilmarnock		A	L1	6000	1-7	Leckie	Pitcairn	Hopewell	McAllister	Good	Batchelor	Beath	Galloway	Pigg	Bruton 1	Turner	Cunningham (4) Connell (2) Morton
S	15-Dec	Ayr United		A	L1	4000	2-2	Leckie	Pitcairn	Hopewell	McAllister	Hoggan	Batchelor	Beath	Bruton 1	McGorm	Bruton 1	Turner	Stevenson Ferrier
S	22-Dec	Motherwell		H	L1	3000	1-6	Leckie	Pitcairn	Hopewell	McAllister	Hoggan	Batchelor	Beath	Bruton	McGorm	McGorm	Turner	Ness (3) Ballantyne Fraser Torbet
S	29-Dec	Partick Thistle		H	L1	5000	2-2	Leckie	Pitcairn	Hopewell	McAllister	Hoggan	Batchelor	Bloxham	Bruton	McGorm	McGorm	Galloway	Glancy (2)
Tu	01-Jan	Cowdenbeath		H	L1	1383	2-5	Hutton	Hutchison	Hopewell	McAllister	Hoggan	Batchelor	Beath	Bruton	McGorm 1	McGorm	Galloway	McColgan (4) Hamill
S	05-Jan	Third Lanark		H	L1	4500	2-3	Hutton	Hutchison	Hopewell	McAllister	Hoggan	Batchelor	Beath	McBain	McGorm	McGorm 1	Turner 1	Main (3)
S	12-Jan	St Johnstone		H	L1	3000	3-2	Leckie	Hutchison	Hopewell	McAllister	Hoggan	Batchelor	Pigg	McBain	Bruton 2	Galloway	Turner	Smith Bell, D
S	19-Jan	Beith	2	A	SC 1	5000	4-1	Leckie	Hutchison	Hopewell	McAllister	Hoggan	Batchelor	Bloxham	Dorrans	Bruton 1	Galloway	Turner	Bell, J
S	26-Jan	Kilmarnock	3	H	SC 1r		3-1	Leckie	Hutchison	Hopewell	McAllister	Hoggan	Batchelor	Bloxham	Pigg	Bruton 3	Pigg	Turner	Drummond
S	02-Feb	Bathgate	4	A	SC 2		2-2	Leckie	Hutchison	Hopewell	McAllister	Hoggan	Batchelor	Beath	Dorrans	Bruton 1	Pigg	Turner	Fairley Drummond
W	06-Feb	Bathgate		H	SC 2r	5000	1-0	Leckie	Hutchison	Hopewell	Pitcairn	Hoggan	Batchelor 1	Beath	McBain 1	Bruton 5	Dorrans	Turner	
S	09-Feb	Rangers		A	L1	1500	0-3	Leckie	Hutchison	Hopewell	McAllister	Hoggan	Batchelor	Pigg	McBain	Bruton	McGorm	Galloway	Muirhead Fleming McPhail
S	16-Feb	Dumbarton	5	H	SC 3		5-2	Leckie	Hutchison	Hopewell	Pitcairn	Pitcairn	Batchelor	Wilkie	McBain 1	Bruton 1	Galloway 1	Turner 1	Haddow Malloy
W	20-Feb	Aberdeen		A	L1	12000	1-2	Leckie	Hutchison	Hopewell	Pitcairn	Pitcairn	Batchelor	Wilkie	Beath	Bruton	Galloway 2	Turner	Yorston (2)
S	23-Feb	Dundee		H	L1	2000	1-0	Leckie	Hutchison	Hopewell	McAllister	Pitcairn	Batchelor	Dorrans	McBain 1	McBain 1	McBain 1	Turner	
S	02-Mar	Kilmarnock	6	H	SC 4		5-3	Leckie	Hutchison	Hopewell	McAllister	Pitcairn	Batchelor	Pigg	Pigg	Bruton 1	Galloway	Turner	Niblce og 1 — Smith Cunningham Paterson
Tu	05-Mar	Hamilton Academical		H	L1	6000	2-5	Leckie	Hutchison	Hopewell	Good	Good	Hoggan	McBain	McBain	Bruton 1	Galloway	Turner	McNally (3) Jones Howe
S	09-Mar	Celtic		A	L1	2800	1-4	Leckie	Hutchison	Hopewell	McAllister	Hoggan	Good	McBain	Dorrans	Pigg	Galloway	Turner	Scaffle (3) Prentice
S	16-Mar	Airdrie		A	L1	3000	1-3	Leckie	Hutchison	Hoggan	McAllister	Hoggan	Good	Bloxham	McGorm	Pigg	Galloway	Turner 1	Baxter Skinner Bertram
S	23-Mar	Hibernian		A	L1	3000	1-0	Leckie	Hutchison	Hopewell	McAllister	Hoggan	Batchelor	Wilkie	Dorrans	Bruton	Galloway	Turner	
W	27-Mar	Dunfermline Athletic		A	FC 1	3000	1-0	Leckie	Hutchison	Hopewell	McAllister	Hoggan	Batchelor	Wilkie	McGorm	Bruton	Galloway 1	Turner	
S	30-Mar	Falkirk		H	L1	1000	2-0	Leckie	Hutchison	Hopewell	McAllister	Hoggan	Batchelor	Bloxham	Dorrans	Bruton 1p	Galloway 1	Turner	
M	01-Apr	East Fife		H	WC 1r	200	2-4	Leckie	Hutchison 2p	Hopewell	McAllister	Hoggan	Batchelor	Wilkie	Dorrans	Bruton	Galloway	Turner	McGauchie (2) Weir Nairn
S	06-Apr	Clyde		A	L1	4000	2-2	Leckie	Hutchison	Hopewell	Good	Hoggan	Batchelor	Good	Dorrans	Bruton 1	Galloway 1	Turner	Haddow Gibson pen
Tu	09-Apr	St Mirren		H	PC SF	2000	2-5	Leckie	Hutchison	Hopewell	McAllister	Hoggan	Batchelor	Wilkie	Dorrans	Bruton 3	Galloway	Turner	McCrae (3) Rankine (2) both pens
S	13-Apr	Dundee		A	DC SF	2000	2-3	Leckie	Hutchison	Hopewell	Good	Hoggan	Batchelor	Wilkie	Beath 1	Pigg 1	Galloway 1	Turner	Campbell, A Smith Lawley
M	15-Apr	Hearts		H	L1	6000	0-4	Leckie	Hutchison	Hopewell	McAllister	Hoggan	Batchelor	Wilkie	Beath	Bruton	Galloway	Turner	Smith Battles Murray Hutchison og
S	20-Apr	Kilmarnock		A	L1	2284	5-3	Leckie	Hutchison	Hopewell	Good	Hoggan	Batchelor	Wilkie	Beath 1	Pigg 1	Galloway	McGorm	Cunningham Williamson (2)
W	24-Apr	Queen's Park		A	L1	2500	1-1	Leckie	Hutchison 2p	Hopewell	McAllister	Hoggan	Batchelor	Wilkie 1	Beath	Bruton	Galloway	Bloxham	Crawford
S	27-Apr	Hearts	7	A	L1		1-1	Leckie	Hutchison X	Hopewell	McAllister	Hoggan	Batchelor	Wilkie	Galloway	Bruton 3	Batchelor	Turner	Battles
M	29-Apr	Peterborough United	8	A	F		0-6	Leckie	Hutchison	Hopewell	McAllister	Pitcairn	Hoggan	Beath	Beath 1	Bruton	Galloway	Turner	Laycock (5) Wellock
W	01-May	York City		A	F		6-4	Anderson	Hutchison	Hopewell	McAllister	Hoggan	Drain	Pitcairn	Batchelor 1	Bruton 4	Galloway	Turner 1	Fenoughty (2) Cowie (2), 1 pen

Manager : Willie Birrell

(1) 1926/27 Final

(2) Sports Dispatch : "An unusual incident occurred at Beith. A spectator rushed on to the field and knocked down Leckie, the Raith goalkeeper. He was taken charge of by the police."

(3) Receipts £160   (4) Receipts £110

(5) Receipts £200   (6) Receipts £500

(7) McMillan sent off

(8) Part of Leslie Bruton's transfer ; Gate £116

Day	Date	Opponents	Note	Venue	Comp	Res	Att	1	2	3	4	5	6	7	8	9	10	11	Substitutes, own goals, goal times and opponents' scorers
S	10-Aug	Third Lanark		A	L2	2-4	3800	McKendrick	Batchelor	Munro	Campbell	Hoggan	Drain	Beath 1	Galloway	Panther 1	Allison	McArthur	Jack (2) Wilson Wallace
W	14-Aug	East Fife	1	H	FC SF	2-0		McKendrick	Batchelor	Munro	Campbell	Hoggan	Drain	Beath	Feechan	Panther 1	Galloway 1	McArthur	
S	17-Aug	Brechin City		H	L2	6-1	4500	McKendrick	Batchelor	Munro	Campbell 1	Hoggan	Drain	Beath 1	Feechan	Allison 2	Galloway 1	McArthur 1	Gunn
W	21-Aug	Cowdenbeath	1	H	FC F	0-0		McKendrick s	Batchelor	Munro	Campbell	Hoggan	Drain	McCormack	Feechan	Galloway	Beath	McArthur	
S	24-Aug	Queen of the South		A	L2	3-1	3000	McKendrick	Batchelor	Munro	Campbell m	Hoggan	Drain	McCormack 1	Feechan	Galloway 2	Galloway 1	McArthur	Derby
W	28-Aug	Dunfermline Athletic		H	FC 1	3-1		McKendrick	Hutchison	Munro	Campbell	Hoggan	Batchelor 2	McCormack	Allison	Galloway 1	Beath	McArthur	Paterson, A
S	31-Aug	Bo'ness		A	L2	1-2	2000	McKendrick	Newman	Batchelor	Campbell	Hutchison	Drain	Morrison	Feechan	Galloway 1	Newman	Newman	Robertson Hutchison
S	04-Sep	Thornton Rangers	2	A	B	-		McKendrick	Newman	Munro	Newman	Hutchison	McKillop	Beath	Feechan	Panther 4	Beath 1	McArthur	
S	07-Sep	Clydebank		H	L2	6-0	5000	McKendrick	Batchelor	Munro	Campbell	Hoggan	Drain	McCormack	Galloway	McCormack	Beath 1	McArthur	Duff og 1
S	14-Sep	Stenhousemuir		A	L2	2-2	1000	McKendrick	Batchelor	Munro	Campbell	Hoggan	Drain	McCormack	Galloway	McCormack 2	Beath	McArthur	Scottiar pen Robertson
S	21-Sep	Leith Athletic		H	L2	1-2	7200	McKendrick	Hutchison	Munro	Campbell	Hoggan	Batchelor	McCormack	Hoggan	Panther	Beath 1	McArthur	Nicol (2)
S	28-Sep	Forfar Athletic		A	L2	0-2	1200	McKendrick	Hutchison	Munro	Campbell	Batchelor	Hoggan	McCormack	Batchelor	Panther	Beath	Galloway	Forbes McLean pen
S	05-Oct	Montrose		H	L2	1-1	3000	McKendrick	Hutchison	Munro	Hoggan	Gillon	Drain	Beath	Galloway	Panther	Batchelor	Galloway	Pirie
M	07-Oct	Cowdenbeath	1	H	FC Fr	2-3		McKendrick	Hutchison	Munro	Campbell	Hoggan	Drain	Beath 1	Galloway	Panther 1	Batchelor	McArthur	McGirr Glancy Higgins
S	12-Oct	St Bernards		A	L2	2-2	2000	McKendrick	Hutchison	Munro	Hoggan	Gillon	Batchelor	Beath 1	Galloway	Panther 2	Birrell	McArthur	Brown Eadie
S	19-Oct	Dumbarton		H	L2	3-2	2000	McKendrick	Hutchison	Munro	Hoggan	Gillon	Batchelor	Beath 1	Galloway	Panther 2	Birrell	Newman	Brannan Shaw
S	26-Oct	East Fife		H	L2	0-2	8000	McKendrick	Hutchison	Munro	Hoggan	Gillon	Batchelor	Beath	Galloway	Morris	Birrell	McCormack	McGauchie Rarity
S	02-Nov	Arbroath		A	L2	2-0	1000	Leckie	Batchelor	Munro	McKillop	Hoggan	Drain	Beath	Birrell	Hutchison 2	Galloway	McCormack	
S	09-Nov	Alloa Athletic		H	L2	7-2	2900	Leckie	Batchelor	Munro	McKillop	Hoggan 1	Drain	Beath 1	Birrell 1	Panther 3	Galloway 1	McCormack	Junior (2)
S	16-Nov	East Stirling		A	L2	4-1	2500	Leckie	Batchelor	Munro	McKillop	Hoggan	Drain	Beath 1	Birrell	Panther 2	Galloway 1	Newman	Renwick
S	23-Nov	King's Park		A	L2	2-2	500	Leckie	Batchelor	Munro	Campbell	Hoggan	Drain	Beath 1	Birrell	Panther 1	Galloway	McArthur	Ross McGreachan
S	30-Nov	Dunfermline Athletic	3	A	L2	2-2	1000	McKendrick	Batchelor	Munro	Campbell	Hoggan 1	Drain	Beath 2	Birrell 2,1p	Panther	Galloway	McArthur	Howieson Paterson, G
S	07-Dec	Armadale		H	L2	8-0	2500	Leckie	Batchelor	Munro	Campbell	Hoggan 1	Drain	Beath	Birrell	Galloway	Galloway 1	Pryde 3	
S	14-Dec	Albion Rovers		A	L2	0-7	500	Leckie	Batchelor	Munro	Campbell	Hoggan	Drain	Beath 2	Birrell	Reynolds	Galloway	Pryde m	Weir (3) Harkins (3) Lindsay
S	21-Dec	Third Lanark		H	L2	1-1	1500	Leckie	Batchelor	Munro	Campbell	Hoggan	Drain	Beath	Feechan	McKillop	Galloway 1	Pryde	McPherson
S	28-Dec	Brechin City		A	L2	3-0	2000	Leckie	Hutchison	Munro	Batchelor	Hoggan	Drain	McCormack	Beath	Feechan	Galloway	McKillop	
W	01-Jan	East Fife		A	L2	2-0	6000	Leckie	Hutchison	Munro	Batchelor	Hoggan	Batchelor	Beath	Beath 1	Birrell 1	Galloway	Pryde 1	
Th	02-Jan	Dumbarton		H	L2	1-2	1500	Leckie	Hutchison	Munro	Batchelor	Hoggan	Drain	Beath 1	Feechan	Birrell	Galloway	Pryde	Hutchison og Junior
S	04-Jan	Queen of the South		A	L2	0-1	2000	Leckie	Batchelor	Munro	Campbell	Hoggan	Drain	Feechan	McLaren	Drysdale	Galloway	Pryde	Newman
S	11-Jan	Bo'ness		H	L2	4-2	1000	Leckie	Batchelor	Munro	Campbell	Hoggan	Drain	McLaren	Galloway	Panther 2	Birrell 1	Pryde	Fleming (2)
S	18-Jan	Aberdeen	4	H	SC 1r	3-3	10000	Leckie	Hutchison	Batchelor	Campbell	Hoggan	Drain	Beath	Galloway	Panther 2	Birrell 1p	Pryde	Love Cheyne Yorston
W	22-Jan	Aberdeen		A	SC 1r	0-7	10000	Leckie	Hutchison	Batchelor	Campbell	Hoggan	Drain	Beath	Galloway	Panther	Birrell	Pryde	Yorston (3) McLaren Cheyne McDermid Smith
S	25-Jan	Clydebank		A	L2	1-1	900	Leckie	Hutchison	Batchelor	Campbell	Hoggan	Drain	McCormack	Beath 1	Panther	Galloway	Morrison	Walker
S	01-Feb	Stenhousemuir		H	L2	6-2	1000	McLeary	Hutchison	Batchelor	Campbell	Hoggan	Drain	Beath 1	McLaren 1	Galloway	Galloway	Robertson 2	Hunter McCallum
S	08-Feb	Leith Athletic		A	L2	1-4	5000	Leckie	Hutchison	Batchelor	Campbell	Hoggan	Drain	Beath	McLaren	Panther 3	Birrell 1p	McGuigan	Marshall Nicol (2.1p) Young
S	15-Feb	Forfar Athletic		H	L2	1-4	1000	Leckie	Mathers	Batchelor	Campbell 1	Hoggan	Drain	Beath	McLaren 1	Panther	Galloway	Pryde	Kilgour (3) McLean
S	22-Feb	Montrose		A	L2	2-1	3000	Leckie	Batchelor	Munro	McKillop 1	Hoggan	Sharp	Beath	McLaren 1	Panther 1	Fitzpatrick	Galloway	Breslin
S	01-Mar	St Bernards		H	L2	2-1	2000	Leckie	Batchelor	Munro	McKillop	Hoggan	McKillop	Beath	McLaren 1	Panther 1	Galloway	Drain	Eadie
S	08-Mar	Arbroath		H	L2	3-1	2500	Leckie	Batchelor 1p	Munro	McKillop	Hoggan	Sharp	Beath	McLaren	Panther 1	Hood	McGuigan 1	Jarvis
S	15-Mar	Alloa Athletic		A	L2	3-2	2000	Leckie	Batchelor	Hoggan	Henderson	Hoggan	Sharp	Beath	McLaren 1	Birrell 3	McKillop	Garland	McArthur Sharp og
S	22-Mar	East Stirling		H	L2	1-3	2000	Leckie	Batchelor	Munro	Campbell	Hoggan	Sharp	Beath	McLaren 1	Panther 1	Galloway	McKillop	McMillan Aitken Munro og
S	29-Mar	King's Park		H	L2	1-3	1500	Leckie	Batchelor	Munro	Campbell	Hoggan	Sharp	Beath	McLaren 1	Panther	Hazel	Ferguson	Dyer, J McGreechan Duffy
S	05-Apr	Dunfermline Athletic		A	L2	3-1	2500	Leckie	Batchelor	Munro	Campbell 1	Hoggan	Sharp	Beath	McLaren 1	Panther 3	Birrell 1	Drysdale	Gilfillan
M	07-Apr	Dundee		H	PC	2-1		Leckie	Batchelor	Munro	Campbell	Hoggan	Drain	McCormack	McLaren	Panther 1	Beath	Beath	McKay
W	09-Apr	St Andrews University		H	FC SF	5-0		Leckie	Batchelor	Munro	Campbell	Hoggan	Drain	McCormack	McLaren	Panther 3	Galloway	Birrell 1	
S	12-Apr	Armadale		A	L2	2-1	3000	Leckie	Batchelor	Munro	McKillop	Hoggan	Sharp	Campbell	McLaren 1	Panther	Beath	Galloway	Polland, John
M	14-Apr	Hibernian		A	DC	0-6	500	Leckie	Batchelor	Munro	McKillop	Hoggan	Drain	Birrell 1p	McLaren	Panther	Galloway	Young	Brown (3) Dobson (2) Taylor
S	19-Apr	Albion Rovers		H	L2	6-2	3000	Leckie	Batchelor	Munro	Campbell	Hoggan	Sharp	McCormack	McLaren 1	Panther 3	Birrell 1	Beath	Hart Harkins
W	23-Apr	Dunfermline Athletic		A	WC SF	1-4		Leckie	Batchelor	Munro	Campbell	Hoggan	Drain	Beath	McLaren	Panther 1	Galloway	Galloway	Marshall og 1
S	26-Apr	East Fife		A	FC F	3-2	3000	Leckie	Batchelor	Munro	Campbell	Hoggan	Drain	Beath	McLaren	Panther	Birrell 1	Galloway 2	McGauchie Weil
W	30-Apr	Fife Junior League	N	H	F	4-1		Newman	Batchelor	Munro	McKillop	Hoggan	Drain	Junior	Galloway	Amateur 1	Beath 2	Stranger	Philp

Manager : Willie Birrell

Goalkeepers to stand still as penalties were taken

(1) 1928/29 Competition

(2) Match abandoned at half time - with Rovers winning 1-0

(3) Dunfermline missed penalty

(4) Receipts £500

(N) Reserve match not included in summary statistics

Day	Date	Opponents	Note	Venue	Comp	Res	Att	1	2	3	4	5	6	7	8	9	10	11	Substitutes, own goals, goal times and opponents' scorers
S	09-Aug	Albion Rovers		A	L2	3-3	5000	Leckie	Batchelor	Munro	McKillop	Hoggan	Sharp	Beath	McLaren 1	Panther 1	Birrell 1	Galloway	Walls Weir Harkins
S	16-Aug	Dumbarton		A	L2	1-3	2000	Leckie	Batchelor	Munro	McKillop	Hoggan	Henderson	Beath	McLaren 2	Panther	Birrell	Galloway 1	Shaw (2) Parlane, W.
W	20-Aug	St Andrews University		H	FC 1	15-2		Leckie	Batchelor	Hoggan	McKillop 1	Henderson	Sharp	Forrest 2	McLaren 2	Jarvis 9	Beath	Michie 1	Cowan Downie
S	23-Aug	Arbroath		H	L2	3-2	3500	Leckie	Batchelor	Hoggan	Birrell	Henderson	McIlwraith	Forrest	McLaren	Panther 3	Beath	Michie 1	Mathieson Gibb
S	30-Aug	Dunfermline Athletic		A	L2	1-3	3500	Leckie	Batchelor	Townley	Birrell	Henderson	Hoggan	Forrest	McLaren	Panther	Beath	Michie1	Gallacher Sclater Junior
W	03-Sep	St Johnstone		H	PC 1	3-1		Leckie	McLean	Brown	Beath	Henderson	Hoggan	Panther	McLaren 2	Jarvis 1	Birrell	Michie	McBain
S	06-Sep	King's Park		H	L2	5-6	2500	Leckie	Brown	Townley	Beath	Henderson	Hoggan 1p	Forrest	McLaren	Panther 1	Jarvis 3	Michie	Duffy Martin (4), one pen. McGreachan
S	13-Sep	Brechin City		A	L2	2-2	1100	Leckie	Bell	Townley	Beath	Henderson 1	Hoggan	Forrest	Birrell	Jarvis 1	Jarvis	Birrell	Burns Moffat
S	20-Sep	St Bernards		H	L2	4-2	4000	Leckie	Bell	Batchelor 1p	Beath	Hoggan	Henderson	Forrest 1	McLaren	Jarvis 2	Galloway	Drysdale	Duff Imrie
S	27-Sep	Bo'ness	1	A	L2	2-3	3700	Leckie	Bell	Townley	Batchelor	Hoggan	Henderson	Panther	McLaren	Jarvis 2	Galloway	Michie	Clark pen Brannan McLaren
S	04-Oct	Queen of the South		H	L2	2-0	5000	Leckie	Bell	Batchelor	Beath	Hoggan	Henderson	Panther 1	McLaren	Jarvis	Birrell 1	Wallace	
M	06-Oct	Dunfermline Athletic		H	WC 1	6-2		McArthur	Bell	Batchelor	Beath	Hoggan 1	Sharp	Panther 1	McLaren 1	Jarvis 3	McLeod	Galloway	Paterson McAndrew
S	11-Oct	Dundee United	2	A	L2	2-1	4000	Leckie	Bell	Batchelor	Beath	Hoggan	Sharp	Panther 1	McLaren	Jarvis 1	Birrell	Galloway	Kay pen
S	18-Oct	Montrose		H	L2	1-2	1500	Leckie	Bell	Batchelor	Beath	Hoggan	Henderson	Panther	Birrell 1	Jarvis	McLeod	Galloway	Gentles Muir
S	25-Oct	Stenhousemuir		H	L2	5-2	3000	Leckie	Bell	Batchelor	Beath	Henderson	Hoggan 1p	Panther	McLaren 1	Jarvis 2	Birrell 1	Pratt	Walker (2)
S	01-Nov	St Johnstone		A	L2	3-2	5000	Leckie	Bell	Batchelor	Beath	Henderson	Hoggan	Panther	McLaren 1	Jarvis 2	Birrell	Pratt	Deuchar Cameron
S	08-Nov	Third Lanark		A	L2	0-6	6000	Leckie	Bell	Batchelor	Beath	Henderson	Hoggan	Panther	McLaren	Jarvis 2	Birrell	Galloway	Dewar (4) Jack Lynas
S	15-Nov	Alloa Athletic		H	L2	7-0	2000	Leckie	Bell	Batchelor	Beath	Hoggan	Henderson	Panther	McLaren 1	Jarvis 5	Birrell 1	Galloway 1	
S	22-Nov	Armadale		H	L2	4-0	1000	Leckie	Bell	Batchelor	Beath	Hoggan	Sharp	Panther	McLaren 1	Jarvis	Birrell 1	Galloway 1	
S	29-Nov	Forfar Athletic		A	L2	0-1	1100	Leckie	Bell	Batchelor	Beath	Hoggan	Sharp	Panther	McLaren	Jarvis	Birrell	Galloway	McLean
S	06-Dec	East Stirling		H	L2	2-1	1500	Leckie	Bell	Batchelor	Beath	Hoggan	Sharp	Panther 1	McLaren	Jarvis 2	Birrell	Townley	Junior
S	13-Dec	Clydebank		H	L2	5-0	2000	Leckie	Bell	Batchelor	Beath	Hoggan	Sharp	Panther 1	McLaren 2	Jarvis 2	Galloway	Chalmers	
S	20-Dec	Albion Rovers		A	L2	0-2	2500	Leckie	Bell	Batchelor	Beath	Hoggan	Sharp	Panther	McLaren	Jarvis	McDonell	Galloway	Harkins Radcliffe
S	27-Dec	Dumbarton		H	L2	2-0	2000	Wallace	Bell	Batchelor	Beath	Hoggan	Sharp	Panther	McLaren	Jarvis 1	McDonell 1	Galloway	
Th	01-Jan	St Bernards		A	L2	1-1	2000	Leckie	Bell	Batchelor	Beath	Hoggan	Sharp	Panther 1	McLaren	Jarvis	Henderson	Galloway	Forrest
F	02-Jan	Bo'ness		H	L2	2-0	2200	Leckie	Bell	Batchelor	Beath	Hoggan	Henderson	Panther 1	McLaren	Jarvis 1	Forrest	Galloway	
S	03-Jan	Arbroath		A	L2	1-0	1600	Leckie	Bell	Batchelor	Beath	Hoggan	Sharp	Panther	McLaren 1	Jarvis	McKenzie	Galloway	
S	10-Jan	Dunfermline Athletic		H	L2	1-1	6000	Leckie	Bell	Batchelor	Beath	Hoggan	Sharp	Panther	McLaren	Jarvis	McKenzie 1	Galloway	Rarity, W
S	17-Jan	Morton	3	A	SC 1	1-1	8400	Leckie	Bell	Batchelor	Beath	Hoggan	Sharp	Panther 1	McLaren	Jarvis	McKenzie	Galloway	McKeenan
W	21-Jan	Morton	4	H	SC 1r	1-1	6000	Leckie	Bell	Batchelor	Beath	Hoggan	Sharp	Panther	McLaren	Jarvis 1	McKenzie	Galloway	Black
S	24-Jan	King's Park	5	A	L2	1-5	1500	Leckie s	Bell	Batchelor	McKillop	Hoggan	Townley	Forrest	Henderson	Jarvis	McKenzie 1	Galloway	Rose (2) Jamieson Duffy Crickett
M	26-Jan	Morton	6	N	SC 1r2	0-2	6000	Leckie	Bell	Batchelor	Beath	Hoggan	Sharp	Panther	McLaren	Jarvis	McKenzie	Galloway	McKeenan (2)
S	31-Jan	Brechin City		H	L2	2-1	700	Wallace	Bell	Batchelor	Beath	Hoggan	Sharp	Panther 1	Forrest	Jarvis 1	McKenzie	Galloway	Saunders
S	07-Feb	Queen of the South		A	L2	1-4	2800	Wallace	Bell	Batchelor	Beath	Hoggan	Sharp	Panther 1	McLaren	Jarvis	McKenzie	Galloway 1	Dyer Rutherford McDonald Anderson
S	14-Feb	Dundee United		H	L2	0-0	3000	Wallace	Bell	Batchelor	Beath	Hoggan x	Sharp	Forrest	McLaren	Panther	McKenzie	Galloway	
S	21-Feb	Montrose		H	L2	2-1	2000	Wallace	Bell	Batchelor m	Beath 1	Henderson	Sharp	Forrest	McLaren 1	Jarvis	McKenzie 1	Galloway	Scoullar
S	28-Feb	Stenhousemuir		A	L2	6-3	1000	Leckie	Bell	Batchelor	Beath	Hoggan 2p	Sharp	Panther	McLaren 1	Jarvis 1	McKenzie 1	Galloway	Robertson (2, 1 pen) Sutton
S	07-Mar	St Johnstone		H	L2	4-2	1000	Leckie	Bell	Batchelor	Beath	Hoggan 1p	Sharp	Panther 1	McLaren	Jarvis 2	McKenzie	Galloway 1	Nicholson Tierney
S	14-Mar	Third Lanark	7	H	L2	3-1	4000	Leckie	Bell	Batchelor 1p	Beath	Hoggan x	Sharp	Panther	McLaren 1	Jarvis 1	McKenzie	Galloway	Breslin
S	21-Mar	Alloa Athletic		A	L2	2-3	1500	Leckie	Bell	Batchelor	Beath	Hoggan	Sharp	Panther 1	McLaren	Jarvis 1	McKenzie	Galloway	Martin Junior Borland
S	28-Mar	Hibernian		A	DC	0-4	1000	Wallace	Bell	Batchelor	Beath	Hoggan	Sharp	Panther	McLaren	Jarvis	McKenzie	Galloway	Wallace McColl (2) Bradley
S	04-Apr	Armadale		A	L2	3-4	700	Leckie	Bell	Batchelor	Beath	Hoggan	McKillop	Panther	McLaren 1	Burt 1	McKenzie	Galloway 1	Russell (2, 1 pen) Fleming (2)
M	06-Apr	Cowdenbeath		H	WC SF	0-2		Wallace	Bell	Hoggan	Beath	Sharp	McKillop	Panther	McLaren	Jarvis	McKenzie	Galloway	Paterson Venters
S	11-Apr	Forfar Athletic	8	H	L2	4-3	1000	Leckie	Bell	Batchelor	Beath 1	Hoggan	Sharp	Panther	McLaren	Jarvis 3	McKenzie	Galloway	Kilgour (2) Black
S	18-Apr	East Stirling		A	L2	1-1	1600	Wallace s	Bell	Batchelor	Beath	Hoggan	Sharp	Galloway	McLaren	Panther 1	McKenzie	Drysdale	Renwick
W	22-Apr	Rosslyn Select	9	A	B	0-4													Morris (2) Bell Philip
S	25-Apr	Clydebank		A	L2	5-1	1000	Wallace	Bell	Batchelor	McKillop	Hoggan 1p	Sharp	Beath	McLaren	Panther 4	McKenzie	Chalmers	McCartney

Manager : Willie Birrell to 3rd December ; James Logan from 8th December

(1) Receipts £150
(2) "Prior to the kick off the local Boys Brigade band played the 'Flowers of the Forest' and the crowd observed two minutes' silence in tribute to the R101 airship heroes."
(3) Receipts £340
(4) after extra time
(5) Leckie saved Baird's penalty, and later saved a second penalty, but Crickett netted from the rebound
(6) at Firhill
(7) Blair ordered off
(8) Wallace saved McCabe penalty, and Renwick sent another penalty past the post
(9) Benefit for Jimmy Penman who had been injured all season

Day	Date	Opponents	Note	Venue	Comp	Res	Att	1	2	3	4	5	6	7	8	9	10	11	Substitutes, own goals, goal times and opponents' scorers
S	08-Aug	Arbroath		A	L2	1-3	3000	Wallace	Bell	Gay	Beath	Hoggan	Sharp	McKay 1	Batchelor	Cowan	McKenzie	Archibald	Oliphant Stewart (2)
W	12-Aug	East Fife	1	H	FC F	2-2		Wallace	Bell	Gay	Beath	Hoggan	Sharp	McKay	Batchelor 1	Cowan 1	McKenzie	Archibald	Weir Mitchell
S	15-Aug	Dunfermline Athletic		H	L2	0-2	5000	Wallace	Bell	Batchelor	McKillop	Hoggan	Sharp	McKay	Beath	Jarvis	McKenzie	Archibald	McGarry Young
W	19-Aug	Armadale		H	L2	5-1	2500	Wallace	Bell	Batchelor	Beath	Hoggan 1p	Sharp	McKay	McDonough	Cowan 3	McKenzie 1	Archibald	Stout
S	22-Aug	King's Park		A	L2	1-1	3000	Wallace	Bell	Batchelor	Beath	Hoggan	Sharp	McKay	McDonough	Cowan 1	McKenzie	Archibald	Temple
W	26-Aug	Edinburgh City		H	L2	7-2	2000	Wallace	Bell	Gay	Beath	Hoggan	Batchelor	McKay	McDonough 1	Cowan 2	McKenzie 1	Archibald 3	Cummings (2 pens)
S	29-Aug	Brechin City		H	L2	1-3	2000	Wallace	Bell	Gay	Beath	Hoggan	Batchelor	McKay	McDonough 1	Cowan	McKenzie	Archibald	Stewart (2) Allardyce
S	05-Sep	East Fife		A	L2	4-1	4500	Wallace	Bell	Batchelor	Beath	Hoggan	Sharp	Campbell	McLaren 1	Cowan 2	McDonough	Archibald 1	Liddell
S	12-Sep	Bo'ness		H	L2	3-1	2000	Wallace	Bell	Batchelor	Beath	Hoggan	Sharp	Campbell	McLaren	Cowan 1	McDonough 1	Archibald 1	Carruthers
S	19-Sep	Queen of the South		A	L2	1-3	3500	Wallace	Bell	Batchelor	Beath	Hoggan	Sharp	McKay	McLaren	Cowan	McDonough	Archibald 1	Rutherford Jenkins McDonald
S	26-Sep	Hibernian		H	L2	1-2	4000	Wallace	Bell	Batchelor	Beath	Hoggan	Sharp	McKay	McLaren	Cowan	McDonough 1	Archibald	Reid Friar
S	03-Oct	Albion Rovers		A	L2	3-1	2000	Wallace	Bell	Batchelor	Beath	Hoggan	Sharp	Cowan 2	McLaren	Jarvis 1	McDonough	Archibald	Anderson pen
M	05-Oct	Cowdenbeath		H	FC 1	1-5	2000	Wallace	Bell	Batchelor	Beath	Hoggan 1p	Sharp	Cowan	McLaren	Jarvis	McKenzie	Archibald	Paterson (3) Campbell Venters
S	10-Oct	Dumbarton		H	L2	4-2	2500	Wallace	Bell	Batchelor	Beath	Hoggan	Sharp 1	Cowan 1	McLaren	Allan	McDonough 1	Archibald 1	Lang (2)
S	17-Oct	St Bernards		H	L2	4-3	2500	Wallace	Bell	Batchelor	Beath	Hoggan	Sharp	Allan	McLaren	Cowan 2	McDonough 1	Archibald 1	Murray (3)
S	24-Oct	Stenhousemuir		A	L2	3-3	1300	Wallace	Bell	Batchelor	Beath	Hoggan	Sharp	Allan	McLaren	Cowan	McDonough 2	Archibald 1	Cowan Cowie Robertson pen
S	31-Oct	Alloa Athletic		H	L2	2-1	2000	Wallace	Bell	Batchelor	Beath	Hoggan	Sharp 1	Allan	McLaren	Cowan 1	McDonough	Archibald	Junior
S	07-Nov	Forfar Athletic		A	L2	1-2	2000	Wallace	Bell	Batchelor	Beath	Hoggan	Sharp	Allan	McLaren	Cowan 1	McDonough	Archibald	Garvie Black
S	14-Nov	Montrose		A	L2	4-3	1000	Wallace	Bell	Batchelor	Beath	Hoggan	Sharp	Allan 1	McLaren	Cowan 2	McDonough	Archibald 1	McDonald (2) Gibb
S	21-Nov	St Johnstone		H	L2	1-1	3000	Wallace	Bell	Batchelor	Beath	Hoggan	Sharp	Allan	McLaren	Cowan 1	McDonough	Archibald	Nicholson
S	28-Nov	East Stirling		H	L2	4-2	4000	Wallace	Bell	Batchelor	Beath	Hoggan 1p	Sharp	McKay 1	McLaren	Cowan 1	McDonough 1	Archibald 1	Hart Turnbull
S	05-Dec	Armadale		A	L2	2-1	1000	Wallace	Bell	Batchelor	Beath	Hoggan	Sharp	McKay	McLaren	Cowan 1	McDonough	Archibald 1	Donnelly
S	12-Dec	Edinburgh City		A	L2	4-2	200	Wallace	Bell	Batchelor	Beath	Hoggan	Sharp	McKay	McLaren	Cowan 2	McDonough	Archibald 2	Hall Parry
S	19-Dec	Arbroath		H	L2	5-1	3500	Wallace	Bell	Batchelor	Beath	Hoggan	Sharp	McKay	McLaren	Cowan 2	McKenzie 1	Archibald 2	Lowe
S	26-Dec	Dunfermline Athletic		A	L2	3-0	5000	Wallace	Bell	Batchelor	Beath	Hoggan	Sharp	McKay	McLaren	Cowan 2	McKenzie 1	Archibald 1	
F	01-Jan	East Fife		H	L2	2-1	6000	Wallace s s	Bell	Batchelor	Beath	Hoggan	Sharp	McKay	McLaren	Cowan 1	McKenzie	Archibald 1	McGauchie pen
S	02-Jan	Bo'ness		A	L2	3-4	2000	Wallace	Bell	Batchelor	Beath	Hoggan	Sharp	Allan	McLaren	Cowan 1	McKenzie 1	Archibald 1	Wallace (2, 1pen) Tallis (2)
S	09-Jan	King's Park		H	L2	2-0	2000	Wallace	Bell	Batchelor	Beath	Hoggan	Sharp	Allan	Black	Cowan 2	McKenzie	Archibald	
S	16-Jan	Inverness Thistle	2	H	SC 1	8-1	4100	Wallace	Bell	Batchelor	McKenzie	Hoggan	Sharp 1	Archibald,R 2	McLaren	Cowan 2	McDonough 2	Archibald 1	Gowe
S	23-Jan	Brechin City		H	L2	1-0	2000	Wallace	Bell	Batchelor	Beath	Hoggan	Sharp	Archibald,R	McLaren	Cowan	McDonough 1	Archibald	
S	30-Jan	Rangers		A	SC 2	0-5	18052	Wallace	Bell	Batchelor	Beath	Hoggan	Sharp	Archibald,R	McLaren	Cowan	McDonough	Archibald	Archibald English (30 Fleming
S	06-Feb	Hibernian	3	H	L2	1-0	4000	Wallace s s	Bell	Batchelor	Allan	Hoggan	Sharp	Beath	McLaren	Cowan	McKenzie	Archibald	Watson og 1
S	13-Feb	Albion Rovers		A	L2	4-0	2500	Wallace	Bell	Batchelor	Beath	Hoggan	Sharp	Pullar	McLaren	Cowan 2	McKenzie 2	Archibald	
S	20-Feb	Dumbarton		A	L2	1-6	2000	Wallace	Bell	Batchelor	Beath	Hoggan	Sharp	Pullar	McLaren	McDonough 1	McDonough	Archibald	Parlane, W. (2) Parlane, J. (2) Hendry Lang
S	27-Feb	St Bernards		H	L2	0-2	2000	Wallace	Bell	Batchelor	Beath	Hoggan	Sharp	Pullar	McDonough	Cowan	McKenzie	Archibald	Murray Marley
S	05-Mar	Stenhousemuir		H	L2	0-0	1000	Wallace	Bell	Morrison	McKillop	Hoggan	Batchelor	Pullar	McKay	Cowan	McKenzie	Archibald	
S	12-Mar	Alloa Athletic		H	L2	0-0	2000	Wallace	Bell	Batchelor	Beath	Hoggan	Hunter	Pullar	McLaren	Cowan	McKenzie	Archibald	
S	19-Mar	Forfar Athletic		H	L2	0-2	1000	Wallace	Bell	Batchelor	Beath	Hoggan	Batchelor	Pullar	McLaren	McDonough	Sharp	Archibald	Black (2)
S	26-Mar	Montrose		H	L2	2-2	1500	Wallace	Bell	Batchelor	Beath	Hoggan	McKenzie 1	McKay	McLaren	Ouchterlonie 1	Sharp	Archibald	McDonald, R Paterson
S	02-Apr	St Johnstone		A	L2	0-2	6000	Wallace	Bell	Batchelor	Beath	Hoggan	Sharp	McKay	McLaren	Cowan	McDonough	Chalmers	Benson (2)
S	09-Apr	East Stirling		H	L2	1-5	1000	Wallace	Bell	Batchelor	Beath	Hoggan	Sharp	McKay	McLaren 1	Cowan	McKenzie	Archibald	Turnbull Black Mason Kemp (2)
S	16-Apr	Queen of the South		A	L2	2-0	400	Wallace	Allan	Batchelor	Beath	McKillop	Hoggan	Aitken 1	McLaren	Cowan m 1	McKenzie	Archibald	
M	18-Apr	Hearts		A	DC	0-1		Wallace	Bell	Morrison	Beath	Hoggan	Sharp	Pullar	McLaren	Cowan	McKenzie	Chalmers	White
W	20-Apr	Cowdenbeath		A	WC 1	1-8		Wallace	Allan	Bell	Beath	Hoggan	Sharp	Newman	McDonough	Cowan 1	McKenzie	Chalmers	Hamill (2) Aston Paterson (4) Venters
W	27-Apr	Dunfermline Athletic		H	PC SF	4-1		Wallace	Allan	Batchelor	Beath	Hoggan	Sharp	Pullar 1	McDonough	Cowan 3.1p	McKenzie	Archibald	Hogg

Manager : James Logan
(1) 1930/31 Final ; lost 8-5 on corners
(2) Receipts £170
(3) Wallace saved two penalties

Day	Date	Opponents	Note	Venue	Comp	Res	Att.	1	2	3	4	5	6	7	8	9	10	11	Substitutes, own goals, goal times and opponents' scorers
S	13-Aug	King's Park		H	L2	9-1	3000	Wallace	Allan	McGuire	Beath	Hoggan	Dick	Ovenstone	Prentice 2	Cowan 4	Bain 1	Archibald 1	Haddow
W	17-Aug	Burntisland Shipyard		A	FC	8-4		Wallace	Allan	McGuire	Beath	Hoggan	Dick	Ovenstone	Prentice 2	Cowan 4	Bain 1	Archibald 1	Connell (2) Arnot Adair
S	20-Aug	Brechin City	1	A	L2	4-2	2000	Wallace	Allan	McGuire	Beath	Hoggan	Dick	Ovenstone	Prentice 2	Cowan 2	Bain	Archibald	McHaffie (2)
Th	25-Aug	Forfar Athletic		A	L2	1-4	800	Wallace	Allan	McGuire	Beath	Hoggan	Dick	Ovenstone	Prentice 1	Cowan 2	Bain	Archibald 1	Ogilvie Black. R. (2) Duncan
S	27-Aug	Dundee United		H	L2	4-1	4000	Wallace	Allan	McGuire	Beath	Hoggan	Dick	Ovenstone	Prentice	Cowan m 3	Bain	Archibald 1	Whyte
S	03-Sep	Leith Athletic		A	L2	0-1	2000	Wallace	Allan	McGuire	Beath	Hoggan	Dick	Ovenstone	Prentice	Cowan	Bain	Archibald	McGirr
S	10-Sep	East Fife		H	L2	3-1	5000	Wallace	Allan	McGuire	Beath	Hoggan	Dick	Ovenstone 1	Prentice	Cowan	McKenzie	Archibald	Herbert
W	14-Sep	St Bernards		H	L2	4-2	1800	Wallace	Allan	McGuire	Beath	Hoggan 2p	Sharp	Ovenstone 1	Prentice	Cowan 1	McKenzie 1	Archibald 2	Murray Eadie
S	17-Sep	Bo'ness	1	H	L2	2-1	1000	Wallace	Allan	McGuire	Beath	Hoggan m	Dick	Ovenstone	Lavan 1	Cowan 1	Bain	Archibald	Pratt
S	24-Sep	Dunfermline Athletic		A	L2	1-1	4000	Wallace	Allan	McGuire	Beath	Hoggan	Dick	Ovenstone	Prentice	Cowan 1	McKenzie	Archibald	Weir
S	01-Oct	Albion Rovers		A	L2	2-1	3000	Wallace	Allan	McGuire	Beath	Hoggan	Dick	Ovenstone	Prentice	Cowan 1	McKenzie 1	Archibald 1	McGillivary
M	03-Oct	Cowdenbeath		H	FC SF	5-3	3000	Wallace	Allan	McGuire	Beath	Hoggan	Dick	Ovenstone	Prentice 1	Cowan 3	McKenzie 1	Archibald	Jones (2) Campbell
S	08-Oct	Edinburgh City		A	L2	5-0	1500	Wallace	Allan	McGuire	Beath	Hoggan	Dick	Ovenstone	Prentice 2	Cowan 2	McKenzie 1	Archibald	
S	15-Oct	Arbroath		A	L2	3-1	2000	Wallace s	Allan	McGuire	Beath	Hoggan	Dick	Ovenstone	Prentice	Cowan 3	McKenzie	Archibald	White
S	22-Oct	Montrose		A	L2	4-2	1500	Wallace	Allan	McGuire	Beath	Hoggan	Dick	Ovenstone	Prentice 1	Cowan 1	McKenzie 1	Archibald 1	Bennett (2)
S	29-Oct	Hibernian		A	L2	1-2	12000	Wallace	Allan	McGuire	Beath	Hoggan	Dick	Ovenstone	Prentice	Cowan 1	McKenzie	Archibald	Wallace (2)
S	05-Nov	Forfar Athletic		A	L2	2-1	2000	Wallace	Allan	McGuire	Beath	Hoggan	Dick	Ovenstone	Prentice	Cowan 2	McKenzie	Archibald	Black
S	12-Nov	St Bernards		A	L2	2-3	5000	Wallace	Allan	McGuire	Beath	Hoggan 1	Dick	Ovenstone	Prentice	Cowan 1	McKenzie	Archibald	Murray Marshall Eadie pen
S	19-Nov	Armadale	2	A	L2	5-1	300	Wallace	Allan	McGuire	Beath	Hoggan	Sharp	Ovenstone	Cox	Cowan 3	Dick 2	Archibald	Michie
S	26-Nov	Queen of the South		H	L2	1-3	3000	Wallace	Allan	McGuire	Beath	Hoggan	Dick	Ovenstone	Cox	Cowan	Prentice	Archibald 1	Anderson Bell McCall
S	03-Dec	Stenhousemuir		A	L2	1-3	1500	Wallace	Allan	McGuire	Beath	Hoggan	Bain	Ovenstone	Prentice	Dick	McKenzie	Archibald	Knox Hart Cowan
S	10-Dec	Alloa Athletic		A	L2	1-4	1700	Wallace	Allan	Newman	Newman	Hoggan	Dick	Cox	Prentice	Cowan	Innes	Archibald	Bell (2) Gilliland (2)
S	17-Dec	Dumbarton	3	H	L2	-	1000	Wallace	Allan	McGuire	Beath	Hoggan	Dick	Ovenstone	Campbell	Cowan 1	Innes 1	Archibald	Parlane, W. Lang
S	24-Dec	King's Park		A	L2	0-6	1000	Wallace	Allan	McGuire	Beath	Hoggan	Dick	Ovenstone	Campbell	Cowan	Innes	Archibald	Haddow (6)
S	31-Dec	Brechin City		A	L2	5-3	1500	Wallace	Allan	McGuire	Beath	Hoggan 1	Dick	Ovenstone	Campbell	Prentice 3	Innes 1	Archibald	Pryde Pyper Jenkins
M	02-Jan	East Fife		A	L2	1-2	6000	Wallace	Allan	McGuire	Beath	Hoggan 1	Dick	Panther	Campbell	Cowan 1	McKenzie	Archibald	Weir Marshall
Tu	03-Jan	Scottish Junior Select		H	F	3-1	1000	Wallace	Allan	Morrison	Reid	Hoggan	Hardie	Leitch	Moyes	Parlane	McKenzie	Vallance	Watt
S	07-Jan	Dundee United		A	L2	1-2	2000	Wallace	Allan	McGuire	Beath	Hoggan m	Dick	Panther	Prentice	Cowan	Innes 1	Ovenstone	Kay Laing
S	14-Jan	Leith Athletic		H	L2	3-0	1000	Wallace	Allan	McGuire	Beath	Hoggan	Dick m	Panther	Campbell	Cowan 2	Innes 1	Ovenstone	Bertram (2)
S	21-Jan	Falkirk		H	SC 1	1-2	7500	Wallace	Allan	McGuire	McKenzie 1	Hoggan	Dick	Ovenstone	Prentice	Cowan	Innes 1	Archibald	Garland
S	28-Jan	Dunfermline Athletic		A	L2	0-1	3000	Wallace	Allan	McGuire	McKenzie	Hoggan	Dick	Beath	Campbell	Cowan	Innes	Archibald	McGauchie pen McCartney Hope
S	04-Feb	East Fife		H	WC	5-3	700	Wallace	Allan	Dick	Beath	Hoggan	McKenzie	Ovenstone 1	Prentice	Cowan 2	Innes	Archibald 2	Duke
S	11-Feb	Albion Rovers		H	L2	2-1	1500	Wallace	Allan	Dick	McKenzie	Hoggan	Parlane	Ovenstone	Newman	Prentice 1	Innes	Archibald 1	Hups Parlane, W Kennedy
S	18-Feb	Dumbarton		A	L2	2-3	1300	Wallace	Allan	Dick	McKenzie	Hoggan	Parlane	Ovenstone 1	Newman 1	Prentice	Innes 1	Archibald	Cumming pen Bradley
S	25-Feb	Edinburgh City		A	L2	5-2	500	Wallace	Allan	McGuire	McKenzie	Hoggan	Parlane	Ovenstone 1	Panther 1	Parlane 1	Innes 1	Archibald	
S	04-Mar	Arbroath	4	H	L2	4-0	800	Wallace s	Allan	Dick	McKenzie	Hoggan	Parlane	Ovenstone	Prentice	Cowan 3	Innes 1	Archibald	
S	11-Mar	Montrose		A	L2	2-4	500	Wallace	Allan	Dick	Newman	Hoggan 1p	Newman	Ovenstone 1	Prentice	Newman	Cowan 2	Newman	Stoddart (2) Ross Robertson
S	18-Mar	Hibernian		H	L2	1-2	3500	Wallace	Allan	Dick	McKenzie	Hoggan 1p	McKenzie	Ovenstone	Prentice	Panther	McKenzie	Innes	Watson Connelly
S	25-Mar	East Fife		A	FC F	1-2	2000	Wallace	Allan	Dick	McKenzie	Hoggan 1p	McKenzie	Ovenstone	Panther 1	Panther	Innes	Innes	Weir (2)
S	01-Apr	Hibernian	5	A	DC	2-4	3500	Wallace	Allan	Dick	McKenzie	Hoggan 1	McKenzie	Ovenstone 1	Prentice	Cowan 3	Archibald	Archibald	Walls Connelly (2) Hart
S	08-Apr	Queen of the South		A	L2	2-2	3000	Wallace	Allan	Dick	Beath	Hoggan	Parlane 1	Panther	Prentice	Cowan	Ovenstone	Ovenstone	Bell McDonald
W	12-Apr	Burntisland Shipyard		A	WC	2-0	1500	Wallace	Allan	McGuire	Beath	Hoggan 1p	McKenzie	Beath	Prentice	Cowan 1	McKenzie	Ovenstone	
S	15-Apr	Stenhousemuir		H	L2	1-1	1500	Newman	Allan	McGowan	Newman	Newman	Newman	Ovenstone 1	Innes	Cowan	Newman	Newman	Hart
W	19-Apr	St Monance Swifts		A	F	4-1	600	Wallace	Newman	Masson	Dick	Hoggan	Parlane	Newman	Kinnaird 1	Panther 1	Cowan 2	Archibald	Marr
S	22-Apr	Alloa Athletic		H	L2	4-3	1000	Wallace	Allan	Dick	Beath	Hoggan	McKenzie	Ovenstone 1	Harvie 1	Cowan 2	Innes	Archibald	Hamilton Bill Reid
W	26-Apr	Dunfermline Athletic	6	A	WC F	1-3	1000	Wallace	Allan	McGuire	Beath	Hoggan	McKenzie	Ovenstone	Prentice	Parlane 1	Innes	Henderson	Archibald (2) Cowie
S	29-Apr	Dumbarton		H	L2	2-2	500	Wallace	Allan	Dick	Beath	Hoggan	McKenzie	Ovenstone	McNaughton 1	Parlane	Prentice	Byrne	Parlane, W. Kennedy

277

Manager : James Logan

(1) Brechin missed penalty
(1) Record expunged, Bo'ness resigned from League
(2) Record expunged, Armadale resigned from League
(3) Match abandoned after 77 minutes with score at 2-2
(4) Wallace saved twice taken penalty
(5) Parland playing for Scotland Amateurs v England
(6) Parlane playing for Scotland Amateurs v Wales

Day	Date	Opponents	Note	Venue	Comp	Res.	Att.	1	2	3	4	5	6	7	8	9	10	11	Substitutes, own goals, goal times and opponents' scorers
S	12-Aug	Stenhousemuir		H	L2	1-3	3000	Wallace	Allan	Cunningham	McIlwraith	Hoggan,M	Parlane	Ovenstone	Black	Cowan	Oliphant 1	Eadie	Cowan Howie (2)
S	19-Aug	East Stirling		A	L2	1-5	1500	Wallace	Allan	Hoggan,R	Crichton	Hoggan,M	Parlane	Ovenstone	Black	Cowan 1	Oliphant	Newman	Jordan (2) Kemp (2) Smith pen
S	26-Aug	Montrose		H	L2	5-0	2000	Wallace	Allan	Hoggan,R	McKenzie	Hoggan,M	Crichton	Ovenstone	Black	Cowan 5	Oliphant	Callaghan	
W	30-Aug	Lochgelly United		A	WC	0-1		Wallace	Allan	Hoggan,R	Robertson	Crichton	Cunningham	Ovenstone	McKenzie	Cowan	Oliphant	Callaghan	Allan og
S	02-Sep	Morton	1	A	L2	1-2	4000	Wallace	Allan	Hoggan,R	McKenzie	Hoggan,M 1p	Crichton	Eadie	Black	Cowan	Oliphant	Callaghan	Clark Mooney pen
S	09-Sep	East Fife		H	L2	0-1	4500	Wallace	Allan	Hoggan,R	McKenzie	Hoggan,M	Crichton	Black	Black	Cowan	Oliphant	Callaghan	Walker
S	16-Sep	Dumbarton		A	L2	0-2	1300	Wallace s	Allan	Hoggan,R	Parlane	Hoggan,M	Crichton	Ovenstone	Black	McCrae	McMillan	Callaghan	McGonagle Ballantyne
S	23-Sep	Alloa Athletic		H	L2	2-2	2000	Wallace	Allan	Hoggan,R	Parlane	Hoggan,M	Crichton	Young	McKenzie	McCrae 1	Herbert 1	Callaghan	Silater Borland
S	30-Sep	St Bernards		A	L2	1-0	1500	Wallace	Allan	Hoggan,R	McKenzie	Hoggan,M	Hoggan,M	Callaghan	Black	Cowan 1	Oliphant	Kinnear	
M	02-Oct	Cowdenbeath		H	FC 1	2-4		Wallace	Allan	Hoggan,R	McAndrew	Crichton	Crichton	Callaghan	Oliphant	Cowan 1	Herbert 1	Kinnear	Cameron (2) Renfrew Hamil
S	07-Oct	Forfar Athletic		H	L2	3-0	1500	Wallace	Allan	Hoggan,R	McKenzie 1	Hoggan,M	Parlane	Ovenstone	Oliphant 2	Cowan	Herbert	Callaghan	
S	14-Oct	Dunfermline Athletic		H	L2	1-1	4000	Wallace	Allan	Hoggan,R	McKenzie	Hoggan,M m	Crichton	Ovenstone	Oliphant 1	Cowan 1	Black	Callaghan	Laidlaw
S	21-Oct	Edinburgh City		A	L2	2-1	300	Wallace	Allan	Hoggan,R	McKenzie	Hoggan,M	Crichton	Ovenstone	Oliphant	Penman 3	Black	Kinnear 1	Rose
S	28-Oct	Brechin City		H	L2	5-1	1000	Wallace	Allan	Hoggan,R	McKenzie	Crichton	Cunningham	Ovenstone	Oliphant 2	Penman	Black	Kinnear	O'Hare
S	04-Nov	Leith Athletic		A	L2	0-2	1500	Wallace	Allan	Hoggan,R	Scott	Crichton	McKenzie	Ovenstone	Oliphant	Penman	Black	Kinnear	Howieson Grant
S	11-Nov	Arbroath		A	L2	0-1	2000	Wallace	Allan	Cunningham	Scott	Hoggan,M	Crichton	Ovenstone	Oliphant	Penman 1	McKenzie	Kinnear	Brand
S	18-Nov	Albion Rovers		H	L2	2-0	500	Wallace	Allan	Cunningham	Scott	Hoggan,M	Crichton	Ovenstone	Oliphant	Penman 1	McKenzie	Kinnear 1	
S	25-Nov	King's Park		A	L2	1-3	2500	Wallace	Allan	Cunningham	Scott	Hoggan,M	Crichton	Ovenstone	Oliphant	Penman	McKenzie	Kinnear	Bryse Dyer Laird
S	02-Dec	Dundee United		H	L2	4-1	1000	Wallace	Allan	Cunningham	Scott	Hoggan,M	Crichton	Oliphant 1	Barnes	Penman 1	McKenzie	Kinnear 1	Willis og 1 Ochterlonie
S	09-Dec	Montrose		A	L2	1-2	1000	Wallace	Allan	Cunningham	Scott	Hoggan,M	Crichton	Penman	Black	Oliphant 1	Smith	Kinnear	Gibb (2)
S	16-Dec	Morton		H	L2	3-1	1500	Wallace	Allan	Cunningham	Scott	Hoggan,M	Crichton	Christie	Black	Oliphant 1	Smith 1	Kinnear 1	Stoddart
S	23-Dec	Alloa Athletic		A	L2	1-3	1000	Wallace	Allan	Cunningham	Scott	Hoggan,M	Benvie	Ovenstone 1	Oliphant	Oliphant	Smith	Kinnear	Bell Borland Brown
S	30-Dec	St Bernards		H	L2	3-1	2000	Wallace	Allan	Cunningham	Scott	Hoggan,M	Crichton	Ovenstone	Oliphant 1	Penman 3	Oliphant	Kinnear	Bow
Tu	02-Jan	East Fife		A	L2	6-2	5000	Wallace	Allan	Cunningham	Scott	Hoggan,M	Crichton	Ovenstone 1	Oliphant	Penman 4	Smith	Kinnear	Hay McCartney
S	06-Jan	Brechin City		A	L2	0-0	1500	Wallace	Allan	Cunningham	Scott	Hoggan,M	Crichton	Hoggan,R	Oliphant	Penman	Smith	Kinnear	
S	13-Jan	Arbroath		H	L2	0-1	3000	Wallace	Allan	Cunningham	Scott	Hoggan,M	Crichton	Cowan	Oliphant	Penman	Smith	Kinnear	Carver
S	20-Jan	Aberdeen		A	SC 1	0-1	12959	Wallace	Allan	Cunningham	Scott	Hoggan,M	Crichton	Ovenstone	Oliphant 1	Penman	Smith	Kinnear	Moore
S	27-Jan	King's Park		H	L2	4-2	2000	Wallace	Allan	Cunningham	Scott	Hoggan,M	Crichton	Ovenstone 1	Oliphant 1	Penman	Smith	Kinnear 2	Bryce (2)
S	03-Feb	Rosyth Dockyard		H	F	3-5	400	Wallace 1	Allan	Hoggan,R	Scott	Hoggan,M	Crichton	McCrae	Oliphant	Cowan	Cowan	Kinnear 2	Thomson (2) Garland Turnbull Gallacher
S	10-Feb	Albion Rovers	2	A	L2	2-2	1500	Wallace	Allan	Hoggan,R	Scott	Hoggan,M	Crichton	Ovenstone	Oliphant 1p	Penman	Oliphant 1p	Kinnear	Bruce pen Beath, J
S	17-Feb	East Fife		H	PC	3-3	1000	McIlwraith	Allan	Cunningham	Scott	Hoggan,M	Crichton 1	Ovenstone 1	Oliphant 1	Penman 1	Oliphant 1	Kinnear	Scott Dougan (2)
S	24-Feb	Edinburgh City		H	L2	6-0	1000	Murray	Allan	Cunningham	Scott	Hoggan,M	Crichton	Ovenstone	Oliphant	Cowan 1	Smith 1	Kinnear 3	
S	03-Mar	East Stirling		H	L2	3-0	1000	Murray	Allan	Cunningham	Scott	Hoggan,M	Crichton	Ovenstone	Newman	Cowan 2	Newman	Newman	
S	10-Mar	Forfar Athletic		A	L2	0-3	800	Murray	Allan	Cunningham	Main	Hoggan,M	Crichton	Ovenstone	Oliphant	Cowan	Oliphant	Oliphant	Black Dunsire Cabrelli
S	17-Mar	Fife Junior Select		H	F	1-3	300	Murray	Newman	Hoggan,R	Oliphant	Newman	Crichton 1	Penman	Newman	Newman	McKenzie	Ovenstone	Sneddon (2) Allison
S	24-Mar	Leith Athletic		H	L2	3-1	1000	Murray	Allan	Cunningham	Scott	Hoggan,M	Cunningham	Ovenstone 1	Newman	Cowan 1	Oliphant 1	Kinnear 1	Morrish
S	31-Mar	Dunfermline Athletic		A	L2	3-1	2500	Murray	Allan	Cunningham	Main	Hoggan,M	Crichton	Ovenstone	Sneddon	Cowan	Oliphant	Kinnear 2	Garland
S	07-Apr	Dumbarton		H	L2	1-1	500	Murray	Allan	Cunningham	Main	Hoggan,M	Crichton 1	Ovenstone	Scott	Penman	Oliphant	Kinnear	Ritchie
S	14-Apr	Stenhousemuir		A	L2	4-5	800	Murray	Allan	Hoggan,R	Scott	Hoggan,M	Crichton	Ovenstone	Oliphant	Cowan 4	Newman	Slater	Fraser pen Hart (3) Cowan
S	21-Apr	Dundee United		A	L2	2-5	700	Murray	Allan	Hoggan,R	Scott	Hoggan,M	Crichton	Ovenstone	Smith	Cowan	Junior 2	Newman	Corbett Brown Ochterlonie Gardiner Laing
S	28-Apr	East Fife		A	PC 1r	0-3	1100	Murray	Allan	Cunningham	Scott	Hoggan,M	Crichton	Penman	Oliphant	Cowan	Smith	Ovenstone	Munro Scott Weir

Manager : James Logan to 22nd October. Bob Bennie from 22nd October

(1) Bourhill missed penalty

(2) Beath missed penalty for Albion Rovers

Day	Date	Opponents	Note	Venue	Comp	Res.	Att.	1	2	3	4	5	6	7	8	9	10	11	Substitutes, own goals, goal times and opponents' scorers
S	11-Aug	Brechin City		H	L2	7-0	2000	Murray	Allan	Cunningham	Main,W	Hoggan,M	Crichton	Colquhoun 3	Millar	Ouchterlonie 2	Main,A 1	Brown 1	
S	18-Aug	Edinburgh City	1	H	L2	2-1	1500	Murray	Allan	Cunningham	Main,W	Hoggan,M	Scott	Colquhoun 1	Millar	Brown 1	Main,A	Ovenstone	Scott Dunsire
W	22-Aug	East Fife		H	FC 1	5-2		Murray	Allan	Cunningham	Main,W	Hoggan,M	Crichton	Colquhoun 2	Millar 2	Brown 1	Main,A	Ovenstone	
S	25-Aug	Leith Athletic		H	L2	1-0	3000	Murray	Allan	Cunningham	Main,W 1	Hoggan,M	Scott	Colquhoun	Millar	Brown	Main,A	Ovenstone	
S	01-Sep	Dundee United		A	L2	0-4	7000	Murray	Allan	Cunningham	Main,W	Hoggan,M	Crichton	Colquhoun	Millar	Morrison	Main,A	Ovenstone	Gardiner (2) Hart Kay
S	08-Sep	Stenhousemuir		H	L2	3-1	1800	Murray	Allan	Cunningham	Main,W	Hoggan,M	Crichton	Colquhoun 2	Millar	Morrison 1	Brown	Ovenstone	Hart
S	15-Sep	East Stirling		A	L2	1-2	2300	Murray	Allan	Cunningham	Main,W	Hoggan,M	Crichton	Colquhoun 1	Millar	Brown 1	Main,A	Ovenstone	Thomson, A Percy
S	22-Sep	Arbroath		H	L2	3-4	1500	Murray	Allan	Cunningham	Scott	Hoggan,M	Crichton	Colquhoun	Main,W	Fulton 2	Main,A	Ovenstone	Briggs (2) Brand (2)
S	29-Sep	Cowdenbeath		A	L2	3-3	2000	Murray	Allan	Cunningham	Main,W	Hoggan,M 1p	Crichton	Colquhoun	Main,A	Fulton 2	Harrower	Ovenstone 1	Newman Craigie Garland
M	01-Oct	Dunfermline Athletic		H	WC 1	4-3		Murray	Allan	Hoggan,R	Main,W	Hoggan,M	Crichton	Ovenstone	Colquhoun	Fulton 2	Main,A	Brown 2	Watson Dobson Main, W og
S	06-Oct	East Fife		A	L2	2-4	4000	Murray	Allan	Hoggan,R	Main,W	Hoggan,M	Crichton	Ovenstone	Colquhoun	Fulton 2	Main,A	Brown	Gillies Cowan Sharp Weir
S	13-Oct	Montrose		A	L2	2-3	400	Murray	Allan	Hoggan,R	Main,W	Hoggan,M	Crichton	Colquhoun	Millar	Fulton 1	Main,A	Brown 1	Stoddart Oliphant Moffat
S	20-Oct	Forfar Athletic		A	L2	2-2	2000	Murray	Allan	Hoggan,M	Main,W	Main,W	Crichton 1	Baxter	Walker	Fulton 1	Millar	Brown	Cochrane (2)
S	27-Oct	Morton		H	L2	1-5	2500	Murray	Allan	Warden	Scott	Hoggan,M	Crichton	Colquhoun	Millar	Fulton 1	Main,A	Brown	Keyes (4) Collins
S	03-Nov	Cowdenbeath		H	L2	2-3	1500	Murray	Allan	Cunningham	Main,W	Hoggan,M	Scott	Archibald 1	Main,A	Fulton 1	Crichton	Colquhoun	Hamill (2) Garland
S	10-Nov	St Bernards		A	L2	2-6	2000	Murray	Allan	Cunningham	Main,W	Crichton	Scott	Archibald	Millar 1	Fulton	Denholm 1	Ovenstone	Eadie (2) Igoe Murray Noble (2)
S	17-Nov	King's Park		A	L2	1-2	2000	Murray	Allan	Millar	Scott	Crichton	Hoggan,M	Archibald	Main,W	Fulton 1	Denholm	Brown	Bryce Temple pen
S	24-Nov	Third Lanark		H	L2	0-1	1200	Murray	Allan	Millar	Main,W	Crichton	Crichton	Archibald	Ouchterlonie	Fulton	Denholm	Brown	Stewart
S	01-Dec	Dumbarton		H	L2	4-2	1000	Murray	Allan	Sneddon	Scott	Crichton 1	Hoggan,M	Ouchterlonie	Millar 1	Fulton 2	Denholm 1	Ovenstone	Haddow Wallace
S	08-Dec	Alloa Athletic		H	L2	3-0	500	Murray	Allan	Cunningham	Scott	Hoggan,M	Hoggan,M	Ouchterlonie	Millar	Fulton 2	Denholm	Ovenstone	
S	15-Dec	Arbroath		A	L2	0-2	500	Murray	Crichton	Cunningham	Main,W	Hoggan,M	Scott	Ouchterlonie	Millar	Fulton	Denholm	Ovenstone	Lowe Carver
S	22-Dec	Forfar Athletic		A	L2	1-3	500	Murray	Crichton	Cunningham	McGirr	Scott	Hoggan,M	Kennedy 1	Millar	Fulton 1	Denholm	Ovenstone	Ward Black, R Newman
S	29-Dec	Montrose		H	L2	1-0	1500	Murray	Allan	Crichton	McGirr	Hoggan,M	Scott	Fulton	Millar	Fulton	Denholm	Ovenstone	
Tu	01-Jan	East Fife		H	L2	0-3	5000	Murray	Allan	Sneddon	Scott	Hoggan,M	Hoggan,M	Newman	Millar	Ouchterlonie	Denholm	Ovenstone	Gillies Cowan (2)
W	02-Jan	Third Lanark		A	L2	3-5	6000	Murray	Allan 1p	Sneddon	Main,W	Hoggan,M	Crichton	Wallace 1	Millar 1	Fulton 1	Denholm	Ovenstone	McLellan (2) Hay Kennedy + another
S	05-Jan	Stenhousemuir		A	L2	1-2	800	Murray	Allan	Sneddon	Denholm	Hoggan,M	Crichton	Wallace 1	Millar	Fulton	Sneddon	Ovenstone	Howie Cowan, P
S	12-Jan	Edinburgh City		A	L2	3-1	50	Murray	Allan	Sneddon	Scott	Hoggan,M	Crichton	Wilson	Fulton 1	Ouchterlonie	Denholm 1	Ovenstone	McCormack (2) O'Rawe
S	19-Jan	Leith Athletic		A	L2	0-3	500	Murray	Allan	Sneddon	Newman	Hoggan,M	Crichton	Wilson	Scott	Fulton	Denholm	Ovenstone	Peat
W	23-Jan	East Stirling		A	SC 1	2-1	3500	Murray	Allan	Sneddon	Scott	Hoggan,M	Crichton	Wilson	Millar	Fulton 1	Denholm 1	Ovenstone	
S	02-Feb	East Stirling		H	L2	1-0	500	Murray	Allan	Cunningham	Scott	Hoggan,M	Crichton	Wilson	Millar	Fulton 3	Denholm	Ovenstone	Douglas
S	09-Feb	Brechin City		A	SC 2	1-1	1855	Murray	Allan	Cunningham	Scott	Hoggan,M	Crichton	Wilson 1	Millar	Fulton	Denholm 1	Ovenstone	Douglas Malloy (2) Osborne, pen
W	13-Feb	Brechin City		H	SC 2r	2-4	5500	Murray	Allan	Cunningham	Scott	Hoggan,M	Crichton 1	Wilson	Millar	Fulton	Denholm	Ovenstone 1	Carruthers (3) Rutherford Guthrie
S	16-Feb	Alloa Athletic		A	L2	2-5	600	Murray	Allan	Cunningham	Scott	Hoggan,M	Crichton	Wilson	Newman	Fulton	Denholm	Ovenstone 2	Hamil Garland (2)
S	23-Feb	Cowdenbeath		H	WC SF	0-3	500	Murray	Allan	Sneddon	Main,W	Hoggan,M	Crichton	Fulton	Fulton	Ouchterlonie	Denholm 1	Ovenstone	Milne (2) King
S	02-Mar	Dundee United		H	L2	0-3	1300	Murray	Allan	Sneddon	Main,W	Crichton	Crichton	Wilson	Fulton	Fulton	Denholm	Ovenstone	
S	09-Mar	Brechin City		A	L2	0-0	300	Paterson	Allan	Sneddon	McNeil	Hoggan,M	Scott 1	Wilson	Main,A	Fulton	Denholm 1	Ovenstone	
S	16-Mar	Morton		H	L2	6-0	500	Paterson	Allan	Sneddon	McNeil	Hoggan,M	Crichton	Wilson 1	Main,A 1	Fulton 2	Denholm 1	Ovenstone	McCombe Pringle (2)
S	23-Mar	Hearts 'A'		H	F	3-3		Paterson	Allan	Sneddon	Scott	Hoggan,M	Crichton	Wilson 1	Main,A 1	Fulton 1	Denholm	Ovenstone	McCombe Pringle (2)
S	30-Mar	St Bernards		H	L2	3-0	1200	Paterson	Allan	Sneddon	Scott	Hoggan,M	Crichton	Wilson 1	Main,A	Fulton 2	Denholm 1	Ovenstone	
S	06-Apr	King's Park		H	L2	2-0	1500	Paterson	Allan	Sneddon	Scott	Hoggan,M	Crichton	Wilson 1	Main,A	Fulton	Denholm 1	Ovenstone	
S	13-Apr	Dumbarton		A	L2	4-3	1300	Paterson	Allan	Sneddon	Scott	Hoggan,M	Crichton	Wilson	Main,A	Fulton 1	Denholm 1	Ovenstone	Haddow Speedie (2)
S	20-Apr	Cowdenbeath		A	FC SF	0-3	1000	Paterson	Allan	Sneddon	Scott	Hoggan,M	Crichton	Wilson	Main,A	Fulton	Denholm	Ovenstone	Watson (2) Kean

Manager : Bob Bennie to 2nd November. Sandy Archibald from 5th November.
Friday April 30th, Rosslyn Juniors and Rovers drew 0-0 in a Benefit match at Station Park, Dysart. Joyner, Scott, Allan, Crichton and trialist centre half Smith all played.. The match was arranged after the McNeill transfer to Rovers.
(1) match kicked off 15 minutes late, Edinburgh City were late in arriving

Day	Date	Opponents	Note	Venue	Comp	Res.	Att.	1	2	3	4	5	6	7	8	9	10	11	Substitutes, own goals, goal times and opponents' scorers
S	10-Aug	Forfar Athletic		A	L2	2-3	500	Paterson	Allan 1p	Sneddon	McNeil	Crichton	Gilbert	Wilson	Denholm	Fulton 1	Philip,H	Dobbie	Black, W Black, R Cameron pen
S	17-Aug	Cowdenbeath		H	L2	4-0	5000	Paterson	Allan	Sneddon	McNeil	Paterson	Gilbert	Wilson 1	Denholm 2	Fulton 1	Philip,H	Dobbie	
S	24-Aug	Stenhousemuir		A	L2	2-1	1000	Paterson	Allan	Sneddon	McNeil	Paterson	Gilbert	Wilson 1	Denholm	Fulton 1	Philip,H	Dobbie	Morrison
S	31-Aug	East Stirling		H	L2	1-6	4000	Paterson	Allan	Sneddon	Crichton	Paterson	Gilbert	Wilson	Denholm	Fulton	Philip,H	Dobbie 1	Gordon Brown Hart (2) McPhail Meechan
W	04-Sep	Dunfermline Athletic		H	FC 1	5-2		Paterson	Allan	Sneddon	McNeil 1	Paterson	Gilbert	Wilson	Denholm 3	Fulton 1	Philip,H	Dobbie	McGowan (2)
S	07-Sep	Leith Athletic		A	L2	1-2	2700	Paterson	Allan	Sneddon	McNeil	Paterson	Gilbert	Wilson	Denholm 1	Fulton	Philip,H	Dobbie	McCormack (2)
S	14-Sep	Dundee United		H	L2	1-1	2000	Paterson	Allan	Sneddon	McNeil	Paterson	Crichton	Philip,H	Denholm	Wilson 1	Gilbert	Dobbie	Corbett
S	21-Sep	Montrose		A	L2	1-3	1000	Paterson	Allan	Sneddon	McNeil	Paterson	Gilbert	Wilson	Denholm	Fulton 1	McIntosh	Dobbie	Osborne pen Allan Malloy
S	28-Sep	Edinburgh City		H	L2	4-2	1500	Paterson	Allan	Sneddon	McNeil	Paterson	Gilbert	Wilson	Denholm	Fulton 3	Philip,H	Dobbie 1	Hope (2)
S	05-Oct	East Fife		A	L2	1-3	3000	Paterson	Allan	Sneddon	McNeil	Paterson	Gilbert	Dawson	Denholm 1	Fulton	Philip,H	Dobbie	Scott Cowan (2)
M	07-Oct	Rangers		H	F	1-4	5000	Paterson	Allan	Sneddon	McNeil	Watson	Gilbert	Wilson	Davie	Fulton 1	Philip,H	Dobbie	Wallace Galloway (2) Kinnear
S	12-Oct	Alloa Athletic		H	L2	1-2	1500	Paterson	Allan	Sneddon	McNeil	Watson	Gilbert	Dawson	Denholm	Fulton	Philip,H 1	Dobbie	Kerr pen McMillan
S	19-Oct	Leith Athletic		H	L2	2-4	1600	Paterson	Allan 1p	Sneddon	McNeil	Watson	Gilbert	Lynas	McGoldrick	Fulton 1	Philip,H	Dobbie	Peat (3) Paterson
S	26-Oct	St Mirren		A	L2	0-6	4000	Simpson	Crichton	Sneddon	Watson	Allan	Gilbert	Lynas	McGoldrick	Fulton	Philip,H	Wilson	Kelly McGregor (2) McGammon Gall (2) — Tait 1 og
S	02-Nov	Dumbarton		H	L2	1-3	1000	Simpson	Allan	Sneddon	Watson	Paterson	Crichton	Lynas	McGoldrick	Fulton	Philip,H	Gilbert	Haddow Cook (2)
S	09-Nov	St Bernards		A	L2	2-6	1000	Simpson	Allan	Sneddon	McNeil	Paterson	Crichton	Lynas	Denholm 2	Fulton	Philip,H	Gilbert	Brookes Russell Murray (3) Hay
S	16-Nov	Falkirk		H	L2	2-3	2000	Paterson	Allan	Sneddon	Philip,J	Watson	Crichton	Wilson	Denholm	Fulton	Philip,H	Dobbie 2	Dawson (2) Newman
S	23-Nov	Forfar Athletic		H	L2	4-0	1000	Paterson	Allan 1	Sneddon	Denholm	Philip,J	Crichton 1	Wilson 1	Brownlie 1	Fulton	Philip,H	Dobbie	
S	30-Nov	King's Park		A	L2	0-3	1000	Paterson	Allan	Sneddon	Denholm	Philip,J	Crichton	Wilson	McNeil	Fulton	Philip,H	Dobbie	Bryce (2) McPherson
S	07-Dec	Brechin City		A	L2	1-2	900	Paterson	Allan	Sneddon	Denholm	Philip,J	Crichton	Gilbert 1	Brownlie	Fulton	Philip,H	Dobbie	Wann (2, 1pen)
S	14-Dec	St Mirren		H	L2	1-3	1500	Paterson	Allan 1	Sneddon	Denholm	Philip,J	Crichton	Brownlie	Craigie	Fulton	Philip,H	Dobbie	Latimer McGregor Allan og
S	28-Dec	Cowdenbeath		A	L2	0-2	2000	Simpson	Allan	Sneddon	Denholm	Philip,J	Crichton	Brownlie	Craigie	Fulton	McGill	Dobbie	Rougvie Whitelaw
W	01-Jan	East Fife		H	L2	1-2	6000	Simpson	Allan	Sneddon	Denholm	Philip,J	Crichton	Brownlie 1	Craigie	Fulton	McGill	Philip,H	Adams Downie
S	04-Jan	East Stirling		A	L2	2-4	1000	Simpson	Allan	Crichton	Denholm	Philip,J	Gilbert	Brownlie 1	Craigie	Fulton 1	McGill 2	Philip,H	McPhail (2) Hart (2)
S	11-Jan	Stenhousemuir		H	L2	3-1	1500	Simpson	Allan	Millar	Gilbert	Philip,J	Crichton	Brownlie 1	Craigie 1	Fulton 1	McGill	Philip,H	Malcolm
S	18-Jan	Dundee United		A	L2	3-4	5000	Reeder	Allan 1	Sneddon	Gilbert	Philip,J	Crichton	Philip,H	Craigie 1	Fulton 1	McGill	Dobbie	Gardiner (2) Milne Hutchison
S	25-Jan	St Johnstone		H	SC 1	2-4	6500	Simpson	Allan	Sneddon	Gilbert	Philip,J	Crichton	Brownlie	Craigie	Fulton 2	McGill	Philip,H	Tennant (3) Caskie
S	01-Feb	Brechin City		H	L2	2-2	1000	Paterson	Allan	Sneddon	Gilbert	Philip,J	Crichton	Brownlie	Craigie 1	Fulton	McGill 1	Philip,H	Wann Boland
S	15-Feb	Edinburgh City		A	L2	0-1	1200	Paterson	Allan	Crichton	Gilbert	Watson	Philip,H	Brownlie	Craigie	Fulton	McGill	Dobbie	Halliday
S	29-Feb	Edinburgh City		H	L2	3-2	500	Paterson	Allan	Philip,J	Gilbert	Watson	Crichton	Dewar	Craigie	Fulton 2	Dobbie	Wardlaw 1	Gallacher Hamilton
S	07-Mar	St Bernards		A	L2	4-1	500	Paterson	Allan	Philip,J	Gilbert	Watson	Crichton	Sneddon	Denholm	Fulton 2	McGill 2	Wardlaw	Paterson
S	14-Mar	Falkirk		A	L2	0-6	6000	Paterson	Allan	Philip,J	Gilbert	Watson	Crichton	Craigie	Denholm	Fulton	McGill	Dobbie	Carruthers Keyes (2) Cowan (2) Dawson
S	21-Mar	Montrose		H	L2	2-0	1200	Paterson	Allan	Philip,J	Gilbert	Watson	Crichton	Philip,H	Craigie 1	Fulton 1	McGill	Dobbie	
S	28-Mar	Morton		H	L2	2-2	1000	Paterson	Allan	Millar	Philip,J	Watson	Crichton 1	Philip,H	Craigie 1	Fulton	McGill	Newman 1	Calder Ferguson
M	04-Apr	King's Park		H	L2	1-2	1000	Paterson	Allan	Sneddon	Gilbert	Watson	Crichton	Dewar	Craigie	Fulton 1	Philip,H	Newman	Bryce Strathie
M	06-Apr	Dundee		H	PC SF	2-2	1000	Paterson	Allan 1p	Crichton	Denholm	Watson	Gilbert	Dewar	Craigie	Fulton	McGill	Dobbie 1	Linton Reid
S	11-Apr	Dumbarton		A	L2	4-3	1200	Paterson	Allan	Philip,J	Denholm	Watson	Crichton	Philip,H 1	Craigie	Fulton 1	McGill 1	Dobbie	Watson Wallace Speedie
W	15-Apr	Dundee	1	A	PC SFr	2-2	800	Paterson	Allan	Philip,J	Denholm 1	Watson	Crichton	Philip,H 1	Craigie	Fulton	McGill 1	Dobbie	Baxter Reid
S	18-Apr	Morton		A	L2	2-11	1000	Paterson	Allan	Philip,J	Denholm	Watson	Crichton	Philip,H	Craigie 1	Fulton 2	McGill	Dobbie	Calder (8) Benzie Ferguson (2)
S	25-Apr	East Fife		A	WC SF	1-5	400	Paterson	Allan	Philip,J	Denholm	Watson	Crichton	Gilbert	Philip,H	Fulton 1	McGill	Dobbie	Philip, J og Cowan (3) Adams

Manager : Sandy Archibald
(1) won on corners

Day	Date	Opponents	Note	Venue	Comp	Res.	Att.	1	2	3	4	5	6	7	8	9	10	11	Substitutes, own goals, goal times and opponents' scorers
S	08-Aug	Stenhousemuir		H	L2	2-1	2500	Crosskey	Allan	Peattie	Baxter	Morrison	Philip,H	Glen	McDonald 1	Bryce 1	Gilmour 1	Whyte	Murray, R
W	12-Aug	Cowdenbeath	1	H	WC	3-3		Crosskey	Allan 1	Peattie	Baxter 1	Morrison	Philip,H	Glen	McDonald	Bryce 1	Gilmour	Whyte	Malloy (2) Boag
S	15-Aug	East Stirling		A	L2	3-0	2000	Crosskey	Allan	Peattie	Baxter	Morrison	Philip,H	Glen	McDonald	Bryce 2	Gilmour	Whyte 1	
W	19-Aug	East Fife	(1)	H	FC F	0-3	3000	Paterson	Allan	Peattie	Baxter	Morrison	Philip,H	Glen	McDonald	Cabrelli	Gilmour	Philip,J	Cowan (2) Downie
S	22-Aug	Leith Athletic		A	L2	1-0	3000	Crosskey	Allan	Peattie	Baxter	Morrison	Cabrelli	Glen 1	Philip,H	Pollock 1	Gilmour	Whyte	
S	29-Aug	Dundee United		H	L2	4-2	6000	Crosskey	Allan	Peattie	Baxter	Morrison	Cabrelli	Glen	McDonald	Fulton 2	Gilmour 1	Whyte	Bain (2)
S	05-Sep	East Fife		A	L2	2-2	12177	Crosskey	Allan 1	Peattie	Baxter	Morrison	Cabrelli	Glen	McDonald 1	Fulton 1	Gilmour 1	Whyte	Adams Scott
W	12-Sep	Edinburgh City		H	L2	3-1	700	Crosskey	Allan	Peattie	Baxter	Morrison	Philip,J	Glen	McDonald 1	Fulton 1	Gilmour 1	Whyte	Anderson
S	16-Sep	Dunfermline Athletic		A	FC SF	0-1		Paterson	Allan	Peattie	Baxter	Morrison	Cabrelli	Glen	Philip,H	Fulton 2	Gilmour 1	Hutchison	Morris
S	19-Sep	Montrose		H	L2	3-0	6000	Crosskey	Allan	Peattie	Baxter	Morrison	Cabrelli	Glen	McDonald	Fulton 1	Gilmour	Whyte	
S	26-Sep	Cowdenbeath		A	L2	1-4	10000	Crosskey	Allan	Peattie	Baxter	Morrison	Cabrelli	Glen	McDonald	Fulton 1	Gilmour 1	Whyte	Malcolm (2) McCurley Craigie
S	03-Oct	Forfar Athletic		H	L2	1-6	5000	Crosskey	Black	Black	Baxter	Morrison	Cabrelli	Glen	Brownlie r35	Fulton	Gilmour	Philip,H	Black, W. (4) McLean Preston
M	05-Oct	Hearts		H	F	1-5	2000	Paterson	Blyth	Peattie	Baxter	Morrison 1	Gilmour	Glen	McDonald 1	Fulton	Gilmour	Hutchison 1	Walsh (4) Black / Philip,H u35
S	10-Oct	King's Park		A	L2	1-5	1500	Crosskey	Blyth	Peattie	Baxter	Morrison	Gilmour	Glen	Cabrelli	Fulton 1	Cabrelli	Hutchison 1	Haggart (2) McDowall, J McDonnell Clark
S	17-Oct	Dumbarton		H	L2	3-0	2000	Crosskey	Robson	Peattie	Baxter	Morrison	Blyth	Glen	Cabrelli	Fulton 3	Cabrelli	Fraser 1	
S	24-Oct	Brechin City		H	L2	3-2	2000	Crosskey	Robson	Peattie	Baxter	Morrison	Blyth	Glen	Cabrelli	Fulton	Gilmour 1	Fraser	Junior (2)
S	31-Oct	St Bernards		A	L2	0-3	4000	Crosskey	Robson	Peattie	Baxter	Morrison	Blyth	Glen	Cabrelli	McLennan 1	Gilmour	Fraser	Grant (2) Pinkerton
S	07-Nov	Dundee United		H	L2	2-3	2500	Crosskey	Robson	Peattie	Baxter	Morrison	Cabrelli	Glen	Philip,H	Fulton	Gilmour	Fraser 1	Milne (2) Paterson
S	14-Nov	Leith Athletic		A	L2	0-3	1000	Crosskey	Robson	Peattie	Baxter	Morrison	Cabrelli	Glen	McDonald 1	Fulton	Gilmour	Fraser	Haddow (2) Murphy
S	21-Nov	Alloa Athletic		H	L2	4-3	3000	Crosskey	Peattie	Smith	Baxter 1	Morrison	Cabrelli	Glen	McDonald	Fulton 2	Philip,H	Bain	Bryer Halliday (2)
S	28-Nov	Brechin City		A	L2	1-3	800	Crosskey	Peattie	Smith	Baxter	Morrison	Cabrelli	Glen	McDonald	Fulton 1	Fraser	Bain	Quigley (2) McDowall
S	12-Dec	Airdrie		H	L2	0-0	3000	Crosskey	Peattie	Smith	Baxter	Morrison	Cabrelli	Glen	Gilmour	Fulton	Gilmour	Gilmour	
S	19-Dec	Stenhousemuir		A	L2	7-2	1000	Crosskey	Peattie	Smith	Baxter	Morrison	Cabrelli	Glen	McDonald	Fulton 5	Steele 1	Fraser 1	Howie (2)
S	26-Dec	East Stirling		H	L2	5-0	3000	Crosskey	Peattie	Smith	Baxter	Morrison 1	Cabrelli	Glen	Gilmour 1	Fulton 2	Steele 1	Fraser 1	
F	01-Jan	East Fife		A	L2	4-3	9200	Crosskey	Allan	Peattie	Baxter	Morrison	Cabrelli	Glen 1	Gilmour	Fulton 1	Steele 1	Fraser	McLeod Adams Young
S	02-Jan	Cowdenbeath		H	L2	1-3	8000	Crosskey	Allan 1	Peattie	Baxter	Morrison	Cabrelli	Glen	Gilmour	Fulton 1	Steele 1	Fraser	Boag (2) Craigie
S	09-Jan	Forfar Athletic		A	L2	1-1	1000	Crosskey	Allan	Peattie	Baxter	Morrison	Cabrelli	Glen	Philip,H	Philip,H	Steele	Fraser	Caroer
S	16-Jan	Ayr United		A	L2	0-1	5000	Paterson	Peattie	Smith	Baxter	Morrison	Cabrelli	Glen	Gilmour	Fulton	Steele	Fraser	Gemmel
S	23-Jan	Morton		H	L2	0-2	4000	Paterson	Peattie	Smith	Baxter	Morrison	Cabrelli	Glen	Gilmour	Fulton	Steele	Fraser	Calder Smith
W	03-Feb	St Johnstone		H	SC 1	0-5	5500	Crosskey	Peattie	Smith	Baxter	Morrison	Cabrelli	Glen	Gilmour	Fulton	Steele	Fraser	Tennant (2) Beattie McCall Casker
S	06-Feb	Dundee United		A	L2	3-1	2000	Paterson	Peattie	Smith	Baxter	Morrison	Cabrelli	Glen	Gilmour 1	Fulton 1	Steele 1	Fraser	Halliday
S	13-Feb	Morton		A	L2	1-5	5000	Paterson	Peattie	Smith	Baxter	Morrison	Cabrelli	Glen	Gilmour	Fulton 1	Steele 1	Fraser	Calder (3) McGarry Smith
S	20-Feb	St Bernards		H	L2	0-1	2500	Paterson	Peattie	Smith	Baxter	Morrison	Cabrelli	Glen	Gilmour	Fulton	Steele 1	Fraser	Flucker
S	27-Feb	Dundee United		A	PC 2	4-4	1000	Paterson	Peattie	Smith	Baxter	Morrison	Cabrelli	Glen	Gilmour 1	Fulton 3	Steele 1	Fraser	Reid Hutchison McFarlane Paterson
S	06-Mar	Edinburgh City		H	L2	6-0	700	Paterson	Peattie	Smith	Baxter	Morrison	Cabrelli	Glen	McIntosh	Robertson 1	Steele 3	Fraser 2	
S	20-Mar	Dumbarton		A	L2	1-3	1000	Paterson	Peattie	Smith	Baxter	Morrison	Cabrelli	Glen	Gilmour 1	Fulton	Steele	Fraser	Murray (2) Duffy
S	27-Mar	Montrose		A	L2	2-0	800	Paterson	Peattie	Smith	Baxter	Morrison	Cabrelli	Glen	Gilmour 1	Fulton 1	Steele 1	Fraser	Gemmell Torbet
S	03-Apr	Ayr United		H	L2	2-2	1500	McKay	Peattie	Smith	Baxter 1	Morrison	Cabrelli	Glen	Gilmour 1	Fulton	Steele	Fraser	Skilligan
M	05-Apr	Dundee United		H	PC 2r	4-1		Paterson	Peattie	Smith	Baxter 1	Morrison	Cabrelli	Glen	Gilmour 3	Fulton 1	Steele	Fraser	Stewart Moffat Newman
S	10-Apr	Airdrie		A	L2	2-3	2000	McKay	Peattie	Smith	Baxter	Morrison	Cabrelli	McDonald	Gilmour	Fulton 2	Steele	Fraser	Rougvie Malloy Malcolm Peattie og
W	14-Apr	Cowdenbeath		A	WC SF	2-4	200	McKay	Peattie	Smith	Baxter	Morrison	Cabrelli	Fraser	Gilmour	Fulton	Steele 1	Fraser 1	McDowall
S	17-Apr	King's Park		H	L2	3-1	1200	McKay	Peattie 1p	Philip,J	Baxter	Morrison	Cabrelli	Glen	Gilmour	Fulton 3	Steele	Joyner	
W	28-Apr	Alloa Athletic		H	PC F	2-0	500	McKay	Peattie	Philip,J	Baxter	Morrison	Cabrelli	Glen	Gilmour	Fulton 1	Steele	Fraser	

Manager : Sandy Archibald

Foul throw-in reverts to the other side rather than a free kick being awarded ; goal kick to leave the penalty area (previously it was permissable to tap into the goalkeeper's hands)

(1) 1935/36 Final

Substitutes, own goals, goal times and opponents' scorers

Day	Date	Opponents	Note	Venue	Comp	Res	Att	1	2	3	4	5	6	7	8	9	10	11	Substitutes, own goals, goal times and opponents' scorers
S	14-Aug	Leith Athletic		A	L2	4-3	1000	McKay,	Peattie	Smith	Baxter	Morrison	Cabrelli	Glen	Gilmour 1	Haywood 2	Whitelaw 1	Joyner	Peat Herbert (2)
S	21-Aug	Dundee United		H	L2	4-2	4000	McKay,	Peattie	Smith	Baxter	Morrison	Cabrelli	Glen	Gilmour 1	Haywood 2	Whitelaw	Joyner 1	Clarkson (2)
W	25-Aug	Dunfermline Athletic	1	A	WC SF	3-2	1200	McKay,	Allan	Smith	Baxter	Morrison	Cabrelli	Glen	Gilmour 1	Haywood 2	Whitelaw	Joyner 1	Robertson, R. Gilbert
S	28-Aug	Brechin City		A	L2	8-2	1300	McKay,	Allan	Smith	Baxter	Morrison	Cabrelli	Glen	Gilmour	Haywood 4	Whitelaw 3	Joyner 1	Laing Cargill
S	04-Sep	Airdrie		H	L2	2-0	10000	McKay,	Allan	Smith	Baxter	Morrison	Cabrelli	Glen	Gilmour	Haywood 1	Whitelaw 1	Joyner	
S	11-Sep	East Fife		A	L2	5-3	10000	McKay,	Allan	Smith	Baxter	Morrison	Cabrelli	Glen	Gilmour 2	Haywood 2	Whitelaw 1	Joyner 1	McLeod (2) Sneddon
S	18-Sep	East Stirling		H	L2	1-1	9000	McKay,	Allan	Smith	Baxter	Morrison	Cabrelli	Glen	Gilmour	Haywood 1	Whitelaw	Joyner	Bulloch
S	25-Sep	Stenhousemuir		H	L2	2-2	1800	McKay,	Allan	Smith	Baxter	Morrison	Cabrelli	Glen	Gilmour	Haywood	Whitelaw	Joyner 2	Allan Hill
S	02-Oct	Forfar Athletic		H	L2	3-0	4000	McKay,	Allan	Smith	Baxter	Morrison	Cabrelli	Glen	Gilmour	Haywood	Whitelaw 1	Joyner 2	
M	04-Oct	East Fife		H	PC 1	4-1	7000	McKay,	Peattie	Smith	Meikleham	Morrison	Cabrelli	Glen 1	Gilmour	Haywood 1	Whitelaw 1	Fraser	McCartney
S	09-Oct	Cowdenbeath		A	L2	3-4	11800	McKay,	Allan	Smith	Baxter	Morrison	Cabrelli	Glen	Gilmour	Haywood	Whitelaw	Joyner	Gray og 1 Wilkie (3) Walls
S	16-Oct	Dumbarton		A	L2	2-2	5000	McKay,	Allan	Smith	Baxter	Morrison	Cabrelli	Glen	Gilmour 1	Haywood	Whitelaw	Joyner 1	Smith, J. Robertson
S	23-Oct	King's Park		H	L2	5-1	5000	McKay,	Allan	Smith	Baxter	Morrison	Cabrelli	Glen	Gilmour 3	Haywood 1	Whitelaw 1	Joyner	McDowal
S	30-Oct	Leith Athletic		H	L2	3-1	6000	McKay,	Allan	Smith	Baxter	Morrison	Cabrelli	Glen	Gilmour 3	Haywood 1	Whitelaw 2	Joyner	Peat
S	06-Nov	Edinburgh City		A	L2	6-1	1500	McKay,	Allan	Smith	Baxter 1	Morrison	Cabrelli	Glen	Gilmour 3	Haywood 2	Whitelaw 1	Joyner 2	Walker
S	13-Nov	Montrose		H	L2	6-0	5000	McKay,	Allan	Smith	Baxter	Morrison	Cabrelli	Glen	Gilmour 1	Haywood 1	Whitelaw 1	Joyner 2	
S	20-Nov	St Bernards		H	L2	4-2	8000	McKay,	Allan	Smith	Baxter	Morrison	Cabrelli	Glen	Gilmour 1	Haywood 2	Whitelaw	Joyner 1	Grant Hucker
S	27-Nov	Albion Rovers		A	L2	5-1	7000	McKay,	Allan	Smith	Baxter	Morrison	Cabrelli	Glen	Gilmour 1	Haywood 1	Whitelaw	Joyner 3	Trotter
S	04-Dec	Stenhousemuir	2	H	L2	6-2	4000	McKay,	Allan 1	Smith	Meikleham	Morrison	Cabrelli	Glen 1	Gilmour 1	Haywood 3	Whitelaw 1	Joyner	Hill (2)
S	18-Dec	Alloa Athletic		H	L2	6-3	5000	McKay,	Allan	Smith	Baxter 1	Morrison	Cabrelli	Glen 1	Gilmour 1	Haywood 3	Whitelaw 2	Joyner	Carson Nisbet Conaboy
S	25-Dec	Dundee United		A	L2	4-4	1400	McKay,	Allan	Smith	Baxter	Morrison	Cabrelli	Glen 1	Gilmour	Haywood	Whitelaw 1	Joyner 1	Skillegeour (2) Hutchison Clarkson
S	01-Jan	East Fife		H	L2	1-3	19500	McKay,	Allan	Smith	Baxter	Morrison	Cabrelli	Glen	Gilmour	Haywood	Whitelaw 1	Joyner	McLeod Cowan Morrison og
M	03-Jan	Airdrie		A	L2	3-2	11000	Watson	Allan	Smith	Baxter	Morrison	Cabrelli	Glen	Gilmour	Haywood 2	Whitelaw	Joyner 1	Murrray O'Rawe
S	08-Jan	East Stirling		A	L2	8-1	2000	Watson	Allan	Smith	Baxter	Morrison	Cabrelli	Glen	Gilmour 4	Haywood 1	Whitelaw 2	Joyner 1	Keith
S	15-Jan	Dunfermline Athletic		H	L2	4-1	12000	Watson	Allan	Smith	Baxter	Morrison	Cabrelli	Glen	Gilmour 1	Haywood 3	Whitelaw	Joyner 1	Robertson, R
S	22-Jan	Montrose	3	H	SC 1	1-0	8500	Watson	Allan	Peattie	Baxter	Morrison	Cabrelli	Glen	Gilmour 1	Haywood	Whitelaw	Joyner	
S	29-Jan	Cowdenbeath		H	L2	6-2	11000	Watson	Allan	Smith	Baxter	Morrison	Cabrelli	Glen 1	Gilmour 1	Haywood 2	Whitelaw 1	McKay,R 1	Rougvie og 1 Walls Boag
S	05-Feb	Montrose		A	L2	2-2	1500	Watson	Allan	Smith	Baxter	Morrison	Cabrelli	Glen	Gilmour 1	Haywood	Whitelaw 1	McKay,R	Ferguson (2)
S	12-Feb	Edinburgh City		H	SC 2	9-2	7400	Watson	Allan	Smith	Baxter	Morrison	Cabrelli	Glen 1	Gilmour 1	Haywood 3	Whitelaw 1	Joyner 1	McLeod Walker
S	19-Feb	Dumbarton		H	L2	7-0	6100	Watson	Allan	Smith	Baxter	Morrison	Cabrelli	Glen 1	Gilmour 3	Haywood 3	Whitelaw 1	Joyner	
S	26-Feb	St Bernards		A	L2	3-0	9000	Watson	Allan	Smith	Baxter	Morrison	Cabrelli	Glen 1	Gilmour 1	Haywood 1	Whitelaw	Joyner	
S	05-Mar	Partick Thistle	4	A	SC 3	2-1	32497	Watson	Allan	Smith	Baxter	Morrison	Cabrelli	Glen	Gilmour 1	Haywood 1	Whitelaw m	Joyner	McKeenan pen
S	12-Mar	Albion Rovers		H	L2	4-1	10000	Watson	Allan	Smith	Baxter	Morrison	Cabrelli	Glen	Gilmour 1	Haywood 1	Whitelaw 3	McKay,R 1	Liddell
S	19-Mar	East Fife	5	A	SC QF	2-2	18642	Watson	Allan	Smith	Baxter	Morrison	Cabrelli	Glen	Gilmour	Haywood	Whitelaw 1p	Joyner 1	Millar Morrison og
W	23-Mar	East Fife	6	H	SC QFr	2-3	25528	Watson	Allan	Smith	Meikleham	Morrison	Cabrelli	Glen	Gilmour	Haywood 1	Whitelaw	Joyner	Tait 1 og Herd (2) 2 pens McCartney
S	26-Mar	Forfar Athletic		A	L2	3-2	500	Watson	Allan	Smith	Peattie	Morrison	Cabrelli	Glen	Gilmour	Haywood 1	Whitelaw 2	Joyner 2	McLean Newman
S	02-Apr	Alloa Athletic		A	L2	8-3	1200	Watson	Allan	Smith	Anderson	Morrison	Cabrelli	Glen	Gilmour 2	Haywood	Whitelaw 2	Joyner 3	Jamieson (2) McKinlay
M	04-Apr	Cowdenbeath		H	FC 1	0-0	4000	McKay,	Peattie	Smith	Anderson	Morrison	Cabrelli	McKay,R	Gilmour	Haywood	Whitelaw	Joyner	
S	09-Apr	Edinburgh City		H	L2	3-1	5000	Watson	Allan	Smith	Baxter	Morrison	Cabrelli	Glen 1	Gilmour	Haywood 1	Whitelaw m	McKay,R 1	Cuthbert
W	13-Apr	King's Park		H	L2	4-1	1000	Watson	Allan	Smith	Baxter	Morrison	Cabrelli	Glen	Gilmour 2	Haywood 1	Whitelaw 3	McKay,R 1	Holland
W	20-Apr	Hearts		H	F	3-2	5000	Watson	Allan	Smith 1p	Baxter	Morrison	Cabrelli	Glen	Gilmour 1	Haywood	Gay 1	McKay,R	Walker pen Allan og
S	23-Apr	Brechin City		H	L2	3-0	4000	Watson	Allan	Smith	Baxter	Morrison	Cabrelli	Glen	Gilmour	Haywood 2	Whitelaw 1	McKay,R	
S	30-Apr	Dunfermline Athletic		A	L2	4-1	3000	Watson	Allan	Smith	Baxter	Morrison	Cabrelli	Glen	Gilmour	Haywood 3	Whitelaw 1	McKay,R	Robertson. R

Manager : Sandy Archibald

Free kick to leave the penalty area (previously tapped into goalkeeper's hands) ; weight of ball increased by one ounce ; penalty circle introduced

Wednesday September 1st, Dunnikier Juniors 2 Raith Rovers XI 1 at Beatty Crescent, attendance 1,500. The Raith team was : Ferris, Allan, Whitelaw, Meikleham, Smith, Kinnear, Maule, Gay, Cairns, Ednie, Fraser. Gay scored Rovers' goal.

(1) 1936/37 competition
(2) Clark sent off
(3) Receipts £250
(4) Rovers largest ever crowd to date
(5) £1527 at 1/6d a time ; first all-ticket match Fife
(6) 1/- admission, all ticket

Day	Date	Opponents	Note	Venue	Comp	Res	Att	1	2	3	4	5	6	7	8	9	10	11	Substitutes, own goals, goal times and opponents' scorers
S	13-Aug	Ayr United		A	L1	1-2	10000	McCreadie	Allan	Smith	Baxter	Low	Cabrelli	Glen	Gilmour	Haywood	Whitelaw 1	McKay	Yardley (2)
W	17-Aug	Burntisland Shipyard		H	FC SF	7-2		McCreadie	Allan	Stuart	Anderson	Morrison	Campbell	Hamilton	Watson,W 1	McKay 2	Sharp 3	Hamilton	Patterson Shaw
S	20-Aug	Partick Thistle		H	L1	2-4	15000	McCreadie	Allan	Smith	Baxter	Low	Cabrelli	Glen	Gilmour 1	Haywood	Whitelaw 1	McArthur 1	McSpadyen McKeenan Wallace Picken
W	24-Aug	Ayr United		H	L1	3-1	10000	McCreadie	Allan	Smith	Baxter	Low	Cabrelli	Glen 1	Gilmour 1	Haywood	Whitelaw 1	McArthur	Dimmet
S	27-Aug	Third Lanark		A	L1	0-5	4000	McCreadie	Allan	Smith	Baxter	Watson,W	Cabrelli	Glen	Gilmour	Haywood	Whitelaw	McArthur	Jones (3) Dewar Allan og
S	03-Sep	Falkirk		H	L1	0-1	10000	Watson,D	Allan	Smith	Campbell	Low	Cabrelli	Glen	Gilmour	Haywood	Whitelaw	McArthur	Bolt
Tu	06-Sep	St Monance Swifts		A	B	9-3		Ferguson	Allan	Morrison	Baxter	Whitelaw	Campbell 1	Hamilton 1	Gilmour 3	Peattie 3	McArthur	McKay 1	Archer (3)
S	10-Sep	St Johnstone		A	L1	2-1	6500	Watson,D	Allan	Smith	Campbell	Low	Cabrelli	Glen 1	Sharp 1	Anderson	Whitelaw	McArthur	Asak
Tu	13-Sep	Partick Thistle		A	L1	1-2	5000	Watson,D	Allan	Smith	Campbell	Low	Cabrelli	Glen	Sharp	Gilmour 1	Whitelaw	McArthur	McCrindle (2)
S	17-Sep	St Mirren		H	L1	1-3	5000	Watson,D	Allan	Smith	Campbell	Low	Cabrelli	Glen	Sharp	Gilmour	Whitelaw 1p	McArthur	McLintock (2) Rankine
S	24-Sep	Celtic		A	L1	1-6	8000	Watson,D	Allan	Smith	Baxter	Low	Cabrelli	Glen	Sharp	Gilmour	Whitelaw 1	McArthur	McDonald (2) Crum (3) Murphy
S	01-Oct	Motherwell		H	L1	0-1	9300	Watson,D	Allan	Smith	Baxter	Low	Cabrelli	Glen	Gilmour	Dunn	Whitelaw	McArthur	Mathie
S	08-Oct	Arbroath		A	L1	4-0	5000	Watson,D	Allan	Smith	Till	Low	Cabrelli	Glen	Whitelaw 1	Dunn 2	Sharp	McArthur 1	Milne Nutley
S	15-Oct	Hibernian		H	L1	1-2	16000	Watson,D	Allan	Smith	Till	Morrison	Cabrelli	Glen	Whitelaw 1	Dunn 1p	Sharp	McArthur	Wilson
S	22-Oct	Hamilton Academical		H	L1	2-1	10000	Watson,D	Allan	Smith	Till	Morrison	Cabrelli 1	Glen	Whitelaw	Dunn m	Sharp	McArthur	Venters (3) Thornton
S	29-Oct	Rangers		A	L1	0-4	12000	Watson,D	Allan	Smith	Till	Morrison	Cabrelli	Glen	Whitelaw	Heywood	Dunn	Haywood	Thomson Reid Collins McAvoy
S	05-Nov	Kilmarnock		A	L1	2-4	3500	Watson,D	Allan	Smith	Till	Morrison	Cabrelli	McKay	Whitelaw	Dunn 2	Gilmour	McArthur	Wallace Martin
S	12-Nov	Clyde		A	L1	3-2	5000	Ferguson	Allan	Smith	Till	Morrison	Cabrelli	McKay	Whitelaw	Dunn 2	Gilmour 1	McArthur	Kyle (4) Wright
S	19-Nov	Queen's Park		H	L1	4-5	7000	Ferguson	Allan	Smith 1p	Till	Morrison	Cabrelli	McKay	Whitelaw 2	Dunn	Gilmour	McArthur 1	Brown Briscoe
S	26-Nov	Hearts	1	H	L1	1-2	15000	Ferguson	Allan	Smith	Till	Low	Cabrelli	Glen	Whitelaw 1	Dunn	Sharp	McKay	Hamilton Biggs Brady (2), 1 pen Strauss (2)
S	03-Dec	Aberdeen		A	L1	3-6	9000	Ferguson	Allan	Smith	Till	Low	Cabrelli	Glen	Whitelaw 1	Dunn 1	Sharp	O'Keefe 1	Dawson (2) Lang (2)
S	10-Dec	Queen of the South		A	L1	2-4	5000	Ferguson	Allan	Peattie	Till	Low	Cabrelli	Glen	Gilmour	Dunn 1	Whitelaw	O'Keefe 1	Bell
S	17-Dec	Albion Rovers		H	L1	1-1	5000	Ferguson	Allan	Peattie	Baxter	Low	Cabrelli	Glen	Whitelaw m	Dunn 1	Cabrelli	O'Keefe	Dewar (2)
S	24-Dec	Third Lanark		H	L1	2-2	5000	Ferguson	Allan	Peattie	Baxter	Low	Cabrelli	McArthur	Whitelaw	Haywood 1	Dunn	O'Keefe 1	Dawson (2) Stewart (3) Carruthers
S	31-Dec	Falkirk		A	L1	1-6	7000	Ferguson	Allan	Peattie	Baxter	Low	Cabrelli	Kerr 1	Till	Haywood 1	Dunn	O'Keefe 1	McCall (3) Mathers McIntosh Simpson
M	02-Jan	St Johnstone		H	L1	5-6	16000	Ferguson	Allan	Peattie	Baxter	Low	Cabrelli	Kerr 1	Till	Haywood 1	Dunn	O'Keefe 3,2p	McIntyre Nutley
Tu	03-Jan	Hibernian		A	L1	1-2	12000	McCreadie	Allan	Peattie	Baxter	Low	Cabrelli	Kerr	Till	Haywood 1	Dunn	McArthur	
S	07-Jan	Celtic		H	L1	4-0	11500	McCreadie	Allan	Morrison	Till 1	Baxter	Cabrelli	Kerr	Whitelaw 2	Haywood	Dunn	O'Keefe 1	
S	14-Jan	Motherwell		A	L1	4-2	7000	McCreadie	Allan	Morrison	Till	Baxter	Cabrelli	Kerr	Whitelaw 2	Haywood	Dunn 1	O'Keefe	Wales Allan og
S	21-Jan	Rangers		H	SC 1	0-1	21747	McCreadie	Allan	Morrison	Till	Baxter	Cabrelli	Kerr	Whitelaw	Haywood	Dunn	O'Keefe	Venters
S	28-Jan	Arbroath		H	L1	1-3	12000	McCreadie	Allan	Morrison	Till	Baxter	Cabrelli	Kerr	Whitelaw 1	Haywood 1	Dunn	O'Keefe m	Adams Christie (2)
S	04-Feb	East Fife		H	WC 1	1-1	3000	Ferguson	Allan	Morrison	Till	Baxter	Cabrelli	Kerr	Whitelaw	Haywood 1	Gilmour 1	O'Keefe m	McKerrell
S	11-Feb	St Mirren		A	L1	2-1	4000	McCreadie	Allan	Morrison	Till	Low	Cabrelli	Glen	Whitelaw 1	Haywood	Dunn 1	O'Keefe 1	McLintock
S	25-Feb	Hamilton Academical		A	L1	3-1	3000	McCreadie	Allan	Morrison	Till	Low	Cabrelli	Glen	Whitelaw	Haywood 2	Dunn 1	O'Keefe	Thomson
S	04-Mar	Rangers		A	L1	0-2	15000	McCreadie	Allan	Morrison	Till	Low	Cabrelli	Kerr	Whitelaw	Haywood	Dunn	O'Keefe	Thornton Venters
S	11-Mar	Kilmarnock		H	L1	2-3	6000	McCreadie	Allan	Peattie	Till	Low	Cabrelli	Kerr	Whitelaw 1	Haywood 1	Dunn	O'Keefe	Ross McGrogan (2) 2 pens
S	18-Mar	Clyde		H	L1	0-2	5000	McCreadie	Allan	Peattie	Till	Low	Baxter	Dunn	Whitelaw	Haywood	McKay	O'Keefe	Taylor (2)
S	25-Mar	Queen's Park		A	L1	0-3	7000	Ferguson	Allan	Morrison	Till	Low	Cabrelli	Glen	Gilmour	Haywood	Dunn	O'Keefe	Sleigh Christie Wright
S	01-Apr	Hearts		A	L1	1-2	12000	Ferguson	Allan	Morrison	Till	Low	Cabrelli	Glen	Whitelaw 1	Haywood	Dunn 1	O'Keefe 1	Garrett (2)
M	03-Apr	Cowdenbeath		H	WC SF	2-1	2000	Ferguson	Allan	Morrison	Cooper	Campbell	Baxter	Maule	Whitelaw 1	Kerr	Dunn	O'Keefe 1	Walls Cooper 1 og
S	08-Apr	Aberdeen		H	L1	3-2	7000	Ferguson	Allan	Peattie	Till	Campbell	Cabrelli	Glen	Dunn 1	Kerr	Whitelaw	O'Keefe 1	Hamilton Biggs
S	22-Apr	Queen of the South		H	L1	1-3	6000	Ferguson	Allan	Peattie	Till	Campbell	Cabrelli	Glen	Dunn	Kerr	Whitelaw 1	O'Keefe	Dawson Hay Savage
W	26-Apr	Dunfermline Athletic		H	FC F	1-1		Ferguson	Allan	Low	Cooper	Campbell	Cabrelli	Maule	Haywood	Kerr 1	Whitelaw	McKay	Whyte
S	29-Apr	Albion Rovers		A	L1	1-2	5000	Ferguson	Allan	Peattie	Till	Campbell	Cabrelli	Glen	Dunn	Haywood 1	Whitelaw	McKay	Burke (2)

Manager : Sandy Archibald
(1) Tommy Walker missed penalty

Day	Date	Opponents	Note	Venue	Comp	Res.	Att.	1	2	3	4	5	6	7	8	9	10	11	Substitutes, own goals, goal times and opponents' scorers
S	12-Aug	Dundee		A	L2	1-5	15000	Moodie	Peattie	Low	Till	Baxter	Cabrelli	Dunn	Whitelaw 1	Haywood	Smith,W	Kerr	Adam Coats McGilvary (3)
W	16-Aug	Dunfermline Athletic	1	A	FC F	1-1		Moodie	Peattie	McAulay	Baxter	Low	Smith,W	Maule	Campbell	Haywood	Whitelaw	Duncan	Johnston
W	19-Aug	Brechin City		H	L2	2-0	3000	Moodie	Peattie	McAulay	Baxter	Low	Cabrelli	Maule	Campbell 1	Dunn 1	Whitelaw	Duncan 1	Peattie (2 own goals)
W	23-Aug	Dunfermline Athletic	2	H	WC F	4-2		Moodie	Peattie	McAulay	Till	Low	Cabrelli	Maule	Whitelaw 1	Kerr 1	Dunn 1	Duncan 1	Kyle Mitchell
S	26-Aug	Queen's Park		A	L2	1-2	11000	Moodie	Peattie	McAulay	Baxter	Low	Smith,W	Maule	Campbell 1	Haywood	Dunn	Duncan	Laing Adamson
Tu	29-Aug	Peebles Rovers		A	F	2-2		Moodie	Peattie	McAulay	Baxter	Low	Cabrelli	Maule	Smith,W	Kerr 1	Dunn 1	Duncan	
W	30-Aug	Burntisland Shipyard		H	FC 1	6-0		Moodie	Peattie	McAulay	Till	Low	Cabrelli	Maule	Whitelaw 1	Kerr 1	Dunn 1	Duncan	Junior (3) 21, 76, 85
S	02-Sep	Stenhousemuir		H	L2	1-3	5000	Moodie	Peattie	McAulay	Baxter	Low	Cabrelli	Maule	Till	Haywood	Whitelaw 1	Duncan	Wilkie McCartney Wilson
S	30-Sep	East Fife		A	PC 1-1	0-3	3000	Moodie	Peattie	McAulay	Cooper 1	Low	Cabrelli	Maule 1	Till	Kerr	Whitelaw	Duncan 2	35
S	07-Oct	East Fife		H	PC 1-2	5-0	3000	Moodie	Peattie	McAulay	Cooper	Low	Cabrelli	Maule 1	Till	Haywood 1	Smith,W	Duncan 1	Taylor (pen) Smith Pattillo Williams (2)
S	14-Oct	Dunfermline Athletic		H	FC SF	2-0		Moodie	Peattie	McAulay	McAulay	Low	Campbell	Maule	Till	Haywood 1	Smith,W	Duncan 2	
S	21-Oct	Aberdeen		A	NEL	1-5	5000	Moodie	Peattie	McAulay	Cooper	Low	Cabrelli	Maule	Till	Haywood	Smith,W 1p	Duncan 1	Garrett (2) Phillips Donaldson Robson
S	28-Oct	Hearts		H	NEL	1-5	5500	Mathieson	Peattie	McAulay	McAulay	Low	Cabrelli	Maule	Hume	Haywood	Brown 1	Duncan	Buchan (3) Rodi Fenner
S	04-Nov	Stenhousemuir		A	NEL	0-5		Mathieson	Peattie	Murray	Till	Low	Cabrelli	Maule	Hume	Haywood	Brown	Duncan	
S	11-Nov	Dundee		H	NEL	2-1	2000	Mathieson	Low	Peattie	Baxter	Murray	Cabrelli	Maule	Till	Brown	Whitelaw 1p	Duncan 1	Adam
S	18-Nov	Cowdenbeath		A	NEL	3-5		Mathieson	Low	Peattie	Baxter	Low	Cabrelli	Maule	Till	Brown 1	Whitelaw m 2	Duncan	McLellan (2) McDowall Gillies (2)
S	25-Nov	King's Park		H	NEL	1-2	1000	Moodie	Peattie	Smith (LU)	Murray	Low	Cabrelli	Maule	Hume	Hume	Brown 1	Duncan	Stewart Ferguson
S	02-Dec	Arbroath		H	NEL	6-0	2000	Moodie	Peattie	Tulip	Murray	Low	Cabrelli	Maule 1	Hume	Hume 2	Brown	Duncan 2	
S	09-Dec	Alloa Athletic		A	NEL	1-3		Moodie	Peattie	Tulip	Murray	Low	Cabrelli	Maule	Till 1	Hume 1	Brown	Duncan	Rice Gillan Fitzsimmons
S	16-Dec	Falkirk		A	NEL	0-5		Moodie	Peattie	Tulip	Till	Low	Cabrelli	Maule	Till	Broadley	Broadley	Duncan 1	McPhee pen Carruthers Stewart (2) Dawson
S	23-Dec	Dundee United		H	NEL	1-1		Moodie	Peattie	Tulip	Baxter	Low	Cabrelli	Kerr	Whitelaw	Broadley	Broadley	Duncan	Gardiner
S	30-Dec	Dunfermline Athletic		H	NEL	0-3		Moodie	Peattie	Tulip	Hume	Murray	Cabrelli	Maule	Till	Hume	Brown	Duncan	Johnston Black Dryan
M	01-Jan	East Fife		A	NEL	2-5		McKay	Peattie	Mackie	Hume	Campbell	Cabrelli	Brown	Whitelaw	Brown	Smith	Duncan 1	Adams Westbrook (2) Morrison (2)
Tu	02-Jan	St Johnstone		A	NEL	3-10	700	Moodie	Peattie	Tulip	Till	Low	Campbell	Maule	Kinnear 1	Kinnear 2	Hume	Duncan	Lorimer (3) Smeaton (3) Cook (3) Campbell og
S	06-Jan	Hibernian		A	NEL	1-4		Moodie	Pope	Tulip	Till	Low	Cabrelli	Maule 1	Murray 1	Broadley 2	Hume	Duncan	Rice Mayes Keen Nutley
S	13-Jan	St Bernards		H	NEL	6-0		Moodie	Pope	Tulip	Till	Low	Cabrelli 1	Maule 1	Murray 1	Kinnear 1	Hume	Duncan 1	
S	10-Feb	Dundee		A	NEL	3-2	2500	Moodie	Pope m	Tulip	Till	Low	Cabrelli 1	Maule 1	Murray 1	Kinnear 3	Hume	Duncan 1	Easson Cook
S	17-Feb	Rangers A		H	F	3-3	1300	Moodie	Pope	Rougvie	Cooper	Low	Cabrelli	Maule 1	Till	Kinnear	Murray 2	Duncan	Gilmour McPhail Kinnear
S	24-Feb	Celtic		A	SC 1-1	2-4	6201	Moodie s	Pope	Tulip	Till	Low	Cabrelli	Maule	Murray 1	Kinnear 1	Hume	Duncan	Crum (2) Divers Gould / Lyon og 1
S	02-Mar	Celtic	3	H	SC 1-2	3-0	6431	Moodie	Pope	Rougvie	Till	Low	Campbell 1	Maule	Tulip 1	Kinnear 1	Hume	Duncan	
S	09-Mar	Hearts		A	NEL	1-2	9551	Moodie	Pope	Rougvie	Till	Murray	Campbell 1	Maule	Tulip 1	Kinnear 1	Hume	Duncan	Walker Phillips
S	16-Mar	Falkirk		H	NEL	2-2		Moodie	Pope	Rougvie	Till	Murray	Cabrelli	Maule	Tulip 1	Kinnear 1	Hume	Duncan 1	Keyes Dawson
S	23-Mar	Stenhousemuir		A	NEL	5-2		Moodie s	Pope	Rougvie	Till	Low	Cabrelli	Maule	Price	Kinnear 2	Tulip 2	Duncan 1	Roughead Mauchline
S	30-Mar	Dunfermline Athletic		A	NEL	4-3		Moodie	Pope	Rougvie	Till	Low	Cabrelli	Maule 1	Price	Kinnear 1	Tulip 1	Duncan 1	Fisher Callan Johnston
M	01-Apr	Aberdeen		H	NEL	4-1		Moodie	Pope	Rougvie	Campbell	Low	Cabrelli	Maule	Tulip	Kinnear 2	Tulip 2	Duncan	Pattillo
S	06-Apr	East Fife		A	NEL	2-3		Moodie	Pope	Rougvie	Till	Murray	Cabrelli	Maule	Brown	Wilkie 1	Tulip	Duncan 1	Adams pen McLeod Watson
W	10-Apr	Hearts		H	NEL	3-4		Mathieson	Pope	Rougvie	Till	Low	Cabrelli	Maule	Murray 1	Price 2	Tulip	Duncan	McCartney (4)
S	13-Apr	St Johnstone		H	NEL	3-4		Mathieson	Pope	Rougvie	Till	Low	Cabrelli	Maule	Murray	Price 2	Tulip	Duncan 1	McIntosh (2) Smeaton Boyd
S	20-Apr	Hibernian		H	NEL	1-1		Moodie	Pope	Rougvie	Cooper	Low	Cabrelli	Maule 1	Murray	Wilkie	Brown	Duncan	Gallacher
W	24-Apr	King's Park		A	NEL	6-5		Moodie	Pope	Rougvie	Campbell	Low	Cabrelli	Maule	Hastie 3	Tulip 1	Murray	Duncan 1	McDowall (3) Black Burrell / Rae og 1
S	27-Apr	St Bernards		A	NEL	0-1		Moodie	Pope	Rougvie	Till	Murray	Cabrelli	Maule	Hastie	Cooper	Tulip	Duncan	Newman
W	01-May	Alloa Athletic		H	NEL	1-3		Moodie	Pope	Rougvie	Campbell	Low	Cabrelli	Maule	Hastie	Murray 1	Till	Duncan	Conway (2) Fitzsimmons
S	04-May	Arbroath		A	NEL	2-0		Moodie	Pope	Rougvie m	Till	Murray	Low	Cooper 1	Maule	Campbell 1	Cabrelli	Duncan	
W	08-May	Dundee United		H	NEL	5-0		Moodie	Pope	Rougvie	Till	Low	Cabrelli	Kerr 1	Maule 1	Wotherspoon 3	Linton	Duncan	

Manager : Sandy Archibald to 14th October. Willie Reekie from 21st October

War was declared on Germany on Sunday September 3rd

(1) 1938/9 Final - lost on toss of a coin

(2) 1938/9 Final

(3) £357 excluding stand & tax

Day	Date	Opponents	Note	Venue	Comp	Res.	Att.	1	2	3	4	5	6	7	8	9	10	11	Substitutes, own goals, goal times and opponents scorers
S	09-Aug	Aberdeen		H	NEL 1	2-4	2000	Keogh	Abbie	Rougvie	Fleming	Murray,R	Martin	Summers	Stewart	Falconer	McNaught 1	Duncan	3, 60 — McCall (2) 74, 87 Donaldson 84 McLeod 76
S	16-Aug	Rangers		A	NEL 1	1-8	3000	Keogh	Abbie	Martin	Fleming	Rougvie	Cabrelli	Summers	Dougal	Falconer	McNaught 1	Joyner	81 — Thornton 49 Hunter Grant (2) 33, 67 Waddell (2) 31, 52 Marshall 47
S	23-Aug	St Bernards		H	NEL 1	3-4	2000	Keogh	McDermott	Rougvie	Leivesley	Low	McDonnell	Duncan 1	Fleming	Newman	McNaught 1	Joyner 1	10, 22, 40 — Dingwall 75 Wilkie, J. (2) 6, 85 Wilkie, W. 80
S	30-Aug	East Fife		H	NEL 1	1-2	4000	Keogh	Masson	Rougvie	Leivesley	Low	McDonnell	Gould	Fleming	Newman	McNaught	Duncan 1	63 — Simpson, W. 61 Simpson, P. 70
S	06-Sep	Dunfermline Athletic		A	NEL 1	4-4	2500	Keogh	McDermott	Rougvie	Leivesley	Low	McDonnell	Gould	Mathieson 1	Whalley 2,1p	McNaught	Duncan 2	31, 13, 60. 75 — Smith 79 Hart 84 pen Smeaton 50 Kinnear 89
S	13-Sep	Dundee United		H	NEL 1	2-1	1500	Keogh	Abbie	Rougvie	McDonnell	Low	Masson	Gould	Stirling	Whalley 4	McNaught	Joyner	50p 70 — Junior 10
S	20-Sep	Leith Athletic		H	NEL 1	9-5	1200	Keogh	McDermott	Rougvie	McDonnell	Low	McDonnell	Gould 1	McLuskie	Whalley 1	McNaught 1p	Joyner 2	5, 48, 31, 33, 34, 61, 35, 17, 20 — Broadley (3) 32, 59, 63 Alexander (2) 44, 74
S	27-Sep	Aberdeen	1	A	NEL 1	1-7	3000	Keogh	Masson	Rougvie	Kelly	Low	Masson	Gould	Murray,R	Whalley	McNaught	Duncan	72 — Dunbar 50 McLeod (3) 5, 87, 89 Dixie 35 McCall 70 Donaldson 83
S	04-Oct	Dunfermline Athletic		H	NEL 1	3-4	2000	Rodgers	Kelly	Rougvie	McDonnell	McDonnell	McDonnell	Gould 1	Mathieson	Whalley 1	McNaught 60,2,1p	Duncan	46, 14p, 24 — Hart (2) both pens 58, 78 Kinnell (2) 44, 56
S	11-Oct	Rangers		A	NEL 1	2-3	3000	Keogh	McDermott	Masson	Kinnear	Low	McDonnell	Gould 1	Maule	Newman	McNaught	Joyner 1	16, 80 — Waddell 11 McKillop 75 Galloway 21
S	18-Oct	East Fife		H	NEL 1	1-5	3500	Keogh	McDermott	Masson	Newman	Masson	McDonnell	Gould	Newman	Whalley 1	Newman	Joyner	63 — Mudie (2) 44, 55 James 80 Simpson, W. 8 Simpson, P. 23
S	25-Oct	Leith Athletic		H	NEL 1	0-4	1000	Keogh	Moodie	Rougvie	Mackie	Low	McDonnell	Gould	Mathieson	Newman	Ferguson	Newman	— Robertson 80 Heywood 65 Laing 20 Slater 55
S	01-Nov	St Bernards		A	NEL 1	2-3	600	Keogh	McDermott	Rougvie	Murray	Low	McDonnell	Gould 2	Murray,J	Whalley	Ferguson	Louden 1	35, 39 — Duffy 31 Wilkie, J. 46 Junior 87
S	08-Nov	Dundee United	2	H	NELC 1-1	9-3	4000	Westland	McDermott	Rougvie	Murray	Low	McNaught	Duncan 2	Murray,J	Gould 4	Ferguson 2	Louden	49, 89, 53, 62, 73, 85, 11, 35, 40 — Ross 41 Juliusson (2) 15, 46
S	15-Nov	East Fife		A	NELC 1-2	0-4	2500	Westland	McDermott	Rougvie	McDonnell	Low	McNaught	Duncan m	Murray,J	Gould	Ferguson	Louden	— Mudie 52 Simpson, W. 5, 61 Simpson, P. 72
S	22-Nov	East Fife	3	A	NELC 1-2	2-5	2800	Westland	McDermott	Rougvie	McDonnell	Low	McNaught	Gould 1	Murray,J	Murray,R 1	Ferguson	Duncan	12, 88 — Smile 85 Mudie 36 James 62 Simpson, W. 10 Simpson, P 64
Th	27-Dec	Raith Athletic		H	F	3-4													Woon (2) Syme, W Livingstone
Th	01-Jan	East Fife		H	NEL 2	7-2	5000	Keogh	Martin	Jones	Phypers	Low	McDonnell	Duncan	Hurrell	Whalley 3	McNaught	Joyner 4	17. 32 — Junior 10
S	03-Jan	Dunfermline Athletic		A	NEL 2	2-3	2000	Westland	Kelly	Miller	Phypers	Low	McDonnell	Stewart 1	Hurrell 1	Whalley	Newman	Joyner	8, 35, 42, 44 — Hunter 10 Smeaton 57 Kinnear 70
S	10-Jan	Rangers		H	NEL 2	4-3	4000	Westland	Martin	McDermott	McDonnell	Low	McDonnell	Stewart	Foxall 2	Leslie 2	McNaught 2	Duncan	65, 29, 82, 1, 77 — McKillop 40 Dempster 20 Beattie 65
S	17-Jan	Aberdeen		A	NEL 2	5-3	2000	Westland	Martin	Miller	Newman	Low	Newman	Stewart 1	Newman	Markie	Duncan	Joyner 2	63, 75 — Armstrong 55 Lyon (2) 51 pen, 81 pen
S	21-Feb	East Fife		H	NEL 2	2-1	2500	Westland	Martin	Jones	McDonnell	Low	Miller	Stewart 1	Miller	Markie	McNaught 1	Joyner	36 — Newman 84
S	28-Feb	Rangers		H	NEL 2	1-6	1000	Westland	Martin 1p	Miller	McDonnell	Low	Miller	Stewart	Hurrell	Conway	McNaught	Joyner	36 — Milleron 89 Sneddon 40 pen Paris (3) 20, 21, 39 Simpson P 7
S	14-Mar	Leith Athletic		H	NEL 2	3-6	3000	Keogh	Martin	Miller	McDonnell	Newman	Aitken	Stewart	Hurrell	King	Whalley 1	Joyner 2	44, 1, 23 — McKillop 38 Grant 53 McIntosh (2) 68, 74 Dempster 13
S	21-Mar	St Bernards		H	NEL 2	1-2	1500	Keogh	Martin	Jones	McDonnell	Low	Conway	Stewart	Hurrell	Adams 1	Conway	Joyner 2	65 — Allan 23 Cairns 50 pen
S	28-Mar	Dundee United		A	NEL 2	0-0	200	Keogh	Martin	Miller	Newman	Low	Miller	Stewart	Hurrell	King	Handley	Duncan	
S	04-Apr	Leith Athletic		A	NEL 2	1-5	1000	Keogh	Martin	Miller	Newman	Low	McDonnell	Stewart 1	Handley	King	Hurrell	Maule	10 — Low 86 Wann (2) 16, 53 Glassey 56 Smart 54
S	11-Apr	Dundee United		A	NEL 2	2-4	300	Keogh	Martin	Miller	McLean	Low	Conway	Stewart	Kinnear 2	Whalley	Hurrell	Newman	60, 63 — Wilson (2) 34, 44 Newman (2) 22, 75
S	18-Apr	St Bernards		H	NEL 2	1-1	1000	Keogh	Martin	Jones	Murphy	Low	McLean	Stewart	Hurrell	Newman	Smith	Beatson 1	89 — Juliusson 43
S	25-Apr	Dunfermline Athletic		H	NEL 2	5-2	1000	Keogh	Martin	Jones	McLean	Low	Conway	Stewart 2	Gordon 1	Whalley	Smith	Beatson 2	5, 88, 40, 85, 88 — Wilkie (2) 44, 78
S		Dunfermline Athletic		H	NEL 2	4-0	2000	Keogh	Martin	Jones	McLean	Low	Conway	Stewart 2	Hurrell	Wotherspoon 1	Smith 1	Beatson	46, 76, 5, 53

Rovers did not play a fixture during 1940/41

1941/42

Manager : Willie Reekie

(1) Aberdeen arrived late and 2 x 40 minutes were played, the result standing

(2) Juliussen missed penalty

(3) Mudie missed penalty

Day	Date	Opponents	Note	Venue	Comp	Res.	Att.	1	2	3	4	5	6	7	8	9	10	11	Goal times	Substitutes, own goals and opponents' scorers
S	08-Aug	Aberdeen		H	NEL 1	1-3	2000	Westland	Martin	Cairns	Phypers	Low	Conway	Stewart 1	Smith	Hurrell	Duncan	Beatson	75	Pattillo (2) 37, 57 Dryden 85
S	15-Aug	Dundee United		A	NEL 1	2-3	2000	Westland	Hickman	Cairns	Phypers	Low	Conway	Stewart	Walker	McDowell 2	Donald	Duncan	15, 40	Singleton 49 Glassey (2) 5, 10
S	22-Aug	East Fife	1	H	NEL 1	0-2	2000	Westland	Martin	Cairns	Phypers	Low	Campbell	Stewart	Smith	McDowell	Hampson	Duncan		Simpson, P. 77 Smith 76
S	29-Aug	Hibernian		A	NEL 1	2-3	2500	Keogh	Cairns	Eden	Hickman	Low	Phypers	Stewart 1	Lowe 1	McFadyen	Hampson	Duncan 1	18, 80	Banks 38 McCormack (2) 9, 41
S	05-Sep	Rangers		H	NEL 1	3-1	3000	Keogh	Cairns	Eden	Hickman	Low	Phypers	Stewart 1	Wilkie	Wilkie	Hampson	Duncan 1	84, 10, 44	Beattie 65
S	12-Sep	Hearts		H	NEL 1	2-1	2500	Keogh	Calpworthy	Cairns	Hickman 1	Low	Conway	Stewart	Wilkie	Wilkie	Smith	Duncan 1	40, 38	Mathieson 28
S	19-Sep	Dunfermline Athletic		A	NEL 1	1-2	2500	Keogh	Cairns	Eden	Phypers	Low	Conway	Stewart	Hurrell	Wilkie	Smith	Duncan 1	64	McGilvary (2) 8, 75
S	26-Sep	East Fife		A	NEL 1	1-4	4000	Keogh	Cairns	Eden	Hickman	Low	Phypers	Stewart	Hurrell 1	Wilkie	Smith	Duncan	71	Woods 36 Ross 48 Duncan 65 Smith 35 pen
S	03-Oct	Dundee United		H	NEL 1	4-0	2000	Keogh	Cairns	Eden	Donald	Low	Donald	Maule 1	Hurrell	Wilkie 2	Conway 1	Duncan	40, 30, 44, 2	
S	10-Oct	Aberdeen		A	NEL 1	1-8	10000	Keogh	Hickman	Cairns	Donald	Low	Phypers	Stewart	Hurrell	Wilkie 1	Conway	Duncan	80	Pattillo (3) 15, 43, 49 Gourlay (4) 1, 9, 14, 72 Ferguson 45
S	17-Oct	Rangers		H	NEL 1	1-3	1000	Keogh	Cairns	Eden	Hickman	Low	Phypers	Stewart	Hurrell	Wilkie 1	Conway	Duncan	37	McIntosh 35 Beattie 34 Williamson 67
S	24-Oct	Hearts	2	H	NEL 1	3-2	2000	Robinson	Hickman	Phypers	Hickman	Low	Conway	Hurrell	Brand 1	Mackie	Smith	Duncan 1	47, 27, 89	Moore 15 Junior 6
S	31-Oct	Dunfermline Athletic		H	NEL 1	1-4	2000	Keogh	Cairns	Jones	Donald	Low	Conway	Hurrell	Smith,W	Smith,W	McNaught 1	Duncan	37	Logie (2) 73, 75 McGilvray 48 Harrower, J. 78
S	07-Nov	Hibernian		H	NEL 1	1-1	1000	Gage	Hickman	Jones	Donald	Low	Phypers	Stewart	Hurrell	Mackie 1	Smith	Duncan	80	Newman 44
S	21-Nov	East Fife		A	NEC 1-1	4-1	2000	Gage	Martin	Jones	Phypers	Low	Phypers	Stewart 1	Hurrell	Cairns 1	Donald 1	Duncan 1	12, 47, 3, 89	Adams 30 pen
S	28-Nov	East Fife		A	NEC 1-2	1-2	2000	Gage	Martin	Jones	Hickman	Low	Phypers	Stewart	Wilson	Cairns 1	Donald	Duncan	15	Skinner (2) 32, 55
S	05-Dec	Aberdeen		H	NEC SF-1	2-6	2000	Gage	Donald	Jones	Hickman	Low	Phypers	Stewart	Robertson 1	Cairns	Hurrell	Duncan 1	56, 16	Taylor 43 Ancell 8 Pattillo (2) 14, 66 Ferguson 81 Dryden 6
S	12-Dec	Aberdeen		A	NEC SF-2	1-5	8000	Gage	Pope	Jones	Giblin	Low	Phypers	Stewart	Hurrell	Hickman 1	Donald	Duncan	52	Ancell 39 Pattillo (2) 12, 57 Ferguson (2) 30,70
F	01-Jan	East Fife		H	NEL 2	3-2	3000	Gage	Pope	Hickman	Imrie	Low	Phypers 1	Stewart	Hurrell	Junior 1	Donald	Maule 1	70, 57, 52	Wilkie (2)
S	02-Jan	Hearts		A	NEL 2	3-5	2500	Moodie	Pope x	Hickman 1	Giblin	Low	Phypers	Stewart 1	Mackie	Donald 1	Hurrell	Maule 1	12, 77	Harvey (2) 35, 58 pen Jackson 18 Lamb (2) 17, 25
S	09-Jan	Aberdeen		A	NEL 2	0-2	5000	Moodie	Hickman	Westwater	Dutch	Low	Phypers	Stewart	Hurrell	Robertson	Glassey	Kelly		Pattillo (2) 12, 77
S	16-Jan	Dunfermline Athletic		H	NEL 2	5-3	1000	Moodie	Donald	Brown	Dutch	Low 2, 1p	Phypers	Stewart	Hurrell 2	Junior 2	Newman	Linton	89p, 91, 59, 60, 50	Neil (2) 40, 87 Harrower 54
S	23-Jan	Dundee United		H	NEL 2	3-1	2000	Moodie	Donald	Hickman	Dutch	Low	Phypers	Kelly 2	Hurrell 1	Stewart	Glassey	Penman	19, 23, 67	Nelson 84
S	30-Jan	Rangers		A	NEL 2	4-5	3000	Moodie	Donald	Martin	Dutch	Low	Kelly	Kelly	Hurrell 2	Stewart	Glassey 1	Penman 1	1, 88, 68, 59	McIntosh 41 Smith (4) 26,79,65,85
S	06-Feb	Hibernian		H	NEL 2	5-3	1500	Moodie	Donald	Phypers	Dutch	Low 1p	Stewart	Kelly	McIntosh	Hurrell 2	Glassey 1	Penman 1	13, 35, 80, 46, 64	Junior 47 Smith, R. (2) 6, 74
S	13-Feb	Dunfermline Athletic		A	NEL 2	0-3	1500	Moodie	Millburn	Hickman	Dutch	Low	Phypers	Kelly	Hurrell	Stewart	Stead	Penman	52	Cairns 14 McGilvray 9 Harrower 34
S	20-Feb	East Fife		H	NEL 2	2-0	2000	Moodie	Millburn	Hickman	Dutch	Low	Phypers	Kelly	Hurrell 2	Stewart	Glassey 2	Penman	55, 63	
S	27-Feb	Hibernian		A	NEL 2	3-2	500	Moodie	Millburn	Hickman	Dutch	Low	Phypers	Stewart	Hurrell 2	Mackie	Glassey 1	Penman	61, 67, 36	Smith, W. 1 Anderson 85 pen
S	06-Mar	Rangers		H	NEL 2	3-2	3000	Moodie	Donald	Hickman	Dutch	Low 2p	Phypers	Stewart	Hurrell	Mackie	Glassey	Penman 1	35, 60, 25	Watkins 26 Kinnear 85 pen
S	13-Mar	Aberdeen		H	NEL 2	1-1	3000	Moodie	Millburn	Hickman	Dutch	Low	Phypers	Stewart	Hurrell	Burnett 1	Glassey	Penman 1	15	Mortensen 25
S	20-Mar	Hearts		A	NEL 2	6-2	2000	Anderson	Millburn	Hickman	Dutch	Low	Phypers	Stewart	Hurrell 2	Ryan 2	Glassey	Penman 2	65, 88, 49, 60, 25, 78	McFarlane 36 Winters 40 pen
S	27-Mar	Dundee United		H	MC 1-1	4-3	4000	Moodie	Millburn	Donald	Dutch	Low	Phypers	Stewart	Hurrell 1	Ryan	Glassey 1	Penman 2	31, 57, 2, 48	Martin 36 pen Nevins 54 Nelson 34
S	03-Apr	Dundee United		A	MC 1-2	5-0	3500	Moodie	Millburn	Donald	Dutch	Low	Phypers	Stewart	Hurrell	Payne 3	Hurrell 2	Penman 1	3, 26, 87, 17, 71	
S	10-Apr	Aberdeen		A	MC Fr	3-4	3500	Moodie	Donald	Hickman	Dutch	Low	Phypers	Stewart	McIntosh	Payne	Payne	Penman 1	7, 21, 6	Elder 70 pen Wann 9 Ross (2) 46, 89
S	24-Apr	East Fife		H	MC SF-1	3-2	5000	Moodie	Shufflebottom	Dutch	Aird	Low	Phypers	Gould 2	Hurrell	Stewart	Glassey 1	Penman	4, 27, 80	Wilkie, J. (2) 15, 72
S	01-May	East Fife		H	MC SF-2	2-1	10000	Moodie	Donald	Higgins	Dutch	Low m	Aird	Stewart 1	Hurrell 1	Payne	Glassey	Penman	5, 44	Carabine 65
S	08-May	Aberdeen		H	MC F	0-0	2000	Moodie	Dutch	Cook,W	Phypers	Low	Aird	Stewart	Hurrell	Payne	Glassey	Penman		
S	15-May	Aberdeen	3	H	MC F	1-1	9000	Moodie	Donald	Cook,W	Dutch	Low	Aird	Stewart	Hurrell	Campbell	Glassey 1	Inglis	50	Ferguson 39
S	29-May	Aberdeen		A	MC Fr	2-6	14000	Moodie	Donald	Cook,W	Dutch	Low 1p	Harvey	Stewart	Hurrell	Payne 1	Glassey	Penman	35, 30	Dyer 43 pen McSpadyen 29 Pattillo (2) 68, 79 Dryden 2 Mortensen 28

Manager : Willie Reekie

(1) Martin missed penalty
(2) Smith missed penalty
(3) Abandoned after 46 minutes due to storm

Day	Date	Opponents	Note	Venue	Comp	Res.	Att.	1	2	3	4	5	6	7	8	9	10	11	Substitutes, own goals, goal times and opponents' scorers
S	14-Aug	East Fife		A	NEL 1	3-2	3000	Moodie	Shufflebottom	Donald	Dutch	Low	Fletcher	Stewart,J 1	Hurrell	Payne 1	Glassey	Kelly 1	85, 3, 35 Sneddon 72 pen Duncan 68
S	21-Aug	Aberdeen		H	NEL 1	3-2	3000	Bruce	Shufflebottom	Donald	Dutch	Low 1p	Fletcher	Stewart,J 1	Hurrell	Payne	Glassey 1	Kelly	28, 80, 63 Ancell 38 Ferguson 50
S	28-Aug	Dundee United		A	NEL 1	1-2	3000	Moodie	Shufflebottom	Donald	Dutch	Low	Fletcher	Stewart,J 1	Hurrell	Payne 1	Conway	Connell	40 Wann 80 Nevins 13
S	04-Sep	Falkirk		H	NEL 1	6-0	3000	Bruce s	Shufflebottom	Donald	Dutch	Low	Fletcher	Stewart,J 1	Hurrell 2	Hay 1	Glassey 1	Penman 1	58, 6, 86, 52, 83, 25
S	11-Sep	Rangers		H	NEL 1	3-2	5000	Bruce	Shufflebottom	Donald	Dutch	Low 1	Fletcher	Stewart,J	Hurrell	Lamb	Glassey 2	Penman	24, 25, 40 McIntosh (2) 5, 53
S	18-Sep	Hearts		A	NEL 1	3-2	4000	Bruce	Shufflebottom	Donald	Dutch	Low	Fletcher	Stewart,J 1	Hurrell 1	Lamb 1	Glassey	Penman 1	61, 30, 26 Hamilton 48 McCrae 73
S	25-Sep	Dunfermline Athletic		H	NEL 1	4-2	7000	Bruce	Shufflebottom	Donald 1	Dutch	Low 1p	Fletcher	Stewart,J	Hurrell 1	Lamb 1	Glassey	Penman 2	86, 16, 88, 74 Logie 36 Dougan 70
S	02-Oct	East Fife		H	NEL 1	4-2	6000	Bruce	Shufflebottom	Donald 1	Dutch	Low	Fletcher	Stewart,J	Hurrell 1	Lamb	Fletcher	Penman 2	86, 16, 47, 85
S	09-Oct	Dunfermline Athletic		A	NEL 1	1-2	5000	Bruce	Dutch	Donald	Phypers	Low m	Phypers	Stewart,J	Hurrell	Lamb	Hunter	Penman	66 Brown 60 Hunter 63
S	16-Oct	Aberdeen		A	NEL 1	1-4	5000	Bruce	Shufflebottom	Donald	Phypers	Low	Phypers	Stewart,J	Hurrell	Lamb	Glassey	Kelly	66 Taylor (2) 53 pen, 89 pen Green (2) 21, 24
S	23-Oct	Dundee United		H	NEL 1	3-0	4000	Bruce	Shufflebottom	Donald	Dutch	Low	Phypers	Stewart,J 2	Hurrell	Lamb	Waldron	Fletcher 1	4, 50, 42
S	06-Nov	Falkirk		A	NEL 1	5-3	3000	Bruce	Shufflebottom	Donald	Dutch	Low	Phypers	Stewart,J	Waldron	Fletcher 1	Glassey 1	Penman 2	26, 44, 12, 3, 49 McGeachie 78 pen Murray 19 Rooney 24
S	13-Nov	Rangers		A	NEL 1	2-1	500	Bruce	Donald	Stewart,S	Dutch	Sneddon	Fletcher	Stewart,J	Waldron	Anderson	Glassey 1	Penman 1	78, 61 Parlane 89 pen
S	20-Nov	Hearts		H	NEL 1	3-0	7000	Bruce	Shufflebottom	Donald	Dutch	Low	Fletcher	Stewart,J 2	Waldron 1	Anderson	Harrower	Penman	58, 43, 71
S	27-Nov	Aberdeen		A	NELC 1-1	1-6	5000	Bruce	Shufflebottom	Donald	Dutch	Low	O'Brien	Stewart,J	Robertson 1	Lamb	McFeat	Fletcher	40 Dyer 51 pen Dunlop 63 Pattillo 84 Green 76 Ancell (2) 77, 88
S	04-Dec	Aberdeen		H	NELC 1-2	2-1	3000	Bruce	Shufflebottom	Donald	Dutch	Low	Kelly	Stewart,J 1	McFeat	Martin 1	Haywood	Penman	70, 17 Pattillo 80
S	25-Dec	East Fife	1	A	B	3-1	2500	Penman	Donald	Stewart,JC	Kelly	Low	Fletcher	Stewart,J	McFeat	Wotherspoon	Haywood 1	Urquhart 2	40, 53, 72 Fotheringham 65
S	01-Jan	East Fife		H	NEL 2	0-4	3000	Bruce	Donald	Stewart,JC	Dutch	Low	Fletcher	Stewart,J	Hurrell	Waldron	Haywood	Maule	Wilkie (2) 65, 77 Duncan (2) 35, 70
M	03-Jan	Dundee United		A	NEL 2	1-3	5000	Bruce	Donald	Stewart,JC	Dutch	Low	Drysdale	Maule	Hurrell 1	Stewart,J	Waldron	Penman	34 Wann 32 Karlsen 40 Brand 76
S	08-Jan	Hearts		A	NEL 2	2-2	2000	Bruce	Dutch	Stewart,JC	Kelly	Low 1p	Kelly	Stewart,J	Hurrell	Waldron 1	Maule 1	Urquhart	55, 1 Anderson 51 Hamilton 75
S	15-Jan	Dunfermline Athletic		H	NEL 2	1-4	2000	Bruce	Shufflebottom	Stewart,JC	Dutch	Low m	Donald	Stewart,J	McFeat	Fletcher	Waldron 1p	Penman	30 Logie 60 Hunter (2) 20, 74 Syme 65
S	22-Jan	Rangers		A	NEL 2	1-3	3000	Bruce	Dutch	Donald	Dutch	Low	Fletcher	Stewart,J	Fletcher	Mullaney	McFeat	Penman 1	6 Newman 37 Smith 55 Kinnear 52
S	29-Jan	Falkirk		A	NEL 2	3-4	2500	Bruce	Shufflebottom b	Stewart,JC	Dutch	Low	Fletcher	Stewart,J	Bain	Mullaney	Waldron b 1	Penman 2	75, 27, 43 McGeachie 80 Ogilvie 30 Rooney 66 Murray 15
S	05-Feb	Dundee United		H	NEL 2	2-0	2000	Bruce	Shufflebottom	Donald	Stewart,JC 1	Low	Fletcher	Stewart,J 1	Waldron	Forbes	Ventre	Penman	42, 75
S	12-Feb	Dunfermline Athletic		A	NEL 2	2-2	2000	Bruce	Shufflebottom	Donald	Stewart,JC 1	Low m	Fletcher	Stewart,J	Bain	Waldron 2, 1p	Ventre	Penman	85, 70 Brown 52 Hunter 30
S	19-Feb	Falkirk		H	NEL 2	3-1	2000	Bruce	Shufflebottom	Donald	Dutch	Low	Fletcher	Fletcher	Feechan 1	Waldron	Ventre	Amos	2, 14, 60p McGeachie 29
S	04-Mar	Hearts		H	NEL 2	1-0	1000	Bruce	Fotheringham	Donald	Dutch	Low	Kelly	Stewart,J	Conway	Fletcher	Ventre 1	Amos	30
S	11-Mar	Aberdeen		A	NEL 2	0-1	5000	Bruce	Shufflebottom	Donald	Dutch	Low	Kelly	Stewart,J	Waldron	Kinnear	Ventre	Penman	Bremner 18
S	18-Mar	Aberdeen		H	NEL 2	2-0	2000	Bruce	Dutch	Donald	Stewart,JC	Low	Kelly	Stewart,J	Maule	Waldron 1	Ventre	Henry 1	38, 57
S	25-Mar	Rangers		H	NEL 2	2-2	4000	Bruce s	Dutch	Donald	Stewart,JC	Low	Fletcher	Stewart,J	McIntosh	Waldron 2p	Ventre	Henry	71, 89 Williamson 44 Venters 4 pen
S	01-Apr	Falkirk		A	MC 1-1	4-2	4000	Bruce	Shufflebottom	Donald	Dutch	Low	Kelly	Stewart,J	Ventre	Waldron 2	Henry	Penman 2	40, 70, 80, 87 Rooney 5 Dawson 20 pen
S	08-Apr	Falkirk	2	H	MC 1-2	3-4	4500	Bruce	Dutch	Donald	Dutch	Low	Fletcher	Stewart,J 2, 1p	Ventre	Cook	Henry	Penman 1	55p, 80, 110 Stannage 1 Ogilvie 28 Dawson (2) 34, 70
S	15-Apr	Aberdeen		A	MC SF	2-2	8000	Bruce	Dutch	Donald	Stewart,JC	Low	Kelly	Stewart,J	Ventre	Waldron 1	Henry	Penman 1	34, 2 Pattillo (2) 58, 73
S	22-Apr	East Fife		A	MC SFr	0-4	1000	Bruce	Dutch	Donald	Dutch	Low	Stewart,JC	Stewart,J	Ventre	Brand	Henry	Penman	Newman 2 Dalziel 33 Wilson (2) 25, 35
S	29-Apr	Aberdeen		H	MC SFr	2-1	5740	Bruce	Dutch	Donald	Stewart,JC	Low	Fletcher	Stewart,J 1	Ventre 1	Waldron 1	Henry	Penman 1	80, 62 Pattillo 32
S	06-May	Rangers		A	MC F-1	2-3	10000	Bruce	Shufflebottom	Donald	Dutch	Low	Kelly	Stewart,J 1	Ventre 1	Waldron	Henry	Penman 1	43, 11 McIntosh (2) 5, 23 McCormack 14
S	13-May	Rangers		H	MC F-2	2-3	8944	Bruce	Shufflebottom	Donald	Dutch	Low	Kelly	Stewart,J	Ventre	Waldron 1p	Henry	Penman 1	31, 42 Venters (2) 55, 59 Rutherford 83
S	03-Jun	Morton		H	SmC 1-1	1-2	4000	Bruce	Shufflebottom	Donald	Dutch	Low	Kelly	Fletcher	Ventre	Stewart,J	Henry	Penman 1	64 Steel 21 Aird 86
S	10-Jun	Morton	2	A	SmC 1-2	3-3	5000	Bruce	Shufflebottom	Donald	Dutch	Low	Stewart,JC	Stewart,J	Ventre 1	Haywood 2	Henry	Penman	37, 79, 115 Gallacher 30 Crum 91 Garth 111

Manager : Willie Reekie
(1) Benefit for Sneddon
(2) after extra time

Substitutes, own goals, goal times and opponents' scorers

Day	Date	Opponents	Note	Venue	Comp	Res	Att	1	2	3	4	5	6	7	8	9	10	11	Substitutes, own goals, goal times and opponents' scorers
S	12-Aug	Dundee		H	NEL 1	2-4	5000	Bruce	Shufflebottom	Donald	Dutch	Low	Lumby	Stewart,J	Ventre	Kelly 2	Henry	Penman	53, 82 Newman 57 Turnbull (2) 15, 43 Roberts 42
S	19-Aug	Dunfermline Athletic		A	NEL 1	2-3	4000	Thomson	Shufflebottom	Donald	Lumby	Low	Stewart,JC	Stewart,J	Hurrell 1	Granville	Ventre 1	Penman 2	79, 84 Forbes 25 Hunter (2) 4, 7
S	26-Aug	Falkirk		H	NEL 1	4-1	3000	Thomson	Shufflebottom	Donald	Stewart,JC	Low	Kelly	Granville	Stewart,J 2	Connor	Jones	Penman 1	3, 49, 67. 73 Sharp 89
S	02-Sep	East Fife		A	NEL 1	2-2	3000	Thomson	Shufflebottom	Donald	Stewart,JC	Low	Kelly	Stewart,J 1	Connor	Wilkie	Jones	Penman 1	35, 55 Aitken 10 Wilson 43
S	09-Sep	Arbroath		H	NEL 1	2-0	3000	Bruce	Shufflebottom	Donald	Stewart,JC	Low	Kelly	Stewart,J	Hurrell	Ruse 2	Glassey	Penman	5, 68
S	16-Sep	Hearts		H	NEL 1	3-0	3000	Bruce	Shufflebottom	Donald	Dutch	Low	Stewart,JC	Kelly	Stewart,J	Gorman 2	Connor 1	Penman 1	65, 80, 73
S	23-Sep	Arbroath		A	NEL 1	5-3	3000	Bruce	Shufflebottom	Donald	Dutch	Low	Kelly	Stewart,J	Connor	Ruse 3	Glassey 1	Penman 1	25, 29, 73, 65, 80 Dryden (2) 26, 67 Junior 42
S	30-Sep	Rangers		A	NEL 1	4-1	5000	Bruce	Shufflebottom	Donald	Dutch	Low	Kelly	Stewart,J 1	Connor	Briscoe 3	Glassey	Penman 1	78, 15, 40, 81 Cargill 5
S	07-Oct	Dundee United		A	NEL 1	1-5	9000	Bruce	Shufflebottom	Donald	Dutch	Low	Kelly	Stewart,J 1	Connor	Briscoe	Henry	Penman 1	55 McKay 49 McGilvary 75 Juliusson 47 Sveenson 58 Nevins 56
S	14-Oct	Aberdeen		H	NEL 1	2-1	3000	Bruce	Shufflebottom	Donald	Stewart,JC	Low	Kelly	Stewart,J	Maule	Connor	Connor	Penman 1	54, 2 Buchan 67
S	21-Oct	Dundee	1	A	NEL 1	6-4	10042	Bruce s	Shufflebottom	Donald	Stewart,JC	Low	Kelly	Stewart,J 1p	Maule 1	Woon 3	Connor	Penman 1	85, 76, 34, 39, 49, 32 Gray 70 pen Collins 88 Turnbull 74 Hill 68
S	28-Oct	Falkirk		A	NEL 1	1-0	3000	Bruce	Shufflebottom	Donald	Stewart,JC	Low	Kelly	Stewart,J	Hurrell 1	Woon	Connor	Penman	40
S	04-Nov	Dunfermline Athletic		H	NEL 1	3-1	2000	Bruce	Shufflebottom	Donald	Stewart,JC	Low	Kelly	Stewart,J 2	Love	Briscoe 1	Henry	Paterson	35, 80, 87 Syme 75
S	11-Nov	Hearts		A	NEL 1	2-0	7000	Bruce	Shufflebottom	Donald	Stewart,JC	Low	Kelly	Stewart,J 1	McKenzie	Woon	Turner	Beattie 1	83, 81
S	18-Nov	Rangers		A	NEL 1	1-2	2000	Bruce	Shufflebottom	Donald	Stewart,JC	Low	Kelly	Beattie	Edmunds 1	Ruse	Turner	Beattie	29 Cargill 73 Watkins 89
S	25-Nov	Dundee United		H	NEL 1	1-1	4000	Bruce	Dutch	Donald	Stewart,JC	Low	Kelly	Beattie	Stewart,J	Ruse 1	Taylor	Penman	21 Juliusson 70
S	02-Dec	East Fife		H	NEL 1	1-2	4000	Bruce	Dutch	Donald	Kelly	Currie	Stewart,JC	Stewart,J	Hurrell	Woon	Glassey	Beattie 1	89 Laird 47 Brown 26
S	09-Dec	Aberdeen		A	NEL 1	0-2	5000	Bruce	Dutch	Donald	Stewart,JC	Low	Kelly	Stewart,J	Maule	Ruse	Beattie	Penman	Dunlop 52 Pattillo 76
S	16-Dec	Dundee		A	NESC SF-1	1-2	4127	Bruce	Shufflebottom	Donald	Stewart,JC	Low	Kelly	Stewart,J 1	Maule	Beattie	Glassey	Penman	37 Moir 11 Anderson 63 pen
S	23-Dec	Dundee		H	NESC SF-2	0-2	6000	Bruce	Shufflebottom	Donald	Stewart,JC	Low	Kelly	Stewart,J	Kinnear	Beattie	McKenzie	Penman	Turnbull 12 Hill 57
S	01-Jan	East Fife		A	NEL 2	1-4	3000	Bruce	Shufflebottom	Donald	Stewart,JC	Low	Kelly	Stewart,J	Hurrell 1	Beattie	Fletcher	Tivendale	19 McDonald 43 Longmuir (2) 17, 33
Tu	02-Jan	Rangers		H	NEL 2	1-2	5000	Bruce s	Dutch	Donald	Stewart,JC	Low	Kelly	Tivendale	Stewart,J	Cairns	Beattie	Penman 1	50 Rutherford 65 McLellan 18
S	06-Jan	Dunfermline Athletic		H	NEL 2	5-2	3000	Bruce	Shufflebottom	Donald 1p	Dutch	Low	Stewart,JC	Beattie 1	Beattie 1	Cairns 1	Kelly	Penman 1	40, 50, 60, 51, 80 Kelly 85 McKeenan 52
S	13-Jan	Dundee United		A	NEL 2	2-5	5000	Bruce	Shufflebottom	Donald	Dutch	Low	Stewart,JC	Beattie 1	Beattie	Cairns 1	Kelly	Penman	30, 57 Scott (2) 34, 44 Juliusson (3) 8, 15, 20
S	10-Feb	Arbroath		H	NEL 2	1-2	2000	Bruce	Shufflebottom	Donald	Stewart,JC	McAlpine	Kelly	Beattie	Young	McMillan	Glassey 1	Penman	65 Yeoman 35 Ferguson 50
S	17-Feb	Arbroath		A	NEL 2	0-8	5000	Bruce	Dutch	Donald	Stewart,JC	Low	Kelly	Stewart,J	Maule	Petrie	Young	Slessor	Pattillo (2) 4, 86 Waldron (2) 6, 49 Green (4) 2, 39, 41, 51
S	24-Feb	Dundee United		H	NEL 2	5-2	1000	Bruce	Dutch	Donald m	Stewart,JC	Low	Kelly	Stewart,J	Maule	Lindsay 3	Young 1	Penman 1	40, 49, 61, 35, 41 Scott (2) 48, 86
S	03-Mar	Rangers		A	NEL 2	0-3	1500	Bruce	Dutch	Donald	Stewart,JC	Low	Montgomery	Stewart,J	Young	Beattie	Glassey	Penman	McMaster 82 McLellan 26 Johnstone 31
S	10-Mar	Dunfermline Athletic	2	A	NEL 2	2-2	3500	Bruce	Dutch	Donald	Stewart,JC	Low	Montgomery	Stewart,J	Hurrell	Anderson	Young 1	Penman	85, 41 Kelly (2) 60, 75
S	17-Mar	Dundee		H	NEL 2	1-4	3500	Bruce	Dutch	Donald	Stewart,JC	Low	Kelly	Stewart,J	Young 1p	Wotherspoon	Montgomery	Penman	80 Miller 70 Bremner 50 pen Pattillo (2) 30, 65
S	24-Mar	Dundee		H	NEL 2	2-1	4000	Bruce	Dutch	Donald	Stewart,JC	Low	Young	Stewart,J 1	Rodgers	Malcolm	Wotherspoon	Penman 1	13, 57 Ewan 10
S	31-Mar	Hearts		H	NEL 2	6-0	3000	Bruce	Dutch	Donald	Kelly	Low	Montgomery	Stewart,J 2	Young 1	Cairns 1	Glassey 2	Penman	33, 75, 83, 57, 15, 27
S	07-Apr	Falkirk		A	NEL 2	4-2	3000	Bruce	Dutch	Donald	Stewart,JC	Low	Montgomery	Tivendale	Stewart,J	Kelly 1	Young 1	Penman 2	82, 63, 16, 26 Newman 85 Bagan 73
S	14-Apr	East Fife		H	NEL 2	0-3	2000	Bruce	Dutch	Donald	Stewart,JC	Low	Montgomery	Tivendale	Stewart,J	Wotherspoon	Young	Penman	Adamson (2) 15, 65 Duncan 13
S	21-Apr	Arbroath		A	NEL 2	4-1	2000	Bruce	Dutch	Donald	Kelly	Low	Montgomery	Stewart,J	Young 2	[Glasgow Am]	Glassey	Penman 1	2, 59, 48, 73 Shirley 12
S	28-Apr	Falkirk		H	NEL 2	5-1	3000	Bruce	Dutch	Donald	Young 1p	Low	Montgomery	Stewart,J	Stewart,J	Campbell	Glassey 1	Penman 2	61, 51, 86, 8. 81 Morrison 40
S	05-May	Dundee		A	NEL 2	0-4	8000	Bruce	Dutch	Donald	Young	Low	Montgomery	Tivendale	Stewart,J	Campbell	McLennan	Penman	Turnbull (3) 3, 32, 66 Smith 51
S	12-May	Hearts		A	NEL 2	0-2	2000	Bruce	Stewart,JC	Donald	Dutch	Low	Montgomery	Stewart,J	Young	Marshalsay	Benson	Penman	McLure 13 pen Urquhart 58
S	19-May	Arbroath		A	MC 1-1	4-1	2800	Bruce	Dutch	Donald	Stewart,JC	Low	Stewart,J	Stewart,J	Young	Benson	Glassey 1	Penman 3	30, 46, 56, 81 Yeoman 48
S	26-May	Arbroath		H	MC 1-2	4-2	3000	Bruce	Dutch	Donald	Stewart,JC	Low	Montgomery	Stewart,J	Marshalsay	Wotherspoon 2	Young	Penman 2	70, 87, 57, 65 Oram (2) 23, 33
S	02-Jun	Aberdeen		A	MC 2	1-3	8000	Thomson	Dutch	Donald	Fletcher	Low	Montgomery	Kelly	Young	Wotherspoon 1	Glassey	Penman	85 Pattillo (2) 61, 66 Cocker 72

Manager : Willie Reekie
(1) Gray missed penalty ; Bruce saved another one
(2) Rovers wore "unfamiliar red and white striped jerseys"

Day	Date	Opponents	Note	Venue	Comp	Res	Att	1	2	3	4	5	6	7	8	9	10	11	Substitutes, own goals, goal times and opponents' scorers
S	11-Aug	Arbroath		H	L2	3-2	3000	Bruce	Dutch	Donald	Kelly	Low	Montgomery	Strachan	Stewart,J 1	Gillfillan	Wallace 1	Penman 1	65, 65, 44 Gould 20 Lamb 46
S	18-Aug	Cowdenbeath		A	L2	1-2	6000	Bruce	Dutch	Donald	Kelly	Low	Montgomery	Strachan	Stewart,J	Wotherspoon 1	Wallace	Penman	70 Moodie 25 Doig 35
S	25-Aug	Ardrie		H	L2	4-0	3000	Bruce	Doyle	Donald	Dutch	Low	Montgomery	Stewart,J 2	Johnston	Woon 1	Wotherspoon	Penman 1	12, 59, 62, 65
S	01-Sep	Dumbarton		A	L2	3-6	3000	Bruce	Doyle	Donald	Dutch	Low	Montgomery	Stewart,J 1	Kelly	Woon 1	Wotherspoon	Penman 1	40, 75, 35 Marshall (2), 5, 87 McDonald (2), 71, 78 McGowan (2) 36,63
S	08-Sep	East Fife		H	L2	0-2	4000	Bruce	Dutch	Donald	Kelly	Low	Montgomery	Stewart,J	Maule	Woon	Adamson	Penman	Wilson 40 Duncan 44
S	15-Sep	Dundee United		A	L2	7-0	5500	Bruce	Bremner	Donald	Dutch	Low	Young 1p	Strachan 1	Johnston	Woon 1	Wotherspoon 1	Penman 3	89, 6, 54, 85, 78, 82, 88
S	22-Sep	Dunfermline Athletic		H	L2	3-2	6000	Bruce	Bremner	Donald	Dutch	Low	Young 1p	Strachan	Johnston 1	Woon 1	Hurrell	Penman	16, 75, 12 Juliussen 2 Anderson 44 Hill (2) 64, 81 Ancell 33
S	29-Sep	Dundee		H	L2	0-5	9000	Bruce	Bremner	Donald	Dutch	Low	Young	Stewart,J	Johnston	Woon	Hurrell	Penman	Kelly (2) 41pen, 53 pen
S	06-Oct	St Johnstone		A	L2	3-5	4000	Bruce	Bremner	Donald	Dutch	Low	Young 1p	Stewart,J	Kelly	Middleton 1	Johnston	Penman 1	88, 27, 15 McIntosh 86 McGeachie 35 Soutar (2) 44, 83 Newman 57
S	13-Oct	Alloa Athletic		H	L2	1-2	5000	Bruce	Hogg	Bremner	Whyte	Low	Montgomery	Stewart,J	Young 1	Woon	McNaught	Penman	18 Dolan 16 McKay 52
S	20-Oct	Ayr United		A	L2	1-1	8000	Bruce	Hogg	Donald	Dutch	Low	Young	Stewart,J	Johnston 1	McNaught	Mullaney	Penman	6 Smith 75
S	27-Oct	Stenhousemuir		H	L2	1-2	3000	Bruce	Hogg	Donald	Dutch	Low	Young	Stewart,J 1	Johnston	Parsons	McNaught	Penman	30 Buchan 35 pen Ormond 88
S	03-Nov	Albion Rovers		H	L2	0-1	2000	Bruce	Hogg	Donald	Dutch	Low	Young	Stewart,J	Maule	Strachan	Mullaney	Penman	Browning 65
S	10-Nov	Cowdenbeath		H	L2	3-2	2000	Bruce	Dutch	Donald	Young	Low	McNaught	Stewart,J	Maule 1	Woon 1	Johnston	Penman 1	15, 70, 44 White (2) 80, 85
S	17-Nov	Arbroath		A	L2	1-2	2500	Bruce	Dutch	Donald	Young	Low	McNaught	Stewart,J	Maule	Woon	Hunter	Penman 1	79 Gould 6 Fright 70
S	24-Nov	Ardrie		A	L2	2-4	3000	Bruce	Watson	Watson	Young	Low	McNaught	Stewart,J 1	Maule	Woon 1	Johnston	Penman	55, 42 Aitken (4) 15,30,40,48
S	01-Dec	Dumbarton		H	L2	1-4	3000	Moreland	Dutch	McLure	Young	Donald	McNaught	Stewart,J	Maule	Woon 1	Dawson	Penman	79 McMillan (3) 43, 61, 70 Timmins 75
S	08-Dec	Dunfermline Athletic		A	L2	1-8	2500	Bruce	Hogg	McLure	Till	Low	Young	Stewart,J	Young	Wotherspoon 1	Dawson 1	Maule	48 Walsh (2) 42, 80 Gilmour (3) 12, 75, 88 Forbes (3) 24, 60, 85
S	15-Dec	Dundee United		H	L2	5-0	2000	Bruce	Hogg	McLure	Till	Montgomery	Young	Stewart,J	Blain	Wotherspoon 2	Dawson 2	Henderson 1	40, 70, 2, 75, 44
S	22-Dec	Dundee		A	L2	0-7	6209	Bruce	Watson	McLure	Dutch	Montgomery	Young	Strachan	Blain	Wotherspoon	Dawson	Henderson	Gallacher (2) 11, 68 Juliussen (3) 28, 36, 89 Cox 37 Turnbull 88
S	29-Dec	Dundee United		H	L2	4-5	3000	Bruce	Marshall	Marshall	Stewart,J	Stark	Bonomy	Stewart,J	Hurrell 1	Woon 2	Dawson 1	Henderson	43, 42, 83, 50 Boyd (2) 41, 82 McIntosh (3) 69, 71, 84
Tu	01-Jan	East Fife		A	L2	0-4	6200	Bruce	Watson	Watson	Johnstone.R	Stark	Bonomy	Paterson	Argue	Wotherspoon	Dawson	Paterson	Paris (3) 15,40,80 Canavan 20
W	02-Jan	Albion Rovers		A	L2	0-3	5400	Bruce	Watson	Hogg	Johnstone.R	Stark	Young	Hurrell	Paterson	Woon	Dawson	Maule	Hannah 88 Keeble (2) 15,17
S	05-Jan	Alloa Athletic		H	L2	0-6	4000	Bruce	Watson	Hogg	Watson	Stark	Young	Paterson	Dawson	Garrett	Rutherford	Charlton	Stephenson (3) 17,40,57 Dolan (3) 30,63,88
S	12-Jan	Ayr United		H	L2	2-3	1500	Bruce	Donald	McLure	Johnstone.R	Stark	Bonomy	Stewart,J 1	Hurrell 1	Kinnear	McNaught	Young 1	65, 30 Morrison (3) 44,50,35
S	19-Jan	Stenhousemuir		A	L2	2-2	1000	Bruce	Watson	McLure	Young	Stark	McNaught	Stewart,J	Morgan	Kinnear 1	Morgan	Paterson 1	76, 49 Arbuckle 75 Cowie 66
S	26-Jan	Dundee United		A	BDSC 1-1	4-1	9000	Bruce	Watson	McLure	Young	Stark	McNaught 1p	Maule	Dawson 1	Dickson 1	Johnston	Paterson 1	39, 3, 85, 78 Buchan 60
S	02-Feb	Dundee United		H	BDSC 1-2	0-3	3000	Bruce	Watson	McLure	Young	Stark	McNaught	Stewart,J	Maule	Dickson	Johnston	Paterson	Pacione 3 Mackay 25 Buchan 52
W	06-Feb	Dundee United	1	N	BDSC 1r2	3-3	9500	Reekie	Watson	McLure	Young	Stark	McNaught	Stewart,J	Maule	Montgomery 1	Johnston 1	Paterson 1	16, 26, 68 Buhan 35 Pacione 28 Smith 40
S	09-Feb	Ardrie		H	BDSC 2	0-4	4000	Bruce	Watson	McLure	Young	Stark	Montgomery	Stewart,J	Maule	Montgomery	Johnston	Paterson	Clapperton 11 McCulloch (2) 27,80 Aitken 42
S	23-Feb	Cowdenbeath		H	LCS	4-2	6000	Bruce	Watson	McLure	Young 1p	Wright	McNaught	Maule	Colvan 1	Stewart,J 1	McPherson 1	Rodgers	82, 18, 21, 81 McCormack 11 McDowall 46
S	02-Mar	East Fife		A	LCS	2-4	4000	Bruce	Watson	McLure	Till	Wright	Young	Maule	Colvan	Stewart,J 1	Johnston 1	Rodgers	8, 18 Simpson 44 Duncan (2) 60, 84 Adamson 67
S	09-Mar	Alloa Athletic		A	LCS	0-3	5000	Bruce	Watson	McLure	Young	Johnstone,R	McNaught m	Maule	Colvan	Stewart,J	Till	Colville	Main 53 Stephenson 61 Dolan 67
S	16-Mar	Ayr United		H	LCS	4-2	9000	Bruce	Watson	McLure	Till	Wright	Young 1p	Maule	Colvan 1	Stewart,J 2	McPherson	Colville	65, 5, 82, 33 Browning 15 Turnbull 57
S	23-Mar	East Fife		A	LCS	3-2	3000	Bruce	Watson	McLure	Till	Wright	Young	Maule	Colvan 1	Stewart,J 1	Johnston	Colville 1	18, 19, 86 Adamson 20 Aikman 53
S	30-Mar	Alloa Athletic		A	LCS	2-3	2000	Bruce	Watson	McLure	Till	Wright	Young	Maule 1	Colvan 1	Stewart,J	Paterson	Colville	78, 70 Malcolm 33 Stephenson 48 Currie 80
S	06-Apr	Stenhousemuir		H	PC 1	0-1	3500	Bruce	Johnston	McLure	Till	Johnstone,R	Young	Maule	Colvan	Stewart,J	McNaught	McNaught	Douglas 34
S	20-Apr	Arbroath		A	VC 1-1	4-3	3000	Bruce	Watson	McLure	Till 1	Johnstone,R	Young	Maule	Colvan 2	Gilmour 1	Gilmour 1	Colville	39, 16, 79, 49 Hill (3) 17, 25, 55
S	27-Apr	Arbroath		H	VC 1-2	3-1	3000	Bruce	Watson	McLure	Till	Young 1p	McNaught	Maule	Colvan	Gilmour 2	Gilmour	Morrison	38, 36, 58 Neilson 78
S	04-May	St Mirren		H	VC 2	2-1	8000	Bruce	Muir	McLure	Till	Johnstone,R	Young	Maule	Colvan 1	Stewart,J 2	Gilmour	McNaught	53, 80 Young 61
S	11-May	East Fife		H	FC SF	0-0	7000	Bruce	Watson	McLure	Till	Johnstone,R	Young	Maule	Colvan	Turnbull	Gilmour	McNaught	
S	18-May	Celtic	2	H	VC 3	0-2	18898	Bruce	Watson	McLure	Till	Johnstone,R	Young	Stewart,J	Maule	Turnbull	Gilmour	McCulloch	Rae 30 Sirrell 77

Manager : Bert Herdman
(1) at Dens Park ; Rovers won on toss of coin
(2) Receipts £1100

Day	Date	Opponents	Note	Venue	Comp	Res.	Att.	1	2	3	4	5	6	7	8	9	10	11	Substitutes, own goals, goal times and opponents' scorers	
S	10-Aug	Arbroath		A	L2	3-2	5000	Bruce	Watson	McLure	Till	Johnstone,T	Young	Stewart	Colvan 2	McKay	Gilmour	Mackie 1	40, 54, 66	Miller 52 Hill 84
W	14-Aug	Arbroath		A	BDSC,1-1	3-2		Bruce	Watson	McLure	Till	Johnstone,T	Young 2	Stewart	Colvan	Muir 1	Gilmour	Mackie	27, 85, 46	Coats (2) 44, 63
S	17-Aug	Dumbarton		H	L2	5-1	8000	Bruce	Watson	McLure	Young	Johnstone,T	McNaught	Stewart 1	Colvan	Muir 2	Gilmour 1	Mackie 1	88, 32, 54, 53, 72	Bootland 82
W	21-Aug	Arbroath		H	BDSC 1-2	1-0	5000	Bruce	Watson	McLure	Young	Johnstone,T	McNaught	Stewart 1	Colvan	Muir	Gilmour	Mackie	8	
S	24-Aug	East Fife		A	L2	4-4	12000	Bruce	Watson	McLure	Till	Johnstone,T	McNaught	Stewart	Colvan	Muir 1	Young 2,1p	Maule 1	43, 51p, 65, 63	Morris (2) 14, 51 Canavan 24 Adams 87
W	28-Aug	St Johnstone		H	BDSC 2	2-1	7000	Bruce	Watson	McLure	Young 1	Johnstone,T	McNaught	Stewart	Colvan	Muir 1	Gilmour	Maule	3, 7	Herd 43 pen
S	31-Aug	Cowdenbeath		H	L2	3-0	14000	Bruce	Watson	McLure	Young	Johnstone,T	McNaught	Stewart	Till	Muir 2	Gilmour 1	Maule	21, 83, 20	
W	04-Sep	Alloa Athletic		H	BDSC SF	2-1	10000	Bruce	Watson	McLure	Young x	Johnstone,T	McNaught	Stewart	Colvan	Muir 2	Gilmour	Maule	12, 75	Connor 86
S	07-Sep	Airdrie		A	L2	1-1	5000	Bruce	Watson	McLure	Till	Young 1p	McNaught	Stewart	Colvan	Muir	Gilmour	Maule	59	Picken 65
W	11-Sep	East Fife		H	BDSC F-1	2-3	18000	Bruce	Watson	McLure	Till	Young	McNaught	Stewart 1	Colvan	Muir	Gilmour	Maule 1	89, 29	Davidson 15 Morris 44 Adams 85
S	14-Sep	Dundee United		H	L2	1-1	7000	Brown	Watson	McLure	Till	Young	McNaught	Stewart	Colvan	Muir	Gilmour 1	Maule	21	McKinnon 17
W	18-Sep	East Fife		A	BDSC F-2	1-4	14000	Brown	Watson	McLure	Young	Johnstone,T	McNaught	Stewart 1	Gilmour	Muir	Colvan	Penman	59	Duncan (2) 13, 61 Morris 32 Davidson 48
S	21-Sep	Dundee		H	LC S	0-2	10000	Brown	Watson	McLure	Till	Johnstone,T	McNaught	Stewart	Colvan	Stewart	Gilmour	Colville		Patillo (2) 8, 76
S	05-Oct	Stenhousemuir		A	LC S	2-1	1600	Brown	Muir	McLure	Till	Johnstone,T	Young 1	Stewart 1	Colvan	Gilmour	Maule	Colville	32, 74	Morrison 78
S	12-Oct	Dundee		A	LC S	1-3	15000	Bruce	Muir	McLure	Till	Johnstone,T	Young	Maule	Colvan	Stewart	Gilmour	McCarthy 1	21	McEwan 29 Patillo (2) 61, 87
S	19-Oct	Stirling Albion		A	F	1-1	2000	Brown s	Muir	France	Malcolm	Johnstone,T	Young	Maule	Colvan	Nugent	Mitchell	Hamilton 1	26	Black 72
S	26-Oct	Stenhousemuir		H	LC S	2-4	4000	Bruce	Muir	Watson	Young	Johnstone,T	McNaught	Stewart	Colvan 1	McIntyre 1	Maule	Penman	8, 29	Morrison 23 O'Dell (2) 32, 49 Ormond 78
S	02-Nov	Dundee		H	L2	1-4	7000	Bruce	Muir	McLure	Young	Johnstone,T	McNaught 1p	Stewart	Maule	McIntyre	Lawson	Hamilton	52	Juliussen (2) 25, 86 Gunn 50 Patillo 60
S	09-Nov	Dunfermline Athletic		H	L2	1-4	5000	Bruce	Muir	McNaught	Till	Johnstone,T	Young	Stewart	Maule	McIntyre 1	Lawson	Colville	38	Wallace (2) 13, 46 Aitken 62 Munro 89
S	16-Nov	Albion Rovers		A	L2	1-2	4000	Bruce	Gilmour	McLure	Till	Young	McNaught	Stewart	McIntyre	Muir	Lawson 1	Colville	46	Doonan 29 McLure, W 16
S	23-Nov	Stenhousemuir		H	L2	1-1	3000	Bruce	Johnstone	McLure	Till	Young	McNaught m	Maule	McIntyre	Muir	Gilmour 1	Middlemas	65	Newman 22
S	30-Nov	Ayr United		H	L2	4-1	3000	Bruce	Johnstone	McLure	Till	McGillivray	Lawson	Maule	Stewart	Muir 1	Young 3,2p	McIntyre	68, 10, 43p, 85p	Morrison 50
S	07-Dec	Alloa Athletic		A	L2	1-4	2500	Bruce	Johnstone	McLure	Till	McGillivray	McNaught	Maule	Stewart	Muir	Young	Oatman 1	42	Stewart (2) 40, 72 Wilson 70 Anderson 78
S	14-Dec	St Johnstone		A	L2	0-2	4000	Brown	Watson	McLure	Till	McGillivray	McNaught	Maule	Stewart	McIntyre	Young	Oatman		Brown 7 Robbie 15
S	21-Dec	Arbroath		H	L2	1-0	3000	Bruce	Watson	McLure	Till	Henderson,R	Lawson	Maule	Stewart	Muir	Gilmour 1	Oatman	41	
S	28-Dec	Dumbarton		A	L2	1-1	2500	Bruce	Watson	McLure	Young	Johnstone,T	McNaught	Maule	Stewart	McIntyre	Gilmour 1	Oatman	13	Morrison 27
W	01-Jan	East Fife		H	L2	0-0	8000	Bruce	Watson	McLure	Lawson	Henderson,R	McNaught	Maule	Young	Stewart	Gilmour	Oatman		
Th	02-Jan	Cowdenbeath		A	L2	4-3	6000	Brown	Watson	McLure	Lawson	Henderson,R	McNaught	Maule	Young 1	Stewart 1	Gilmour 1	Oatman 1	14, 10, 55 3	Jones (2), 7, 73 Boyd 79
S	04-Jan	Albion Rovers		H	L2	2-0	4000	Brown	Watson	McLure	Lawson	Henderson,R	McNaught	Maule	Young 2	Stewart	Gilmour	Colville	57, 79	
S	11-Jan	Dunfermline Athletic		A	L2	1-4	1500	Brown	Watson	McLure	Lawson 1	Henderson,R	McNaught	Maule	Young	Stewart	Gilmour	Colville	76	Kinnell (2) 14, 34 Kinnear 42 Irvine 47
S	18-Jan	Alloa Athletic		H	L2	3-2	5500	Bruce	Muir	McLure	Lawson	Henderson,R	McNaught	Maule	Young 1	Stewart 2	Gilmour	Oatman	70, 21, 60	Dolan 18 Anderson 78
S	25-Jan	Queen of the South	1	A	SC 1	4-3	10100	Bruce	Muir	McLure	Lawson	Henderson,R	McNaught	Maule	Young	Stewart 2	Gilmour	Penman 2	19, 44, 40, 48	Oakes 1 Law (2) 8, 30
S	01-Feb	Ayr United		A	L2	1-0	8000	Bruce	Muir	Gilmour	Till	Henderson,R	McNaught	Maule	Lawson	Stewart	Dysart	Colvan 1	75	
S	22-Feb	Arbroath	2	A	SC 2	4-5	6000	Bruce	Muir	McDonald,P	Lawson	Henderson,R	McNaught	Maule	Young 1	Stewart 1	Gilmour 1	Penman 1	15, 66, 59, 87	Hill 9 Carrie 23 Smith 52 McMullen (2) 67, 83
S	22-Mar	Stenhousemuir		A	L2	1-4	1200	Bruce	Watson	Cougher	Till	Henderson,R	McNaught	Maule	Young 1p	Stewart	Gilmour	McLure	30	Montgomery 24 Fleming (2) 35, 48 Hope 51
S	29-Mar	St Johnstone		H	L2	2-1	3000	Bruce	Watson	McLure	Till	Young	McNaught	Maule	McDonald 1	Stewart	Mackie 1	Oatman	22, 68	Simpson
S	05-Apr	East Fife	3	A	FC SFr	2-7	500	Bruce	Watson	McLure	Till	Henderson,R	McNaught	Maule	McDonald	Stewart	Young	Penman 2	9, 80	Morris (3) 1, 27, 74 Aitken 28 Duncan 54 pen Davidson 65 Canavan 77
M	07-Apr	Airdrie	4	H	L2	1-2	5000	Bruce	Muir	McLure	Gilmour	Henderson,R	Young	Stewart	Maule	O'Donnell	McDonald 1	Oatman	88	Cunningham 86 Dalgleish 30
M	14-Apr	Dundee United		A	L2	0-3	8000	Brown	Muir	Gilmour	Watson	Henderson,R	Young	Stewart	O'Donnell	McKay	McDonald	Brown		Pacione 16 Crothers (2) 19, ...
S	19-Apr	Dundee A		H	F	2-1	3000	Brown	Muir	McLure	Young 1p	Henderson,R	McNaught	Stewart	Maule	O'Donnell	McDonald	Penman	60, 43 Cowie og	Marshall 46
W	23-Apr	Dundee		A	L2	2-5	10000	Brown	Muir	McLure	Young	Henderson,R	McNaught	Stewart	Maule	McKay 1	McDonald 1	Gilmour	10,50	Juliussen (3) 34,39,65 Ewen 22 Patillo 23
S	26-Apr	Stirling Albion		H	F	2-2	3000	Stobbie	Muir	McLure	Garry	Henderson,R	Till	Stewart	Mitchell	McKay 2	Maule	Penman	13, 30	Watson (2) 5, 55
Tu	06-May	East Fife		A	FC SF-1	2-3	5000	Brown	Muir	McLure	Stewart	Henderson,R	McNaught	Maule	McIntyre	Arthur	Airlie	Penman 2	22, 66	Canavan (2) 6, 86 Morris
S	17-May	East Fife		H	FC SF-2	1-5	7000	Brown	Maxwell	Lamb	Kelly	Henderson,R	McNaught	Stewart	Henderson,G 1	Shields	Maule	Penman	27	Morris (2) 15, 58 Davidson (2) 34, 47 Duncan pen 85

Manager : Bert Herdman

(1) Receipts £750

(2) Receipts £350

(3) 1945/46 competition

(4) played on a muddy pitch at Stark's Park. Rovers changed to blue and white stripes at half time, to help distinguish the mud-splattered teams. McNaught missed the match (played on holiday Monday afternoon) as he was engaged in essential building work.

Day	Date	Opponents	Note	Venue	Comp	Res.	Att.	1	2	3	4	5	6	7	8	9	10	11	Goal times	Substitutes, own goals, goal times and opponents' scorers
S	09-Aug	Dunfermline Athletic		A	LC S	2-0		Brown	McAra	McLure	Till	Henderson	Young	Dalziel	Stewart 1	Dolan	Brady 1	Penman	40, 38	
W	13-Aug	Dumbarton		H	L2	2-1	8000	Brown	McAra	McLure	Young 1	Henderson	McNaught	Dalziel 1	Stewart	Dolan	Brady	Penman	89, 50	Cantwell 56
S	16-Aug	Alloa Athletic		H	LC S	4-2	6000	Brown	McAra	McLure	Till	Henderson	McNaught	Dalziel	Young 1	Stewart 1	Brady 1	Joyner 1	13, 43, 29, 44	Stewart,R (2) 60,70
S	23-Aug	Hamilton Academical		H	LC S	3-1	8000	Brown	McAra	McLure	Till	Henderson	McNaught	Dalziel	Young 1,2p	Stewart	Brady 1	Joyner 1	22, 67p, 2	Martin 75
W	27-Aug	Kilmarnock		A	L2	1-7	9700	Brown	McAra	McLure	Till	Henderson	McNaught	Dalziel	Young 1p	Stewart	Brady	Joyner	48	Walsh (3) 22 .... Collins (3) .... Turnbull pen
S	30-Aug	Dunfermline Athletic		H	LC S	6-1	7000	Brown	McAra	McLure	Till	Weir	McNaught	Dalziel 1	Stewart 2	Stewart	Brady 1	Joyner 2	57, 14, 35, 89, 52, 71	Kinnell 36
S	06-Sep	Alloa Athletic		A	L2	2-1	5000	Brown	Muir 1	McLure	Till	Weir	Young	Dalziel 1	Young	Joyner 1	Maule	Joyner	8, 30	Black 65
M	08-Sep	East Fife		A	PC 1	2-1	4000	Harper	McAra	Harper	Kelly	Weir	McNaught	Dalziel	Stewart	Muir	Maule	Penman	28, 60	Duncan 55 pen
S	13-Sep	Hamilton Academical		A	LC S	1-6	8000	Brown	Brown	McAra	Till	Henderson	McNaught	Dalziel	Stewart	Stewart	Brady	Joyner 1	66	Devin 34 McIntosh 83 Martin 75 Wright 30 Anderson 81 Devine 88
S	20-Sep	East Fife		H	L2	0-4	9000	Harper s	Muir	McLure	Till	McAra	McNaught	Dalziel	Brady	Stewart 1	Maule	Joyner 1		Morris 38 Duncan (2) 77, 78 D. Davidson 89
S	27-Sep	Stirling Albion		A	L2	3-3	7000	Harper	Muir	McLure	Till	McAra	McNaught	Stewart 2	Maule	Walker	Brady	Joyner 1	60, 88, 44	Henderson (3) 11,27,80
S	04-Oct	Cowdenbeath		H	L2	3-5	6000	Harper	Muir	McLure	Till	McAra	McNaught	Stewart	Maule	Dolan	Brady	Joyner 1	20, 29, 28	McCready 7 Jones (4) 9, 12, 34, 44
S	11-Oct	Albion Rovers		A	L2	1-1	4000	Brown	Muir	McLure	Till	McNaught	Brady 1	Stewart 2	Dolan	Penman 3	Maule	Joyner	65	Hunter 4
S	18-Oct	Alloa Athletic		H	L2	7-1	4100	Harper	McAra	McLure	Till	McNaught	Brady 1	Stewart 3	Dolan 1	Penman 1	Maule 1	Joyner 1	14, 11, 59, 13, 3, 48, 71	Stewart pen 76
S	25-Oct	Arbroath		A	L2	6-1	3000	Brown	McAra	McLure	Kelly	McNaught	Brady	Stewart 1	Dolan	Penman 3	Maule	Joyner 1	65, 74, 84, 47, 36, 72	Colvan 38
S	01-Nov	St.Johnstone		A	L2	5-2	7000	Brown	McAra	McLure	Till	McNaught	Till	Stewart 2	Dolan 1	Penman 1	Maule 1	Joyner 1	49, 28, 70, 79, 84	Brown 8 Mayes 56
S	08-Nov	Leith Athletic		H	L2	5-1	3800	Brown	Muir	McLure	Till	McNaught	Brady 1	Stewart	Dolan	Penman 2	Maule	Joyner 1	40, 9, 13, 60, 48	Skinner 88
S	15-Nov	Hamilton Academical	1	A	L2	2-1	5000	Brown	Muir	McLure	Till	McNaught	Brady	Stewart 1	Dolan	Penman 1	Maule	Todd	20, 78	Martin 30
S	22-Nov	Ayr United		A	L2	4-2	5000	Brown	Muir	McLure	Till	McNaught	Brady	Stewart 2	Dolan 1	Penman 1	Maule	Joyner 2	55, 10, 65, 73	Beattie 16 Morrison 44
S	29-Nov	Dundee United		H	L2	5-1	6290	Brown	Muir	McLure	Till	McNaught	Brady	Stewart 3	Dolan 1	Penman 1	Maule	Joyner 1	21, 60, 75, 40, 85	Crothers 52
S	06-Dec	Stenhousemuir		H	L2	6-2	5300	Brown	Muir	McLure	Till	McNaught	Brady 1	Stewart	Dolan 1	Penman 2	Maule	Joyner 1	35, 44, 64, 9, 22, 87	Anderson (2) 51p, 68
S	13-Dec	Dunfermline Athletic		A	L2	4-2	8000	Harper	Muir	McLure	Till	McNaught	Brady 1	Stewart 1	Dolan	Penman 1	Maule 1	Joyner 1	16, 67, 79, 44	Wright 4 Keith 15
S	20-Dec	Dumbarton		A	L2	2-4	5500	Brown	Muir	McLure	Till	McNaught	Brady 1	Stewart	Dolan 1	Penman 1	Maule	Joyner	87, 42	Bootland (2) 20, 84 Wardlaw 27 Cantwell 61
S	27-Dec	Kilmarnock		H	L2	4-3	5000	Smith	Muir	McLure	Till	McNaught	Brady 1	Stewart	Dolan	Penman 1	Maule	Joyner 1	64, 56, 60, 80	Cavin (2) 17, 59 Turnbull 75p
Th	01-Jan	East Fife		A	L2	2-3	14000	Smith	Muir	McLure	Till	McNaught	Brady 1p	Stewart	Dolan	Penman	Maule	Joyner 1	83, 17	Davidson Duncan 47 pen McLennan 79
S	03-Jan	Stirling Albion		H	L2	0-1	7000	Smith	Muir	McLure	Till	McNaught	Brady	Maule	Dolan	Penman	Maule	Joyner		Henderson 31
S	10-Jan	Cowdenbeath		A	L2	1-1	6500	Smith	Muir	McLure	Till	McNaught	Brady	Maule	Dolan	Penman	Young	Joyner 1	10	Shankland 40p
S	17-Jan	Albion Rovers		H	L2	2-3	6000	Smith	Muir	McLure	Till 1	McNaught	Young	Maule	Dolan	Penman	Young	Young	21, 33	Smith 20 Carrie (2) 65, 80
S	24-Jan	Aberdeen		A	F	1-3	8000	McKenzie	Muir	McLure	Till	McNaught	Young	Maule	Young	Findlay 1	Kerr	Joyner	7	Baird 28 Williams (2) 42, 87
S	31-Jan	Alloa Athletic		A	L2	2-5	4200	Harper	Muir	McLure	Till	McNaught	Brady	Maule 2	Dolan	Findlay	Young	Penman 1	49, 74	Barclay (2) 40, 73 Paris (2) 42, 57 Mackie 70
S	07-Feb	Stirling Albion		A	SC 2	4-2	9000	Harper	McAra	McLure	Till	McNaught	Brady	Maule	Young	Findlay	Venters	Penman	55, 71, 8, 35 Sherrington og	Henderson 25 Moffat 53
S	14-Feb	Arbroath		H	L2	2-0	5000	Harper	McAra	McLure	Kelly	McNaught	Till	Muir	Maule 2	Penman	Venters 1	Joyner	54, 80	
S	21-Feb	Kilmarnock		A	SC 3	0-3	12000	Harper	Muir	McLure	Till	McNaught	Brady	Muir	Maule 1	Findlay 1	Venters	Joyner		Parfane 3 Duncan 21 Stevenson 86
S	28-Feb	Leith Athletic		A	L2	1-1	3000	Harper	Muir	McLure	Till	McNaught	Brady	Dalziel 1	Maule	Penman	Venters	Penman 1	88	Robertson 44
S	06-Mar	Hamilton Academical		H	L2	3-3	5000	Harper	Muir	McLure	Till	McNaught	Brady	Maule 1	Dolan 2	Young	Young	Penman 1	72, 3, 23	McVinish (2) 26, 80 Martin 34
S	13-Mar	Ayr United		H	L2	2-0	5000	Harper	Muir	McLure	Till	McNaught	Brady	Maule	Dolan	Rae	Venters	Penman	68, 87	
S	20-Mar	Dundee United		A	L2	0-3	12000	Harper	Muir	McLure	Till	McNaught	Brady	Maule	Dolan	Rae	Young	Joyner 2		Pacione (2) 10, 20 Henderson 34
W	24-Mar	Dunfermline Athletic		A	FC 1	1-0	1000	Smith	Muir	Todd	Kelly	McNaught	Young	Maule	Brady	Dolan	Young	Penman 1	27	
S	27-Mar	Stenhousemuir		A	L2	1-1	5000	Smith	Muir	McLure	Kelly	McNaught	Young	Maule	Dolan	Dolan	Venters	Penman 1	43	Gray 70
S	03-Apr	Dunfermline Athletic		H	L2	1-3		Harper	Muir	McLure	Kelly	McNaught	Brady	Maule	McGurn	Rae	Brady	Penman 1	22	Keith (2) 47, 89 Kinnear 55
M	05-Apr	Albion Rovers		H	BDSC 1	1-2	5000	Harper	Muir	McLure	Till	McNaught	Brady	Maule 1	Dolan	Penman	Penman 1	Joyner	73	Stein pen Kerr 89
S	17-Apr	Cowdenbeath		A	FC SF	3-2		Smith	Muir	McLure	Till	Young	Young	Maule 1	Joyner 1	Joyner 1	Venters	Joyner	57, 60, 75	Shankland (2) 70p 80p
W	21-Apr	Cowdenbeath		H	PC 2	4-3	1500	Smith	Muir	McLure	Till	McNaught	Young 1p	Menzies 1	Dolan	Joyner	Brady 1	Penman 1	30, 55, 54, 44	McCreadie 14 Elliott 42 Jones
S	24-Apr	St.Johnstone		H	L2	6-1	3500	Westland	Haddow	Eden	Till	Young	Brady 1	Dalziel 1	Dolan	Penman 2	Maule	Joyner 2	54, 31, 6, 62, 44, 47	Peat 30 pen
Tu	27-Apr	East Stirling		H	PC SF	3-0	2500	Westland	McLure	Eden	Till	McNaught	Young	Till	Dolan	Penman 2	Maule	Joyner	65, 12, 88	

Manager : Bert Herdman

(1) Anderson missed penalty

2 9 2

Substitutes, own goals, goal times and opponents' scorers

Day	Date	Opponents	Note	Venue	Comp	Res.	Att.	1	2	3	4	5	6	7	8	9	10	11	Substitutes, own goals, goal times and opponents' scorers
S	14-Aug	Queen's Park		H	L2	3-1	7000	Westland	McLure	Eden	Young	McNaught	Brady	Menzies 1	Collins	Stockdale	Maule	Penman 2	62, 16, 20 / Cunningham 23
W	18-Aug	Cowdenbeath		A	L2	1-2	5000	Westland	McLure	Eden	Till	Young	Brady	Menzies 1	Collins	Stockdale	Maule	Penman	25 / Jones 10 McGurn 11
S	21-Aug	East Stirling		H	L2	5-1	4100	Westland	McLure	Eden	Till	McNaught	Brady 1	Menzies 1	Young	Penman 2	Maule	Joyner 1	80, 49, 56, 81, 40 / Newman 26
W	25-Aug	Hearts		A	PC F	2-1	6000	Westland	McLure	Eden	Ellis	Young	Brady	Menzies	Collins 2	Penman	Maule	Joyner 1	29, 39 / Martin 60
S	28-Aug	Hamilton Academical		A	L2	4-1	7500	Westland	McLure	Eden	Ellis	McNaught	Brady	Menzies	Collins	Penman 3	Maule	Joyner 1	60, 66, 85, 2 / Cummings 30
W	01-Sep	Stenhousemuir		H	L2	3-0	8000	Westland	Muir	Eden	Young	McNaught	Young	Menzies	Collins	Penman 1	Maule	Joyner 2	28, 30, 77
S	04-Sep	Arbroath		A	L2	2-1	5000	Westland	McLure	Eden	Till	McNaught	Young	Menzies 1	Collins	Penman 1	Maule	Joyner 1	57, 44 / McLure og 62
W	08-Sep	East Fife	1	H	FC F	3-2	8835	Westland	McLure	Eden	Till	Young m	Ellis	Menzies 1	Collins	Penman 1	Ellis	Joyner 1	40, 35, 18 / Henderson 46 Weir 57
S	11-Sep	Cowdenbeath		H	LC S	3-3	7000	Westland	McLure	Eden	Till	McNaught	Brady	Menzies	Young 1p	Penman	Maule	Joyner 2	40, 43, 56 / Jones (2), 9, 39 Shankland 65 pen
S	18-Sep	Stirling Albion		A	LC S	7-1	5000	Westland	McLure	McNaught	Till	Young	Brady	Menzies	Maule	Penman 6	Ellis 1	Colville	13, 21, 56, 69, 84, 86, 89 / Henderson 22
S	25-Sep	Dunfermline Athletic		H	LC S	2-1	12000	Westland	McLure	McNaught	Till	Young	Brady	Stockdale	Maule 1	Penman 2	Ellis	Joyner 1	9, 47 / Keith 15
S	02-Oct	Cowdenbeath		A	LC S	6-0	8000	Westland	McLure	McNaught	Till	Young	Brady 1	Stockdale	Maule	Penman 3	Ellis	Joyner	88, 28, 53, 58, 80, 46
M	04-Oct	East Stirling		H	BDSC 1	2-0	5000	Westland	McLure	McNaught	Till	Young	Brady 2	Stockdale	Maule	Penman	Ellis	Joyner	68, 69
S	09-Oct	Stirling Albion		H	LC S	6-2	7000	Westland	McLure	McNaught	Collins	Young	Brady	Menzies 1	Maule	Penman 4	Ellis 1	Joyner	81, 11, 46, 70, 82, 12 / Henderson (2) 10, 12
S	16-Oct	Dunfermline Athletic		A	LC S	0-1	8000	Westland	McLure	McNaught	Young	Young m	Kelly	Menzies	Maule	Penman	Gavin	Joyner	Roy 88
S	23-Oct	Dumbarton		A	LC S	4-3	7000	Westland	McLure	McNaught	Collins	Young	Brady 1	Menzies	Collins	Penman 3	Ellis 1	Joyner	3, 65, 83, 82 / Donegan 16 Goldie 23 Bootland 46 pen
H	30-Oct	East Fife		H	LC QF	5-3	24000	Westland	McLure	McNaught	Till	Young m	Brady 1	Collins	Maule 1p	Penman 1	Ellis 1	Joyner 2	44, 19, 72, 37, 77 / Morris (3) 61, 75, 77
S	06-Nov	Dundee United		A	L2	4-1	12000	Westland	McLure	McNaught	Till	Young	Collins	Menzies	Maule	Penman	Ellis 1	Joyner 3	50, 20, 28, 31 / McKay 77
S	13-Nov	Ayr United		H	L2	6-0	7000	Westland	McLure	McNaught	Till	Colville	Brady 1	Collins	Maule	Penman 4	Ellis 1	Joyner	48, 10, 53, 57, 85, 33
S	20-Nov	Hamilton Academical	2	N	LC SF	2-0	16750	Westland	McLure	McNaught	Till	Young	Brady	Carson	Maule	Penman 1	Ellis 1	Joyner 1	46, 35
S	27-Nov	Dunfermline Athletic		A	L2	5-1	6000	Westland	McLure	McNaught	Till	Young	Brady	Carson 1	Maule	Penman 2	Ellis 1	Joyner	14, 65, 78, 77, 50 / Kinnear (2) 30p, 65
S	04-Dec	Alloa Athletic		A	L2	3-2	7200	Westland	Muir	McLure	Till	McNaught	Brady	Carson	Maule 2,1p	Penman 1	Collins	Joyner	30, 49p, 79 / Newman 60
S	11-Dec	Kilmarnock		H	L2	2-5	10000	Westland	McLure	McNaught	Till	Young	Brady	Carson	Maule 1p	Penman 2	Ellis	Joyner	54, 61 / Aitken 23 McLaren 43
S	18-Dec	Stirling Albion		H	L2	3-2	7000	Westland	Muir	McLure	Till	McNaught	Brady	Carson	Maule 1	Penman 2	Ellis	Joyner	76, 54, 89 / Whiteford 3 pen Guy 60 Dick 85 Stirling, A. (2) 3.23
S	25-Dec	Cowdenbeath		A	L2	5-1	2600	Westland	McLure	McNaught	Till	Young	Leigh	Carson	Brady 1	Penman 1	Maule 1p	Joyner 2	76, 75, 18, 36, 83 / Jones 5 McGurn 82
S	01-Jan	East Stirling		H	L2	3-0	12000	Westland	McLure	McNaught	Till	Young	Leigh	Menzies	Brady 3	Penman	Maule	Joyner	6, 30, 61 / Crawford 52
S	03-Jan	Hamilton Academical		A	L2	1-1	9169	Westland	McLure	McNaught	Till	Young	Leigh	Menzies	Brady	Penman	Maule	Joyner	59 / Douglas 2
S	08-Jan	Queen's Park		H	L2	3-1	6000	Westland	McLure	McNaught	Leigh	Young	Leigh	Carson	Maule	Penman 3	Ellis	Joyner	17, 34, 55 / Ross 87
S	15-Jan	Arbroath		A	L2	1-0	11625	Westland	McLure	McNaught	Till	Young	Brady	Carson	Maule	Penman	Brady 1	Joyner	59
S	22-Jan	Leith Athletic	3	A	SC 1	1-3	3000	Smith	McLure	McNaught	Till	Young	Leigh	Doherty	Maule	Penman s	Brady 1	Joyner	8 / Anderson 3 Garvie 30 Montgomery 87
S	29-Jan	Stenhousemuir		A	L2	1-1	26538	Westland	McLure	McNaught	Till	Young	Brady	Carson	Maule	Penman	Ellis 1	Joyner	87 / Plumb 9
S	05-Feb	Hibernian	4	A	SC 2	3-4	20400	Westland	McLure	McNaught	Till	Colville	Leigh	Stockdale	Maule	Penman 1	Collins 1	Joyner	48, 36, 77 / Ormond 23 Plumb 8 Kean 82 Colville og 84
W	09-Feb	Hibernian		H	SC 2r	2-0	11200	Westland	Muir	McNaught	Till	Colville	Brady m	Maule m	Brady m	Penman	Collins 2	Joyner	18 / Partane 18 Bannan 42 Murray 56
S	12-Feb	Airdrie		H	L2	1-3	9000	Westland s	McLure	McNaught	Till	Young 1	Ellis	Collins	Maule	Penman	McInnes	Joyner	70, 72, 75 / Quinn 5 Crothers 10 McKay 2nd half
S	19-Feb	Dundee United		A	L2	3-2	4000	Westland s	Eden	McNaught	Till	Young	Brady	Collins 3	Maule	Penman	McInnes	Colville	4, 8, 69 / Beattie 33 Morrison 43
S	26-Feb	Ayr United		A	L2	3-5	4000	Westland	McLure	McNaught	Till	Young	Brady	Maule	Collins 1	Penman	McInnes 1	Joyner 1	37, 56, 75, 86, 89 / Craig 10 Smeaton 39 Buckley (3) 56.85.89
S	05-Mar	St.Johnstone		H	L2			Westland	McLure	McNaught	Young	Young	Leigh	Maule	Maule	Penman 5	Brady	Joyner	
S	12-Mar	Rangers	5	N	LC F	0-2	56450	Westland	McLure	McNaught	Young	Colville	Leigh	Stockdale	Collins	Penman	Maule	Menzies	46 / Gillick 46 Paton 59
S	19-Mar	Alloa Athletic		A	L2	5-0	6000	Westland	McLure	McNaught	Young	Colville	Leigh	Stockdale	Collins	Penman	Maule	McInnes 1	31, 76 / Smith 12 McLaren (2) 25, 75
S	26-Mar	Kilmarnock		H	L2	1-3	6000	Westland	McLure	McNaught	Young	Colville	Leigh	Stockdale	Collins	Penman	Maule	Brady	57
S	02-Apr	Stirling Albion		A	L2	2-0	10104	Westland	McLure	McNaught	Young	Colville	Leigh	Kelly	Collins	Penman m78 2	Maule	Stirling 1	40, 46, 49
M	04-Apr	Airdrie		H	BDSC 2	1-0	6180	Westland	McLure	McNaught	Young	Colville	Leigh	Till	Maule	Collins	McInnes	Stirling 1	49
S	09-Apr	Dumbarton		A	L2	2-0	1500	Westland	McLure	McNaught	Young	Colville	Leigh	Stockdale	Maule	Penman 2	Collins 1	Stirling	40, 56, 15, 62
S	16-Apr	Airdrie		H	L2	3-0	12500	Westland	McLure	McNaught	Young	Colville	Leigh	Stockdale	Maule	Penman 1	Maule	Stirling	
S	23-Apr	St.Johnstone		A	L2	1-0	9500	Westland	McLure	McNaught	Young	Colville	Leigh	Stockdale	Collins 2	Penman	Collins 2	Stirling 2	
S	30-Apr	Dunfermline Athletic		H	BDSC SF	4-0	24150	Westland	McLure	McNaught	Young	Colville	Leigh	Stockdale	Maule	Penman 1	Collins 1	Stirling	
W	04-May	Kilmarnock		H	BDSC SF	5-1	5889	Westland	Kelly	McLure	Young 2	Colville	Leigh	Stockdale 1	Maule	Penman 1	Collins 1	Stirling	62, 73, 49, 76, 15 / McLaren 75
S	07-May	St.Johnstone		H	BDSC F-1	1-2	6500	McEwan	Kelly	McLure	Young	Colville	Leigh	Stockdale	Maule	Penman 1	Collins	Stirling	30 / Craig 30 McRoberts 17

Manager : Bert Herdman

(1) 1947/48 Final
(2) at Celtic Park
(3) Receipts £856
(4) Receipts £1771
(5) at Hampden Park

Day	Date	Opponents	Note	Venue	Comp	Res	Att	1	2	3	4	5	6	7	8	9	10	11	Substitutes, own goals, goal times and opponents' scorers
S	13-Aug	East Fife		H	L	CS 0-3	23000	McGregor	McLure	McNaught	Young	Colville	Leigh	Stockdale	Maule	Penman	Collins	Joyner	78; Black 80 Brown 86 Fleming 89
W	17-Aug	Hearts		A	L	CS 1-5	32000	McGregor	McLure	McNaught	Young	Colville	Till	Maule	Crawford 1	Penman	Collins	Joyner	Swan (2) 8, 49 Conn (2) 50, 89 Bauld 49
S	20-Aug	Stirling Albion		H	L	CS 6-2	15000	Westland	McLure	McNaught	Till	Colville	Young 1	Smith 1	Crawford	Penman 2	Maule m 1	Stirling 1	50, 40, 58, 71, 63, 70; Keith (2) 15, 72
W	24-Aug	St Johnstone	1	A	BDSC	F-2 0-2	9000	Westland	McLure	McNaught	Young	Colville	Young	Smith	Maule	Penman	Murray	Stirling	Munro 34 pen McRoberts 61
S	27-Aug	East Fife		A	L	CS 2-3	15000	Westland	McLure	McNaught	Till	Colville	Young	Smith	Collins 1	Penman 1	Murray	Stirling	87, 67; Duncan (2) 2, 54 Davidson 18
W	31-Aug	Hearts		H	L	CS 1-2	18000	Westland	McLure	McNaught	Kelly	McNaught	Young	Smith	Crawford	Murray b 1	Collins	Penman	72; Conn (2) 49, 89
S	03-Sep	Stirling Albion		A	L	CS 1-4	14000	Westland	McLure	Colville	Kelly	McNaught 1p	Young	Smith	Crawford	Collins	Murray	Joyner	61; Keith 15 Jones 20 Dick (2) 38, 40
S	10-Sep	Hibernian		H	L1	0-6	22000	McGregor	McLure	McNaught	Young	Colville	Leigh	Smith	Maule	Crawford	Collins	Penman	Smith 48 Reilly (2) 61, 87 Turnbull (2) 19, 63 Combe 84
S	17-Sep	Falkirk	2	A	L1	1-1	12000	McGregor	McLure	McNaught	Young	Colville	Till	Smith	Maule 1	Collins	McLaughlin	Penman	68; Inglis 73
S	24-Sep	East Fife		A	L1	4-4	23000	McGregor	McLure	McNaught	Young	Colville	Till	Smith 1	Maule 1	Collins	McLaughlin 1	Penman 1	8, 84, 80, 72; Morris (2) 32, 37 Brown (2) 42, 46
S	01-Oct	Celtic		A	L1	2-2	32000	Westland	McLure	McNaught	Young	Colville	Till	Smith 1	Maule	Goldie	McLaughlin 1	Penman 2	35, 44; Taylor 4 Haughney 37
S	08-Oct	Partick Thistle	3	H	L1	1-3	12000	Westland	McLure	McNaught	Young	Colville	Till	Smith	Maule	Goldie	McLaughlin 1	Penman	39; Davidson 3 Walker 72 Wilson 77
S	15-Oct	St Mirren		H	L1	0-2	12000	McGregor	McLure	McNaught	Young	Colville	Till	Smith	Maule	Penman	McLaughlin	Joyner	Blyth 46 Guthrie 53
S	22-Oct	Motherwell		A	L1	1-1	12000	McGregor	McLaughlin	McNaught	Young	Colville	Collins	Smith	Collins	Goldie 1	Maule	Penman 1	44; Aitkenhead 12
S	29-Oct	Stirling Albion		H	L1	2-0	15000	McGregor	McLure	McNaught	Till	Colville	Woodcock	Smith	Collins 1	Goldie 1	Maule	Penman 1	14, 89
S	05-Nov	Dundee	4	A	L1	1-2	25000	McGregor	McLure	McNaught	Till	Colville	Woodcock	Smith	Collins 1	Goldie 1	Maule	Penman	81; Gerrie (2) 52, 75
S	12-Nov	Third Lanark		H	L1	1-1	10000	McGregor	McLaughlin	McNaught	Till	Colville	Woodcock	Smith	Collins 1	Goldie	Maule	Penman	50; McLeod 44
S	19-Nov	Rangers	5	H	L1	1-3	24800	McGregor	Farrell	McNaught	Till	Woodcock	Colville	Smith	Maule 1	Penman	McLaughlin	Joyner	77; Williamson (2) 42, 89 Thornton 66
S	26-Nov	Aberdeen		A	L1	0-3	16000	McGregor	Kelly	McNaught	Till	Woodcock	Brown	Goldie	Maule	Colville	Collins	Penman	Hamilton (2) 9, 84 Hather 38
S	03-Dec	Queen of the South		A	L1	0-0	8000	McGregor	McLure	McNaught	Till	Colville	Leigh	Maule	Collins	Penman	Garth	Joyner	
S	10-Dec	Clyde	6	H	L1	7-1	12000	McGregor	McSpadyen	McNaught	Till 1	Colville 1	Leigh	Smith 1	Maule 1	Collins 2	Garth	Penman 1	89, 8, 72, 46, 36, 70, 80; Linwood 74
S	17-Dec	Hearts		A	L1	0-2	25000	McGregor	McSpadyen	McNaught	Till	Woodcock	Colville	Smith	Maule	Collins	Garth	Stirling	Bauld 17 Conn 72
S	24-Dec	Hibernian		A	L1	2-4	20000	McGregor	McSpadyen	McNaught	Till	Woodcock	Colville	Kelly	Maule 1	Collins	Garth 1	Stirling	35, 18; Johnstone 9 Reilly (2) 14, 23 Smith 62
S	31-Dec	Falkirk	7	H	L1	6-4	17000	McGregor	McSpadyen	McNaught	Till	Woodcock	Colville	Kelly 1	Maule 2	Collins 2	Garth 1	Stirling	60, 26, 58, 21, 37, 16; Inglis 14 Plumb 18 Dawson 16 McCue 48
M	02-Jan	East Fife		A	L1	0-3	22500	McGregor	McSpadyen	McNaught	Till	Woodcock	Colville	Kelly	Maule	Collins	Garth	Stirling	Aitken, R. 25 Brown (2) 51, 61
Tu	03-Jan	Celtic		H	L1	1-1	22000	McGregor	McSpadyen	McNaught	Till	Colville	Leigh	Smith	Maule	Collins	McLaughlin 1	Stirling	19; Haughney 12
S	07-Jan	Partick Thistle		A	L1	0-1	15000	Johnstone	McSpadyen	McNaught	Till	Colville	Leigh	Smith	Maule	Collins	McLaughlin	Stirling	Walker 74
S	14-Jan	St Mirren		H	L1	2-1	12000	Johnstone	McSpadyen	McNaught	Till b	Colville	Leigh	Kelly	Maule	Collins 1	Garth	Murray 1	35, 17; Lesz 64
S	21-Jan	Motherwell		A	L1	0-2	14000	Johnstone	McSpadyen	McNaught	Till	Colville	Leigh	Kelly	Maule	Collins	Garth	Murray	Watson (2) 4, 65
S	28-Jan	Airdrie	8	H	SC 1	3-0	9286	Johnstone	McSpadyen	McNaught	Till	Colville	Leigh	Maule	McLaughlin 2	Garth	Penman 1		84, 87, 85; Millar 9
S	04-Feb	Stirling Albion	9	A	L1	2-1	12000	Johnstone	McSpadyen	McNaught m	Till	Colville	Leigh	Young 1	Maule	McLaughlin 1	Garth	Penman 1	65, 76
S	11-Feb	Clyde	10	H	SC 2	3-2	13180	Johnstone	McSpadyen	McNaught	Till	Colville	Leigh	Young	Maule	McLaughlin 1	Garth	Penman 1	Milgan 14, Mennie 64, Campbell og 7, Balletty 12 Ackerman 63
S	18-Feb	Third Lanark		A	L1	1-0	15000	Johnstone	McSpadyen	McNaught	Till	Colville	Leigh	Young	Maule	McLaughlin	Garth	Penman	65
S	04-Mar	Aberdeen	11	A	L1	0-2	35000	Johnstone	McSpadyen	Young	Till	Colville	Leigh	Smith	Maule	McLaughlin m88	Collins	Penman	Williamson 12 Waddell 64
S	11-Mar	Rangers	12	A	SC QF	1-1	43080	Johnstone	McSpadyen	Young	Till	Colville	Leigh	Maule	Crawford	Penman 1	McLaughlin 1	Stirling	Baird 1 Hamilton 25
W	15-Mar	Rangers	13	H	SC QFr	1-1	28743	Johnstone	McSpadyen	Young	Till	Colville	Young	Maule	Crawford	Penman	McLaughlin 1	Urquhart	Findlay 31
S	18-Mar	Clyde		H	L1	1-2	12000	Johnstone	Kelly	McLure	Till	Colville	Young	Collins	McLaughlin	Penman	McLaughlin	Urquhart	75; Williamson 21
S	25-Mar	Hearts		H	L1	2-0	20000	Johnstone	McSpadyen	McLure	Till	Colville	Young	Young	McLaughlin	Collins 2	McLaughlin	Penman	77, 80; Deakin 70
M	27-Mar	Rangers	14	A	SC QFr2	0-2	63900	Johnstone	McSpadyen	Young	Till	Colville	Young	Smith	McLaughlin	Collins	Urquhart	Penman	Findlay 25 Cox 36
S	08-Apr	Dundee		H	L1	4-1	9500	Johnstone	McSpadyen	McLure	Till	Colville	Young	Maule	Crawford	Goldie	Urquhart 1	Penman 3	88, 19, 54, 84; Boyd 17
S	22-Apr	Queen of the South		H	L1	2-0	7000	Johnstone	McSpadyen	McLure	Till	Colville	Young	Maule	Crawford	Collins	Urquhart 1	Penman	15, 75 Sharpe og
H		Alloa Athletic		PC	Pr	3-3	3000	Johnstone	Stockdale	McLure	Till	Colville	Young	Henderson	Mitchell 1	Penman	Goldie	Collins 1	Brander	5, 13, 2; Gordon 32 Masterton 38 Pow 77
W	03-May	Alloa Athletic		A	PC	Pr 2-4	3000	Johnstone	Kelly	McLure	Till	Colville	Young	Henderson 1	Maule	Collins 2	McLaughlin	Penman	19, 34; Gordon 6 Pow 32 Davidson pen 44 Flaherty 63
S	06-May	East Fife		A	FC	SF 0-1	5000	Johnstone	Kelly	McLure	Till	Colville	Young	Kelly	McLaughlin	McLaughlin	Crawford	Penman	Duncan 19

Manager : Bert Herdman

(1) 1948/49 Final
(2) Dawson sent off ; Inglis and Logan booked
(3) Young broke ankle in the first minute ; Goldie, McLure injured
(4) McLure broke leg
(5) Over 26000 tickets sold
(6) Rovers highest score in the top league to date
(7) Rival captains Telfer and Till were both booked after an incident late in the game
(8) Receipts £ 631
(9) Referee R. Main of Glasgow knocked out by stone after game
(10) Receipts £896
(11) Smith injured after 15 minutes
(12) Receipts £2,580
(13) after extra time ; Receipts £1900. Record attendance
(14) Receipts £4725
The players spent the weekend before the Rangers second replay at Ibrox at Balloch, at a cost to the club of £61 15/6d

Day	Date	Opponents	Note	Venue	Comp	Res	Att	1	2	3	4	5	6	7	8	9	10	11	Opponents' scorers	Goal times
S	12-Aug	Third Lanark		H	LC S	3-2	15000	Johnstone	McLure	McNaught	Till	Colville	Young	Brander 1	Maule 1	McLaughlin	Keith 1	Penman 1	Henderson 66 Cuthbertson 71	89, 13, 1
W	16-Aug	East Fife		A	LC S	3-3	12000	Johnstone	McLure	McNaught	Till	Colville	Young	Leigh	Maule 1	McLaughlin	Keith 1	Penman 1	Duncan 27 Black 33 Morris 66	28, 12, 7
S	19-Aug	Celtic		A	LC S	1-2	35000	Johnstone	McLure	McNaught	Till	Colville	Young	Leigh 1	Maule	McLaughlin	Keith	Penman	McPhail (2) 33, 88	42
S	26-Aug	Third Lanark		A	LC S	0-1	10000	Johnstone	McLure	McNaught	Till	Colville	Young	Henderson	Maule	Keith	McLaughlin	Penman	Staroscik 51	
W	30-Aug	East Fife		H	LC S	1-4	15000	Johnstone	McLure	McNaught	Till	Colville	Leigh	Henderson 1	Mitchell	Keith	Maule	Penman 1	Fleming 41 Bonthrone (3) 46, 70, 89	38
S	02-Sep	Celtic		H	LC S	2-2	16000	Johnstone	McLure	McNaught	Till	Colville	Leigh	Henderson 1	Mitchell	Young 2	Maule	Penman	Collins 22 Peacock 30	57, 65
S	09-Sep	Partick Thistle		H	L1	2-5	15000	Clark	McLure	McNaught	Till	Colville	Leigh	Maule	Mitchell	Young 2	McLaughlin	Penman	McCalman (2) 17, 89 [overlapping text]	40, 50
S	16-Sep	Third Lanark		H	L1	4-0	11000	Clark	McLure	McNaught	Till	Colville	Leigh	Stockdale	Mitchell	Young 2	Maule	Penman 2		30, 87, 42, 57
S	23-Sep	East Fife		A	L1	1-3	17500	Johnstone	McLure	McNaught	Till	Colville	Leigh	Stockdale 1	Mitchell	Young	Maule	Penman 1	Fleming 18 Bonthrone (2) 20, 73	31
S	30-Sep	Celtic		H	L1	1-2	13500	Johnstone	McLure	McNaught	McLaughlin	Colville	McLaughlin	Mitchell	Keith	Young	Maule	Brander	Peacock 37 Weir, J. 12	4
M	02-Oct	Dunfermline Athletic		H	FC	6-3	5500	Johnstone	McLure	McNaught	McLaughlin 1	Woodcock	Coville	Brander 1	Maule 2	Young 2	Murray	Penman 1	Clark (2) 38, 56 Kirk 63	68, 85, 26, 33, 19, 69
S	07-Oct	Celtic		A	L1	3-2	20000	Johnstone	McLure	McNaught	McLaughlin 2	Woodcock	McLaughlin	Brander	Maule	Young	Murray	Penman 1	Peacock (2) 11, 36	78, 83, 23
S	14-Oct	St Mirren		H	L1	2-0	15000	Johnstone	McLure	McNaught	McLaughlin	Colville	Leigh	Brander	Maule	Young 1	Murray 1	Penman		85, 23
S	21-Oct	Morton		H	L1	1-1	15000	Johnstone	McLure	Condie	McLaughlin	Colville	Leigh	Brander	Maule 1	Young 1	Murray	Penman 1	Cupples 2	46
S	28-Oct	Falkirk		A	L1	3-2	10000	Johnstone	McLure	McNaught	McLaughlin	Colville	Leigh	Brander	Maule 1	Young 1	Murray	Penman 1	Morrison 20 Brown 2	74, 21, 57
S	04-Nov	Dundee		H	L1	0-1	25000	Johnstone	McLure	McNaught	McLaughlin	Colville	Leigh	Brander	Maule	Young	Murray	Penman	Gerrie 49	40
S	11-Nov	Airdrie		A	L1	5-2	5000	Johnstone	McLure	McNaught	McLaughlin	Colville	Leigh	Stockdale 1	Maule	Young 1	Collins	Brander 3	Welsh 37 McMillan 47	76, 62, 21, 52, 74
S	18-Nov	Rangers	1	A	L1	1-4	25000	Johnstone	McLure	McNaught	McLaughlin	Colville	Leigh	Stockdale	Maule	Young 1	Collins 1	Brander	Williamson (2) 8, 47 Young 88 pen Paton 36	34
S	25-Nov	Aberdeen		H	L1	1-0	18000	Johnstone	McLure	McNaught	McLaughlin	Colville m	Leigh	McIlhatton	Maule	Young 1	Collins 1	Brander		26
S	02-Dec	Motherwell		A	L1	3-4	13000	Johnstone	McLure	McNaught	McLaughlin	Colville 1p	Leigh	McIlhatton	Maule	Young 1	Murray 1	Brander	Forrest 10 Watson 63 Kelly (2) 68, 89	35, 14, 61
S	09-Dec	Clyde		A	L1	0-1	7000	Johnstone	McLure	McNaught	McLaughlin	Colville	Leigh	McIlhatton	Maule	Young	Murray	Brander	Buchanan 6	
S	16-Dec	Hearts		H	L1	2-0	12000	Johnstone	McLure	McNaught	McLaughlin	Colville	Leigh	McIlhatton	Maule	Young 2	Murray	Penman		12, 89
S	23-Dec	Partick Thistle		A	L1	2-2	10000	Johnstone	McLure	McNaught	McLaughlin	Colville	Leigh	McIlhatton	Maule	Young 1	Murray 1	Penman	McCreadie 12 Stott 44	88, 68
S	30-Dec	Third Lanark		A	L1	2-1	9000	Johnstone	McLure	McNaught	McLaughlin	Colville	Leigh	McIlhatton	Maule	Young 1	Murray 1	Penman	Dick 19	21, 8
M	01-Jan	East Fife		H	L1	3-0	12000	Johnstone	McLure	McNaught	McLaughlin 2	Colville	Leigh	McIlhatton	Maule	Young	Murray	Penman 1		2, 55, 6
S	06-Jan	Hibernian		A	L1	1-3	22000	Johnstone	McLure	McNaught	McLaughlin	Colville 1p	Leigh	McIlhatton	Maule	Young	Murray	Penman	McVinish 14 Cupples 89	4
S	20-Jan	Morton		A	L1	0-2	14000	Clark	Woodcock	McLure	McLaughlin	Colville	Leigh	McIlhatton	Collins	Young	Murray	Penman	Stott 64	
S	27-Jan	Partick Thistle	2	A	SC 1	1-1	21600	Johnstone	McLure	McNaught	McLaughlin	Colville	Leigh	Maule	Collins	Young 1	Murray	Penman		14
W	31-Jan	Partick Thistle		H	SC 1r	1-0	11500	Johnstone s	McLure	McNaught	McLaughlin	Colville	Leigh	Maule	Collins	Young 1	Murray	Penman		76
S	03-Feb	Falkirk		H	L1	3-0	12000	Johnstone	McLure	McNaught	McLaughlin	Colville	Leigh	Maule	Collins 1	Young 2	Murray 1	Penman		33, 60, 85
S	10-Feb	Brechin City	3	H	SC 2	5-2	12000	Johnstone	McLure	McNaught	McLaughlin	Colville	Leigh	Maule 2	Collins 1	Young	Murray 1	Penman 1	Skinner 26 Broadley 58	70, 87, 42, 2, 60
S	17-Feb	Airdrie		H	L1	0-1	9000	Johnstone	McLure	McNaught	McLaughlin 2	Colville	Leigh	Maule	Waller	Young 2	Murray	Penman 1	Docherty 87	
S	24-Feb	Rangers		A	L1	2-1	24000	Johnstone	McLure	McNaught	McLaughlin	Colville	Leigh	Maule 2	Young	Penman 2	Murray	Brander 1	Waddell 35	87, 22, 46
S	03-Mar	Aberdeen		A	SC 3	2-1	15000	Johnstone	McLure	McNaught	McLaughlin	Colville	Leigh	Maule	Young	Penman 2	Murray	Brander	Delaney 75	27, 66
S	10-Mar	Dundee		H	L1	2-1	40920	Johnstone	Wilkie	McNaught	McLaughlin	Colville	Leigh	Maule	Young	Penman 1	Murray	Brander	Christie 31	3, 61
S	17-Mar	Clyde		H	L1	4-1	9000	Johnstone	Till	McNaught	McLaughlin	Colville	Leigh	Maule	Young	Penman 1	Murray 1	Brander	Campbell 12	13, 29, 72, 10
S	24-Mar	Hearts		A	L1	1-3	23000	Johnstone	McLure	McNaught	McLaughlin	Colville	Leigh	Maule	Young 2	Penman 1	Murray	Condie	Wardhaugh 40 Urquhuart 60 Cumming 88	52
S	31-Mar	Celtic	4	N	SC SF	2-3	83019	Johnstone	Kelly	McNaught	McLaughlin	Colville	Leigh	Maule	Young	Penman 1	Murray	Brander	Weir 2 McPhail 40 Tully 81	80, 35 Boden og
M	02-Apr	Dundee		A	L1	0-2	14000	Johnstone	McLure	McNaught	McLaughlin	Colville	Young	Maule	Young	Penman	Murray	Brander	Williams 11 Hill 50	
W	25-Apr	Hibernian		A	L1	0-3	20000	Johnstone	McLure	McNaught	McLaughlin	Colville	Leigh	Maule	Young	Penman	Murray	Brander	Turnbull 41 pen Combe 74 Reilly 89	
S	28-Apr	St Mirren		A	L1	0-2	10000	Johnstone	McLure	McNaught	McLaughlin	Colville	Leigh	Maule	Cockburn	Collins	Collins	Brander	Stewart 15 Telfer 51	
W	02-May	Motherwell		A	L1	2-3	4000	Johnstone	Till	McNaught	Young	Colville	Leigh	Maule	Young	Penman 1	McLaughlin 1	Murray	Watson 6 Humphries 50 Aitken 42	52, 57
F	04-May	Fraserburgh	5	A	F	0-1		Johnstone	McLure	McLure	Till	Colville	Leigh	Maule	Mitchell 1	Penman	Cockburn	Murray	Russell 43	
S	05-May	Brechin City		A	F	2-1		Johnstone	Clunie	McNaught	McLaughlin	Colville	Young	Maule	Mitchell	Penman	Murray	Brander	Paris 25	78, 20
M	07-May	Elgin City		A	F	4-1		Johnstone	Till	McLure	Young	Colville	Leigh	Maule 1	Maule 1	Cockburn 1	McLaughlin 2	Murray	Auld 17	60, 84, 14, 25
W	09-May	Inverness Thistle		A	F	1-1		Johnstone	Till	McLure	Leigh	Clunie	Colville	Murray	Maule 1	McLaughlin	Young	Brander	McKenzie 30	37
S	14-Jul	Queen's Park		H	SM 1	9-0	9000	Johnstone	McLure	McNaught	McLaughlin	Colville 1	Leigh	McEwan	Young	Penman 5	Maule	McIntyre		77, 41, 9, 40, 44, 57, 87, 62, 26 Bell og
Tu	17-Jul	Queen of the South	6	N	SM 2	2-2	5000	Gray	McLure	McNaught	McLaughlin	Colville	Leigh	McEwan 1	Young 1	Penman 1	Maule	McIntyre	Paterson 7 Inglis 14	44, 35
W	18-Jul	Queen of the South	6	N	SM 2r	2-2	6000	Gray	McLure	McNaught	McLaughlin	Colville	Leigh	McEwan 1	Young 1	Penman	Maule	McIntyre		82, 5
S	28-Jul	Celtic	4	N	SM SF	1-3	48897	Gray	McLure	McNaught	McLaughlin	Colville	Leigh	McEwan	Young	Penman	Maule	McIntyre	Walsh (3) 24, 52, 65	McGrory og 46

Manager : Bert Herdman

(1) Waddell missed penalty
(2) Receipts £1400
(3) Receipts £780
(4) at Hampden Park
(5) John Dutch Benefit
(6) at Celtic Park

Substitutes, own goals, goal times and opponents' scorers

Day	Date	Opponents	Note	Venue	Comp	Res	Att	1	2	3	4	5	6	7	8	9	10	11		Substitutes, own goals, goal times and opponents' scorers
S	11-Aug	Hearts		A	LCS	0-1	30000	Johnstone	McLure	McNaught	McLaughlin	Colville	Leigh	McEwan	Maule	Penman	Young	McIntyre		Bauld 50
W	15-Aug	St Mirren		H	LCS	3-2	9500	Johnstone	McLure	McNaught	McLaughlin	Colville	Leigh	McEwan 1	Maule	Penman 2	Young	McIntyre	48, 31, 59	Lesz 2 Rice 23
S	18-Aug	Dundee		A	LCS	0-5	21000	Gray	McLure	McNaught	McLaughlin	Colville	Leigh	Maule	Young	Penman	Murray	McIntyre		Steel 42 Toner (3) 53, 74, 85 Colville og 87
W	25-Aug	Hearts		H	LCS	2-0	15000	Gray	McLure	McNaught	McLaughlin	Colville	Leigh	Wood	Maule	Young 1	Murray	Penman	27, 9	
S	29-Aug	St Mirren		A	LCS	0-2	12000	Gray	Wilkie	McNaught	McLaughlin	Colville	Leigh	McEwan	Maule	Penman	Young	Penman		Blyth 57 Crowe 72
S	01-Sep	Dundee		H	LCS	1-3	14000	Gray	Wilkie	McNaught	Till	Colville m	McLaughlin	McEwan	Maule 1	Penman	Young	Penman 1	51	Christie (2) 37, 47 Williams 80
S	08-Sep	Hibernian		H	L1	0-2	17500	Johnstone	McLure	McNaught	Young	Colville	Leigh	McEwan	Maule	Penman	McLaughlin	McIntyre		Johnstone 8 Smith 44
S	15-Sep	St Mirren	1	A	L1	0-3	10000	Gray	McLure	McNaught	McLaughlin	Colville	Leigh	McEwan	Mitchell	Young	Maule	Penman		Goldthorpe 25 Lapsley 32 Colville og 70
S	22-Sep	East Fife		H	L1	2-3	18000	Gray	McLure	McNaught	McLaughlin	Clunie	Leigh	McEwan	Murray	Young 1	Young	Maule	59, 66	Gardiner 4 Stewart, J 47 Duncan 48
S	29-Sep	Queen of the South		A	L1	2-2	10500	Gray	Wilkie	McNaught	Till	Colville	Leigh	McEwan	McLaughlin	Young	Maule 1p	McIntyre	70, 89	Patterson 74 McKeown 78
S	06-Oct	Partick Thistle		H	L1	1-2	10000	Johnstone	Wilkie	McLure	Till	Colville	Leigh	McEwan	McLaughlin 1	Young	Kelly	Maule	76	Walker (2) 29, 46
S	13-Oct	Airdrie	2	A	L1	1-2	11000	Johnstone	Wilkie	McNaught	Young	Colville m	Leigh 1	McEwan	McLaughlin 1	Copland 1	Kelly	Murray	15	Lennox 4 Shankland 65 pen
S	20-Oct	Morton		H	L1	4-1	7000	Johnstone	Wilkie	McNaught	Young	Colville	Leigh 1	McEwan	Maule	Copland 1	Kelly 1	McIntyre 1	25, 15, 40, 50	Linwood 20
S	27-Oct	Stirling Albion		A	L1	3-0	12000	Johnstone	Wilkie	McNaught	Young	Colville	Leigh	McEwan	Maule	Copland 1	Kelly	McIntyre 1	85, 53, 15	
S	03-Nov	Dundee		A	L1	0-2	21000	Johnstone	Wilkie	McNaught	Young	Colville	Leigh	McEwan	Maule	Copland 1	Kelly	McIntyre		Flavell (2) 6, 8
S	10-Nov	Airdrie		H	L1	1-1	8000	Johnstone	Wilkie	McNaught	Young	Colville	Leigh	McEwan	Maule	Copland 1	Kelly	McIntyre	89	McCulloch 79
S	17-Nov	Rangers		H	L1	3-1	20000	Johnstone	Wilkie	McNaught	Young	Colville	Leigh	Wood	McEwan 1	Copland	Maule 1	Brander 1	58, 52, 6	Liddell 60
S	24-Nov	Aberdeen		A	L1	2-2	15000	Johnstone	Wilkie	McNaught	Young 1p	Colville	Leigh	Wood 1	McEwan	Copland	Kelly	Brander	50, 60	Yorston 6 Hamilton 40
S	01-Dec	Motherwell		A	L1	3-1	8000	Johnstone	Wilkie	McNaught	Young	Colville	Leigh	Wood	McEwan 2	Copland	Maule	Brander 1	43, 53, 45	Aitkenhead 74 pen
S	08-Dec	Third Lanark		H	L1	1-0	12000	Johnstone	Wilkie	McNaught	Young 1	Colville	Leigh	Wood	McEwan	Copland	Maule	Brander	77	
S	15-Dec	Hearts		A	L1	2-4	25000	Johnstone	McLure	McNaught	Young	Colville	Leigh	McIntyre	McEwan 1	Copland	Maule	Brander	42, 78 Brown og	Whittle 25 Conn 81 Rutherford (2) 30, 89
S	22-Dec	Hibernian		A	L1	0-5	24500	Johnstone	McLure	McNaught	Young	Colville	Leigh	Wood	McEwan	Kelly	Kelly	Brander		Reilly 7 Combe (2) 24, 68 Johnstone (2) 55, 57
S	29-Dec	St Mirren		H	L1	2-1	12000	Johnstone	McLure	McNaught	Young	Colville	Leigh	McIntyre	McEwan	Kelly 1	Kelly	Penman 1	70, 67	Duncanson 47
Tu	01-Jan	East Fife		A	L1	1-0	16425	Johnstone	McLure	McNaught	Young	Colville	Leigh	Maule	McEwan	Penman	Kelly	McIntyre	40	
W	02-Jan	Queen of the South		H	L1	0-0	12000	Johnstone	McLure	McNaught	Young	Colville	Leigh	Maule	Maule	Penman	Kelly	McIntyre		
W	09-Jan	Partick Thistle		A	L1	1-1	3000	Johnstone	McLure	McNaught	Young	Colville	Leigh	Wood	McEwan	Copland	Kelly	Penman	49	Hewitt 80
S	12-Jan	Celtic		H	L1	1-0	20000	Johnstone s	McLure	McNaught	Young	Colville	Leigh	Wood	Maule	Copland	Kelly	Penman	32	
S	19-Jan	Morton		H	L1	2-0	9000	Johnstone	McLure	McNaught	Young	Colville	Leigh	Wood 1	Maule	Copland 1	Kelly	McIntyre	30, 20	
S	26-Jan	Hibernian		H	SC 1	0-0	32867	Johnstone	McLure	McNaught	Young	Colville	McLaughlin	Maule	McEwan	Copland	McEwan	Penman		
W	30-Jan	Hibernian	3	A	SC 1r	0-0	30259	Johnstone	McLure	McNaught	Young	Colville	Leigh	Wood	McEwan	Copland	McEwan	Penman		
S	02-Feb	Stirling Albion		A	L1	2-1	4500	Johnstone	Sharpe	McNaught	Young	Colville	Leigh	McIntyre 1	Maule	Copland	Cockburn 1	Brander	14, 21	Anderson 83
M	04-Feb	Hibernian	4	N	SC 1r2	4-1	33614	Johnstone	McLure	McNaught	Young	Colville	Leigh	McEwan	Maule	Penman 2	Kelly 1	McIntyre 1	2, 57, 61, 14	Reilly 46
S	09-Feb	Hearts	5	A	SC 2	1-2	47152	Johnstone	McLure	McNaught	Young	Clunie	Colville	McEwan	Maule	Penman	Kelly	Brander 1	41	Bauld 85
W	13-Feb	Dundee		H	L1	1-2	4500	Johnstone	McLure	McNaught	Nee	Colville	Leigh	Maule	McEwan	McEwan	McLaughlin	Penman		Toner 7 Ewan 50
S	16-Feb	East Fife		A	FC SF	0-4	6000	Johnstone	McLure	McNaught	Young	Colville	Leigh	Wood	McEwan	Penman	Kelly	Penman		Gardiner (2) 7, 57 Stewart 14 Bonthrone 82
S	23-Feb	Celtic		A	L1	1-0	22000	Johnstone	McLure	McNaught	Young	Colville	Leigh	Maule	McEwan	Penman	Kelly 1	McIntyre	21	
W	27-Feb	Rangers		H	L1	0-1	20000	Johnstone	McLure	McNaught	Young	Colville	Williamson	Maule	McEwan	Copland	Kelly	McIntyre		Thornton 1
S	01-Mar	Aberdeen		H	L1	2-1	7000	Johnstone	McLure	McNaught	Young	Colville	Leigh	Maule	McEwan	Copland 1	Kelly	McIntyre	46, 89	Rodger 27
S	15-Mar	Third Lanark		A	L1	1-3	14000	Johnstone	McLure	McNaught b	Young	Colville	Leigh	McEwan	McEwan	Copland 1	Kelly	McIntyre 1	54	Dick (2) 30, 62 Henderson 83 pen
S	22-Mar	Hearts		H	L1	2-1	11000	Johnstone	McLure	McNaught	Young 1	Colville	Leigh	Wood	McEwan	McEwan	Cockburn	Penman	57, 15	Whittle 28
S	29-Mar	East Fife		H	F	2-2	1000	Drummond	McLure	Condie	Young	Colville	Leigh	Wood	Sibbald	Penman	Cockburn 2	Maule	26, 67	Gardiner 33 Duncan 61 pen
S	19-Apr	Queen of the South		A	F	3-0	4000	Johnstone	McLure	McNaught	Young	Colville	Leigh	Wood	McEwan 1	Copland 1	Kelly 1	McIntyre	17, 77, 28	
W	23-Apr	Dunfermline Athletic		A	PC	1-0	4000	Johnstone	McLure	McNaught	Young	Colville 2p	Williamson	Wood	McEwan	Copland 1	Cockburn	Penman	44	
S	26-Apr	St Mirren		A	F	0-2	7500	Stewart	McLure	McNaught	Young	Colville	Leigh	Maule	McEwan	Penman	Maule	Penman		Goldthorpe 50 Wilson 80
W	28-Apr	Motherwell		H	L1	2-0	10000	Johnstone	McLure	McNaught	Young	Colville	Leigh	Maule	McEwan	Copland	Cockburn	Penman	75, 85	
S	03-May	Millwall		A	F	3-3	10034	Johnstone	McLure	McNaught	Young	Colville	Leigh	Wood	McEwan	Penman	Cockburn 1	McIntyre 2	McLaughlin u25 50, 15, 80	Monkhouse (3) 18, 24, 51
M	12-May	Hearts		A	PC SF	1-1		Johnstone	McLure	Condie	Young	Colville	Leigh	Maule	McEwan	Penman r	Cockburn	Allan	64	Whittle 29
W	14-May	Hearts		H	PC SFr	0-2	4000	Johnstone	McLure	Condie	Williamson	Colville	Leigh	Maule	McEwan	Young	Cockburn	Allan		Whittle 24 Bauld 60

Manager : Bert Herdman

Obstruction punishable by indirect free kick ; length of studs could be 1/4 of an inch longer

(1) Jimmy Mitchell broke leg after 8 minutes play
(2) McCulloch missed penalty
(3) after extra time receipts £2473
(4) at Tynecastle, receipts £2999
(5) receipts £3340

Substitutes, own goals, goal times and opponents' scorers

Day	Date	Opponents	Note	Venue	Comp	Res	Att	1	2	3	4	5	6	7	8	9	10	11	Goal times	Opponents' scorers etc.
S	09-Aug	Dundee		A	LC S	1-2	20000	Johnstone	McLure	McNaught	Young	Colville	Leigh	Maule	McEwan	McDonald	McIntyre	Penman	42	Burrell 12 Christie 17
W	13-Aug	Clyde		H	LC S	4-3	12000	Johnstone	McLure	McNaught	Young	Colville	Leigh	Maule 1	McEwan 1	McDonald 2	McIntyre	Scott	70, 86, 54, 81	McPhail 25 Buchanan 46 Ring 48
S	16-Aug	Airdrie		A	LC S	1-0	6500	Johnstone	McLure	McNaught	Young	Colville	Leigh	McEwan	Maule	McDonald	McIntyre	Penman	53	
S	23-Aug	Dundee		H	LC S	1-2	18000	Johnstone	McLure	McNaught	Young	Colville	Leigh	McEwan 1	Maule	McDonald 1	McIntyre	Penman	62	Steel (2) 61, 84
W	27-Aug	Clyde		A	LC S	1-6	7000	Johnstone	McLure	McNaught	Young	Colville	Leigh	McEwan 1	Maule	McDonald	McIntyre	Penman	81	Buchanan (2) 10, 59 Ring 25 McPhail (2) 31, 82 Baird 76
S	30-Aug	Airdrie		H	LC S	1-1	8000	Stewart	McLure	McNaught	Young	Colville	Williamson	Wood	McEwan	Williamson,P	McIntyre	Penman 1	64	Welsh 75
S	06-Sep	Airdrie		A	L1	1-3	9000	Stewart	McLure	McNaught	Young 1	Colville	Leigh	Wood	McEwan	Penman	Maule	Scott	74	McGurn 17 McMillan 38 pen Brown, W. 43
S	13-Sep	Celtic		H	L1	1-1	18000	Stewart	McLure	McNaught	Young	Colville	Leigh	Wood	McEwan	Penman	Cockburn	McIntyre	54	Tully 60
S	20-Sep	East Fife		A	L1	0-2	15000	Stewart	McLure	McNaught	Young	Colville	Leigh	Wood	McEwan	Penman	Cockburn	McIntyre		Wright 41 Fleming 2nd half
S	27-Sep	St Mirren		A	L1	0-1	9000	Stewart	McLure	Condie	Young	Colville	Williamson	McEwan	Cockburn	McDonald	Kelly	McIntyre		Telfer 42
S	11-Oct	Dundee		H	L1	1-1	11000	Stewart	McLure	McNaught	Leigh	Colville	Williamson	McIntyre	McEwan	Young 1	Kelly	Scott	31	Henderson 16
S	18-Oct	Partick Thistle		A	L1	1-4	6000	Stewart	McLure	McNaught	Leigh	Colville	Williamson	McEwan	McIntyre	Young 1	Kelly 1	Scott	44	Stott (4) 18, 59, 64, 69
S	25-Oct	Third Lanark		H	L1	3-4	6000	Stewart	McLure	McNaught	Leigh	Colville	Williamson	McEwan	McIntyre 1	Young 1	Maule 1	Scott	22, 72, 9	Dobbie (2) 30, 85 Cuthbertson 63 Henderson 47
S	01-Nov	Clyde		A	L1	2-3	8000	Johnstone	McLure	McNaught	Young	Clunie	Leigh	McEwan	Maule	Copland 2	Kelly	Scott	70, 85	Buchanan 14 McPhail (2) 49, 77
S	08-Nov	Aberdeen		H	L1	2-1	8500	Johnstone	McLure	McNaught	Young	Clunie	Leigh	Maule	McIntyre 1	Copland 1	Kelly	Penman	6, 57	Buckley 64
S	15-Nov	Motherwell		H	L1	1-1	8000	Stewart	McNaught	McNaught	McNaught	Colville	Williamson	Maule	McIntyre	Copland 1	Kelly	Penman	30	Aitkenhead 26
S	22-Nov	Rangers		A	L1	2-3	25000	Stewart	McLure	McNaught	Young	Condie	Williamson	Maule	McIntyre	Copland 2	McEwan	Penman	25, 35	Prentice 16 Grierson (2) 57, 60
S	29-Nov	Hearts		H	L1	1-1	11000	Stewart	McLure	McNaught	McNaught	Condie	Williamson	Maule	Taylor	Copland 1	Scott	Penman	54	Urquhart 55
S	06-Dec	Falkirk		A	L1	2-3	10000	Johnstone	McLure	McNaught	Young	Condie	Williamson	Maule	Taylor	Copland 1	Scott	Penman 1	12, 38	Dunlop (2) 17, 25 Campbell 28
S	13-Dec	Queen of the South		H	L1	1-1	5500	Johnstone	McLure	McNaught	Young	Colville m	Williamson	Maule	Taylor	Copland	Scott	Penman 1	70	Patterson 40
S	27-Dec	Celtic		A	L1	1-0	20000	Johnstone	McLure	McNaught	Young	Colville	Williamson	Maule	Kelly	Copland 1	McEwan	Penman	24	
Th	01-Jan	East Fife		H	L1	0-0	20000	Johnstone	McLure	McNaught	Young	Colville	Williamson	Maule	Kelly	Copland	McEwan	Penman		
S	10-Jan	Hibernian		H	L1	4-2	17000	Johnstone s	McLure	McNaught	Young	Colville	Williamson	McDonald	Maule	Copland 3	McIntyre 1	Penman	37, 60, 63, 10	Ormond 27 Combe 62
S	17-Jan	Dundee		A	L1	3-2	22500	Johnstone	McLure	McNaught b	Young	Colville	Williamson	Maule	Kelly	Copland 2	McIntyre	Penman 1	20, 68, 6	Steel 55 Boyd 74 pen
S	24-Jan	Clachnacuddin	1	H	SC 1	5-0	25000	Stewart	McLure	McNaught	Young	Colville	Williamson	Maule	Kelly 1	Copland 4	Kelly	Penman	80, 14, 40, 55, 70	
S	31-Jan	Partick Thistle		H	L1	2-2	8500	Johnstone	McLure	McNaught	Young	Colville	Williamson	Maule	Kelly	Copland	McIntyre	Penman 2	21, 50	Howitt 27 Walker 37
S	07-Feb	Hearts	2	H	SC 2	0-1	31306	Johnstone	McLure	McNaught	Young	Colville	Leigh	Maule	Kelly	Copland	McIntyre	Penman		Bauld 36
S	14-Feb	Third Lanark	3	A	L1	1-2	13500	Johnstone	McLure	McNaught	Leigh	Colville	Williamson	McIntyre	McIntyre	Copland 1	Maule	Penman 1	18	Henderson 26 Dick 43
S	28-Feb	Aberdeen		A	L1	2-0	18000	Johnstone	McLure	McNaught	Leigh	Colville	Williamson	McEwan x89	McIntyre	Copland 1	Young 1	Penman	18, 9	
S	07-Mar	Motherwell		A	L1	1-2	12200	Johnstone	McLure	McNaught	Leigh	Colville	Williamson	Wood	McEwan	Copland	Young	Penman 1	73	Williams 49 Humphries 68
S	14-Mar	Airdrie		H	L1	3-0	10000	Johnstone	McLure	McNaught	Leigh	Colville	Williamson	Wood	Young	Copland	Kelly	Penman 3	27, 40, 85	
W	18-Mar	Rangers	4	H	L1	3-1	17800	Johnstone	McLure	McNaught	Leigh	Colville	Williamson	Wood	Young 2,1p	Copland	Kelly	Penman 1	5p, 32, 41	Simpson 85
S	21-Mar	Hearts		A	L1	2-1	23450	Johnstone	McLure	McNaught	Leigh	Colville	Williamson	Maule	Young	Copland	Kelly 2	Penman	76, 79	Conn 52
S	28-Mar	Falkirk		A	L1	0-2	8500	Johnstone	McLure	McNaught	Leigh	Colville	Williamson	Maule	Young	Copland	Maule	Penman		Brown 46 Plumb 66
S	04-Apr	Queen of the South		A	L1	1-1	8500	Johnstone	McLure	McNaught	Leigh	Colville	Williamson	Maule	Young	Copland 1	Kelly	Penman	15	Black 1
S	11-Apr	Clyde		H	L1	3-2	7000	Johnstone	McLure	McNaught	Leigh	Colville	Williamson	Maule	Young	Copland	Kelly	Penman 2	65, 67, 70	Keogh 37 Baird 57 pen
M	20-Apr	Millwall		A	F	3-2	7680	Johnstone	McLure	McNaught	Leigh	Colville	Williamson	McIntyre	Young 1	Copland	McIntyre 1	Penman	Thrippleton og 1. 50, 35, 70	Green 5 Neary 78
S	25-Apr	St Mirren		A	L1	2-3	8000	Johnstone	McLure	McNaught	Leigh	Colville	Williamson	McEwan 1	Young 1	Copland	McIntyre	Penman 1	15, 18	Gemmell 19 Stewart 20 Telfer 80
W	29-Apr	Hibernian		A	L1	1-4	10000	Johnstone	McLure	McNaught	Leigh	Colville	Williamson	McEwan 1	Young 1	Copland	McIntyre	Penman	55	Johnstone (2) 38, 47 Ormond 84 Turnbull 89
S	02-May	Burntisland Shipyard	N1	H	FC SF-1	6-0		Stewart	McLaughlin	Condie	Cockburn	Wilkie	Archibald	Livingstone 2	Mitchell 1	Currie 1	Taylor 2	Scott	75,85,7,5,27,41	
S	02-May	Falkirk		A	PC 1	2-3	4000	Johnstone	McLure	McGowan	Young	Colville	Leigh	McEwan	Wood	Copland 1	Williamson 1	Penman	12, 44	Campbell 10 Brown 60 McCrae 69
W	13-May	East Fife		H	FC F	1-1	2000	Johnstone	Scobie	McGowan	Young m	Colville	Leigh	McEwan 1	Scott	Copland	McNaught	Penman	55	Bonthrone 81

Manager : Bert Herdman

(1) Receipts £584

(2) 31306 tickets were sold for the Hearts cup tie, but the actual attendance was 26929 Ground , 1729 enclosure, 67 uncovered seats, 878 C Stand plus 1000 season tickets.   There were 692 transfers to B Stand

(3) Henderson ordered off with McEwan in 89 minutes

(4) First time a white ball was used at Stark's Park

(N1) fixture fulfilled by reserve team, not included in summary statistics. Livingstone a trialist from Hibs.   The second leg of the Fife Cup semi final was due to be played in Burntisland on 5th May, but they scratched as they could not raise a team because of injuries.

Day	Date	Opponents	Note	Venue	Comp	Res.	Att.	1	2	3	4	5	6	7	8	9	10	11	Substitutes, own goals, goal times and opponents' scorers	
S	08-Aug	Rangers		H	LC S	0-4	24807	Johnstone	McLure	McNaught	Young	Colville	Leigh	McEwan	McDonald	Copland	Kelly	Penman	Young 20 pen Simpson 75 Grierson 89 Prentice 23	
W	12-Aug	Hamilton Academical		A	LC S	2-1	12000	Johnstone	McLure	McNaught	Young	Colville	Leigh	McEwan	McIntyre	Copland	Kelly	Penman	Todd 19	8,70
S	15-Aug	Hearts		A	LC S	0-2	25000	Johnstone	Kirk	McNaught	Young	Colville	Williamson	McEwan	Clunie	Copland	Williamson	McIntyre	Wardhaugh 7 Urquhart	
W	22-Aug	Rangers		A	LC S	1-3	38000	Johnstone	Kirk	McNaught	Leigh	Colville	Williamson	McEwan	Young	Copland	Kelly 1	McIntyre	McCulloch 38 Paton (2) 49, 73	10
W	26-Aug	Hamilton Academical		H	LC S	2-0	6000	Johnstone	Kirk	McNaught	Leigh	Colville	Williamson	McEwan	Young 1	Copland 2	Kelly 1	McIntyre		35,55
S	29-Aug	Hearts		H	LC S	3-1	9000	Stewart	McLure	McNaught	Leigh	Colville	Williamson	McEwan	Young 2	Copland 1	Kelly	McIntyre	Wardhaugh 11	42,58,74
S	05-Sep	Hibernian	1	H	L1	4-0	15200	Johnstone	Kirk	McNaught	Leigh	Colville	Williamson	McEwan	Young	Copland 1	Kelly 1	Penman		13,17,15,29
S	12-Sep	Dundee		H	L1	0-0	23000	Johnstone	Kirk	McNaught	Leigh	Colville	Williamson	McEwan	Young	Copland 1	Kelly 1	Penman		
S	19-Sep	East Fife		H	L1	2-2	17000	Johnstone	Kirk	McNaught	Leigh	Colville	Williamson	McEwan	Young	Copland 1	Kelly 1	Scott	Fleming 11 Bonthrone 74	47,52
S	26-Sep	St Mirren		A	L1	0-3	12000	Johnstone	Kirk	McNaught	Leigh	Colville	Williamson	McEwan	Young	Copland	Kelly	Scott	Gemmell 13 Stewart (2) 35, 55	
S	03-Oct	Airdrie		H	L1	5-1	10000	Johnstone	Kirk	McNaught	Leigh	Colville	Williamson	McEwan	Young 1	Copland 3	Kelly 1	Scott	Baird 79	75,12,21,82,89
S	10-Oct	Celtic		A	L1	0-3	20000	Johnstone	Kirk	McNaught	Leigh	Colville	Williamson	McEwan	Young	Copland	Kelly 1	Scott	Fernie (2) 6, 67 Collins 68	
S	17-Oct	Partick Thistle		H	L1	4-1	10000	Johnstone	Kirk	McNaught	Williamson	Colville	Leigh	McEwan	Young 1	Copland 2	Kelly	Scott	Walker 80	73,7,88,56
S	24-Oct	Stirling Albion		A	L1	3-1	14000	Johnstone	Kirk	McNaught	Williamson	Colville	Leigh	McEwan	Young	Copland 3	Kelly 1	Scott	Swanson 10	60,71,74
S	31-Oct	Queen of the South		A	L1	1-5	9500	Johnstone	Kirk	McNaught	McIntyre	Colville	Leigh	McEwan	Young 1	Copland	Kelly	Scott	Rothera (2) 10, 88 Black 16 McGill (2) 52, 75	4
M	02-Nov	Carlisle United		A	F	4-1	8100	Johnstone	McLure	McNaught	Young	Colville	Leigh	McEwan	Maule	Copland 2	Kelly	Scott 2	Atkinson 60	20,44,8,85
S	07-Nov	Falkirk		H	L1	0-2	8000	Johnstone	McLure	McNaught	Young	Colville	Leigh b	McEwan	Maule	Copland	Kelly	Scott	Sinclair 5 Delaney 62	
S	14-Nov	Hearts		A	L1	1-5	22000	Johnstone	McLure	McNaught	Young	Colville	Leigh	McEwan	Napier	Copland	Kelly	Scott	Wardhaugh (3) 18sec, 13, 80 Conn (2) 44, 73	20
S	21-Nov	Rangers		H	L1	1-2	15500	Drummond	Kirk	McNaught	Williamson	Colville	Leigh	McEwan	Young 1	Copland	Kelly	Scott	Thornton 35 Simpson 54	83
S	28-Nov	Hamilton Academical		A	L1	1-2	6000	Drummond	Kirk	McNaught	Clunie	Colville	Williamson	Copland	Young	Penman 1	Kelly	Scott	Scott 50 Young 53	33
S	05-Dec	Aberdeen		A	L1	0-4	14000	Johnstone	Kirk	McNaught	Williamson	Colville	Leigh	McEwan	Young	Copland	Kelly	Penman	Leggatt 35 Buckley 79	
S	12-Dec	Clyde		H	L1	3-4	6000	Johnstone	Kirk	McNaught	Williamson	Clunie	Colville	McEwan	Young	Copland 2	Scott 1	Penman	Ring 19 Buchanan (2) 50, 70 Baird 36	17,60,6
S	19-Dec	Hibernian		A	L1	0-5	16000	Drummond	Clunie	McNaught	Young	Colville	Williamson	McDonald	McEwan	Copland	Scott	McIntyre b	Reilly 13 Turnbull (2) 14, 26 Smith (2) 31, 64	
S	26-Dec	Dundee		A	L1	1-2	10000	Drummond	McLure	McNaught	McNeil	Colville	Williamson	McEwan	Young	Copland 1	Kelly	McIntyre	Toner (2) 49, 85	18
F	01-Jan	East Fife		H	L1	1-1	12000	Drummond	McLure	McNaught	Young	Colville	Williamson	Rice	McNeil	Copland 1	Kelly	Scott 1	Fleming 72	70
S	02-Jan	St Mirren		H	L1	1-2	12000	Drummond	McLure	McNaught	Young	Colville	Leigh	McEwan	McNeil	Copland 1	Kelly	Scott	Telfer 60 Blyth 78	23
S	09-Jan	Airdrie		A	L1	2-1	12000	Drummond	McLure	McNaught	McNeil	Colville	Leigh	McEwan	Young 1	Copland 1	Kelly	Duncan	McMillan pen 26	67,75
S	16-Jan	Celtic		H	L1	2-0	13000	Drummond	McLure	McNaught	McNeil	Colville	Leigh	McEwan	Young 1	Copland 1	Kelly	Duncan		84,14
S	23-Jan	Partick Thistle		A	L1	3-5	15000	Drummond	McLure b	McNaught	McNeil	Colville	Leigh	McEwan 1	Young 1	Copland	Kelly 1	Duncan	Crawford 3 McKenzie 40 Davidson 44 pen Howitt 45 Sharp 53	49,62,30
S	06-Feb	Stirling Albion		H	L1	1-1	8000	Drummond	McLure	McNaught	McNeil	Colville	Leigh	McEwan 1	Young	Copland	Kelly 1	Duncan	Chalmers 16 pen	27
S	13-Feb	Coldstream	2	A	SC 2	10-1	1115	Drummond	McLure	McNaught	McNeil 1	Colville	Leigh	McEwan 1	McNeil	Copland 3	Kelly 1	Duncan 2	Robertson 66	29,85,56,79,1,5,55,66,40,50
S	20-Feb	Queen of the South		H	L1	1-1	9000	Drummond	McLure	McNaught	McNeil	Colville	Leigh	McEwan	Young 2	Copland	Kelly	Duncan 1	Rothera 68	13
S	27-Feb	Motherwell	3	A	SC 3	1-4	18000	Drummond	McLure	McNaught	McNeil	Colville	Leigh	McEwan	Young	Copland 1	Kelly	Duncan	McNaught og 1 Humphries 10 Hunter 15 Forrest 85	60
S	06-Mar	Hearts	4	H	L1	4-2	20000	Drummond	McLure	McNaught	McNeil	Colville	Leigh	McEwan 1	McNeil	Copland	Kelly	Duncan 2.1p	Souness 67 Conn 86	25, 2, 56p, 64
S	13-Mar	Cowdenbeath		A	FC SF	0-2	3000	Drummond	McLure	McNaught	Young	Colville	Leigh	McEwan	McNeil	Copland	Kelly	Duncan	Simpson 5 Inglis 70	
W	17-Mar	Rangers		H	L1	2-2	12000	Drummond	Kirk	McLure	Young	Colville	Leigh	McEwan	McNeil 1	Copland	Kelly 1	Duncan	Caldow 48 pen Paton 58	7,76
S	20-Mar	Hamilton Academical		H	L1	5-0	8000	Johnstone	McLure	McNaught	McNeil	Colville	Young	McEwan	Young	Copland 3	Kelly	Duncan 1p		35,46,56,69,27
S	27-Mar	Aberdeen		A	L1	3-1	9000	Drummond	McLure	McNaught	McNeil	Colville	McIntyre	McEwan 2	Rice 1	Copland	Kelly	Duncan 1p	Wishart 13	81,85,37
S	03-Apr	Clyde		A	L1	2-4	5000	Drummond	McLure	McNaught	Young	Colville	Leigh	McIntyre	Rice	Copland 2	Kelly	Duncan		16,60
S	10-Apr	Falkirk		A	L1	3-0	8000	Drummond	McLure	McNaught	Young	Colville	Leigh	McIntyre	Scott 1	Copland 2	Thomson	Duncan	Buchanan 8 Hill 28 Ring (2) 60, 89	63,16,60
S	17-Apr	Cowdenbeath		H	L1	5-1	4000	Drummond	McLure	McNaught	McNeil	Colville	Leigh	McIntyre 1	Scott	Copland 1	Thomson 2	Duncan 1	Inglis 71	49,53,58,70,80
W	21-Apr	Montrose		A	F	7-1	1500	Johnstone	Kirk	McNaught	Young 1	Colville	Leigh	Scott 2	Young	Copland 1	McNeil 1	Duncan 1	Taylor	80,10,21,61,16,32,56
M	26-Apr	Stenhousemuir	5	H	PC SF	1-1	1000	Drummond	McLure	McNaught	McNeil	Colville	Leigh	McIntyre	Napier 1	Copland 1	Kelly	Duncan 1	Hendry 2	20
W	28-Apr	East Fife	6	H	FC F	2-2	6000	Drummond	McLure	McNaught	Young	Colville	Leigh	Scott	Scott	Copland 2	Thomson	Duncan	Fleming 46 Stewart, J 52	40,43
Th	06-May	Bury		H	F	1-2	5500	Drummond	McLure	McNaught	Young	Colville	Leigh	McIntyre	Scott 1	Copland	Thomson	Duncan	May 37 Clarke 88	38

Manager : Bert Herdman

(1) Turnbull sent off
(2) Receipts £108.; Coldstream received £19 12/3d including Rovers donation of £15 of their share
(3) Receipts £1245
(4) Parker missed penalty
(5) Rovers scratched from the competition
(6) There was surprise that there was no extra time ; the referee signalled it, but the players protested, and left the field. It was later decided that the trophy would be shared

Manager : Bert Herdman

Day	Date	Opponents	Note	Venue	Comp	Res.	Att.	1	2	3	4	5	6	7	8	9	10	11	Substitutes, own goals, goal times	Opponents' scorers
S	14-Aug	Kilmarnock		A	LC S	2-3	18000	Drummond	McLure	McNaught	Young	Colville	Leigh	McEwan	Rice	Copland 2	Thomson	Duncan	55, 75	Harvey 39 Middlemas 47 pen Curlett 76
W	18-Aug	St Mirren		H	LC S	2-2	9000	Drummond	McLure	McNaught 1	Young 1	Colville	Leigh	McEwan	McNeil	Copland	Thomson	Duncan	54, 56	McGrory 71 Holmes 80
S	21-Aug	Motherwell		A	LC S	1-1	10000	Drummond	McLure	McNaught	Young	Colville	Leigh	McEwan 1	Kelly	Copland	Thomson	Duncan	15	Aitken 75
W	25-Aug	Cowdenbeath		A	PC 1	1-3		Stewart	Kirk	McNaught	Young	Colville	Leigh	McEwan	Weir	Copland	Scott	Duncan	Judge og 20	Buchan (2) 35, 43 Young 88 pen
S	28-Aug	Kilmarnock		H	LC S	0-1	11000	Stewart	McLure	McNaught	Young	Colville	Leigh	McEwan	Kelly	Copland	Thomson	Duncan		Mays 37
W	01-Sep	St Mirren		A	LC S	1-3	10000	Stewart	McLure b	McNaught	Young	Colville	Leigh	McEwan	Rice	Copland	Scott	Scott	12	Gemmell (2) 37, 44 McGrory 53
S	04-Sep	Motherwell		H	LC S	3-0	10000	Stewart	Kirk	McNaught	Archibald	Colville	Leigh	McEwan 1	Young 1	Copland 1	Kelly	Duncan	3, 19, 83	
S	11-Sep	Dundee		H	L 1	0-3	14000	Stewart	Kirk	McNaught	Young	Colville	Leigh	McEwan	Kelly	Buchan	Buchan	Duncan		Fleming 35 Gardiner 87 Wilson 88
S	18-Sep	East Fife		A	L 1	1-0	15000	Stewart	Kirk	McNaught	Young	Colville	Leigh	McEwan 1	Kelly	Copland	Buchan	Duncan	6	
S	25-Sep	Celtic		H	L 1	1-3	16000	Drummond	Kirk	McNaught	Young	Colville	Leigh	McIntyre	Kelly	Copland	Buchan	Duncan	75	Haughney (2) 55 pen, 70 pen Mochan 67
S	02-Oct	Partick Thistle		A	L 1	1-1	14000	Drummond	McLure	McNaught	Archibald	Colville	Leigh	Copland 1	Kelly	Copland	Buchan	Duncan	57	McParland 42
M	04-Oct	Scottish Command XI		H	F	4-1	5000	Drummond	Weir	McNaught	Archibald	Colville	Leigh	Hanlon 1	Thomson	Young 1	Buchan 1	Smith 1	72, 48, 13, 31	Bell 85
S	09-Oct	St Mirren		H	L 1	4-0	9000	Drummond	McLure	McNaught	Archibald 1	Colville	Leigh	Copland	Kelly	Young	Copland 2	Duncan 1	27, 7, 35, 22	
S	16-Oct	Hibernian		A	L 1	1-2	18000	Drummond	McLure	McNaught	Archibald	Colville	Leigh	Copland 1	Kelly	Young	Buchan	Duncan	11	Buchanan 27 Ward 88
S	23-Oct	Stirling Albion		H	L 1	5-1	8000	Drummond	McLure	McNaught	Archibald	Colville	Leigh	Scott	Rice 1	Young 1	Buchan 1	Duncan 2	3, 85, 75, 58, 80	Smith 86
S	30-Oct	Motherwell		A	L 1	2-3	10000	Drummond	McLure	McNaught	Archibald	Colville	Leigh	Scott	Rice	Young 2	Buchan	Duncan	19, 87	Williams 35 Hunter 61 Aitken 73
S	06-Nov	Clyde		A	L 1	0-3	12500	Drummond	McLure	McNaught	Archibald	Colville	Leigh	Rice	Young	Copland	Buchan	Duncan		Buchanan (3) 18, 40, 50
S	13-Nov	Aberdeen		H	L 1	1-2	9000	Drummond	McLure	McNaught	Archibald	Colville	Leigh	Kirk	Kelly 1	Young	Buchan	Duncan	75	Allister 32 Yorston 40
S	20-Nov	Queen of the South		H	L 1	3-1	7000	Drummond	McLure	McNaught	Archibald 1	Colville	Leigh	Kirk	Young	Copland 2	Thomson	Duncan	72, 24, 65	Rothera 57
S	27-Nov	Rangers		A	L 1	0-1	25000	Drummond	McLure	McNaught	Young	Colville	Leigh	Kirk	Thomson	Buchan	Buchan	Duncan		Hubbard 23 pen
S	04-Dec	Hearts		H	L 1	0-6	12000	Drummond	McLure	McNaught	Young	Colville	Leigh	Kirk	Thomson	Copland 1	Campbell	Duncan		Urquhart 16 Bauld (2) 37, 53 Conn 40 Souness 77 Wardhaugh 82
S	11-Dec	Falkirk		A	L 1	1-2	9000	Johnstone	Kirk	McLure	Young	Colville	Leigh	McEwan	Scott	Copland	Kelly	Duncan	13	Davidson 51 Campbell 54
S	18-Dec	Kilmarnock		H	L 1	0-0	6500	Johnstone	Kirk	McLure	Young	Colville	Leigh	McEwan 1	Scott	Copland	Kelly	Duncan 1p		
S	25-Dec	Dundee		A	L 1	1-4	12500	Johnstone	Kirk	McLure	Young	Colville	Leigh	McEwan	Bain	Copland 1	Young 1	Duncan 1p	66	Merchant (2) 23, 84 Henderson 53 Christie 71
S	01-Jan	East Fife		H	L 1	4-1	12000	Johnstone	Kirk	McLure	Bain	Colville	Leigh	Archibald 1	McEwan	Copland 1	Young 1	Duncan	70, 54, 10, 27	Gardiner 66
M	03-Jan	Celtic		A	L 1	1-4	21000	Johnstone	Kirk	McLure	Bain	Colville	Leigh	Rice	Thomson	Copland	Young 2	Duncan	51	Evans 22 Collins 34 Walsh 50 Tully 68
S	08-Jan	Partick Thistle		H	L 1	2-3	10000	Johnstone	Kirk	McLure	Bain	Colville	Leigh	Rutherford	Rice	Copland	Young	Duncan 1p	11, 81	Howitt 15 Wright 30 Leigh 42
S	29-Jan	Stirling Albion		A	L 1	1-2	6000	Johnstone	Kirk	McLure	Bain	Colville	Leigh	Rutherford	McEwan	Stewart,J	Young	Duncan	69	Smith 6 McGill 18
S	05-Feb	Morton	1	A	SC 5	3-1	6395	Johnstone	Kirk	McLure	Young	Colville	Leigh	McEwan	Stewart,J	Copland 3	Kelly	Duncan	4, 15, 80	Hannigan 32
S	12-Feb	Motherwell		H	L 1	3-2	7500	Johnstone	Kirk	McLure	Young	Colville	Bain	McEwan	Stewart,J	Copland 1	Kelly 1	Duncan 1p	44, 60, 8	McSeveney 56 Redpath 88
S	19-Feb	Clyde	2	A	SC 6	1-3	12000	Johnstone	Kirk	McLure	Young	Colville	Bain	Rutherford 1	Stewart,J	Copland 1	Kelly	Duncan m	31	Robertson 28 Hill 47 McPhail 70
S	26-Feb	Clyde		H	L 1	2-3	8000	Johnstone	Kirk	McLure	Young	Colville	Bain	McEwan	Stewart,J	Copland	Kelly 2	Scott	39, 55	Ring 20 Hill (2) 80, 88
S	05-Mar	Third Lanark		H	F	3-2	2000	Drummond	Kirk	McNaught	Young	Colville	Bain	Stewart,J	Murney	Copland 1	Kelly 2	Scott	58, 35, 48	Armstrong 27 McLeod 81
S	12-Mar	Queen of the South		A	L 1	0-2	8000	Stewart	Kirk	McNaught	Young	Colville	Leigh	Stewart,J	Young	Copland	Kelly	Scott		Rothera 11 Patterson 63
M	14-Mar	Carlisle United		A	F	2-5	4000	Stewart	McLure	McLure	Young	McNaught	Leigh	Kirk 1	Stewart,J	Copland 1	Kelly	Duncan	58, 50	Atkinson 1 Kinloch 10 pen Whitehouse (2) 65, 40 Jackson 40
S	19-Mar	Rangers		H	L 1	1-0	13500	Stewart	Kirk	McLure	Young	McNaught	Leigh	Rutherford	Stewart,J	Copland 1	Hutchison	Scott	10	
M	21-Mar	Coventry City		A	F	1-1	6280	Stewart	Kirk	McLure	Young 1	McNaught	McNeil	Stewart,J	Thomson	Copland	Kelly	Scott	84	Hill 77
S	26-Mar	Hearts		A	L 1	0-2	17000	Stewart	Kirk	McLure	Young	McNaught	Leigh	Rutherford m	Stewart,J	Copland	Kelly	Duncan		Urquhart 25 Mackenzie 65
S	02-Apr	Falkirk		H	L 1	3-0	9000	Stewart	Kirk	McLure	Bain 1	McNaught	Leigh	McEwan	Young 1	Copland 1	Kelly	Duncan	52, 72, 24	
S	09-Apr	Kilmarnock		A	L 1	2-2	12000	Stewart	Kirk 1p	McLure	Bain 1	McNaught	Leigh	McEwan 1	Young 1	Copland 1	Kelly	Duncan	81, 53	Flavell 17 Clark 20
S	16-Apr	St Mirren		A	L 1	2-0	9000	Stewart	Weir	McLure	Bain	McNaught	Leigh	McEwan 1	Young	Copland 2	Kelly	Duncan	44, 67	
S	23-Apr	Aberdeen		A	L 1	2-3	10000	Stewart	Weir	McLure	Bain	McNaught	Leigh	McEwan	Young	Copland 2	Kelly	Duncan	43, 85	Buckley (2) 11, 32 Hather 44
S	30-Apr	Hibernian		H	L 1	2-1	15000	Stewart	Weir	McLure	Bain	McNaught	Williamson	McEwan	Young	Copland 1	Kelly 1	Scott	14, 3	Turnbull 71
S	07-May	East Fife	3	H	FC SF	4-3	4000	Stewart	Weir	McLure	Stewart,J	McNaught	Bain	McEwan 1	Young 2	Copland 1	Kelly	Duncan	Emery og 1, 23, 112, 34, 11	Stewart, J 23 Leishman 66 Gardiner 83
S	14-May	Dunfermline Athletic	4	A	FC F-1	1-1	6500	Stewart	Weir	McLure	Bain	McNaught	Leigh	McEwan 1	Young	Copland	Kelly	Duncan	14	O'Brien 63

Ball not to be changed unless referee permits

(1) Gate Receipts £495
(2) Gate Receipts £854
(3) after extra time
(4) Fife Cup shared with Dunfermline after uninspiring final "A Cup Final in Name only"

Former goalkeeper George Johnstone was first team coach, and Andy Young was named local Sportsman of the Year, with Andy Leigh runner up

Day	Date	Opponents	Note	Venue	Comp	Res.	Att.	1	2	3	4	5	6	7	8	9	10	11	Goal times	Substitutes, own goals, goal times and opponents' scorers
S	13-Aug	East Fife		H	LC S	2-4	18000	Drummond	McLure	McNaught	Bain	Weir	Leigh	McEwan 1	Young	Copland	Kelly 1	McMillan	1, 15	Leishman 1 1/2 Matthew 21 Stewart, J. 78 Plumb 46
W	17-Aug	Hearts		A	LC S	0-5	25000	Drummond	Archibald	McLure	Bain	McNaught	Leigh	Hutchison	McEwan	Young	Kelly	Scott		Conn (2) 14, 88 Leigh og 42 Souness 67 Urquhart 84
S	20-Aug	Partick Thistle		A	LC S	0-4	15000	Drummond	Bain	McLure	Young	McNaught	Leigh	Hutchison	McEwan	Cuthbert	Kelly	McMillan		Crowe 10 McParland (2) 34, 35 Sharp 88
W	27-Aug	East Fife		H	LC S	2-0	10000	Stewart	Weir	McLure	Bain	McNaught	Leigh	Scott	McEwan 1	Copland	Young 1	Thomson	35, 73	
S	31-Aug	Hearts		H	LC S	0-2	6000	Stewart	Weir	McLure	Archibald	McNaught	Leigh	Hutchison	McEwan	Copland	Young	Thomson		Parker per 32 Young 86
S	03-Sep	Partick Thistle		H	LC S	0-1	6000	Stewart	Weir	McLure	Bain	McNaught	Leigh	Hutchison	McEwan	Thomson	Young	Scott		McKenzie 61
S	10-Sep	St Mirren	1	H	L1	2-2	7000	Drummond	Weir	McLure	Bain	McNaught	Leigh	McEwan	Young 1	Copland	Thomson 1	Scott	6, 36	Rodger 10 Archdeacon 67
S	17-Sep	Queen of the South		A	L1	1-0	7500	Drummond	Weir	McLure	Bain	McNaught	Leigh	McMillan	McEwan	Copland	Thomson	Scott	55	
S	24-Sep	East Fife		H	L1	4-0	9500	Drummond	Weir	McLure	Bain	McNaught	Leigh	McMillan	Murney	Copland 3,1p	Young	Scott	6, 23p, 33, 54	
S	01-Oct	Celtic		A	L1	0-2	20000	Drummond	Weir	McLure	Bain	McNaught	Leigh	McMillan	McEwan	Copland	Thomson	Scott		McVittie 7 Sharkey 86
S	08-Oct	Stirling Albion		H	L1	2-0	6000	Drummond	Weir	Leigh	Bain	McNaught	McEwan	McMillan 1	Young 1	Thomson	Kelly	Scott	80, 46	
S	15-Oct	Dundee		H	L1	3-6	13000	Drummond	McLure	McLure	Bain	McNaught	Leigh	McMillan 1	Young	Copland 1	Thomson 1	Scott	11, 76, 42	Smith (4) 15, 19, 57, 58 Malloy 49 pen Chalmers 83
S	22-Oct	Airdrie		H	L1	3-3	9000	Drummond	Polland	McLure	Bain	McNaught	Leigh	McMillan	McEwan	Copland 1	Thomson 2	Scott	62, 5, 89	Bain og 10 Baird 23 McMillan 47
S	29-Oct	Partick Thistle		A	L1	2-1	12000	Drummond	Polland	McLure	Bain	McNaught	Leigh	McMillan 1	McEwan	Copland 1	Thomson	Scott	65, 83	Sharp 3
S	05-Nov	Hibernian		H	L1	0-4	12000	Drummond	Polland	McLure	Bain	Weir	Leigh	McMillan	McEwan	Copland	Kelly	Scott		Turnbull (2) 4 pen, 44.5 Reilly 10 Combe 23
S	12-Nov	Kilmarnock		A	L1	2-1	8000	Drummond	Polland	Leigh	Bain	Weir	McNaught	McEwan 1	Murney 1	Allan	Thomson	Scott	17, 49	Mackay 28
S	19-Nov	Falkirk		A	L1	1-3	10000	Drummond	Polland	Leigh	Bain	Weir	McNaught	McEwan b	Murney	Allan	Bain	Scott	89	O'Hara 45 Wright 69 Sinclair 77
S	26-Nov	Aberdeen		H	L1	1-1	10000	Drummond	Polland	Weir	McMillan	McNaught	McMillan	McEwan	Young	Copland	Thomson	Scott	73	Buckley 6
S	03-Dec	Rangers		A	L1	0-4	25000	Drummond	Polland	McLure	Young	McNaught	Leigh	McEwan	Young	Copland	Thomson	Scott		Kitchenbrand 9 Simpson (2) 39, 85 Scott 75
S	10-Dec	Dunfermline Athletic		H	L1	1-1	8000	Drummond	Polland	McLure	McMillan	McNaught	Leigh	McEwan 1	Young	Copland	Thomson	McEwan	44	O'Brien 53
S	17-Dec	Clyde		H	L1	1-3	6000	Drummond	Polland	McLure	McMillan	McNaught	Leigh	McEwan	Kelly	Young 1p	Young 1p	Scott	68	Gallagher 10 Robertson 19 Ring 65
S	24-Dec	Motherwell		A	L1	1-5	7000	Drummond	Polland	McLure	McMillan	McNaught	Leigh	McEwan	Young	Copland	McMillan	Scott	65	Bain 12 Humphries (2) 33, 71 Reid 46 Gardiner 69
S	31-Dec	Hearts		H	L1	1-1	12000	Drummond	Weir	McLure	Williamson	McNaught	Leigh	McEwan 1	Kelly	Bain	Kelly	Copland	Glidden 22 og	Bauld 26
M	02-Jan	East Fife		A	L1	0-3	14000	Stewart	Weir	Weir	Williamson	McNaught	Leigh	McEwan	Kelly	Bain	Young	Copland		Bonthrone 32 Matthew 47 Plumb 66
S	07-Jan	Queen of the South		H	L1	3-1	8000	Stewart	Polland	McLure	Young	McNaught	Leigh	McEwan 1	Kelly	Copland 1	Thomson 1	McMillan 1	33, 46, 40	Jenkins 57
S	21-Jan	Celtic		H	L1	1-1	15000	Stewart	Polland	McLure	Young	McNaught	Leigh	McEwan	Kelly	Copland 1	Kelly	McMillan	41	Mochan 25
W	08-Feb	Hibernian	2	A	SC 5	1-1	26024	Stewart	Polland	McLure	Young	McNaught	Leigh	McEwan 1	Kelly	Copland	Kelly 1	McMillan	71	Turnbull 86
S	11-Feb	Dundee		H	L1	1-1	10000	Stewart	Polland	McLure	Young	McNaught	Leigh	McEwan 1	Murney	Copland	Kelly	McMillan 1	78	O'Hara 44
M	13-Feb	Hibernian		H	SC 5r	3-1	14000	Stewart	Polland	McLure	Young m	McNaught	Leigh	McEwan 1	Thomson	Copland 2	Kelly 1	McMillan	15, 29, 50	Reilly 56
S	18-Feb	Queen's Park	3	H	SC 6	2-2	14986	Stewart	Polland	McLure	Young	McNaught	Leigh	McEwan 1	Kelly 1	Copland 1	Kelly	McMillan	15, 61	McCann 12 McLean 66
W	22-Feb	Queen's Park	4	A	SC 6r	2-1	16872	Stewart	Polland	McLure	Young	McNaught 1p	Leigh	McEwan 1	Thomson	Copland 1	Thomson	McMillan	72, 113	Omand 40
S	25-Feb	Airdrie		A	L1	3-4	9300	Stewart	Polland	McLure	Wallace	McNaught	Leigh	McEwan 1	Kelly	Copland 1	Young	McMillan	70, 80, 43	Rankin 46 McMillan (2) 81, 85 Price 89
S	03-Mar	Partick Thistle	5	H	SC QF	2-1	18264	Stewart	Polland	McLure	Young	McNaught	Leigh	McEwan 1	Kelly	Copland	Thomson 1	McMillan	5, 80	Crowe 56
W	07-Mar	Partick Thistle	6	N	SC SF	2-2	54364	Stewart	Polland	McLure	Young	McNaught	Leigh	McEwan 1	Kelly	Copland 2	Thomson	McMillan	12, 44	Ewing 56 Crowe 63 McKenzie 82
		Partick Thistle	7	N	SC SFr	0-0	58643	Stewart	Polland	McLure	Young	McNaught	Leigh	McEwan 1	Kelly 1	Copland	Thomson	McMillan		
S	10-Mar	Hibernian		A	L1	2-2	25000	Stewart	Polland	McLure	Young	McNaught	Leigh	McEwan 1	Kelly	Copland	Thomson	McMillan 1	34, 76	Ormond 49 Smith 57
S	17-Mar	Kilmarnock		H	L1	1-1	10000	Stewart	Polland	McLure	Young	McNaught	Leigh	McEwan 1	Kelly	Copland	Thomson	McMillan	39	Beattie 19
S	24-Mar	Hearts		A	L1	5-3	20000	Stewart	Polland	McLure	Young	McNaught	Leigh	McEwan	Kelly	Copland	Kelly	McMillan	38, 5, 41, 49, 87	Wardhaugh (2) 1, 73 Crawford 86
W	28-Mar	Aberdeen		A	L1	2-0	10000	Stewart	Polland	Bain	Young	McNaught	Leigh	Carr	Kelly	Copland 4	Kelly	McMillan	Parker og 1	Leggatt 20 Boyd (2) 30, 89
M	02-Apr	Falkirk		H	L1	2-0	10000	Stewart	Polland	Bain	Young	McNaught	Leigh	Carr	McEwan	Copland	Kelly	McMillan	49, 5	Murray (2) 47, 81 Hubbard (2) 48 pen, 84 Leigh 58 og
F	07-Apr	Rangers		A	L1	0-5	20000	Stewart	Polland	Bain	Young	McNaught	Leigh	Carr	McEwan	Copland	Kelly 1	McMillan	20	
W	13-Apr	St Mirren		A	L1	1-0	13000	Stewart	Polland	Bain	Young	Wallace	Leigh	McEwan	Murney 1	Copland	Kelly 1	McMillan	Walters og 79	Dickson 30 Duthie 36 pen Miller 68
S	18-Apr	Dunfermline Athletic		H	L1	2-3	5000	Stewart	Polland	Bain	Young	Wallace	Leigh	McEwan	Murney 1	Copland	Kelly 1	McMillan 1	11, 19, 79	Kemp 43
S	21-Apr	Clyde		A	L1	3-1	11600	Drummond	Polland	Bain	Young 1	McNaught	Leigh	McEwan 1	Murney 1	Copland	Kelly 1	Scott	41, 86	Kerr 18 Quinn 44 Aitkenhead 89
Th	26-Apr	Motherwell		H	L1	4-3	18000	Drummond	Bain	Bain	Young 1	McNaught	Leigh	McEwan 1	Murney 1	Copland	Kelly 1	Urquhart	52, 66, 47, 60	Bauld (2) 3, 58 Wardhaugh (3) 22, 29, 61 Kirk 72 pen Mackay 85
S	28-Apr	Hearts		A	L1	2-7	18000	Drummond	Bain	Bain	Young	McNaught	Leigh	McEwan 1	Murney	Copland	Kelly	Urquhart	Mackenzie og 1 38, 50	Walters og 79
M	30-Apr	Stirling Albion		A	L1	1-0	3000	Drummond	Polland	Young	Wallace	McNaught	Leigh	McMillan	McEwan 1	Copland	Kelly	Urquhart	14	
S	05-May	Cowdenbeath		H	FC F	1-0	2000	Drummond	Polland	Knox	Young	McNaught	Leigh	McMillan	Kelly	McEwan 1	Wallace	Urquhart	37	
S	12-May	East Fife		A	FC SF	2-1	2000	Drummond	Polland	Holton	Bain	McNaught	Leigh	McEwan	Murray	Young	Wallace	Urquhart 2	61, 86	Bonthrone 22

Manager : Bert Herdman

(1) Lapsley's penalty hit the post, he netted the rebound, but the 'goal' was disallowed
(2) One of two Scottish Cup ties that evening permitted under lights for the first time ; receipts £2409
(3) Receipts £1200
(4) after extra time
(5) Receipts £1349
(6) at Easter Road, receipts £5615
(7) at Easter Road

Day	Date	Opponents	Note	Venue	Comp	Res.	Att.	1	2	3	4	5	6	7	8	9	10	11	Substitutes, own goals, goal times and opponents' scorers
S	11-Aug	Airdrie		H	LCS	4-2	18000	Drummond	Polland	McLure	Young	McNaught	Leigh	McEwan 1	Kelly 1p	Copland 2	Williamson	Urquhart	85, 51, 46, 79 / Baird 24 McMillan 86
W	15-Aug	Dundee		A	LCS	0-1	16000	Drummond	Polland	McLure	Young b	McNaught	Leigh	McEwan b	Kelly b	Copland	Williamson	Urquhart	Merchant 55
S	18-Aug	Motherwell		H	LCS	4-2	9000	Drummond	Polland	McLure	Young	McNaught	Leigh	McEwan 1	Kelly	Williamson 1	Murney	Urquhart 2	82, 12, 40, 46 / Gardiner 51 Hunter 55
S	25-Aug	Airdrie		A	LCS	1-3	9000	Drummond	Polland	McLure	Bain	McNaught	Leigh	McEwan	Kelly	Copland 1	Kerray 1	Urquhart	50 / McCulloch (2) 35, 47 Baird 85
W	29-Aug	Dundee		H	LCS	2-2	8500	Drummond	Polland	McLure	Young	McNaught	Leigh	McEwan	Kelly 2,1p	Williamson	Kerray	Urquhart	54p, 86 / Black 38 Merchant 77
S	01-Sep	Motherwell		A	LCS	1-0	7000	Drummond	Polland	Beath	Young	McNaught	Leigh	McEwan 1	Kelly 1p	Bain	Williamson	Urquhart	55
S	08-Sep	Ayr United		A	L1	3-0	10000	Drummond	Polland	Beath	Young	McNaught	Leigh	McEwan 1	Kelly 1	Copland 1	Urquhart	Buchan	43, 71, 80
M	10-Sep	Stenhousemuir		A	PC1	2-1	1000	Drummond	Polland	McNaught	Young	Bruce	Leigh	McEwan	Kelly	Copland 1	Kerry 1	Urquhart	59, 22 / Jack 58
S	15-Sep	Airdrie		H	L1	4-6	10000	Drummond	Polland	Beath	Young	McNaught	Leigh	McEwan	Kerry 1	Copland	Urquhart 2	Buchan 1	26, 61, 83, 73 / Baird (2) 17, 49 McCulloch (2) 19, 35 McMillan 38 Welsh 70
S	22-Sep	East Fife		A	L1	3-2	12000	Drummond	Polland	Bain	Young	McNaught	Leigh	McEwan 1	Kelly 1	Copland 1	Urquhart	Buchan	71, 26, 18 / Plumb 10 Leishman 33
S	29-Sep	Dunfermline Athletic		H	L1	2-2	15000	Drummond	Polland	McNaught	Young	Bruce	Leigh	McEwan	Kelly	Copland 2	Urquhart	Buchan	19, 33 / McWilliams 10 Dickson 25
S	06-Oct	Queen of the South		A	L1	5-1	7000	Drummond	Polland	Bain	Young	McNaught	Leigh	McEwan 1	Kelly 1p	Copland 1	Williamson 2	Urquhart	13, 75, 43, 20, 51 / Black 21
S	13-Oct	Hibernian		H	L1	1-1	13000	Drummond	Polland	Bain	Young	McNaught	Leigh	McEwan	Kelly 1p	Copland	Williamson	Urquhart	74 / Ormond 44
S	20-Oct	Celtic		A	L1	1-1	12000	Drummond	Polland	McLure	Young	McNaught	Leigh	McEwan	Kelly	Copland	Williamson 1	Urquhart	40 / McPhail 25
S	27-Oct	St Mirren		A	L1	3-3	8000	Stewart	Polland	McLure	Young	McNaught	Leigh	McEwan	Kelly 1	Copland 2	Williamson	Urquhart	65, 30, 67 / McNaught 24 og McGill 62 Devine 79
S	03-Nov	Aberdeen		H	L1	3-2	11000	Drummond	Polland	McLure	Young	McNaught	Leigh	McEwan	Kelly	Copland 1	Williamson 2	Urquhart	26, 55, 78 / Wishart 6 Allan 9
S	10-Nov	Hearts		H	L1	2-3	20000	Drummond	Polland	McLure	Young	McNaught	Leigh	McEwan 1	Kelly	Copland	Williamson 1	Urquhart	20, 75 / Wardhaugh (2) 4, 83 Crawford 54
S	17-Nov	Motherwell		A	L1	2-0	15000	Stewart	Polland	Bain	Young	McNaught	Leigh	McEwan	Kelly 1p	Copland 1	Williamson	Urquhart	77, 60
S	24-Nov	Kilmarnock		A	L1	0-3	8000	Stewart	Polland	Bain	Young	McNaught	Leigh X45	McEwan	Kelly b	Copland	Williamson 1	Urquhart	Beattie (2) 4, 50 Mays 44
S	01-Dec	Queen's Park		H	L1	3-0	9000	Stewart	Polland	Bain	Young	McNaught	Leigh	McEwan 1	Kelly 1	Copland	Williamson 1	Urquhart	54, 46, 48
S	08-Dec	Rangers		H	L1	5-1	20000	Stewart	Polland	Bain	Young	McNaught	Leigh	McEwan	Kelly 1	Copland 2	Williamson	Urquhart 2	19, 61, 63, 89, 90 / Simpson 14
S	22-Dec	Falkirk		A	L1	4-0	10000	Stewart	Polland	Bain	Young	McNaught	Leigh	McEwan	Kelly 1	Copland 2	Williamson	Urquhart 1	80, 14, 55, 82 / Ewing 36
Tu	25-Dec	Partick Thistle		A	L1	1-1	14000	Stewart	Polland	Bain	Young	McNaught	Leigh	McEwan	Kelly 1	Copland 1	Williamson	Urquhart	48 / Christie 54 Reid 78
S	29-Dec	Dundee		H	L1	1-2	16000	Stewart	Polland	Bain	Young	McNaught	Leigh	McEwan	Kelly 1	Copland 1	Williamson	Urquhart	44 / Stewart, J. 2
Tu	01-Jan	East Fife		H	L1	4-1	15000	Stewart	Polland	Bain	Young	McNaught	Leigh	McEwan	Kelly 2	Copland 1	Williamson 1	Urquhart	5, 88, 15, 44 / McMillan 86 peh Baird 88
S	02-Jan	Airdrie		A	L1	2-2	10000	Stewart	Polland	Bain	Williamson	McNaught	Leigh	Carr	Kelly 1	Copland 1	Urquhart	Buchan	18, 83 / Price 9 Whittle 80
S	05-Jan	Ayr United		H	L1	5-2	10000	Stewart	Polland	Bain 1	Young 1	McNaught	Leigh	Carr 1	Kelly 2,1p	Copland 1	Williamson	Urquhart	15, 72, 67, 63p, 70 / Tighe 7 Dickson 44
S	12-Jan	Dunfermline Athletic		A	L1	2-2	12000	Stewart	Polland	Bain	Young	McNaught	Leigh	Carr 1	McEwan	Copland 1	McMillan	Urquhart	57, 6 / Wright 7 Smith 56 Ewing 77
S	19-Jan	Partick Thistle		H	L1	0-3	11000	Stewart	Polland	Bain	Young	McNaught	Leigh	McEwan	McEwan	Copland	McMillan	Urquhart	Reilly 34
S	26-Jan	Inverness Caledonian		A	SC 5	4-1	15000	Drummond	Polland	Bain	Young	McNaught	Leigh	McEwan	Kelly	Copland 1	Williamson 2	Urquhart 1	31, 60, 72, 86 / Christie 85 Mackenzie 89
S	02-Feb	Inverness Caledonian		H	SC 5	3-2	6301	Drummond	Polland	Bain	Young	McNaught	Leigh	McEwan	Kelly 2,1p	Copland 2	Williamson 1	Urquhart	10, 72p, 3 / Fernie 38
S	09-Feb	Celtic		A	L1	3-1	22446	Drummond	Polland	Bain	Young	McNaught	Leigh	McEwan	Kelly	Copland	Williamson 2	Urquhart	84, 33, 16
S	16-Feb	Dundee United	1	H	SC 6	7-0	12000	Drummond	Polland	Bain	Young	McNaught	Leigh	McEwan 1	Kelly 3,1p	Copland 2	Williamson 1	Urquhart 2	35, 5, 54p, 59, 38, 16, 85
S	23-Feb	St Mirren		H	L1	7-0	8000	Drummond	Polland	Bain	Young	McNaught	Leigh	McEwan 1	Kelly 2	Copland 2	Williamson 2	Urquhart 2	75, 61, 89, 51, 68, 3, 49
S	02-Mar	Dumbarton	2	A	SC QF	4-0	18001	Drummond	Polland	Bain	Young	McNaught	Leigh	McEwan 1	Kelly 1	Copland 2	Williamson	Urquhart	67, 20, 64, 77
W	06-Mar	Aberdeen		A	L1	0-1	5000	Stewart	Polland	Bain	Young	McNaught	Leigh	McEwan	Kelly	Copland	Williamson	Urquhart	Leggatt 4
S	09-Mar	Hearts		H	L1	1-2	30000	Stewart	Polland	Bain	Young	McNaught	McMillan	McEwan 1	Kelly 1	Copland 2	Williamson 1	Urquhart	35 / Wardhaugh 24 Bauld 68
S	16-Mar	Motherwell		H	L1	3-2	10000	Drummond	Polland	Bain	Young	McNaught	McMillan	McEwan	Kelly	Copland	Williamson	Urquhart	57, 73, 11 / Hunter (2) 12, 44
S	23-Mar	Falkirk	3	N	SC SF	2-2	48275	Drummond	Polland	Bain	Young	McNaught	Leigh	McEwan 1	Kelly	Copland 1p	Williamson 1	Urquhart	40, 35 / Grierson 17 Leigh og 46
W	27-Mar	Falkirk	4	N	SC SFr	0-2	25296	Drummond	Polland	Bain	Young	McNaught	Leigh	McEwan	Kelly	Copland	Williamson	Urquhart	Moran 11 O'Hara 83
Tu	02-Apr	Rangers		A	L1	1-3	41000	Drummond	Polland	Knox	Young	McNaught	Leigh	McEwan	Kelly	Copland 1	Williamson 1	Urquhart	69 / Morrison 9 Scott 25 Simpson 52
M	08-Apr	Fulham		A	F	3-1	3400	Drummond	Polland	Knox	Young	McNaught	Leigh	McEwan	Kelly	Copland 1	Williamson	Urquhart	43, 6 / Hill (2) 16, 43 Stevens Bentley
Tu	09-Apr	Reading		A	F	2-3	4530	Drummond	Polland	Knox	Young	McNaught	Leigh	McEwan	Hutchison	Copland	Williamson 1	Urquhart	11, 53p, 67 / Kirkup 8 Webb (2)
S	13-Apr	Queen of the South		H	L1	4-2	4500	Drummond	Polland	Knox	Young	McNaught	Leigh	McEwan 1	Kelly 2,1p	Copland	Williamson 1	Urquhart	8p, 67, 68, 33 / Whitehead 63
M	15-Apr	Kilmarnock		H	L1	6-0	6000	Drummond	Polland	Knox	Young	McNaught	Leigh	McEwan 1	Kelly 2,1p	Copland 1	Williamson	Hutchison 1	Mays (2) 63, 72
F	26-Apr	Falkirk		H	L1	2-3	5000	Drummond	Polland	Knox	Young	McNaught	McMillan	McEwan 1	Kelly	Copland 1	Williamson 1	Urquhart	58, 69 / Sinclair 17 Merchant 77 Grierson 82
S	27-Apr	Dundee	5	A	L1	0-3	7000	Drummond	Polland	Knox	Young	McNaught	Wallace	McEwan	Kelly	Copland	Hutchison	Urquhart	Easson 39 Cowie 45 Black 56
Tu	30-Apr	Queen's Park		A	L1	0-1	2801	Drummond	Polland	Knox	Young	McNaught	Wallace	McEwan	Kelly	Copland	Hutchison	Urquhart	McEwan 61
M	13-May	Inverness Caledonian	6	A	F	7-1	3000	Drummond	Polland	Williamson	Young	McNaught	Wallace	McEwan	Kelly 2	Hutchison 3	Campbell 1	Urquhart	Smith og 1 / Clyne

Manager : Bert Herdman

(1) Gate receipts £915
(2) Gate receipts £1347
(3) at Tynecastle, gate receipts £5945
(4) at Tynecastle, gate receipts £3577
(5) The match kicked off 25 minutes late as three players of each side, and two match officials, were delayed due to a train problem.
(6) Rovers goal times 40, 82, 10, 20, 87, 65, 5

Day	Date	Opponents	Note	Venue	Comp	Res	Att	1	2	3	4	5	6	7	8	9	10	11	Goal times	Substitutes, own goals & opponents' scorers
S	10-Aug	Partick Thistle		H	LC S	1-0	11756	Drummond	Polland	Knox	Young	McNaught	Leigh	McEwan	Kelly,B	Copland	Williamson,J	Urquhart	19	McGill 87
Tu	13-Aug	St Mirren		A	LC S	0-1	10800	Drummond	Polland	Knox	Young	McNaught	Leigh	McEwan	Kelly,B	Copland	Williamson,J	Urquhart		
S	17-Aug	Rangers		A	LC S	3-4	45000	Drummond	Polland	Knox	Young	McNaught	Leigh	McEwan	Kelly,B	Copland	Williamson,J	Urquhart	84, 53, 69	Scott 5 Leigh og 11 Murray 48 Simpson 52
S	24-Aug	Partick Thistle		H	LC S	4-1	8000	Drummond	Polland	Kelly	Young	McNaught	Leigh	McEwan	Kerray	Williamson,J	Kelly,B	Urquhart	22, 66, 69, 81	Ewing 24
W	28-Aug	Rangers		H	LC S	4-1	7290	Drummond	Polland	Kelly	Young	McNaught	McMillan	McEwan	Kerray	Williamson,J	Kelly,B	Urquhart	66, 68, 27, 42	Higgins 83
S	31-Aug	Rangers		H	LC S	4-3	23824	Drummond	Polland	Bain	Young	McNaught	Leigh	McEwan	Kerray	Williamson,J	Kelly,B	Urquhart	80, 11, 34, 80	Scott (2) 6, 27 Hubbard 28 pen
S	07-Sep	Third Lanark		A	L1	4-2	8224	Drummond	Polland	Bain	Young	McNaught	Leigh	McEwan	Kerray	Williamson,J	Kelly,B	Urquhart	73, 16, 50, 53	Allan 24 Lewis 68 pen
S	14-Sep	Dundee		H	L1	2-0	16000	Drummond	Polland	Bain	Young	McNaught	Leigh	McEwan	Kerray	Williamson,J	Kelly,B	Urquhart	77, 83	
S	21-Sep	East Fife		H	L1	0-2	11932	Drummond	Polland	Knox	Young	McNaught	Leigh	McEwan	Kerray	Williamson,J	Williamson,J	Urquhart		Leishman 3 Bonthrone 87 pen
S	28-Sep	Queen of the South		A	L1	1-1	8000	Drummond	Polland	Hughes	Young	McNaught	Leigh	McEwan	Kerray	Copland	Kelly,B	Urquhart	55	Patterson 90
M	30-Sep	Dunfermline Athletic	1	H	FC F	1-1	3000	Drummond	Polland	Knox	Bain	McNaught	Leigh	McEwan	Kerray	Copland	Williamson,J	Urquhart		Watson 89
S	05-Oct	St Mirren		A	L1	4-1	7644	Drummond	Polland	Williamson,J	Young	McNaught	Leigh	McEwan	Kerray	Copland	Williamson,J	Urquhart	85, 83, 27, 51	
S	12-Oct	Celtic		H	L1	1-1	20000	Drummond	Polland	Williamson,J	Young	McNaught	Leigh	McEwan	Kerray	Copland	Kelly,B	Urquhart	15	Mochan 9
S	19-Oct	Queen of the South		A	L1	3-1	6958	Drummond	Polland	Williamson,J	Hughes	McNaught	Leigh	McEwan	Kerray	Copland	Kelly,B	Urquhart	50, 68, 35	Patterson 64 pen
S	26-Oct	Hibernian		A	L1	2-2	20000	Drummond	Polland	Williamson,J	Hughes	Polland	Leigh	McEwan	Kerray	Copland	Kelly,B	Urquhart	51, 55	Harrower 26 Turnbull 78 pen
S	02-Nov	Clyde		H	L1	5-0	11049	Drummond	Polland	Williamson,J	Young	McNaught	Leigh	McEwan	Kerray	Copland	Kelly,B	Urquhart	66, 19, 83, 23, 25	
S	09-Nov	Motherwell		A	L1	2-0	10600	Drummond	Polland	Williamson,J	Young	McNaught	Leigh	McEwan	Kerray	Copland	Kelly,B	Urquhart	13, 17	
S	16-Nov	Falkirk		A	L1	4-1	14000	Drummond	Polland	Williamson,J	Young	McNaught	Leigh	McEwan	Kerray	Copland	Kelly,B	Urquhart	18, 85, 14, 73	Moran 87
S	23-Nov	Queen's Park		A	L1	3-2	6409	Drummond	Polland	Williamson,J	Young	McNaught	Leigh	McEwan	Kerray	Copland	Kelly,B	Urquhart	61, 53, 86	McEwan 31 Smith 62
S	30-Nov	Aberdeen		H	L1	0-1	12000	Drummond	Polland	Williamson,J	Young	McNaught	Leigh	McEwan	Kerray	Copland	Kelly,B	Urquhart		Brownlie 3
S	07-Dec	Hearts		H	L1	0-3	20000	Drummond	Polland	Williamson,J	Young	McNaught	Leigh	McEwan	Kerray	Copland	Kelly,B	Urquhart		Wardhaugh (2) 5, 57 Murray 11
S	14-Dec	Partick Thistle		A	L1	2-3	10000	Drummond	Polland	Williamson,J	Young	McNaught	Leigh	McEwan	Kerray	Copland	Kelly,B	Urquhart	4, 74	Smith 6 McParland 51 Kerr 61
S	21-Dec	Airdrie		A	L1	1-2	4000	Drummond	Bain	Williamson,J	Young	McNaught	Leigh	McEwan	Kerray	Copland	Kelly,B	Urquhart	26	Baillie 62 Rankin 66
S	28-Dec	Kilmarnock		H	L1	1-1	8000	Stewart	Polland	Knox	Young	McNaught	Leigh	McEwan	Kerray	Copland	Kelly,B	Urquhart	63	McBride 51
W	01-Jan	East Fife		A	L1	2-2	15000	Drummond	Polland	Knox	Young	McNaught	Leigh	McEwan	Kerray	Williamson,J	Murney	Urquhart	31, 15	Neilson 24 Bonthrone 47
Th	02-Jan	Dundee		H	L1	4-0	10000	Drummond	Polland	Knox	Young	McNaught	Leigh	McEwan	Kelly,B	Copland	Kelly,B	Urquhart	24, 36, 71, 48	
S	04-Jan	Third Lanark		A	L1	0-2	10000	Drummond	Polland	Knox	Young	McNaught	Leigh	McEwan	Kelly,B	Williamson,J	Williamson,J	Urquhart		Gray 14 Allan 28
S	11-Jan	Cowdenbeath		H	FC SF	4-1	2000	Thorburn	McGregor	Knox	Young	McNaught	Leigh	McEwan	Kelly,B	Williamson,T	Williamson,J	Urquhart	56, 57, 59, 30	Miller 43
S	18-Jan	St Mirren		A	L1	4-0	6000	Thorburn	McGregor	Polland	Young	McNaught	Leigh	McEwan	Kelly,B	Copland	Williamson,J	Urquhart	26, 12, 28, 40	
S	25-Jan	Celtic		H	L1	1-2	10000	Thorburn	McGregor	Polland	Young	McNaught	Leigh	McEwan	Kelly,B	Copland	Williamson,J	Urquhart	49	Collins 2 Byrne 12
W	29-Jan	Waterschei-Thor		H	F	3-1	12000	Thorburn	McGregor	Polland	Young	McNaught	Leigh	McEwan	Kelly,B	Copland	Williamson,J	Urquhart	38, 81, 87	Meyers 67
S	01-Feb	Peebles Rovers	2	H	SC 1	4-0	5068	Thorburn	Wallace	Williamson,J	Young	Polland	Leigh	McEwan	Kelly,B	Copland	Kerray	Urquhart	13, 40, 89, 9	Kerray u45 1
S	15-Feb	Dundee	3	H	SC 2	2-6	12649	Thorburn	Williamson,J	Williamson,J	Young	Polland	Leigh	McEwan	Murney	Copland	Kelly,B	Urquhart		Cousin 3
S	22-Feb	Clyde		A	L1	0-5	10000	Drummond	Young	Young	Wallace	Polland	Leigh	McEwan	Murney	Copland	Kelly,B	Urquhart		Currie 7 Coyle (3) 33, 61, 63 Robertson 41 Herd 69
S	01-Mar	Leeds United		A	F			Drummond	Polland	Knox	Young	Williamson,J	Leigh	McEwan	Kerray	Copland	Williamson,J	Urquhart	9, 70	Baird (2) 4, 55 Meek 47 Peyton 60 McConnell 67
W	05-Mar	Motherwell		H	L1	1-1	7000	Drummond	Wallace	Wallace	Young	McNaught	Leigh	McEwan	Wallace	Williamson,J	Kelly,B	Urquhart		McSeveney 28
S	08-Mar	Falkirk		A	L1	2-3	9000	Drummond	Wallace	Lockerbie	Young	McNaught	Leigh	McEwan	Polland	Williamson,J	Kelly,B	Urquhart	11, 34	Grierson 27 McCole 66 pen Lockerbie 89 og
S	15-Mar	Queen's Park		H	L1	3-1	5000	Drummond	Polland	Lockerbie	Young	McNaught	Leigh	Tainsh	Polland	Williamson,J	Kelly,B	Urquhart	44, 61, 80	Chalmers 21
S	22-Mar	Aberdeen		A	L1	2-3	7000	Drummond	Polland	Lockerbie	Young	McNaught	Leigh	McEwan	Kerray	Williamson,J	Kelly,B	Urquhart	78, 39	Mulhall 23 Davidson 73 Hay 79
S	29-Mar	Hearts		A	L1	1-4	15000	Drummond	Polland	Lockerbie	Young	McNaught	Leigh	McEwan	Kerray	Kerray	Kelly,B	Urquhart	74	Murray (2) 3, 26 Wardhaugh 7 Young 34
S	05-Apr	Partick Thistle		H	L1	3-2	7000	Drummond	Polland	Lockerbie	Young	McNaught	Leigh	McEwan	Kerray	Kelly,B	Williamson,J	Urquhart	43, 78, 85	Ewing 58 McParland 68
S	12-Apr	Airdrie		A	L1	4-0	5000	Drummond	Polland	Lockerbie	Young	McNaught	Leigh	McEwan	Kerray	Williamson,J	Baxter	McMillan	47, 43, 15, 44	
W	16-Apr	Rangers		H	L1	1-4	15000	Drummond	Polland	Lockerbie	Young	McNaught	Leigh	McEwan	Kelly,B	Baxter	Williamson,J	McMillan	25	Hubbard 2 Murray (2) 42, 55 Miller 55; Shearer og 25
S	23-Apr	Rangers		H	L1	1-3	10000	Thorburn	Polland	Lockerbie	Young	McNaught	Leigh	McEwan	Kelly,B	Williamson,T	Williamson,J	McMillan	26	Miller (2) 12, 65 Baird 14
S	26-Apr	Kilmarnock		H	PC 3	1-1	4000	Thorburn	Polland	Knox	Young	McNaught	Leigh	McEwan	Kelly,B	Williamson,T	Williamson,J	Baxter	88	Black 18
M	28-Apr	Alloa Athletic		H	PC 3	2-1	2000	Thorburn	Polland	Hughes	Young	McNaught	Leigh	McEwan	Kelly,B	Williamson,T	Kelly,B	McMillan	65, 86	White 24
W	30-Apr	Hibernian		H	L1	2-0	7000	Thorburn	Polland	Beath	Young	McNaught	Leigh	McEwan	Kelly,B	Copland	Kelly,B	McMillan		
S	03-May	Falkirk		A	PC SF	4-3		Thorburn	Polland	Beath	Young	McNaught	Baxter	McEwan	Kelly,B	Heenan	Kelly,B	Baxter	61, 50, 18, 38	Grierson (2) 9, 13 O'Hara 19 pen
W	07-May	Dunfermline Athletic		H	FC F-1	3-2		Drummond	Beath	Beath	Young	McNaught	Leigh	McEwan	Kelly,B	Heenan	Williamson,J	Kerray	71, 85, 79	Dickson (2) 8, 19
S	10-May	Dunfermline Athletic	4	A	FC F-2	1-3	6000	Thorburn	Polland	Beath	Young	McNaught	Leigh	McEwan	Kerray	Heenan	Kelly,B	McMillan	87	Dickson (2) 9, 98 Harvey 43
S	10-May	Stirling Albion		A	PC F	0-5	1500	Robertson	McGregor	Lockerbie	Hughes	Thomson	Baxter	Wallace	Williamson,T	Heenan	Murray	Ness		Gilmour (2) 35, ... Benvie 40 Spence Newman

Manager : Bert Herdman

(1) 1956/57 Final
(2) Gate receipts £434
(3) In the week following the match, McEwan was told by the Dundee management that he couldn't train at Dens Park, after a clash with Albert Henderson in which both probably deserved to be sent off. McEwan has been booked three times in 18 months, all against Dundee
(4) after extra time

Day	Date	Opponents	Note	Venue	Comp	Res	Att	1	2	3	4	5	6	7	8	9	10	11	Substitutes, own goals, goal times and opponents' scorers
S	09-Aug	Third Lanark		A	LC S	2-4	10000	Thorburn	Polland	Lockerbie	Young	McNaught	Leigh	McEwan 1	French	Dobbie 1	Williamson	Urquhart	34, 47	Allan 10 Craig, R. 46 Gray 71 McInnes 78
W	13-Aug	Rangers	1	H	LC S	3-1	12000	Thorburn	Polland	Lockerbie	Leigh	McNaught	Baxter	McEwan	Ward	Dobbie 1	Williamson 1	Urquhart 1	30, 87, 85	Hubbard pen 65
S	16-Aug	Hearts		A	LC S	1-3	18000	Thorburn	Polland	Lockerbie	Leigh	McGregor	Baxter	McEwan	Ward	Dobbie 1	Williamson	Urquhart	74	Young (2) 36, 37 Hamilton 66
W	20-Aug	Stirling Albion		H	L1	0-1	7000	Thorburn	Young	Lockerbie	Leigh	McGregor	Baxter	McEwan	Kerray	Dobbie	Williamson	Urquhart		Gilmour 83
S	23-Aug	Third Lanark		H	LCS	3-1	7000	Thorburn	Young	Lockerbie	Leigh	McGregor	Baxter	McEwan	Kerray	Dobbie 3	Ward	Urquhart	36, 42, 67	Craig, R. 84
W	27-Aug	Rangers		A	LC S	0-6	25000	Thorburn	Young	Lockerbie	Leigh	McGregor	Baxter	McEwan	Kerray	Dobbie	Ward	Urquhart		Murray 5 Simpson (3) 9, 36, 68 Wilson 15 Hubbard 88 pen
S	30-Aug	Hearts		H	LCS	1-3	16000	Thorburn	Young	Lockerbie	Leigh	McNaught	Baxter	McEwan	Hughes	Dobbie 1	Kerray	Urquhart	15	Crawford 36 Mackay 78 Hamilton 84
S	06-Sep	Dunfermline Athletic		H	L1	1-1	5000	Thorburn	McGregor	Lockerbie	Leigh	McNaught	Baxter	McEwan	Kerray	Dobbie	Hughes	Urquhart	8	Dickson 29
S	13-Sep	Dundee	2	A	L1	4-1	10000	Thorburn	McGregor	Lockerbie	Leigh b	McNaught	Baxter	McEwan 1p	Kerray 1	Dobbie b	Hughes	Urquhart 1	1, 71, 48, 72	Hill 17
S	20-Sep	Celtic		A	L1	1-3	30000	Thorburn	Polland	McGregor	Leigh	McNaught	Baxter	McEwan 2	Kerray	Dobbie	Wallace	Urquhart	23	Fernie (2) 12, 70 Smith 63
S	27-Sep	Hibernian		H	L1	5-2	15000	Thorburn	Polland	McFarlane	Leigh	McNaught	Baxter	McEwan 1	Kerray 1	Dobbie 1	Young 2	Urquhart	83, 85p, 16, 41, 77	Baker 12 Preston 28
M	29-Sep	Dunfermline Athletic		A	L1	3-3	8000	Thorburn	Polland	McFarlane	Leigh	McNaught	Baxter	McEwan 2,1p	Kerray 1	Dobbie 1	Young 1	Urquhart	61, 39, 34	Melrose (2) 16 pen, 26 Dickson 67
S	04-Oct	Dumbarton		A	L1	2-3	6000	Drummond	Polland	McFarlane	Leigh	McNaught	Baxter	McEwan 1	Kerray 1	Dobbie 1	Young	Urquhart	53, 79	Gray (2) 2, 22 Hilley 71
M	06-Oct	Dumbarton		H	L1	1-1	3000	Thorburn	Polland	McFarlane	Young	McNaught	Baxter	McEwan 1	Kerray	Dobbie	Conn 1	Urquhart	18	Whalen 30 pen
S	11-Oct	Partick Thistle		H	L1	2-2	13000	Drummond	Polland	McFarlane	Young	McNaught	Baxter	McEwan 1p	Kerray	Dobbie	Conn	Urquhart 1	32, 65	Wilson 2 Mathers 74 pen
S	18-Oct	Rangers		A	L1	4-4	35000	Thorburn	Polland	Williamson	Ward	McNaught	Baxter	McEwan 1	Kerray 1	Dobbie	Young	Urquhart 1	82, 42, 44, 72	McMillan 36 Baird 41 Scott 59 Hubbard 66
S	25-Oct	Kilmarnock		H	L1	1-0	8000	Drummond	Polland	Williamson	Ward	McNaught	Baxter	Leigh	Kerray	Dobbie 1	Young	Urquhart	69	
W	29-Oct	Hearts	3	H	L1	0-5	6000	Drummond	Polland	Williamson	Leigh	McNaught	Baxter	McEwan	Kerray	Dobbie	Young	Urquhart		Murray 45 secs Bauld 36 Wardhaugh 64 Mackay 81 Thomson 87 pen
S	01-Nov	St Mirren		H	L1	2-1	5500	Drummond	Polland	McFarlane	Leigh	McNaught	Baxter	McEwan 1p	Kerray	Williamson	Conn	McMillan	9, 76	Gemmell 72
S	08-Nov	Motherwell		A	L1	3-3	14000	Drummond	Polland	McFarlane	Leigh	McNaught	Baxter	McEwan	Young 1	Dobbie 1	Urquhart	McMillan	26, 22, 46	St John 19 Weir, A. 33 Aiken 56
S	15-Nov	Aberdeen		A	L1	2-2	17000	Drummond	Polland	McFarlane	Leigh	McNaught	Baxter	McEwan b	Young	Dobbie 1	Urquhart 1	McMillan	51, 48	Hather 41 Little 47
S	22-Nov	Queen of the South		H	L1	2-1	4500	Drummond	Polland	McFarlane	Leigh	McNaught	Baxter	McEwan	Young 1	Dobbie 1	Urquhart 1	McMillan	67, 37	McGill 81
M	24-Nov	Leicester City		A	F	3-3	7000	Thorburn	Polland	McFarlane	Leigh	McNaught	Baxter	McEwan 1	Young 1	Dobbie 1	Urquhart	Kerray 1	86, 70, 50	McNeill 12 Leek 60 Lornie 76
S	29-Nov	Clyde		A	L1	1-4	7500	Drummond	Polland	McFarlane	Leigh	McNaught	Baxter	McEwan 1	Young	Dobbie	Urquhart	Kerray	63	Currie (2) 11, 26 Coyle (2) 81, 89
S	06-Dec	Airdrie		A	L1	0-4	6000	Drummond	Polland	McFarlane	Leigh	McNaught	Baxter	McEwan	Young	Williamson	Young	Kerray		McGill (2) 26, 89 Sharkey 39 Rankin 48
S	13-Dec	Kilmarnock		A	L1	0-2	7000	Drummond	Polland	McFarlane	Leigh	McNaught	Baxter	McEwan	Young	Dobbie	Urquhart	Perry		McBride (2) 47, 60
S	20-Dec	Falkirk		H	L1	1-2	5000	Drummond	Polland	McFarlane	Leigh	McNaught	Baxter	McEwan	Kerray	Young 1	Baxter	Perry	16	Grierson 44 Moran 70
S	27-Dec	Stirling Albion		A	L1	1-2	5000	Drummond	Williamson	McFarlane	Leigh	McNaught	Baxter	McEwan	Young	Dobbie	Young	Perry	70	Gilmour (2) 1st half, 43
Th	01-Jan	Dunfermline Athletic		H	L1	2-2	9000	Drummond	Polland	McFarlane	Williamson	McNaught	Baxter	Kerray 1	Young	Young	Urquhart 1	Prior	9, 49	Melrose 10 Watson 16
S	03-Jan			A	L1	0-2	14000	Drummond	Polland	McFarlane	Williamson	McNaught	Baxter	Kerray	Kerray	Young	Urquhart	Prior		Curlett 21 Bonthrone 39
W	21-Jan	Hibernian		A	L1	2-4	10000	Bennett	McFarlane	Williamson	Polland	McNaught	Leigh	McEwan	Conn 1	Gardiner	Urquhart	Prior 1	14, 23	Ormond 40 Baxter (2) 43, 73 Gibson 80
S	24-Jan	Third Lanark		A	L1	2-4	6000	Bennett	McFarlane	Williamson	Polland	McNaught	Baxter	McEwan	Conn	Dobbie	Kerray 1	Prior	42, 27	Gray (3) 46, 66, 85 Goodfellow 50
S	31-Jan	Hibernian	4	H	SC 1	1-1	16642	Drummond	Polland	McFarlane	Young	McNaught	Baxter	McEwan 1	Conn 1	Dobbie	Kerray	Urquhart	51	Smith 57
S	07-Feb	Partick Thistle		A	SC 1r	1-2	21000	Drummond	Polland	McFarlane	Young	McNaught	Baxter	McEwan	Conn 1	Dobbie 1	Kerray	Urquhart	24, 43, 40	McParland 54
W	14-Feb	East Fife		H	FC SF	1-1	8000	Drummond	Polland	Lockerbie	Ward	McGregor	Baxter	McEwan 2	Conn	Taylor 1	Gardiner	Urquhart	62	Turnbull 31 pen Fox 35
W	18-Feb	Rangers		A	L1	2-2	12000	Drummond	Polland	McFarlane	Young	McNaught	Baxter	Arnott	McEwan	Dobbie	Gardiner	Urquhart	28	Duchart 55
S	21-Feb	Hearts		A	L1	3-0	5000	Drummond	Polland	Lockerbie	Ward	McGregor	Baxter	McEwan 2	Conn	Dobbie	Kerray	Gardiner	2, 18	
S	28-Feb	Airdrie		H	L1	1-3	9000	Drummond	Polland	McFarlane	Young	McGregor	Leigh	McEwan 1	Conn	Kerray	Ward 1	Urquhart 1	29, 72, 83	Mackay 50 Thomson 62 pen
W	04-Mar	St Mirren		A	L1	1-2	8000	Drummond	Polland	McFarlane	Young	McNaught	Leigh	McEwan 1	Conn	Kerray	Ward	Urquhart 1	52	Rodger 12 Gemmell 51 Baker 86
S	07-Mar	Motherwell		H	L1	3-0	8000	Drummond	Polland	McFarlane	Young 1	McNaught	Leigh	McEwan 1	Conn	Dobbie	Gardiner	Urquhart 1	58, 66, 75	
W	11-Mar	East Fife		A	FC SFr	3-4	4000	Drummond	Thomson	McFarlane	Young 1	McNaught	Leigh	Arnott	Ward	Kerray 1	Gardiner	Urquhart 1	52, 85, 53	Boyd 21 Watson 31 Reilly (2) 72, …
W	18-Mar	Aberdeen		H	L1	0-1	4000	Drummond s	Polland	McFarlane	Young	McNaught	Leigh	McEwan	Conn	Gardiner	Gardiner	Urquhart		Baird 50
S	21-Mar	Queen of the South		A	L1	1-1	3500	Drummond	Polland	McFarlane	Baxter	McNaught	Leigh	McEwan	Ward	Young	Kerray	Urquhart 1	63	Ewing 35
S	28-Mar	Clyde		H	L1	1-0	8300	Drummond	Polland	McFarlane	Young	McNaught	Leigh	McEwan	Kerray	Young	Urquhart 1	Perry	72	
M	06-Apr	Celtic		H	L1	3-1	8000	Drummond	Polland	McFarlane 1	Young	McNaught	Baxter	McEwan	Conn	Kerray	Gardiner	Perry	70, 17, 73	Mochan 71 pen
M	13-Apr	Millwall		A	F	2-3		Drummond	Polland	McFarlane	Young	McNaught	Leigh	McEwan 2	Conn 1	Kerray 1	Leigh	Perry	71, 72, 80	Moyse 24 Heckman 52 Crowshaw 55
S	18-Apr	Falkirk		A	L1	2-2	10500	Drummond	Polland	McFarlane	Young	McNaught	Baxter	McEwan 2	Conn 1	Kerray 1	Urquhart	Leishman	12, 48	White, (2) 24, 89
S	25-Apr	Dunfermline Athletic		A	PC SF	1-1		Drummond	Polland	McFarlane	Young	McNaught	Baxter	McEwan	Conn 1	Kerray 1	Urquhart	Leishman	81	Smith 71
S	02-May	Dunfermline Athletic		H	PC SFr	8-2		Drummond	Polland	Leigh	Williamson	McNaught	Baxter	McEwan 4,2p	Conn 3	White	Urquhart 1	Leishman	7,15p,65,73p,33,42,62,21	Reid (2) 43, 58

Manager : Bert Herdman

(1) Baird sent off 58 minutes
(2) Abandoned after 31 mins, thunder storm
(3) The team wore a brand new strip presented by the Supporters Club, white with two hoops and navy shorts, inspired by the Hungarians
(4) Gate receipts £2000
(5) The re-arranged League match against Rangers had the kick off moved from 3pm to 3.30pm to give shift workers finishing at 2pm a better opportunity to see the match. On the same day,

At the Board Meeting of 15th July 1958, it was decided to terminate the employment of the scouts in Ayrshire (Allan Collins), Lanarkshire (Tommy Brady) and Stirlingshire (John Duncan), because players could not travel to train at Stark's Park. Leeds were approached to sell George O'Brien, but it was turned down. George Johnstone played outfield for the Barry, Ostlere & Shepherd team which won the SISA Summer Football League. Monday 15th December, Willie McNaught played left back for the International Select in Lawrie Reilly's Testimonial match. On Saturday 27th June 1959, the World Pipe Band Championship were held at Stark's Park. Jimmy McEwan was on the transfer list at his own request, and in mid September Falkirk offered Tommy Murray in exchange. In early November, Jackie Williamson was placed on the transfer list at his request. Scunthorpe's offer of £4,000 a month later was £1,000 below Rovers' valuation, and was followed by an enquiry by Falkirk.. In late February, Williamson and Willie Polland were offered in exchange for Bernie Kelly, whom Leicester were prepared to transfer. While Liverpool and Hearts were showing an interest in McEwan, Williamson was sold to Dunfermline for £1500. Alex Whitelaw was sacked as trainer at the end of June 1959. On 11th December 1958 it was agreed to donate funds to buy a chair in the Scots Kirk in Paris. Jim Baxter attended a Scotland International training session at Turnbery on 2nd November 1958.

Day	Date	Opponents	Note	Venue	Comp	Res.	Att.	1	2	3	4	5	6	7	8	9	10	11	Substitutes, own goals, goal times and opponents scorers
S	08-Aug	Celtic		H	LC S	2-1	18000	Drummond	Polland	McFarlane 1p	Young	McNaught	Leigh	Kerray	Conn 1	White	McKinven	Urquhart	23, 44 — Mackie 60
W	12-Aug	Airdrie		A	LC S	3-2	6000	Drummond	Polland	McFarlane	Young 1	McNaught	Leigh	Kerray 1	Conn 1	White 1	McKinven	Urquhart	14, 40, 8 — Rankin 31 McGill 74
S	15-Aug	Partick Thistle		H	LC S	2-0	8000	Drummond	Polland	McFarlane	Young	McNaught	Leigh	Kerray	Conn 1	White	McKinven 1	Urquhart	79, 2
W	19-Aug	Airdrie		A	L1	2-1	6000	Drummond	Polland	McFarlane	Young	McNaught	Leigh	Kerray	Conn	White 1	McKinven	Urquhart 1	59, 15 — McGill 20
S	22-Aug	Celtic		A	LC S	0-1	24000	Drummond	Polland	McFarlane	Young	McNaught	Leigh	Kerray	Conn	White	McKinven	Urquhart	McFarlane og 36
W	26-Aug	Airdrie		H	LC S	3-0	9000	Drummond	Polland	McFarlane 1p	Young	McNaught	Leigh	Kerray	Conn 1	White	McKinven	Urquhart 2	80, 31, 32
S	29-Aug	Partick Thistle		H	LC S	3-1	10000	Drummond	Polland	McFarlane	Hughes	McNaught	Baxter	Kerray	Conn 1	White	Leishman 1	Urquhart	Wright og 1 88, 42, 20 — Keenan 1
M	31-Aug	East Stirling	1	H	PC F	5-2	3000	Drummond	Polland	McFarlane	Young	McNaught	Baxter	Kerray	Conn	Leishman 3	McKinven 1	Urquhart 1	19, 35, 36, 6, 67 — Boyd, A. 28 McCreadie 66
S	05-Sep	Dunfermline Athletic		A	L1	3-2	13000	Drummond	Polland	McFarlane 1p	Young	McNaught	Baxter	Kerray	Conn 1	White	McKinven 1	Urquhart 1	36, 74, 28 — Mailer 73 Dickson 81
W	09-Sep	Arbroath		H	LC QF-1	2-2	9000	Drummond	Polland	McFarlane	Young	McNaught	Baxter	Kerray	Conn 1	White	McKinven	Urquhart	58, 76 — Hay 4 Brown 77
S	12-Sep	Dundee		A	L1	2-0	10000	Drummond	Polland	McFarlane	Leigh	McNaught	Baxter	Kerray 1	Hughes	White	Conn 1	Urquhart	22, 74
S	16-Sep	Arbroath	2	A	LC QF-2	1-2	6598	Drummond	Polland	McFarlane	Leigh	McNaught	Baxter	Kerray	Conn	Mochan 1	McKinven	Urquhart	65 — Brown (2) 74, 95
S	19-Sep	Celtic		H	L1	0-3	13000	Drummond	Polland	McFarlane	Leigh	McNaught	Baxter	Kerray	Conn	White	Mochan	Urquhart	Jackson 20 Chalmers (2) 52, 84
S	26-Sep	St Mirren		A	L1	2-3	14000	Drummond	Polland	McFarlane	Young	McNaught	Baxter	Kerray	Hughes	Mochan 1	Conn 1	Urquhart	52, 25 — Bryceland 4 Riddell 10 Rodger 11
S	03-Oct	Stirling Albion		A	L1	0-1	7000	Drummond	Polland	McFarlane	Young	McNaught	Baxter	Kerray	Hughes	Mochan	Conn	Urquhart	Colquhoun 39
S	10-Oct	Ayr United		A	L1	0-4	12000	Drummond	Polland	Lockerbie	Young	McNaught	Baxter	Kerray	Conn	White	McKinven	Urquhart	Price (2) 20, 24 Fulton (2) 68, 70
S	17-Oct	Partick Thistle		H	L1	1-2	5000	Drummond	Polland	Mochan	Young	McNaught	Baxter	Murphy 1	Conn	Baxter 1	Urquhart	McKinven	53 — McPartland 22 Smith 81
S	24-Oct	Clyde		H	L1	3-1	5000	Drummond	Polland	Mochan	Young	McNaught	Baxter	Wallace	Spence	Kerray 2	Spence	Urquhart	48, 64, 82 — Robertson 46
W	28-Oct	Aston Villa		A	F	1-5	15000	Drummond	Polland	Mochan	Young	McNaught	Baxter	Wallace	McKinven 78	Kerray 2	McKinven	Urquhart	White u65 — McPartland 6 Price (2) 34, 79 McEwan 66 Crowe 75
S	31-Oct	Third Lanark		A	L1	3-1	7000	Drummond	Polland	Mochan	Young	McGregor	Baxter	Wallace 1	Conn 1	Kerray	Spence	Urquhart 1	80, 52, 28 — Hilley 4
S	07-Nov	Arbroath		H	L1	5-0	5000	Drummond	Polland	Mochan	Young	McNaught	Baxter	Wallace	Conn 1	Kerray	Spence	Urquhart	McLevy og 1 77, 5, 11, 41, 37
M	09-Nov	Dunfermline Athletic		A	PC 2	0-2	5000	Drummond	Polland	Mochan	Young	McNaught	Baxter	Wallace 1	Conn	Kerray X	Spence	Urquhart 1	Dickson 13 Melrose 81
S	14-Nov	Hibernian		H	L1	4-2	8000	Drummond	Polland	Mochan	Young	McNaught	Baxter	Wallace	Conn 1	Kerray	Spence	Urquhart 1	39, 81, 54, 62 — Baker 30 Preston 79
S	21-Nov	Rangers		H	L1	3-2	30000	Drummond	Polland	Mochan	Young	McNaught	Baxter 1	Wallace 1	Conn	Kerray 2	Spence 1	Urquhart 1	17, 16, 56 — Wilson 2 Scott 13
S	28-Nov	Aberdeen		A	L1	5-1	9000	Drummond	Polland	Mochan	Young	McNaught	Baxter	Wallace	Conn 2	Kerray	Spence	Urquhart	67, 74, 76, 69, 19 — Wishart 89
S	05-Dec	Motherwell		H	L1	1-1	9000	Drummond	Polland	Mochan	Young	McNaught	Baxter	Wallace 1	Conn	Kerray	Spence	Urquhart	20 — Baxter 26 og
S	12-Dec	Kilmarnock		A	L1	0-1	9000	Drummond	Polland	Mochan	Young	McNaught	Baxter	Wallace	Conn	Kerray	Spence	Urquhart	McInally 88
S	19-Dec	Hearts		H	L1	1-4	24000	Drummond	Polland	Mochan	Young	McNaught	Baxter b	Wallace 1	Conn	Kerray	Spence	Urquhart	51 — Cumming 24 Young 46 Blackwood 62 Smith 54
S	26-Dec	Airdrie		H	L1	2-3	5000	Drummond	Polland	Mochan	Young	McNaught	Baxter	Wallace 1	Spence	Kerray	Spence	Urquhart	2, 82 — Sharkey 3 Duncan 8 Storrie 58
F	01-Jan	Dunfermline Athletic		A	L1	2-0	11000	Thorburn	Polland	Mochan	Young 1p	McNaught	Baxter	Wallace	Spence	Kerray 1	Spence 1	Urquhart	69, 5
S	02-Jan	Dundee		H	L1	1-1	18000	Thorburn	Polland	Mochan	Young	McNaught	Baxter	Spence	Spence	Kerray	Spence	Murphy	70 — Bonthrone 75
S	09-Jan	Celtic		A	L1	0-1	7000	Drummond	Polland	Mochan	Young	McNaught	Baxter	Wallace	Conn	Kerray	Urquhart	Urquhart	Mochan 64
S	16-Jan	St Mirren	3	H	L1	6-1	7000	Thorburn	McFarlane	Mochan	Young	McNaught	Baxter	Wallace 3	Conn 1	Kerray 2	Spence	Urquhart	53, 80, 83, 49, 55, 65 — Baker 33
S	23-Jan	Stirling Albion		A	L1	2-4	2150	Thorburn	McFarlane 1p	McFarlane 1p	Young	McNaught	Baxter	Wallace	Conn	Kerray	Spence 1	Urquhart	57, 30 — Martin 17 Glancy 23 Gilmour 70 Colquhoun 77 pen
S	30-Jan	Queen's Park	4	A	SC 1	0-2	2742	Thorburn	McFarlane	McFarlane	Young	McNaught	Baxter	Wallace	Conn	Kerray	Spence	Urquhart	Church 7 Omand 60
S	06-Feb	Ayr United		H	L1	2-0	4500	Thorburn	Stevenson	Mochan	Young 1p	Polland	McNaught	Wallace	French 1	Spence	Baxter	Murphy	30, 58 — Devine 15
S	20-Feb	Partick Thistle		A	L1	1-6	7000	Drummond	Stevenson	Mochan	Young	Polland	Baxter	Wallace	French	McKinven	Spence	Urquhart	55 — McLaughlin (3) 20, 49, 58 Boyd 48 Robertson 48 Herd 62
S	27-Feb	Clyde		H	L1	2-3	6000	Thorburn	Polland	Mochan	Young	McNaught	Baxter	Wallace 1	French	McKinven	Spence	Murphy	70, 27 — Gray 34 Hilley (2) 50, 63
S	05-Mar	Third Lanark		H	L1	2-1	4000	Thorburn	Stevenson	Mochan	Young	McGregor	Baxter	Wallace 1	French	White	Spence 1	Urquhart 1	57, 64 — Easson 55
S	12-Mar	Arbroath		A	L1	3-0	3500	Thorburn	Stevenson	Mochan	Young	McGregor	Baxter	Wallace 1p	French 1	Lawson	Spence 1	Urquhart	9, 47, 21
S	19-Mar	Hibernian		H	L1	1-2	8000	Thorburn	Stevenson	Mochan	Polland	McGregor	Baxter	Wallace 1	French 1	Lawson	Spence 1	Urquhart	75 — McMillan 73 Baird 86
S	26-Mar	Rangers		A	L1	2-4	12000	Thorburn	Stevenson	Mochan	Polland	McGregor	Duffy	Wallace	French	Lawson	Spence	Urquhart 1	Kinnell og 1 66, 13 — Little (2) 6, 88 Brownlee 32 Glen 87
S	02-Apr	Aberdeen		A	L1	2-4	6000	Thorburn	Stevenson	Mochan	Polland	McGregor	Baxter	Wallace 1p	French	Lawson	Spence	Urquhart	St John 25 Young 62
S	16-Apr	Motherwell		A	L1	1-2	8500	Thorburn	Stevenson	Mochan	Polland	McGregor	Baxter	Wallace	French	McDonald	Spence	Urquhart	48 — Black 38 Wentzel 58
W	20-Apr	Burntisland Shipyard		H	FC 1	10-0	1000	Drummond	Stevenson	Mochan	Young 1	McGregor	Baxter 1	Menzies 1	Wallace 1	McDonald 2	Spence 4	Urquhart	21, 76, 67, 70, 13, 20, 28, 48, 53, 73
W	27-Apr	Kilmarnock		H	L1	0-2	6000	Thorburn	Stevenson	Mochan	Young	Polland	Baxter	Menzies	Wallace	McDonald	Spence	Urquhart	Young 72 Smith 78
S	30-Apr	Hearts		H	L1	2-2	5000	Thorburn	Stevenson	Mochan	Polland	McGregor	Baxter	Wallace	French	White 1	Spence	Urquhart	37, 76 — Smith 37
S	07-May	East Fife		H	FC SF	3-0		Thorburn	Stevenson	Mochan	Polland	McGregor	Duffy	Duncan	Spence	White	Spence	Wallace	13, 60, 59
W	11-May	Dunfermline Athletic		A	FC F-1	1-1		Thorburn	Stevenson	Mochan	Young 1	McGregor	Duffy	Duncan 1	Young 1p	White	Urquhart	Urquhart	65 — Miller 76
S	14-May	Dunfermline Athletic		H	FC F-2	1-1		Thorburn	Stevenson	Mochan	Polland	McGregor	Duffy	Duncan	Spence	White	Spence	Urquhart	48

Manager : Bert Herdman

(1) 1958/59 Final
(2) after extra time
(3) Rovers complained to the Daily record about their reporting of the match
(4) Gate receipts £306

Season 1960-61 — *Substitutes, own goals, goal times and opponents' scorers*

Day	Date	Opponents	Note	Venue	Comp	Res	Att	1	2	3	4	5	6	7	8	9	10	11	Substitutes, own goals, goal times and opponents' scorers
S	13-Aug	Dundee		A	LC S	0-5	16000	Thorburn	Stevenson	Mochan	Polland	McNaught	Leigh	Wallace	French	Easson	Spence	Urquhart	Penman 6 Gilzean (3) 8, 44, 89 Robertson 65
W	17-Aug	Aberdeen		H	LC S	4-1	6000	Thorburn	Stevenson	Mochan	Polland	McGregor	Duffy	Wallace 1	Wood	Easson	Spence 1	Urquhart 1	Brownlie og 1 86, 76, 44, 61 Little 89
S	20-Aug	Ayr United		H	LC S	1-1	8000	Thorburn	Stevenson	Mochan	Polland	McGregor	Duffy	Wallace	Wood	Easson 1	Kelly 1	Urquhart	2 McGhee 41
W	24-Aug	Dundee		H	L1	2-1	7000	Thorburn	Stevenson	Mochan	Polland	McGregor	Leigh	Wallace	Spence	Easson 1	Kelly 1	Urquhart	23, 75 Cousin 8
S	27-Aug	Dundee		H	LC S	0-3	8000	Thorburn	Stevenson	Mochan	Polland	McGregor	Leigh	Malcolm	Spence	Easson	Kelly	Urquhart	Gilzean (2) 19, 57 Waddell 57
W	30-Aug	Aberdeen		A	LC S	0-3	10000	Thorburn	McGregor	Mochan	Wilson	McGregor	Leigh	Malcolm	Spence	Peebles	Kelly	Urquhart	Davidson (2) 16, 57 Mulhall 18
S	03-Sep	Ayr United		A	LC S	2-1	6000	Thorburn	Stevenson	Mochan	Spence	Polland	Leigh	Wallace 1	Easson 1	French	Kelly	Urquhart	8, 34 Fulton 73 pen
Th	08-Sep	Petach Tikva		H	F	4-1	4500	Thorburn	Stevenson	Mochan m	Spence	Polland	Leigh	Wallace 2	Easson	French	Kelly	Urquhart 1	Razabi 76
S	10-Sep	Dunfermline Athletic		A	L1	2-3	10000	Thorburn	Stevenson	Mochan	Spence	Polland	Leigh	Wallace 1	Easson	French 1	Matthew 1	Urquhart 1	32, 42 Dickson (2) 58, 88 Melrose 89
S	17-Sep	St Mirren		H	L1	5-2	7000	Thorburn	Stevenson	Mochan m	Spence	Polland	Leigh	Wallace 2	Kelly m 1p	French 1	Matthew 1	Matthew 1	2, 41, 53, 56, 76 Bryceland (2) 3, 17
S	24-Sep	Hibernian		A	L1	1-0	12000	Thorburn	Wilson	Mochan	Spence	Polland	Leigh	Wallace	Kelly	French	Matthew 1	Urquhart	27
Tu	27-Sep	Aston Villa	1	H	F	2-1	10110	Thorburn	Wilson r18	Mochan	Spence	Polland	Leigh	Wallace 1	Kelly 1	French	Matthew 1	Urquhart	58 McEwan 85
S	01-Oct	Kilmarnock		H	L1	1-1	5000	Thorburn	Stevenson	Mochan	Spence	Polland	Leigh	Wallace	Kelly 1	French	Matthew 1	Urquhart	McIlroy 41
S	08-Oct	Motherwell		A	L1	1-2	10000	Thorburn	Stevenson	Mochan	Spence	Polland	Leigh	Wallace	Kelly	French 1	Matthew	Urquhart 2	Martis og 50 St John 13 McCann 38
M	10-Oct	Leeds United		H	F	4-1		Thorburn	Stevenson	Mochan	Spence	Polland	Leigh	Wallace	Kelly b 1	French	Matthew	Urquhart	19, 81, 8, 79 Cameron pen 89
S	15-Oct	Dundee United		H	L1	0-2	7000	Thorburn	Wilson	Mochan	Spence	Polland	Leigh	Wallace	Kelly	French 1	Matthew	Urquhart	McLeod 76 Reid 89
S	22-Oct	Aberdeen		H	L1	0-3	5000	Thorburn	Stevenson	Wilson	Stein	Polland	Leigh	Wallace	Kelly	French	Matthew	Urquhart	Mulhall 34 Cooke 55 Little 87
F	28-Oct	Gateshead		A	F	4-2		Thorburn	Wilson	Mochan	Polland	McNaught	Leigh	Wallace 1	Kelly	French	Spence 1	Urquhart 1	75, 67, 69, 65 Wimshurst 88 Heron 89
M	31-Oct	Hearts	2	A	B	2-2	6000	Thorburn	Wilson	Mochan	Polland	McNaught	Duffy	French	Kelly	Peebles 1	Spence 1	Urquhart	21, 19 Hamilton 7 Crawford 74
W	02-Nov	Rangers		A	L1	0-3	10000	Thorburn	Wilson	Mochan	Polland	McNaught	Duffy	French	Easson	Peebles	Matthew	Matthew	McNaught 27 og McMillan 57 Wilson 79
S	05-Nov	Celtic		H	L1	2-2	13000	Thorburn	Wilson	Mochan	Polland	McNaught	Duffy	Spence 2	Easson	Matthew	Kelly	Matthew	63, 69 Fernie 17 Chalmers 78
S	12-Nov	Clyde		H	L1	1-0	5000	Thorburn	Wilson	Mochan	Polland	McNaught	Urquhart	Urquhart	Spence	Easson 1	Kelly	Matthew	69
S	19-Nov	Third Lanark		A	L1	3-4	9000	Thorburn.	Wilson	Mochan	Polland	McNaught	Duffy	Wallace	Easson 1	White 1	Kelly 1	Matthew	8, 49, 26 Gray 37 Reilly (2) 48 pen, 82 Cunningham 78
S	26-Nov	Hearts		A	L1	0-1	17000	Thorburn	Wilson	Mochan	Polland	McNaught	Duffy	Wallace c	Spence	Easson	Kelly 1	Urquhart	Blackwood 18
S	03-Dec	Partick Thistle		H	L1	1-3	3000	Thorburn	Polland	Mochan	Polland	McNaught	Duffy	Wallace	Easson 1	French	Malcolm	Urquhart m	44 McParland 28 Closs 7 McBride 74
S	10-Dec	Ayr United		A	L1	1-1	3500	Thorburn	Polland	McNaught	Leigh	McGregor	Stein	Spence	Spence	Easson	Malcolm	Urquhart 1	89 Price 89 1/2
S	17-Dec	Airdrie		H	L1	2-0	6000	Thorburn	Polland	Mochan	Leigh	McNaught	Stein	Cooper	Easson	Wallace	Malcolm	Urquhart 2,1p	4p, 89
S	24-Dec	St Johnstone		A	L1	2-0	9000	Thorburn	Polland	Mochan	Leigh	McNaught	Stein	Cooper	Easson 1	Wallace 1	Malcolm	Urquhart	59, 39 Henderson 26 Cousin 61
S	31-Dec	Dundee		H	L1	3-2	8000	Thorburn	Polland	Mochan	Leigh	McNaught	Stein	Cooper	Easson 2	Wallace 2	Malcolm	Urquhart	34 Dickson 58
M	02-Jan	Dunfermline Athletic		H	L1	1-1	9000	Thorburn	Polland	Mochan	Leigh	McNaught	Stein	Cooper	Easson	Wallace	Malcolm 1	Urquhart	55 Gemmell 32 Kerrigan 59 Rodger 88
M	09-Jan	St Mirren		A	L1	0-3	7000	Thorburn	Polland	Mochan	Leigh	McNaught	Stein	Cooper	Easson	Wallace	Wood	Urquhart	Baker (2) 69, 72
S	14-Jan	Hibernian		H	L1	0-2	11000	Drummond	Polland	Mochan	Leigh	McNaught	Stein	Menzies	Easson	Wallace	Malcolm	Urquhart 1	Davidson 12 Kerr (3) 16, 21, 57 McInally 55 Brown 81
S	21-Jan	Kilmarnock		A	L1	0-6	11000	Drummond	McDonald	Stein	Leigh	McNaught	Urquhart	Menzies	Easson	Wallace	Malcolm	Matthew	85 Hunter 28 St John 51 Weir 53
S	04-Feb	Motherwell		H	L1	1-3	7000	Drummond	McDonald	McNaught	Leigh	Polland	Stein	French	Wallace	Malcolm	Matthew	Urquhart 1	2, 87 Neilson 7 Mochan 16 McDonald 25 og Carlyle 82
S	11-Feb	Buckie Thistle	3	A	SC 2	2-0	5436	Thorburn	McDonald	McNaught	Leigh	Polland	Stein	Wallace 2	Kelly	Malcolm	Matthew	Urquhart	13
S	18-Feb	Dundee United		A	L1	1-4	10000	Thorburn	McDonald	McFarlane	Polland	McNaught	Leigh	Malcolm	Easson	Wallace	Kelly	Urquhart 1	10 Chalmers 7 Leigh 14 og Fernie 24 Hughes 89
S	25-Feb	Celtic	4	H	SC 3	1-4	19633	Thorburn	McDonald	McNaught	Leigh	Polland	Duffy	Peebles	Easson	Wallace	Malcolm	Matthew	71, 56
W	01-Mar	Aberdeen		A	L1	1-4	7000	Thorburn	McDonald	McNaught	Stein	Polland	Leigh	Wallace	Fox 1p	Buchanan	Benvie	Urquhart	9, 84
S	04-Mar	Rangers		A	L1	2-3	14000	Thorburn	McDonald	McNaught	Stein	Polland	Leigh	Buchanan	Fox 1p	Buchanan	Benvie	Urquhart	71, 56 Brand (2) 9, 35 Wilson 80
S	18-Mar	Clyde		A	L1	2-0	6000	Thorburn	McDonald	McNaught	Stein	Polland	Leigh	Wallace 1	Fox 1	Wallace 1	Benvie 1	Urquhart	74
M	20-Mar	Celtic		H	L1	1-1	7000	Thorburn	McDonald	McNaught	Stein	Polland	Leigh	Buchanan	Fox 1	Wallace	Benvie	Urquhart 1	74 Chalmers 22
S	25-Mar	Third Lanark		H	L1	3-6	4000	Thorburn s	McDonald	McNaught	Stein	Polland	Leigh	Buchanan	Fox 1	Wallace 2	Benvie	Urquhart 1	80, 83, 87 Gray (3) 8, 27, 78 Harley 57 Hilley 63 McInnes 66
S	01-Apr	Hearts		H	L1	1-1	5000	Thorburn	McDonald	McNaught	Stein	Polland	Leigh	Buchanan	Fox	Wallace	Benvie	Urquhart 1	28 Johnston 7
S	08-Apr	Partick Thistle		A	L1	2-2	5000	Thorburn s	McDonald	McNaught	Stein	Polland	Leigh	Buchanan 1	Fox 1p	Wallace 1	Benvie	Urquhart 1	74, 40 McBride 14 Duffy 63
W	12-Apr	Ayr United		H	L1	3-1	2500	Thorburn	McDonald	McNaught	Stein	Polland	Leigh r70	Buchanan 1	Fox	Wallace 1	Benvie 1	Urquhart	72, 6, 58 McIntyre. A. 62
M	17-Apr	Leeds United		A	F	0-3	3000	Thorburn	McDonald	McNaught	Stein	Polland	Leigh	Buchanan 1	Fox	Wallace	Benvie 1	Urquhart	McConnell (2) 5, 40 McCole 30
S	22-Apr	Airdrie		A	L1	0-1	2200	Miller	Wilson	McNaught	Stein	Polland	Leigh	Benvie	Fox	Wallace	Fox	Urquhart	McGuire u70 Storrie 60
S	29-Apr	St Johnstone		H	L1	1-3	3000	Thorburn	Wilson	Stevenson	Stein	McNaught	Leigh	Cooper	Easson	White	Benvie	Urquhart	31 Gilfillan 12 pen Walker 48 McVittie 60
S	06-May	Cowdenbeath		H	FC SF	2-1	1500	Thorburn	McDonald	Wilson	Wilson	McNaught	Leigh	Cooper	Fox 1	White	Fox 1	Urquhart	8, 43 Mill 79
W	10-May	Dunfermline Athletic		H	FC F-1	3-1	700	Miller	Thorburn	Stein	Maguire	McNaught	Leigh	Malcolm 1	Finlay	Buchanan	Benvie	Urquhart	16, 61, 10 Melrose 60
S	13-May	Dunfermline Athletic		A	FC F-2	0-4	4050	Thorburn	McDonald	Stein	Maguire	McNaught	Leigh	Adamson	Fox 2	White	Benvie	Urquhart	Dickson (2) 26, 65 Peebles 71 Melrose 81

Manager : Bert Herdman

(1) Official floodlight opening
(2) George Dobbie Benefit
(3) Gate receipts £600
(4) Gate receipts £2097

Day	Date	Opponents	Note	Venue	Comp	Res.	Att	1	2	3	4	5	6	7	8	9	10	11	Substitutes, own goals, goal times and opponents' scorers
S	12-Aug	Hearts		A	LC S	0-1	17264	Thorburn	McDonald	Mochan	Reid	McNaught	Clinton	Malcolm	Sharkey	Adamson	Fox	McNamee	Wallace 15
W	16-Aug	St Mirren		H	LC S	0-3	5190	Thorburn	McDonald	Mochan	Reid	McNaught	Clinton	Malcolm	Sharkey	Adamson	Fox	McNamee	Bryceland 75 Rodger 79 Kerrigan 87
S	19-Aug	Kilmarnock		H	LC S	1-7	4437	Thorburn	McDonald	Mochan	Reid	McNaught	Clinton	Malcolm	Adamson	Sharkey 1	Benvie	McNamee	75 — Kerr (2) 16, 44 Mulroy, 21 Clinton og 47 Mulroy (3) 62, 64, 89
S	23-Aug	St Johnstone		H	L1	1-1	5113	Thorburn	McDonald	Mochan	Stein	Forsyth	Clinton	Benvie	Adamson	Sharkey	Malcolm	McNamee 1	89 — Bell 2
S	26-Aug	Hearts		H	LC S	3-1	5499	Thorburn	McDonald	Mochan	Stein	Forsyth	Clinton	Malcolm	Fox 2	White	Benvie	McNamee 1	11, 44, 5 — Ross 38
W	30-Aug	St Mirren		A	LC S	2-0	10687	Thorburn	McDonald	Mochan	Stein	Forsyth	Clinton	Malcolm	Fox 1	White	Benvie	McNamee 1	60, 65
S	02-Sep	Kilmarnock		A	LC S	1-4	6549	Thorburn	McDonald	Mochan	Stein	Forsyth	Clinton	Malcolm	Fox 1p	White	Benvie	McNamee	63 — McDonald og 15 secs McInally (2) 25, 57 McIlroy 59
S	09-Sep	Hibernian		A	L1	2-3	11117	Cunningham	McDonald	Mochan	Stein	Forsyth	Clinton	Sharkey	Fox 1	White 1	Benvie	McNamee	85, 41 — McGlynn 37 Fraser 44 Stevenson 57
S	16-Sep	Dunfermline Athletic		H	L1	2-2	6351	Cunningham	McDonald	Mochan	Stein	Forsyth	Clinton	Sharkey	Fox	White 2	Benvie	McNamee	34, 52 — Melrose 65 Smith 87
S	23-Sep	Partick Thistle		A	L1	2-3	6599	Cunningham	McDonald	Mochan	Stein	Forsyth	Clinton	Lourie	Fox m	White 1	Benvie 1	Watson	64, 47 — McParland 15 McBride 40 Duffy 73
S	30-Sep	St Mirren		H	L1	4-0	3971	Cunningham	McDonald	Mochan	Stein	Forsyth	Clinton 1	Lourie	Malcolm	White 2	Benvie 1	Watson	68, 4, 56, 58
S	07-Oct	Motherwell		H	L1	0-3	6258	Cunningham	McDonald	Mochan	Stein	Forsyth	Clinton	Lourie	Malcolm	White	Benvie	Watson	Roberts (2) 17, 57 Stevenson 24
S	14-Oct	Rangers		A	L1	0-6	37040	Cunningham	McDonald	Mochan	Stein	Forsyth	Clinton	Malcolm	White	Adamson	Benvie	Watson	McMillan 29 Brand (4) 30, 68, 87, 89 Wilson 34
M	16-Oct	Cowdenbeath		H	FC SF	7-0		Cunningham	McDonald	Mochan	Clinton	Forsyth	Maguire	McDonald	Fox 2	White	Benvie 2	Watson 2	12, 61, 21, 57, 29, 7, 33 — Stirling og 1
S	21-Oct	Third Lanark		A	L1	1-2	5520	Cunningham	Wilson	Mochan	Stein	Forsyth	Clinton	McDonald	Fox	White	Benvie	Watson 1	58 — Hilley (2) 54, 62
S	28-Oct	Dundee United		H	L1	0-0	3895	Cunningham	Wilson	Mochan	Stein	Forsyth	Clinton	White	Benvie	Bolton	Fox	Watson	
M	30-Oct	East Fife		A	FC F-1	3-0		Cunningham	Wilson	Mochan	Stein	Forsyth	Clinton	Watson 1	Benvie 1	White 1	McNamee	Urquhart	30, 1, 59 — Ormond (2) 8, 78
S	04-Nov	Falkirk		H	L1	1-2	2935	Cunningham	Wilson	Mochan	Stein	Forsyth	Clinton	Watson	Benvie 1	White	McNamee	Urquhart	88
M	06-Nov	East Fife		H	FC F-2	1-0		Cunningham	Wilson	Mochan	Stein	Forsyth	Leigh	Benvie	White	Adamson 1	Urquhart	Watson	79
S	11-Nov	Kilmarnock		A	L1	3-2	8252	Thorburn	Wilson	Mochan	Stein	Forsyth	Leigh	Adamson 1	White 1	Benvie	Clinton	Watson 1	89, 51, 59 — Black 18 McInally 22
W	18-Nov	Dundee		A	L1	4-5	14236	Thorburn	Wilson	Mochan	Stein	Forsyth	Leigh 1	Lourie	Fox	White 2	Clinton 1	Watson	22, 60, 63, 58 — Gilzean (2) 50, 52 Wishart 69 Seith 86 Smith 88
S	25-Nov	Hearts		H	L1	0-1	4149	Thorburn	Wilson	Mochan	Stein	Forsyth	Leigh	Lourie	White	White	Clinton	Watson	Gordon 38
S	02-Dec	Ardrie		A	L1	4-2	5264	Thorburn	Wilson	Mochan	Clinton	Forsyth	Leigh	Adamson	Fox 2	White 1	Benvie	Watson	65, 85, 46, 40 — Johnstone og 1 — Storrie 63 Reid 87
S	09-Dec	Queen's Park		H	SC 1	1-1	2275	Thorburn	Wilson	Mochan	Clinton	Forsyth	Leigh	Adamson	Fox	White 1	Benvie	Watson	55 — Buchanan 41
W	13-Dec	Queen's Park		A	SC 1r	4-1	2839	Thorburn	Wilson	Mochan	Clinton	Forsyth	Leigh	Adamson 1	Fox 1	White 2	Malcolm	Watson	66, 23, 60, 78 — Logan 11
S	16-Dec	Stirling Albion		A	L1	3-0	3496	Thorburn	Wilson	Mochan	Clinton	Forsyth	Leigh	Adamson 2	Fox	White	Benvie	Malcolm 1	24, 80, 88
S	23-Dec	Celtic		H	L1	0-4	9404	Thorburn	Wilson	Mochan	Clinton	Forsyth	Leigh	Adamson	Fox	White	Benvie	Malcolm	Chalmers 28 Carroll 42 Divers (2) 57, 59
Tu	02-Jan	Hibernian		H	L1	0-2	5625	Thorburn	Wilson	Mochan	Clinton	Forsyth	Leigh	Adamson	Fox	White	Benvie	Watson	Stevenson 68 Gibson 72
S	06-Jan	St Johnstone		A	L1	0-0	7479	Thorburn	Wilson	Mochan	Stein	Forsyth	Leigh	Adamson	Fox	Price	Benvie	Watson	
S	13-Jan	Partick Thistle		H	L1	1-0	3529	Thorburn	Wilson	Mochan	Stein	Forsyth	Leigh	Adamson	Benvie	Price 1	Watson	Fox	29
M	15-Jan	Dunfermline Athletic		A	L1	0-3	6130	Thorburn	Wilson	Mochan	Stein	Forsyth	Leigh	Benvie	Fox	Price	Malcolm	Watson	Melrose (2) 55, 60 Smith 73
S	20-Jan	St Mirren		A	L1	1-5	8131	Thorburn	Wilson	Mochan	Stein	Forsyth	Leigh	Benvie	White	Price	Malcolm	Watson 1	81 — Beck (4) 31, 60, 73, 83 McLean 67
Tu	23-Jan	Aberdeen		A	L1	3-3	5156	Thorburn	Wilson	Mochan	Stein	Forsyth	Clinton	Adamson 1	Fox 2	Price	Clinton	Watson 1	8, 43, 40 — Callaghan 27 Cooke 55 Mulhall 85
S	27-Jan	Alloa Athletic		A	SC 2	2-1	3982	Thorburn	Stevenson	Mochan	White	Forsyth	Maguire	Adamson	Fox 1	McDonald	Price 1	Watson	10, 42 — Jamieson 40
S	03-Feb	Motherwell		H	L1	0-3	5803	Thorburn	Wilson	Mochan	Stein	Forsyth	Leigh	Adamson	Fox	Price	Clinton	Watson	Aitken 33 Young 69 Roberts 89
S	10-Feb	Rangers		H	L1	1-3	11983	Thorburn	Wilson	Mochan	Stein	Forsyth	Leigh	Adamson	Fox 1	Price	Clinton	Watson	71 — Brand (2) 10, 59 Scott 22
S	17-Feb	St Mirren		H	SC 3	1-1	10630	Thorburn	Stevenson	Mochan	Stein	Forsyth	Maguire	Watson	Russell 1	Russell	Maguire	Urquhart	2 — Fernie 6
Tu	20-Feb	St Mirren		A	SC 3r	0-4	16500	Thorburn	Stevenson	Mochan	Stein	Forsyth	Maguire	Adamson	Russell	Russell	Maguire	Watson	Stewart 22 Kerrigan (2) 42, 87 Beck 79
S	24-Feb	Dundee United		A	L1	2-4	6686	Thorburn	Stevenson	Mochan	Stein	Forsyth	Leigh	Adamson	Fox 1	Price	Clinton 1	Watson	36, 57 — Gillespie 25 Mochan 76 pen Howieson 80 Irvine 86
W	28-Feb	Third Lanark		H	L1	4-3	2230	Thorburn	Stevenson	Mochan	Clinton	Forsyth	Leigh	Adamson	White 1	Price	McFadzean 1	Urquhart 1	55, 83, 23, 85 — Reilly 17 Harley 19 Forsyth og 82
S	03-Mar	Falkirk		H	L1	0-3	5694	Thorburn	Stevenson	Mochan	Clinton	Forsyth	Leigh	Adamson	White	Price	McFadzean	Urquhart	Duchart 30 Thomson 82 Murray 87
S	10-Mar	Berwick Rangers		A	F	1-1	1500	Thorburn	Stevenson	Mochan	Stein 1	Forsyth	Maguire	Adamson b	Kerr 1	Gilfillan	McFadzean	Urquhart	80 — McCulloch 32
W	14-Mar	Kilmarnock		H	L1	2-2	2621	Thorburn	Stevenson	Mochan	Stein	Forsyth	Leigh	Adamson	Kerr 1	Gilfillan 1	McFadzean	Urquhart	28, 78 — Kerr (2) 49, 67
S	17-Mar	Dundee		H	L1	2-3	5299	Thorburn	Stevenson	Mochan	Stein 1	Forsyth	Leigh	Adamson 1	Kerr	Gilfillan 2	McFadzean	Urquhart	3, 56 — Cousin 13 Penman (2) 63, 82
S	24-Mar	Hearts		H	L1	1-0	7465	Thorburn	Stevenson	Mochan	Stein	Forsyth	Leigh	Adamson 1	Kerr 1	Gilfillan 2	McFadzean	Urquhart	21
S	31-Mar	Ardrie		H	L1	1-1	3305	Thorburn	Stevenson	Mochan	Stein	Forsyth	Leigh	Adamson b	Kerr 1	Gilfillan	McFadzean	Urquhart	15 secs — Duncan 42 pen
S	07-Apr	Stirling Albion		H	L1	2-1	3155	Thorburn	Stevenson	Mochan	Stein	Forsyth	Clinton	Adamson 1	Kerr 2	Gilfillan	McFadzean	Urquhart	60, 64 — Gilmour 59
S	21-Apr	Celtic		A	L1	1-0	12565	Thorburn	Stevenson	Mochan	Stein	Forsyth	Leigh	Adamson	Kerr 2	Gilfillan	McFadzean	Urquhart 1	76
S	28-Apr	Aberdeen		H	L1	3-1	3780	Thorburn	Stevenson	Mochan	Stein	Forsyth	Leigh	Adamson	Kerr 2	Gilfillan 1	McFadzean	Urquhart	11, 81, 4 — Mulhall 49
M	30-Apr	Dunfermline Athletic	1	H	B	1-1		Thorburn	Stevenson	McNaught	Stein	Forsyth	Leigh	Adamson	Kerr	Gilfillan 1	Russell	Urquhart	69 — Duffy 40

Manager : Bert Herdman to 19th October. Hugh Shaw from 20th October
Following a court case involving George Eastham, some restrictions in players contracts were lifted in England
(1) McNaught/Urquhart Testimonial

Substitutes, own goals, goal times and opponents' scorers

Day	Date	Opponents	Venue	Comp	Res	Att	1	2	3	4	5	6	7	8	9	10	11	Goal times	Substitutes, own goals and opponents' scorers
S	11-Aug	Dunfermline Athletic	H	LC S	2-2	8592	Thorburn	Stevenson	Wilson	Stein	Forsyth	Leigh 1	Adamson 1p	Kerr	Gilfillan	McFadzean	McGrogan	15, 38	McDonald 20 McLindon 87
W	15-Aug	Airdrie	A	LC S	1-1	1785	Thorburn	Stevenson	Wilson	Stein	Forsyth	Leigh	Adamson	Kerr 1	Gilfillan	McFadzean	McGrogan	16	Tees 47
S	18-Aug	Kilmarnock	H	LC S	2-3	5470	Thorburn	Stevenson	Wilson	Stein	Forsyth	Leigh	Adamson	Kerr	Gilfillan 1	McFadzean 1	McGrogan	27, 38	Sneddon 17 Kerr 54 pen Brown 80
W	22-Aug	Third Lanark	H	L1	1-1	3833	Thorburn	Stevenson	Wilson	Stein	Forsyth	White	Adamson 1	Kerr	Gilfillan	McFadzean	McGrogan	44	Stenhouse 21
S	25-Aug	Dunfermline Athletic	A	LC S	1-1	9518	Thorburn	Stevenson	Wilson	Stein	Forsyth	Burrows	Adamson 1	White	Gilfillan	McFadzean	McGrogan	24	Melrose 80
W	29-Aug	Airdrie	H	LC S	3-1	3196	Thorburn	Stevenson	Wilson	Stein 1	Forsyth	Leigh	Adamson m	Kerr 1	Gilfillan 1	McFadzean	McGrogan	14, 66, 84	Tees 45 1/2
S	01-Sep	Kilmarnock	A	LC S	0-6	5891	Thorburn	Stevenson	Wilson	Stein	Forsyth	Leigh	Adamson	Kerr	Russell	McFadzean	Gilfillan	23	Forsyth 8 og McIlroy 10 Kerr 76
S	08-Sep	Dunfermline Athletic	A	L1	0-6	8613	Muirhead	Wilson	Maguire	Stein	Forsyth	Leigh	Adamson	Kerr	White	McFadzean	McGrogan		Peebles (3) 17 pen, 19, 86 pen Dickson (2) 23, 24 Edwards 46
S	15-Sep	St Mirren	H	L1	0-1	3753	Muirhead	Wilson	Maguire	Stein	Forsyth	Leigh	Adamson	Kerr	White	McFadzean	McGrogan		Bryceland 77
S	22-Sep	Airdrie	A	L1	1-8	2762	Muirhead	Wilson	Maguire	Stein	Forsyth	Leigh	Adamson	Smith,J	Menzies	McFadzean	Lourie	83	Tees 13 Duncan (3) 18, 24, 85 Rowan (2) 22, 88 Murray 43 Coats 53
S	29-Sep	Celtic	H	L1	0-2	9699	Thorburn	Wilson	Maguire	Stein	Burrows	Burrows	Lourie	Smith,J	Menzies	McFadzean	McNamee		Murdoch 30 McNeill 77 pen
S	06-Oct	Hibernian	A	L1	0-1	7111	Thorburn	Wilson	Maguire	Haig	Forsyth	Burrows	Lourie	Stein	Kerr	Smith,J	Adamson		Stevenson, . 37 pen
M	08-Oct	East Fife	H	FC SF	0-1		Thorburn	Wilson	Maguire	Stein	Clinton	Burrows	Adamson	Kerr	Menzies	McFadzean	McNamee		Walker 83
S	13-Oct	Aberdeen	A	L1	0-10	10072	Thorburn	Wilson	Maguire	Stein	Burrows	Leigh	Adamson	Kerr	Lourie	McFadzean	McNamee		Winchester (3) 1, 73, 80 Cummings (4) 30, 44, 57, 64 Cooke 8 Little 61 Kinnell pen 82
S	20-Oct	Clyde	H	L1	1-1	2837	Thorburn	Stevenson	Wilson	Stein	Forsyth	Clinton	Lourie	Smith,J	Adamson 1	McFadzean	Aitken	38	McLean 64
S	27-Oct	Dundee United	H	PC 1	1-8	5391	Thorburn	Stevenson	Wilson	Stein	Clinton	Leigh	Boner	Forsyth	Gilfillan	McFadzean 1	Adamson	69	Gillespie (3) 28, 71, 80 Carlyle (2) 30 pen, 64 Neilson 35 Mitchell 52 Irvine 63
S	03-Nov	Falkirk	H	L1	1-3	3081	Thorburn	Stevenson	Haig	Stein	Forsyth	Leigh	Boner	Smith,J	Menzies	McFadzean	Adamson 1	1	Stevenson 33 og Fulton 36 Davidson 55
S	10-Nov	Kilmarnock	A	L1	1-3	7306	Thorburn	Stevenson	Haig	Wilson	Forsyth	Smith,W	Boner	Kerr	Caven	McNamee	Adamson	32	Brown 15 Beattie 75 Kerr 84 pen
M	12-Nov	Dunfermline Athletic	H	PC 1	3-1	1803	Thorburn	Stevenson b	Haig	Wilson 1p	Forsyth	Smith,W	Boner	Kerr	Caven	Aitken 1	Adamson 1	46, 57, 83	Lunn 36
S	17-Nov	Partick Thistle	A	L1	2-3	5187	Thorburn	Stevenson	Haig	Stein	Forsyth	Smith,W	Boner	Kerr 1	McNamee	Aitken 1	Adamson	26, 85	Whitelaw 61 Smith 65 Hainey 70
S	24-Nov	Queen of the South	A	L1	1-5	4976	Thorburn	Stevenson	Haig	Stein	Forsyth	Smith,W	Adamson	Kerr	Aitken	McFadzean	McNamee 1	61	Murray 15 Smith 21 og Anderson 52 Frye 57 Martin 89
S	01-Dec	Hearts	H	L1	0-3	3083	Thorburn	Stevenson	Haig	Wilson	Forsyth	Smith,W	Adamson	Kerr	Gilfillan	McFadzean	Aitken		Hamilton, W 38 Gordon 74 Wallace 79
S	08-Dec	Motherwell	A	L1	2-5		Thorburn	Stevenson	Haig	Wilson	Forsyth	Clinton	Lourie 1	Smith,W	Gilfillan	Aitken	Adamson 1	63, 27	McBride 8 Russell (3) 3, 32, 62, 67 Roberts 82
M	10-Dec	Cowdenbeath	H	PC 2	3-0		Thorburn	Stevenson	Haig	Stein	Forsyth	Clinton	Boner	Smith,W	Caven 1	Aitken 1	Adamson 1	60, 72, 74	
S	15-Dec	Rangers	A	L1	2-4	19748	Thorburn	Stevenson	Haig	Stein	Forsyth	Clinton	Boner	Smith,W 1	Caven 1	Aitken	Adamson	12, 27	Wilson 11 Brand (3) 17 pen, 22, 23
S	22-Dec	Dundee	H	L1	2-4	3300	Thorburn	Stevenson	Haig	Stein	Forsyth	Clinton 1p	McDonald	Smith,W	Caven 1	Aitken	Adamson	87	Grant 20 Gray 85
S	29-Dec	Third Lanark	A	L1	1-2	2634	Thorburn	Stevenson	Haig b	Stein	Forsyth	Clinton	McDonald	Smith,W 1	Caven	Aitken	Adamson	24, 44	Beck 20
W	02-Jan	St Mirren	H	L1	2-1	4711	Thorburn	Stevenson	Haig	Wilson	Bolton	Clinton	McDonald	Smith,W	Caven	Aitken 1	Adamson	11, 65	Tees 25
S	05-Jan	Airdrie	H	L1	0-1	3179	Thorburn	Stevenson	Haig	Wilson	Bolton	Clinton	McDonald	Smith,W	Caven	Aitken	Adamson		
S	12-Jan	Eyemouth United	H	SC 1	2-0	2000	Thorburn	Stevenson	Haig	Wilson	Bolton	Leigh	Lourie	Smith,J	Caven	McDonald 2	Aitken	31, 70	
S	26-Jan	Clyde	A	SC 2	3-2	4674	Thorburn	Stevenson	Haig	Clinton	Bolton	Leigh	McDonald 1	Aitken 2	Caven 1	McFadzean	McNamee 1	31, 70, 69	Currie (2) 62, 79
S	02-Mar	Dundee United	A	L1	2-7	4314	Thorburn	Stevenson	Haig	Clinton	Bolton	Burrows 1	McDonald 1	Aitken	Caven 1	McFadzean 1	Adamson	9, 60	Irvine (2) 26, 83 Gillespie (2) 30, 89 Mitchell 49 Carlyle 80 Fraser 72
S	09-Mar	Falkirk	H	L1	3-2	3726	Thorburn	Wilson	Haig	Stein	Bolton	Burrows	McDonald	Caven 1	Adamson	McNamee 1	Lourie	50, 9, 58	Fulton 51 Lambie 65
W	13-Mar	Third Lanark	A	SC 3	1-0	2451	Thorburn	Wilson	Haig	Stein	Bolton	Burrows	McDonald	Caven	Adamson	McNamee	Lourie	80	
S	16-Mar	Kilmarnock	H	L1	1-4	9974	Thorburn	Wilson	Clinton	Stein	Bolton	Burrows	McDonald	Caven	Adamson 1	McNamee	Lourie	84	Kerr (3) 25, 72, 88 O'Connor 78
Tu	19-Mar	Celtic	H	L1	1-4	7874	Muirhead	Wilson	Haig	Stein	Bolton	Burrows	Lourie	Menzies	Gilfillan	McFadzean 1	McNamee	47	Brogan (2) 60, 65 McNamee 69 Chalmers 88
S	23-Mar	Partick Thistle	A	L1	1-4	1920	Thorburn	Wilson	Haig	McFadzean 1	Bolton	Burrows	Lourie	Menzies	Adamson	Aitken	McNamee	19	Duffy 8 Gourlay (2) 14, 31 Whitelaw 85
W	27-Mar	Aberdeen	H	L1	2-4	5000	Thorburn	Stevenson	Haig	Wilson	Bolton	Burrows	McNamee	Aitken	Caven	McFadzean	Adamson 1	46, 44	McLean 10 Reid 25 Ferguson 32 Finlay 39 pen
S	30-Mar	Aberdeen	H	SC QF	2-1	5575	Thorburn	Stevenson	Haig	Wilson	Bolton	Burrows	Lourie	McDonald	Gilfillan 2	Smith,W	Adamson	15, 88	Cummings 27
S	06-Apr	Hearts	A	L1	1-2		Thorburn	Stevenson	Haig	Wilson	Bolton	Burrows	Lourie	Smith,W	Gilfillan 1	McFadzean	Adamson	54	Gordon 49 Hamilton, J. 59
S	13-Apr	Celtic	N (1)	SC SF	2-5	35681	Thorburn	Stevenson	Clinton	Wilson	Bolton	Burrows	Lourie	McDonald 1	Gilfillan 1	Smith,W	Adamson	16, 65	Divers 10 McKay (2) 52 pen, 58 pen Chalmers 70 Brogan 65
S	20-Apr	Rangers	H	L1	2-2	10222	Thorburn	Stevenson	Haig	Wilson	Bolton	Burrows	Lourie	McDonald	Gilfillan 1	Menzies	McGrogan 1	24, 1	Baxter 51 Millar 55
S	27-Apr	Dundee	A	L1	1-1	8683	Thorburn	Stevenson	Haig	Wilson	Bolton	Burrows	Lourie 1	McDonald	Gilfillan	Menzies	McGrogan	62	Gilzean 40
W	01-May	Dunfermline Athletic	H	L1	1-2	1824	Thorburn	Stevenson	Haig	Wilson	Bolton	Stein	Lourie	McDonald	Gilfillan	Menzies 1	McGrogan	43	Edwards 18 Sinclair 36
S	04-May	Aberdeen	A	L1	0-4	1232	Thorburn	Stevenson	Haig	Wilson	Bolton	Burrows	McDonald	Stein	Gilfillan	Menzies	McGrogan		Kinnell (2) 23, 73 Little (2) 37, 83
S	11-May	Queen of the South	H	L1	1-1	1254	Thorburn	Stevenson	Haig	Wilson	Bolton	Burrows	Boner	McDonald	Gilfillan	Menzies 1	McGrogan	68	Frye 35
W	15-May	Motherwell	A	L1	1-5	1709	Thorburn	Stevenson	Haig	Wilson	Bolton	Burrows	McDonald	Boner	Gilfillan	McGrogan 1	Menzies	66	Lonie 10 Roberts 30 Weir 60 McBride (2) 80, 81
S	18-May	Hibernian	H	L1	0-4	3458	Thorburn	Stevenson	Haig	Wilson	Bolton	Burrows	Lourie	McDonald	Gilfillan	Menzies	McGrogan		Fraser 18 Baxter (2) 44, 87 Baker 22

Manager : Hugh Shaw

(1) at Ibrox

Day	Date	Opponents	Note	Venue	Comp	Res.	Att.	1	2	3	4	5	6	7	8	9	10	11	Substitutes, own goals, goal times and opponents' scorers		
S	10-Aug	East Fife		H	LC S	1-1	4460	Reid	Stevenson	Haig	Wood	Burrows	Stein	Lourie	Thoms 1	Mochan	Menzies	McGrogan	27		McWatt 4
W	14-Aug	Dumbarton		A	LC S	0-3	3058	Reid	Stevenson	Gray	Wilson	Burrows	Stein	Lourie	Thoms	Mochan	Menzies	McGrogan			Coyle 31 Hodgson 48 Halliday 53
S	17-Aug	Arbroath		H	LC S	3-4	2408	Reid	Wilson	Gray	Wood	Stein	Burrows	Lourie	Thoms 1	Mochan 2	Menzies	McGrogan	12, 10, 80		Murray (2) 35, 81 Tulloch 64 Morrison 74
W	21-Aug	Brechin City		A	L2	1-2	1122	Reid	Wilson	Gray	Wood	Stein	Burrows	Lourie	Thoms 1	Mochan	Menzies	McGrogan	20		Sharp 4 Tocher 11
S	24-Aug	East Fife		A	LC S	0-3	3869	Prentice	Haig	Gray	Stein	Wilson	Burrows	Lourie	Thoms	Mochan	Gilpin	McGrogan			Gray og 61 Stewart (2) 35, 42
W	28-Aug	Dumbarton		H	LC S	1-2	1678	Prentice	Haig	Gray	Wilson	Finlay	Burrows	McNiven	Thoms	Mochan	Gilpin 1	McGrogan	64		Bowie 43 Black 77
S	31-Aug	Arbroath		A	LC S	0-2	1408	Reid	Haig	Gray	Wilson	Finlay	Burrows	McGrogan	Thoms	McNiven	Gilpin	Mochan			Soutar (2) 20, 40
W	04-Sep	Albion Rovers		H	L2	3-0	1659	Reid	Haig	Gray	Burrows	Finlay	Menzies	McGrogan 1	McNiven	Thoms	Gilpin 1	Mochan	McLeod og 1	72. 77, 83	
S	07-Sep	East Fife		H	L2	1-1	4006	Reid	Haig	Gray	Burrows	Finlay	Menzies	McGrogan	McNiven	Thoms	Gilpin 1	Mochan	16		Aitken 23
W	11-Sep	Albion Rovers		A	L2	0-1	803	Reid	Haig	Craig	Burrows	Finlay	Menzies	McGrogan	McNiven	Mochan	Gilpin	Lourie			Haig og 37
F	13-Sep	Gateshead		H	F	4-2		Reid	Haig	Gray	Menzies	Burrows	McNiven	Lourie	McGrogan 2	Thoms 2	Gilpin	Mochan	20, 26, 82, 88		Laird 43 Steel 62
W	18-Sep	Arbroath		H	L2	2-3	1617	Reid	Haig	Gray	Burrows	Finlay	McNiven	Lourie	McGrogan 1	Thoms	Gilpin 1	Mochan	54, 31		Tulloch 50 Junior 62 Murray 70
S	21-Sep	Stirling Albion		H	L2	7-0	2192	Reid	Wilson	Gray	Burrows	Finlay	McNiven	Lourie 2	McGrogan 1	Menzies 4	Gilpin	Mochan	40, 82, 86, 27, 58, 61, 81		
Tu	24-Sep	Arbroath		A	L2	1-8	2064	Reid	Wilson	Gray	Burrows	Finlay	McNiven	Lourie	McGrogan 1	Menzies	Gilpin	Thoms	11		Eason (2) 19, 86 Donnelly 21 Tulloch 41 Murray 69 Kennedy (2) 63 pen, 66 Soutar 89
S	28-Sep	Montrose		A	L2	0-1	1896	Reid	Wilson	Forrest	Burrows	Finlay	McNiven	Lourie	McGrogan	Menzies	Gilpin	Mochan			Sim 50
S	05-Oct	Ayr United		H	L2	0-1	1815	Reid	Wilson	Forrest	Burrows	Finlay	McNiven m	Lourie	Menzies,J	McGrogan	Gilpin	Mochan			Jones 53
W	09-Oct	Burntisland Shipyard		H	FC 1	11-0		Reid	Wilson	Gray	Selfridge	Finlay	Burrows	Menzies	Gilpin 3	Hutton 5	McNiven 2	Lourie	Hutton,D og 1		
S	12-Oct	Hamilton Academical		A	L2	5-1	1687	Reid	Wilson	Forrest	Menzies	Finlay	Stein	Lourie 2	Gilpin 1	Hutton 1	McNiven 1	Mochan	43, 76, 40, 48, 88		Anderson 86
S	19-Oct	Dumbarton		A	L2	0-4	1291	Reid	Wilson	Forrest	Menzies	Finlay	Stein	Lourie	Gilpin	Hutton	McNiven	Mochan			Lawlor 9 Bingham 19 Hodgson (2) 77, 79
S	26-Oct	Alloa Athletic		H	L2	1-2	1609	Reid	Wilson	Haig	McMillan	Finlay	Stein	Menzies	Gilpin 1	Hutton	McNiven	Mochan	44		Walker 56 Nellies 68
S	02-Nov	Stenhousemuir		A	L2	0-1	421	Reid	Wilson	Haig	McMillan	Finlay	McNiven	Lourie	McGrogan	Buist	Bell	Mochan			Watters 75
S	09-Nov	Clyde		H	L2	1-2	1884	Reid	Wilson	Haig	Stein	Burrows	McNiven	Lourie	Bell	Mochan 1	Gilpin	McGrogan	20		Hood (2) 8, 29
S	16-Nov	Berwick Rangers		H	L2	2-0	1446	Reid	Wilson	Haig	Menzies	Burrows	McNiven	Lourie	Bell	Mochan 1	Gilpin	McGrogan	Junior og 1	61, 35	
S	23-Nov	Stranraer		A	L2	3-2	1056	Reid	Wilson	Haig	Stein	Burrows	McNiven	Lourie 2	Menzies	McGrogan 1	Bell	Gilpin	43, 63, 36		Wallace 44 King, S. 50
Tu	26-Nov	Dunfermline Athletic		A	FC SF	2-3		Reid	Wilson	Haig	Stein	Burrows	McNiven	Lourie	Menzies	McGrogan 1	Bell	Gilpin 1	58, 61		Peebles 13 Millar (2) 60, 64
S	30-Nov	Queen's Park		H	L2	2-3	1789	Reid	Wilson	Haig	Stein	Burrows	McNiven	Lourie	Menzies	McGrogan 2,1p	Bell	Gilpin	59p, 61		Buchanan 28 Hopper 87 Grant 89 pen
S	07-Dec	Cowdenbeath		H	L2	2-0	1585	Reid	Wilson	Haig	Stein	Burrows	McNiven	Lourie	Menzies	McGrogan 1p	Bell	Gilpin 1	42, 32		
S	14-Dec	Forfar Athletic		A	L2	1-0	808	Reid	Wilson	Haig	Stein	Burrows	McNiven	Wood	Menzies	McGrogan	Bell	Gilpin 1	20		
S	21-Dec	Morton		H	L2	0-3	3550	Reid	Wilson	Haig	Stein	Burrows	McNiven	Menzies	Wood	McGrogan	Bell	Gilpin			Burrows og 6 Caven 58 McGraw 73
S	28-Dec	Brechin City		H	L2	2-0	1505	Reid	Wilson	Briggs	Stein	Burrows	McNiven	Wood	Bell	Menzies 1	Gilpin	McGrogan 1	56, 29		
W	01-Jan	East Fife		A	L2	0-3	5051	Reid	Wilson	Briggs	Stein	Burrows	McNiven	Wood	Bell	Menzies	Gilpin	McGrogan			Dewar 65 McWatt 68 Aitken 79
S	04-Jan	Stirling Albion		A	L2	0-3	1214	Reid	Wilson	Gray	Stein	Burrows	McNiven	McGrogan	Bell	Hutton	Gilpin	Mochan			McBeth (3) 20 secs, 36, 57
S	11-Jan	Dumbarton		A	SC 1	0-4	3200	Reid	Wilson	Haig	Stein	Burrows	McNiven	Lourie	Menzies	McGrogan	Bell	Gilpin			Black 2 Callaghan 68 Bowie (2) 70, 80
S	18-Jan	Montrose		H	L2	6-1	1395	Reid	Wilson	Stein	Bell	Burrows	McNiven	Lourie	McGrogan	Park	Gilpin	Mochan			McNamee 66
S	25-Jan	Dundee United Res.	1	H	F	5-3		Reid	Wilson r*	Stein	Bell r***	Burrows	McNiven r**	Lourie 2	McGrogan	Park r**** 1	Gilpin 1	Buist 1	Gray u*	Selfridge u**	Allan 1 Soutar 16 Reddington 80
S	01-Feb	Ayr United		A	L2	1-1	2082	Reid	Wilson	Stein	Bell	Burrows	McNiven	Lourie	McGrogan	Park 1	Gilpin	Mochan	8		Kilgannon 54
S	08-Feb	Hamilton Academical		H	L2	4-0	1527	Reid	Wilson	Stein	Bell	Burrows	McNiven	Lourie	McGrogan 1	Park 1	Gilpin 1	Mochan 1	78, 89, 37, 28		
S	15-Feb	Dumbarton		H	L2	2-1	1580	Reid	Wilson	Stein	Bell	Burrows	McNiven 1	Lourie 1	McGrogan	Park	Gilpin	Brown	44, 85		McNiven 5 og
S	22-Feb	Alloa Athletic		A	L2	6-0	424	Reid	Wilson	Stein	Bell	Burrows	McNiven	Lourie 2	Brown 1	Park	Gilpin 1	McGrogan 2	37, 40, 50, 16, 35, 56		
S	29-Feb	Stenhousemuir		H	L2	2-2	1815	Reid	Wilson	Stein	Bell	Burrows	McNiven	Lourie	Brown 2	Park	Gilpin	McGrogan	22, 31		Henderson 58 Dackers 68
S	07-Mar	Clyde		A	L2	3-3	1598	Reid	Wilson	Stein	Bell	Burrows	McNiven	Lourie 1	Brown 1	Park	Gilpin 1	McGrogan	74, 86, 89		Morrison 25 Hood 35 Reid 42
S	21-Mar	Stranraer		H	L2	2-1	1093	Reid	Wilson	Stein	Bell	Burrows	McNiven	Lourie	Brown 1	Park 1	Gilpin	McGrogan	55, 14		McDonald 11
W	01-Apr	Queen's Park		A	L2	3-2	888	Reid	Wilson	Stein	Bell 1	Burrows	McNiven	Lourie	Brown	Park 1	Gilpin 1	McGrogan	89, 55, 64		Buchanan 44 Millar 76
S	04-Apr	Cowdenbeath		A	L2	3-0	1149	Reid	Wilson	Stein	Bell	Burrows	McNiven	Lourie	Brown	Park 1	Gilpin 1	McGrogan 1	52, 77, 58		
W	08-Apr	Berwick Rangers		A	L2	1-1	1300	Reid	Wilson	Stein	Bell	Burrows	McNiven	Lourie	Brown	Park	Gilpin 1	McGrogan	57		Williamson 37
S	18-Apr	Forfar Athletic		H	L2	1-4	1583	Reid	Wilson	Stein	Bell	Burrows	McNiven	Lourie	Brown	Park 1	Gilpin	McGrogan	15		Dick (2) 11, 60 McMurdo (2) 72, 88
F	24-Apr	Morton		A	L2	2-4	7682	Reid	Wilson	Stein	Bell	Ross	McNiven	Lourie 1	Brown	Park 1	Gilpin	McGrogan	5, 40		McGraw 6 Reilly 17 Caven 29 Wilson 47

Manager : Doug Cowie

*(1) additional substitites, Newman u***, Hutton u****, goal times 1, 37, 22, 70, 27*

Day	Date	Opponents	Note	Venue	Comp	Res	Att	1	2	3	4	5	6	7	8	9	10	11	Goal times	Substitutes, own goals, goal times and opponents' scorers
S	08-Aug	East Fife		H	LC S	1-4	4288	Reid	Wilson	Stein	Kerr	Burrows	McNiven	Lourie	Murray	McGrogan 1	Bell	Gilpin	59	Christie (3) 35, 78, 85 Aitken 47
W	12-Aug	Montrose		A	LC S	4-2	1197	Reid	Wilson	Stein	Kerr	Burrows	McNiven	Lourie	Murray 1	Brown 2	Bell	McGrogan 1	37, 14, 85, 9	Napier pen 44 Riddle 55
W	15-Aug	Queen of the South		A	LC S	1-1	2767	Reid	Wilson	Stein	Kerr	Burrows	Haig	McGrogan	Murray 1	Brown	Bell	McNiven	33	Coates 44
W	19-Aug	Brechin City		H	L2	2-1	1645	Reid	Park	Stein	Haig	Burrows	McNiven	Lourie	Murray 1	Brown 1	Bell	McNiven	33, 78	Thoms 28
S	22-Aug	East Fife		A	LC S	5-1	2973	Reid	Wilson	Stein	Haig	Burrows	McNiven	Lourie	Murray 1	Park 2	Bell 1	McGrogan 2	9, 53, 28, 33, 41	Aitken 89
W	26-Aug	Montrose	1	H	LC S	7-0	2378	Brown	Wilson	Stein	Haig	Burrows	McNiven	Lourie 1	Murray 1	Park 1	Bell 1	McGrogan 2		Ogilvie og 1
W	29-Aug	Queen of the South		H	LC S	2-3	4029	Brown	Wilson	Stein	Wilson	Burrows	McNiven	Lourie	Murray	Park	Bell	McGrogan 1	71, 17	Coates (2) 25, 54 Law, J. 69
W	02-Sep	Alloa Athletic		H	L2	0-0	1620	Brown	Wilson	Stein	Haig	Burrows	McNiven	Lourie	Murray	Park	Brown	McGrogan		
S	05-Sep	East Fife		A	L2	1-2	2774	Brown	Wilson	Stein	Kerr	Burrows	Haig	Lourie	Murray 1p	Park	Bell	McNiven	49	Dewar (2) 24, 79
W	09-Sep	Stranraer		H	L2	0-4	1187	Brown	Wilson	Stein	Murray	Burrows	Haig	Lourie	Murray	Brown	Brown	McNiven		Logan (3) 14, 48, 70 McDonald 32
S	12-Sep	Stirling Albion		H	L2	0-1	1906	Reid	Grant	Wilson	Selfridge	Burrows	Porterfield	McGrogan	Gardner	Park	Gilpin	McGrogan		McTurk 78 pen
W	16-Sep	Alloa Athletic		H	L2	2-4	1683	Reid	Grant	Wilson	Selfridge	Burrows	Stein	Blues	Gardner	Brown 1	Gilpin	Buist	62, 9	Rutherford (4) 7, 19, 30, 57
S	19-Sep	Stranraer		A	L2	3-3	1277	Reid	Park	Kerr	Kerr	Grant	Burrows	Lourie	Gardner 1	Gardner 1	McGrogan 1	McGrogan 1	2, 15, 52	McDonald 4 Logan (2) 53, 77
W	23-Sep	Cowdenbeath		A	L2	1-1	794	Reid	Stein	Whitnall	Wilson	Grant	Burrows	Lourie	Brown 1	Gardner	McGrogan	Gilpin	33	Rolland 68
S	26-Sep	Stenhousemuir		H	L2	1-2	1355	Reid	Burrows	Whitnall	Wilson	Grant	McNiven	Lourie	Brown	Gardner	Bell 1	McGrogan	20	Whitnall 53 og Bryce 60
W	30-Sep	Cowdenbeath		H	L2	0-1	1171	Reid	Grant	Whitnall	Stein	Burrows	Porterfield	McDonald, W	Bell	Brown 2	Gilpin	McGrogan		Matthew 54 pen
S	03-Oct	Montrose	2	A	L2	3-8	1233	Reid	Grant	Whitnall	Stein	Burrows	Porterfield	Wilson 1	Gardner	Brown	Gilpin	Lourie	68, 1, 75	
S	10-Oct	Arbroath		H	L2	1-1	1295	Reid	Grant	Whitnall	Whitnall	Selfridge	Porterfield	Wilson	Gardner	Brown	Gardner	Blues 1	63	Henderson 31
S	17-Oct	Albion Rovers		H	L2	1-2	823	Reid	Grant	Selfridge	Whitnall	Selfridge	Porterfield	Gardner 1	Brown	Wilson	Glen	Fisher	30 secs	Dillon 8 McIlwraith 81
S	24-Oct	Hamilton Academical		A	L2	2-2	1525	Reid	Grant	Selfridge	Stein	Burrows	Porterfield	Lourie	Gardner	Park 2	McLean	Fisher	59, 72	Forsyth (2) 59, 73
S	31-Oct	Ayr United		A	L2	4-0	1952	Reid	Grant	Selfridge	Stein	Burrows	Porterfield	Lourie	Gardner	Park 2	Wishart 2	McLean	29, 71, 24, 64	
S	07-Nov	ES Clydebank		A	L2	3-0	1923	Reid	Grant	Selfridge	Stein	Burrows	Porterfield	Lourie	Gardner	Park 2	McLean 1	Fisher	5, 56, 72	
S	14-Nov	Queen of the South		H	L2	1-1	2778	Reid	Grant	Selfridge	Stein	Burrows	Porterfield	Lourie	Gardner 1	Park	McLean	Fisher	65	Dickson 46
S	21-Nov	Berwick Rangers		A	L2	3-2	1280	Reid	Grant	Selfridge	Stein	Burrows	Porterfield	Lourie	Gardner	Park 2	McLean	McLean	80, 25, 40	Jackson (2) 28, 36
S	28-Nov	Queen's Park		H	L2	4-2	1657	Reid	Grant	Selfridge	Stein	Burrows	Porterfield	Lourie	Gardner 2	Park 1	Wishart	McLean	56, 83, 33, 46	Breslin 4 Ingram 8
S	05-Dec	Forfar Athletic		A	L2	3-2	951	Reid	Wilson	Selfridge	Stein	Burrows	Porterfield	Lourie 1	Gardner	Park 2	Wishart 1	McLean	15, 32, 84	Gray 33 Mackie 85
S	12-Dec	Dumbarton		H	L2	0-3	2188	Reid	Grant	Wilson	Stein	Selfridge	Porterfield	Lourie	Gardner	Park	Wishart	McLean		Veitch 64 Nelson (2) 73, 82
S	26-Dec	Brechin City		A	L2	3-3	526	Reid	Grant	Gray	Stein	Burrows	Porterfield	Gardner	Gardner	Park 1	Wishart	McLean	38, 53, 78	Cooper (2) 18, 37 Reid 77
F	01-Jan	East Fife		H	L2	1-1	3962	Reid	Grant	Gray	Stein	Burrows	Porterfield	Fisher	Murray 1	Gardner	Bell 1	McLean	46	Dewar 75
S	02-Jan	Stirling Albion		A	L2	1-2	3424	Reid	Grant	Gray	Stein	Burrows	Porterfield	Lourie	Murray	Gardner	Bell 1	McLean	55	Thoms 1 Fleming 67
S	09-Jan	Montrose		H	L2	0-0	1517	Reid	Grant	Gray	Stein	Burrows	Porterfield	Lourie	Murray	Park	Bell 1	McLean		
S	16-Jan	Stenhousemuir		A	L2	0-0	373	Reid	Grant	Gray	Wishart	Stein	Porterfield	Lourie	Gardner	Gardner	Bell	McLean		
S	23-Jan	Inverness Caledonian		A	SC 2P	1-2	4500	Reid	Wilson	Gray	Wishart	Stein	Porterfield	Wilson	Murray	Gardner 1	Murray	McLean	43	Grant 28 McInnes 55
S	30-Jan	Arbroath		A	L2	1-0	1529	Reid	Wilson	Gray	Wishart	Grant	Porterfield	Fisher	Murray	Richardson	Bell	McLean	27	
S	13-Feb	Albion Rovers		H	L2	0-3	680	Reid	Wilson	Gray	Wishart	Grant	Porterfield	Fisher	Murray	Richardson	Gardner	McLean		McCallum 23 Mallan 57 Boyle 81
S	27-Feb	Hamilton Academical		H	L2	0-2	1497	Reid	Wilson	Gray	Gardner	Grant	Wishart	Fisher	Murray	Richardson	Porterfield	McDonald, J		Currie (2) 38, 84
S	13-Mar	ES Clydebank		H	L2	2-2	1728	Reid	Grant	Gray	Gardner	Grant	Porterfield	Fisher	Murray 1	Porterfield	Lyall 1	McDonald, J	47, 70	Roxburgh 2 Jones 13
S	20-Mar	Queen of the South		A	L2	1-1	1164	Reid	Grant	Gray	Stein	Stein	Porterfield	Gardner	Gardner	Richardson	Lyall	McDonald, J	78	Davison 17
S	27-Mar	Berwick Rangers		H	L2	3-0	991	Reid	Grant	Gray	Stein	Burrows	Porterfield	Hutchison 1	Murray	Gardner 1	Lyall 1	Buist	50, 35, 49	
M	05-Apr	Cowdenbeath		H	FC SF	0-0	1000	Reid	Grant	Gray	Stein	Burrows	Porterfield	Hutchison	Murray	Gardner	Lyall 1	Lyall		
W	07-Apr	Forfar Athletic		H	L2	5-2	897	Reid	Grant	Gray	Stein	Burrows	Porterfield	Hutchison 1	Gardner	Richardson 2	Lyall 2	McLean	25, 21, 76, 44, 50	Watt 34 Soutar 79
S	17-Apr	Dumbarton		A	L2	1-2	917	Reid	Grant	Gray	Stein	Stein	Porterfield	Hutchison	Gardner	Richardson	Lyall 1	McLean	30	Nelson 56 Kelly 77
Tu	20-Apr	Queen's Park		A	L2	0-0	1016	Reid	Gray	McKeown	Stein	Burrows	Porterfield	Hutchison	Gardner	Richardson	Lyall 1	McLean		
M	26-Apr	Cowdenbeath		A	FC SFr	3-0	200	Reid	Gray	McKeown	Stein	Burrows	Porterfield 1	McLean	Gardner 1	Richardson	McDonald	McDonald	40, 30, 20	
W	28-Apr	Ayr United		H	L2	1-1	983	Reid	Gray	McKeown	Stein	Burrows	Porterfield 1	Hutchison	Gardner 1	Richardson	Lyall	McLean	5	McAnespie 10

Manager : George Farm

(1) Goal times 81, 49, 64, 35 secs, 25, 45, 89

(2) Montrose goalscorers Jones (5) 20, 44p, 48, 52, 82 Wallace 22 Dougan 54 Elliott 80

Day	Date	Opponents	Note	Venue	Comp	Res.	Att.	1	2	3	4	5	6	7	8	9	10	11	Substitutes, own goals, goal times and opponents' scorers
S	14-Aug	Stirling Albion		H	LC S	3-1	2485	Reid	McKeown	Gray	Stein	Evans	Porterfield	Hutchison	Gardner	Richardson 2	Lyall 1	McLean	12, 88, 48 Fleming 66
W	18-Aug	Arbroath		A	LC S	2-2	1695	Reid	McKeown	Gray	Stein	Evans	Porterfield	Hutchison	Gardner	Richardson 1	Lyall 1	McLean	30, 73 Herron (2) 46, 80
S	21-Aug	Queen's Park		A	LC S	1-1	1549	Reid	McKeown	Gray	Stein	Evans	Porterfield	Hutchison	Gardner 1	Richardson	Lyall 1	McLean	38 Mackay 65
W	25-Aug	East Stirling		H	L2	3-1	2214	Reid	McKeown	Gray	Stein	Evans	Porterfield	Hutchison 1	Gardner 1	Richardson	Lyall 1	McLean	25, 59, 75 Smith 31
S	28-Aug	Stirling Albion		A	LC S	2-1	1969	Reid	McKeown	Gray	Stein	Evans	Porterfield	Hutchison	Gardner	Richardson	Lyall 1	McLean	32, 18 Fleming 8
W	01-Sep	Arbroath		H	LC S	4-2	3234	Reid	McKeown	Gray	Stein	Evans	Porterfield	Hutchison	Gardner 1	Richardson 1	Lyall 3	McLean	7, 58, 86, 88 Henderson 16 Hughes 84
S	04-Sep	Queen's Park		H	LC S	3-0	3984	Reid	McKeown	Gray	Stein	Evans	Porterfield	Hutchison	Gardner 1	Richardson 1	Lyall 1	McLean	85, 21, 86
W	08-Sep	Cowdenbeath		A	L2	0-0	1400	Reid	McKeown	Gray	Stein	Evans	Porterfield	Hutchison	Gardner	Richardson	Lyall	McLean	
S	11-Sep	Airdrie		A	L2	2-1	2187	Reid	McKeown	Gray	Stein	Evans	Porterfield	Hutchison	Gardner 1	Richardson	Lyall 1	McLean	89, 12 Murray 54
W	15-Sep	Celtic	3	H	LC QF-1	1-8	14520	Reid	McKeown	Gray	Stein	Evans	Porterfield	Hutchison	Gardner	Richardson 1	Lyall	McLean	21
S	18-Sep	East Fife		H	L2	1-3	3624	Reid	McKeown	Gray	Stein	Evans	Porterfield	Hutchison	Gardner	Glen	Lyall 1	Christie	81 Christie (2) 12, 28 Dewar 49
W	22-Sep	Celtic	3	A	LC QF-2	0-4	8296	Reid	Selfridge	Gray	Stein	Evans	Porterfield	Christie	Gardner	Richardson	Lyall	McLean	Murdoch 49 Auld (2) 50, 53 Chalmers 83
S	25-Sep	Stranraer		A	L2	1-2	952	Reid	Selfridge	Gray	Stein 1	Evans	Porterfield	Hutchison	Gardner	Richardson	Lyall	McLean	82 Evans og 12 Hanlon 89
W	29-Sep	Third Lanark		H	L2	6-1	1386	Brown	Gray	Selfridge	Stein	Evans	Porterfield	Hutchison	Gardner 1	Lyall 4	McLean	Christie 1	66, 27, 29, 80, 90, 55 McLaughlin 4
S	09-Oct	Arbroath		A	L2	1-3	1879	Reid	Gray	Selfridge	Stein	Evans	Porterfield	Hutchison	Gardner 1	Lyall	McLean	Christie	76 Morrison 56 Donnelly 60 Henderson 67
M	11-Oct	Dunfermline Athletic	1	H	FC F-1	1-5		Reid	McKeown	Gray	Gardner	Evans	Porterfield	Hutchison b x	Lyall	Richardson	McLean 1	McDonald	28 Edwards (2) 2 pen, 75 Hunter (2) 28, 32 Smith 38
S	16-Oct	Stenhousemuir		H	L2	2-0	1695	Reid	Stein	Gray	Gardner	Evans	Porterfield 1p	Hutchison	Lyall 1	Richardson	McLean 1	McDonald	68, 26
M	23-Oct	Dunfermline Athletic	1	A	FC F-2	3-4		Brown	Stein	Gray	Gardner	Evans	Porterfield	Hutchison 1	Lyall 1	Richardson	McLean	McDonald 1	75, 9, 20 Smith 15 Paton 61 Wilson 63 Callaghan, T. 68
S	23-Oct	Ayr United		A	L2	2-2	5851	Brown	Stein	Gray	Gardner	Evans	Porterfield x	Hutchison 1	Lyall	Richardson 2	McLean	McDonald	73, 37 McMillan 69 Monan 83
S	30-Oct	Queen of the South		A	L2	0-1	1731	Reid	McKeown	Gray	Gardner	Evans	Porterfield	Hutchison	Lyall	Richardson	McLean	McDonald	Dick 35
S	06-Nov	Forfar Athletic		H	L2	1-1	845	Reid	McKeown	Gray	Stein 1	Evans	Porterfield 1	Christie	Gardner	Richardson	McLean	McDonald	80 Knox 35
S	13-Nov	Queen's Park		H	L2	5-1	1399	Reid	McKeown 1	Gray	Stein	Evans	Porterfield 1	Christie	Gardner	Richardson	Lyall 2	McLean 1	87, 31, 20, 53, 23 Buchanan 13
S	20-Nov	Montrose		A	L2	2-1	1001	Reid	McKeown 1	Gray	Stein	Evans	Porterfield	Christie 1	Gardner	Richardson 1	Lyall	McLean	49, 11 Wallace 57
S	27-Nov	Dumbarton		H	L2	4-0	1562	Reid	McKeown	Gray	Stein	Evans	Porterfield 1p	Christie 1	Gardner	Richardson 1	Lyall 1	McLean	86, 40, 37, 52
S	11-Dec	Albion Rovers		A	L2	0-1	808	Reid	McKeown	Gray	Stein	Evans	Porterfield	Christie	Gardner	Richardson 1	Lyall	McLean	Reilly 85
S	18-Dec	Brechin City		H	L2	1-1	1338	Reid	McKeown	Gray	Stein	Evans	Porterfield	Christie	Gardner	Richardson 1	Lyall 1	McLean	34 Sneddon 89 1/2
S	25-Dec	Alloa Athletic		A	L2	2-1	632	Reid	McKeown	Gray	Selfridge	Evans	Porterfield	Christie	Gardner	Richardson 2	Lyall	McLean	10, 15 St John 50
M	03-Jan	Airdrie	4	H	L2	0-8	3291	Reid	McKeown	Gray	Stein	Evans	Porterfield	Christie	Lyall	Richardson	Lyall	McLean	68
S	08-Jan	Inverness Caledonian		H	SC 1P	1-0	2302	Reid	Selfridge	Ross	Stein	Evans	Gardner	McLean	Lyall	Richardson	Porterfield 1	McDonald	42, 55, 28, 70, 26
S	15-Jan	Stranraer	2	H	SC 2P	5-0	1389	Reid	Gray	Gray	Stein	Evans	Gardner	Glen	McLean	Lyall 2	Porterfield 2	Tulloch 1	68 Rutherford 85
S	22-Jan	Alloa Athletic		H	L2	0-1	2090	Reid	Selfridge	Gray	Stein	Evans	Gardner	Tulloch	McLean	Lyall	Porterfield	McDonald	Kennedy 16 pen Donnelly 20 Wilkie 56
S	29-Jan	Arbroath		H	L2	0-3	1425	Reid	Selfridge	Gray	Stein	Evans	Porterfield	Glen	Richardson	Tulloch	Gardner	McDonald	Wallace 57
S	05-Feb	Brechin City		A	L2	8-1	580	Coates	Selfridge	Gray	Stein 1	Evans	Porterfield 1	Christie	Richardson 4	Gardner 1	McKeown 1	McDonald	72,16,34,46,63,81,77,65 Black 66
S	12-Feb	Stenhousemuir		A	L2	1-1	267	Coates	Selfridge	Gray	Stein	Evans	Porterfield	Christie	Richardson 1	Gardner	McKeown	McKeown 1	24 Smith 60 pen
S	26-Feb	Queen of the South		A	L2	2-1	1870	Coates	McKeown	Gray	Stein 2	Evans	Porterfield 1p	Gardner	Richardson	Lyall	Lyall	McDonald 1	88, 20
S	05-Mar	Forfar Athletic		A	L2	6-0	800	Coates	Selfridge	Gray	Stein	Evans	Porterfield 1	Gardner	Richardson 2	Lyall 2	McLean 1	McDonald	87,31,55,41,83,89
W	09-Mar	Berwick Rangers		H	L2	1-0	1270	Coates	Selfridge	Gray	Stein	Evans	Porterfield	Gardner	Richardson 1	Lyall	McLean	McDonald	53
Tu	15-Mar	Queen's Park		A	L2	1-1	797	Coates	Selfridge	Gray	Stein	Evans	Porterfield	Gardner	Richardson 1	Lyall	McLean 1	McDonald	71 Mulgrew 15
S	19-Mar	Montrose		H	L2	3-0	1237	Coates	Selfridge	Gray	Stein	Evans	Porterfield 1p	Glen 1	Duncan 1	Glen	McLean	McDonald	76, 27, 19
S	26-Mar	Dumbarton		A	L2	2-0	942	Coates	Selfridge	Gray	Stein	Evans	Porterfield 2	Glen	Richardson	Gardner	McLean	McDonald	7, 74 Christie 29
Tu	29-Mar	East Fife		H	L2	1-1	2524	Coates	Selfridge	Gray	Stein	Evans	Porterfield	McKeown	Richardson 1	Gardner	McLean	McDonald 1	2
F	01-Apr	Cowdenbeath		H	L2	4-0	1548	Coates	Selfridge	Gray	Stein 2	Evans	Porterfield 1p	McKeown	Richardson 1p	Gardner	McLean	McDonald	62, 76, 81, 42
W	06-Apr	Third Lanark		A	L2	0-1	434	Coates	McKeown	Gray	Stein	Evans	Porterfield	McKeown	Richardson	Gardner	McLean	McDonald	Kilgannon 83 pen
W	09-Apr	Berwick Rangers		A	L2	2-2	780	Coates	Selfridge	Gray	Selfridge	Evans	Porterfield	Richardson	Richardson 1	Gardner	Garland	McDonald 1	1, 55 Forsyth 11 Kilgannon 89
W	14-Apr	Ayr United		H	L2	0-2	1856	Coates	Selfridge	Gray	Stein	Evans	McLean	McDonald 1	Richardson	Gardner	Bruce	McDonald	McMillan 14 Hawkshaw 40
S	16-Apr	Albion Rovers		H	L2	1-1	1502	Coates	McKeown	Gray	Selfridge	Evans	McLean	McDonald	Richardson 1	Gardner	Porterfield	McDonald	64 Green 66
M	18-Apr	East Fife		H	FC SF	4-1	1120	Coates	Selfridge	Gray	Stein 1	Evans	Porterfield	McKeown	McLean	Richardson 1	Porterfield	McLean	90, 79, 48, 65 Watt 70
W	27-Apr	East Stirling		A	L2	0-0	405	Coates	Selfridge	McKeown	Stein	Evans	Porterfield	Ford	Spilarewicz	Glen	Gardner 2	McDonald	Keddie 31 pen
S	30-Apr	Alloa Athletic		H	L2	1-1	1161	Coates	Selfridge	McKeown	Davidson	Evans	Porterfield	Gray	Spilarewicz	Richardson 1	Gardner	McLean	56

Manager : George Farm
(1) 1964/65 Final
(2) Gate receipts £200
(3) Celtic goalscorers McBride (3) 17, 58, 88 Lennox 19 Johnstone 44 Hughes (3) 66pen, 77, 80
(4) Airdrie goalscorers Marshall (3) 11, 22, 70 Ferguson 40 Murray (3) 45, 53, 79 Phillips 71

Substitutes, own goals, goal times and opponents' scorers

Day	Date	Opponents	Note	Venue	Comp	Res	Att	1	2	3	4	5	6	7	8	9	10	11	Substitutes, goal times & opponents' scorers
S	06-Aug	Stirling Albion		H	F	2-0	500	Coates	Selfridge	Gray	Stein	Evans	Rennie	Lister	Richardson	Gardner 1	Porterfield	Spilarewicz 1	McLean 30. 24 — 56 — Clark (2) 32, 74
S	13-Aug	Cowdenbeath		H	LCS	1-2	2250	Coates	Selfridge	Gray	Stein	Evans	Rennie	Lister	Richardson	Gardner 1	Porterfield	Spilarewicz	Spilarewicz 56 — Lumsden 86 pen
W	17-Aug	Ayr United	1	A	LCS	0-0	3500	Reid	Selfridge	Gray	Stein	Evans	Rennie	Lister x74	Richardson	Gardner	Gardner	McDonald b	McLean 43
S	20-Aug	Berwick Rangers		A	LCS	1-1	1137	Reid	Selfridge	Rennie	Stein	Evans	Rennie	Lister	Richardson 1	Gardner 1	Gardner	McDonald	Spilarewicz 45 — Wallace 36
W	24-Aug	Montrose		H	L2	1-1	1872	Reid	Gray	Gray	Rennie	Evans	Porterfield	Lister	Richardson	Gardner,R	Gardner,R	McDonald	Selfridge 65 — Clark (2) 55, 83
S	27-Aug	Cowdenbeath		A	LCS	1-2	1134	Reid	Stein 1	Gray	Davidson	Evans	Porterfield 1p	Lister	Richardson 2	Gardner	Gardner	McDonald	Selfridge 80, 37, 45 — Grant 68
W	31-Aug	Ayr United		H	LCS	3-1	1582	Reid	Stein	Gray b	Davidson r45	Evans	Porterfield	Lister 1	Richardson 1	Spilarewicz	McLean	McDonald	McLean u45 2, 74 — McGowan 36 Kirk 37
H	03-Sep	Berwick Rangers		H	LCS	2-0	1697	Reid s	Stein 1	Gray	McLean	Evans	Porterfield	Lister	Richardson 1	Spilarewicz 1	Gardner	McDonald	Selfridge 72, 51, 14 — Lawlor 20
W	07-Sep	Dumbarton		A	L2	3-2	1022	Reid	Stein 1	Gray	Davidson b	Evans	Porterfield	Lister 1	Richardson 1	Spilarewicz	Gardner 1	McDonald 1	Selfridge 72, 25
S	10-Sep	East Fife		A	L2	2-1	2265	Reid	Stein	Gray	Davidson	Evans	Porterfield	Lister	Gardner 1	Gardner	McLean	McDonald	Selfridge 25, 64
W	14-Sep	Dumbarton		H	L2	2-0	1713	Reid	Stein	Gray	Davidson	Evans	Porterfield	Lister	Richardson 1	Gardner	McLean	McDonald	Selfridge 49, 65, 88
S	17-Sep	Clydebank		H	L2	3-0	2086	Reid	Stein	Gray	Davidson	Evans	Porterfield	Lister	Gardner 3	Richardson 1	McLean	McDonald	McLean 38, 72 — Carlyle 64
S	24-Sep	East Stirling		A	L2	2-1	621	Reid s	Stein	Gray	Davidson	Evans	Porterfield	Selfridge	Gardner 2	Richardson	Selfridge	McDonald	Selfridge 76, 81, 88, 90 — Henderson 44 1/2
S	01-Oct	Third Lanark		H	L2	4-1	1832	Reid	Stein	Gray	Davidson b	Evans	Porterfield 1p	Lister	Richardson	Gardner,R 2	Gardner 1	McLean	Rennie 54 — Bolton 7
S	08-Oct	Morton		A	L2	0-1	6949	Reid	Stein	Gray	Davidson	Evans	Porterfield	Selfridge	Richardson	McLean	Gardner	Gardner,R	Rennie — Edwards 23 Paton 87
W	12-Oct	Dunfermline Athletic		H	FC F-1	1-2	1106	Reid	Selfridge	Gray	Stein	Evans	Porterfield 1p	Lister	McLean	Richardson	Gardner	Gardner,R	Selfridge u45 80, 32, 71, 8, 35 — Matthews 82 pen
S	15-Oct	Forfar Athletic		A	L2	5-4	3196	Reid	Stein 1	Gray	McLean	Evans	Porterfield	Lister	Richardson r45 1	Wallace 1	Gardner	Gardner,R 1	Selfridge u110 50, 30, 52, 65, 78 — Hunter (2) 29, 62 Maxwell 48 Edwards 51
W	19-Oct	Dunfermline Athletic	2	A	FC F-2	3-1	1251	Reid	Stein 1	Gray	Rennie	Evans	Porterfield	Lister	Richardson r110 1	Wallace 4	Gardner	Glen	Selfridge 90, 54, 84 — Keddie 76
S	22-Oct	Alloa Athletic		H	L2	1-1	2187	Reid	Selfridge	Gray	Rennie	Evans	Porterfield	Lister	Richardson 1	Wallace	McLean 1	McDonald 1	Selfridge 40 — Jenkins 75
S	29-Oct	Albion Rovers		A	L2	2-1	646	Reid	Selfridge	Gray	Stein	Evans	Porterfield 1p	Lister	Richardson	Wallace	Gardner 1	Gardner 1	McLean 80, 76 — Hannon 77
S	05-Nov	Stranraer		H	L2	2-1	2030	Reid	Stein	Gray	McLean	Evans	Porterfield	Lister	Richardson 1	Wallace	Gardner 1	Horne	Selfridge 83, 6 — Halliday 18 secs
S	12-Nov	Brechin City		A	L2	4-2	1536	Reid	Stein	Gray	McLean	Evans	Porterfield	McDonald	Wallace 1	Richardson	Gardner 3	Horne	Selfridge 56, 17, 49, 72 — Lumsden 36 Christie 46
S	19-Nov	Berwick Rangers		H	L2	2-1	2416	Reid	Stein	Gray	McLean	Evans	Porterfield 1p	McDonald r45	Wallace	Richardson 1	Gardner	Horne	Selfridge u45 45, 56 — Mackay 4
S	26-Nov	Queen's Park		A	L2	2-1	1654	Reid	Selfridge	Gray	McLean	Evans	Porterfield	Wallace	Richardson 2	Richardson	Gardner	Horne	Lister 75, 83 — Clark 27
S	03-Dec	Cowdenbeath		H	L2	1-5	2262	Reid	Stein	Gray	McLean	Evans	Porterfield	Lister	Wallace	Richardson	Gardner 1	Horne	Selfridge 57
S	10-Dec	Arbroath		A	F	2-1	2511	Reid	Selfridge	Gray	Davidson	Evans	Porterfield	Horne	Richardson	Wallace 1	Gardner 1	McDonald	Selfridge 27, 65 — Grant 1
S	17-Dec	Hibs Reserves		H	L2	3-1	8223	Reid	Stein b	Gray	McLean	Evans	Porterfield	Millar	Richardson 2	Wallace	Gardner b 1	McDonald	Horne 15 secs. 80, 43 — Vint 23
S	24-Dec	Hamilton Academical		A	L2	0-2	3083	Reid	Stein	Gray	McLean	Evans	Porterfield	Millar	Richardson 1	Wallace	Gardner	McDonald	Newman — Dick 32 McChesney 89 pen
M	31-Dec	Queen of the South		H	L2	1-0	1209	Reid	Stein	Gray	McLean	Evans	Porterfield	Millar	Richardson	Wallace 1	Gardner b 1	McDonald	Lister 6
Tu	02-Jan	East Fife	3	A	L2	2-3	7760	Reid	Stein	Gray	McLean	Evans	Porterfield	Millar r60	Richardson 2	Wallace 1	Gardner	McDonald	Lister 33, 56 — Moy (2) 15, 82 Rankin 87
S	03-Jan	Clydebank		H	L2	6-1	3186	Reid	Stein b	Gray	McLean	Evans	Porterfield	Lister	Richardson	Wallace	Gardner 2	Lourie 2	Lister u60 69,79,90,52,43 secs, 44 — Kilgannon 54
S	14-Jan	Third Lanark		A	L2	2-3	2269	Reid	Stein b	Gray	McLean	Evans	Porterfield	Millar	Richardson	Wallace	Gardner 2	Lourie b	Millar 77, 73 — Mason 86
S	21-Jan	Montrose		H	L2	5-1	1302	Reid	Stein	Gray	McLean	Evans	Porterfield	Lister	Stein	Wallace	Gardner x80 1	Lourie u45	Millar u45 65, 82, 16, 21, 46 — Hopper (2) 12, 56 Watson 89
S	28-Jan	Queen's Park	3	A	SC 1	3-2	2638	Reid	Stein b	Gray	McLean	Evans	Porterfield	Lourie	Richardson 1	Wallace	Gardner 2	Lourie 1	Lister 65, 37, 75 — Knox 89
S	04-Feb	Forfar Athletic		H	L2	6-1	2696	Reid	Stein b	Gray	McLean	Evans	Porterfield 1p	Millar	Richardson b 3	Wallace 1	Gardner 2	Mackle	Lister 62,13,35,68,38,85 — Keddie 55 Marshall 79
S	11-Feb	Alloa Athletic		A	L2	2-1	1000	Reid	Stein	Gray	McLean	Evans	Porterfield	Millar	Richardson 2	Wallace	Gardner	Mackle	Lister 33, 60 — Jones 32
S	18-Feb	East Stirling		H	L2	5-1	2115	Reid	Selfridge	Gray	McLean	Evans	Porterfield	Millar	Stein	Wallace 2	Richardson	Mackle	Lister 36, 82 — Murphy 43
S	25-Feb	Albion Rovers		A	L2	0-2	1120	Reid	Stein	Gray	McLean	Evans	Porterfield	Millar	Richardson 1	Wallace 1	Gardner 1	Mackle 2	Selfridge 50, 47, 82, 39, 63 — McQueen 30
S	04-Mar	Stranraer		H	L2	4-0	2878	Reid	Stein	Gray	McLean	Evans	Porterfield	Millar	Richardson	Wallace 3	Gardner	Mackle 1	McLean 51, 78, 87, 47 — Irvin 88
S	11-Mar	Brechin City		A	L2	1-0	2569	Reid	Stein	Gray	McLean	Evans	Porterfield	Millar	Richardson r40	Wallace	Gardner	Mackle	McLean u40 Mowbray og 88
S	18-Mar	Berwick Rangers		H	L2	0-1	7122	Reid	Stein	Gray	Polland	Evans	Porterfield	Millar	Richardson r72	Wallace	Gardner	Mackle	McLean u72 — Ainslie (2) 83, 85
S	25-Mar	Queen's Park		A	L2	1-1	2322	Reid	Stein	Gray	Polland	Evans	Porterfield	Millar 1	Lister	Wallace	Gardner	Mackle	McLean 81 — Donnelly 70
S	01-Apr	Cowdenbeath		H	L2	4-0	856	Reid	Stein	Gray	Polland	Evans	Porterfield	Millar	Lister	Wallace	Gardner 3	Mackle 1	McLean 5, 19, 70, 44 — Black 90 secs
S	08-Apr	Arbroath		A	L2	3-1	1291	Reid	Stein	Gray	Polland	Evans	Porterfield	Millar r62	Lister 1	Wallace	Gardner 1	Mackle 1	McLean u62 38, 6, 60 — Thomson 67
W	12-Apr	Stenhousemuir		H	L2	1-1	2657	Reid	Stein 2	Gray	Polland	Evans	Porterfield	Millar	Lister	Wallace	Gardner	Mackle	Selfridge 90 — Livingstone 45
S	15-Apr	Stenhousemuir		A	L2	7-2	5921	Reid	Stein	McLean	Polland	Evans	Porterfield	Millar r35	Lister 1	Wallace 3	Gardner 1	Mackle 1	Selfridge 60,63,82,32,36,70,19 — Law, L 25 McMurdo 67
Tu	02-May	Burntisland Shipyard	4	H	FC SF	5-1	500	Reid	Selfridge	McLean	Stein	Polland	Porterfield	Millar r35 1	Lister	Richardson 1	Gardner	McDonald	Wallace u35 Clark og 1 — Tulloch 26 Crawford 57
S	06-May	East Fife		H	FC F	5-1	500	Reid	Stein	McLean	Polland	Evans	Porterfield m37	Millar r45	Lister 1	Wallace 3	Gardner 1	Mackle	Spilarewicz u45 69,50,57,88,72 — Gardner 66
S	13-May	Morton		H	F	5-2	2000	Reid	Stein	McLean	Polland	Evans	Porterfield	Spilarewicz	Lister 1	Wallace 1	Gardner 3	Mackle	Selfridge 40, 63, 14, 20, 88 — Bartram 12 Stein og 52

Manager : George Farm

(1) Thomson sent off with Lister after 74 minutes
(2) after extra time
(3) Watson sent off 89 minutes
(4) goal times 12,8,23,42,85,52

Manager : Tommy Walker

Day	Date	Opponents	Note	Venue	Comp	Res.	Att.	1	2	3	4	5	6	7	8	9	10	11	Substitutes, own goals, goal times and opponents' scorers
S	05-Aug	Nottingham Forest		H	F	1-5	7500	Reid	Selfridge	Gray	Polland r10	Evans	Paterson	Lister 1p	Stein	Wallace	Falconer	Millar,A r45	Hislop u10, Spilarewicz u45; 62; Baker (2) 37, 82 Hinton 47 pen Kea 44½ Wignall 81
S	12-Aug	Dumbarton		H	LCS	2-0	2490	Reid	Selfridge	Gray	Stein	Evans	McLean	Lister 2	Wallace	Richardson	Falconer	Mackie	Spilarewicz; 7, 60
W	16-Aug	Morton	4	A	LCS	1-3	3980	Reid	Selfridge	Gray	Bolton	Evans	Porterfield	Lister	Stein	Wallace 1	Richardson	Falconer r45	McLean u45; 25; Sweeney 35 Allan 44½ Bartram 80 pen
S	19-Aug	Queen of the South		H	LCS	2-5	2615	Reid	Selfridge	Gray	Kinloch	Evans	Porterfield	Millar,A	McLean	Richardson 1	Lister 1	Wallace 1	Falconer; 45 secs, 47; Dick (2) 14, 54 Davidson (3) 27, 44, 84
S	26-Aug	Dumbarton		A	LCS	1-1	871	Reid	Stein	Gray	Kinloch	Evans	Porterfield	Lister	Murphy	Wallace 1	Richardson r85	Falconer	Spilarewicz u85; 20; McGoldrick 24
W	30-Aug	Morton		A	LCS	2-3	1892	Reid	Stein	Gray	Kinloch	Evans	Porterfield	Lister	Murphy 1	Wallace	Richardson 1	Falconer	Spilarewicz; 18, 47; Bartram (2) 54, 87 Evans og 74
S	02-Sep	Queen of the South		A	LCS	2-3	2120	Reid	Stein b+X 78	Gray	Kinloch	Evans	Porterfield	Lister 2,1p	Murphy	Wallace	Richardson	Falconer	Davidson; 4, 83p; Pollock 15 Law 41 Davidson 51
S	09-Sep	Dunfermline Athletic		A	L1	1-2	7094	Reid	Stein	Gray	Kinloch	Evans	Porterfield	Lister 1p	Sneddon	Wallace	Murphy	Falconer	Richardson; 46; Delaney 78 Gardner 85
S	16-Sep	Hibernian		H	L1	0-3	7840	Reid	Stein	Gray	Kinloch	Evans	Porterfield	Lister	Sneddon	Wallace	Murphy	Falconer	Richardson; Kinloch og 6 Cormack 22 Stein 40
S	23-Sep	Stirling Albion	6	H	L1	7-1	3183	Reid	Stein	Gray	Kinloch	Evans	Porterfield	Lister 1p	Sneddon 2	Wallace 3	Murphy	Falconer	Richardson; Reid og 1; Hall 82 (goal times — see note 6)
S	30-Sep	St Johnstone	1	A	L1	0-1	5470	Reid	Bolton	Gray	Kinloch	Evans	Porterfield	Lister	Sneddon	Wallace	Murphy x51	Falconer	McLean; Aird 61
W	04-Oct	Cowdenbeath		H	F	4-1	1500	Reid	Bolton	Gray	Davidson b	Evans	Porterfield	Lister 1	Sneddon 1	Cunningham 2	Murphy	Wallace	McLean; 65, 46, 12, 60; Connolly 25 secs
S	07-Oct	Airdrie		H	L1	1-1	3383	Reid	Bolton	Gray	Kinloch	Davidson	Porterfield	Lister r60	Sneddon	Wallace 1	Cunningham	Mackie	Murphy u60; 80; Marshall 3½
S	14-Oct	Hearts		H	L1	2-4	6962	Reid	Bolton	Gray	Kinloch	Davidson	Porterfield	Wallace 1	Stein	Cunningham 1	Sneddon	Mackie	McLean u60; 49, 17; Jensen (2) 6, 78 Traynor 10 Ford 20
S	21-Oct	Kilmarnock		A	L1	2-1	3417	Reid	Bolton r70	Gray	Kinloch	Davidson	Porterfield	Wallace 1	Stein	Cunningham 1	Sneddon	Mackie r60	Lister u70; 90, 34; Cameron 27
S	28-Oct	Partick Thistle		H	L1	3-3	3765	Reid	Bolton	Gray 1	Kinloch	Davidson	Porterfield	Wallace 2	Stein	Cunningham 1	Sneddon	Mackie	Lister; 62, 15; McParland 46½ O'Neill 58 Coulston 72
S	04-Nov	Morton		A	L1	3-3	5338	Reid	Bolton	Gray	Kinloch	Davidson	Porterfield	Wallace 2	Stein	Cunningham	Sneddon	Mackie	Lister; 50, 56, 71; Stevenson (2) 24, 37 Jensen 81
S	11-Nov	Aberdeen	8	A	L1	2-6	9420	Reid	Hislop	Gray	Stein	Davidson	Porterfield	Wallace	Sneddon	Cunningham	Falconer	Mackie	Falconer; 30, 85; (Aberdeen goalscorers — see note 8)
S	18-Nov	Dundee United		H	L1	0-1	4596	Reid s	Hislop	Gray	Stein	Davidson	Porterfield	Murphy	Sneddon	Wallace	Richardson	Falconer	Cunningham; Gillespie 28
S	25-Nov	Celtic		A	L1	0-2	16536	Reid	Hislop	Gray	Stein	Davidson	Porterfield	Murphy	Sneddon 2	Wallace 2	Richardson	Falconer	Cunningham; Gemmell 57 pen Wallace 65
S	02-Dec	Motherwell		H	L1	2-2	2931	Gray,J	Hislop	Gray	Stein	Davidson	Porterfield	Murphy	Sneddon	Wallace	Richardson	Falconer	Cunningham; 73, 89; Hogg 9 Campbell 41
S	09-Dec	Falkirk		A	L1	1-1	3177	Gray,J	Hislop	Gray	Stein	Davidson	Porterfield	Lister	Sneddon	Cunningham 1	Lister	Falconer	Murphy; 83; Graham 81
S	16-Dec	Rangers	9	A	L1	2-10	26432	Gray,J	Hislop	Gray	Stein	Davidson	Porterfield	Lister 1	Sneddon	Cunningham	Cunningham	Mackie	Murphy; Smith og 1 26, 80; (Rangers goalscorers — see note 9)
S	23-Dec	Dundee		A	L1	0-4	5548	Aitken	Selfridge	Gray	Stein	Davidson	Sneddon	Lister	Falconer	Falconer	Richardson	Mackie	Murphy; Gray,A og 37 McLean,J 57 Houston 61 McLean,G 66 pen
S	30-Dec	Clyde		H	L1	1-1	3778	Reid	Hislop	Gray	Stein	Gray	Sneddon	Wallace	Falconer	Murphy 1	Falconer	Wallace	Richardson; 28; Hood 8
M	01-Jan	Dunfermline Athletic		A	L1	0-6	6373	Reid	Selfridge	Gray	Stein	Gray	Sneddon	Murphy	Lister	Falconer	Richardson	Mackie	Cunningham; Paton (3) 38, 78, 81 Robertson (3) 43 pen, 70, 80
Tu	02-Jan	Hibernian		A	L1	2-2	6619	Reid	Hislop	Gray	Stein	Kinloch	Sneddon	Murphy	Wallace 1	Wallace	Richardson	Falconer	Cunningham; 80, 51; Cormack 16 Grant 63
S	20-Jan	Airdrie		A	L1	1-4	2347	Reid	Hislop	Gray	Bolton	Kinloch	Judge	Murphy	Wallace	Wallace	Mackie	Gillespie	Falconer; 43; Marshall 30 Goodwin (2) 32, 84 pen Jarvie 76
S	27-Jan	Aberdeen	2	A	SC 1	1-1	10719	Reid	Hislop	Gray	Bolton	Kinloch	Judge	Wallace	Wallace	Cunningham	Mackie	Gillespie 1	Judge; 10; Robb 23
W	31-Jan	Aberdeen		H	SC 1r	0-1	9000	Reid	Selfridge	Gray	Bolton	Davidson	Gray	Stein	Wallace	Wallace	Sneddon m	Gillespie	Judge; Reid og 68
S	10-Feb	Kilmarnock		H	L1	1-2	2986	Reid	Hislop	Gray	Stein	Davidson	Bolton	Mackie	Stein	Wallace 1	Sneddon	Gillespie 2	Judge; 84; Queen 64 pen Cameron 82
S	17-Feb	Stirling Albion	7	A	L1	7-0	1464	Reid	Hislop	Gray	Stein	Bolton	Sneddon	Wilson	Falconer 1	Wallace 2	Sneddon	Gillespie 2	Sneddon; (goal times — see note 7)
W	28-Feb	Partick Thistle		H	L1	0-3	3103	Reid	Hislop	Gray	Stein	Bolton	Millar,D	Wilson	Falconer 1	Wallace 2	Sneddon	Gillespie	Sneddon; Gallagher 6 Gibb 44 Coulston 50
S	02-Mar	Morton		H	L1	3-1	3572	Reid	Hislop	Gray	Stein	Polland	Millar,D	Wilson	Falconer 1	Wallace 2	Judge	Gillespie	Sneddon; 11, 19, 37; Allan 42 pen
M	04-Mar	Hearts		A	L1	2-0	6290	Reid	Hislop	Gray	Stein	Polland	Millar,D	Wilson	Falconer 1	Wallace 2	Judge	Gillespie r	Sneddon; 7, 75
S	09-Mar	Aberdeen		A	L1	3-1	5045	Reid	Hislop	Gray	Stein	Polland	Millar,D	Wilson	Falconer 1	Wallace 2	Judge	Gillespie 1	Sneddon; 36, 45, 63; Taylor 27 secs
S	16-Mar	Dundee United		H	L1	3-3	4455	Reid	Hislop	Gray	Stein	Polland	Millar,D	Wilson 1	Falconer	Wallace 3	Judge 1	Gillespie	Sneddon; 10, 17, 34; Mitchell 29 Wilson 58 Gillespie 84 pen
W	20-Mar	St Johnstone		H	L1	3-2	6122	Reid	Hislop	Gray	Stein	Polland	Millar,D	Wilson	Falconer 1	Wallace	Judge 1	Gillespie	Sneddon; 62, 55, 7; McCarry 2 Aitken 35
S	23-Mar	Celtic		A	L1	0-5	21477	Reid	Hislop	Gray	Bolton	Polland	Millar,D	Wilson r	Falconer 1	Wallace 3	Judge	Gillespie	Sneddon u; 51, 72, 73; Wallace (3) 17, 70, 74 Hughes 50 Lennox 54
S	30-Mar	Motherwell		H	L1	3-1	5161	Reid	Hislop	Gray	Stein	Polland	Millar,D	Millar,A r	Falconer 1	Wallace	Judge	Gillespie	Sneddon u 1; 61, 81; McInally 68
S	06-Apr	Falkirk		A	L1	2-3	3770	Reid	Hislop	Gray	Bolton	Polland	Millar,D	Falconer	Falconer 1	Wallace	Judge 2	Gillespie	Sneddon u; 66, 85; Georgeson 8 McLean, G. 18
S	13-Apr	Rangers	2	H	L1	2-3	18888	Reid	Hislop	Gray	Stein	Polland	Bolton	Millar,A r	Falconer	Wallace	Judge x	Gillespie	Sneddon u; Smith 23 Willoughby 38 Penman 84
S	20-Apr	Dundee		A	L1	0-2	5085	Reid	Hislop	Gray	Bolton	Polland	Bolton	Millar,A r	Stein	Wallace	Judge 2	Gillespie r	Bolton; 40, 58
Tu	30-Apr	Clyde		A	L1	0-5	1114	Reid	Hislop b	Gray	Stein b	Polland	Millar,D	Gillespie	Falconer	Wallace	Judge	Gillespie	Bolton; Slater (3) 14, 53, 56 Hastings 24 Glasgow 25 pen
Th	02-May	East Fife	5	A	FC F-1	2-1	—	Reid	Hislop	Gray	Millar,D 1	Polland	Sneddon	Cunningham	Falconer 2,1p	Wallace	Sneddon 2	Gillespie	Bolton; 75p, 87, 17, 78; Waddell 67
S	04-May	East Fife		H	FC F-2	2-2	3000	Reid	Hislop	Gray	Millar,D 1	Polland	Sneddon	Cunningham	Falconer 2	Wallace	Sneddon	Gillespie	Bolton; 90, 88; Dewar (2) 4, 43
S	18-May	Ross Co-Brora Select	3	A	F	4-2	2000	Reid	Gray	Hislop	Millar,D	Polland	Clifford	Gillespie	Falconer 2,1p	Sneddon 2	Murphy	Millar,A	Aitken u45; 24, 30, 44, 80; MacLennan (2) 39, 46
W	22-May	Inverness Select		A	F	4-2	—	Reid r45	Gray	Hislop	Millar,D	Bolton	Clifford	Millar,A	Falconer 2	Wallace 2	Judge	Wallace u45	Brownlee Allan 89
S	25-May	Moray-Nairn Select		A	F	6-2	—	Reid	Hislop	Gray	Millar,D	Davidson	Bolton 1	Millar,A	Falconer 2	Wallace	Richardson 1	Gillespie 1	Laing og 1; 65, 42, 50, 10, 63, 75; Thomson 85 Anderson 88

(1) Miller sent off 58 minutes

(2) Gate Receipts £2290

(3) Roddy Georgeson sent off

(4) The match was put back three days because of the Scottish Cup Final at Hampden (won by George Farm's Dunfermline, who included former Rovers Bobby Kinloch, Ian Lister and Pat Gardner),

(5) Dunfermline, with Cup and forthcoming American tour commitments, scratched from the final and East fife took their place.

(6) Goal times 80,35,88,18,70,86,69   (7) Goal times 39,70,71,74, 80,20,62   (8) Aberdeen goalscorers Johnston pen 42 Little 58 Petersen (2) 68 pen, 82 Mackie og 72 Wilson 87   (9) Rangers goalscorers Johnston (2) 2, 89 Ferguson (3) 34, 48, 77 Persson (2) 6, 84 Greig (2) 17, 73 pen Willoughby 35

Own goals scored by Stirling players Reid and Rogerson

Substitutes, own goals, goal times and opponents' scorers

Day	Date	Opponents	Note	Venue	Comp	Res	Att	1	2	3	4	5	6	7	8	9	10	11	Sub	Goals	Opponents' scorers
Th	01-Aug	Queens Park Rangers		H	F	1-3		Reid	Hislop	Gray	Stein	Poland	Millar,D	Wilson	Falconer 1p	Wallace	Sneddon	Gillespie	Bolton u 1	50	Clarke 19 Leitch 88 Morgan, I. 42
S	03-Aug	Wigan Athletic	4	A	F	4-4		Reid	Hislop	Gray	Stein	Poland	Millar,D 1	Wilson	Judge 1	Falconer 1	Sneddon	Gillespie	Stein	Aitken u	Ryan (2) 40 secs, 24 Sealey 43 Cairney 44
S	10-Aug	Falkirk		A	LCS	1-1	3606	Reid	Hislop	Gray	Millar,D	Poland	Bolton	Wilson	Falconer 1	Wallace	Sneddon	Gillespie	Stein	19	Young 33
W	14-Aug	Hibernian		H	LCS	0-1	6654	Reid	Hislop	Gray	Millar,D	Poland	Bolton	Wilson	Falconer b	Wallace	Sneddon	Gillespie	Stein		O'Rourke 14
S	17-Aug	St Johnstone		A	LCS	0-0	3956	Reid	Hislop	Gray	Millar,D	Poland	Bolton	Wilson	Falconer	Wallace	Sneddon	Gillespie	Stein		
S	24-Aug	Falkirk		H	LCS	4-2	4402	Reid	Hislop	Gray	Millar,D	Poland	Bolton	Wilson	Judge 2	Wallace	Sneddon x40	Gillespie	Stein	96, 51, 74, 29	Young 11 Frickleton 22
W	28-Aug	Hibernian	1	A	LCS	0-3	7929	Reid	Hislop	Gray	Millar,D	Poland	Bolton	Wilson	Falconer	Wallace	Sneddon	Gillespie	Stein		Stanton Marinello (2) 65, 70
S	31-Aug	St Johnstone		H	LCS	2-1	3693	Reid	Hislop	Gray	Millar,D	Poland	Bolton	Wilson	Judge r84	Wallace	Sneddon	Gillespie	Stein u84	6, 84	Whitelaw 40
S	07-Sep	Dunfermline Athletic		A	L1	2-3	7461	Reid	Stein	Gray	Millar,D	Poland	Bolton	Wilson	Falconer 1p	Wallace	Judge 1	Gillespie	Stein	20, 55	Paton (2) 9, 67 Lister pen 82
S	14-Sep	Hibernian	2	H	L1	2-0	5610	Reid	Stein	Gray	Millar,D	Poland	Bolton	Wilson	Falconer 1	Wallace	Judge 1	Gillespie r5	Hislop u5	44, 26	
S	21-Sep	Clyde		A	L1	2-3	2267	Reid	Hislop	Gray	Millar,D 1	Poland	Bolton	Wilson	Falconer 1	Wallace	Judge	Gillespie	Hislop	57, 65	Hood 18 Staite 32 Hastings 48
S	28-Sep	Morton		H	L1	0-1	4248	Reid	Hislop	Gray	Millar,D	Poland	Bolton	Wilson	Falconer	Wallace	Sneddon	Purcell r64	Stein u64		Harper 86
S	05-Oct	St Mirren		A	L1	2-2	5576	Reid	Hislop	Gray	Millar,D 1	Poland	Bolton r45	Wilson	Falconer	Wallace 2	Judge	Sneddon	Weir u45	17, 76	Kane (2) 2, 78
S	12-Oct	Arbroath		H	L1	3-1	3365	Reid	Hislop	Gray	Millar,D	Poland	Davidson	Wilson	Falconer 1	Wallace	Judge	Sneddon	Millar,A	34, 16, 41	Bruce 65
S	19-Oct	Partick Thistle		A	L1	3-0	4128	Reid	Hislop	Gray	Millar,D	Poland	Bolton	Wilson 1	Falconer 2	Wallace	Sneddon	Gillespie 1	Judge	27, 54, 57	
S	26-Oct	Kilmarnock		A	L1	4-4	4461	Reid	Hislop	Gray	Millar,D	Poland	Bolton	Wilson	Falconer 2	Wallace 1	Sneddon	Gillespie 1	Judge	8, 23, 33, 44	McLean, T (2) 57 pen, 89 Morrison 67 McIlroy 84
S	02-Nov	Aberdeen		H	L1	1-2	8414	Reid	Hislop	Gray	Millar,D	McDonald	Bolton	Wilson	Falconer	Wallace	Judge	Gillespie	Sneddon	24	Forrest 23 Craig 60 pen
S	09-Nov	Dundee United		A	L1	1-2	5069	Reid	Hislop	Gray	Millar,D	Poland	Bolton	Wilson 1	Falconer	Wallace	Sneddon	Gillespie u80	Judge u80	85	Mitchell 57 Cameron, K 60
S	16-Nov	Celtic		H	L1	0-2	31220	Reid x	Hislop	Weir b	Millar,D	Poland	Bolton	Wilson	Falconer	Wallace	Sneddon	Gillespie	Richardson		Murdoch (2) 12, 74
S	23-Nov	Falkirk		H	L1	3-1	3808	Reid	Hislop	Weir	Millar,D	Poland	Bolton	Wilson	Falconer	Sneddon	Wallace 1	Gillespie	Judge	76, 44, 89	Gibson 81
S	30-Nov	St Johnstone		A	L1	0-3	3644	Reid	Hislop	Weir b	Millar,D	Poland	Bolton	Wilson	Falconer	Sneddon r67	Wallace	Gillespie	Judge u67		Hall 4 Aitken 16 Whitelaw 42
S	07-Dec	Rangers	3	H	L1	0-3	13470	Reid	Hislop	Weir	Millar,D	Poland	Bolton	Wilson	Wallace	Sneddon	Watt	Gillespie	Judge		McDonald 47 Stein 75 Watson 83
S	14-Dec	Hearts		A	L1	0-1	6898	Reid	Hislop	Weir	Millar,D	Poland	Bolton	Wilson	Wallace	Judge r81	Watt	Sneddon	Falconer u81		Gordon 63
S	21-Dec	Airdrie		H	L1	1-2	3086	Reid	Hislop	Gray	Millar,D	Poland	Bolton	Wilson	Falconer	Wallace 1	Judge	Gillespie	Sneddon	25 secs	McPheat 29 Jarvie 48
W	01-Jan	Dunfermline Athletic		H	L1	0-3	10071	Reid	Hislop	Gray	Stein	Poland	Bolton	Wilson	Falconer	Wallace	Wallace	Wallace	Sneddon		Edwards 55 Gardner (2) 59, 77
Th	02-Jan	Hibernian		A	L1	0-3	11499	Reid	Hislop	Gray	Millar,D	Bolton	Millar,D	Wallace	Falconer	Wallace	Sneddon	Gillespie	McDonald		McBride (2) 13, 42 Cormack 67
S	04-Jan	Clyde		H	L1	1-1	3909	Whiteside	McDonald b	Gray	Millar,D	Poland	Bolton	Wilson	Wallace	Richardson	Sneddon	Watt r34	Stein u34 1	59	McHugh 67
S	11-Jan	Morton		A	L1	2-3	4909	Whiteside	McDonald	Gray	Millar,D	Poland	Bolton	Cunningham	Stein	Wallace 2	Richardson	Sneddon	Watt	36, 63	Bartram (2) 16, 22 Harper 70 pen
S	18-Jan	St Mirren		H	L1	0-2	3647	Reid	McDonald	Gray	Millar,D	Poland	Bolton	Cunningham	Falconer	Wilson	Sneddon r	Watt	Gillespie u		McLaughlin 44 Blair 81
S	25-Jan	Dunfermline Athletic		H	SC 1	0-2	10500	Whiteside	McDonald b	Gray b	Millar,D	Poland	Bolton	Cunningham	Stein b	Stein b	Wallace	Watt	Falconer		Gardner 67 Paton 80
S	01-Feb	Arbroath		A	L1	1-0	2305	Reid	McDonald	Gray	Millar,D	Poland	Bolton x	Cunningham	Falconer 1	Wallace	Sneddon	Wilson	Stein	30	
Tu	11-Feb	Partick Thistle		H	L1	1-2	2274	Reid	McDonald	Gray	Millar,D	Poland	Bolton	Cunningham	Falconer	Wallace b	Sneddon	Wilson 1	Stein	44	Flanagan (2) 33, 89 pen
W	26-Feb	Kilmarnock		H	L1	0-0	2846	Reid	McDonald	Gray	Millar,D	Poland	Bolton	Cunningham	Falconer	Wallace 1	Sneddon	Wilson 1	Millar,A		
W	05-Mar	Dundee United		H	L1	1-3	3769	Reid	McDonald	Gray b	Millar,D m	Poland	Bolton	Cunningham	Falconer	Wallace 1	Sneddon	Wilson	Judge	8	Wood 1 Cameron, K (2) 36, 64
S	08-Mar	Celtic		A	L1	1-3	14292	Reid	McDonald	Gray	Millar,D	Poland	Bolton	Cunningham	Falconer	Wallace 1	Sneddon	Wilson	Judge u83	46	Wallace (2) 63, 89 Auld 80
S	15-Mar	Falkirk		H	L1	3-1	5532	Reid	McDonald	Gray	Millar,D	Poland	Bolton	Millar,A b	Falconer 2	Wallace	Sneddon r83 1	Wilson	Judge u62	19, 81, 21	Graham 65
W	19-Mar	Aberdeen		H	L1	3-2	3559	Reid	McDonald	Gray	Millar,D 1	Poland	Bolton	Millar,A	Falconer r62	Wallace 1	Sneddon 1	Wilson	Judge u60	61, 3, 77	Johnston 4 Forrest 52
S	22-Mar	Dundee		H	L1	1-5	6029	Reid	McDonald	Gray	Millar,D m	Poland	Bolton	Millar,A	Falconer r60	Wallace 1	Sneddon 1	Wilson	Judge u75	35	Hall (3) 20, 27, 89 Connelly 33 Aitken 47
W	26-Mar	Dundee		A	L1	2-2	4783	Reid	McDonald	Gray	Millar,D	Poland	Bolton	Wilson r75 1	Falconer	Wallace 1	Sneddon	Gillespie	Stein u69	20, 53	Bryce 3 Duncan 50
S	29-Mar	Rangers		H	L1	1-2	27671	Reid	McDonald	Gray	Millar,D	Poland	Bolton	Millar,A r69	Falconer 1	Wallace	Sneddon	Gillespie	Judge	58	Penman 46 Johnston 88
S	05-Apr	Hearts		H	L1	0-3	6242	Reid	McDonald	Gray	Millar,D	Poland	Bolton	Wilson	Wilson	Wallace	Sneddon	Gillespie	Judge		Irvine 35 Traynor 74 Ford 87
S	12-Apr	Airdrie		A	L1	0-2	3187	Reid	McDonald	Gray	Millar,D	Poland	Bolton	Wilson	Falconer	Wallace	Sneddon	Gillespie	Stein		Marshall 63 Whiteford, D 80
S	19-Apr	Dundee		H	L1	4-0	4791	Reid	McDonald	Gray	Millar,D	Poland	Bolton	Cunningham	Falconer 1p	Wallace 2	Sneddon	Wilson 1	Judge	55, 44, 71, 30	
W	23-Apr	Cowdenbeath		H	FC SF	2-0		Whiteside	McDonald	Gray	Cooper	Bolton	Polland	Wilson	Judge	Wallace 2	Watt r75	Falconer	Selfridge u75	44, 52	
Tu	29-Apr	East Fife		H	FC F-1	2-1		Reid	McDonald	Gray	Bolton	Buchanan	Cooper	Millar,A 2	Judge	Wallace	Sneddon	Wilson	Falconer	63, 78	
F	02-May	East Fife		A	FC F-2	2-0	2000	Reid	McDonald	Gray	Bolton	Buchanan	Polland	Millar,A	Watt	Wallace 1	Falconer r45	Wilson r45	Judge u45	45, 50	Dewar 48

Manager : Tommy Walker to 29th January. Jimmy Miller from 9th February

(1) Quinn sent off along with Sneddon in 40 minutes
(2) Colin Stein sent off
(3) John Greig missed penalty 53 minutes
(4) Goal times 78, 21, 28, 82

Day	Date	Opponents	Note	Venue	Comp	Res	Att	1	2	3	4	5	6	7	8	9	10	11	Substitute	Goal times	Opponents scorers
S	26-Jul	Millwall	3	A	F	1-4		Reid	McDonald	Weir	Millar,D	Polland	Bolton	Millar,A r	Falconer	Wallace	Sneddon r	Wilson,P r	Davidson u	16	Possee (3) 7, 12, 70 Dear 82
M	28-Jul	Brentwood		A	F	1-1		Whiteside	McDonald	Gray	Polland	Bolton	Watt	Sinclair 1	Falconer	Wallace	Davidson	Sneddon	Gray		Loughton 47
S	02-Aug	Millwall		H	F	1-2		Whiteside	McDonald	Gray	Millar,D	Polland	Bolton	Millar,A r	Falconer	Wallace	Sneddon	Watt r45 1	McManus u45	21	Weller 15 Dear 31
S	09-Aug	Rangers		H	LCS	2-3	17784	Reid	McDonald r	Gray	Millar,D	Polland	Bolton	Millar,A 1	Sinclair 1	Wallace	Sneddon	Wilson,P	Davidson u b		Johansen 15 Stein 36 McDonald 72
W	13-Aug	Airdrie		A	LCS	1-3	2152	Reid	Hislop	Gray	Millar,D b	Polland	Bolton	Millar,A	Sinclair	Wallace	Sneddon	Wilson,P	Watt	12	Fyfe 32 Marshall 55 Menzies 88
S	16-Aug	Celtic		A	LCS	0-5	34436	Reid	Hislop	Gray	Millar,D	Polland	Davidson	Millar,A	Sinclair	Wallace	Sneddon	Wilson,P	Watt		Wallace (2) Hood McNeill Hughes
W	20-Aug	Airdrie		H	LCS	2-1	2907	Reid	Hislop	Gray	Millar,D	Polland	Davidson	Millar,A 1	Sneddon r	Wallace 2	Sinclair 1	Wilson,P	Watt u	29, 28	Marshall 16
S	23-Aug	Rangers		H	LCS	3-3	38040	Reid	Hislop	Gray	Millar,D	Polland	Davidson b	Millar,A 1	Lindsay	Wallace 2	Sinclair b 1	Wilson,P	McDonald	39, 71, 81	Polland og 31 Penman 57 McDonald 83
W	27-Aug	Celtic		H	LCS	2-5	17733	Reid	Hislop	Gray	Millar,D r	Polland	Davidson	Millar,A 1	Sneddon	Wallace 1	Sinclair 1	Wilson,P	McDonald	68, 80	Chalmers (2) 2, 87 Hood (2) 17, 56 Brogan 50
S	30-Aug	Airdrie		H	L1	1-0	4245	Reid	Hislop	Gray	Millar,D	Polland	Davidson	Millar,A	Sneddon	Wallace	Sinclair 1	Brand	Lindsay u	21	
W	03-Sep	Morton		H	L1	1-2	5565	Reid	Hislop	Gray	Millar,D	Polland	McDonald	Millar,A	McDonald	Wallace	Sinclair 1	Watt r	Lindsay u	15	Harper 10 Mason 49
S	06-Sep	Kilmarnock		A	L1	0-1	3884	Reid	Hislop	Gray	Millar,D	Polland	McDonald r45 b	Millar,A r	Falconer	Wallace	Brand	Watt	Wilson,J		Mathie
S	13-Sep	Dundee		H	L1	0-0	4741	Reid	Gray	Gray	Cooper	Polland	Lindsay	Millar,A	Brand	Sinclair 1	Brand	Sinclair	Lindsay u45		
S	20-Sep	Hibernian		A	L1	1-3	8477	Reid	Gray	Gray	Millar,D	Polland	Lindsay	Millar,A r	Brand	Sinclair 1	Sinclair	Falconer	Sneddon u	46	Marinello 17 Sheviane 53 McBride 65
S	27-Sep	Dunfermline Athletic		H	L1	1-1	7639	Reid	Hislop	Gray	Millar,D	Polland	Cooper	Millar,A	Falconer	Mitchell	Brand	Wilson,P r	Wilson,P u	12	McLean 24
S	04-Oct	Celtic	4	A	L1	1-7	31933	Reid	McDonald	Lindsay b	Millar,D	Polland	Cooper	Millar,A	Brand 1	Sinclair 1	Watt	Gillespie	McManus u	41	
S	11-Oct	St Mirren		H	L1	1-3	3891	Reid	Hislop	Lindsay	Cooper	Polland	Cooper	Falconer	Brand	Sinclair	Sinclair 1	Gillespie r60	Bolton u	33	Blair (3) 24, 30, 84
W	15-Oct	Cowdenbeath		H	FC SF	0-2	2000	Reid	McDonald	Gray	Cooper	Polland b	Millar,D	Millar,A r	McGuire	Sinclair	Brand	Gillespie	Millar,A u60		Bostock 8 Dickson 87
S	18-Oct	Partick Thistle		A	L1	1-1	4225	Reid	Hislop	Gray	Davidson	Polland	Cooper b	Falconer	McGuire	Brand	Brand	Mitchell 1	Millar,A u	79	Bone 17
S	25-Oct	Motherwell		H	L1	2-2	3513	Reid	Gray	Weir	Davidson	Polland	Cooper	Millar,A	McGuire	Mitchell 2	Brand	Sinclair	Millar,D	67, 72	Murray 32 Murphy 70
S	01-Nov	Hearts		A	L1	2-3	6231	Reid	Gray	Weir	Bolton	Polland b	Cooper	Millar,A	McGuire	McGuire	Judge 2	Brand	Millar,D	62, 75	Moller 35 McDonald (2) 55, 61
S	08-Nov	St Johnstone		H	L1	1-0	4894	Reid	Gray	Weir	Bolton	Polland	Cooper	Millar,A	McGuire	Judge 1	Sinclair	Sneddon	Sneddon u65	86	
S	15-Nov	Ayr United		A	L1	1-2	5973	Reid	Gray	Weir	Millar,D b	Polland 1	Millar,D b	Millar,A r	McGuire	Judge	Brand	Sneddon	Lindsay	89	Hood 63 Ingram 70
S	22-Nov	Dundee United		H	L1	0-1	2771	Reid	McDonald	McDonald	Bolton	Polland	Bolton	Brand	McGuire	Judge	Falconer	Sneddon	Wilson,P u		Wilson 20
S	29-Nov	Rangers		A	L1	0-3	23948	Reid	Lindsay	Lindsay	Bolton	Polland	Bolton	Brand	McGuire	Judge	Falconer	Falconer	Millar,D		Johnston 8 Stein 37 McDonald 62
S	06-Dec	Clyde		H	L1	1-1	2037	Reid	McDonald	Weir x	McDonald	Polland	Cooper r75	Brand	McGuire b	Judge 1	Sinclair	Falconer	Sneddon u75	41	Hulston 22
S	13-Dec	Airdrie	1	A	L1	2-1	3178	Reid	McDonald	Lindsay	Bolton	Polland	Sneddon	McGuire	Judge	Sneddon	Falconer	Brand 1	Cooper	49, 48	Marshall 43
S	20-Dec	Morton		H	L1	0-1	3743	Reid	McDonald	Lindsay	McDonald	Polland r30	Buchanan	McGuire	Judge 1	Sneddon	Bolton b	Brand 1	Wilson,P		Osborne 23
S	27-Dec	Aberdeen		H	L1	0-3	7510	Reid	McDonald	Lindsay	McDonald	Bolton	Buchanan	McGuire	Judge	Sneddon	Sinclair	Millar,A r72	Sinclair		Murray 30 Harper (3) 33 pen, 78, 81 Robb 63
Th	01-Jan	Dunfermline Athletic		A	L1	0-3	5644	Reid	Hislop	Lindsay	McDonald	Bolton	Buchanan	Hislop	Judge	Vincent	McGuire	Bolton	Polland u72		Gillespie (2) 30, 73 Edwards 51
S	03-Jan	Hibernian		H	L1	1-5	8336	Reid	Hislop	Lindsay	Hislop	Buchanan	Gray r53	Judge	McGuire	Vincent	McGuire	Falconer	Cooper u53	6	Graham (2) 37, 89 Cormack 60
S	10-Jan	Aberdeen		A	L1	0-0	4561	Reid	Hislop b	Lindsay	Cooper	Buchanan	Buchanan	Judge	Millar,A	Judge	McGuire	Vincent	Wilson,J		
S	17-Jan	Dundee		H	L1	0-3	6893	Whiteside	Hislop	Lindsay	Cooper	Polland	Bolton	Millar,A	Millar,D r55	Sinclair	McGuire	Brand	McGuire		Waddell, R. 12 Finlayson (2) 52, 56
S	24-Jan	East Fife		A	SC 3	2-3	2313	Whiteside	Hislop	Lindsay	Cooper r60	Polland	Bolton	Millar,A r1	Millar,D	Sinclair	McGuire	Brand 1	Judge u55	23, 16	McDonald 84 Morrison 85 Mathie 88
S	31-Jan	Kilmarnock		H	L1	1-1	1711	Whiteside	Hislop	Weir	Cooper	Polland	Bolton b	Millar,A	Millar,D	Sinclair	McGuire	Brand 1	Sneddon u60	9	Hulston 14
S	07-Feb	Clyde		A	L1	0-2	3743	Whiteside	Hislop	Weir b	Cooper	Buchanan	Bolton	Millar,A	Millar,D	Sinclair	McGuire	Brand 1	Sneddon u30		Hamilton 5
W	25-Feb	Celtic		H	L1	0-2	8324	Whiteside	Hislop	Weir	Cooper	Bolton	Sneddon	Wilson,P	Sinclair	Sinclair	McGuire	Brand	Buchanan		McNeill 2 Gemmell 59
S	28-Feb	St Mirren		A	L1	3-3	4288	Whiteside	Hislop	Weir	Cooper	Bolton	Sneddon	Wilson,P	McCarthy	Sinclair	McGuire 2	Brand	Buchanan	40, 19, 38	Blair (2) 60, 85 Lister 78 pen
W	04-Mar	Hibernian		A	L1	0-3	2370	Whiteside	Hislop	Weir	Cooper	Bolton	Sneddon	McCarthy	McCarthy r60	Judge r	McGuire b	Brand	Buchanan		Cowan 4 Jarvie 48 Goodwin 52
S	07-Mar	Partick Thistle		H	L1	1-1	2596	Reid	Brown	Lindsay b	Cooper	Bolton	Sneddon	Millar,A	Wilson,J	Judge r75	McGuire	Wilson,P 1	Watt u60	88	Flanigan 84
W	11-Mar	Rangers		A	L1	1-1	6380	Reid	Brown	Lindsay	Bolton	Buchanan	Sneddon	Millar,A r1	Cooper 1	Judge	McGuire	Wilson,P	Watt u75	42	Penman 26
S	14-Mar	Motherwell		A	L1	0-1	4848	Reid	Brown	Lindsay	Bolton	Buchanan	Sneddon	Millar,A	Cooper 1	Judge r	McGuire	Wilson,P	McCarthy u		Muir 27
S	21-Mar	Hearts		H	L1	0-3	4936	Reid	Brown	Lindsay	Bolton	Buchanan	Sneddon	Brand	Watt	Judge	McGuire	Wilson,P	Watt u b		Townsend (2) 10, 60 Traynor 89
S	28-Mar	St Johnstone		A	L1	1-1	3572	Reid	Gray r50	Lindsay	Bolton	Polland	Sneddon	Falconer 1	Cooper	Judge	Brand 1	Wilson,P	McCarthy	89	Wilson 83
S	04-Apr	Ayr United	2	H	L1	1-1	1995	Reid	Gray	Weir	Bolton x88	Polland b	Sneddon	Millar,A r60	Cooper	Wilson,P	Sinclair	Falconer m	McGuire u60 x88	88	Malone 58
S	18-Apr	Dundee United		A	L1	2-4	3757	Reid	Brown b	Lindsay b	Wilson,J	Polland b	Cooper	Wilson,P 1	McGuire	Mitchell	Sinclair	Falconer 1p	Hislop	73, 59	Mitchell (3) 3, 42, 57 pen Henry 31

Rovers goal 83

Manager : Jimmy Millar

(1) abandoned half time

(2) Quinton Young sent off 88 minutes

(3) Substitute Sinclair u***

(4) Celtic goalscorers Johnstone (2) 13, 20 Lennox (2) 37, 63 Callaghan 67 Wallace 38 Hughes 73

Substitutes, own goals, goal times and opponents' scorers

Day	Date	Opponents	Note	Venue	Comp	Res.	Att.	1	2	3	4	5	6	7	8	9	10	11	Substitutes, goal times & opponents' scorers
S	01-Aug	Hartlepool	8	A	F	1-2		Reid r 45	Gray	Lindsay	Wilson,J	Wilkinson	Sneddon	Hogg	Wallace	Falconer	Cooper	Wilson,P	McDermott u45 · Sinclair u · Sharkley (2)
W	05-Aug	Hartlepool		H	F	1-4		Reid r**	Gray	Lindsay	Millar,D	Wilkinson	Sneddon	Hogg	Wilson,P r*	Wallace 1	Cooper	Falconer	McDermott u** · Mitchell u** 30 · Young (2) 42, 48 Dawes 62 Clarke 82
S	08-Aug	Montrose		H	LCS	1-0	2350	Reid	Gray	Lindsay	Millar,D	Wilkinson	Sneddon	Wilson,P	Sinclair 1	Wallace	Sneddon 1	McCarthy	Falconer 62
W	12-Aug	East Stirling		A	LCS	0-2	800	Reid	Gray	Lindsay	Millar,D r30	Wilkinson	Sneddon	Wilson,P	Sinclair	Wallace	Clark	McCarthy	Brown u30 · Miller 55 Harper 79
S	15-Aug	Cowdenbeath		A	LCS	1-3	2168	Reid	Brown	Lindsay	Wilkinson	Gray	McGuire	Wilson,P	Sneddon	Mitchell	Mitchell	Wallace	McCarthy 79 · Dickson 22 Mullen 56 Kinnell 60 pen
W	19-Aug	East Stirling		H	LCS	2-1	1991	Reid	Brown	Lindsay	Gray	Wilkinson	Sneddon	Wilson,P 1	McGuire	Wallace	Clark 1	Sinclair 1	McCarthy 66, 11 · Sinclair og 60
S	22-Aug	Montrose		H	LCS	1-4	1280	Reid	Brown	Lindsay	Gray	Wilkinson	Sneddon	Wilson,P	McGuire	Wallace	Clark	Sinclair	McCarthy 71 · Crammond 39 Livingstone 41 Kemp (2) 76, 84
W	26-Aug	Cowdenbeath		H	LCS	0-2	3077	Reid	Gray	Lindsay	Millar,D	Wilkinson	Wood	Wilson,P	McCarthy	Wallace	McGuire 1	Sinclair	McCarthy · Dickson 43 Ross 70
W	02-Sep	Arbroath		H	L2	1-1	1757	Reid	Gray	Lindsay	Millar,D	Cooper	Sneddon	Wilson,P	McCarthy 1	Wallace	McGuire	Cormack	Sinclair 68 · Jack 41
S	05-Sep	East Fife	9	A	L2	1-5	4288	Reid x	Gray	Lindsay	Millar,D	Cooper	Sneddon	Wilson,P	McCarthy r	Wallace r	McGuire x	Cormack 1	Sinclair u 19 · [9] Finlayson (2) 14, 31 Miller 34 pen Honeyman 39 Cooper og 47
W	09-Sep	Clydebank		A	L2	0-3	1042	Reid	Gray	Lindsay	Millar,D	Brown	Cooper	Wilson,P	McGuire	Wallace	Sinclair	Cormack	McCarthy · Gray og Kane Munro
S	12-Sep	Stenhousemuir		H	L2	4-1	1597	Reid	Gray	Lindsay	Millar,D	Brown	Cooper	Wilson,P	McGuire	Wallace	Sinclair 4	Cormack	McCarthy 35, 55, 57, 67 · Murdoch 32
W	16-Sep	Clydebank		H	L2	1-1	1651	Reid	Gray	Lindsay	Millar,D	Brown	Cooper	Wilson,P	McGuire	Wallace 1	Sinclair	Cormack	McCarthy 6 · Caskie 84
S	19-Sep	Forfar Athletic		A	L2	3-3	1487	Reid	Gray	Lindsay	Millar,D	Brown	Cooper	Georgeson	McGuire 1	Wallace 2,1p	Sinclair	Cormack	Wilkinson 18, 61p, 73 · Stewart 23 Kinner 25 Reid 40
W	23-Sep	Arbroath		A	L2	0-4	1725	Reid	Gray	Lindsay	Millar,D	Brown	Cooper	Georgeson	McGuire	Wallace	Sinclair	Cormack	Wilkinson · Cant 40 Bruce (3) 42, 73, 75
S	26-Sep	Brechin City		H	L2	2-0	1909	McDermott	Gray	Lindsay	Millar,D	Brown	Cooper	Georgeson	McGuire 1p	Wallace	McGuire 1p	Sinclair	Wilson,P 57, 74
S	03-Oct	Stirling Albion		A	L2	1-0	1447	McDermott	Gray	Lindsay	Millar,D	Wilkinson	Sneddon	Georgeson	Georgeson	Wallace	Georgeson	Cormack	Millar,Do 82
S	10-Oct	East Stirling		H	L2	1-1	1960	McDermott	Gray	Lindsay	Millar,D	Wilkinson	Lindsay	Wilson,P	Georgeson	Wallace 1	Georgeson	Cormack	Hislop 68 · Hamill 19
S	17-Oct	Dumbarton		H	L2	0-2	2323	McDermott	Gray	Lindsay	Millar,D	Wilkinson	Lindsay	Wilson,P 1	Georgeson	Wallace	McGuire	Sinclair	Millar,Do · Gallagher, B. 65 McCormack 81
S	24-Oct	Albion Rovers		H	L2	2-2	1933	McDermott	Hislop	Gray	Millar,D	Wilkinson	Lindsay	Wilson,P 1	Georgeson	Wallace	McGuire b 1p	McGuire	Sneddon 90, 11 · McCallan 85
S	31-Oct	Alloa Athletic		H	L2	4-1	1990	McDermott	Hislop	Lindsay	Millar,D	Wilkinson	Cooper	Wilson,P 1	Mitchell 2	Mitchell	Mitchell 2	McGuire	Cormack 1 25, 82, 9, 51 · Coulston 71
S	07-Nov	Partick Thistle		A	L2	0-1	3827	McDermott	Hislop	Gray	Millar,Do 65	Lindsay	Cooper	Wilson,P 1	Mitchell	Wallace	Georgeson 1	McGuire	Beveridge · Campbell (Thistle scored)
S	14-Nov	Queen's Park		H	L2	6-4	2213	McDermott	Hislop	Gray	Millar,D	Lindsay	Cooper	Wilson,P 1	Wallace 2	Mitchell	Georgeson 1	McGuire 1p	Cormack u65 38, 48, 55, 90, 86, 21 · Campbell 57 Bill 63 Fearn 84 Morrison 88
S	21-Nov	Queen of the South		A	L2	1-0	1732	McDermott	Hislop	Gray	Cooper	Innes	Lindsay	Wilson,P	Wallace 1	Mitchell	Georgeson b	McGuire	Millar,Do 60
S	28-Nov	Montrose		H	L2	2-2	2468	McDermott	Hislop	Gray	Cooper	Innes	Lindsay 1	Wilson,P	Wallace 1	Mitchell	Georgeson 1	McGuire r70	Sinclair u70 18, 37 · Young 48 Crammond 64
S	05-Dec	Berwick Rangers		A	L2	2-0	801	McDermott	Brown	Gray	Cooper	Innes	Lindsay	Wilson,P	Wallace 1	Mitchell	Georgeson 1	McGuire	Sinclair u 89, 60 · [8 Clark u scored 89]
M	07-Dec	Celtic XI		H	F	2-2	3000	McDermott	Gray	Beveridge	Cooper	Wilkinson	Lindsay	McGuire	Main	Mitchell	Sinclair b	McGuire b 2,1p	Hislop 26, 44p · Wilson 15 Wallace 58
S	12-Dec	Stranraer		A	L2	0-1	2454	McDermott	Wilkinson	Beveridge	Cooper	Wilkinson	Lindsay	McGuire	Wallace	Mitchell	Georgeson	Sinclair	Hislop · Collings 32
S	26-Dec	Hamilton Academical		H	L2	1-0	848	McDermott	Gray	Gray	Cooper	Thomson	Lindsay	McGuire	Wallace r55	Mitchell 1	Georgeson	McGuire	McCarthy u55 71
F	01-Jan	East Fife		H	L2	2-1	8737	McDermott	Gray	Beveridge	Cooper	Thomson b	Lindsay	McGuire	Wallace	Mitchell 1	Georgeson 1	Wilson,P r70	Innes u70 45, 57 · Miller 11
S	02-Jan	Stenhousemuir		A	L2	3-3	1223	McDermott	Gray	Beveridge r50	Innes 1	Thomson	Lindsay	Cooper	Wallace	Mitchell 1	Georgeson 1	Wilkie	Briggs u50 74, 57, 67 · Jamieson 63 McPaul 88 Thomson og 90
S	09-Jan	Forfar Athletic		H	L2	3-2	2610	McDermott	Wilkinson	Beveridge	Innes	Thomson	Lindsay	Wilson,P r55	Wallace 1	Mitchell	Georgeson 2,1p	Wilkie	Cooper u55 17, 10p, 50 · Stewart 60 McInnes 90
S	16-Jan	Brechin City		A	L2	4-1	504	McDermott	Wilkinson	Beveridge	Innes 1	Thomson	Lindsay	Sneddon	Sneddon	Mitchell	Georgeson 1p	Wilkie	Cooper u 1 70, 84, 12, 87 · Reid 61
S	23-Jan	St Johnstone		A	SC 3	2-2	5187	McDermott	Wilkinson	Gray	Hislop	Thomson	Lindsay	Mitchell r	Wallace	Sinclair	Georgeson 1	Innes 1	Mitchell 77, 79 · Pearson 37 Aird 51
Tu	26-Jan	St Johnstone	1	H	SC 3r	4-3	8438	McDermott	Wilkinson	Gray	Innes	Thomson	Lindsay	Cooper	Wallace 1	Sinclair 3	Georgeson 1	Hislop	Mitchell u60 8, 16, 50, 63 · Rooney 14 Connelly 45 Hall 81
S	30-Jan	Stirling Albion		H	L2	1-2	3799	McDermott	Wilkinson r60	Gray	Hislop	Thomson	Lindsay	Cooper	Wallace 1	Sinclair 1	Georgeson	Innes	Innes u77 65 · Dowds 43 McMillan 60
S	06-Feb	East Stirling		A	L2	2-4	587	McDermott	Gray	Beveridge	Innes r	Thomson	Lindsay	Wilson,I	Wilson,I	Sinclair	Clark	Wilkie 1	Clark 45, 72 · Donachie (2) 20, 25 Miller 59 McQuade 84
S	13-Feb	Clyde	2	H	SC 4	1-1	5902	McDermott	Gray	Beveridge	Cooper	Thomson	Lindsay	Wilson,P 1	Wallace r77	Sinclair 1	Georgeson	McGuire	Mitchell 49 · Hastings 69
W	17-Feb	Clyde	3	A	SC 4r	2-0	2656	McDermott	Gray	Beveridge	Cooper	Thomson	Lindsay	Hislop	Wallace 2	Sinclair 1	Georgeson	McGuire	Mitchell 57, 55
S	20-Feb	Dumbarton		H	L2	3-0	2889	McDermott	Beveridge	Beveridge	Cooper	Thomson r24	Lindsay	Hislop	Wallace	Sinclair r	Georgeson	McGuire 1p	Wilkinson u45 55, 84, 81
S	27-Feb	Albion Rovers		A	L2	0-2	608	McDermott	Innes	Gray	Cooper	Thomson r	Lindsay b	Hislop r45	McGuire	Mitchell r45	Mitchell 1	Wilkie r45	Wilkinson · Corrigan 2 Ferris 30
Tu	02-Mar	Dundee United XI	7	H	F	1-1		Reid	Hislop	Gray	Beveridge	Thomson	Lindsay	Wallace	Sinclair	Mitchell r45	Sinclair 1	McGuire	Wilkinson 65 · Innes og 40 · Wilson,I u45
Tu	06-Mar	Celtic	4	A	SC QF	1-7	32000	Reid	Hislop	Gray	Dempsey	Innes	Lindsay	Marshall	Wallace	Innes	Georgeson 1	Sneddon	Wilkie u54 · [4] Celtic: Lennox (3) 22, 27, 82 Wallace 72 Gemmell 37 pen Callaghan 53 Davidson 75 · Sinclair's goal 88
S	13-Mar	Partick Thistle		H	L2	0-2	3606	McDermott	Hislop	Gray	Dempsey	Innes	Lindsay	Wallace r4	Dempsey	Sinclair r54	Mitchell	Wilkie	Wilkie u54 · Lawrie 7 Coulston 56
S	20-Mar	Queen's Park	5	A	L2	1-0	850	McDermott s80	Hislop 1	Gray b 1	Wilkinson	Lindsay x62	Thomson	Clark r70	Dempsey	Georgeson	Wilkinson	Wilkie	Wilson,P u4 78
S	27-Mar	Queen of the South		H	L2	1-1	1849	McDermott	Hislop 1	Gray	Wilkinson	Thomson	Thomson	Wilson,P 2	Wilkinson	Georgeson	Wilson,I 40	McGuire	Mitchell u70 19 · McChesney 37 pen
S	03-Apr	Montrose		H	L2	2-6	1606	McDermott	Gray	Scott	Dempsey 1	Wilkinson	Lindsay	Millar,Do	Millar,Do	Georgeson	McGuire 2,1p	McGuire	Wilkie u40 30, 78 · Barr 24 Crammond (3) 44, 60, 72 Third 45 Young 67
S	10-Apr	Berwick Rangers	6	H	L2	2-1	1403	McDermott	Gray	Scott	Dempsey	Thomson	Lindsay b	Millar,Do	Georgeson 1	Georgeson	McGuire 2,1p	Cormack	Beveridge 52, 64p · McGuckin 17
S	17-Apr	Stranraer		A	L2	5-3	1115	McDermott	Gray	Beveridge	Dempsey 1	Innes	Lindsay	Millar,Do	Georgeson	Donnelly	Millar,Do	Mitchell 1	Urquhart 18, 82, 32, 47, 75 · Collings 44 Blackwood 64 Letford 65
W	21-Apr	Alloa Athletic		H	L2	1-2	1003	McDermott	Wilkinson	Gray	Dempsey	Innes	Lindsay	Gallazzi r70	Mitchell	Georgeson	McGuire	McGuire	Georgeson u70 1 80 · Thomson 56 Wodecki 70
S	24-Apr	Hamilton Academical		H	L2	0-0	1314	McDermott	Hislop	Gray	Dempsey	Wilkinson	Wilkinson	Millar,Do	Devlin	Georgeson	Lindsay	McGuire	Innes
M	26-Apr	Dunfermline Athletic		A	FC SF	1-4		McDermott	Gray	Jamieson	Dempsey	Innes	Wilkinson r17	Millar,Do	Sinclair	Hislop	Lindsay	McGuire 1p	Georgeson u17 78 · Paton 18 Thomson 47 Mitchell 70 Miller 86

Manager : Jimmy Millar to 28th September.   Bill Baxter from 20th October

(1) Gate receipts £2119   (2) Gate receipts £1413   (3) Gate receipts £500

(4) Gate receipts £8500   Celtic goalscorers Lennox (3) 22, 27, 82 Wallace 72 Gemmell 37 pen Callaghan 53 Davidson 75

(5) Malcolm Mackay sent off 34 minutes

(6) Gordon Haig booked and sent off

(7) Substitutes Clark u45, Newman u45, Newman u   *Sinclair's goal scored in 88 minutes*

(8) Substitutes McGuire u, Clark u who scored in 89 minutes

(9) East Fife goalscorers Finlayson (2) 14, 31 Miller 34 pen Honeyman 39 Cooper og 47

Day	Date	Opponents	Note	Venue	Comp	Res.	Att.	1	2	3	4	5	6	7	8	9	10	11	Substitutes, own goals and goal times
M	02-Aug	Barnsley		H	F	1-2		McDermott r	Wilkinson r	Lindsay	Dempsey	Staite	Thomson,J	McLeod	Georgeson r	Wallace r 1	Cooper	Robertson r	Hislop, McGuire; Jamieson 26, Reid 62
S	07-Aug	East Fife		A	F	1-2		McDermott	Hislop	Jamieson r**	Dempsey	Staite	Thomson,J	McLeod	Innes r*	Wallace	McGuire 2p	Robertson 1	Fraser u*, Lindsay u**; 56, 65
W	14-Aug	East Fife		H	LCS	2-1	5623	McDermott	Wilkinson	Hislop	Dempsey	Staite	Thomson,J	McLeod	Georgeson	Wallace	McGuire 2p	Robertson	Innes
S	18-Aug	Arbroath		A	LCS	0-4	1982	McDermott	Hislop	Wilkinson r	Dempsey	Staite	Thomson,J	McLeod	Georgeson	Wallace	McGuire	Robertson	Cooper u
W	21-Aug	Partick Thistle		H	LCS	1-1	3377	McDermott	Hislop	Lindsay	Dempsey	Staite	Thomson,J	McLeod	Georgeson 1	Wallace	McGuire	Robertson	Cooper u; 31
W	25-Aug	Arbroath		H	LCS	1-1	2808	McDermott	Hislop	Lindsay	Dempsey	Staite	Thomson,J	McLeod r	Georgeson 1	Boyack r	McGuire	Robertson	Cooper u; 87
W	28-Aug	East Fife		A	LCS	0-5	4527	McDermott	Hislop r	Lindsay	Dempsey	Staite	Thomson,J	Robertson	Cooper	Wallace	McGuire	McGuire	Cooper u; 60
W	01-Sep	Partick Thistle		A	LCS	1-1	2497	McDermott	Hislop	Jamieson	Dempsey	Staite	Thomson,J r	Robertson 1	Cooper 1	Wallace 1	McGuire	McGuire	Wilson u
S	04-Sep	Cowdenbeath		A	L2	1-1	2242	McDermott	Hislop	Hislop	Dempsey	Staite	Cooper	Robertson	Georgeson r	Wallace 1	McGuire b	Lister	Wilkinson u x; 71
W	08-Sep	Arbroath		A	L2	0-4	2057	McDermott	Hislop	Hislop	Dempsey	Staite	Cooper	Robertson	Georgeson	Wallace 1	Lister	Robertson	Miller u
S	11-Sep	Albion Rovers		H	L2	3-1	2257	McDermott	Hislop 1	Hislop 1	Dempsey	Staite	Cooper	Lister	Georgeson r	Wallace 1	McGuire b	Lister	Innes; 18, 49, 25
W	15-Sep	Alloa Athletic		H	L2	1-1	2277	McDermott	Hislop	Hislop	Dempsey	Staite	Cooper 1	Robertson	Georgeson r	Wallace	McGuire 1	Robertson	Miller; 55
S	18-Sep	Queen's Park		A	L2	0-1	959	McDermott	Hislop	Jamieson	Dempsey	Staite	Cooper	Lister	Georgeson r	Wallace 1	McGuire	Lister	Beveridge u
S	22-Sep	Queen's Park		A	L2	2-3	1006	McDermott	Hislop	Jamieson x	Dempsey	Staite 1	Cooper	Gardner r	Georgeson r	Wallace 1	McGuire	McGuire	Georgeson u; 5, 30
W	25-Sep	Dumbarton		H	L2	6-1	2270	Reid	Hislop	Jamieson	Dempsey	Thomson,A b	Cooper	Robertson	Georgeson r	Stevenson r 18	McGuire	McGuire	Lister u, Wallace u 18 1; 65, 71, 75, 26, 53, 24
S	29-Sep	Arbroath		H	L2	1-1	2469	Reid	Hislop	Thomson,J	Dempsey	Thomson,A	Cooper	McLeod 2	Cooper	Staite r 18	McGuire 1p	Robertson 2	Stevenson u; 77
S	02-Oct	Montrose		H	L2	1-3	1652	Reid	Hislop	Thomson,J	Dempsey	Thomson,A	Cooper	McLeod 1	Cooper	Wallace	McGuire	Robertson r	Georgeson u; 60
S	09-Oct	St Mirren		H	L2	2-0	2721	Reid	Hislop b	Beveridge	Dempsey	Thomson,A	Cooper	McLeod 1	Cooper r	Wallace 1	McGuire	Lister	Beveridge; 22, 65
S	16-Oct	Berwick Rangers		H	L2	1-0	723	Reid	Hislop	Lindsay	Dempsey	Thomson,A	Cooper	McLeod 1	Cooper	Staite	McGuire 1p	McGuire	Beveridge; 18
S	23-Oct	Queen of the South		A	L2	1-2	2508	Reid s	Thomson,J	Lindsay	Dempsey	Thomson,A 1	Cooper	McLeod r	Georgeson	Staite 1	Staite r66	Robertson	Thomson,J; 27
S	30-Oct	Hamilton Academical		H	L2	1-2	2074	McDermott	Hislop	Beveridge	Dempsey	Thomson,J	Cooper	Lister	Cooper 1	Staite 1	Cooper 1	Robertson	Tront u
S	06-Nov	Stranraer		A	L2	1-2	1101	McDermott	Thomson,J	Lindsay	Dempsey	Innes	Lindsay	Robertson	Lister	Georgeson	Georgeson	McGuire	Robertson u 66; 65
S	13-Nov	Clydebank		H	L2	1-3	2086	McDermott	Thomson,J	Lindsay	Dempsey	Innes	Fraser	McLeod	Cooper 1	Tront r	Georgeson	McGuire	Lister u; 54
S	20-Nov	Brechin City		A	L2	4-0	268	McDermott	Thomson,J	Lindsay	Dempsey	Innes	Cooper	McLeod	Georgeson	Wallace 1	Cooper 1	Lister	Lister; Littlejohn og 1; 30, 22, 76, 69
S	27-Nov	Stirling Albion		A	L2	2-5	2209	McDermott	Hislop 1	Lindsay	Dempsey	Thomson,A	Innes	McLeod	Georgeson	Wallace 2	Cooper	Robertson	Tront; 66, 55
S	04-Dec	Stenhousemuir		A	L2	1-0	511	Reid r	Hislop	Lindsay	Dempsey	Thomson,A	Thomson,A	McLeod r	Georgeson 1	Wallace 1	Cooper	Lister	Robertson u 1; 30
S	11-Dec	East Stirling	1	H	L2	3-1	1880	Duff	Hislop	Lindsay	Dempsey	Thomson,A	Cooper	Lister	Georgeson 1	Wallace 1	McGuire	Lister	McLeod u; 50, 18, 64
S	18-Dec	Forfar Athletic		A	L2	1-0	1198	McDermott	Reid r	Lindsay	Dempsey	Dempsey	Cooper	Lister r	Georgeson	Wallace 1	McGuire	McGuire	McLeod; 21
M	27-Dec	Celtic XI		H	F	2-2	2000	McDermott	Hislop	Jamieson	Lindsay	Dempsey	Cooper	Lister r	Georgeson 1	Wallace 2	McGuire	Robertson 2	Tront; 28, 75
S	01-Jan	Brechin City		H	L2	1-1	5845	McDermott	Hislop	Beveridge	Lindsay	Dempsey 1	Cooper	Dempsey	Georgeson	Wallace 1	McGuire	Robertson 1	Thomson,A u; 85
S	03-Jan	Montrose		A	L2	1-3	839	McDermott	Hislop	Beveridge	Lindsay	Dempsey	Cooper	Tront	Dempsey	Staite	McGuire b	Robertson 2	Thomson,A u; 90
S	08-Jan	Queen's Park		H	SC 2	1-1	2135	McDermott	Hislop	Beveridge	Lindsay	Dempsey 1	Cooper	Lister	Dempsey 1	Staite	McGuire	Robertson r	Lister u; 2
S	15-Jan	Brechin City		H	SC 2	2-1	1670	Reid	Hislop	Beveridge	Lindsay	Dempsey	Cooper	Lister r	Dempsey	Jamieson	McGuire	Robertson r	Staite; 31, 71
M	22-Jan	Montrose		A	L2	4-0	1985	McDermott	Hislop	Beveridge	Lindsay	Staite	Cooper	McGuire	Georgeson	Wallace 2	Dempsey	Robertson	Staite u; 12, 40, 49, 7
S	29-Jan	St Mirren		A	L2	0-2	4668	McDermott	Hislop	Beveridge	Lindsay	Staite	Cooper	McGuire	Georgeson	Wallace	Dempsey r	Robertson	Lister u
S	05-Feb	Dunfermline Athletic		H	SC 3	2-0	7483	McDermott	Hislop	Beveridge	Lindsay	Staite b	Cooper	McGuire 1p	Georgeson	Wallace b	Dempsey r	Robertson 1	Lister u; 21, 56
S	12-Feb	Berwick Rangers		H	L2	3-1	2328	McDermott	Hislop	Beveridge	Lindsay	Staite	Thomson,A	McGuire 1p	Georgeson 1	Wallace 1	Dempsey	Robertson b	Lister u; 68, 7, 66
S	19-Feb	Queen of the South		A	L2	1-1	2589	McDermott	Jamieson	Beveridge	Lindsay	Staite b	Cooper	Lister 1	Georgeson 1	Wallace x	Dempsey	Robertson 1	Tront; 73
S	26-Feb	Dumbarton		A	SC 4	3-0	6236	McDermott	Hislop	Beveridge	Lindsay	Staite	Cooper	McGuire	Georgeson	Wallace 1	Dempsey	Robertson	Thomson,A u; 72, 47, 75
M	04-Mar	Hamilton Academical		A	L2	1-1	1171	McDermott	Hislop	Lindsay 1	Lindsay	Staite	Cooper	McGuire	Georgeson 1	Wallace	Dempsey	Robertson 1	Lister u; 69
S	11-Mar	Stranraer	2	A	L2	0-0	2071	Reid	Hislop b	Jamieson	Lindsay	Staite	Cooper	McGuire	Georgeson	Wallace	Dempsey r	Robertson 1	Lister u
S	18-Mar	Kilmarnock		H	SC QF	1-3	10815	McDermott	Hislop	Beveridge r	Lindsay	Staite	Cooper	Brown	Georgeson	Wallace r 3	Dempsey b	McGuire	Lister u; 57
S	25-Mar	Brechin City		H	L2	0-1	1190	Brown	Hislop b	Lindsay	McLeod	Staite b 1	Cooper	McGuire	Georgeson	Wallace	Dempsey r	McGuire	Boyack u
S	01-Apr	Stirling Albion		A	L2	0-3	1303	Reid	Hislop	Scott	McLeod	Staite	Cooper	McGuire	Georgeson	Wallace	Dempsey	Robertson r	Lister u
S	08-Apr	Stenhousemuir		H	L2	4-0	1291	McDermott	Hislop	Scott r	McLeod	Staite	Cooper	Brown,T	Georgeson b	Miller	McGuire	Robertson r	Thomson,Jo u; 67, 54p, 56, 52
Tu	11-Apr	Clydebank		H	L2	1-3	977	Reid	Hislop	Scott	McLeod	Staite	Cooper	McGuire 2, 1p	Georgeson	Wallace	Urquhart r	Robertson r	Jamieson u; 12
S	15-Apr	East Stirling		A	L2	1-2	551	McDermott	Hislop	Beveridge	McLeod	Staite	Staite	Lister	Georgeson	Wallace 1	Robertson 1	Robertson 1	McGuire; 21
Tu	18-Apr	Dumbarton		A	L2	0-5	4715	Reid	Hislop	Beveridge	McLeod	Staite	Staite	Newman	Wallace	Wallace 1	Georgeson b	McGuire	Georgeson
S	22-Apr	Forfar Athletic		H	L2	4-2	1086	Brown	Newman	Hislop 1	Dempsey	Dempsey	Cooper	Robertson	Wallace 2	Wallace 2	Lindsay 1	McGuire	Staite u; 47, 33, 77, 63
W	26-Apr	Cowdenbeath		H	FC SF	0-0	650	McDermott	Hislop	Beveridge	Lindsay	Staite	Cooper	McGuire	Georgeson	Wallace	Dempsey	Robertson	Lister

Manager : Bill Baxter to 28th November. George Farm from 29th November

Goal difference used instead of goal average

(1) With Reid and McDermott injured, Willie Duff came out of retirement (aged 36) to play in goal. He had previously played under George Farm at Dunfermline

(2) Hopkins sent off

Opponents goalscorers, overflow substitute appearances, and overflow goal times, are listed together for seasons 1971-72 to 2007-08 inclusive, on pages 352 to 356.

Day	Date	Opponents	Note	Venue	Comp	Res.	Att.	1	2	3	4	5	6	7	8	9	10	11	Substitutes, own goals and goal times
S	05-Aug	Bolton Wanderers		H	F	2-1	3000	Reid	Hislop	Urquhart	Dempsey	Staite	Cooper	Wallace r 1	McLaren r**	Baker 1p	Selway	Robertson	Brown u* Georgeson u** 52, 41
S	12-Aug	St Johnstone		A	LCS	0-2	3131	Reid	Hislop b	Urquhart	Dempsey	Staite	Cooper	Wallace r	McLaren	Georgeson	Selway	Robertson	Brown u
W	16-Aug	Montrose		H	LCS	1-2	2144	Reid	Hislop	Urquhart	Dempsey	Staite b 1	Cooper	Wallace	McLaren r	Georgeson	Selway	Robertson	Brown u 3
S	19-Aug	Falkirk		A	LCS	0-1	3608	McDermott	McLaren	McLaren	Dempsey	Staite b	Cooper	Brown	Wallace	Baker r15	Selway b	Robertson	Georgeson u15
W	23-Aug	Montrose		A	LCS	1-2	1551	McDermott	McLaren x	McLaren	Dempsey	Staite	Cooper	Brown r	Wallace	Baker	Selway 1	Robertson	Georgeson u 25
S	26-Aug	St Johnstone		H	LCS	3-0	2961	Reid	Hislop	McLaren	Dempsey	Staite	Cooper b	Brown 1	Wallace 1	Baker 1p	Selway	Robertson	Georgeson u 43, 18, 49
W	30-Aug	Falkirk		H	LCS	1-0	2351	Reid	Hislop	McLaren	Dempsey	Staite	Cooper	Brown 1	Wallace	Baker	Selway	Robertson	Georgeson 12
S	02-Sep	Albion Rovers		A	L2	2-0	692	Reid	Hislop b	McLaren	Dempsey	Staite b	Cooper	Brown 1	Wallace	Baker 1p	Selway	Robertson	Georgeson 38, 88
S	09-Sep	Forfar Athletic		H	L2	3-2	2061	Reid	Hislop	McLaren	Dempsey r	Staite	Cooper	Brown 1	Georgeson	Baker 3,2p	Selway	Robertson	Georgeson u 15p, 38p, 75
W	13-Sep	Montrose		A	L2	2-3	1222	Reid	McLaren	Hislop	Dempsey b 1	Dempsey	Cooper	Brown	Georgeson 1	Baker	Selway	Robertson	Urquhart 36, 27
S	16-Sep	Clydebank		H	L2	1-1	1415	Reid	Urquhart	Hislop	McLaren	Staite	Cooper	Brown r	Georgeson	Baker	Selway	Robertson	Markie u 63
W	20-Sep	Montrose		H	L2	1-0	1691	McDermott	Urquhart	Hislop	Dempsey	Staite	Cooper	Brown	Georgeson	Georgeson 1	Selway	Robertson	McLaren 68
S	23-Sep	Berwick Rangers		H	L2	8-1	2086	McDermott	Urquhart	Hislop	Dempsey	Staite	Cooper	Brown 1	Georgeson 1	Baker 5	Selway	Robertson r	Wallace u Melrose og 1 1,85,16,31,56,72,77,30
W	27-Sep	Alloa Athletic		H	L2	1-0	1156	McDermott	Urquhart	Hislop	Dempsey b	Staite	Cooper	Brown	Georgeson	Georgeson 1	Selway	Robertson	Wallace 52
S	30-Sep	East Stirling		H	L2	3-0	920	McDermott	Urquhart	Hislop	Dempsey	Staite	Cooper	Brown	Georgeson	Baker x 1p	Selway	McLaren 2	Reid 63, 1, 21
S	07-Oct	Stirling Albion		A	L2	1-1	4148	McDermott	Urquhart	Hislop	Dempsey	Staite b	Cooper	Brown	Georgeson	Wallace 1	McLaren	Robertson	McLaren u 71
S	14-Oct	Clyde		A	L2	0-3	2175	McDermott	Urquhart	Hislop	Dempsey	Staite	Cooper	Wallace	Wallace	Baker 1p	McLaren	Robertson	Brown u
S	21-Oct	Dunfermline Athletic		H	L2	1-2	5883	McDermott	Urquhart	Hislop	Dempsey 1	Staite	Cooper	Brown	Dempsey	Baker	McLaren	Robertson	Selway 67
M	30-Oct	Dundee United		H	F	2-0			Selway	Hislop	Staite	Staite	Cooper	Brown	Dempsey 1	Baker	McLaren	Robertson	Wallace u 1 30, 68
W	04-Nov	Brechin City		A	L2	6-4	595	McDermott	Selway	Hislop	Hannigan	Staite	Cooper	Brown	Dempsey	Baker 1	McLaren	Robertson	Wallace u 76,11,18,42,63,82
Tu	07-Nov	Cowdenbeath	2	H	FC SFr	3-0		McDermott	Selway	Hislop 1	Hannigan r	Staite	Cooper	Wallace 1	Georgeson 2	Baker 1	McLaren	Robertson	Georgeson u 65, 15, 36
S	11-Nov	Stranraer		H	L2	5-1	1841	McDermott	Urquhart	Hislop	Hannigan	Dempsey	Cooper	Brown	Georgeson	Wallace 1	McLaren 1	Robertson	Donaldson Duffy og 1 28,71,24,73,87
S	18-Nov	Hamilton Academical		A	L2	3-3	1540	McDermott	Selway	Hislop	Hannigan 1	Dempsey b 1	Cooper	Brown r	Georgeson	Baker	McLaren 1	Robertson r	Urquhart u 75, 87, 65
S	25-Nov	Stenhousemuir		H	L2	0-2	2070	McDermott	Selway b	Hislop	Dempsey	Staite b	Cooper	Hannigan	Georgeson 1	Georgeson	Wallace u	Robertson	Wallace u
S	02-Dec	St Mirren		H	L2	3-0	2399	McDermott	Selway	Hislop	Dempsey b	Gray	Cooper	Hannigan	Georgeson	Baker 2	Wallace 1	Robertson	Urquhart 35, 88, 15
F	08-Dec	Queen's Park		H	L2	2-1	1739	McDermott	Selway	Hislop	Gray	Gray	Cooper	Dempsey b	Georgeson	Baker	McPhee r	Robertson b 1	Donaldson u 68, 63
S	16-Dec	Cowdenbeath		H	L2	2-2	2499	McDermott	Selway	Hislop	Urquhart r	Gray	Cooper	Brown	Georgeson	Baker 2,1p	McPhee	Robertson	McLaren u 32, 72p
S	23-Dec	Queen of the South		A	L2	1-1	1064	McDermott	Donaldson	Selway	Whitelaw	Gray	Cooper	Wallace	Georgeson	Baker 1p	McPhee 1	Robertson r	Brown u 33
W	27-Dec	Albion Rovers		H	L2	4-0	1919	McDermott	Donaldson	Selway	Dempsey	Gray	Cooper	Wallace	Georgeson	Wallace	McPhee	Robertson r	Georgeson 20, 56, 10, 72
M	01-Jan	Stenhousemuir		A	L2	0-1	1578	McDermott	Wallace	McLaren	Dempsey b	Gray	Cooper	McLaren	McLaren	Baker	Dempsey	Robertson 2	Reid
S	13-Jan	Stenhousemuir		A	SC 2	0-0	1361	McDermott	Donaldson b	Selway	Whitelaw	Gray	Cooper	Brown 1	Wallace	Baker	Dempsey b	Robertson	Georgeson u
W	17-Jan	Stenhousemuir		H	SC 2r	3-0	2506	McDermott	Donaldson 1	Selway	Wallace 1	Gray	Cooper	Brown r	Georgeson	Baker r	Dempsey	Robertson	Urquhart u 55, 70, 68
S	20-Jan	East Stirling		A	L2	2-2	1711	McDermott	Donaldson	Selway	Donaldson	Gray	Cooper	Donaldson	Georgeson r	Georgeson r	Dempsey	Robertson	Urquhart u 46, 71
S	27-Jan	Stirling Albion		H	L2	2-1	2425	McDermott	Hislop	Urquhart r	Donaldson	Gray	Cooper	Urquhart r	Dempsey	Robertson	Selway	Robertson b	McLaren u Carr og 1 73, 84
S	03-Feb	Motherwell	3	A	SC 3	1-2	5621	McDermott	Hislop r	Selway	Dempsey	Gray	Cooper	Brown	Baker 1p	Robertson	Dempsey	Wallace	McLaren u 73
S	10-Feb	Clyde		H	L2	0-0	3396	McDermott	Hislop	Hislop	Dempsey	Gray	Cooper	Brown r	Baker	Baker 2	Dempsey	Wallace	McLaren u
S	24-Feb	Berwick Rangers		A	L2	3-1	482	McDermott	Donaldson	Hislop	Selway	Gray	Cooper	Brown	Baker 2	Baker 1p	Georgeson 1	Hislop	Hislop 70. 75, 23
S	28-Feb	Clydebank		H	L2	2-0	1698	McDermott	Donaldson	Hislop	Selway r	Gray	Cooper	Brown	Baker 1p	Baker	Georgeson 1	Hislop u	Hislop u 37, 13
W	07-Mar	Dunfermline Athletic	2	A	FC F-1	1-1		McDermott	Hislop	Hislop	Hislop	Dempsey	Cooper	Robertson	Wallace r	Baker	Georgeson 1	Brown	Brown u 58
S	10-Mar	Brechin City		H	L2	3-1	2188	McDermott	Donaldson	Hislop	Dempsey	Selway	Cooper	Robertson	Wallace 1	Baker 2p	Baker	Brown 1	Brown u 1 61, 90, 74
W	14-Mar	Dunfermline Athletic	2	H	FC F-2	3-1	968	McDermott	Donaldson	Hislop	Selway	Selway	Cooper	Brown 2	Georgeson	Baker	Baker 1	Robertson	Urquhart 44. 72, 68
S	17-Mar	Stranraer		A	L2	4-1	2085	McDermott	Hislop	Hislop	Dempsey	Selway	Cooper	Brown 2	Baker	Baker r	Wallace 1	Robertson	Urquhart McAuley og 1 10, 19, 41, 77
S	24-Mar	Hamilton Academical	4	H	L2	2-0	2707	McDermott	Donaldson	Hislop	Dempsey b	Selway	Cooper	Brown	Georgeson 1	Urquhart	Wallace	Robertson	Urquhart u 33, 87
W	28-Mar	Alloa Athletic		H	L2	1-1	654	McDermott	Urquhart	Hislop	Dempsey	Gray u	Cooper	Brown	Georgeson 1	Georgeson	Wallace r	Robertson	Gray u 90
S	31-Mar	Stenhousemuir		A	L2	0-3	2364	McDermott	Donaldson r	Hislop	Dempsey	Groves	Cooper	Brown	Selway	Georgeson	Clelland	Robertson	McLaren
S	07-Apr	St Mirren		A	L2	1-3	596	McDermott	Donaldson	Hislop	Dempsey	Selway	Cooper	Urquhart r	McLaren	Brown	Clelland	Robertson 1	Urquhart u 34
S	14-Apr	Queen's Park		A	L2	1-0	1840	McDermott	Donaldson	Hislop	Dempsey	Selway	Cooper	Brown	McLaren	Georgeson r	Wallace	Robertson 1	Georgeson u 68
S	21-Apr	Cowdenbeath		H	L2	1-1	6630	McDermott	Donaldson	Hislop b	Dempsey	Rogerson	Selway	Brown	Cooper	Wallace	Wallace 1	Robertson 1	Groves u 25
W	25-Apr	Dunfermline Athletic		A	L2	0-1	1840	McDermott	Donaldson	Hislop	Dempsey	Rogerson	Selway	Robertson	Cooper	Wilson r	McLaren	Duncan r	Georgeson u
S	28-Apr	Queen of the South		H	L2	2-0	1433	McDermott	Donaldson	Hislop	Dempsey	Rogerson	Selway	Brown	Cooper	Wilson	Wallace 1	Robertson 1	Urquhart u 79, 25

Manager : George Farm

(1) Goalkeeper Bobby Reid was pressed into service as an (unused) substitute in two matches, such was the small player pool.

(2) 1971/72 competition (3) A dog on the pitch held up the first half for four minutes, evading all attempts to capture it.

(4) In the wake of the League match at home to Hamilton, George Farm used his programme notes to condemn the visitors' "disgraceful exhibition". "Their conduct was an insult to paying customers, a constant threat to our players, and reflected no credit whatsoever on their new manager, Eric Smith. No wonder the usual courtesies exchanged by competing managers did not take place after the game. At least Mr Smith had the good sense to leave without attempting to explain or justify his team's tactics." An enterprising journalist showed the programme to Eric Smith, who retorted : "Of course it is an accepted fact that from time to time we have such outbursts from Mr Farm. Controversy of the right type is good for football and for Mr Farm's TV image."

Day	Date	Opponents	Note	Venue	Comp	Res.	Att.	1	2	3	4	5	6	7	8	9	10	11	Substitutes, own goals and goal times
S	28-Jul	Dundee	1	A	DrC	0-1	4000	McDermott	Brown,W	Hislop,T	Dempsey	Rogerson	Selway	Rice r 105	Baker	Jack	Cooper	Duncan r 90	Wallace u 90, Brown,T u 105
S	04-Aug	Dunfermline Athletic		H	F	2-1	3000	McDermott	Brown,W	Hislop,T	Dempsey	Rogerson	Selway	Rice r 2	Baker	Jack	Cooper r 65	Duncan	Wallace u 45, Graham u 65 — 5, 15
W	11-Aug	Stirling Albion		A	LCS	0-1	2484	McDermott	Donaldson b	Brown,W	Wallace r 39	Rogerson	Selway	Rice	Baker	Jack r b	Cooper	Duncan	Cleland u, Graham u 39
W	15-Aug	Cowdenbeath		H	LCS	5-1	3012	McDermott	Donaldson	Brown,W	Wallace r 45	Rogerson	Selway	Rice	Baker 2	Graham 2	Cooper	Duncan 1	Brown,T u 45 — 30, 75, 34, 59, 55
S	18-Aug	Queen of the South	2	H	LCS	2-2	3138	McDermott	Brown,W	Hislop,T	Wallace r	Rogerson	Selway	Rice	Baker 2,1p	Graham	Cooper	Duncan	Brown,T u r — 19, 60
W	22-Aug	Cowdenbeath	3	A	LCS	1-0	2013	McDermott	Cleland	Cleland	Brown,W	Rogerson	Selway	Rice	Baker m 1	Graham	Cooper	Duncan	Brown,T — 40
S	25-Aug	Queen of the South		A	LCS	2-1	2006	McDermott	Brown,W	Cooper	Dempsey r50	Rogerson	Selway	Rice*	Baker r*	Graham 1	Wallace 1	Duncan	Hislop,T u50, Jack u* — 72, 20
M	27-Aug	Cowdenbeath		H	LCS	0-1	2100	McDermott	Brown,T	Brown,W	Wallace	Rogerson	Selway b	Rice*	Brown,T r	Graham 1	Cooper	Duncan	Jack u*, Cleland u
W	29-Aug	Stirling Albion		H	LCS	1-0	3270	McDermott	Hislop,T	Brown,W	Wallace	Rogerson	Selway	Wallace	Jack 1	Graham	Cooper b	Duncan r70	Robertson u70 — 57
S	01-Sep	Airdrie		A	LCS	0-4	3057	McDermott	Hislop,T	Brown,W	Wood	Rogerson	Selway	Wallace	Baker	Graham	Cooper r60	Duncan r60	Jack u60
W	05-Sep	Hamilton Academical		A	L2	1-2	1897	McDermott	Hislop,T	Cleland	Wood	Rogerson b	Selway	Graham	Baker	Wallace r60	Brown,W r80	Duncan 1	Robertson u60, Donaldson u80 — 50
S	08-Sep	Cowdenbeath		H	L2	2-2	1704	Blair	Hislop,T 1	Cleland	Wood	Rogerson	Selway	Wallace b 1	Baker	Graham r25	Brown,W	Duncan r45	Rice u60, Jack u25 — 16, 18
W	12-Sep	Hibernian	4	A	LC 2-1	10693	Blair	Donaldson	Hislop,T	Wood	Selway	Cooper	Wallace	Graham	Baker 1	Brown,W	Duncan r45	Cooper, Cleland, Bremner og 1 — 3, 50
S	15-Sep	Queen of the South		H	L2	3-0	2358	McDermott	Donaldson	Hislop,T	Wood	Selway	Cooper	Wallace r70	Robertson	Baker m	Brown,W	Duncan	Cleland, Robertson u60 2 — 45, 71, 84
W	19-Sep	Queen's Park		A	L2	0-1	689	McDermott	Donaldson	Hislop,T	Wood	Rogerson	Cooper	Wallace r70	Robertson	Baker r60	Brown,W 45	Duncan	Graham u70
S	22-Sep	Clydebank		A	L2	1-1	1426	McDermott	Donaldson	Hislop,T	Wood	Rogerson	Cooper	Robertson r75 1	Graham	Baker	Selway r80	Duncan	Rogerson u45, Brown,W u80 — 4
Tu	25-Sep	Hamilton Academical		H	L2	0-3	2117	McDermott	Donaldson	Hislop,T	Wood	Rogerson	Cooper	Rice r59	Wallace r59	Baker	Brown,W b	Duncan	Rice u75, Robertson u59
S	29-Sep	St Mirren		A	L2	2-4	1712	McDermott	Brown,W	Hislop,T	Wood	Selway	Cooper	Robertson	Jack 1	Baker r	Brown,T r80	Duncan	Jack u59, Graham u80 — 65, 25
S	06-Oct	Montrose		A	L2	3-1	998	McDermott	Brown,W	Hislop,T	Wood	Selway	Cooper	Robertson r	Jack 2	Baker r	Brown,T	Duncan	Wallace u, Clelland — 14, 57, 20
W	10-Oct	Hibernian		H	LC 2-2	7493	McDermott	Brown,W	Hislop,T	Wood	Rogerson	Cooper	Robertson 1p	Jack	Baker	Brown,T	Duncan	Wallace u, Rogerson
S	13-Oct	Alloa Athletic		H	L2	3-2	1646	McDermott	Brown,W b	Hislop,T	Wood	Rogerson	Cooper	Robertson 1p	Jack 2	Baker	Brown,T	Duncan	Rogerson, Wallace — 65, 14, 71
S	20-Oct	Berwick Rangers		A	L2	0-1	665	McDermott	Brown,W	Hislop,T	Wood	Selway r80	Cooper	Robertson r80	Jack	Baker	Brown,T	Duncan	Rogerson u80, Rice u80
M	22-Oct	Burntisland Shipyard		H	FC 1	5-0	500	McDermott	Brown,W	Hislop,T	Wood 1	Selway	Cooper	Robertson 1	Jack 1	Wallace 1	Brown,T 1	Duncan r55	Cleland, Urquhart — 58, 17, 52, 24, 89
S	27-Oct	Kilmarnock		A	L2	1-1	4181	McDermott	Brown,W	Hislop,T	Wood	Selway	Cooper b	Robertson r60	Jack	Wallace 1	Brown,T 1	Duncan r45	Rogerson, Urquhart u60 — 25
S	03-Nov	Stranraer		H	L2	1-0	1532	McDermott	Brown,W	Hislop,T	Wood	Selway	Cooper	Robertson 1p	Jack r	Wallace	Brown,T 1	Duncan 1	Rogerson u45, Graham u — 33
M	05-Nov	Cowdenbeath		H	FC SF	0-1	400	McDermott	Brown,W	Hislop,T r	Wood	Selway	Cooper	Robertson	Wallace	Wallace	Brown,T	Duncan	Rogerson u45, Urquhart u
S	10-Nov	Forfar Athletic		A	L2	4-1	862	McDermott	Donaldson	Brown,W	Wood	Selway	Cooper	Robertson 2p	Jack r45	Wallace 1	Brown,T 1	Duncan	Rogerson, Graham u45 — 64, 89, 57, 68
S	17-Nov	Albion Rovers		H	L2	3-0	1552	McDermott	Donaldson	Brown,W	Wood 1	Selway	Cooper	Robertson 73	Wallace	Baker 1	Brown,T b	Duncan	Rogerson, Graham u73 — 47, 59, 36
S	24-Nov	Brechin City		A	L2	4-0	401	McDermott	Donaldson	Brown,W	Wood 1	Selway	Cooper	Robertson b 3,1p	Wallace	Baker b 1	Brown,T b	Duncan	Simpson, Graham — 3, 36, 61p, 84
S	29-Dec	Airdrie	4	A	L2	0-4	2320	McDermott	Donaldson	Brown,W x	Wood	Selway	Cooper	Robertson	Simpson b	Simpson b	Brown,T r60	Duncan	Simpson, Urquhart u60 — 18
Tu	01-Jan	Cowdenbeath		H	L2	1-2	2546	McDermott	Graham	Brown,W	Wood	Selway	Cooper	Robertson	Simpson	Baker 1	Brown,T	Duncan	Rogerson, Urquhart u55
S	05-Jan	St Mirren		A	L2	0-0	1708	Blair	Selway b	Brown,W	Dempsey	Rogerson b	Cooper	Lindsay	Simpson*	Baker	Brown,T	Duncan r	Graham u*, Robertson u
S	12-Jan	Celtic	5	H	F	6-2	987	Blair	Selway r 45	Hislop,T	Dempsey	Rogerson	Cooper	Lindsay 1	Wood r 45	Baker 2	Mitchell r 45 1	Duncan r 45	Wallace u 45 1, Brown,T u 45, Robertson u 45 1
S	19-Jan	Hearts		H	F	3-1	200	Blair	Brown,W	Hislop,T	Dempsey	Rogerson	Cooper	Lindsay r 60	Rice	Baker 1	Mitchell	Robertson 1p	Wallace u 60, Oliver og 1 — 32, 70, 80
Sn	27-Jan	Morton		H	SC 3	2-2	5209	McDermott	Brown,W	Breen	Dempsey	Rogerson	Cooper	Lindsay r	Wallace	Baker 1	Rice	Robertson 1p	Mitchell, Brown,T u — 7, 20
Tu	29-Jan	Morton	1	A	SC 3r	0-0	1586	McDermott	Brown,W	Hislop,T	Dempsey bx	Rogerson b	Cooper	Robertson	Brown,T	Baker r45	Mitchell x	Duncan r72	Rice u72, Simpson u45 b
Tu	02-Feb	Montrose		A	L2	2-2	1355	Blair	Donaldson	Hislop,T	Wood	Dempsey	Cooper	Lindsay	Brown,T	Graham r74	Mitchell r*	Duncan 1	Simpson u74, Urquhart u45 — 29, 54
Sn	03-Feb	Morton	6	N	SC 3r2	0-1	5645	McDermott	Brown,W	Hislop,T	Wood	Dempsey	Cooper	Lindsay	Wallace	Baker	Brown,T	Duncan	Hislop,T, Rice u
S	09-Feb	Alloa Athletic		A	L2	4-0	464	McDermott	Brown,W	Breen	Wallace	Rogerson	Cooper	Robertson r	Wallace	Baker 1	Clelland	Duncan	Hislop,T, Dempsey u — 4, 30, 50, 76p
S	16-Feb	East Stirling		H	L2	1-0	588	McDermott	Brown,W	Hislop,T	Wallace	Rogerson	Cooper	Robertson	Mitchell	Baker 60	Wallace	Duncan	Hislop,T, Lindsay u75 1 — 88
S	23-Feb	Berwick Rangers		H	L2	1-1	1675	McDermott	Brown,W	Breen	Wallace	Rogerson	Cooper	Robertson b	Dempsey	Baker r60	Wallace	Duncan	Dempsey u, Lindsay u60 — 85
S	02-Mar	Kilmarnock		H	L2	3-1	2081	McDermott	Hislop,T	Brown,W	Dempsey	Rogerson	Cooper	Robertson b	Brown,T 1	Mitchell 2	Mitchell r60	Duncan 1	Lindsay u60, Simpson — 44, 4, 57
S	09-Mar	Stranraer		A	L2	3-2	910	McDermott	Hislop,T	Brown,W	Dempsey	Rogerson	Cooper 1	Robertson 2,1p	Mitchell	Dempsey	Dempsey	Duncan	Donaldson, Lindsay — 18, 37p, 25
S	16-Mar	Forfar Athletic		H	L2	4-1	1639	McDermott	Hislop,T	Brown,W 1	Dempsey	Rogerson	Cooper	Lindsay 1	Brown,T 1	Mitchell r60	Mitchell r30	Duncan	Simpson u60 1, Donaldson — 22, 31, 6, 75,
S	23-Mar	Albion Rovers		A	L2	1-0	464	McDermott	Donaldson	Brown,W 1	Dempsey	Rogerson	Cooper b	Robertson 1p	Brown,T	Wallace 1	Clelland	Duncan	Rice — 52
S	30-Mar	Brechin City	7	H	L2	1-1	1428	McDermott	Hislop,T 1	Brown,W	Cleland	Rogerson	Cooper	Robertson 1p	Baker	Mitchell r73	Wood	Duncan	Lindsay u73 — 38
Tu	02-Apr	Stenhousemuir		H	L2	3-0	1148	McDermott	Hislop,T	Brown,W	Wood	Rogerson	Cooper	Robertson 1	Baker 1	Mitchell 2	Wallace	Duncan 1	Brown,T — 40, 25, 8
S	06-Apr	Stenhousemuir		A	L2	1-0	462	McDermott	Hislop,T	Brown,W	Brown,T	Rogerson	Cooper	Robertson b	Baker	Mitchell r30	Wallace	Duncan 1	Urquhart u30 — 70
W	10-Apr	Queen of the South		A	L2	0-3	2351	McDermott	Hislop,T	Brown,T	Brown,T	Rogerson	Cooper	Robertson b	Baker r*	Hislop,J r30	Wallace	Duncan	Dempsey u*
S	13-Apr	East Stirling		H	L2	5-0	1593	McDermott	Hislop,T	Brown,W b	Dempsey	Rogerson	Cooper	Lyall	Wallace 2	Baker 1	Wallace	Robertson 1	Rice u72 — 58, 60, 44, 35, 72
Tu	16-Apr	Stirling Albion		H	L2	5-4	1654	McDermott	Hislop,T	Brown,W	Dempsey	Rogerson b	Cooper	Lyall r80 1	Wallace 1	Baker 1	Brown,T 1	Robertson r72 2p	Duncan u80 — 13, 89, 65, 52, 40
S	20-Apr	Stirling Albion		A	L2	1-1	1333	McDermott	Rice	Brown,W	Dempsey	Rogerson	Cooper	Lyall r60	Wallace	Brown,T	Wood	Robertson 1p	Hislop,T, Duncan u60 — 35
Tu	23-Apr	Queen's Park		H	L2	3-1	1438	McDermott	Rice	Hislop,T	Dempsey	Rogerson	Cooper	Lyall	Brown,T 2	Wallace	Wood	Robertson 1p	Mitchell, Duncan u60 — 55, 65, 31
W	01-May	Clydebank		H	L2	2-2	1239	McDermott	Rice	Hislop,T	Dempsey	Rogerson	Cooper	Lyall r60	Brown,T 1	Wallace	Wood	Robertson 1	Graham, Duncan u60 — 25, 81

Manager : George Farm

(1) after extra time   (2) Tom Brown substituted for the out-of-form Gordon Wallace in 50 minutes.   36 minutes later, George Farm, deciding that Brown's appearance had not had the desired effect, replaced him with Peter Donaldson.   (3) Abandoned half time, floodlight failure   (4) McCann sent off   (5) Impressive Friendly match results have often to be tempered by the strength of the opposition, but the 6-2 victory over Celtic on Saturday 12th January was against a team which included Connaghan, Hay, Quinn, McDonald, Connelly, Johnstone, Callaghan, Davidson, Lynch, Lennox and substitute Wilson.   Goal times 42,54,73,44,61,81   (6) at Tynecastle   (7) Clark sent off

Day	Date	Opponents	Note	Venue	Comp	Res.	Att.	1	2	3	4	5	6	7	8	9	10	11	Substitutes, own goals and goal times
S	03-Aug	Morton		H	F	1-1	1424	McDermott r*	Brown,Jr**	Brown,W	Wallace r**	Gillespie	Cooper	Rice r***	Brown,T	Hislop,J 1 48mins	Wood r****	Duncan	Mackie u* · Devlin u** · Urquhart u*** · Hislop,T u**** Boyle u*****
W	07-Aug	Preston North End		H	F	0-4	3553	McDermott	Brown,W	Hislop,T r*	Wood r***	Dempsey	Cooper	Robertson r*	Hislop,Jr**	Baker r****	Wallace	Duncan r	Brown,Ju** · Urquhart u** · Graham u*** · Brown,T u**** · 76
S	09-Aug	Queen of the South		H	LCS	1-1	1567	McDermott	Brown,W	Hislop,T	Wallace 1	Dempsey	Urquhart	Robertson r*	Brown,T	Hislop,J	Cooper	Lindsay 45	Lindsay u* · Graham u
W	13-Aug	Berwick Rangers		A	LCS	0-2	438	McDermott	Brown,W	Hislop,T	Wallace	Dempsey	Urquhart	Robertson b	Brown,T	Hislop,J r60	Cooper	Duncan r	Graham u60 · Duncan u45
S	17-Aug	Hamilton Academical		A	LCS	0-1	2361	McDermott	Brown,J	Hislop,T	Urquhart b	Dempsey	Cooper	Robertson b	Brown,Wr*b	Wallace	Wood	Duncan r	Graham u · Brown,T u*
W	20-Aug	Berwick Rangers		H	LCS	1-0	1182	McDermott	Brown,W	Hislop,T	Dempsey	Rogerson	Cooper	Brown,T	Urquhart 1	Wallace	Hislop,J	Robertson 1p	Wood · Brown,J · 64
S	24-Aug	Hamilton Academical		H	LCS	2-1	1809	McDermott	Brown,W	Hislop,T	Dempsey	Rogerson	Cooper	Brown,T	Urquhart 1	Wallace r	Hislop,J	Robertson 1p	Wood · Rice · 40, 54
W	28-Aug	Queen of the South		A	LCS	0-2	1250	McDermott	Brown,W	Hislop,T	Dempsey	Rogerson	Dempsey	Boyle r45	Brown,T	Wallace r	Wood	Robertson	Duncan u45 · Graham u
S	31-Aug	Cowdenbeath	1	A	L2	2-0	1553	McDermott	Brown,W	Hislop,T b	Dempsey	Rogerson	Cooper	Brown,T 1	Brown,T	Robertson b 1	Hislop,J r	Duncan	Boyle u · Wood · 34, 84
S	07-Sep	East Fife		H	L2	0-2	3442	McDermott	Brown,W	Hislop,T	Dempsey	Rogerson	Cooper b	Brown,T r*	Urquhart	Robertson	Hislop,J r	Duncan r	Wood u* · Boyle u
W	11-Sep	Stranraer		A	L2	0-0	1264	McDermott	Brown,J	Hislop,T	Hislop,T	Rogerson b	Brown,J	Brown,T	Conn	Boyle r	Urquhart	Robertson b	Hislop,J u · Duncan
S	14-Sep	Montrose		H	L2	2-1	1216	McDermott	Brown,W	Hislop,T	Wood	Rogerson	Brown,J	Brown,T	Urquhart	Brown,T	Brown,T	Robertson b	Boyle · Duncan
W	18-Sep	Stranraer		H	L2	1-2	1277	McDermott	Brown,W	Hislop,T	Hislop,T	Rogerson	Brown,W	Conn	Brown,T	Wallace	Hislop,J r70	Robertson	Conn u62 · Duncan u78 · 14, 88
W	25-Sep	Forfar Athletic		A	L2	0-2	643	McDermott	Brown,W	Hislop,T	Urquhart r62	Rogerson b	Wood	Brown,T r78 1	Brown,T	Wallace r	Hislop,Jr*	Duncan	Jobson u70 · Conn
S	28-Sep	Berwick Rangers		A	L2	1-2	566	McDermott	Brown,W	Hislop,T	Brown,T	Dempsey	Wood	Robertson	Brown,T	Wallace	Wallace r	Jobson r	Brown,J u* · Brown,Ju · 45
S	05-Oct	Hamilton Academical		A	L2	0-2	1996	McDermott	Brown,W 1	Hislop,T	Brown,T	Rogerson	Wood	Robertson 1p	Conn	Wallace r	Wallace	Duncan r80	Brown,Ju · Mollison u
S	12-Oct	Queen's Park		H	L2	2-2	1241	McDermott	Brown,W	Hislop,T	Dempsey	Rogerson	Wood	Mercer r58	Conn r62	Wallace	Wallace	Duncan r80	Duncan u58 · Mollison · 42, 65
S	19-Oct	Stirling Albion		A	L2	1-2	1258	McDermott	Brown,W	Hislop,T	Dempsey	Taylor	Brown,J	Robertson	Wallace	Hislop,J1	Hislop,J1	Robertson x 1p	Graham u80 · Mollison · 6
S	26-Oct	Stenhousemuir	2	H	L2	2-0	1291	McDermott	Brown,W	Hislop,T	Wood r20	Taylor	Cooper	Urquhart	Brown,T b	Hislop,J1	Hislop,J1	Robertson 1	Brown,T u20 · Graham · 80, 70
S	02-Nov	East Stirling	3	A	L2	1-1	1150	McDermott	Brown,W	Hislop,T	Brown,J	Taylor	Cooper	Graham r20	Urquhart	Hislop,J	Wallace	Robertson 1	Brown,T u20 r85 · Duncan u85 · 75, 78
M	04-Nov	East Fife		H	FC SF	2-4	600	McDermott	Brown,W	Hislop,T	Brown,J	Rogerson	Cooper	Boyle b 1	Taylor	Hislop,J	Miller	Robertson 1	Graham u60 · Conn · 88
S	09-Nov	Albion Rovers		H	L2	1-2	1313	McDermott	Brown,J b	Hislop,T	Taylor	McCallum	Cooper	Urquhart r60	Wallace	Hislop,J	Urquhart	Robertson 1	Brown,T · Lindsay · 43
S	16-Nov	St Mirren	4	A	L2	1-0	1964	McDermott	Brown,J	Hislop,T	Taylor	McCallum	Cooper	Robertson	Wallace 1	Graham	Urquhart	Duncan	Brown,W · Hislop,J · 75
S	23-Nov	Clydebank		H	L2	1-2	1111	McDermott	Brown,J	Hislop,T	Taylor	McCallum	Cooper	Robertson b	Wallace 1	Graham	Wood	Hislop,J b 1	Lindsay · Urquhart · 81, 76, 26, 30, 65
S	30-Nov	Brechin City	5	H	L2	5-2	995	McDermott	Brown,W	Hislop,T 1	Taylor 1	McCallum	Cooper	Robertson b	Wallace 1	Graham 1	Wood	Hislop,J r75	Urquhart · Urquhart · 67, 62
S	07-Dec	Alloa Athletic		A	L2	2-0	551	McDermott	Brown,W	Hislop,T	Taylor	McCallum	Cooper	Duncan r45	Wallace r	Dailey	Wood	Robertson	Urquhart · Urquhart
S	14-Dec	Falkirk		H	L2	1-0	1751	McDermott	Brown,W b	Hislop,T b	Taylor b	McCallum	Cooper	Duncan	Wallace b	Graham	Wood	Duncan r80	Urquhart u b · Lindsay · 72
S	21-Dec	Queen of the South		A	L2	1-1	1492	McDermott	Brown,W r80	Hislop,T	Taylor 1	McCallum	Cooper	Duncan r75	Wallace	Graham	Wood	Robertson	Brown,T u80 · Robertson · 27
S	28-Dec	Cowdenbeath		H	L2	1-0	1844	McDermott	Brown,J	Hislop,T	Taylor	McCallum r51	Cooper	Robertson r60	Wallace 1	Graham	Wood	Urquhart r45	Brown,T u51 · Robertson · 26
W	01-Jan	East Fife		A	L2	1-2	5292	McDermott	Brown,J	Hislop,T	Taylor b	McCallum b	Cooper	Robertson b	Wallace	Graham 1	Wood r70	Hislop,J	Dempsey u70 · Brown,W · 49
S	04-Jan	Meadowbank Thistle		H	L2	3-1	1804	McDermott	Brown,J	Dempster	Taylor	McCallum	Cooper r45	Duncan	Wallace	Graham r45	Conn 1	Hislop,J 1p	Dailey u45 1 · Urquhart u45 · 9, 40, 54
S	11-Jan	Meadowbank Thistle		A	L2	0-1	1335	McDermott	Brown,J	Hislop,T	Taylor	McCallum	Cooper	Duncan 1	Wallace	Graham	Wood r	Hislop,J r75	Dailey u80 · Urquhart
S	18-Jan	Berwick Rangers		H	L2	2-0	1619	McDermott	Brown,W r89	Hislop,T	Taylor	McCallum	Cooper	Duncan r*	Wallace r	Dailey	Wood	Robertson	Urquhart u89 · Graham u75 · 84, 54
S	25-Jan	Queen of the South	6	A	SC 3	0-2	2793	McDermott	Brown,J	Hislop,T	Brown,T	McCallum	Cooper	Robertson b	Wallace b	Graham	Wood	Duncan r80	Urquhart u* b · Hislop,Ju
S	01-Feb	Hamilton Academical	7	H	L2	1-0	1895	McDermott	Brown,W b	Hislop,T	Taylor b	McCallum	Cooper	Duncan r75	Wallace b	Graham	Hislop,J 1	Robertson	Brown,T u80 · Wood · 59
S	08-Feb	Queen's Park	8	A	L2	1-1	663	McDermott	Brown,J	Hislop,T	Taylor	McCallum	Cooper	Robertson r60	Brown,T	McMillan	Hislop,J 1	Robertson	Wood u75 · McMillan u60 · 73
S	15-Feb	Montrose		H	L2	0-4	2286	McDermott	Brown,J	Dempster	Taylor	McCallum	Cooper	Robertson b	Brown,T	McMillan	Hislop,J	Urquhart r45	Graham u60 · Wood u45
S	22-Feb	Stirling		H	L2	3-0	1740	McDermott	Urquhart	Hislop,T	Taylor b	McCallum 1	Cooper	Robertson b	McMillan	McMillan b	Graham 1	Hislop,J	Wood · Duncan · 88, 63, 86
S	01-Mar	Stenhousemuir		A	L2	0-1	596	McDermott	Urquhart b	Hislop,T	Dempster	McCallum	Cooper	Robertson b	Brown,T r*	McMillan b	Graham 1	Hislop,J r	Lindsay u* · Brown,J u · 15
S	08-Mar	East Stirling		H	L2	1-1	1450	McDermott	Wood	Cairns	Taylor b	McMillan	Hunter	Brown,J1	Brown,T 1 45	Graham	Graham 1	Duncan r67	Wood u45 · Brown,J u56
S	15-Mar	Albion Rovers		A	L2	1-2	483	McDermott	Wood	Cairns	Urquhart	Hunter	Cooper	Robertson 1	Brown,T 1	Graham	Wallace	Robertson	Brown,T · Dempster · 31
S	22-Mar	St Mirren		H	L2	1-2	1557	McDermott	Brown,J	Cairns	Brown,T	Taylor	Cooper	Robertson	Brown,T 1	Graham	Wallace	Hislop,J	Brown,T · Duncan · 58
S	29-Mar	Clydebank		A	L2	2-3	1126	McDermott	Brown,J	Cairns	Brown,T	Taylor	Cooper	Robertson 1	Wallace	Hislop,J r	Urquhart b	Duncan 1	Jobson u · Hunter · 5, 12
S	05-Apr	Brechin City		A	L2	1-1	402	McDermott	Brown,J	Cairns	Brown,T	Taylor	Cooper	Hislop,J	Jobson r*	Wallace b 1	Urquhart r	Duncan b	Graham u* · Hunter u · 12
S	12-Apr	Alloa Athletic		H	L2	3-1	938	McDermott	Brown,J	Cairns	Brown,T 2	Taylor	Cooper	Hislop,J 1p	Graham	Wallace	Urquhart r73	Duncan	Hunter u73 · Jobson u · 47, 77, 85
W	19-Apr	Falkirk	9	A	L2	0-1	2665	McDermott	Brown,J	Cairns	Brown,T 1	Cooper	Cooper	Hislop,Jb	Wallace r	Graham	Urquhart x	Duncan r*	Hunter u* · Jobson u
W	23-Apr	Forfar Athletic		H	L2	2-0	816	McDermott	Brown,J	Brown,J	Brown,T 1	Taylor	Cooper	Hislop,J	Graham	Wallace 1	Urquhart	Duncan r	Hunter · Jobson · 56, 41
S	26-Apr	Queen of the South		H	L2	2-2	1310	McDermott	Brown,J	Brown,T	Brown,T	Taylor	Cooper	Hislop,J b	Graham x 1	Wallace 1	Urquhart	Duncan r	Hunter u · Jobson · 13, 55

Manager : George Farm to 17th October. Bert Paton from 22nd October to 24th March. Andy Matthew from 22nd April

(1) Stewart booked for a tackle on Robertson and sent off for kicking the ball away
(2) Wight booked and later sent off
(3) Bobby Stein sent off ; Bert Graham was taken off with a broken nose in 20 minutes, to be replaced by Tom Brown. In 85 minutes, Brown sustained a leg injury, and the substitute was substituted by Ronnie Duncan.
(4) St Mirren manager Alex Ferguson reported to SFA for remarks made to the referee
(5) Weir booked and later sent off
(6) Gate receipts £824
(7) Young sent off
(8) at Lesser Hampden
(9) Urquhart and Lawson sent off

Day	Date	Opponents	Note	Venue	Comp	Res	Att	1	2	3	4	5	6	7	8	9	10	11	Substitutes, own goals and goal times
S	02-Aug	Hartlepool		H	F	2-2	700	McDermott	Brown,J	Cairns r45	Brown,T 69 1	Urquhart	Cooper	Robertson	Graham r58	Hislop,J 1	Wallace	Duncan	Brown,W u45 Hunter u45 Robertson,L u45 17, 75
Tu	05-Aug	Southend United	1	H	F	3-0	700	McDermott	Brown,J	Cairns	Brown,T	McKenzie	Cooper	Robertson	Wallace r80	Hislop,J 2	Hunter	Duncan r85	Brown,W u80, Jobson u85, Urquhart, Graham. Jobson u58 Cunningham og 1 19, 77, 46
W	09-Aug	Montrose		H	LCS	2-1	1804	McDermott	Brown,J	Brown,W	Brown,T	Cairns	Cooper	Robertson 1	Wallace	Hislop,J	Hunter	Duncan 1	Jobson Dempster 65p 9
S	13-Aug	East Fife		A	LCS	2-2	3014	McDermott	Brown,J	Brown,W b	Brown,T	Cairns	Cooper	Robertson 2,1p	Wallace b	Hislop,J r	Graham	Duncan	Hunter u Dempster 3, 80p
S	16-Aug	St Mirren		H	LCS	1-0	2345	McDermott	Brown,J	Brown,W b	Brown,T	Cairns	Cooper	Robertson	Wallace 45	Hislop,J 1	Graham	Duncan r80	Urquhart u45 Hunter 89
S	20-Aug	East Fife		H	LCS	0-2	3247	McDermott	Brown,J	Brown,W b	Brown,T	Cairns	Cooper	Robertson	Wallace	Hislop,J	Graham	Duncan	Taylor u80 Urquhart
S	23-Aug	St Mirren		A	LCS	1-1	2441	McDermott	Brown,J r 80	Brown,W 45	Taylor	Cairns	Cooper	Robertson 1	Brown,T	Graham	Urquhart r70	Duncan	Hislop,J u45 Hunter u80 89
W	27-Aug	Montrose		A	LCS	1-2	2113	McDermott	Brown,J b	Cairns	Taylor	Cairns	Cooper	Robertson 1	Wallace	Graham	Urquhart	Duncan b 1	Hunter u70 65
S	30-Aug	Stranraer		H	L3	3-3	1575	McDermott	Brown,J	Cairns	Brown,T	Taylor	Cooper	Robertson	Wallace	Graham	Urquhart 1	Duncan	Jobson Heap og 1 80, 65, 35
S	06-Sep	Cowdenbeath		A	L3	1-1	1366	McDermott	Brown,J	Brown,W	Brown,T	Taylor	Cooper	Robertson	Wallace	Graham	Urquhart 1	Duncan x73	Hunter 57
S	13-Sep	Stenhousemuir	3	H	L3	2-0	1443	McDermott	Brown,J	Brown,W	Taylor	Cairns	Cooper	Robertson 1	Brown,T	Wallace 1	Urquhart b	Duncan	Hunter 36, 30
S	20-Sep	Queen's Park	4	A	L3	3-2	712	McDermott	Brown,J	Brown,W	Taylor r80	Cairns	Cooper	Robertson 1	Brown,T r83 1	Wallace 1	Urquhart b	Duncan 1	Hislop,J u83 Hunter u80 15, 22, 79
S	27-Sep	Forfar Athletic		H	L3	2-2	1237	McDermott	Brown,J	Brown,W	Taylor r	Cairns	Cooper	Robertson	Brown,T	Wallace r	Urquhart	Duncan 1	Hunter u Graham 32, 70
Tu	30-Sep	Dunfermline Athletic	5	H	FC SF	1-1		McDermott	Brown,J	Dempster	Urquhart	Cairns	Cooper	Robertson	Wallace	Graham 1	Hunter	Duncan	Jobson Brown,T 23
S	04-Oct	Clydebank		A	L3	1-1	1413	McDermott	Brown,J	Dempster	Urquhart	Cairns b	Cooper	Robertson 1	Wallace b	Graham b	Hunter r	Duncan	Brown,T u Taylor 50
S	11-Oct	Alloa Athletic		H	L3	1-0	1864	McDermott	Brown,J	Dempster	Urquhart	Cairns	Cooper	Robertson 1p	Brown,T	Graham r56	Hunter	Duncan	Wallace u56 Taylor 79
S	18-Oct	Meadowbank Thistle	6	A	L3	1-0	946	McDermott	Brown,J	Dempster	Taylor	Cairns	Cooper 1	Robertson	Brown,T r65	Wallace	Hunter	Duncan	Hislop,J u65 Urquhart 44
Tu	21-Oct	East Fife		H	FC F-1	3-0		McDermott	Brown,J	Brown,W	Brown,T	Taylor	Cooper	Robertson r69 1	Jobson	Wallace r76 1	Urquhart	Hislop,J 1	Graham u76 Duncan u69 33, 75, 38
S	25-Oct	Albion Rovers		A	L3	1-1	1852	McDermott	Brown,J	Brown,W	Brown,T	Taylor	Cooper	Robertson 1p	Jobson r60	Wallace	Hunter	Duncan	Duncan u60 Graham 30
Tu	28-Oct	East Fife		A	FC F-2	0-2	2147	McDermott	Brown,J	Brown,W	Urquhart r70	Taylor	Cooper	Robertson	Brown,T	Wallace	Urquhart b	Duncan	Graham Hislop,J
S	01-Nov	Stirling Albion		H	L3	2-2	918	McDermott	Brown,J	Brown,W	Brown,T	Taylor	Cooper	Robertson 2	Brown,T	Wallace	Hunter	Duncan	Hislop,J u70 Graham 35, 39
S	08-Nov	East Stirling		A	L3	1-1	362	McDermott	Brown,J	Brown,W	Brown,T	Taylor	Cooper	Robertson	Wallace	Graham r45	Hunter	Duncan	Hislop,J u45 1 Cairns 74
S	15-Nov	Berwick Rangers		A	L3	3-1	1682	McDermott	Brown,J	Brown,W b	Brown,T r75	Taylor	Cooper	Robertson 2,1p	Wallace	Hislop,J 1	Hunter b	Duncan 1	Urquhart u75 Jobson 44p, 89, 44
S	22-Nov	Brechin City		H	L3	1-1	725	McDermott	Brown,J	Brown,W	Brown,T	Taylor	Cooper	Robertson	Wallace	Hislop,J	Hunter	Duncan 1	Urquhart Jobson 64
S	29-Nov	Forfar Athletic		A	L3	0-0	2539	McDermott	Brown,J	Brown,W	McFarlane	Taylor	Cooper	Robertson	Wallace b	Hislop,J r63	Hunter b	Duncan	Jobson u63 Urquhart
S	06-Dec	Clydebank		H	L3	1-0	2169	McDermott	Brown,J b	Brown,W	McFarlane	Taylor	Cooper	Hislop,J 1p	Wallace	Graham	Hunter r86	Duncan	Jobson u86 Brown,T 84
S	13-Dec	Peterhead		A	SC 1	2-0	1624	McDermott	Brown,J	Brown,W	McFarlane r80	Taylor	Cooper	Hislop,J	Wallace 2	Graham	Hunter r45	Duncan	Urquhart u45 Brown,T u80 43, 80
H	20-Dec	Meadowbank Thistle		H	L3	3-2	669	McDermott	Brown,J	Brown,W 1	Urquhart 1	Taylor	Cooper	Hislop,Jr	Wallace 2	Graham 1	Hunter	Duncan	Brown,T u Jobson 60, 50, 56
S	27-Dec	Albion Rovers		A	L3	2-1	3080	McDermott	Brown,J	Brown,W	Urquhart	Taylor r11	Cooper	Hislop,Jr	Wallace 2	Graham 1	Hunter b	Duncan	Brown,T u11 Jobson 44, 45
Th	01-Jan	Cowdenbeath		H	L3	2-1	1162	McDermott	Brown,J	Brown,W	Urquhart	Taylor	Cooper	Hislop,J	Wallace 1	Graham 1	Hunter	Duncan	Brown,T Jobson 80, 20
S	03-Jan	Stenhousemuir		A	SC 2	3-0	3899	McDermott	Brown,J	Brown,W	Brown,T	Taylor	Cooper	Hislop,J r67 1	Wallace 2	Graham r75	Hunter	Duncan	Brown,T u67 Jobson u75 44, 40, 77
S	10-Jan	Clydebank		H	L3	3-1	697	McDermott	Brown,J	Brown,W	Urquhart r*	Taylor	Cooper	Hislop,J	Wallace 87 b 1	Graham 1	Hunter 1	Duncan	McFarlane u87 Brown,T 67, 86, 6
S	17-Jan	Brechin City		A	L3	4-0	6626	McDermott	Brown,J 1	Brown,W	Urquhart	Taylor	Cooper	Hislop,J r73	Wallace 1	Graham r	Hunter r	Duncan 1	McFarlane u Brown,T u* 43, 60, 79, 41
S	24-Jan	Arbroath		H	SC 3	1-0	2801	McDermott	Brown,J	Brown,W	McFarlane	Taylor	Cooper	Hislop,J r74 1p	Wallace 1	Graham r80	Hunter 1	Duncan	McFarlane u80 Brown,T 64
S	31-Jan	Queen's Park		A	L3	0-2	920	McDermott	Brown,J	Brown,W r76	McFarlane	Taylor	Cooper	Hislop,J r73	Wallace	Graham r78	Hunter 1	Duncan	McFarlane u78 Brown,T u60
S	07-Feb	Stranraer		A	L3	3-1	4170	McDermott	Brown,J 1p	Cairns	McFarlane	Taylor b	Cooper	Brown,T	Wallace 1	Graham	Hunter r85 1	Duncan	Cairns u75 Hislop,J u85 63, 35, 82
S	14-Feb	Montrose	8	A	SC 4	1-2	1597	Reid	Urquhart	Brown,W r76	McFarlane	Taylor	Cooper	Brown,T r60	Wallace 80	Graham r77 1	Hunter	Duncan	Jobson u77 Jobson u60 6
S	28-Feb	East Stirling		H	L3	0-0	1761	McDermott	Brown,J m	Urquhart	McFarlane	Taylor	Urquhart	Hislop,J	Wallace m 1	Graham	Hunter	Duncan 1	Candlish u76 Hislop,J u80 33
S	06-Mar	Stirling Albion		A	L3	1-0	1000	McDermott	Brown,J	Urquhart	McFarlane	Taylor	Cooper	Hislop,J	Wallace 80	Graham	Hunter	Duncan	Brown,T Candlish 55, 82, 33, 83
W	10-Mar	Queen of the South		H	SpC S	4-2	2575	McDermott	Brown,J	Urquhart	McFarlane	Taylor	Cooper	Hislop,J	Jobson 1	Jobson 1	Hunter	Duncan 1	Brown,T u80 Graham u77 1 11, 71
S	13-Mar	Clydebank		H	SpC S	2-1	1008	McDermott	Brown,J	Urquhart	McFarlane	Taylor	Cooper	Hislop,J	Jobson 80	Jobson 80	Hunter	Duncan 1	Brown,T u45 Graham u76 28, 36, 81
W	17-Mar	Berwick Rangers		H	SpC S	3-0	2529	McDermott	Brown,J	Urquhart	McFarlane	Taylor	Cooper	Hislop,J	Wallace 77 1	Jobson r76 2	Hunter r45	Duncan	Graham u80 Brown,T 67, 57
S	20-Mar	Clyde		A	SpC S	2-2	3403	McDermott	Brown,J	Brown,W	McFarlane	Taylor	Cooper	Hislop,J 1p	Wallace 1	Jobson 80	Hunter r45	Duncan	Graham u78 Brown,T u74 6, 60
S	27-Mar	Clyde		H	SpC S	2-1	580	McDermott	Brown,J	Urquhart	McFarlane	Taylor	Cooper	Hislop,J 1p	Jobson 80	Jobson r78	Hunter 1	Duncan	Graham u73 Brown,W 64
S	31-Mar	Alloa Athletic		H	L3	1-0	2675	McDermott	Brown,J	Urquhart 2	McFarlane b	Taylor	Cooper	Hislop,J	Wallace	Jobson r78	Hunter 1	Duncan	Graham u Graham u59 74
W	03-Apr	Queen of the South		A	SpC S	0-2		McDermott	Brown,J r32	Brown,W	McFarlane	Taylor	Cooper	Jobson	Wallace	Graham	Hunter r45	Duncan	Brown,W u45 Jobson 59, 74
S	10-Apr	Clydebank		H	SpC S	2-1	3093	McDermott	Brown,J	Brown,W	McFarlane	Taylor	Cooper	Brown,T	Wallace	Graham	Hunter	Duncan	Brown,T u32 Jobson 24, 12
S	17-Apr	Dumbarton		H	SpC 1-1	2-2	2248	McDermott	Brown,J	Brown,W	Urquhart	McFarlane	Cooper	Hislop,J m	Wallace 1	Wallace	Hunter	Duncan	Jobson u80
M	19-Apr	Dumbarton		H	SpC 1-2	0-4		McDermott	Urquhart	Brown,W	Brown,T	McFarlane	Cooper	Hislop,J m	Wallace	Graham r80	Hunter r52	Duncan	Candlish u52

Manager : Andy Matthew

(1) Cunningham sent off 54 minutes
(2) Johnson sent off 43 minutes
(3) McCullie and Duncan sent off 73 minutes
(4) at Lesser Hampden
(5) won 3-2 on penalties
(6) Davidson sent off 88 minutes
(7) Franchetti sent off 64 minutes
(8) The fourth round draw for the Scottish Cup was held in the boardroom at Stark's Park, immediately after the third round match against Arbroath. 14 year old Stewart Reid, son of Director Bobby, and 13 year old Brian Leigh, son of former player and Development Club organiser Andy, drew the numbered balls which saw Rovers travel to Montrose in the fourth round, when Stewart's dad came out of retirement to play in goal.

Day	Date	Opponents	Note	Venue	Comp	Res.	Att.	1	2	3	4	5	6	7	8	9	10	11	Substitutes, own goals and goal times
M	02-Aug	Hartlepool		H	F	0-1	1500	McDermott	Brown,J	Mathieson	Wheatley m	Taylor	Cooper	Hislop	Urquhart r*	Jobson	Hunter r**	Duncan	Robertson,L u*, Graham u*, Brown,W, Brown,T
Th	05-Aug	Rangers XI		H	F	0-1	2911	McDermott	Brown,J	Mathieson	Wheatley r*	Taylor	Cooper	Hislop	Wallace r***	Jobson r****	Hunter r**	Duncan	Urquhart u*, Brown,W u**, Graham u***, Brown,T u****
S	07-Aug	Partick Thistle		H	ASC 1-1	1-2	2303	McDermott	Brown,J x	Mathieson	Wheatley b	Taylor	Cooper	Hislop	Wallace 1	Jobson r*	Hunter r**	Duncan	Graham u*, Urquhart u**, McFarlane; 7
W	11-Aug	Partick Thistle		A	ASC 1-2	1-3	2000	McDermott	Brown,J	Mathieson	Wheatley 1	Taylor b	Cooper	Urquhart	Wallace	Jobson r75	Hunter	Duncan	Graham u75, Brown,T u; 28
S	14-Aug	Clyde		A	LCS	1-1	986	McDermott	Brown,J	Mathieson	McFarlane	Taylor	Cooper	Urquhart r	Wallace	Graham 1	Hunter	Duncan	Brown,T u*, Brown,T; 81
W	18-Aug	Airdrie		H	LCS	1-4	2170	McDermott	Brown,J	Mathieson	McFarlane	Taylor	Cooper	Urquhart 1p	Wallace	Graham	Hunter r79	Duncan	Jobson u79; 89
S	21-Aug	Queen's Park		H	LCS	0-1	1661	McDermott	Brown,J	Mathieson	McFarlane	Taylor r34	Cooper	Urquhart b	Wallace 1	Graham	Hunter r79	Duncan	Wheatley u34, Jobson u79
W	25-Aug	Airdrie		A	LCS	1-7	2156	McDermott	Brown,J r	Mathieson	Wheatley	Taylor	Cooper	Urquhart 2	Wallace	Graham	Hunter r70	Duncan	Brown,W u70, Candlish u70
S	28-Aug	Queen's Park		A	LCS	4-0	724	McDermott	Brown,J r	Mathieson	Wheatley	McFarlane	Cooper	Urquhart 2	Wallace	Hislop 2	Hunter	Duncan	Jobson, Brown,W; 24, 81, 13, 67
W	01-Sep	Clyde		H	LCS	1-1	1292	McDermott	Brown,J	Mathieson	Wheatley	McFarlane	Cooper	Urquhart	Wallace	Hislop	Hunter	Duncan 1	Jobson, Brown,W; 36
S	04-Sep	Falkirk		H	L2	1-1	2553	McDermott	Brown,J	Mathieson	Wheatley	Taylor	Cooper	Urquhart	Wallace	Hislop 1	Hunter	Duncan	Jobson, Hunter; 68
Tu	07-Sep	Clydebank		A	L2	0-3	2153	McDermott	Brown,J	Mathieson	Wheatley	Taylor	Cooper r*	Urquhart	Wallace r**	Hislop	McFarlane	Duncan	Jobson u**, Hunter u*
S	11-Sep	St Johnstone		A	L2	0-2	2058	McDermott	Brown,W r77	Mathieson	Wheatley	Taylor 65	Cooper	Urquhart	Wallace	Hislop	Hunter	Duncan	Jobson u65, Wheatley u77
S	15-Sep	Montrose		H	L2	0-2	1397	McDermott	Brown,J	Mathieson	Urquhart	McFarlane	Cooper	Hislop	Wallace b	Graham	McFarlane	Duncan r8	Brown,T u8, Jobson
S	18-Sep	Arbroath		H	L2	1-0	2027	McDermott	Brown,J	Mathieson	Urquhart	McFarlane	Cooper 1	Brown,T	Wallace r78	Graham	Hunter	Hislop	Jobson u78, Wheatley; 85
W	22-Sep	St Mirren		A	L2	1-1	2006	McDermott	Brown,J	Mathieson	Urquhart	McFarlane	Cooper 1	Brown,T	Wallace r* 1	Graham	Hunter r	Hislop	Taylor u, Wheatley u*; 54
S	25-Sep	Queen of the South		A	L2	0-1	1862	McDermott	Brown,J r	Mathieson	Urquhart	Taylor	Cooper	Brown,T r75	Urquhart	Graham	Hunter r70 b	Hislop b	Wheatley u, Duncan u75
W	29-Sep	Morton		A	L2	1-3	956	McDermott	McCullie	Mathieson	McFarlane	Taylor	Cooper 1	Urquhart x	Wallace	Graham	Hunter r70 b	Hislop b	Brown,T u70, Wheatley; 3
S	02-Oct	Dumbarton		H	L2	1-1	1553	McDermott	McCullie	Mathieson	McFarlane	Taylor	Cooper	Wallace r27	Urquhart 1	Graham	Hunter	Hislop	Brown,T u27, Wheatley; 62
W	06-Oct	Morton		H	L2	3-3	1338	McDermott	McCullie	Mathieson	Wheatley	Taylor	Cooper	Brown,T 2	Urquhart	Graham 1	Hunter 1	Hislop	Wheatley u, Wheatley; 9, 54, 41
S	09-Oct	Dundee		A	L2	1-3	5372	McDermott s	McCullie	Mathieson	McFarlane	Taylor	Cooper	Brown,T	Urquhart r 1	Graham u85	Hunter b	Hislop	Wheatley u, Jobson u85; 22
S	16-Oct	Hamilton Academical		H	L2	0-2	2234	McDermott	Brown,J	Mathieson	McFarlane	Taylor b	Cooper	Wallaceb b	Urquhart	Harrow	Hunter b	Duncan r56	Hislop u56, Graham
S	23-Oct	Airdrie		A	L2	0-1	1938	McDermott	Brown,J	Mathieson	McFarlane r*	Taylor	Cooper	Hislop	McFarlane r*	Wallace r**	Hunter	Harrow	Wheatley u*, Brown,T u**; 43
S	30-Oct	East Fife	1	H	L2	1-0	3522	McDermott	Brown,J	Brown,W	Urquhart b	Taylor b	Cooper b x	McFarlane	Wallace b x	McCullie r70	Hunter	Harrow	Robertson,J, Wheatley; 62, 53
S	06-Nov	Falkirk		A	L2	2-1	1903	McDermott	Brown,J	Brown,W	McFarlane	Taylor	Cooper	Wallace 1	Urquhart	Graham 1	Hunter b	Harrow	Jobson u73, Wheatley; 84
Tu	09-Nov	Burnisland Shipyard		H	FC 1	1-0	250	McDermott	Brown,J	Wheatley	Urquhart	Taylor	Cooper	Wallace	Urquhart	Graham 1	Hunter b	Harrow 1	Wheatley u79, Jobson u75; Milne og 76
S	13-Nov	St Johnstone		H	L2	1-1	2322	McDermott	Brown,J	Brown,W	McFarlane	Taylor	Cooper	Wallace	Urquhart r73	Graham 1	Hunter	Harrow	Jobson u73, Jobson u75; 85
S	20-Nov	Arbroath		A	L2	1-2	1462	McDermott	Brown,J r79	Brown,W	McFarlane	Taylor	Cooper	Wallace r75	Urquhart	Graham	Hunter b	Harrow	Wheatley u79, McFarlane u75; 4
S	27-Nov	Queen of the South		A	L2	3-3	1799	McDermott	Wheatley b	Brown,W b	Urquhart 2	Taylor	Cooper	Harrow	Wallace r45	Graham	Hunter b	Duncan	Jobson u45 1, Wheatley u; Milne og 76
W	15-Dec	Falkirk		H	L2	1-2	1645	McDermott	Urquhart	Brown,W	McFarlane	Taylor	Cooper	Hislop	Wallace	Harrow	Hunter r	Duncan 1	Wheatley u, Graham; 44
S	18-Dec	Hamilton Academical		A	L2	0-0	1324	McDermott	Urquhart	Brown,W	McFarlane	Taylor	Cooper	Wallace	Urquhart	Harrow	Hunter	Duncan	McFarlane u34, Cant u; 34
S	01-Jan	East Fife		A	L2	1-2	4503	McDermott	Brown,J b	Brown,W	Urquhart m 1	Taylor	Cooper r34	Wallace	Wallace	Graham 1	Hunter	Duncan	Cant u50, Graham u78
S	08-Jan	Albion Rovers		A	SC 2	1-2	1500	McDermott	Brown,J	Brown,W	Urquhart r78	Taylor	Cooper	McFarlane b	Wallace 1	Harrow	Hunter r50	Duncan	Candlish, Wheatley; 75, 62, 65
S	22-Jan	Queen of the South		A	L2	3-3	1789	McDermott	Brown,W b	Brown,W b	Urquhart	Taylor	Cooper	McFarlane b	Wallace 1	Harrow	Hunter 1	Duncan	Candlish u78, Wheatley; 37, 76, 34
Tu	25-Jan	St Johnstone		A	L2	3-3	1445	McDermott	Brown,J 1	Brown,W r77	McFarlane	Taylor 1	Cooper 1	Wallace 1	Urquhart	Harrow	Hunter	Duncan r78	Candlish, Wheatley; 51, 55, 15
S	05-Feb	Dumbarton		H	L2	3-1	1613	McDermott	Brown,J 1	Brown,W 1p	McFarlane	Taylor	Cooper 1	McFarlane b	Urquhart	Harrow r71	Hunter	Duncan	Candlish u75, Candlish
Tu	08-Feb	Arbroath		H	L2	0-1	1910	McDermott	Houston b	Hunter	Candlish	McFarlane	McFarlane	McFarlane	Wallace b	Hislop 2	Hunter	Duncan	Hislop u71, Candlish
S	12-Feb	Dundee		A	L2	0-4	5088	McDermott	Houston	Hunter	Urquhart b	McFarlane	Cooper b	McFarlane	Wallace 1	Hislop 1	Candlish b	Duncan	Hunter u65, Candlish; 10, 47
W	16-Feb	Airdrie		H	L2	2-2	1688	McDermott	Houston	Brown,W	Urquhart b	Taylor	Cooper	McFarlane	Wallace	Hunter	Candlish	Duncan	Hunter u65, Candlish; 22
S	19-Feb	Hamilton Academical		H	L2	1-1	1734	McDermott	Houston	Brown,W r65	Urquhart	Taylor	Cooper 1	McFarlane	Wallace r45	Harrow 1	Wheatley b	Harrow	Duncan u65, Candlish u45, Candlish u78
S	23-Feb	Dumbarton		H	L2	0-2	934	McDermott	Houston	Brown,W	Urquhart 2	Taylor	Cooper	McFarlane	Wallace b	Hislop 1	Wheatley b	Harrow	Hunter u65, Candlish u45
S	26-Feb	Falkirk		A	L2	3-0	1792	McDermott	Houston	Brown,W	Urquhart	Taylor 45	Cooper b	Hislop	Wallace b	Hunter	Wheatley	Duncan b 1	Hunter u77, Pettie; 17, 86, 46
S	05-Mar	Airdrie		A	L2	3-3	993	McDermott	Houston	Brown,W r77	Urquhart	McFarlane	Cooper b	Hislop	Wallace 2	Harrow 1	Hunter b	Duncan	Wheatley, Pettie; 48, 62, 24
S	12-Mar	Montrose		H	L2	1-0	1564	McDermott	Houston b	Brown,W 1p	Candlish	McFarlane	Cooper	Hislop 1	Wallace 1	Harrow 1	Hunter b	Duncan	Wheatley u, Pettie; 18
W	23-Mar	East Fife		A	L2	2-1	3228	McDermott	Houston	Hunter	Urquhart	McFarlane	Cooper	Hislop 1	Wallace 1	Harrow 1	Candlish	Duncan	Wheatley, Pettie; 71, 82
S	26-Mar	Montrose		A	L2	1-2	1228	McDermott	Houston	Hunter	Urquhart	McFarlane	Cooper	Hislop	Wallace	Harrow r71	Candlish	Duncan	Wheatley u45, Pettie; 34
S	02-Apr	St Mirren		A	L2	0-2	5660	McDermott s	Houston	Brown,W	McFarlane	Taylor b x	Cooper	Hislop	Wallace r45	Harrow	McFarlane	Duncan r	Wheatley u45, Candlish u
S	09-Apr	Airdrie		H	L2	1-3	3779	McDermott s	Houston	Brown,W b	Urquhart b	Taylor r72	Cooper	Hislop	Urquhart b	Harrow r71	Hunter b	Duncan 1	Jobson u72, Candlish u; 35
S	16-Apr	Clydebank		H	L2	2-1	2524	McDermott	Brown,J	Hunter	McFarlane	Taylor	Cooper	Hislop	Urquhart 1p	Harrow 1	Candlish	Duncan	Pettie u70, Candlish; 10, 28
S	23-Apr	Clydebank	2	A	L2	0-2	2660	McDermott	Brown,J	Brown,W	McFarlane	Taylor	Cooper	Hislop	Urquhart	Harrow 1	Candlish r70	Duncan	Pettie u70, Houston
S	30-Apr	Morton		H	L2	3-4	3252	McDermott	Brown,J	Brown,W 1p	Candlish u81 b	McFarlane	Cooper	Hislop 1	Wallace 1	Harrow	Hunter	Duncan r82	Houston u81, Whyte u82; 10, 89, 85

Manager : Andy Matthew
(1) Dave Clarke sent off 68 minutes
(2) McColl missed penalty

Day	Date	Opponents	Note	Venue	Comp	Res	Att	1	2	3	4	5	6	7	8	9	10	11	Substitutes, own goals and goal times
M	01-Aug	Cowdenbeath		A	FC SF	0-1	1000	Frame	Houston	Hunter	Urquhart	Taylor	Thomson b	Purvis r	Pettie	Hislop	Harrow	Duncan	McKay u / McComb
S	06-Aug	Dundee		H	F	1-0	1201	Frame s	Houston	Hunter r45	Urquhart r*	Taylor	Thomson	Pettie u**	Hislop 1	Harrow	Candlish	Duncan r***	Brown,J u45 / McComb u* / Purvis u** — McKay u*** 33, Purvis, 44
Tu	09-Aug	Hibernian XI		H	F	1-2	845	Frame	Brown,J	Houston	McComb	Taylor	Thomson	Pettie	Hislop 1	Harrow	Candlish	Duncan	McKay / McDonough
S	13-Aug	Forfar Athletic		A	L3	0-1	960	Frame	Houston	Houston	McComb	McFarlane	Thomson	Pettie	Hislop 1	Harrow	Candlish r	Duncan	McKay u / McDonough
S	20-Aug	Cowdenbeath		A	L3	2-2	1613	Frame s	Brown,J	Houston	Urquhart m 1	Taylor	Thomson	Pettie	Hislop 1	Hislop	McFarlane b	Duncan r64	Wallace u64 / Candlish / 50, 55
S	27-Aug	Stenhousemuir		A	L3	1-1	575	McDermott	Houston	Hunter	McFarlane	Taylor	Thomson	Pettie 1	Wallace,G	Hislop	Urquhart r80	Harrow	Candlish u80 / Duncan / 75
W	31-Aug	Arbroath		H	LC 2-1	2-1	1542	McDermott	Houston	Hunter	McFarlane	Taylor	Thomson	Pettie	Wallace,G	Hislop r	Urquhart	Harrow	Duncan / Candlish
S	03-Sep	Arbroath		A	LC 2-2	2-2	1339	McDermott	Houston	Hunter	McFarlane	Taylor 1	Thomson	Pettie r	Wallace,G r35	Harrow	Urquhart	Hislop	Candlish u / Candlish u / 85
S	10-Sep	East Stirling		H	L3	1-0	1081	McDermott	Houston	Hunter	McFarlane	Taylor b	Thomson	Pettie	Wallace,G r35	Hislop 1	Urquhart	Duncan	Candlish u85 / Harrow / 60
W	14-Sep	Berwick Rangers		A	L3	0-0	426	McDermott	Houston	Hunter	McFarlane	Taylor	Thomson	Pettie	Urquhart r**	Hislop	Harrow r*	Duncan	Candlish u* / Moffat u**
S	17-Sep	Stranraer		H	L3	1-1	1443	McDermott	Houston	Hunter	McFarlane	Taylor b	Thomson	Pettie 1	Wallace,G r45	Hislop	Urquhart	Duncan r75	Harrow u45 1 / Candlish u75 / 71
S	24-Sep	Queen's Park		H	L3	3-0	727	McDermott	Houston	Hunter	McFarlane	Taylor	Thomson	Pettie	Harrow	Hislop r75	Urquhart r80	Duncan 2	McComb u75 / Candlish u80 / 52, 34, 41
W	28-Sep	Meadowbank Thistle		H	L3	1-0	1249	McDermott	Houston r68	Hunter 1	McFarlane	Taylor	Thomson	Pettie	Harrow	Hislop	Urquhart	Duncan	Candlish u68 / McComb / 60
S	01-Oct	Falkirk	1	A	L3	2-2	2449	McDermott b	McDonough	Hunter	McFarlane	Taylor b	Thomson r82	Pettie 1	Wallace,G	Harrow 1	Urquhart	Duncan b	Candlish u82 / Hislop / 54, 20
S	08-Oct	Clyde		A	L3	0-0	1193	Frame	McDonough	Hunter b x	McFarlane	Taylor	Thomson	Pettie r	Harrow	Harrow	Urquhart	Duncan b	Hislop u82 / McComb
S	15-Oct	Dunfermline Athletic		H	L3	2-1	3053	Frame	McDonough	Hunter r b	McFarlane	Taylor	Thomson	Pettie	Harrow	Wallace,G 1	Urquhart 73p	Duncan r9	Hislop u9 / McComb u / 38, 73
W	19-Oct	East Stirling		H	L3	1-1	1546	McDermott	McDonough	Hunter	McFarlane	Taylor	Thomson	Pettie	Harrow	Wallace,G 1	Urquhart	Duncan 1	McComb / Hislop / 16
S	22-Oct	Brechin City		A	L3	0-4	534	Frame	McDonough	Hunter b	McFarlane	Taylor	Thomson	Pettie	Harrow	Hislop r*	Urquhart	Candlish r**	McComb* / Wildridge u*
S	29-Oct	Cowdenbeath		A	L3	2-1	1462	McDermott	Houston	McDonough	Urquhart	Taylor	McFarlane	Pettie	Harrow	Hislop	Hunter	Duncan 2	Wildridge / Candlish / 21, 55
S	05-Nov	Stenhousemuir		H	L3	3-0	1247	McDermott	Houston	McDonough	Urquhart	Taylor	McFarlane	Pettie	Harrow 1	Hislop 1	Hunter	Duncan 1	Wildridge / Candlish / 76, 72, 74
S	12-Nov	East Stirling		A	L3	2-1	700	McDermott	Houston	Urquhart 1	Urquhart 1	Taylor	McFarlane	Pettie	Harrow	Hislop	Hunter	Duncan 1	Moffat / Thomson / 89, 42
S	19-Nov	Stranraer		A	L3	4-1	1000	McDermott	Houston	McDonough	Urquhart	Taylor	McFarlane	Pettie 1	Harrow	Hislop	Candlish 2	Duncan 1	Wildridge / Thomson / 89, 38, 56, 90
S	26-Nov	Queen's Park		H	L3	1-1	1812	McDermott	Houston	McDonough	Urquhart r80 b	Taylor	McFarlane	Pettie	Harrow	Hislop r75	Candlish	Duncan r60 1	Thomson u75 1 / McComb u80 / 78
S	10-Dec	Clyde		H	L3	1-1	1835	McDermott	Houston	McDonough	Urquhart	Taylor	McFarlane	Pettie	Candlish	Harrow	Hunter	Duncan r60 1	Thomson / Thomson / 31
S	17-Dec	Stenhousemuir		H	SC 1	1-0	1412	McDermott	Houston	McDonough	Urquhart	Taylor	McFarlane	Pettie	Moffat	Harrow b 1	Hunter	Hislop	Thomson / Candlish / 17
S	24-Dec	Dunfermline Athletic		H	L3	0-1	2937	McDermott	Houston	McDonough	Urquhart	Taylor	McFarlane	Pettie	Moffat	Harrow	Hunter	Wildridge	Thomson u20 / Candlish
S	31-Dec	Forfar Athletic		H	L3	1-2	2002	McDermott	Houston	McDonough	Urquhart	Taylor	McFarlane	Pettie r70	Moffat	Harrow	Hunter r20	Duncan 1	Candlish u70 / Hislop / 73
M	02-Jan	Stenhousemuir		A	L3	2-1	725	Frame	Houston	McDonough	Urquhart	Taylor 1	McFarlane	Pettie	Hislop	Harrow 1	Hunter	Duncan b	Thomson u / Thomson / 13, 53
S	07-Jan	Berwick Rangers		A	SC 2	0-6	1771	McDermott	Houston r	McDonough r	Urquhart	Taylor	Thomson	Forrest 3	Hislop	Harrow	Hunter 1	Duncan r	Hislop u 1 / Candlish
S	14-Jan	Berwick Rangers		H	L3	7-1	2022	McDermott	Urquhart	McDonough m 1	McFarlane	Taylor	Thomson	Forrest	Pettie 1	Harrow	Hunter 1	Duncan 1	Hislop / Dunn / 41,20,65,87,61,68,89
Tu	24-Jan	Dundee United		H	F	0-3	741	McDermott	Urquhart	Brown,W	McFarlane	Taylor	Thomson	Forrest	Pettie	Harrow	Hunter	Duncan	Candlish u 2 / Brown,W
S	28-Jan	East Stirling		A	L3	2-2	558	McDermott	Urquhart	McDonough	McFarlane	Taylor	Thomson	Forrest r	Pettie	Harrow 2	Wallace,GG	Duncan	Brown,W u / Houston / 3, 27
S	18-Feb	Falkirk		A	F	2-0	100	McDermott	Brown,W	McDonough	McFarlane	Taylor	Thomson	Forrest r	Pettie	Harrow 1	Wallace,GG	Duncan	Forrest u45 / Brown,W
S	25-Feb	Meadowbank Thistle		H	L3	4-0	1775	McDermott	McDonough	McDonough h r	McFarlane	Taylor	Thomson	Candlish	Pettie 1	Harrow	Wallace,GG 2	Duncan 80	Forrest u80 / Brown,W / 30, 89, 34, 64
S	04-Mar	Meadowbank Thistle		A	L3	0-0	921	McDermott	McDonough	McDonough	McFarlane	Taylor	Thomson	Candlish r45	Pettie r	Harrow	Wallace,GG	Duncan	Forrest u45 / Brown,W
S	11-Mar	Cowdenbeath		H	L3	2-2	2080	McDermott	McDonough	Candlish 1p	McFarlane	Taylor	Thomson r*	Forrest	Pettie	Harrow	Wallace,GG 1	Duncan r**	Hunter u* / Hislop u** / 14, 89
S	18-Mar	Albion Rovers		A	L3	2-1	694	McDermott	McDonough	Candlish	McFarlane	Taylor	Thomson r*	Forrest	Pettie	Harrow	Hunter	Hunter	Duncan u32 1 / McDonough / 49, 82
Tu	21-Mar	Queen's Park		A	L3	0-0	616	McDermott	McDonough b	Candlish	McFarlane	Taylor	Thomson r73	Forrest	Pettie	Harrow	Wallace,GG	Duncan r66	Murray u66 / Hunter u73
S	25-Mar	Brechin City		H	L3	3-1	1915	McDermott	Urquhart	Candlish m	McFarlane	Taylor r75 1	Hunter	Pettie r70	Pettie r70	Harrow 1	Wallace,GG	Hislop	Forrest u70 / Forrest / McDonough u75 / 25, 40, 44
W	29-Mar	Falkirk		H	L3	1-1	2498	McDermott	Urquhart	Candlish m 1	McFarlane	Taylor	Thomson	Pettie	Pettie	Harrow b	Wallace,GG	Duncan	Hunter u / Forrest / 66
S	01-Apr	Stranraer		A	L3	0-1	957	McDermott	Urquhart	Candlish	McFarlane	Taylor	Thomson b	Pettie r65	Hunter u80	Harrow	Wallace,GG	Duncan	Murray u65 / Hunter u
Tu	04-Apr	Falkirk		A	L3	2-2	2189	McDermott	Urquhart	Candlish	McFarlane	Taylor	Thomson	Murray u80	Murray r33	Harrow	Hunter	Duncan	McDonough u33 / Forrest u80 / 44, 48
S	08-Apr	Forfar Athletic		H	L3	2-0	2034	McDermott	Urquhart	Candlish	McFarlane	Taylor	Thomson	Pettie r	Murray 1	Harrow 1	Urquhart	Duncan	Forrest u 1 / Hunter / 52, 62
W	12-Apr	Albion Rovers		A	L3	2-0	1964	McDermott	McDonough	Candlish	McFarlane	Taylor	Thomson	Wallace,GG 1	Wallace,GG	Harrow 1	Murray r* 1	Duncan 1	Urquhart u* / Hunter u** / 90, 9
S	15-Apr	Berwick Rangers		A	L3	2-1	1643	McDermott	McDonough	Candlish	McFarlane	Taylor	Thomson	Forrest r**	Murray	Harrow r	Hunter 1	Duncan 1	Hunter u* / Forrest / 2, 46
S	22-Apr	Brechin City		H	L3	1-0	2139	McDermott	McDonough	Candlish	McFarlane	Taylor	Thomson	Wallace,GG	Murray 1	Harrow r	Hunter	Duncan	Forrest u / Forrest / 59
W	26-Apr	Clyde		H	L3	1-0	1934	McDermott	McDonough	Candlish	McFarlane	Taylor	Thomson	Wallace,GG	Murray	Harrow 1	Hunter	Duncan	Forrest / Pettie
S	29-Apr	Dunfermline Athletic		A	L3	2-0	3197	McDermott	McDonough	Candlish	Pettie	Taylor r58 b	Thomson	Wallace,GG	Murray	Harrow 1	Hunter r63	Duncan	Houston u58 / Forrest u63 1 / 24, 72

Manager : Andy Matthew to 10th January. Willie McLean from 30th January.
(1) George Watson, Falkirk goalkeeper, sent off in 67 minutes for a foul on Pettie

Day	Date	Opponents	Note	Venue	Comp	Res	Att	1	2	3	4	5	6	7	8	9	10	11	Substitutes, own goals and goal times
S	29-Jul	Dundee United		H	F	0-3	1659	Frame r68	McDonough	Candlish	Taylor r45	Forsyth	Thomson	McComb	Urquhart r 52	Harrow	Murray	Duncan	Mallin u68; Houston u54; Hunter u52 r54; Forrest u45; Coleman — 21, 70, 5
M	31-Jul	Cowdenbeath		H	FC SF	3-2	693	Mallin s	McDonough	Candlish	Urquhart	Forsyth	Thomson	Forrest 1	McComb	Harrow 1	Murray	Duncan 1	Coleman u; Forrest u72; McComb u86; Forrest u25; Taylor — 85
S	05-Aug	Morton		H	ASC 1-1	1-2	2045	Mallin	McDonough	Candlish	Forsyth	Taylor	Thomson r86	Houston	Urquhart r72	Harrow	Murray r5	Duncan 1	Forrest u72; McComb u5 r25; Forrest u25 — 3
Tu	08-Aug	Morton		A	ASC 1-2	1-4	3000	McDermott	McDonough b	Candlish	Forsyth	Taylor	Thomson	Houston	Urquhart b	Harrow	Murray r5	Duncan	Coleman u*; Wildridge u** — 50
S	12-Aug	Clyde		A	L2	1-3	951	McDermott	McDonough	Candlish	Urquhart	Houston b	McFarlane	Forrest r*	McComb r**	Harrow 1	Murray r45	Duncan	Wildridge u**
S	19-Aug	Clydebank		H	L2	4-2	1982	McDermott	McDonough 1	Candlish	Houston	Taylor	McFarlane	Wallace 2, 1p	Urquhart	Harrow	Murray	Duncan	Wildridge u45 — 8, 4, 37p, 7
S	26-Aug	Stirling Albion		A	L2	1-0	1577	McDermott	Urquhart	Candlish b	Forsyth	Houston b	McFarlane	Wallace	Urquhart	Harrow	Murray r60	Duncan r75	Forrest u75 1 — 87
S	30-Aug	Queen's Park		H	LC 2-1	4-2	1632	McDermott	McDonough	Candlish	Forsyth	Houston	McFarlane	Wallace 4, 1p	Thomson	Harrow	Hunter r62 1	Forrest 1	Hunter; Thomson — 17, 35, 43p, 74
S	02-Sep	Queen's Park	1	A	LC 2-1	2-4	804	McDermott	McDonough r75	Candlish	Forsyth	Houston	McDonough r75	Wallace	Urquhart	Harrow	Hunter r52	Forrest 1	Duncan u60; Thomson u75 — 28, 93
W	06-Sep	Hamilton Academical		A	L2	1-1	1916	McDermott	Houston	Candlish	Forsyth	Taylor	McFarlane	Wallace	Urquhart	Harrow	Hunter r*	Duncan	Murray u62; Forrest — 32
S	09-Sep	Ayr United		H	L2	0-0	2249	McDermott	Houston	Candlish	Forsyth	Taylor	McFarlane	Wallace	Urquhart	Harrow	Hunter r*	Duncan	Forrest u52; Murray u78
W	13-Sep	Dundee		H	L2	2-4	4488	McDermott	Houston	Candlish	Forsyth	Taylor	McFarlane	Wallace 1	Urquhart	Harrow	Murray	Duncan 1	Forrest u*; Murray u** — 33, 11
S	16-Sep	Airdrie		A	L2	0-3	1690	McDermott	Houston b	Candlish r73	Forsyth	Taylor	McFarlane	Wallace 1	Urquhart	Harrow	Hunter r*	Duncan r60	Thomson u60; Thomson u73
S	23-Sep	Queen of the South		H	L2	4-0	1897	McDermott	Houston b	Candlish r70	Forsyth r45	Taylor	McFarlane	Wallace 1	Urquhart	Harrow r79	Murray r	McDonough	Pettie u45; Forrest u70 3 — 25, 68, 76, 89
W	27-Sep	St Johnstone		A	L2	1-1	1412	McDermott	McDonough	McDonough	Forsyth	Taylor	McFarlane	Wallace 2	Urquhart 1	Harrow 2	Murray	Forrest	Pettie u; Thomson — 13
S	30-Sep	Arbroath		H	L2	5-0	1292	McDermott	Houston	McDonough	Forsyth	Taylor b	McFarlane r60	Wallace	Urquhart 1	Harrow	Murray	Forrest 1	Thomson u60 1; Pettie u79 — 25, 61, 41, 34, 82
W	04-Oct	Montrose		H	LC 3-1	3-0	2310	McDermott	Houston b	Candlish	Forsyth	Taylor b	McFarlane	Wallace	Urquhart	Harrow	Murray r62	Forrest 1	Pettie u62; Thomson — 6, 80, 33
S	07-Oct	Dumbarton		H	L2	1-2	2720	McDermott	Houston b	Candlish	Forsyth	Taylor r65	McFarlane	Wallace	Urquhart	Harrow	Murray	Forrest	Pettie u; Thomson u65
W	11-Oct	Montrose		A	LC 3-2	1-5	1428	McDermott	Houston b	Candlish	Forsyth b	Taylor	McFarlane	Wallace 1	Urquhart	Harrow	Murray	Forrest r b	Pettie u; Thomson — 5
S	14-Oct	Kilmarnock		A	L2	0-3	2621	McDermott	Thomson	Candlish	Forsyth	Taylor r75	McFarlane r45	Wallace	Houston	Harrow	Murray	Urquhart	Forrest u45; Pettie u75
S	21-Oct	Montrose		H	L2	3-1	1894	McDermott	McFarlane	Candlish b	Forsyth	Taylor b 1	Pettie	Wallace 1p	Urquhart b	Harrow	Murray r48	Forrest	Thomson u48; Duncan — 37, 69, 6
S	28-Oct	Clydebank	2	A	L2	1-2	1553	McDermott	Houston	Candlish	Forsyth	Taylor	McFarlane r85	Wallace	Urquhart b	Harrow x89 1	Thomson r	Pettie	Forrest u; McDonough u85 u85 60 — 2
S	04-Nov	Stirling Albion		H	L2	1-2	1755	McDermott	Houston	Candlish 1	Forsyth b	Taylor	McDonough	Pettie	Urquhart	Forrest	Murray r68	Duncan	Hunter u68; McFarlane
Tu	07-Nov	East Fife		A	FC F-1	0-0	500	McDermott	McDonough	Candlish	Myles	Houston	Thomson	Forrest	Pettie	Harrow	Hunter	Duncan r70	Urquhart; Murray
S	11-Nov	Ayr United		A	L2	0-3	3733	McDermott	McDonough b	Candlish	Forsyth b	Houston	McFarlane	Wallace	Urquhart	Harrow	Pettie	Duncan	Pettie u70; Thomson — 56, 22
S	18-Nov	Airdrie		H	L2	2-0	1781	McDermott	McDonough	Candlish b	Forsyth	Houston	McFarlane 1	Wallace 1p	Urquhart r77	Harrow	Murray	Duncan	Pettie u77; Forrest — 65
S	25-Nov	Queen of the South		A	L2	1-2	1255	McDermott	McDonough	Candlish	Houston	Taylor	McFarlane	Wallace	Urquhart r78	Harrow	Murray	Duncan	Pettie u78; Thomson
S	09-Dec	Dumbarton		A	L2	3-1	820	McDermott	McDonough 1	Candlish	Houston	Thomson	McFarlane	Wallace	Urquhart r85	Harrow	Murray	Duncan r25	Pettie u25 1; Forrest — 57, 18, 33
S	16-Dec	Kilmarnock		H	L2	1-3	1843	McDermott	McDonough	Candlish	Houston	Thomson	McFarlane r70	Wallace 1	Urquhart r65	Harrow	Murray	Pettie	Pettie u70; Taylor u85 — 38
S	23-Dec	Montrose		A	L2	0-0	585	McDermott	McDonough	Candlish	Houston	Thomson	McFarlane	Wallace	Thomson	Harrow	Murray	Thomson,R	Pettie u65; Forsyth
S	20-Jan	Queen of the South		H	L2	3-0	1138	McDermott	McDonough	Candlish	McFarlane	Houston	Thomson	Wallace 1p	Urquhart	Harrow 1	Thomson,R r65	Duncan r65	Forrest u65; Murray — 22, 39, 83
S	27-Jan	Hearts		H	SC 3	0-2	9998	McDermott	McDonough	Candlish	Houston	Forsyth	Thomson b	Wallace	Urquhart r17	Harrow	McFarlane b	Thomson,R r80	Murray u17; Forrest u80
S	24-Feb	Kilmarnock		H	L2	1-2	3267	McDermott	McDonough	Candlish	McFarlane	Forsyth	Thomson	Wallace	Urquhart	Harrow	Thomson,R 1	Duncan	Houston; Forrest — 36
W	28-Feb	Dumbarton	3	A	L2	0-1	700	McDermott	McDonough	Candlish	McFarlane	Forsyth r60	Thomson	Wallace	Urquhart	Harrow	Thomson,R	Duncan r45	Forrest u45; Houston u60
S	03-Mar	Clyde		H	L2	1-2	1370	McDermott	Houston	Candlish	McFarlane	Forsyth	Thomson	Wallace r45	Urquhart	Harrow	Thomson,R	Forrest 1	Pettie u45; Murray — 14
W	07-Mar	Stirling Albion		A	L2	0-3	898	McDermott	Houston	Candlish	Houston	Forsyth	Thomson b	Wallace	Urquhart	Harrow	Thomson,R	Forrest	Pettie u; Murray
S	10-Mar	Hamilton Academical		H	L2	0-1	1364	McDermott	McDonough	Candlish	Houston	Forsyth r55	Thomson	Wallace	Murray r75	Harrow	Thomson,R	Duncan	Pettie u55; Forrest u75 — 20
W	14-Mar	Ayr United		H	L2	2-0	1147	McDermott	McDonough	Candlish	Urquhart	Forsyth	Thomson	Wallace	Murray 1	Harrow	Murray 1	Duncan r1	Pettie u; Duncan r1 — 74
W	28-Mar	Dumbarton		A	L2	0-3	585	McDermott	McDonough	Candlish	Ford	Forsyth	Thomson	Wallace	Urquhart	Harrow	Thomson,R	Duncan	Forrest; Murray
S	31-Mar	Clyde		A	L2	1-1	630	McDermott	McDonough r73	Candlish	Ford	Forsyth b	Thomson	Wallace 1p	Urquhart	Harrow 1	Thomson,R	Duncan r68 b	Forrest u68; Murray
W	04-Apr	Airdrie		A	L2	1-0	897	McDermott	Houston	Candlish	Ford	Forsyth	Thomson	Wallace	Urquhart	Harrow 1	Thomson,R	McComb r	Forrest u; Murray u60
S	07-Apr	St Johnstone		A	L2	0-3	1632	McDermott	Houston	Candlish	Ford	Forsyth	Thomson	Wallace	Urquhart	Harrow r60	Thomson,R	McComb	Forrest u60; Murray u73
W	11-Apr	Dundee		H	L2	1-2	2769	McDermott	Ford	Candlish	Urquhart	Forsyth	Thomson	Wallace	McComb r75	Harrow 1	Thomson,R	Duncan	Houston u75; Forrest — 89
S	14-Apr	Arbroath		H	L2	1-2	1593	McDermott	Urquhart	Candlish	Ford	Houston	Thomson 1	Wallace	Murray	Harrow	Thomson,R	Duncan r61	Forrest u61; McComb — 83
W	18-Apr	Arbroath		A	L2	1-0	1026	McDermott	Houston	Candlish	Ford	Forsyth	Forrest	Forrest	McComb r	Harrow	Thomson,R	Duncan r79	Urquhart u; Wallace u79 1p — 87
S	21-Apr	Montrose		A	L2	1-1	1001	McDermott	Houston	Candlish	Ford	Forsyth	Thomson	Forrest u63	Urquhart	Harrow	Thomson,R	McComb r65 1	Urquhart u; Murray — 2
S	28-Apr	Hamilton Academical		H	L2	2-0	1443	McDermott	Houston	Candlish	Ford 1	Forsyth b	Thomson	Wallace	Urquhart b	Harrow 1	Thomson,R	Duncan	Wallace u65; McComb
W	02-May	Clydebank		H	L2	1-2	1333	McDermott	Campbell	Candlish	Ford	Houston	Thomson	Forrest 1p	Urquhart	Harrow 1	Thomson,R	Duncan r85	Wallace u63; McComb — 79, 82
S	05-May	East Fife	4	A	FC F-2	2-2	1304	McDermott	Houston	Candlish	Ford	Houston	Thomson b	Forrest 1p	Urquhart b	McComb r65	Harrow	Duncan r	Forrest u85; McComb — 32
Tu	08-May	Dundee		A	L2	0-2	6450	McDermott	Houston	Candlish	Ford	Thomson	Forsyth	Wallace	Urquhart b	Harrow	Thomson,R	Duncan r	Wildridge u65; Myles; Forrest u — 32, 44

Manager : Willie McLean to 28th January. Gordon Wallace from 30th January
(1) after extra time, won 4-2 on penalties
(2) Harrow and Fanning sent off in the final minute
(3) Abandoned (snow shower) after 61 minutes
(4) lost 4-2 on penalties

Day	Date	Opponents	Note	Venue	Comp	Res.	Att.	1	2	3	4	5	6	7	8	9	10	11	Substitutes, own goals and goal times
S	28-Jul	Preston North End		H	F	0-1	1320	McDermott	McDonough r**	Candlish	Ford*	Forsyth	McFarlane	Wallace r***	Steen r70	Harrow	Thomson,R	Miller	Urquhart u*, Houston u**, Myles u70, Mitchell
Th	02-Aug	Swansea City		H	F	0-2	1751	McDermott	Houston	Candlish	Ford	Forsyth	McFarlane	Wallace	Steen r	Harrow	Thomson,R	Miller	Thomson,D u*, McDonough, Forrest, Urquhart, Thomson,R
F	03-Aug	Keith	7	A	F	2-2	300	McDermott	McDonough	Steen	Ford r*	Houston	Thomson,D	Mitchell 1	Myles	Forrest	Urquhart	Wallace r** 1	Candlish u*, Miller u**, Forsyth, Thomson,R, Wallace
Sn	05-Aug	Huntly	8	A	F	7-2	200	McDermott	McDonough	Steen r**	Urquhart 1	Forsyth b	Thomson,D	Forrest 2	Myles r*	Harrow 2	Thomson,R	Miller	Thomson,D u*, Candlish u**, Houston
S	11-Aug	Clyde		H	L2	0-0	1543	McDermott	McDonough	Candlish	Ford	Forsyth b	Thomson,D	Wallace	Urquhart	Harrow	Thomson,R	Miller	Forrest u75, Steen, Urquhart
S	18-Aug	Airdrie		A	L2	0-0	1875	McDermott	Houston	Candlish	Ford	Forsyth	Thomson,D	Wallace	Urquhart	Harrow	Thomson,R	Miller	Forrest, Urquhart
S	25-Aug	Dunfermline Athletic		H	L2	0-0	2898	McDermott	Houston	Candlish	Ford	Forsyth b	Thomson,D	Forrest b	Urquhart	Harrow	Thomson,R	Miller	Forrest u63 b, Urquhart u63
W	29-Aug	East Fife		H	LC 2-1	1-0	2151	McDermott	Houston	Candlish	Ford	Forsyth b	Thomson,D	Forrest b	Urquhart	Harrow r67 b	McFarlane 1	Miller	Wallace u67, McComb u85, 21
Sa	01-Sep	East Fife		A	LC 2-2	2-0	2355	McDermott	Houston b	Candlish b	Ford	Forsyth b	Thomson,D	McFarlane r76 1	Urquhart r76	Forrest m	Forrest	Miller r76 1	McComb u76, Wallace u76, 4, 65
W	05-Sep	Berwick Rangers		A	L2	0-0	1227	McDermott	Houston	Candlish	Ford	Forsyth b	Thomson,D	Forrest r*	Urquhart	Harrow	McFarlane r**	Miller	Wallace u*, Thomson,R u**
S	08-Sep	St Johnstone		H	L2	2-2	2725	McDermott	Houston	Candlish b	Ford 1	Forsyth	Thomson,D	Wallace	Urquhart b	Harrow 1	McFarlane	Miller 1	Forrest b, Thomson,R, 10, 76
Tu	11-Sep	Hearts		H	L2	3-2	4632	McDermott	Houston	Candlish	Ford	Forsyth b	Thomson,D	Wallace	Urquhart	Harrow 1	McFarlane	Miller 1	Forrest, Thomson,R, 84, 40, 67
S	15-Sep	Motherwell		H	L2	5-2	3097	McDermott	Houston	Candlish	Ford	Forsyth	Thomson,D	Wallace 2	Urquhart	Harrow 2	McFarlane b	Miller	Thomson,R u1, Thomson,R u74, Forrest u74, 8, 25, 73, 82, 70
W	19-Sep	Hamilton Academical		A	L2	3-1	2111	McDermott	Houston	Candlish r81 b	Ford	Forsyth 1	Thomson,D	Wallace r74 m 2	Urquhart r	Harrow	McFarlane 1	Miller 1	Forrest u79, Candlish u***, Thomson,R u81, 1, 68, 77
S	22-Sep	Clydebank		H	L2	2-4	3040	McDermott	Houston b	McDonough b	Ford	Forsyth b 1	Thomson,D	Wallace r79 1	Urquhart	Harrow	McFarlane	Miller	Forrest, Thomson,R, 43, 34
W	26-Sep	St Johnstone		H	LC 3-1	1-1	3479	McDermott	Houston	McDonough b	Ford	Steel	Thomson,D b	Wallace 1p	Urquhart	Harrow	Carroll	Miller	Forrest u72, Steen, 46
S	29-Sep	Ayr United		H	L2	2-2	2265	McDermott	Houston	McDonough	Ford 1	Steel	Thomson,D	Wallace r72	Urquhart	Harrow	Carroll r80	Miller 1	Forrest u75, McFarlane u80, 65, 57
Tu	02-Oct	Dunfermline Athletic	1	H	FC SF	1-1	849	McDermott	Houston	McDonough	McFarlane	Forsyth	Steel	Wallace r75	Urquhart	Forrest 1	Carroll	Duncan	Harrow u*, Thomson,R u**, 38
S	06-Oct	Arbroath		A	L2	1-3	1340	McDermott	Houston	McDonough	Ford	Forsyth	Thomson,D b	Harris r*	Urquhart	Harrow r45	Carroll 1	Miller	Forrest u45 r59, McFarlane u59, 73
W	10-Oct	St Johnstone		A	LC 3-2	3-1	4035	McDermott	Houston b	McDonough	Ford 1	Forsyth	Thomson,D	Wallace	Urquhart	Harrow 1	McFarlane	Miller 1	Carroll u80, Forrest, 20, 73, 62
S	13-Oct	Dumbarton		A	L2	2-4	1339	McDermott	Houston	McDonough	Ford b 1	Forsyth b	Thomson,D	Wallace r60 b 1p	Urquhart	Harrow	McFarlane	Miller	Carroll, Steen, 85, 51
S	20-Oct	Stirling Albion		H	L2	1-1	2113	McDermott	Houston	Candlish	Ford	Forsyth	Thomson,D	Wallace r70	Urquhart b	Harrow	Carroll 1	Miller	Forrest u70, McFarlane, 3
S	27-Oct	Airdrie		H	L2	1-2	2809	McDermott	Houston	Candlish	Ford	Forsyth	Thomson,D	Wallace	Urquhart	Harrow	Carroll r75	Miller	Duncan u75, Forrest, Lapsley og 50
W	31-Oct	Dundee United		A	LC QF-1	0-0	7426	McDermott	Houston	Candlish	Ford	Forsyth	Thomson,D	Wallace	Urquhart	Harrow	Carroll	Miller	McFarlane, Duncan
S	03-Nov	Dunfermline Athletic		A	L2	1-1	3529	McDermott	Houston b	Candlish	Ford b	Forsyth	Thomson,D	Wallace	Urquhart	Harrow	Carroll	Miller r58	Duncan u58, Forrest u65, 7
S	10-Nov	St Johnstone		H	L2	1-2	1863	McDermott	Houston	McDonough	Ford 1	Forsyth	Thomson,D	McComb r65	Urquhart	Harrow	Carroll	Duncan r75	Harris u70, Wallace
W	14-Nov	Dundee United		H	LC QF-2	0-1	6838	McDermott	Houston	Candlish b	Ford 1	Forsyth	Thomson,D	Miller	Urquhart b	Harrow	Carroll r70	Miller	Thomson,R u70, Duncan u70, 7
S	17-Nov	Motherwell	2	A	L2	2-1	2123	McDermott	McDonough	Candlish	McFarlane	Forsyth b	Thomson,D	Wallace r70	Urquhart b	Harrow r****	Carroll	McFarlane r**	Thomson,R, Harris, Thomson,D u*** 32, 12, 56
Sa	24-Nov	Partick Thistle		A	L2	0-2	500	McDermott	McDonough	Candlish b	Ford	Forsyth	Thomson,D r79	Urquhart r74	Urquhart b	Harrow b	Carroll r*	Miller	Carroll u, Harris u*, Martin u67, Steen u74
S	01-Dec	Ayr United		A	L2	0-3	2766	McDermott	McDonough bx	McDonough	Ford	Forsyth	Thomson,D	Ballantyne	Urquhart b	Harrow b	Carroll	Miller	Thomson,R, Harris, 37
S	08-Dec	Arbroath		H	L2	1-1	1333	McDermott	Houston	Candlish	Ford	Forsyth	Thomson,D	Ballantyne	Urquhart	Harrow 1	Carroll	Miller	Thomson,R, Harris, 34
M	10-Dec	Dundee		H	F	1-3	300	McDermott	Houston	Candlish	Ford	McFarlane	Thomson,D	Ballantyne	McFarlane r70	Harrow	Carroll	McFarlane r**	Urquhart u*, Miller u*, Duncan u***
S	15-Dec	Dumbarton		H	L2	0-1	1223	McDermott	Houston	Candlish	Ford	Forsyth	Thomson,D	Ballantyne	McFarlane	Harrow	Carroll	Miller	Carroll u, McFarlane
S	29-Dec	Airdrie		A	L2	3-0	1990	McDermott	Houston	Candlish	Ford 1	Forsyth	Thomson,D	Ballantyne b	Urquhart b	Harrow	Carroll	McFarlane	Thomson,R, Miller, 25, 35, 88
Tu	01-Jan	Dunfermline Athletic	3	H	L2	1-0	4077	McDermott	Houston	Candlish	Ford r81	Forsyth 1	Thomson,D	Ballantyne 3	Urquhart	Harrow 1	Carroll 1	McFarlane	Duncan u70, Miller, 37
S	12-Jan	Motherwell	4	H	L2	0-1	2259	McDermott	Houston	Candlish b	Ford b	Forsyth	Thomson,D	Ballantyne 1	Urquhart	Ballantyne x44	Carroll 1	Miller	Duncan u75, Duncan u70
S	19-Jan	Hamilton Academical		A	L2	1-1	1802	McDermott	Houston	Candlish	Ford 1	Forsyth 1	Thomson,D	Steen	Urquhart	Ballantyne	Thomson,R	Miller r85	Carroll u55, Duncan, 40
Sa	26-Jan	Celtic		A	SC 3	1-2	18000	McDermott	Houston	Candlish	Ford	Forsyth	Thomson,D	Urquhart	McFarlane	McFarlane	Thomson,R	Miller	Duncan, Steen, 57
S	09-Feb	Arbroath		H	L2	2-1	1485	McDermott	Houston	Candlish	Ford 1	Forsyth	Thomson,D	Ballantyne 1	Urquhart b	Harrow	Thomson,R r55	Miller 1	Duncan u68, Forrest, 76, 75
S	16-Feb	Hamilton Academical		H	L2	2-1	1483	McDermott	Houston	Candlish	Ford 1	Forsyth	Thomson,D	Ballantyne 1	Urquhart	Harrow 1	Carroll 1	Miller	Duncan, McFarlane u81, 25, 70
Sa	23-Feb	Dumbarton		A	L2	4-0	1899	McDermott	Houston	Candlish	Ford r81	Forsyth b	Thomson,D	Ballantyne 2,1p	Urquhart b	Harrow 68 1	Carroll 1	Miller	Duncan, McFarlane, 10, 77p, 33, 41
S	01-Mar	Clyde		A	L2	4-0	735	McDermott	Houston	Candlish	Ford 1	Forsyth b	Thomson,D b	Ballantyne 2p	Urquhart	Harrow 2	Carroll	Miller	Duncan u75, McFarlane, 52, 68, 80, 82
S	08-Mar	St Johnstone	5	A	L2	2-2	2033	McDermott	Houston	Candlish	Ford b	Forsyth	Thomson,D	Ballantyne b x63	Urquhart b x63	Harrow 78	Carroll 1	Miller	Duncan u1, Thomson,R, 43, 74
S	15-Mar	Hearts		H	L2	0-0	4010	McDermott	Houston	Candlish	Ford	McFarlane	Thomson,D	Ballantyne	Urquhart	Harrow 1	Carroll r74	Miller	McComb u32, Urquhart, 12, 66
W	19-Mar	Berwick Rangers		H	L2	2-1	1242	McDermott	Houston	Candlish	Ford	McFarlane	Thomson,D	Ballantyne 1p	McFarlane r74	Harrow r75	Carroll r70	Miller 1	Harris u74, Thomson,R, 12, 66
S	25-Mar	Clydebank		A	L2	0-1	652	McDermott	Houston b	Candlish	Ford	Steel	Thomson,D	Miller	Steen	Harrow	Carroll 1	Duncan r32	Urquhart, Thomson,R, 8
S	29-Mar	Clyde		H	L2	1-1	1397	McDermott	Houston	Candlish	Ford 1	Forsyth	Thomson,D	Martin	Steen	Ballantyne	Carroll	Miller	Urquhart, McFarlane, 68
W	02-Apr	Stirling Albion		A	L2	1-0	932	McDermott	Houston	Candlish	Ford 1	Forsyth	Thomson,D	Steen	McFarlane	Ballantyne 1p	Carroll	Miller	Martin u70, Harris u70, 68
S	05-Apr	Clydebank		H	L2	3-0	902	McDermott	Houston	Candlish 2	Ford 1	Forsyth	Thomson,D	Steen	McFarlane	Ballantyne	Carroll 1p	Miller	Urquhart u88, Martin u70
W	09-Apr	Hearts		A	L2	2-2	6133	McDermott	Houston	Candlish	Ford 1	Forsyth	Thomson,D	Steen 1	McFarlane	Harrow 88	Carroll	Miller r85	Urquhart u68 b, Harrow, 56, 81, 72
S	12-Apr	Ayr United		H	L2	2-0	2140	McDermott	Houston	Candlish	Ford 1	Forsyth b	Thomson,D	Steen	McFarlane r68	Harrow 78	Carroll m b	Miller	Harrow u74, Martin u85, 76, 71
S	19-Apr	Stirling Albion		A	L2	0-0	1038	McDermott	Houston	Candlish	Ford 1	Forsyth	Thomson,D	Steen	McFarlane r74	Ballantyne	Carroll r74	Miller	Harrow u70, Martin u78, 72, 50
S	26-Apr	Berwick Rangers		A	L2	3-3	1124	McDermott	Houston	Candlish	Ford 1	Forsyth	Thomson,D	Steen 2	Urquhart	Ballantyne	Carroll r70	Miller 1	Harrow 1, Harris, 31, 42, 34
S	04-May	Fife All Stars XI	6	H	B	3-4	1711	McDermott	Houston	Candlish	Ford 1	Forsyth	Thomson,D	Steen	Urquhart	Ballantyne	Carroll 1	Miller 1	Harrow 1, McIntosh, Duncan, 83, 60, 68

Manager : Gordon Wallace

(1) Lost 5-4 on penalties
(2) Soutar sent off 83 minutes
(3) Williams sent off in 83 minutes
(4) Smith and Harrow sent off 44 minutes
(5) Rutherford missed penalty 89 minutes
(6) Murray McDermott Testimonial
(7) Rovers goal times 47, 44
(8) Rovers goal times 67, 41, 73, 36, 40, 37, 87

1980-81

Day	Date	Opponents	Note	Venue	Comp	Res.	Att.	1	2	3	4	5	6	7	8	9	10	11	Substitutes, own goals and goal times
S	26-Jul	Lincoln City		H	F	1-1	500	McDermott	Steen r*	Candlish	Ford	Houston	Thomson,D	Harris r*** 1	Urquhart	Lawson	Carroll	Duncan r**	McIntosh u*, Martin u**, Anderson u***
M	28-Jul	Chelsea		H	F	3-2	1862	McDermott	Houston	Candlish	Ford 1	Forsyth	Thomson,D	Lawson 1	Urquhart	Harrow	Carroll	Miller r50	McFarlane, Steen, Duncan; 15, 65, 55; 36; Harris
S	02-Aug	Swansea City		H	F	0-2	1074	McDermott	Houston 63 b	Candlish	Ford	Steel	Thomson,D	Lawson	Urquhart	Harrow	Carroll	Duncan 2	Steen u63, Duncan u50; Harris
Tu	05-Aug	Burntisland Shipyard		H	FC 1	6-0	132	Walker	McIntosh	Candlish	Ford	Forsyth	Thomson,D	Ballantyne 1	Harris 1	Harrow 3	Carroll	Duncan 2	Anderson, Martin; Harris; 47, 30, 52, 57, 76, 86
S	09-Aug	Hibernian		A	L2	1-0	4846	McDermott	Houston b	Candlish 1	Ford	Forsyth	Thomson,D	Ballantyne 1p	Urquhart u	Harrow	Carroll	Lawson	McFarlane, Duncan; 88
W	13-Aug	Falkirk		H	L2	3-2	1856	McDermott	Houston	Candlish	Ford 1	Forsyth	Thomson,D b	Ballantyne	Urquhart	Harrow b	Carroll 1	Lawson	McFarlane, Duncan; 83, 18, 9
S	16-Aug	Clydebank		H	L2	0-4	1901	McDermott	Houston	Candlish	Ford 1	Forsyth	Thomson,D	Ballantyne	Urquhart b	Harrow	Carroll r62	Lawson	Duncan u62, Steen
W	20-Aug	Falkirk		A	LC 1-2	2-0	1594	McDermott	Houston	Candlish 1	Ford 1	Forsyth b	Thomson,D	Ballantyne	Urquhart r85	Harrow r85	Steen 1	Lawson	Steen, Carroll u85; 17, 79
S	23-Aug	Dunfermline Athletic		A	L2	2-0	3816	McDermott	Houston	Candlish	Ford	Forsyth	Thomson,D	Ballantyne	Urquhart	Harrow b	Steen	Lawson	McFarlane u85, Carroll; 16, 19
W	27-Aug	Dumbarton		A	LC 2-1	1-0	831	McDermott	Houston	Candlish 1	Ford	Forsyth	Thomson,D	Ballantyne	Urquhart	Harrow	Steen	Lawson	McFarlane, Carroll; 52
S	30-Aug	Dumbarton	1	H	LC 2-2	1-1	1946	McDermott s	Houston b	Candlish	Ford	Forsyth b	Thomson,D	Ballantyne r57	Urquhart r	Harrow	Steen	Lawson 1	Steel, Carroll; 110
W	03-Sep	Clydebank		H	LC 3-1	0-1	1763	McDermott	Houston	Candlish	Ford	Forsyth b	Thomson,D	Ballantyne r**	Urquhart	Harrow	Steen	Lawson r*	Carroll u, Miller u57
S	06-Sep	St Johnstone		H	L2	2-1	1695	McDermott	Houston	Candlish	Ford	Forsyth b	Steel	Ballantyne m	Urquhart	Harrow	Carroll r70	Steen	Duncan u*, Harris u**; 69, 20
Tu	09-Sep	Falkirk		H	L2	2-1	1428	McDermott	Houston	Candlish 1	Ford	Forsyth b	Steel	Ballantyne	Urquhart b	Harrow b 1	Steen	Miller r88	Miller u70, Lawson; 34
S	13-Sep	Motherwell		A	L2	1-1	2230	McDermott	Houston	Candlish	Ford	Forsyth	Steel	Ballantyne	Urquhart b	Harrow 1	Steen	Miller	Lawson u88, Martin; 10, 14
W	17-Sep	Stirling Albion		H	L2	2-0	851	McDermott	Houston	Candlish	Ford	Forsyth	Steel	Ballantyne r	Urquhart	Harrow 2	Steen	Miller	Lawson u, Carroll; 47, 49, 35, 8
S	20-Sep	Dumbarton		H	L2	4-1	1694	McDermott	Houston	Candlish	Ford r68	Forsyth	Steel	Lawson 2	Urquhart 1	Harrow r68 1	Steen	Miller	Carroll u68, Ballantyne u68
W	24-Sep	Clydebank		A	LC 3-2	0-1	1022	McDermott	Houston	Candlish	Ford	Thomson,D	Steel	Lawson r**	Urquhart b	Harrow	Steen r*	Miller	Carroll u*, Ballantyne u**
S	27-Sep	Hamilton Academical		A	L2	1-3	2185	McDermott	Houston	Candlish	Ford	Thomson,D	Steel b	Lawson	Carroll	Ballantyne	Steen	Miller r65	Harris u65 1, Berry; 67
W	01-Oct	Ayr United		H	L2	0-1	2498	McDermott	Houston	Candlish	Ford	Thomson,D	Steel b	Ballantyne	Steen	Harris	Carroll	Miller b	Miller, Miller
S	04-Oct	East Stirling		H	L2	2-1	1395	McDermott	Houston	Candlish	Ford	Houston b	Steel	Ballantyne	Steen	Lawson	Berry	Miller r62	Harris u62 2, Martin; 68, 75
M	06-Oct	Cowdenbeath	2	A	FC SF	4-4	566	Walker 1	McDonough	Berry	Steen 1	Levein	Thomson,D	Ballantyne	Matthew	Harris	Martin 1	Miller 1	Lowe, Robertson; 63, 64, 74, 83
S	11-Oct	Dundee		H	L2	0-0	3255	McDermott	Houston	Candlish	Ford	Forsyth	Steel	Ballantyne	Urquhart b	Harris	Steen	Lawson r77	Miller u77, Berry
S	18-Oct	Berwick Rangers		A	L2	4-1	1061	McDermott	McDonough	Candlish	Ford	Forsyth	Steel	Ballantyne 2	Urquhart	Harris 1	Steen 1	Miller	Lawson, Berry; 6, 65, 55, 12
S	25-Oct	Motherwell		H	L2	2-0	2498	McDermott	McDonough	Candlish	Ford 1	Forsyth	Steel	Ballantyne 2	Urquhart	Harris r	Steen	Miller	Lawson u, Berry; 14, 22
S	01-Nov	St Johnstone		A	L2	3-0	2956	McDermott	McDonough	Candlish	Ford 1	Forsyth 1	Steel	Harris r	Urquhart	Harris r	Steen	Miller	Lawson u, Carroll; 67, 57, 47
S	08-Nov	Stirling Albion		A	L2	3-0	1978	McDermott	McDonough	Candlish	Ford	Forsyth	Steel	Ballantyne 2,1p	Urquhart	Harris r71 1	Steen	Miller u71	Lawson u71, Carroll; 29, 34p, 68
S	15-Nov	Dumbarton		H	L2	2-2	968	McDermott	McDonough	Candlish	Ford	Forsyth b	Steel	Ballantyne 1	Martin	Harris r	Carroll	Lawson	Lawson, Carroll; 72, 27
M	17-Nov	Dunfermline Athletic		H	FC F-1	2-0	733	Walker	Houston	McDonough	Steen	Thomson,D	Thomson,D 1	Lawson	Martin	Ballantyne	Carroll 1p	Berry b	Levein u, Lawson; 81, 29
S	22-Nov	Hamilton Academical		H	L2	1-0	2342	McDermott	McDonough	Candlish	Ford	Forsyth	Steel	Harris m	Urquhart	Harris 1	Steen r	Miller r68	Carroll u, Lawson u68; 87
S	22-Nov	Motherwell		A	L2	3-0	2953	McDermott s	McDonough	Candlish	Ford 1	Forsyth	Steel	Ballantyne r81 2	Urquhart	Harris 1	Steen	Miller r68	Carroll u68, Lawson u81; 36, 57, 13
S	13-Dec	Berwick Rangers		H	L2	2-1	1772	McDermott	McDonough	Candlish	Ford	Forsyth 1	Steel	Ballantyne r67	Urquhart	Harris	Steen r75	Miller r88 1	Lawson u88, Carroll; 52, 79
S	20-Dec	Ayr United	3	H	L2	2-1	2359	McDermott	McDonough	Candlish	Ford 1	Forsyth b	Steel	Ballantyne b 1p	Urquhart b	Harris 1	Carroll	Miller	Lawson u15, Carroll u65; 85
Th	01-Jan	Dunfermline Athletic		H	L2	1-1	4763	McDermott	Houston	Candlish	Ford	Forsyth b	Steel	Ballantyne r15	Urquhart	Harris b	Steen 1	Miller r65	Carroll u85, Miller; 53, 29
S	03-Jan	Falkirk		A	L2	0-1	3188	McDermott	McDonough	McDonough	Ford	Forsyth 1p	Steel	Lawson	Urquhart b	Harris	Steen 1	Mitchell r85	Miller u80, Carroll
S	10-Jan	Hibernian		H	L2	2-0	9603	McDermott	McDonough	Candlish	Ford	Forsyth b	Steel	Lawson r80	Urquhart	Harris 1	Steen	Mitchell	Carroll u75, Lawson u75; 53, 29
S	24-Jan	Aberdeen	4	H	SC 3	1-2	9656	McDermott	McDonough	Candlish	Ford	Forsyth	Steel	Lawson r82	Urquhart b	Harris 1	Carroll	Mitchell	Lawson u67, Carroll u75; 62
S	31-Jan	Motherwell		H	L2	1-0	1652	McDermott	Houston	Candlish	Ford	Forsyth	Steel	Ballantyne r75	Urquhart	Harris	Steen r75	Mitchell r75	Lawson u77, Carroll
S	07-Feb	Dumbarton		A	L2	3-0	1884	McDermott	Houston	Candlish	Ford	Forsyth 1	Steel	Ballantyne r67	Urquhart	Harris	Steen r75	Mitchell	Ballantyne u*, Miller u**; Jackson og 89; 22
S	14-Feb	Berwick Rangers	5	H	L2	1-1	6315	McDermott	Houston	Candlish	Ford	Forsyth b	Steel	Ballantyne r77	Urquhart	Harris 1	Carroll	Mitchell r57	Ballantyne u82, Mitchell; 90
S	21-Feb	Stirling Albion		A	L2	1-0	1148	McDermott	Houston	Candlish	Ford	Forsyth 1	Steel	Lawson r*	Urquhart b	Harris b	Steen	Mitchell r**	Lawson, Mitchell
S	28-Feb	East Stirling		H	L2	0-0	1652	McDermott	McDonough	Candlish	Ford	Forsyth 1	Steel	Lawson r82	Urquhart b	Harris	Steen	Miller	Mitchell, Mitchell u76
S	07-Mar	Hamilton Academical		A	L2	2-0	1884	McDermott	McDonough	Candlish	Ford	Forsyth 1	Steel	Ballantyne	Urquhart	Harris 1	Steen r64	Miller 1	Thomson,D u33, Thomson,D; 65
S	14-Mar	Ayr United		H	L2	1-3	6315	McDermott	McDonough b	Candlish	Berry	Forsyth	Steel	Ballantyne x65	Thomson,D r76	Harris b	Steen	Miller 1	Ford u62, Harris u81; 68
S	21-Mar	Ayr United		H	L2	1-1	2389	McDermott	McDonough b	Candlish	Berry	Forsyth	Steel	Russell	Steen	Harris	Carroll 1	Miller	Miller u64, Lawson u75
Tu	24-Mar	East Stirling		H	L2	1-0	1140	McDermott	McDonough	Candlish r33	Berry	Forsyth b	Steel	Russell r81 b 1	Steen	Ballantyne	Carroll	Miller	Mitchell u32 1, McDonough u82 51
S	28-Mar	Falkirk		A	L2	0-0	2702	McDermott	McDonough b	McDonough	Berry r75	Forsyth	Steel	Russell b	Steen	Harris r62	Carroll	Miller	Steen u72, Steen u72
W	01-Apr	Dundee		A	L2	1-2	6178	McDermott	McDonough	Candlish 1	Ford r82	Forsyth	Steel	Russell b	Steen	Harris b	Carroll	Berry r64	Steen u74, Steen u74; 51
S	04-Apr	Clydebank		H	L2	1-1	2361	McDermott	McDonough b	Candlish 1	Ford	Forsyth b	Steel	Russell	Urquhart b	Lawson r32	Carroll b	Miller	Harris u64, Steel u75; 62
S	11-Apr	St Johnstone		A	L2	0-2	4926	McDermott	McDonough b	Candlish	Ford	Forsyth b	Steel	Russell b	Urquhart	Ballantyne	Carroll r72	Mitchell r72	Mitchell u26, Harris u45
S	18-Apr	Hibernian		A	L2	0-2	8071	McDermott	McDonough	Candlish	Ford	Thomson,D	Steel	Russell b	Urquhart	Ballantyne	Carroll r74	Mitchell r57	Miller, Harris; 49
W	22-Apr	Clydebank		A	L2	0-3	690	McDermott	McDonough	Candlish	Ford	Thomson,D r75	Thomson,D r75	Russell	Urquhart x71	Russell	Steen r64	Miller	
S	25-Apr	Dunfermline Athletic		A	L2	1-0	2535	McDermott r45	McDonough r26	Candlish	Ford	Houston	Steel	Russell	Carroll	Russell 1	Steen	Miller	
W	29-Apr	Dunfermline Athletic		A	FC F-2	0-0	200	Walker	Ford	Candlish	Berry	Houston	Mitchell	Ballantyne	Carroll	Ballantyne	Steen	Mitchell	

Manager : Gordon Wallace

(1) after extra time
(2) won 4-2 on penalties ; goalkeeper Tommy Walker scored with a clearance from his hands
(3) Shanks missed penalty 56 minutes
(4) Gate receipts £16200
(5) Berwick manager Frank Connor cautioned by referee for dissent 3 minutes before half time

Day	Date	Opponents	Note	Venue	Comp	Res.	Att.	1	2	3	4	5	6	7	8	9	10	11	Substitutes, own goals and goal times
S	25-Jul	St Mirren	1	N	T	3-5		Walker	Houston	McDonough	Robinson	Forsyth	Steel	Ballantyne	Urquhart	Russell	Carroll	Mitchell	Irvine, Houston, Martin; Steel; Russell 1, Martin u; Miller
Sn	26-Jul	Keith	2	A	T	2-2		Walker	McDonough	Berry	Robinson 1	Forsyth	Irvine	Martin 1	Russell	Ballantyne 1	Steen	Mitchell	Houston, Steel, Steen; Robinson
Tu	28-Jul	Elgin City		A	F	2-4	200	Walker	McDonough	Berry	Robinson 1	Houston	Steel	Irvine	Russell	Ballantyne	Carroll	Miller 1	Forsyth, Steen, Miller; 17, 80
M	01-Aug	Stenhousemuir		A	FC SF	1-2		Walker	McDonough	Berry	Urquhart	Forsyth	Forsyth	Ballantyne	Urquhart	Matthew	Lowe	Mitchell	Candlish, McIntosh, Robinson; Levein
S	03-Aug	East Fife		A	LC S	2-1	5362	Walker	Ford	Candlish	Thomson	Houston	Steel	Harris 1	Urquhart	Russell b 2	Carroll r73	Miller	Steen u73, Harris u; 9, 79
S	08-Aug	Dundee		H	LC S	2-5	2627	Walker	Ford	Candlish	Robinson	Houston	Steel b	Ballantyne	Urquhart	Russell r53	Carroll	Mitchell r	Harris u53, Houston; 3, 27
W	12-Aug	Morton		A	LC S	1-8	14419	Walker	Houston	Candlish	Robinson	Forsyth 1	Steel	Ballantyne 1	Urquhart r73	Russell 1	Carroll	Mitchell	Steen u73, Mitchell; 25
S	15-Aug	Rangers		A	LC S	0-2	2321	Walker	Houston	Candlish	Robinson	Forsyth b	Steel	Ballantyne	Urquhart	Russell	Carroll	Ballantyne	Harris, Steen
W	19-Aug	Morton		H	LC S	1-1	1858	Walker	Houston	Candlish	Robinson	Forsyth b	Steel	Ballantyne 1	Urquhart	Russell	Berry	Mitchell	Irvine u82, Miller u; 66
S	22-Aug	Dundee		A	LC S	1-3	6640	Walker	Houston	Candlish	Robinson	Forsyth r82	Steel	Ballantyne	Urquhart	Russell 1	Berry	Mitchell r	Ford u75, Harris u75; 29
W	26-Aug	Rangers		H	LC S	0-1	1352	Walker s	Houston b	Candlish	Robinson	Forsyth	Steel	Ballantyne	Urquhart r75	Russell	Berry	Mitchell r75	Ford u55, Harris u74, Robinson
S	29-Aug	Hamilton Academical		A	L2	0-3	2018	Walker	McDonough	Candlish	Robinson r74	Forsyth	Houston	Ballantyne	Urquhart r55	Russell	Berry	Mitchell	Harris u62, Robinson
S	05-Sep	Falkirk		H	L2	0-0	2527	Walker	Houston	Candlish	Ford	Houston	Houston	Ballantyne r62	Berry b	Russell	Berry b	Miller	Ballantyne u76, Robinson
Tu	08-Sep	Dunfermline Athletic		A	L2	0-0	820	Walker	McDonough	McDonough	Ford	Forsyth	McDonough	Ballantyne	Urquhart	Steen	Steen	Mitchell r76	Ballantyne u73, Robinson u55
S	12-Sep	Queen's Park		A	L2	1-1	1859	Walker	Houston	McDonough	Ford 1	Forsyth x73	Houston	Harris	Urquhart r55	Russell r73	Steen r73	Mitchell	Robinson u75, Ballantyne; 41
W	16-Sep	Dumbarton		H	L2	1-3	1181	Walker	Houston	McDonough	Robinson 1	Forsyth	Houston	Harris	Urquhart	Russell	Steen	Mitchell r75	Ford u43, Miller u64
S	19-Sep	East Stirling		H	L2	1-0	1189	Walker	Houston	McDonough	Robinson	Forsyth	Steel	Ballantyne	Berry 43	Russell r64	Steen	Harris	Berry, Miller; 68
S	23-Sep	Motherwell		A	L2	0-3	2102	Walker s	Houston	Candlish	Robinson	Forsyth	Steel	Russell	Urquhart	Ballantyne	Steen	Harris	Miller u75, Miller
S	26-Sep	St Johnstone		A	L2	0-2	1718	Walker	McDonough	Candlish	Robinson	Forsyth	Steel	Russell 1	Berry	Ballantyne	Steen r84	Harris	Russell u75, Urquhart u84
S	03-Oct	Ayr United		H	L2	0-1	1399	Walker	McDonough	Candlish	Robinson	Forsyth b	Steel	Ballantyne	Irvine	Harris r75	Steen r69	Miller	Urquhart u69, Ballantyne u86
S	10-Oct	Clydebank		A	L2	0-2	1325	Walker	Houston	Candlish	Ford	Forsyth b	Steel	Harris r86	Urquhart	Gibson	Steen	Miller	Ballantyne u76, Steen; 52
S	17-Oct	Hearts		A	L2	1-2	5001	Walker	Robertson	Candlish	Ford	Forsyth	Irvine b 1	Irvine b 1	Urquhart	Gibson	Russell	Robinson r76	Ballantyne u32 2, Steen; 87, 88
S	24-Oct	Queen of the South		H	L2	2-1	1402	Walker	Robertson	Candlish	Ford	Forsyth	Steel	Russell r72	Urquhart	Gibson 1	Russell r32	Robinson	Mitchell, Mitchell; 60
S	31-Oct	Kilmarnock	3	A	L2	1-1	1859	Donaldson	Robertson	Candlish	Ford	Forsyth	Steel b	Ballantyne b 2	Urquhart r84	Gibson 1	Irvine 1	Robinson	Steen u84, Mitchell; 61, 10
S	07-Nov	Falkirk		H	L2	2-0	1901	Donaldson	Robertson	Candlish r66	Ford 1	Forsyth	Candlish	Ballantyne 1	Berry	Gibson 1p	Irvine	Robinson	Carroll u66, Carroll; 88, 43
S	14-Nov	Hamilton Academical		A	L2	2-0	1803	Donaldson	Houston	McDonough	Ford 1	Forsyth	Candlish	Ballantyne r84	Urquhart	Gibson 1	Irvine r70	Robinson	Carroll u70, Mitchell; 57
S	21-Nov	Dumbarton		A	L2	1-1	231	Donaldson	Houston r70	McDonough	Ford	Forsyth r73	McDonough	Ballantyne	Urquhart	Gibson 1p	Irvine r70	Robinson	Ford u, Ballantyne
S	28-Nov	St Johnstone		H	L2	0-4	2332	Donaldson	Houston	McDonough 68	Ford	Steel	McDonough	Ballantyne	Urquhart	Gibson	Irvine r70	Robinson	Ballantyne u70, Irvine u80
S	05-Dec	Ayr United		A	L2	0-2	2124	Walker	Robertson	McDonough	Steen u	Steel	Thomson	Russell b	Urquhart	Gibson r70	Carroll	Mitchell	Carroll u80, Mitchell u80
S	02-Jan	Dundee United		H	F	0-3	1006	Donaldson	Houston	McDonough	Ford r80	Steel	Thomson	Ballantyne	Urquhart	Gibson r70	Carroll	Robinson	Mitchell u85, Ballantyne u72; Steen
Tu	05-Jan	Celtic	4	A	SC 3	0-1	756	Donaldson	Robertson	McDonough	Ford	Steel	Thomson	Ballantyne	Irvine r80	Gibson	Harris r80	Robinson r76	Carroll, Mitchell; 35, 81, 57
S	23-Jan	Dundee		A	L2	3-2	5474	Donaldson	Robertson	McDonough	Ford r85	Steel	Houston	Russell r72	Urquhart	Russell b x40	Carroll	Robinson	Russell u83, Addison; 85
S	30-Jan	Queen of the South		A	L2	1-0	785	Donaldson	Robertson	McDonough	Ford	Steel	Houston	Ballantyne	Urquhart	Gibson 1	Mitchell r83	Robinson	Russell u83, Carroll u83; 26, 14, 51
W	03-Feb	Clydebank		A	L2	1-0	575	Donaldson	Robertson	McDonough	Ford	Steel	Houston	Ballantyne 1	Urquhart	Mitchell r83	Mitchell	Robinson	Russell u58, Carroll; 64
S	06-Feb	Dunfermline Athletic		A	L2	1-4	2053	Donaldson	Robertson	McDonough	Ford 1	Houston	Houston 1	Ballantyne r83	Urquhart	Gibson 1	Mitchell	Robinson	Carroll u68, Robertson; 30
Tu	09-Feb	Queen's Park		A	L2	0-2	1160	Donaldson	Houston	McDonough b	Ford	Forsyth	Houston	Ballantyne m 1	Urquhart r58	Gibson	Mitchell 1	Robinson	Carroll u55, Robertson
S	13-Feb	Partick Thistle		A	F	0-4	800	Donaldson	Houston	McDonough	Ford	Forsyth	Steel	Ballantyne	Urquhart	Gibson	Mitchell	Robinson	Russell u78, Harris u79; 88
S	20-Feb	Motherwell		H	L2	1-0	3205	Donaldson	Robertson r57	McDonough	Ford	Forsyth	Houston	Ballantyne	Urquhart r79	Mitchell r79	Mitchell r79	Robinson r55	Spence u70, Lowe; 25
S	27-Feb	Hearts		A	L2	1-2	3999	Donaldson	Ford	McDonough	Ford	Forsyth b	Steel	Ballantyne b	Urquhart	Gibson	Carroll	Mitchell r78	Spence u61, Russell; 10
W	03-Mar	East Stirling		H	L2	0-3	242	Donaldson	Ford	McDonough b	Ford	Forsyth	Houston	Ballantyne 1	Urquhart	Gibson 1	Carroll	Lowe	Ford u76, Ford u73; 72
S	06-Mar	Hamilton Academical		A	L2	1-1	1270	Donaldson	Ford	McDonough	Urquhart b	Forsyth	Houston	Ballantyne 1	Urquhart	Gibson r83 1	Carroll	Russell	Ford u57, Gibson u76
S	13-Mar	Kilmarnock		H	L2	0-1	1220	Donaldson	Houston	McDonough b	Urquhart b	Steel	Steel	Ballantyne 1	Russell	Gibson r69	Carroll	Ford u73	Harris u45, Gibson; 36, 90
S	20-Mar	East Stirling		A	L2	2-3	411	Donaldson	Robertson	McDonough x70	Urquhart r76	Forsyth r77	Houston	Ballantyne	Russell r88	Ballantyne r73	Lowe	Spence r77	Carroll, Spence; 10, 30, 41
S	27-Mar	Dunfermline Athletic		H	L2	1-3	2063	Donaldson	Ford	Berry	Berry	Forsyth b	Steel	Ballantyne 1	Russell	Lowe	Lowe	Spence	Spence u83, Carroll; 10
W	31-Mar	Hearts	5	H	FC SF	1-0	2460	Walker	Ford	McDonough	Berry	Forsyth	Steel	Ballantyne 2	Russell	Lowe	Carroll	Spence r45	Spence u59, Russell u69
S	03-Apr	Dumbarton		H	L2	3-3	365	Walker	McDonough	McDonough	Berry	Forsyth	Steel	Ballantyne 2	Urquhart	Carroll	Carroll	Harris	Russell u77, Ford u77
Tu	06-Apr	Kilmarnock		A	L2	1-2	1401	Walker	Houston	McDonough	Berry r59	Forsyth	Houston	Ballantyne b	Russell	Gibson r83 1	Steen	Harris	Ford u73, Gibson u73
S	10-Apr	Queen of the South		H	L2	0-0	1380	Walker	Houston	McDonough b	Robinson	Forsyth r77	Houston	Ballantyne 1	Urquhart	Gibson r69	Steen	Harris 1	Gibson u 2.1p, Steen; 47p, 73
S	17-Apr	Clydebank		A	L2	0-1	682	Walker	Houston	McDonough	Robinson	Forsyth	Steel	Harris	Urquhart	Ballantyne r73	Steen s73	Spence r77	Urquhart u70, Martin u81; 2
W	21-Apr	Motherwell		H	L2	1-3	1950	Walker	McDonough	McDonough	Berry r81	Forsyth	Thomson	Russell r	Urquhart x65	Ballantyne r73	Steen r70	Spence	Russell u, Steen; Ahern og 77
S	24-Apr	Falkirk		A	L2	2-3	1288	Walker	Walker	Robertson	Robinson	Levein	Ford	Ford	Gibson 1	Addison	Steen r70	Harris	Gibson; 47p, 73
Tu	27-Apr	Dunfermline Athletic	6	H	FC SF	1-0	406	Walker	Houston	McDonough	Berry r81	Forsyth	Thomson	Ballantyne r	Ford	Ford	Steen r70	Harris	Urquhart u70, Steen; Martin u81
S	01-May	Ayr United		H	L2	1-0	890	Walker	Houston b	Ford	Robinson	Forsyth	Thomson	Ballantyne r	Berry	Gibson	Lowe	Harris	Russell u, Steen
S	08-May	Queen's Park		A	L2	0-2	719	Walker	Houston	Ford	Robinson	Forsyth	Thomson r66	Ballantyne	Urquhart	Gibson	Berry	Spence r48	Mitchell u42, Russell u66; Steen
S	15-May	St Johnstone		H	L2	0-1	1276	Walker	Robertson	Robinson	Robinson	Forsyth	Harris	Harris	Urquhart	Addison r62	Addison r62	Mitchell	Russell u62, Steen

Manager : Gordon Wallace

(1) Keith Tournament
(2) Keith Tournament ; St Mirren beat Brechin City 5-4 on penalties after a 0-0 draw in the Final
(3) Wilson missed penalty
(4) Gate receipts £5872.50
(5) McNeill sent off 85 minutes
(6) Oliver sent off in 60 minutes

Day	Date	Opponents	Note	Venue	Comp	Res.	Att.	1	2	3	4	5	6	7	8	9	10	11	Substitutes, own goals and goal times
S	31-Jul	Cowdenbeath		A	F	2-2	500	Cramb	Houston	Candlish	Robinson	Forsyth	More	Russell	Urquhart r75	Gibson 1	Carroll	Mitchell r59	Harris u59 1; McDonough u75 Walker, Thomson; Robertson; 83, 63
Tu	03-Aug	Sheffield United	1	H	B / F	0-3	1000	Cramb	Houston	McDonough	McCulloch	More	Thomson	Steen r70	Russell	Gibson r57	Candlish	Harris	Carroll u57; Spence u57; Robinson; Urquhart
S	07-Aug	Swansea City		H	F	0-4	1181	Walker	Houston	Candlish	Robinson	Forsyth	Steel	Harris r70	Urquhart b	Gibson	Carroll r83	Mitchell r78	Russell u70; McCulloch u83; Spence u78
S	14-Aug	Falkirk		H	LC S	0-0	1163	Walker	Houston	Candlish	Robinson	Forsyth	More	Harris r76	Urquhart r74	Ballantyne	Gibson r74	Mitchell r76	Thomson u76; Spence u76
W	18-Aug	St Johnstone		A	LC S	0-5	1623	Walker	Houston	Candlish	Robinson	Forsyth	More	Harris	Thomson	Ballantyne	Gibson r72	Mitchell	Thomson u74; Russell u74
S	21-Aug	Dundee United		A	LC S	1-5	5039	Walker	Houston	Candlish	Robinson	Forsyth	More	Steen	Russell b 1	Ballantyne	McCulloch	Harris 1	Russell u72; Urquhart; 44
W	25-Aug	St Johnstone	2	H	LC S	3-3	1310	Walker	Robertson	Candlish	Robinson	More	Thomson	Steen	Russell	Ballantyne m 1	McCulloch	Harris r69 b	Gibson u69 1; Urquhart; 71, 38, 90
S	28-Aug	Falkirk		A	LC S	0-2	902	Walker	Robertson	Candlish	Robinson	More	Thomson	Steen	Russell	Ballantyne	McCulloch	Harris r59	Gibson u59; Forsyth
W	01-Sep	Dundee United		H	LC S	1-3	1934	Walker	Robertson	Candlish	Thomson	Forsyth	More	Robinson	Gibson r74	Harris 1	McCulloch r74	Mitchell	Urquhart u74; Spence u74; 47
S	04-Sep	Clydebank		A	L2	1-1	631	Walker	Robertson	Candlish r32	Thomson	Forsyth	More 1	Robinson	Gibson	Harris	McCulloch	Mitchell	Urquhart u32; Ballantyne; 60
W	08-Sep	St Johnstone		H	L2	0-3	1388	Walker	Robertson	Candlish	Thomson	Forsyth r45	More	Robinson	Gibson	Harris	McCulloch	Mitchell r61	Urquhart u45; Ballantyne u61
S	11-Sep	Airdrie	3	H	L2	0-3	1109	Walker	Robertson	Sweeney	Thomson	Houston	Thomson	Robinson	Gibson	Harris	McCulloch r60	Mitchell r45	Ballantyne u45; Urquhart u60 b
Tu	14-Sep	Dunfermline Athletic		A	L2	2-1	1288	Walker	Houston	McDonough	Urquhart	More	Thomson	Robinson	Gibson r70	Ballantyne r70	Steen	Harris 2	Spence u70; McCulloch; 41, 85
S	18-Sep	Queen's Park		H	L2	3-1	1051	Walker	Houston	McDonough	Urquhart r53	More	Thomson	Robinson	Russell b 1	Ballantyne r79 1	Steen	Harris 1p	McCulloch u53; Spence u79; 5, 52, 35
W	22-Sep	Alloa Athletic		A	L2	0-3	777	Walker	Houston	McDonough	Forsyth	Forsyth	Thomson	Robinson r78	Russell	Ballantyne	McCulloch r65	Harris b	Robertson u65; Gibson u78
S	25-Sep	Partick Thistle		A	L2	1-2	1785	Walker	Houston b	McDonough b	Urquhart	More	Thomson	Robinson	Russell b	Ballantyne r73	Steen	Harris 1	Spence u73; Forsyth; 85
S	02-Oct	Hearts		H	L2	1-0	3543	Walker	Houston	McDonough	Urquhart	More	Thomson	Robinson	Russell r78	Harris 1	Steen	Spence	Ballantyne u78; Gillespie; 63
S	09-Oct	Clyde		A	L2	2-0	549	Walker	Houston	McDonough	Urquhart b	More	Thomson	Robinson	Russell 1	Harris r83 1	Steen r58	Spence	Kerr u58; Ballantyne u83; 80, 60
S	16-Oct	Dumbarton		H	L2	3-0	1095	Walker	Houston	McDonough	Urquhart	More b	Thomson	Robinson 1	Russell 1	Harris 1	Steen	Spence 1	Steen; Ballantyne; 15, 65, 52
S	23-Oct	Hamilton Academical		H	L2	4-1	1436	Walker	Houston	McDonough	Urquhart	More	Thomson	Robinson 1	Russell 1	Harris m 1	Kerr	Spence 1	Steen; Ballantyne; 13, 80, 64, 90
S	30-Oct	Ayr United		A	L2	4-0	1007	Walker	Houston	McDonough	Urquhart r85	More	Thomson	Robinson	Russell 2	Harris 1	Kerr 1	Spence 1	Steen u85; Ballantyne; 42, 89, 53, 62
S	06-Nov	Falkirk		H	L2	2-1	1792	Walker	Houston	McDonough	Urquhart	More	Thomson b	Robinson	Russell	Harris 1p	Kerr	Spence 1	Steen; Ballantyne; 41, 77
S	13-Nov	St Johnstone		A	L2	1-2	3123	Walker	Houston b	Candlish	Urquhart	Forsyth	Thomson b	Robinson	Russell r80	Harris 1	Kerr	Spence	Steen; Ballantyne u80; 57
Tu	16-Nov	East Fife	4	A	FC SF	0-0	300	Cramb	Robertson	McDonough	McCulloch r66	More r35	Steel	Steen	Gibson	Ballantyne	Kerr b	Mitchell	Spence u66; Sweeney
S	20-Nov	Queen's Park		A	L2	2-0	753	Walker	Houston b	McDonough	Urquhart b	Forsyth r37	Thomson	Robinson	Russell r30	Harris	Kerr 1	Spence r77	Ballantyne u30 1; Steen; 44, 47
S	27-Nov	Alloa Athletic		H	L2	0-1	1499	Walker	Houston	McDonough	Urquhart	Steel	Thomson	Steen	Russell r71	Ballantyne	Kerr	Spence	Steen u35; Gibson u71
S	04-Dec	Hearts		A	L2	0-2	4190	Walker	Houston	McDonough	Robinson	Steel	Thomson	Steen	Ballantyne r74	Harris b	Kerr	Spence r54	Candlish u37; Gibson u74
S	11-Dec	Partick Thistle		H	L2	2-2	1644	Walker	Robertson	McDonough	Robinson	More b	Thomson	Steen r75	Russell 2	Harris r80	Kerr	Spence	Candlish u54; Ballantyne u80; 4, 62
S	18-Dec	Clydebank		H	L2	0-3	1046	Walker	Houston	McDonough	Robinson r45	More	Thomson	Marshall	Ballantyne u75	Ballantyne	Kerr	Spence	Candlish u45; Ballantyne u75
M	27-Dec	Airdrie		A	L2	2-1	1502	Walker	McDonough	Candlish	Houston	More	Thomson b	Marshall	Russell 2	Harris 1	Kerr b	Spence 1	Steen; Ballantyne; 20, 60
S	01-Jan	Dunfermline Athletic	6	H	L2	6-0	2611	Walker	McDonough	Candlish 1	Houston	More	Thomson b	Marshall	Russell 1	Harris	Kerr 1	Spence r77	Ballantyne u77 1; Steen; 50, 1, 26, 72, 43, 78
M	03-Jan	Falkirk		A	L2	0-2	2061	Walker	McDonough	Candlish	Houston	Thomson	Thomson	Marshall	Russell	Harris	Kerr	Spence	Robinson; Steen
M	08-Jan	Dumbarton	5	A	L2	1-2	403	Walker b	McDonough	Candlish b	Houston b	Thomson	Gillespie r53	Marshall	Russell 1	Russell r71	Kerr	Spence r75	Steen u53; Ballantyne u75; 39
S	15-Jan	Clyde		H	L2	1-2	1183	Walker	Robertson	McDonough	Houston	More b	Thomson	Marshall	Ballantyne r61	Ballantyne	Kerr	Spence	Smith u61 1; Steel; 65
S	22-Jan	Ayr United		H	L2	0-1	1131	Cramb	Robertson	Candlish	Houston	More	Thomson	Marshall	Russell	Russell 1	Kerr b	Spence	Robinson; Robinson
S	29-Jan	East Fife	6	A	SC 3	2-2	5760	Walker	Robertson r70	Candlish b	Houston	More	Thomson b	Marshall r86	Russell	Smith	Kerr	Robinson	Ballantyne u70; Robinson u86; 83, 71
S	05-Feb	Hamilton Academical		A	L2	2-2	734	Walker	Robertson	Candlish 1	Houston	More	Thomson 1	Urquhart	Urquhart	Smith	Kerr 1	Spence	Robinson u45; Robinson; Carson og 1; 43, 62
Tu	22-Feb	Motherwell		H	F	2-3	800	Cramb	Robertson	Candlish	Urquhart r65	More	Urquhart	Thomson 1	Smith r45	Russell r65	Kerr	Marshall	Spence; Houston u65; Spence u65; 58, 65, 84
S	26-Feb	Alloa Athletic		H	L2	3-1	1060	Walker	Robertson	Candlish	Urquhart	More	Forsyth	Harris 1	Smith 1	Russell 1	Kerr	Marshall	Houston u51; Houston og 1; Thomson og 1
S	05-Mar	St Johnstone		A	L2	0-1	2174	Walker	Robertson r45	Sweeney	Urquhart	More	Forsyth r51	Harris b	Smith	Harris	McCulloch	Russell	Candlish u45; Spence; 62
M	14-Mar	St Mirren Reserves		H	F	1-1	500	Walker	Robertson	McCulloch	McCulloch	More	Forsyth r45	Marshall	Smith r53	Harris 1	Kerr 1p	Marshall 2	Spence u72; Gillespie u45; Urquhart u53
S	19-Mar	Hamilton Academical		A	L2	5-0	824	Walker	Robertson	Candlish	Urquhart	More	Forsyth	Harris 1	Russell 1p	Russell 1p	Kerr r82 1p	Marshall 2	Spence; Houston; 57, 84, 81, 19, 58
Tu	22-Mar	Partick Thistle		A	L2	0-1	1494	Walker	Robertson	Candlish	Urquhart	More	Forsyth	Harris	Russell	Russell 1	Kerr	Marshall	Houston u7; Thomson; 63
S	26-Mar	Clydebank		H	L2	1-3	1010	Walker	Robertson	Candlish b	Houston u68	More 1	Forsyth	Harris 1	Smith	Harris	Kerr 1p	Marshall 1	Thomson u68; McCulloch; 80, 24, 57, 69
Tu	29-Mar	Hearts	7	H	L2	4-2	3306	Walker	Robertson	McDonough	Urquhart	More 1	Forsyth	Harris 1	Urquhart	Russell r71	Kerr 1p	Marshall 1	Gillespie u71; Thomson; McCathie og 1 Crawford og 1; 18, 84
S	02-Apr	Dunfermline Athletic		A	L2	2-2	1935	Walker	Robertson	McDonough	Urquhart	More 1	Forsyth	Harris	Smith	Smith	Kerr	Marshall r78	Russell u78; Thomson; 54, 24
S	09-Apr	Dumbarton		A	L2	0-0	845	Walker	McDonough	Candlish	Robertson	More 1	Forsyth	Smith	Urquhart	Russell b	Kerr	Harris 1	Marshall; Thomson
S	16-Apr	Airdrie		A	L2	2-4	762	Cramb	Gillespie	Candlish	Robertson	More 1	Smith	Smith	Smith	Smith	Kerr	Marshall r61	Spence u61; Robinson; 62, 70, 86
S	23-Apr	Falkirk		A	L2	3-3	835	Cramb	Robertson	Thomson	Urquhart	More	Forsyth	Harris	Russell	Harris	Kerr	Marshall 2	Ballantyne u80; Robinson u67; 85, 79
S	30-Apr	Clyde		A	L2	2-3	503	Walker	Robertson	Kerr b x75 1p	Urquhart b	More	Forsyth	Robinson u80	Smith b	Russell	McCulloch r67	Marshall r67	Ballantyne u80; Robinson u67; 85, 79
S	07-May	Ayr United		A	L2	2-3	1142	Walker	Robertson	Thomson 1	Urquhart	More	Forsyth	Harris b 1	Smith b	Russell	McCulloch r67	Marshall 1	Robinson u67; 62, 70, 86
S	14-May	Queen's Park		H	L2	2-2	604	Walker	Robertson	Thomson	Urquhart	More	Forsyth b	Harris 1	Smith	Russell	McCulloch	Marshall 1	Ballantyne; Robinson; 62, 52

Manager : Gordon Wallace

(1) Donald Urquhart Testimonial

(2) Kennedy sent off 84 minutes

(3) Miller sent off 80 minutes

(4) Won 4-1 on penalties

(5) Donnelly missed penalty 65 minutes

(6) Gate receipts £6500

(7) Hearts player manager Alex McDonald booked and sent off 77 minutes

Day	Date	Opponents	Note	Venue	Comp	Res.	Att.	1	2	3	4	5	6	7	8	9	10	11	Substitutes, own goals and goal times
S	30-Jul	Keith	1	A	T	3-1		Westwood	Robertson r*	Sweeney **	More	Forsyth	Kerr	Urquhart	Marshall 1	Russell 1	Smith	Harris	Galloway u*; Kerr u*; Spence 22, 55, 80
Sn	31-Jul	Forfar Athletic	2	N	T	1-1		Westwood	Galloway	Robertson r*	Urquhart	More	Marshall r**	Marshall 1	McCulloch	Spence	Harris	Russell	Kerr u61; Hill u**; Wright 62
M	08-Aug	Swansea City	3	H	F	2-2		Westwood	Robertson	Sweeney	Urquhart r76	More	More	Smith r50	Kerr 1p	Harris b	Spence	Spence	Spence u61; Thomson u67; Wright 74, 84
S	13-Aug	Dunfermline Athletic		H	FC F	1-2	743	Graham	Robertson	Sweeney	Urquhart 1	More	Thomson	Smith	Kerr	Robertson Ch 68	Robertson 1	Robertson 1	Wright u50; McCulloch; 73
S	20-Aug	Brechin City		A	L2	0-9	9773	Graham	Ferguson	Sweeney	Urquhart	More	Thomson	Smith	Kerr m	Marshall	Hill 61	Robertson	Wright u68; Blackie; 22
W	24-Aug	Aberdeen		H	LC 2-1	0-3	3117	Graham	Ferguson	Sweeney	Urquhart r88	More	Thomson	Smith	Robertson	Harris	Hill	Marshall	Spence u61; Wright
S	27-Aug	Aberdeen		H	LC 2-2	1-2	1622	Graham	Ferguson r77	Sweeney	Urquhart	More	Robertson	Smith	Kerr	Harris	Kerr	Spence r79	Hill u77; Spence u88; 68
S	03-Sep	Falkirk		A	L2	1-2	915	Graham	Ferguson	Sweeney	Urquhart	More	Robertson	Smith b 1	Marshall	Harris	Smith b 1	Wright r81	Wright u79; Hill
S	10-Sep	Clydebank		H	L2	0-0	907	Graham	Ferguson	Robertson	Urquhart	Forsyth b	More	Smith	Marshall	Harris	Kerr b	Wright	Wright u81; Hill; 27
W	14-Sep	Hamilton Academical	4	H	L2	1-2	2197	Graham	Ferguson b x70	Robertson	Urquhart	Forsyth	More	Smith	Marshall	Harris	Kerr	Wright	Spence; Spence
S	17-Sep	Partick Thistle	5	A	L2	0-2	1075	Graham	Houston r63 b	Robertson	Urquhart	Forsyth	More	Smith	Marshall	Harris	Kerr r63	Thomson	Wright u63; Spence u63; 83
S	24-Sep	Morton		H	L2	1-3	1065	Graham	Robertson	Thomson	Urquhart	Forsyth	More x65	Smith	Marshall 1	Harris 1	Kerr	Wright 1	Hill; McCulloch; 49, 76
W	28-Sep	Ayr United		H	L2	2-2	421	Graham	Thomson b	Robertson	Urquhart	Forsyth b	More	Smith	Marshall	Harris 1	Kerr b 1	Wright	Hill; McCulloch; 4
S	01-Oct	Dumbarton		H	L2	1-2	839	Graham	Thomson r*	Thomson r*	Urquhart	Forsyth	Spence	Smith b	Marshall r89	Harris	Kerr b 1	Wright	More u*; Hill u**; 17, 67
S	08-Oct	Clyde	6	A	L2	2-1	874	Walker	Robertson	Sweeney	Urquhart b	Forsyth	Spence r**	Smith	Marshall 1	Spence 2	Kerr 1p	Wright	Thomson u89; Thomson; 50, 59
S	15-Oct	Alloa Athletic		H	L2	0-0	1324	Walker	Robertson	Sweeney	Urquhart b	Forsyth	More	Smith	Marshall	Spence r80	Kerr b	Wright r65	Hill u80; Hill
S	22-Oct	Airdrie		H	L2	1-2	1397	Walker	Robertson	Sweeney	Urquhart	More	More b	Smith	Marshall	Spence	Kerr	Wright r70	Harris u65; Hill; 85
S	29-Oct	Kilmarnock		H	L2	3-1	928	Walker	Robertson	Sweeney 1	Urquhart	More	Spence	Smith	Marshall b	Harris 1	Kerr 2, 1p	Wright	Houston u70; Thomson; 67, 30, 88p
S	05-Nov	Meadowbank Thistle	7	H	L2	0-0	976	Walker b	Robertson	Sweeney	Urquhart	More	Houston b	Smith b	Marshall	Harris x68	Kerr	Wright r69	Houston; Thomson
S	12-Nov	Hamilton Academical		A	L2	1-2	1667	Walker	Robertson	Sweeney	Urquhart	More	Spence	Smith	Marshall	Spence	Kerr 1p	Wright r64	Candlish; McCulloch; 35
S	19-Nov	Partick Thistle		H	L2	0-5	621	Walker	Robertson	Sweeney	Urquhart	More	Spence r64	Smith b 1	Marshall	Harris	Kerr	Wright	Candlish u69; McCulloch u64
S	26-Nov	Clyde		A	L2	1-3	791	Walker	Robertson r47	Sweeney	Urquhart b	More	Spence	Smith	Marshall	Harris	Kerr	Wright	Candlish u64; McCulloch u64; 67
S	03-Dec	Dumbarton	8	H	L2	0-0	1440	Walker	Candlish	Sweeney	Urquhart b	More	Robertson	Smith	Spence	Harris	Kerr r65	Wright r60	Candlish u47; McCulloch u65
S	10-Dec	Morton		A	L2	1-3	680	Walker	Candlish	Sweeney	Marshall b	More	Robertson	Smith	Spence	Harris	Kerr	Marshall	Hill; Spence
S	17-Dec	Ayr United		H	L2	1-1	813	Walker s	Candlish b	Sweeney	Houston	More	Candlish	Urquhart b	Urquhart	Harris	Urquhart b	Wright	Livingstone u60; McCulloch; 70
M	26-Dec	Clydebank		A	L2	2-2	1287	Walker	Candlish	Sweeney	Houston	Marshall b	Candlish	Smith b	Marshall b	Harris b	Kerr r86	Wright	Spence; Spence; 60
S	31-Dec	Falkirk		A	L2	1-1	1396	Walker	Candlish r45	Sweeney r67	Houston	Houston b	Candlish	Smith	Marshall b	Harris b	Kerr r86	Wright	Spence u86; Hill; 50, 89
M	02-Jan	Brechin City		A	L2	0-1	1147	Walker	Houston	Sweeney	Houston	Houston	Robertson	Smith b	Ramsay	Harris	Urquhart b	Wright	Ramsay u45 1; Kerr u67; 89
S	07-Jan	Airdrie		H	L2	3-1	562	Walker	Houston	Sweeney	Urquhart	More	Robertson	Smith 1	Marshall	Harris r78	Kerr r86	Marshall	Spence u78; Wright
S	04-Feb	Meadowbank Thistle		A	L2	1-4	940	Walker	Houston r67	Sweeney	Urquhart 1	More b	Robertson	Smith 1	Spence r74	Spence r74	Kerr	Wright b	Hill u74; McCulloch; 13, 64, 40
M	06-Feb	Dumbarton		H	SC 3	2-3	941	McArthur	Robertson	Robertson	Urquhart	More	Houston	Smith 2	Spence	Spence	Kerr	Wright r66	Hill u67 b; McCulloch; 70
S	11-Feb	Airdrie		H	L2	1-1	1109	McArthur	Robertson r80	Robertson r80	Urquhart	More	Marshall	Smith 1	Marshall	Harris	Kerr	Wright r67	Spence u66; More u86; 16, 85
F	17-Feb	Alloa Athletic		H	L2	1-3	640	McArthur	Houston	Sweeney	Urquhart	More	Marshall b	Smith b	Ritchie	Ramsay	Kerr 1p	Wright	Spence u67; Candlish; 43
S	25-Feb	Dumbarton		A	L2	2-1	768	McArthur	Houston	Sweeney	Urquhart	More	Marshall	Smith	Ritchie r88	Ramsay	Kerr 1p	Wright b	Candlish u80; Candlish u88; 15
W	29-Feb	Morton		H	L2	0-2	995	McArthur	Houston	Sweeney	Urquhart	More b	Marshall	Smith	Ritchie	Ramsay 1	Kerr b 1p	Wright 1	Spence; Hill u88
S	03-Mar	Morton		H	L2	3-4	529	McArthur	Houston	Sweeney u68	Philip r67	Corstorphine	Robertson	Marshall	Ritchie	Ramsay 1	Kerr 1p	Wright	Spence u70; Candlish
S	10-Mar	Clydebank		H	L2	1-2	300	McArthur	Houston	Sweeney	Urquhart	Houston	Robertson	Smith	Ritchie r83 1	Ramsay 1	Kerr 1p	Wright 1	Philip u68; Robertson u70; 49, 57
Tu	13-Mar	East Fife		H	FC SF	1-2	1111	Walker	Houston b	Robertson	Urquhart	More	Marshall 1	Smith	Ritchie r85	Ramsay	Kerr	Wright	Urquhart u67; Spence u83; 42, 49, 71
S	17-Mar	Partick Thistle	9	H	L2	2-1	680	McArthur	Houston	Robertson	Urquhart b	More	Marshall 1	Smith	Ritchie r89	Ramsay r89	Kerr b 1p	Wright 1	Sweeney u89; Hill u85; 56
S	24-Mar	Kilmarnock		A	L2	2-2	904	McArthur	Houston	Robertson	Urquhart	More	Marshall 1	Smith	Ritchie	Ramsay 1	Kerr 1p	Wright	Sweeney; Philip u89; 5, 28
S	31-Mar	Clyde		H	L2		839	McArthur	Houston	Robertson	Urquhart	More	Marshall 1	Smith	Ritchie r56	Ramsay r66	Kerr 1p	Wright 1	Sweeney u56; Philip; 28, 69
S	07-Apr	Ayr United	10	H	L2	5-0	1274	McArthur	Houston	Robertson	Urquhart	More	Marshall 1 b	Smith 1	Ritchie	Ramsay	Kerr r69 2,1p	Wright 1	Philip u66; Philip u66; 87, 81p
S	14-Apr	Falkirk		A	L2	0-1	722	McArthur	Houston r63	Robertson	Urquhart	More	Marshall	Smith	Ritchie	Ramsay r69	Kerr r69 2,1p	Wright 1	Philip u69; Candlish u88; 50, 54, 5, 15p, 28
S	21-Apr	Alloa Athletic		A	L2	0-2	864	McArthur	Marshall r85	Robertson 1	Urquhart	More	Marshall	Smith	Ritchie r45 b	Ramsay r55	Kerr m	Wright	Philip u69; Candlish
S	28-Apr	Hamilton Academical		H	L2	0-2	651	Walker	Marshall b 1	Robertson	Urquhart	More	Philip	Smith	Ritchie r45 b	Marshall	Kerr	Wright 1	Philip u55; Candlish
S	05-May	Brechin City	11	H	L2	6-0	1283	Walker	Robertson 1	Robertson 1	Urquhart	More	Philip	Smith	Ritchie	Ramsay	Kerr 4,2p	Wright 1	Ramsay u63; Sweeney u45; 20, 14, 43p, 68, 83p, 88
S	12-May	Meadowbank Thistle		A	L2	2-1	—	Walker	Robertson	Robertson	Urquhart	More	Philip	Smith	Ritchie r45	Ramsay	Kerr 1	Wright	Houston; Sweeney u45; 3, 83

Manager : Bobby Wilson from 11th September

(1) Keith Tournament

(2) Lost 5-4 on penalties ; Keith Tournament

(3) Wilcox sent off in 87 minutes

(4) Hutchison sent off in 88 minutes

(5) Holmes sent off in 73 minutes

(6) Garner missed penalty

(7) Godfrey sent off in 68 minutes

(8) Robertson sent off in 73 minutes

(9) McDowell sent off in 79 minutes

(10) Armour sent off in 70 minutes

(11) Mackie sent off in 70 minutes

1984-85

Day	Date	Opponents	Note	Venue	Comp	Res.	Att.	1	2	3	4	5	6	7	8	9	10	11	Substitutes, own goals and goal times
S	28-Jul	Forfar Athletic	1	N	T	2-2		Blair	Houston	Candlish	Urquhart	More	Philip	Smith	Ritchie	Ramsay 2	Marshall 1	Robertson	Wright, Kerr, Herd, Livingstone
Sn	29-Jul	Keith	2	A	T	3-2		Blair	Houston	Candlish	Urquhart	More	Philip	Smith 1	Ritchie r	Ramsay	Marshall	Robertson 2	Wright, Kerr, Herd, Livingstone
W	01-Aug	Meadowbank Thistle		A	F	1-2		Blair*	Houston r	Candlish r	Urquhart r	More	Philip	Smith 3	Ritchie r	Ramsay 2	Marshall	Robertson 2	Inglis u*, Kerr u, Herd u, Sweeney u, Livingstone u, 5, 56, 80, 47, 59
W	04-Aug	Lossiemouth		H	F	5-0		Blair	Houston	Candlish	Urquhart	More	Philip	Smith	Robertson	Ramsay	Marshall r	Wright	Ritchie u, Kerr u, Livingstone, Livingstone u, 40
Tu	07-Aug	Leeds United		H	F	0-2	686	Blair	Houston	Candlish	Urquhart	Corstorphine	Philip	Smith r	Marshall r	Ramsay	Kerr r	Wright	Ritchie u, Herd, Sweeney
S	11-Aug	Berwick Rangers		A	L3	1-2		Blair	Robertson	Candlish	Urquhart	Corstorphine	Robertson 1	Smith	Marshall	Marshall	Marshall	Wright 1	Houston, Houston, 64
Tu	14-Aug	Burntisland Shipyard		H	FC 1	9-2		Blair	Houston	Candlish 1	Urquhart	Corstorphine 1	Philip	Smith 2	Ritchie 1	Ramsay	Kerr r67	Wright 2	Livingstone u67, Ramsay, Young og 1
S	18-Aug	Dunfermline Athletic		H	L3	1-3	2004	Blair	Houston	Candlish	Urquhart	Corstorphine	Philip b	Smith b	Marshall	Robertson	Kerr	Wright 1	Livingstone, Ritchie, 51
Tu	21-Aug	Clydebank		H	LC 2	2-0	906	Blair	Robertson	Candlish r74	Urquhart	Corstorphine	Philip	Smith 2	Marshall	Ramsay r79	Kerr b	Wright	Houston u74, Ritchie u79, 2, 82
S	25-Aug	Cowdenbeath		A	L3	1-5	877	Blair	Robertson	Houston b	Urquhart	Corstorphine	Philip	Smith	Marshall 1	Ramsay r53	Kerr	Wright r76	Ritchie u53, Livingstone u76, 39
W	29-Aug	Rangers		A	LC 3	0-4	10123	Blair	Robertson	Houston	Urquhart	Corstorphine r73	Philip	Smith	Marshall	Ramsay r60	Kerr	Wright	Sweeney u60, Livingstone u76, Ritchie u73
S	01-Sep	Arbroath		H	L3	2-0	775	Blair	Houston	Houston	Urquhart	Philip	Philip	Smith	Marshall	Marshall	More	Wright 2	Falls u65, Ritchie u73, 25, 48
S	08-Sep	Stirling Albion		H	L3	1-1	963	Blair	Robertson	Houston r85	Urquhart b	More	Philip	Ritchie r65	Ritchie	Marshall	Sweeney r84	Wright 1	Ramsay u62, Herd u85, 12
S	15-Sep	Stranraer		A	L3	2-1	501	Blair	Robertson	Sweeney	Urquhart	More	Philip	Smith	Ritchie	Marshall b	Sweeney r62	Wright	Ramsay u, Livingstone, 32, 46
S	22-Sep	Queen's Park		H	L3	0-2	1003	Blair	Herd	Sweeney	Urquhart	Philip	Philip	Smith r76	Elvin	Marshall	Robertson 2	Wright 1	Bavidge u58, Ritchie u76, Livingstone
S	29-Sep	East Stirling		H	L3	2-0	660	Blair s	Herd	Sweeney r45	Urquhart r58	More	Philip	Smith r60	Elvin	Bavidge 1	Robertson 1	Wright	Corstorphine u45, Ritchie u60, 20, 76
S	06-Oct	Stenhousemuir		A	L3	1-1	527	Blair	Herd r58 b	Sweeney	Urquhart	More	Philip	Smith	Elvin	Bavidge	Robertson 1	Wright	Corstorphine u58, Ritchie u58, 66
S	13-Oct	Alloa Athletic	3	A	L3	1-1	921	Blair	More	Sweeney	Urquhart r58 b	Corstorphine	Philip	Smith x85	Elvin	Falls r69	Robertson	Wright 1	Urquhart u69, Ritchie, 31
S	20-Oct	Montrose		H	L3	0-1	849	Blair	More r73	Sweeney	Marshall	Corstorphine	Philip	Marshall	Elvin	McNeill r57	Robertson	Wright	Ritchie u57, Herd u73
S	27-Oct	Albion Rovers		H	L3	3-0	718	Blair	More r76	Sweeney	Urquhart	Marshall	Philip	Smith 2	Elvin	Ramsay r76	Robertson 1	Wright 1	Urquhart u76, Ritchie u76, 37, 71, 54
S	03-Nov	Queen of the South		A	L3	5-3	534	Blair	Herd	Urquhart	Marshall	Urquhart	Philip	Smith 1	Elvin	Ramsay 1	Robertson 1	Wright 1	Corstorphine u82, Ritchie, 2, 43, 57, 66, 54
S	10-Nov	Stirling Albion		A	L3	1-1	659	Blair	Herd	Sweeney	Marshall 2	More r82	Philip	Smith	Elvin	Ramsay	Robertson 1	Wright 1	Corstorphine u45, Ritchie, 76
S	17-Nov	Stranraer		H	L3	1-2	729	Blair	Houston	Sweeney	Marshall r45 b	Urquhart b	Philip	Smith 1	Elvin	Ramsay r73	Robertson	Wright 1	Bavidge u73, Ritchie u77, 88
S	24-Nov	Queen's Park	4	A	L3	1-1	540	Blair	Houston b	Sweeney	Urquhart r77	Corstorphine b	Philip	Smith 1	Elvin	Ramsay r85 1	Robertson 1	Wright 1	Bavidge u85, Urquhart, 70
S	01-Dec	Stenhousemuir		H	L3	3-0	656	Blair	Houston r45	Sweeney	Ritchie	More	Philip	Smith 1	Elvin	Ramsay r45 1	Robertson	Wright 1	Herd u45, Sokoluk u45, 50, 44, 65
W	05-Dec	Hearts		H	F	4-1		Blair	Houston 1	Sweeney	Ritchie	Philip r81	Philip	Smith 1p	Elvin 1	Ramsay r55 1	Robertson r55 1	Wright 1	Elvin u55, McNeill u81, 30, 6, 1, 75
S	15-Dec	East Stirling		A	L3	3-1	366	Blair	Houston	Sweeney b	Ritchie	More	Philip	Smith 1	Elvin	Ramsay	Robertson b	Wright 1	Bavidge u68, Urquhart, 65, 2, 78
S	22-Dec	Cowdenbeath		H	L3	0-3	1068	Blair	Houston r45 b	Sweeney	Ritchie r68 b	More	Philip	Smith m	Elvin	Ramsay	Robertson b	Wright	Sweeney u45, Ritchie u68, 76
S	29-Dec	Arbroath		A	L3	1-2	543	Blair	Urquhart	Sweeney	Marshall	More	Philip	Smith	Elvin	Bavidge	Robertson	Wright r68	Herd u70, McNeill, 57, 35
W	02-Jan	Dunfermline Athletic		A	L3	2-1	4035	Blair	Urquhart b x30	Sweeney r70	Marshall	More	Philip	Smith	Elvin 1	Bavidge r70	Robertson 1	Wright	Ramsay u70, Herd u83
S	05-Jan	Queen's Park		H	SC 2	0-0	1028	Blair	Houston	Sweeney	Marshall r83	More	Philip	Smith 1	Elvin	Bavidge r70	Robertson	Wright	Ritchie u62, Ritchie, 57
M	21-Jan	Queen's Park		H	SC 2r	1-0	1032	Blair	Houston r62	Sweeney	Marshall	More	Philip	Smith 1	Elvin	Ramsay r83 b	Robertson 1	Wright	Ritchie u71, Herd u62, 4, 89
S	26-Jan	Clyde		H	SC 3	1-2	2012	Blair	Candlish	Sweeney	Marshall	More	Philip	Smith 1	Elvin	Bavidge r62	Robertson 1	Wright	Herd u65, Bavidge, 37
S	02-Feb	Alloa Athletic		H	L3	2-1	1120	Blair	Candlish	Candlish	Marshall	More	Philip	Smith 1	Elvin	Bavidge	Robertson	Wright	Herd u82, Ritchie, 21, 74
M	04-Feb	Clyde	5	A	SC 3r	2-1	1239	Blair	Candlish	Candlish	Marshall	More	Philip	Smith 1	Elvin	Leitch	Robertson 1	Wright	Herd, Ritchie, 37
W	09-Feb	Montrose		A	L3	0-2	450	Blair	Candlish	Candlish	Marshall	More	Philip	Smith	Elvin	Ramsay r65	Robertson	Wright	Ritchie, Ritchie
S	16-Feb	Aberdeen		H	SC 4	1-2	10000	Inglis	Robertson	Urquhart b	Urquhart	More b	Philip	Smith 1p	Elvin	Leitch	Robertson	Wright r82	Falls u82, Herd, Muir og 1
W	20-Feb	Berwick Rangers		H	L3	2-1	651	Blair	Herd 1	Candlish	Marshall	More	Philip	Smith	Elvin b	Marshall b	Robertson	Leitch 1	Urquhart u82, Herd u82, 42, 62
S	23-Feb	Cowdenbeath		A	L3	0-0	776	Inglis	Herd	Sweeney	Marshall	More	Philip	Smith b 1p	Elvin b	Leitch r82	Robertson r82	Wright	Urquhart u71, Corstorphine
S	02-Mar	East Stirling		A	L3	1-2	392	Blair	Candlish r45	Sweeney	Marshall	More r60	Philip	Smith r52	Elvin	Leitch	Robertson	Wright 1	Urquhart u45, Herd, 66
W	06-Mar	Stenhousemuir		H	L3	1-2	574	Glynn	Candlish	Sweeney	Urquhart	More r60	Philip	Smith 1	Elvin 1	Leitch	Robertson	Wright 1	Sweeney u52, Herd u77, 57, 35
S	09-Mar	Stirling Albion		A	L3	2-4	706	Blair	Candlish r77	Sweeney	Urquhart r75	Urquhart	Philip r42	Smith 2p	Elvin	Leitch r84 b	Robertson 1	Wright b	Marshall u48, Herd u77, 38, 36
S	16-Mar	Queen of the South		A	L3	0-3	551	Inglis	Robertson	Sweeney	Urquhart r76 b	More 1	Philip	Smith 2.1p	Elvin r71	Leitch	McNeill r61	Wright	Marshall u61, Wright u75
S	23-Mar	Stranraer		H	L3	4-1	434	Blair	Herd 1	Candlish	Ritchie	More	Philip	Smith 1	Marshall	Leitch	Robertson 1	Wright 2	Marshall, Urquhart, 60, 31, 1, 47
Tu	26-Mar	Queen of the South		A	L3	3-0	543	McLafferty	Herd	Sweeney	Ritchie r78	More	Philip	Smith 3	Elvin b	Leitch	Robertson	Wright 3	Marshall u78, Urquhart, 48, 62, 70
Tu	02-Apr	Albion Rovers		A	L3	6-0	401	McLafferty	Herd	Sweeney	Ritchie r79	More	Philip	Smith 1	Elvin	Leitch	Robertson	Wright b	Urquhart u78, Marshall u79 b, 60, 86, 87, 3, 4, 23
Tu	09-Apr	Alloa Athletic		H	L3	2-0	1243	McLafferty	Herd	Sweeney	Ritchie r77	Philip r76	Philip	Smith 1	Elvin	Leitch	Robertson 1	Wright 1	Urquhart u76, Marshall u79 b, 13, 51
S	13-Apr	Arbroath		H	L3	2-1	767	Inglis	Herd	Sweeney b	Ritchie r69	Philip r42	Philip	Smith 2p	Marshall	Leitch	Robertson 1	Wright	Urquhart u60, Marshall u77, 33, 83
W	17-Apr	Cowdenbeath	6	H	FC SF	3-3	324	McLafferty	Herd	Sweeney	Marshall b	Urquhart	Philip	Smith 2.1p	Elvin b	Leitch r84 b	Robertson	Wright	McNeill u42 b, Herd u77, 30, 79, 33
Tu	20-Apr	Queen's Park	7	A	L3	3-2	527	McLafferty	Herd	Sweeney	Marshall 1	Urquhart r76 b	Philip	Smith 1	Elvin	Leitch	Robertson b 1	Wright	Candlish u76, Candlish u69, 19p, 27
Tu	23-Apr	Dunfermline Athletic		A	L3	3-2	3028	McLafferty	Herd	Sweeney	Marshall 1	Corstorphine r81	Philip	Smith 2.1p	Elvin	Leitch	Robertson 1	Wright	Candlish u76, McNeill, 11, 82, 77
S	27-Apr	Albion Rovers		A	L3	4-2	509	McLafferty	Herd	Candlish	Marshall	Candlish	Philip	Smith 2.1p	Elvin r79	Leitch	Robertson r75	Wright 3	Urquhart u75, Candlish u81, 58, 11, 59, 75
S	04-May	Berwick Rangers		A	L3		740	McLafferty	Herd	Sweeney b	Marshall	More	Philip	Smith 2.1p	Elvin r79	Leitch	Robertson b	Wright	Urquhart, McNeill, 48, 85p, 87
S	11-May	Montrose		H	L3	1-3	1194	McLafferty	Herd	Sweeney	Marshall	More	Philip	Smith 1p	Elvin r79	Leitch	Robertson	Wright b	Urquhart u79, Candlish, 37

Manager : Bobby Wilson

(1) Lost on penalties ; Keith Tournament

(2) Keith Tournament

(3) Thompson sent off in 80 minutes

(4) Loughran sent off in 82 minutes

(6) lost 1-3 on penalties

(5) Deans sent off in 89 minutes

(7) Walker sent off in 73 minutes

(8) Goal times 89, 59, 12, 5, 65, 78, 72, 87, 17

Substitutes, own goals and goal times

Day	Date	Opponents	Note	Venue	Comp	Res.	Att.	1	2	3	4	5	6	7	8	9	10	11	Substitutes, own goals and goal times
S	27-Jul	Gala Fairydean		A	F	5-3		McLafferty	Herd	Sweeney	McNeill	More	Philip r65	Smith 2	Elvin 1	Leitch	Robertson	Wright 2	Candlish u, Voy u, Livingstone u, Walker u; Falls 74, 73, 86
W	31-Jul	Hearts		H	F	3-2		McLafferty	Herd	Sweeney	Marshall r85 1	More r58	Philip r65	Smith	Elvin	Leitch r65	Robertson	Wright 2	Voy u65 Candlish, McNeill u65, Walker u85, Livingstone; Philip 73, 20, 89, 87
S	03-Aug	Ross County		A	F	4-1		McLafferty	Candlish	Sweeney	McNeill r70	More r58	Voy	Smith r83 1p	Livingstone r64 1	Walker r64 1	Robertson r48	Wright 1	Herd u58 Falls u70, Leitch 64, Fairgrieve u83, Elvin u64 1; Smith u59 60, 89
Sn	04-Aug	Forres Mechanics		A	F	2-1		McLafferty	Herd r70	Sweeney r30	McNeill r48	Philip r57	Voy	Falls	Livingstone r85	Walker r59	Robertson r48	Wright 2	Candlish u70, Fairgrieve u85, Livingstone u70, Robertson u48
Tu	06-Aug	East Fife		H	F	2-1		McLafferty	Herd	Candlish r63	Marshall	More	Voy	Smith 1	McNeill	Leitch	Robertson 1	Wright	Candlish u30, Voy u57, Livingstone, Elvin; Walker 75, 52
S	10-Aug	St.Johnstone		A	L3	0-2	1600	McLafferty	Herd	Robertson	Marshall	More	Voy	Smith	McNeill	Leitch	Robertson	Wright	Walker u63, Livingstone; Elvin
W	14-Aug	East Stirling		A	LC 1	3-1	458	McLafferty	Herd b	Sweeney	Marshall 1	More	Voy	Smith 1	Elvin	Walker r70 1	Robertson r33	McNeill b 1	Livingstone u70, Wright; 87, 11, 14
S	17-Aug	Stranraer		A	L3	2-3	594	Thomson	Herd b	Sweeney	Marshall b	More	Voy 1	Smith	McNeill	Leitch b	Robertson	Wright 1	Walker u33, Candlish; 44, 78
W	21-Aug	Clydebank		A	LC 2	2-7	1065	McLafferty	Herd	Sweeney	Marshall r62 1	More	Voy	Smith 1	Elvin b	McNeill	Robertson r62 1	Wright r75	Leitch u62, Walker u75; 16, 79
S	24-Aug	Cowdenbeath		A	L3	4-1	1032	McLafferty	Herd b	Sweeney	Marshall r86	More	Gavine	Smith 2,1p	Elvin b	Elvin b	Robertson	Wright 1	McNeill u86, Voy; Cochrane og 1; 17, 23p, 68, 86
S	31-Aug	Stirling Albion		H	L3	1-1	1040	McLafferty	Herd b	Sweeney	Marshall	More	Gavine	Smith 1	Elvin	Leitch	Robertson	Wright	McNeill u73, Voy; 44
S	07-Sep	Meadowbank Thistle		H	L3	1-1	896	McLafferty	Herd r61	Sweeney	Marshall	More r67	Gavine	Smith 1p	Elvin b	Leitch	Robertson	Wright 1	McNeill u61, Voy u67 b; 45
S	14-Sep	Dunfermline Athletic		A	L3	3-3	3119	McLafferty	Candlish b	Sweeney	Marshall	Voy r5	Gavine b 2	Smith 2	Elvin b	Leitch r73 b	Robertson r82	Wright r82	Herd u5, McNeill u82; 30, 72, 22
Tu	24-Sep	Queen's Park		H	L3	3-1	811	McLafferty	Herd	Sweeney	Marshall b	Candlish	Gavine b	Smith x75	Elvin	Leitch r80	Robertson r88	Wright r88	McNeill u80, Walker u88; 17, 65, 50
S	28-Sep	Albion Rovers	1	A	L3	0-2	481	McLafferty	Herd b	Sweeney	Candlish	Candlish	Gavine r63 b	McNeill 1	Elvin	Leitch	Robertson	Wright	McNeill u63, Voy
S	05-Oct	Arbroath		H	L3	2-1	1083	McLafferty	Candlish	Sweeney 1	Marshall	More	Gavine b	Candlish 1	Elvin b	Walker r65	Robertson	Wright	Herd u65 b, Leitch; 6, 71
S	12-Oct	Berwick Rangers		A	L3	3-4	649	McLafferty	Candlish	Sweeney r79	Marshall	More	Gavine b	Smith 1	Elvin r80	McNeill r80	Robertson	Wright 2	Herd u79, Voy u80; 17, 21, 42
S	19-Oct	Queen of the South		H	L3	0-1	1291	McLafferty	Candlish	Candlish	Marshall	More	Philip b	Smith 2	Elvin	McNeill	Walker r60 b	Wright	Fairgrieve u80, Gavine u60
S	26-Oct	East Stirling		A	L3	2-0	454	McLafferty	Candlish	Candlish	Marshall	More	More	Smith	Elvin	McNeill	Robertson	Wright 1	Voy, Walker; 47, 88
S	02-Nov	Stenhousemuir		H	L3	9-2	756	McLafferty	Candlish	Candlish	Marshall	More	Philip	Smith 1	Elvin	McNeill	Robertson	Wright 5	Herd u77, Walker; 21, 1, 8, 50p, 32, 36, 38, 53, 65 [3]
S	09-Nov	Meadowbank Thistle		A	L3	0-6	550	McLafferty	Candlish	Candlish	Marshall	More	Philip	Smith 3,1p	Elvin r83	Marshall 1	Robertson r80	Wright	Herd u74, McNeill u83
S	16-Nov	Dunfermline Athletic		H	L3	1-2	3448	McLafferty	Candlish	Candlish	Marshall r77 1	More	Philip	Smith	Elvin	Marshall	Robertson	Wright	Leitch u38, McNeill u51; 25
S	23-Nov	Queen's Park		A	L3	0-0	548	McLafferty	Herd	Sweeney r74	Marshall	More	Philip	Smith	Elvin	Marshall b	Robertson	Wright r75	Leitch u62, McNeill u75
S	07-Dec	Dunfermline Athletic		A	SC 1	0-2	5558	McLafferty	Herd b	Sweeney r17	Reid b	Voy	Philip	Smith x26	Elvin r62	Walker	Robertson	Wright	McNeill u68, Philip
S	14-Dec	Arbroath		A	L3	2-2	620	McLafferty	Herd b	Sweeney r38	Reid r51	Voy	Philip	Smith x26	Marshall r68 b	Walker	Robertson	Wright	McNeill u45, Fairgrieve u87; 22, 37p
S	28-Dec	Arbroath		A	L3	1-4	1461	McLafferty	Philip	Sweeney	Gavine	Voy	More	Leitch r87	Marshall b	Walker	Robertson b 1	Wright	McNeill u43, Fairgrieve u80; 89
S	11-Jan	Cowdenbeath		A	L3	0-1	579	McLafferty	Anderson	Sweeney 2,1p	Gavine r45	Voy	More	Leitch r43	Gavine r80	McNeill	Robertson	Robertson b 1	Corstorphine, Fairgrieve u45
S	18-Jan	Queen of the South		A	L3	0-2	1378	McLafferty	Herd	Sweeney	Philip	Voy	More	McNeill	Gavine	Walker	Robertson r45	Wright	Walker u67, Hynd u79
Tu	04-Feb	Albion Rovers		H	L3	1-0	369	McLafferty	Philip	Sweeney r81	Anderson	Voy	Philip	Smith	McNeill r79	Walker	Wright	Fairgrieve r67	McNeill u81, Gavine; 5
S	15-Feb	Dunfermline Athletic		H	L3	3-3	2663	McLafferty	Philip	Philip	Herd	Voy	More	Marshall	Anderson	Smith 1	Wright	Leitch r81	Corstorphine u53, Walker u80; 21, 84, 53
Tu	18-Feb	Berwick Rangers		H	L3	3-1	519	McLafferty	Philip	Philip	Herd 2	Voy	More	Marshall b	Anderson	Smith 1	Wright 2	Leitch	McNeill, Fairgrieve; 29, 27, 86
S	05-Mar	Meadowbank Thistle		H	L3	3-0	366	McLafferty	Philip	Philip	Herd	Voy	More	Anderson r53	Marshall r80	Smith 2	Wright 2	Leitch	Corstorphine, Walker u75; 9, 30, 58
S	08-Mar	St.Johnstone		A	L3	3-1	1130	McLafferty	Hynd	Philip	Philip	Voy	More	Marshall 1	Herd	Smith 2	Wright 1	Leitch	McNeill u70, Corstorphine; 75, 52, 79
Tu	11-Mar	Stranraer		H	L3	1-0	534	McLafferty	Hynd	Philip	Philip	Voy	More	Marshall	Herd	Smith b	Wright 1	Leitch r70	Fairgrieve u83, Walker u83; 21
S	15-Mar	Arbroath		A	L3	1-2	611	McLafferty	Hynd	Sweeney	Philip	Voy	More b	Marshall b	Herd b	Smith	Wright r83 b	Leitch r83	Falls u78, McNeill; 12
S	22-Mar	Cowdenbeath		H	L3	2-1	713	McLafferty	Hynd	Sweeney	More	Voy	More b	Marshall x62	Herd	Smith 2	Wright	Leitch	Robertson u62, Walker; 66, 77
Tu	25-Mar	East Stirling		H	L3	1-4	557	McLafferty	Hynd	Sweeney	More	Voy	Philip	Robertson r78	Herd b	Smith b	Wright 1	Leitch r62	Corstorphine u62, Walker u81; 77
S	29-Mar	Berwick Rangers		A	L3	0-1	570	McLafferty	Philip r81	Robertson	More	Voy b	Robertson	Marshall	Herd	Smith b	Wright r39	Leitch	Corstorphine u55 b, Walker u68
Th	03-Apr	Cowdenbeath		A	FC SF	2-3	238	McLafferty	Philip r55	Sweeney	Herd	Voy	More	Marshall r68 1	McNeill	Smith 1	Fairgrieve	Leitch b	McNeill, Corstorphine; 28, 10
S	05-Apr	East Stirling		A	L3	2-0	472	McLafferty	Hynd	Sweeney	Herd	Voy	More	Marshall	Robertson 1	Wright	Wright	Leitch b	McNeill u45, Walker u75; 44, 6
W	09-Apr	Queen of the South	2	H	L3	0-2	840	McLafferty	Hynd r75	Robertson	Robertson	Voy	More b	Robertson 1	Herd b	Smith 1	Wright	Leitch r45	Fairgrieve u, Corstorphine; 86
S	12-Apr	Stenhousemuir		A	L3	0-1	390	McLafferty	Hynd	Robertson r	Robertson r	Voy	More b	Marshall	Herd	Smith b	Wright	McNeill	Walker, Leitch
Tu	15-Apr	Stirling Albion		H	L3	1-1	276	McLafferty	Hynd	Sweeney	Herd	Voy	More b	Marshall	McNeill	Smith	Wright	Fairgrieve 1	Fairgrieve u29, Walker; 86
S	19-Apr	Stirling Albion		A	L3	1-3	409	McLafferty	Hynd	Sweeney	Philip r29	Voy	Philip	Marshall b	Herd	McNeill	Wright	McNeill	Walker u29, Robertson; 6
Tu	22-Apr	Stranraer		H	L3	4-1	267	McLafferty	Hynd	Sweeney	More	Voy	Fairgrieve	Marshall	Herd r77	Smith 1	Wright	McNeill 2	Walker u77, Robertson; 8, 87, 30, 53
S	26-Apr	Queen's Park		H	L3	2-1	556	McLafferty	Hynd	Sweeney	More	Voy	Fairgrieve r85	Marshall	Herd	Smith 2	Wright 2	McNeill	Walker u85, Corstorphine; 27, 36
S	03-May	Albion Rovers		H	L3	5-2	510	McLafferty	Hynd	Sweeney	More	Voy 1	Fairgrieve	McNeill 1	Herd	Smith 1	Leitch b	Wright 1	Walker, Corstorphine; 12, 71, 83, 70, 5

Manager : Bobby Wilson to 22nd January. Frank Connor from 21st March
(1) Deakin sent off along with Paul Smith in 75 minutes
(2) Dick sent off in 63 minutes
(3) Goal times 21,1,8,50p,32,36,38,53,65

Day	Date	Opponents	Note	Venue	Comp	Res	Att.	1	2	3	4	5	6	7	8	9	10	11	Substitutes, own goals and goal times
Tu	29-Jul	Dundee United		H	F	2-1	1026	McAlpine	Hynd	Sweeney	Herd	Voy	Robertson	Marshall r87	Harrow	Wright 2	Gordon	Fairgrieve r57	Simpson u57, McNeill u87, McLafferty, Spence, Sheach; 16, 22
S	02-Aug	Burntisland Shipyard	1	H	FC SF	5-1	1535	McAlpine	Hynd	Sweeney	Herd 1	Voy	Robertson	Simpson r68	Marshall 1	Wright 2	Gordon r72	Harrow 1	McNeill u66, Fairgrieve u72; 35, 88, 25, 54, 28
Sn	03-Aug	East Fife	1	H	FC F	3-1	898	McAlpine	Hynd	Sweeney r78	Herd	Voy	Robertson	Simpson r66	Marshall	Wright 1	Gordon	Harrow 1	Simpson u66, Fairgrieve u78; 70, 39p, 89
W	06-Aug	Rangers XI		H	F	2-1	841	McAlpine r76	Hynd	Sweeney	Robertson	Voy	Voy	Simpson	Marshall	Wright 1	Gordon r75	Harrow 1	McLafferty u65, Fairgrieve u75; 80, 44
S	09-Aug	Stranraer	2	A	L3	1-1	539	McAlpine	Hynd	Sweeney	Robertson	Brash	Voy	Simpson 1	Gordon	Wright b	Fairgrieve	Harrow	McNeill, Kerr; 25 secs
W	13-Aug	Arbroath		A	LC 1	1-2	738	McAlpine	Hynd	Sweeney r22	Robertson	Brash b	Voy	Simpson 1	McNeill	Wright b	Gordon b	Harrow	Candish u22, Fairgrieve; Hill og 24
S	16-Aug	Ayr United		H	L3	5-0	1207	McAlpine	Voy	Candish	Robertson	Brash	Kerr	Simpson	Gordon 1	Wright 1	Sweeney r78	Harrow 3,1p	Fairgrieve u78, McNeill; 68, 44, 35, 49, 89p
S	23-Aug	Meadowbank Thistle		A	L3	1-0	742	McAlpine	Voy	Robertson	Brash b X55		Kerr r89 b	Simpson	Marshall b	Wright 1	Gordon r83	Harrow	Fairgrieve u83, Candish u89; 44
S	30-Aug	Queen's Park		H	L3	2-2	1342	McAlpine	Robertson	Sweeney	Herd 1	Voy	Robertson	Simpson	Marshall	Wright 1	Gordon r50	Harrow	Candish u50, Fairgrieve; 43, 67
S	06-Sep	Stirling Albion		H	L3	0-0	1539	McAlpine	Voy	Sweeney	Robertson r71	Brash b	Kerr	Simpson	Herd	Wright	Gordon	Marshall b	Wilson u71, Candish
S	13-Sep	Cowdenbeath		A	L3	2-1	1019	McAlpine	Voy	Sweeney r88	Robertson	Brash b	Kerr	Simpson 1	Herd 1	Wright 1	Gordon	Harrow r38	McNeill u38 b, Candish u88; 44, 13
S	20-Sep	Berwick Rangers		H	L3	1-1	1324	McAlpine	Herd b	Sweeney	Robertson	Brash	Kerr	Simpson	Marshall	Wright 1	Gordon	Harris	Candish u88, Candish; 64
S	27-Sep	East Stirling		H	L3	5-0	497	McAlpine	Candish	Sweeney	Herd	Robertson	Kerr	Simpson 1	Marshall r80	Wright 1	Gordon b	Harris 3,1p	Harrow u80, Fairgrieve; 54, 57, 34p, 63, 77
S	04-Oct	Stenhousemuir	3	A	L3	2-1	757	McLafferty	Candish	Candish r76	Herd 1	Robertson	Kerr b	Marshall r43	Harris	Harrow m68	Gordon	Harris	Harrow u77 b 1, Fairgrieve; 10, 88
S	11-Oct	St Johnstone	4	H	L3	2-2	1775	McAlpine	Voy	Sweeney	Herd X20	Brash	Kerr	Simpson 1	Marshall 1	Wright 2	Harrow	Wright 2	Simpson u43, Fairgrieve; 31, 58
S	18-Oct	Alloa Athletic		A	L3	2-2	1282	McLafferty	Voy	Candish	Marshall	Brash	Kerr	Simpson	Harrow	Harrow	Harrow	Harris	Candish, Wilson; 20, 40
S	25-Oct	Arbroath		H	L3	3-0	1488	McAlpine	Voy	Sweeney	Herd	Brash	Kerr b	Simpson	Marshall 1	Wright 1	Sweeney r87	Harris 2	Wilson u76, McNeill u87; 86, 16, 40
S	01-Nov	Albion Rovers		A	L3	4-2	812	McAlpine	Voy	Sweeney	Robertson	Brash	Kerr	Simpson 1	Marshall 1	Wright 1	Harrow r36 1	Harris 1	Candish u36, McNeill; 6, 87, 12, 90
S	08-Nov	Ayr United		H	L3	3-3	1558	McLafferty	Voy	Sweeney	Robertson	Brash	Kerr	Simpson	Marshall	Wright	Harrow	Harris 1	Wilson, McNeill; 84, 73, 23
S	15-Nov	Stranraer		H	L3	2-1	1516	McAlpine	Voy b	Sweeney b	Robertson	Brash	Kerr	Simpson	Marshall	Wright	Harrow	Harris 2,1p	Wilson, Candish; 44, 89
S	22-Nov	Meadowbank Thistle		H	L3	2-3	1791	McAlpine	Voy b	Sweeney b	Robertson	Brash b 1	Kerr	Simpson	Marshall b	Harrow b	Harrow	Harris 2	Wilson, Candish; 23, 81p
S	29-Nov	Queen's Park		A	L3	2-2	789	McAlpine	Voy	Sweeney	Robertson	Brash	Kerr	Simpson	Wilson	Harrow	Wilson	Harris 1	McNeill, Candish; 11, 41
S	13-Dec	St Johnstone		H	L3	1-1	1677	McAlpine	Voy	Sweeney	Robertson	Brash	Kerr	Simpson	Marshall	Harrow	Wilson	Harris 1	Simpson u65, Gordon; 85
S	17-Dec	Alloa Athletic		H	L3	0-0	1073	McAlpine	Voy	Sweeney b	Robertson	Brash	Kerr	Simpson	Marshall	Harrow	Gordon r65	Harris 1	Candish, Candish
S	20-Dec	Arbroath		A	L3	1-2	669	McAlpine	Voy	Sweeney	Robertson	Brash	Kerr	Marshall	Marshall 1	Harrow 1	Gordon	Harris 1	Spence, Wilson; 82
S	27-Dec	Albion Rovers		H	L3	2-0	1560	McAlpine	Voy	Sweeney	Robertson	Brash	Kerr	Simpson	Marshall	Harrow 1	Gordon	Harris 1	Spence u81, Wilson; 84, 26
Th	01-Jan	Cowdenbeath	5	H	L3	2-2	1424	McAlpine	Voy	Sweeney	Robertson 1	Brash	Kerr	Simpson	Marshall	Harrow r81	Gordon	Harris 1	Spence u81, Voy; 40, 75
S	24-Jan	East Stirling		A	L3	2-0	1095	McAlpine	Herd	Sweeney b	Robertson	Brash	Kerr	Simpson	Marshall	Harrow r81	Gordon	Harris 2,1p	Spence u56, Voy u73; 50p, 72
M	26-Jan	Vale of Leithen	6	H	SC 2	4-0	1247	McAlpine	Herd	Sweeney	Robertson	Brash	Kerr	Simpson 1	Marshall 1	Harrow	Herd	Harris r73 2,1p	Spence, Candish; 61, 29, 47, 70p
S	31-Jan	Queen of the South		A	SC 3	1-0	1800	McAlpine	Voy	Sweeney	Robertson	Brash	Kerr	Simpson	Marshall	Harrow	Herd	Harris 1	Spence u67, Candish; 8
Tu	03-Feb	Stirling Albion		A	L3	1-1	778	McAlpine	Voy b	Sweeney	Robertson	Brash	Kerr	Simpson	Marshall	Harrow	Herd r60	Harris r67 1p	Spence u58, Candish; 4
S	07-Feb	Stenhousemuir		H	L3	1-0	1344	McAlpine	Voy	Sweeney b	Robertson	Brash	Kerr	Simpson	Marshall	Harrow	Sweeney r86	Harris r58 1	Wright u60, Candish u45; 24
Tu	10-Feb	Berwick Rangers		H	L3	4-2	408	McAlpine	Herd 1	Candish 1	Robertson 1	Brash b 1	Kerr	Spence 45	Spence b	Harrow 2	Sweeney r84	Harris	Wright u86, McNeill u85; 90, 25, 70, 43
S	14-Feb	Alloa Athletic		A	L3	4-2	1160	McAlpine	Herd	Candish 1	Robertson 1	Brash b 1	Kerr	Simpson	Marshall b	Harrow	Gordon r110	Harris r85 1p	McNeill u84, Gordon u53; 41, 31
S	21-Feb	Peterhead	7	H	SC 4	2-2	3529	McAlpine s82	Herd	Candish 1	Robertson	Brash b 1	Kerr	Simpson	Marshall	Harrow	Marshall	Harris r53 m17	McNeill u110, Wright; 4, 6, 30
W	25-Feb	Peterhead	7	A	SC 4r	3-3	5600	McAlpine	Candish	Sweeney	Robertson 2	Brash	Kerr	Simpson	Herd b x70	Harrow X42	Gordon	Marshall	McNeill u67, Wright; 10, 55
S	28-Feb	Stirling Albion	8	H	L3	3-0	1688	McAlpine	Candish	Candish b	Robertson 1	Brash b	Kerr	Simpson	Marshall	Harrow	Sweeney r85	Dalziel r67 1	McNeill u65, Wright u85; 84, 21, 34
M	02-Mar	Peterhead	9	N	SC 4r2	3-0	6000	McAlpine	Herd	Sweeney r45	Robertson	Brash	Kerr	Gordon	Gordon	Marshall 1	Gordon b	Harris r65 1	McNeill, Herd u45
S	07-Mar	Cowdenbeath	10	A	L3	2-2	1428	McAlpine	Kerr b	Sweeney	Robertson	Brash b	Purdie	Marshall	Marshall	Harrow	Gordon	Harris	McNeill u65, Wright u45; 71, 73
S	14-Mar	St Mirren		H	SC QF	0-2	8392	McAlpine	Candish	Sweeney	Marshall r65	Robertson	Kerr	Simpson	Harrow	Harrow	Gordon	Harris r45	McNeill u61 1, Wright u77
Tu	17-Mar	Arbroath		H	L3	2-2	1177	McAlpine	Candish	Sweeney r77	Purdie	Archibald	Kerr	Simpson	Robertson	Dalziel	Gordon	Harrow	McNeill u61 1, Wright; 31, 52, 80
S	21-Mar	Berwick Rangers		A	L3	3-2	1120	McAlpine	Candish	Sweeney	Purdie	Brash	Harrow	Simpson	Robertson	Dalziel 2	Gordon	Marshall r61 2	McNeill, Candish; 42
W	25-Mar	East Stirling		A	L3	1-1	640	McAlpine	Kerr	Kerr b	Purdie b	Brash 1	Harrow	Simpson	Robertson	Dalziel	Gordon	Marshall	McNeill u67, Candish; 72
S	28-Mar	Meadowbank Thistle		H	L3	1-1	1845	McAlpine	Herd	Kerr b	Purdie	Brash	Robertson	Simpson	Marshall	Dalziel r67	Sweeney	Harrow 1	Wright, Candish; 42
S	04-Apr	Queen's Park		H	L3	2-1	522	McAlpine	Kerr	Kerr b	Purdie b	Brash	Robertson	Simpson	Marshall	Harrow	Sweeney	Harris 1	Harrow u63 1, Candish; 79
S	11-Apr	Stenhousemuir		H	L3	1-0	1296	McAlpine	Kerr	Kerr	Purdie b	Brash	Herd	Simpson	Marshall	Dalziel r63	Sweeney	Harris	Harris u67, Gordon; 4, 69
S	18-Apr	Albion Rovers		A	L3	2-1	694	McAlpine	Candish	Sweeney	Sweeney	Brash	Kerr	Robertson	Robertson	Marshall 1	Sweeney	Dalziel r72 1	Purdie u67, Candish u78
S	25-Apr	Ayr United		A	L3	0-0	3022	McAlpine	Herd	Sweeney	Robertson	Brash	Kerr	Marshall	Dalziel	Dalziel	Gordon	Dalziel r83	Harrow u66, Purdie u83; 55
S	02-May	St Johnstone		A	L3	2-2	1177	McAlpine	Herd	Sweeney	Robertson	Brash	Kerr	Simpson r66	Marshall	Harrow r78	Gordon	Dalziel 2	Harrow u66, Purdie; 51, 52, 32, 49
S	09-May	Stranraer		A	L3	4-1	625	McAlpine	Herd	Sweeney	Robertson	Brash	Kerr	Simpson r45	Marshall 1	Harris 1	Gordon r45	Harris 1	Harrow u68, Purdie
M	11-May	Dunfermline Athletic	11	H	B	2-1	1814	McAlpine 45	Herd	Candish	Kerr	Kerr	Herd	Wright r68	Wright r68	Smith 2	Sweeney	Wright	Harris u68, McLafferty u45, Marshall u45; 4, 8

Manager : Frank Connor
(1) The Fife Cup was played as a four-team tournament on the weekend of 2nd and 3rd August at Stark's Park.
(2) Watt missed penalty kick
(3) Smith sent off
(4) Crawley and Billy Herd sent off in 20 minutes
(5) Paxton missed penalty
(6) Thorpe missed penalty
(7) after extra time
(8) Gavin sent off in second half
(9) at Gayfield Park
(10) Paxton and Proudfoot sent off
(11) Candlish Testimonial ; former players Paul Smith and Keith Wright guested for Rovers

Day	Date	Opponents	Note	Venue	Comp	Res.	Att.	1	2	3	4	5	6	7	8	9	10	11	Substitutes, own goals and goal times
S	25-Jul	Falkirk		H	F	1-0	879	McAlpine	Herd	McStay	Purdie	Kerr	Sweeney r74	Marshall r45	Gibson r73	Harrow	Dalziel	Harris r81 1p	Wright u73, Fairgrieve u74, Strachan u81, Archibald; 5
M	27-Jul	Hibernian XI		H	F	0-1	535	McAlpine	Herd	Sweeney	Purdie	Kerr r45	McStay	Marshall r45	Gibson	Harrow	Dalziel r45	Harris r59	Fairgrieve u45, Wright u45, Ferguson u74, Archibald u45, Strachan u59
W	29-Jul	East Fife	1	N	FC SF	2-0	1353	McAlpine	Herd b	McStay	Purdie	Archibald	Kerr	Marshall	Ferguson 1	Harrow	Sweeney	Harris r65 1	Wright u65, Fairgrieve, Fairgrieve u45; 77, 41
S	01-Aug	Dunfermline Athletic	1	N	FC F	2-2	818	McAlpine	Herd b	McStay 1	Purdie	Archibald	Sweeney 1	Marshall	Marshall	Harrow	Dalziel r65 1	Ferguson	Archibald; 70, 23
Sn	02-Aug	Cowdenbeath	1	N	FC F	2-2	479	McAlpine	Herd	McLeod r45	Purdie	Kerr	Kerr	Gibson	Wright	Harrow	Harrow r45	Sweeney r72	Strachan u65, Fairgrieve u72; 33
Tu	04-Aug	Dundee United		H	F	0-2	1698	McLafferty	Herd	McLeod	Kerr	Kerr	Fairgrieve	Ferguson r84	Ferguson r84	Harrow	Harrow r45	Harrow	Strachan u45, Archibald u45, McLeod u45, Wright u84
S	08-Aug	Forfar Athletic		A	L2	1-4	1329	McAlpine	Herd	McLeod	Kerr	Brash	Sweeney	Marshall	Harrow	Harris	Dalziel	Harris	Archibald u79, Ferguson u78/79 b; Clark og 83
W	12-Aug	Queen of the South		A	L2	3-0	1988	McAlpine	Archibald	McLeod	Kerr	Brash	Fairgrieve	Marshall 1	Harrow	Harris 2, 1p	Dalziel	Harris 2, 1p	Wright u80, Strachan; 70, 9p, 68
S	15-Aug	Partick Thistle		H	L2	0-0	1685	McAlpine	Archibald	McLeod	Kerr	Brash	McStay b	Simpson	Herd	Harris	Dalziel	Harris	Wright
W	19-Aug	Clydebank		A	L2	2-1	2139	McAlpine	Archibald	McLeod	Kerr	Brash	McStay	Simpson	Marshall	Harris b	Dalziel 1	Sweeney r85	Gibson u85, Harrow u86; 71, 16
S	22-Aug	Hamilton Academical		H	L2	1-2	6217	McAlpine	Archibald	McLeod	Kerr	Brash b	Gibson	Simpson	Marshall	Harris 1p	Dalziel r80	McStay r57	Wright u57, Harrow u71; 41
Tu	25-Aug	Dundee United		H	LC 2	1-2	2104	McAlpine	Archibald	McStay	Kerr	Brash b	Gibson	Simpson	Marshall	Harris	Dalziel r80	McLeod	Harrow u80, Wright; 62
S	29-Aug	East Fife		A	L2	1-2	1674	McAlpine	McStay r80	McLeod	Kerr	Brash	Gibson	Simpson	Marshall	Harris	Dalziel 1	McLeod	Harrow u80, Wright; 74
S	05-Sep	Clyde		H	L2	1-3	1436	McAlpine	McStay	McLeod	Kerr	Brash	Gibson	Simpson	Wright	Harris	Dalziel 1	Sweeney	Purdie; 34
S	12-Sep	Kilmarnock		A	L2	4-3	1111	McAlpine	McStay	McLeod	Kerr b	Brash b	Gibson 1	Simpson	Wright	Harris 1p	Dalziel 1	Sweeney r45 1	Harrow, Fairgrieve u45; 79, 43, 57, 39
Tu	15-Sep	Meadowbank Thistle		H	L2	2-0	1012	McAlpine	McStay b	McLeod	Kerr	Brash	Gibson	Simpson	Wright	Harris r72 1	Dalziel 1	Sweeney	Lloyd u72, Fairgrieve; 17, 74
S	19-Sep	Clydebank		H	L2	2-1	2048	McAlpine	McStay r75	McLeod	Kerr	Brash	Gibson	Simpson r50	Wright r50	Lloyd 2	Dalziel	Sweeney	Fairgrieve u75, Harrow u50; 27, 30
S	26-Sep	Airdrie		H	L2	3-2	1788	McAlpine	Archibald	McLeod	Kerr	Brash	Gibson 2	Simpson 1	Purdie r68 b	Harris r75	Dalziel	Sweeney	Fairgrieve u68, Harrow u75; 45, 52, 59
Tu	29-Sep	Dumbarton		H	L2	4-1	1079	McAlpine	Archibald	McLeod r77	Kerr	Brash	Gibson	Simpson r72	Purdie	Harris r79 2, 1p	Dalziel 2	Sweeney r72	Lloyd u79, Lloyd u75; 11pm, 62, 78, 88
S	03-Oct	Forfar Athletic		A	L2	0-3	1127	McAlpine	Archibald	McLeod r77	Kerr	Brash	Gibson	Simpson	Purdie	Harris r57	Dalziel	Sweeney	Lloyd u57, Fairgrieve u77
S	07-Oct	Queen of the South	2	H	L2	3-1	1925	McAlpine	Archibald	McLeod r65 b	Kerr b	Brash	Gibson	Simpson	Purdie 1	Harris	Dalziel r80 2	Sweeney	Lloyd u80, Harrow u65; 20, 22, 71
S	10-Oct	Hamilton Academical		A	L2	2-0	2276	McAlpine	Archibald	McLeod	Kerr b	Brash	Gibson r78 b 1	Simpson 1	Purdie	Harris	Dalziel r86	Sweeney	Lloyd u86, McStay u78; 51, 86
S	17-Oct	Kilmarnock		H	L2	0-2	921	McAlpine s	Archibald	McLeod	Kerr	Brash	Gibson r*	Simpson	Purdie r	Harris x70	Dalziel	Sweeney	Lloyd u*, McStay u
Tu	20-Oct	Meadowbank Thistle		A	L2	3-4	2063	McAlpine	Archibald r82	McLeod	Kerr	Brash	McStay r* 1	Simpson 1	Purdie r	Lloyd	Dalziel 1	Sweeney 1	Harrow u*, Wright u; 67, 83, 18
S	24-Oct	Partick Thistle		A	L2	4-3	695	McAlpine	McStay	McLeod	Kerr	Brash	Wright 1	Simpson 1	Wright r85	Harris 1p	Dalziel 2	Sweeney	Harrow u82, Lloyd u82; 11, 46, 51, 58
Tu	27-Oct	Dumbarton		A	L2	3-1	950	McAlpine	McStay	McLeod	Fraser	Brash 1	Wright	Simpson	Marshall r66	Harris r80	Dalziel r80 1	Sweeney b	Harrow u66, Lloyd u80; 90, 60, 11
S	31-Oct	Clyde		H	L2	2-3	3148	McAlpine	McStay	McLeod	Fraser b	Brash 1	Wright	Simpson	Marshall r75	Harris 2	Dalziel b 1p	Sweeney	Lloyd u75, Lloyd u80; 26, 88
S	07-Nov	East Fife	3	H	L2	7-1	2230	McAlpine	McStay 1	McLeod	Fraser	Brash 1	Gibson	Simpson r78	Marshall r78	Harris	Dalziel 3	Sweeney	Lloyd u78, Harrow u78; 63, 15, 67, 80, 48, 49, 60
S	14-Nov	Clydebank		A	L2	1-0	2035	McAlpine	McStay 1	Harrow	Fraser	Brash	Wright	Simpson	Marshall	Harris r76	Dalziel r69	Sweeney r85	Lloyd u76 1, Purdie; 79
S	21-Nov	Airdrie		A	L2	0-3	1808	McAlpine	McStay	Harrow	Fraser	Brash	Gibson r85 b	Simpson	Marshall	Harris	Dalziel	Sweeney	Lloyd u69, Wright u85
S	28-Nov	Forfar Athletic		H	L2	0-0	1006	McAlpine b	McStay	Harrow	Fraser	Brash	Gibson	Simpson	Marshall	Harris	Dalziel 2	Sweeney	Lloyd, Purdie
S	05-Dec	Queen of the South		A	L2	5-1	1654	McAlpine	McStay 1	Harrow	Fraser	Brash	Gibson	Simpson r82	Purdie	Harris 1p	Dalziel 2	Sweeney 1	Lloyd u82, Wright; 75, 49, 22, 79, 61
S	12-Dec	Kilmarnock		A	L2	1-1	2029	McAlpine	McStay	Harrow	Fraser	Brash	Gibson	Simpson	Purdie r77 b	Harris	Dalziel	Sweeney	Marshall u77, Ferguson; 50
S	19-Dec	Meadowbank Thistle		H	L2	4-0	3317	McAlpine	McStay	Harrow b	Fraser r65	Brash	Gibson 1	Simpson 1	Marshall 1	Harris 1	Dalziel	Sweeney	Ferguson u45 2, Kerr u65, Hendrie og 1; 80, 53, 62, 30
S	26-Dec	Clyde		A	L2	2-0	4609	McAlpine	McStay b	Harrow b	Fraser r88	Brash b	Gibson 1	Lloyd r45	Marshall	Harris b	Dalziel 1	Sweeney	Wright u64, Kerr u88; 35, 71
S	02-Jan	East Fife		A	L2	2-1	1333	McAlpine	McStay b	Harrow b	Fraser	Brash b	Gibson b	Ferguson r64	Marshall	Harris r79	Dalziel 1	Sweeney	Lloyd u79, Wright; 53, 89
S	09-Jan	Clydebank		A	L2	1-3	5327	McAlpine	McStay	Sweeney b	Fraser	Kerr	Gibson b	Simpson 1	Marshall	Lloyd r83	Dalziel	Coyle	Wright u83, Archibald; 6
S	16-Jan	Ardrie		H	L2	2-2	1766	McLafferty	McStay	Harrow	Fraser	Kerr	Coyle	Simpson 1	Coyle	Lloyd r79	Dalziel 1	Coyle	McLeod, Marshall; 88, 19
S	06-Feb	Partick Thistle		A	L2	0-5	1901	McAlpine	McStay b	Harrow	Fraser b	Archibald b x65	Gibson	Simpson r78	Harrow	Harris	Dalziel r64	Sweeney r78	Lloyd u78, Kerr u85
M	08-Feb	Rangers		H	SC 3	0-0	9500	McAlpine	McStay b	Harrow b	Fraser	Brash b	Gibson	Simpson	Coyle	Harris	Lloyd r65 1	Sweeney	Lloyd u64, Marshall
W	10-Feb	Rangers		A	SC 3r	1-4	35144	McAlpine	McStay b	Harrow b	Fraser	Brash b	Gibson r75	Simpson	Coyle b	Harris	Lloyd r70 1	Lloyd r70 1	McLeod u75, Marshall u65; 50
S	13-Feb	Dumbarton		H	L2	2-2	876	McAlpine	McStay	McLeod	Fraser	Brash	McLeod	Simpson 1	Coyle b	Lloyd r70 1	Dalziel r60 1	Sweeney b	McLeod u70, Marshall u70; 46
S	20-Feb	St Mirren		H	F	3-2	1056	McLafferty	McStay r56	Harrow r73	Fraser	Brash	Gibson	Simpson 1	Coyle	Harris r79	Dalziel r60 1	Sweeney r45	Marshall u45, McLeod u45, Wright u73, Lloyd u79, Spence u60; 51, 3, 68
W	27-Feb	Forfar Athletic		A	L2	2-2	2586	McAlpine	Coyle	Harrow	Fraser b 1	Brash b	Gibson	Simpson	Marshall 1	Harris 1	Dalziel r76	Sweeney b	Lloyd u76, McLeod; 87, 45
S	02-Mar	Hamilton Academical		H	L2	0-1	1536	McAlpine	McStay	Harrow	Fraser	Brash	Gibson r80	Simpson	Coyle	Harris	Dalziel r70	Sweeney	Lloyd u70, McLeod u80
S	05-Mar	Kilmarnock		A	L2	2-2	978	McLafferty	McStay	McLeod	Fraser	Brash b	Coyle 1	Simpson	Wright	Harris b 1	Lloyd	Sweeney r64 b	Dalziel u45, Dalziel; 38, 59
S	12-Mar	Meadowbank Thistle		H	L2	0-3	702	McLafferty	McStay	McLeod	Fraser b	Brash b	Coyle b	Simpson	Wright	Harris r45	Dalziel 1	Sweeney r64 b	Marshall u76, Gibson u64
S	19-Mar	Clyde		A	L2	2-1	2466	McLafferty	McStay	McLeod	Fraser	Brash	Gibson	Simpson 1	Coyle	Lloyd r76	Dalziel 1	Sweeney r64 1	Kerr u79, Harrow u79; 87, 27
S	26-Mar	East Fife		H	L2	0-1	1579	McLafferty	McStay	McLeod	Fraser	Brash	Gibson	Simpson 1	Coyle b	Lloyd r79	Dalziel	Sweeney r79	Spence u63, Wright u80
S	02-Apr	Partick Thistle		H	L2	1-2	1833	McLafferty	McStay	Harrow	Kerr	Archibald	Gibson	Simpson	Coyle b 1	Ferguson r63	Dalziel b 1	Sweeney b	Ferguson u73, Wright; 85
S	09-Apr	Hamilton Academical		A	L2	1-2	876	McLafferty	McStay b 1	Harrow	Kerr	Archibald	Gibson	Simpson r45	Coyle	Harrow r73	Dalziel 1	Sweeney	Wright u85, Lloyd; 42
S	16-Apr	Airdrie		H	L2	2-1	1109	McLafferty s	McStay	McLeod	Fraser	Archibald b	Wright	Simpson	Coyle	Ferguson	Dalziel r73	Fairgrieve r67	Kerr u67, Lloyd u73 1; 57, 24
S	23-Apr	Clydebank		H	L2	2-3	942	McLafferty	McStay	Harrow	Fraser	Brash b	Coyle	Simpson 1	Marshall r87	Ferguson 1	Dalziel r71 2, 1p	Sweeney	Spence u71, Kerr u87; 53, 76
S	30-Apr	Queen of the South		H	L2	4-2	795	McLafferty	McStay	Harrow	Fraser	Brash b	Coyle	Simpson 1	Marshall	Ferguson 1	Dalziel r72 2, 1p	Sweeney b	Spence u72, Kerr; 40, 64, 61, 71p
S	07-May	Dumbarton		A	L2	0-3		McAlpine	McStay	McLeod	Fraser	Brash	Coyle	Simpson	Marshall	Ferguson	Dalziel r72	Sweeney b	Kerr

Manager : Frank Connor

(1) The Fife Cup was played as a four-team tournament on the weekend of 2nd and 3rd August at Stark's Park.

(2) Hughes missed penalty in 54 minutes

(3) Reid sent off 29 minutes

Substitutes, own goals and goal times

Day	Date	Opponents	Note	Venue	Comp	Res.	Att.	1	2	3	4	5	6	7	8	9	10	11	Substitutes, own goals and goal times
S	30-Jul	Rangers		H	F	1-2	9500	Arthur	McStay	Murray	Fraser	Dennis	Gibson	Ferguson,I r70	Coyle	Ferguson,	Dalziel r80 1	Sweeney r75	Spence u70, Strachan u75, Buchanan u80, Archibald, Paterno 17
Tu	02-Aug	Motherwell		H	F	0-1	800	Paterno	McStay	Sweeney r45	Fraser	Dennis	Gibson	Simpson r62	Coyle	Ferguson, r68	Dalziel r73	Wright r62	Buchanan u45, Archibald u62, Ferguson,I u68, Spence u62
S	06-Aug	Dunfermline Athletic	1	A	FC SF	1-2		Main	McStay	Murray	Coyle	Dennis	Gibson	Simpson	Coyle	Ferguson,I r5	Dalziel	Sweeney 1	Ferguson,I u5, Spence u68, Wright 23
S	13-Aug	St.Johnstone		A	L2	1-3	2634	Arthur	McStay	Murray b	Coyle	Dennis b	Gibson	Simpson	Coyle	Ferguson,I r68	Dalziel	Sweeney 1	Spence u85, Strachan 24
W	17-Aug	Falkirk	2	A	LC 2	1-1	2751	Arthur	McStay b	Murray	Coyle	Dennis b x58	Gibson	Simpson	Wright r86 1	Ferguson,I r95	Dalziel 85 1p	Sweeney	Spence u80, Strachan u95, Archibald u86, 4
S	20-Aug	Queen of the South		H	L2	2-1	1402	Arthur	Archibald b	Murray	Coyle	Dennis	Gibson	Simpson	Wright r86 1	Ferguson,I r80	Dalziel	Sweeney	Logan u79, Archibald u86, Wright, Mills og 1, 31, 53
S	27-Aug	Dunfermline Athletic		A	L2	1-2	6388	Arthur	Archibald	Murray b	Coyle b	Archibald	Gibson	Simpson 1	McStay	Simpson 1	Dalziel r79	Sweeney b	Logan u60, Strachan u78, Wright, 83
S	03-Sep	Clyde		H	L2	0-0	1522	Arthur	McStay	Murray 1	Coyle b	Archibald	Gibson	Simpson r78	Wright b	Ferguson,I r60	Dalziel	Sweeney b	Logan u60, Wright, 74
S	10-Sep	Meadowbank Thistle		A	L2	1-2	1420	Arthur	McStay	Murray	Coyle b	Dennis	Gibson b	Romaines	Romaines	Ferguson,I r60	Dalziel r60 m	Sweeney b	Ferguson,I, Wright u60, Wright, 82
S	17-Sep	Airdrie		H	L2	1-2	1679	Arthur	Archibald r60	Murray	Coyle b	Archibald	Gibson	Simpson, r67	Romaines	Ferguson,	Dalziel	Sweeney b	Wright u60, Loigan u67, Buchanan u81
S	24-Sep	Forfar Athletic		A	L2	0-1	816	Arthur	McStay	Murray	Coyle	Archibald	Gibson	Romaines	Wright r61	Logan r68	Dalziel	Strachan	Ferguson,I u68, Buchanan u81, Dennis
S	01-Oct	Ayr United		H	L2	0-0	1894	Arthur	McStay	Murray	Fraser	Brash	Coyle	Simpson	Coyle	Ferguson, b	Dalziel	Sweeney r77	Strachan u77, Dennis
S	08-Oct	Morton		A	L2	1-0	1719	Arthur	McStay	Murray	Fraser	Brash	Gibson b	Simpson 1	Romaines	Ferguson,	Dalziel	Sweeney	Strachan, Wright, 70
M	10-Oct	Dundee United XI		H	F	2-1		Arthur	McStay	Murray	Fraser	Brash r73	Gibson	Simpson r45	Coyle	Ferguson,I r69 2	Dalziel r78	Sweeney	Dennis u73, Ferguson,I u78, Strachan u45, Logan u69
S	15-Oct	Clydebank		H	L2	1-3	1726	Arthur	McStay 1p	Murray	Fraser r64	Brash b	Coyle	Simpson	Romaines	Ferguson,	Dalziel r66	Sweeney	Wright u64, Logan u66, 86
S	22-Oct	Kilmarnock		A	L2	1-1	1965	Arthur	McStay b	Murray	Fraser	Brash	Gibson 1	Simpson	Coyle r72	Ferguson,I r60	Logan	Sweeney	Marshall u72, Dalziel u60, 25
S	29-Oct	Falkirk		A	L2	1-3	2993	Arthur	McStay	Murray	Fraser b	Brash r76 b	Gibson 1	Simpson	Coyle	Ferguson,I r71	Logan	Sweeney	Dalziel u71, Marshall u76, 25
S	05-Nov	Partick Thistle		H	L2	5-3	1682	Arthur	McStay	Murray	Fraser 2	Brash	Gibson 1	Marshall r71	Coyle	Ferguson,l 2	Dalziel r76	Sweeney	Simpson u71, Logan u76, 59, 85, 30, 14, 63
S	12-Nov	Meadowbank Thistle		H	L2	1-0	1549	Arthur	McStay b	Murray 1	Fraser b	Brash r27	Gibson	Marshall r86 b	Coyle	Ferguson,I 1	Dalziel	Sweeney b	Simpson u27, Romaines u86, 55
S	19-Nov	Airdrie		A	L2	1-3	1838	Arthur	McStay	Murray	Fraser b	Coyle b	Gibson	Simpson	Marshall b	Ferguson,I r45	Dalziel	Sweeney	Dennis, Romaines, 86
S	26-Nov	Forfar Athletic		H	L2	2-1	1305	Arthur	McStay	Murray	Fraser	Dennis	Gibson	Simpson	Dalziel r86 1	Logan 1	Coyle	Sweeney	Logan u45 1, Romaines u86, 3, 48
S	03-Dec	Queen of the South		A	L2	1-0	734	Arthur	McStay	Murray	Fraser b	Dennis	Gibson	Simpson r50	Dalziel r75	Logan	Romaines	Sweeney	Marshall u50, Ferguson,I u75, 9
S	10-Dec	Falkirk		H	L2	1-3	3046	Arthur	McStay	Murray	Fraser b	Dennis b	Gibson 1	Marshall	Dalziel	Ferguson,I r64	Romaines r65 b	Sweeney	Logan u35, Simpson u65, 75
S	17-Dec	Kilmarnock		H	L2	0-0	1514	Arthur	McStay	Murray	Fraser	Dennis	Gibson	Simpson	Dalziel	Logan	Coyle	Sweeney r69	Marshall u69, Romaines
S	24-Dec	Clydebank	3	A	L2	1-3	1197	Arthur	McStay	Murray b	Fraser b	Brash b	Gibson	Romaines r72	Logan 1	Ferguson, r64	Coyle b	Sweeney	Simpson u64, Marshall u72, 10
S	31-Dec	Clyde		A	L2	1-0	688	Arthur	McStay	Murray b	Fraser	Brash	Gibson	Simpson r23	Dalziel r72 1	Logan	Coyle b	Sweeney	Marshall u23, Romaines u72, 44
Tu	03-Jan	Dunfermline Athletic		H	L2	1-3	9331	Arthur	McStay b	Murray	Fraser r56 b	Brash b	Gibson	Marshall	Dalziel r75 1	Logan	Coyle	Strachan 1	Romaines u56, Ferguson,I u75, 36
S	07-Jan	Partick Thistle		A	L2	1-1	2167	Arthur	McStay	Murray	Coyle	Brash	Gibson	Romaines	Dalziel x50	Logan r68	Sweeney b	Sweeney	Ferguson,I u68, Wright u86, 36
S	14-Jan	St.Johnstone		H	L2	1-1	5041	Arthur	McStay 1p	Murray	Coyle	Glennie	Gibson	Marshall	Romaines	Strachan r77	Romaines r59	Sweeney	Ferguson,I u77, Wright u89, 39
S	21-Jan	Morton		H	L2	1-0	1553	Arthur	McStay	Murray	Coyle	Glennie	Gibson	Ferguson,l	Dalziel r73 1	Ferguson,I r89 1	Strachan r59	Sweeney	Simpson u59, Wright u89, 75
S	28-Jan	Rangers		A	SC 3	1-1	9422	Arthur	McStay	Murray	Fraser	Glennie	Gibson	Ferguson,I r75	Dalziel r82	Logan r79	Coyle b	Sweeney	Marshall u73, Romaines u79, 53
W	01-Feb	Rangers		A	SC 3r	0-3	40307	Arthur b s	McStay b	Murray b	Fraser b	Glennie	Gibson	Simpson r58	Dalziel 2	Logan	Coyle	Sweeney r24	Marshall u75, Romaines u82
S	04-Feb	Ayr United		A	L2	1-1	2375	Arthur	McStay	Murray	Fraser	Glennie	Gibson b	Ferguson,l	Dalziel	Ferguson,I r78 1	Coyle	Sweeney r84	Romaines u24, Logan u58, 32
S	11-Feb	Meadowbank Thistle		A	L2	3-1	889	Arthur b s	McStay	Murray	Fraser	Glennie	Gibson	Ferguson,I r81	Dalziel 2	Logan r78 1	Coyle	Sweeney	Strachan u78, Romaines u84, 35, 40, 46
S	18-Feb	Dundee		H	F	2-2	968	McCloy	Glennie r77	Murray r84	Fraser	Brash	Gibson	Ferguson,I r81	McStay r45 1p	Logan r73 1	Dalziel	Dalziel	Marshall u45, Ferguson, u73, Romaines u61 Dennis u77 Buchanan u84, 13, 36
W	01-Mar	Airdrie		H	L2	1-1	1633	Arthur	Glennie	Sweeney	Fraser	Brash	Gibson	Simpson r71	Dalziel	Logan 1	Coyle	Marshall	Ferguson,I u71, Strachan, 67
S	04-Mar	Queen of the South		H	L2	4-1	1295	Arthur	Murray	Murray	Fraser	Brash 2	Gibson r57	Simpson r45	Dalziel r57	Logan 1	Coyle b	Sweeney 1	Marshall u45, Marshall u57, 4, 23, 11, 51
S	11-Mar	St.Johnstone		A	L2	1-0	6814	Arthur	McStay	Murray	Fraser	Glennie	Gibson	Simpson r71	Dalziel 1	Logan	Coyle	Sweeney	Ferguson,I u71, Marshall, 85
S	18-Mar	Aberdeen		H	F	3-1	1583	Arthur	McStay r70	Murray	Fraser r77	Glennie	Gibson	Simpson r79 1	Dalziel r57	Logan	Coyle 1	Sweeney r45	Ferguson,I u57 1, Romaines u70, Dennis u77 Marshall u65 Strachan u79, 65, 9, 90
S	25-Mar	Ayr United		A	L2	2-2	2774	Arthur	McStay b 1p	Murray	Marshall r89	Glennie b	Gibson	Simpson r67	Dalziel 1	Logan	Coyle	Nelson b	Ferguson,I u67, Romaines u89, 9, 60
S	01-Apr	Clyde		H	L2	2-0	1412	Arthur	McStay 1p	Murray	Marshall r51	Glennie	Gibson	Simpson r75	Dalziel 1	Logan	Coyle	Nelson	Ferguson,I u75, Romaines u51, 5, 59
W	05-Apr	Morton		A	L2	0-2	1840	Arthur	McStay m	Murray	Romaines	Glennie	Gibson	Simpson r68	Romaines	Logan	Coyle	Nelson	Ferguson,I u68, Romaines u68, Dennis
S	08-Apr	Falkirk		A	L2	0-3	2932	Arthur	McStay	Murray	Glennie	Dennis b	Gibson	Simpson r68	Dalziel	Ferguson,I	Coyle	Simpson r68	Strachan u64, Nelson u66
S	15-Apr	Kilmarnock		A	L2	2-1	2218	Arthur	McStay	Murray b	Fraser	Glennie	Gibson	Simpson 1	Dalziel 1	Ferguson,I r80	Coyle b	Nelson	Marshall u80, Romaines, 68, 74
S	22-Apr	Forfar Athletic		H	L2	2-3	1087	Arthur	McStay	Fraser	Fraser	Glennie	Gibson 1	Simpson r66	Dalziel 1	Ferguson,I	Coyle 1	Nelson r74	Marshall u66, Romaines u74, 37, 85
S	29-Apr	Clydebank		H	L2	3-0	1032	Arthur	McStay	Murray	Fraser 1p	Glennie	Gibson	Simpson r83	Burn	Ferguson,I	Coyle 1	Nelson 1	Burn u83, Buchanan, 75, 59, 38
S	06-May	Morton		A	L2	1-0	1070	Arthur	Buchanan	Murray	McStay	Glennie r75	Gibson	Simpson r83	Burn	Ferguson,I	Coyle	Nelson 1	Marshall u73, Dennis u75, 17
S	13-May	Partick Thistle		H	L2	1-1	1656	Arthur	McStay	Murray	Coyle	Glennie	Gibson	Simpson	Burn	Marshall 1	Dalziel r82	Nelson 1	Romaines u82, Raeside, 52

Manager : Frank Connor

(1) The Fife Cup was played as a four team tournament on the weekend of 6th and 7th August at Dunfermline.

(2) after extra time, lost 8-9 on penalties

(3) Auld sent off 75 minutes

Day	Date	Opponents	Note	Venue	Comp	Res	Att	1	2	3	4	5	6	7	8	9	10	11	Substitutes, own goals and goal times
M	31-Jul	Colchester United		H	F	3-4	990	Arthur	McStay	Murray	Fraser	Glennie	Gibson 1	Simpson 1	Dennis	Ferguson	Coyle	Nelson	McLeod, Burn u45, Romaines; Burn 9, 5, 66
W	02-Aug	Rangers		H	F	1-2	1510	Arthur	McStay r45	Murray	Fraser 1p	Glennie	Gibson r72	McLeod	Dennis	Ferguson	Dalziel 1	Nelson	Burn u45, Romaines u72, Buchanan; Marshall 72
S	05-Aug	Cardiff City		H	F	3-2	722	Arthur	Buchanan r56	McLeod	Fraser r69	Glennie r69	Gibson r70	Simpson r56	Dennis r45	Simpson	Dalziel 1	Burn	Murray u45, McStay u56 1, Nelson u56; Romaines u70 73, 89, 86
Tu	08-Aug	Newcastle United		H	F	0-4	1959	Arthur	McStay	Murray	Fraser 1p	Glennie	Gibson r13	McLeod	Coyle	Simpson	Dalziel	Nelson r74	Burn u13, Dennis u63, Romaines u69; Ferguson u74
S	12-Aug	Morton		H	L2	2-0	1529	Arthur	McStay	Murray	Fraser b	Glennie	McLeod	Simpson	Dalziel	Ferguson	Coyle r50 1	Nelson r74	Romaines u50, Burn u85; 35, 46
Tu	15-Aug	Dunfermline Athletic		A	LC 2	0-3	6331	Arthur	McStay b	Murray b	Fraser b	Glennie b	Dennis b	Simpson r76	Dalziel	Ferguson	McLeod r85 b	Romaines r70	Nelson u70 b, Burn u85
S	19-Aug	Falkirk		A	L2	2-0	3527	Arthur	McStay	Murray	Fraser b	Glennie b	Dennis	Simpson r70	Dalziel 1	Ferguson 1	McLeod	Romaines b	Nelson u76, Gibson; 86, 55
S	26-Aug	Meadowbank Thistle		A	L2	2-1	854	Arthur	McStay	Murray	Fraser	Glennie	Dennis	Simpson	Dalziel	Ferguson 2	McLeod	Romaines b	Nelson u70, Burn; 46, 67
Tu	02-Sep	St Johnstone		H	L2	0-2	4979	Arthur r69	McStay	Murray b	Fraser m	Glennie	Dennis	Simpson r75	Dalziel r70 1	Ferguson b	McLeod	Romaines r78	Nelson u69, Burn u78
S	05-Sep	Partick Thistle		A	L2	1-3	3436	Arthur	McStay	Murray b	Fraser x60	Glennie	Dennis b	Simpson r52	Dalziel	Ferguson r71	McLeod	Romaines	Nelson u75, Logan u70; 58
S	09-Sep	Airdrie		H	L2	0-4	1807	Arthur b	McStay	Murray	Coyle	Glennie	McLeod	Romaines	Dalziel 1	Burn b	Burn b	Nelson r79	Logan u70, Nelson u52
S	16-Sep	Albion Rovers		A	L2	2-1	1218	Arthur	McStay	Murray	Fraser	Glennie	McLeod	Romaines b	Dalziel 1	Logan r70 1	McLeod	Nelson	Ferguson u70, Scobie u79; 34, 36
S	23-Sep	Forfar Athletic		A	L2	2-2	757	Arthur	McStay	Murray	Fraser	McStay	Burn	Romaines r80 2	Dalziel r80 2	Logan 52	Burn	Nelson	Sorbie u52, Ferguson u80; 56, 65
S	30-Sep	Clydebank		H	L2	1-0	1316	Arthur	McStay	Murray b	Fraser	Glennie	McLeod b	Romaines	Dalziel 1	Logan 60	McLeod	Nelson 1	Ferguson u80, Sorbie; 47
S	07-Oct	Alloa Athletic		A	L2	0-2	1675	Arthur	McStay	Murray b	Fraser	McGeachie	McLeod	Romaines r72	Dalziel 1	Logan r58	Coyle	Nelson	Ferguson u60, Sorbie
S	14-Oct	Ayr United		H	FC 1	2-0	1571	Arthur	McStay	Murray	Fraser	McGeachie b	McLeod	Simpson r73	Sorbie	Ferguson 1	Romaines	Nelson r49	Simpson u72, Ferguson u58; 18, 40
W	18-Oct	East Fife		H	FC 1	2-1	747	Arthur	Buchanan	Murray	Fraser r19	McGeachie b	McLeod	Simpson r61	Dalziel	Ferguson 1	Burn 1	Burn 1	Sorbie u73, Donald u61; 55, 76
S	21-Oct	Clyde		H	L2	0-2	1543	Arthur	McStay b	Murray	Coyle	McGeachie	McLeod	Simpson r64	Sorbie	Logan 1	Sorbie	Sorbie	McStay u19, Buchanan
S	28-Oct	Hamilton Academical		A	L2	2-3	1311	Arthur	McLeod	Murray	Buchanan	McGeachie	Coyle	Ferguson r73	Dalziel m 2	McDonald	Romaines	Burn	Ferguson u64, Simpson u73; 6, 51
S	04-Nov	Partick Thistle		H	FC SF	1-1	2433	Arthur	McStay	Murray	Coyle	McGeachie r45	McLeod	Simpson r77	Dalziel	McDonald	Romaines	Burn	Simpson u73, Sorbie; 60
W	08-Nov	Cowdenbeath		A	L2	0-1	554	Arthur	Thomson	Murray	Buchanan	Coyle	McLeod	Donald 1p	Dalziel r81 1	McDonald 1	Romaines	Burn r50	Sorbie u45 1, Ferguson u77
S	11-Nov	Airdrie		A	L2	2-3	2217	Arthur	McStay	Murray	Fraser r44	McStay	McLeod	Simpson	Sorbie	McDonald 1	Ferguson	Sorbie	Logan u45 1, Baxter u50; 72, 69
Tu	14-Nov	Celtic		H	F	1-2		Arthur	Buchanan	Murray r75	Coyle	McStay	McLeod	Ferguson r52	Dalziel r57	McDonald 1	Romaines	Sorbie	Buchanan u44, Donald u52; 41
S	18-Nov	Albion Rovers		A	L2	2-2	621	Arthur	Buchanan	McLeod	Coyle	McStay	Nelson	Simpson r73	Dalziel 1	McDonald 1	Romaines	Sorbie	Donald u52, Logan u57; 58, 85
S	25-Nov	Forfar Athletic		A	L2	1-0	1249	Arthur	McLeod	Murray	Fraser	McGeachie	McLeod	Ferguson r60	Dalziel	McDonald 1	Romaines	Nelson r80	Logan u73, Burn; 75
S	02-Dec	Morton		A	L2	1-3	1050	Arthur	McLeod	Murray r45	Coyle	McGeachie r87	McLeod	Romaines	Dalziel	McDonald 1p	Burn	Nelson r78	Simpson u60, Sorbie u80; 43
W	06-Dec	Burntisland Shipyard		A	SC 3	7-0	682	Arthur	Buchanan	Murray 1	Buchanan	Coyle	McLeod	Sorbie	Dalziel 1	McDonald r65	Burn 1	Nelson r77 2	Simpson u78, Sorbie u87; 62, 77, 47, 8, 51, 68, 80
S	09-Dec	Alloa Athletic		H	SC 3r	1-1	1118	Arthur	McStay	Murray	Coyle	McGeachie	McLeod	Romaines r78	Dalziel	McDonald r70	Burn 1	Nelson	Logan u65 2, Donald u77; 83
S	16-Dec	Ayr United		A	L2	0-1	1745	Arthur	McLeod	Murray	McGeachie	McStay	Burn	Romaines	Dalziel	McDonald	Romaines	Nelson	Logan u70 1, Sorbie
W	23-Dec	Morton		H	L2	4-0	1227	Arthur	McLeod	Murray	McGeachie	McStay	Burn	Romaines	Dalziel	McDonald	Romaines	Nelson	Ferguson u78, Sorbie; 87, 35, 68, 73
S	30-Dec	Falkirk		H	L2	1-2	2765	Arthur	McLeod	Murray	McGeachie r8	McStay 1	Coyle	Logan r25 1	Dalziel 1	McDonald 1p	Romaines	Nelson	Ferguson u75, Sorbie; 13
S	02-Jan	Meadowbank Thistle		H	L2	2-1	1897	Arthur	McLeod	Murray	Coyle	McStay	Coyle	Logan r63	Dalziel 1	McDonald 2	Burn	Nelson	Ferguson u63, Sorbie u70; 25, 61
S	06-Jan	St Johnstone		A	L2	1-3	5293	Arthur	McLeod	Murray	Fraser	McStay	Coyle	Simpson r72	Dalziel 2	McDonald 1p	Coyle	Burn	Ferguson u72, Sorbie u84; 44, 18
S	13-Jan	Hamilton Academical		H	L2	2-2	1575	Arthur	McLeod	Murray r45	Fraser	McGeachie	Coyle	Simpson r78	Dalziel 1	McDonald	Sorbie u80	Nelson 1	Ferguson u45, McDonald u70; 16
M	20-Jan	Morton		A	SC 3	1-3	3100	Arthur	McLeod	McLeod	Fraser	McStay	McLeod	Logan r73	Dalziel r87	McDonald	Sorbie	Nelson	McDonald u73 1, Ferguson u78
S	29-Jan	Morton		H	SC 3r	2-2	2740	Arthur	McStay 1	McLeod	Fraser 1	McStay	Coyle r1	Simpson r80	Dalziel r83	McDonald 1	Burn	Nelson	Ferguson u1, McDonald; 83, 33
S	03-Feb	Forfar Athletic		H	L2	2-2	717	Arthur	McStay	McLeod	Fraser 1	McStay	Coyle	Simpson r66	Dalziel r87	McDonald 2	Burn	Nelson 1	Ferguson u80, Logan u87; 28, 75, 61
S	10-Feb	Albion Rovers		A	L2	3-0	1035	Arthur	McStay	McLeod	Fraser	Dennis	Coyle	Logan r75 1	Dalziel r70 1	McDonald 1	Burn	Nelson 1	Logan u66, Ferguson u83; 64, 59, 37
S	17-Feb	Meadowbank Thistle		H	L2	0-0	729	Arthur	McStay	McGeachie	Fraser	Dennis	Coyle 1	Simpson	Dalziel r70 1	McDonald	Burn	Burn	Logan u70, Sorbie u80
S	03-Mar	St Johnstone		A	L2	2-1	3852	Arthur	McStay	McLeod	Fraser	Dennis	Coyle	Simpson	Dalziel r89	McDonald	Ferguson r80	Sorbie	Ferguson u89, Logan; 5, 85
S	10-Mar	Morton		H	L2	2-1	1182	Arthur	McStay 1	McLeod	Fraser r53	Dennis	McGeachie r53	Simpson	Dalziel	McDonald 1	Sorbie	Nelson	Logan u53, Murray
S	17-Mar	Clyde		A	L2	0-0	497	Arthur	McStay	McLeod	Fraser	Dennis	Coyle	Logan r70	Dalziel	McDonald	Coyle	Nelson	Logan u70, Murray
W	21-Mar	Clyde		H	L2	0-0	381	Arthur	McStay	McLeod	Fraser	Dennis	Coyle	Logan	Dalziel	McDonald r73	Burn	Nelson	Ferguson u70, Murray
S	24-Mar	Clydebank		A	L2	2-2	776	Arthur	McStay	McLeod	Fraser	Dennis	Coyle	Logan 1	Dalziel	McDonald r80 1p	Burn r85	Nelson 1	Ferguson u80, Murray u85; 10, 9
S	31-Mar	Ayr United		H	L2	5-2	1117	Arthur	McStay	McLeod	Fraser	Dennis	Coyle	Ferguson 1	Dalziel r28 2	McDonald	Burn 81	Nelson 1	Simpson u28 1, Romaines u81; 62, 10, 20, 11, 31
S	07-Apr	Hamilton Academical		H	L2	0-0	1191	Arthur	McStay	McLeod	Fraser	Dennis	Coyle	Simpson	Dalziel r65	McDonald	Burn	Nelson 1	Ferguson u65, Romaines u80
S	14-Apr	Alloa Athletic		A	L2	4-0	760	Arthur	McStay	McLeod	Coyle	Dennis	Romaines	Logan 1	Dalziel r80	McDonald	Burn 1	Nelson 1	Ferguson u80 1, McDonald u70; 50, 67, 65, 88
S	21-Apr	Airdrie		A	L2	1-0	1770	Arthur	McStay	McLeod	Coyle	Dennis	Romaines	Logan 1	Dalziel 1	McDonald	Burn	Nelson	Ferguson, Buchanan; 64
S	28-Apr	Falkirk		H	L2	1-1	1733	Arthur	McStay	Murray	McLeod	Dennis	Romaines	Logan r75	Dalziel 1	McDonald	Burn	Nelson	Simpson u75, Buchanan; 62
S	05-May	Partick Thistle		A	L2	1-1	2002	Arthur	McStay	McLeod	McLeod	Dennis	Romaines	Logan r58	Dalziel 1	McDonald	Burn	Nelson	Simpson u58, Sinclair; 86

Manager : Frank Connor to 5th November. Jimmy Nicholl from 20th November

Day	Date	Opponents	Note	Venue	Comp	Res	Att	1	2	3	4	5	6	7	8	9	10	11	Substitutes, own goals and goal times
M	31-Jul	Hearts		H	F	2-3	2541	Arthur	McStay	McLeod	Fraser r66	Dennis	McGeachie r80	Simpson r58	Dalziel r74	McDonald 1	Coyle	Nelson 1	Ferguson u58 Burn u66 Logan u74 Banner, Donald 70, 43
Th	02-Aug	Rangers		H	F	2-1	1390	Arthur r85	McStay	McLeod	Fraser	Dennis	McGeachie r60	Ferguson r60	Burn 1	McDonald r60 1	Dalziel	Nelson	Simpson u60 Logan u60 Sinclair u80 Banner u85 88, 52
S	11-Aug	Wimbledon		H	F	0-2	1092	Arthur	McStay	McLeod	Fraser	Dennis	Coyle	Ferguson r79	Dalziel r63	McDonald	McGeachie	Nelson r45	Burn u45 Sinclair u63 Strang u79 Murray
F	17-Aug	Dundee United		H	F	2-1	771	Banner	McStay	McLeod	Fraser r74	Dennis 1	McGeachie 45	Simpson r72	Dalziel r56	McDonald	McGeachie 45	Burn 45	Ferguson u45 Murray u45 Logan u56 1 Henderson u74 63, 71
Tu	21-Aug	Forfar Athletic		A	LC 2	2-1	1114	Arthur	McStay	McLeod	Fraser	Dennis	McGeachie 1	Simpson r72	Dalziel 2	McDonald	Ferguson	Burn	Logan u72 Murray 76, 90
S	25-Aug	Brechin City		A	L2	4-0	850	Arthur	McStay	McLeod	Fraser	Dennis	McGeachie r80	Simpson r67	Dalziel 2	McDonald r45	Coyle	Nelson 1	Logan u67 1 Ferguson u80 40, 60, 55, 84
W	29-Aug	Hibernian		A	LC 3	1-0	4631	Arthur	McStay	McLeod	Fraser	Dennis	McGeachie 1	Logan	Dalziel	McDonald r45	Coyle	Nelson r85	Ferguson u45 Burn u85 24
S	01-Sep	Clyde		H	L2	1-1	1410	Arthur	McStay	McLeod	Fraser	Dennis	McGeachie	Logan	Dalziel 1	Ferguson r75	Coyle	Nelson	Burn u75 Murray 10
Tu	04-Sep	Rangers		A	LC QF	2-6	31320	Arthur	McStay	McLeod r44	Fraser	Dennis	McGeachie r70	Coyle 1	Dalziel	Logan r60	Burn r80	Nelson	Ferguson u60 Murray u80 Butcher og 1 32, 71
S	08-Sep	Morton		H	L2	1-0	1395	Arthur	McStay	Murray	Fraser	Dennis	McGeachie	Simpson	Dalziel 1	Ferguson	Coyle	Nelson	Burn u44 Logan u70 57
S	15-Sep	Meadowbank Thistle		A	L2	1-1	750	Arthur	McStay	Murray	Fraser	Dennis	McGeachie	Simpson r72	Dalziel 1	McDonald r73	Coyle r84	Nelson	Logan u73 Burn u84 61
Tu	18-Sep	Forfar Athletic		H	L2	2-1	1053	Arthur	McStay	Murray	Fraser	Dennis	McGeachie r62	Simpson r85	Dalziel 1	McDonald 1	Coyle r8	Nelson	Burn u62 Logan u72 Lorimer og 1 52, 43
S	22-Sep	Clydebank		H	L2	2-0	1535	Arthur	McStay	Murray	Fraser	Dennis	McGeachie	Simpson r78	Dalziel 1	McDonald 1p	Coyle	Nelson	Burn u45 Logan u85 44, 71
S	29-Sep	Ayr United		A	L2	0-2	1888	Arthur	McStay	Murray	Fraser r45	Dennis	McGeachie	Simpson	Dalziel	McDonald	Coyle	Nelson	Logan u78
Tu	02-Oct	Falkirk		A	LCC 1	3-0	2000	Arthur	McStay	Murray	Coyle	Dennis	Romaines r65	Logan	Dalziel	McDonald 1	Ferguson r85	Nelson	Sinclair u65 Burn u85 1 Whittaker og 1 86, 89, 24
Tu	06-Oct	Hamilton Academical		H	L2	1-0	1138	Arthur	McStay	Murray	Coyle	Dennis	Romaines r70	Logan r80	Dalziel	Ferguson 1	Ferguson 1	Burn	Sinclair u70 Simpson u80 73
Tu	09-Oct	Kilmarnock		A	L2	1-1	4003	Arthur	McStay	Murray	Coyle	Dennis	McGeachie	Logan r75	Dalziel r85 1	McDonald	Romaines	Burn	Ferguson u75 Sinclair u85 58
S	13-Oct	Dundee		A	L2	1-1	3494	Arthur	McStay	Murray	Fraser	Dennis	McGeachie r70	Logan	Dalziel	McDonald r77	Coyle 1	Nelson	Burn u70 Ferguson u77 66
Tu	16-Oct	Hamilton Academical		H	LCC 2	3-2	1416	Arthur	McStay	McLeod	Coyle	Dennis	Burn 1	Logan 2	Dalziel 2	McDonald	Ferguson r83	Nelson	Murray u83 McGeachie 57, 31, 34
S	20-Oct	Airdrie		A	L2	5-1	2500	Arthur	McStay	McLeod	Coyle	Dennis	McGeachie r82	Logan 2	Dalziel r75	McDonald	Burn	Nelson	Ferguson u75 2 Murray u82 Conn og 1 88, 9, 80, 83, 53
Tu	23-Oct	Dundee	1	H	LCC 3	0-1	4161	Arthur	McStay	McLeod	Coyle	Dennis	Murray	Logan	Dalziel	McDonald r91	Ferguson	Nelson	Sinclair u75 Logan u91
S	27-Oct	Partick Thistle		H	L2	0-0	3052	Arthur	McStay	McLeod	Coyle	Dennis	Murray r65	Logan	Dalziel	McDonald r60	Ferguson	Nelson	Simpson u60 Sinclair u65
S	03-Nov	Falkirk		A	L2	1-7	3963	Arthur	McStay	McLeod	Coyle	Dennis	McGeachie r63	Logan r70	Dalziel 1	Ferguson	Romaines	Nelson	Sinclair Simpson u70 40
S	10-Nov	Clyde		A	L2	2-1	650	Arthur	McStay	McLeod	Coyle	Dennis	Ferguson	Simpson	Dalziel 2	Logan 1	Coyle	Nelson	Murray Murray 51, 87
S	17-Nov	Brechin City		H	L2	1-1	1461	Arthur	McStay	McLeod	Coyle	Dennis	Ferguson	Simpson r73	Dalziel	Logan 1	Coyle	Nelson	Romaines u73 Murray 40
S	24-Nov	Kilmarnock		H	L2	1-1	2260	Arthur	McStay	McLeod r28	Fraser	Dennis	Romaines	Simpson 1	Dalziel r50	Logan	Ferguson	Murray	Sinclair u28 McDonald u50 8
S	01-Dec	Hamilton Academical		A	L2	2-2	1464	Arthur	McStay	Murray	Fraser	Dennis	McGeachie	Simpson r85	Dalziel 2.1p	Logan	Romaines 1	Nelson	Sinclair u85 Cowan 36, 35p
S	08-Dec	Ayr United		H	L2	3-0	1179	Arthur	McStay	Murray	McStay	McGeachie r15	McGeachie r80	Ferguson 1	Dalziel	Logan	Romaines	Nelson	Strang u80 Cowan 89, 4, 44
S	15-Dec	Clydebank		A	L2	1-1	961	Arthur	McStay	Murray	Nicholl	Dennis	McLeod	Ferguson	Dalziel 1	Ferguson 1	Fraser	Nelson	Nelson McLeod 64
S	29-Dec	Falkirk		H	L2	1-4	3764	Arthur	McStay	Murray	Nicholl	McGeachie	McLeod	Romaines r80	Dalziel 1	Ferguson	Fraser r65	Nelson	Logan u75 Strang 3
Tu	01-Jan	Dundee		A	L2	1-2	4815	Arthur	McStay	McLeod	Nicholl r45	Dennis	McGeachie r50	Logan	Dalziel	Ferguson	Fraser	Nelson 1	Sinclair u65 Logan u80 33
S	05-Jan	Airdrie		H	L2	1-1	2075	Arthur	McStay	McLeod	Coyle	Dennis	McGeachie	Logan	Dalziel	Ferguson	Murray	Nelson 1	Romaines u50 Sinclair 42
S	26-Jan	Hamilton Academical		H	SC 3	0-1	2266	Arthur	Nicholl	McLeod r57	Raeside	McGeachie	Nicholl	Fraser r	Dalziel	Ferguson	Sinclair	Nelson 1	Sinclair u Logan u
S	02-Feb	Forfar Athletic		A	L2	1-3	826	Arthur	McStay	McGeachie	Coyle	McGeachie	McGeachie	Simpson r57	Dalziel 1p	Ferguson	Romaines	Nelson 1	Murray u57 Romaines 61
S	16-Feb	Falkirk		A	FC SF	2-0	4560	Arthur	McStay 1	Murray	Coyle	McGeachie r80	Raeside	Dunleavy	Dalziel	Ferguson	Sinclair	Nelson 1	Murray u80 Logan 50, 43
Tu	19-Feb	Brechin City		H	L2	1-0	1074	Arthur	McStay	McGeachie	Nicholl	McGeachie r15	Dennis	Dunleavy	Dalziel 1	Ferguson 1	Sinclair	Nelson	Raeside u15 Logan 18
S	23-Feb	Partick Thistle		A	L2	3-0	3600	Arthur	McStay	McLeod	Nicholl	Dennis	Raeside	Dunleavy r73	Dalziel 2	Ferguson 1	Sinclair r77	Nelson	Sinclair u77 Murray 10, 40, 52
S	02-Mar	Ayr United		A	L2	3-5	2386	Arthur	McStay	McLeod r12	Nicholl	Dennis	Raeside	Dunleavy r80	Dalziel 1	Ferguson 2	Coyle	Nelson	McGeachie Logan 82, 30, 53
W	06-Mar	Meadowbank Thistle		H	L2	1-3	1000	Arthur	McStay	Raeside	Nicholl	Dennis 1	McGeachie	Dunleavy r80	Dalziel 1	Logan 60	Coyle 45	Nelson	Logan u80 Murray 2
S	09-Mar	Partick Thistle		H	L2	1-5	2255	Arthur	McStay	McLeod 1	Coyle	Dennis	McGeachie	Dunleavy 1	Fraser	Henderson	Coyle	Nelson	Romaines u45 Romaines 36
S	16-Mar	Clyde		H	L2	1-0	1013	Arthur	McStay	McLeod	Raeside	Dennis	Raeside	Dunleavy 1	Dalziel 1	Ferguson	Sinclair	Nelson	McGeachie u57 Logan 89
S	23-Mar	Meadowbank Thistle		A	L2	1-4	300	Banner	McStay	McLeod	Raeside	Dennis	Nicholl	Dunleavy 1	Dalziel	Ferguson	Sinclair	Nelson	McStay Romaines 75
Tu	26-Mar	Dunfermline Athletic		A	FC SF	2-1	1254	Arthur	McStay	Murray	Coyle	Raeside	Sinclair r55	Dunleavy 1	Fraser	Ferguson 1	Romaines	Logan 1	Strang u55 Cowan 71, 89
S	30-Mar	Morton		A	L2	0-4	1761	Banner	McStay 1	McLeod	Coyle	Dennis	Raeside r68	Dunleavy	Dalziel	Ferguson	Sinclair r68	Nelson	Logan u68 Romaines u68
S	06-Apr	Kilmarnock		H	L2	1-2	881	Arthur	McStay	McLeod	Coyle	Dennis	Raeside	Dunleavy 1	Dalziel	Logan r75	McGeachie	Nelson	Strang u73 Romaines 57
S	13-Apr	Forfar Athletic		A	L2	1-2	2453	Banner	McStay	McLeod	Nicholl	Dennis 1	Raeside	Dunleavy	Dalziel	Logan 60	McGeachie	Nelson	Sinclair u12 Ferguson u75 12
Tu	16-Apr	Morton		H	L2	2-1	1140	Arthur	McStay	McLeod	Coyle	McGeachie	Coyle	Dunleavy	Dalziel 1	Ferguson	Sinclair	Nelson	Ferguson u60 Romaines 40, 41
S	20-Apr	Hamilton Academical		H	L2	1-5	453	Arthur	McStay	McLeod	Raeside	Dennis	Raeside	Dunleavy	Dalziel 1	Henderson	Sinclair	Nelson r45	Strang Romaines 59, 33
M	22-Apr	East Fife	2	A	FC F	1-1	3756	Arthur s s	McStay	McLeod	Coyle	McGeachie	Romaines	Dunleavy	Strang	Ferguson 1p	Murray	Nelson	Burn u45 Coyle 75
S	27-Apr	Clyde	3	A	L2	1-1	875	Arthur r80	McStay	McLeod	Coyle	Dennis r82	McGeachie	Dunleavy	Dalziel	Ferguson	Sinclair	Nelson	Strang u82 Raeside
S	04-May	Clydebank	4	H	L2	1-2	4152	Arthur r80	Young	McLeod	Raeside	Dennis	McGeachie	Dunleavy	Raeside	Ferguson	Sinclair	Burn r85	Strang u85 Coyle u80 35
S	11-May	Airdrie		H	L2	0-1		Banner	McStay r65	McLeod	Coyle	Dennis r57	McGeachie	Dunleavy	Dalziel	Ferguson	Sinclair	Nelson	Raeside u57 Logan u65

Manager : Jimmy Nicholl

(1) after extra time
(2) won 4-1 on penalties
(3) Gordon Arthur saved two penalty kicks from Billy Dodds, in 60 and 85 minutes.
(4) David Sinclair took over from the injured Gordon Arthur in goal.

Day	Date	Opponents	Note	Venue	Comp	Res.	Att.	1	2	3	4	5	6	7	8	9	10	11	Substitutes, own goals and goal times
S	27-Jul	Aberdeen		H	F	1-2	1684	Arthur	McLeod r62	McGeachie	Coyle	Dennis r45	Raeside r45	Dunleavy r34	Dalziel r45	Ferguson r73	Sinclair r41	Burn	Brewster u31 1, McStay u41, Strang u45, Meldrum u73, Banner 48
M	29-Jul	Swansea City		H	F	2-2	504	Banner	McLeod r77	Meldrum	Burn	Dennis	Raeside	Logan 1	Strang	Logan 1	Abercromby 1	Simpson	Coyle u45, McStay u45, Strang u45, Young u62, McNab u34, Nicholl 27,55
W	31-Jul	Hearts		H	F	1-4	2207	Arthur	McLeod	McGeachie	Nicholl r58	Dennis	McGeachie	Logan 1	Dalziel r87	Ferguson	Brewster	Burn r80	McStay u58, Simpson u80, Abercromby, Strang u87, Coyle 24
S	03-Aug	Cliftonville		H	F	4-1	573	Banner	McLeod	Abercromby r77	Coyle	Dennis	McGeachie	Ferguson 3	Dalziel r59 1	Quinn r73	Brewster	Sinclair	Strang u59, Logan u73, Young u77, Meldrum u77, Burn, 27,39,58,75
S	10-Aug	Meadowbank Thistle		A	L2	0-2	703	Arthur	Nicholl	McGeachie	Sinclair	Dennis	McGeachie	Williamson	Dalziel	Ferguson	Brewster	Nelson	Williamson u45, Logan u73, Meldrum u77, Burn
Tu	13-Aug	Clydebank		A	L2	2-0	738	Arthur	Nicholl	McLeod	Sinclair	Dennis	McGeachie	Williamson 1	Dalziel 1	Ferguson 1	Brewster 1	Nelson 1	Coyle, Burn, 37,33
S	17-Aug	Forfar Athletic		H	L2	2-0	1175	Arthur	Nicholl	McLeod r35	Sinclair	Dennis	McGeachie	Williamson 1	Ferguson 1	Ferguson 1	Brewster 1	Nelson	Coyle u35, McKenzie, 5,36
Tu	20-Aug	Motherwell		H	LC 2	4-1	3204	Arthur	Nicholl	McLeod	Sinclair	Dennis	McGeachie	Williamson	McKenzie	Ferguson	Brewster 2	Nelson	Coyle, Quinn, 7,76,78,58
S	24-Aug	Ayr United		A	L2	0-1	3270	Arthur	Nicholl r75	McLeod r86	Sinclair	Dennis	McGeachie	Williamson r80	McKenzie	Ferguson	Brewster	Nelson	Quinn u86, Coyle
Tu	27-Aug	Celtic		A	LC 3	1-3	21081	Arthur	Nicholl	McLeod	Sinclair	Dennis	McGeachie	Williamson r80	McKenzie r60	Ferguson	Brewster	Nelson	Burn u75, Dalziel u80, 22
S	31-Aug	Dundee		H	L2	0-1	3122	Arthur	Nicholl	McLeod	Sinclair	Dennis	McGeachie	Williamson	Dalziel	Ferguson 1	Brewster	Nelson	Dalziel u60, McStay
S	07-Sep	Stirling Albion		H	L2	1-0	1252	Arthur	Young	McLeod	Sinclair	Dennis	McGeachie	Williamson	Dalziel	Ferguson 1	Brewster 1	Nelson	Ferguson, Raeside, 29
S	14-Sep	Partick Thistle		A	L2	0-5	3477	Arthur	Young	McLeod	Sinclair r46	Dennis	McGeachie	Williamson	Dalziel	McKenzie	Brewster	Nelson	Burn u46, Raeside
S	21-Sep	Morton		H	L2	1-1	1219	Arthur	Nicholl	McLeod	Burn	Dennis	Coyle	Ferguson	Dalziel	McKenzie 1	Brewster r78	Williamson	Dunleavy u78, McStay, 54
S	28-Sep	Kilmarnock		A	L2	0-1	3385	Arthur	Nicholl	McLeod	Coyle	Dennis	McGeachie	Williamson r67	Ferguson	McKenzie	Burn	Nelson	Strang u67, McStay
Tu	05-Oct	Hamilton Academical		A	L2	1-3	1007	Arthur	Nicholl	McLeod	Burn	Dennis	McGeachie r17	Williamson	Dalziel 1	Brewster	Brewster	Nelson r32	Coyle u17, Ferguson u32, 4
Tu	08-Oct	Montrose		A	L2	3-0	681	Arthur	McStay	McLeod 1	Coyle	Dennis	Raeside	Dunleavy	Dalziel r50 1	McKenzie	Brewster 1	Burn	Williamson u50, Nicholl, 37,43,85
S	12-Oct	Meadowbank Thistle		H	L2	1-1	766	Arthur	McStay r77	McLeod	Coyle	Dennis	Raeside	Dunleavy	Dalziel	McKenzie	Brewster 1	Burn	Young u77, Williamson u77, 85
Tu	15-Oct	Clydebank	1	A	LCC 2	1-1	350	Arthur	McStay	McLeod	Coyle	Raeside	Young r105	Burn	McKenzie	Hetherston r90	Brewster 1	Nelson r45	Dunleavy u105, Nicholl, 37
S	19-Oct	Forfar Athletic		A	L2	1-0	559	Arthur	McStay	McLeod	Coyle	McGeachie r23	Raeside	Burn	Dalziel 1	Strang	Brewster 1	Nelson r45	Sinclair u23, Dunleavy u45, 55
Tu	22-Oct	Morton		A	LCC QF	3-2	1767	Arthur	McStay	McLeod	Coyle	Dennis	Raeside	Dunleavy	Dalziel 3	Strang	Brewster r54	Burn r76	Strang u76, Young u90, 24,67,88
S	26-Oct	Stirling Albion		A	L2	3-1	650	Arthur	McStay	McLeod	Coyle	Dennis	Raeside	Nicholl	Dalziel 3	Hetherston	Brewster	Burn	Strang u54, Young, 27,40,88
Tu	29-Oct	Partick Thistle		H	L2	1-0	2027	Arthur	McStay r86	McLeod	Coyle	Dennis	Raeside	Sinclair	Dalziel	Hetherston r54	Brewster	Nelson r49	Strang u49 1, Young u86, 79
S	02-Nov	Dundee		A	L2	1-1	2937	Arthur	McStay	McLeod	Coyle	Dennis	Raeside	Nicholl	Dalziel 1	Hetherston	Brewster 1	Burn	Strang, Young, 24
Tu	05-Nov	Hamilton Academical		A	LCC SF	0-0	2306	Arthur	McStay	McLeod	Coyle	Dennis	Raeside	Nicholl r70	Dalziel 1p	Hetherston r83	Brewster r83	Burn r82	Young u75, Young u82, 58
S	09-Nov	Hamilton Academical		H	L2	0-0	1441	Arthur	McStay	McLeod	Coyle	Dennis	Raeside	Nicholl	Dalziel	Hetherston	Brewster	Burn	McKenzie u70, Strang u83
S	16-Nov	Hamilton Academical		A	L2	1-4	1433	Arthur	McStay	McLeod	Coyle	McGeachie	Raeside	Nicholl	Dalziel 1	Strang r75	Brewster	Hetherston	Young u75, McGeachie, 49
Tu	19-Nov	Montrose		H	L2	2-1	812	Arthur	McStay	McLeod	Coyle	Dennis	McGeachie	Nicholl	Dalziel r88 1p	Williamson	Brewster 1	Hetherston	Strang u88, Young, 55,74
S	23-Nov	Morton		A	L2	2-0	1280	Arthur	McStay	McLeod	Coyle	Dennis	McGeachie	Hetherston	Dalziel 1	Williamson	Brewster	Nelson	Strang, Young, 8,51
Tu	30-Nov	Clydebank		H	L2	4-0	1195	Arthur	McStay	McLeod	Coyle	Dennis	McGeachie r20	Hetherston	Dalziel 3	Williamson r80	Brewster 70 1	Nelson	Strang u70, Young, 5,34,61,27
Tu	03-Dec	Kilmarnock		H	L2	1-1	2280	Arthur	McStay 1	McLeod	Coyle	Dennis	McStay	Hetherston	Dalziel r58 1	Williamson	Brewster	Nelson	Young u20, Sinclair, 28
S	07-Dec	Meadowbank Thistle		A	L2	1-0	549	Arthur	Young	McLeod	Coyle	Dennis	McStay	Hetherston r80	Dalziel 1	Williamson r80	Strang	Nelson	Strang u58, Sinclair u80, 56
S	14-Dec	Stirling Albion		H	L2	1-2	1199	Arthur	McStay r77	McLeod	Sinclair 1	Dennis	Sinclair	Williamson	Dalziel	Williamson	Brewster 1	Nelson	Dunleavy u77, Cameron, 43
S	21-Dec	Partick Thistle		A	L2	2-0	2558	Arthur	McStay	McLeod	Nicholl	Dennis	Nicholl	Dunleavy	Hetherston	Brewster r77	Brewster r77	Nelson	Young, Strang, 17
S	28-Dec	Ayr United		A	L2	0-1	2257	Arthur	McStay	McLeod	Coyle	Dennis	Nicholl	Dunleavy 1	Dalziel r56 1	Brewster	Brewster	Nelson	Sinclair, Strang, 56
W	01-Jan	Dundee		H	L2	1-0	3976	Arthur	McStay	McLeod	Coyle r60	Dennis	Nicholl	Dunleavy r51	Hetherston	Sinclair	Brewster 1	Nelson	Williamson u56, Burn, 49
S	04-Jan	Hamilton Academical		H	L2	2-1	2299	Arthur	McStay	McLeod	Nicholl	Dennis	Nicholl	Sinclair	Hetherston	Sinclair	Brewster 1	Nelson	Burn u60, Williamson u51, 74,52
S	11-Jan	Montrose		A	L2	2-2	1200	Arthur	McStay 1	McLeod	Coyle	Dennis	Raeside	Burn	Dalziel 2	Strang r84 1	Brewster	Nelson 2	Young u84, Dunleavy, 34,14
S	18-Jan	Clydebank		A	L2	1-1	740	Arthur	McStay 1	McLeod	Coyle	Dennis	Nicholl	Burn	Dalziel 1	McKenzie	Brewster	Nelson	Strang, Dunleavy, 62
S	25-Jan	St Johnstone		H	SC 3	0-2	7166	Arthur	McStay	McLeod r75	Coyle	Dennis	Raeside r65	Nicholl	Dalziel	McKenzie	Brewster	Nelson	Williamson u63, Strang u75
S	01-Feb	Forfar Athletic		H	L2	1-0	142	Arthur	McStay	McLeod	Coyle	Dennis	Raeside r57	Hetherston	Dalziel 1	McKenzie 1	Brewster r77	Nelson	Burn u57, Williamson, McKenna og 1, 90,50
S	08-Feb	Morton		H	L2	2-0	1703	Arthur	McStay	McLeod	Coyle	Dennis	Raeside	McKenzie	Dalziel 2	McKenzie	Brewster r77	Nelson	Burn u77, Nicholl, 16,28
W	26-Feb	Kilmarnock		A	L2	0-1	3657	Arthur	McStay	McLeod	Coyle	Dennis	McGeachie	Nicholl r67	McKenzie	Dalziel	Hetherston	Nelson	Brewster u67, Sinclair
S	29-Feb	Hamilton Academical		A	L2	0-1	1885	Arthur	McStay	McLeod	Coyle	Dennis	McGeachie	Nicholl	Dalziel	McKenzie	Hetherston	Nelson r68	Brewster u68, Sinclair, 49
S	07-Mar	Montrose		H	L2	5-0	1090	Arthur	McStay	McLeod	Coyle	Dennis	McGeachie	Nicholl r48 1	Dalziel 2	McKenzie	Brewster 2	Hetherston	Nelson u48, Williamson, 46,13,44,52,84
S	14-Mar	Ayr United		H	L2	2-4	1473	Arthur	McStay	McLeod	Coyle	Dennis	McGeachie r69	Nicholl	Dalziel	McKenzie	Brewster	Nelson	Sinclair u69, Williamson, 17,50
S	21-Mar	Dundee		A	L2	2-3	4458	Arthur	McStay	McLeod r37	Coyle	Dennis	Sinclair	Burn	Dalziel	McKenzie r65	Brewster	Hetherston	Nelson u37, Williamson u65 1, Chisholm og 1, 66,5
S	28-Mar	Meadowbank Thistle		H	L2	3-0	885	Arthur	McStay r70	McLeod	Nicholl	Dennis	Dair	Williamson	Dalziel 3	Hetherston	Brewster	Nelson r65	McKenzie u70, Dair u86, 47,83,84
M	30-Mar	Cowdenbeath		H	FC 1	1-3	323	Banner	Young	Nicholl	Herrick	Sinclair	Sinclair	Crawford	Burn	Nelson	Nelson	McNab r46	Davis u46, Johnston, 45
S	04-Apr	Forfar Athletic		A	L2	2-1	609	Arthur	McStay	McLeod	Nicholl	Dair	Sinclair	Williamson r69	Brewster r82 1	Brewster r77	Brewster r82 1	Nelson 1	McKenzie u82, Dair u86, 40,36
Tu	07-Apr	Stirling Albion		A	L2	2-1	880	Arthur	McStay	McLeod	Nicholl	Dennis	Sinclair	Hetherston	Dalziel 1	Hetherston	Brewster	Nelson 1	McKenzie u69, Burn, 25,31
S	11-Apr	Partick Thistle		H	L2	0-0	3514	Arthur	McStay	McLeod	Nicholl	Dennis	Sinclair	Hetherston	Dalziel 1	Hetherston	Brewster r76	Nelson r65	Dair u65, Williamson u76
S	18-Apr	Morton		A	L2	1-0	1432	Arthur	McStay	McLeod	Nicholl r78	Dennis	Sinclair	Hetherston	Dalziel r46	McKenzie	Brewster	Nelson	Burn, Williamson, 19
S	25-Apr	Clydebank		H	L2	0-0	939	Arthur	McStay	McLeod	Nicholl r78	Dennis	Sinclair	Hetherston	Dalziel	McKenzie	Brewster	Nelson	Dunleavy u46, Dair u78
S	02-May	Kilmarnock		H	L2	1-1	1960	Arthur	McStay	McLeod	Nicholl r81	Dennis	Sinclair	Hetherston	Dalziel	McKenzie 1	Brewster	Nelson r85	Dunleavy u85, Dair u81, 15

Manager : Jimmy Nicholl

(1) after extra time, won 4-3 on penalties

Day	Date	Opponents	Note	Venue	Comp	Res	Att	1	2	3	4	5	6	7	8	9	10	11	Substitutes, own goals and goal times
S	18-Jul	Hearts		H	F	1-2	1519	Arthur	McStay	McLeod	Raeside	Dennis	Sinclair	Nicholl	Dalziel 1p	McKenzie	Brewster	Hetherston	Burn u45 Aertshilling u45 Coyle u60 Strang u60 60
Tu	21-Jul	Hibernian		H	F	0-3	874	Arthur	McStay	Thomson	Coyle	Cowan	Heddle r60	Williamson r45	Burn r57	Strang	Brewster r45	Dair	Cameron u45 Aertshilling u45 Crawford u57 McNab u60
F	24-Jul	Rangers XI	1	A	FC SF	1-0	1198	Arthur	McStay	McLeod	Sinclair	Dennis	Raeside r12	Hetherston	Dalziel	McKenzie	Brewster r37	Thomson r63	Dair u37 Cameron u47 1 Crawford u63 Coyle 58
Sn	25-Jul	East Fife	2	N	FC F	3-1		Arthur	Young	Meldrum	Nicholl	McGeachie r12	Burn	Hetherston	Cameron 1	Strang 1	Thomson	Dair r64	Sinclair u64 Raeside u12 43, 65, 29
M	27-Jul	Dunfermline Athletic			F	3-1	1383	Arthur	Young	Meldrum	Nicholl	Sinclair	Burn	Williamson	Cameron 1	Strang	Brewster	Dair	Raeside 30
S	27-Jul	Aberdeen XI		H	F	0-0		Arthur	McStay	McLeod	Coyle	Dennis	Raeside	Williamson r70	Dalziel	Crawford	Brewster	Thomson	Cowan Dunleavy Davis
S	01-Aug	St Mirren		H	L2	7-0	2254	Arthur	McStay	McLeod	Coyle b 1	Dennis	Sinclair	Nicholl r77 b	Dalziel 3	Hetherston r70	Brewster 2	Dair 1	Thomson u70 McKenzie u77 35,15,64,75,70,83,17
Tu	04-Aug	Stirling Albion		H	L2	0-0	1513	Arthur	McStay	McLeod	Coyle	Dennis	Sinclair	Nicholl	Dalziel	Hetherston	Brewster	Dair r68 b	Thomson McKenzie
S	08-Aug	Kilmarnock		A	L2	1-1	4566	Arthur	McStay b	McLeod	Coyle b	Dennis b X62	Raeside	Nicholl	Dalziel 1	Hetherston	Brewster r70	Dair r68 b	Thomson u68 McKenzie u70 19
W	12-Aug	Hibernian		A	LC 2	1-4	7292	Arthur	McStay 1	McLeod	Coyle 76 b	Raeside	Nicholl	Thomson r62	Dalziel	Hetherston	Brewster r70	Dair	Cameron u76 McKenzie u70 69
S	15-Aug	Ayr United		H	L2	1-0	1417	Carson	McStay	McLeod	Coyle	Dennis	Nicholl	Thomson	Dalziel	Hetherston	Brewster 1	Dair	Cameron McKenzie u62 72
S	22-Aug	Dunfermline Athletic		H	L2	1-0	6377	Carson	McStay	McLeod	Coyle X38	Dennis	Nicholl b	Thomson 1	Dalziel p90 b	Hetherston	Brewster b	Dair 52	McGeachie u52 McKenzie u90 54
S	29-Aug	Dumbarton		A	L2	2-1	1105	Carson	McStay	McLeod	Nicholl	Dennis	McGeachie b	Thomson 1	Dalziel 2	Hetherston	Brewster	Dair r77	Sinclair u83 46, 56
S	05-Sep	Hamilton Academical		A	L2	2-1	2384	Carson	McStay 1	McLeod	Nicholl	Dennis	McGeachie	Thomson 1	Dalziel	Hetherston	Brewster r61 1	Dair r79	Sinclair u79 83, 11
S	12-Sep	Morton		H	L2	2-1	2613	Carson s	McStay r56	McLeod	Nicholl r77	Dennis	McGeachie	Thomson b	Dalziel 1	Hetherston b	Brewster 1	McKenzie	Sinclair u77 b Williamson 4, 53
S	19-Sep	Cowdenbeath		A	L2	3-0	1974	Carson	McStay	McLeod b	Nicholl	Dennis	McGeachie b	Thomson	Dalziel	Hetherston 3	Brewster	McKenzie	Sinclair u56 Cameron 37, 76, 86
S	26-Sep	Meadowbank Thistle		H	L2	2-0	1142	Carson	McStay	McLeod	Nicholl	Dennis	McGeachie	Thomson	Dalziel	Hetherston	Brewster	McKenzie 1	Sinclair u45 Dair 22, 55
S	03-Oct	Clydebank		H	L2	2-2	2424	Carson	McStay 1	McLeod	Nicholl	Dennis b	Nicholl	Thomson	Dalziel 1	Hetherston	Brewster	McKenzie r73	Williamson u73 Sinclair 87, 48
S	10-Oct	St Mirren		A	L2	1-1	6194	Carson s80	McStay X80	McLeod b	Coyle	Dennis b X62	McGeachie u52	Nicholl	Dalziel	Hetherston 1	Brewster	Thomson	Williamson McKenzie u75 36
S	17-Oct	Kilmarnock		H	L2	1-1	3718	Carson	Nicholl b	McLeod	Coyle	Raeside r45	McGeachie r62	Sinclair b	Dalziel	Hetherston 1	Brewster	Thomson	Williamson u45 McKenzie u62 1 73
Tu	20-Oct	Meadowbank Thistle	3	H	LCC 2	0-0	1203	Arthur	McStay	McLeod	Coyle	Herrick	Coyle r102	Williamson	Cameron r72	McKenzie	Brewster	Dair	Crawford u72 Young u105 19, 6
S	24-Oct	Hamilton Academical		H	L2	2-2	2303	Arthur	McStay 1	McLeod	Coyle	Dennis	McGeachie	Williamson	Dalziel r85 1	Hetherston	Brewster 1	Thomson	McGeachie u85 16, 21, 32 secs, 88
S	31-Oct	Dumbarton		H	L2	4-1	1990	Carson b	McStay 1	McLeod	Coyle	Dennis	McGeachie r45	Nicholl 1	Dalziel 2	Hetherston r81	Brewster r81	Thomson r59	Sinclair u45 Crawford u81 78
S	07-Nov	Ayr United		A	L2	1-1	2160	Carson	McStay	McLeod	Coyle	Dennis	McGeachie r41	Nicholl 1	Dalziel	Hetherston 1	Brewster 1	Thomson r59	Crawford u41 Crawford u59 48
S	14-Nov	Dunfermline Athletic		H	L2	1-0	5794	Carson	McStay	McLeod	Coyle b	Raeside b	Sinclair	Nicholl	Dalziel	Hetherston	Brewster	Crawford r84 1	Thomson u84 82, 90, 35
S	21-Nov	Cowdenbeath		H	L2	3-0	2002	Carson	McStay	McLeod	Coyle	Raeside	Sinclair	Nicholl	Dalziel 2	Hetherston 1	Brewster	Crawford	Cameron McKenzie 14, 56, 73, 52
S	28-Nov	Morton		A	L2	4-3	2583	Carson	McStay	McLeod	Coyle b	Raeside	Sinclair	Nicholl	Dalziel 2	Hetherston	Brewster 1	Crawford r66	Thomson u66 McKenzie 14, 56, 73, 52
Tu	01-Dec	Clydebank		A	L2	0-3	1316	Carson	McStay	Thomson	Coyle	Raeside r49 b	Sinclair	Nicholl	Dalziel	Hetherston	Brewster	Crawford r75	Dair u49 McKenzie u75
S	05-Dec	Meadowbank Thistle		A	L2	5-0	1930	Carson	McStay 1	McLeod	Coyle	McGeachie	Sinclair	Nicholl 1	Dalziel 1	Hetherston	Brewster r70 1	Crawford	Dair McKenzie u62 1 57, 64, 41, 68, 73
S	12-Dec	St Mirren		H	L2	3-1	3211	Carson	McStay 1	Thomson	Coyle	McGeachie	Sinclair	Nicholl r33	Dalziel r65 1	Hetherston	Brewster r70 1	Crawford	McLeod u33 b McKenzie u65 38, 46, 74
S	26-Dec	Ayr United		H	L2	1-1	3119	Carson	McStay 1	Thomson	Coyle	McGeachie b	Sinclair	Nicholl	Dalziel	Hetherston	Brewster 1	Crawford	McLeod McKenzie u65 66
Tu	29-Dec	Stirling Albion		H	L2	3-0	1251	Carson	McStay	Thomson 1	Coyle	McGeachie	Sinclair	Nicholl r10	Dalziel 2	Hetherston	Brewster b	Crawford r71	McLeod u71 McLeod u10 r79 19, 5, 69
S	02-Jan	Dunfermline Athletic		A	L2	0-5	10798	Carson	McStay	McLeod	Coyle r81	McGeachie	McGeachie b X29	McKenzie	Dalziel	Hetherston	Brewster	Thomson	Crawford u10 r79 McKenzie u79
S	09-Jan	Dunfermline Athletic		A	SC 3	4-2	7309	Carson r20	McStay	McLeod	Coyle	Sinclair	Thomson 1	McKenzie	Dalziel r84 1	Hetherston	Brewster	Crawford 1	Crawford u20 McKenzie u84 23, 78, 89, 6
Tu	26-Jan	Clydebank	4	A	L2	4-2	2016	Carson	McStay x37	McLeod	Coyle	Dennis b	Sinclair 75 b	Cameron r78	Dalziel 1	Hetherston	Brewster 1 b	Thomson	McKenzie u84 Crawford u78 23, 78, 89, 6
S	30-Jan	Kilmarnock		H	L2	0-3	7003	Carson	McStay	Thomson	Coyle	Dennis b	Sinclair 75 b	Nicholl r84	Dalziel	Hetherston	Brewster	Dair	Crawford u61 Cameron u84 67
Tu	02-Feb	Hamilton Academical		H	L2	1-1	2690	Carson	McStay	Thomson	Coyle	Dennis	Sinclair	Nicholl r36	Dalziel 1p	Hetherston	Brewster	McKenzie r68	McLeod u36 Crawford u68 78, 8
S	06-Feb	Dumbarton		A	L2	2-1	1201	Carson	McStay	Thomson	Coyle	Dennis	Sinclair	Cameron	Dalziel 1p	Hetherston r83	Brewster 1	Crawford r81 1	Thomson u83 Dair 54, 34
S	13-Feb	Stirling Albion		A	L2	2-0	2103	Arthur	Sinclair	McLeod 1	Coyle	Dennis	McGeachie	Cameron	Dalziel 1	Hetherston	Brewster	Sinclair	Thomson u83 Dair 41
S	20-Feb	Meadowbank Thistle		A	L2	1-1	998	Arthur	McStay	McLeod 1	Coyle b	Dennis	McGeachie	Cameron 1	Dalziel	Hetherston	Brewster	Sinclair	Thomson u80 Crawford 40, 67
S	27-Feb	Cowdenbeath		A	L2	2-0	1978	Arthur	McStay	McLeod r80	Coyle b	Dennis	McGeachie	Cameron r72	Dalziel 1	Hetherston	Brewster 1	Sinclair	Crawford u72 Thomson u83 22, 52
S	06-Mar	Morton		H	L2	2-0	1938	Arthur	McStay	McLeod b	Coyle	Dennis	McGeachie	Nicholl	Dalziel 1	Hetherston	Brewster 1	Sinclair	McGeachie u72 Cameron 32
W	10-Mar	St Mirren		A	L2	1-1	2700	Arthur	McStay	McLeod 1	Coyle	Dennis	McGeachie	Nicholl r72 b	Dalziel	Hetherston	Brewster 1	Sinclair	McKenzie u66 Cameron u72 7, 57
S	13-Mar	Kilmarnock	5	H	L2	4-1	4738	Arthur	McStay	McLeod	Coyle	Dennis	McGeachie	Nicholl 2	Dalziel r66 1	Hetherston	Brewster 1	Cameron	McKenzie u66 Raeside 60, 79
S	20-Mar	Dunfermline Athletic		H	L2	1-2	6985	Arthur	McStay	McLeod	Coyle	Dennis	McGeachie	Nicholl 1	Dalziel 48	Hetherston	Brewster	Sinclair r28	McKenzie u48 Cameron 60, 79
S	27-Mar	Ayr United		A	L2	0-0	2664	Arthur	McStay	McLeod b	Coyle	Sinclair	McGeachie b	Nicholl	Dalziel	Hetherston	Brewster	Cameron	McKenzie u28 Crawford u68
S	03-Apr	Hamilton Academical		A	L2	2-2	3014	Arthur	McStay	McLeod 1	Coyle	Dennis	McGeachie b	Nicholl	Dalziel 1	Hetherston	Brewster 1	Cameron	Raeside Crawford 58, 83
S	10-Apr	Dumbarton		H	L2	2-0	4893	Arthur	McStay r65	McLeod	Coyle	Dennis	Raeside	Nicholl	Dalziel 1	Hetherston	Brewster 2	Crawford	Crawford u65 Crawford u19 r75 27, 48
S	17-Apr	Morton		A	L2	1-1	1792	Arthur	McStay b	McLeod r19	Nicholl	Dennis	Raeside	Nicholl	Dalziel r71 m30	Hetherston	Brewster 2	Dair r71	Crawford u19 r75 1 Dair u71 48
S	24-Apr	Cowdenbeath		A	L2	4-1	2752	Arthur	McStay 1	McLeod	Raeside	Dennis	Raeside	Cameron	Dalziel	Hetherston r79 1	Brewster r79 1	Cameron	Cusick u61 Dair u79 42, 54, 23, 9
S	01-May	Stirling Albion		H	L2	1-2	1746	Arthur	McStay	Thomson r65	Coyle	Dennis 1	McGeachie	Nicholl	Dalziel	Hetherston	Brewster	Dair	Dair u65 Raeside 84
W	08-May	Meadowbank Thistle	6	H	B	3-2	1961	Arthur	McStay 1	Thomson r58	Cameron	Dennis	Raeside r58	Nicholl r45 1	Dalziel 1	Hetherston	Brewster 2	Dair r80	Thomson u58 Crawford u80 Murray og 1 40, 81, 75
S	12-May	St Johnstone		A	L2	4-2	1473	Carson r45	McStay	Thomson	Coyle	Dennis	McGeachie	Nicholl r45 1	Dalziel 1	Hetherston	Brewster r45 1	Harris	Arthur u45 Cameron u45 Raeside Cusick u75 33, 65, 36, 3
S	15-May	Clydebank		A	L2	1-4	1090	Carson	McStay 1	Thomson	Coyle	Dennis	McGeachie	Nicholl	Dalziel r75	Hetherston	Brewster	Dair 45	Cameron u45 McKenzie u75 90

Manager : Jimmy Nicholl

(1) Fife Cup played as a tournament at Bayview Park on the weekend of 25th and 26th July ; Smith sent off   (2) at Bayview

(3) after extra time, lost 2-4 on penalties ; Rovers subsequently fined £1000 by the Scottish League for fielding a weakened team

(4) McCluskey sent off 37 minutes

(5) Highlights shown on BBC TV   (6) Gordon Dalziel Testimonial

Day	Date	Opponents	Note	Venue	Comp	Res.	Att.	1	2	3	4	5	6	7	8	9	10	11	Substitutes, own goals and goal times
Sn	18-Jul	St Patricks Athletic		A	F	1-4		Carson	McStay	McLeod	Coyle	Dennis	Sinclair	Dair	Dalziel 1	Hetherston	Hawke	Broddle	Cameron u / Crawford u / Rowbotham u 41
Tu	20-Jul	Shelbourne		A	F	4-3		Carson	Rowbotham	McLeod 1	Coyle	Dennis 1	Sinclair	Cameron 1	Dalziel	Hetherston	Hawke	Crawford	Dair u 43, 33, 38, 60 / Hawke u 3
Th	22-Jul	Drogheda		A	F	1-1		Carson	Rowbotham	McLeod	Coyle	Dennis 1	Sinclair	Cameron	Dalziel	Hetherston	Crawford	Broddle r	Dair u / Hawke u 3
S	24-Jul	Carrick Rangers		A	F	3-1	1744	Carson	McStay	Broddle	Coyle	Dennis	McGeachie	Sinclair	Dalziel 1	Hetherston	Hawke	Cameron 1	McStay u68 / McLeod u / Mooney u 1 / Pollock u / Cameron 15, 35, 89
W	28-Jul	Luton Town		H	F	0-0	733	Arthur	McStay	McLeod	Coyle	Dennis	McGeachie	Nicholl	Cameron 1	Crawford	Thomson,I	Dair 1	Dair u / Thomson,I / Sinclair / Cameron
S	31-Jul	Burntisland Shipyard	1	H	FC SF	3-1	573	Carson	Rowbotham	McLeod	Coyle	Dennis r68	McGeachie 1	Nicholl r74	Dalziel 1	Hetherston 1	Crawford 1	Dair	McNab u68 / Broddle u74 47, 40, 85
Sn	01-Aug	Cowdenbeath	1	H	FC F	5-2	4628	Arthur	McStay 1	Broddle	Coyle	Dennis 1	McGeachie R45	Nicholl r62	Dalziel 2	Hetherston 1	Crawford 1	Cameron	Sinclair u45 / Cameron u62 34, 8, 90, 58, 88
W	07-Aug	St Johnstone	2	H	LC 2	1-2	1957	Carson	McStay	McLeod	Coyle	Dennis	McGeachie R61	Nicholl	Dalziel r64	Hetherston	Hawke	Cameron	Sinclair u61 / Rowbotham 37
S	11-Aug	Arbroath		H	LC 2														
S	14-Aug	Hearts		A	L1	0-1	8587	Carson	McStay	McLeod	Coyle	Dennis b	Sinclair r71	Nicholl r85	Dalziel	Hetherston b	Cameron	Broddle	Broddle u64 / Sinclair u85 18
S	21-Aug	Partick Thistle		A	L1	2-2	3814	Carson	McStay	McLeod	Coyle	Dennis 1	McGeachie	Rowbotham	Dalziel	Hetherston	Cameron	Cameron r88 b	Hawke u71 / Cameron u64 / Nicholl
S	28-Aug	Motherwell		H	L1	1-4	5644	Arthur	McStay	McLeod	Coyle 1	Dennis 1	Sinclair b	Nicholl	Dalziel 1p	Hetherston	Crawford	Cameron	Broddle u88 / Sinclair 27, 61
S	04-Sep	Dundee United		H	L1	1-1	5304	Carson	McStay	McGeachie r67	Coyle 1	Dennis	McGeachie	Nicholl	Dalziel	Hetherston	Crawford	Dair	Broddle u67 / Sinclair 96
S	11-Sep	Celtic		H	L1	1-4	8114	Carson	McStay	Rowbotham	Coyle b	Dennis	McGeachie	Nicholl 1	Crawford	Hetherston	Crawford	Dair	Dair / Broddle 90
M	13-Sep	Glenavon		A	F	4-1		Carson r45	McStay	Rowbotham	Coyle	Dennis b	McGeachie	Nicholl	Crawford 1	Hetherston	Cameron	Cameron r56 2	Dalziel / Broddle 69
S	18-Sep	Dundee		A	L1	1-0	4654	Carson	McStay 1	Broddle	Coyle	Dennis r60	McGeachie	Sinclair	Dalziel	Hetherston r62 1	Crawford 1	Dair 1	Mooney u56 / Thomson u45 / Buist u60 39, 40, 9, 46
S	25-Sep	Aberdeen		A	L1	1-4	11472	Carson	McStay	Rowbotham	Coyle	Dennis 1	McGeachie	Nicholl	Cameron	Hetherston	Crawford r60	Dair	Sinclair u82 / Dalziel 65
S	02-Oct	Rangers		H	L1	1-1	8161	Thomson	McStay 1	Rowbotham	Coyle	Dennis	McGeachie	Nicholl r79	Graham r21	Cameron	Crawford	Cameron	Graham u60 / Sinclair 87
Tu	05-Oct	Hibernian		A	L1	2-3	9203	Thomson	McStay	Rowbotham	Coyle	Dennis	McGeachie	Nicholl r80	Graham	Hetherston	Crawford	Dair 1	Cameron u21 / Sinclair u79 29
S	09-Oct	Kilmarnock		H	L1	2-2	4482	Thomson	McStay	Rowbotham	Coyle	Dennis	McGeachie	Nicholl r27	Dalziel r69	Hetherston	Crawford	Dair 1	Sinclair u80 / Cameron u69 52, 40
S	16-Oct	Hearts		H	L1	1-0	5276	Thomson	McStay	Rowbotham r70	Coyle	Dennis	McGeachie	Nicholl	Dalziel r79	Hetherston 1	Crawford	Dair 1	Sinclair u27 / Cameron u70 7, 26
S	23-Oct	St Johnstone		A	L1	1-1	4411	Thomson	McStay	Rowbotham b	Coyle	Dennis	McGeachie	Nicholl r89	Cameron u60	Hetherston	Crawford	Dair 1	Sinclair u79 / Cameron u70 22
S	30-Oct	Partick Thistle		A	L1	0-3	4774	Thomson	McStay	Rowbotham	Coyle	Dennis	Sinclair	Nicholl	Graham	Cameron 1	Graham	Dair 1	Crawford u60 / Sinclair u89 69
S	06-Nov	Motherwell		A	L1	2-2	4443	Thomson	McStay b	Rowbotham b	Coyle b	Dennis b&X76	Sinclair	Nicholl	Graham b	Cameron r78	Graham 1	Dair r65	Crawford / Sinclair u60 65
S	09-Nov	Dundee United		A	L1	2-2	5775	Thomson	McStay	Rowbotham	Coyle	Dennis	Cameron r51	Nicholl	Dalziel r66	Hetherston r66	Graham	Dair 1	Broddle / Crawford
S	13-Nov	Rangers		A	L1	0-2	42611	Thomson	McStay	Rowbotham	Coyle	Dennis	Sinclair	Nicholl r31	Dalziel r69 1p	Hetherston	Graham 1	Dair	Crawford u78 / Dalziel u65
S	27-Nov	Celtic		A	L1	1-1	17453	Thomson	McStay	Rowbotham	Coyle	Dennis	Sinclair	Nicholl r83	Dalziel	Hetherston	Graham r13	Broddle	Cameron u31 / Broddle
W	01-Dec	Dundee		H	L1	2-1	3609	Thomson	McStay	Broddle	Coyle	Dennis	Sinclair	Nicholl r77	Dalziel 1	Hetherston r52	Graham	Dair	Crawford u69 / Cameron u52 6, 42
S	04-Dec	Hibernian		H	L1	1-2	4407	Thomson	McStay	Broddle	Coyle	Dennis	Sinclair	Nicholl r45	Dalziel r72	Cameron	Graham 1	Dair	Crawford u72 / McGeachie u45 28
Tu	07-Dec	Aberdeen		A	L1	1-1	4205	Thomson	McStay	Broddle	Coyle	Dennis	McGeachie	Sinclair	Dalziel 1	Rowbotham	Graham	Dair	Crawford / Rowbotham u69 40
S	11-Dec	Kilmarnock		A	L1	0-1	6012	Thomson	McStay b	Broddle	Coyle	Dennis	McGeachie r45	Sinclair r77	Dalziel	Hetherston	Graham	Dair	Crawford u77 / Cameron u65
S	18-Dec	Hearts		A	L1	1-0	6227	Thomson	McStay	Broddle	Coyle	Dennis	Sinclair 1	Nicholl	Dalziel r62	Crawford	Graham	Dair	McGeachie / Cameron u62 25
W	12-Jan	Partick Thistle		A	L1	2-2	3599	Thomson	Rowbotham	Broddle	Coyle	Dennis	Sinclair	Nicholl r72	Crawford r72	Crawford r72	Graham b	Dair	McGeachie / Cameron u72
S	15-Jan	Dundee United		A	L1	1-3	5150	Thomson	Rowbotham	Broddle	Coyle	Dennis	Sinclair	Nicholl r83	Dalziel	Cameron	Sinclair	Dair	Crawford u83 / McGeachie
W	19-Jan	St Johnstone		H	L1	2-0	3693	Thomson	McStay	Broddle	Coyle	Dennis	McGeachie	Cameron	Dalziel 1	Sinclair	Graham	Dair r75	McStay u75 / Crawford
S	22-Jan	Dundee		A	L1	0-0	3934	Thomson	Rowbotham	Broddle r22	Coyle	Dennis	McGeachie b	Cameron b	Dalziel 1	Crawford	Graham b	Dair r69	McStay u22 b&35 / Crawford u69 / Blake og 1 84, 20
Tu	25-Jan	Motherwell		A	L1	0-4	5076	Thomson	McAnespie	McGeachie	Coyle	Dennis	McGeachie b	Nicholl r77	Dalziel r67	Sinclair	Graham b	Cameron 1	Kelly u77 / Crawford u67 42
S	29-Jan	Brechin City		H	SC 3	0-1	2846	Thomson	McStay 1	McGeachie	Coyle	Dennis	Sinclair	Nicholl r87	Dalziel	Crawford	Graham	Dair 1	Kelly u87 / Crawford 31, 24
S	05-Feb	Celtic		H	L1	0-0	7678	Thomson	McStay	Rowbotham	Coyle	Dennis	Cameron	Nicholl r78	Graham	Cameron	Cameron	Dair	McAnespie / Dalziel
S	12-Feb	Aberdeen		A	L1	0-4	10553	Thomson	McStay	Rowbotham	Coyle b	Dennis	Sinclair b	Cameron b	Graham b	Crawford r78	Crawford	Dair	McAnespie u78 / Dalziel u78 m81
S	19-Feb	Aberdeen		H	SC 4	0-1	13740	Thomson	McStay	Rowbotham	Coyle	Dennis	Sinclair	Nicholl	Cameron	Crawford r70	Crawford 1	Dair	McAnespie / Graham u70
Tu	26-Feb	Rangers		A	L1	1-2	8988	Thomson	McStay	Rowbotham	Coyle r45	Dennis	Sinclair r60	Nicholl r62	Lennon r84	Hetherston r83	Crawford	Dair	McAnespie u62 / Nicholl u83 15
S	05-Mar	Hibernian		A	L1	0-3	6039	Thomson	McStay	Broddle	Cameron	Dennis	Sinclair	Cameron	Graham r56	Hetherston	Crawford	Dair	Rowbotham / Dalziel u56
F	11-Mar	Ards		A	F	3-0		Thomson	McStay r45	Rowbotham	Coyle	Sinclair	Cameron r45	de Gefrouwe r57	Dalziel r68 1	Hetherston 1p	Graham	Dair	Crawford u57 1 / McAnespie u45 / Kelly u45 / Nicholl u68 44, 30, 75 / 67, 45, 78
Tu	15-Mar	Kilmarnock		H	L1	3-2	3585	Thomson	McStay	Rowbotham b	Coyle	Dennis	Sinclair b	Nicholl	Graham 1	Hetherston 1p	Crawford b	Dair	Kelly / Dalziel 44, 30, 75
S	19-Mar	Hearts		H	L1	2-2	5697	Thomson	McStay 1	Rowbotham b	Coyle	Dennis	Sinclair	Nicholl	Graham b	Hetherston b	Crawford 1	Dair	McAnespie / Dalziel u63 27, 57
S	26-Mar	St Johnstone		A	L1	0-2	4550	Thomson	McStay	Sinclair	Coyle	Dennis	Cameron	Nicholl 1	Graham	Hetherston	Crawford	Dair r63 b	Rowbotham / Dalziel u63 31
W	30-Mar	Celtic		H	L1	1-2	14140	Thomson	McStay	Rowbotham	Coyle	Dennis b	Sinclair b	Nicholl	Graham	Hetherston	Crawford 1	Cameron r69	Kelly u69 / Dalziel u69 31
S	02-Apr	Dundee		H	L1	1-2	3245	Thomson	McStay	Sinclair b	Coyle	Dennis	Cameron	Nicholl	Lennon r84	Hetherston	Crawford 1	Dair	Kelly u84 / Kelly 51
S	16-Apr	Rangers		A	L1	0-4	42545	Thomson	McStay	Rowbotham	Coyle r45	Dennis	McGeachie	Nicholl r62	Cameron	Hetherston r83	Crawford	Dair	Rowbotham / Cameron u62
S	23-Apr	Kilmarnock		H	L1	0-0	7426	Thomson	McStay	Broddle	Coyle	Dennis	Lennon	Cameron	Graham	Hetherston	Crawford	Dair	Rowbotham / Kelly
Tu	26-Apr	Hibernian		H	L1	1-1	3040	Thomson	McStay r70	Broddle	Coyle	Dennis	Sinclair	Cameron 1 b	Graham	Hetherston	Crawford r70	Dair	Rowbotham r70 / Kelly r70 72
S	30-Apr	Partick Thistle		A	L1	2-2	4541	Thomson	Rowbotham	Broddle	Coyle	Dennis	Sinclair	Kelly r76	Graham	Hetherston 1p	Cameron 1	Lennon r76	Crawford r70 / Kelly r76 2, 27
Tu	03-May	Aberdeen		A	L1	0-2	2798	Thomson	Rowbotham	Broddle	Coyle	Dennis	Lennon	Nicholl r58 b	Graham	Hetherston 1	Graham	Cameron	Dair u76 / Sinclair 76
S	07-May	Motherwell		H	L1	3-3	3449	Carson	McAnespie	Broddle	Coyle	Dennis	Lennon	Rowbotham r79	Dalziel r53 1	Hetherston 1	Graham 1	Dair	Dair u58 / Crawford u79 26, 90, 23
S	14-May	Dundee United		A	L1	3-2	5335	Potter	McStay	Broddle r80	Coyle	Dennis	Sinclair 1	Lennon	Graham r76	Hetherston	Crawford	Dair 2	Sinclair u53 / Rowbotham u80 45, 10, 34

Manager : Jimmy Nicholl

Last season of two points for a win

(1) Fife Cup played as a tournament at Stark's Park over the weekend of 31st July and 1st August

(2) Turner booked and sent off

1994-95

Day	Date	Opponents	Note	Venue	Comp	Res.	Att.	1	2	3	4	5	6	7	8	9	10	11	Substitutes, own goals and goal times				
S	30-Jul	Middlesbrough		H	F	1-0		Thomson	McAnespie r75	Broddle	Coyle	Dennis r75	Sinclair	Lennon	Dalziel r66	Graham r66	Cameron 1	Dair	Crawford u66	McStay u66	Kelly u75	Raeside u75	Potter
Tu	02-Aug	Larne		A	F	2-0		Thomson	McStay	Broddle	Coyle	Dennis	Sinclair	Lennon r58	Cameron r68	Crawford 1	Kelly	Dair 1	McAnespie u58	Raeside u68	68, 37		
Th	04-Aug	Banbridge Town		A	F	2-0		Potter	McAnespie	Broddle	Raeside	Sinclair	McMillan	Kirkwood	Dalziel 1	Graham 1	Kelly	Cameron	Coyle	Dennis	Dair	Crawford	McStay
S	06-Aug	Bangor		A	F	2-0		Thomson	McStay r69	Kirkwood	Coyle r69 1	Dennis	Sinclair	Lennon	Kelly	Crawford	Graham 1	Dair	McAnespie u69	Raeside u69	37, 3		
Tu	09-Aug	Hearts	1	H	F	2-0	2172	Thomson	Rowbotham	Kirkwood r73	Coyle r65	Raeside	Sinclair	Lennon r68	Dalziel r45 1	Graham r75	Cameron	Dair 1	Crawford u45	Broddle u65	Kelly u68	McStay u73	McAnespie u75
S	13-Aug	St Johnstone		H	L2	1-1	4374	Thomson	Rowbotham	Kirkwood	Coyle	Dennis	Sinclair	Lennon	Dalziel	Graham	Cameron 1	Dair r74	Raeside u46	Crawford u74	Potter	54	
W	17-Aug	Ross County		A	LC 2	5-0	2288	Thomson	Rowbotham	Kirkwood r	Coyle	Raeside	Sinclair	Lennon b	Dalziel r 1	Graham 3	Cameron r	Dair	Broddle u	Crawford u	Potter		
S	20-Aug	Hamilton Academical		H	L2	1-1	2825	Thomson	Rowbotham b,b&X75	Broddle	Coyle	Raeside r55	Sinclair	Lennon	Dalziel	Graham 1	Cameron	Dair r75	Crawford u55	McAnespie u	Potter	39	
S	27-Aug	Dunfermline Athletic		A	L2	0-1	7372	Thomson	McAnespie	Broddle	Coyle	Sinclair	Redford r62	Lennon	Cameron	Graham	Dair	Crawford	Dalziel u62	Kelly	Potter		
W	31-Aug	Kilmarnock		H	LC 3	3-2	4181	Thomson	McAnespie b	Broddle b	Rowbotham	Narey	Sinclair	Lennon	Dalziel r69	Graham	Cameron 3	Redford r81	Crawford u69	Coyle u81	Potter	35, 41, 77	
S	03-Sep	Clydebank		H	L2	1-1	2861	Thomson	McAnespie	Broddle	Rowbotham	Narey	Sinclair b	Lennon	Dalziel r68	Graham	Cameron 1	Redford	Crawford u68	Kelly	Potter	26	
S	10-Sep	Stranraer		A	L2	0-0	1505	Thomson	McAnespie	Broddle	Rowbotham r	Narey	Sinclair	Lennon	Dalziel	Graham	Cameron	Redford r	Kirkwood u	Wilson u	Potter		
S	17-Sep	Queen of the South		A	LCC 1	2-0	1376	Thomson	McAnespie	Rowbotham	Lennon	Narey	Sinclair b	Nicholl	Crawford 1	Graham	Cameron 1	Wilson r81	Dair u81	Dennis	Potter	14,2	
Tu	20-Sep	St Johnstone		A	LC QF	3-1	6287	Thomson	McAnespie	Broddle	Rowbotham	Dennis 1	Sinclair	Nicholl	Dalziel r81	Graham 1	Cameron	Lennon 1	Dair u81	Redford	Potter	19, 30, 83	
S	24-Sep	St Mirren		A	L2	2-1	2953	Thomson	McAnespie	Broddle	Rowbotham	Dennis	Redford	Lennon	Crawford r86 1	Graham 1	Cameron	Dair r75	Wilson u75	Dalziel u86	Potter	10, 83	
Tu	27-Sep	Airdrie	2	A	LCC 1	1-1	1360	Thomson	McAnespie	Redford r66	Lennon	Dennis	Narey	Wilson	Dalziel r78 1	Crawford	Cameron	Dair	Broddle u66	Sinclair u78 b	Potter	17	
S	01-Oct	Ayr United		H	L2	3-0	2854	Thomson	McAnespie	Broddle	Lennon	Dennis b	Sinclair	Nicholl	Crawford 1	Graham	Cameron	Dair r73	Dalziel u73 2,1p	Redford	Potter	32, 75, 84p	
S	08-Oct	Airdrie		A	L2	0-0	2096	Thomson	McAnespie	Broddle	Lennon r76	Dennis	Sinclair	Nicholl r59 b	Dalziel	Graham	Cameron	Crawford	Kirkwood u59	Wilson u76	Potter		
S	15-Oct	Dundee		H	L2	1-1	3834	Thomson	McAnespie	Broddle	Narey	Dennis b	Sinclair	Lennon b,b&X72	Dalziel r78	Graham b	Cameron 1 b	Crawford r85	Rowbotham u78	Dair u85	Allan	45	
S	22-Oct	St Johnstone		A	L2	1-3	3925	Thomson	McAnespie b	Broddle	Sinclair b	Dennis b	Narey	Kirkwood r69	Dalziel 1	Graham	Cameron	Dair r45	Wilson u45	Crawford u64	Potter	86	
Tu	25-Oct	Airdrie	3	N	LC SF	1-1	7260	Thomson	McAnespie	Broddle r90	Sinclair	Dennis	Narey	Lennon	Dalziel r51	Graham 1	Cameron	Kirkwood r69	Crawford u51	Potter u69	Rowbotham u90	39	
S	29-Oct	Dunfermline Athletic		H	L2	2-5	5965	Allan	McAnespie	Broddle	Sinclair	Dennis	Redford r63	Lennon r63	Crawford	Graham	Cameron	Wilson 2	Dalziel u63	Kirkwood u63	Potter	2, 25	
S	05-Nov	Hamilton Academical	4	A	L2	3-0	1112	Thomson	McAnespie	Broddle	Sinclair r70	Dennis	Narey	Wilson	Dalziel r75 1	Graham	Cameron	Crawford 2	Kirkwood u70	Dair u75	Potter	75, 79. 88	
Tu	08-Nov	Cowdenbeath	N	A	FC SF	2-0	188	Allan	Rowbotham	Quinn r85	McMillan	Sinclair	Raeside	Lennon 1	Redford	Dair	Kirkwood r82	Weatherston 1	McKinlay u82	Buist u85		7, 11	
S	12-Nov	Stranraer		H	L2	4-2	2556	Thomson	McAnespie	Broddle	Lennon	Dennis	Narey	Wilson	Dalziel r56 3,1p	Graham r72 1	Cameron	Crawford	Dair u56	Rowbotham u72	Potter	24, 34, 53p, 55	
S	19-Nov	Clydebank		A	L2	3-0	1090	Thomson	McAnespie	Broddle	Rowbotham	Dennis r81	Narey 1	Redford r35	Dalziel 1	Graham 1	Cameron	Crawford	Dair u35	McMillan u81	Potter	56, 6, 53	
Sn	27-Nov	Celtic	5	N	LC F	2-2	45384	Thomson	McAnespie	Broddle r93	Narey	Dennis	Sinclair	Crawford 1	Dalziel r112 1	Graham	Cameron	Dair	Rowbotham u93	Redford u112	Potter	18, 88	
S	03-Dec	Ayr United		A	L2	1-1	2216	Thomson	McAnespie r80	Broddle b	Sinclair	Dennis	Narey	Redford	Dalziel 1	Crawford	Cameron	Wilson r84	Rowbotham u80	Kirkwood u84	Potter	65	
Tu	06-Dec	St Mirren		H	L2	1-1	4084	Thomson	McAnespie	Broddle	Sinclair r60	Dennis	Narey	Redford	Dalziel r70 1p	Crawford	Cameron	Wilson	Kirkwood u70	Rowbotham u60	Potter	34	
S	10-Dec	Dundee		A	L2	1-2	3482	Thomson	McAnespie	Broddle	Rowbotham b	Narey	Sinclair r81	Nicholl b	Dalziel 1p	Crawford	Cameron	Redford	Wilson u81	Kelly	Allan	63	
M	26-Dec	Airdrie		H	L2	3-2	4338	Thomson	McAnespie	Broddle	Narey	Dennis	Redford	Nicholl	Dalziel r78 1	Graham	Cameron 1	Crawford	Sinclair u78 1	Wilson	Allan	30, 16, 89	
S	31-Dec	St Johnstone		H	L2	2-0	4973	Thomson	McAnespie	Broddle 1	Sinclair	Dennis	Narey	Redford r66	Dalziel 1	Graham b	Cameron	Crawford r80	Kirkwood u66	Wilson u80	Allan	6, 79	
S	07-Jan	Hamilton Academical		H	L2	2-0	3130	Thomson	McAnespie	Broddle r74	Sinclair 1	Dennis	Narey	Nicholl	Dalziel	Graham	Cameron 1	Kirkwood	Wilson u74	Crawford	Allan	3, 62	
W	11-Jan	Dunfermline Athletic		A	L2	1-0	8414	Thomson	McAnespie	Rowbotham	Narey	Dennis	Sinclair	Nicholl	Dalziel r73	Graham 1	Cameron	Kirkwood	Wilson u73	Crawford	Allan	82	
S	14-Jan	Clydebank		H	L2	1-0	3129	Thomson	McAnespie	Rowbotham	Lennon	Dennis 1	Narey	Nicholl	Dalziel r75	Crawford	Cameron	Wilson	Dair u75	Kirkwood	Allan	90	
Tu	24-Jan	Stranraer		A	L2	4-2	460	Thomson	McAnespie	Broddle	Sinclair	Raeside	Narey	Nicholl	Dalziel 1	Crawford 1	Lennon	Wilson 2 r86	Kirkwood u86	Dair	Allan	69, 58, 24, 84	
S	28-Jan	Ayr United		H	SC 3	1-0	4156	Thomson	McAnespie	Broddle	Coyle	Raeside	Sinclair	Nicholl	Dalziel	Crawford r84 1	Lennon	Wilson	Graham u84	Kirkwood	Allan	21	
S	04-Feb	Ayr United		H	L2	2-1	2799	Thomson	McAnespie	Broddle r67	Coyle r67	Dennis	Raeside	Sinclair 1	Dalziel	Crawford 1	Lennon	Wilson	Rowbotham u67	Graham u67	Allan	19, 71	
S	11-Feb	St Mirren		A	L2	2-1	2516	Thomson	McAnespie	Broddle	Coyle	Dennis	Raeside	Wilson r61	Sinclair	Graham	Crawford 2	Lennon	Cameron u61	Rowbotham	Allan	4, 44	
S	18-Feb	Dundee		A	SC 4	2-1	7622	Thomson	McAnespie	Broddle r73	Coyle	Dennis	Raeside r35	Sinclair	Cameron	Graham 1	Lennon	Crawford	Wilson u35	Rowbotham u73 1	Allan	71, 81	
S	25-Feb	Dundee		H	L2	0-0	5885	Thomson	McAnespie	Rowbotham	Coyle	Dennis	Sinclair	Wilson	Cameron r41	Graham	Crawford r80	Dair	Broddle u41	Dalziel u80	Allan		
M	06-Mar	Airdrie		A	L2	2-1	1726	Thomson	McAnespie	Rowbotham	Lennon	Dennis	Sinclair	Wilson	Cameron	Graham 1	Crawford	Dair 1	Broddle	Dalziel	Allan	81. 70	
S	14-Mar	Airdrie		H	SC QF	1-4	7130	Thomson	McAnespie	Rowbotham	Cameron 1	Dennis	Sinclair	Wilson r58	Crawford	Graham	Lennon r45	Dair	Broddle u45	Dalziel u58	Allan	84	
S	18-Mar	Stranraer		H	L2	1-1	2197	Thomson	Kirkwood	Rowbotham	Narey	Sinclair	Cameron	Nicholl	Dalziel 1	Graham	Crawford u88	Rougier	Wilson u88	Lennon	Allan	17	
S	01-Apr	Ayr United		A	L2	1-0	1995	Thomson	McAnespie	Rowbotham	Coyle	Dennis	Raeside	Dair r31	Rougier r31	Crawford	Kirkwood 1	Sinclair	Graham u31	Cameron u80	Allan	45	
Tu	04-Apr	Clydebank		A	L2	2-1	1421	Thomson	McAnespie	Rowbotham	Coyle	Dennis	Sinclair	Kirkwood r73	Graham	Crawford 1	Lennon	Cameron 1	Wilson u73	Redford	Allan	88, 57	
S	08-Apr	St Mirren		H	L2	2-1	3669	Thomson	McAnespie	Kirkwood	Coyle	Dennis b	Sinclair	Cameron 2	Rougier r66	Graham	Crawford u84	Lennon	Wilson u66	Broddle u84	Allan	35, 38	
Tu	11-Apr	Ross County	6	A	F	3-0	1800	Thomson	McAnespie	Kirkwood r**	Lennon	Dennis	Sinclair	Rougier	Crawford 1	Graham 2	Cameron r b	Wilson	Robertson u	Quinn u**		29. 64, 78	
S	15-Apr	Airdrie		H	L2	0-1	4494	Thomson	McAnespie	Kirkwood	Lennon b	Dennis	Sinclair b	Nicholl r66 b	Cameron	Graham b,b&X44	Crawford	Dair r71	Dalziel u66	Redford u71	Allan		
S	22-Apr	Dundee		A	L2	2-0	7826	Thomson	McAnespie	Broddle u86	Sinclair b	Raeside	Narey	Nicholl b	Dalziel	Crawford 1	Cameron	Wilson r81 1	Dair u81	Kirkwood u86	Allan	68, 78	
S	29-Apr	St Johnstone		A	L2	2-1	5092	Thomson	McAnespie	Broddle	Narey	Raeside r62	Sinclair	Nicholl r88	Dalziel	Crawford 1	Cameron	Wilson	Rougier u62	Rowbotham u88	Allan	Preston og 1	90, 63
S	06-May	Dunfermline Athletic		H	L2	0-0	9300	Thomson	McAnespie	Broddle	Narey	Raeside	Sinclair	Wilson r90	Dalziel r88	Crawford	Cameron	Dair	Kirkwood u88	Lennon u90	Allan		
S	13-May	Hamilton Academical		A	L2	0-0	5333	Thomson	McAnespie	Broddle	Narey	Dennis	Raeside	Nicholl	Dalziel	Dair r64	Cameron	Sinclair	Wilson u64	Kirkwood	Allan		

Manager : Jimmy Nicholl

First season for three points for a win ; Substitute goalkeepers permitted as a third substitute on the bench, although only two could be selected

(1) Hogg and Levein sent off in 44 minutes for fighting

(2) after extra time, lost 5-3 on penalties ; played at Broadwood Stadium

(3) after extra time, won 5-4 on penalties, at McDiarmid Park

(4) McNulty sent off 63 minutes

(5) at Ibrox, after extra time, won 6-5 on penalties

(6) Match in aid of the British Heart Foundation

(N) Fixture fulfilled by reserve team, not included in summary statistics

Stevie Crawford and Colin Cameron were nominated in the SPFA Division One Player of the Year awards (which Crawford won), Crawford nominated for the young Player of the Year (won by Charlie Miller of Rangers) and Jimmy Nicholl was voted Manager of the year by the Scottish Football Writers' Association.

Tony Rougier was signed from Trinity Pros in mid January, but his work permit did not come through until 8th March

Day	Date	Opponents	Note	Venue	Comp	Res.	Att.	1	2	3	4	5	6	7	8	9	10	11	Substitutes, own goals and goal times				
Sn	23-Jul	Derry City		A	F	4-1	2000	Thomson,SY	McAnespie	Broddle r	McInally r	Dennis	Sinclair	Wilson 1	Dair r	Crawford 1	Cameron	Taylor r 2	Graham u	Lennon u90	Coyle u r	Kirkwood	Rougier
Tu	25-Jul	Distillery		A	F	4-0	1000	Fridge	Kirkwood	Broddle	Coyle	Dennis	Raeside	Rougier 1	Crawford 2	Lennon	Graham	Dair 1	19, 60, 29, ...				
Th	27-Jul	Moyola Park		A	F	10-0	700	Thomson,SY	McAnespie	Broddle	McInally	Raeside	Sinclair	Wilson 2	Crawford 1	Taylor	Rougier 3	Coyle	Dennis u	Cameron u	Graham u 4		
S	29-Jul	Glentoran		A	F	1-3	1500	Thomson,SY	Kirkwood	Broddle	Coyle	Dennis	Sinclair 1	Taylor	Dair	Lennon	Graham	Rougier	12				
Tu	01-Aug	Oldham Athletic		H	F	2-0	2394	Thomson,SY	McAnespie	Broddle r71	Coyle	Raeside	Sinclair	McInally	Cameron 1	Crawford	Taylor r71	Wilson 1	Dair u71	Kirkwood u71	Graham	Lennon	Fridge
Tu	08-Aug	Goto Itrottarfelag		H	Uc Pr-1	4-0	5082	Thomson,SY	McAnespie 1	Broddle	McInally	Dennis	Sinclair	Rougier r65 1	Cameron 1	Crawford r79	Taylor	Dair 1	Graham u65	Lennon u79	Coyle	Kirkwood	Fridge
Th	10-Aug	Manchester City		H	F	2-2	1846	Fridge r75	Kirkwood r43	Rowbotham	Coyle	McMillan	Raeside	Rougier r78	Lennon 1p	Graham	Cameron r60	Crawford r75	Buist u43	Forrest u60 1	Potter u75	Robertson u78	McKinlay u75
Tu	15-Aug	Dunfermline Athletic	1	H	FC F	1-0	1604	Fridge	McAnespie r87	Buist	Coyle r30	Raeside	McMillan r69	Forrest	Kirkwood	McKinlay	Graham	Robertson 1	Drummond u30	Nicholl u69	Black u87	38	
S	19-Aug	Arbroath		H	LC 2	2-1	3046	Thomson,SY	Kirkwood 2p b	Broddle b	McInally r54	Dennis	Sinclair	Rougier	Cameron	Crawford	Taylor	Dair r74	Lennon u54	Graham u74	Fridge	10, 53	
Th	22-Aug	Goto Itrottarfelag		A	UC Pr-2	2-2	500	Thomson,SY	Kirkwood	Broddle	Lennon 1	Dennis r85	Sinclair	Rougier	Graham	Crawford 1	Taylor r77	Cameron	Forrest u77	Raeside u85	Fridge	Robertson	McKinlay
S	26-Aug	Celtic		H	L1	0-1	9300	Thomson,SY	Kirkwood	Broddle	McInally r83	Dennis	Sinclair b	Wilson	Cameron	Graham b	Crawford r19	Rougier b	Lennon u19	Raeside u83	Fridge		
Th	31-Aug	Celtic	2	A	LC 3	1-2	27546	Thomson,SY	Kirkwood	Broddle b	McInally r60 b	Dennis r100	Sinclair	Rougier 1	Cameron b	Crawford	Lennon	Dair r60	Wilson u60	Graham u60	Coyle u100	78	
S	09-Sep	Rangers		A	L1	0-4	43535	Thomson,SY	Kirkwood	Broddle	McInally r45	Dennis	Sinclair	Wilson r45	Cameron r74	Crawford	Lennon	Rougier	Coyle u45	Graham u45	McAnespie u74		
Tu	12-Sep	IA Akranes		H	UC 1-1	3-1	5284	Thomson,SY	McAnespie	Broddle b	Kirkwood b	Dennis	Sinclair	Wilson r85 1	Cameron	Crawford r59	Lennon 2	Rougier r27	Dair u27	Graham u59	Coyle u85	Fridge	Nicholl
S	16-Sep	Kilmarnock		H	L1	2-0	4441	Thomson,SY	McAnespie	Broddle	Coyle	Sinclair	Kirkwood	Wilson r74	Cameron r84	Graham 1	Lennon	Dair r84 1	Rougier u74	Crawford u84	McInally u84	52, 84	
S	23-Sep	Partick Thistle		H	L1	3-1	4342	Thomson,SY s88	McAnespie	Broddle	Coyle	Sinclair b	Kirkwood r53	Rougier r75	Cameron 2	Graham r55	Lennon b	Dair 1	McInally u53	Crawford u55	Wilson u75	5, 64, 38	
Tu	26-Sep	IA Akranes		A	UC 1-2	0-1	4000	Thomson,SY	McAnespie	Broddle	Coyle b	Dennis	Sinclair	Kirkwood	Cameron	Crawford r75	Lennon	Dair r87	Wilson u75	McInally u87	Fridge	Raeside	Nicholl
S	30-Sep	Aberdeen		A	L1	0-3	13983	Thomson,SY	Kirkwood r84	Broddle	McInally b	Dennis	Sinclair	Wilson r45	Cameron	Crawford r66	Lennon	Dair	Coyle u45 b	Raeside u66	Nicholl u84		
W	04-Oct	Hibernian		H	L1	3-0	6051	Thomson,SY	Kirkwood	Broddle	Coyle	Dennis	Sinclair 1	McInally	Cameron 2	Graham	Lennon	Dair	Crawford	Taylor	Raeside	53, 13, 55	
S	07-Oct	Motherwell		A	L1	2-0	5727	Thomson,SY	Kirkwood b	Broddle	Coyle	Dennis	Sinclair 1	McInally	Cameron r90	Graham	Lennon	Dair 1	Crawford u90	Taylor	Raeside	68, 42	
S	14-Oct	Hearts		A	L1	2-4	10133	Thomson,SY	Kirkwood	Broddle	Coyle r43 b	Dennis	Sinclair	McInally r60	Cameron r80	Graham 1	Lennon	Dair	Crawford u43 1	Taylor u60	McMillan u80	63, 80	
Tu	17-Oct	Bayern Munich	3	H	UC 2-1	0-2	12818	Thomson,SY	Kirkwood	Broddle	Coyle	Dennis	Sinclair	McInally r75 b	Cameron	Graham	Lennon	Dair r74	Crawford u74	Rougier u75	Taylor	Fridge	Raeside
S	21-Oct	Falkirk		H	L1	0-1	4715	Thomson,SY	Kirkwood r58	Broddle	Coyle	Dennis	Sinclair	McInally r74	Cameron	Graham	Lennon	Dair	Rougier u58	Crawford u74	McMillan		
S	28-Oct	Rangers		H	L1	2-2	9300	Thomson,SY	Buist r75	Broddle	Coyle	McMillan	Sinclair	Dair	Cameron 1	Crawford	Lennon 1	Rougier r71	Graham u71	Taylor u75	Raeside	66, 50	
Tu	31-Oct	Bayern Munich	4	A	UC 2-2	1-2	27000	Thomson,SY	Taylor r64	Broddle	Coyle r80 b	Dennis	Sinclair b	Rougier r60	Cameron	Crawford	Lennon 1	Dair	Graham u60	Kirkwood u64	McInally u80	Fridge	McMillan
S	04-Nov	Kilmarnock		A	L1	1-5	6440	Thomson,SY	Kirkwood	Broddle r52 b	Coyle	Dennis r67 b x71	Sinclair	McInally	Cameron r72 1	Crawford	Lennon	Dair	Graham u52	McMillan u67	Taylor u72	46	
W	08-Nov	Celtic		A	L1	0-0	31119	Thomson,SY	Kirkwood b	Broddle	Coyle b	Dennis b	Sinclair	McInally b	Cameron r58	Crawford b	Lennon	Dair	Graham u58	Wilson	Raeside		
S	11-Nov	Motherwell		H	L1	0-0	4293	Thomson,SY	Kirkwood	Broddle	Coyle	Dennis	Sinclair	McInally	Cameron	Crawford	Lennon r68	Dair r81	Graham u68	Rougier u81	Taylor		
S	18-Nov	Aberdeen		H	L1	1-0	5786	Thomson,SY	McInally	Broddle	Coyle b	Dennis	Sinclair	Crawford	Cameron b	Graham r84	Lennon 1p	Dair	Wilson u84	Taylor	Kirkwood	16	
S	25-Nov	Partick Thistle		A	L1	2-0	3503	Thomson,SY	McInally	Broddle	Coyle	Dennis	Sinclair	Crawford 1	Cameron	Graham 1	Lennon r79	Dair r68	Kirkwood u68	Taylor u79	Rougier	31, 6	
S	02-Dec	Falkirk		A	L1	1-2	4404	Thomson,SY	McInally	Broddle	Coyle r71	Dennis	Sinclair	Crawford	Cameron	Graham 1	Lennon r71	Wilson	Taylor u71	Rougier u71	Kirkwood	57	
S	09-Dec	Hearts	5	H	L1	1-1	6348	Thomson,SY	McInally	Broddle	Coyle	Sinclair b	Humphries b	Crawford	Cameron	Graham b	Lennon r60 1p b	Wilson	Rougier u60	Kirkwood	Taylor	28	
S	16-Dec	Hibernian		A	L1	2-1	8985	Thomson,SY	McKilligan r58	Broddle	Coyle	Dennis	Humphries r80 b	Crawford 1	Cameron	Graham 1	Lennon	Rougier r84	Kirkwood u58 b	Sinclair u80	Wilson u84	57, 60	
S	06-Jan	Kilmarnock	8	H	L1	1-1	4781	Thomson,SY	Sinclair	Broddle b	Coyle	Dennis	Humphries x86	Crawford	Cameron	Graham b	Lennon r67 1 b	Kirkwood	Wilson u67	Taylor	McKilligan	33	
Tu	09-Jan	Celtic		H	L1	1-3	9300	Thomson,SY	McKilligan	Broddle	Coyle r56	Dennis b	Sinclair	Wilson r75	Cameron 1	Graham	Lennon r65	Crawford	Taylor u65	Forrest u75	McKilligan u56	81	
S	13-Jan	Rangers		A	L1	0-4	42498	Thomson,SY	McInally	Humphries	Coyle r45	Dennis	Sinclair	Wilson r59	Cameron	Graham	Lennon	Crawford	Broddle u45	McMillan u59	McKilligan		
S	20-Jan	Falkirk		H	L1	1-0	4123	Thomson,SY	McMillan	Humphries	Lennon	Dennis	Sinclair 1	Rougier	Cameron	Graham	Crawford	Dair r69	Broddle u69	Coyle	McKilligan	70	
Tu	23-Jan	Partick Thistle		H	L1	0-2	3651	Thomson,SY	McMillan	Humphries	Lennon r68	Dennis	Sinclair	Dair r68	Cameron b	Graham	Crawford	Rougier	Broddle u68	Kirkwood u68	Coyle		
S	27-Jan	Queen's Park		H	SC 3	3-0	2665	Fridge	McMillan r52	Humphries	Kirkwood	Dennis	Sinclair r89 b	Rougier	Cameron 2	Graham	Lennon 1	Crawford	McKilligan u52	Coyle u89	Buist	71, 87, 78	
S	03-Feb	Hearts		A	L1	0-2	10183	Fridge	Kirkwood	Broddle r60	Coyle	Dennis b	Humphries b	Crawford	Cameron	Graham r75	Rougier	Dair	McMillan u60	McKilligan u75	Buist		
W	07-Feb	Aberdeen		A	L1	0-1	6628	Geddes	Kirkwood b	Broddle r82	Coyle	Dennis b	Sinclair	Dair	Cameron	Crawford	Lennon	Rougier r82	Broddle u82	Graham u82	McMillan		
S	10-Feb	Hibernian		H	L1	1-0	4832	Geddes	Kirkwood 1	Broddle	Coyle	Dennis	Sinclair	Rougier b	Cameron	Crawford r59	Lennon	Dair b	Graham u59	McInally	Humphries	39	
S	17-Feb	Celtic		A	SC 4	0-2	33415	Geddes	Kirkwood	Broddle	Coyle	Dennis	Sinclair	Rougier	Cameron	Crawford r48	Lennon r24	McInally	Dair u24	Graham u48	Fridge		
S	24-Feb	Motherwell		A	L1	0-1	5569	Geddes	McCulloch b	Broddle r86 b	Coyle	Raeside	Sinclair	Rougier	Cameron	Dair	Kirkwood	McInally r80 b	Taylor u80	Wilson u86	Humphries		
S	02-Mar	Partick Thistle		A	L1	3-0	2320	Geddes	McCulloch	Kirkwood 1p	McInally	Raeside	Sinclair	Thomson,SM	Cameron 1	Crawford	Duffield 1	Kirk	Dair	Rougier	Humphries	68, 39, 63	
S	16-Mar	Aberdeen	6	H	L1	2-2	4932	Geddes	McCulloch	Kirkwood	McInally	Raeside	Sinclair b	Thomson,SM	Cameron 1	Duffield r82	Lennon r67	Kirk 1	Crawford u67	Rougier u82	Taylor	35, 10	
S	23-Mar	Kilmarnock		A	L1	0-2	6143	Geddes	McCulloch	Kirkwood	McInally	Raeside	Sinclair b	Thomson,SM	Cameron r79	Duffield	Lennon	Kirk	Crawford u79	Dair	Taylor		
S	30-Mar	Rangers		H	L1	2-4	9300	Geddes	McCulloch	Kirkwood 1p	McInally b	Krivokapic b	Raeside	Thomson,SM	Kirk r76	Duffield 1	Lennon	Rougier r76	Dair u76	Taylor u76	McMillan	68, 29	
S	06-Apr	Falkirk		A	L1	3-2	3766	Geddes b s58	McCulloch	Kirkwood r71	McInally	Krivokapic	Raeside 1	Thomson,SM	Miller	Duffield 1	Lennon	Rougier 1 b	Bonnar u71	Dair	McMillan	69, 79, 25	
S	13-Apr	Hearts		H	L1	1-3	4765	Geddes	McCulloch	Bonnar	Krivokapic	McMillan r54	Buist	Thomson,SM	Miller b	Duffield	Lennon 1p	Rougier	Kirk u54	Thomson,SY	Kirkwood	74	
Tu	16-Apr	Cowdenbeath	N	A	FC 1	2-3	200	Logan x89	Bogie	McPherson r74	Buist	McMillan	Landells	Sellars r70 1	Mauchlen x89	Smart	Kirk	Stein	Dargo u74	McKinlay u70 1	Drummond	53, 75	
S	20-Apr	Hibernian		A	L1	1-1	7671	Thomson,SY	Kirkwood	Bonnar b	Krivokapic b	Dennis	Sinclair b	Thomson,SM	Kirk r70 b	Duffield	Miller 1	Rougier	Lennon u70	Wilson	Raeside	47	
S	27-Apr	Motherwell	7	H	L1	2-0	3685	Thomson,SY	Kirkwood	Bonnar	Krivokapic	Dennis	Sinclair	Thomson,SM 1	Kirk	Duffield 1	McInally r85	Rougier	Lennon u85	Wilson	Raeside	55, 33	
S	04-May	Celtic		A	L1	1-4	37423	Thomson,SY	Kirkwood	Bonnar r76	McInally	Dennis	Sinclair	Lennon	Taylor r68	Duffield 1	Thomson,SM	Rougier r81	Landells u68	Dargo u76	Sellars u81	50	

Manager : Jimmy Nicholl to 8th February. Jimmy Thomson from 9th February.
(1) 1994/5 Final (2) after extra time (3) at Easter Road (4) Papin missed penalty kick
(5) Berry sent off 30 minutes ; Locke booked and sent off 77 minutes (6) Windass booked and sent off 89 minutes (7) McCart sent off 58 minutes
(8) Rovers successfully appealed against the sending off of Mark Humphries, admitting that Shaun Dennis was the guilty party. On 22nd January the disciplinary committee of the SFA took no action against either player. (N) Fixture fulfilled by reserve team, not included in summary statistics ; McMahon sent off 38 minutes ; Kirk replaced Logan in goal in 89 minutes

Substitutes, own goals and goal times

Day	Date	Opponents	Note	Venue	Comp	Res	Att	1	2	3	4	5	6	7	8	9	10	11	Substitutes, own goals and goal times
M	15-Jul	Billingham Town		A	F	3-0	100	Thomson,SY	McCulloch	Bonnar	Krivokapic	Dennis	Browne	Thomson,SM 1	McNally	Dargo r70	Millar 2	Harvey	Kirk u70, Geddes, McCulloch u45, McPherson, Dargo u
Tu	16-Jul	Shildon		A	F	5-0	200	Geddes	McCulloch	McPherson	McNally	Craig	Millar 2	Twaddle	Kirkwood	Dargo 3	Kirk	Harvey	Harvey u45, Millar u64, Geddes, Twaddle, McPherson, Craig; 15, 27, 3, 25, 75
Th	18-Jul	Bishop Auckland		A	F	1-0	250	Thomson,SY 65	McNally	Craig r45	Krivokapic	Dennis	Browne	Thomson,SM	Kirkwood	Dargo 3	Millar r45	Twaddle r	McCulloch u311, Thomson,SM u91, Dargo u, Millar u64, Harmison og 1; 11, 87...
F	19-Jul	Ashington		A	F	3-0	400	Thomson,SY 45	Kirkwood r31	McPherson	McNally	Dennis	Browne	Thomson,SM	McNally	Duffield	Harvey r49	Williams	Geddes u45, Dargo u63, Millar u64, Dargo u; 23, 44, 66
S	27-Jul	Brechin City		A	F	3-0	300	Thomson,SY r45	Kirkwood b	Bonnar	Krivokapic	Dennis	Browne	Rougier r66	McNally	Kirk r63 2	Lennon	Harvey r61	Kirkwood u53, Geddes u65, Dargo u65, Millar u66, Kirk u76; 19, 29, 38, 67
Tu	30-Jul	Ayr United		A	F	4-0	800	Thomson,SY	McCulloch b	Bonnar	Browne	Dennis	Browne	Thomson,SM r651	McNally r53	Rougier r76 3	Kirkwood m74	Harvey	Kirkwood u53, Millar u61, Thomson,SM u61, Stein u76
S	03-Aug	Falkirk		A	F	0-3	1454	Thomson,SY	Bogie r53	McPherson r76	Browne	Dennis	Craig	Thomson,SM	McNally	Dargo r58	Lennon	Harvey	Francis u53, Mauchlen u58, Millar u61, Stein u76, Geddes
S	10-Aug	Rangers		A	L1	0-1	46221	Thomson,SY	Kirkwood	Bonnar	Browne b	Dennis	Craig	Thomson,SM	Rougier	Rougier 2 b	Lennon	Harvey r57	Francis u53, Mauchlen u58, Duffield u65, Dargo u82, Geddes
Tu	13-Aug	Airdrie	1 A	LC 2	2-3	1985	Thomson,SY	Kirkwood	Bonnar r27	Browne b	Dennis	Browne	Thomson,SM r96	McNally	Rougier 2 b	Lennon	Harvey r75	Twaddle u57, Millar u27, Twaddle u96; 13, 71
S	17-Aug	Celtic		A	L1	1-4	47200	Thomson,SY	Kirkwood r54	Bonnar	Browne	Dennis b	Craig	Thomson,SM r54	McNally b	Rougier r68	Lennon	Millar b	Twaddle u54, Duffield u75, Twaddle u54 1, Harvey u68; 67
Th	22-Aug	Cowdenbeath	N1 A	FC SF	1-1	150	Thomson,SY	Francis	McPherson	Landells	Craig	Kirkwood	Byers	Mauchlen	Sellars 1	Dargo	Stein	McInally, Kirk; 33
S	24-Aug	Motherwell	2 H	B	2-2	2000	Geddes u45	McInally	Bonnar	Browne b	Dennis	Browne b	Rougier	Harvey r63	Duffield 1	Lennon m32	Stein	Thomson,SM u63, Thomson,SY u45, Kirk, Craig
W	28-Aug	Coventry City		H	F	0-5	4863	Geddes	Taylor	Millar	Krivokapic	Craig	Johnston	Byers	Mauchlen	Duffield 1	Harvey	Twaddle r81	Thomson,SM,SY u45, Francis u45, Stein u81; McPherson
Th	29-Aug	Dunfermline Athletic	N A	FC F	0-5	250	Geddes	McInally	McPherson	Humphries	Francis	Johnston	Byers	Mauchlen	Dargo	Sellars r45	Stein	Thomson,SM,SY u45
S	07-Sep	Aberdeen		H	L1	1-4	5055	Thomson,SY	McInally b	Bonnar 1	Krivokapic b	Dennis	Browne r45	Thomson,SM r77	Kirkwood r77	Duffield r77	Lennon	Rougier	Millar u45 b, McCulloch u77, Kirk u77 b; 3
S	14-Sep	Hibernian		H	L1	0-1	8671	Geddes	McCulloch	Bonnar r78	Krivokapic b	Dennis	Mitchell	Thomson,SM r83	Kirk	Duffield 1	Lennon	Rougier	Millar u70, Twaddle u78, Harvey u83
S	21-Sep	Dundee United	3 H	L1	3-2	5077	Thomson,SY	Kirk	Bonnar	Krivokapic	Dennis	Mitchell	Kirk r45	Millar	Duffield	Lennon	Rougier	Twaddle u78 1, Harvey u78, McCulloch; 5, 60, 86
S	28-Sep	Dunfermline Athletic		A	L1	1-3	8634	Geddes	Kirk b	Bonnar r77	Krivokapic	Dennis	Mitchell	Twaddle	Millar	Duffield	Lennon r50	Rougier r78	Thomson,SM,SY u50, Harvey u77, McCulloch u77; 47
W	12-Oct	Hearts		H	L1	1-1	6240	Thomson,SY	Kirk	Millar	Krivokapic b	Dennis	Mitchell	Twaddle	Harvey	Thomson,SM r78	Duffield r73	Rougier r78	Twaddle u73, Bonnar u78, Lorimer; 70
S	19-Oct	Kilmarnock		A	L1	0-1	5829	Scott	Taylor	Rougier	Krivokapic r65	Dennis b	Mitchell	Harvey r81	Harvey	Thomson,SM,SY r84	Lennon r65	Rougier 1	Kirk u65, Duffield u65, Bonnar u84; 2
S	26-Oct	Rangers		H	L1	0-1	11200	Scott	Taylor r45	Rougier	Millar	Dennis	Mitchell	Twaddle	Harvey r81	Duffield	Lennon	Rougier	Kirk u45, Thomson,SM,SY u81, Lorimer u81
S	02-Nov	Rangers		A	L1	2-2	9705	Scott	Kirk	Millar	Andersen,V r68	Dennis	Mitchell	Twaddle r62 1	Thomson,SM,SY 1	Rougier	Lennon	Bergerson	Duffield u62, Bonnar u68, Browne; 25, 76
S	16-Nov	Dunfermline Athletic		H	L1	1-2	6762	Thomson,SY	Craig	Millar b	Andersen,V b	Dennis x44	Mitchell	Rougier	Duffield	Thomson,SM	Lennon	Bergerson	Duffield u72 1, Lorimer; 78
S	23-Nov	Dundee United		A	L1	2-1	8028	Thomson,SY b	Kirk 1 x80	Millar	Andersen,V b	Craig	Mitchell	Twaddle b,b&87	Duffield r81	Thomson,SM	Lennon	Bergerson r811 b	McCulloch u81, Bonnar u81; 52, 24
S	30-Nov	Dundee United	3 H	L1	1-0	3749	Thomson,SY	Taylor	Bonnar	Andersen,V b	Craig	Mitchell	Rougier	Duffield r81	Thomson,SM	Lennon 1	Bergerson	McGill u81, Bonnar u81, Harvey; 89
S	07-Dec	Hearts		A	L1	0-0	10719	Thomson,SY	Kirk	Bonnar r77	Andersen,V b	Craig	Mitchell	Twaddle	Duffield r86	Thomson,SM	Lennon	Bergerson r86	Harvey u86, Taylor u86, Lorimer
W	11-Dec	Motherwell		H	L1	1-0	4040	Thomson,SY	Kirk r76	Rougier	Andersen,V	Dennis	Mitchell	Twaddle r70	Duffield	Thomson,SM 1	Lennon 1	Bergerson	Taylor u76, Harvey, Krivokapic; 89
S	21-Dec	Hibernian		A	L1	0-4	4224	Thomson,SY	Kirk	Rougier	Andersen,V	Dennis b	Mitchell b	Twaddle r70	Duffield	Thomson,SM b	Lennon b	Bergerson	Taylor u70, Harvey, Krivokapic
Th	26-Dec	Dundee United		A	L1	0-1	48322	Thomson,SY	Kirk	Rougier	Andersen,V r62	Dennis	Mitchell	Twaddle	Taylor b	Thomson,SM,SY r62	Lorimer r70	Rougier	Duffield u62, McGill u62, Kirkwood
S	28-Dec	Dundee United		H	L1	0-2	5762	Thomson,SY	Kirk	Craig b	Andersen,V r61	Dennis	Mitchell	Twaddle r76	Duffield	Thomson,SM	Lennon b	Rougier	McGill u76 b, Kirkwood, Taylor
W	01-Jan	Dunfermline Athletic		A	L1	0-2	7236	Scott	Kirk b	Craig	Andersen,V r61	Dennis	Mitchell	Taylor r61	Thomson,SM b	McGill r85 b	Lennon	Millar	Rougier u61, Harvey u76, Kirkwood
S	04-Jan	Hearts		H	L1	1-2	6460	Scott	Kirk r41	Millar	Andersen,V	Dennis	Craig	Thomson,SM	Duffield	McGill r76	Lennon 1	Rougier	Harvey u68, Thomson,SM,SY u72, Duffield u87
S	11-Jan	Kilmarnock		H	L1	1-2	5505	Scott	Taylor	Millar	Andersen,V b	Millen	Millen	Twaddle r72 1 b	Andersen,S b	Hallum	Lennon	Rougier	Taylor u41, Duffield u72, Duffield u87
Tu	14-Jan	Kilmarnock		A	L1	1-2	8544	Thomson,SY	Taylor	Millar	Andersen,V b	Millen	Millen b	Twaddle	Andersen,S 1	Hallum	Lennon	Rougier	Bonnar, Duffield; 14
S	18-Jan	Aberdeen		H	L1	2-2	3950	Thomson,SY	Taylor	Millar	Andersen,V	Millen	Millen b	Twaddle r82	Andersen,S r45	Hallum	Lennon 1p	Rougier r68	Kirkwood u68, Lorimer; 16, 85
Tu	21-Jan	Bayern Munich		H	F	1-0	4780	Thomson,SY	Kirkwood 1 b	Millar	Andersen,V	Millen	Millen	Twaddle	Andersen,S 1	Hallum 45	Lennon m39	Rougier 1 b	Bonnar u36, Duffield u45 1, Lorimer u78; 56
M	27-Jan	Airdrie	A	SC 3	4-1	3112	Thomson,SY	Kirkwood	Millar	Andersen,V	Millen	Millen	Twaddle r72	Andersen,S 1	Hallum	Lennon	Rougier	Duffield, Scott, Bonnar; 58, 49, 89, 82
S	01-Feb	Hibernian		A	L1	1-0	9424	Thomson,SY	Kirkwood	Millar b	Andersen,V	Millen	Millen	Twaddle r72	Andersen,S r73	Hallum 88	Lennon 1	Rougier	Duffield u72, McGill u88, Bonnar; 69
Th	06-Feb	Celtic		A	L1	0-2	45233	Thomson,SY	Kirk b	Millar b	Andersen,V	Millen	Millen	Twaddle	Duffield	Hallum 86	Lennon	Rougier	Duffield u73, McGill u86, Kirkwood
S	15-Feb	Brechin City	A	SC 4	2-1	2203	Thomson,SY	Kirk 66 1	Millar	Andersen,V	Millen	Millen	Twaddle	Andersen,S r76 1	Duffield	Lennon	Rougier	Kirkwood u66, Hallum u76, Lorimer; 49, 66
S	18-Feb	Motherwell		A	L1	1-5	3052	Thomson,SY	Taylor r62	Bonnar	Andersen,V	Millen	Millen	Twaddle r84	Duffield 1	Hallum r84	Lennon	Rougier	Lorimer u62, Bonnar u84; 79
Tu	22-Feb	Hearts		A	L1	2-3	10341	Thomson,SY	Kirk r80	Makela 1	Andersen,V	Millen	Millen	Twaddle r76	Duffield	Kirkwood r80	Lennon b	Andersen,S	Rougier u80, Bonnar u80, Andersen,V; 41, 4
W	05-Mar	Kilmarnock	4 H	L1	2-1	3305	Thomson,SY	Kirk r82 b	Makela	Andersen,V b	Millen	Millen	Twaddle	Duffield	Kirkwood 1p	Lennon	Andersen,S	Rougier u68, Andersen,V u82 Harvey; 60, 10
S	08-Mar	Falkirk	A	SC QF	0-2	6692	Thomson,SY	Kirk r66	Mitchell r66	Andersen,V	Craig	Millen x77	Twaddle	Duffield	Kirkwood	Lennon	Andersen,S r68 1	Rougier u66, Harvey u66
S	15-Mar	Dunfermline Athletic	5 H	L1	0-1	5882	Scott	Makela b	Millar b	Mitchell	Craig	Millen	Twaddle	Duffield	Kirkwood r64	Lennon	Harvey	Kirk u64, Rougier u66, Browne; 1
S	22-Mar	Dundee United		H	L1	1-1	8372	Thomson,SY	Makela r77	Millar b	Harvey	Craig	Mitchell	Twaddle b	Duffield 1	Kirkwood	Lennon	Rougier	Kirk u77, Dargo, Andersen,V; 81
S	05-Apr	Celtic		A	L1	1-1	7912	Thomson,SY	Makela	Taylor	Harvey	Craig 1	Mitchell	Dargo r72	Andersen,S	Kirkwood	Lennon	Rougier b	Kirk u72, McCulloch, Stein; 89
S	12-Apr	Motherwell		A	L1	0-5	4691	Thomson,SY	Taylor r51	Millen	Millen	Craig	Mitchell	Harvey r51 b	Duffield	Kirkwood	Lennon	Rougier	Kirk u51, Bonnar u51, Dargo
Tu	15-Apr	Rangers		A	L1	0-6	9745	Thomson,SY	Bonnar	Millen	Millen	Craig 1	Mitchell	Makela r66	Harvey r79	Rougier	Anderson,V r45	Kirk	Dargo u66, Kirkwood u45, Harvey u59, Browne
S	03-May	Aberdeen		H	L1	0-2	10763	Thomson,SY	Makela	Millen	Millen	Craig	Mitchell	Twaddle r79	Duffield	McGill r59	Lennon b	Millar b	Dargo u79, Harvey u59, Stein u79
S	10-May	Hibernian		H	L1	1-1	6274	Thomson,SY	McCulloch	Kirkwood r75 b	Millen	Craig	Mitchell	Twaddle r78	Duffield 1	Kirk 68	Lennon	Millar b	Dargo u68, Harvey u75, Stein u75; 7

Manager : Jimmy Thomson to 27th August. Tommy McLean 3rd September to 10th September. Iain Munro 16th September to 14th April

(1) after extra time

(2) Andy Leigh Testimonial

(3) McIntyre sent off 39 minutes

(4) McGowne booked and sent off 60 minutes

(5) Petrie sent off 77 minutes

(N) Fixture fulfilled by reserve team, not included in summary statistics

(N1) Fixture fulfilled by reserve team, not included in summary statistics. Won 5-4 on penalties

Day	Date	Opponents	Note	Venue	Comp	Res.	Att.	1	2	3	4	5	6	7	8	9	10	11	Substitutes, own goals and goal times				
S	19-Jul	Limavady United	11	A	F	5-0	250	Van de Kamp	McEwan r	Thomson r 1	Kirkwood r	Craig r	Millen r	Lennon r 1	Harvey r	Duffield r 1	Wright r	Cameron r	McCulloch u	Fotheringham u	Millar u	Browne u	Twaddle u
Tu	22-Jul	Dundalk	12	A	F	2-0	300	Van de Kamp	McEwan r71	Thomson r71	Kirkwood r45	Craig r45	Millen	Lennon r58	Harvey r45	Duffield r58 2	Wright r58	Cameron r58	McCulloch u71	Fotheringham u71	Millar u45	Browne u71	Twaddle u58
Th	24-Jul	Cliftonville		A	F	2-1	200	Van de Kamp	McEwan	Fotheringham	Millen	Mitchell	Craig r*	Harvey r**	Millar r***	Duffield r****	Dair,L	Twaddle r*****	Browne u*	Lennon u**	McPherson u***	McGill u**** 1	Stein u*****
S	26-Jul	Stranraer	1	A	F	4-0	200	Van de Kamp	Browne r80	Millar	Kirkwood	Millen r45	Craig	Lennon	Harvey r80 1	Duffield r70 1	Wright r70 1	Cameron	Dair,L u70	Kirk u70 1	Mitchell u45	McCulloch u80	Twaddle u80
S	02-Aug	Stirling Albion		A	L2	1-1	2159	Van de Kamp	McEwan	Thomson	Kirkwood	Craig	Millen b	Lennon	Harvey r83	Duffield 1	Wright r83	Cameron	Twaddle u83	Kirk u83	Mitchell	26	
S	09-Aug	Forfar Athletic		H	LC 2	5-0	2945	Van de Kamp	McEwan	Fotheringham r75	Kirkwood r65	Craig	Millen 1	Lennon	Twaddle	Duffield r65 3	Wright	Cameron 1	Dair,L u65	Kirk u65	Mitchell u75	48, 25, 27, 43, 56	
Tu	12-Aug	Clyde		A	LCC 1	4-2	897	Van de Kamp s80	McEwan	Fotheringham r84 b	Kirkwood b	Craig	Millen	Lennon 1	Twaddle r70	Duffield	Wright 1	Cameron 1	Dair,L u70 1	Mitchell u84	Kirk	65, 13, 18, 74	
S	16-Aug	Airdrie		H	L2	1-1	3413	Van de Kamp	McEwan b	Fotheringham r74	Kirkwood r61	Craig b	Millen	Lennon	Dair,L r61	Duffield	Wright 1	Cameron	Mitchell u61	Millar u61	Kirk u74	78	
Tu	19-Aug	Hearts	2	H	LC 3	1-2	7146	Van de Kamp	McEwan r68	Fotheringham	Kirkwood r68	Craig	Millen	Lennon x75	Millar	Duffield	Wright 1	Cameron	Twaddle u68	Kirk u68	Mitchell	55	
S	23-Aug	Hamilton Academical		A	L2	0-2	1177	Van de Kamp	Mitchell r63	Fotheringham	Kirkwood	Craig	Millen	Twaddle	Millar b	Duffield r63	Wright	Cameron	Dair,L u63	Kirk u63	Browne		
Tu	26-Aug	Stranraer		H	LCC 2	0-1	1972	Van de Kamp	McEwan	Thomson	Kirkwood	Craig	Millen	Lennon	Twaddle r72	Hartley r81	Kirk	Cameron r72	Duffield u72	Dair,L u72	Browne u81		
S	30-Aug	Dundee		A	L2	2-2	4461	Van de Kamp	McEwan	Fotheringham r78	Kirkwood	Mitchell r29	Millen	Hartley	Lennon	Wright	Cameron r45	Thomson,SM	Dair,L u29	Duffield u45	McGill u78	Irvine og 1	84, 79
S	13-Sep	St Mirren		H	L2	2-1	3311	Van de Kamp	McEwan	Thomson	Kirkwood b	Fotheringham	Millen	Dair,L 1	Lennon	Duffield r80	Cameron	Dair,J r70	Wright u70 1	Hartley u80	McCulloch	63, 77	
S	20-Sep	Ayr United		A	L2	0-1	1987	Van de Kamp	McEwan b	Thomson	Kirkwood	Fotheringham	Millen r79	Dair,L	Lennon	Duffield r69	Wright	Dair,J r69	Browne u69	Hartley u69	Cameron u79		
Tu	23-Sep	Dunfermline Athletic	N	A	FC 1	3-0	300	Scott	McCulloch r45	Thomson	Miller	Browne	Fotheringham	Hartley r87	Cameron r87	McGill b	Dargo 2,1p	Stein 1	Byers u45	Smart u87	Venables u87	63p,80,83	
S	27-Sep	Falkirk		H	L2	2-0	3564	Van de Kamp	McEwan 1	Thomson	Millar	Fotheringham	Browne	Hartley r86	Lennon	McGill r63	Dargo r76	Dair,L 1 b	Duffield u63	Kirkwood u76	Dair,J u86	23, 20	
S	04-Oct	Morton		A	L2	3-1	2309	Van de Kamp	McEwan	Kirkwood	Millar	Browne	Fotheringham	Hartley	Lennon b	McGill r81 1	Dargo r81 1	Dair,L r84 1	Duffield u81	Wright u81	Dair,J u84	61, 29, 11	
Tu	14-Oct	East Fife	N	A	FC SF	2-1	200	Scott	McCulloch b	Thomson	Harvey	Hynd	Mitchell	Twaddle	Wright	Duffield 1	Cameron 1	Dair,J	Byers	Venables	Maughan	43,65	
S	18-Oct	Partick Thistle		H	L2	2-0	3417	Van de Kamp	McEwan	Kirkwood b	Millar	Browne	Fotheringham	Hartley 1 b	Lennon 1	Dargo r59	McGill x55	Dair,L r64	Wright u59	Dair,J u64	Duffield	13, 90	
S	25-Oct	Stirling Albion		H	L2	2-0	3280	Van de Kamp	McEwan	Kirkwood	Millar	Browne	Fotheringham b	Hartley 1	Lennon	Dargo r63	Dair,J	Dair,L r75	Thomson,SM u63 b	Wright u75 1	Duffield	38, 84	
Tu	28-Oct	Cowdenbeath	N	H	FC F	6-0	1142	Scott	McCulloch	Thomson r80	Harvey	Mitchell	Cameron 1	Twaddle	McGill r74 1	Duffield 2	Wright r68 1	Stein	Venables u68	Byers u74 1	Hynd 80	80,10,53,85,65,89	
S	01-Nov	Airdrie		A	L2	0-1	1945	Van de Kamp	McEwan	Thomson	Kirkwood b	Browne	Fotheringham	Hartley	Lennon	McGill r86	Wright r78	Millar r72	Dair,L u72	Dair,J u78	Duffield u86		
S	08-Nov	Dundee	3	H	L2	0-1	4763	Van de Kamp	McEwan	Thomson b	Kirkwood b	Browne	Fotheringham b	Hartley b	Lennon	Dargo r72	McGill r72	Twaddle r79	Wright u72	Dair,L u72	Dair,J u79		
S	15-Nov	St Mirren		A	L2	3-2	2476	Van de Kamp	McEwan	Thomson r65	Kirkwood	Browne	Fotheringham	Hartley 1 b	Lennon 1	McGill r69	Dair,L 1	Dair,J r80	Twaddle u65	Dargo u69	Millar u80	76, 79, 44	
S	22-Nov	Falkirk		A	L2	1-0	3162	Van de Kamp	McEwan b	Thomson	Cameron	Browne	Fotheringham b	Hartley r56	Lennon	Dargo r78	Dair,L r87	Dair,J	Twaddle u56	Millar u78	McGill u87	McGowan og 16	
S	29-Nov	Ayr United		H	L2	0-1	3015	Van de Kamp	McEwan	Thomson b	Cameron r63	Browne b	Fotheringham	Hartley	Lennon	Dargo	Dair,L r70 b	Dair,J	McGill u70	Twaddle u63	Millar		
S	06-Dec	Morton		H	L2	0-0	2792	Van de Kamp	McEwan	Thomson	Dair,J r65	Browne	Fotheringham b	Hartley	Lennon	Dargo	McGill r81	Dair,L	Stein u65	Millar u81	McCulloch		
S	13-Dec	Partick Thistle	4	A	L2	3-1	3214	Van de Kamp b	McEwan	Thomson	Millar	Browne 1	Fotheringham	Hartley x80	Lennon	Dargo r79 b	Wright 2	Twaddle r85	Dair,L u79	McCulloch u85	McGill	39, 71. 72	
S	20-Dec	Hamilton Academical		H	L2	3-1	2789	Van de Kamp	McEwan r90	Thomson	Millar b	Browne b	Fotheringham	Dair,L r68	Lennon b	Dargo	Wright 2	Twaddle r64	Stein u64	Dair,J u68	McCulloch u90	McQuade og 1	85, 90, 76
S	27-Dec	Stirling Albion		A	L2	2-3	2087	Van de Kamp	McEwan b	Thomson	Millar	Browne	Fotheringham	Dair,J	Lennon	Dargo r63	Wright 2	Stein r83	Dair,L u63	Twaddle u83		8, 24	
S	03-Jan	Dundee		A	L2	1-1	5241	Van de Kamp	McEwan	Thomson	Kirkwood	Browne	Fotheringham b	Dair,J	Millar	Dargo	Wright b	Stein r82	Twaddle u82	McCulloch	Dair,L	Kelly og 44	
S	10-Jan	St Mirren		H	L2	4-1	3612	Van de Kamp s25	McEwan	Thomson	Kirkwood b	Browne b	Fotheringham r83	Hartley 1	Lennon r75	Dargo r78 3	Wright	Millar	Stein u75	Dair,J u78	Galloway u83	42, 33, 47, 74	
S	24-Jan	Hibernian	5	A	SC 3	2-1	11411	Van de Kamp	McEwan b,b&x84	Thomson	Kirkwood r52	Browne	Fotheringham	Hartley r87	Lennon	Dargo r75	Wright	Millar 2	Galloway u52	Dair,J u75	Stein u87	10, 21	
S	31-Jan	Ayr United		A	L2	0-0	1989	Van de Kamp	McEwan	Thomson b	Kirkwood r20	Browne	Fotheringham b	Hartley	Lennon	Dargo	Wright r70	Millar b	Stein u20	Dair,J u70	Galloway		
Tu	03-Feb	Falkirk	6	H	L2	2-0	4666	Van de Kamp	McEwan	Thomson b	Millar b	Browne	Fotheringham b	Hartley r82 b	Lennon 1p	Dargo 1	Wright r78	Dair,J r70	Galloway u70	Stein u78	Dair,L u82	29, 70	
S	07-Feb	Partick Thistle	7	H	L2	2-0	3675	Van de Kamp s88	McEwan	Thomson	Millar 1	Browne	Fotheringham	Hartley	Lennon m44	Dargo 1	Wright r80	Dair,J	Stein u80	Dair,L	Galloway	68, 59	
S	14-Feb	Falkirk		H	SC 4	1-3	6259	Van de Kamp	McCulloch r55	Thomson 1	Millar	Browne	Fotheringham	Hartley b	Lennon	Dargo r68	Wright	Dair,J r55	Galloway u55	Dair,L u55	Stein u68	84	
S	21-Feb	Morton		A	L2	1-3	2289	Van de Kamp	McEwan	Thomson 1	Millar b	Browne	Galloway r74	Hartley	Lennon	Dargo	McGill r84	Dair,L r84	Wright u74	Stein u74	McCulloch u84	63	
S	07-Mar	Airdrie		H	L2	1-1	2638	Van de Kamp	McEwan	Thomson	Millar b	Andrews b	Browne	Hartley	Lennon	Dargo r85	Fotheringham 1	Stein r73	Dair,L u73	McGill u85	Dair,J	23	
S	14-Mar	Falkirk		A	L2	1-0	3512	Van de Kamp b	McEwan b	Thomson	Millar	Andrews b	Browne	Hartley	Lennon	McGill r89	Walker r75 1p	Fotheringham b	Dair,J u89	Dargo u75	Stein		
Tu	17-Mar	Hamilton Academical	8	A	L2	4-1	711	Van de Kamp	McEwan	Thomson	Millar	Andrews r88	Browne	Hartley 1	Lennon	McGill 2	Walker r82 1p	Fotheringham b	Dair,J u82	Stein u88	Dargo	17, 79, 86, 57	
S	21-Mar	Ayr United		H	L2	0-0	2881	Van de Kamp	McEwan	Thomson	Dair,J	Andrews	Browne	Hartley	Lennon	McGill r60	Walker r82 b	Fotheringham	Stein u60	McCulloch u82	McPherson		
S	28-Mar	Partick Thistle		A	L2	2-1	2457	Van de Kamp	McEwan r28	Thomson	McCulloch	Andrews x50	Browne b	Hartley 2	Lennon	Walker r81	Dair,J r86	Fotheringham b	Stein u28	Dargo u81	Galloway u86 b	28, 65	
S	04-Apr	Morton	9	H	L2	1-2	2401	Van de Kamp	McCulloch	Thomson	Tosh	Browne 1	Fotheringham	Hartley	Lennon	Walker r53	Dair,J r53	Stein	Dargo u53	Blunt u53	Galloway	84	
S	11-Apr	Dundee		H	L2	1-1	6984	Van de Kamp	McEwan	Thomson	McCulloch	Browne	Fotheringham b	Hartley 1	Lennon	Dargo r69	Tosh	Stein r78	Wright u69	Walker u78 b	Blunt	52	
S	18-Apr	St Mirren		A	L2	2-0	2285	Van de Kamp	McEwan	McCulloch b	Tosh	Browne	Fotheringham	Hartley	Lennon	Wright r80 1	Thomson	Stein r60	Dargo u60 1	Millar u80	McGill	30, 89	
S	25-Apr	Stirling Albion		H	L2	0-1	2326	Van de Kamp	McEwan r84	McCulloch	Tosh	Browne	Millar	Hartley	Lennon r62	Wright	Dargo r62	Thomson	Stein u62	Walker u62	McGill u84 b		
S	02-May	Airdrie	10	A	L2	0-1	1173	Van de Kamp	McEwan	McCulloch	Tosh	Andrews	Browne	Hartley b	Thomson r66	Wright b	McPherson r45	Stein r45	Dair,L u45	Dargo u45	Venables u66		
S	09-May	Hamilton Academical		H	L2	2-1	2054	Van de Kamp	McCulloch	McPherson r74	Tosh	Browne	Fotheringham b	Hartley 1	Venables r60	Dair,L r60	Dargo 1 b	Dair,J b	Byers u60	Smart u60	Stein u74	87, 70	

Manager : Jimmy Nicholl

(1) Black missed penalty 89 minutes
(2) Adam sent off 75 minutes
(3) Eddie Annand booked & sent off 60 minutes
(4) Boyle missed penalty 16 minutes
(5) Dods sent off 80 minutes
(6) Craig missed penalty 60 minutes
(7) Kevin Gaughan sent off 44 minutes
(8) Ferguson sent off 57 minutes. Rovers League match with Hamilton Accies at Cliftonhill on 28th February was cancelled the day before. Although work had been completed to repair electrical faults, a safety certificate for various electrical appliances (eg kettle, fax, etc.) had not been issued by the Council. When the game was eventually played, it was staged at Firhill.
(9) Kevin Twaddle sent off 81 minutes
(10) Jimmy Nicholl sent to stand 12 minutes
(11) Additional substitutes : Kirk u 2 ; Dair,L u; Byers u ; Stein u ; Mitchell u Rovers' goal times 17, 24, 40, 78, 80
(N) Fixture fulfilled by reserve team, not included in summary statistics
(12) Additional substitutes : Dair,L u45 ; Kirk u58 ; Byers u58 ; Stein u58. Rovers' goal times 23, 27

1998-99

Day	Date	Opponents	Note	Venue	Comp	Res.	Att.	1	2	3	4	5	6	7	8	9	10	11	Substitutes, own goals and goal times				
S	18-Jul	Deveronvale		A	F	5-0	250	Van de Kamp	McEwan	McPherson	McCulloch	Browne	Bowman	Hartley	Fotheringham	Wright 1	Tosh 1	Dair,J 1	Stein 1	Cameron u 1	Venables	Byers	Wilson
M	20-Jul	Lossiemouth		A	F	6-1	200	Van de Kamp	McEwan	Dair,J 1	McCulloch	Browne	Fotheringham	Hartley 1	Bowman b	Wright 1	Tosh	Cameron 1	McPherson	Stein	Smart	Venables	Hynd u 1
W	22-Jul	Ross County		A	F	1-0	350	Van de Kamp	Dair,J	McPherson r64	McCulloch	Browne	Fotheringham r83	Hartley	Bowman	Wright r82	Tosh r82	Cameron 1	Stein u82	Smart u82	Venables u64	Hynd u83	Byers
S	25-Jul	Fulham		H	F	1-4	1521	Van de Kamp r70	McEwan	Dair,J r80	McCulloch	Browne r45	Fotheringham	Hartley	Bowman	Wright r70	Tosh	Cameron r75 1	McPherson r45	Stein u75	Venables u80	Reid u70	Dair,L u70
Th	30-Jul	Hearts Reserves		H	F	4-2	1422	Van de Kamp	McEwan	Dair,J	McCulloch	Browne	Fotheringham	Hartley r66	Bowman r71 b	Wright r66 1	Tosh 1	Cameron r63 1	McPherson u63	Smart u66	Dair,L u66	Robertson u71 1	8, 44, 35, 83
Tu	04-Aug	Hamilton Academical	1	H	L2	0-2	2328	Van de Kamp	McEwan	McPherson r65	McCulloch r27	Browne	Fotheringham	Hartley	Bowman	Wright	Tosh	Dair,J b	Stein u27	Dair,L u65	Venables		
S	08-Aug	Clydebank	2	H	LC 2	2-0	1560	Van de Kamp	McEwan b, x64	McPherson	Venables	Browne	Fotheringham	Hartley	Bowman	Wright r82 1 b	Tosh b	Dair,J r73 1	Smart u73	Robertson u82	Byers	63, 50	
S	15-Aug	St Mirren		A	L2	1-2	2106	Van de Kamp	Dair,J r76	McPherson r58	Venables	Browne	Fotheringham b	Hartley	Bowman b	Wright	Tosh r76 b	Cameron 1	McCulloch u58	Smart u76	Dair,L u76	7	
W	19-Aug	Hearts	3	A	LC 3	2-4	12238	Van de Kamp b	McEwan r86	Dair,J	Bowman	Browne b	Fotheringham b	Hartley 1	Shields r62 1	Wright	Tosh r114 b	Cameron b	McCulloch u86	Venables u14	Robertson u62	87, 41	
S	22-Aug	Ayr United		H	L2	0-0	2022	Van de Kamp	McEwan	Dair,J	Bowman	Browne	Fotheringham	Hartley	Shields r76	Wright r69	Tosh	Cameron r76	McCulloch u76 b	Smart u76	Robertson u69		
S	29-Aug	Airdrie	4	A	L2	1-0	2800	Van de Kamp	McEwan b	Dair,J	Venables r69	Browne b	Fotheringham b	Hartley 1 b	Bowman	Robertson r67	Tosh b	Cameron	McCulloch u69	Shields u67	Stein	75	
S	05-Sep	Morton		H	L2	0-0	1894	Van de Kamp	McCulloch	Dair,J	Robertson r76	Browne	Fotheringham b	Hartley	Bowman	Shields r61	Tosh	Cameron	Wright u76	Stein u61	McPherson		
S	12-Sep	Falkirk		H	L2	1-1	3073	Van de Kamp	McEwan	Dair,J	Bowman	Browne	Fotheringham b,x75	Hartley	McPherson r68	Dargo r73 1	Tosh r89	Cameron	McCulloch u73	Robertson u89	Shields u68	44	
S	19-Sep	Hibernian		A	L2	1-3	8850	Van de Kamp	McEwan	Dair,J	McCulloch r86	Browne b	Andrews	Hartley	Bowman r45	Dargo b, b&x 79	Tosh	Cameron	Wright u45 1	Shields u86	McPherson	60	
S	26-Sep	Stranraer		A	L2	2-2	622	Van de Kamp	McEwan	Dair,J 1 b	Fotheringham	Browne	Andrews	Hartley 1	Bowman b	Wright r78	Tosh r63	Cameron b	Smart u78	Lennon u63	McCulloch	70, 49	
S	03-Oct	Clydebank		H	L2	0-1	1676	Van de Kamp	McEwan r53	Dair,J	Browne	Andrews	Fotheringham b	Hartley b	Bowman	Dargo	Lennon r65	Cameron r59	McCulloch u65	Wright u53	Tosh u59		
Sn	11-Oct	St Mirren		H	L2	1-0	1973	Van de Kamp	McCulloch	Dair,J	Lennon	Browne	Fotheringham b	Hartley	Byers	Wright 1	Smart r67	Stein r87	Andrews u87	Fotheringham u67	McPherson	77	
S	17-Oct	Hamilton Academical	5	A	L2	2-3	790	Van de Kamp	McCulloch	Dair,J	Bowman	Andrews	Browne b	Hartley b	Tosh 2	Wright	Dargo r78	Lennon r78	McEwan u78	Stein u78	Byers	15, 35	
W	28-Oct	Dunfermline Athletic	N1	H	FC 1	2-2	300	Coyle	Maughan	McInally	Taylor	Ellis	McPherson 1	Fotheringham,G	Byers	Smart 1p	Shields r82	Stein	Stewart u82	Morrison	Clark	11, 41	
S	31-Oct	Morton		A	L2	0-2	1468	Van de Kamp	McCulloch r74	Dair,J	Bowman	Browne b	Andrews	Hartley	Smart r45	Dargo r74	Tosh b	Lennon	Cameron u45	Byers u74	Shields u74		
Tu	03-Nov	Airdrie		H	L2	1-3	1420	Van de Kamp	Bowman	Dair,J	Lennon r66	Browne b	Andrews r66	Hartley	Wright	Dargo r69	Tosh	Cameron 1	McCulloch u66	Byers u66 b	Fotheringham,G u69	25	
S	07-Nov	Hibernian		H	L2	1-3	4926	Van de Kamp	McEwan r62 b	Dair,J	Byers r57	Browne	Fotheringham r76 b	Hartley	Bowman b, b&X51	Dargo 1	Lennon b	Cameron	Wright u62	Stein u76	Andrews u57	87	
S	14-Nov	Falkirk		A	L2	1-1	3611	Van de Kamp	McEwan	Dair,J	Byers r67	Browne b	Fotheringham b	Lennon	Tosh r83	Dargo 1	Cameron	Wright	McCulloch u83	Stein u67	McPherson	24	
S	21-Nov	Stranraer		H	L2	2-0	1949	Van de Kamp	McCulloch	Dair,J	Byers r72	Browne	Fotheringham	Hartley 1p	Lennon	Dargo 1	Britton	Cameron	Tosh u72	Stein	Andrews	20, 90	
S	28-Nov	Clydebank	6	A	L2	1-1	417	Van de Kamp	McCulloch	Dair,J	Tosh	Andrews	Fotheringham	Hartley r65 1p	Lennon	Britton	Byers r65	Cameron	McPherson u65	Stein u65	Ellis	39	
Tu	08-Dec	Hamilton Academical	7	H	L2	1-1	1943	Van de Kamp	McCulloch b	Dair,J	Tosh x47	Andrews r40	Fotheringham b	Hartley m13 b	Lennon b	Dargo b	Britton 1 b	Cameron r20	McEwan u40	Byers u20	Stein	80	
S	12-Dec	Ayr United	8	A	L2	2-0	2245	Van de Kamp	McEwan	Dair,J 1	McCulloch	Browne b,b&x 69	Fotheringham b	Hartley	Lennon	Britton	Bowman	Byers r78	Stein u78	Smart	Ellis	Welsh og 1	45, 12
S	19-Dec	Morton		H	L2	1-3	2731	Van de Kamp	McEwan	Dair,J	Byers r62	McCulloch	Fotheringham	Smart r62	Lennon	Britton	Bowman b	Cameron r82 1	Stein u62	Shields u62	Ellis u82	13	
S	26-Dec	Airdrie		H	L2	2-2	2673	Van de Kamp	McEwan	Dair,J	Bowman x38	Browne	McCulloch b	Byers r45	Lennon	Dargo r81	Shields r73	Cameron 1 b	Stein u73 1	Robertson u81	Ellis u45	11, 75	
S	02-Jan	Hibernian		A	L2	1-5	14703	Van de Kamp	McEwan b	Dair,J	McCulloch	Browne	Robertson r72	Byers r63	Lennon	Dargo 1	Cameron r45	Stein	Shields u45	Ellis u72	Brownlie u63	39	
S	09-Jan	Falkirk		H	L2	2-1	3393	Van de Kamp b	McEwan	Dair,J	McCulloch r62	Andrews	Browne b	Bowman	Lennon r84	Dargo	Holmes 1	Tosh r75	Cameron u75 1	Brownlie u62	Kirkwood u84	89, 65	
S	16-Jan	Stranraer		A	L2	0-2	586	Van de Kamp	McEwan	Dair,J	Bowman	Andrews	Browne	Kirkwood r66	Lennon	Dargo b	Holmes r74	Cameron	McCulloch u74	Brownlie u66	Byers		
S	23-Jan	Clyde		H	SC 3	0-4	2599	Van de Kamp	McEwan	Dair,J	Bowman b	Browne b	Fotheringham	Byers r45	Lennon r58	Dargo	Robertson r45	Cameron	McCulloch u58 x88	Stein u45	Andrews u45		
S	30-Jan	Clydebank	9	H	L2	2-1	1819	McGeown	McEwan r45	Dair,J 1	Bowman	Andrews	Browne	Tosh r83 1	Fotheringham b	Shields r85	Holmes	Cameron	Stein u83	Lennon u45	Fotheringham,G u85	9, 49	
S	06-Feb	St Mirren		A	L2	1-3	1648	McGeown	Browne b	Dair,J r71	Bowman	Andrews 1	Fotheringham b	Tosh b	Holmes	Shields r81	Cameron	Stein r61	Brownlie u61	Ellis u71	Fotheringham,G u81	22	
M	15-Feb	Hearts XI		H	F	0-3	1107	Van de Kamp r45	McCulloch r80	Cormack	Dair,J	Browne	Andrews	Brownlie	Tosh	Shields r65	Cameron r80	Fotheringham	Stein u65	Byers u80	Fotheringham,G u80	Dargo u65	McGeown u45
S	20-Feb	Ayr United		H	L2	2-4	1888	McGeown	Dair,J	Cormack	Bowman r50 b	Browne	Andrews b	Tosh r79	Holmes 2	Dargo r65	Cameron	Fotheringham b	Shields u79	Lennon u50	Brownlie u65	2, 8	
Tu	23-Feb	East Fife		A	FC SF	2-1	423	Van de Kamp	McEwan	Cormack	McCulloch	Taylor b	Lennon	Fotheringham,G r71	Shields 2	Dargo r88	Nicol r77	Brownlie	McInally u71	Clark u88	McLeish u77	72, 80	
S	27-Feb	Airdrie		H	L2	0-1	1913	Van de Kamp	McEwan	Fotheringham	Tosh	Andrews	McCulloch	Brownlie	Lennon r75	Shields r90	Holmes r60	Cameron	Browne u75	Stein u60	Dargo u60		
S	06-Mar	Aberdeen		H	F	3-0	1121	Van de Kamp	McEwan	Fotheringham	Bowman	Browne	Andrews r72	McCulloch r72	Tosh r72	Dargo r57 1	Brownlie	Cameron r57	Stein u57 1	Byers u72	Holmes u57 1	Cormack u72	Taylor u72
S	13-Mar	Morton		A	L2	1-1	1795	Van de Kamp	McEwan	Fotheringham b	McCulloch	Browne	Andrews	Bowman	Tosh r75	Dargo 1p	Brownlie r45	Cameron r81	Stein u81	Lennon u75	Holmes u45	60	
S	20-Mar	Clydebank	10	A	L2	0-0	300	Van de Kamp	McEwan	Fotheringham b	McCulloch	Browne	Andrews	Bowman b	Tosh	Holmes	Cameron	Stein r70	Shields u70	Lennon	Byers		
W	24-Mar	Rangers		H	F	1-0	4815	Van de Kamp	McCulloch	Ellis r70	Tosh 1	Browne	Fotheringham	Fotheringham,G r66	Lennon	Shields,P r66	Holmes r75	Stein	Bowman u66	Byers u75	Kirkwood u70	Cameron u66	Coyle
S	03-Apr	Stranraer		H	L2	3-2	1883	Van de Kamp	Tosh	Fotheringham 1	Browne b	Andrews	Cameron r75	McCulloch	Lennon	Dargo 1	Holmes	Stein r29	McEwan u75	McQuade u29 1	Byers	19, 90, 37	
Tu	06-Apr	Burntisland Shipyard	N	H	FC F	5-0	331	Coyle	Maughan	McInally	Kirkwood	Ellis	Byers	Fotheringham,G r75	Smart r70	Brownlie	McQuade	McLeish r70	Craig u75	Nicol u70	Stewart u70		
S	10-Apr	Hibernian	11	H	L2	1-3	5740	Van de Kamp	McEwan	Fotheringham	Tosh	Browne	Andrews	McCulloch r61	Lennon r83	Dargo	Holmes 1	Cameron r61	Ellis u61	McLeish u83	McQuade u61	29	
S	17-Apr	Falkirk		A	L2	0-1	2532	Van de Kamp	McEwan b	Ellis r85	Kirkwood r80	Browne	Fotheringham b	McCulloch	Lennon	Dargo	Holmes	McQuade r68	Byers u68	Andrews u85	Brownlie u80		
S	24-Apr	Hamilton Academical	12	A	L2	2-1	1398	Van de Kamp	McEwan	Ellis	Kirkwood	Browne b	Fotheringham	McCulloch	Lennon r49	Dargo r89 1	Holmes 1	McQuade r68	Stein u49	Byers u73	Andrews u89	31, 89	
S	01-May	St Mirren		H	L2	1-1	2396	Van de Kamp	Maughan r59	Ellis	Kirkwood	Browne	McCulloch	Nicol r80	McLeish	Dargo r53	Holmes 1	Stein	Brownlie u80	McQuade u53	Andrews u59	26	
S	08-May	Ayr United		A	L2	0-1	1886	Van de Kamp	McEwan r60	Ellis	Kirkwood	Andrews	McCulloch	Fotheringham,G	Byers	McQuade r60	Holmes r69	McInally	Stein u60	Clark u60	Nicol u69		

Manager : Jimmy Nicholl

(1) Hamilton goalkeeper replaced after half time
(2) Clydebank goalkeeper replaced after 18 minutes
(3) after extra time
(4) McGrillen missed penalty 89 minutes
(5) at Firhill
(6) at Boghead
(7) Nicholl sent to stand 61 minutes
(8) Lyons sent off 48 minutes
(9) Brannigan sent off 70 minutes
(10) Anthony missed penalty 4 minutes ; Wishart booked & sent off 43 minutes
(11) McGinlay sent off 25 minutes
(12) at Firhill ; Darren Henderson sent off 56 minutes
(N) Fixture fulfilled by reserve team, not included in summary statistics
(N1) won 3-1 on penalties, fixture fulfilled by reserve team not included in summary statistics

Day	Date	Opponents	Note	Venue	Comp	Res	Att	1	2	3	4	5	6	7	8	9	10	11	Substitutes, own goals and goal times
S	17-Jul	Albion Rovers		A	F	4-0	319	Van de Kamp s80	Hamilton r55	McCulloch r45	Andrews	Gaughan r45	Black r60	Tosh,S 2	Agnew	Dargo r73	Shields,P 1	Stein r45	McEwan u55, Ellis u45, McKenzie u60, McInally u45
M	19-Jul	Cardiff City		H	F	2-0	900	Van de Kamp	Hamilton	McCulloch	Andrews	Gaughan	Black r58	Tosh,P r57	Tosh,S r78	Dargo r73	Burns 2	Stein r77	Agnew u78, Shields,P u73, Kirkwood u77, Browne
W	21-Jul	Sheffield United		H	F	1-0	1248	Van de Kamp	Hamilton	McCulloch	Andrews	Gaughan	Black r58	Tosh,P r72	Tosh,S r82	Dargo 1p	Burns r54	Stein r63	Agnew u58, Shields,P u72, Kirkwood u82, Hetherston u63
S	24-Jul	Rochdale		H	F	0-2	921	Van de Kamp	Hamilton	McCulloch	Andrews r17	Gaughan	Black r49	McEwan r52	Tosh,S	Dargo	Burns	Stein r52	Agnew u49, McEwan u52, Hetherston u52, Browne
S	31-Jul	Stranraer	1	A	LC 1	1-0	625	Van de Kamp	Hamilton	McCulloch	Andrews r17	Gaughan	Black	Agnew	McEwan	Tosh,P r63 b	Burns	Stein	Shields,P u62 r70, Browne u17, Kirkwood u70, Shields,P
S	07-Aug	Livingston		A	L2	1-1	4128	Van de Kamp	McEwan	McCulloch	Andrews	Gaughan	Black r70	McEwan r67	Agnew	Tosh,P r85 1	Burns	Stein	Agnew u70, Shields,P u67, Hetherston u85, 55
Tu	10-Aug	Ayr United		A	LCC 1	1-0	1881	Van de Kamp	Hamilton	Ellis	Andrews	Browne	Black r70	Kirkwood	Agnew	Shields,P r85	Clark r89 1	Hetherston b	McCulloch u89, Shields,D u85, McInally, 44
S	14-Aug	St Mirren		H	L2	0-6	2787	Van de Kamp	McEwan	McCulloch	Andrews	Gaughan b	Black r45	Tosh,S	Tosh,S	Tosh,P r45	Burns	Stein r45	McEwan u45, Kirkwood u45, Clark u45
W	17-Aug	Motherwell	2	H	LC 2	2-2	2392	McConidchie	McEwan r61	Ellis	Andrews	Browne b	Black r71 b	Tosh,P b	Tosh,S r60	Shields,P r45	Burns 1 b	Stein r45	Agnew u60, Dargo u60 1, Hamilton u71, 75, 88
S	21-Aug	Clydebank	3	A	L2	1-1	232	Coyle s5	McCulloch r73	Kirkwood	Andrews	Browne	Black r71 b	Hamilton	Agnew r72	Dargo r60	Burns 1 b	Stein r67	McCulloch u61, Black u72, Clark u67, 7
Tu	24-Aug	Stranraer		A	LCC 2	2-1	422	Coyle	McEwan	Ellis	Andrews 1	Browne	Black r60	Tosh,P	Agnew	Dargo 1	Clark	Hetherston r70 b	Hamilton u73, Tosh,S u60 b, Stein u70, 32, 88
S	28-Aug	Airdrie	4	A	L2	4-1	1653	Coyle	McEwan	Kirkwood	Andrews 1	Browne	Black r60	Agathe r88 3	Tosh,S b	Dargo 1	Clark	Stein r70	Hamilton u85, Agnew u76, Clark u88, 3, 37, 65, 72
S	04-Sep	Ayr United		H	L2	5-1	2368	Coyle	McEwan	Kirkwood	Andrews	Browne	Black r85 1 b	Agathe r87 1	Tosh,S r82	Dargo 2	Burns r76 b	Stein	Tosh,P u82, Clark u87 1, Hamilton, 64, 7, 63, 61, 89
S	11-Sep	Morton	5	A	L2	0-2	970	Van de Kamp	McEwan b	Kirkwood	Andrews	Browne b	Black	Agathe	Tosh,S r82	Dargo r77	Burns 1	Stein r64	Hetherston u64, Clark u86
Tu	14-Sep	Livingston		A	LCC QF	1-3	2233	Van de Kamp	McEwan	Kirkwood	Andrews	Browne b	Black r86 b	Tosh,P r61	Tosh,S	Dargo r77	Burns b	Stein r64	Shields,P u85, Hetherston u64, Clark u86
S	18-Sep	Dunfermline Athletic		H	L2	2-2	6087	Van de Kamp	McEwan r15	Ellis	Andrews	Browne	Hamilton	Agathe	Berthe r45	Dargo 2	Burns	Stein	Agathe u61, Tosh,S u56 b, Hamilton u66, McManus og 81
S	25-Sep	Inverness Caledonian Thistle		A	L2	2-0	2961	Van de Kamp	McEwan	Ellis	Andrews	Browne	Black	Agathe 1	Tosh,S	Dargo 2	Burns	Stein 1	Shields,P, Hamilton, 57, 80
S	02-Oct	St Mirren		H	L2	2-1	3182	Van de Kamp	McEwan	Ellis	Andrews 1	Browne	Black r78	Agathe 1	Tosh,S	Dargo r45 b	Burns	Stein 1	Tosh,P u78, Hetherston, 8, 24
S	16-Oct	Livingston		A	L2	2-3	3850	Coyle	Waldie	Preget	Andrews	Browne	Black 1p	Agathe r75 b	Tosh,S b,b&X88	Hamilton b,b&X44	Burns 1 b	Stein b	Shields,P u83, Craig u15 r83, 15, 59
S	23-Oct	Livingston	6	H	L2	3-1	2949	Van de Kamp	McEwan	Preget	Andrews	Browne 1 b	Black 1p	Agathe	Tosh,P b	Dargo r34	Burns	Stein 1	Shields,P u34 1, McCulloch, 44, 80
S	30-Oct	Morton		H	L2	3-1	2664	Van de Kamp	McEwan	Hamilton	Andrews	Browne b	Black	Agathe 1	Tosh,S b	Shields,P r45	Burns 1 b	Stein 1	McCulloch u82, Clark u45, 22, 34, 75
S	06-Nov	Dunfermline Athletic		A	L2	1-1	6953	Van de Kamp	McEwan b	Hamilton	Andrews	Browne b	Black	Agathe	Tosh,S	Clark r73	Burns	Stein 1	Tosh,P u73, Hetherston, 72, 77, 83
W	10-Nov	Burntisland Shipyard	N	H	FC sf	2-1	200	Coyle	McEwan b	Ellis r75	Webster	Penman	Nicol	Fotheringham,K r75	McKenzie r75	Shields,D 2	Stewart	McInally	Hampshire u75, Rushford u75, 81
S	14-Nov	Ayr United		A	L2	1-0	1769	Van de Kamp b	McEwan	Hamilton b	Andrews	Browne	Black	Agathe b	Tosh,P	Clark r89	Burns b	Stein r62	McCulloch u89, Kirkwood, 30, 58
Sn	20-Nov	Airdrie		A	L2	1-1	2359	Van de Kamp	McEwan	Hamilton	Andrews	Browne	Black b	Agathe	Tosh,P r61	Clark r85	Burns	Stein	Clark u85, McCulloch u62 1, Kirkwood, 84
S	27-Nov	Falkirk		A	L2	1-2	2611	Van de Kamp	McEwan b	Hamilton r58	Andrews	Browne r84 b	Black	Agathe 1	Tosh,S	Roberts r85	Burns	Stein	Clark u84, Hetherston u61 1, McCulloch, 64
S	04-Dec	Inverness Caledonian Thistle		H	L2	4-2	1971	Van de Kamp	McEwan b	Hamilton	Andrews	Browne 1	Black r88	Agathe	Tosh,S	Roberts r86 1	Burns 2	Hetherston r72	McCulloch u88, Stein u58, Begue u86, 82
M	27-Dec	Morton		A	L2	0-1	1056	Van de Kamp	McEwan b	Opinel	Andrews	Browne	Black	Hamilton	Tosh,S r61	Dargo b	Burns	Stein	Clark u61, McKenzie, 73, 3, 38, 39
M	03-Jan	Dunfermline Athletic	7	H	L2	3-0	7463	Van de Kamp	McEwan	Opinel r73 b	Andrews b	Browne 1	Black	Agathe	McKenzie r75	Dargo b	Burns 1	Stein r86	McCulloch u73, Tosh,P, 21, 89, 1
S	08-Jan	Airdrie		H	L2	2-0	2583	Van de Kamp	McEwan	Opinel	Andrews b	Browne	Black	Agathe r75	Tosh,P	Dargo r86 1p	Burns 1	Stein r86	McCulloch u75, Shields,P u86, Clark u86, 47, 18
S	15-Jan	Airdrie		A	L2	2-0	1935	Van de Kamp b	McEwan	Opinel b	Andrews	Browne	Black	Agathe r88	Tosh,P	Dargo b, b&X77	Burns r86	Stein r81 1	McCulloch u81, Shields,P u81, Shields,P, 50, 66
Tu	18-Jan	Clydebank		H	L2	1-0	2754	Van de Kamp	McEwan	Opinel r77	Andrews	Browne b	Black b	Agathe	Tosh,S 1	Clark r55	Burns b	Stein r73	Shields,P u55, McCulloch u77, McCulloch, 90
S	22-Jan	Inverness Caledonian Thistle		A	L2	1-0	2302	Van de Kamp b	McEwan	Opinel b	Andrews	Browne b	Black b	Agathe b	Tosh,S	Dargo 1	Burns	Stein r73	Javary u73 b, Clark, 44
S	29-Jan	Clyde		A	SC 3	1-3	1831	Van de Kamp	McEwan	Opinel b	Andrews b	Browne	Black	Agathe b	Tosh,S b,b&X45	Dargo 1	Burns	Stein r85	Hetherston u80 b, Clark, 35
S	05-Feb	Falkirk	8	H	L2	0-1	4191	Van de Kamp b	McEwan	McCulloch	Andrews	Browne r70	Javary r80 b	Agathe b	Tosh,S b,b&X45	Dargo b	Burns	Stein	Hetherston u80 b, Clark u70, Opinel
S	19-Feb	Dundee		H	F	1-0	516	Van de Kamp	Maughan	McCulloch r79	Hamilton	Browne	Nicol r60	Agathe r82 1	Shields,P r52	Dargo	Burns r78	Hetherston	Stein u60, Ellis u79, Cameron u52
S	26-Feb	St Mirren		H	L2	1-2	4662	Van de Kamp	McCulloch b	Opinel r77 b	Gaughan	Browne	Javary b,b&X80	Agathe	Tosh,P 1	Dargo b	Burns r88 b	Stein r72	Hamilton u77, Shields,P u88, 85
S	04-Mar	Morton	9	H	L2	3-0	2026	Van de Kamp	McCulloch b	Opinel r71	Gaughan	Browne	Tosh,S 1	Agathe r66	Tosh,P r83 1	Dargo	Burns 1	Stein 1	McEwan u71, Hetherston u72, Owusu u66, 84, 62, 44
Tu	07-Mar	Clydebank	3	A	L2	1-2	265	Van de Kamp	McCulloch	Opinel b	Gaughan r73	Browne	Javary b	Tosh,P	Tosh,P 1	Dargo r60 b	Burns	Stein r50	McEwan u71, Hetherston u83, Owusu v50, 25
S	11-Mar	Livingston		A	L2	0-0	3160	Van de Kamp	McEwan	Opinel r45 b	Andrews	Black	Javary b	Agathe	Tosh,P r87	Owusu	Tosh,S	Stein r87	Owusu u50, McEwan u45, McEwan u87
S	18-Mar	Dunfermline Athletic	7	H	L2	2-0	6694	Van de Kamp	Hamilton 1	Opinel	Andrews	Browne 1	Black	Agathe	Owusu r76	Dargo 1	Burns b	Stein	Tosh,S u76, Hetherston u87, Gaughan, 77, 78
S	25-Mar	Airdrie		H	L2	2-0	2046	Van de Kamp	McEwan	Opinel	McCulloch	Browne 1	Javary b	Agathe r81 b	Owusu 1 b	Dargo 1	Burns	Stein	Tosh,S u88, Tosh,P u81, Gaughan, 25, 10
S	01-Apr	Ayr United		A	L2	1-0	1841	Van de Kamp	McEwan	Opinel	McCulloch	Browne	Javary r80 b	Agathe r12	Owusu 1 b	Dargo 1	Tosh,S	Stein r58	Tosh,S u74, Gaughan u88, Tosh,P u58, 26
S	08-Apr	Inverness Caledonian Thistle		H	L2	2-0	2538	Van de Kamp	McCulloch u53	Opinel r88	Gaughan	Maughan	Kirkwood r58	Agathe	Owusu r67	Dargo 1	Burns	Stein	Gaughan u88, McEwan u53, Tosh,P u67, 60, 78
S	15-Apr	Falkirk		A	L2	0-1	4686	Van de Kamp	McEwan	Opinel	Fenwick	Browne r75	Javary	Agathe	Owusu	Dargo	Burns b	Stein r55	Tosh,S u12 1, Tosh,S u55, McEwan u53
S	22-Apr	Livingston		H	L2	1-3	2129	Van de Kamp	McEwan	Opinel	Andrews	Browne	Fenwick	Agathe r87	Owusu 1	Dargo b	Burns	Stein	Tosh,S u55, Tosh,P u75 x88, McCulloch u87, 23
S	29-Apr	St Mirren		A	L2	0-3	8386	Van de Kamp	McEwan b	Opinel b, b&X90	Andrews	Browne	Javary r60 b	Tosh,S	Owusu	Dargo r60 b	Burns	Stein 1	McCulloch u87, Tosh,S u57, Fenwick
M	01-May	Cowdenbeath	N	H	FC F	2-1	150	Coyle	Hamilton 1	Ellis r82	Gaughan	Maughan	Kirkwood r58	Fotheringham,K r58	Nicol 1	Tosh,P	Clark	Stein	Stein u60, Craig u58, Shields u58, 39, 75
S	06-May	Clydebank		H	L2	0-0	1510	Van de Kamp	McEwan	McCulloch	Gaughan	Browne	Nicol	Agathe r45	Tosh,P	Dargo r45	Burns	Stein r68	Hampshire u82, Shields,D u45, Clark u45, Craig u68

Manager : John McVeigh to 1st December. Peter Hetherston from 1st December.

(1) after extra time

(2) after extra time, lost 5-4 on penalties

(3) at Cappielow

(4) Evans booked & sent off 88 minutes

(5) Kenny Black booked in 3 seconds for a foul on Keith Wright

(6) McCaldon sent off 34 minutes

(7) Coyle sent off 32 minutes

(8) Peter Hetherston sent to stand at half time

(9) Derek Anderson sent off

(10) Reynolds sent off 69 minutes

(N) Fixture fulfilled by reserve team, not included in summary statistics

Day	Date	Opponents	Note	Venue	Comp	Res	Att.	1	2	3	4	5	6	7	8	9	10	11	Substitutes, own goals and goal times
M	17-Jul	Dundee		H	F	1-2	1405	Van de Kamp	McCulloch	Opinel r54	Gaughan	Browne	Javary r32 b	Clark r45	Tosh,S r60	Tosh,P r45	Burns 1	Stein	Hamilton u54, Nicol u32, Creaney u45, Coyle
Th	20-Jul	East Stirling	1	A	F	3-0	100	Coyle	McEwan	McNally	Hamilton	Ellis	Black r60	Shields,D	Tosh,P r76	Clark r45 1	Creaney 2p	Hampshire	Rushford u60, Niven u76, Craig u45, 20, 6, 15
	22-Jul	Blackpool		A	F	0-2	1232	Van de Kamp	McCulloch	Opinel r70	Gaughan r60	Browne	Black r60	McEwan	Nicol r45	Clark r65	Creaney 45	Stein	Tosh,P u45, Hamilton u60, Hampshire u65, McEwan u45, McNally u70
W	26-Jul	Walsall		A	F	1-3	895	Van de Kamp	McEwan	McCulloch r70	Gaughan	Browne r45	Miller,M	Kiriakov r	Tosh,S	Clark 65	Creaney 45	Creaney r59	Clark u20, Stein u, Hamilton u59, Ellis, McInally u70
S	29-Jul	Rochdale		H	F	4-1	1002	Van de Kamp	McCulloch	Opinel r60	Gaughan	Browne	Miller,M 1	McEwan r75	Tosh,S	Clark 60	Tosh,P 20	Stein r71	Hamilton u75, Hetherston u86, Creaney u60, Mballa u60 2, Ellis
S	05-Aug	Alloa Athletic		H	L2	1-2	2123	Van de Kamp	McCulloch	Opinel b,b&X 58	Gaughan	Browne	Javary r75	McEwan	Tosh,S	Clark 45	Burns	Stein	Mballa u45 1, Andrews u75, Coyle, Tosh,P, Mballa u60 2
	08-Aug	East Fife		A	LC 1	2-1	1429	Van de Kamp	McCulloch	Ellis	Andrews	Browne	Black	McEwan	Tosh,S	Mballa r88	Burns 1 b	Stein	Clark u73, Shields,D u88, Coyle, McEwan, Tosh,P
Tu	12-Aug	Airdrie		A	L2	1-1	3011	Van de Kamp	McCulloch b	Ellis r68	Gaughan b	Browne	Black r60	Tosh,P r73 1 b	Tosh,S	Clark	Burns 1 b	Stein	Clark u68, Creaney u57, Gaughan, Coyle, McEwan
	15-Aug	Morton		H	LCC 1	0-4	1160	Van de Kamp	McCulloch	Ellis r73	Gaughan	Browne	Black r60	McEwan	Tosh,S	Clark	Burns b	Creaney r60	Stein u73, Hetherston u60, Mballa u60, McEwan, Coyle
Tu	22-Aug	Arbroath		H	LC 2	2-1	1354	Van de Kamp	McCulloch	Opinel b, b&X61	Andrews r38 b	Browne	Black	Tosh,S r55 b	McKinnon b	Tosh,P r83	Burns 2,1p	Stein	Gaughan u38, Clark u55, Creaney u83, Coyle
S	26-Aug	Inverness Caledonian Thistle		H	L2	4-1	1615	Van de Kamp	McCulloch	Opinel	Gaughan	Browne	Black r75	Tosh,S	McKinnon r86 1	Tosh,P r66 1	Burns 1 b	Stein 1	Clark u75, Creaney u66 1, Mballa u86, Coyle
	02-Sep	Ross County		A	L2	4-1	1759	Van de Kamp	McCulloch	Opinel b	Dennis	Browne	Black	Tosh,S	McKinnon r80	Tosh,P r69 1 b	Burns 1 b	Stein 1	Clark u89, Creaney u80, Mballa u69 1, Ellis
Tu	05-Sep	Celtic		A	LC 3	0-4	32307	Van de Kamp	McCulloch	Opinel b	Andrews	Browne b	Black r89 b	Tosh,S	McKinnon x24	Tosh,P r62	Burns b,b&X47	Stein r83	Clark u77, Creaney u83, Mballa u62, Ellis
S	09-Sep	Falkirk		A	L2	1-2	2762	Van de Kamp	McCulloch b	Dennis	Andrews 1	Browne r67	Black b	Tosh,S	Opinel r85	Tosh,P r56	Burns b	Opinel	Clark u56 b, Stein u67, Mballa u67, Creaney
	16-Sep	Livingston		H	L2	4-0	4010	Van de Kamp	McCulloch	Dennis	Andrews 2	Browne	Black	Tosh,S b	Opinel	Tosh,P r711 1 b	Burns 83 1	Stein	Clark u83, Creaney u71, Ellis u83, Creaney
	23-Sep	Morton		A	L2	0-1	2078	Van de Kamp	McCulloch	Dennis	Andrews	Browne	Black	Tosh,S	Ellis b	Tosh,P r74	Burns	Stein r67	Clark u74, Hetherston u84, Hetherston u67, Ellis
	30-Sep	Clyde		A	L2	0-0	1153	Van de Kamp	McCulloch	Dennis b	Hamilton	Browne	Black	Ellis b	Ellis b	Tosh,P r43	Clark	Stein b	Nicol u12, Shields,D d43, Hampshire, Creaney
S	07-Oct	Ayr United		H	L2	1-3	1858	Van de Kamp	McCulloch	Dennis	Hamilton r55	Browne	Black	Nicol	Ellis	Creaney r55	Clark	Stein r79	Hetherston u79, Shields,D d55, Mballa u55 1, Hampshire
	14-Oct	Alloa Athletic		A	L2	1-0	987	Van de Kamp	McCulloch	Dennis	Hamilton	Browne	Black	Hetherston r73	Ellis b	Clark r84	Clark	Stein	Nicol u73 b, Shields,D d84, Hampshire, Creaney
	21-Oct	Airdrie		H	L2	1-1	1930	Van de Kamp	McCulloch	Dennis	Hamilton r77	Browne	Black b	Hetherston r77	Ellis	Clark	Shields,D 1	Stein 1	Creaney u77, McInally, Hampshire, Nicol
	28-Oct	Inverness Caledonian Thistle	2	A	L2	2-1	1723	Van de Kamp	McCulloch	Dennis	Hamilton r55	Browne	Black r85	Hetherston r82	Ellis	Clark r76	Clark	Stein 1	Nicol u82, Hampshire u85, Shields,D d76, Coyle
S	04-Nov	Falkirk		H	L2	0-2	3120	Van de Kamp	McCulloch	Dennis	Hamilton	Browne	Black b,b&X78	Hetherston	Ellis r75	Clark r79	Clark	Stein	Tosh,P u55 b, Nicol u79, Hampshire u75, Coyle
	11-Nov	Morton		A	L2	2-1	650	Van de Kamp	McCulloch	Dennis b	Hamilton	Browne	Nicol 1	Hetherston b	Ellis r76 b	Mballa	Bayne	Stein b	Opinel u76 b, x90, Tosh,P u80, Hampshire, Coyle
	25-Nov	Ayr United		A	L2	2-4	2212	Van de Kamp	McCulloch	Dennis	Hamilton r57 b	Browne	Nicol r57	Hetherston r72	Ellis 1	Mballa r80 1	Bayne	Stein b	Tosh,P u57, Agnew u57, Black u72, Coyle
	02-Dec	Clyde		H	L2	1-2	1810	Van de Kamp	McCulloch	Ellis r79	Dempsie	Browne	Black	Clark r63	Ellis	Mballa 1	Bayne	Stein b	Tosh,P u63, Shields,D u79, Nicol, Coyle
Tu	05-Dec	Livingston		H	L2	1-2	1626	Van de Kamp	McCulloch	Ellis	Dempsie r45	Browne b	Black b	Hamilton	Nicol b	Mballa r72	Bayne r58	Stein 1	Shields,D u45 b, Mballa u72, Hampshire, Coyle
	09-Dec	Ross County		A	L2	0-0	2578	Van de Kamp	McCulloch	Hampshire	Ellis	Browne	Black	Hamilton	Hetherston	Tosh r58 b	Bayne b	Stein	Clark u58, Mballa u58, Shields,D, Nicol
	16-Dec	Alloa Athletic		A	L2	2-1	1267	Van de Kamp	McCulloch	Hampshire	Ellis b	Browne	Black	Hamilton r70	Hetherston	Mballa r77 1	Bayne b	Stein	Clark u77, Tosh,P u70 1 b, Shields,D, Coyle
	06-Jan	Morton		H	L2	0-2	3214	Van de Kamp	McCulloch b	Hampshire	Ellis r45	Browne	Nicol	Hamilton	Hetherston	Mballa r45	Bayne	Stein	Clark u45 b, Tosh,P u45, Niven, Coyle
S	13-Jan	Clyde		A	L2	0-0	1721	Van de Kamp	Hamilton	Ellis b	McCulloch	Browne	Hampshire r81	Tosh,P	Nicol	Clark	Bayne	Stein	Hetherston u81, Niven, Maughan, Coyle
Tu	23-Jan	Dunfermline Athletic		H	F	1-3	1304	Coyle	McCulloch	Ellis	Tosh,P 1 b	Browne	Black r85	Nicol	Hampshire	Clark b	Bayne r73	Stein	Hetherston u85, Mballa u73, Hamilton, Van de Kamp
	27-Jan	Stirling Albion		A	SC 3	0-2	1075	Coyle	McCulloch	Hampshire	Ellis r66	Browne	Hampshire	Tosh,P r45	Nicol r78	Clark 45	Clark	Stein	Bayne u45, Hamilton u45, Niven u78, Van de Kamp
	03-Feb	Ross County		H	L2	0-4	1402	Monin	McCulloch b	Hampshire	Inglis	Browne	Black	Clark	Nicol	Bayne r66	Bayne r66	Stein	McInally u24, Hamilton u66, Niven, Kane
	10-Feb	Airdrie		A	L2	0-3	1380	Monin	Hamilton	Hampshire	Inglis r17	Dennis	Black r61	Hetherston	Nicol	Mballa r24	Clark	Stein r76	McInally u76, Niven u61, Ellis, Kane
	17-Feb	Ayr United		A	L2	1-4	1753	Coyle	Kelly	Ellis r26	Ellis	Inglis 62	Black r80	Black r75	Blackadder b	Jones	Clark 65	Stein	Ellis u17, Mballa u65, Bayne, Kane
Tu	20-Feb	Cowdenbeath	N1	H	FC SF	1-1	1217	Coyle	Hamilton	Hampshire	Maughan	Ross	Niven	Cauley r80	Blackadder b	Scarborough	Clark	Cunningham r76 1	Clark u57, Hetherston u75, Hamilton, Kane
S	10-Mar	Inverness Caledonian Thistle		H	L2	1-1	200	Monin s89	Kelly	Hampshire	Inglis	Browne r56	Dennis	Nicol	Nanou r68	Mballa r68	Jones 1	Stein	Wheelwright u80, McKenzie, 44, Coyle
	17-Mar	Morton		A	L2	1-1	1342	Monin	Kelly	Hampshire b	Dennis	Browne r45	Ellis	Nicol r63	Nanou	Mballa r45	Jones	Stein	Tosh,P u61, Ellis u56, Clark, Coyle
F	31-Mar	Inverness Caledonian Thistle	3	H	L2	1-1	908	Monin	Kelly r68	Hampshire b,b&X66	Inglis r34	Inglis	Black r80	Nicol	Nanou b	Jones r54	Jones 2	Stein r75	Clark u45, Tosh,P u45 1, Black u68, Coyle
S	03-Apr	Livingston		A	L2	0-2	1299	Monin	Alfonso	Ellis r26	Dennis b	Browne	Black	Nicol r80	Capin b	Smith r80	Jones	Stein r86 3	Clark u54, Hamilton u34, Black u63, Black
	07-Apr	Ayr United		H	L2	2-0	1794	Monin	Alfonso	Hampshire	Dennis	Browne	Black	Nicol r80	Capin b,b&X89	Jones 2	Jones r64	Stein	Tosh,P u80, Hamilton u26, Mballa u68, Mballa
Tu	10-Apr	Falkirk		A	L2	0-0	1586	Monin s89	Alfonso r68	Hampshire	Dennis	Browne	Black b	Hamilton	Smith b	Jones r80	Tosh,P	Tosh,P r64	Tosh,P u62, Mballa u80, Nanou u80, Hamilton
	14-Apr	Clyde		H	L2	0-2	2026	Monin	Inglis 62	Ellis 89	Dennis	Browne	Black b	Nicol r80	Smith b	Smith	Tosh,P	Stein r88	Stein u64, Ellis u68, Nanou u80, Nanou
	21-Apr	Alloa Athletic	4	A	L2	1-1	1634	Monin	Inglis b	Ellis 89	Dennis	Browne	Black r80	Kelly	Capin	Smith r80 b	Tosh,P	Stein	Mballa u88, Ellis u68, Mballa u64 b, Nanou
	28-Apr	Airdrie		H	L2	2-1	1817	Monin	Inglis	Ellis	Dennis	Browne	Black b	Alfonso	Capin	Smith r80 b	Tosh,P m53	Stein r75	Mballa u62, Nanou, Nanou u80, Ellis
W	02-May	Dunfermline Athletic		A	FC F	5-0	1953	Coyle	McCulloch	Ellis	Hamilton	Browne r80	Black r80	Nanou	Niven	Mballa b	Tosh,P 2	Hampshire	Hetherston u75, Mballa u80 b, Alfonso, Hetherston
S	05-May	Ross County		A	L2	0-4	2186	Monin	Capin	Ellis	McCulloch r85 b	Alfonso r45	Nicol	Nanou	Hampshire r60	Smith x70	Smith	Stein	Nicol u86, Hampshire u80, Alfonso u89, Hampshire
							400	Coyle											Ross u45 b, Cauley u, Cunningham
							3004	Monin											Hamilton u85, Mballa u60, Black

Manager : Peter Hetherston

(1) Clarke sent off 34 minutes

(2) Murie, booked and sent off 44 minutes

(3) Anderson sent off 32 minutes

(4) McManus sent off 53 minutes ; Evans sent off 67 minutes

(N1) won 4-2 on penalties, fixture fulfilled by reserve team not included in summary statistics

Day	Date	Opponents	Note	Venue	Comp	Res	Att	1	2	3	4	5	6	7	8	9	10	11	Substitutes, own goals and goal times
S	21-Jul	Livingston		H	F	1-3	890	Monin	McCulloch	Hampshire	Dennis r80	Browne	Henderson,D	Nanou r61	Mathieson r69	Smith 1	O'Boyle	Stein	Ellis u80 · Niven u69 · Black · Miotto
Tu	24-Jul	York City		H	F	1-0	724	Monin 45	McCulloch	Hampshire r45	Dennis	Browne	Henderson,D r45	Nanou	Mathieson	Smith r45	O'Boyle 1	Stein	Ellis u45 · Miotto u45 · Zoco u45 · Novo u45 · Black
S	28-Jul	Halifax Town		H	F	1-0	869	Monin r58	McCulloch b	Ellis	Dennis r63	Browne r63	Zoco r54	Nanou	Mathieson	Novo 1	O'Boyle r58	Stein r63	McCulloch u63 · Henderson,D u41 · Hampshire u63 · Smith u58 · Miotto u58
Tu	04-Aug	Airdrie		A	L2	2-2	1229	Monin	Clark,J	Ellis	Dennis 1	Browne	Henderson,D	Nanou 2	Mathieson	Novo 1	O'Boyle	Stein	Hampshire u84 · McCulloch · Nicol · Miotto
S	07-Aug	East Fife	1	A	LCC 1	3-2	1085	Miotto	Zoco r73	Ellis	Dennis	Browne b	Henderson,D b	Novo 2	Mathieson b	Crabbe 1	O'Boyle b	Stein b	Nanou u73 · Nicol · Clark,J · Miotto
S	11-Aug	Partick Thistle		H	L2	1-2	3134	Miotto	McCulloch	Zoco	Dennis b	Browne b	Henderson,D r40 b	Novo b X67	Mathieson 1	Smith b	Crabbe r85 b	Stein b	Hampshire u85 · O'Boyle u60 · Clark,J · McCulloch · Nanou · Miotto
Tu	14-Aug	Partick Thistle	2	H	LCC 2	3-5	1650	Miotto	McCulloch	Zoco r74 b	Dennis	Browne r69	Zoco	Novo 1	Nanou	Crabbe	Crabbe	Henderson,D	Stein u69 · Clark,A 45 · Hampshire · Monin
S	18-Aug	Ross County		A	L2	0-1	2099	Miotto b	McCulloch	Ellis	Dennis	Browne b	Henderson,D	Zoco	Mathieson	Smith	Mathieson	Stein	Clark,A u74 · Nanou · Ellis · Monin
S	25-Aug	Ayr United		A	L2	1-1	2410	Miotto	McCulloch	Zoco b	Dennis	Browne	Henderson,D 1	Novo 2,1p	Mathieson r66 b	Smith r66 b	Crabbe 1	Stein 1	O'Boyle u66 · Clark,A u79 · Nanou · Clark,J · Monin
S	09-Sep	Falkirk		H	L2	5-2	2360	Monin b	McCulloch b	Zoco b	Dennis r87 b	Browne	Henderson,D b	Novo b	Mathieson r64	Smith r79	Crabbe r81 2	Stein b	O'Boyle u64 · Nanou · O'Boyle · Monin
Tu	11-Sep	Montrose		H	LC 1	1-0	1099	Miotto	McCulloch	Zoco	Dennis	Browne	Henderson,D 1	Novo 2	Mathieson	Smith	Crabbe	Stein 1	Nanou · Ellis · O'Boyle · Monin
S	15-Sep	Arbroath		H	L2	3-1	1698	Miotto	McCulloch b	Zoco	Dennis b	Browne	Henderson,D b	Novo 2	Mathieson r64	Smith 1	Crabbe 1	Stein b	Clark,A u64 · Ellis · Nanou · Monin
W	19-Sep	Inverness Caledonian Thistle		A	L2	2-5	984	Monin	Zoco	Ellis r89	McCulloch	Browne	Henderson,D b	Novo r89 2 b	Mathieson b	Smith 1	Crabbe 1	Stein 1 p b	Clark,J u89 · Nanou u76 · Clark,J · Miotto
S	22-Sep	St Mirren	3	H	L2	3-0	2465	Monin	Zoco r80 b	Ellis	McCulloch	Browne r84	Henderson,D	Novo r73 1 b	Mathieson r76 b	Smith 1	Crabbe	Stein	Hampshire u80 · Hampshire · Clark,J · Miotto
Tu	25-Sep	Falkirk	4	A	LC 2	2-0	1572	Monin	Zoco b	Ellis b	McCulloch	Browne	Henderson,D b	Novo 1	Mathieson	Smith 1	Crabbe	Stein	Clark,A u84 · Nanou · Nanou · Miotto
S	29-Sep	Clyde		A	L2	2-3	1220	Monin	Zoco	Ellis	McCulloch	Browne	Henderson,D b	Novo r61 1	Mathieson r72 b	Smith 1	Crabbe	Stein	Nanou u61 · Clark,A u72 · Hampshire · Miotto
S	06-Oct	Airdrie		H	L2	2-2	2077	Monin	Zoco	Ellis	McCulloch b	Browne r77 b	Henderson,D b	Novo b	Mathieson r62	Smith	Crabbe	Stein	Dennis u77 · Clark,A u62 · Nicol · Miotto
Tu	09-Oct	Hibernian		H	LC 3	0-2	4601	Monin	Zoco r79	McCulloch	Ellis b	Browne b	Henderson,D r45 b	Novo r82	Nanou	Smith 1	Crabbe	Stein b	Hampshire u45 · O'Boyle u82 · Matheson · Miotto
S	20-Oct	Partick Thistle		A	L2	1-2	3129	Monin	Zoco r45	McCulloch	Ellis	Browne	Henderson,D r45 b	Novo	Nanou r76	Smith b	Crabbe b	Stein b	Hampshire u45 · O'Boyle u76 · Matheson · Miotto
S	27-Oct	Falkirk	5	H	L2	2-1	2391	Monin	McCulloch	McCulloch	Dennis 1	Browne	Hampshire	Novo b	Zoco r54	Smith	Mathieson	Stein b	Nanou · Ellis · Ellis · Miotto
S	03-Nov	Ayr United		H	L2	1-1	1781	Miotto	McCulloch	Tejero	Dennis	Browne	Hampshire b	Novo 1 p b	Zoco r54	Smith	Jones r72	Stein	Nanou u54 · Clark,A u69 · Niven · Miotto
S	10-Nov	Inverness Caledonian Thistle		H	L2	1-5	1468	Monin	McCulloch b	Tejero	Dennis	Browne b	Zoco	Novo 1 p b	Hampshire b	Smith b	Jones r62	Henderson,D r28	Ellis u28 b · Miller,J u72 · Ellis · Miotto
S	17-Nov	Arbroath		A	L2	1-1	1034	Monin	McCulloch	Tejero b	Dennis	Browne	Javary	Novo 1 b	Paquito r84	Smith	Jones r67	Stein	Miller,J u62 · Clark,A · Clark,A · Miotto
S	24-Nov	Clyde		H	L2	1-2	1556	Monin	McCulloch	Tejero	Dennis b	Zoco	Javary	Novo	Paquito	Smith 1	Novo	Stein	Nanou u78 · Clark,A u67 · Ellis · Miotto
S	01-Dec	St Mirren		A	L2	3-3	3417	Monin	McCulloch r20	Tejero	Dennis	Browne	Javary b	Miller,J r78 1	Paquito b	Smith 2	Novo 1	Stein	Nanou u20 · Clark,A u60 1 · Hampshire · Miotto
S	08-Dec	Ross County		A	L2	1-3	1449	Monin	McCulloch	Zoco	Zoco	Browne b	Javary b	Miller,J r60	Paquito	Smith	Novo 1	Stein b	Nanou u79 · Clark,A u64 · Ellis · Miotto
S	15-Dec	Partick Thistle		H	L2	1-1	1566	Miotto	McCulloch	Tejero 1	Browne b	Browne	Javary b	Novo r79 b	Paquito	Smith b	Novo 2	Stein b	Miller,J u63 · Clark,A · Miller,J · Miotto
S	29-Dec	Ayr United		A	L2	1-3	2033	Monin	McCulloch b	Tejero b b&X42	Ellis	Browne	Javary	Novo r63	Nanou r68 b	Smith	Jones r64 1	Stein	Novo u79 · Clark,A u68 · Dennis · Sweeney
Tu	08-Jan	Hamilton Accies		A	SC 3	0-1	1727	Monin	McCulloch	Hampshire	Ellis	Browne	Zoco r79 b	Zoco r79 b	Nanou r68 b	Smith	Jones r45	Stein	Hampshire u45 b · Novo u79 · Paquito · Monin
S	12-Jan	Inverness Caledonian Thistle		H	L2	0-5	1822	Monin	Zoco	Tejero	Dennis	Browne	Javary r65 b	Henderson,R	Henderson,D	Smith	Clark r69	Henderson,D	Jones u69 · Nanou u65 · Ellis · Sweeney
S	19-Jan	St Mirren		H	L2	1-0	1849	Monin	Zoco	Tejero	Dennis	Browne	Henderson,R	Novo 1 b	Javary b	Smith 1	Paquito r88	Henderson,D b	McGarty u88 · Jones · Stein · Miotto
S	26-Jan	Arbroath	6	H	L2	0-0	1737	Monin b	McCulloch	Tejero	Dennis	Browne	Henderson,R b	Novo	McGarty	Smith	Davidson	Henderson,D	McCulloch · Javary · Paquito · Jones · Miotto
S	02-Feb	Clyde		H	L2	2-1	1095	Monin	McCulloch b	McCulloch b	Dennis	Browne	Henderson,R b	McGarty	Miller,M	Smith 2	Novo	Henderson,D 1 b	Nanou · Stein u78 · Jones u66 · Davidson · Miotto
S	09-Feb	Ross County		A	L2	2-4	2592	Monin b	McCulloch	Henderson,R 1	Dennis	Browne	Henderson,R r b	McGarty r66	Miller,M r66	Smith 2	Novo 1	Henderson,D	McGarty u70 · Jones · Stein · McCulloch · Miotto
S	16-Feb	Partick Thistle		H	L2	2-0	2729	Monin	Miller,M	Henderson,R r78	Dennis	Browne	Nanou b	Davidson	Paquito r70	Smith 1	Novo 1	Henderson,D r82	Stein u82 · Jones u89 · McGarty u89 · Ellis · Miotto
S	23-Feb	Falkirk		A	L2	5-1	2511	Monin	Miller,M	Hampshire r85	Dennis	Browne	Nanou	Paquito r70	Paquito r89	Smith	Novo 2	Henderson,D	McCulloch u78 · McGarty u89 · Jones · Stein · Miotto
S	02-Mar	Ayr United		A	L2	3-3	2010	Monin	Miller,M b	Ellis r75	Ellis	Browne	Nanou	Davidson r89 1	Paquito 1	Smith 2	Novo 1	Henderson,D b	Stein u85 · Jones u67 · McGarty u85 · McCulloch · Miotto
S	09-Mar	Falkirk		H	L2	1-2	2680	Monin b	McCulloch b	Ellis	Dennis	Browne	Nanou	Davidson	Paquito r89	Smith 1	Novo r89	Henderson,D	Tejero u64 · Paquito u61 · Matheson · McGarty · Miotto
S	16-Mar	Inverness Caledonian Thistle		H	L2	0-0	1590	Monin	Davidson x87	Ellis	Dennis 1	Browne	Nanou	Davidson r85 b	Paquito r67	Smith	Novo 1	Henderson,D	Matheson · Stein u75 · Jones · Jones · Miotto
S	23-Mar	Arbroath		A	L2	2-2	1185	Monin	Miller,W r78	Dennis 1	Dennis	Browne	Nanou r64	Davidson	Jones r61	Smith	Novo 1	Henderson,D r73	Jones u84 · Matheson u73 · Stein · Nanou · Miotto
S	30-Mar	St Mirren		H	L2	0-1	4014	Miotto	Miller,M	Ellis	Dennis	Browne	Ellis	Miller,M	Paquito b	Smith	Novo	Henderson,D	Stein u64 · Miller,W · Jones u78 · McCulloch · Miotto
S	06-Apr	Clyde		H	L2	0-1	1621	Monin	Miller,M b	Ellis	Dennis	Browne	Nanou r86	Tejero r64	Paquito b	Smith b	Novo b	Stein	Matheson u86 · Davidson u78 · Hampshire · Matheson · Miotto
S	13-Apr	Airdrie		H	L2	2-1	1138	Monin	Miller,W r33	Ellis	Dennis	Browne	Nanou	Novo 1	Henderson,D	Smith 1	Novo b	Brown	Davidson u78 · Brown · Jones u85 · Hampshire · Miotto
S	20-Apr	Partick Thistle		A	L2	0-1	6028	Miotto	Zoco	McCulloch	Dennis	McCulloch	Henderson,D	Davidson r85	Matheson r68	Smith	Novo b	Stein	Browne u68 · Nanou u33 · Ross · Hampshire · Sweeney
Tu	23-Apr	Cowdenbeath	N1	H	FC SF	1-1	185	Sweeney	Rushford 1	Hampshire	Brown	Tejero	Rushford	Paliczka r78 1	Paquito	Jones	Clark	Blackadder	Miller,S u78 · Ross · Crumlish · Scarborough
S	27-Apr	Ross County		H	FC F	1-1	1216	Miotto	McCulloch	Ellis	Dennis	Browne	Nanou	Davidson r75	Nanou	Clark	Scarborough 1 r90	Blackadder	Clark,A u75 · Crumlish · Brown · Hampshire
M	29-Apr	Dunfermline Athletic	N	H	FC F	2-1	332	Sweeney	Rushford 1	Hampshire	Brown,I	Ellis	Paliczka	Paliczka	Paquito	Clark r88	Scarborough	Blackadder	Crumlish u90 · Miller,S u88 · Ross u45 · Dickson

Manager : Peter Hetherston to 11th December. Jocky Scott from 19th December

(1) Herkes sent off 81 minutes
(2) after extra time
(3) Ross sent off 79 minutes
(4) Kerr sent off 37 minutes ; Christie booked and sent off 81 minutes
(5) The match kicked off 30 minutes late while a lineman was found. The match officials were one short as the Scottish League had omitted to appoint a replacement for referee Kenny Clark.
(6) Paul Brownlie missed penalty 40 minutes
(N) Fixture fulfilled by reserve team not included in summary statistics
(N1) won 3-1 on penalties, fixture fulfilled by reserve team not included in summary statistics

Day	Date	Opponents	Note	Venue	Comp	Res.	Att.	1	2	3	4	5	6	7	8	9	10	11	Substitutes, own goals and goal times
Su	14-Jul	Dundee	6	H	F	1-1	1978	Raul r85	McCulloch r45	Parkin r45	Dennis r45	Brown r81	Nanou r45	Carrigan r45 1p	Paquito r65	Smith r45	Hampshire r45	Prest r77	Ellis u45, Sweeney u85, Matheson u45, Miller,S u81, Browne u45
Th	18-Jul	St Mirren	7	H	F	3-3	710	Monin	McCulloch r45	Moffat r45	Browne r45	Ellis r45	Brady u45	Carrigan	Paquito r80	Prest r85 1	Hampshire r45 1	Mas r73	Parkin u45, Dennis u45 r60, Brown u45, Nanou u45, Matheson u45
S	20-Jul	Gretna	8	H	F	2-0	607	Raul	Ross	Parkin r68	Brady	Browne	Nanou	Matheson	Prest	Carrigan r80	Hampshire 1	Prest r65 1	McCulloch u80, Ellis u68, Paliczka u70, Ellis, Mas u68
S	27-Jul	East Fife	A	FC	SF	1-0	834	Raul	Ross	Parkin	Brady	Browne	Nanou	Matheson r70	Paquito	Smith r68	Hampshire	Mas r	Blackadder u, Paliczka u70, Mas u74, Miller,S, Monin
S	03-Aug	Stranraer		H	L3	1-1	1790	Raul	Ross	Ellis r45	Brady	Browne	Nanou b	Carrigan r57 1p	Paquito	Smith r57	Hampshire	Prest b&X80	Blackadder u68, Paliczka u57, Matheson, Ellis, Monin
Tu	06-Aug	Airdrie United	A	LCC	1	0-3	1649	Raul	Brown r74	Parkin	Brady	Browne	Nanou b	Matheson b	Paquito	Smith	Hampshire	Prest	Carrigan u45, Carrigan u70, Mas u74, Ross, Monin
S	10-Aug	Berwick Rangers		H	L3	1-1	804	Raul	Ross	Parkin r61	Brady	Dennis	Moffat b	Matheson r70	Paquito	Smith r60	Hampshire	Boylan r83 1	Prest u61, Prest u60, Blackadder u83, Ellis, Monin
S	17-Aug	Dumbarton	A	L3	1-0	1866	Raul	Brown	Ellis	Moffat r63	Dennis	Brady	Matheson r45	Paquito	Smith r61 1	Hampshire	Boylan	Nanou u60 b, Blackadder u63 1, Hawley u63 1, Browne, Monin
S	24-Aug	Cowdenbeath		H	L3	1-3	1678	Raul	Brown x32	Ellis	Brady r60	Dennis	Moffat r45	Boylan 1	Paquito	Smith r59	Hampshire	Hawley	Prest u60, Prest u61, Blackadder u45 b, Browne, Monin
F	30-Aug	Stenhousemuir	A	L3	1-0	1701	Raul	Brown b	Hampshire	Dennis	Dennis b	Calderon r73 b	Boylan r82	Paquito	Smith r26	Hawley	Hawley	Miller,S u82, Brady u73, Blackadder u61, Ross, Monin
Tu	10-Sep	Alloa Athletic	1	H	L3	2-3	1342	Monin	Ross r59	Hampshire	Dennis b	Dennis	Nanou	Boylan 45	Paquito	Nanou	Hawley	Prest 1	Carrigan u59 1p, Blackadder u45, Boylan u45, Brady, Raul
S	14-Sep	Airdrie United		H	L3	0-0	2028	Raul	Brown b	Ellis	Brady	Dennis	Nanou	Hawley	Paquito	Hawley	Calderon r81	Calderon r81	Carrigan u26, Calderon u59, Calderon u59, Smith, Monin
S	21-Sep	Hamilton Academical		A	L3	4-0	1961	Raul	Brown	Ellis	Brady	Dennis	Nanou 1	Carrigan r65 2,1p	Paquito	Hawley 2	Blackadder r59 b	Boylan r65 1	Hampshire u59, Calderon u65, McManus u85, Smith, Monin
S	28-Sep	Brechin City		A	L3	3-1	2007	Raul	Brown	Ellis	Brady 1	Dennis	Nanou	Carrigan r85 b	Paquito	Hawley r80	Blackadder	Boylan r71 1	Calderon u71, McManus u85, Smith, Hampshire, Monin
S	05-Oct	Forfar Athletic		A	L3	2-1	1075	Raul	Patino	Parkin r62	Brady r62	Dennis	Nanou	Carrigan	Paquito b	Hawley 1	Blackadder b	Boylan r75	Hampshire u75, Hampshire u75, Smith u80, Parkin, Sweeney
S	19-Oct	Berwick Rangers		H	L3	1-2	1906	Raul	Ellis r80	Calderon	Brady r81	Patino	Nanou b	Carrigan	Paquito	Hawley	Blackadder	Boylan	Smith u80, Smith u80, Calderon u62, Smith, Sweeney
S	26-Oct	Stranraer		A	L3	2-2	585	Raul	Ellis	Ellis	Brady	Patino	Nanou r66	Carrigan 1	Paquito	Hawley r69	Calderon r45	Blackadder	Prest u66, Prest u45 b, Ross, Smith, Sweeney
S	02-Nov	Stenhousemuir	2	A	L3	1-0	1045	Raul	Patino r45	Ellis	Brady	Dennis b	Nanou 1	Blackadder	Paquito 1	Smith r69	Blackadder	Hampshire b	Smith u69, McManus u69, Boylan u45, Ross, Sweeney
S	09-Nov	Cowdenbeath		H	L3	4-1	2428	Raul	Patino	Ellis	Brady	Dennis	Nanou	Blackadder r78 2	Paquito	Smith r70	Blackadder r82	Hampshire	Boylan u78, Boylan u51, Prest u45 b, Brown, Monin
S	16-Nov	Airdrie United		A	L3	0-0	1718	Raul	Ellis	Calderon	Ellis	Dennis	Nanou r51	Hampshire r86	Paquito	Smith r70	Smith r70	Hawley	Prest u86, Prest u45, McManus u70, Moffat, Monin
S	23-Nov	Hamilton Academical		A	L3	1-1	1897	Raul x70	Ellis	Ellis	Brady r61	Dennis	Blackadder r45	Boylan 1	Paquito 1	Smith r70	Hampshire	Hawley	Carrigan u59, Monin u70, McManus u61, Moffat, Ross
S	30-Nov	Forfar Athletic	3	H	L3	5-1	1779	Monin	Ellis	Parkin b	Hampshire	Dennis 1	Nanou r89	Blackadder r75 1p	Paquito	Smith r75 b	Calderon b	McManus 2	Carrigan u75, Brady u89, Hawley u75, Smith, Gonet
S	07-Dec	Dumbarton		H	SC	1	1-0	1639	Monin	Patino	Parkin	Brady	Dennis	Nanou r89	Blackadder 1	Paquito	Smith r78	Calderon	McManus r83	Miller,S u89, Boylan u83 b, Hawley u78, Patino, Raul
S	14-Dec	Brechin City		A	L3	2-1	734	Raul	Patino	Ellis b	Brady b	Dennis	Nanou b	Blackadder	Paquito	Smith b	Calderon r45	McManus r88 2	Carrigan u87, Prest u88 b, Hawley, Moffat, Ross
S	21-Dec	Dumbarton		A	L3	3-0	1244	Raul	Patino	Ellis r84	Brady r62	Dennis	Nanou	Blackadder r87	Paquito	Smith 2	Calderon r89	Hawley 1	Carrigan u82, Hampshire u84, Prest u89, Parkin, Rovde
W	01-Jan	Cowdenbeath		A	L3	1-1	1919	Raul	Patino	Ellis r82	Brady r81	Dennis b	Nanou	Blackadder	Paquito b	Smith r82	Fyfe r60	Hawley 1 b	Prest u65, Hampshire u60, Prest u82, Parkin, Sweeney
M	13-Jan	Montrose		H	SC	2	3-1	1514	Raul	Patino	Calderon r45 b	Brady	Dennis	Nanou 1	Carrigan r65 1	Paquito	Smith 1	Hampshire	Hawley r65 1	Blackadder u65, Moffat u45, McManus u65, Ellis, Sweeney
S	18-Jan	Airdrie United		A	L3	1-0	2247	Raul	Patino 1 b	Calderon	Brady	Dennis	Nanou r81	Carrigan r65	Paquito	Smith 1	Hampshire r45	Hawley r77 b	Carrigan u81, McManus u77, Fyfe u45, Prest, Sweeney
S	25-Jan	Inverness Caledonian Thistle		A	SC	3	0-2	2146	Sweeney	Patino b	Ellis	Brady r81	Dennis	Nanou	Blackadder	Paquito	Smith	Calderon	McManus	Parkin u82, Carrigan u45, Shields u62, Hampshire, Gonzales
S	01-Feb	Hamilton Academical		A	L3	0-0	1292	Raul	Patino r66	Ellis	McKinnon	Dennis	Nanou r45	Blackadder	Paquito 1	Smith b	McKinnon	McManus r62	Prest u67, McManus u78, Ellis, Hampshire, Gonzales
S	08-Feb	Brechin City		H	L3	1-2	1776	Raul	Patino r82	Calderon	Brady	Dennis	McKinnon 1	Nanou 45	Paquito 1	Smith	Fyfe r78	Shields r67	Carrigan u68, Calderon u68, McManus u58, Prest, Sweeney
S	22-Feb	Berwick Rangers	4	A	L3	1-1	820	Raul	Patino	Calderon	McKinnon	Dennis 1	Nanou	Blackadder	Paquito	Prest r58 1	Fyfe r68	Shields r68 1	Carrigan u65, Calderon u72, McManus u85, Calderon, Sweeney
S	01-Mar	Stranraer		A	L3	2-1	1790	Raul b	Patino	Parkin r45	Brady	Dennis 1	McKinnon	Blackadder	Paquito b	Prest r85 1	Fyfe	Shields r45	Carrigan u45, Hampshire u45, Parkin, Parkin, Sweeney
Tu	04-Mar	Stranraer		H	L3	3-0	1448	Raul	Patino	Calderon	McKinnon	Dennis b	Nanou	Carrigan r73	Paquito	McManus r63 1	Fyfe 1	Prest r84	Carrigan u63 b, McKinnon u76, Shields u84, Parkin, Sweeney
S	08-Mar	Cowdenbeath		H	L3	2-1	1900	Raul	Patino 1 b	Ellis r72 b	Brady b	Dennis	Hampshire	Carrigan r65	Paquito 1	McManus r82	Fyfe r76	Prest 2,1p	Carrigan u66, McKinnon u82, Shields u72, Gonzales, Gonzales
S	11-Mar	Forfar Athletic		A	L3	2-4	688	Sweeney	Patino b	Calderon	Brady	Dennis	Hampshire	Carrigan	Paquito 1	Carrigan r73	Fyfe r65	McManus	Nanou u66, Nanou u66, Fyfe, Hampshire, Gonzales
Tu	15-Mar	Stenhousemuir	5	A	L3	3-1	1135	Raul	El Khebir	Parkin 1	McKinnon	Dennis	Brady	Matheson	Paquito	Prest	McKinnon	Blackadder r80	Fyfe u63, Shields u80, Ellis, Hampshire, Gonzales
S	22-Mar	Hamilton Academical		A	L3	1-1	1762	Raul	El Khebir	Calderon	Brady r55	Dennis	McKinnon r25	Blackadder	Paquito	Prest r47	McKinnon r61	Shields	Blackadder u61, McManus u72, McManus u85, Calderon, Gonzales
W	26-Mar	Stenhousemuir		H	L3	0-1	1627	Raul	Nanou	Ellis	Brady	Dennis	Hampshire r45	Carrigan	Paquito	McManus r66	Hampshire	Shields	Carrigan u66, Sweeney u45, Parkin, Parkin, Davidson
S	29-Mar	Livingston		H	F	0-4	425	Gonzales r45	Ross	Parkin	Ellis r45	Brown r74	Brady r72	Matheson	Valdez r66	Smith	Hampshire	Fyfe r45	Nanou u74, Nanou u84, McKinnon, McKinnon, Davidson
S	05-Apr	Airdrie United		A	L3	0-1	1788	Gonzales	Patino	Calderon	Brady	Brown	Brady	Blackadder	Paquito	Smith r84 1	Calderon	Prest	Nanou u66, Shields u75, Fyfe u45, Ellis, Sweeney
S	12-Apr	Forfar Athletic		A	L3	0-1	2036	Gonzales	Patino	Parkin r45	McKinnon	Ellis	Hampshire	Blackadder	Paquito 1	Smith	Calderon	Prest r75	Nanou u25, Blackadder u37 b, Shields u55, Ellis, Sweeney
S	19-Apr	Brechin City		A	L3	0-1	1830	Gonzales	Hampshire	Ellis	Hampshire	Dennis	McKinnon r25	Valdez x85	Paquito	Smith r37	Calderon	Prest r37	Matheson u45, Prest u72, McManus u81, Brown, Brown
S	26-Apr	Stranraer		A	L3	0-1	725	Gonzales	Patino	Ellis	Brady	Dennis	Nanou	Nanou	Paquito	Shields	Calderon r81	Shields	Matheson u85, McManus u85, Valdez, Valdez, Sweeney
S	03-May	Berwick Rangers		H	L3	1-4	2746	Gonzales	Ross r45	Parkin	Brady b	Dennis	Nanou	McManus r81	Valdez	Smith r85 1	Calderon	Prest	Correia u80, Shields u41, Calderon, Paquito, Gonzales
Tu	06-May	Dunfermline Athletic		A	FC	F	1-4	950	Sweeney	Valdez	Parkin b	Brown	Davidson	Moffat	Matheson	Valdez	Paliczka r80	Fyfe	Blackadder	Paliczka u56, Davidson u45, Shields u56, Brown, Sweeney
S	10-May	Dumbarton		A	L3	1-4	1501	Gonzales	Valdez	Ellis	Ross	Ellis r56	Moffat	McManus	Matheson	Smith r56	Blackadder 1p	Fyfe r45	Davidson u45, Shields u56, Brown

Rovers' goal times 33, 16

Manager : Antonio Calderon

(1) after extra time

(2) McKenzie sent off

(3) Paul Tosh sent off 41 minutes

(4) Burke's goal in 7 seconds believed to match the Scottish record

(5) Coulter sent off 88 minutes

(6) Additional substitutes : Brady u45 ; Blackadder u45 ; Ross u65 ; Mas u45 ; Moffat u45 ; Paliczka u77 ; Monin

(7) Additional substitutes : Miller,S u73 ; Blackadder u45 ; Ross u45 ; Paliczka u60 1 ; Whyte u85 ; Sweeney ; Davidson

(8) Additional substitutes : Paliczka u65 ; Monin ; Whyte. Rovers' goal times 33, 16

Day	Date	Opponents	Note	Venue	Comp	Res.	Att.	1	2	3	4	5	6	7	8	9	10	11	Substitutes, own goals and goal times				
W	16-Jul	Annan Athletic		A	F	1-0	100	Gonzales r	Talio	McKeown	Brown	Dennis r	Brittan	Peers 1 65mins	Paquito	Sutton r	Blackadder r	Prest r	Sweeney u	Patino u	Brady u	Maxwell u	Smith u
S	19-Jul	St Andrews United	8	A	F	5-0	130	Gonzales r45	Talio r45	McKeown	Brown r45	Patino	Maxwell r45	Peers r64 1	O'Donoghue r62	Sutton r45 2	Henry r78	Jordan r45	Sawyers u45	Ritchie u78	Sweeney u45	Brady u45	Blackadder u45
Tu	22-Jul	Bradford City		H	F	2-0	1110	Gonzales	Patino	McKeown r45	Brady	Dennis r45	Brittan	Peers	Paquito r45	Sutton 1	Blackadder r45	Prest 1	Brown u45	Henry u45	O'Neill u45	Stanley u45	
S	26-Jul	Dundee		H	F	1-4	1822	Gonzales r80	Patino r45	O'Neill	Brady	Brown	Stanley	Peers r45	Paquito	Sutton r45 1	Brittan	Prest r45	McKeown u45	Sweeney u80	Blackadder u45	Boukraa u45	Obimili u45
Tu	29-Jul	Albion Rovers	1	A	F	0-2	310	Sweeney	Talio	Driana	McKeown r58	Brown r45	Henry	Peers r45	Marchio-Vechio r34	Sutton r45	Blackadder m65	Boukraa	McCann u34	Devlin u45	Martin u45	Richardson u58	Gonzales
S	02-Aug	East Stirling		A	LCC 1	5-2	556	Gonzales	Patino b	Calderon	Brady	Dennis	Stanley 1	Peers r74 1	Paquito	Sutton r74 2	Brittan r71	Prest r77 1	Brown u77	Blackadder u71	Martin u74	Sweeney	Smith
Tu	05-Aug	Cowdenbeath	N	A	FC SF	2-1	250	Sweeney	Devlin	McKeown	McCann	Brown	Ritchie r45	Blackadder 1	Raffel	Martin x76	Boyle	Richardson r59	Haddow u59	Malcolm u45 1	Stanley	Gonzales	
S	09-Aug	St Mirren	2	H	L2	1-1	3090	Gonzales b	Patino	Calderon r63	Talio r45	Dennis	Brady	Stanley	Paquito	Sutton	Brittan r70 1	Prest	Brown u45	Peers u63	Blackadder u70	Malcolm	Sweeney
Tu	12-Aug	Stranraer		H	LCC 2	2-0	1369	Gonzales	Patino	Talio r45	Brady	Brown b	Stanley	Peers r71	Paquito	Sutton 1	Brittan	Prest r81 b	Blackadder u71	McCann u81	Calderon u45 1 b&X	McKeown	Sweeney
S	16-Aug	Brechin City	3	A	L2	3-0	1021	Gonzales	Patino	Calderon	Brady	Dennis	Stanley	Peers r65	Paquito	Sutton r88 3,1p	Brittan	Prest r75	Talio u83	Blackadder u65	Martin u75	Brown	Sweeney
S	23-Aug	Ayr United		H	L2	1-1	2364	Gonzales	Patino	Calderon	Brittan b	Dennis 1	Stanley	Peers r59	Paquito	Sutton r74	Henry r45	Prest *	Blackadder u59	Stanik u45	Evans u74	Talio	Brown,R
Tu	26-Aug	St Mirren		H	LCC QF	3-2	1949	Gonzales b	Patino	Stanik b	Brittan	Brown b	Henry	Stanley	Paquito	Sutton	Blackadder	Prest r74 2	Boyle u74	Talio	Peers	Evans	Carroll
S	30-Aug	Falkirk		H	L2	0-1	4232	Gonzales b	Patino r79	Stanik	Brittan	Dennis b&x 89	Henry r45	Stanley r80	Paquito	Sutton b	Calderon b&x 83	Prest	Brady u45	Blackadder u79	Evans u80	Talio	Carroll
Tu	02-Sep	Arbroath		A	LC 1	0-1	879	Gonzales	Talio	Stanik r15 b	Brown r71	Dennis	Brady b	Brittan	Henry	Hawley	Calderon	Evans r73	Peers u71	Blackadder u15	Prest u73	Sutton	Carroll
S	13-Sep	Queen of the South		A	L2	2-0	2142	Gonzales b	Patino	Talio r83	Brady	Brown	Stanley	Brittan	Paquito	Sutton 2	Blackadder	Prest r45 b	Henry u83	Hawley u45	Raffel	Martin	Sweeney
Tu	16-Sep	Inverness Caledonian Thistle	4	H	LCC SF	0-4	2110	Gonzales	Patino	Stanik b	Brady r45 b	Dennis	Brittan r67	Stanley	Paquito	Sutton	Blackadder r45 b	Prest	Calderon u45	Hawley u67	Robb u45	Henry	Sweeney
S	20-Sep	St Johnstone		A	L2	1-0	2983	Gonzales	Brown	Stanik	Brady	Dennis	Stanley	Blackadder	Paquito	Sutton	Calderon 1	Robb r71	Hawley u71	Henry u45	Brittan	Prest	Sweeney
S	27-Sep	Ross County		H	L2	1-7	2292	Gonzales	Brown r54 1	Stanik b	Brady r45 b	Dennis	Stanley	Blackadder	Paquito	Sutton	Calderon r27	Robb	Brittan u45 b	Prest u27	Hawley u54	Patino	Sweeney
S	04-Oct	Inverness Caledonian Thistle		A	L2	1-2	1707	Gonzales	Patino	Stanik b	Brady	Brown b	Stanley	Brittan r61	Paquito	Sutton 1	Calderon	Robb r75	Peers u75	Hawley u61	Prest	Blackadder	Sweeney
S	18-Oct	Clyde		H	L2	0-1	1765	Gonzales	Patino b	Stanik	Brittan	Talio r70	Brady r86	Stanley	Paquito	Sutton	Calderon b	Robb r45	Peers u70	Blackadder u86	Hawley u45	Evans	Sweeney
S	25-Oct	Brechin City		H	L2	2-1	1685	Gonzales	Patino	Stanik	Talio r58	Brown b	Brittan	Stanley	Paquito	Sutton 1	Calderon	Hawley 1	Blackadder u58	Brady	Evans	Robb	Sweeney
S	01-Nov	St Mirren		A	L2	1-2	3005	Gonzales	Patino	Stanik b	Talio r82	Brown	Brittan	Stanley	Paquito 1	Sutton r72	Calderon r78 b	Hawley	Blackadder u82	Prest u72	Robb u78	Brady	Sweeney
S	08-Nov	Queen of the South		H	L2	0-1	1944	Gonzales	Patino b	Stanik	Jack	Brown r45	Brady r51	Stanley	Paquito	Hawley	Calderon	Prest r51	Sutton u51	Brittan u45	Robb u51	Blackadder	Sweeney
F	14-Nov	Falkirk		A	L2	2-3	3237	Gonzales	Patino	Stanik b	Jack b	Talio	Brady r69	Blackadder 1 b	Paquito	Sutton 1 b	Calderon r63	Robb r69	Prest u69	Stanley u63	Evans u69	Hawley	Sweeney
S	22-Nov	Ross County		A	L2	2-3	2803	Gonzales	Patino r77	Stanik	Brady r67	Jack	Stanley	Blackadder	Paquito	Sutton 1	Calderon 1	Robb r61	Brown u77	Brittan u67	Hawley u61	Talio	Sweeney
S	29-Nov	St Johnstone		H	L2	1-4	1996	Langfield	Brown	Stanik	Jack r67	Dennis	Stanley	Blackadder r64	Paquito	Sutton	Calderon r67	Hawley 1	Brittan u64	Robb u67	Carranza u67	Brady	Sweeney
S	06-Dec	Clyde		A	L2	0-0	1375	Langfield	Patino	Stanik b	Brown b	Dennis	Jack	Stanley b	Paquito b	Sutton	Carranza r75	Prest	Blackadder u75	Martin	Hawley	Brady	Sweeney
S	13-Dec	Inverness Caledonian Thistle		H	L2	1-3	1432	Langfield	Patino r60	Stanik r72	Jack	Dennis	Brady	Blackadder r72	Paquito	Sutton 1 b	Robb	Prest	Brown u60	Stanley u72	Calderon u72	Hawley	Sweeney
S	27-Dec	Ayr United		A	L2	0-1	1791	Langfield	Patino	Stanik r45	Calderon	Dennis	Stanley	Blackadder r80	Paquito b	Sutton	Carranza r28	Robb	Brady u28	Martin u80	Hawley u45	Talio	Gonzales
S	03-Jan	Falkirk	5	H	L2	2-0	2885	Langfield	Patino	Calderon b	Talio	Dennis	Brady	Stanley 1	Paquito	Sutton 1p	Boyle r86 b	Evans r77	Martin u77	Young u86	Prest	Blackadder	Gonzales
S	10-Jan	Kilmarnock		H	SC 3	1-3	3610	Gonzales	Patino	Stanik	Talio r82 1	Calderon	Brady	Stanley	Paquito	Sutton	Boyle r62	Evans r45	Prest u62	Martin u82	Pereira u45	McKeown	Sweeney
S	17-Jan	Queen of the South		A	L2	1-1	2098	Gonzales	Patino	Calderon	Brady r64	Brown	Stanley	Talio r80 b	Paquito	Sutton 1	Pereira b	Stanik r64	Blackadder u80	Boyle u64	Evans u64	Prest	Sweeney
S	24-Jan	St Johnstone		A	L2	2-5	2636	Gonzales	Patino 1	Stanik	Calderon	Brown r57 b	Brady r57	Talio	Paquito	Sutton 1	Pereira	Young	Boyle u57	Evans u57	Martin	Prest	Sweeney
S	07-Feb	Ross County		H	L2	0-0	1562	Berthelot	Patino r45	Stanik	Bornes	Dennis b	Calderon	Nieto	Paquito b	Ferrero r74	Pereira b & X	Young r89	Brady u89	Evans u74	Boyle u45	Brown	Gonzales
S	14-Feb	Inverness Caledonian Thistle		A	L2	0-3	1879	Berthelot	Smart	Stanik	Bornes	Dennis	Calderon b	Young r80	Nieto	Ferrero	Boyle r45	Evans r45	Brady u45	Malcolm u80	Miller u45	Maxwell	Gonzales
S	21-Feb	Clyde		H	L2	0-3	1871	Berthelot	Smart	Stanik	Bornes	Brown r45	Brady	Nieto r63	Paquito	Ferrero	Calderon	Dow r75	Malcolm u63	Young u75	Capin u45	Maxwell	Gonzales
S	06-Mar	St Mirren		H	L2	2-0	1882	Berthelot	Patino r45	Dow r51	Bornes b	Dennis	Stanik b	Nieto	Paquito	Ferrero 1	Pereira r80 1 b	Capin	Brady u51 b	Boyle u80	Smart u45	Young	Gonzales
W	10-Mar	Brechin City		A	L2	1-1	925	Berthelot	Capin	Stanik	Calderon 1	Dennis	Smart b	Brady	Paquito r12	Ferrero	Pereira r83 b	Dow r79	Boyle u79	Malcolm u83	Young u12	Martin	Gonzales
S	13-Mar	Ayr United		H	L2	2-1	2231	Berthelot	Smart r63	Dow r55	Bornes	Dennis	Brady	Young r82	Capin	Ferrero	Pereira 2,1p	Stanik	Boyle u55	Calderon u63	Nieto u82	Malcolm	Gonzales
Tu	23-Mar	Queen of the South	6	H	L2	3-1	1482	Berthelot	Capin	Calderon b	Bornes b	Dennis	Brady	Nieto r86	Paquito 1	Ferrero	Pereira 1	Young r78	Maxwell u86	Boyle u78	Malcolm	Smart	Gonzales
S	27-Mar	Falkirk		A	L2	0-1	2386	Berthelot	Capin b	Stanik	Bornes	Dennis	Brady r36	Nieto r82 b	Paquito	Ferrero b	Pereira	Young r57	Maxwell u82	Calderon u57	Smart u36	Martin	Gonzales
S	03-Apr	Ross County		A	L2	1-1	2413	Berthelot r64	Capin	Stanik	Bornes	Dennis	Brady x70	Nieto	Paquito	Calderon	Pereira 1 b	Young r59	Gonzales u64	Boyle u82	Martin u59 r82	Smart	Maxwell
S	10-Apr	St Johnstone		H	L2	1-1	2676	Berthelot	Capin b	Stanik	Bornes b	Smart	Calderon b	Nieto	Paquito	Ferrero	Pereira 1 b	Dow r76	Maxwell u76	Young	Miller	Leiper	Gonzales
S	17-Apr	Clyde		A	L2	1-4	1533	Berthelot	Capin b	Stanik b24 X25	Bornes	Dennis	Brady	Nieto r81	Paquito	Ferrero 1	Dow r81	Calderon u68	Maxwell u68	Boyle u81	Smart u81	Young	Gonzales
S	24-Apr	Inverness Caledonian Thistle		H	L2	0-1	1748	Berthelot	Capin	Smart r77	Bornes r40	Dennis	Brady	Nieto r55	Paquito	Ferrero	Maxwell b	Dow	Boyle u40	Young u77	O'Reilly u55	Martin	Gonzales
S	01-May	St Mirren		A	L2	1-1	2372	Berthelot	Smart	Stanik b	Bornes b	Dennis	Brady	Nieto r67	Paquito r45	Ferrero 1	Dow r45	Capin	Boyle u67	Young u45	O'Reilly u45	Maxwell	Gonzales
S	08-May	Brechin		H	L2	1-1	2311	Berthelot	Smart	Stanik	Bornes	Dennis	Brady r89	Capin b	Paquito	Dow r58	O'Reilly r85 1	Young	Maxwell u53 b	Boyle u85	Malcolm u89	Brown	Gonzales
W	12-May	Dunfermline Athletic	7	A	FC F	1-1	542	Gonzales	Smart r60	Stanik	Bornes	Brown	Maxwell	Miller	Young	O'Reilly	Boyle	Malcolm r81 1	Martin u60	Irons u81	Glynn	Leiper	Berthelot
S	15-May	Ayr United		A	L2	0-1	1283	Gonzales b	Glynn	Brown	Smart	Boyle r83	Martin r70	Maxwell	Young	Miller r75	O'Reilly	Malcolm	Raffel u75	Leiper u83	Irons u70	Fox	Hall

Manager : Antonio Calderon

(1) Yardley sent off 89 minutes

(2) Broadfoot sent off

(3) Clark booked and sent off

(4) Robertson booked and sent off

(5) Ferguson sent off 6 minutes

(6) Reid sent off 60 minutes

(7) won 4-3 on penalties

(8) Additional substitutes : Brittain u 45 ; Boyle u 66 ; McCann u65 ; Prest u45 2. Rovers' goal times 15, 25, 27, 51, 72

(N) Fixture fulfilled by reserve team not included in summary statistics

Day	Date	Opponents	Note	Venue	Comp	Res	Att	1	2	3	4	5	6	7	8	9	10	11	Substitutes, own goals and goal times
S	03-Jul	Huntly		A	F	3-3	230	Pounosammy r45	Smart	Paquito •	Hajovsky	Brady r45	Benaissa r45	Outtara r45	Hagan	McAlpine r45	Fraser r55	Ebanda r45 2	Berthelot u45, Young u45, Maxwell u45, Eloujdi u45, Cochrane u45
S	10-Jul	Berwick Rangers		A	F	1-3	150	Berthelot r45	Benaissa	Smart	Hajovsky	Outtara r45	Boyle r45	Young r45	Ocovan	Sacko r45	Tchimbakala	Fraser r45	Pounosammy45, Paquito r45, Maxwell u45, McAlpine u45, Ebanda u45 1
Tu	13-Jul	East Fife		A	F	3-2		Pounosammy r45	Paquito	Hajovsky	Benaissa r45	Maxwell r45	Brady	Outtara r45	McAlpine	Ebanda r45	Eloujdi r65	Ebanda r57 2	Young u45, Outtara u73, Hagan u65, Boyle u45, O'Reilly u57 1p
Sn	17-Jul	Gretna Under 19s	1	N	T SF	0-0	200	Pounosammy r71	Benaissa r73	McAlpine r45	Hajovsky	Guellai r45	Davidson r71	Outtara r45	McAlpine	Ebanda r45	Linn r45	Hagan r70	Young u45, Brady u73, Eloujdi u45, Boyle u70, Davidson u45
Sn	18-Jul	Stranraer	2	N	TF	1-0	300	Pounosammy	Smart	McAlpine	Maxwell	Hajovsky	Davidson r45	Young r45	Outtara	Ebanda	Eloujdi	Boyle r45	Berthelot u71, Benaissa u45, Outtara u45, Sacko u45 1, Linn u45
W	21-Jul	Dundee United		H	F	1-1	1301	Pounosammy	Paquito	McAlpine	Hajovsky r47	Davidson r45	Maxwell r45	Brady r58	Benaissa r45	Sacko 1	Tchimbakala r58	Ebanda	Smart u45, Outtara u45, Young u58, Eloujdi u45, Boyle u58
Th	22-Jul	Rochdale		H	F	2-3	620	Berthelot	Smart	Benaissa r37	Hajovsky	Davidson	Young r45	Outtara r60	McAlpine	Sacko	Sacko 1	Boyle r74	Maxwell u47, Outtara u37, Young u58, Hagan u45, Stewart u74
S	31-Jul	Albion Rovers		H	LCC 1	0-2	1207	Berthelot	Smart r80 b	McAlpine b	Hajovsky	Davidson	Brady	Outtara r60	Sacko b	Ebanda	Young	Hagan r60	Eloujdi u60, Boyle u60, Malcolm u80, Benaissa, Berthelot
S	07-Aug	Hamilton Academical		A	L2	0-2	2176	Pounosammy	Outtara r89	McAlpine	Hajovsky b	Davidson r57	Brady	Brady	Bartholeme	Hagan r40	Ebanda	Lusamba r45	Smart u45, Outtara u57, Boyle u40, Malcolm u80, Berthelot
Tu	10-Aug	Stranraer		A	LC 1	1-2	420	Berthelot	Outtara r89	Benaissa r45	Benaissa r45	Smart	Paquito 1	Brady	Paquito	Young r68	Sacko	O'Reilly	Hagan u68, Boyle u45, Leiper u89, Malcolm, Berthelot
S	14-Aug	Clyde		H	L2	2-3	1784	Pounosammy	Perry	McAlpine	McAlpine	Bartholeme	Brady	Young	Davidson b	Sacko 1	O'Reilly	O'Reilly	Boyle u60, Malcolm u66, Bartholeme, Smart, Pounosammy
S	21-Aug	Airdrie United		A	L2	1-1	2009	Berthelot	Perry	Perry	Hajovsky	Smart	Brady b	Young	Paquito b	Sacko 1	McAlpine	McAlpine	Boyle u60, Tagro, Mendy, Young, Pounosammy
S	28-Aug	St Johnstone		H	L2	0-1	2574	Berthelot	Perry r80	Outtara	Hajovsky	Smart	Brady b	Daly	Davidson b	Ebanda r74	Sacko 1	McAlpine	Boyle u81, Young u74, Davidson, Maxwell, Pounosammy
S	04-Sep	Ross County		A	L2	1-2	1540	Pounosammy	Perry r60	Outtara b	Hajovsky r86	Smart	Brady	Daly	Paquito r76	Martin	Sacko	McAlpine r81	Young u80, Tagro u86, Davidson, Young, Hall
S	11-Sep	Falkirk		A	L2	2-4	3449	Berthelot	Perry	Outtara	Hajovsky b	Smart	Bartholeme	Daly	Davidson r64	Martin r45	Sacko	McAlpine	Maxwell u76, Miller u64 1, Tagro u86, Martin, Pounosammy
S	18-Sep	St Mirren		H	L2	0-3	2111	Berthelot	Maxwell b	Miller	Hajovsky b	Bartholeme	Bartholeme	Daly	Davidson r69	Tagro r82	Ebanda	Sacko 1	Young u64 1, McAlpine u69, Martin u82, Martin, Young
S	25-Sep	Queen of the South		H	L2	1-2	1491	Berthelot	Outtara b	Miller	Brady	Smart	Bartholeme r84	Perry r56	Paquito	Ebanda r68 1	Sacko	Sacko b	McAlpine u84, Martin u68, Brady u56, Outtara, Pounosammy
S	02-Oct	Partick Thistle		A	L2	0-2	3059	Pounosammy	Outtara	Miller r80	Brady	Davidson	Davidson	Maxwell r79	Bartholeme r25	Ebanda	Sacko	Daly	McAlpine u25, Martin u79, Tagro, Boyle, Smart
M		Cowdenbeath		A	FC SF	4-1	155	Berthelot	Paquito	Miller	Brady	Davidson	Bartholeme	Young r45	Paquito	Ebanda r72 1	Sacko 2	Daly	Maxwell u72, Boyle u80, Young, Smart, Boyle
S	16-Oct	Clyde		A	L2	0-2	3002	Pounosammy	Paquito r28	Miller	Brady b	Davidson	Bartholeme	Outtara r59	Davidson b	Ebanda	Sacko 1	McAlpine r88	Daly u59, Young, Smart, Boyle, Pounosammy
S	23-Oct	Hamilton Academical		H	L2	0-1	1193	Berthelot	Mendy	Miller	Brady	Dennis	Bartholeme	Young	Brady b	Ebanda r22	Sacko	Daly b	Martin u88, McAlpine u22 r72, Raffel u52, Malcolm, Pounosammy
S	30-Oct	St Johnstone	3	A	L2	0-2	2452	Berthelot	Mendy b	Miller	Smart r45	Davidson	Bartholeme	Young	Brady	Martin 1	Sacko	Raffel r81	McAlpine u45, Boyle u81, McQuade, Malcolm, Boyle
S	13-Nov	Falkirk		H	L2	0-2	1646	Berthelot r71	Mendy	Miller	Raffel b	Davidson	Bartholeme	Young r65	Young	Martin	Sacko	Daly r45	Ebanda u45, Malcolm, Tulloch, Mendy, Hall
S	20-Nov	St Mirren		A	L2	0-1	1371	Berthelot	Mendy r64 b	Miller	Davidson	Dennis	Bartholeme	Davidson	Raffel r55	Martin	Sacko	Outtara	Ebanda u65, Young u55, Mendy u28, Malcolm, Pounosammy
S	23-Nov	Ross County		A	L2	1-1	1795	Pounosammy	Mendy	Miller b	Smart	Dennis	Bartholeme	Brady r66	Raffel r55	Ebanda	Martin r68	Outtara 1	Young u55, Sacko u68, Malcolm, Tagro, Pounosammy
S	27-Nov	Partick Thistle		A	L2	0-2	2579	Berthelot	Mendy b	Miller	Smart	Dennis	Bartholeme	Davidson	Paquito	Outtara	Sacko r75	Outtara	Davidson u66, Martin u75, Raffel, Tagro, Pounosammy
S	04-Dec	Queen of the South		A	L2	1-4	1127	Berthelot	Paquito	Miller	Smart r76 b	Dennis	Bartholeme	Brady	Outtara	Ebanda	Sacko	Outtara	Young u76, Young u71, Martin u45, Raffel, Mendy
S	11-Dec	Hamilton Academical		A	L2	0-2	3516	Pounosammy	Mendy	McMullen b	Davidson b	Dennis	Bartholeme	Davidson b	Brady	Martin	Sacko	Brady	Sacko u69, Malcolm u45, Hall, Young, Hall
S	18-Dec	St Johnstone		H	L2	0-2	1545	Pounosammy	Pounosammy	McMullen r88	Raffel r45	Dennis	Bartholeme	Sacko	Sacko r72	O'Reilly r45 b	Ebanda r67 b	Brady	Ebanda u45, Malcolm u65, Martin u45, Young, Berthelot
S	26-Dec	Ross County		A	L2	0-2	1393	Pounosammy	Outtara	McMullen	Davidson	Smart	Bartholeme	Brady 1 b	Raffel r75	O'Reilly r82	Martin 1	Miller b	O'Reilly u72, Malcolm u67, McGowan, Leiper, Pounosammy
W	29-Dec	Falkirk		H	L2	2-0	1534	Pounosammy	Mendy	McMullen	Davidson	Smart	Bartholeme b	Davidson	Raffel r69	O'Reilly r82	Martin 1	Miller b	Young u75, Murtagh u69, Malcolm u82, Tulloch, Pounosammy
S	01-Jan	Alloa Athletic		H	L2	0-1	3181	Mendy	Outtara	McMullen r54	Davidson	Smart b	Bartholeme	Jablonski	Murtagh 1	Martin	Crabbe	Miller r88	Malcolm u88, Murtagh u82, McGowan u45, Raffel, Hall
S	08-Jan	St Mirren		H	SC 3	0-2	1394	Pounosammy	Outtara	Fullerton	Davidson	Smart	Bartholeme	Murtagh	Jablonski	Crabbe r73	Clarke 2 b	Fullarton r77	O'Reilly u77, Tulloch u54, Raffel, Casey, Hall
S	15-Jan	Queen of the South	4	H	L2	1-2	1599	Pounosammy	Outtara b	Tulloch r45 1	Davidson	Smart b	Bartholeme	Murtagh	Jablonski	Clarke	Clarke 1	Crabbe r80	Young u80, Tulloch u54, O'Reilly, Leiper, Hall
S	22-Jan	Partick Thistle		H	L2	3-3	1403	Berthelot	Outtara	McMullen	Jablonski	Smart	Bartholeme r35	Murtagh r53	Tulloch 1 b	Martin r88 b	Martin	Fullarton	Leiper, Leiper, Martin u45, Malcolm, Hall
S	29-Jan	Airdrie United		A	L2	1-2	1361	Berthelot	Outtara	McMullen 1	Davidson b	Smart	Bartholeme	Jablonski	Jablonski	Clarke r75	Crabbe	Tulloch	O'Reilly u73, Malcolm u83, Fullarton u35, Murtagh, Casey
S	12-Feb	Ross County		A	L2	0-2	1474	Berthelot	Outtara	McMullen r84	Davidson	Smart b	Bartholeme	Murtagh	Bartholeme	Clarke 1	Clarke 1	Crabbe b	Martin u53, Malcolm u63, Fullarton u84, Leiper, Hall
S	19-Feb	Hamilton Academical		H	L2	2-1	1122	Berthelot	Outtara	Tulloch	Jablonski	Smart r29	Bartholeme	Murtagh	Murtagh	Martin r88 b	Clarke 1	Tulloch r65	Fullarton u84, Martin u29 2, Fullarton u65, Murtagh, Hall
S	05-Mar	St Mirren		A	L2	2-3	244	Berthelot x50	Outtara	Tulloch r87	Davidson b	Davidson	Martin r66	Martin r66	Martin r66	Clarke r75	Crabbe	McMullen	Malcolm u45, Fullarton u66, Raffel u73, Leiper, Hall
S	07-May	Airdrie United		H	L2	0-1	1296	Hall	Outtara	Fullerton r59	Davidson	Smart	Leiper	Murtagh r68	Jablonski	Clarke r82	Crabbe	Martin b	Tulloch u59, Malcolm u68, Gilfillan u82, Woods, Raffel

Manager : Claud Anelka to 8th October.   Gordon Dalziel from 11th October
(1) Annan Tournament ; won 8-7 on penalties
(2) Annan Tournament
(3) Anderson sent off
(4) Baird sent off 77 minutes

Day	Date	Opponents	Note	Venue	Comp	Res.	Att.	1	2	3	4	5	6	7	8	9	10	11	Substitutes, own goals and goal times				
S	09-Jul	Dunfermline Athletic		H	F	0-5	1656	Brown	Silvestro r45	Ellis	Davidson r69	Lumsden	McLeod	Ferguson r61	Jablonski	Annard r45	Jaconelli r45	Crilly r39	McManus u45	Leiper u69	Clarke u61	Crabbe u45	Martin u45
Th	14-Jul	Bloomfield	1	A	F	7-0		Brown r	Davidson	Ellis 2	Silvestro	Lumsden	McLeod	Jablonski 2	Ferguson r	Annand r 2	Crabbe r	Crilly r 1	Hall u	McManus u	Leiper u	Clarke u	Tulloch u
S	16-Jul	Cliftonville	2	A	F	0-0		Brown r76	Davidson r63	Ellis	Silvestro r70	Lumsden	McLeod	Jablonski	Ferguson r45	Annand r45	McManus r60	Crilly	Hall u76	Leiper u63	Clarke u70	Tulloch u45	Crabbe u45
W	20-Jul	Dundee		H	F	0-2	1050	Brown	Davidson	Ellis	Silvestro	Lumsden	McLeod	Jablonski r66	Ferguson r78	Annand r72	McManus r80	Crilly	Tulloch u66	Martin u78	Clarke u72	Jaconelli u80	Leiper
S	23-Jul	East Fife		A	F	4-2	489	Brown	Davidson	Ellis r85 1	Silvestro r36	Lumsden	McLeod r89	Jablonski r89	Ferguson	Crabbe r80	Annand r45	Crilly	Tulloch u36	Leiper u89	Clarke u89	Jaconelli u80 1	McManus u45 2
S	30-Jul	Elgin City	3	H	LCC 1	3-1	1418	Brown	Davidson	Leiper r45	Crilly	Lumsden	McLeod	Jablonski	Ferguson r72	Crabbe r87 1	McManus 1	Ellis	Silvestro u72	Annand u87	Fairbairn u45	Jaconelli	Hall
S	06-Aug	Morton		A	L3	0-2	3222	Brown	Lyle	Ellis	Silvestro	Lumsden	McLeod	Jablonski r45	Ferguson	Crabbe r45	McManus r79 b	Crilly	Annand u45	Fairbairn u45	Jaconelli u79	Davidson	Hall
Tu	09-Aug	Airdrie United		H	LC 1	2-0	1237	Brown	Lyle	Ellis	Silvestro	Lumsden	McLeod	Crilly	Ferguson	Annand r87 b 1	McManus r75	Jablonski 1	Fairbairn u75	Jaconelli u87	Davidson	Tulloch	Hall
S	13-Aug	Gretna		H	L3	1-3	2124	Brown b	Lyle b	Ellis	Silvestro	Lumsden b	McLeod	Crilly b 1	Ferguson	Annand r	McManus	Jablonski r45	Fairbairn u45 r81	Jaconelli u81	Tulloch	Davidson	Hall
S	20-Aug	Alloa Athletic	4	A	L3	2-1	931	Brown	Lyle	Ellis b	Silvestro b	Lumsden 1	McLeod	Crilly b	Ferguson r59	Annand r78 1p	McManus r89	Jablonski	Fairbairn u59	Davidson u78	Jaconelli u89	Tulloch	Hall
Tu	23-Aug	Livingston		H	LC 2	1-2	2077	Brown	Lyle	Tulloch r73	Silvestro	Lumsden	McLeod	Fairbairn r63	Crilly b	Annand r57	McManus 1	Ellis	Annand u57	Jaconelli u63	Davidson u73	Leiper	Hall
S	27-Aug	Partick Thistle		A	L3	3-1	2577	Brown	Lyle b	Hilland	Silvestro	Lumsden	McLeod b 1	Crilly	Davidson	Crabbe r71	McManus r85 1	Ellis	Fairbairn u71 1	Annand u85	Jablonski	Tulloch	Hall
Tu	30-Aug	Dumbarton	3	H	LCC 2	2-1	1382	Brown b	Lyle	Hilland	Davidson r106	Lumsden	McLeod	Fairbairn r73	Crilly	Annand r90	McManus 1	Ellis	Crabbe u45	Silvestro u73	Jablonski u106	Tulloch	Hall
S	10-Sep	Stirling Albion		H	L3	5-2	1997	Brown	Lyle	Hilland	Silvestro r55	Lumsden	McLeod	Crilly 1	Jablonski 1	Fairbairn	McManus r84 2	Ellis 1	Davidson u55	Annand u84	Batchelor	Leiper	Hall
Tu	13-Sep	St Johnstone	5	A	LCC qf	1-5	1672	Brown	Lyle	Hilland r45	Davidson	Lumsden	McLeod	Crilly r62	Jablonski	Fairbairn	McManus 1	Ellis r76	Annand u62	Tulloch u76	Jaconelli u45	Crabbe	Hall
S	17-Sep	Ayr United		H	L3	3-3	1846	Brown	Lyle	Hilland b X61	Davidson	Lumsden b	McLeod	Fairbairn r89	Silvestro r34	Crabbe r84 b 1	McManus 1	Ellis	Jablonski u34 b 1	Tulloch u84	Annand u89	Jaconelli	Hall
S	24-Sep	Peterhead		A	L3	1-0	740	Brown	Lyle	Ellis	Wilson r62	Lumsden	McLeod	Fairbairn	Silvestro r55	Annand b	McManus r76 1	Davidson	Jablonski u55	Jaconelli u62	Leiper u76	Batchelor	Hall
S	01-Oct	Forfar Athletic		H	L3	0-2	1809	Brown	Lyle	Ellis	Wilson r30	Lumsden	McLeod	Fairbairn b	Silvestro r68	Annand	McManus r45	Davidson	Jaconelli u45	Hilland u30	Ferguson u68	Bagan	Hall
S	15-Oct	Dumbarton		A	L3	2-1	852	Brown	Lyle	Ellis 1	Wilson	Lumsden	McLeod 1	Crilly r59	Ferguson r85	Fairbairn b	McManus r76	Davidson	Silvestro u59	Annand u76	Bagan u85	Hilland	Hall
S	22-Oct	Morton		H	L3	1-2	2446	Brown	Lyle	Ellis	Wilson r45 b	Lumsden	McLeod	Crilly	Ferguson b	Crabbe r79	McManus	Davidson r45	Fairbairn u45	Hilland u45	Annand u79	Silvestro	Hall
Tu	25-Oct	Gretna		A	L3	1-5	1074	Brown	Lyle r70 b	Hilland r45	Silvestro	Lumsden	McLeod	Crilly	Ferguson r45	Crabbe X53	McManus	Ellis 1	Ferguson u45	Wilson u45	Lyle u70	Annand	Hall
S	29-Oct	Stirling Albion		A	L3	0-1	868	Brown	Lyle b	Hilland r60	Jablonski r60	Lumsden b	McLeod b	Fairbairn	Davidson r76 b	Crilly	McManus	Ellis	Annand u60	Silvestro u60	Bagan u76	Ferguson	Hall
S	05-Nov	Partick Thistle		H	L3	1-1	2039	Brown	Lyle	Ellis	Silvestro r87	Lumsden	McLeod b	Fairbairn 1	Ferguson	Annand b	McManus r75	Crilly r36	Jablonski 36	Crabbe u75	Bagan u87	Wilson	Hall
Tu	22-Nov	Ayr United		A	L3	1-2	930	Brown b	Lyle r76	Ellis	Silvestro b	Lumsden	McLeod b	Fairbairn	Crabbe	Annand b 1	McManus	Jablonski	Bagan u76	Davidson	Leiper	Jaconelli	Hall
S	26-Nov	Peterhead		H	L3	0-2	1202	Brown b	Lyle r60	Ellis	Silvestro	Lumsden	McLeod	Fairbairn	Crabbe	Annand r68	McManus	Jablonski r68	Bagan u60	Davidson u68	Jaconelli u68	Leiper	Hall
S	03-Dec	Dumbarton		H	L3	3-2	1060	Brown s89	Lyle	Tulloch r54	Silvestro	Lumsden	McLeod r61	Fairbairn	McManus 1	Crabbe r77	Jablonski 1	Ellis	Davidson u54 1	Bagan u61	Annand u77	Jaconelli	Hall
S	10-Dec	Queen's Park		A	SC 2	0-2	721	Brown	Lyle	Stirling	Silvestro b	Lumsden	Davidson r 45	Fairbairn	McManus b	Crabbe	Jablonski r64 b	Ellis	McLeod u45	Annand u64	Tulloch	Jaconelli	Hall
M	26-Dec	Morton		A	L3	0-2	2812	Brown	Lyle b bX 70	Ellis	Silvestro	Lumsden	Davidson	Crilly r	McManus	Fairbairn	Crabbe r72	Jablonski	McLeod u72 x72	Jaconelli u	Stirling	Wilson	Hall
S	31-Dec	Alloa Athletic	6	H	L3	3-2	1637	Brown	Silvestro	Ellis	Jaconelli r85	Lumsden	Davidson	Fairbairn	McManus 3	Crilly	Crabbe r72	Jablonski r56 1	Tulloch u85	Bagan u72	Stirling u56	Wilson	Hall
M	02-Jan	Partick Thistle		A	L3	0-1	2428	Brown	Lyle r86	Ellis	Silvestro b	Lumsden	Davidson	Fairbairn b	McManus	Crilly	Bagan r60	Stirling r45	Clarke u45	Crabbe u60	McLeod u86	Jaconelli	Hall
S	14-Jan	Stirling Albion		H	L3	2-3	2236	Brown	Silvestro	Ellis	Davidson r88 b	Lumsden	McLeod	Fairbairn	McManus 1	Crilly r67	Crabbe r79	Jablonski	Bagan u88	Jaconelli u67 b	Clarke u79	Wilson	Hall
S	21-Jan	Ayr United		H	L3	1-1	1467	Brown	Silvestro b	Ellis	Davidson r	Lumsden b	Wilson	Jablonski r81	McManus	Crilly 1	Crabbe r69	Fairbairn	Bagan u81	Clarke u69	Jaconelli	Tulloch	Hall
S	28-Jan	Peterhead	7	A	L3	0-0	702	Hall	Lyle	Ellis	Silvestro	Lumsden	McLeod	Jablonski r65	McManus	Clarke r83	Davidson b	Crilly	Fairbairn u65	Crabbe u83	Bagan	Jaconelli	Tulloch
S	04-Feb	Forfar Athletic		H	L3	1-0	1409	Brown	Davidson	Ellis	Silvestro	Campbell	Lumsden	Bonar r54	McManus r54	Crabbe b	Adam r85	Crilly	Lyle u65	Fairbairn u54	Jablonski u85	McLeod	Hall
S	11-Feb	Dumbarton		A	L3	1-0	812	Brown	Lyle	Ellis	Silvestro	Campbell	Lumsden	Crilly r66	McManus r89 1	Jablonski r76	Davidson	Adam	Bonar u66	Crabbe u89	Fairbairn u76	McLeod	Hall
S	18-Feb	Gretna		H	L3	0-1	1745	Brown	Lyle r61	Ellis	Silvestro	Campbell	Lumsden	Crilly	McManus	Fairbairn r70	Davidson b	Adam r45	Jablonski u70	McLeod u45	Bonar u61	Clarke	Hall
S	25-Feb	Alloa Athletic		A	L3	1-1	749	Brown	Lyle r72	McLeod	Silvestro	Campbell b	Lumsden	Davidson 1	McManus r82	Jablonski r90	Crilly	Ellis	Fairbairn u72	Adam u82	Crabbe u90	Bonar	Hall
S	11-Mar	Stirling Albion		A	L3	2-2	1079	Brown	Lyle	McLeod	Silvestro	Campbell	Lumsden	Crilly 1	McManus 1	Crabbe r55	Davidson	Ellis r45	Fairbairn u45 r81	Clarke u55	Bonar	Leiper	Hall
S	18-Mar	Ayr United		A	L3	0-0	1010	Brown	Lyle	McLeod b	Silvestro r74	Campbell	Lumsden	Bonar	McManus	Crilly	Davidson	Fairbairn r59	Ellis u74	Jablonski u59	Bonar	Leiper	Hall
Tu	21-Mar	Partick Thistle		H	L3	1-2	1112	Brown	Lyle	McLeod	Bonar	Campbell	Lumsden 1	Fairbairn	McManus	Clarke r60	Davidson	Ellis r70	Jablonski u60	Adam u70	Jaconelli	Leiper	Hall
S	25-Mar	Peterhead		H	L3	1-0	1098	Brown	Lyle	McLeod	Bonar r57	Campbell	Lumsden	Fairbairn r67	McManus	Crilly	Davidson	Adam r60 1	Jablonski u57	Ellis u60	Clarke u67	Jaconelli	Hall
Tu	28-Mar	Forfar Athletic		A	L3	2-5	437	Brown	Lyle r32	McLeod r45	Silvestro	Campbell 1	Lumsden	Bonar	McManus b 1	Crilly	Davidson b	Adam r68	Tulloch u45 b	Fairbairn u32	Jaconelli u68	Jablonski	Hall
S	01-Apr	Forfar Athletic		A	L3	2-0	581	Brown	Bonar b	Ellis	Silvestro	Campbell b	Lumsden	Fairbairn	McManus 1	Jablonski r86 b 1	Davidson	Crilly	Jaconelli u86	Lyle	Tulloch	Adam	Hall
S	08-Apr	Dumbarton		H	L3	0-0	1055	Brown	Bonar	Ellis	Silvestro	Campbell	Lumsden	Fairbairn b	McManus	Jablonski r71	Davidson	Crilly	Crabbe u71	Lyle	McLeod	Jaconelli	Hall
S	15-Apr	Morton		H	L3	1-1	1395	Brown	Lyle	Ellis	Silvestro	Campbell	Lumsden	Fairbairn	McManus 1	Crabbe r71	Bonar	Crilly	Jablonski u71	Adam	Lieper	Jaconelli	Hall
S	22-Apr	Gretna		A	L3	1-2	2201	Brown	Bonar	McLeod	Silvestro 1	Campbell	Lumsden	Fairbairn r57	McManus	Crabbe r68	Jablonski r60	Ellis	Jaconelli u57	Adam u60	Lyle u68	Leiper	Hall
S	29-Apr	Alloa Athletic		H	L3	0-1	1506	Brown	Bonar	Ellis	Silvestro	Campbell	Lumsden	Fairbairn	McManus	Crabbe r57	Davidson	Crilly r66	Jablonski u57	McLeod u66	Hall	Leiper	Tulloch
S	06-May	East Fife		A	FC sf	0-1	450	Hall	Liddle	Tullloch	Smith r74	Campbell	Leiper	Batchelor	Darling	Sargeant	Halley r84	Richardson r57	Gray u54	Thomson u84	Cunningham u57		

Manager : Gordon Dalziel

(1) Shine a Light Charity Trophy *(2) Shine a Light Charity Trophy ; won 4-2 on penalties*

(3) after extra time

(4) McGlynn sent off 89 minutes

(5) Paul McManus opened the scoring in the 5-1 Challenge Cup quarter final defeat at Perth, and a bad night got worse when he was arrested after the match – for being in Perth. He was on conditional bail from a charge of taking part in a brawl outside a Perth nightclub, and one of the conditions was that he was not to set foot in Perth until the trial. Once the nonsense of his re-arrest had been tossed out of court, he returned in February and was sentenced to 240 hours community service.

(6) Ovenstone sent off 70 minutes

(7) YTS goalkeeper Hall played following Alistair Brown's thumb injury sustained while training at Hibs, and kept a clean sheet, the last 15 minutes of which were in semi darkness due to a partial failure of the floodlights at Balmoor Stadium.

Day	Date	Opponents	Note	Venue	Comp	Res.	Att.	1	2	3	4	5	6	7	8	9	10	11	Substitutes, own goals and goal times				
S	08-Jul	Dundee United		H	F	1-4	1176	Brown	Bonar r82	Leiper	Silvestro r84	Campbell	Lumsden	Fairbairn	McManus	One r74	Davidson	Kilgannon r82	Batchelor u82	Darling u84	Bouadji u74	Tulloch u82	Fahey
S	15-Jul	Livingston		H	F	2-1	775	Brown r68	Bonar	Leiper r62	Silvestro	Campbell r62	Lumsden	Fairbairn r77	McManus	One r62	Davidson	Kilgannon r66	Fahey u68	Tulloch u62	Sergeant u77	Harty u62	Bouadji u62
W	19-Jul	Falkirk		H	F	1-4	1054	Brown	Bonar 1	Fotheringham r73	Silvestro	Campbell	Lumsden	Fairbairn r85	McManus r85	One r62	Davidson r79	Kilgannon r84	Dair u69 r84	Leiper u69	Bouadji u45	Harty u85	Sergeant u84
S	22-Jul	Stenhousemuir		A	F	2-1	500	Brown	Bonar	Fotheringham r86	Silvestro r45	Campbell	Lumsden	Fairbairn r20	McManus r45 1	One r78 1	Davidson	Tulloch r69	Manson u20	Bouadji u45	Leiper u69	Harty u45	Sergeant u78
S	29-Jul	East Fife		A	F	2-1	700	Fahey	Bonar	Fotheringham r75	Silvestro	Campbell r83	Lumsden	Fairbairn r69	McManus r66 1	Harty r64	Davidson r83	Kilgannon 1	One u66	Manson u69	Leiper u75	Tulloch u83	Boudaji u83
S	05-Aug	Morton		A	L3	0-2	2596	Brown	Bonar	Fotheringham r81	Silvestro	Campbell	Lumsden	Fairbairn r70	McManus	Harty r64	Davidson b	Kilgannon	One u64	Tulloch u81	Manson u70	Boudaji	Fahey
Tu	08-Aug	Airdrie United		H	LC 1	1-2	1260	Brown s36	Bonar	Leiper r73	Silvestro	Campbell	Lumsden	Harty r64	McManus	One b 1	Davidson	Kilgannon r76	Fairbairn u64	Tulloch u73	Manson u76	Batchelor	Fahey
S	12-Aug	Forfar Athletic		H	L3	0-0	1437	Brown	Bonar	Fotheringham	Silvestro	Campbell	Lumsden	Manson r76	McManus	One b	Davidson	Tulloch r55	Fairbairn u55	Kilgannon u76	Harty u70	Batchelor	Fahey
Tu	15-Aug	St Johnstone	1	A	LCC 1	1-3	1261	Brown	Bonar	Fotheringham	Silvestro	Campbell	Lumsden	Tulloch r84	Harty	One r65 1	Davidson	Kilgannon r98	Manson u65	Fairbairn u87	Leiper u84	Batchelor	Fahey
S	19-Aug	Peterhead		A	L3	1-0	718	Brown	Bonar	Fotheringham 1	Silvestro	Campbell	Lumsden	Tulloch r67	Harty b	One r86	Davidson	Kilgannon r88	Manson u86 b	Fairbairn u67	Leiper u88	Batchelor	Fahey
S	26-Aug	Cowdenbeath		H	L3	1-3	2457	Brown	Bonar b	Fotheringham	Silvestro	Campbell 1	Lumsden	Janczyk r66	Harty	One b	Davidson b	Kilgannon r84	Manson u59	Xavier u54 b	Tulloch	Leiper	Fahey
Sn	03-Sep	Stranraer		A	L3	4-1	986	Brown	Bonar b	Tulloch r32	Silvestro	Campbell 1	Lumsden	Fotheringham b	Davidson	Harty r66 2	McManus 1	Manson	Janczyk u32	One u85	Sargent	Leiper	Fahey
S	09-Sep	Stranraer		A	L3	4-1	452	Brown	Bonar	Fotheringham r32	Silvestro	Campbell 1	Lumsden	Fotheringham r59	Davidson	Harty	McManus 1	Manson	Kilgannon u55	Davidson u59	One u67	Janczyk u72 b	Fahey
S	16-Sep	Brechin City		H	L3	1-1	1818	Brown	Bonar	Fotheringham b	Campbell	Lumsden	Janczyk	Fairbairn r55 b	Davidson r85	One	McManus 1	Manson	One u67	Janczyk u72 b	Thorarinsson u69	Kilgannon u62	Fahey
S	23-Sep	Alloa Athletic		H	L3	0-0	1517	Brown	Bonar	Fotheringham r80	Campbell	Lumsden	Silvestro	Manson r67	Davidson r72	Harty	McManus	Kilgannon r59	Davidson u59	Janczyk u77	Bannerman		Fahey
S	30-Sep	Ayr United		A	L3	0-1	745	Brown	Bonar	Fotheringham	Campbell	Lumsden	Silvestro r77	McManus	Davidson b	One	Harty b	Manson r62	Harty u73	Tansey u63	Bannerman		Fahey
S	14-Oct	Morton		H	L3	1-3	1330	Brown	Wilson	Fotheringham b	Andrews	Lumsden	Silvestro r39	McManus	Davidson r63	One r73 1	Thorarinsson	McManus	Tansey u68	Janczyk u81	Kilgannon	Tulloch	Fahey
S	21-Oct	Forfar Athletic		A	L3	1-1	754	Brown	Wilson	Fotheringham	Andrews	Lumsden	Davidson b 1	Currie,P	Bonar	Thorarinsson b	One r81 b 1	Manson r68	Fairbairn u66	Kilgannon u80	Tansey u86	Tulloch	Fahey
S	28-Oct	Stirling Albion		H	L3	1-3	1656	Brown	Bonar	Wilson	Fotheringham 1p	Campbell b	Davidson	Fairbairn r80	Silvestro b	One	Thorarinsson	Batchelor r66	Bonar u78	Tulloch	Lumsden	Bannerman	Currie,P
S	04-Nov	Cowdenbeath		A	L3	2-1	1487	Brown	Wilson	Fotheringham	Andrews	Campbell b b	Davidson	Fairbairn r84	Silvestro	One b 1	Thorarinsson	Currie,P 62	One u64 b 1	Currie,P u77	Lumsden	Kilgannon	Fahey
S	11-Nov	Brechin City		H	L3	0-1	745	Brown	Bonar	Fotheringham	Andrews	Campbell b	Davidson b 1	Wilson r77	Silvestro	One	Thorarinsson	Currie,P r60	Fahey u43	One u85	Bonar u62	Lumsden	Lumsden
S	25-Nov	Stranraer		A	L3	1-1	1458	Brown	Bonar	Fotheringham b	Andrews	Campbell	Davidson b	Fairbairn X65	Silvestro b	McManus	Thorarinsson r64	Fairbairn	One u60	Tulloch u87	Lumsden	Kilgannon	Currie,P
S	02-Dec	Alloa Athletic		A	L3	2-1	786	Brown r43	Bonar b	Fotheringham X65	Andrews	Campbell b	Davidson 1	Fairbairn X65	Silvestro b	McManus	Thorarinsson r85 1	Currie,P r62	Harty u60 b	Manson u75	Currie,P u45	Andrews	Currie,D
S	09-Dec	Dumbarton		H	SC 2	0-1	1186	Fahey	Bonar b	Fotheringham	Campbell 1	Campbell b	Davidson	Fairbairn X65	Silvestro	McManus	Thorarinsson	Currie,P r60	Silvestro u61	Halley u85	Tulloch	Andrews	Currie,D
S	16-Dec	Ayr United		H	L3	0-1	2368	Fahey	Wilson	Pelosi b	Campbell	Lumsden	Silvestro	Thorarinsson r45	Bonar	McManus	One r87 b	Kilgannon r75	Tulloch u45	One u61	Manson u75	Andrews	Currie,D
S	23-Dec	Morton		A	L3	0-1	1538	Fahey b	Wilson	Pelosi	Campbell	Lumsden	Manson r60	Thorarinsson	Bonar b	McManus	One r85 b	Kilgannon b	Fotheringham u85	Ciani u61	Manson	Halley	Currie,D
S	30-Dec	Peterhead		H	L3	5-2	2744	Fahey	Wilson	Pelosi	Campbell	Lumsden	Davidson r75	Fairbairn 1	Bonar r61	McManus 3	Harty r61 1	Thorarinsson	Bonar u60 1	Fairbairn u71	Halley		Currie,D
Tu	02-Jan	Cowdenbeath		H	L3	1-2	922	Fahey	Wilson	Pelosi	Campbell	Lumsden	Silvestro	Fairbairn	One	McManus	Harty r61	Davidson r45	Whateley u83	Playle	Richardson	O'Neill	Halley
S	13-Jan	Stirling Albion		A	L3	1-0	495	Currie,D	Batchelor	Pelosi r85	Dingwall	Bonar	Darling r83	Manson 1	Mackie	One	Fairbairn	Kilgannon r60	Playle				Halley
Tu	16-Jan	Dunfermline Athletic	2	A	FC sf	2-2	1445	Fahey	Wilson	Pelosi	Campbell 1	Andrews	Lumsden b	Davidson 1	Silvestro	One	McManus b	Pirret 1	Fairbairn u72	Carcary u54	Fotheringham	Bonar	Currie,D
S	20-Jan	Brechin City		H	L3	1-0	327	Fahey	Wilson	Fotheringham	Campbell 1	Andrews	Lumsden b	Davidson 1	Silvestro	McManus b	McLaughlin r72	Kilgannon r54	Fairbairn u70	One u81	Kilgannon	Bonar	Currie,D
S	27-Jan	Stranraer		A	L3	2-0	1763	Fahey	Wilson	Fotheringham r73b2	Campbell b 1	Andrews	Lumsden b	Davidson r84 1	Silvestro	McManus	McLaughlin r70	Carcary r81 1	Hislop u57 1	Fairbairn u77	Pelosi		Currie,D
S	03-Feb	Alloa Athletic		H	L3	3-0	2161	Fahey	Wilson	Fotheringham r78	Campbell b 1	Andrews	Lumsden b	Davidson r84 b 1	Silvestro	McManus r77 1p	McLaughlin r57	Carcary	McLaughlin u78	Fairbairn u78	Pelosi u85	McLaughlin u75	Currie,D
S	17-Feb	Peterhead		A	L3	2-1	909	Fahey	Wilson	Pelosi	Andrews b	Lumsden	Bonar b	Fairbairn	Silvestro	McManus	Hislop r85 1	Carcary r70	McLaughlin u85	McManus u64	Kilgannon	Mackie	Currie,D
W	21-Feb	Ayr United		H	L3	2-0	862	Fahey b	Wilson b 1	Fotheringham 67	Campbell	Andrews	Lumsden	Davidson b	Silvestro	Bonar	Hislop 67	Pelosi 64	Hislop u65	Fairbairn u69 1	Fotheringham u82	Bonar	Currie,D
S	24-Feb	Forfar Athletic		H	L3	2-1	1945	Fahey	Wilson	Fotheringham r82	Campbell	Andrews b	Lumsden	Davidson b	Silvestro	McManus r69	McLaughlin r65	Carcary	Fairbairn u69 1	Fotheringham u82	Bonar		Currie,D
S	03-Mar	Cowdenbeath		A	L3	5-1	2249	Fahey	Wilson	Fotheringham 73b2	Campbell b 1	Andrews b	Lumsden 1	Davidson b	Bonar	McManus	Hislop 1	Carcary 73	Fairbairn u75	McLaughlin u75	Silvestro		Currie,D
S	10-Mar	Stirling Albion		H	L3	0-1	2161	Fahey	Wilson	Fotheringham 78	Campbell b 1	Andrews b	Lumsden b	Davidson b+X89	McLaughlin r57	McManus r77 1p	Hislop r75 b	Carcary	McLaughlin u73	Fairbairn u78	McLaughlin u75	Silvestro	Currie,D
S	17-Mar	Brechin City		A	L3	2-1	909	Fahey	Wilson	Pelosi	Andrews b	Lumsden	Bonar b	Fairbairn	Silvestro	McManus	Hislop r85 1	Carcary	McLaughlin u85	Dingwall	Mackie		Currie,D
S	31-Mar	Stranraer		H	L3	0-0	1645	Fahey	Wilson b	Fotheringham	Andrews	Lumsden b	Silvestro	Davidson b	Neil	McManus	Hislop 67	Pelosi r64	Pelosi u40	Kilgannon	Dingwall	Mackie	Ellison
Tu	03-Apr	Ayr United		H	L3	3-2	825	Fahey	Wilson	Fotheringham	Campbell r69 b	Andrews 1	Lumsden b	Davidson b	McManus	Hislop b 1	McLaughlin	Carcary r40	Pelosi u51	Kilgannon u69	Dingwall	Mackie	Ellison
S	07-Apr	Alloa Athletic		H	L3	2-0	4327	Fahey	Wilson	Pelosi	Lumsden b 1	Andrews	Silvestro	Davidson 88 b	McManus 1	Hislop b 1	McLaughlin	Neil b	Silvestro u41	Kilgannon u88	Kilgannon u88	Mackie u82	Ellison
S	14-Apr	Morton		A	L3	2-1	699	Fahey	Wilson	Pelosi b b+X 68	Lumsden b 1	Andrews	Davidson r76	Davidson	Bonar b	Hislop r41	McLaughlin r61	Neil r82	Silvestro u41	Kilgannon u61	Silvestro	Mackie	Ellison
S	21-Apr	Forfar Athletic		H	L3	2-1	1589	Fahey	Wilson	Fotheringham	Andrews b 1	Davidson r76	Bonar	Fairbairn 1	Neil	McManus	McLaughlin r72	Carcary r112	Silvestro u12	Dingwall u72	Dingwall u72	Mackie u76	Currie,D
W	02-May	Peterhead		H	L3 PO-1	2-0	3043	Fahey	Wilson b	Fotheringham	Campbell	Andrews	Silvestro	Davidson r70	Silvestro	McManus	McLaughlin r63	Neil	Hislop u63	Bonar u70	Fairbairn	Pelosi	Currie,D
S	05-May	Stirling Albion		A	L3 PO-2	1-3	2656	Fahey	Wilson b	Fotheringham	Campbell b	Andrews	Lumsden	Davidson b	Fairbairn r75 1	Hislop	Neil r75	Carcary r75	Silvestro u75	McLaughlin u75	McLaughlin u75	Pelosi	Currie,D

Manager : Gordon Dalziel to 31st August. Craig Levein from 5th September to 30th October. John McGlynn from 21st November.

(1) after extra time ; Stevenson sent off 83 minutes
(2) lost 6-4 on penalties
(3) Lunan sent off 68 minutes

Day	Date	Opponents	Note	Venue	Comp	Res.	Att.	1	2	3	4	5	6	7	8	9	10	11	Substitutes, own goals and goal times
S	14-Jul	Southport		A	F	1-3	100	Fahey 45	Wilson	Pelosi 1	Dingwall	Lumsden	Davidson	Borris r75	Winter r45	Hislop 68	Weir	Carcary 45	Renton u45, Dingwall u78, Weir u60, Darling u75, Silvestro u45, Halley u68, Sloan u45
W	18-Jul	Kilmarnock		H	F	2-1	962	Fahey	Wilson	Pelosi r78	Andrews	Campbell r64	Silvestro	Borris r79	Borris r60	Weir r61 1	Tod	Sloan 1	Dingwall u60, Lumsden u64, Winter u60, Silvestro u60, Carcary u60, Hislop u61
Sn	22-Jul	Dundee United		H	F	2-2	1370	Renton	Wilson	Pelosi	Andrews	Lumsden r60	Silvestro r60	Borris r79	Hislop	Hislop	Tod 1	Carcary r60	Weir u60, Davidson u60, Dingwall u79, Sloan u60, Fahey
W	25-Jul	Burntisland Shipyard		A	FC sf	5-0	250	Renton	Dingwall	Main r15	Wedderburn	Spalding	Darling 1	Whatley r82	Davidson r65	Halley 2	Graham	Thomson r73	Mackie u14, Beveridge u82, Bryce u73 1, Dingwall u79, Paterson, Amos
S	28-Jul	Forfar Athletic		A	F	1-0	350	Fahey r65	Wilson r80	Pelosi	Campbell	Andrews 1	Davidson r45 b	Borris r70	Silvestro	Weir	Weir b b+X 88	Sloan r65	Renton u65, Wedderburn u80, Darling u70 1, Winter u65, Halley u77
S	04-Aug	Airdrie United		A	L3	3-0	1645	Fahey	Wilson	Pelosi	Campbell	Andrews b	Silvestro	Borris r70	Winter	Hislop	Weir r88 1	Sloan	Winter u45 b, Carcary u70, Dingwall u70 1, Darling, Renton
Tu	07-Aug	Clyde		A	LC 1	3-0	892	Fahey	Wilson	Pelosi	Campbell	Andrews 1	Silvestro b+X90	Carcary r84 1	Winter	Hislop	Borris 1	Sloan	Darling u84, Halley u88, Borris, Darling –, Renton
S	11-Aug	Berwick Rangers		H	L3	3-1	2020	Fahey r33	Wilson	Pelosi	Tod 1	Andrews	Silvestro	Carcary r45	Andrews b	Tod 1	Weir	Sloan r83	Halley u45, Halley u83, Renton u33, Dingwall, Mackie
Tu	14-Aug	St Johnstone	1	H	LCC 1	1-1	1801	Renton	Wilson	Pelosi	Tod	Andrews	Silvestro	Borris r113	Andrews 1	Hislop r21	Weir r84 b	Sloan	Campbell u21, Darling u113, Dingwall, Darling, Renton
S	18-Aug	Alloa Athletic		H	L3	2-1	1978	Renton	Wilson	Dingwall	Campbell	Andrews b	Davidson m52	Borris	Andrews 1	Tod 1	Weir	Sloan r69	Darling u69, Halley u84, Mackie, Whatley, Amos
S	25-Aug	Cowdenbeath		H	L3	0-1	1953	Renton	Wilson	Pelosi	Campbell	Andrews	Silvestro 1	Borris	Andrews b	Tod r20	Tod 1	Sloan r67	Hislop u20, Carcary u67, Dingwall, Halley, Fahey
W	29-Aug	Motherwell		A	LC 2	5-2	1015	Renton	Wilson	Pelosi	Davidson	Andrews	Silvestro	Borris r68	Andrews	Hislop	Hislop	Carcary r73 1	Davidson u73, Sloan u68, Dingwall, Darling, Renton
S	01-Sep	Queen's Park		H	L3	1-0	2101	Fahey b	Wilson	Pelosi	Campbell	Andrews	Silvestro r62 b	Borris r67	Andrews	Hislop 1	Weir r83 3,1p	Carcary	Campbell u62, Tod u69, Sloan u38, Dingwall, Amos
S	15-Sep	Ross County		H	L3	2-3	1760	Fahey	Wilson	Pelosi	Campbell	Andrews	Tod	Davidson	Winter r84	Hislop r69	Weir r69	Carcary	Sloan u67, Halley u83, Tod, Dingwall, Amos
S	22-Sep	Ayr United		A	L3	1-0	668	Fahey	Wilson	Pelosi	Campbell	Andrews	Silvestro	Sloan r75	Davidson	Hislop 2,1p	Weir	Silvestro	Carcary u69, Sloan u84, Dingwall, Halley, Amos
S	29-Sep	Brechin City		A	L3	2-1	855	Fahey	Wilson	Pelosi	Campbell	Andrews	Tod	Borris r67	Davidson b	Hislop r60	Weir r85 b	Carcary 1	Tod u60, Winter u75, Lumsden, Dingwall, Amos
S	06-Oct	Peterhead		H	L3	1-2	1729	Fahey	Wilson	Pelosi	Campbell b	Andrews	Tod	Campbell b	Davidson	Hislop	Weir	Carcary 1	Winter u85, Dingwall u90, Lumsden, Thomson, Brown
S	20-Oct	Airdrie United		A	L3	1-2	1053	Fahey	Wilson	Pelosi	Campbell	Lumsden	Tod r76	Davidson	Davidson	Silvestro r90	Weir r79 b 1p	Sloan 1	Carcary u79 r88, Lumsden u88, Dingwall, Darling, Brown
S	27-Oct	Alloa Athletic		H	L3	2-0	2357	Fahey	Wilson	Pelosi	Campbell	Andrews	Davidson	Davidson b	Davidson 1	Hislop	Weir 45	Sloan 1	Walker u76, Carcary u45, Dingwall, Winter, Brown
S	03-Nov	Cowdenbeath		H	L3	0-2	1860	Fahey	Wilson	Dingwall r77	Campbell b	Andrews	Davidson r45	Borris r61 b	Davidson	Hislop b 1	Goodwillie r67 1	Sloan	Carcary u61, Tod, Winter, Weir u67, Tod, Winter, Brown
S	10-Nov	Queen's Park		H	L3	3-0	3571	Fahey	Wilson	Dingwall	Dingwall	Andrews	Winter r79	Borris r62	Winter r79	Hislop	Goodwillie	Sloan	Weir u62, Winter u45, Tod, Weir u77, Brown
Th	15-Nov	Hearts		H	F	3-0	1200	Brown 62	Wilson	Dingwall	Lumsden	Andrews r71	Sloan r80 b	Borris r83	Campbell r77	Weir 1	Tod 1	Carcary r83 1	Renton u62 s67, Walker u69, Whatley u83, Thomson u83, Renton
S	24-Nov	Threave Rovers		A	SC 3	5-0	629	Fahey	Wilson	Dingwall	Campbell	Andrews	Walker b	Borris	Davidson	Hislop 2	Weir r83	Carcary 2	Tod u83, Weir u68 1, Lumsden u77, Winter u80, Whatley
S	01-Dec	Ross County		A	L3	3-2	2729	Fahey	Wilson	Dingwall	Campbell	Andrews	Walker	Borris	Davidson b	Hislop r88 b 2,1p	Goodwillie r68	Sloan	Weir u68 1, Winter u88, Tod, Lumsden
S	08-Dec	Brechin City		H	L3	1-1	1475	Fahey	Wilson	Dingwall	Campbell	Andrews 1	Walker r81	Borris r85	Davidson 1	Hislop	Goodwillie r70	Sloan 1	Tod u85, Winter u68, Weir u70
S	15-Dec	Peterhead		A	L3	3-0	1044	Fahey	Wilson	Dingwall	Campbell 1	Andrews	Walker r62	Borris r85	Davidson 1	Hislop	Goodwillie r70	Sloan	Winter u81, Carcary u73, Tod, Renton
S	22-Dec	Airdrie United		A	L3	2-2	1454	Renton	Wilson	Dingwall	Campbell	Lumsden	Sloan	Borris	Henderson r76	Hislop r67	Goodwillie 2	Carcary r63	Carcary u45, Winter u63, Tod, Renton
W	26-Dec	Berwick Rangers		A	L3	1-2	570	Renton	Wilson	Dingwall	Campbell	Andrews	Winter	Borris	Henderson	Hislop r67	Goodwillie r67	Sloan 1	Tod u67, Hislop u35, Winter u63, Weir u67 b, Winter, Renton
S	29-Dec	Alloa Athletic		H	L3	3-2	1896	Renton	Wilson	Dingwall b	Lumsden	Lumsden r88	Winter	Sloan r45	Henderson	Hislop r58	Goodwillie 1	Sloan 1	Tod u45, Borris u78, Hislop u41 1, Whatley u88, Thomson
S	02-Jan	Cowdenbeath	2	A	L3	0-2	712	Renton	Wilson	Dingwall r60	Campbell	Tod	Tod	Sloan r78 b 1	Winter r76	Hislop r67	Goodwillie r41	Templeton 75 1	Hislop u41 1, Goodwillie u75, Carcary u62, Hislop u71 1, Fahey
S	05-Jan	Ross County	3	A	L3	4-1	2319	Renton	Wilson b	Dingwall	Campbell r32	Tod	Tod	Sloan	Henderson	Weir r71	Hislop	Templeton	Lumsden u32 c39, Borris u39, Walker u69, Thomson, Renton
S	12-Jan	St Johnstone		A	L3	0-1	2113	Renton	Wilson	Dingwall	Tod	Andrews	Winter	Sloan r73	Silvestro r86	Weir 1	Hislop r68	Templeton r83	Borris u73, Carcary u68, Halley u83, Wedderburn, Renton
S	19-Jan	Queen's Park		A	SC 4	1-3	1466	Renton	Wilson	Dingwall	Davidson b	Andrews	Walker	Carcary r68 b	Sloan	Hislop b	Goodwillie r75	Templeton 45 1	Borris u45 b, Winter u68, Halley u76, Tod, Renton
S	26-Jan	Berwick Rangers	4	A	L3	1-0	743	Fahey	Wilson	Pelosi	Campbell 1	Andrews 1	Walker r81	Sloan	Davidson b	Weir	Goodwillie r66	Templeton r70	Winter u45, Weir u75 1, Tod, Renton
S	02-Feb	Airdrie United		A	L3	3-0	1252	Renton	Wilson	Pelosi	Campbell	Lumsden	Davidson r45	Borris r66	Sloan	Hislop r79	Goodwillie r66	Templeton	Tod u79, Weir u81, Weir u66
S	09-Feb	Brechin City		A	L3	0-3	656	Renton	Wilson	Pelosi	Campbell	Lumsden r35	Sloan	Sloan	Henderson	Hislop r58	Goodwillie r72	Templeton	Tod u58, Borris u76, Carcary u66, Winter
S	16-Feb	Peterhead	5	H	L3	2-3	1513	Fahey	Wilson	Pelosi	Tod	Davidson	Henderson	Templeton 1	Henderson	Weir	Goodwillie r35	Sloan	Hislop u35, Borris u90, Carcary u72 1, Winter, Amos
S	23-Feb	Ayr United		A	L3	1-2	712	Fahey	Wilson	Pelosi	Lumsden	Tod	Silvestro	Templeton r79	Silvestro	Hislop r72	Goodwillie	Sloan	Borris u79, Goodwillie u72, Carcary u35 r90, Winter, Fahey
S	01-Mar	Cowdenbeath		A	L3	1-1	545	Renton	Wilson	Pelosi	Campbell	Tod	Davidson b	Davidson 2	Henderson	Weir	Weir	Sloan	Hislop u64, Goodwillie u72, Henderson u73, Winter, Wedderburn
S	08-Mar	Peterhead		A	L3	0-2	1349	Renton	Wilson	Pelosi	Henderson r76	Tod	Davidson b	Winter	Henderson r76	Weir r73	Winter r73	Goodwillie r69	Hislop u64, Borris u86, Carcary u77, Dingwall, Renton
S	15-Mar	Airdrie United		A	L3	3-2	1607	Renton	Wilson	Pelosi	Campbell	Davidson	Tod	Borris r85	Silvestro	Hislop	Weir	Goodwillie r77 1	Sloan u76, Weir u59, Carcary u69, Dingwall, Fahey
S	22-Mar	Ross County		A	L3	0-1	751	Renton	Wilson	Pelosi	Campbell b	Davidson	Silvestro r65	Borris r83	Henderson	Hislop	Weir 1	Goodwillie r69	Carcary u77, Henderson u65, Carcary u55, Weir, Renton
S	29-Mar	Queen's Park		H	L3	1-0	1458	Fahey	Wilson	Pelosi	Campbell	Davidson	Silvestro	Borris b b+X 89	Silvestro b	Hislop	Goodwillie b 1	Templeton r55	Winter u77, Henderson u69, Carcary u83, Weir, Renton
S	05-Apr	Ayr United		A	L3	3-2	2973	Renton	Wilson	Pelosi b	Campbell	Tod	Davidson	Henderson r84 b	Henderson	Weir 72	Goodwillie 2	Templeton r77 1	Weir u60, Carcary u66, Dingwall, Winter, Amos
S	12-Apr	Brechin City		H	L3	0-1	1386	Renton	Wilson	Pelosi	Campbell	Davidson	Tod	Templeton r85	Silvestro b	Hislop	Goodwillie r60	Templeton r69	Hislop u72, Carcary u66, Bryce u72, Winter, Amos
S	19-Apr	Berwick Rangers		H	L3	1-0	1212	Renton	Wilson	Pelosi	Tod	Tod	Silvestro	Templeton r73 1	Henderson	Weir 1	Weir 1	Sloan	Carcary u68, Bryce u85, Borris, Dingwall, Amos
S	26-Apr	Peterhead		H	L3	1-1	1955	Renton r33	Wilson	Pelosi	Tod r45	Davidson	Silvestro r68	Templeton r73 1	Winter r45	Hislop	Goodwillie r57 1p	Sloan 1	Carcary u45 1, Borris u45, Silvestro u66, Whatley, Wedderburn
W	30-Apr	Airdrie United		H	L3 PO-1	0-2	2831	Fahey	Wilson b	Pelosi	Campbell b	Davidson	Henderson r66	Borris	Henderson	Borris	Goodwillie	Sloan	Fahey u33, Bryce u73 1, Silvestro u66, Bryce u57 1, Templeton u75, Tod, Bryce, Brown
S	03-May	Airdrie United		A	L3 PO-2	2-2	2007	Brown	Wilson	Pelosi	Campbell b	Davidson	Silvestro r74	Henderson b	Tod	Weir b 2,1p	Goodwillie r61	Sloan b	Carcary u74, Weir u20 b, Templeton, Borris, Fahey

Manager : John McGlynn

(1) after extra time, lost 5-4 penalties
(2) Gilfillan sent off 58 minutes
(3) Lawson sent off 85 minutes
(4) Fairbairn sent off 80 minutes
(5) Henderson sent off 43 minutes

Fixture dates	opponents' scorers and goaltimes		
1971/72			
02-Aug	Seal (2) 87, 89	Campbell 3 Goldthorp 52	
07-Aug	Waddell (2) 68, 69	Hall 78	
14-Aug	McPhee 66		
21-Aug	Coulston 75	McLardy 55	
25-Aug	Christiansen 8	Miller 59	
28-Aug	Bernard 40	Edmonds 44	
01-Sep	Rae, T (2) 18, 44 Bone 34 Wilson 64 og Forsyth 81	Hay 3	
08-Sep	Newman 13	Wilson 29	
15-Sep	Campbell 21	Hughes 53 Wight 67	
22-Sep	Currie 81	McLeod, A. 15 Redburn 47 McKean 88	
29-Sep	Wodecki 31 Johnstone 42 Brown 85	Bostock 64	
	Graham 88	Hughes 43	
1973/74			
02-Oct	Crammond 53 Young 61 Barr 73	Selway 107 og	
09-Oct		Sinclair 16	
16-Oct		Mc Alpine 78	
23-Oct	Dempster 36 Hood 77	Blackadder 85	
30-Oct	McIlroy 24	Dempster (2) 17, 85 pen	
06-Nov	Campbell 34 Traynor 60		
13-Nov	Munro 76 McGhee 80 Currie 87		
27-Nov	McMillan 22 Lawson (2) 60, 82 McPhee (2) 65, 84	Bostock 37	
04-Dec	Thomson, A og 69	Mullen 83	
11-Dec		Sermani (2) 59, 65	
18-Dec	McKechnie 60 secs McPhee 12 Steele 86	Third 81 Lawrie 85	
01-Jan		Caskie 40 Cooper 43 Hall 75	
15-Jan	Franchetti 60 Brogan 85	Campbell 47 Bostock 74	
22-Jan	Mullen 48	Smith 11 Stanton 60 Higgins 87	
05-Feb	Rutherford 46 Daily 70 Gray 89	Ness 72	
19-Feb	I. Campbell 90	Whiteford, J. 63	
26-Feb	Harrier 84 pen	Thomson 38	
1975/76			
29-Mar	McKean 50 Borland 87	McInally 12 Hegarty 28 Hood 58	
06-Oct		Hughes (2) 47, 82 Third 60 Dickson 84	
13-Oct	Hall 18	Livingstone 16	
20-Oct	Hood 58	Schaedler 38 Gordon 70	
27-Oct		Wilson 82 Campbell, J. 88	
03-Nov	Harper 32	Armstrong 23	
11-Mar		Maxwell 88 pen	
18-Mar	Cook 34 Maxwell 54 Morrison 80	Lyall 33	
25-Mar	Cunningham 4	Cooper 82 og	
01-Apr			
08-Apr			
15-Apr	Fallon 25 pen Currie 51 McPaul 65	Franchetti (2) 35, 59 McCann 51 McRoberts 90	
15-Apr	Stein 31 Scanlon 85	Laing (2) 17, 51	
18-Apr	Wilson (5) 15, 29, 53, 71, 78	Scott 77	
22-Apr	Porter (2) 6, 27	Goodwin 77	
1972/73			
05-Aug	Byrom 79	Brogan 4	
12-Aug	Pearson (2) 39, 72	O'Connor 63 Rutherford 72	
16-Aug	Martin 54 Crammond 70	Lawson (2) 8, 85 Muir 36	
23-Aug	Johnston 44 Livingstone 61	Meakin 33	
26-Aug		Georgeson 8	
02-Sep	Finlayson 31 pen Bojczuk 47	Morton 51	
09-Sep	Third (2) 29, 33 Livingstone 85		
13-Sep		Fotherington 44 Davidson 76	
20-Sep	Currie 57	McGuigan 47	
27-Sep	Lister 33 pen	Murphy 82	
10-Oct		Lumsden 19	
14-Oct	Steele 76	Lawson (3) 27, 29, 68 Murphy 37	
17-Oct	Sullivan 10 McVie 21 Boyle 30	Lawson 73	
20-Apr	Nelson 43 Shaw 80	Fallis 69	
01-May		McGovern (2) 17, 77	
1974/75			
03-Aug	Evans 48	Anderson 37	
07-Aug	Hood (2) 20, 80 Lawless 35	Burns 13 Coleman 20 Elwiss 42 Charlton 44	
13-Aug	Hughes (2) 35, 85	Urquhart og 47 Dailey 55	
17-Aug		Bonnyman 68	
20-Aug	Franchetti 89	McNicholl 12	
24-Aug	Laing 45 secs Campbell 66	Hegarty 65	
23-Dec	Hamilton 22	Reid 35 O'Hara 38	
01-Jan	Finlayson 15	Cooper 18	
03-Apr		Bryce (2) 7, 37	
10-Apr	O'Connor (2) 14, 80	Brown, A. 47 Cooper 77 og	
17-Apr		Bourke (2) 2, 22 Graham 19 Wallace 26	
1976/77			
02-Aug		Bielby 68	
11-Sep	Miller 76		
18-Sep	Robertson (2) 20, 67	Phinn 49 Kyles 60	
25-Sep	Duffin 66 pen		

Fixture dates	opponents' scorers and goaltimes		
05-Aug	Stein 89	Marshall 5 Harley 27	
07-Aug	Anderson 40 Houston 50		
11-Aug	Hansen, A. (2) 47, 58 Craig, Joe 68	Morton 52 pen	
14-Aug	McCaig 17	Leetion 60	
18-Aug	Anderson (2) 22, 65 Cairney 39 Whiteford, D. 90	Frye 75	
25-Aug	Cairney 31 Jarvie 37 pen Whiteford (2) 42, 68 Clark 89 Clark 89 Marsh 912	McRoberts (2) 65, 90	
28-Aug			
01-Sep	Hood 60		
04-Sep	Holt 19	Laing 4	
07-Sep	Larnach (2) 5, 14 McCallan 44		
11-Sep	Lambie 7 Sellars 80		
15-Sep	Stewart 27 Street 37		
22-Sep	McDowell 25		
25-Sep	Reid 31		
1978/79			
29-Jul	Payne 52 Sturrock 58 Dodds 67		
31-Jul	Harley (2) 40, 59		
05-Aug	Ritchie 44 Rooney 72		
12-Aug	Myles og 14 O'Neill 20 Ward 35		
19-Aug	Miller (2) 39, 47		
30-Aug	Ballantyne 11 McDonald 58		
02-Sep	Horn 21 Wilkie 83 Ballantyne (2) 89, 110		
06-Sep	Graham 35		
09-Sep			
13-Sep	McGregor 61	Redford (2) 20, 77 Barr 25 MacDougall 75	
16-Sep	Bone (2) 64, 69	Goldthorp (2) 34, 88 Houston 62 og	
27-Sep	Dempster 25 Reid 76	McNeill 44	
30-Sep	Hutchison 12 Robinson 65		
04-Oct			
07-Oct	Gillies (2) 34, 50 pen		
11-Oct	Dickson, G. 3 Dickson, P. (2) 30, 89 pen	Mair 14 Lowe 39 pen Robb 75 Harl 79 Livingstone 81	
14-Oct	Borthwick 49 Taylor 57 O'Connor 90	Cairney 27 Hughes 29 Bourke 71	
21-Oct	Brown 29	Livingstone 3	
28-Oct	Fletcher 32	McCormick 41 pen McDougall 70	
04-Nov	Hoggan 35 Pirie (2) 63, 78 Sinclair 85	Armstrong 54 Steele 90	
11-Nov	Whiteford (2) 23, 53		
18-Nov	Young 27	Crammond 23 McCall 35 Reilly 76	
25-Nov	Whiteford, J. 22 Bourke 58	Coughlin 78 Bryce 84	
16-Dec	McDowell 29	Houston og 74	
23-Dec		Bourke (2) 6, 87 Maxwell 65	
20-Jan	Gray 45		
23-Mar	Street 49 Daun 60		
26-Mar	Murphy 89		
02-Apr	McGarvey (2) 55, 60	Robertson (2) 43, 49	
09-Apr	McGarvey 28 Mowat 68 Hyslop 86	Maxwell 64 Street 71	
16-Apr	McCallan 4	Whiteford, D. 54	
23-Apr	McCallan 14 Cooper 19	Houston 81 og McCabe 82	
30-Apr	Anderson 56 Ritchie 70 Hutchison 78 McGhee 88	Steele (2) 77, 83 Gray 85	
1977/78			
01-Aug	Moore 56	McCulloch 18	
06-Aug		Whiteford, J (3) 2, 56, 81	
09-Aug	McComb og Newman 64	Marshall 53	
13-Aug	Graham 75		
20-Aug	Hunter 51 pen Graham 75	Pelosi 19 Brogan 24 Ward 61	
27-Aug	Scott 52 pen	McLaren 47 Redford 80	
31-Aug	Bone 53	Fletcher 43 Yule 64	
03-Sep	Cargill 22 Bone (2) 36, 42		
10-Sep		Robb 23	
14-Sep			
17-Sep	Frye 67 pen		
24-Sep		McDougall 23 McIntyre 84	
28-Sep		Methven 10 Neilson 62	
01-Oct	Kinnear (2) 40, 53	Redford 51 McLaren 55	
08-Oct			
15-Oct			
19-Oct	Shields 63	Baxter 50	
22-Oct	Gillespie 18 Thomson og 20 Robb (2) 55, 88	Waddle (2) 42, 88	
29-Oct	Markey 16 pen	O'Hare 75 Fettes 83	
12-Nov	Docherty 15	Nicoll 14 Reid 16	
19-Nov	Frye 1		
26-Nov	Ballantyne 51		
10-Dec	Marshall 25		
24-Dec	Georgeson 85		
31-Dec	Clark 52 Brash 57	Goldthorpe 35 Brogan 71	
02-Jan	Wilson 3	O'Connor (2) 6, 43	
07-Jan	Wight (2) 6, 77 Smith, I (3) 20, 55, 65 Laing 30 pen	McLaughlin 42 Clelland 51	
14-Jan	Wight 40	Graham 40	
28-Jan	Wallace, G. 18 Payne 28 Kirkwood 70	Miller 2 Sweeney 15 Given 48 Ronald 81	
18-Feb	Renwick 44 1/2 Stirling 70	Hamilton 54	
25-Feb		Mullen 15	
04-Mar		Myles (2) 17, 34 Kydd 30	
		Brogan 83	

	opponents' scorers and goaltimes		
13-Oct	McCluskey (3) 18, 72pen, 75 pe Blair 76		
20-Oct	Kennedy, A. 35		
27-Oct	McCulloch 60 Clark 89		
31-Oct			
03-Nov	Robertson 18		
10-Nov	Pelosi 20 Rutherford 85		
14-Nov	Hegarty 70		
17-Nov	McLaughlin 52		
24-Nov	Melrose 27 McDonald 70		
01-Dec	McSherry 23 Frye 44 Connor 66 pen		
08-Dec	Myles 81		
10-Dec	Pirie 23 pen Ferguson 79 Mackie 81		
15-Dec	Sharp 44		
29-Dec			
01-Jan	Kidd 63		
12-Jan	Alexander 20		
19-Jan	Lennox 15 Doyle 34		
26-Jan	Yule 12		
16-Feb	Fairlie 27 pen		
23-Feb			
01-Mar			
08-Mar	Brogan (2) 19, 72		
15-Mar			
19-Mar	Smith 38 pen		
29-Mar	Colgan 89		
02-Apr	Kean 26		
05-Apr			
12-Apr			
19-Apr	Fraser 70 Gibson 81		
04-May	Tait 4 McDowell 65 Smith, D. 80 pen		
	Fraser 18 Robertson 55 Gibson 62 Harris 80		
1980/81			
26-Jul	Keeley 5		
28-Jul	Fillery 40 Droy 44		
02-Aug	Charles 10 Giles 53		
05-Aug			
09-Aug			
13-Aug	Coyle, J. 75	Leetion 36 Perry 45	
16-Aug	Wright 12 McDougall 43 McDowell 51	McGorm (2) 18, 75 McCabe 21 Miller 83	
20-Aug	Blair 72		
23-Aug	McCathie 35 Forrest 48 Rolland 56 pen Liddell 70		
27-Aug	Gallagher, B. 80		
30-Aug	Houston 30		
03-Sep			
06-Sep			
09-Sep	Mackie 65		
13-Sep	Kidd 6		
17-Sep	Wallace 45		
20-Sep			
25-Oct			
08-Nov			
15-Nov	Donnelly 5 McGowan 77		
17-Nov			
22-Nov			
13-Dec	Morris 25		
20-Dec			
01-Jan	Oliver 48		
03-Jan			
10-Jan			
24-Jan	Jarvie 10 McGhee 68		
31-Jan			
07-Feb			
14-Feb	Black 84		
21-Feb			
28-Feb			
07-Mar			
14-Mar	Geddes (2) 62, 81 Scrimgeour 63		
21-Mar	McCutcheon 72		
24-Mar			
28-Mar			
04-Apr	Sinclair 42 Fraser 55		
	McGorm 43		
11-Apr	McNeil 20 Morton 84		
18-Apr	Murray 40 Callachan 48		
22-Apr	Miller 1 McGorm 75 Given 81pen		

Fixture dates	*opponents' scorers and goaltimes*
25-Apr	
29-Apr	
1981/82	
25-Jul	McDougall (2) 40, 75 Stark (2) 65 pen, 83 Somner 88
26-Jul	
28-Jul	Kellas, Blacklaw
01-Aug	Bremner 28 Murray (2) 47, 52 Junior 81
03-Aug	
08-Aug	Fleming 27
12-Aug	Hutchinson 54 McNeill 88 Ritchie 10 Rooney 46 Busby 46
15-Aug	Redford (4) 30,71,86,89 Jardine 8 Russell 49 McAdam 28
19-Aug	Thomson 32 Rooney 84 pen
22-Aug	Stephen 44
26-Aug	Redford 62 Johnstone 63 McDonald 72
29-Aug	Brown 21
05-Sep	Smith 78 Herd (2) 44, 77
08-Sep	
12-Sep	
16-Sep	Brown 26 Coyle, J. (2) 78, 79
19-Sep	
23-Sep	McLaughlin (2) 16, 38 Irvine 41
26-Sep	Caldwell 17 McDonald 77
03-Oct	Frye 35
10-Oct	Coyne 8 Miller 69
17-Oct	McDonald 23 Liddell 44
24-Oct	Robertson 37
31-Oct	Gallagher 27
07-Nov	Oliver 44
14-Nov	
21-Nov	Coyle, J. 16
28-Nov	Morton 36 Brogan (3) 39, 59, 89
05-Dec	Morris (2) 49, 53
02-Jan	Bannon 58 pen Milne 87
05-Jan	McAdam 15 Nicholas (2) 24, 83
23-Jan	Stephen 80
30-Jan	Cloy 25 pen Gordon 60
03-Feb	
06-Feb	Hegarty 23 McNaughton 64
09-Feb	
13-Feb	Dunlop 87 Doyle 17 O'Hara 65 Higgins 68
20-Feb	Irvine 24 Cleland 58
27-Feb	Robertson 41 McCoy (2) 43, 83 Bowman 89
03-Mar	
06-Mar	Craig 51 Wright 57
13-Mar	Mauchlen 25 Bourke 61 McDicken 89
20-Mar	Rennie 89
27-Mar	Stewart 28
31-Mar	McCoy (2) 46, 63 McDonald 82
03-Apr	
06-Apr	Bryson 1 Clarke 45 Bourke 76
10-Apr	Alexander (2) 19, 31
17-Apr	
21-Apr	McLaughlin pen 49
24-Apr	Ward 1 Smith 33 Hoggan pen 82
27-Apr	Bowie 26 Morrison (2) 75, 77
01-May	
08-May	Houston og 21 Nicholson 47
15-May	Brogan 5
1982/83	
31-Jul	Fairley 8 pen Hyslop 75
03-Aug	Edwards 30 Trusson (2) 66, 79
07-Aug	Charles (2) 12, 73 Kennedy 30 James 89
14-Aug	
18-Aug	Addison 2 Brogan (3) 38, 56, 75 Morton 82
21-Aug	Narey (2) 9, 78 Payne 11 Britton 52 Milne 65
25-Aug	Brogan (2) 28, 60 Beedie 88
28-Aug	Herd (2) 25, 50
01-Sep	Bannon 45 pen Dodds 69 Sturrock 72
04-Sep	Hughes 28
08-Sep	Morton 20 Brogan (2) 47, 86
11-Sep	Miller (2) 29, 57 McKeown 43
14-Sep	Considine 44
18-Sep	Gilmour 80
22-Sep	Garner 13 McComb 26 Houston 50
25-Sep	Jardine 66 O'Hara 75
02-Oct	
09-Oct	
16-Oct	
23-Oct	Wright 44
30-Oct	
06-Nov	Oliver, M 78
13-Nov	Brogan 35 Morton 63
16-Nov	
20-Nov	Grant 57 Houston og 68
27-Nov	Campbell 21
04-Dec	Mackay 14 Johnstone 70 pen
11-Dec	Johnston 64 Jardine 69
18-Dec	Given 4 Coyne 74 Ronald 75
27-Dec	Rodger 26
01-Jan	
03-Jan	Houston 67 Herd
08-Jan	Stevenson 43 Close 48
15-Jan	O'Neill 17 Reilly 62
22-Jan	Larnach 89
29-Jan	Thomson 45
05-Feb	McLaughlin 33 Phillips 43
22-Feb	Mauchlan 64 Gahagan (2) 72, 82
26-Feb	McComb 14
05-Mar	Brogan 71
14-Mar	Charnley 11
19-Mar	
22-Mar	McDowall 6
26-Mar	Coyne (2) 40, 77 Williamson 52
29-Mar	Johnstone (2) 7, 73 pen
02-Apr	Morrison (2) 67 pen, 68
09-Apr	
16-Apr	Millar, B (2) 11, 25 Anderson 53 Walker 81
23-Apr	Herd 14 Jobson 24 Forrest 89
30-Apr	Sinclair 48 O'Neill 63 Masterton 67
07-May	Connor (3) 37, 54, 65
14-May	Quinn 37 Grant 68
1983/84	
30-Jul	Davidson 28
31-Jul	McDonald 20
08-Aug	Marustik 47 Walsh 89
13-Aug	Perry 44 McCathie 48
20-Aug	Campbell 44 pen
24-Aug	Stark (3) 19, 62, 79 Porteous 29 Black (4) 44, 52 pen, 65, 69 Hewitt 59
27-Aug	Hewitt (2) 35, 69 Stark 86
03-Sep	Ferguson 47 og Grant 49
10-Sep	
14-Sep	Phillips (2) 48, 83
17-Sep	Kay 9 Johnston 17
24-Sep	McNeil (3) 9, 44, 49
28-Sep	McInally 11 McNaughton 54
01-Oct	McNeill 11 Ashwood 52
08-Oct	Frye 73
15-Oct	Thomson 25
22-Oct	
29-Oct	Clark 48 Clarke 60
05-Nov	Korotkich
12-Nov	
19-Nov	Jardine 34 pen Doyle, J. 49
26-Nov	Frye (3) 33, 53, 83 Ahern 74 Deans 79
03-Dec	Ashwood 32 Bourke 51 Coyle, J. 55
10-Dec	
17-Dec	Murray (2) 7, 57 Connor 20
26-Dec	Larnach 9
31-Dec	Houston, P. 52 McAllister 70
02-Jan	Campbell 28 pen
07-Jan	McGuire 70
04-Feb	Armstrong pen 72
06-Feb	Coyle, J. 10 Bourke 57 Ashwood (2) 72, 89
11-Feb	Yule 39 McGuire 49 Lawrie 57
17-Feb	Paterson 46
25-Feb	Bourke (2) 8, 71 Craig 42
29-Feb	Gallagher 81
03-Mar	Robertson 41 Docherty 60
10-Mar	Given 2 pen Murray 14 McCabe 56 Ronald 74
13-Mar	Durie (2) 13, 42 pen
17-Mar	Herd 57
24-Mar	Brown 27
31-Mar	Willock 41 Deans 59
07-Apr	
14-Apr	Houston 63
21-Apr	Paterson 43 Lloyd 65 pen
28-Apr	Somner (2) 43, 77
05-May	
12-May	Robertson 5
1984/85	
28-Jul	
29-Jul	
01-Aug	Sprott 50 Smith 75
04-Aug	
07-Aug	Wright 19 Philip og 31
11-Aug	Davidson 81 McComb 89
14-Aug	
18-Aug	McCathie (2) 10, 24 Jenkins 64
21-Aug	
25-Aug	Mitchell 32 Christie 73 Williamson 66 Paterson (2) 76, 86
29-Aug	McCoist (2) 5, 17 Paterson 44 Redford 79
01-Sep	
08-Sep	Watt 10
15-Sep	Higgins 89
22-Sep	Caven 8 Nicholson 58
29-Sep	
06-Oct	Gillen 5
13-Oct	Harris 54
20-Oct	Sheran 40
27-Oct	
03-Nov	Cloy (2), 1pen 5, 15 Campbell,P
10-Nov	Thompson 45
17-Nov	Murdoch 74 Logan 76
24-Nov	Nicholson 9
01-Dec	
05-Dec	
15-Dec	Gibson 42
22-Dec	Paterson 35 Oliver (2) 67, 83
29-Dec	Kennedy 51 Paterson 56 pen
02-Jan	McCathie 68
05-Jan	
21-Jan	
26-Jan	Quinn 34 Reilly 85
02-Feb	Thomson 44 Murray 72
04-Feb	Frye 32
09-Feb	Caithness (2) 55, 65
16-Feb	McDougall (2) 30, 43 pen
20-Feb	Davidson 80
23-Feb	
02-Mar	Steel 31 Rennie 51
06-Mar	Wilson 52 Reid 89
09-Mar	Irvine (2) 53, 62 Thomson 68 Ormond 75
16-Mar	Robertson 49 Oliver 78 Muir 82
23-Mar	Sweeney 37
26-Mar	
02-Apr	
09-Apr	
13-Apr	Young 89
17-Apr	Mitchell 41 pen Hacket 63 Oliver 73
20-Apr	Caven 23
23-Apr	Watson 72 Jenkins 75
27-Apr	Kasule 7 Slaven 87
04-May	
11-May	Duffy 24 Caithness (2) 76, 85
1985/86	
27-Jul	(49) (85) (87)
31-Jul	Cherry 10 Downie 42 pen
03-Aug	(60)
04-Aug	(80)
06-Aug	Kirk 53
10-Aug	Gibson 35 Ward 56
14-Aug	Maskrey 60
17-Aug	Mauchlen (2) 17, 51 McGuire 26
21-Aug	Moore 23 Larnach (3) 48, 52, 87 Lloyd (2) 60, 72 McCabe 89
24-Aug	Williamson 11 pen
31-Aug	Walker 39
07-Sep	Jackson 60
14-Sep	Watson (2) 26, 48 Jenkins 32
24-Sep	Brannigan 89 pen
28-Sep	McKay 77 Kasule 85
05-Oct	McWalter 24
12-Oct	Sokoluk (2) 13, 32 McCann 72 pen Cavanagh 87
19-Oct	Dick 16
26-Oct	
02-Nov	Sinnett (2) 46, 86
09-Nov	Tierney (2) 50, 83 McGachie 55 Armstrong 65 pen Scott 85 Jackson 77
16-Nov	Jenkins (2) 22 pen, 81
23-Nov	
07-Dec	Heddle 1 Watson 46
14-Dec	Torrance 64 Glover 85
28-Dec	Johnston 4 Barron 25 McGurn 29 Millen 53
11-Jan	McGlashan 10
18-Jan	Bryce 34 McBride 47
01-Feb	Bateman 8 Grant 40
04-Feb	
15-Feb	Campbell 3 Watson (2) 14, 78
18-Feb	Sokoluk 14
05-Mar	
08-Mar	Barron 5
11-Mar	
15-Mar	Fotheringham 55 McWalter 81
22-Mar	Grant 74
25-Mar	McGonigle (2) 22, 68 Gaffney (2) 50, 68
29-Mar	Newman 68
03-Apr	Rutherford 26 Grant 35 Armour 65
05-Apr	
09-Apr	Cochrane 57 Bryce 60
12-Apr	Sinnett 24
15-Apr	Irvine 51
19-Apr	Irvine (2) 3, 19 Thompson 26
22-Apr	McCurdy 11
26-Apr	Caven 8
03-May	Kasule 2 Rodgers 17 pen
1986/87	
29-Jul	Coyne 67
02-Aug	McAndrew 55
03-Aug	Kirkwood 15
06-Aug	Russell 75
09-Aug	McGonigle 82
13-Aug	Morrison (2) 1, 20
16-Aug	
23-Aug	
30-Aug	Caven 32 O'Brien 44
06-Sep	
13-Sep	McGlashan 85
20-Sep	Tait 58
27-Sep	
04-Oct	Erwin 85
11-Oct	Gibson 44 Payne 89
18-Oct	Sorbie 18 Sullivan 89
25-Oct	
01-Nov	Conn 30 Voy og 70
08-Nov	McCracken (2) 2, 33 Sludden 18
15-Nov	Clelland 13
22-Nov	Armstrong 50 Leetion 73 McGachie 76
29-Nov	Armstrong 29 pen Ward 64
13-Dec	Lloyd 72
17-Dec	
20-Dec	McWalter 55 Brannigan 80
27-Dec	
01-Jan	Grant, R. (2) 28, 38
24-Jan	
26-Jan	
31-Jan	
03-Feb	Harrow og 70
07-Feb	
10-Feb	Cavanagh 8
14-Feb	Nelson 19 McDonald 29
21-Feb	Loch 24 Bell 83
25-Feb	Walker (2) 23, 77 Bain 81
28-Feb	Gavin 22 Kemp 75
02-Mar	
07-Mar	Grant, R. 56 Paxton 82
14-Mar	Godfrey 18 Chalmers 89
17-Mar	Duff 48 Brannigan 86
21-Mar	Cavanagh 44 Marshall 64
25-Mar	McGonnigal 28
28-Mar	McGachie 36
04-Apr	Caven 65
11-Apr	
18-Apr	Gallagher 25
25-Apr	
02-May	Millen 87
09-May	Creaney 4
11-May	Jenkins 29
1987/88	
25-Jul	
27-Jul	McGovern 40
29-Jul	
01-Aug	Jenkins (2) 12, 16
02-Aug	Proudfoot 35 Williamson 40 Grant, R. 83
04-Aug	Ferguson (2) 48 pen, 73
08-Aug	McDonald (3) 30pen, 88, 89 Blackie 40
12-Aug	
15-Aug	
19-Aug	Bryce 45
22-Aug	Jamieson 5 McCabe 75
25-Aug	Sturrock 43 Malpas 69
29-Aug	Hunter 66 McCafferty 72
05-Sep	Henderson 18 Walker 56 McGlashan 74
12-Sep	Cuthbertson 7 Harkness 11 McInnes 61
15-Sep	
19-Sep	Dickson 61
26-Sep	Campbell 17 Moore 23
29-Sep	Houston 84
03-Oct	Scott (2) 9, 39 McDonald 85 pen
07-Oct	Doherty 69
10-Oct	
17-Oct	Gilmour 30 Harkness 50
20-Oct	Tierney 30 McGonigal 40 Kasule 42 McGachie 63
24-Oct	Gallacher (2) 59, 82 Logan 65
27-Oct	Coyle, O. 33 pen
31-Oct	Willock (2) 8, 76 Walker 61 pen
07-Nov	Graham 90
14-Nov	
21-Nov	Black 7 McCabe (2) 26, 45
28-Nov	
05-Dec	Frye 36
12-Dec	Reid 72
19-Dec	
26-Dec	
02-Jan	Hunter 67
09-Jan	Davies 39 Irons 63 Bryce 86
16-Jan	Parlane 44 McCabe 51
06-Feb	Gallagher (2) 6, 22 Kelly (2) 40, 78 Law 81
08-Feb	
10-Feb	Durrant (2) 15 pen, 80 Walters 81 McCoist 85
13-Feb	McLeod 20 og
20-Feb	Chalmers 18 McGarvey 27
27-Feb	Ward 27 Brown 44 pen
02-Mar	Thomson 62
05-Mar	Davidson 80 Cuthbertson ....
12-Mar	Boyd 12 Reilly 19 Logan 64
19-Mar	Millar 67
26-Mar	Perry 64 pen
02-Apr	Kelly (2) 2, 74
09-Apr	Harris 3 Sprott 39
16-Apr	Flood 36
23-Apr	Davies (2) 14, 65 Bryce 44
30-Apr	Frye 80 Hetherington 87
07-May	Rooney 24 Coyle 40 Docherty 70
1988/89	
30-Jul	McCoist 36 Gough 84
02-Aug	Smith 72
06-Aug	Watson (2) 12, 86
13-Aug	Watters 15 Maskrey 38 McVicar 88 pen
17-Aug	Burgess 39 pen
20-Aug	Moore pen 6
27-Aug	Robertson, C. 41 Smith, T. 48
03-Sep	
10-Sep	Reilly 14 Sprott 53
17-Sep	Conn 30 McDonald, K. 42
24-Sep	Clark 32
01-Oct	
08-Oct	
10-Oct	
15-Oct	Eadie 60 Coyle (2) 64, 68
22-Oct	Wylde 9
29-Oct	McNair 30 Rae 47 Houston 69
05-Nov	McCoy 1 Kelly (2) 50, 66
12-Nov	
19-Nov	Campbell (2) 40, 80 Grant 44
26-Nov	Ward 57
03-Dec	
10-Dec	Hetherston 26 Burgess 39 Rae 84
17-Dec	
24-Dec	Auld 11 Caffrey 28 Treanor 66 pen
31-Dec	
03-Jan	Jack 16 Brash 48 og Smith, T. 66
07-Jan	Flood 10
14-Jan	Maskrey 25
21-Jan	
28-Jan	Ferguson, I. 67
01-Feb	Walters 35 Drinkell 46 Fraser og 79
04-Feb	Walker 49
11-Feb	Armstrong 87
18-Feb	Coyne 8 McBride 87
01-Mar	Conn 90
04-Mar	McGuire 61
11-Mar	
18-Mar	Nicholas 66
25-Mar	Templeton (20 28, 35 pen
01-Apr	
05-Apr	Coyle 8 pen Johnston 50
08-Apr	Gallacher (2) 7, 21 Houston 80
15-Apr	Harkness 15
22-Apr	McNaughton (2) 25, 69 Ward 48
29-Apr	
06-May	
13-May	Peebles 9
1989/90	
31-Jul	Scott (2) 16, 23 Allinson 17 Bennett 62
02-Aug	Spencer 43 McSwegan 70
05-Aug	Morgan 14 Curtis 72
08-Aug	Glennie 13 og Quinn (2) 17 pen, 18 Brazil 76 pen
12-Aug	
15-Aug	Rougvie Abercromby Jack
19-Aug	
26-Aug	Inglis 76
02-Sep	Moore 27 Grant 41
05-Sep	Wright 30 Campbell 46 Charnley 84 pen
09-Sep	Gray 43 McDonald (2) 67, 72 Butler 80
16-Sep	McAnenay 10
23-Sep	Morton 29 Brewster 40
30-Sep	
07-Oct	Lee, I. 33 Lamont 86
14-Oct	
18-Oct	Brown 29
21-Oct	Clarke 43 McGlashan 48
28-Oct	Harris 24 pen Miller 44 Morrison 69
04-Nov	Campbell 73
08-Nov	
11-Nov	Balfour 44 McPhee 59 Harvey 74
14-Nov	Walker 30 pen Fulton 72
18-Nov	McTeague 34 Watson 83
25-Nov	
02-Dec	Coyle, O. 4 Coyle, T. 10 Eadie 80
06-Dec	
09-Dec	Irvine 56
16-Dec	Templeton 51
23-Dec	Alexander 5
30-Dec	
02-Jan	Roseburgh 25 Inglis 30
06-Jan	Grant 87
13-Jan	McLeod og 28 McGachie (2) 37, 89
20-Jan	Alexander 55 O'Hara 62
29-Jan	Fowler 42 Alexander (2) 47, 90
03-Feb	Clark 29 Clinging 75
10-Feb	Clark (2) 68, 77
17-Feb	
03-Mar	
10-Mar	Roberts 53
17-Mar	Speirs
21-Mar	
24-Mar	Harvey 41 Kelly 67
31-Mar	Bryce pen 4 McCracken 74
07-Apr	
14-Apr	
21-Apr	
28-Apr	Baptie
05-May	English
1990/91	
31-Jul	Robertson (2) 22 pen, 89 McPherson 48
02-Aug	Tromboli 6
11-Aug	Cork 6 Fairweather 67
17-Aug	Ferguson 89
21-Aug	Brewster 27 pen
25-Aug	
29-Aug	
01-Sep	Gilmour
04-Sep	McCoist (3) 43, ... Johnston 53 Butcher 72 Steven 89
08-Sep	
15-Sep	Roseburgh 53
18-Sep	White 34
22-Sep	
29-Sep	Bryce (2) 52 pen, 76
02-Oct	
06-Oct	
09-Oct	Watters 27
13-Oct	Campbell 85
16-Oct	Harris 9 pen McCluskey 49
20-Oct	Lawrence 67
23-Oct	Dodds 106
27-Oct	
03-Nov	McWilliams (2), Hetherston (2) Taylor McGiven Cody
10-Nov	Mallan 64
17-Nov	Ritchie 25 Lees 50
24-Nov	Burns 44
01-Dec	McCluskey 14 Hillcoat 38
08-Dec	
15-Dec	Kelly 24
29-Dec	McWilliams (2) 49, 75 Stainrod (2) 57, 80
01-Jan	Chisholm 57 Jamieson 79
05-Jan	Harvey 22
26-Jan	McCluskey 85
02-Feb	Adam 7 Brewster 47 Petrie 49
16-Feb	
19-Feb	
23-Feb	
02-Mar	Fraser (4) 6, 39, 56, 74 Bryce 32
06-Mar	Prentice (3) 16, 36, 85
09-Mar	Buckley 46 Roche 18 McGlashan 55 Elliott 42 Charnley pen 44
16-Mar	
23-Mar	Little (2) 62, 81 Roxburgh 79 Logan 64
26-Mar	O'Brien 77
30-Mar	McInnes 21 McCabe 44 Deeney 63 Fowler 74

Fixture dates Goal times, own goals, opponents' scorers and goaltimes

Date	Goal times / own goals	Opponents' scorers and goaltimes
06-Apr	Williamson 42 Campbell 58	English 33 Dennis og 73
13-Apr	Campbell 64 Petrie 84	Roddie 26 Shearer 82
16-Apr	Kelly 46	Martin 9
20-Apr	McCluskey 64	Lambert (2) 1, 53 Kirk 40
22-Apr	Scott 62	Hannah 86 Brewster 88
27-Apr	Jamieson 2 McMartin 73	
04-May	Mair 78 Eadie 88	
11-May	Balfour	
1991/92		
27-Jul	Gilhaus 20 Booth 77	
29-Jul	Davey 77 Legg 86	Irons 22
31-Jul	Crabbe 14 Robertson 55 McPherson 59 McKinlay 55	
03-Aug	Drake 25	Chalmers 23
10-Aug	Young 18 Little 39	French 57 pen
13-Aug		Montgomerie 31 Williamson 79
17-Aug	Kirk 52	Currie 47
20-Aug	Smith 84	
24-Aug	Miller 33 Creaney 72 Fulton 74	ONeil 50
27-Aug	Craig 67	Lavety 90 secs
31-Aug		Lawrence 35
14-Sep	Flannigan (3) 18, 40, 44 McGlashan 49 English 89	
21-Sep	Mathie 71	Anderson 88
28-Sep	Campbell 2	
05-Oct	Reid 24 McCluskey (2) 34, 64	Curran 39 O'Boyle (2) 58, 80 pen
08-Oct		Cooper 74
12-Oct	Logan 44	Petrie (2) 17, 62 Ward (2) 31, 61 French 55
15-Oct	Dickson 90 secs	
19-Oct		
22-Oct	Mathie 14 Doak 58	Ferguson 73 Walker 88
26-Oct	Armstrong 84	Walker 32 Nicholas 84
29-Oct	Dodds 37	Hood 6
05-Nov	Miller 71 Weir 80	Hamilton 67 pen Weighorst 76
1993/94		Cooper 20 Boyle 82
09-Nov	36 54 22 76	
16-Nov	26 60 2nd half	
22-Nov	48	Gallagher 31 Sinclair og 57
24-Nov	56	Moore 64
28-Nov		McWhirter 89
31-Jan	Roxburgh 49	Shaw 30
07-Aug	Harris 10 Callaghan 27	
14-Aug	Wright 29	Cooper 64
21-Aug	Elliot 12 Martin 47	Harvey (2) 22, 80 Davies 38 Black pen 60
28-Aug	Robertson 49	Cody 62
04-Jan	Britton 34 Grant 54	
11-Jan	McKinlay 4	Robertson 59
18-Jan	Nicholas (2) 9, 27 Payton (2) 66, 89	Lavety 24
01-Feb	McBride 54	Cooper 45
08-Feb	Shearer 31 Jess 56 Richardson (2) 77, 83	
26-Feb	Hetherston og 13	McMartin 59
09-Oct	Jackson 22 O'Neill 49 McAllister 70	
09-Dec	Williamson 71 Mitchell 75	
16-Oct	Grant 46	
23-Oct	Torfason 37	
30-Oct	Craig 26	
06-Nov	Arnott (2) 21, 81 O'Donnell 76	
09-Nov	Bowman 26 Rowbotham og 33	
13-Nov	Hateley (2) 61 pen, 73	
25-Jan	Collins (2) 2, 61	
04-Dec	Wieghorst 17	
02-Oct	Wright 21 Findlay 34	
07-Feb	Miller 31	
11-Dec	Brown 24	

(additional Goal times / own goals entries, left section)

Williamson 88 · Watters (2) 48, 63 · Walker 68 · Stark 80 · Den Bieman 57 McKay 87 · Wright 57 Moore 71 · McPherson 64 · Napier 14 · Graham (3) 30, 35, 85 Walker 32 · NcCall (2) 26, 76 Dodds 49 · Torfason 37 · Craig 26 · Winter 60 Lamont (2) 64, 74 · Winter 73 pen · Reilly 82 · **1995/96** · Mitchell 75 · Evans (2) 18, 29 Hamilton 73 pen McGinlay 90 · Gibson 72 · McDonald 5 · Alexander 3 · **1992/93** · Porteous 75 · Foster 23 Crabbe 71 · Hamilton 20 pen Evans (2) 38, 50 · Elliott 17 · Flannigan 58 Eadie 68 · McLeod og 86 · Reilly 50 pen · Wright 31

Date	Goal times / own goals	Opponents' scorers
30-Apr	Alexander 9 / Robertson 33	
03-May	Watson 20 Armstrong 71 pen	Ferguson 73 Walker 88
07-May	Roseburgh 11 Rutherford 53	Walker 32 Nicholas 84
14-May	Torfason 40 Maskrey 83	Hood 6
1994/95	Flannigan (3) 41, 73, 85 Eadie 86	Hamilton 67 pen Weighorst 76
30-Jul 73		Cooper 20 Boyle 82
02-Aug		
04-Aug		
06-Aug		
09-Aug 30, 66		
13-Aug		Gallagher 31 Sinclair og 57
17-Aug		Moore 64
20-Aug		McWhirter 89
27-Aug		Shaw 30
31-Aug		
03-Sep		Cooper 64
10-Sep	Nicholas (2) 9, 27 Payton (2) 66, 89	Harvey (2) 22, 80 Davies 38 Black pen 60
17-Sep	McBride 54	Cody 62
20-Sep		
24-Sep	Shearer 31 Jess 56 Richardson (2) 77, 83	Robertson 59
01-Oct	Hetherston og 13	Lavety 24
08-Oct	Jackson 22 O'Neill 49 McAllister 70	Cooper 45
15-Oct	Williamson 71 Mitchell 75	
22-Oct	Grant 46	McMartin 59
25-Oct	Brewster (2) 11, 57	
29-Oct	Torfason 83 pen	
05-Nov	Shaw 31 pen Blake 57	
13-Nov	Coyne 31 Kirk 59 McGrillen 77	
12-Sep 79, 14, 66	Paatelainen (2) 43, 77 Shearer 74 Booth 77	McCormack 40 pen
16-Sep	Miller 80	Jarnskor, H. 78 Jarnskor, M. 87
23-Sep	Ferguson 70 Durie 78	Van Hooydonck 78
30-Sep	Findlay 23 Wright (2) 34, 45	Van Hooydonck 52 Donnelly 119
04-Oct		McCoist (2) 16, 87 Miller 23 Robertson 29
07-Oct		Thordarson, O. 44
14-Oct	McSkimming 51 Mitchell 53	McDonald 78
17-Oct	Colquhoun 18 Levein 85	Gunlaugsson 50
21-Oct	Dodds (2) 15, 82 pen	Booth (2) 6, 71 Miller 25
28-Oct	Donnelly (2) 18, 60	Smith, T. (3) 23, 39, 85 pen
31-Oct 43	Shaw 13	Millar 9 Lawrence (2) 11, 76 Robertson 66
08-Nov	Robertson 18 McCoist 43 Ferguson, D. 46 Michaltchenko 51	Klinsmann (2) 6, 73
23-Apr		McGrillen 44
26-Apr	Wright 31	Gough 55 Petric 65
		Klinsmann 51 Babbel 63
		Henry (2) 18, 42 Wright (2) 54, 68 Brown 62
		Tait 40

(right section)

Date	Goal times / own goals	Opponents' scorers
12-Aug	McGrillen (2) 52, 59	Ganley 36 Gibson 62
16-Aug		Cooper 37
19-Aug		Weir 58 Adam 65
23-Aug	Robertson 53	Sherry 53 Ritchie 67
26-Aug	McGinlay 17	Young 69
30-Aug	Black 87 pen	Grady 20 Annand 27
13-Sep	O'Donnell 16 Collins 38 Van Hooydonck.....	Mendes 89
20-Sep	McCoist 24 Durie (2) 39, 42 Ferguson 82	Ferguson 35
23-Sep	McDonald, R. (2) 73, 89	
27-Sep		Blaikie 85
04-Oct		Fisher 19
14-Oct	Robertson 44 pen Locke 53	
18-Oct	Windass 16	
25-Oct		Cooper
28-Oct		
01-Nov	Thom 9 Donnelly 24	
08-Nov	Falconer 59	McInally 65
15-Nov		Watson 4 Yardley 10
22-Nov		Dick 85
29-Nov	Miller 24 Buchan 84	
06-Dec	McKee 67 Wright 75	Morgan pen 80
13-Dec	McCoist (3) 38 pen, 83, 89 Durie 92 pen	Clark 21
20-Dec	James 12 Craig 31	Bennett 44 Price 61 Paterson 84
27-Dec	Cameron 42 Pointon 47 Mackay 73	Anderson 47
03-Jan	McMahon 33, Wood 76, Winter 88	Turner 35
10-Jan	McGinlay 82	McGinlay 22
24-Jan	Cadette (2) 1, 60 Gray 37 Grant 42	
31-Jan		
03-Feb		Keith 21 Crabbe 38 McAllister 63
07-Feb		Collins 6 Mahood 10 Duffield 86
14-Feb		McEwan og 88
21-Feb		
07-Mar		Clark 12
14-Mar	Hamilton 10 Hagan 23 McGrillen 49	
17-Mar	Steven 24	Stirling pen 50
21-Mar	Cooper 27 Hetherston 76 Eadie 111	Duffield 9 McPherson 86
28-Mar	Van Hooydonck 16 Thom (2) 25, 50 Donnelly 87	Annand 60
04-Apr	McKinnon 3	
11-Apr	Van Den Gaag (2) 21, 57 Arnot 30	Lorimer 89
18-Apr	Isias (2) 53, 63	McPhee 12
25-Apr	Shaw (3) 15, 26, 71, Petrie 49, Millar pen 69	Fotheringham og 14
02-May	Windass 11 Dodds (3) 19 pen, 26, 84 pen	
09-May	Kirk og 54	
1998/99	McSwegan 2 McLaren 58	More 50
18-Jul Smart	35, 6, 60, 77, 89	Masson og 1
22-Jul Wilson 17	Britton 44 French 51 Miller, M. 89	17
25-Jul 12	Robertson 2	
30-Jul	Brown, 36 Wright.....	
04-Aug	Miller 77	
08-Aug	Van Vossen 58 McCoist 65	
15-Aug	Millar og 12 French 24	
19-Aug	Duffy 85	
22-Aug		
29-Aug		
05-Sep	Jackson (2) 61, 79 McGinlay 67	Duffield 33
12-Sep	Gough 29 Gascoigne 35 Albertz 46 McCoist 79	Crawford (2) 68 pen, 89 Guggi 78
19-Sep	Olafsson 2	Cameron 34 Young 61
26-Sep	Britton (2) 55, 57	McDonald 58
03-Oct	Robertson 4 Hamilton 73	
11-Oct		
17-Oct	Cadete 73 Hay 89	McCormick (2) 58, 60 Wales 70
28-Oct	Rowson 26 Miller 46	Templeman (2) 5, 44
31-Oct		McCormick 10 Hawke 44
03-Nov	Sandison 34	Cooper 4 McCann 22 Black 61
07-Nov	Kirkwood og 15	McGinlay 60 Crawford 62 pen Paataleinen 78
14-Nov	De Canio 47 Cadete 79	Keith 22
21-Nov	Brand 2	
28-Nov	Coyle 27 Van Der Gaag 40 Coyne (2) 48, 54 May 81	Smith 32
19-Sep	Weir 24 McCann (2)	Tait 10
08-Dec	McIntyre 87	
12-Dec	Robertson 4 Hamilton 73	
19-Dec	James 43 Hagan 81	Thomas 3 Curran 36 Evans 6 Black 38 pen
26-Dec	Smith 29	Crabbe 1
02-Jan	Millar og 57 Winters 72	Young (2) 68, 83
09-Jan	De Canio 88	Andrews og 70 Carrigan 87 Convery 8 McCusker 16 pen
16-Jan	Coyne (2) 54, 75 Coyle 77 Falconer 18 Weir 46	McDonald 18
23-Jan	Petric 10 Durie (2) 21, 23 Robertson 28 Lavelty... McCoist 81	McLaughlin 16 McGarry 49 Yardley 60
30-Jan	Millen og 9 Dodds 34	Hamilton (3) 20, 73, 89
06-Feb	McGinlay 26	Ferguson 11 Lyons (2) 46, 88 Craig 52
15-Feb		Dair, L. pen 60
20-Feb		
23-Feb		Evans 56
27-Feb		
06-Mar 34, 60. 75		
13-Apr		Thomas 20
20-Mar	Tait 40	
24-Jul Donnelly og 1		
26-Jul 25, 48, 65, 88	20, 55 Toland 75	
02-Aug		
09-Aug		

Fixture dates	Goal times, own goals,	opponents' scorers and goaltimes		

The pages which follow contain summary statistics on the Raith Rovers' players who have played for the first team between 1883 and May 2008.   The appearances total includes all first team matches, including friendlies and local cup ties in which a recognised first team was fielded, and it includes appearances as substitutes.   Not included are substitutes who did not take the field.   The goals total follows the same criteria.

GOALS

356

Fixture dates	Goal times, own goals, opponents' scorers and goaltimes	
25-Mar	15	Jackson (2) 1, 35 Sellars 27 Lombardi 33 Gribben 65
28-Mar	45, 62	
01-Apr	41, 79	
08-Apr		
15-Apr	20	McLaren 88
22-Apr	53	Deuchar 9 Skelton 74
29-Apr		Brown 66
06-May		Fortune 34
2006/07		
08-Jul	49	Miller (2) 34,73 Hunt (2) 38,77
15-Jul	Dingwall u66	Shields pen 8
19-Jul	Bouadji u79 56	Moutinho 11 Lima 21 Craig 26 Barr 64
22-Jul	Dingwall u86 28, 53	Templeton 52
29-Jul	14, 64	Smart 80
05-Aug		Templeman 21 Campbell og 51
08-Aug	41	McLaren 47 Prunty 71
12-Aug		Sheerin James 97 Milne 112
15-Aug	8	Clarke (2) 12,90 Paatelainen 87
19-Aug	53	Cramb 69
26-Aug	73	Hamilton 3
03-Sep	88	Fairbairn og 18
09-Sep	88, 60, 68, 55	
16-Sep	74	
23-Sep		Pettigrew 80
30-Sep		McLaughlin 69 Lilley 72 pen Templeman 89
14-Oct	30	Tosh 89
21-Oct	11	Tomana 1 Cramb 83 Shields 89
28-Oct	34	Clarke 65
04-Nov	62, 74	King 3
11-Nov		Wright 22
25-Nov	71	Brown 51
02-Dec	18, 61	Gemmell 51
09-Dec		
16-Dec	84	Stevenson 52
23-Dec		Linn 82 Maccauley 88
30-Dec	77, 15, 68, 86, 53	Buchanan 73 Paatelainen 83
02-Jan	71	Williamson 39 McIntyre 46
13-Jan	75	
16-Jan	24, 54	
20-Jan	76	
27-Jan	70, 27	Tosh 44
03-Feb	56, 20, 82	Buchanan pen 25
17-Feb		Cramb 84
21-Feb	74, 72	Ferguson 81
24-Feb	15, 80	
03-Mar	20, 31, 42, 64, 45	Robertson 68
10-Mar		McAnespie 56 Sloan 62
17-Mar	79, 28	Wilson og 55
31-Mar		
03-Apr		Aitken (2) 30 pen 69 Cramb 80
07-Apr	10, 15, 32	Gray 10 Ferguson 18 Mackie 75
14-Apr	69, 75	Wright 42
21-Apr	67, 31	Flood 90 secs Robson 55
28-Apr	8, 59	Kerrigan 20
02-May		
05-May	29	
2007/08		
14-Jul	85	Little 31
18-Jul	12, 84	Sheerin pen 14
22-Jul	41, 6	Brown 85
25-Jul	85, 27, 10, 73, 77	Deasly 37
28-Jul	Carcary u65 70, 76	Mclean 44 McCormack 76 Porter 90
04-Aug	10	Cairney 49 Trouten 51 pen
07-Aug	70, 21, 80	
11-Aug	25, 79, 64	Williams 10 Robertson 19 Stevenson 59
14-Aug	89	
18-Aug	Fleming og 1 81, 53	McKeown 21
25-Aug		Agnew 10 Ferguson 64
28-Aug	48	
01-Sep	64, 69, 32, 45p, 62	Cairney (2) 49,90
15-Sep		
22-Sep	89, 90p	
29-Sep	5	
06-Oct	27	
20-Oct	65, 85	Barrowman 47 Scott 93
27-Oct	72	Smith 41
03-Nov	15, 29	
10-Nov		
15-Nov	38, 46, 65	
24-Nov	29, 77, 89, 62, 72	Lumsden og 18 Istead 70
01-Dec	2, 58p, 89	Diack 20 Little 56
08-Dec	69	Ferguson 14 McKeown pen 90
15-Dec	39, 21, 53	
22-Dec	10, 79	
26-Dec	21	
29-Dec	5, 78, 84	

Fixture dates	Goal times, own goals, opponents' scorers and goaltimes	
02-Jan	10, 85, 68, 67	Ramsey 23
05-Jan		Higgins 37
12-Jan	80	Jackson 19 Milne 49 Sheerin pen 57
19-Jan	23	
26-Jan	34, 69, 83	Smith 50 Prunty 69 Russell 75
02-Feb		Byers 1 Diack (2) 2, 69
09-Feb	Walker og 1 90, 25	Williams (2) 15, 39
16-Feb	68	Coakley 49 Buist 66
23-Feb		Fahey og 36 McQuade 62
01-Mar	36, 80, 25	McKay 44
08-Mar		
15-Mar	21	Barrowman 18 Scott 20
22-Mar	29, 68, 25	Ferry 64
29-Mar		
05-Apr	90	Diack 12
12-Apr	72	McLaren 12 Gemmill 28
19-Apr	42, 64, 80, 71, 86	Bavidge 53 Mann pen 56 Ross (2) 68,76 Sharp 57
26-Apr	21, 61	Russell (2) 30,38
30-Apr		Prunty 10 Donnelly 77
03-May	19p, 89	

In August 1999, Goldenacre Bowling Club in Edinburgh held a Sportsman's Dinner, and guests included several former football players, a number of whom had a Raith Rovers connection. Pictured are, back row, left to right : Willie King (president Goldenacre BC), Bobby Kirk (Raith Rovers and Hearts), Willie McFarlane (Hibs and Raith Rovers), Freddie Glidden (Hearts), Alan Muir (vice president Goldenacre BC). Front row : John Cumming (Hearts), Lawrie Reilly (Hibs), Joe Baker (Hibs and Raith Rovers), Jackie Hunter (Motherwell) and Jimmy Millar (Rangers player and Raith Rovers manager)

First Team Player	Position	Date Signed	Signed from	Date Left	Next Club	Total Appearances	Goals
Abbie, John L	RB	16/07/1941	St Bernards	13/09/1941	Partick Thistle	3	
Abbott, James	IF	03/01/1916		30/04/1921		72	21
Abercromby, Billy	M	29/07/1991	East Stirling	03/08/1991	Trialist	2	1
Adam, Stephen	M	31/01/2006	Livingston	30/05/2006	Loan	8	1
Adams	CF	14/03/1942		14/03/1942	Trialist	1	1
Adamson	LB	01/08/1887	Dunnikier	30/04/1890		57	0
Adamson	IL	08/09/1945	Lochgelly St Andrews	08/09/1945	Trialist	2	0
Adamson, Robert T	F	11/05/1961	Dundee	30/04/1963	Morton	74	23
Addison, Brian G	M	20/08/1981	Stobswell	15/05/1983	Lochee United	2	0
Addison, Thomas	CH	03/09/1887	Burntisland Thistle	23/08/1890		12	0
Aertschilling, Lionel	M	18/07/1992	Sparta Rotterdam	23/07/1992	Trialist	2	0
Agathe, Didier	F	31/08/1999	Montpellier Herault	30/06/2000	Hibs	33	8
Agnew, Paul	M	08/07/1999	Ayr United	30/04/2001	Freed	13	0
Aird, William	WH	23/04/1943	Morton	15/05/1943	War Guest	3	0
Airlie, Seton	IF	03/05/1947	Celtic	05/06/1947	Cancelled	1	0
Aitken	IR	30/05/1903		30/05/1903	Trialist	1	0
Aitken	OR	16/04/1932	Rosyth	16/04/1932	Trialist	1	1
Aitken, George	LH	21/02/1942	Lochgelly Albert	21/02/1942	Trialist	1	0
Aitken, J	OR	29/09/1917	KOSB	27/04/1918	Trialist	3	0
Aitken, Morris	IL	22/11/1962	Dundonald Bluebell	30/05/1963	East Fife	18	6
Aitken, Robert J	G	23/12/1967	Oakley United	01/05/1969	Valleyfield Colliery	4	0
Aitken, Samuel	HB	09/08/1910	Middlesbrough	24/08/1912	Ayr United	80	2
Alexander	CF	07/04/1919		07/04/1919	Trialist	1	0
Alexander,	OL	26/08/1908		05/10/1908	Trialist	2	1
Alfonso Lopez, Miguel	D	30/03/2001	Airdrie	15/05/2001	Badajoz	6	0
Allan	IR	06/01/1909		06/01/1909	Trialist	1	0
Allan	OL	15/02/1896		22/02/1896	Trialist	2	2
Allan, James	CF	10/11/1955	East Stirling	17/01/1956	East Stirling	2	0
Allan, Raymond George Kyle	G	14/10/1994	Motherwell	24/07/1995	Brechin City	1	0
Allan, Robert	RB	14/09/1931	St Andrews United	25/07/1939	Dundee	273	12
Allan, William	OL	12/05/1952	Hibs	23/05/1952	Stirling Albion	2	0
Allison, William S	IL	16/12/1925	Kettering Town	30/04/1933		81	33
Allister	OR	12/10/1895		12/10/1895	Trialist	1	1
Amos, Liam	G	17/07/2007				0	0
Amos, William	OL	19/02/1944	Hall & Co	04/03/1944	War Guest	2	0
Amphlett	IL	04/04/1910	Dunfermline	04/10/1910	Trialist	1	0
Andersen, Soren	F	10/01/1997	Hvidovre	11/03/1997	AB Copenhagen	11	5
Andersen, Vetle	M	29/11/1996	Vigor	10/05/1997	Inverness CT	22	0
Anderson	G	12/05/1902		12/05/1902	Trialist	1	0
Anderson	G	01/05/1929		01/05/1929	Trialist	2	0
Anderson, Alasdair	FB	10/03/1945		10/03/1945	Trialist	2	0
Anderson, Alex	G	15/07/1984	Newburgh	15/05/1987	Newburgh	5	0
Anderson, Gary	CF	24/07/1979	Cupar YM	21/11/1981	St Andrews United	1	0
Anderson, George	IL	26/07/1943	Dundee	24/03/1943	War Guest	1	0
Anderson, Harry A	LH	24/05/1912	Hibernian	20/08/1915	Lochgelly United	55	7
Anderson, Harry A		10/05/1912	St Mirren	26/06/1920	Third Lanark	171	14
Anderson, John	LB	19/12/1902	Musselburgh Fern	30/04/1904	St Mirren		
Anderson, John	CF	21/08/1907		06/01/1909	Hearts	34	6
Anderson, Neil Paterson	RH	02/12/1937	Blairhall Colliery	27/07/1939	Guest	4	0
Anderson, P	IL	15/08/1905		15/08/1905	Trialist	1	0
Anderson, William Ross	CF	13/11/1943	Hibs	20/11/1943	War Guest	2	0
Andrews	RH	22/04/1908		05/01/1909		2	0
Andrews, Marvin Anthony	CH	11/02/1998	Carib	05/10/2000	Livingston	133	14

First Team Player	Position	Date Signed	Signed from	Date Left	Next Club	Total Appearances	Goals
Andrews, Marvin Anthony	CF	04/10/2006	Dumbarton	10/05/2008	Bathgate Thistle	27	5
Annand, Edward	OR	28/06/2005	Dunfermline Juniors	21/01/2008		43	5
Archibald, Alexander	OR	16/03/1916	Rangers	15/08/1917	Rangers	2	1
Archibald, Alexander	RH	02/11/1934	Rangers	14/10/1939	Dunfermline	8	1
Archibald, David	CH	18/09/1952	Glencraig Colliery	30/04/1956	Arbroath	13	3
Archibald, Eric	OL	07/08/1986	Hill of Beath Hawthorn	18/11/1988	Hill of Beath Hawtho	32	0
Archibald, John (Jacky)	OR	15/05/1931	Denny Hibs	30/04/1933		78	32
Archibald, Robert	OL	12/01/1932	Clydebank	30/04/1932		3	2
Archibald, Robert F	M	05/05/1920	Aberdeen	01/07/1924	Third Lanark	198	18
Areld, Odd	IR	16/11/1996		22/11/1996	Trialist	1	0
Argue	OR			28/12/1945	Trialist	1	0
Arnott, John	OR	06/08/1958	Dalkeith Thistle	30/04/1959	East Fife	2	5
Arthur	CF	22/01/1887		12/03/1887		2	0
Arthur, Alex.M.	G	03/05/1947	Hibs	06/06/1947	Cancelled	1	0
Arthur, Gordon George	F	17/05/1988	Dumbarton	08/09/1993	Forfar Athletic	220	0
Axford, David	WH	14/06/1907	Hearts	30/04/1913		75	44
Bacon	OR	13/04/1918		20/04/1918	Trialist	2	0
Bagan, David	CF	02/09/2005	St Johnstone	30/01/2006		10	0
Bain	IR	20/08/1898	Inverkeithing Thistle	03/09/1898		2	4
Bain	FB	07/02/1903		07/02/1903	Trialist	2	0
Bain, Alexander	IL	17/06/1927	Buckie	26/10/1927	Cancelled	3	0
Bain, George C	FB	27/05/1932	Dundee United	21/01/1933	Lochgelly FC	8	2
Bain, Ian D	OR	24/12/1954	Stirling Albion	11/01/1958	Dunfermline Athletic	90	3
Bain, James Clark	OL	20/09/1909	Kirkcaldy Albion	30/04/1913		36	9
Bain, Peter	CH	11/06/1928	Dundee United	07/12/1928	Cancelled	4	0
Bain, Peter	CF	21/11/1936	Dundee United	12/12/1936	Trialist		
Baird, J	CF	01/04/1912		01/04/1912	Trialist	1	0
Baker, Joe	G	26/06/1972	Hibernian	07/10/1974	Free transfer	75	50
Ballantyne, John Ian	D	12/11/1979	Dundee United	14/02/1983	East Stirling	143	48
Banner, Alan	LB	21/07/1990	East Fife	30/04/1992	Camelon	11	0
Bannerman, Gordon	OL	02/01/1908	Coupar Angus	09/08/1913	St Johnstone	37	7
Bannerman, Scott John	CF	11/10/2006	Dumbarton	03/01/2007		1	0
Barclay, A	IR	23/05/1892	Kirkcaldy Newton XI	31/05/1895		7	0
Barclay, James	IL	28/10/1899	Broxburn Athletic	30/04/1900		7	5
Barker, James	M	07/09/1889		07/09/1889		3	0
Barnes, Arthur	IR	02/12/1933	Hearts of Beath	02/11/1933		1	0
Barns, J	IL	29/09/1889		29/09/1889		1	0
Barrau, Xavier	M	26/08/2006	FC Meyrin (Switz)	03/09/2006	Trialist	2	0
Bartholome, Anthony	D	20/08/2004	Valence	07/05/2005		28	0
Barton, George McIntosh	RB	26/05/1921	Newtongrange Star	22/05/1928	Bristol Rovers	208	1
Batchelor, Blair	M	26/07/2005	St Johnstone	30/04/2007		3	0
Batchelor, Mark	LH	05/04/2005		30/04/2005		0	0
Batchelor, Thomas	LH	22/03/1926	Newburgh West End	01/01/1932	Falkirk	289	33
Bauld, Robert	IF	04/01/1921	Glencraig Celtic	07/12/1923	Dundee Hibs	96	22
Bauldie, James	CF	02/10/1919	Bowhill	30/04/1921		11	7
Bavidge, Mitchell	F	19/09/1984	Keith	30/04/1985	Caledonian	10	1
Baxter, Andrew	HB	24/08/1894		29/09/1895		11	2
Baxter, David Sparks Seath	RH	16/05/1936	St Johnstone	19/03/1940		109	6
Baxter, James Curran	LH	17/04/1957	Crossgates Primrose	23/06/1960	Rangers	84	4
Baxter, John	M	09/02/1990	Dundonald Bluebell	30/04/1991		1	0
Baxter, Robert	HB	20/11/1902		30/04/1908		50	1
Baxter, Robert	OR	27/10/1934	Inverkeithing	27/10/1934	Trialist	1	0
Bayne, Graham	F	01/12/2000	Dundee	28/02/2001	Loan	10	0
Beath, John R	RH	12/10/1927	Anstruther Rangers	30/04/1933	Albion Rovers	213	28

First Team Player	Position	Date Signed	Signed from	Date Left	Next Club	Total Appearances	Goals
Beath, Robert Hay	LB	15/08/1955	Nairn Thistle	30/04/1959	St Mirren	7	1
Beatson, P	OL	11/04/1942	Lochgelly	25/04/1942	Trialist	4	3
Beattie, Alexander	OL	09/11/1944	Rangers	30/03/1945	Loan	13	3
Begue, Yannis	M	01/12/1999	[France]	21/03/2000	Albion Rovers	2	0
Bell, Andrew	RB	11/09/1930	Denbeath Star	24/08/1932		82	0
Bell, James	CF	24/08/1904	HMS Caledonia Q'fery	30/04/1908		25	7
Bell, John	OL	31/12/1898	Raith Athletic	30/04/1900		2	3
Bell, John	OL	18/07/1900	Leith Athletic	30/04/1902		29	11
Bell, Peter Norton	IF	02/11/1963	St Johnstone	10/02/1965	Emigrated	42	8
Bell, W	OR	30/12/1922	Darlington	23/09/1926	Manchester City	176	13
Bell, William	IL	31/12/1898	Raith Athletic	02/01/1899		3	1
Benaissa, Amar	CF	28/10/1920	Rosslyn Juniors	19/01/1922	East Fife	16	7
Bennett, Ian	M	02/07/2004	AS Choisy le Roi	17/01/2005		8	0
Bennie, Robert H B	G	06/06/1958	Pumpherston	30/04/1959		2	0
Benson, James	LH	18/12/1933	Hearts	02/11/1934	Resigned	1	0
Benvie, William	CF	12/04/1945	St Johnstone	09/05/1945	War Guest	2	0
Bergersen, Kent	IF	16/02/1961	Dunfermline Athletic	01/08/1962	Cowdenbeath	39	8
Berry, David Hunter	OL	30/11/1996	Valerengen	30/12/1996		6	1
Berry, Richard	M	26/09/1980	East Fife	15/05/1982	Kelty Hearts	28	0
Berthe, Mohammed	CH	07/07/1919	Kinglassie Hearts	14/07/1921	Lochgelly United	22	1
Berthelot, David	CF	18/09/1999	Hearts	19/09/1999	Trialist	1	0
Bett	G	13/07/2004	Louans Cuiseaux	30/04/2005		50	0
Bett	CF	07/12/1895		14/12/1895	Trialist	2	0
Beveridge, William	OR	12/09/1896	Methil Rovers	30/04/1897		33	14
Beveridge, William	LB	05/11/1970	Clackmannan	30/04/1972	Sauchie Juniors	31	0
Bird, George	RB	09/09/1893	Lochgelly United	04/10/1894	Lochgelly United	12	0
Birrell, D	OL	10/08/1895	Methil Rovers	10/08/1895	Trialist	2	0
Birrell, William	IR	14/06/1919	Kirkcaldy United	31/01/1921	Middlesbrough	148	47
Birrell, William		17/11/1927	Middlesbrough	01/12/1930	Bournemouth (Manager		
Black	IL	02/01/1912		02/01/1912	Trialist	1	0
Black, A	LB	14/04/1900		21/04/1900	Trialist	2	0
Black, Crawford	FB	23/09/1936	Aston Villa	08/10/1936		2	0
Black, Derek John	F	26/08/1994	Livingston U15	30/04/1996	Whitburn	1	0
Black, Henry	IR	09/01/1932	Wallyford	09/01/1932	Trialist	1	0
Black, Kenneth George	M	02/07/1999	Airdrie	30/04/2002	Edinburgh University	69	4
Black, William	CF	08/05/1907		08/05/1907	Trialist	1	2
Black, William	OL	20/05/1903		05/10/1904		6	1
Black, William	G	24/02/1920	Hearts	28/02/1920	Loan	3	0
Black, William	G	18/08/1921	Hearts	02/12/1922	Loan		
Black, William	IR	28/06/1933	East Stirling	10/01/1934	Cancelled	14	0
Blackadder, Ryan Robert	M	10/07/2000	Form D Under 16	30/01/2004	Hamilton Accies	66	8
Blackburn, Robert	OR	14/07/1903	Hearts	30/04/1904	Hamilton Accies	28	6
Blackie, William	OR	20/08/1983	Dunfermline Athletic	20/08/1983	Musselburgh Athletic	0	0
Blackstock	RB	24/04/1901		27/04/1901	Trialist	1	0
Blain, Peter	IR	15/12/1945	Albion Rovers	22/12/1945	War Guest	2	0
Blair, Alan	G	31/08/1973	Kirkcaldy YMCA	30/04/1974	Free transfer	47	0
Blair, Alan		05/07/1984	Dundee	15/04/1985	Free transfer		
Bloxham, Albert	OR	05/10/1928	Chesterfield	30/04/1930	Yeovil & Petters U	11	2
Blues, George	OR	30/09/1964		12/10/1964	Trialist	2	1
Blunt, Jason	M	31/03/1998	Leeds United	30/04/1998	Loan	1	0
Blyth	CF	20/05/1916	Loanhead	20/05/1916	Trialist	1	0
Blyth, Alex	IR	15/08/1899		30/04/1900		1	0
Blyth, Andrew	F	12/08/1893	Raith Athletic	10/05/1906		92	20
Blyth, John	RH	28/09/1895	Kirkcaldy	22/02/1896		19	0

First Team Player	Position	Date Signed	Signed from	Date Left	Next Club	Total Appearances	Goals
Blyth, William	LH	29/10/1936	Dunfermline Athletic	18/11/1936	Cancelled	6	0
Bogie, Alexander	F	01/08/1890		30/04/1892	Ardwick	42	48
Bogie, Graeme	RB	11/10/1995	Glenrothes Strollers	30/12/1996	East Fife	1	0
Bolton, John McCaig	CH	15/02/1961	Nairn Thistle	06/07/1963	Ipswich Town	114	2
Bolton, John McCaig		23/06/1967	Morton	04/09/1970	Dumbarton		
Bonar, Paul	LB	31/03/1996	Airdrie	22/07/1997	Ayr United	26	1
Bonar, Steven Andrew	D	31/01/2006	Forfar Athletic	30/05/2007		44	2
Boner, David	OR	23/07/1962	Dundee United	30/04/1963	Freed	9	0
Bonnella	RB	07/08/1892	Pathhead United	07/08/1892	Trialist	1	0
Bonomy, John	LH	02/01/1946	Motherwell	12/01/1946	War Guest	2	0
Bonthron, Robert	RB	30/06/1900	Raith Athletic	30/04/1902	Dundee	68	1
Borland, John Thompson Mathieson	OR	03/05/1922	Rutherglen Glencairn	30/04/1923	Kilmarnock	24	3
Bornes Rincon, Joaquim	D	04/02/2004	Huelva	15/05/2004		14	0
Borris, Ryan	M	23/05/2007	Dumbarton	30/05/2008	Free Transfer	38	1
Borthwick, Adam	LB	24/08/1909	Raith Rovers Juniors	11/09/1909		5	0
Bouadji, Romauld	M	12/07/2006	Clyde	31/07/2003	Trialist	5	0
Boukraa, Karim	M	01/07/1998	Dundee United	30/06/1999	Yee Hote (Hong Kong)	33	0
Bowman, David	F	17/07/1971	Arbroath	30/04/1972	Freed	2	0
Boyack, David	M	09/08/2002	Dundee	30/12/2003	Dundee	16	5
Boylan, Colin Hugh	M	24/07/2003	Youths	27/01/2005	East Fife	35	0
Boyle, John Paul	OR	07/08/1974	Stenhousemuir	13/11/1974	Alloa	6	1
Boyle, Martin	CF	15/08/1903	Hibs	30/04/1904		4	2
Boyle, Peter	M	18/07/2002	Livingston	27/01/2005	Partick Thistle	110	2
Brady, Darren	LH	17/07/1947	Falkirk	01/05/1949	Inverness Thistle	70	22
Brady, Thomas	IR	24/10/1942		24/10/1942	Trialist	1	0
Brand	CF	22/04/1944	Dundee United	22/04/1944	War Guest	1	0
Brand, Norman Roger	IF	18/08/1969	Sunderland	22/04/1970	Hamilton Accies	25	5
Brand, Ralph	OL	18/10/1949	Aberdeen East End	21/03/1952	Newcastle United	32	9
Brander, George Milne	CH	17/07/1986	Forfar Athletic	17/03/1989	Brechin City	96	8
Brash, Alexander Y	FB	09/02/1973	Lochgelly Albert	23/02/1974	Trialist	2	0
Breen, Thomas	RB	15/09/1945	Liverpool	13/10/1045	War Guest	5	0
Bremner, W	F	26/07/1991	Forfar Athletic	05/08/1993	Dundee United	103	38
Brewster, Craig James	F	05/10/1963		05/10/1963	Trialist	2	0
Briggs, Willie	F	01/12/1970		01/12/1970	Trialist	1	0
Briggs, Wilson	IR	30/09/1944	Sheffield Wednesday	04/11/1944	War Guest	3	4
Briscoe, James Patrick	F	22/07/2003	Livingston	31/12/2003	Livingston	22	1
Brittain, Richard	CF	20/11/1998	Dunfermline	20/12/1998	Loan	5	1
Britton, Gerard Joseph	G	14/12/1939	Leith Athletic	02/01/1940	War Guest	3	2
Broadley, Edward	LB	14/07/1993	Partick Thistle	14/03/1996	East Fife	108	1
Broddie, Julian	CH	06/04/1903		06/04/1903	Trialist	1	0
Bromwell	OL	14/04/1947	Hamilton Accies	14/04/1947	Trialist	1	0
Brown	IR	16/07/1887		25/02/1893		4	0
Brown	CH	05/05/1902		05/05/1902	Trialist	1	0
Brown	CH	04/03/1905		04/03/1905	Trialist	2	0
Brown, Alexander	LB	16/01/1943		16/01/1943	Trialist	1	0
Brown, Alistair	G	04/08/1964	Morton	30/04/1965		16	8
Brown, Allan W	G	25/07/2005	Hibs	30/05/2006	Loan	46	0
Brown, Andrew	CF	25/11/1925	Hamilton Accies	31/12/1926	Partick Thistle	23	17
Brown, Edwin A (Eddie)	OL	07/08/1934	Lochgelly	19/12/1934	Cancelled	13	7
Brown, George McA	OR	25/05/1922	Hearts	30/04/1923		4	0
Brown, Gordon	G	01/02/1925	Dunnikier Juniors	30/04/1926		2	0
Brown	G	22/04/1972	Lochore Welfare	15/05/1973	Provisional	2	0
Brown, Henry (Harry)	OL	19/12/1907	Brechin City	04/08/1911	St Johnstone	18	3

First Team Player	Position	Date Signed	Signed from	Date Left	Next Club	Total Appearances	Goals
Brown, Henry S	OL	25/10/1939	Reading	20/04/1940	War Guest	13	3
Brown, Ian	D	10/07/2000	Greig Park Rangers	30/06/2004	Glenrothes	39	1
Brown, James	G	04/11/1915	Airdrie	01/08/1924	Dunfermline	227	0
Brown, James	LH	24/08/1949	Ardrossan W.R.	30/04/1951		1	0
Brown, James Andrew	RB	26/06/1974	Dunfermline	01/11/1977	Newburgh	117	5
Brown, Jamie		17/08/2004		22/09/2004		0	0
Brown, John L	RB	02/08/1947	Forfar Athletic	23/09/1947	Cancelled	1	0
Brown, John Kenneth	LB	09/06/1969	Penicuik Athletic	05/01/1971	Penicuik Athletic	16	0
Brown, Michael	G	07/07/2006	Forfar Athletic	30/05/2008	East Fife	30	0
Brown, Robert	G	21/09/1946	Montrose	27/03/1948	Cancelled	32	0
Brown, Russell	G	23/08/2003	Lochee United	23/08/2003	Trialist	0	0
Brown, Tom	M	04/01/1972	Lochgelly Albert	27/11/1976	Montrose	167	34
Brown, William	HB	09/07/1919		17/01/1920	St Bernards	13	7
Brown, William		04/03/1920	St Bernards	06/03/1920	St Bernards		
Brown, William	IF	15/02/1964	Blairgowrie Juniors	30/04/1965	Freed	5	0
Brown, William	LB	01/06/1973	Motherwell	30/04/1978	Newtongrange Star	140	5
Brown, William B		16/06/1900	Airdrie	30/04/1901		11	5
Brown, William J	RB	02/09/1930	Rochdale	30/04/1931		2	0
Browne, Paul Gerard	CH	03/07/1996	Aston Villa	30/05/2002	Arbroath	225	6
Brownlie, Paul Jack	F	29/12/1998	Clyde	31/07/1999	Arbroath	12	1
Brownlie, Richard	F	10/01/1936	Dundee St Josephs	30/04/1937		11	3
Brownlie, Thomas	IF	13/11/1911		24/07/1912	Cowdenbeath	22	3
Bruce	CF	27/04/1908		27/04/1908	Trialist	1	0
Bruce, Bobby	OL	14/04/1966	Lochgelly Albert	14/04/1966	Trialist	1	0
Bruce, Eric Gaul	CH	13/08/1955	Nairn Thistle	20/01/1959	Cancelled	2	0
Bruce, J	G	28/04/1917	Partick Thistle	28/04/1917	Trialist	1	0
Bruce, John	LB	28/10/1899	Buckhaven United	30/04/1900	Left back	8	0
Bruce, William S.	G	28/08/1943	Banks o Dee Juvenile	30/07/1947	Aberdeen	142	0
Bruton, Leslie	CF	29/11/1928	Peterborough United	13/05/1929	Blackburn Rovers	28	31
Bryce	CF	17/02/1894		17/02/1894	Trialist	1	0
Bryce, Kieran		17/08/2004		24/08/2004	Alloa	0	0
Bryce, Lee		29/05/2007				5	2
Bryce, Robert	CF	08/08/1936		20/08/1936	Trialist	3	3
Buchan, Robert	OL	27/08/1954	Cowdenbeath	30/04/1958	Trialist	18	5
Buchanan, Alexander	CH	07/03/1968	Valleyfield Colliery	30/04/1970	Oakley United	10	0
Buchanan, G. C.	HB	09/03/1889		26/04/1890		21	4
Buchanan, John	OR	05/06/1925	Hibernian	12/11/1925	Bournemouth & Bos.	4	2
Buchanan, James	OR	24/02/1961	Hibernian	01/06/1961	Newport County	10	1
Buchanan, Neil	FB	01/01/1988	Lochgelly Albert	30/04/1990	Armadale Thistle	13	0
Buist, David B	OL	30/01/1964	Blairgowrie Juniors	30/04/1965		5	1
Buist, Mark	CH	20/07/1993	Glenrothes Strollers	16/08/1996	Stirling Albion	5	0
Burn, Philip	M	05/08/1988	Lochgelly Albert	06/11/1992	Ballymena United	87	6
Burnett, John	CF	13/03/1943	Hall & Co	13/03/1943	Trialist	1	1
Burns	IR	04/01/1904		04/01/1904	Trialist	1	1
Burns	IR	04/04/1910		04/04/1910	Trialist	1	0
Burns	CF	22/08/1923		22/08/1923	Trialist	1	0
Burns, Alexander	M	06/07/1999	Southend United	29/09/2000	Livingston	56	17
Burrows, Frank	CH	06/07/1961	Fishcross Juveniles	04/05/1965	Scunthorpe United	99	1
Burt	IR	23/10/1886		23/10/1886	Trialist	1	1
Burt, George R	CF	04/04/1931	Camelon	04/03/1931	Trialist	1	0
Burton	IL	15/05/1902		15/05/1902	Trialist	2	0
Butler, Matthew	OL	14/08/1915	Kelty Rangers	04/12/1915	Kirkcaldy United	6	0
Byers, Kevin	M	09/07/1996	Glenrothes Strollers	30/06/1999	Inverness C.T.	22	0
Byrne,	OL	29/04/1933	Musselburgh Bruntonian	29/04/1933	Trialist	1	0

First Team Player	Position	Date Signed	Signed from	Date Left	Next Club	Total Appearances	Goals
Cabrelli, Peter	LH	15/08/1936	Falkirk	29/09/1943	Dundee United	162	2
Cairney	RH	19/08/1925		19/08/1925	Trialist	1	0
Cairns	CF	02/01/1945	Lochgelly Violet	31/03/1945	Trialist	4	3
Cairns, David	D	10/08/1925	Wellesley Juniors	28/12/1926	Kettering Town	25	1
Cairns, David	FB	07/03/1975	Cowdenbeath	24/08/1976	Berwick Rangers	28	0
Cairns, John	G	20/07/1895	Kirkcaldy	02/03/1899	Linthouse	153	1
Cairns, John	FB	08/08/1942	Leith Athletic	01/01/1943	War Loan	16	2
Cairns, Thomas	IL	17/06/1902		05/05/1904	Glossop	30	3
Calderon, Antonio	M	05/07/2002	Airdrie	19/05/2004	Cadiz	60	4
Calderwood	LH	05/05/1888		05/05/1888	Trialist	1	0
Caldwell, John	LH	10/05/1924		10/05/1924	Trialist	1	0
Callaghan, Thomas Tallett	OL	26/08/1933	Third Lanark	02/11/1933	Cancelled	10	0
Calpworthy	RB	12/09/1942	Chelsea	12/09/1942	War Guest	1	0
Cameron, Colin	M	13/07/1990	Lochore Welfare	31/03/1996	Hearts	168	42
Cameron, David	F	19/02/2000	Brighton	19/02/2000	Trialist	1	0
Cameron, Ian	M	17/07/1997	Hibernian	30/06/1999	Clydebank	53	12
Cameron, John	IR	01/08/1888	Kirkcaldy FC	30/04/1893		51	17
Campbell	IR	10/09/1892		10/09/1892	Trialist	1	0
Campbell	CH	25/04/1903		25/04/1903	Trialist	1	0
Campbell	LH	22/08/1942	Luton	22/08/1942	War Guest	1	0
Campbell	CF	28/04/1945	Stirling	05/05/1945	Trialist	2	1
Campbell, Andrew	IR	14/12/1932	Dundee	11/02/1933	Lincoln City	4	0
Campbell, David S	OR	10/08/1931	Denbeath	26/10/1931	Cancelled	1	0
Campbell, Donald	LH	31/08/1954	Lochore Welfare	30/04/1956		1	0
Campbell, Gary W	FB	05/01/1979	Blackpool	30/11/1979	amateur football	1	0
Campbell, George	OL	22/08/1907	Falkirk	30/04/1909		9	0
Campbell, John	IF	10/05/1957	Hibernian	28/09/1957	Cancelled	1	1
Campbell, Mark Thomas	CH	31/01/2006	St Johnstone			87	8
Campbell, Richard	D	01/09/2004	Edina Hibs			0	0
Campbell, Robert	CH	13/09/1922		27/09/122	Trialist	3	0
Campbell, Robert S	WH	07/05/1938	Rangers	03/12/1945		23	5
Campbell, William	RB	06/08/1919		23/01/1920	St Bernards	2	0
Campbell, William R	RH	15/07/1929	Huddersfield Town	03/04/1933		37	2
Candlish, Christopher	LB	02/12/1975	Lochore Welfare	15/05/1987	Brechin City	312	17
Cant, Andrew	M	14/02/1920	Dunfermline D&D.S&S.	30/04/1921	East Fife	9	1
Cant, Jimmy	M	27/11/1976	Montrose	30/04/1977	Arbroath Vics	3	0
Capin Martino, Salvador	M	30/03/2001	Airdrie	30/05/2004	Poli Ejido	19	0
Capin Martino, Salvador	M	18/02/2004	Livingston	30/05/2004			
Carcary, Derek	OL	19/01/2007	Rangers	30/05/2008	Free Transfer	52	10
Carmichael	LB	15/08/1899	Raith Athletic	15/08/1899	Trialist	1	0
Carr, James	OR	28/01/1956	Douglasdale Juniors	30/04/1958	Freed	8	2
Carranza, Luis Alberto	F	29/11/2003	Dundee	04/01/2004	Quilmes (Argentina)	3	0
Carrigan, Brian Eric	F	12/07/2002	Clydebank	30/05/2003	Hamilton	30	6
Carroll	IR	26/04/1902		03/02/1902	Trialist	3	1
Carroll, Patrick	M	24/09/1979	Hibernian	14/09/1982	Falkirk	93	7
Carroll, Richard	G	26/08/2003	Elmwood	26/09/2003	Loan	0	0
Carson, George	M	12/08/1948	Vale of Leven	01/07/1949	Dumbarton	8	1
Carson, Thomas	G	05/08/1992	Dundee	30/04/1993	Vale of Leven	44	0
Carter	CH	16/10/1915		16/10/1915	Trialist	1	0
Casey, Mark	IR	12/02/2005		19/02/2005	Trialist	3	1
Cassells	RB	05/05/1894	Black Watch	19/05/1894	Trialist	2	0
Cassidy	G	01/04/1912		01/04/1912	Trialist	1	0
Caven, John Brown	CF	03/08/1959	Airdrie	10/10/1959	Bellshill Athletic	16	5
Caven, John Brown	CF	01/11/1962	Brighton	30/04/1963	Morton	1	0

First Team Player	Position	Date Signed	Signed from	Date Left	Next Club	Total Appearances	Goals
Cooper, James Thomson	OR	10/12/1960	Ardeer Thistle	30/04/1962	Airdrie	8	0
Cooper, Robert Brian	WH	06/08/1968	Aberdeen	21/12/1977	East Fife	350	12
Cooper, Thomas Scott	RH	11/10/1938	Kirkwall	30/04/1945		9	2
Chaplin	CF	11/10/1951	Dundee	30/04/1959	Emigrated	243	150
Copeland, Ernest	LB	01/01/1999	Morton	31/03/1999	Stirling Albion	4	0
Cormack, Peter Robert	OL	20/08/1970	Dundee	30/04/1971	Broxburn Athletic	13	2
Cormack, Raymond	D	28/01/2003	Aberton (South Africa)	30/04/2003		2	0
Correira, Marco Sergio	RH	27/04/1895	Crail Union	27/04/1895	Trialist	1	1
Corstorphine	CH	13/08/1984	Preston Athletic	15/05/1986	Freed	19	1
Corstorphine, Steven	OL	10/04/1924		10/04/1924	Trialist	1	0
Cowan	CH	30/12/1899		30/12/1899	Trialist	1	1
Cowan, Daniel	CF	07/05/1931	Celtic	30/06/1934	East Fife	99	106
Cowan, Joseph	CH	14/10/1989	Armadale Thistle	15/05/1993	Armadale Thistle	1	0
Cowan, Mark	CF	01/08/1890	Kirkcaldy Albion	30/04/1900		58	54
Cowan, William	RH	12/06/1924	Ashfield	26/02/1926	Broxburn United	9	1
Cowie, Alexander	CF	16/10/1926	Keith	25/01/1928	Arbroath	29	13
Cowie, James G	LH	01/08/1893	Kirkcaldy Albion	30/04/1897	Leith Athletic	178	13
Cowper, John	IR	02/07/1932	Falkirk	10/01/1933	Cancelled	3	0
Cox, William				30/05/2001	Morton	9	0
Coyle, Craig Robert	G	01/07/1998	Salveson BC	30/05/2001	Morton	9	0
Coyle, Ronald	D	08/01/1988	Rochdale	22/03/1996	Ayr United	327	13
Crabbe, Scott	F	07/08/2001	Livingston	02/11/2001	Ayr United	58	8
Crabbe, Thomas		31/01/2005	Albion Rovers	30/05/2006			
Craig, David William	CH	10/05/1996	Hamilton Accies	09/09/1997	Hamilton Accies	49	3
Craig, Robert M	IF	11/09/1963	St Mirren	11/09/1963	Trialist	1	0
Craig, Steven	M	02/07/1998	Hutchison Vale BC	30/05/2000	Falkirk	3	0
Craigie, Alexander McC	IR	11/12/1935	Morton	30/04/1936		19	4
Cramb, Peter	G	01/05/1982	Methil Rovers	15/05/1983	Freed	7	0
Cranston, Thomas	OR	25/05/1912	Ardrossan Celtic	17/03/1914	Third Lanark	73	12
Crawford, David	D	14/04/1903		04/05/1903	Rangers	3	1
Crawford, John Campbell (Ian)	IF	20/06/1949	East Stirling	30/04/1950	Ayr United	8	1
Crawford, Stephen	F	03/07/1991	Castlebridge	30/06/1996	Millwall	160	37
Creaney, Gerard Thomas	F	05/08/2000	Notts County	30/10/2000	Queen of the South	14	3
Crichton	RH	31/01/1892	Raith Athletic	01/04/1893		9	0
Crichton	RB	19/04/1916		16/04/1916	Trialist	1	0
Crichton, William	LH	18/08/1933	East Stirling	30/04/1936	East Stirling	107	8
Cricket, Thomas M	RB	29/06/1926	St Rochs	27/08/1928	Kings Park	6	0
Crilly, Mark Patrick	M	22/06/2005	St Mirren	30/05/2006		38	5
Crosskey, Thomas R	G	08/06/1936	Albion Rovers	30/04/1937	Montrose	27	0
Crumlish, Sean	M	09/07/2001	Barrhead BC	30/05/2003	Vale of Leithen		
Cumming, Arthur	LB	26/07/1904	Dunnikier Athletic	30/04/1917		343	4
Cummings	RH	21/05/1890		21/05/1890	Trialist	1	0
Cunningham, William	G	11/08/1961	Dundee	30/04/1962	Stenhousemuir	14	0
Cunningham, William	F	02/06/1967	Kirkcaldy Travel Clu	30/04/1969	Glenrothes	23	7
Cunningham, William J	LB	14/06/1933	Hearts	30/04/1935		44	0
Curley, John	IL	03/11/1925	St Anthonys	11/09/1926	Kilmarnock	11	0
Currie	G	16/03/1889	Pathhead United	16/03/1889	Trialist	2	0
Currie, David		12/07/2006		30/04/2007		0	0
Currie, Edward	CH	30/11/1944	Third Lanark	15/12/1944	War Guest	1	0
Currie, Paul	M	13/10/2006	Musselburgh Athletic	09/01/2007	Temporary transfer	9	1
Currie, Walter	WH	23/12/1916	East Fife	26/12/1919	Leicester City	61	6
Cusick, John James	M	01/03/1993	St Johnstone	31/07/1993	Dundonald Bluebell	3	0
Cuthbert, James	G	13/08/1955	Nairn Thistle	30/04/1956	Freed	4	1
Dailey, Douglas	CF	13/11/1974	Berwick Rangers	05/03/1975	Barrow		
Dair, Jason	OL	03/07/1991	Castlebridge	30/06/1996	Millwall	199	23

First Team Player	Position	Date Signed	Signed from	Date Left	Next Club	Total Appearances	Goals
Chalmers, David C	CF	15/08/1911	Third Lanark	01/09/1912	East Fife	21	4
Chalmers, Tom	F	01/08/1885		30/04/1890		131	64
Chalmers, William Ritchie	OL	11/08/1931	Newburgh West End	01/08/1931	Bournemouth	5	0
Chaplin	CH	29/09/1924		29/09/1924	Trialist	1	0
Chapman, G	G	19/12/1885		1/5/1886		12	0
Chapman, George A	LH	21/05/1924	Hearts	30/04/1925	Bathgate	19	3
Chapman, George R	CH	11/06/1907	Hearts	30/04/1908	Blackburn Rovers	43	8
Charlton	OL	05/01/1946	RAF Donibristle	05/01/1946	Trialist	1	0
Christie	OR	16/12/1933	Thornton Hibs	16/12/1933	Trialist	1	0
Christie, James	IF	03/05/1919	Dysart	30/04/1921		6	0
Christie, Terence	OR	16/08/1965	Dundee	26/02/1966	Hawick RA	13	2
Ciani, Amick	M	02/01/2007	Ross County	02/01/2007	Trialist	1	0
Clark	LH	12/05/1902		12/05/1902	Trialist	1	0
Clark	OR	24/08/1889	Burntisland Thistle	24/8/1889	Trialist	1	0
Clark, Andrew Alexander	F	01/07/1998	Hutchison Vale BC	30/05/2002	Trialist	77	4
Clark, David	OL	16/07/1887		12/05/1888		83	37
Clark, Frank	G	26/05/1919	Denbeath Star	22/12/1919	Lochgelly United	4	0
Clark, Ian	IF	21/07/1970	Links United	30/04/1971		7	2
Clark, James Edward	G	04/07/1950	Morton	30/04/1951	Glentoran	2	0
Clark, James Sutherland	D	06/08/2001	Falkirk	30/05/2002		3	0
Clark, Thomas	LH	06/08/1902		30/04/1903		3	0
Clark, William	RB	01/08/1885		12/05/1888		82	2
Clarke, Patrick	F	31/01/2005	Dunfermline (Berwick loan)	31/08/2005	Arbroath	24	5
Clarkston, Thomas	OR	15/08/1903	Morton	30/04/1905		47	19
Clelland, Robert (Bobby)	M	01/12/1972	Haddington Athletic	30/04/1974	Cowdenbeath	8	0
Clifford, John	LH	18/05/1968	Motherwell	27/05/1968	Trialist	2	0
Clinton, Michael	LH	25/07/1961	Clyde	30/04/1963	Inverness Caley	49	4
Clunie, Henry	G	01/08/1889		21/04/1900		58	0
Clunie, James Robertson	CH	27/07/1950	Raith Athletic	28/12/1953	Aberdeen	12	0
Coats, Thomas S	G	02/03/1966	Larkhall Thistle	21/01/1967	Third Lanark	18	0
Cobban, William L	OL	10/12/1915		30/04/1922		18	3
Cochrane, James		03/07/2004	Sunday League Amateur	03/07/2004	Trialist	1	0
Cockburn, James B.R.	IF	06/03/1951	Clyde	30/04/1953	Brechin City	14	5
Coleman, Jack	OR	28/11/1977	Oakley United	30/04/1979	Glenrothes	2	0
Collier, Walter	OR	01/08/1893	Raith Athletic	30/04/1894		2	1
Collier, William	LH	14/02/1912	Army football	09/06/1924	Retired	205	10
Collins, Allan	IF	16/06/1948	Kilmarnock	30/04/1951	Stenhousemuir	72	29
Colquhoun, Duncan Morton	OR	19/06/1934		22/11/1934	Dumbarton	14	9
Colvan, Hugh	IR	21/02/1946	Hibernian	30/04/1946	Loan	28	9
Colville, Henry	LB	09/03/1946	Falkirk	13/06/1955	Falkirk	291	9
Conaty, Thomas Philip	RH	08/08/1927		29/09/1927	South Shields	2	0
Condie, David Matthew	LB	06/07/1950	Markinch Victoria Rgs	30/04/1953		10	0
Conn, Alfred	IF	26/09/1958	Hearts	30/04/1960	Retired	51	26
Conn, Robert	M	05/09/1974	Hearts	12/03/1975	England	7	1
Connell	OL	28/08/1943	Donibristle	28/08/1943	Trialist	1	0
Connell, Peter	IR	01/08/1895		26/09/1896		11	1
Connor, John	IF	26/08/1944	Queen of the South	28/10/1944	Loan	9	1
Conquer, Andrew D	LB	22/03/1947	Haddington Athletic	22/03/1947	Trialist	1	0
Conway, John	IF	19/02/1942	Celtic	30/04/1942	Loan	17	1
Cook	LB	16/10/1912		16/10/1912	Trialist	1	0
Cook	CF	08/04/1944				1	0
Cook, Robert C	OL	15/05/1943	St Johnstone	15/05/1943	War Guest	1	0
Cook, Thomas	OL	01/08/1888	Raith Athletic	07/12/1891		12	3
Cook, William	LB	15/05/1943	Everton	29/05/1943	War Guest	2	0

First Team Player	Position	Date Signed	Signed from	Date Left	Next Club	Total Appearances	Goals
Dair, Jason	M	12/09/1997	Millwall	26/02/1999	Dunfermline Athletic	35	5
Dair, Lee	M	27/06/1997	Rangers	08/10/1997	Cowdenbeath	222	146
Dall, William	CH	01/08/1893		25/03/1895	Sheffield United	66	35
Dalrymple, George	IF	20/06/1905	Hibs	15/05/1906	Loan		
Dalrymple, George		25/10/1906	Hibernian	28/05/1907	Ayr Parkhouse		
Daly, Wesley James Patrick	M	20/08/2004	Queens Park Rangers	15/01/2005	Loan	11	1
Dalziel, David G.	OR	12/07/1947	Newtongrange Star	30/04/1948	Edinburgh City	13	3
Dalziel, Gordon	CF	25/02/1987	East Stirling	09/08/1995	Ayr United	378	202
Dargo, Craig Peter	F	11/10/1995	Links United	06/06/2000	Kilmarnock	102	37
Darling, Jason	D	04/07/2006		30/04/2008		8	1
Davidson	CH	05/01/1909		05/01/1909		1	0
Davidson, Alan Martin	D	09/07/2001	Raith Youth	30/04/2003	Falkirk	3	0
Davidson, Hugh Norman	M	27/03/2002	Dundee United	28/04/2002	Loan	10	1
Davidson, Ian	D	29/07/2004	Scarborough			148	8
Davidson, Joseph	HB	09/06/1913	Petershill	13/01/1915	Abercorn	8	0
Davidson, Thomas	CH	25/05/1966	Armiston Rangers	22/04/1970	Berwick Rangers	39	0
Davie, John	FB	01/02/1912	Hamilton Accies	03/02/1912	Loan	1	0
Davie, John	IR	07/10/1935	Hibs	07/10/1935	Trialist	1	0
Davis, Michael	M	03/07/1991	Glenrothes Strollers	30/04/1993	Newburgh	1	0
Dawson, Alexander	OL	01/08/1894	Cupar Athletic	30/04/1896		29	26
Dawson, David	IF	29/03/1921	Lochgelly Wednesday	20/05/1922	Dunfermline Athletic	15	7
Dawson, Joseph	IL	01/12/1945	Forfar Athletic	28/02/1946		8	4
Dawson, Peter	OR	05/10/1935	Blairhall Juniors	12/10/1935	Trialist	2	0
Day	RB	27/04/1908		27/04/1908	Trialist	1	0
de Getrouwe, Erwin	OR	11/03/1994	[Belgium]	11/03/1994	Trialist	1	0
Dempsey, James	WH	06/03/1971	Hamilton Academical	23/01/1975	Stirling Albion	135	7
Dempsie, Mark William	M	01/12/2000	Hibs	01/01/2001	Loan	2	0
Dempster, Chris	FB	23/11/1974	Castlehill	30/04/1976	Halbeath	8	0
Denholm, David	LB	31/08/1901	Parkmore (Dundee Jns)	30/04/1908		54	0
Denholm, George Anderson	WH	13/11/1934	Hearts of Beath	30/04/1936		53	20
Dennis, Shaun	CH	03/08/1988	Lochgelly Albert	10/01/1997	Hibs	453	16
Dennis, Shaun		23/02/2001	Hibs	30/06/2004	Brechin City		
Dennis, Shaun		15/10/2004	Brechin City	01/07/2005	retired		
Deuchars, Neilson	HB	13/09/1894	Kirkcaldy Albion	30/04/1895		115	25
Deuchars, William S	RH	04/10/1924	St Johnstone YMCA	03/09/1928	Dundee United	96	7
Devine, Archie	IF	21/06/1901	Lochgelly United	30/04/1904	Falkirk	43	15
Devine, James	IR	30/06/1901	St Bernards	19/04/1902	Lochgelly United	16	10
Devlin	M	24/04/1971			Trialist	1	0
Devlin, William John	D	09/07/2003	S Form	20/04/2004		2	0
Dewar, James	OR	29/02/1936	Kirkcaldy Boys Club	04/04/1936		2	0
Dick	FB	26/04/1906		05/01/1910		5	0
Dick, William R	WH	10/08/1932	Hibernian	30/04/1934		41	2
Dickson, James	G	10/12/1919	St Bernards	30/04/1923		40	0
Dickson, Peter	CF	22/01/1946	Army	30/04/1946		2	1
Dillon, Bernard	F	26/05/1903	St Mirren	30/04/1904		43	8
Dingwall, Joseph Michael	D	04/07/2006		30/05/2008	Free Transfer	27	0
Dobbie, George	CF	14/07/1958	Hearts	30/04/1960	Freed	29	14
Dobbie, William S.R.	OL	03/08/1935	Denbeath Star	30/04/1936	Montrose	29	5
Docherty, Hugh	OR	13/01/1949	Blackpool	01/07/1949		1	0
Doig, George	IR	23/04/1887	Kirkcaldy Wanderers	21/05/1887		6	3
Dolan, Andrew	IR	14/06/1947	Alloa Athletic	14/08/1948	Bury	29	6
Don, James	G	14/05/1903		30/04/1911		51	0
Donagher, Michael	WH	07/05/1908	Barnsley	30/04/1913		94	3
Donald	OR	22/04/1908		22/04/1908	Trialist	2	0

First Team Player	Position	Date Signed	Signed from	Date Left	Next Club	Total Appearances	Goals
Donald, Anderson	LB	23/02/1990	Armadale Thistle	30/04/1990		4	1
Donald, John	LB	18/11/1942		21/02/1946		115	4
Donaldson, Alastair	G	24/10/1981	Hibernian	30/04/1982	Montrose (A/Man)	22	0
Donaldson, Peter	FB	01/11/1972	Haddington Athletic	17/04/1974	Berwick Rangers	37	1
Donaldson, Robert	OR	06/02/1886		13/03/1886		5	1
Donnelly	F	21/04/1971		21/04/1971	Trialist	1	0
Dorrans, Owen	IF	21/05/1925	Cowdenbeath	10/06/1929	Morton	114	26
Dorward, John	G	04/09/1899		30/05/1903	Cowdenbeath	30	8
Dougal	IR	23/08/1941		23/08/1941		1	0
Dougall	CF	11/04/1927		11/04/1927	Trialist	1	0
Douglas, A	IR	24/08/1895		28/09/1895		4	1
Douglas, Peter	CF	29/11/1900	Hibernian	23/03/1901	Loan	17	9
Dow, Andrew	LB	17/02/2004	Arbroath	15/05/2004	Lochee United	9	0
Dowie, William	G	26/07/1905	Dunnikier Athletic	30/04/1915		130	2
Doyle	RB	25/08/1945	Crosshill Hearts	01/09/1945		2	0
Drain, George	LH	25/09/1928	Lochgelly Celtic	16/09/1930		37	0
Driana	LB	29/07/2003		29/07/2003		1	0
Drummond	LH	28/03/1942	Dundonald	28/03/1942		1	0
Drummond, Charles	G	30/03/1952	Lochore Welfare	01/07/1961	Cowdenbeath	202	0
Drummond, George	CF	14/08/1899	Cowdenbeath	30/04/1901		66	32
Drummond, John George	F	21/07/1994	Inverkeithing United	30/04/1995		1	0
Dryburgh	CF	07/04/1900		07/04/1900	Trialist	1	0
Drysdale	OL	04/01/1930	Newburgh West End	20/09/1930		4	0
Drysdale, John	LH	03/01/1944	Kilmarnock	08/01/1944	War Guest	1	0
Duff	CH	01/01/1889		01/01/1889	Trialist	1	0
Duff, William	G	05/01/1972	Dunfermline	01/07/1972	Trialist	2	0
Duffield, Peter	CF	29/02/1996	Airdrieonians	08/11/1997	East Stirling	1	1
Duffus, John	LH	01/08/1889		03/11/1894	Morton	65	20
Duffy, Charles	CH	17/08/1916		30/04/1917		13	0
Duffy, John	LH	10/03/1960	Nairn Thistle	18/11/1960	Cancelled	4	0
Dunbar, Henry	LH	19/08/1914		30/04/1915	Dumbarton Harp	14	0
Duncan, Alexander Ronald	OL	01/04/1973	Whitburn	15/10/1980	Cowdenbeath	4	0
Duncan, David Miller	OL	17/05/1939	Lochgelly Albert	23/12/1942	Celtic	260	36
Duncan, David Miller		06/01/1954	East Fife	30/04/1955	Crewe Alexandra	132	47
Duncan, George	OR	04/05/1960	Rangers	31/05/1960	Cancelled	3	1
Duncan, James	OL	26/02/1916		29/04/1916		2	0
Duncan, Jim	CF	15/03/1966	Eyemouth United	15/03/1966	Trialist	1	1
Duncan, John	OL	21/02/1918	Lochgelly United	29/07/1922	Leicester City	161	37
Duncan, Thomas	OR	19/04/1920		29/07/1922	Leicester City	72	10
Dunleavy, Damien	IF	12/02/1991	Sligo Rovers	31/07/1992	Derry City	32	3
Dunn, John	OL	27/06/1919	Leith Benburb	04/08/1921	Broxburn United	33	5
Dunn, Tony	LB	01/11/1977	Glenrothes United	30/04/1978	Halbeath	0	0
Dunn, William	IF	29/09/1938	Southampton	03/04/1942	Albion Rovers	38	18
Dunsire, Andrew	IF	24/01/1920	Kinghorn Ath. Juvs.	26/12/1925	Broxburn United	5	1
Dutch, John	RB	17/02/1943	A.Hall & Co. Ltd.	01/11/1943	East Fife	101	1
Dysart	IL	01/02/1947	Sauchie Juveniles	01/02/1947	Trialist	1	0
Eadie, Donald McCallum	CF	12/08/1933	Leith Athletic	09/09/1933		2	0
Eardley, George	F	29/11/1902	Leith Athletic	30/04/1903		7	2
Easson, David S	F	21/05/1960	Arbroath	01/07/1961	Morton	25	9
Ebanda, Herve	F	28/07/2004	Beaucaire	17/02/2005	Alloa	25	8
Eckford, John	F	01/08/1893	Raith Athletic	30/04/1896		202	119
Eden, Terrance R	LB	27/04/1948	Harrow Town	01/07/1949		18	0
Edmunds	IR	18/11/1944	Cardiff			1	1
el Khebir, Karim	RB	15/03/2003	Valence	22/03/2002	Trialist	2	0

Players (Foster – George)

First Team Player	Position	Date Signed	Signed from	Date Left	Next Club	Total Appearances	Goals
Foster, Alexander	LH	14/08/1915	Montraive	30/04/1919		24	0
Foster, Thomas	CF	11/05/1903	Kirkcaldy FC	13/05/1903	Trialist	2	0
Fotheringham	RB	04/03/1944	Hill of Beath Star	04/03/1944	Trialist	1	0
Fotheringham, George Thomas	F	01/07/1998	Catkin United	30/05/2000	Dunfermline Ath	8	1
Fotheringham, James	F	06/05/1902	Leith Athletic	10/05/1902	Loan	1	1
Fotheringham, Kevin George	D	07/08/1997	Hamilton Accies	30/05/1999	Hill of Beath Hawtho	114	7
Fotheringham, Kevin George		26/07/2006	St Johnstone	30/05/2007	East Fife	39	21
Fox, Desmond W	IF	24/02/1961	Hibernian	30/04/1962		0	0
Fox, Mark	M	26/08/2003	Raith Rovers Form D	31/01/2005	Free Transfer	2	2
Foxall	IR	10/01/1942		21/03/1942	War Guest	11	0
Frame, Calum	G	27/09/1976	Pumpherston	18/08/1978	Berwick Rangers	40	0
Frame, David B	RB	06/06/1925	Third Lanark	10/09/1926	Dykehead	1	0
France, Louis	LB	19/10/1946	St Johnstone YM	19/10/1946	Dundee United		
Francis, Christopher Douglas	F	11/10/1995	Valleyfield	30/05/1997	Thornton Hibs	2	0
Fraser, Alan	WH	30/07/1971	Dunfermline Railway	01/03/1972	Cowdenbeath	2	0
Fraser, Campbell Grant	M	23/10/1987	Rangers	29/03/1991	Dundee	109	7
Fraser, Gary	F	03/07/2004	Rangers	10/07/2004	Trialist		
Fraser, Norman	OL	21/10/1936	Forthill Athletic	18/03/1938	Montrose	2	0
Fraser, Richard	IL	02/04/1906	Dunfermline Violet	16/11/1906	Dunfermline Athletic	28	7
Fraser, Richard	IL	13/06/1908	Dunfermline Athletic	05/01/1909	Cowdenbeath	16	0
French, James W M	IF	06/08/1958	Peebles Rovers	30/04/1961		29	4
Frew, Michael Anthony	M	31/08/2004	Ballingry Rovers	06/07/2005	Free Transfer	0	0
Frew, Thomas	CF	25/08/1896	Hearts of Beath	30/04/1897	Hearts of Beath	13	1
Fridge, Leslie Francis	G	05/07/1995	Clyde	30/05/1996	Dundalk	5	0
Fullerton, Eamon	D	28/01/2005	Livingston	31/05/2005	Loan	11	0
Fulton, George H	CF	22/09/1934	St Johnstone	01/09/1937	St Johnstone	107	85
Fyall, George	LH	08/11/1910		28/03/1912	Cowdenbeath	1	0
Fyfe, A	IR	19/08/1899		24/08/1905	Loan	3	1
Fyfe, Graham	M	01/01/2003	Celtic	30/05/2003	Loan	15	1
Fyfe, J	OR	24/08/1904		24/08/1904	Trialist	1	0
Gage, Albert	G	21/11/1942	Fulham	02/01/1943	War Guest	7	0
Gallazzi, Norman	F	21/04/1971		21/04/1971	Trialist	1	0
Gallocher, Patrick	CH	24/08/1897	Burnley	28/02/1898	Berwick Rangers	17	3
Galloway	CF	03/12/1887		02/01/1888		3	0
Galloway, Andrew Douglas	M	12/12/1997	[Australia]	15/05/1998	Cancelled	6	0
Galloway, David Wilson	IL	29/10/1927	Wellesley	22/04/1931	Aberdeen	132	27
Gardiner, Michael	M	30/07/1983	Berwick Rangers	31/07/1983	Trialist	2	0
Gardiner, James Ian	OL	10/01/1959	Motherwell	30/04/1959	East Fife	9	1
Gardiner, William	IF	15/05/1900	Kirkcaldy FC	24/04/1901		2	0
Gardner	OR	18/09/1971			Trialist	1	0
Gardner, Patrick	IF	08/09/1964	Airdrie	31/07/1967	Dunfermline	135	57
Gardner, Robert	G	23/08/1966	Stirling Albion	28/10/1966	Stirling Albion	5	3
Garland, Alex	OL	09/04/1966	Newburgh	09/04/1966	Ayr United	1	0
Garland, Charles	OL	15/03/1930	St Andrews Athletic	13/03/1930	Trialist	17	3
Garrie, James	CF	29/10/1946	Markinch Victoria Rgs	30/04/1947		30	2
Garriock, W	CF	05/01/1946	Arniston	05/01/1946	Trialist	6	2
Garth, James	IL	01/12/1949	Clyde	10/05/1950	Morton	1	0
Gaughan, Kevin	D	02/07/1999	Partick	30/05/2000	Stirling Albion	12	2
Gavin, George R	IL	29/05/1948	Hearts	01/07/1949	Ayr United	21	0
Gavine, William James	M	23/08/1985	St Johnstone	17/03/1986	Berwick Rangers	1	0
Gay	IL	20/04/1938	Pittenweem Rovers	30/03/1938		15	2
Gay, James McL	LB	30/06/1931	Watford	30/04/1932		1	1
Geddes, Alexander Robert	G	26/01/1996	Kilmarnock	30/05/1997	Linfield	4	0
George	OR	26/04/1909		26/04/1909	Trialist	18	0

Players (Elder – Forsyth)

First Team Player	Position	Date Signed	Signed from	Date Left	Next Club	Total Appearances	Goals
Elder, A	IF	06/02/1886		07/04/1886		2	0
Ellis	OR	22/04/1944	Peebles Athletic	22/04/1944		1	0
Ellis, James	IR	07/07/1948	Airdrie	11/03/1949	Cowdenbeath	18	9
Ellis, Laurence	LB	02/07/1998	Links United	30/05/2003	St Mirren	164	7
Ellis, Laurence		27/05/2005	St Mirren	30/05/2006	Stirling Albion	0	0
Ellison, Steven	G	31/03/2007	Bonnyrigg Rose	30/04/2007		7	0
Eloujdi, Mehdi	M	02/07/2004	US Ivry	02/08/2004		61	5
Elvin, Charles	M	21/09/1984	Brechin City	17/01/1986	Berwick Rangers	10	0
Evans, David Charles	F	22/08/2003	Tayport	30/03/2004	Tayport	112	0
Evans, Scot	CH	07/07/1965	Third Lanark	01/12/1967	Retired	0	0
Ewart, Scot	F	17/08/2004	East Kilbride Burgh United	30/04/2005		127	0
Ewing, James	G	30/06/1908	Newtongrange Star	01/03/1912	Third Lanark	54	0
Fahey, Christopher	G	11/07/2006	Stenhousemuir	30/05/2008	Free Transfer	1	0
Fair	RB	25/08/1894	Cupar Athletic	25/08/1894	Trialist	73	7
Fairbairn, Brian	F	29/07/2005	East Fife	30/07/2007		1	0
Fairbairn, David	OL	20/11/1900	Inch Boys Club	23/02/1901	Leith Athletic	33	1
Fairgrieve, George	F	17/03/1985	Inch Boys Club	30/04/1989	St Bernards	3	1
Falconer, Douglas	CF	23/08/1941	Army	24/03/1942	Dundee	93	33
Falconer, George	IF	18/05/1967	Montrose	02/10/1970	St Andrews United	6	0
Falls, Thomas	F	15/07/1984	Newburgh	30/04/1986	Freed	1	0
Farrell, Thomas	RB	13/06/1949	Falkirk	30/04/1950	Trialist	1	1
Feechan	IR	19/02/1944	Denbeath	19/02/1944	Cancelled		
Feehan, James	IR	21/06/1929	St Andrews United	11/01/1930	Hibs	9	1
Fenwick, Paul Joseph	D	31/03/2000	Morton	30/05/2001		2	0
Ferguson, Archibald	G	03/10/1938	Crossgates Primrose	27/04/1939	Hamilton Accies	18	0
Ferguson, Charles	IL	25/10/1941	Aberdeen	08/12/1941	Albion Rovers	5	2
Ferguson, Derek	M	27/05/2005	Hamilton Accies	14/02/2006	Cowdenbeath	16	0
Ferguson, Eric	F	01/07/1988	Dunfermline	27/02/1989	Hearts	12	0
Ferguson, Ian	OL	06/08/1987	Lochgelly Albert	09/10/1991	Trialist	151	30
Ferguson, James	RB	29/03/1930	Maryhill Hibs	29/03/1930	Loan	1	0
Ferguson, Keith John	CF	19/08/1983	Cowdenbeath	18/09/1983	Darlington	6	0
Ferrero Gallardo, Sebastian Alejandro		04/02/2004	Celta Vigo	30/05/2004	Furness FC	12	3
Findlay, Alex	CF	26/10/1897		22/03/1898	Freed	11	8
Findlay, John B	IR	18/12/1947	Auchterarder Juveniles	30/04/1948	Cancelled	4	2
Finlay, Allan J	CH	05/05/1961	Hearts	09/05/1961	retired	1	0
Finlay, William	OR	26/07/1963	Clyde	30/04/1964	Downfield	15	0
Fisher, David	OR	28/09/1964	Downfield	30/04/1965	Trialist	9	0
Fisher, John	F	05/04/1897	Raith Athletic	17/04/1897		8	4
Fitzpatrick, Stephen	IL	08/09/2004	Hearts	30/04/2005	Trialist	0	0
Fitzpatrick, Thomas	LB	22/02/1930	Anstruther	22/02/1930	Dunfermline	1	0
Flanders, John	RH	22/02/1902	Hibernian	22/02/1902	Freed	58	1
Fleming, James W S	LH	27/09/1941	Hibs	27/09/1941	Morton	4	0
Fletcher, Alex	CF	14/08/1943	Ardeer Juveniles	02/05/1945	Stirling Albion	30	2
Forbes, Alexander Rooney	CH	05/03/1944	Dundee North End	05/02/1944	Hearts	1	0
Ford, Alex	M	02/03/1935	Kirkford Juniors	02/03/1935		1	0
Ford, Robert Alan Cameron	OR	17/03/1979	Montrose	15/05/1982	Dunfermline	153	16
Ford, Robert G	IL	12/07/1966	Frances Colliery	30/04/1967	Freed	1	0
Forrest, George	M	13/06/1930	York City	30/04/1931	Morton	11	3
Forrest, Gordon Iain	LB	21/07/1993	Rosyth Recreation	05/09/1996	Livingston	4	1
Forrest, John (Jackie)	F	28/09/1963	Arbroath	20/10/1963	Cancelled	4	0
Forrest, Robert Gordon	CH	12/01/1978	Alloa Athletic	08/02/1980	Cowdenbeath	71	18
Forrest, Samuel	CH	12/08/1916	Watford	30/04/1917		29	1
Forsyth, Allan Barrie	G	19/07/1978	Dundee United	26/10/1983	Dunfermline	205	11
Forsyth, John Finnie	OR	28/06/1961	Newburgh	30/05/1963	Alloa	69	0

First Team Player	Position	Date Signed	Signed from	Date Left	Next Club	Total Appearances	Goals
George, Matthew	CF	07/10/1903	Dundee	07/10/1903	Trialist	1	0
Georgeson, Roderick	IF	18/09/1970	Dundee	15/05/1973	Berwick Rangers	118	31
Giblin, James	RH	12/12/1942	Dundee North End	02/01/1943	Trialist	2	0
Gibson	RH	02/01/1906		05/01/1906	Trialist	3	0
Gibson, Frederick Thomas Bertrand	OL	06/06/1910	Sunderland	09/08/1917	Hearts	204	56
Gibson, Ian	M	30/04/1987	St Johnstone	25/08/1989	Arbroath	88	11
Gibson, James B	HB	18/05/1912		30/04/1915		31	2
Gibson, William	CF	09/10/1981	Partick Thistle	16/12/1982	Cowdenbeath	49	12
Gilbert, John	HB	06/10/1935	Kirkford Juniors	30/04/1936		30	1
Gilfillan	CF	11/08/1945	Hill of Beath	11/08/1945	Trialist	0	0
Gilfillan, Jamie	F	17/08/2004	Burntisland Shipyard	30/04/2006	Kirkcaldy YMCA Juns	2	0
Gilfillan, Robert I	CF	07/03/1962	St Johnstone	30/04/1963	Southend United	32	9
Gilhooley	CH	02/04/1917		02/04/1917	Trialist	1	0
Gillan, Felix T	CH	02/10/1929		15/11/1929	Cancelled	4	0
Gillespie, Edward	CH	24/01/1898	Polton Vale			36	4
Gillespie, Eric	CH	03/08/1974	Hamilton Accies	03/08/1974	Albion Rovers	1	0
Gillespie, Ewan	CH	20/09/1982	Edinburgh University	15/05/1983	Spartans	7	0
Gillespie, James	OL	02/02/1968	East Stirling	24/12/1969	Dunfermline	47	5
Gillespie, Robert	RH	16/10/1912	Kirkcaldy United	16/10/1912	Trialist	1	0
Gillies	CF	07/10/1895	Lochgelly	07/10/1895	Trialist	1	0
Gilmour, A	OL	01/01/1918		01/01/1918	Trialist	1	0
Gilmour, Alexander	IL	10/10/1922		30/04/1923		22	6
Gilmour, George	WH	15/11/1910	Hearts	04/09/1912	St Bernards	50	1
Gilmour, George Reynolds	IL	16/04/1946	Third Lanark	30/04/1947	East Fife	35	10
Gilmour, James	OL	24/08/1899	Raith Athletic	30/04/1901		46	21
Gilmour, Thomas	IR	06/07/1936	Albion Rovers	21/04/1939	Rangers	98	59
Gilmour, W	IL	01/01/1918	Balgonie	01/01/1918	Trialist	1	0
Gilpin, James	IF	30/08/1963	Nairn Thistle	30/04/1965	Bradford PA	50	20
Glassey, Robert	IL	09/01/1943	Third Lanark	02/06/1945	War Guest	36	20
Glen, Alexander Moir Spalding	OR	05/08/1936	Forthill Athletic	28/08/1942	Dundee United	107	11
Glen, Ian	F	26/08/1964	Nairn Thistle	30/04/1967		10	1
Glennie, Robert	CH	01/01/1989	Dundee	25/09/1989	Forfar Athletic (pm)	32	0
Glynn, Daniel	D	29/10/2003		31/08/2004	Cowdenbeath	1	0
Glynn, Mark	G	06/03/1985	Ormiston Primrose	06/03/1985	Trialist	1	0
Goldie, Hugh	CF	29/09/1949	Dumbarton	04/07/1950	Ayr United	8	2
Gonet, Stefan	G	30/11/2002	Ross County	30/11/2002	Trialist	0	0
Gonzalez, Ramiro Daniel	G	24/01/2003	Real Aliva	30/05/2004	Dumbarton	46	0
Good, Hugh Jardine	CH	10/08/1928	Bristol City	01/12/1929	Bo'ness	17	0
Goodwillie, David	F	02/11/2007	Dundee United	30/05/2007	Loan	23	9
Gordon	IR	18/04/1942		18/04/1942	Trialist	1	1
Gordon, Ian F	M	02/07/1986	Dunfermline Ath.	15/05/1987	Livingston United	33	1
Gordon, Steven	D	17/08/2004	St Johnstone	09/03/2005		0	0
Gorman	CF	16/09/1944	Lumphinnans	16/09/1944	Trialist	1	2
Gould, John Daniel	OR	24/01/1943	Arbroath	24/04/1943	Dumbarton	14	12
Goulden, John	WH	06/08/1927	Hull	30/04/1928		7	0
Gourlay, Henry	G	09/08/1890	Kirkcaldy Wanderers	09/08/1890	Trialist	1	0
Gourlay, James C	IF	22/08/1905		23/10/1913	Kirkcaldy United	301	111
Gourlay, James William Main	OR	14/08/1914	Leith Athletic	30/04/1919		8	1
Gow	RH	26/04/1906		26/04/1906	Trialist	1	0
Graham	LB	23/11/1889		23/11/1889	Trialist	1	0
Graham, Alastair	CF	23/09/1993	Motherwell	01/03/1996	Falkirk	120	30
Graham, Andrew	G	11/08/1983	Dundee United	08/10/1983	Loan	12	0
Graham, Harry	IR	21/08/1912	Birmingham City	01/06/1913	Hearts	42	12
Graham, Robert	IF	10/08/1973	Armadale Thistle	30/04/1977	Cowdenbeath	114	20
Graham, William A	LB	15/08/1927	Rosslyn Juniors	30/04/1928		12	0
Grant, Archibald	RB	20/05/1899	Buckhaven	09/11/1899	Berwick Rangers	2	0
Grant, John	RB	10/09/1964	Hibernian	30/04/1965		30	0
Grant, Walter	IF	29/07/1925	Aberdeen	19/06/1926	Crystal Palace	28	4
Granville, Norman	OR	19/08/1944	Parkhead	26/08/1944		2	0
Gray, Alexander W	LB	08/12/1962	Nairn Thistle	01/08/1971	Australia	290	2
Gray, George	G	02/04/1951	Balgonie Scotia	30/04/1953	Colchester United	9	0
Gray, James B	G	08/08/1967	Partick Thistle	30/04/1968		3	0
Gray, John	IL	03/05/1903	Kirkcaldy FC	30/04/1906	Motherwell	124	39
Gray, William	CH	01/12/1972	Dundee United	15/05/1973	Stranraer	17	0
Green, John	OL	15/10/1902		30/04/1908		17	4
Greig, Andrew	CF	17/02/1917	Aberdeen	17/02/1917	Loan	1	0
Grierson, Alexander (Sandy)	LH	31/07/1901	Raith Athletic	13/06/1911	Kirkcaldy United	343	23
Grierson, Alexander (Sandy)	CH	11/11/1914		11/11/1914			
Grieve, Andrew	G	01/08/1893	Kirkcaldy Albion	04/08/1896	Kirkcaldy	145	0
Grieve, Andrew	CH	24/05/1899		10/05/1900			
Grieve, Peter	CH	16/08/1917		06/04/1918		14	0
Groves, Edward Andrew	CH	19/01/1971	Glenrothes	15/05/1973		3	0
Guellai	CH	17/07/2004		18/07/2004	Trialist	1	0
Haddow, David	RB	24/04/1948	Vale of Clyde	24/04/1948	Trialist	1	0
Haddow, Mark Lyle	M	09/07/2003	Youths	14/01/2004	Albion Rovers	1	0
Hagan, Phillip	M	29/07/2004	Dundee Violet	10/09/2004	Lochee United	8	0
Haig, Gordon Montgomery	LB	02/05/1962	Ormiston Primrose	29/10/1964	Berwick Rangers	53	0
Hajovsky, Tomas	D	30/07/2004	SK Tatran Postoma	10/11/2004		14	0
Haldane	CF	11/04/1914		11/04/1914	Trialist	1	0
Hall, Alexander Robertson	RH	01/08/1893	Dundee Wanderers	01/08/1894	Hearts	107	18
Hall, Stuart Matthew	G	13/07/2004	Ballingry Rovers	30/05/2006	Thornton Hibs	5	0
Halley, John Edgar	M	04/07/2006		30/04/2008		9	0
Halliday, J	CH	10/04/1886		01/05/1886		2	0
Hallum, Carsten	F	10/01/1997	Hvidovre	25/02/1997	Loan	9	0
Hamill, Jamie Peter		17/08/2004		22/09/2004		0	0
Hamilton	G	21/06/1902		21/06/1902	Guest	1	0
Hamilton	OL	19/10/1946	Newcastle	02/04/1946	Brechin City	2	1
Hamilton, Alexander	RB	10/01/1907	Clyde	11/05/1907	Clyde	7	0
Hamilton, Donald Smart	IR	17/06/1938	Thornton Hibs	27/04/1939		2	1
Hamilton, Steven James	D	13/07/1999	Kilmarnock	30/05/2001	Albion Rovers	48	1
Hampshire, Paul Christopher	M	02/07/1998	Hutchison Vale BC	30/05/2003	Berwick Rangers	69	2
Hampson	IL	22/08/1942	Stoke	12/09/1942	War Guest	4	1
Handley, Fred	IR	21/03/1942	Jeanfield	28/03/1942	Trialist	2	0
Hanlon, Thomas	OR	12/07/1954	Muirkirk	30/04/1955		1	1
Hannigan, Ernie	RH	01/11/1972	Queen of the South	01/12/1972	Hong Kong	7	2
Hardie, John	IR	22/04/1933	Hearts of Beath	22/04/1933	Trialist	1	1
Harley	G	19/08/1899	Scotia	19/08/1899	Trialist	1	0
Harley, Charles	RB	04/04/1910	Kirkcaldy United	30/04/1910	Guest	4	0
Harper	OR	24/04/1915		24/04/1915	Trialist	1	0
Harper	RH	10/04/1924		24/04/1924	Trialist	1	0
Harper, Frank P.	G	07/07/1947	St Johnstone	30/04/1948	Dunfermline Athletic	14	0
Harris	IR	30/04/1925	Hearts of Beath	30/04/1925	Trialist	1	1
Harris, Colin	F	30/04/1979	Exit Thistle	15/02/1984	Dundee	217	83
Harris, Colin		18/09/1986	Hibernian	19/03/1988	Hamilton Accies		
Harrow, Andrew	CF	15/10/1976	Cowdenbeath	25/09/1980	Luton Town	276	74
Harrow, Andrew	G	27/05/1986	Motherwell	15/05/1988	East Fife		
Harrower	OL	29/09/1934	Hearts of Beath	29/09/1934	Trialist	1	0
Harrower	IL	20/11/1943	Dunfermline Ath	20/11/1943	War Guest	1	0

First Team Player	Position	Date Signed	Signed from	Date Left	Next Club	Total Appearances	Goals
Hislop, Thomas	RB	20/02/1967	Clackmannan	19/03/1975	Freed	268	8
Hogg, Alexander	FB	01/11/1945	Burnbank Athletic	19/03/1946		9	0
Hogg, David	OR	01/08/1970	Dumbarton	05/08/1970	Berwick Rangers	2	0
Hoggan, Matthew	CH	19/11/1927	Grange Rovers	30/04/1935	East Stirling	320	24
Hoggan, Richard Philip	LB	16/08/1933	Grange Rovers	05/11/1934	East Stirling	23	0
Holburn, Alick	IF	01/08/1885		10/09/1887		40	20
Holmes, Derek	CF	09/01/1999	Hearts	09/05/1999	Loan	16	7
Holton, Patrick	LB	10/05/1956	Hamilton Accies	24/05/1956	Loan	1	0
Hood	RB	23/05/1892	Kirkcaldy Newton XI	31/05/1892	Loan	6	0
Hood, Peter	OL	01/03/1930	Rosslyn	01/03/1930	Trialist	1	0
Hope, James	IR	01/06/1912	Balgonie Scotia	01/08/1914	Stoke City	26	5
Hope, James		09/11/1916	Stoke City	25/11/1916	Loan		
Hopewell, David	LB	21/12/1927	Cowdenbeath	16/01/1930	Dundee	76	0
Horne, William	OL	05/11/1966	Clydebank	30/04/1967	Free Transfer	7	0
Hough	IR	22/04/1914	Maryhill	22/04/1914	Trialist	2	1
Houston, Thomas Alexander	D	01/09/1976	Kirkcaldy YM Juniors	15/05/1985	Glenrothes (20/7)	281	2
Howieson	CH	02/01/1906		20/01/1906	Trialist	1	0
Howitt, Kyle	F	26/08/2003	Cowdenbeath	20/01/2005	Cowdenbeath	1	0
Hughes, John	OL	05/01/1954	Linlithgow BC	30/04/1960	Freed	6	0
Hughes, Robert	OL	09/08/1890	Glencraig Colliery	09/08/1890		1	1
Hume, William C S	IF	04/11/1939	Kirkcaldy Wanderers	01/03/1940	Hearts	17	4
Humphries, Mark	FB	01/12/1995	Aberdeen	22/11/1996	Ayr United	10	0
Hunter	LH	19/03/1932	Bristol City	19/03/1932	Trialist	1	0
Hunter	LL	09/10/1943	Dunfermline Juvenile	09/10/1943	Trialist	1	0
Hunter	IL	17/11/1945	ITC Perth	17/11/1945	Trialist	1	0
Hunter, Alexander	IL	01/09/1920	Oakley United	10/08/1921	Trialist	2	0
Hunter, Andrew	IR	15/09/1896		30/04/1897		54	14
Hunter, David Thomas	IR	04/03/1975	Oakley United	19/01/1979	Dunfermline Athletic	139	11
Hunter, Henry	M	31/01/1911	Kirkcaldy YM Juniors	30/04/1912	Trialist	4	0
Hunter, John	G	14/03/1912	Falkirk	30/04/1915	Trialist	14	2
Hurrell, William	OL	17/04/1942	Dundee Stobswell	18/01/1946	Millwall	68	26
Hutchison, Daniel	IR	19/09/1936	St Josephs (Dundee)	05/10/1936	Dundee United	2	1
Hutchison, David	OL	28/04/1954	Nairn Thistle	05/10/1957	Montrose	6	4
Hutchison, Thomas	OR	30/12/1889	Raith Athletic	30/12/1889	Trialist	3	1
Hutchison, David	IL	10/01/1929	Peterborough	30/04/1933		44	4
Hutchison, John T	RB	29/07/1915	Peterborough	30/04/1921		76	2
Hutchison, Robert	RH	13/08/1954	Lochore Welfare	30/04/1957		3	0
Hutchison, Robert Forbes	OR	31/03/1965	Comrie Colliery	23/12/1967	Freed	26	4
Hutchison, Ronald	OR	05/07/1963	Newburgh	30/04/1964		6	6
Hutton, Donald M	CF	22/12/1928	Lochgelly Celtic	18/02/1929	Cancelled	2	0
Hutton, Robert	G	02/08/1902	Black Watch	19/03/1903	Scone FC	14	4
Hynd, Alexander	D	26/06/1996	Glenrothes Strollers	30/04/1999		1	0
Hynd, Alistair	RB	10/03/1986	Inverkeithing United	02/12/1986	Crossgates (dt)	21	0
Hynd, John	RH	11/01/1943	St Johnstone	11/01/1943	Loan	1	0
Imrie, William	G	26/10/1984	Halbeath	30/04/1985	Halbeath	3	0
Inglis, Alexander Seaton	RB	05/07/1904	Kelty Rangers	30/04/1913		229	8
Inglis, Anderson	OL	14/05/1943	Falkirk	31/08/1943	Falkirk	1	0
Inglis, James M	CH	19/01/2001	Aberdeen	10/05/2001		13	0
Inglis, John	RB	13/08/1914		28/06/1924	Sheffield Wednesday	281	13
Inglis, William W	CF	31/10/1886		15/09/1909		1	1
Innes	LB	08/05/1907		08/05/1907	Trialist	3	0
Innes	IL	17/12/1932	Clackmannan Juniors	30/04/1933	Alloa	20	7
Innes, George	CH	16/10/1970	Bathgate Thistle	10/01/1972	St Johnstone	27	3
Innes, George							
Innes, James	FB	08/11/1924	Wellesley Juniors	01/08/1925	Forfar Athletic	7	0

First Team Player	Position	Date Signed	Signed from	Date Left	Next Club	Total Appearances	Goals
Hartley, Paul	OR	22/08/1997	Millwall	23/12/1998	Hibernian	58	15
Harty, Ian McGuinness	CF	01/08/2006	Stranraer	12/01/2007	Stirling Albion	18	4
Harvey, John	LH	29/05/1943	Kilmarnock	23/08/1943	Hearts	1	0
Harvey, Paul Edward	M	03/07/1996	Airdrie	30/06/1999	Queen of the South	33	1
Hastie	IR	24/04/1940		01/05/1940	Trialist	3	3
Hastie, John	IL	12/07/1911	Celtic	01/05/1912	Celtic	25	4
Hawke, Warren Robert	F	03/08/1993	Sunderland	15/08/1993	Berwick Rangers	8	0
Hawley, Karl Leon	F	09/08/2002	Walsall	30/01/2003	Loan	33	10
Hawley, Karl Leon	F	29/08/2003	Walsall	31/12/2003	Loan		
Haxton	OL	24/04/1902	Lochgelly Juniors	10/05/1902	Trialist	2	0
Hay, I.M.	CF	01/04/1943	Hall & Co	01/04/1943	Trialist	1	1
Hayles	LH	14/04/1888		14/04/1888	Trialist	1	10
Haywood, Norman Scott Carmichael	CF	28/05/1937	Peebles Rovers	16/06/1941	Leith Athletic	83	70
Hazel, A	IF	22/03/1930	Crossgates Primrose	29/03/1930	Trialist	2	0
Hazells, Peter	LH	01/08/1885		26/10/1889		79	2
Heddle, Ian Alexander	M	21/07/1992	St Johnstone	21/07/1992	Forfar Athletic	1	0
Heenan, Thomas	CF	03/05/1958	Stirling Albion	24/05/1958	Bradford PA	3	2
Henderson, Thomas	CH	15/03/1930	Newtongrange Star	15/03/1930	Trialist	1	0
Henderson	OL	01/01/1933		26/03/1933		1	0
Henderson, A	IL	09/11/1889		15/12/1890		8	6
Henderson, Darren Ronald	M	09/07/2001	Ross County	30/05/2002	Forfar Athletic	37	4
Henderson, G	IR	17/05/1947		17/05/1947		1	1
Henderson, James	CH	09/08/1890		30/04/1891		9	0
Henderson, John	OL	15/12/1945	Wishaw	22/12/1945	Trialist	2	1
Henderson, Niall	LH	24/08/1889	Burntisland Thistle	30/04/1890		24	3
Henderson, Nicholas Sinclair	F	18/01/2008	Gretna (loan to Dumbarton)	30/05/2008	Free Transfer	16	0
Henderson, Peter	M	06/09/1990	Broxburn Athletic	18/09/1992	Cowdenbeath	2	0
Henderson, Peter S	RH	07/08/1915		30/04/1919		16	0
Henderson, Richard	CH	08/05/1930	Newtongrange Star	30/04/1931		18	1
Henderson, Robbie Matthew	M	09/01/2004	Lochee Harp	26/01/2005	Free Transfer	0	0
Henderson, Ronald W	D	11/01/2002	Kilmarnock	30/05/2002	Loan	8	0
Henderson, Thomas	CH	04/01/1947	Markinch Victoria Ra	30/04/1948	Dundalk	25	0
Henderson, W	OR	14/03/1950	Brechin City	09/12/1950	Montrose	7	3
Hendretta	F	01/08/1887	Union	20/04/1889		34	31
Hendry, Alexander	IR	01/09/1913		01/09/1913	Trialist	1	0
Henry	IL	18/03/1944	Lewis United	04/11/1944	War Guest	14	1
Henry, James	IL	21/04/1909		21/04/1909	Trialist	1	0
Hepburn, Andrew	M	26/08/2003	Carnoustie Panmure	29/10/2003	Dundee North End	9	1
Hepburn, David	OR	12/11/1887		10/11/1888		2	0
Herbert, John	RH	01/08/1886		10/11/1889		17	0
Herd, David	IL	20/09/1933	East Fife	02/11/1933	Brechin City	3	1
Herd, William David	CH	22/03/1919	Kirkcaldy United	22/03/1919	Trialist	1	0
Herrick, Mark John	RB	15/07/1984	Newburgh	05/09/1987	Cowdenbeath	116	9
Hetherston, Brian	M	15/10/1991	Peterborough United	30/04/1993	Ards	2	0
Hetherston, Peter	M	20/07/1999	Sligo Rovers	30/05/2001	Freed	45	2
Hickman	M	17/10/1991	Falkirk	04/07/1994	Aberdeen	126	14
Higgins, Charles	FB	15/08/1942	Aston Villa	10/04/1943	War Guest	25	3
Higgins, James	LB	01/05/1943	Morton	26/08/1943	Cancelled	1	0
Hill, John	IR	27/08/1954	Ardrossan Winton Rov	10/12/1959	Ardrossan Winton R	5	0
Hilland, Paul	OR	01/05/1983	Musselburgh Windsor	15/05/1984		11	0
Hilley, Cornelius	LB	26/08/2005	Clyde	31/10/2005		9	0
Hislop, John	WH	28/05/1923	St Rochs	01/06/1925	Third Lanark	64	10
Hislop, Steven	CH	16/10/1970	Tranent	30/04/1978		144	35
	F	31/01/2007	Livingston			56	16

First Team Player	Position	Date Signed	Signed from	Date Left	Next Club	Total Appearances	Goals
Ireland, Lee	D	26/08/2003	Whitburn BC	06/10/2003		0	0
Irons, Stuart	M	01/08/2003	Youth team	03/09/2004	Hamilton Accies	2	0
Irvine, Lloyd	M	02/07/1981	Stirling Albion	13/04/1982	Petershill	14	2
Irvine, Magnus	IR	26/12/1896	Kirkcaldy FC	26/12/1896	Trialist	1	0
Jablonski, Neil		28/01/2005	Dundee	30/05/2007		34	10
Jack, James	CF	02/07/1973	Falkirk	11/12/1973	Bath City	18	7
Jack, Matthias	Def	08/11/2003	Iceland	06/01/2004		6	0
Jaconelli, Emilio	M	22/06/2005	Queen of the South	30/05/2007		36	1
James, Alexander	IL	27/05/1922	Ashfield	23/09/1925	Preston North End	151	41
Jamieson, Alexander	LB	23/04/1971	East Fife	30/04/1972	Dundee Osborne	12	0
Janczyk, Neil	M	23/08/2006	St Johnstone	01/01/2007	loan	7	0
Janes, James Towns	CH	23/08/1904	Trainer	30/04/1905		5	1
Jarvis, David	LB	01/08/1885		30/04/1889		98	54
Jarvis, John T	CF	19/07/1930	Arbroath	20/11/1931	Arbroath	41	50
Jarvis, Sidney	LB	22/12/1926	Kettering Town	11/11/1927	Middlesbrough	35	1
Jarvis, William	CH	01/08/1885	Kirkcaldy	30/04/1889	Kirkcaldy	104	9
Javary, Jean Philipe	M	20/01/2000	Montpellier	19/08/2000	Brentford	22	0
Javary, Jean Philipe		23/11/2001	Partick Thistle	30/01/2002	Bradford City		
Jeffreys	OL	03/09/1887	Ravenscraig	02/11/1887		5	4
Jennings, Thomas Hamilton Oliver	CF	04/01/1921	Cadzow St Annes	20/03/1925	Leeds United	196	127
Jessiman, James F	IL	27/12/1919		30/04/1920	Arthurlie	14	3
Jobson, John	F	24/08/1974	Lochgelly Albert	30/04/1977	Cowdenbeath	33	4
Johnston	IR	24/04/1901	Auchtermuchty Junior	27/04/1901	Trialist	7	2
Johnston, Anthony C.M.A.	CH	01/05/1946	Partick Thistle	30/04/1947	Freed	20	0
Johnston, George		03/07/1991	Castlebridge	30/04/1992	Lochgelly Albert	0	0
Johnston, William	IF	18/09/1945	Clydebank Juniors	30/04/1946		16	5
Johnstone	RH	17/03/1921		20/09/1922		2	1
Johnstone, George	G	05/01/1950	Dunfermline Ath.	30/04/1955	Dumbarton	168	0
Johnstone, Patrick	IL	28/01/1911	Kirkcaldy United	28/01/1911	Trialist	1	0
Johnstone, Robert	CH	02/03/1946	Linfield	30/05/1946	Tranmere Rovers	9	0
Jones	LB	01/01/1942	Bradford	25/04/1942		12	0
Jones	CH	27/04/1907		27/04/1907	Trialist	1	0
Jones	IR	28/04/1905		28/04/1905	Trialist	1	0
Jones	IL	26/08/1944	Everton	02/09/1944	War Loan	2	0
Jones, Dean M	CF	15/01/2004		30/04/2004		0	0
Jones, Mark		09/02/2001	Chesterfield	09/04/2001	Loan	25	5
Jones, Mark		17/11/2001	Chesterfield	30/05/2002	Free Transfer		
Jordan, Franco		19/07/2003	Argentina			1	0
Jordan, Norman	OL	30/03/1921	Rosslyn	30/04/1922		2	0
Joyner, Francis McNab	OL	17/05/1937	St Andrews United	08/04/1938	Sheffield United	124	76
Joyner, Francis McNab		11/08/1947	Dundee	07/01/1950	Hamilton Accies		
Judge, Michael	IF	09/09/1967	Dunfermline Ath.	22/04/1970	Berwick Rangers	56	14
Kane, Barry	G	03/02/2001	Clyde	17/02/2001	Trialist	0	0
Kane, Edward	OL	19/12/1902		27/12/1902	Trialist	2	0
Kaye, William	RB	29/08/1891	Burntisland Thistle			213	4
Keay	OL	15/04/1912		30/04/1912	Trialist	3	0
Keith, William Y	IF	27/05/1950	Stirling Albion	15/12/1950	Cowdenbeath	6	1
Kelly	RB	27/09/1941		03/01/1942	War Guest	3	0
Kelly, Bernard	IF	05/10/1951	Muirkirk	23/07/1958	Leicester City	254	109
Kelly, Bernard		12/08/1960	Aberdeen	15/08/1961			
Kelly, Edward	LB	26/11/1956	Newtongrange Star	01/11/1957		3	0
Kelly, Frank	HB	15/05/1947	Celtic	20/06/1947	Cancelled	1	0
Kelly, Norman	M	19/01/1994	Glenavon	10/02/1995	Brunei	11	0
Kelly, Patrick	D	16/02/2001	Livingston	30/05/2001	Partick Thistle	7	0

First Team Player	Position	Date Signed	Signed from	Date Left	Next Club	Total Appearances	Goals
Kelly, Robert	WH	09/01/1943	Dunnikier	21/02/1946	Millwall	56	6
Kelly, Thomas	OL	20/05/1916	Hearts of Beath	20/05/1916	Trialist		
Kelly, Walter M	RH	19/08/1947	Hill of Beath Ramble	09/08/1952	Bury	23	1
Kelly, William	LH	30/01/1943	Hill of Beath	30/01/1943	Trialist	1	0
Kemp, George W	IR	01/08/1908	Dunblane	30/08/1908		3	2
Kennedy	OR	29/12/1934		29/12/1934	Trialist	1	1
Kennedy, jnr	RB	08/10/1892	Woodburn	22/10/1892		3	0
Kennedy, John	RB	10/09/1892		24/09/1892		3	0
Keogh, James	IF	15/02/1928	Falkirk	30/04/1928		5	0
Kerr, Alex	G	06/07/1942	Thornton Hibs	01/09/1943	Cancelled	29	0
Kerr, Alexander	IL	30/08/1902		30/04/1903		1	0
Kerr, David	IR	27/02/1962	Inverness Thistle	22/03/1963	Montrose	27	12
Kerr, Glenn Michael	D	15/08/1986	St Andrews United	10/06/1988	Cowdenbeath	81	0
Kerr, James	M	06/10/1982	Airdrie	21/09/1984	Brechin City	87	25
Kerr, James Wilson	F	29/12/1938	Leith Athletic	21/12/1945	Cancelled	22	5
Kerr, Walter	G	01/08/1917	Falkirk	19/11/1918	Falkirk	40	0
Kerr, Walter		22/03/1919	Falkirk	30/04/1919	Broxburn United		
Kerr, William	RH	05/11/1964	Queen's Park	16/12/1964	Airdrie	6	0
Kerray, James	F	10/08/1956	Dunipace Juniors	08/02/1960	Dunfermline Athletic	111	37
Kilgannon, Sean David	M	11/07/2006	Partick Thistle	30/05/2007		22	1
Kilpatrick, Samuel	RB	18/09/1916		04/11/1916		7	1
King		01/04/1912		01/04/1912	Trialist	2	0
King, Arthur M	CF	28/02/1942	East Stirling	28/03/1942		2	0
King, Robert	LH	16/03/1926	Hearts	30/04/1926	Loan	8	0
Kinloch, Robert	RH	12/08/1967	Toronto Stars	17/02/1968	Dunfermline Athletic	15	0
Kinnaird, Thomas	IR	19/04/1933	St Andrews Athletic	19/04/1933	Trialist	1	1
Kinnear, David	OL	02/04/1934	Burntisland United	11/04/1934	Rangers	28	18
Kinnear, David		11/10/1941	War Guest		Rangers		
Kinnear, David		10/01/1940	Dunnikier Juniors	21/02/1946		15	15
Kiriakov, Ilian	IF	26/07/2000	Aberdeen	26/07/2000	Trialist	1	0
Kirk, Robert P	M	02/07/1953	Dunfermline	02/06/1955	Hearts	48	3
Kirk, Stephen David	RB	01/03/1996	Falkirk	14/01/1998	East Fife	51	10
Kirkwood, David Stewart	M	10/08/1994	Airdrie	30/05/2000	Retired	137	9
Knox, William J	LB	19/07/1955	Annbank United	30/04/1958	Third Lanark	18	0
Krivokapic, Miodrag	D	29/03/1996	Motherwell	30/05/1997	Hamilton Accies	15	0
Laing, T	RB	19/09/1885		19/09/1885	Trialist	1	0
Lamb, Robert Basey Smith	CF	11/09/1943	Hearts	16/12/1943	Hearts	9	4
Lambert, John Philp	CH	01/08/1893	Raith Athletic	30/04/1901		238	26
Landels, Graeme John	D	11/10/1995	ICI Juveniles	30/04/1997	LinlithgowRose	1	0
Lang, William	RH	10/08/1901	Edinburgh Rosebery	17/08/1902		9	1
Langfield, James	G	29/11/2003	Dundee	04/01/2004	Partick Thistle	5	0
Latimer, Ross James Alexander	LB	24/02/2004		30/04/2004		0	0
Lavery, William J	LB	24/01/1914	Middlesbrough	12/07/1919	St Mirren	68	1
Lavin, Patrick	IR	17/09/1932	Shotts	17/09/1932	Trialist	1	1
Law	OR	27/04/1910		27/04/1910	Trialist	1	0
Lawson, George	WH	01/11/1946	Polkemmet Juniors	01/07/1949	Freed	13	2
Lawson, John	IR	22/04/1905	Dunnikier Athletic	22/04/1905	Trialist	1	1
Lawson, John H	CF	13/11/1958	Ballingry Rovers	30/04/1960	Free Transfer	4	0
Lawson, Michael	F	06/06/1980	St Johnstone	20/06/1981	Berwick Rangers	36	4
Leck, William	FB	04/05/1903	Lochgelly United	30/04/1904	East Fife	24	1
Leckie, John T (Jack)	G	08/12/1927	Alloa	01/03/1932	Port Vale	131	0
Lee	OL	03/10/1904	Edinburgh Myrtle	03/10/1904	Trialist	1	0
Lees	IR	10/08/1895	Edinburgh Casuals	24/08/1895	Trialist	2	0

Players (continued)

First Team Player	Position	Date Signed	Signed from	Date Left	Next Club	Total Appearances	Goals
Macdonald, W	IR	28/09/1901	Edinburgh Renton	30/04/1902	Trialist	4	1
Mackay	OR	06/05/1897		23/05/1903	Trialist	4	1
Mackay, Eric	G	22/05/1937	Irish Football	30/04/1938	Freed	28	0
Mackay, Robert	OL	21/01/1938	Army	01/05/1939	Stenhousemuir	18	6
Mackay, William H	CH	01/08/1890	Hearts	06/10/1994		102	30
Mackenzie, Alan	F	16/08/1991	Cowdenbeath	03/12/1993	Clyde	55	9
Mackenzie, Alexander	IL	14/01/1931	Old Kilpatrick Jnrs	29/03/1934	Aldershot	93	21
Mackenzie, Stewart	CF	05/08/1975	Glenrothes	05/08/1975	Trialist	1	0
Mackie	IR	29/10/1942	Freuchie	06/03/1943	Trialist	4	2
Mackie	RH	02/01/1943	Raith Athletic	02/01/1943	Trialist	1	0
Mackie	CF	25/10/1941	Raith Athletic	25/10/1941	Trialist	1	0
Mackie, Alexander	F	16/08/1899	Raith Athletic	01/05/1902	Rangers	79	65
Mackie, James	G	14/06/1900		30/04/1917		134	0
Mackie, Jamie	F	28/04/2007	Tayport Thistle			2	0
Mackie, Robert	OL	10/08/1946	Sauchie Juniors	12/10/1946	East Stirling	4	2
Mackie, Thomas F	LB	02/01/1940	St Johnstone	02/01/1940	Trialist	1	0
Mackie, Thomas J	OL	08/02/1967	Forfar Athletic	19/03/1968	Forfar Athletic	32	7
MacLean, William M	IF	30/07/1919	Denbeath Star	26/06/1920	St Mirren	38	3
MacLeod, Alastair F	IF	24/07/1987	Kilmarnock	15/05/1988	Retired	35	0
Macleod, Ian Murdo	LB	26/07/1989	Falkirk	01/11/1993	Meadowbank	189	5
MacLeod, Robert	G	04/05/1911	Scottish Rifles	01/08/1913	Newport County	90	0
MacNeill, Duncan	F	13/06/1910		16/02/1916	Motherwell	71	20
MacNiven, Alex (Sandy)	LH	03/09/1963	Brechin City	30/04/1965	Montrose	52	5
Macrae, James	CF	23/09/1933	St Andrews United	03/02/1934	Centre forward	2	1
Main, Alan David	G	06/08/1988	Dundee United	06/08/1988	Loan	1	0
Main, Alex	IF	06/08/1934		01/11/1934		20	2
Main, Daniel	IR	29/05/2007	Anstruther Amateurs	30/05/2008		1	0
Main, Gordon	D	05/11/1970	Rangers East	20/12/1971	Released	1	0
Main, Ross	RH	26/08/2003		06/10/2003	Released	0	0
Main, William Gay	RB	07/05/1934		30/04/1935		24	1
Makela, Janne	RH	27/02/1997	Finland	30/05/1997	Loan	8	1
Malcolm	CF	19/10/1946		19/10/1946	Loan	1	0
Malcolm (St Johnstone YM)	M	24/03/1945	St Johnstone YM	24/03/1945	Trialist	1	0
Malcolm, Craig	OR	24/07/2003	Raith Rovers Form D	30/04/2005	Airdrie	21	4
Malcolm, Walter Grant Lees	G	20/07/1960	Newcastle United	30/04/1962	Airdrie	29	3
Mallin, Michael	CH	25/07/1978	Methil Rovers	30/04/1979	Glenrothes	3	0
Mann, Alex	CH	31/08/1889		28/09/1899		6	1
Manning, John	M	22/05/1905	Kirkcaldy United	01/05/1907	Blackburn Rovers	88	4
Manson, Stephen	M	03/08/2006	Berwick Rangers	23/01/2007	Clydebank	17	3
Marchbank, Walter	M	26/11/1924	Hearts	25/12/1925	Clydebank	23	1
Marchio-Vechio	IF	29/07/2003		29/07/2003	Trialist	1	0
Markie	IF	14/02/1942	Australian AF	14/02/1942	War Guest	1	0
Markie, Peter	LH	17/05/1971	Lawside Academy	15/05/1973	Lochee Harp	1	0
Marr	RH	22/04/1905		28/04/1905	Trialist	2	0
Marr	F	01/09/1913		01/09/1913	Trialist	1	0
Marshall	CH	13/03/1971			Trialist	1	0
Marshall	HB	02/10/1905		02/10/1905	Trialist	1	0
Marshall, Andrew	IL	01/08/1888	Union	30/04/1895		38	12
Marshall, Andrew (2nd)	CH	24/11/1889		30/04/1890		11	2
Marshall, Harry (Henry James Hall)	RB	11/10/1900	Alloa	30/04/1901	Celtic	29	3
Marshall, Henry	M	24/11/1900		24/11/1900	Trialist	1	0
Marshall, James Henderson	M	16/12/1982	Cowdenbeath	30/10/1989	Arbroath	251	42
Marshall, Richard	FB	02/07/1989	Dundee	30/04/1990		0	0
Marshall, Walter	LB	01/01/1946	Arbroath Vics	01/01/1946	Trialist	1	0

First Team Player	Position	Date Signed	Signed from	Date Left	Next Club	Total Appearances	Goals
Leigh, Andrew Black	LH	25/12/1948	Dunoon Athletic	30/04/1963	Retired	489	5
Leiper, Colin	M	26/08/2003	Youths	30/04/2007	Whitburn	23	0
Leishman, Robert	F	24/04/1959	East Fife	30/04/1960		8	5
Leitch	OR	01/08/1889		16/09/1893		63	40
Leitch, Alex	LH	04/10/1911		30/04/1912		4	1
Leitch, Gordon Robert	F	31/01/1985	Forfar Athletic	15/05/1986	Berwick Rangers25/6	52	2
Lennon, Daniel Joseph	M	31/03/1994	Hibernian	30/06/1999	Ayr United	200	23
Leslie	CF	17/01/1942	Lumphinnans	17/01/1942	Trialist	1	2
Leslie, William	LH	16/11/1910		29/12/1910	Elgin City	1	0
Levein, Paul Reginald	CH	04/02/1980	Lochore Welfare	15/05/1982	Lochore Welfare	3	0
Liddle, Christopher	RH	29/09/2004		29/09/2004	Loan	0	0
Lievesley, Leslie	IR	30/08/1941	Crystal Palace	13/09/1941	War Guest	3	0
Lindsay, Alex. Findlay	OR	02/11/1916	Dundee Violet	30/04/1917	Tottenham Hotspur	30	9
Lindsay, Archie	RH	05/01/1974	Dundonald Bluebell	30/04/1975	Lochgelly Albert	14	3
Lindsay, Frederick Todd	CF	04/05/1921	Amateur	30/04/1923		6	0
Lindsay, John	LH	24/02/1945	Morton	24/02/1945	Loan	1	3
Lindsay, Kenneth	LH	09/06/1969	Penicuik Athletic	30/07/1972	Australia	110	4
Lindsay, Thomas	G	14/08/1899	Cowdenbeath	30/04/1900		18	0
Lindsay, W	LB	24/08/1895		24/08/1895	Trialist	1	0
Linn, Robert	F	17/07/2004	Dundee	22/07/2004	St Johnstone	3	1
Linton, David Halley	IL	08/05/1940	Partick Thistle	16/01/1943	War Guest	2	0
Lister, Ian T	OR	01/07/1966	Aberdeen	10/02/1968	Dunfermline Athletic	80	15
Lister, Ian T	F	30/08/1971	St Mirren	30/04/1972	Berwick Rangers		
Litster, John R	LH	01/08/1885		18/08/1888		76	51
Livingstone	M	28/04/1905		28/04/1905		1	0
Livingstone, Iain Thomas	F	08/12/1983	Raith Colts	24/09/1985	Montrose	8	0
Lloyd, David A	LB	13/09/1987	St Johnstone	22/06/1988	Stranraer	32	7
Lockerbie, John	OR	04/03/1958	Peebles Rovers	30/04/1960	Eyemouth United	20	0
Lockhart, Thomas	F	24/08/1895		31/08/1895		4	0
Logan, Alan	WH	26/08/1988	Partick Thistle	21/07/1992	Montrose	104	27
Logan, James H	M	18/05/1912	Bradford PA	30/04/1920	Retired (Manager)	102	4
Lorimer, David James	OL	10/10/1996	Hamilton Accies	30/04/1997	Clydebank	4	0
Loudon, George	OR	08/11/1944	Albion Rovers	15/11/1944	War Guest	2	1
Laurie, John Clifton (Ian)	M	19/08/1961	Linlithgow Rose	22/01/1965	ES Clydebank	90	22
Laurie, John Clifton (Ian)	OL	05/01/1967	Airdrie	30/04/1967	Stirling Albion		
Love, John F	IR	04/11/1944	Leith Athletic	04/11/1944	War Guest	1	0
Low, Alexander	CH	23/07/1938	Falkirk	02/05/1942	Dundee United	218	10
Low, Alexander	CH	08/08/1942	Dundee United	30/04/1946			
Lowe, Alexander Cameron	OR	28/01/1980	Eastbank	15/05/1982	Lochore Welfare	7	0
Lowe, Henry Pratt	IR	29/08/1942	QPR	29/08/1942	War Guest	1	1
Lowther	WH	16/10/1912		16/10/1912	Trialist	1	0
Lowther, James	WH	16/08/1917		27/04/1918		9	0
Lumby, Walter Charles William	CH	12/08/1944	Stockport County	19/08/1944	War Guest	2	0
Lumsden	OL	22/08/1923		22/08/1923	Trialist	1	0
Lumsden, Todd	OR	18/05/2005	Hamilton Accies	18/05/2005		99	5
Lusamba, Nsinba	IF	07/08/2004	Ilkeston Town	07/08/2004	Trialist	1	0
Lyall, Bobby	OR	15/04/1974	Cowdenbeath	08/05/1974	Tranent	5	1
Lyall, George	IF	20/03/1965	Bell Baxter HS	17/03/1966	Preston NE	41	31
Lyall, Peter	G	19/09/1885		07/10/1890		33	0
Lyle, William	FB	09/08/2005	Ayr United	30/05/2007		36	0
Lynas, John	OR	19/10/1935	Third Lanark	15/11/1935	cancelled	4	0
Macbain, Lawrence D	IR	08/01/1929	St Johnstone	30/04/1929	Loan	10	3
MacDonald, Hector	M	18/08/1901	Lochgelly United	30/04/1902	Leith Athletic	70	24
Macdonald, Kenneth Stewart	CF	19/10/1989	Airdrie	08/12/1990	St Johnstone	50	16

First Team Player	Position	Date Signed	Signed from	Date Left	Next Club	Total Appearances	Goals
Marshall, William	OL	14/04/1925	Townhill Juniors	30/04/1925		9	2
Marshalsay, George	CF	26/05/1945	St Johnstone	29/06/1945	Trialist	2	0
Martin	CF	04/12/1943		04/12/1943	Trialist	1	1
Martin, Fred	CF	12/02/1913	Sunderland	30/04/1921		74	35
Martin, John	F	09/07/2003	East Fife	29/07/2005	East Fife	48	4
Martin, Joseph D	LB	09/08/1941	Lochgelly	16/08/1941	Trialist	2	0
Martin, Peter	FB	05/01/1942	Lochgelly Albert	16/02/1943	Dundee United	18	1
Martin, William	IF	15/04/1979	Kirkcaldy YMCA	15/05/1982	Forfar Athletic	11	2
Mas Farre, Javier	M	26/07/2002	UD Barbastro	15/08/2002		5	0
Masson, William C	LB	22/04/1933	Whifflet Emerald	26/11/1938	Dundee	8	1
Mathers, William	RB	15/02/1930	Dundee Juniors	15/02/1930	Trialist	1	0
Matheson, Ross	M	13/06/2001	Morton	30/05/2003	Cowdenbeath	34	1
Mathie	LB	07/03/1896	Raith Athletic	14/05/1896		7	0
Mathieson, Alex	IR	06/09/1941	Benburb	01/11/1941		3	1
Mathieson, James	G	21/11/1922	Colinsburgh United	01/01/1926	Middlesbrough	141	0
Mathieson, James		04/11/1939	Queen of the South	30/04/1940			
Mathieson, William	LB	11/06/1976	Arbroath	01/04/1977	retired (injury)	31	0
Matthew, Andrew	OL	12/09/1960	Rangers	01/08/1961	Dunfermline Athletic	16	3
Matthew, Derek William	IR	15/09/1980	Rangers	12/02/1982	Kirkcaldy YM	2	0
Mauchlen, Iain		11/10/1995	Leicester City	30/04/1996	Lochee United	1	0
Mauchline, Robert	OR	09/08/1941	Accrington	09/08/1941	War Guest	1	0
Maughan, Roderick Edward Alexander	M	18/08/1997	Granton BC	30/03/2001	Arbroath	2	0
Maule, John F	F	23/12/1938	Lochore Welfare	19/02/1954	Third Lanark	371	58
Maxwell	CF	07/12/1901		07/12/1901	Trialist	1	0
Maxwell, Charles	RB	15/05/1947	Morton	14/06/1947	Cancelled	1	0
Maxwell, Daniel Ryan	M	30/01/2004	Hamilton Academical	13/01/2005	Dagenham & Redbridge	21	0
Maxwell, John	IL	05/07/1904	Kelty Rangers	03/02/1905	East Fife	5	0
Mballa, Ivan	F	04/08/2000	Vindelle ASFC	30/05/2001	Aldershot Town 1/9	37	10
McAinsh, Thomas	OL	07/02/1908	Bonnyrigg Thistle	06/06/1910	East Stirling	80	19
McAllister, William	RH	17/11/1927	Middlesbrough	14/05/1929	Hearts	77	1
McAlpine, Andrew C	CH	10/02/1945	Dumbarton	10/02/1945	War Guest	1	0
McAlpine, Hamish	G	24/06/1986	Dundee United	01/05/1988	Arbroath	93	1
McAlpine, Joseph Charles	M	30/07/2004	Queen of the South	21/01/2005	Forfar Athletic	20	0
McAndrew, Hamish	RH	02/10/1933	St Andrews Athletic	02/10/1933		1	0
McAnespie, Stephen	FB	25/01/1994	Vasterhaninge IF	28/09/1995	Bolton Wanderers	63	1
McAra, Athol	RB	14/06/1947	Hearts	30/04/1948	Albion Rovers	17	0
McArthur, Edward Stanley Smith	OL	10/08/1929	Crossgates Primrose	08/01/1930	Alloa Athletic	32	5
McArthur, James Jones	G	14/02/1984	Hibernian	15/05/1984	Kirkcaldy RFC	12	0
McArthur, Peter S	G	06/10/1930	Morton	18/10/1930	Loan	1	0
McAulay, Archibald	IF	12/06/1909	Maryhill	17/08/1911	Abercorn	80	26
McAulay, Hugh	OR	16/09/1895	Hearts of Beath	30/04/1896		3	1
McAulay, Robert	LB	16/08/1939	Rangers	19/03/1940		12	0
McAvoy, Robert	LB	25/11/1926	St Mirren	26/01/1927	St Bernards	4	0
McBeath, Alexander	LH	10/08/1921	Broomhall	15/08/1924	Hamilton Accies	34	0
McBride, Hugh	RB	12/08/1924	East Fife	24/10/1924	Hamilton Accies	6	0
McCaig, David	RH	26/10/1926	Law Scotia	19/07/1928	Bristol Rovers	27	1
McCallum, William	CH	04/11/1974	Dunfermline Athletic	30/04/1975	Released	19	1
McCann, Liam	M	09/07/2003	Pollok United	17/10/2003	Queen's Park	4	0
McCann, William	Mid	01/09/2003	Dundee United	06/10/2003		0	0
McCarthy, Edward	IR	08/08/1968	Salveson Boys Club	19/01/1971	Peebles Rovers	9	0
McCarthy, Philip	OL	12/10/1946	Cork	12/11/1946	Trialist	1	1
McClelland, James	CF	10/10/1922	Rosslyn Juniors	30/04/1923	Southend United	1	0
McCloy, Peter	G	18/02/1989	Hearts	18/02/1989	Temporary	1	0
McComb, Leonard Kerr	IF	01/06/1977	Currie Juveniles	30/04/1980	Alloa	22	1

First Team Player	Position	Date Signed	Signed from	Date Left	Next Club	Total Appearances	Goals
McCondichie, Andrew Morrison	G	21/08/1999	Maryhill	18/09/1999	Albion Rovers	1	0
McCondochie, John	OL	10/04/1922	Newtongrange Star	30/04/1923	Released	2	0
McCormack, Andrew	OR	20/08/1929	Denny Hibs	30/04/1930	Released	17	1
McCreadie, Richard	G	22/07/1938	East Stirling	28/06/1939	East Stirling	15	0
McCullie, Colin	RB	01/09/1976	Stenhousemuir	30/04/1977	Bonnybridge	5	0
McCulloch	OL	18/05/1946		18/05/1946	Trialist	1	0
McCulloch, Alastair	M	01/05/1982	Melbourne Thistle	24/02/1984	Cowdenbeath	18	0
McCulloch, Alexander	IF	25/06/1913	Coventry City	30/04/1915	Hearts	8	0
McCulloch, Greg	RB	24/02/1996	Aberdeen	09/08/2002	Brechin City	176	1
McCulloch, J	IR	05/05/1902	Raith Athletic	07/05/1902	Trialist	5	1
McCusker	IL	27/04/1901	Dunfermline Athletic	27/04/1901	Trialist	1	0
McDermott, Charles M	RB	23/08/1901	Bradford City	10/01/1942	War Guest	10	0
McDermott, Murray J	G	22/10/1969	Penicuik Athletic	21/08/1981	Berwick	494	0
McDonald	LB	19/08/1925		19/08/1925	Trialist	1	0
McDonald, Alex	G	22/03/1919	Balgonie Scotia	30/04/1920		18	0
McDonald, Alex J	IR	15/09/1917	Rosslyn Juniors	22/09/1917	Trialist	2	0
McDonald, Andrew	IF	07/08/1952	Petershill	30/04/1954	Irvine Meadow	9	4
McDonald, James	IL	30/04/1920	Bradford City	30/04/1922	Reserve trainer	19	3
McDonald, James	IR	08/06/1936	Queen of the South	30/04/1937		16	5
McDonald, John	OR	30/09/1901	Vale of Wemyss	15/02/1907	Rangers	147	51
McDonald, John		05/09/1919	Rangers	08/11/1919	Loan		
McDonald, John S	OL	14/03/1965	Blairgowrie Juniors	30/04/1968	Montrose	49	4
McDonald, Kenneth M	RB	30/10/1968	Detroit Cougars	23/01/1970	Hakoa, Australia	33	0
McDonald, Patrick	IF	14/02/1947	Celtic	30/04/1947	Dunfermline	7	3
McDonald, Robert L	FB	10/10/1959	Musselburgh Athletic	30/04/1962	Nottingham Forest	35	3
McDonald, Thomas	OR	21/12/1962	Dunfermline Athletic	30/04/1963	Queen of the South	19	4
McDonald, William	OL	24/09/1964	Dundee United	26/10/1964	Cancelled	1	0
McDonell, Alex	WH	14/11/1941	Alloa Athletic	30/04/1942	War Guest	22	0
McDonnell, Donald	IL	20/12/1930	Newburgh West End	27/12/1930	Trialist	2	1
McDonough, Brian R.W.	FB	10/06/1976	Glenpark United	15/05/1983	Cowdenbeath	165	3
McDonough, Michael	IF	21/08/1931	Denny Hibs	30/04/1932	Juniors	27	11
McDougall, Allan	RB	04/03/1905	Coatbridge	30/04/1905	Released	8	0
McDougall, John Lindsay	CF	17/10/1922	Wellesley Juniors	16/03/1923	Forfar Athletic	26	0
McDougall, John Lindsay	IR	30/04/1923	Forfar Athletic	14/12/1928	Aldershot		
McDowall, Isaac	IR	15/08/1942	Cowdenbeath	22/08/1942	Loan	0	2
McEwan	IR	21/06/1902		21/06/1902	Guest	11	2
McEwan, Alexander	G	25/02/1913		30/04/1914		1	0
McEwan, Alexander	RB	28/04/1949	Sauchie Juveniles	05/08/1950	East Stirling		
McEwan, Craig George	OR	16/07/1997	Clyde	22/09/2000	Ayr United	127	1
McEwan, James	CF	15/06/1951	Arbroath	23/04/1959	Aston Villa	314	92
McFadyen, William	IL	29/08/1942	Motherwell	29/08/1942	War Guest	1	0
McFadzean, James	IL	27/02/1962	St Mirren	30/04/1963	Kilmarnock	33	6
McFarlane	LB	08/05/1907		08/05/1907	Trialist	1	0
McFarlane, James	RH	03/08/1927		14/11/1927	Cancelled	1	0
McFarlane, Thomas	WH	12/07/1901		24/04/1902		8	0
McFarlane, Thomas Haxton	LB	24/11/1975	Comrie Colliery	30/08/1980	Cowdenbeath	177	4
McFarlane, William	IF	25/09/1958	Hibernian	22/09/1958	Morton	54	5
McFeat, Andrew	OR	06/04/1944	Polmont Juveniles	30/04/1945		5	0
McGaffney	IL	15/05/1900	Inverkeithing Thistle	15/05/1900	Trialist	1	0
McGarry, Chris	LB	05/04/2005					
McGarty, Mark	D	18/01/2002	Dunfermline	18/04/2002	Loan	8	0
McGeachie, George	CH	03/11/1989	Dundee	26/07/1994	Stenhousemuir	138	3
McGeown, Mark	G	29/01/1999	Stirling Albion	28/02/1999	Loan	4	0
McGibbon, Donald Alex.	IL	26/06/1922	Rangers	23/01/1923	St Bernards	3	0

First Team Player	Position	Date Signed	Signed from	Date Left	Next Club	Total Appearances	Goals
McGill, Derek	CF	22/11/1996	Hamilton Accies	30/06/1998	Queens Park	27	5
McGill, Patrick	IL	23/12/1935	Hearts	30/04/1936	Freed	17	7
McGillivray, Angus	CH	01/11/1946	Arbroath	21/12/1946	Dundee United	3	0
McGirr, William	RH	19/12/1934	Cowdenbeath	30/04/1935	Released	2	0
McGlone	LH	01/09/1913		01/09/1913	Trialist	1	0
McGoldrick, Edward	IR	15/10/1935	Dundee	12/11/1935	Trialist	3	0
McGorm, James	IL	10/10/1928		23/02/1929	St Johnstone	14	1
McGowan, Aloysius	LB	11/05/1953	St Johnstone	15/05/1953	Cancelled	1	0
McGowan, Michael	M	22/01/2005	Dundee	29/01/2005	Clyde	1	0
McGown, James		19/04/1933	Dunnikier	19/04/1933	Trialist	1	0
McGregor, Alexander	G	21/05/1949	Albion Rovers	30/04/1950	Arbroath	19	0
McGregor, Ian	CH	17/08/1957	Lochore Welfare	30/04/1961	Cowdenbeath	29	0
McGregor, John	IF	15/10/1902		30/04/1907		7	0
McGrogan, Felix	OL	02/06/1962	Pollok	03/10/1964	St Johnstone	73	29
McGuigan, Joseph	OL	08/02/1930	Stoneyburn	08/03/1930	Trialist	2	1
McGuire, Bernard	F	14/10/1969	East Stirling	01/12/1972	Clydebank	109	23
McGuire, George	LB	30/06/1932	Morton	30/04/1933	Released	30	0
McGuire, Vincent	FB	15/02/1961	Nairn Thistle	30/04/1963	Released	15	0
McGurn, William	CF	27/03/1948	Thornton Hibs	27/03/1948	Trialist	1	0
McIlhatton, John	OR	23/11/1950	Dundee	30/04/1951	Barry Town	9	0
McIlwraith, Archibald Torrance	LH	23/08/1930	Grange Rovers	12/08/1932	Trialist	3	0
McInally, David	LH	01/07/1998	Cathkin United	30/05/2001	Arbroath	8	0
McInally, James Edward	M	07/07/1995	Dundee United	02/10/1996	Dundee United	47	0
McInnes, David	LB	24/06/1920	St Johnstone	05/08/1921	Dundee Hibernian	13	0
McInnes, John	IL	18/02/1949	Partick Thistle	01/07/1949	Loan	5	2
McIntosh, Alex	IR	06/02/1943	Wolves	10/04/1943	War Guest	4	0
McIntosh, Alex	IL	21/09/1935	Hearts of Beath	06/03/1937	Trialist		
McIntosh, James Mercer	LB	30/04/1979	Warout Thistle	21/11/1981	Released	3	0
McIntyre	LH	04/04/1910		30/04/1910	Trialist	4	0
McIntyre, Elgin M	IL	01/10/1946	Lochgelly Albert	30/04/1947	Freed	9	2
McIntyre, John	OL	12/06/1951	Irvine Meadow	22/11/1954	Irvine Meadow	66	14
McKay	OL	01/04/1911		01/04/1911	Trialist	1	0
McKay, Graham S	M	28/06/1977	Glenrothes United	30/04/1978	Released	3	0
McKay, James	CF	10/08/1946	Celtic	10/08/1946	Portadown	4	3
McKay, John	G	30/12/1939	St Bernards	01/05/1940	Loan	1	0
McKay, Joseph	OR	15/05/1931	Denny Hibs	30/04/1933	Released	21	2
McKechnie, James	OR	28/12/1922	Partick Thistle	16/04/1923	Hamilton Accies	3	0
McKendrick, Robert	G	04/07/1929	Newtongrange Star	30/04/1930	Released	17	0
McKennan, Peter S	F	07/11/1936	Partick Thistle	05/05/1945	Loan	2	1
McKenzie	IL	11/04/1914	Perth Kinnoull	11/04/1914	Trialist	1	0
McKenzie, James	G	05/02/1948	Slateford Athletic	05/02/1948	Trialist	1	0
McKenzie, Jamie	M	08/07/1999	Partick	31/03/2000	Albion Rovers	2	0
McKenzie, John	IR	25/03/1944	Dundee East Craigie	25/03/1944	Trialist	2	0
McKenzie, John A	IF	11/11/1944	Ayr United	23/12/1944	War Guest	2	0
McKenzie, Reverend John H.	G	06/12/1924		06/12/1924		1	0
McKeon, Thomas M	FB	30/01/1965	St Andrews United	30/04/1967		34	2
McKeown, Frank	D	16/07/2003	St Mirren Youth	31/07/2004	Partick Thistle	7	0
McKerley, James	WH	30/07/1915	Armadale	09/08/1916	Airdrie	29	0
McKilligan, Neil	FB	24/11/1995	Ayr United	21/09/1996	Albion Rovers	4	0
McKillop, Alistair R	RH	16/06/1930	Kirkcaldy Waverley	30/04/1932	Rosslyn	19	2
McKinlay, Craig	M	13/08/1993	ICI Grangemouth	30/04/1996	Released	2	0
McKinlay, Hamilton	G	07/09/1927	Lochgelly Celtic	07/08/1927	Trialist	2	1
McKinnon, Matthew	OL	11/08/1917	Cliftonville	11/08/1919	Lochgelly United	33	0
McKinnon, Raymond	M	21/08/2000	Livingston	24/11/2000	East Fife	17	3

First Team Player	Position	Date Signed	Signed from	Date Left	Next Club	Total Appearances	Goals
McKinnon, Raymond	M	16/01/2003	Montrose	30/04/2003	Lochee United	15	3
McKinven, John James	IF	24/11/1958	Bathgate Thistle	30/04/1960	Southend United	0	0
McKnight, John	M	17/08/2004	Polbeth BC	27/10/2004	Alloa Athletic	72	0
McLafferty, Ronald	G	15/04/1985	Newtongrange Star	15/05/1988	Edinburgh United	92	23
McLaren, Gardner J (Jacky)	IR	31/01/1930	Grange Rovers	05/09/1933	Stenhousemuir	34	4
McLaren, William R	M	01/06/1972	East Fife	15/05/1973	Queen of South	82	17
McLaughlan, Joseph	WH	12/09/1949	Aberdeen	17/04/1950	Airdrie	18	2
McLaughlin, Denis	LB	11/01/2007	Hearts	30/05/2007	Loan	107	8
McLay, George	RH	13/06/1910	Glencraig		died in war		
McLean	RH	04/04/1942		25/04/1942	Trialist	4	0
McLean, David	IL	02/01/1907	Kirkcaldy United	02/01/1907	Trialist	1	0
McLean, James	FB	17/03/1900	Kirkcaldy	17/03/1900	Trialist	10	0
McLean, John	RB	02/09/1930	Rhyl	06/11/1930	cancelled	1	0
McLean, Thomas	IR	01/09/1917		23/03/1918	St Mirren	21	6
McLean, William	M	22/10/1964	Alloa	30/04/1968	retired	106	6
McLeary	F	24/08/1895		25/04/1896		3	0
McLeary, Edward	G	01/02/1930	Dundee North End	01/02/1930	Trialist	1	0
McLeish, Kevin Michael	IL	01/07/1998	Edina Hibs	31/03/2000	Dunfermline Athletic	3	0
McLeod	LB	22/04/1914	Loanhead	20/05/1916	Trialist	2	0
McLeod	LH	11/08/1894		25/08/1894	Trialist	4	0
McLeod, Christopher	CH	01/06/2005	Arbroath	30/05/2006	Montrose	40	2
McLeod, James	IL	04/10/1930	Carlisle United	14/11/1930	Cancelled	2	0
McLeod, John Murdoch	OR	12/07/1971	KV Mechelen	30/04/1972	Newtongrange Star	21	5
McLeod, Stuart	M	17/08/2004	Bathgate BC			0	0
McLure, Malcolm	FB	29/11/1945	Hearts	30/04/1957	Hamilton Accies	387	0
McLuskie	IR	20/09/1941		20/09/1941	Trialist	1	0
McLuskie, James	G	16/10/1909		15/09/1910	Released	4	0
McManus, Brian M	IF	29/03/1969	Peebles Rovers	22/04/1970	Released	2	0
McManus, Paul John	F	31/08/2002	East Fife	30/05/2003	Albion Rovers	110	36
McManus, Paul John	F	06/07/2005	Stranraer	30/05/2007	East Fife		
McMillan	IL	23/09/1933		23/09/1933	Trialist	1	0
McMillan, Alex .	CF	10/02/1945	Shettleston	10/02/1945	Trialist	1	0
McMillan, Angus	CF	23/01/1975	Stirling Albion	21/10/1975	Released	5	0
McMillan, Hamish	OL	06/08/1955	Rangers	13/01/1959	Stranraer	49	10
McMillan, Ian	CH	31/03/1993	Armadale Thistle	30/04/1996	Linlithgow Rose	13	0
McMillan, William	RH	15/10/1963	Arbroath	13/11/1963	Montrose	2	0
McMullen, Paul	D	07/01/2005	Inverness Caledonian Th	02/05/2005	Australia	11	1
McMurray, John Michael	D	17/08/2004	Hareleeshill BC	14/12/2005	Released	0	0
McMurray, Stuart		31/10/2003				0	0
McNab, Gary	FB	14/08/1992	Dundonald Bluebell	23/11/1993	South Africa	5	0
McNamee, John James	OL	30/03/1961	Thornton Hibs	30/04/1963	Montrose	24	7
McNaught, William	LB	23/08/1941	Army football	30/04/1962	Brechin City	658	15
McNaughton	OL	30/04/1933		29/04/1933	Trialist	1	2
McNeil	LB	11/05/1903		13/05/1903	Trialist	2	0
McNeil, John	CF	18/01/1927	Hearts	29/04/1927	Loan	7	6
McNeil, Ronald	WH	13/07/1953	Irvine Victoria	30/04/1955	Northampton Town	19	3
McNeill, Michael	RH	29/03/1935	Rosslyn Juniors	30/04/1935	Freed	16	1
McNeill, William John	M	15/07/1984	Musselburgh Athletic	02/04/1987	Sepsi 78 (Finland)	58	6
McNicoll, George	CF	30/08/1906	Aberdeen	30/04/1913	Released	35	22
McPhee, Ian	IL	01/12/1972	St Johnstone	01/01/1973	Albion Rovers	4	1
McPherson, Dean	D	06/08/1994	Hutchison Vale	30/06/1999	Berwick Rangers	15	1
McPherson, William	IL	23/02/1946	Hearts	16/03/1946	Trialist	2	1
McQuade, John	G	31/03/1999	Port Vale	09/05/1999	Stirling Albion	6	3
McQuade, Paul	M	15/07/2004	Dundonald Bluebell	01/06/2005	Released	0	0

First Team Player	Position	Date Signed	Signed from	Date Left	Next Club	Total Appearances	Goals
McQueen, John	IR	14/05/1898	East Stirling	30/04/1900		45	10
McSpadyen, Thomas S	RB	30/11/1949	Hearts	26/04/1950	Loan	22	0
McStay, John	RB	03/07/1987	Motherwell	19/08/1994	Falkirk	334	32
McTavish, Robert	IF	09/09/1915	Third Lanark	30/04/1916	Loan	14	2
Meagher, James H	IR	25/09/1928	Dundee	03/11/1928	St Bernards	2	0
Mearns, William	OR	10/07/1901		07/12/1901		3	0
Meikleham, Andrew	RH	03/09/1937	Leith Athletic	30/04/1938	Dundee United	4	0
Meldrum, Graham Ian	FB	10/07/1991	Gairdoch United	08/02/1993	Bo'ness United	5	0
Mendy, Maurice	D	28/07/2004	AS Orly	02/03/2005	Released	11	0
Menzies, Brian	F	20/07/1961	Nairn Thistle	21/02/1964	Montrose	35	7
Menzies, David	IL	01/08/1895		30/04/1897		26	9
Menzies, James	OR	03/06/1948	Coltness United	30/04/1949	St Johnstone	18	6
Menzies, James	OR	07/09/1959	Lochore Welfare	30/04/1961	Trialist	4	1
Menzies, Jim	IR	05/10/1963		05/10/1963	Trialist	2	0
Mercer	OR	12/10/1974		12/10/1974	Trialist	1	0
Mercer, W	OL	30/03/1901		27/04/1901	Trialist	4	0
Messer, James	F	04/06/1904	Tayport	30/04/1908	Freed	12	1
Michie, Harry	OL	09/08/1930	Dundee United	04/10/1930	Cancelled	6	2
Middlemas, William	OL	23/11/1946	New Stevenston	23/11/1946	Trialist	1	0
Middleton	CF	06/10/1945	Blackpool	06/10/1945	Trialist	1	0
Millar, David A	WH	14/02/1968	Aberdeen	12/11/1970	St Mirren	102	7
Millar, James	CF	31/01/1920	Alloa			5	1
Millar, James	LB	21/05/1890	Kirkcaldy Wanderers	09/08/1890	Trialist	2	0
Millar, John	M	31/03/1996	Hearts	30/06/1998	Livingston	73	8
Millar, John	LB	11/02/1893	Kinghorn / Kirkcaldy	11/02/1893	Trialist	1	0
Millar, Marc	M	01/02/2002	Ross County	30/05/2003	Brechin City	11	1
Millar, Paul Thomas	M	13/02/2004	Derby County	30/05/2005	Released	25	0
Millburn, James	RB	13/02/1943	Leeds United	03/04/1943	War Guest	7	0
Millen, Andrew Frank	D	10/01/1997	Hibernian	04/10/1997	Ayr United	31	1
Miller	IR	01/08/1887		14/01/1888		1	0
Miller	LB	03/01/1942	Third Lanark	04/04/1942		9	0
Miller, Adam	CF	11/08/1906		30/04/1907		2	0
Miller, Alan James Webster	OR	22/12/1966	Camelon	22/04/1970	East Stirling	67	10
Miller, Andrew B	LB	11/06/1934	Bowhill	30/04/1935		23	5
Miller, Douglas Robert	F	21/07/1970	Loanhead United	30/04/1972	Livingston United	9	2
Miller, George P	IR	25/07/1922	Hearts	17/01/1925	Hearts	120	35
Miller, Hugh	LB	11/02/1926		11/02/1926	Trialist	40	1
Miller, Ian	IL	06/11/1974	Dundee	30/04/1975	Sauchie	1	0
Miller, James	LH	24/04/1925	Maryhill	01/10/1926	Preston NE	31	7
Miller, John	G	27/07/1960	Thornton Hibs	14/08/1961	Released	1	0
Miller, John	OL	09/08/1890		09/08/1890		1	0
Miller, Joseph	M	07/12/2001	Australia	07/01/2002	Clydebank	5	1
Miller, Robert	OR	16/06/1979	Montrose	12/02/1982	Cowdenbeath	95	16
Miller, Steven	D	11/01/1936	Bowhill	28/03/1936		3	0
Miller, Thomas	IF	09/07/2001	Barrhead BC	20/01/2003	Livingston	5	0
Miller, William Nisbit	D	16/12/1926	Hamilton Accies	30/04/1928		1	0
Milliken	RH	28/03/2002	Dundee	30/05/2002	Cowdenbeath	3	0
Milne, John	IR	01/01/1918		01/01/1918	Trialist	1	0
Milne, Robert	IL	26/11/1898	Kirkcaldy Wanderers	04/03/1899	Trialist	2	0
Milne, Robert		12/04/1930	Montrose	12/04/1930	Trialist	1	0
Miotto, Simon Jonathan	G	09/07/2001	Blackpool Mechanics	30/5/2002		14	0
Mitchell	G	28/04/1905		30/04/1905	Trialist	1	0
Mitchell	HB	31/12/1906		02/01/1907	Trialist	2	0
Mitchell, A	LB	20/12/1897		20/12/1897	Trialist	1	0

First Team Player	Position	Date Signed	Signed from	Date Left	Next Club	Total Appearances	Goals
Mitchell, Graham Lee	D	11/10/1996	Bradford City	30/05/1998	Cardiff City	29	0
Mitchell, Henry George K	F	25/10/1905	Dunnikier Athletic	22/07/1911	Albion Rovers	111	28
Mitchell, James (1)	IR	14/08/1946	Bo'ness United	30/04/1953	Released	12	2
Mitchell, John Alexander	OR	10/01/1981	Falkirk	17/12/1982	Cowdenbeath	45	2
Mitchell, Robert	OR	30/04/1979	Kelty United	30/04/1981	Oakley United	1	1
Mitchell, William	WH	26/06/1907	Pathhead United	30/04/1911		66	0
Mitchell, William J	CF	23/06/1969	Leven Hibs	14/06/1971	Celtic	41	16
Mitchell, William J	CF	11/01/1974	Dunfermline Athletic	30/04/1974	Alloa	5	0
Mochan, Denis	LB	01/09/1959	East Fife	12/06/1962	Nottingham Forest	119	2
Mochan, Neil	F	29/06/1963	Dundee United	10/02/1964	Celtic (trainer)	25	6
Moffat, Adam	IR	15/08/1977	Oakley United	30/04/1979	Cowdenbeath	4	0
Moffat, Adam	M	08/07/2002	Livingston	30/04/2003	Cowdenbeath	8	0
Moir, John	CF	03/12/1904		03/12/1904	Trialist	1	1
Mollison, Drew	CH	21/08/1974	Lochgelly Albert	30/04/1975	Lochgelly Albert	1	0
Monaghan, Patrick	OR	14/08/1915	Maryhill	30/04/1919	Abercorn	35	2
Monin, Samuel	G	06/03/2001	AS Monaco	30/05/2005		49	0
Montgomery		03/01/1906		03/01/1906	Trialist	1	0
Montgomery, William	LH	26/03/1945	Ashfield	21/02/1946	Released	25	1
Moodie	RB	25/10/1941	Reading	25/10/1941	Trialist	1	0
Moodie, Charles Chalmers	RH	11/11/1895	Raith Athletic	30/04/1912	East Fife	420	35
Moodie, John	G	11/08/1939	Hearts	11/08/1939	Aberdeen	57	0
Moodie, Thomas	WH	18/05/1905	Dundee	01/01/1908		42	3
Mooney, Stephen	M	18/09/1993	Airdrie	30/04/1994	Dumbarton	2	1
More, Colin David	CH	12/07/1982	Hearts	15/05/1986	Berwick Rangers	171	5
Moreland, Alexander	G	25/09/1945	Dromyne Amateurs	30/04/1946		1	0
Morgan	CF	01/04/1911		01/04/1911	Trialist	2	1
Morgan	LB	11/04/1931	Bowhill	11/04/1931		1	0
Morgan	IL	12/01/1946	Freuchie	19/01/1946	Trialist	2	0
Morris	WH	21/06/1902	Norwood	21/06/1902	Guest	1	0
Morris, Archibald	LB	01/09/1921	Edinburgh Emmet	20/01/1925	Alloa	22	0
Morris, Charles	CH	29/08/1901		15/05/1902	Dundee	42	1
Morris, Colin		01/09/2004		22/09/2004	Dundee	0	0
Morris, David	CH	09/12/1920	Newtongrange Star	22/12/1925	Preston North End	263	9
Morris, Robert	CF	26/10/1929	Newburgh West End	26/10/1929	Trialist	1	0
Morrison	LB	12/03/1932		16/04/1932	Trialist	2	0
Morrison	OL	04/09/1929		04/09/1929	Trialist	1	0
Morrison, Allan S	OL	27/04/1946	Clyde	27/04/1946	Trialist	1	0
Morrison, James R	CH	13/05/1936	Brechin City	27/04/1939		105	2
Morrison, John	LB	28/08/1934	Bo'ness	25/09/1934	Cancelled	2	1
Morrison, William	FB	14/05/1912	Clyde	27/08/1915	Morton	91	4
Morton	G	07/10/1889		01/01/1898		23	0
Moyes, David	LB	27/12/1919	Kingseat Juniors	18/08/1926	Leicester City	291	12
Muir	LB	27/02/1897	Dunfermline	27/02/1897	Trialist	1	0
Muir	G	09/03/1889		09/03/1889	Trialist	1	0
Muir	OR	05/01/1909		05/01/1909	Trialist	1	0
Muir, Henry (Harry)	LB	05/09/1916	Rangers	30/04/1920	Rangers	78	0
Muir, Henry (Harry)	RB	01/05/1946	Lochore Welfare	31/07/1949	Stirling Albion	68	12
Muir, James	G	03/05/1927	Dunfermline Athletic	30/04/1929		65	0
Muirhead, William	G	18/08/1962	Hibernian	30/04/1963	Toronto City	3	0
Mullaney, Hugh	IL	20/10/1945	Tranent	03/11/1945	Trialist	1	0
Mullaney, Robert	CF	22/01/1944	Dundee Anchorage	29/01/1944	Trialist	2	0
Munro, James	CF	22/02/1928	St Johnstone	26/04/1928	St Johnstone	3	1
Munro, Thomas F	LB	29/05/1929	Partick Thistle	30/04/1931		44	0

First Team Player	Position	Date Signed	Signed from	Date Left	Next Club	Total Appearances	Goals
Murney, Bernard	IR	30/10/1954	Saltcoats Victoria	30/04/1958	Johnstone Burgh	14	4
Murnin, William	LH	04/04/1891	Bathgate Rovers	04/04/1891	Trialist	1	0
Murphy	RH	11/04/1942	Burntisland	11/04/1942	Trialist	1	0
Murphy, Andrew	OR	16/05/1959	Celtic	30/04/1960	Albion Rovers	4	1
Murphy, James	RH	05/10/1900		30/04/2001	Cowdenbeath	31	2
Murphy, James	F	23/08/1967	Hearts	24/02/1968	Notts County	15	3
Murray, Derek R	LB	19/07/1988	Motherwell	30/04/1991	Oakley United	110	3
Murray, James	HB	06/08/1964	Hearts	30/04/1965		22	7
Murray, John	HB	01/11/1939	Plymouth Argyle	22/11/1941	War Guest	31	8
Murray, John	IR	25/10/1941	Manchester United	22/11/1941	War Guest	4	0
Murray, Leslie	OL	31/03/1949	Lochgelly Albert	02/11/1951	Arbroath	46	10
Murray, Leslie	IL	08/05/1958	Cowdenbeath	13/05/1958	Trialist	0	0
Murray, Mark				05/04/2005		0	0
Murray, Matthew	IR	11/05/1956	Kilmarnock	17/05/1956	Ayr United	1	0
Murray, Thomas Dickson	G	14/03/1934	Newburgh West End	30/04/1935		45	0
Murray, Tommy	IF	14/03/1978	Arbroath	30/04/1980	Bo'ness United	41	4
Murtagh, Conall	M	22/01/2005	Hearts	22/05/2005	Loan	11	1
Myles, John	OR	01/01/1889	Kirkcaldy	01/01/1889	Trialist	1	0
Myles, John S	IF	01/08/1978	Dundee United	30/04/1980	Bonnyrigg Rose	5	1
Nairn, James	RB	01/10/1906	Bowhill Thistle	30/04/1908		12	0
Nanou, Wilfred	M	09/03/2001	FC Vaulx-en-Vein	30/05/2003		74	4
Napier, Alexander	IR	16/02/1951	Dalkeith Thistle	11/03/1952	Montrose	2	1
Narey, David	CH	31/08/1994	Dundee United	30/06/1995	Retired	26	1
Nee, Robert R	RH	20/06/1950	Dalkeith Thistle	30/04/1955	Freed	1	0
Neil, Boyd Perrie Jackson (John)		31/03/2006	Armadale Sporting Club	03/07/2007	Free Transfer	8	0
Neilson, Adam	OL	31/01/1920		17/04/1920		2	0
Neilson, D	CH	06/10/1888		06/10/1888	Trialist	1	0
Neilson, James	F	20/02/1892	St Bernards	03/04/1900		159	90
Neilson, John	RH	03/05/1904	Kirkcaldy United	02/11/1905	Kirkcaldy United	64	6
Neish, James B	IF	08/11/1924	Dunnikier Juniors	19/12/1925	East Fife	25	7
Neish, John	G	11/06/1913	Denbeath Star	30/04/1919	East Fife	57	0
Nelson, Martin	IR	23/03/1989	Hamilton Accies	04/12/1992	Montrose	131	17
Nelson, Thomas	RB	01/08/1885	Thistle	30/04/1896		213	60
Ness	RB	05/05/1902		05/05/1902	Trialist	2	0
Ness, Daryl	D	17/08/2004	Salvesen BC			0	0
Ness, Hugh P	OL	04/04/1957	Cowdenbeath Royals	30/04/1959	Accrington Stanley	1	0
Ness, John	G	30/09/1907	[Fife juniors]	20/11/1911	Cowdenbeath	11	0
Newbigging, Henry	CF	16/12/1915	Hamilton Accies	30/04/1916	Hamilton Accies	5	3
Newbould	RH	24/09/1924		24/09/1924	Trialist	1	1
Newton	IR	10/04/1924		10/04/1924	Trialist	1	0
Niblo, John	CF	03/01/1905	Kirkcaldy	30/04/1905		1	0
Niblo, Thomas Bruce	OL	13/08/1909	Aberdeen	30/04/1910		33	5
Nicholl, William	IR	20/11/1900		30/04/1901	Lochgelly United	1	0
Nicholl, James Michael	M	20/11/1990	Dunfermline Athletic	08/02/1996	Millwall	149	7
Nicholson, Robert	CH	19/03/1895		27/02/1904		24	5
Nicol, Kevin Andrew	M	01/07/1998	Hill o' Beath	17/01/2002	Hibs	32	2
Nicol, Robert	IR	02/03/1935	Kirkford Juniors	02/03/1935	Trialist	1	0
Nicol, William M	IR	07/09/1927	Lochgelly Celtic	07/08/1927	Trialist	1	0
Nieto Martos, Juan Manuel	D	30/01/2004	Palamos	01/05/2004		12	0
Nisbet, George	G	26/06/1926	Ayr United	30/04/1927		2	0
Nisbet, Peter	LB	03/03/1899	Cowdenbeath	21/03/1999	Loan	1	0
Niven, Derek	M	10/07/2000	Stenhousemuir	24/11/2001	Bolton Wanderers	4	0
Norval, J	RH	01/08/1885		01/01/1890		30	24
Notman, Archibald	OR	28/02/1931	Inverkeithing	28/02/1931	Trialist	1	1

First Team Player	Position	Date Signed	Signed from	Date Left	Next Club	Total Appearances	Goals
Novo, Ignacio Javier Gomez	F	31/07/2001	SD Huesca	09/07/2002	Dundee	40	24
Nugent, M.A.	CF	19/10/1946	Bowhill Hearts	19/10/1946	Hearts	1	0
Oag, Alexander	LB	05/11/1894	North Western	27/01/1896	Newton Heath	62	1
Oag, Alexander		22/12/1897	Newton Heath	30/4/1898			
Oatman, James R.	OL	09/12/1946	Rosslyn Juniors	30/04/1947	Bowhill Rovers	9	2
Obidele, Emeke Aboy	M	26/07/2003	Panseraikos	26/07/2003	Dumbarton	1	0
O'Boyle, George	F	18/07/2001	St Johnstone	02/11/2001	Brechin City	10	1
O'Brien	LH	27/11/1943	Hull City	27/11/1943	Trialist	1	0
Ocovan, Peter	M	12/08/2004	Nitra (Slovakia)	10/11/2004		1	0
O'Donnell, Frank	IF	07/04/1947	Nottingham Forest	30/04/1947	Buxton	3	0
O'Donoghue, Ross	M	17/07/2003	Aberdeen	17/07/2003	Trialist	1	0
O'Hara, Shane	D	26/08/2003	Broxburn Colts	29/10/2003		0	0
Ojeda, Raul	G	26/07/2002	Balaguer CF	30/05/2003		34	0
O'Keefe, Timothy James	OL	02/12/1938	Hibs	28/04/1939	Hibs	21	10
Oliphant, Henry (Harry)	IF	23/06/1933	Keith (player coach)	30/04/1934	Montrose	38	15
O'Mara, Craig	M	22/09/2004	Livingston	31/03/2007	Released	0	0
One, Armand	CF	22/07/2006	Cowdenbeath	27/03/2007	Turun Palloseura	29	7
O'Neil, Steven	M	26/08/2003	Youths			2	0
O'Neill, James	RH	12/08/1916	Blackburn Rovers	30/04/1917		6	0
Opinel, Sacha	D	06/01/2000	Stockport County	12/01/2001	Leyton Orient	27	0
O'Reilly, Craig	CF	10/12/2003	Berwick Rangers	28/06/2005	Dundee	19	2
Orr, Ronald	IL	17/01/1912	Vale of Leithen	01/03/1913	South Shields	7	1
Orrock, James	RH	16/06/1902	Vale of Wemyss	30/04/1906	Cowdenbeath	24	0
Oswald, James	LB	31/07/1901	Leith Athletic	15/08/1902	Leith Athletic	46	0
Ouattara, Moussa	M	31/07/2004	AS Orly	30/04/2005		42	1
Ouchterlonie, William WM	CF	26/06/1934	Dundee United	01/05/1935	Portadown	9	3
Ovenstone, David G	OR	01/09/1932	Rosslyn Juniors	30/04/1935	Q.P.R.	107	17
Owens, William	RB	06/08/1903		30/04/1913		12	1
Owusu, Ansah	F	01/03/2000	Wimbledon	30/04/2000	Loan	10	3
Page, Samuel	G	28/02/1928	St Johnstone	26/04/1928	St Johnstone	7	0
Paliczka, Sean	F	04/09/2001	Hibs	30/04/2003	Vale of Leithen	9	1
Panther, Frederick G	OR	29/05/1929	Folkestone	24/08/1932	cancelled	44	45
Panther, Frederick G		02/01/1933		30/04/1933	Free Transfer		
Park, John	CF	04/01/1964	Stirling Albion	20/02/1965	East Fife	32	24
Parkin, Paul	D	19/07/2002	Hearts	30/05/2003	Free Transfer	17	0
Parlane, John McKenzie	LH	01/02/1933	Dumbarton	24/10/1933	cancelled	15	2
Parsons	CF	27/10/1945	Oakley United	27/10/1945	Trialist	2	0
Paterno, John	G	05/07/1985	Leven Royals	30/06/1989	Lochgelly Albert	1	0
Paterson, Andrew H	G	29/07/1915	Kirkcaldy United	18/11/1915	Kirkcaldy United	11	0
Paterson, John	RH	25/08/1909	Kirkcaldy United	15/09/1909	Trialist	2	0
Paterson, John Watson	G	11/03/1935	Thornton Hibs	30/04/1937		49	0
Paterson, Thomas	OL	04/11/1944	Lochore Welfare	24/01/1946	Montrose	10	2
Paterson, William	CH	22/06/1935	Arbroath	28/02/1936	Stenhousemuir	11	0
Patino, Cristian Fabian	D	20/09/2002	Jorge Newbury	30/05/2003		56	3
Paton, James	WH	02/05/1896	Cowdenbeath	30/04/1900		23	3
Patterson, Gordon C	LH	05/08/1967	Rangers	10/02/1968	Cancelled	1	0
Payne, James	CF	30/08/1928	Anstruther Rangers	27/10/1928	Armadale	4	1
Payne, Joseph	CF	03/04/1943	Chelsea	28/08/1943	Loan	7	6
Pearson	LH	25/12/1906		06/01/1909		2	0
Pearson	G	25/04/1928		25/04/1928	Trialist	3	0
Peattie, William	FB	19/05/1936	St Monance Swifts	08/05/1940	Dundee	89	4
Peebles, James	CF	27/07/1960	Greenock Juniors	30/04/1961		4	1
Peers, Mark	F	22/07/2003	Liverpool	12/01/2004		14	3
Peggie	CF	02/04/1906	Vale of Wemyss	26/04/1906	Trialist	2	2

First Team Player	Position	Date Signed	Signed from	Date Left	Next Club	Total Appearances	Goals
Pelosi, Marco Giancarlo	M	14/12/2006	Hearts			45	0
Pender, Robert	LH	22/09/1916	Dumbarton Harp	15/05/1919	Middlesbrough	13	0
Penman, James C	CF	07/11/1933	Dunnikier Juniors	30/04/1934		18	13
Penman, William H	CF	08/08/1942	Raith Athletic	29/04/1954	Stirling Albion	328	211
Pereira Gomez, Ramon	CF	09/01/2004	Logrones	30/05/2004	Hearts	11	6
Perry, Edward G.B.	OL	21/11/1958	Falkirk	30/04/1959	Queen's Park	5	0
Perry, Jack Joseph	D	20/08/2004	Queens Park Rangers	02/11/2004	Loan	6	0
Petrie	CF	17/02/1945	Raith Athletic	17/02/1945	Trialist	1	0
Pettie, Gordon	M	22/11/1976	Burnlea	30/04/1980		62	7
Philip, David C	RB	10/06/1910	Leith Athletic	30/04/1917		112	0
Philip, Alexander R	CH	23/05/1903	Lochee United	30/04/1908		70	9
Philip, Iain F	D	12/02/1984	Dundee United	15/05/1986	Arbroath	90	0
Phillips, Charles	CF	26/03/1908	Ayr Parkhouse	30/05/1908	Ayr Parkhouse	3	0
Philp, David	OL	26/05/1899		29/04/1899	Alloa	1	0
Philp, Hector	IF	09/08/1935	Lochgelly Albert	30/04/1937		48	3
Philp, John B	WH	17/12/1935	Leicester City	30/04/1937		24	0
Phypers, Ernest	WH	01/01/1942	Doncaster Rovers	06/11/1943	War Guest	40	1
Pigg, Albert	CF	09/05/1927	Carlisle United	25/09/1929	Barnsley	70	43
Pitblado	RB	21/06/1902		21/06/1902	Guest	2	0
Pitcairn, John W	CH	28/03/1925	Maryhill	30/04/1930		130	2
Polland, William	FB	21/06/1955	Wallhouse Rose Juvs.	27/04/1960	Hearts	372	2
Polland, William	CH	15/03/1967	Hearts	30/04/1970	Retired		
Pollock		24/07/1993		24/07/1993	Trialist	1	0
Pollock, Walter	CF	22/08/1936	Armadale Thistle	22/08/1936	Trialist	1	1
Pope, Alfred Leslie	RB	13/01/1940	Hearts	02/01/1943	Loan	22	0
Porter, James	FB	15/10/1925	East Stirling	30/04/1928	Forfar Athletic	25	3
Porter, William	CH	30/09/1913	Kirkintilloch Rob Roy	04/03/1916	Armadale	144	14
Porter, William	LH	25/06/1919	Hearts	06/10/1920	Hearts		
Porterfield, John (Ian)	LH	06/07/1964	Lochore Welfare	30/12/1967	Sunderland	153	22
Potter, Brian	G	13/08/1993	Rosyth Recreation	30/04/1996	Oakley United	4	0
Pounoussamy, Rudy Jean Francois	G	28/07/2004	FC Capricorne	30/01/2005		17	0
Pratt, Alex	IR	25/10/1930	Ormiston Primrose	01/11/1930	Trialist	2	0
Preget, Antoine	LB	16/11/1999	Chateauroux	16/11/1999	Dundee United	2	0
Prentice, Adam	G	28/08/1963	Thornton Hibs	30/04/1964			
Prentice, David	IR	11/06/1932	Plymouth	30/04/1933	Mansfield Town	36	16
Prest, Martin Hugo	F	04/07/2002	Ross County	02/02/2004		54	13
Price, John	IR	22/03/1940	Hartlepool	13/04/1940	War Guest	4	4
Price, Peter	CF	06/01/1962	Ayr United	30/04/1962	Albion Rovers	10	1
Prior, Peter	OL	30/12/1958	Fauldhouse United	30/04/1959	Dundee United	5	1
Proctor, William	IR	03/10/1904	Dundee juniors	30/04/1913		34	7
Pryde, James G	OL	02/12/1929	Dundee	30/04/1930		11	4
Pullar, William	OR	11/02/1932	Leith Athletic	17/01/1992	Peterborough United	8	1
Purcell, Patrick	F	08/08/1968	Dundee United	30/04/1969	Newtongrange Star	1	0
Purdie, Bryan	D	06/03/1987	Falkirk	19/12/1987	Partick Thistle	26	1
Purvis, George	OR	01/06/1977	Glenrothes United	30/04/1978		2	0
Quinn	CF	02/01/1906	Centre forward	02/01/1906	Trialist	1	0
Quinn, Mark	M	27/02/1993	Strathbock U18s	30/04/1996	Linlithgow Rose	1	0
Quinn, Stephen A	M	09/08/1991	Airdrie	19/12/1999	Loan	3	0
Rae	IL	03/01/1906		08/05/1907		2	0
Rae, J	IR	03/01/1906		03/01/1906	Trialist	1	0
Rae, John	IL	15/09/1900		01/08/1901		20	3
Rae, Joseph	CF	05/03/1948	Celtic	30/04/1948	Rosario	4	0
Raeburn, James	RH	05/01/1921	Tranent Juniors	20/11/1925	Broxburn United	200	4
Raeside, Robert	CH	13/09/1990	St Andrews United	10/07/1996	Dundee	83	1

First Team Player	Position	Date Signed	Signed from	Date Left	Next Club	Total Appearances	Goals
Raffell, Bruce John	M	18/07/2003	Dundee United	30/04/2005		15	0
Ramage	RB	03/12/1887		23/12/1897	Trialist	4	0
Ramsay	CF	02/04/1917		02/04/1917	Trialist	1	1
Ramsay, Aaron	IR	09/09/1910	Kilmarnock	30/04/1911	Loan	30	4
Ramsay, Andrew	IL	20/02/1897	Logrones	27/05/1899		78	53
Ramsay, Charles	CF	01/08/1886		20/09/1890		87	14
Ramsay, George	IF	07/11/1896	Pathhead United	01/05/1901	Cowdenbeath	136	33
Ramsay, Paul Roger	CH	12/12/1983	Musselburgh Athletic	15/05/1985	Newtongrange Star	42	11
Rankin, Simpson	CH	23/07/1902		30/04/1904	Kirkcaldy United	70	14
Rankine, John	OR	19/11/1902	Rangers	22/06/1903	Kirkcaldy United	20	4
Rankine, Peter	G	30/07/1928	Birmingham	30/08/1928		2	0
Rathbone, Edward	CH	15/08/1910	Centre half	15/09/1910		4	0
Rattray, John C	RH	14/05/1913	Falkirk	30/04/1925	Dumbarton	207	27
Reay, George Thompson	OR	06/12/1925	Kettering Town	22/05/1928	Bristol Rovers	70	17
Redford, Ian Petrie	M	26/08/1994	Brechin City	30/05/1995	Retired	15	0
Reeder, George	G	18/01/1936	Bo'ness Cadora	18/01/1936	Trialist	1	0
Reekie, James	G	16/03/1946	Lochgelly Albert	16/03/1946	Trialist	1	0
Reekie, William	OR	19/02/1921	Abbotshall Juniors	19/02/1921	Trialist	1	0
Reid, Brian	D	16/11/1985	Brechin City	23/11/1985	Arbroath Vics	2	0
Reid, Christopher Thomas	M	20/08/1983	Cowdenbeath	20/08/1983	Meadowbank Thistle	1	0
Reid, George	RH	31/07/1961	K.O.S.B.	30/04/1962	Johnstone Burgh	3	0
Reid, Robert B A	G	31/05/1963	Arbroath	26/02/1974	retired	328	0
Rennie	RB	25/08/1909		25/08/1909	Trialist	2	0
Rennie, George B	RH	24/05/1966	Berwick Rangers	30/04/1967	East Stirling	9	0
Renton	RH	04/01/1921	Edinburgh Juniors	04/01/1921	Trialist	1	0
Renton, Keiron	G	01/06/2007	Elgin City	30/05/2008	Free Transfer	23	0
Reynolds	CF	21/12/1929	Windsor H.	21/12/1929	Trialist	1	0
Rice, Alexander	IF	01/04/1973	Fairfield Juveniles	01/09/1974	Brechin City	21	2
Rice, Peter	IR	31/12/1953	St Mirren	30/04/1955	Albion Rovers	13	2
Richardson, Gary Steven	M	18/05/2003	Hearts	14/01/2004	Albion Rovers	2	0
Richardson, James	M	13/10/1894	Hearts	05/01/1895		13	5
Richardson, John	IF	30/01/1965	Lochore Welfare	30/04/1969	Berwick Rangers	109	60
Richmond, William C	OL	27/10/1927	Thornton Rangers	30/04/1928	Dundee United	1	2
Rintoul, Jordan	Mid	17/08/2004	Falkirk Form D	30/04/2005		1	0
Ripley, William S	WH	10/11/1916	Stoke City	30/04/1917		9	0
Ritchie	OR	21/06/1902		21/06/1902	Guest	1	0
Ritchie, Alexander W	OL	29/05/1923	St Bernards	12/03/1926	Dunfermline Athletic	148	46
Ritchie, Brian A	M	24/02/1984	Dundonald Bluebell	15/05/1985	Fife juniors	48	2
Ritchie, Duncan	OR	23/05/1911	Hibs	12/04/1912	Sheffield Wednesday	41	5
Ritchie, Harry	OR	04/11/1899	St Bernards	13/01/1900		4	0
Ritchie, Keiran Owen	F	18/07/2003	Dundee	16/01/2004		2	0
Rivas, Francisco Ortiz (Paquito)	M	06/11/2001	UD Las Palmas	28/01/2005	Hamilton Accies	122	9
Robb	LB	29/02/1896	Lochgelly United	09/05/1896		7	0
Robb, Bryan	OL	19/02/1921		19/02/1921	Trialist	1	0
Robb, Steven	M	29/08/2003	Dundee	31/12/2003	Loan	12	0
Roberts, James Weir	LH	22/04/1908	East Stirling	27/04/1912	East Fife	3	0
Roberts	CF	10/04/1924		10/04/1924	Trialist	1	1
Roberts, Mark Kingsley	MF	19/11/1999	Kilmarnock	19/12/1999	Loan	3	1
Robertson	CF	09/01/1943		09/01/1943	Trialist	1	0
Robertson	LH	14/02/1903	Black Watch	14/02/1903	Trialist	1	0
Robertson	CH	01/02/1908		01/02/1908	Trialist	1	0
Robertson, A	LB	23/11/1895		08/02/1896		1	0
Robertson, Alex	LH	02/11/1889	Kirkcaldy	02/11/1889	Trialist	1	0
Robertson, Alexander	M	30/08/2002	Berwick	30/09/2002	Trialist	0	0

Players (continued)

Table A — Robertson, Christopher J G → Scott, Colin George

First Team Player	Position	Date Signed	Signed from	Next Club	Date Left	Total Appearances	Goals
Robertson, Christopher J G	CF	20/08/1983	Cowdenbeath	Meadowbank Thistle	20/08/1983	1	0
Robertson, Craig Peter	M	25/08/1980	Hearts	Dunfermline	02/06/1987	224	29
Robertson, Frank	OL	01/02/1930	Ormiston Primrose	Trialist	01/02/1930	1	2
Robertson, George B	G	08/05/1958	Cowdenbeath	Cancelled	13/05/1958	1	0
Robertson, Graham	RH	30/08/1933	Cowdenbeath	Alloa	30/08/1933	1	0
Robertson, Graham Stuart	F	03/08/1993	Balgonie Colts U16	Millwall	30/05/1996	13	2
Robertson, Graham Stuart	F	07/08/1998	Millwall	East Fife	05/03/1999	2	2
Robertson, James	IR	05/12/1942	Leith Athletic	War Guest	27/11/1943	0	0
Robertson, John Cameron	IF	12/07/1976	East Fife	Leven Juniors	30/04/1977	2	0
Robertson, Leslie	CH	28/01/1975	Culross BC	Glenrothes	30/04/1975	2	0
Robertson, Malcolm	OR	22/07/1971	Penicuik Athletic	Ayr United	03/12/1975	197	71
Robertson, Peter	CH	19/08/1899	Cowdenbeath	Kirkcaldy	30/04/1901	71	6
Robertson, Robert	HB	06/08/1894	Raith Athletic	Trialist	26/03/1898	20	0
Robertson, Roland Y	CF	06/03/1937	Dunblane Juniors	Dundee	06/03/1937	1	1
Robertson, Samuel	LH	15/06/1901	East Fife	War Guest	15/05/1902	31	2
Robertson, Walter	FB	28/03/1919	East Fife		30/04/1920	2	0
Robinson, John James (Jack)	G	24/10/1942	Manchester City	South Shields	24/10/1942	1	0
Robinson, Robert S	M	22/07/1981	Hearts		15/05/1983	72	4
Robson, Frederick Whelans	RB	19/10/1936	Dunfermline Athletic	South Shields	20/12/1919	5	0
Robson, George A	OR	04/12/1915			26/04/1919	69	0
Rodger	IR	12/04/1919	Newburgh		24/03/1945	2	0
Rodgers	IR	24/03/1945	Ayr United		11/10/1941	1	0
Rodgers, Charles G	G	11/10/1941	Celtic	Guest	02/03/1946	1	0
Rodgers, Patrick	OL	23/02/1946	St Mirren		01/03/1975	2	0
Rogerson, Drew	CH	01/05/1973	Falkirk	Bo'ness United	20/06/1991	54	0
Romaines, Stuart	F	10/09/1988		Alloa	02/04/1917	80	2
Ross	RH	02/04/1917	Derry City	Trialist	05/11/1963	1	0
Ross, Bobby	IR	05/10/1963	Falkirk Youth		09/07/2001	1	0
Ross, David Robert	D	09/07/2001			30/04/2003	10	0
Ross, J	IR	09/03/1889	Inverness Caledonian		27/01/1894	3	0
Ross, Samuel	LB	15/01/1966		Cancelled	15/02/1966	1	0
Roughead	CF	26/04/1906	Trinity Pros		26/04/1906	1	0
Rougier, Anthony Leo	OL	13/03/1995	Denbeath Star	Hibernian	17/07/1997	81	14
Rougvie, David	F	23/01/1917	Cowdenbeath	Denbeath Star	30/04/1919	17	9
Rougvie, Ralph	LB	20/02/1940	Ayr United	Cancelled	24/06/1944	30	0
Rovde, Marius	G	21/12/2002	Plymouth Argyle	Trialist	21/12/2002	0	0
Rowbotham, Jason	LB	31/07/1993	Carnoustie Panmure	Wycombe Wanderers	11/09/1995	72	2
Ruse, Victor J	CF	09/09/1944	Rosyth Rec Colts	Dundee	09/12/1944	5	6
Rushford, John	M	13/07/1999		Trialist	30/04/2002	1	0
Russell	IR	29/09/1924	Kilsyth Rangers	Trialist	29/09/1924	1	4
Russell, Frank M	IL	15/08/1961		Johnstone Burgh	30/10/1962	6	0
Russell, James	HB	01/08/1885	Forthill Athletic		21/05/1890	107	7
Russell, John	OL	08/11/1907	Airdrie	War Guest	30/04/1911	6	1
Russell, Robert S	CH	15/03/1981	Hearts of Beath	Falkirk	20/06/1984	92	23
Russell, William	CF	25/08/1896	Hearts	Hamilton Accies	30/08/1897	25	0
Rutherford, Edward (Ernie)	D	06/01/1955	Arniston	Trialist	30/04/1955	5	1
Rutherford, Norman	IL	05/01/1946	Crystal Palace	Trialist	05/01/1946	1	0
Ryan	CF	20/03/1943	Paris FC	Trialist	27/03/1943	4	0
Sacko, Hamed	F	02/07/2004	Spartans	Trialist	27/01/2005	33	10
Sargeant, Fraser Peter Simon	IL	15/04/2006			30/04/2007	4	0
Sawyers, Patrick	RH	19/07/2003	Rangers	Trialist	19/07/2003	1	0
Scobbie, George	HB	11/05/1953	Montrose	Cancelled	05/05/1953	66	8
Scott, Alex Ian	OL	17/06/1952	Hamilton Academical	Brechin City	01/01/1956	6	0
Scott, Colin George	G	17/10/1996		Clydebank	30/06/1998		

Table B — Scott, James → Smith

First Team Player	Position	Date Signed	Signed from	Next Club	Date Left	Total Appearances	Goals
Scott, James	IF	30/09/1913	Petershill	Killed in action	17/10/1925	72	24
Scott, James F	CF	01/06/1925	Wemyss Athletic	Arbroath	30/04/1935	13	5
Scott, James Ford	RH	13/11/1933	Newburgh West End	Newburgh West End	03/01/1906	53	1
Scott, John	RB	01/09/1899		Cancelled	30/04/1972	72	2
Scott, Thomas	FB	17/08/1970	Tynecastle BC	Newtongrange Star	30/04/1972	6	0
Scott, Walter	RB	16/09/1915	Hearts	St Bernards	09/03/1916	16	0
Seath, John M	OR	01/06/1908	amateur		30/04/1910	5	1
Selfridge, Henry	FB	13/09/1963	Nairn Thistle	Cancelled	28/04/1969	66	0
Sellars, Neil Andrew	CF	03/08/1994	Kirkcaldy YM	Thornton Hibs	30/04/1997	2	0
Selway, Ronald	WH	01/06/1972	Dundee	Retired	26/01/1974	73	1
Semple, Gary	F	27/08/2003	Hibs		30/04/2004	0	0
Shand, Robert	OL	23/08/1909	Glencraig		15/09/1909	14	5
Shand, Robert	CF	23/03/1918			30/04/1919		
Sharkey, James	IF	30/05/1961	Airdrie	Cambridge Town	30/04/1962	6	1
Sharp, Alexander	IF	27/06/1938	Falkirk	Trialist	19/03/1940	10	4
Sharp, Robert	RB	20/09/1951	Rosyth Recreation	Dundee	30/04/1952	1	0
Sharp, Thomas	LH	13/03/1930	Stoneyburn Juniors	Freed	10/01/1933	82	3
Sheach, David	OR	03/06/1986	Kirkcaldy YM	St Andrews United	10/01/1987	0	0
Shields, Dene	F	14/07/1999	Granton BC	Cancelled	21/12/2000	28	6
Shields, Dene	CF	10/01/2003	Sunderland	Sunderland	30/05/2004		
Shields, James	CF	09/05/1947	Celtic	Brechin City	19/06/1947	1	0
Shields, Paul Martin	CF	02/06/1998	Milton Green	Dumbarton	22/03/2000	33	5
Shufflebottom, Frank	RB	24/04/1943	Notts County	Celtic	13/01/1945	47	0
Silvestro, Christopher	M	25/05/2005	Albion Rovers	Dundee United		106	2
Simpson	OL	05/05/1902			12/05/1902	4	0
Simpson, Andrew	G	04/09/1902		Trialist	30/04/1903	6	0
Simpson, Henry	CH	01/08/1893	Raith Athletic		30/04/1896	12	1
Simpson, Henry C (Harry)	IR	29/06/1910	St Bernards	Ayr United	05/10/1910	6	0
Simpson, Hugh	G	13/05/1908	Bo'ness	Leith Athletic	14/08/1912	118	12
Simpson, John	IF	27/11/1973	Whitburn	Bonnyrigg Rose	30/04/1974	6	1
Simpson, Stephen	OR	17/06/1986	Oakley United	Hill of Beath Hawtho	13/01/1992	186	21
Simpson, William C	G	25/10/1935	Dumbarton	Cancelled	14/02/1936	8	0
Sinclair, Colin	IF	06/08/1968	Linlithgow Rose	Darlington	15/06/1971	62	22
Sinclair, David	D	12/03/1990	Kelty Under 21s	Millwall	30/06/1996	235	11
Sinclair, James	OR	21/12/1907	Coupar Angus	Trialist	21/12/1907	1	0
Sinclair, John	RB	19/09/1898	Raith Athletic		21/04/1900	33	1
Skene, Ralph	G	10/02/1906		Trialist	10/02/1906	1	0
Slack, James	OL	13/09/1911	Petershill	Cowdenbeath	15/07/1913	26	5
Slater	RB	05/10/1925		Trialist	05/10/1925	1	0
Slater, John	OL	14/04/1934	Wallyford Bluebell	Trialist	14/04/1934	1	0
Slaven, John	LH	21/01/1922	Dundee Forthill	Forfar Athletic	23/02/1923	56	3
Slaven, John	HB	14/10/1925	Arbroath	Hearts	21/12/1925		
Slessor	OL	17/02/1945	Watford	War Guest	17/02/1945		
Sloan	CH	02/01/1907		Trialist	02/01/1907	1	0
Sloan, P Robertson	CF	21/09/1916	Aberdeen	Trialist	21/09/1916	1	1
Sloan, Robert	D	18/05/2007	Alloa			46	8
Smart	RB	15/08/1906		Trialist	15/08/1906	1	0
Smart, Craig	F	11/10/1995	Valleyfield	Hill of Beath Hawthorn	30/04/2000	10	1
Smart, Jonathan	D	30/01/2004	Dee Club	Rowantree Amateurs	30/05/2005	53	0
Smith	IL	13/04/1895	Crail Union	Hearts	18/05/1895	22	20
Smith	RH	25/12/1906		Trialist	25/12/1906	1	0
Smith	HB	06/11/1909	Guardbridge	Trialist	15/01/1910	4	1
Smith	OL	17/03/1917		Cancelled	03/11/1917	2	0
Smith	LB	25/11/1939	Leeds United	Trialist	25/11/1939	1	0

First Team Player	Position	Date Signed	Signed from	Next Club	Date Left	Total Appearances	Goals
Smith	IL	11/04/1942	Tranmere Rovers	Trialist	25/04/1942	3	
Smith, Andrew Mark	F	09/07/2002	Kilmarnock	Clyde	30/05/2003	81	22
Smith, Charles	OL	13/10/1954	Lochore Welfare	Dundee	30/04/1954	1	1
Smith, Gilbert	IF	18/06/1907	Sauchie	Cowdenbeath	30/04/1908	4	1
Smith, Harry McP	IL	09/12/1933	Dundee	Clapton Orient	30/04/1934	15	2
Smith, James	CF	28/07/1902	Lochgelly Rangers	Lochgelly United	06/12/1902	12	8
Smith, James B	OR	08/03/1928	Hearts	Hearts	26/04/1928	11	6
Smith, John	LB	30/10/1936	Bo'ness Cadora		06/03/1945	92	6
Smith, John D	G	10/08/1962	Salvesen BC	Freed	30/04/1963	6	0
Smith, John Henry	G	10/12/1947	Preston Athletic	Forfar Athletic	01/07/1949	11	0
Smith, Paul McKinnon	F	14/01/1983	Dundee United	Motherwell	27/04/1986	162	74
Smith, Robert	IF	16/10/1895	Lochgelly United		09/11/1895	5	1
Smith, Robert B	IR	28/09/1927		Aldershot	14/12/1929	15	3
Smith, Robert B	OR	29/04/1949	Dalkeith Thistle	Darlington	30/04/1950	20	4
Smith, William	IF	02/10/1962	Banks o' Dee	Darlington	30/04/1963	15	2
Smith, William	CF	31/10/1942	Bournemouth	Trialist	31/10/1942	1	0
Smith, William	CH	17/03/1917	Trainer		17/03/1917	1	0
Sneddon	IR	31/03/1934		Trialist	31/03/1934	1	0
Sneddon, Alex	RB	27/12/1919			30/04/1921	8	0
Sneddon, David	IF	08/09/1967	Kilmarnock	Hurlford United	30/04/1971	115	11
Sneddon, James P	LB	03/01/1935	Dunfermline United		30/04/1936	44	0
Sneddon, John	CH	13/11/1943	East Fife	Loan	13/11/1943	1	0
Snoddy, Thomas Gillespie	FB	27/11/1911	Vale of Clyde	St Mirren	01/08/1912	53	5
Sokoluk, John Anthony	OL	05/12/1984	Tranent	Trialist	05/12/1984	1	0
Sorbie, Stuart Graham	M	19/09/1989	St Johnstone	Arbroath	10/07/1990	20	1
Speedie	OL	05/05/1902		Trialist	12/05/1902	2	0
Spence, Charles Alexander	OL	28/09/1981	Whitburn	Freed	15/05/1984	67	6
Spence, Ian	IF	23/10/1959	Stirling Albion	Stirling Albion	23/12/1960	53	17
Spence, William B	F	14/04/1986	Jubilee Athletic	St Johnstone	24/09/1988	15	1
Spilarewicz, Christopher	IF	05/05/1966	Frances Colliery	Frances Colliery	02/02/1968	12	5
Staite, Dick	CH	01/07/1971	Clyde	Retired	01/11/1972	56	4
Stalker, James	IL	18/04/1903	Kirkcaldy United	Trialist	25/04/1903	2	2
Stanik, Goran	RB	22/08/2003	Rad Belgrade	Livingston	30/05/2004	34	0
Stanley, Craig	M	29/07/2003	Walsall	Loan	21/01/2004	27	2
Stanners	G	12/05/1900	Lochore Rangers	Trialist	15/05/1900	2	0
Stark, David	CH	02/01/1946	Bowhill Rovers	Hamilton Accies	30/04/1946	9	0
Stark, George	OR	27/02/1909	Cupar FC		30/04/1911	20	0
Stead	IL	13/02/1943		Trialist	13/02/1943	1	0
Steel, Derek	CH	01/08/1977	Tynecastle BC	East Stirling	01/01/1983	87	0
Steel, Peter	G	15/03/1922	Tranent	St Bernards	24/03/1923	7	0
Steele, John	IL	18/12/1936	Ayr United	Ayr United	30/04/1937	21	11
Steen, John Matheson (Ian)	IF	01/07/1979	Stranraer	East Stirling	04/02/1983	100	8
Stein, Jay	OL	11/10/1995	Inverkeithing United	Stenhousemuir	30/05/2002	182	17
Stein, Robert Scott	D	05/08/1960	Broxburn Athletic	Montrose	30/04/1969	318	15
Stevenson	LB	21/06/1902		Guest	21/06/1902	2	0
Stevenson, Fraser	CF	22/09/1971	Sauchie	Trialist	22/09/1971	2	1
Stevenson, James	FB	21/07/1959	St Mirren	Cowdenbeath	14/03/1964	81	1
Stewart	CF	24/08/1889	Arbroath	Trialist	24/08/1889	1	0
Stewart, Alex	G	24/02/1917	Falkirk	Loan	24/02/1917	1	0
Stewart, D	OR	08/04/1893	Raith Athletic	Trialist	24/05/1893	3	1
Stewart, David	LH	11/07/1898	Kirkcaldy Wanderers		30/04/1906	49	9
Stewart, George	LB	25/11/1903	Lochee United		30/04/1911	81	0
Stewart, George Scott	G	13/12/1950	Petershill	Stirling Albion	30/04/1958	68	0
Stewart, James	F	27/02/1907	Pathhead United Jun		30/04/1908	13	1

First Team Player	Position	Date Signed	Signed from	Next Club	Date Left	Total Appearances	Goals
Stewart, James C	RH	06/04/1944	Partick Thistle	Cancelled	29/06/1945	46	2
Stewart, John	IF	04/05/1912	Buckie	Dunfermline Athletic	08/07/1913	15	10
Stewart, John G (Jacky)	OR	05/01/1942	Dundonald Bluebell	Birmingham City	10/01/1948	244	89
Stewart, John G (Jacky)		19/01/1955	Birmingham City	retired	30/04/1955		
Stewart, Michael	M	31/01/2004	Dundee North End	Dundee North End	30/04/2005	1	0
Stewart, P	FB	01/08/1917	Denbeath Star		30/04/1918	26	1
Stewart, Sammy	LB	13/11/1943	East Fife	Loan	13/11/1943	1	0
Stirling	IR	13/09/1941	Benburb	Trialist	13/09/1941	1	0
Stirling, James	OL	19/02/1949	Stirling Albion		30/04/1950	17	3
Stirling, Jered	LB	11/12/2005	Ayr United	Elgin City	09/01/2006	3	0
Stobbie	G	26/04/1947	Crossgates Primrose	Trialist	26/04/1947	1	0
Stockdale, Douglas	IR	06/05/1948	Lincoln City	Ayr United	16/03/1951	22	3
Stocks, James	IF	02/07/1898	Burntisland		16/12/1899	42	14
Stoddart, George G	IR	16/06/1914	Inverkeithing United	Hull City	11/11/1920	8	1
Strachan, Alan	OL	16/10/1986	Crossgates Primrose	Arbroath	30/04/1989	16	1
Strachan, James	OR	19/06/1905	Arniston Rangers	Rangers	08/12/1906	10	0
Strachan, William	OR	27/06/1945	Dundonald Bluebell	Rangers	27/06/1945	6	1
Strang	LB	31/12/1898	Dunfermline	Trialist	31/12/1898	1	0
Strang, Shaun Anthony	F	02/08/1990	Dunfermline Ath	Freed	15/05/1993	32	4
Stuart, George McK	LB	11/08/1938	Partick Dolphins		27/04/1939	1	0
Stuart, Richard	RB	25/08/1917	Arbroath	Trialist	30/04/1919	12	2
Sturrock	CH	24/08/1889	Arbroath	Trialist	24/08/1889	1	0
Summers	IR	09/08/1941	Lochgelly Albert	Trialist	16/08/1941	2	0
Sutherland, Benjamin	OR	03/09/1907	Townhill Thistle	Trialist	30/04/1913	27	5
Suttie, Alexander	IL	09/10/1893	Pathhead United		30/04/1897	133	97
Sutton, John William Michael	F	22/07/2003	Leicester City	Millwall	29/01/2004	32	20
Sweeney, Jamie	G	09/07/2001	Raith Youth	Linlithgow Rose	31/01/2004	10	0
Sweeney, Paul Martin F	LB	01/07/1980	Whitburn Centre	Newcastle United	21/03/1989	257	10
Tagro, Baroan	M	20/08/2004	Carshalton Athletic		19/01/2005	5	0
Tainsh, Ronald	OR	12/06/1956	Lochore Welfare	Freed	30/04/1958	3	2
Tait, Jordan	CH	13/07/2004	Ayr United	Freed	13/07/2004	1	0
Talio, Vincent	D	07/08/2003	FC Lugon	Trialist	31/01/2004	16	1
Tansey, Paul	M	13/10/2006	Musselburgh	Qatar	10/11/2006	4	0
Taylor	RH	22/04/1914	Windygates	Musselburgh	22/04/1914	1	0
Taylor	CH	31/12/1898	Dunfermline	Trialist	02/01/1899	2	1
Taylor	IL	25/11/1944	Southend		25/11/1944	2	1
Taylor	IL	16/04/1912		Guest	16/04/1912	1	0
Taylor, Alexander	M	05/07/1995	Partick Thistle	Ross Co 24/7/97	30/06/1997	1	2
Taylor, Archibald	CH	13/08/1902	Dundee	Dundee	15/08/1903	36	4
Taylor, David	RB	01/11/1924			30/04/1925	34	0
Taylor, James Watson	OR	16/10/1974	Forfar Athletic	Freed	30/04/1979	4	0
Taylor, John S	CH	22/06/1926	Bristol City	Freed	30/04/1927	179	7
Taylor, Robert	CH	13/12/1958	Frances Colliery	Freed		3	0
Taylor, Russell Thomas	D	16/07/1996	Glenrothes Strollers	Dunfermline Athletic	30/06/1999	1	1
Taylor, William	IR	22/08/1952	Matrix Juniors	Freed	30/04/1953	2	0
Tchimbakala, Jules	M	23/06/2004	Paris FC		23/02/2005	3	0
Tejero, Alvero Quesada	LB	06/10/2001	Rayo Vallecano	Trialist	30/05/2002	18	1
Temple	CH	15/05/1900	Inverkeithing Thistle	Loan	15/05/1900	1	0
Templeton, David	F	01/01/2008	Hearts	Trialist	30/05/2008	17	5
Tervit, William	CF	20/11/1900	Southampton	Trialist	24/11/1900	1	0
Thompson, James H	OL	07/09/1916		Trialist	30/04/1919	7	1
Thoms, John (Jackie)	IF	08/08/1963	Bath City	Brechin City	18/10/1963	12	5
Thomson	OR	22/08/1910	Petershill	Trialist	22/08/1910	1	0
Thomson	G	19/08/1944	Chesterfield	War Guest	02/09/1944	3	0

Players (Tyrie – Webster)

First Team Player	Position	Date Signed	Signed from	Date Left	Next Club	Total Appearances	Goals
Tyrie	CF	02/11/1889		30/04/1890	Trialist	3	4
Urquhart	IR			30/04/1890		19	10
Urquhart, Donald Henderson	M	13/01/1971	Bell Baxter HS	15/05/1985	Glenrothes	498	25
Urquhart, John	OL	14/03/1950	Hearts	30/04/1950	Loan	258	75
Urquhart, John		20/04/1956	Hearts	30/04/1964	Retired	1	0
Urquhart, R	LB	22/08/1896		22/08/1896	Trialist	4	0
Valdes, Alvaro	M	28/03/2003	Atletico Madrid	30/05/2003			
Van De Kamp, Guido	G	01/07/1997	Dunfermline Athletic	02/02/2001	Alloa Athletic	164	0
Venables, Ross Adam	M	02/09/1997	Millwall	01/08/1999	East Fife	8	0
Venters, Alexander	IL	02/02/1948	Blackburn Rovers	30/04/1948	Alloa	10	1
Ventre, John	IF	06/04/1944	Carluke Rovers	30/08/1944	Falkirk	18	4
Vincent, Stanley W T	CF	12/12/1969	Durban City	19/01/1970	Cancelled	2	0
Voy, Gary W	D	25/07/1985	Dundee United	15/05/1988	Retired injured	65	3
Waite, George	CF	29/04/1920	Bradford City	29/01/1921	Clydebank	24	12
Waldron, Ernest	CF	23/10/1943	Crystal Palace	13/05/1944	War Guest	20	15
Walker	IR	20/10/1934	Perth YMCA	20/10/1934	Trialist	1	0
Walker, Alan B	F	21/01/1985	Hutcheson Vale	23/10/1986	Jubilee Athletic (dt	23	2
Walker, Allan	M	26/10/2007	Livingston	26/01/2008	Loan	8	0
Walker, Andrew	CH	08/02/1916	Chelsea	19/02/1916		2	0
Walker, Andrew Francis	F	13/03/1998	Sheffield United	10/05/1998	Loan	7	2
Walker, Cyril John	IR	15/08/1942	Sheffield Wed	15/08/1942		2	0
Walker, David	F	01/08/1893	Kirkcaldy Wanderers	30/04/1899	Cowdenbeath	225	156
Walker, David	CF	18/10/1947	Lochee Harp	27/02/1948	Cancelled	1	0
Walker, Dawson	OR	23/08/1928	Kilmarnock	13/10/1928	Partick Thistle	2	0
Walker, James	OR	01/08/1893		01/08/1895	St Bernards	145	105
Walker, John	FB	11/11/1903	Maryhill Juniors	30/04/1906	Rangers	20	0
Walker, John	IL	08/08/1908	Motherwell	30/04/1910	Rangers	7	1
Walker, Thomas Tarvit	G	22/12/1978	Methil Rovers	15/05/1984	Falkirk	101	1
Wallace, Brian K S	WH	01/11/1955	Forfar Celtic	01/09/1959	Uganda	19	1
Wallace, George Gordon	IF	14/10/1966	Montrose	04/09/1969	Dundee	224	113
Wallace, George Gordon	IF	09/02/1978	Dundee United	30/07/1983	Dundee United	318	104
Wallace, Gordon	OL	11/04/1970	Penicuik Athletic	20/10/1977	Dundee United	1	1
Wallace, James	IL	04/10/1930	Scone Thistle	04/10/1930		1	1
Wallace, John	G	11/08/1945	Dundee Anchorage	18/08/1945		80	45
Wallace, John Martin	CF	16/01/1931	Wallyford Bluebell	14/02/1934	Blackpool	48	0
Wallace, Joseph	G	12/01/1904	Glasgow Perthshire	01/04/1906	Third Lanark	2	2
Wallace, William	OR	07/06/1913	Vale of Grange	02/09/1915	Airdrie	73	34
Wallace, William	IF	05/01/1935	Lochgelly Albert	12/01/1935	Trialist	1	0
Wallace, William S.B.	IF	22/10/1959	Stenhousemuir	27/04/1960	Hearts	1	1
Waller, Thomas Henry	IR	29/11/1950	Thorntree United	05/01/1952	Freed	12	1
Walters	LH	05/01/1909		05/01/1909	Trialist		
Ward, John	LB	16/05/1958	Aberdeen	30/04/1959	Stranraer	1	0
Warden, James	OL	27/10/1934	Third Lanark	01/11/1934	Trialist	2	1
Wardlaw, William	OR	29/02/1936	Thornton Hibs	07/03/1936	Trialist	63	20
Wardrope, William	CF	12/09/1908	Third Lanark	30/04/1912	Freed	1	0
Watson		19/08/1925		19/08/1925	Trial		
Watson, Andrew	RB	25/12/1945	Armadale Thistle	30/04/1947	Armadale Thistle	48	0
Watson, Brian M	OL	31/05/1961	Broxburn Athletic	30/04/1962	Worcester City	27	7
Watson, David	G	22/10/1937	Dundee United	22/11/1938	Cancelled	31	0
Watson, William Christie	CH	17/10/1935	Renfrew	15/07/1936	Dundee	20	1
Watt, William D	IF	05/12/1968	Aberdeen	15/01/1970	Ross County	20	1
Watters, Charles	IR	29/04/1920	Third Lanark	30/04/1922	Freed	13	0
Waugh, John T	IF	03/09/1913	Dykehead	30/04/1914	Hamilton Accies	34	3
Webster, George	OR	01/08/1887		28/02/1891		34	5

Players (Thomson – Twaddle)

First Team Player	Position	Date Signed	Signed from	Date Left	Next Club	Total Appearances	Goals
Thomson, Andrew	RB	31/12/1956	Burntisland Shipyard	30/04/1959	Brechin City	2	0
Thomson, Arthur	CH	30/12/1970	Oldham Athletic	30/04/1972	Dalkeith Thistle	33	1
Thomson, Charles M	G	12/10/1927	St Johnstone YMCA	09/12/1927	Alloa	4	0
Thomson, David	LB	01/08/1889	Raith Athletic	30/04/1900		4	2
Thomson, David	IF	14/01/1904	Darvel	30/04/1908		7	4
Thomson, David	CH	01/03/1976	Warout Thistle	26/11/1983	Retired	206	7
Thomson, David	CF	26/04/1890		30/04/1891		2	1
Thomson, G		29/05/2007				1	0
Thomson, Gary	M	21/07/1992	Queen of the South	23/10/1993	Clydebank	43	4
Thomson, Ian	M	01/01/1988	Lochgelly Albert	24/08/1990	Alloa	1	0
Thomson, James	G	04/11/1953	Beith	30/04/1956	Southend United	40	9
Thomson, James Donaldson	IF	06/07/1971	Dunfermline Athletic	30/04/1972	Retired	18	0
Thomson, James Smith	LH	01/08/1894		21/04/1900		182	3
Thomson, John	LB	26/12/1914	Hearts	23/01/1915	Trialist	7	1
Thomson, John	IL	01/10/1972	Dundee St Patricks	30/04/1973		1	0
Thomson, John	WH	31/08/1922		30/04/1923		7	2
Thomson, John G	OR	21/11/1944	Ashfield	24/09/1945	Cancelled	1	0
Thomson, John J	G	14/12/1978	Stirling Albion	30/06/1998	East Fife	35	2
Thomson, Robin	IL	01/03/1996	Aberdeen	19/06/1912	Hibs	74	10
Thomson, Scott Munro	OR	08/09/1993	Forfar Athletic	23/05/1963	Ipswich Town	165	0
Thomson, Scott Yuill	G	10/05/1905		14/11/1951	Arbroath	10	0
Thomson, Thomas	IL	05/06/1911	Arthurlie	05/05/1945		8	1
Thomson, William J	IF	29/09/2006	Hearts	15/04/1893	Trialist	12	2
Thorarinsson, Hjalmar	F	15/03/1919		22/08/1923		1	0
Thorburn	OR	29/05/1910	Buckhaven	30/04/1928		12	1
Thorburn, Alexander HR	F	28/01/1956	Douglasdale Juniors	30/04/1920		175	0
Thorburn, James AF	G	21/09/1938	Crossgates Primrose		Killed in action		
Till, Ernest	RH	01/01/1945	Gallatown Sports C.	30/04/1948		229	5
Tivendale,	OR	01/08/1892	Dunfermline Athletic	03/10/1898		6	0
Tod, Andrew	CF	22/08/1923	Raith Athletic	15/12/1900		31	6
Tod, John	IR	09/06/1926		30/05/2001	Trialist	12	1
Todd, A	LH	01/05/1914	Falkirk	29/09/2000		1	0
Todd, Hugh R	LH	06/06/1914	Denbeath Star	21/02/1931		33	1
Todd, James	FB	11/10/1947	Musselburgh	22/02/1896	Freed	3	0
Todd, James	IF	07/09/1896	Auchtermuchty Junior	01/09/1913		27	4
Todd, James B	OL	25/08/1900	Dunfermline Ath Juns	30/04/1921		2	0
Torbet	OL	02/07/1999	Bo'ness	30/04/1972	Forfar Athletic	5	1
Torrance, Henry	LB	31/03/1998	Hibs	21/04/1917	Livingston	9	1
Tosh, Paul James	F	07/09/1930	St Johnstone	30/04/1940		63	14
Tosh, Steven William	M	22/02/1896	Dunnikier Juniors	15/02/1966		95	13
Townley, David M	LB	01/09/1913		23/01/2007		6	0
Traill	CF	10/05/1919		18/05/1946	Trialist	1	0
Traill	IL	06/06/1914		18/11/1944	Trialist	1	1
Traill, William	IL	04/10/1971	Buckhaven	06/09/1902	St Andrews Utd	19	3
Tront, Josef	OR	13/04/1917	Dundee Elmwood	23/12/1916	Trialist	3	0
Trotter	CF	09/12/1939		05/05/1929	Guest	2	1
Tulips, James	LB	06/01/1966	Alloa	17/01/1998	Trial	21	8
Tulloch, George B	F	21/07/2004	Stenhousemuir	15/02/1966	Cancelled	3	1
Tulloch, Stephen	OL	11/05/1946	Dunfermline Athletic	23/01/2007		38	2
Turnbull, Ronald W	CF	11/11/1944	Dundee	18/05/1946	Trialist	2	0
Turner	IL	23/08/1902	Wolves	18/11/1944	War Guest	2	0
Turner, George, Sgt	LB	01/07/1914	St Johnstone	06/09/1902		3	0
Turner, Neil McD	IR	24/04/1924	Leeds City	23/12/1916	St Mirren	65	14
Turner, Thomas S	OL	03/07/1996	St Roch's	05/05/1929	Blackburn Rovers	158	25
Twaddle, Kevin	OR	03/07/1996	St Johnstone	17/01/1998	Morton	53	4

First Team Player	Position	Date Signed	Signed from	Date Left	Next Club	Total Appearances	Goals
Wedderburn, Craig	M	29/05/2007				1	0
Weightman, David	IF	15/08/1917	Gillingham	27/04/1917	East Fife	28	10
Weir, David	LB	06/08/1968	Manchester United	22/04/1970	Australia	18	0
Weir, Edward	CH	02/08/1947	Dunfermline Athletic	30/04/1938	Dundalk	3	0
Weir, Graham	F	01/06/2007	Queen of the South			43	15
Weir, James	OR	07/09/1895	Kirkcaldy	21/09/1895		2	0
Weir, Robert	CF	24/08/1901	Anniston Rangers	30/04/1902		29	13
Weir, Thomas W M	FB	26/05/1954	East Fife	30/04/1956	Retired	25	0
Welsh, Fletcher	CF	04/06/1914	Leith Athletic	17/09/1915	Hearts	52	51
Welsh, Fletcher		29/07/1916			Sheffield Wednesday		
Westland, Douglas G	G	24/05/1948	Stoke City	30/04/1950	Freed	66	0
Westwater	LB	09/01/1943		09/01/1943	Trialist	1	0
Westwood, David	G	30/07/1983	Hill of Beath Hawthorn	10/08/1983	Trialist	3	0
Whalley, George	CF	06/09/1941	Hearts	18/04/1942	Loan	13	13
Whannell, J	CF	01/08/1887	Woodburn	18/08/1888		6	3
Whatley, Mark Christopher	F	27/02/2007	Madras College			2	0
Wheatley, Stewart	M	10/06/1976	Falkirk	30/04/1977	Berwick Rangers	15	1
White	RH	18/09/1897		18/09/1897	Trialist	1	0
White	G	21/04/1917		21/04/1917	Trialist	1	0
White, Thomas	CF	10/06/1958	Bonnyrigg Rose Ath	06/10/1962	St Mirren	51	16
Whiteford	LH	07/04/1917		07/04/1917		1	0
Whitelaw, Gordon	RH	01/12/1972	St Johnstone	15/05/1973	Freed	4	0
Whitelaw, John	IL	14/05/1937	York City	18/09/1941	St Bernards	92	57
Whiteside, William	G	28/09/1968	Ashfield	11/04/1977	Stranraer	13	0
Whitnall, John Iain	LB	13/09/1963	Nairn Thistle	30/04/1965	Freed	6	0
Whyte	RH	13/10/1945		13/10/1945	Trialist	1	0
Whyte, Charles C	OL	15/05/1936	Brechin City	11/03/1937	Montrose	9	1
Whyte, Graeme Brand	F	09/07/2001	Gairdoch United BC	30/04/2003	Freed	1	0
Whyte, Sandy	OR	30/11/1975	Clackmannan	30/04/1978	Sauchie Juniors	1	0
Wildridge, Ian	F	01/06/1977	Glenpark Juveniles	30/04/1980	Forfar Athletic	5	0
Wilkie	CH	18/01/1898		18/01/1898	Trialist	1	0
Wilkie, Adam C	FB	08/06/1907	Townhill	30/04/1915		35	0
Wilkie, Alexander	RB	10/09/1949	Rosslyn Juniors	01/07/1953	Barry Town	17	0
Wilkie, James	RH	29/07/1905		30/04/1908	Kirkcaldy United	109	20
Wilkie, John	CF	05/09/1942	Morton	02/09/1944	Loan	8	5
Wilkie, John	CF	06/04/1940	Hearts of Beath	20/04/1940	Loan	2	1
Wilkie, John Carlin	OL	05/01/1971	Arbroath	30/04/1971	Keith	9	1
Wilkie, William	OR	01/03/1929	Partick Thistle	29/04/1929	Loan	8	1
Wilkinson, Ian	D	03/06/1970	Hibernian	11/11/1971	Hamilton Accies	30	0
Williams	CH	21/04/1924	Dykehead	21/04/1924	Trialist	1	0
Williams	G	27/04/1909		27/04/1909	Trialist	1	0
Williams	OL	19/07/1996		19/07/1996	Trialist	1	0
Williamson	LH	09/03/1889		01/01/1890		6	0
Williamson, John	WH	21/02/1952	Stoneyburn Juniors	07/03/1959	Dunfermline Athletic	156	34
Williamson, Peter B	CF	16/08/1952	Thornton Hibs	30/04/1953		1	0
Williamson, Thomas	CF	10/01/1958	Blairhall Juniors	20/02/1959	Cancelled	5	2
Williamson, Trevor	OR	09/08/1991	Portadown	11/11/1992	Glenavon	34	2
Wilson	CF	01/08/1887		15/02/1890		5	14
Wilson, Barry John	OR	03/09/1994	Ross County	20/07/1996	Inverness CT	51	10
Wilson, Craig	RB	13/10/2006	Dunfermline			77	1
Wilson, David	CF	13/12/1902	Black Watch	30/04/1903	Dundee	12	9
Wilson, David William	G	09/07/1996	Rosyth Recreation	30/04/1999	Released	0	0
Wilson, Derek	M	17/08/2004	Linlithgow BC	06/04/2006	Released	0	0
Wilson, George	IL	08/09/1915	Newcastle United	30/04/1920	East Fife	69	6

First Team Player	Position	Date Signed	Signed from	Date Left	Next Club	Total Appearances	Goals
Wilson, Ian	IF	01/10/1970	Kirkcaldy BB	30/04/1972	Thornton Hibs	4	0
Wilson, James	OR	17/01/1917	St Mirren	07/12/1935	St Mirren	29	10
Wilson, James	IR	23/07/1969	Penicuik Athletic	07/09/1970	Clydebank	3	0
Wilson, John	IR	28/11/1942	Chesterfield	28/11/1942	Trialist	1	0
Wilson, John	F	09/09/1893	Lochgelly United	11/11/1893		8	6
Wilson, John	WH	01/06/1909	Penicuik	30/04/1917		70	0
Wilson, John	LH	15/08/1899	Kirkcaldy	15/08/1899	Trialist	1	0
Wilson, Murray	CF	28/04/1973	Leven Juniors	28/04/1973	Trialist	1	0
Wilson, Patrick	OL	14/02/1968	Aberdeen	21/08/1971	Berwick Rangers	104	16
Wilson, Robert	WH	10/08/1915		30/04/1919		17	1
Wilson, Robert	OR	17/12/1902		17/12/1902	Trialist	4	2
Wilson, Robert B	M	11/06/1986	Hill of Beath Hawthorn	29/01/1987	Hill of Beath Hawtho	5	0
Wilson, Robert L	OR	14/05/1921	Broxburn Athletic	30/04/1923	St Johnstone	8	0
Wilson, Scott William	CH	28/06/2005	Clyde	23/01/2006	Brechin City	6	0
Wilson, William	RB	02/05/1959	Sauchie Juveniles	30/04/1965	Freed	140	3
Wilson, William	IR	02/05/1904	East Fife	04/11/1904	Dundee	5	0
Winning	CH	03/04/1905		03/04/1905	Trialist	1	0
Winning, William	RB	09/06/1913	Parkhead	30/04/1919		102	0
Winter, Craig John	M	10/01/1994	Hibernian	19/07/1994	Cowdenbeath	36	1
Winter, Craig John		01/01/2007	Dumbarton	30/05/2008	Free Transfer		
Wishart	RH	01/08/1889	Raith Athletic	17/02/1894		31	19
Wishart, Robert W	WH	30/10/1964	Airdrie	30/04/1965	Free transfer	10	3
Wood, Albert	OR	29/06/1950	Newtongrange Star	30/04/1954	Brechin City	23	2
Wood, Alexander Douglas	IR	20/07/1960	Sunderland	30/04/1961	Free transfer	3	0
Wood, James	IR	20/08/1970	Salveson Boys Club	19/01/1971	East Fife	1	0
Wood, Ronald S	OR	10/08/1962	St Bernards 'A'	30/04/1964	Free transfer	7	0
Wood, Wilson	WH	13/06/1973	Hearts	30/04/1975	Free transfer	55	2
Woodcock, James	CH	20/08/1949	A.Hall & Co. FC	01/01/1951	St Johnstone	14	0
Woods, Dean	F	31/08/2004	Hearts	26/08/2005	Released	0	0
Woods, Steven		10/11/2004		30/05/2005		5	0
Woon, Arthur	CF	01/09/1945	Dundee United	02/02/1946	Trialist	1	0
Wotherspoon, James	CF	15/03/1945	Markinch VR	02/02/1946	Montrose	18	14
Wright	OL	02/11/1895		09/11/1895	Trialist	18	11
Wright, David	IR	14/08/1923		30/04/1924	East Fife	2	0
Wright, David R.	CH	07/02/1946	HM Forces	30/04/1946	Forfar Athletic	1	0
Wright, John	M	03/06/1986	Kirkcaldy YM Juniors	31/01/1989	Cowdenbeath	5	0
Wright, Keith Arthur	CF	01/05/1983	Melbourne Thistle	06/12/1986	Dundee	42	2
Wright, Keith Arthur		17/07/1997	Hibernian	20/11/1998	Morton	211	96
Wyles	OR	15/08/1899	Buckhaven	15/08/1899	Trialist	1	1
Wylie, James A	OR	09/07/1907	Queens Park	01/11/1907	Hamilton Accies	5	1
Young	OL	12/04/1930		12/04/1930	Trialist	1	0
Young	OL	30/09/1933	Airdrie Juniors	30/09/1933	Trialist	1	0
Young, Andrew	WH	10/02/1945	Celtic	30/04/1961	Retired	622	141
Young, David	G	02/05/1906	Pathhead United	30/04/1907		3	2
Young, David	FB	11/07/1991	Tynecastle BC	15/05/1993	Free Transfer	19	0
Young, James	OR	18/08/1917		16/02/1918	Lochgelly United	17	5
Young, Lloyd Paul	M	13/01/2004	Lochee Harp	17/03/2005	Tayport	40	1
Zoco, Jorge	M	02/08/2001	Badajoz	30/05/2002		27	1

SUPPORTERS CLUB PLAYER OF THE YEAR

55/6 Willie McNaught
56/7 Andy Young
57/8 Jimmy McEwan
58/9 Andy Leigh

59/60 no award

John Nicholson, Chairman of the Supporters Club, writing in the 1960/61 handbook, said : "It was felt that after a few years it was really team spirit that counts and with the consent of the board, we have allowed this event to lapse, but we shall continue to encourage the team in every way possible to give of their best." On 30th September 1958, the Board of Directors had express their unhappiness at the annual award.   The award was resurrected in 1980/81

SUPPORTERS CLUB PLAYER OF THE YEAR

80/1 Bobby Ford
81/2 Willie Gibson
82/3 Bobby Russell
83/4 Paul Smith
84/5 Keith Wright
85/6 Paul Smith
86/7 Glen Kerr
87/8 John McStay
88/9 Cammy Fraser
89/0 Martin Nelson
90/1 Gordon Dalziel
91/2 Gordon Dalziel
92/3 Craig Brewster
93/4 Shaun Dennis
94/5 Steve McAnespie
95/6 David Sinclair
96/7 Danny Lennon
97/8 Guido Van De Kamp
98/9 Kevin Fotheringham
99/0 Marvin Andrews
00/1 Paul Brown
01/2 Nacho Novo
02/3 Paquito
03/4 Antonio Calderon
04/5 David Berthelot
05/6 Paul McManus
06/7 Chris Fahey
07/8 Ian Davidson

Opposite page

In May 1951, the club undertook a three match Highland tour (four if you include Brechin City). As the players relaxed in Inverness and the surrounding countryside, a photographer took several pictures, copies of which were distributed to everyone in the travelling party.

The two photographs opposite show players and officials at leisure in the Highlands (and what was considered to be casual wear in 1951)

PLAYERS' PLAYER OF THE YEAR

81/2 Ian Ballantyne
82/3 Colin More & Colin Harris
83/4 Paul Smith
84/5 Craig Robertson
85/6 Paul Smith
86/7 Stevie Simpson
87/8 John McStay & Paul Sweeney
88/9 Cammy Fraser
89/0 Iain McLeod
90/1 Martin Nelson
91/2 Gordon Dalziel
92/3 Peter Hetherston
93/4 Shaun Dennis
94/5 Steve McAnespie
95/6 Danny Lennon
96/7 Danny Lennon
97/8 Scott M. Thomson
98/9 Paul Browne
99/0 Paul Browne
00/1 Paul Browne
01/2 Nacho Novo
02/3 Pacquito
03/4 Darren Brady & Paquito
04/5 Ian Davidson
05/6 Ian Davidson
06/7 Craig Wilson
07/8 Craig Wilson

YOUNG PLAYER OF THE YEAR

83/4 Billy Herd
84/5 Billy McNeill
85/6 Alasdair Anderson
86/7 John Wright
87/8 Ian Ferguson
88/9 Philip Burn
89/0 Neil Buchanan
90/1 Robert Raeside & David Sinclair
91/2 Jason Dair
92/3 Colin Cameron
93/4 Stevie Crawford
94/5 Steve McAnespie
95/6 Craig Dargo
96/7 Craig Dargo
97/8 Craig Dargo
98/9 Paul Shields
99/0 Kevin Nicol
00/1 Jay Stein
01/2 Ian Brown
02/3 Ryan Blackadder
03/4 Lloyd Young
04/5 Stephen Tulloch
05.6 Colin Leiper
06/7 Jamie Mackie
07/8 Mark Whatley

On pages 378, 379 and 380 are programme covers from historic Rovers' matches.   For more details on collecting programmes, and Raith Rovers items in particular, go to www.pmfc.co.uk, or write to Programme Monthly, PO Box 3236, Norwich, NR7 7BE

Almost certainly the oldest programme involving Raith Rovers, issued by Aberdeen club Orion on 22nd October 1898

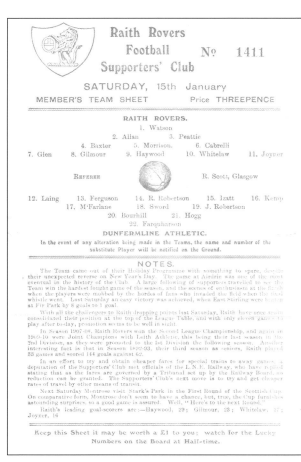

The Supporters Club started issuing single sheet programmes for the second half of 1937/38 season

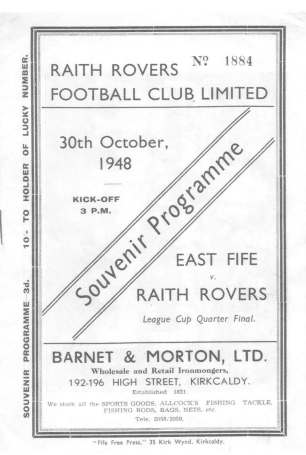

The Club's first Official Programme for a big match in 1948/49 - printed then, as now, by McGilvray Printers

The first regular programme issued by the Football Club, for the opening home match of the 1949/50 season

The club's first Cup Final programme, in March 1949, which ended in an undeserved defeat

There was a record attendance at Stark's Park to see Hibs in the Scottish Cup on 26th January 1952

Rovers' record victory in League or Cup Coldstream 1 Raith Rovers 10

An iconic front page photograph for a memorable game, Raith Rovers 5 Rangers 1 8th December 1956

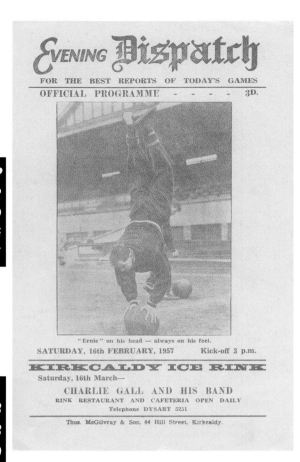

*Those were the days .... Scottish Cup
6th round, 16th February 1957,
Raith Rovers 7 Dundee United 0*

*Back to the First Division, after
Raith Rovers 7 Queen of the South 2
clinched promotion*

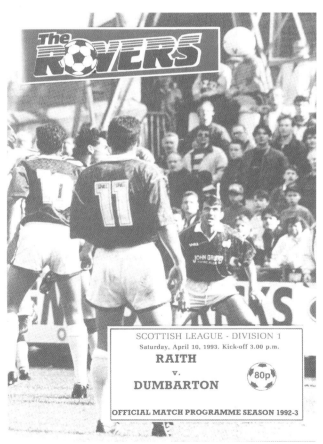

*Another promotion, and a First Division
Championship, as the Premier League
beckoned in April 1993*

Hopefully, this wasn't a one-off in the club's history

ACKNOWLEDGEMENTS AND SOURCES OF INFORMATION

Thanks to

My wife Liz, son Shaun and daughter Vicki (who took some of the photographs), and to Charlie Cant for their help in proof reading and correcting the original draught.

The staff at Kirkcaldy Central and Sinclairtown Libraries, over many years, for their help and forebearance during countless hours of scrutinising old newspapers.

Colin Lobban, Richard McBrearty and all the staff at the Scottish Football Museum at Hampden Park ; David Thomson of the Scottish Football League and Andy Mitchell, former Head of Communications at the Scottish Football Association

John Hutchison, Club Historian of Leicester City FC, for some Rovers-related photographs ; the interviewers and contributors to the fanzine "Stark's Bark" from which several quotations have been taken ; John Drysdale for passing on information from Spain relating to the Canary Islands "shipwreck" ; Peter Napier for passing on his father's papers.

References to Kirkcaldy's History have been taken from

Kirkcaldy in old picture postcards by Carol McNeill, 2001, ISBN 90-288-3537-7
Kirkcaldy Remembered, compiled by Kirkcaldy Civic Society, 1999. ISBN 0-7524-1549-2
Old Kirkcaldy, Central, North & West by Eric Eunson, 1998. ISBN 1-84033-052
Various booklets published by Kirkcaldy Civic Society between 1986 and 2001
Kirkcaldy, A New Illustrated History, by Duncan Glen, 2004. ISBN 0-86142-146-9
A History of Kirkcaldy 1843-1949 by P.K. Livingstone
Kirkcaldy, A History and Celebration by Kirkcaldy Civic Society, 2005, ISBN 1-84567-749-8

The contents of the book have been compiled over a period of 40 years, so please forgive any omissions, through forgetfulness, from the following list of sources.

The Mitchell Library in Glasgow ; National Library in Edinburgh ; British Newspaper Library at Colindale ; and local libraries throughout Scotland, for their newspaper collections.   In Kirkcaldy, primary sources have been The Fife Free Press, The Kirkcaldy Times, The Fifeshire Advertiser and the Kirkcaldy Mail.   Companies House and West Register House in Edinburgh were visited for information on the club's corporate history.   Fife Council's Archive Centre in Markinch provided information on Stark's Park, and on Councillor Robert Stark.

Some photographs have been taken from the first history of club, written by R.M. Connell in the mid 1920s, published by George W. May, London.

Some of the statistical information on players has been taken from two previous publications by the author : "A Record of Post-War Scottish League Players" and "A Record of Pre-War Scottish League Players".   Several football reference and history books were used in compiling these, including :
Rothmans Football Yearbook 1970-71 to 2002-03, succeeded in 2003-04 by Sky Sports Football Yearbook, latterly published by Headline Books. Scottish editor Alan Elliott.
The Scottish Football League Review, 1980-81 to 2005-06.   Published under various sponsors' titles by The Scottish Football League, edited by David Thomson.
The now defunct (and much missed) Soccer Star magazine listed teamlines from the late 1950's until its demise in 1970.
Peter Black's "Football Know-All", published in two editions of the Weekly News every August, was supplemented by the weekling printing of each week's SFL and SFA registrations, until the mid 1980's.
Most of the information on players who plied their trade south of the border, or who were transferred across the border, has been obtained from The PFA Premier & Football League Players Records 1946-2005, edited and compiled by Barry J. Hugman, published in 2005 by Queen Anne Press, £30 hardback, ISBN 1-85291-665-6.
An invaluable help with references to pre-war English League players is Football League Players' Records 1888 to 1939, compiled by Michael Joyce, published by Soccer Data in 2002, ISBN 1-899468-63-3.
Scottish Amateur Internationals and Internationalists 1927-1974 by George Campbell, published in 1985, provided information on Rovers' players capped at that level

There have been a number of superb books devoted to individual clubs, which have been consulted in the course of researches. In (club) alphabetical order :
Aberdeen, The European Era, A Complete Record, by Clive Leatherdale, published in 1997 by Desert Island Books, £16.99 hardback, ISBN 1-874287-11-2.
The Aberdeen Football Companion by Clive Leatherdale, published in 1986 by John Donald Publishers Ltd., £5.95 softback, ISBN 0-85976-182-7.
The Boys from The 'Brig, The Life and Times of Albion Rovers, by R.W. Marwick, published by Monklands Library Services Department in 1986, ISBN 0-946120-19-6.
The Official History of Ayr United Football Club by Duncan Carmichael, Vol. 2 1939-1990, published by the club in 1992.
An Alphabet of The Celts : A Complete Who's Who of Celtic FC by Eugene McBride, Martin O'Connor with George Sheridan. Published in 1994 by ACL & Polar Ltd., £18.95 hardback, ISBN 0-9514862-7-6.

Celtic, A Complete Record 1888-1992, compiled by Paul Lunney, published by Breedon Books, ISBN 1-873626-27-4.
Very detailed match-by-match statistics as a major appendix to a narrative-and-pictorial club history.
The Celtic Football Companion by David Docherty, published in 1986 by John Donald Publishers Ltd., £5.95 softback, ISBN 0-85976-173-8.
"The Miners" A Who's Who of Cowdenbeath FC (Part 1, Abdullah to McWilliams) by David A. Allan. £5 plus 75p p&p from Frank Dillon, 230 Foulford Road, Cowdenbeath, KY4 9AX, cheques made payable to Cowdenbeath Supporters Club.
The Sons of The Rock, The Official History of Dumbarton FC, updated by Jim McAllister and published by himself in 2002. £12.00 softback plus £2 p&p from the author at 23 Kinloch Road, Newton Mearns, Glasgow, G77 6LY
They Wore The Dark Blue, A Complete Record of Dundee FC, by Norrie Price, who published it in 1995, £12.95 hardback, ISBN 0-9521426-2-7.
Dundee United Who's Who by Pat Kelly, published in 1998 by John Donald Publishers Ltd, £8.50 softback, ISBN 0-85976-502-4.
Rags to Riches, The Official History of Dundee United by Mike Watson, published in 1985 by David Winter & Son Ltd., £4.95 hardback.
Hamilton Academical Who's Who by Peter McLeish, published by Soccer Data in 1997, £7.99 softback, ISBN 1-899468-80-3.
Hearts in Art by Andrew Hoggan, published in 1995 by Mainstream, £12.99 hardback, ISBN 1-85158-736-5.
Gritty, Gallant, Glorious, A History and Complete Record of the Hearts 1946-1997 by Norrie Price, who published it in 1997, £15.99 hardback, ISBN 0-9521426-3-5.
Who's Who of Kilmarnock FC, compiled by Bill Donnachie, published by Mainstream in 1989, £9.95 hardback.
Killie, The Official History, by David Ross, published in 1994 by Yore Publications, £15.95 hardback, ISBN 1-874427-75-5.
The Men Who Made Motherwell Football Club 1946-2001, by Jim Jeffrey and Genge Fry, published by Tempus Publishing Ltd in 2001, £15.00 softback, ISBN 0-7524-2191-3.
'Well Again', The Official History of Motherwell Football Club 1886-2004 by Graham Barnstaple and Keith Brown, £20.95 hardback published by Yore Publications in 2001, ISBN 0-9547830-2-6
Partick Thistle Football Club 1876-2002, The Official History, by Robert Reid, Niall Kennedy, Billy Thomson, William Anderson and Stuart Deans, published by Yore Publications in 2001, £20.95 hardback, ISBN 1-874427-593.
The Men With The Educated Feet, A Statistical and Pictorial History of Queen's Park FC by F.H.S. Robertson, published by The Queen's Park Supporters Association, third edition 1992, £5 softback, ISBN 0-9510047-19.
The Rangers Football Companion by David Docherty, published in 1986 by John Donald Publishers Ltd., £5.95 softback, ISBN 0-85976-172-X.
Rangers Player by Player, by Bob Ferrier and Robert McElroy, published in 1990 and 1997 (softback £14.99) by Hamlyn, ISBN 0-600-59275-8.
Rangers The Complete Record by Bob Ferrier and Robert McElroy, published by Breedon Books in 1996, £16.99 hardback, ISBN 1-85983-015-3.
Bristling with possibilities ... The Official History of St Johnstone FC 1885-1997 by Alastair Blair and Brian Doyle, published by the club in 1997, £15 hardback (also softback).
St Johnstone Who's Who 1946 to 1992 by Jim Slater, published by the club in 1992, priced £6.95 softback.
Stirling Albion FC 1945-1988 by Allan Grieve and John Turnbull, published in 1988 by twentynil publications.
Several "Who's Who" publications relating to English League clubs were consulted for information on former Rovers players and managers.
Scotland The Team by Andrew Ward, published by Breedon Books in 1987, ISBN 0-907969-34-8
Scotland : The Complete International Football Record, by Richard Keir, published by Breedon Books in 2001, ISBN 1-85983-232-6
A Scottish Soccer Internationalists' Who's Who, 1872-1986 by Douglas Lamming, published in 1987 by Hutton Press, £5.95 softback, ISBN 0-907033-47-4

For forty years, the author has been recording the club's history as it happened, and researching its past. He has followed in the footsteps of two predecessors. Alex Arnot lived at 64 Ava Street and over a period of 40 years, from the early years of last century, carefully noted the club's affairs, and researched its early history. He passed this information on to Peter Napier, a great servant to Raith Rovers, firstly as an office bearer in the Supporters Club, and then as a Club Director. He wrote the club's second history book, in 1948, and continued to compile its statistics until the early 1960s. He is pictured here with his Supporters Club, and Football Club, colleague Bert Herdman. The statistics compiled by Alex Arnot and Peter Napier are included in this book.

Mentioned above is the fanzine Stark's Bark, which between August 1992 and April 2001, contained a great deal of historical information, as well as contemporary accounts, and many interviews with former players and managers. Back issues of most editions remain available for sale (details are on page 384)

Some of the major topics included in Stark's Bark over the years, with the issue number in parenthesis, include :
Frank Connor interview (1)
Martin Harvey interview (6)
McStay/Duncan Ferguson case ; 1993/94 and 1994/95 round-ups, Rovers abroad (8)
Rovers in the Faroes (9)
Record Signings (10)
Rovers in Iceland and Munich ; Alex Brash interview (11)
Rovers' Internationalists (12)
George McLay (13)
Jimmy Nicholl's resignation (13)

Interviews were conducted by the author, Ally Gourlay and John Greer. Following the demise of Stark's Bark, Ally Gourlay published two editions of "The Wraith", a Raith Rovers History Magazine. Issue 1, Autumn 2002, included interviews with Joe Baker and Colin Harris, and Issue 2, Spring 2003, included a 1960 newspaper interview with Johnny Urquhart, an obituary of Murray McDermott and the club's milestone goals.

The best historical sources are often oral, and it is impossible to quantify or identify the conversations held and stories heard over almost fifty years. A lot of them came from my father, Jack Litster, and uncles Harry Campbell and Willie McLaren ; most came from Charlie Campbell, and if someone hadn't got there first, this book could have been called "Tales of a Grandfather".

Also available

ROVERS RECALLED : RAITH ROVERS IN PICTURES THROUGH THE YEARS

Two books, each of 100 pages, containing hundreds of photographs and illustrations from the 19th century to the end of the 20th century involving players, match action, team groups and many other aspects of the Club's history.

Volume 1 costs £6.95, and Volume 2 costs £7.95, and they are available from Waterstone's bookshop in Kirkcaldy High Street, or by post from John Litster, c/o 4 Ben Ledi Road, Kirkcaldy, KY2 5RP, post free.

The author has a substantial quantity of spare copies of Raith Rovers programmes,

handbooks and photographs. These are available for sale. Please send a list of specific requirements to the above address, or request a catalogue. These items are listed on the website www.pmfc.co.uk, click on Football History and follow the links.

Available from the above address is the quarterly magazine "Scottish Football Historian", which for 26 years has been publishing articles on various aspects of Scottish Football History. Subscriptions are £1.35 per copy (cheques payable to J. Litster) or send 5 x 2nd class stamps for the current issue.

Included in this issue : George Robertson of Motherwell .... Albion Rovers history in a nutshell ... The Early Years of the Scottish Football League .... Charity matches .... Barrie Mitchell Interview .... Berwick Rangers' first League match .... Hearts First Scottish Cup Win ... Jock White .... Obituaries include Charlie Aitken and John Cushley.

No.105   Spring 2008   £1